AMERICAN
COUNCIL
★ OF ★
LEARNED
SOCIETIES
★

DICTIONARY OF AMERICAN BIOGRAPHY

DICTIONARY OF
AMERICAN BIOGRAPHY

DICTIONARY OF AMERICAN BIOGRAPHY

UNDER THE AUSPICES OF THE
AMERICAN COUNCIL OF LEARNED SOCIETIES

EDITED BY
ALLEN JOHNSON
AND
DUMAS MALONE

Cushman — Eberle
VOLUME V

CHARLES SCRIBNER'S SONS
NEW YORK
1930

Prompted solely by a desire for public service the New York Times Company and its President, Mr. Adolph S. Ochs, have made possible the preparation of the manuscript of the Dictionary of American Biography through a subvention of more than $500,000 and with the understanding that the entire responsibility for the contents of the volumes rests with the American Council of Learned Societies.

vii

CONTRIBUTORS TO VOLUME V

Thomas P. Abernethy	T. P. A.	Edward E. Curtis	E. E. C.
LeRoy Abrams	L. R. A.	Robert E. Cushman	R. E. C.
Adeline Adams	A. A.	Marion Dargan	M. D.
James Truslow Adams	J. T. A.	Irwin H. DeLong	I. H. DeL.
Cyrus Adler	C. A.	Davis R. Dewey	D. R. D.
Carroll S. Alden	C. S. A.	Charles A. Dinsmore	C. A. D.
William H. Allison	W. H. A.	Eleanor Robinette Dobson	E. R. D.
Katharine H. Amend	K. H. A.	William E. Dodd	W. E. D.
John C. Archer	J. C. A.	Charles Wright Dodge	C. W. D.
Percy M. Ashburn	P. M. A.	Mary Danforth Dodge	M. D. D.
Frederick W. Ashley	F. W. A.	Elizabeth Donnan	E. D.
Christina H. Baker	C. H. B.	William Howe Downes	W. H. D.
Charles M. Bakewell	C. M. B.	Stella M. Drumm	S. M. D.
Thomas S. Barclay	T. S. B.	W. E. Burghardt DuBois	W. E. B. D.
Howard Barnes	H. B.	Raymond S. Dugan	R. S. D.
Claribel R. Barnett	C. R. B.	W. F. Durand	W. F. D.
Ernest Sutherland Bates	E. S. B—s.	Lionel C. Durel	L. C. D.
William A. Beardsley	W. A. B.	James H. Easterby	J. H. E—y.
Marcus Benjamin	M. B.	Walter Prichard Eaton	W. P. E.
Elbert J. Benton	E. J. B.	Edwin F. Edgett	E. F. E.
Arthur R. Blessing	A. R. B.	J. Harold Ennis	J. H. E—s.
Herbert E. Bolton	H. E. B.	Charles R. Erdman, Jr.	C. R. E., Jr.
Laetitia Todd Bolton	L. T. B.	Marjory Erskine	M. E.
Milledge L. Bonham, Jr.	M. L. B., Jr.	Ethel Webb Faulkner	E. W. F.
Archibald L. Bouton	A. L. B.	Harold U. Faulkner	H. U. F.
Witt Bowden	W. B.	Albert B. Faust	A. B. F.
Sarah G. Bowerman	S. G. B.	G. J. Fiebeger	G. J. F.
Claude G. Bowers	C. G. B.	Byron A. Finney	B. A. F.
Benjamin Brawley	B. B.	Harold N. Fowler	H. N. F.
Robert P. Brooks	R. P. B.	Early Lee Fox	E. L. F.
Everett S. Brown	E. S. B—n.	John H. Frederick	J. H. F.
Roberta B. Burnet	R. B. B.	Claude M. Fuess	C. M. F.
Guy H. Burnham	G. H. B.	George W. Fuller	G. W. F.
Isabel M. Calder	I. M. C.	John F. Fulton	J. F. F.
James M. Callahan	J. M. C.	Ralph Henry Gabriel	R. H. G.
Robert C. Canby	R. C. C—y.	Katharine Jeanne Galla-	
Charles F. Carey	C. F. C—y.	gher	K. J. G.
Frank T. Carlton	F. T. C.	George Harvey Genzmer	G. H. G.
William Glasgow Bruce Car-		W. J. Ghent	W. J. G.
son	W. G. B. C.	Armistead Churchill Gor-	
Wayland J. Chase	W. J. C.	don, Jr.	A. C. G., Jr.
Russell H. Chittenden	R. H. C.	Gladys Graham	G. G.
Robert C. Clark	R. C. C—k.	Charles B. Gulick	C. B. G.
Rudolf A. Clemen	R. A. C.	J. G. deR. Hamilton	J. G. deR. H.
Katherine W. Clendinning	K. W. C.	Talbot Faulkner Hamlin	T. F. H.
Oral S. Coad	O. S. C.	William A. Hamor	W. A. H.
Charles F. Coan	C. F. C—n.	Ralph V. Harlow	R. V. H.
Frederick W. Coburn	F. W. C.	Thomas L. Harris	T. L. H.
R. S. Cotterill	R. S. C.	Mary Bronson Hartt	M. B. H.
E. Merton Coulter	E. M. C.	George E. Hastings	G. E. H.
Isaac J. Cox	I. J. C.	Paul L. Haworth	P. L. H.

Contributors to Volume V

FRED E. HAYNES . . . . . . F. E. H.
ELLWOOD HENDRICK . . . . . E. H.
FRANK I. HERRIOTT . . . . . F. I. H.
J. D. HICKS . . . . J. D. H.
HOMER CAREY HOCKETT . . . H. C. H.
JEAN MACKINNON HOLT . . . J. M. H.
WALTER HOUGH . . . . . . W. H.
L. O. HOWARD . . . . L. O. H.
EDGAR ERSKINE HUME . . . . E. E. H.
ASHER ISAACS . . . . A. I.
JOSEPH JACKSON . . . . . . J. J.
EDWARD H. JENKINS . . . . E. H. J.
ALLEN JOHNSON . . . . . . A. J.
CECIL M. JOHNSON . . . . . C. M. J.
HENRY JOHNSON . . . . . . H. J.
HERBERT ANTHONY KELLAR . H. A. K.
LOUISE PHELPS KELLOGG . . L. P. K.
ALLEN MARSHALL KLINE . . A. M. K.
JAMES O. KNAUSS . . . . . . J. O. K.
RHEA MANSFIELD KNITTLE . R. M. K.
H. W. HOWARD KNOTT . . . H. W. H. K.
RALPH S. KUYKENDALL . . . R. S. K.
LEONARD W. LABAREE . . . . L. W. L.
JAMES MELVIN LEE . . . . . J. M. L.
FRANK GRANT LEWIS . . . . F. G. L.
CHARLES R. LINGLEY . . . . C. R. L.
ELLA LONN . . . . E. L.
LAWRENCE T. LOWREY . . . L. T. L.
ALEXANDER McADIE . . . . . A. M.
THOMAS DENTON McCORMICK T. D. M.
THOMAS McCRAE . . . . . . T. M.
P. B. McDONALD . . . . . . P. B. M.
S. S. McKAY . . . . S. S. M.
DONALD L. McMURRY . . . D. L. M.
BRUCE E. MAHAN . . . . . B. E. M.
DUMAS MALONE . . . . . . D. M.
HELEN JO SCOTT MANN . . . H. J. S. M.
FREDERICK H. MARTENS . . . F. H. M.
FRANK JEWETT MATHER, JR. F. J. M., Jr.
ALBERT P. MATHEWS . . . . A. P. M.
DAVID M. MATTESON . . . . D. M. M.
WILLIAM R. MAXON . . . . W. R. M.
BERNARD MAYO . . . . . . B. M—o.
LAWRENCE S. MAYO . . . . L. S. M.
NEWTON D. MERENESS . . . N. D. M.
GEORGE P. MERRILL . . . . G. P. M.
DOUGLASS W. MILLER . . . . D. W. M.
LOUIE M. MINER . . . . . . L. M. M.
BROADUS MITCHELL . . . . B. M—l.
CARL W. MITMAN . . . . . C. W. M.
FRANK MONAGHAN . . . . . F. M.
HERBERT R. MOODY . . . . H. R. M.
ROBERT E. MOODY . . . . . R. E. M.
ALBERT B. MOORE . . . . . A. B. M.
SAMUEL E. MORISON . . . . S. E. M.
JARVIS M. MORSE . . . . . . J. M. M.
WILLIAM BENNETT MUNRO . W. B. M.
CHARLES E. MUNROE . . . . C. E. M.

GEORGE B. MYERS . . . . . G. B. M.
EDWIN G. NASH . . . . . . E. G. N.
ALLAN NEVINS . . . . . . A. N.
LYMAN C. NEWELL . . . . . L. C. N.
JEANNETTE P. NICHOLS . . . J. P. N.
ROBERT HASTINGS NICHOLS . R. H. N.
ROY F. NICHOLS . . . . . . R. F. N.
HAROLD J. NOBLE . . . . . H. J. N.
JOHN F. NOLL . . . . J. F. N.
WALTER B. NORRIS . . . . W. B. N.
CLARA D. NOYES . . . . . . C. D. N.
GRACE LEE NUTE . . . . . . G. L. N.
FRANK M. O'BRIEN . . . . . F. M. O'B.
MILDRED B. PALMER . . . . M. B. P.
VICTOR H. PALTSITS . . . . V. H. P.
JOHN C. PARISH . . . . . . J. C. P.
FRED LEWIS PATTEE . . . . F. L. P—e.
CHARLES O. PAULLIN . . . . C. O. P.
FREDERIC LOGAN PAXSON . . F. L. P—n.
ROBERT E. PEABODY . . . . R. E. P.
C. C. PEARSON . . . . . . C. C. P.
DONALD C. PEATTIE . . . . D. C. P.
EPAPHRODITUS PECK . . . . E. P—k.
FREDERICK T. PERSONS . . . F. T. P.
A. EVERETT PETERSON . . . A. E. P.
JAMES M. PHALEN . . . . . J. M. P.
FRANCIS S. PHILBRICK . . . F. S. P.
DAVID PHILIPSON . . . . . D. P.
PAUL CHRISLER PHILLIPS . . P. C. P.
JOHN E. POMFRET . . . . . J. E. P.
JULIUS W. PRATT . . . . . . J. W. P.
EDWARD PREBLE . . . . . . E. P—e.
WALTER PRICHARD . . . . . W. P.
HERBERT I. PRIESTLEY . . . H. I. P.
RICHARD J. PURCELL . . . . R. J. P.
ARTHUR H. QUINN . . . . . A. H. Q.
JAMES G. RANDALL . . . . . J. G. R.
BELLE RANKIN . . . . B. R.
P. O. RAY . . . . P. O. R.
RUTH REDFIELD . . . . . . R. R.
THOMAS C. RICHARDS . . . T. C. R.
FRANKLIN L. RILEY . . . . . F. L. R.
HENRY MORTON ROBINSON . H. M. R.
WILLIAM A. ROBINSON . . . W. A. R.
J. MAGNUS ROHNE . . . . . J. M. R.
J. J. ROLBIECKI . . . . . . J. J. R.
CARL P. ROLLINS . . . . . C. P. R.
FRANK EDWARD ROSS . . . . F. E. R.
EDWIN RYAN . . . . E. R.
JOSEPH SCHAFER . . . . . . J. S—r.
JAY FRANK SCHAMBERG . . . J. F. S.
HERBERT W. SCHNEIDER . . . H. W. S.
DON C. SEITZ . . . . D. C. S.
BENJAMIN F. SHAMBAUGH . B. F. S.
MURIEL SHAVER . . . . . . M. S.
WILLIAM B. SHAW . . . . . W. B. S.
LESTER BURRELL SHIPPEE . . L. B. S.
GEORGE N. SHUSTER . . . . G. N. S.

Contributors to Volume V

Wilbur H. Siebert	W. H. S.	Harrison A. Trexler	H. A. T.
Sarah H. J. Simpson	S. H. J. S.	Roland G. Usher	R. G. U.
David Eugene Smith	D. E. S.	William T. Utter	W. T. U—r.
Edgar Fahs Smith	E. F. S.	Mark Van Doren	M. V–D.
Walter M. Smith	W. M. S.	Arnold J. F. van Laer	A. J. F. v–L.
Charles L. Souvay	C. L. S.	Henry R. Viets	H. R. V.
Thomas M. Spaulding	T. M. S.	John D. Wade	J. D. W.
Charles Worthen Spencer	C. W. S.	W. Randall Waterman	W. R. W.
Harris Elwood Starr	H. E. S.	Walter A. Wells	W. A. W.
Martha T. Stephenson	M. T. S.	Abdel Ross Wentz	A. R. W.
Nathaniel Wright Stephenson	N. W. S.	Thomas Jefferson Wertenbaker	T. J. W.
Wayne E. Stevens	W. E. S.	Allan Westcott	A. W.
George R. Stewart, Jr.	G. R. S., Jr.	George F. Whicher	G. F. W.
Anson Phelps Stokes	A. P. S.	W. L. Whittlesey	W. L. W—y.
James Sullivan	J. S—n.	James F. Willard	J. F. W.
Alfred H. Sweet	A. H. S.	Paul Wilstach	P. W.
William Warren Sweet	W. W. S.	John Garrett Winter	J. G. W.
Fletcher Harper Swift	F. H. S.	Thomas Woody	T. W.
Henry P. Talbot	H. P. T.	Ernest H. Wright	E. H. W.
Edwin P. Tanner	E. P. T.	Herbert Francis Wright	H. F. W.
Frank A. Taylor	F. A. T.	Walter L. Wright, Jr.	W. L. W—t., Jr.
David Y. Thomas	D. Y. T.	James Ingersoll Wyer	J. I. W.
Holland Thompson	H. T.	Edna Yost	E. Y.

DICTIONARY OF

AMERICAN BIOGRAPHY

Cushman — Eberle

CUSHMAN, CHARLOTTE SAUNDERS (July 23, 1816–Feb. 17, 1876), actress, was born in Boston. Her father, Elkanah Cushman, merchant, was a direct descendant of Robert Cushman [q.v.] of the Leyden congregation, agent of the Pilgrims in their negotiations with the Adventurers. Her mother was Mary Eliza Babbitt of Sturbridge (now Southbridge), Mass. The Babbitts were gifted musically. Forced by her father's death to earn a living, Charlotte studied for the operatic stage, and joined the company of Clara Fisher (Mrs. Maeder) in Boston and made her début on Apr. 8, 1835, at the Tremont Theatre, Boston, as Countess Almaviva in *The Marriage of Figaro*. She then secured an engagement to sing in New Orleans. Here her voice, a natural contralto, is said to have broken down by being forced by Mr. Maeder into the soprano register, but Mrs. Maeder denied this, saying Charlotte disliked the toil of vocal practise and was "stage struck." At any rate, in New Orleans she switched from the operatic to the dramatic stage, received some instruction from J. H. Barton, a visiting English actor, and on the night of his benefit, at the age of nineteen, appeared as Lady Macbeth. Encouraged by a local success she came North and secured an engagement at the Bowery Theatre, which promptly burned down, destroying her wardrobe. As she had brought her mother and young sister and brother from Boston, she went to Albany to find work while the theatre was being rebuilt, and there was described as "tall, thin and lanky." But she was socially as well as artistically successful, and prospered. Here she acted Romeo for the first time, and many other parts, including the eternal Belvidera in *Venice Preserved*. On May 8, 1837, under the management of James H. Hackett in

New York, she first appeared in one of her most famous impersonations, Meg Merrilies, in *Guy Mannering* (Winter, *The Wallet of Time*, I, 163). It was not at first greatly acclaimed. She joined the Park Company in New York in the fall of 1837, where she made a hit as Nancy Sykes in *Oliver Twist*, another of her famous rôles. From 1842 to 1844 she was stage manager of the Walnut Street Theatre, Philadelphia. Here George Vandenhoff acted with her and records (*Leaves from an Actor's Note-Book*, 1860, pp. 194 ff.) that she then displayed "a rude, strong, uncultivated talent; it was not till after she had seen and acted with Macready,—which she did the next season,—that she really brought artistic study and finish to her performances. . . . Her greatest part, fearfully natural, dreadfully intense, horribly real, was Nancy Sykes; it was too true; it was painful. . . ."

The engagement with Macready, at his request, not only brought her quick mind in contact with a person from whom she could learn, but filled her with an ambition to act in London. Accordingly she made the plunge—the second American actress to do so—and on Feb. 14, 1845, acted Bianca in *Fazio* at the Princess Theatre, London, in support of Edwin Forrest. Her success was decisive. She added, among other rôles, Lady Macbeth and Rosalind. In December 1845, with her sister Susan [q.v.] as Juliet, she acted Romeo. Sheridan Knowles likened her Romeo to Kean's Othello, and described the scene with the Friar as one "of topmost passion; not simulated passion—no such thing; real, palpably real . . . my blood ran hot and cold." She remained in England till 1849, and added during this time perhaps her greatest rôle, Queen Katherine. From 1849 to 1852 she toured America, and, with the prestige of her London success and her added skill, was proclaimed without dispute the leading actress of our stage. Then, and later, she acted not only female rôles, but those of Romeo, Wolsey, Hamlet, and Claude Melnotte. By 1852 she had achieved not only fame but a fortune, and announced her retirement from the stage. Till 1857 she lived in England, acting however more or less frequently. In 1857 she returned to America and appeared as Cardinal Wolsey at Burton's Theatre, New York, and in 1858 gave a series of "farewell performances." She then retired to Rome to live. Two years later she was back. Another year, and she gave a farewell performance in New Haven, and returned to Rome, where she remained for the greater part of the next decade, only returning to America in 1865 to give a series of performances which netted $8,267 for the United States Sanitary Commission. In 1870 she came back to America, and devoted the rest of her life chiefly to public readings of famous plays. She made a good many stage appearances, however, a famous engagement being that at Booth's Theatre in October and November 1874, when she acted Queen Katherine, Lady Macbeth, and Meg Merrilies, three of her greatest parts. This was actually her farewell, so far as New York was concerned, and after the concluding performance of *Macbeth* Richard Henry Stoddard read an ode, and William Cullen Bryant made a speech and presented her with a laurel crown. Her farewell appearance in her native Boston was on May 15, 1875, and her last on any stage at Easton, Pa., June 2, 1875. She died in Boston, Feb. 17, 1876. The immediate cause was pneumonia, but her constitution had long been undermined by cancer. She was buried in Mount Auburn Cemetery, Cambridge.

There can be little doubt that Charlotte Cushman was the most powerful actress America has produced. The contemporary records, over a long period of years, pay almost unvarying tribute to the vividness and moving quality of her effects. She was tall, strong-framed, deep-voiced, almost masculine in some respects, without feminine beauty certainly, and totally unable to conquer audiences by "sex appeal." She had to conquer by the keenness of her intellect in shaping a part, the depth of the feeling expressed, and the vividness and power of execution. That she did so conquer, over a period of forty years, is attested by numerous records. Among the most vivid is William Winter's description of her Queen Katherine (*Other Days*, pp. 155 ff.), when he actually shrank back to the rear of the box from the blaze of her eyes. "Whenever," he says, "the

occasion arrived for liberated power, passionate feeling, poetic significance, dramatic effect, she rose to that occasion and made it superb." Again he speaks of her Meg Merrilies, and says: "Her voice . . . had in it an unearthly music that made the nerves thrill and the brain tremble." As cool an Englishman as Henry Morley (*Journal of a London Playgoer*, 1866, p. 80) says: "Miss Cushman's melodramatic Meg Merrilies has quite as indisputably the attributes of genius about it as any piece of poetry or tragedy could have. Such is her power over the intention and feeling of the part that the mere words of it become a secondary matter." Dissenting voices were largely confined to those who (like Vandenhoff) objected to her male impersonations, chiefly on the ground that even she could not make them quite convincing. She never married. Her celibate life, her long suffering from cancer, and the energy with which she attacked the great melodramatic or tragic rôles in which she excelled, all conspired, probably, to bring about periods of depression when she felt she could act no more. This accounts for her frequent farewells and reappearances, for which she was much blamed. Like a good many other energetic and keen-minded spinsters of her New England heritage, she was somewhat masculine in appearance and dominating in personality, but deeply fond of children and full of kind deeds. The Cushman School in Boston was named after her, greatly to her delight. Her style of acting was formed, of course, on the great tradition of Garrick and Kean; it belonged to the age of huge auditoriums, rhetorical drama, and large, sweeping effects. She was not a pioneer in modern naturalism like Charles Matthews in England, and Jefferson in America. Nor did she seek to develop a native drama. She belonged to the royal line. She brought to our stage, however, not only striking genius, but strong, irreproachable character, a certain social prestige belonging to her ancestry, and a powerful stimulant to all of her sex who sought a wider chance for expression in the arts and in life. She was one of the great American women of the mid-nineteenth century, and so recognized in her own lifetime. The fact that she left behind a fortune of over half a million dollars did nothing in American eyes to lessen her prestige. Such another dominating figure on our stage is hardly likely to arise until the reign of naturalistic drama is ended.

[Emma Stebbins, *Charlotte Cushman: Her Letters and Memories of her Life* (1878); Wm. Winter, *Other Days* (1908) and *The Wallet of Time* (1909–13); H. P. Phelps, *Players of a Century* (1880); B. Matthews and L. Hutton, *Actors and Actresses of Gt. Brit. and the U. S.* (1886); H. W. Cushman, *A Hist. and Biog. Geneal. of the Cushmans* (1855).]   W.P.E.

CUSHMAN, GEORGE HEWITT (June 5, 1814–Aug. 3, 1876), miniature painter and engraver, was a native of Windham, Conn., the son of John H. Cushman and Pamela Webb. Early in his life he desired to be a soldier, but was prevented from entering West Point by a change in family fortunes, and turned his attention to cultivating his natural talent for drawing and painting. After studying drawing under Washington Allston (Baker, *post*), he learned line-engraving with Asaph Willard of Hartford, Conn. He also studied with Seth and John Cheney [*qq.v.*], the latter the distinguished line-engraver with whom he later shared a studio in Boston. In 1843 his name first appeared in the Philadelphia Directory, and for the next two decades he was a resident of that city, being described in the Directory as miniature painter and subsequently as portrait painter. Although regarded as one of the best miniature painters in America in his time, and second only to Malbone, Cushman preferred to follow his art without making any bid for fame, painting chiefly for his friends. He never exhibited his charming miniatures although he did sign his engravings, which were "executed with much taste and ability" (*Ibid.*). He engraved, after designs by F. O. C. Darley [*q.v.*], many of the plates for the thirty-four volume edition of Cooper's novels (1859–61) and for the Household Edition of Dickens (1861); plates for Frances S. Osgood's *Poems* (1850), and the portraits of Forrest in Alger's *Life of Edwin Forrest* (1877). He also engraved, *inter alia,* a portrait of Lord Byron, after Phillips, and "Young America in the Alps," after G. P. A. Healy. But though he made many plates for books, as an engraver he was concerned chiefly with notes for the state banks. The passage of the National Banking Act and the opening of the Bureau of Engraving and Printing at Washington caused him to retire from this work. In 1862 he removed to New York City, and resided there until his death, devoting most of his time after leaving Philadelphia to miniature painting. His miniatures have a delicacy and charm that would have won for him great fame, but he never would exhibit his work in public shows. His general reticence so far as his art was concerned is accounted for by one who knew him (French, *post,* p. 87) as having been due to a sense of modesty which "was so extreme that it became a defect." He underestimated his own genius, which was genuine, and which, pursued with ambition and determination, would have placed him at the head of American miniature painters of his period. Mrs. Lippincott (Grace Greenwood), quoted by French (*Ibid., p.* 86), remarked of Cushman's miniatures that they "were always remarkable for purity and simplicity of character as well as tone." His portrait of himself is reproduced in Anne Hollingsworth Wharton's *Heirlooms in Miniatures* (1898, p. 212). During the latter years of his life he suffered from a painful malady which curbed his ambition as well as his physical energy. He died at a water cure at Jersey City Heights, N. J., and was buried in South Laurel Hill Cemetery, Philadelphia. In 1849 he had married Susan Wetherill, granddaughter of Samuel Wetherill, the "Free Quaker" introduced into S. Weir Mitchell's romance, *Hugh Wynne,* and his funeral was held at the old Wetherill mansion, "Chalkley Hall," Frankford, Philadelphia. The only time his miniatures were publicly exhibited was in 1893 when in the Retrospective Exhibit at the Columbian Exposition in Chicago, a group of them was given the central position. Several examples of his engraving were shown in the exhibition of the works of one hundred notable American engravers, held in the New York Public Library in 1928.

[For many of the dates and particulars, Miss Ida Cushman, a daughter of the artist, has been the authority. See also H. W. French, *Art and Artists in Conn.* (1879), pp. 85–87; W. S. Baker, *Am. Engravers and Their Works* (1875); D. M. Stauffer, *Am. Engravers upon Copper and Steel* (1907). Baker and Stauffer give different birthplaces, and neither notes any work by Cushman.]   J.J.

CUSHMAN, JOSHUA (Apr. 11, 1761–Jan. 27, 1834), Congregational clergyman, congressman from Massachusetts and Maine, was the son of Abner and Mary (Tillson) Cushman of Halifax, Mass., and a descendant in the sixth generation of Robert Cushman [*q.v.*], agent of the Pilgrims in England. Nothing is known of his own early life until the time of his enlistment in the 9th Regiment of the Massachusetts line, Apr. 1, 1777. He saw service at Fort Stanwix and Saratoga, wintered at Valley Forge, and later accompanied Washington's army through the Jerseys to White Plains, N. Y. His honorable discharge came in March 1780, after he had served under Gen. Gates at Fishkill and near West Point. He entered Harvard in 1783, but, owing to his inability to meet the bills of his final quarter, he did not receive the degree of A.B. until 1791. Meanwhile he had studied theology under Rev. Ephraim Briggs, and was approved as a candidate for the ministry by the Worcester Association in January 1789. He was ordained religious teacher of Winslow in the District of Maine in 1795. The liberal covenant which Cushman drew up for the church at Winslow is notable for its lack of insistence upon the sacrament of the Lord's Supper. In 1814, by reason of reduced numbers and financial difficulties brought on by the war, his agreement with the town was terminated. It seems entirely probable that his liberal ideas had also caused some discontent. He represented Kennebec County in the Massachusetts Senate in 1810, and the Town of Winslow in the House in 1811 and 1812. He was elected to the national House of Representatives in the fall of 1818. Though an earnest advocate of the separation of Maine from Massachusetts, he, with three other representatives from Maine, hostile to slavery, voted against Clay's compromise, which admitted Missouri and Maine to the Union at the same time. Later, with them, he defended his action in a pamphlet (M. Kingsley and others, *An Address to the People of Maine,* 1820). After the organization of the state of Maine, he served in the Seventeenth and the Eighteenth Congresses as one of its representatives. He was a state senator in 1828, and representative in 1833. As the senior member of the House he presided over its organization early in January 1834. Later in the same month he died at Augusta, where he lies buried in the state tomb. His sermons show him to have been devout and very liberal in his religious views. A clear thinker and an accomplished speaker, he was much in demand as an orator on public occasions; his printed and manuscript orations are good examples of the grandiloquent oratory of the times. In politics he was a supporter of Jefferson, and later of Jackson. His sympathies with struggling debtors, numerous in his own state, led him to speak in Congress in March 1822 in favor of the Bankrupt Bill. He was a strong advocate of Revolutionary pensions, the benefits of which he himself shared in the last years of his life. He married Lucy, the daughter of Peter and Aurah (Tufts) Jones of Medford, Mass., Sept. 13, 1802.

[H. W. Cushman, *A Hist. and Biog. Geneal. of the Cushmans* (1855), pp. 184–99. *Centennial Hist. of Waterville* (1902), pp. 556–61; the Cushman MSS. in the possession of Mr. F. H. Cushman of Winslow. The date of Cushman's birth is taken from the manuscript Harvard College Faculty Records, V, 124. A brief list of his printed sermons and orations is in Jos. Williamson, *A Bibliography of the State of Me.* (2 vols., 1896), I, 336.]　　　　　　　　R. E. M.

CUSHMAN, PAULINE (June 10, 1835–Dec. 2, 1893), Union spy, actress, the daughter of a Spanish political refugee and a Frenchwoman, was born in New Orleans. In time her father took his large family to Grand Rapids, Mich., where he became a trader. The education of his only daughter was necessarily scanty but it gave her the hardiness to travel to New York in her eighteenth year to earn her own living. She was recruited there by the manager of the New Orleans *Varieties* for his show and soon after her arrival in the South was married to Charles Dickinson, another stage performer. Dickinson enlisted as a musician in the Northern army during the Civil War, and died in the winter of 1862 of dysentery. In March of the following year, she was playing in *The Seven Sisters* at Wood's Theatre in Louisville. At a certain point in the performance she was called on to drink a toast and was urged by certain Southern sympathizers to toast the Southern cause. Making this public avowal of sympathy on the advice of the provost-marshal, she was dismissed from the theatre. She then took an oath of allegiance to the Federal government and was commissioned as secret agent. A supposed rebel, she was subsequently expelled from Nashville, with instructions to penetrate as far South as possible, and to collect all the military information she could, but under no condition to carry notes or plans. Unfortunately, her opportunities to obtain military maps were so great that she violated her instructions. Her uneasy knowledge of the possession of these materials caused her to make an incriminating effort to escape when detained not far from Bragg's headquarters at Tullahoma, Tenn. The papers being discovered, she was tried by a military court and sentenced to be hanged in ten days. Anxiety over her position, added to the strain of her hard journeys, brought on a temporary physical collapse. Removed from the military jail to more comfortable quarters at Shelbyville, Tenn., she was left behind when the Confederates hastily retreated from that place in June 1863. She was able to give the advancing army of Rosecrans much valuable information, but had become so well-known that further spying was impossible.

Sent North, she was treated with great acclaim, fêted as "the spy of the Cumberland," and commended by Lincoln for her services. She returned to the stage, and traveled far and wide, lecturing in a Federal uniform. Her last years were not happy. She was married in 1872 to August Fichtner, who died before many years. Her unhappy marriage to Jerry Fryer in 1879 ended in separation. Her children all died in early childhood, and as she grew older her efforts to make a living by lecturing and sewing were ineffectual. She committed suicide in San Francisco, where the G. A. R., in acknowledgment of her services, gave her a semi-military funeral and burial in their plot.

[F. L. Sarmiento, *Life of Pauline Cushman* (1865), which has some marks of the work of a press-agent, was evidently copied by Frank Moore, *Women of the War* (1866). The War Dept. records, however, and those in the Pension Office, filed as W. C. 362644, bear out the story. See also *San Francisco Call,* Dec. 3, 4,

CUSHMAN, ROBERT (*c.* 1579–1625), one of the organizers of the Pilgrim emigration to America, was born at Canterbury. He married in England, where in 1608 his son Thomas was born, went to Holland about 1609, and at once joined the Pilgrim church at Leyden. He seems to have had some means for, though he earned his living as a wool-comber, he bought two houses there. His wife, Sarah, died in 1616 and he married in June 1617, Mary, widow of Thomas Singleton, herself from Sandwich. In 1617 he went to England with John Carver to seek a patent for the prospective emigrants, and was again in England with Elder Brewster when the first patent was obtained. He and Carver made the financial arrangements with the English merchants which were accepted by the Pilgrims at Leyden in 1620, and organized the group which sailed direct from England on the *Mayflower.* Probably he was responsible for the proposed alterations in the agreement which were rejected by the Pilgrims at Southampton. The resultant quarrel is perhaps the real explanation of Cushman's failure to emigrate to America. Sailing as commander of the *Speedwell,* he and his family remained ashore after that ship put back, though he served as agent of the Pilgrims in England for the rest of his life. On the return of the *Mayflower* in the summer of 1621, Cushman published a pamphlet entitled, *Of the State of the Colony* [of New Plymouth] *and the need of the Public Spirit in the Colonists.* He was instrumental in sending out the *Fortune* with a second contingent of colonists in July 1621, sailing on it himself with his only son, Thomas. He brought with him the agreement with the merchants which the Pilgrims had rejected at Southampton and to which they now consented, an act which they ever after regretted with all their hearts. At Plymouth, though not a minister, he delivered a sermon which was published in London in 1622, the first American religious discourse published anywhere. Leaving his son behind with Bradford, he returned to England on the *Fortune,* Dec. 13, having been in this country only three weeks. He never returned. In 1622 he published a tract entitled, *Reasons and Considerations Touching the Lawfulness of Removing out of England into the Parts of America.* In 1623, he obtained with Edward Winslow a grant of land on Cape Ann, which the Pilgrims long used as a fishing station and which was of great consequence in establishing the economic independence of Plymouth. Cushman died in England in 1625. His son lived his life at Plymouth, dying there in 1691.

[The chief authority is Wm. Bradford, *Hist. of Plimmoth Plantation* (2 vols., 1912). See also H. M. and M. Dexter, *England and Holland of the Pilgrims* (1905); W. H. Burgess, *The Pastor of the Pilgrims: A Biog. of John Robinson* (1920); R. G. Usher, *The Pilgrims and their Hist.* (1918); and H. W. Cushman, *A Hist. and Biog. Genealogy of the Cushmans* (1855). Robert Cushman's tracts are reprinted in Alexander Young, *Chronicles of the Pilgrim Fathers* (1841), and in various facsimile editions.]   R. G. U.

CUSHMAN, SUSAN WEBB (Mar. 17, 1822–May 10, 1859), actress, was born in Boston, the daughter of Elkanah Cushman and Mary Eliza Babbitt, and a younger sister of Charlotte Cushman [*q.v.*]. She remained a younger sister all her professional life, under the protection, and the shadow, of the maternal but mighty Charlotte. She and her mother accompanied the elder sister to New York and Albany in 1836, when Charlotte was getting her feet on the professional ladder, and a year later she made her own début as Laura in Epes Sargent's play, *The Genoese.* She was then only fifteen, but in those days the child actor was more admired than at present and her success was considerable. It is recorded (H. W. Cushman, *A Historical and Biographical Genealogy of the Cushmans,* 1855, p. 511), that she was married, Mar. 14, 1836, to Nelson M. Meriman, in Boston, and that she was left destitute by him, with an infant, and took up acting at her sister's advice, as a means of livelihood. Later she acted Grace Harkaway to Charlotte's Lady Gay Spanker, both in New York and Philadelphia, probably in 1841 or 1842, was acclaimed in *Satan in Paris,* and appeared as Desdemona to the Othello of George Vandenhoff, a man of culture and not apparently much given to over-heated eulogies. He later wrote an autobiographical book, called *Leaves from an Actor's Note-Book,* which contains many criticisms of elder players, valuable to-day for their evident cool-headedness and penetration. Among others is one of Susan Cushman, as well as many of her greater sister. In 1842 Charlotte was stage manager of the Walnut Street Theatre, Philadelphia, and Susan was also a member of the company. Vandenhoff gave six performances with them, receiving $180 as his share for the six nights. "Susan," he wrote, "was a pretty creature, but had not a spark of Charlotte's genius; she pleased 'the fellows,' however, and was the best walking-lady on the American stage. (Walking-ladies, madam, are not pedestrians, necessarily; it is the English term for what they call on the French stage, *ingénues;* young ladies of no particular strength of character, whose business is to look pretty, to dress prettily, and to speak prettily; charmingly innocent, and deliciously insipid.)"

In 1845, Charlotte went to England to seek acclaim there, hoping thus to better her position at home, and took Susan with her. She had already played Romeo in America, and now studied the play again with Susan as Juliet, and the two sisters presented this tragedy to London, at the Haymarket, Dec. 30, 1845. They insisted on using the original version, not the theatre prompt copy, and for so doing the vexed company called them "American Indians." The play ran eighty nights in London, and was then taken on a tour of England, with success. Miss Stebbins says that Charlotte chose this play, to effect her sister's début, so that her sister could have the right support, but the statement is a trifle naïve. Charlotte was a good showman, and she also enjoyed assuming masculine rôles. In the numerous reviews of this production, most of the comment is concerned with Charlotte's Romeo, but several critics spoke pleasantly of "the grace and delicacy" of Susan's acting, and Sheridan Knowles, amid his raptures over Charlotte's Romeo, found breath to speak of the first scene as "admirably personated by her beautiful sister." The sisters also played *Twelfth Night* together. A further record of Susan's theatrical career in England is found in the *Autobiography* of Anna Cora Mowatt (pp. 273 ff.). In 1848 Mrs. Mowatt was to appear in London in *The Lady of Lyons,* and Susan Cushman was engaged for Helen. She did not appear at the first rehearsal, and the manager was furious. He persuaded another actress to try the rôle, but as the next rehearsal was about to begin, in walked Susan. It was now her turn to be furious. "An angry scene ensued," wrote Mrs. Mowatt, "such as I never before, and I rejoice to say never after, witnessed in a theatre." But Susan lost in the encounter, and was forced to leave the house. Her sister would have surely remained. Later that same year, Susan married Dr. James Sheridan Muspratt, "a distinguished chemist and author" of Liverpool, and retired from the stage. She died in Liverpool, May 10, 1859.

[Emma Stebbins, *Charlotte Cushman: Her Letters and Memories of her Life* (1878); Geo. Vandenhoff, *Leaves from an Actor's Note-Book* (1860); Anna Cora Mowatt, *Autobiography of an Actress* (1859).]

W. P. E.

CUSHNY, ARTHUR ROBERTSON (Mar. 6, 1866–Feb. 25, 1926), physician, the son of the Rev. John Cushny of Speymouth, Scotland, by his wife, Catherine Ogilvie Brown, was born at Fochabers (Morayshire). After attending a rural school there he went to the University of Aberdeen, where he received the degree of M.A.

in 1886. He then took up the study of medicine at Marischal College, Aberdeen, from which he graduated in 1889 with highest honors, taking the degrees of M.B. and C.M., and M.D. in 1892. While Cushny was at Aberdeen, J. T. Cash, the physiologist, aroused his interest in the physiological action of drugs, and in order to enlarge his experience in this field, he went to study on the Continent, spending a year in the laboratory of Oswald Schmiedeberg at Strassburg, and several months with Hugo Kronecker, the physiologist of Berne, from whom he learned the elements of physiological technique. He remained abroad until 1893 when, at the instigation of Prof. J. J. Abel, he accepted the chair of pharmacology which the latter had just resigned at the University of Michigan. Though only twenty-seven years of age, he rapidly made a place for himself at Michigan. In addition to bearing heavy responsibilities as a teacher, he was active in research and also found time in 1899 to prepare his *Text-Book of Pharmacology and Therapeutics,* a well-written work which has held the field in English almost without a rival for thirty years, a posthumous edition (the ninth) having been brought out in 1928.

Cushny's contributions to pharmacology were outstanding. He carried out, with modern technique, the first experimental analysis of the action of digitalis on warm-blooded animals, and was thus able to explain its effects and to increase considerably the therapeutic uses of this valuable drug. His first paper appeared in 1897 (*Journal of Experimental Medicine*), and his later observations were summarized in 1925 in a monograph, *The Action and Uses in Medicine of Digitalis and Its Allies.* Cushny was the first to recognize the similarity between clinical and experimental auricular fibrillation. His interest in the physiological action of optical isomers, which extended over many years, also culminated in a monograph, which was published posthumously, *The Biological Relation of Optically Isometric Substances* (1926). He took up the subject of the mechanism of kidney secretion about 1900, and between 1901 and 1904 contributed to it a series of three important papers published in the *Journal of Physiology.* In 1917 he advanced what was termed the "modern theory" of kidney-secretion in a separate monograph, *The Secretion of Urine,* a second edition of which prepared by himself was brought out a few months after his death. In this work he put aside the theories which assigned to the kidneys special vital activities inexplicable in physical terms, and added support to the view, now widely accepted, that the chief structures of the kidney, the glomeruli, are in reality simple filters, and that substances useful to the body are re-absorbed during the passage of the filtrate through the urinary tubules, the waste products being thus allowed to escape.

Cushney stayed at Ann Arbor until 1905, when he accepted the chair of pharmacology at University College, London. There he remained until 1918 when he received a call from Edinburgh to succeed Sir Thomas Fraser. To each of the three chairs which he occupied he brought prestige and dignity. On his removal to Scotland he secured an historic manor house near Edinburgh, the "Dumbiedykes" of the *Heart of Midlothian,* where he was able to withdraw somewhat from public life and to entertain the many students and physicians which an international reputation and a kindly disposition had brought to him in increasing numbers. He was an ardent horticulturist, and his pleasure in his garden grew with advancing years. He died suddenly of an apoplectic stroke at his home. In 1896 he had married Sarah Firbank, an Englishwoman whom he had met abroad.

[H. H. Dale, in *Proc. Royal Soc. of London* (1926), 100B, pp. xix–xxvii; *The Times* (London), Feb. 26, 1926; *Nature,* 1926, pp. 117, 387; *Lancet* (London), 1926, I, 519–20; *Brit. Med. Jour.,* 1926, I, 455–57; *Glasgow Herald,* Feb. 26, 1926; *Edinburgh Weekly Scotsman,* Mar. 6, 1926; private information.]

J.F.F.

CUSTER, GEORGE ARMSTRONG (Dec. 5, 1839–June 25, 1876), soldier, was born in New Rumley, Harrison County, Ohio, the son of Emmanuel H. and Maria (Ward) Custer. His paternal great-grandfather was a Hessian officer named Küster, who after surrendering with Burgoyne settled in Pennsylvania, later moving to Maryland. His father was a farmer and blacksmith. Both parents are praised by Custer, in a letter written in after years, as noble, devoted, and self-sacrificing. The boy attended the local schools until he was about ten, and after that until his seventeenth year divided his time between his parents' home and that of his married half-sister, Lydia Reed, at Monroe, Mich. His ambition from early childhood was to be a soldier. From New Rumley, in the summer of 1857, appointed by the local representative in Congress, he went to West Point. Though a rapid reader, with a quick apprehension and good memory, he was a negligent student; he was, moreover, mischievous and given to pranks—a "big jolly boy," as Gen. Morris Schaff characterized him—and he graduated (June 24, 1861) at the foot of a class of thirty-four. A few days later, on the charge of failing, while officer of the guard, to stop a fist-fight between two cadets, he was court-martialed and found guilty. At Washington, however, the proceedings were pigeon-holed, and he was ordered to report for duty.

As a second lieutenant assigned to the 2nd Cavalry, he reached Bull Run on the morning of the battle. Afterward he served in the defense movements about Washington until October, when he was sent home on sick leave. Returning in February 1862, he was transferred to the 5th Cavalry. He came to the notice of McClellan in the Peninsular campaign, and on June 5 was appointed one of his aides, with the rank of captain of volunteers, but with McClellan's retirement his rank lapsed to that of first lieutenant of the regular army, to which he had been promoted on July 17. Pleasanton, head of Hooker's newly formed Cavalry Corps, saw in him the makings of a cavalry leader, and for gallant conduct at Aldie, June 16, 1863, recommended him for a brigadier-generalship and organized for him a brigade of Michigan regiments. Appointed on June 29, Custer served with distinction through the Gettysburg and Virginia campaigns. Conspicuous in figure and attire and noted for the energy and dash of his operations and their almost unvarying success, he became by the end of the year one of the most celebrated commanders at the front. During the winter he returned to Monroe, where on Feb. 9, 1864, he married his boyhood sweetheart, Elizabeth, the daughter of Judge Daniel S. Bacon. He found favor with Sheridan on the opening of the campaigns of 1864 and became in time his most trusted lieutenant. On May 8 he was made a captain in the regular service; the fight at Yellow Tavern, May 11, brought him the brevet of lieutenant-colonel, and Winchester, Sept. 19, that of colonel. The Shenandoah campaign added greatly to his laurels. On Oct. 2 he was placed at the head of the 3rd Division of the Cavalry Corps, and on Oct. 19 was brevetted major-general of volunteers. But it was in the pursuit of Lee's army from Richmond in April 1865 that he won his greatest glory. His division held the van, and day and night, with little pause for rest or food, it kept relentlessly at its task, striking here and there, crumpling up the lines of defense and capturing prisoners, wagons, and guns until on the morning of Apr. 9 it threw itself across Gordon's front and made further resistance useless. It was to Custer that the Confederate flag of truce, a crash towel, was brought, and it was to him that it afterward came as a present from Sheridan, along with the present to his wife of the small table on which Grant had written the terms of surrender. "I know of no one," wrote Sheridan, "whose efforts have contributed more to this happy result than those of Custer." Two more honorary promotions were to come to Custer—brevets of brigadier-general and of major-general of the regular army, both dated back to Mar. 13. On Apr. 15 he was made a major-general of volunteers.

After the Grand Review he was sent to the Southwest, where Sheridan had preceded him, and on Feb. 1, 1866, he was mustered out of the volunteer service. The disbandment of the volunteer army stripped him of his honorary rank and left him a mere captain in the 5th Cavalry. He applied for a year's leave of absence and with a strong recommendation from Grant offered his services to the Mexican Army of Liberation. President Johnson, however, refused the request for a leave and instead ordered him to accompany the presidential party in its famous "swing around the circle." On July 28 the organization of the 7th Cavalry was authorized, and Custer was assigned to it with the rank of lieutenant-colonel. Early in the following year he joined his regiment at Fort Riley, Kan., and as its first colonel never joined it, and its second did not assume command until after the battle of the Little Big Horn, he remained its active commander until his death. He took an active part in the muddled Indian campaign of 1867 under Hancock and for its failure was made a scapegoat. On charges of deliberate absence from duty he was court-martialed and sentenced to a year's suspension from the army. Sheridan, who succeeded Hancock, recalled Custer to his regiment in the fall of 1868, and on Nov. 27 he won a brilliant victory over Black Kettle's band of Cheyennes, in the battle of the Washita. After two years more of campaigning on the plains the regiment was broken up and scattered at various garrison points, but early in 1873 was reunited at Fort Rice, in the present North Dakota. He took part in Stanley's Yellowstone expedition of that year and on its return was assigned to the command of the newly established Fort Abraham Lincoln, across the river from Bismarck. In the following summer on orders from the War Department, he led through the Black Hills an exploring expedition of 1,200 men—an event which resulted in the discovery of gold and contributed in some measure to the Sioux War a year and a half later.

He was to have commanded the expedition ordered to set out early in 1876 to cooperate with the columns of Crook and Gibbon in rounding up the hostile Sioux and Cheyennes. In the middle of March, however, he was summonsed to Washington to testify before a Congressional committee regarding frauds in the Indian service. His testimony, unfavorable to Belknap, the former secretary of war, gave great offense to President Grant, who not only deprived him of his command, substituting Terry, the district commander, but ordered that he should not even be permitted to accompany the expedition. A storm of popular disapproval, joined with the earnest plea of Terry, caused Grant to relent so far as to restore Custer to the command of his regiment. Leaving the Missouri on May 17, the expedition under Terry reached the Powder on June 7, and later moved on to the mouth of the Rosebud. At noon of June 22, Custer and his regiment, a total force of about 655 men, set out directly for the Little Big Horn, while Terry, with Gibbon, who had joined him from the west, started up the Yellowstone to reach the field by way of the Big Horn. Custer arrived in the vicinity of the village on the 25th, intending to attack early the following morning. Learning, however, that his presence had been discovered, he decided on an immediate attack. Shortly after noon he divided his force into three battalions, sending Benteen to the left, Reno straight ahead across the river into the valley and taking his own five troops on a detour to the right in order to strike the village further down stream. An overwhelming force, variously reckoned at from 2,500 to 4,000 well-armed warriors, was encountered. Reno was soon driven in flight from the valley, taking refuge on the bluffs on the north of the river, where shortly afterward he was joined by Benteen and where a valiant defense was maintained until the departure of the Indians on the afternoon of the 26th. Custer, on reaching the slope of what has since been known as Custer Hill, was surrounded and with every one of his immediate command was killed. Lieut. Bradley, scouting in advance of Terry and Gibbon on the morning of the 27th, found the bodies, most of them stripped and scalped and many otherwise mutilated. The body of Custer, pierced by a bullet in the left temple and in the left side, though stripped, was unmutilated.

The controversy that began immediately thereafter has continued intermittently ever since, with no signs that it will ever be ended. Custer has been charged with disobedience of orders, with having made his attack before the time agreed upon, with a reckless determination to risk the lives of his command in a vain effort to regain the prestige alleged to have been lost through Grant's disfavor and with much else. His defenders have replied that the only orders known to exist gave him full discretion, that there is no evidence of an agreement as to the time of attack, that if his main motive were personal glory he must have known that recklessness was the one thing sure to defeat his aim, and that had his subordinate, Reno, borne a more courageous part the result might have been different. Sherman, in his official report for the year, admitted that the "campaign had been planned on wrong premises" and that until Custer's death there was nothing to indicate that any detachment would encounter more than 500 or 800 Indians. The cause of Custer's defeat was the dispatch of a force inferior in armament and vastly inferior in numbers to the force it encountered.

Custer was tall, slender, and lithe, with a strong physique and an exceptional capacity for endurance. He had blue eyes, and his hair (which he wore long until his last campaign) and mustache were of a golden tint. His dress in the early days of the Civil War had been slouchy and unkempt; but on attaining the rank of general he donned a conspicuous costume of olive-gray corduroy or velveteen, lavishly tinseled with gold braid and set off with a cavalier hat and a long scarlet necktie. On the plains he usually wore buckskin. His manner on the field was brusque and aggressive and his voice sharp and at times rasping; but in hours of relaxation he was genial and companionable. Lawrence Barrett, the actor, who knew him intimately, says that his voice was "earnest, soft, tender and appealing" and that his personality was one of rare charm. In personal habits he was abstemious; except in the peace-pipe ceremony with Indians he did not use tobacco, and there is no evidence, despite malicious stories to the contrary, that save for a brief period during the Civil War he ever drank liquor. He became, in his later days, an avid student, particularly of military science and of belles-lettres, and he spent much of his leisure time in writing. In 1874 he published in book form his fascinating narrative, *My Life on the Plains* (later re-titled *Wild Life on the Plains*), the text of which had appeared serially in the *Galaxy*. His "War Memoirs"—recollections of the Civil War to the time of the battle of Williamsburg—were published in the *Galaxy* in 1876, after his death. He had a high sense of integrity, and he strove earnestly, with results disastrous to himself, to check the then prevalent corruption in the Indian Bureau. His character was positive, and though he won devoted friends he made vindictive enemies, particularly in the army. He may well be likened, in his last days, to the central figure in a Greek tragedy, hemmed in by a closing net of adverse circumstances, while his every movement to extricate himself served only to hasten the inevitable end.

[See G. W. Cullum, *Biog. Reg.* (3rd ed., 1891); Frederick Whittaker, *A Complete Life of Gen. Geo. A. Custer* (1876); F. S. Dellenbaugh, *Geo. Armstrong Custer* (1917); Elizabeth Bacon Custer, *The Boy General* (1901), ed. by Mary E. Burt. The literature of the Little Big Horn battle is voluminous. Especially noteworthy contributions are: E. S. Godfrey, "Custer's Last Battle," *Century Mag.*, Jan. 1892; J. M. Hanson, *The Conquest of the Missouri* (1909); Jas. McLaughlin, *My Friend the Indian* (1910); W. A. Graham, *The Story of the Little Big Horn* (1926); C. F. Bates and Fairfax Downey, *Fifty Years After the Little Big Horn Battle* (pamph., 1926); Edward J. McClernand, "The Indian and the Buffalo in Montana," *Cavalry Jour.*, Jan. 1927; and the appendices to Cyrus Townsend Brady, *Indian Fights and Fighters* (1904) and *Northwestern Fights and Fighters* (1907). See also the impressionistic biography, *Custer, the Last of the Cavaliers* (1928), by Frazier Hunt.]   W.J.G.

CUSTIS, GEORGE WASHINGTON PARKE (Apr. 30, 1781–Oct. 10, 1857), playwright, inherited the traditions of a Southern landholder through his father, John Parke Custis, the stepson of George Washington, and also through his mother Eleanor Calvert, a descendant of Lord Baltimore. Owing to the early death of his father, he grew up under the charge of Washington at Mount Vernon, Va., where he lived until the death of Mrs. Washington, when he made his home at Arlington, Va. After a time spent at Princeton College, he was commissioned in 1799 a cornet of horse in the United States army, and became aide-de-camp to Gen. Charles C. Pinckney, with the rank of colonel. He was not, however, called into active service at this time. In 1804 he married Mary Lee Fitzhugh, and went to live upon his large estate. His daughter, Mary Custis, married Robert E. Lee, thus linking the two great generals in a family connection. In 1803 he inaugurated an annual convention for the promotion of agriculture and especially for the encouragement of the wool industry. During the War of 1812 he served as a volunteer in the defense of the city of Washington. When Lafayette visited the United States in 1824, Custis naturally took an active part in his welcome and was prompted to write his entertaining "Conversations with Lafayette," published in the *Alexandria Gazette*. In 1826 he began in the *United States Gazette* his recollections of Washington, which were continued in the *National Intelligencer,* and were published in 1860. An incident in which Washington was the chief actor became the central motive of Custis's first play, *The Indian Prophecy,* performed at the Chestnut Street Theatre, Philadelphia, July 4, 1827, and published in 1828. His most successful play, *Pocahontas, or the Settlers of Virginia,* produced at the Walnut Street Theatre, Philadelphia, Jan. 16, 1830, and published in the same year, showed his sense of the dramatic, as he violated chronology in the career of Pocahontas in order to make her salvation of Capt. John Smith the climax of the drama. His other plays are known only by contemporary description, for, with the instinct of a Southern gentleman, he published little. *The Railroad,* a "national drama," which was performed at the Walnut Street Theatre, Philadelphia, May 16, 1830, seems to have brought on the stage for the first time a real "locomotive steam carriage." Custis's attitude toward the stage is revealed in a letter to his wife, in which he says, "I had promised the poor rogues of actors, a play for the 12th Sept., the anniversary of the battle of North Point; but finding myself not in the vein, I wrote them to defer it." *North Point,* or *Baltimore Defended,* was, however, finished in nine hours and produced Sept. 12, 1833, in Baltimore (*Recollections,* p. 59). Custis's *Eighth of January* was played Jan. 8, 1834, at the Park Theatre, New York, and there are unconfirmed statements that he wrote another play, *The Pawnee Chief.* He was of medium height, of a fair and somewhat florid complexion, and of great personal charm. He died at Arlington, the last male representative of his family.

[The best source of information concerning Custis is the memoir by his daughter, Mary Custis Lee, published in the *Recollections and Private Memoirs of Washington by his Adopted Son* (1860). For accounts and criticisms of the plays, see Chas. Durang, "Hist. of the Phila. Stage," in the Phila. *Sunday Dispatch,* ser. 2, beginning June 29, 1856, chs. LI and LIII; J. N. Ireland, *Records of the N. Y. Stage* (1866–67), I, 644 and II, 77; A. H. Quinn, *Hist. of the Am. Drama from the Beginning to the Civil War* (1923), pp. 270–73.]

A. H. Q.

CUTBUSH, JAMES (1788–Dec. 15, 1823), chemist, was the son of Edward Cutbush, an English stonecutter in Philadelphia, and his wife Anne Marriat; and younger brother of Edward, a naval surgeon, and of William, a West Point graduate who became a prominent engineer. Where and how he obtained his education is a matter of conjecture. His career is traced chiefly through his publications. In his twentieth year, he wrote a series of fifteen articles which appeared in the Philadelphia *Aurora* (beginning in July 1808), on the "Application of Chemistry to Arts and Manufactures." His purpose was to educate the public in the application of science to practical affairs and to arouse interest in science in general. There is a boyish ardor in his appeal to "you enlightened citizens, men of science and improvement, artists and manufacturers" to seize the auspicious time to develop natural resources by the aid of arts and sciences. In the same year (1808) he published a little volume entitled *A*

Useful Cabinet; and an article in the Philadelphia *Medical Museum* on mercury fulminate. To the same journal he contributed in 1809 an article describing a method of purifying ether and the production of ethylene; also an article (1811) on the value of the hop to brewers. To the *Freemason's Magazine* he contributed (1811) an article on "Subjects and Importance of Chemistry" and a short historical sketch of the science. In this same year was founded the Columbian Chemical Society of which he was the first president. Cutbush was also vice-president of the Linnean Society and a member of the Society for the Promotion of a Rational System of Education, before which in 1811 he delivered an oration advocating the introduction of instruction in the physical sciences in schools (*An Oration on Education,* published in 1812). For a time he gave popular lectures on chemistry, and was professor of chemistry, mineralogy and natural philosophy in "St. John's College" of Philadelphia. In 1813 he published a *Philosophy of Experimental Chemistry* in two volumes, one of the first chemical textbooks published by a native American. In 1814 he was appointed assistant apothecary-general of the United States army. In 1820 he became chief medical officer at West Point, and then acting professor of chemistry and mineralogy. He continued to contribute to various journals: to the *American Journal of Science,* among others, articles on the improvement of the Voltaic electrical lamp (1820) and on the composition and properties of Greek fire (1823) and Chinese fire (1824). In 1821 he published *A Synopsis of Chemistry* and after his death his widow published *A System of Pyrotechny* (1825) in two volumes, a notable contribution based on careful experimental study. He died at the early age of thirty-five and was buried at West Point.

[All that has been ascertained about this pioneer in chemical science is contained in *James Cutbush: an American Chemist* (1919), by Dr. Edgar F. Smith, whose death prevented the revision of this article by his own hand.—Editor.]

E. F. S.

CUTLER, CARROLL (Jan. 31, 1829–Jan. 24, 1894), Congregational clergyman, college president, was born in Windham, N. H., the son of Calvin and Rhoda Bartlett (Little) Cutler. As his father had a large family to rear on the meager salary of a rural Presbyterian clergyman, Carroll was obliged to earn his education. He worked on a farm and taught district school, attended Phillips Andover Academy, and graduated from Yale College in 1854. A year of teaching at Bloomfield, N. J., provided him with sufficient money to carry him through the following year at Union Theological Seminary in New York; he continued his reading of divinity while a tutor at Yale 1856–58, and in January of 1858 was licensed to preach by the Congregational West Association of New Haven. Having attained his professional ambition, he returned to Bloomfield, N. J., to be married on Aug. 10 of that year to Frances, daughter of the Rev. Joseph S. Gallagher, who was secretary and treasurer of Union Seminary. The next year he spent in travel and study abroad, especially in Germany, and in the spring of 1860 he was appointed professor of intellectual philosophy and rhetoric in Western Reserve College at Hudson, Ohio. The college was then a representative "freshwater" institution, nourished chiefly on hopes for the future, but its half-dozen scrimped professors included several men of uncommon ability. Cutler soon proved to be one of them, making his mark as a teacher rather than as an administrator or a productive scholar. For four months of 1862 he was a tall, stalwart first lieutenant of Company B of the 85th Ohio Volunteer Infantry, engaged in escorting prisoners to Vicksburg for exchange. In 1871 he assumed the presidency of the college after assuring himself that his new duties need not interfere with his work in the classroom. In 1876 he published *A History of Western Reserve College during its First Half Century 1826–76.* Cutler's learning, his good sense, his command of English style, and his moral fervor are pleasantly revealed in *The Beginnings of Ethics* (1889), which, appearing in the year before James's *Principles of Psychology,* belongs to the era when philosophy, in American colleges, was still dominated by theology. In 1882 Western Reserve College was raised to comparative affluence by endowments made by Amasa Stone and others, was removed from Hudson to Cleveland, and changed its name to Adelbert College of Western Reserve University. Cutler resigned the presidency in 1886, retaining his professorship, but continued to occupy the office until 1888, when his successor was installed. He soon found himself hopelessly at variance with the new president and in 1889 severed all connection with the college. His last years were spent in the South as a teacher in two negro schools, Biddle University at Charlotte, N. C., and Talladega College at Talladega, Ala. He taught until within a week of his death.

[*Records and Statistics of the Academic Class of '54, Yale Univ., 1854–96* (1896); *Obit. Record Grads. Yale Univ.,* 1894; *One Hundred Years of Western Reserve* (Hudson, Ohio, 1926).]   G.H.G.

CUTLER, JAMES GOOLD (Apr. 24, 1848– Apr. 21, 1927), architect, inventor, banker, son of John Nathan and Mary E. (Goold) Cutler, of English-Dutch descent, was born in Albany, N. Y., where his father and grandfather had a carriage manufactory. He attended the local city schools and completed his education in Albany Academy. Upon graduation he began work in his grandfather's carriage factory but soon took up the study of architecture with a local firm of architects in Albany. On Sept. 27, 1871, he married Anna K. Abbey of Kingston, N. Y. The next year he and his young bride settled in Rochester, N. Y., where he went to work as a draftsman for a local architect. His progress was rapid and in a few years he became a partner of his first employer. He continued to practise his profession for a total of twenty-two years, his architectural work including residences, office and bank buildings, and factories. During this time he devised and patented the familiar mail chutes observed in modern office buildings and extending from the highest to the first floor. His invention was known as a "letter box connection," for which Patent Number 284,951 was granted him on Sept. 11, 1883. The year after he obtained his patent, Cutler, with his brother J. Warren Cutler, formed the Cutler Manufacturing Company, to build and install letter-chutes. The business grew at a prodigious rate and its products were sold throughout the world. In 1908 the company built its own factory and continued, with Cutler as president, until 1915 when the firm was reorganized and he resigned the presidency. He was interested in municipal and civic affairs and as early as 1895 was appointed a member of the White Charter Commission of New York State to draft a uniform charter for second-class cities. He was a presidential elector in 1896 and in 1916. In 1897 he served as consulting architect for the New York state capitol, in 1900 he was commissioner of public safety for Rochester, and in 1903 he was elected mayor, being reëlected two years later. For more than thirty years prior to his death he was prominently connected with several banks in Rochester. He was one of the first presidents of the Rochester Chamber of Commerce, and a member of the Rochester City Planning Advisory Board from the time of its organization until his resignation two years before his death. He was an honorary member of the American Institute of Architects and served three terms as president of the Western New York State Association of Architects. He was a trustee of the University of Rochester and of the Municipal Art Commission and a member of many clubs.

[Direct correspondence with Rochester Chamber of Commerce; Patent Office records; *Who's Who in America,* 1926–27; *Democrat and Chronicle* (Rochester), Apr. 22, 1927; N. S. Cutler, *Cutler Memorial and Geneal. Hist.* (1889).]   C.W.M.

CUTLER, LIZZIE PETIT (1831–Jan. 16, 1902), author, was born in Milton and died in Richmond, Va. Her father's people were "respectable farmers," and her mother was descended from distinguished Anglo-French Virginia landowners. Left motherless as an infant, she was entrusted first to an aunt, a widow much engrossed in social affairs, and later to a grand-aunt, who soon removed from her estate near Charlottesville to Charlottesville itself. The child's education had been irregular, and in her new residence it was made more so by the constant necessity of meeting the social obligations of life in a university environment. In 1855 she published, with half-hearted anonymity, *Light and Darkness, a Story of Fashionable Life*. She chose as her scene places which she had not had the fortune to visit—New York, New Haven, and the expanse of Europe, and she professed "to veil a moral in every scene," but in one essential regard she defied the canons of romance. "I have endeavored," she said, "to portray the bad not as wholly bad nor the good as immaculate, since of human nature either is rarely or never true." The heresy of this view-point was widely and vigorously denounced, and the *Southern Literary Messenger* of October 1855, while admitting the interest of the book, calls it "a story of guilty love," and judges that "it had far better never been published." The author fled to New York. Society there did not blench at receiving her, but the late furore proved so disciplinary that in her next book, *Household Mysteries, a Romance of Southern Life* (1856), she maintained a more seemly attitude. In 1858, she published *The Stars of the Crowd, or Men and Women of the Day*. Soon afterward, a misunderstanding with her publishers made it necessary for her to earn money. She undertook a series of public readings and so won the popular favor that she determined to become an actress. This resolution was defeated by her marriage to Peter G. Cutler, a prominent New York lawyer. During her married life, social activities absorbed most of the energy which she had formerly devoted to writing. When her husband died in 1870 he left her an ample livelihood, but it soon disappeared and she was forced to return to Charlottesville to ask help of friends whom she had long before estranged by the "latitude" of her writings. She sincerely attempted atonement by returning to the stricter ideals of her very young womanhood, and by writing industriously, though not with great success, for any publication that would accept her work. She spoke tenderly of the Confederacy, and people remembered that "during the war, though she was in New York, powerless

to aid her people, she had given them her sympathy and tears." But from 1865 to 1902 is a long while, and the Richmond newspapers, when occasion came, gave brief notice of her sudden, solitary death as that of "an aged, dependent old woman, in a cheap boarding house." She had friends, the reporter added, in South Carolina and in Tennessee.

[In addition to sources already mentioned see J. D. Freeman ("Mary Forrest"), *Women of the South* (1861); J. G. Johnson, *Southern Fiction Prior to 1860* (1909); *Richmond Times,* Jan. 17, 1902; O. F. Adams, *Dict. Am. Authors* (1901); S. A. B. Putnam, *Things and Thoughts* (Mar.–Apr. 1902); I. Raymond, *Southland Writers* (1870).]
            J. D. W.

CUTLER, MANASSEH (May 13, 1742–July 28, 1823), Congregational clergyman, botanist, colonizer, was born in Killingly, Windham County, Conn., and was a direct descendant of John Cutler, who settled in Watertown, Mass., in 1634. He was the third child and oldest son of Hezekiah and Susanna (Clark) Cutler, who had a farm on the borderline between Rhode Island and Connecticut. After some preparatory instruction under Rev. Aaron Brown, he entered Yale College, where he graduated in 1765. Although he showed some aptitude for mathematics and natural science, he won no important collegiate distinctions. During the following winter he taught school in Dedham, Mass. On Sept. 7, 1766, he married Mary, eldest daughter of Rev. Thomas Balch of Dedham, and settled on Martha's Vineyard, where as agent for his wife's aunt, Mrs. Hannah Newman, he opened a store. While residing there, he was admitted to practise as an attorney in the court of common pleas and was employed in several court-room cases. At the Yale Commencement in 1768 he received the degree of A.M. Determining in October 1768 to study divinity, he moved with his family back to Dedham, where he spent the next two years reading theology under the direction of his father-in-law, meanwhile securing a license to preach (1770) and delivering sermons in various towns in the vicinity. On Sept. 11, 1771, he was ordained as pastor of the Congregational church in Ipswich Hamlet (now Hamilton), Mass., and was soon established in that parish, where he was to remain, with frequent absences on business, for the rest of his long life.

Being in sympathy with the Revolution, he was eager to promote the cause of the Patriots. After the battle of Lexington, he addressed the Minute Men of Ipswich Hamlet and then rode with them on horseback to Cambridge. He frequently visited the encampments of Massachusetts militia, and in September 1776 went to Dorchester, on leave from his parish, as chaplain in Col. Ebenezer Francis's 11th Massachusetts Regiment. When that organization broke up in January 1777, Cutler resumed his clerical duties, but in August 1778 he set out with Gen. Titcomb as chaplain in his brigade on its expedition to Rhode Island. When the troops came back in September, Cutler, who needed to add to his meager income, took up the study of medicine under his friend and parishioner, Dr. Elisha Whitney, and soon developed sufficient skill to practise as a physician. In May and June 1779, he had more than forty smallpox patients under his care at Wenham. Meanwhile, his restlessness found outlet in many scientific investigations. He measured the distances of some of the stars with a sextant and telescope; he entered the positions of Jupiter's moons in his journal; he observed hairs and other objects through a microscope; he described a remarkable aurora borealis; he performed experiments with an electrical machine; and he inoculated people for smallpox. One of his preferred avocations was botany, and he was the first to prepare a systematic account of the flora of New England. He examined 350 separate species, classifying them according to the Linnean method. In quest of information, he made an expedition, with six companions, to Mt. Washington in 1784, and was one of those to reach the summit. By means of the crude instruments which he carried, he computed that the top was 9,000 feet above the sea, an error of approximately 2,600 feet. He was elected in 1791 a member of the American Academy of Arts and Sciences and was punctilious in attendance at the meetings, contributing some valuable papers to its *Proceedings*. Among these are descriptions of the transit of Mercury over the sun, Nov. 12, 1782, of the eclipse of the moon, Mar. 29, 1782, and of the sun in the following April, as well as an article called "An Account of Some of the Vegetable Productions Naturally Growing in This Part of America," in which he summarized his conclusions regarding New England flora. He was a member of the American Philosophical Society (1784), the Philadelphia Linnæan Society (1809), the American Antiquarian Society (1813), and the New England Linnæan Society (1815), as well as an honorary fellow of the Massachusetts Medical Society. Yale gave him in 1789 the degree of LL.D. He frequently had pupils under instruction in his house, and in 1782 he opened a private boarding-school, which was continued for more than a quarter of a century. There were years when he had as many as twenty boys, most of them from well-known families in Essex County. One of those whom he prepared for college was

Nathaniel Silsbee, later United States senator from Massachusetts.

Up to the age of forty-five, Cutler had played many parts as teacher, storekeeper, clergyman, physician, soldier, explorer, and scientist. He was now, however, to enter upon a series of adventures of an entirely new kind, which were to give him a little-understood but important place in the history of American expansion. At the close of the Revolutionary War, a group of veterans, headed by Gen. Rufus Putnam, Winthrop Sargent, and others, became interested in a colonization scheme in the Ohio Valley; and on Mar. 1, 1786, in Boston, Cutler joined in forming the Ohio Company and was one of the five men who drafted its original articles of agreement. The company desired particularly to secure from Congress the grant of a choice tract at the junction of the Ohio and Muskingum rivers, which could be settled by "the most robust and industrious people in America." After one agent, Samuel H. Parsons, had failed, Cutler was sent by the company to New York in the summer of 1787 to conduct the negotiations. While the proposals of the Ohio Company were being considered by the Continental Congress, plans were also outlined for the administration of the vast territory involved. The draft of the Ordinance of 1787, which contained elements drawn from many sources, was submitted by Nathan Dane [*q.v.*] to Cutler, who made several suggestions, all but one of which he says were adopted. There has been much debate as to Cutler's share in this noted document, and his precise contribution to it has never been exactly determined.

The Ordinance was adopted July 13, 1787. Cutler, who had arrived in New York July 5 with letters of introduction to many influential people, at once began work with Congress. By means of active lobbying and skilful maneuvering he succeeded in winning over a hostile minority and, on Oct. 27, 1787, signed a contract with the Treasury Board giving the Ohio Company the right to take up one and a half million acres at approximately eight cents specie an acre. Colonization in the territory thus acquired began immediately. In December 1787, Putnam with sixty pioneers set out on the journey West, reaching the junction of the Ohio and Muskingum rivers in the following April. They there established the town of Marietta and began the settlement of Ohio. Cutler himself set out on July 21, 1788, driving in a sulky, and covered a distance of 750 miles in twenty-nine days. During his stay in Ohio he examined various mounds and fortifications in the vicinity of Marietta, and concluded that these were the work of ancient tribes. He returned to Massachusetts in 1789, having seen his colony well established. In 1795 he was offered a commission as judge of the supreme court of Ohio Territory, but declined it.

In 1800 Cutler represented his town in the Massachusetts General Court, and in the autumn was elected to Congress as a Federalist from the Essex District. He served two terms, but declined a renomination in 1804, the strain of congressional activities having proved too much for his health. He returned to Hamilton, where he was still pastor of the church, and on Oct. 27, 1814, delivered a "Century Discourse." His wife died, Nov. 2, 1815, but he, in spite of frequent attacks of asthma, continued to preach until his death nearly eight years later. Cutler's journal, carefully kept over a series of years, is an amazing personal record, revealing his eagerness to get authentic information on all sorts of subjects. One of his favorite extracts from Virgil gives the key to his character, *Felix, qui potuit rerum cognoscere causas.* He had an unbounded curiosity which led him to carry on a tremendous correspondence with authorities in many fields. Neatness was his passion, and everything in his library and about his place was in perfect order. In his prime he was a tall and portly figure, usually attired in a black velvet suit, with black silk stockings and silver knee- and shoe-buckles. His manners were courtly, and he entertained most graciously the many guests who came to his house in Hamilton.

[The basis for any biography of Cutler is necessarily Wm. P. and Julia P. Cutler, *Life, Journals, and Correspondence of Rev. Manasseh Cutler* (2 vols., 1888). For discussions of his part in the Ordinance of 1787, see E. Channing, *Hist. of the U. S.*, vol. III (1912), ch. xvii; Jay A. Barrett, *The Evolution of the Ordinance of 1787* (1891); and F. B. Stone, in *Pa. Mag. of Hist. and Biog.*, Oct. 1889. Manasseh Cutler, *An Explanation of the Map which Delineates that Part of the Federal Lands, Comprehended between Pa. West Line, the Rivers Ohio and Scioto, and Lake Erie, etc.*, published anonymously (1787), published in French (1789), has been reprinted many times because it is an early description of Ohio. See also, Wm. B. Sprague, *Annals Am. Pulpit*, vol. II (1857); *Literary Diary of Ezra Stiles* (1901); N. S. Cutler, *Cutler Memorial and Geneal. Hist.* (1889); Jos. B. Felt, *Hist. of Ipswich, Essex and Hamilton* (1834); E. D. Larned, *Hist. of Windham County, Conn.* (1874–80); *New-Eng. Hist. and Geneal. Reg.*, Oct. 1853, Apr. 1873; *North Am. Rev.*, Apr. 1876; *Mag. of Am. Hist.*, Apr. 1881, Dec. 1889; F. B. Dexter, *Biog. Sketches Grads. Yale Coll.*, vol. III (1903).]
C.M.F.

CUTLER, TIMOTHY (May 31, 1684–Aug. 17, 1765), rector of Yale College, Episcopal clergyman, was born in Charlestown, Mass., a descendant of Robert Cutler who settled in that town prior to Oct. 28, 1636. His father was Maj. John Cutler, an anchorsmith, and his mother, Martha Wiswall. The fact that both his father and grandfather opposed the government formed

after the overthrow of Andros in 1689, and although severely penalized, refused to subscribe to it until it had received royal sanction, suggests a family tendency to conform to the established order at home, which may have had something to do with Timothy's subsequent conversion to the Church of England. When seventeen years old he graduated from Harvard College, and on Jan. 11, 1709/10, having come from Massachusetts to Connecticut with the recommendation of being "one of the best preachers both colonies afforded," he was ordained pastor of the Congregational church in Stratford. On Mar. 21, 1710/11, he married Elizabeth, daughter of Rev. Samuel Andrew [q.v.] of Milford, Conn., then acting rector of Yale College. He served his parish acceptably until March 1718/19 when, conditions at Yale calling imperatively for a resident rector, he undertook that office at the request of the trustees, his appointment being formally approved in September. Although his father-in-law was doubtless instrumental in securing his appointment, Cutler was in general well fitted for the position, being "an excellent Linguist," a "good Logician, Geographer, and Rhetorician," while "in the Philosophy & Metaphysics & Ethics of his Day or juvenile Education he was great. ... He was of an high, lofty, & despotic mien. He made a grand Figure as the Head of a College" (*The Literary Diary of Ezra Stiles*, 1901, II, 339–40).

The new rectorship opened auspiciously and an era of prosperity seemed at hand when, on Sept. 13, 1722, the rector, with Tutor Daniel Browne and several Congregational clergymen, met with the trustees, declared themselves doubtful of the validity of their ordination, and asked advice with regard to entering the Church of England. Upon request they made a written statement of their position, and the meeting was adjourned for a month. In the meantime Gov. Saltonstall arranged a public debate on the matter, held Oct. 16, as a result of which, on the following day, at a special meeting of the trustees, it was voted to "excuse the Rev. Mr. Cutler from all further services as Rector of Yale College," and it was provided that all future rectors and tutors should declare to the trustees their assent to the Saybrook Confession of Faith, and give satisfaction as to their opposition to "Arminian and prelatical corruptions."

Contemporary evidence indicates that Cutler was never whole-heartedly a Dissenter, that he had been converted to Episcopalianism when at Stratford by John Checkley [q.v.], and that in spite of this fact had accepted the rectorship of a Congregational college, publicly declaring what he had privately believed only when a desirable place in the Established Church was assured him (*Collections of the Massachusetts Historical Society,* ser. 2, IV, 299; Josiah Quincy, *History of Harvard University,* 1840, I, 365; F. B. Dexter, *Biographical Sketches of the Graduates of Yale College, with Annals of the College History,* vol. I, 1885, p. 271).

After a visit to London where he was ordained by the Bishop of Norwich in March 1723, and received the degree of D.D. from both Oxford and Cambridge, Cutler became rector of the newly formed Christ Church, Boston. Here he remained until his death, one of the leading Episcopal clergymen of New England, full of polemic spirit, venerated for his learning, but too haughty in manner to be popular. He founded the church at Dedham and took care of Christ Church, Braintree. He was a high Tory, intolerant of Dissenters, and a militant defender of the rights of his fellow believers. With Rev. Samuel Myles of King's Chapel he laid claim to a seat on the Board of Overseers of Harvard, as a minister of the Episcopal church in Boston, maintaining that he was a "teaching elder" as required by the college charter. Both the Overseers and General Court decided against him (Quincy, *supra,* pp. 365–76). He never ceased to urge the appointment of a bishop for the American colonies. With the exception of four sermons, two preached before the Connecticut General Assembly, May 9, 1717, and Oct. 18, 1719, he left no published works.

[W. S. Perry, *Hist. Colls. Relating to the Am. Colonial Ch.* (1870) and John Nichols, *Illustrations of the Lit. Hist. of the Eighteenth Century* (1822) contain Cutler letters; Henry W. Foote, *Annals of King's Chapel* (1882–96) is rich in references. See also Nahum S. Cutter, *A Cutler Memorial and Geneal. Hist.* (1889); Richard Frothingham, *Hist. of Charlestown, Mass.,* no. 5 (1847); Edwin Oviatt, *The Beginnings of Yale* (1916); Samuel Orcutt, *Hist. of the Old Town of Stratford and the City of Bridgeport, Conn.* (1886); Justin Winsor, *Memorial Hist. of Boston,* vol. II (1881); E. E. Beardsley, *Hist. of the Episc. Ch. in Conn.* (1866); Wm. S. Perry, *Hist. of the Am. Episc. Ch.* (1885); Wm. B. Sprague, *Annals of the Am. Pulpit,* vol. V (1859); Henry Burroughs, *An Hist. Account of Christ Church, Boston* (1874); Asa Eaton, *Hist. Account of Christ Church, Boston* (1824).]   H. E. S.

CUTTER, CHARLES AMMI (Mar. 14, 1837– Sept. 6, 1903), librarian, the third son of Charles Champney and Hannah (Biglow) Cutter, was descended on both sides from ancestors who for eight generations had lived and died within a few miles of Boston. Among them were farmers, housewrights, traders, millers, innholders, but no scholars. Cutter was born in Boston, and spent his boyhood in Charlestown and Cambridge. From the Hopkins Grammar School he entered Harvard College at fourteen, graduating third among the eighty-two members of the class of 1855. While in the Harvard Divinity School (1858–59), where he was librarian as well as student, he became so attracted toward librarianship that after preaching a few months he went into the Harvard library, where he served as an assistant from 1860 to 1868. On May 21, 1863, he was married to Sarah Fayerweather Appleton, daughter of Charles John and Sophia (Haven) Appleton of Portsmouth, N. H. In December 1868 he was elected librarian of the Boston Athenæum, the most famous of American proprietary libraries. It is clear evidence of his quality that he held this prized position under such directors as the first and second Charles Francis Adams, Brooks Adams, Oliver Wendell Holmes, Francis Parkman, and Henry Cabot Lodge, and gave satisfaction to such readers as Emerson, Bronson Alcott, Whipple, Palfrey, Bancroft, Charles Sumner, and many other New England "Brahmins" to whom the Athenæum was a literary sanctuary. In such congenial surroundings it would have been easy to let the demands of the hour absorb one's days; but Cutter devoted twelve years of incessant labor to the production of his monumental *Catalogue of the Library of the Boston Athenæum* (5 vols., 1874–82), which Justin Winsor said was "the best catalogue extant." For years it stood almost alone in American bibliographic undertakings in magnitude and thoroughness. As an aid to other libraries there was at that time nothing remotely comparable to it. Out of the difficulties met in compiling this catalogue grew a work of wide usefulness and more permanent value, his *Rules for a Printed Dictionary Catalogue* (1875), intended for the guidance of himself and his associates but recognized at once as so valuable a tool that it was reprinted by the national Bureau of Education in 1876. It immediately became the world's leading text-book in systematic dictionary cataloguing and has not yet been superseded.

Cutter was now reckoned among the half-dozen foremost American librarians, so that in the great library movement which began with the organization of the American Library Association he had a large part. From its first meeting in Philadelphia in October 1876, until his death, he attended more of its annual conferences than any other person. He helped to establish the *Library Journal* (September 1876); was from the beginning in charge of its bibliographic department; and was its general editor from 1881 to 1893. His *Expansive Classification* (1891–1904), "the most logical and scholarly of modern bibliographic schemes," is his best but not his most famous work. In much wider use are his *Rules* and his alphabetic-order tables on which are based the author name-marks now commonly seen on books in American libraries. Declining reëlection at the Athenæum in 1893, he spent the next year and a half in European travel and study. In October 1894 he began to develop the newly founded Forbes Library in Northampton, Mass. His plans for cultivating literary and artistic taste in his younger readers involved the lending of pictures and musical scores as well as books. He aimed, as he said in the last year of his life, to develop "a new type of public library, which, speaking broadly, will lend everything to anybody in any desired quantity for any desired time." While on a driving trip with his wife, he died suddenly at Walpole, N. H., Sept. 6, 1903, having never fully recovered from a severe illness of the preceding spring.

His books disclose unusual power of analysis, exceptionally accurate scholarship, great knowledge. Evidences of his wide culture are to be found in the files of the *Nation* to which he was a contributor for thirty-five years. He was an ardent lover of nature, was keenly interested in music, art, the drama, and dancing, was devoted to rowing, bicycling, mountain-climbing; a man of spontaneous and unconquerable humor, a delightful companion, and of an incorrigible industry that made him eminent in his profession.

[W. E. Foster and Thorvald Solberg in *Lib. Jour.*, Oct., Nov. 1903; Benj. Cutter, *A Hist. of the Cutter Family of New Eng.* (1871); *Forbes Lib. Reports,* 1894–1903; W. C. Berwick Sayers, *A Manual of Classification for Librarians and Bibliographers* (1926); W. E. Foster, in *Bull. of the Am. Lib. Asso.*, Oct. 1926; *Nation* (N. Y.), Sept. 17, 1903; *Springfield Daily Republican,* Sept. 8, 1903.]   F. W. A.

CUTTER, EPHRAIM (Sept. 1, 1832–Apr. 25, 1917), physician, was born at Woburn, Mass., the son of Benjamin and Mary (Whittemore) Cutter. He came of fairly distinguished ancestry, his father being a practitioner at Woburn, and his grandfather, Amos Whittemore, having achieved reputation as an inventor. After preparation at Warren Academy, he entered Yale where he graduated in 1852. Apparently he had a *penchant* for acquiring college degrees, obtaining, from Yale, A.B. (1852), M.D. (1855); from Harvard, M.D. (1856); from the University of Pennsylvania, M.D. (1857). His professional career may be divided into three periods: (1856–74) when he was engaged in practise at Woburn in association with his father; (1875–80) when he practised in Cambridge; (1881–1901) when he practised in New York City. He possessed great ability in medical research and in the invention of medical appliances. His earliest efforts were given to solving some of the problems connected with the examination and photography of the vocal organs. In 1859 an apparatus for viewing the larynx was constructed from his design, and in 1866 he made photographs of the larynx which, it is claimed, went a little further than any of those previously produced, in that they showed the thyroid insertion. Soon after this he published his *Veratrum Viride as a Therapeutical Agent* (1860, 1862). General surgery and gynecology early engaged his attention, and he devised, almost every year, one or more new instruments or new operative procedures. In 1869 he was using a new kind of metallic suture; in 1870 he described an écraseur for removing growths from deep cavities; in 1871 he brought out a new eustachian catheter; in 1873 an invalid chair; in 1874 an inhaler for nascent ammonia chloride; in 1875 a galvanocaustic holder. In 1871 he devoted especial attention to the therapeutic effects of electricity, being one of the first to demonstrate that galvanic currents penetrate the human body. On his removal in 1875 to Cambridge, he returned to his morphological studies, making frequent examinations of the blood and sputum with special reference to their clinical significance. At this time gynecological subjects also claimed his renewed interest, and he wrote *A Contribution to the Treatment of the Versions and Flexions of the Unimpregnated Uterus* (1871–76).

The last period of his life, dating from the beginning of his residence in New York, was largely devoted to the investigation of cancer, tuberculosis, diseases of the heart and blood vessels, and disorders of nutrition. Among his more important contributions of this period were *Partial Syllabic Lists of the Clinical Morphologies of the Blood, Feces, Skin,* etc. (1888, 1892), *Fatty Ills and their Masquerades* (1898), *Fatty and Fibroid Degeneration, Bright's Disease, Apoplexy, Fatty Heart, Puerperal Convulsions,* etc. (1892). He became intensely interested in the subject of food and did much to arouse the public mind against the decorticated and denatured wheat and wheat flours, especially stressing their effect in bringing about an early decay of the teeth. He delved also into the cancer problem and referred to cancer tissue as "being under mob law and rioting in the body systemic," forecasting one of the most prominent theories of the present day as to the origin of malignant growths. On his retirement from practise in 1901, he took up his residence in West Falmouth, Mass., where he died at the age of eighty-four as the result of a cerebral hemorrhage. He was twice married: first, Oct. 7, 1856, to Rebecca Smith Sullivan, and two years after her death in 1899, to Mrs. Anna L. Davidson. There were two sons of his first marriage: Benjamin, and Dr. John Ashburton Cutter who was associated with him in practise and in the writing of some of his later works.

Cutter's writings lacked literary grace and were rather full of arbitrary statements which his arguments failed to support and which subsequent experience has failed to confirm. By virtue of his forceful, positive manner, however, he exercised great influence over the medical opinion of his day, and some of his observations have proved to be strikingly prophetic.

[Jos. M. Toner, *Address before the Rocky Mt. Medic. Asso., June 6, 1877* (1877), with biographies of the members; *Record of the Class of 1852, Yale Coll., for the Quarter Century after Graduation* (1878); Cutter's *Partial Syllabic Lists of the Clinical Morphologies of the Blood, Feces, Skin*, etc. (2 ed. 1892), containing a biographical sketch, and bibliography of his writings; *Trans. Am. Laryngol. Ass.*, 1917; *Boston Medic. and Surgic. Jour.*, CLXXVI, 684; *Va. Medic. Semi-Monthly*, XXII, 128–30; *Obit. Record Grads. Yale Univ.*, 1917; Benj. Cutter, *Hist. of the Cutter Family of New Eng.* (1871); J. W. Leonard, *Men of America* (1908); *Who's Who in America*, 1916–17.] W. A. W.

CUTTER, GEORGE WASHINGTON (1801–Dec. 25, 1865), poet, was born in Quebec, Canada, of a family which had come there from Massachusetts. His education was not extensive but for a time he studied law and, after a residence at Terre Haute, Ind., during which he served in the lower house of the Indiana legislature, 1838–39 (*Complete List of Members*, etc., 1903), he practised in Covington, Ky., until the beginning of the Mexican War stirred his imagination with visions of conquest for his country and of military glory for himself. In 1847 he helped to raise a company of volunteers, which became a part of the 2nd Kentucky Regiment. He was made its captain and joined Taylor's army on the Rio Grande, where he served with distinction until the close of the war. He took part in the battle of Buena Vista during which he helped to carry Col. Clay from a position of danger under the enemy's fire and remained with him until his death. The victory inspired one of his best-known poems, written on the battle-field. At the close of the war he went into politics as a zealous Whig and later became a more or less popular orator in the cause of Know-Nothingism. He was also at one time an earnest advocate and speaker for the temperance cause. Under Taylor's administration he received a clerkship in the Treasury Department at Washington which he held until the close of Fillmore's administration, when he lost it through political changes and left Washington. Early in life he had married Mrs. Frances Ann Drake of Cincinnati, an actress in tragic parts, from whom he was divorced. Later he married again in the West. He published three volumes of verse, *Buena Vista*

and Other Poems (1848), *The Song of Steam and Other Poems* (1857), and *Poems, National and Patriotic* (1857)—all vigorous and unconventional in thought, if conventional in metre. *The Song of Steam*, his best work, is suggestive of Kipling's later poetic apotheosis of machinery. A few years before his death Cutter returned to Washington but found no employment. When stricken with paralysis, he was admitted to Providence Hospital on an order from the Commissioner of Public Buildings, and there he died alone. His funeral was conducted by the St. John's Masonic Lodge and he was buried in the lot owned by the Lodge in the Congressional Cemetery.

[Wm. T. Coggeshall, *Poets and Poetry of the West* (1860); J. W. Townsend, *Ky. in Am. Letters, 1784–1912* (1913); Rufus W. Griswold, *Poets and Poetry of America* (rev. ed. 1874); *Lib. of Southern Literature*, vol. XV (1909); Benj. Cutter, *Hist. of the Cutter Family of New Eng.* (1871); *New-Eng. Hist. and Geneal. Reg.*, Apr. 1866; *Evening Star* (Washington, D. C.), Dec. 27, 1865; *Daily Morning Chronicle* (Washington, D. C.), Dec. 28, 1865.] S. G. B.

CUTTING, JAMES AMBROSE (1814–Aug. 6, 1867), inventor, son of Abijah Cutting, a descendant of a seventeenth-century English immigrant who settled in the central portion of what is now the state of New Hampshire, was born in the village of Hanover, on the western border of the state. Shortly after his birth his parents moved to Haverhill, N.H., where the family lived in straitened circumstances for a great many years, presumably as farmers. It would seem that young Cutting was interested in bee-keeping to the extent of consistently trying to improve the type of hive then in use. He eventually succeeded and on June 24, 1844, received United States Patent No. 3,638 for a beehive. Armed with his patent, Cutting proceeded to engage in the manufacture of his hive and apparently experienced partial financial success during the succeeding decade. It is said, however, that before the end of this period he was again made destitute through poor investments. He next became interested in photography, the daguerreotype then being in vogue. He is first heard of in this connection in April 1854 through correspondence with the Commissioner of Patents in Washington relative to his application for patents on improvements in the collodion process of photography. The broad claims made by him in the original application were rejected because the process was not new, but for certain details of the process, patents numbered 11,213, 11,266, and 11,267 were eventually granted in July 1854. In one of these he styled his process "ambrotype," from the Greek word *ambrotos*, meaning immortal, his claim being that by his process greater permanency of picture was secured than otherwise. The same month a British patent was granted him. Although Cutting is said to have enjoyed considerable prosperity for a time, it seems probable that these patents were of very little value to him, for the commercial photographers of the day were universally of the feeling that he was not entitled to the inventions, and accordingly paid very little regard to them. Cutting continued to reside in Boston engaging in photographic work and apparently experimenting in several allied directions, for on Mar. 16, 1858, he, with L. H. Bradford of Boston, received Patent No. 19,626 for a photolithographic process. This invention seems to have had some merit, for five years after Cutting's death his administrator, A. O. Butman, and Bradford obtained from the Patent Office an extension of the original patent. Cutting's name appears in the Boston city directories until 1862, when, because of his weakened mental state, he was committed to a lunatic asylum at Worcester, Mass., where he died five years later.

[M. H. Ellis, *The Ambrotype and Photographic Instructor* (1856); *Humphrey's Daguerrian Jour.*, 1854–56; *Ann. Cyc.*, 1867; *Worcester Daily Spy*, Aug. 12, 1867; correspondence with the Am. Antiquarian Soc., Worcester, Mass.; U. S. Patent Office records.]

C. W. M.

CUYLER, THEODORE (Sept. 14, 1819–Apr. 5, 1876), lawyer, was descended from Hendrick Cuyler, a native of Hassett, Overyssel, Netherlands, who emigrated to New Netherland some time prior to 1660, and settled at Albany. Fourth in direct line of descent was Cornelis Cuyler, a prominent pastor of the Reformed Dutch Church at Poughkeepsie, N. Y. He married Eleanor, daughter of Isaac de Graaff of Schenectady, and their eldest son, Theodore, was born at Poughkeepsie. His early education was obtained at the public school there, but, on the family removing in 1834 to Philadelphia, he entered the University of Pennsylvania and graduated in 1838, third in his class. After studying in the office of Charles Chauncey he was admitted to the bar, Oct. 7, 1841, and commenced practise in Philadelphia. Developing unusual legal talent, he was retained in many important causes at an early stage of his career. His brilliant advocacy in the celebrated Christiana treason case in the United States circuit court in November 1851, involving a charge against a number of persons for affording assistance to fugitive slaves from Maryland, placed him in the front rank of contemporary trial counsel. Interested in all local matters of public importance he found time to act as director of public schools in Philadelphia, and in 1856 became a member of the Select Council, a position which

he retained for six years, during four of which he was chairman. In April 1857 he was appointed solicitor at Philadelphia for the Pennsylvania Railroad Company, and when, twelve years later, a departmental reorganization took place he became its general counsel. For a number of years the company was involved in heavy litigation, which he conducted with remarkable success, establishing his reputation as the greatest corporation lawyer of the period. He was exceptional in that he was equally effective before a jury or on appeal, and for nearly twenty years he was retained on one side or the other in almost every corporation case of importance in Pennsylvania and the neighboring states. He "was prone to take cases too easily in the initial and middle stages, with the result that, to save the day he was often forced at the end to make herculean efforts. . . . Driven to the last ditch he was most dangerous, and more than once snatched victory out of the very jaws of destruction" (Eastman, *post*). In 1872 he was elected a delegate-at-large from Philadelphia to the Pennsylvania state constitutional convention, and took a prominent part in its discussions. He died in Philadelphia, Apr. 5, 1876. He was married, on Dec. 21, 1853, to Mary Elizabeth, eldest daughter of Rev. Thomas de Witt of New York.

[Maud Churchill Nicoll, *The Earliest Cuylers in Holland and America* (1912); J. T. Scharf and T. Westcott, *Hist. of Phila.* (1884), II, 1546; P. M. Eastman, *Courts and Lawyers of Pa.* (1922), III, 830; *Legal Intelligencer*, Apr. 7, 14, 1876.]

H. W. H. K.

CUYLER, THEODORE LEDYARD (Jan. 10, 1822–Feb. 26, 1909), Presbyterian clergyman, writer, son of Benjamin Ledyard and Louisa (Morrell) Cuyler, was born in Aurora, N. Y., of which town his great-grandfather, Gen. Benjamin Ledyard of New London, Conn., whose daughter Mary married Glen Cuyler, was one of the first settlers. The Cuylers were of Dutch origin, descendants of Hendrick, who came to Albany about 1664 (Maud C. Nicoll, *The Earliest Cuylers in Holland and America and Some of their Descendants*, 1912). Theodore's father died when his son was but four and a half years old, and the latter was brought up on his grandfather Morrell's farm by a deeply religious mother who early determined that he should enter the ministry. Prepared for college by private tutorship and at the Hill Top School, Mendham, N. J., he graduated from Princeton in 1841 at the age of nineteen. The following year he made a trip to Europe where he visited Wordsworth, Dickens, and Carlyle, an interesting description of whom is given in his *Recollections of a Long Life*. In 1846 he graduated from the Princeton Theological Seminary, was licensed by the Second Presbytery of Philadelphia, Apr. 22 of the same year, and ordained by the Presbytery of West Jersey, May 4, 1848. From 1846 to 1849 he supplied the Presbyterian Church at Burlington, N. J., and from 1849 to 1853 he was pastor of the Third Church, Trenton. While here, Mar. 17, 1853, he married Annie E. Mathiot, daughter of Joshua Mathiot of Newark, Ohio. In November of this year he became pastor of the Market Street Dutch Reformed Church of New York, where he remained until 1860 when he began a thirty years' pastorate at the Lafayette Avenue Presbyterian Church, Brooklyn. In April 1890 he became pastor emeritus, continuing to reside in Brooklyn, preaching, lecturing, and writing.

During his long service in Brooklyn, he became one of the most popular preachers of that city and known throughout the country as a public speaker and writer. His sermons were pungent, evangelical in tone, enforced with striking illustrations, and delivered with great earnestness. Preaching he regarded as "spiritual gunnery," and said that his hearers would testify that he had never spared his lungs or their ears. Theologically, he was a conservative, declaring that he had found that "the true things were not new, and most of the new things were not true." In the great revival of 1858 which began in New York he was one of the early leaders. Vigorous in body and abounding in energy, he gave himself to a variety of activities. He was especially interested in the temperance movement, and made his first public address at a welcome to Father Mathew in the City Hall, Glasgow, in 1842. He prepared the constitution for the National Temperance Society and Publication House, founded in 1865, and later was for some years its president. In theory he was a "legal suppressionist," but declared that the only real remedy for the liquor evil lies in removing the desire to use liquor. Without a stiff public sentiment back of legal suppression, he contended, "it may become a delusion and a farce." He wrote for the religious press incessantly, and before his death boasted four thousand articles, many of which were translated into foreign languages. He also published some twenty-two books, several of them widely popular. For the most part they are informally devotional in character, but include two volumes of sermons, *Stirring the Eagle's Nest and other Practical Discourses* (1892) and *A Model Christian* (1903), a volume of foreign travel, *From the Nile to Norway* (1882), and his *Recollections of a Long Life* (1902). The last named has much charm and contains sketches of many famous people at home and abroad whom the author had known.

[In addition to his *Recollections* see, *Necrological Report, Princeton Theol. Sem.* (1909); *Who's Who in America*, 1908–09; *Lafayette Ave. Ch., its Hist. and Commemorative Services* (1885); obituary in *N. Y. Times*, Feb. 27, 1909, editorial, Feb. 28, 1909.]

H. E. S.

DABLON, CLAUDE (Jan. 21, 1619, or Feb. 1618–May 3, or Sept. 20, 1697), Jesuit missionary from Dieppe, began his novitiate at Paris in 1639. From the beginning of his career he had a great desire to enter the foreign field. Sent to Canada in 1655, he was almost immediately designated for the Iroquois mission, the most difficult and dangerous in North America. Dablon was at this time in early middle life, with vigorous intellect and keen powers of observation, and withal physically fit and the possessor of unsurpassed endurance. He left Montreal in the autumn of 1655 together with Father Chaumonot and a party of Iroquois. His diary expresses his delight in the wilderness and in the beauties of nature. "I sleep," he wrote en route, "as well on the ground as I did on a mattress or as I would in a feather bed" (*Jesuit Relations*, XLI, 227). The winter was passed among the Onondaga at the present Liverpool, N. Y. In the spring, it being necessary to consult the authorities in Canada, Dablon went thither on foot, Mar. 2–30, a terrible journey over melting ice and softening snow-fields. At Quebec it was determined to accede to the request of the Iroquois for a French settlement in their midst, and Dablon became leader of a colony of fifty Frenchmen, who for months lived among these Indians in central New York. Then, having learned that the Indians meditated treachery and massacre, the entire group succeeded in escaping in March 1658, and reached Canada in safety.

Dablon remained three years thereafter at Quebec in civilized surroundings. He was, however, always eager for distant explorations and in May 1661, with Father Druillettes, undertook an excursion up the Saguenay and across to Lake St. John on a mission to the Cree tribe. In 1669 he was sent to the Northwest as superior of the Ottawa mission, where Allouez and Marquette were already laboring. He made headquarters at Sault Ste. Marie, and thence he sent Allouez late in the same year to explore the region around Green Bay and begin missions among the tribes there. The next autumn Dablon himself accompanied Allouez on a visit to central Wisconsin. His descriptions of his journey are full of enthusiasm; he likened the passage of the rapids of the lower Fox River to the steps up to Paradise. Into that river the missionaries threw a stone idol, worshipped by the neighboring Indians. Dablon also gave a detailed description of the Lake Superior copper mines, and of the pageant whereby France in June 1671 took possession of the region of the upper Great Lakes. Chosen Superior of all the Canadian missions while still in the Northwest, Dablon returned to Quebec to take office July 12, 1671. It was he who appointed Marquette to accompany Joliet on his voyage of discovery to the Mississippi and who reported that discovery to the authorities in France. Dablon never again left Quebec; his first term as Superior ended in 1680, but he served again in that office 1686-93. He was one of the most energetic, able and conscientious of the Canadian missionaries; his zeal and endurance were notable, and his judgment was excellent; his delight in nature and in the conquering of obstacles distinguished him; and his writings are a source of information about natural phenomena and the habits and customs of the natives. He was a contributor to the *Relations* of 1669-70, reviser of those of 1672-73, 1679, editor of the published *Relations* of 1670-71, 1671-72, and compiler of those from 1673 to 1678. He also edited Marquette's narratives, aided Chaumonot in arranging his autobiography and wrote several diaries of his travels and letters which have been preserved.

[Dablon's writings are in *The Jesuit Relations and Allied Documents* (1896-1901), ed. by R. G. Thwaites, *passim.* See sketch in *The Jesuit Relations*, vol. XLI, p. 257; T. J. Campbell, *Pioneer Priests of North America 1642-1710* (1908), I, 101-24; L. P. Kellogg, *French Régime in Wis. and the Northwest* (1925), 158-63, 169, 188, 191.]

                         L. P. K.

DABNEY, RICHARD (1787-Nov. 25, 1825), poet, was born in Louisa County, Va., a son of Samuel Dabney and his wife Jane Meriwether (aunt of the explorer Meriwether Lewis). His father, member of an old Virginia family of distinguished descent, was a small planter, able to provide his twelve children with only meager educational advantages. Richard, however, when about sixteen entered a classical school where he made astonishing progress with Greek and Latin, and shortly won a position as assistant teacher in a Richmond academy. In 1812 he published at Richmond a small volume of *Poems, Original and Translated,* but, disappointed at the indifference shown it, soon sought its suppression. Seeking a literary career, he moved to Philadelphia, where he remained for a few years in the employ of Mathew Carey [q.v.], the publisher, and is supposed to have written a large part of the latter's powerful plea for party unity in war-time, *The Olive Branch; or Faults on Both Sides, Federal and Democratic* (1814). In 1815 a revised and augmented edition of the *Poems,* likewise a losing venture, was issued by Carey. The original poems consist of "Illustrations of the Simple Moral Emotions" and miscellaneous patriotic or love lyrics; two-fifths of the volume is composed of translations or adaptations from the Greek, Latin, and Italian, with one piece from the French. Of the original compositions with their naïve prefaces and notes, shadowy abstractions, and amateurish refrains, little needs to be said; many are didactic and funereal, others echo recent English poets. The translations, the work of a scholar rather than a poet, are better, although undistinguished. His rendering of Greek and Latin lacks the simple lucidity of the classics; his sonnets from the Italian show a prosodical concern unusual in his writings, save in his blank verse, yet similarly fail to "touch the magic string." Intellectual range and vigor are more noticeable in his verse than metrical talent; too often his product is marred by unnatural syntax, limping rhythms, or impossible rhymes. His claim to poetic attainment seemingly lies in the mere fact that his book was twice printed; it is incredible that any one should examine the poems thoughtfully and yet overestimate them so grossly as has customarily been done. From Philadelphia Dabney returned to Louisa County, where he read extensively, enjoyed freely the convivial social life of the region, and, at the instigation of neighbors, taught a small school. To him was erroneously attributed, in 1818, over his disclaimer, the authorship of a widely admired classical poem, *Rhododaphne.* His increased dependence upon opium, first prescribed in consequence of painful injuries contracted at the burning of the Richmond Theatre, Dec. 26, 1811, and his lifelong fondness for drink rendered his last years creatively barren. He died, unmarried, at his birthplace, after considerable bodily suffering, fruit of his infirmities and indulgence, and a no less acute mental anguish born of disappointed hopes and the consciousness of abilities squandered.

[*Dabneys of Va.* (1888), by W. H. Dabney, gives the genealogy of the family. The single authoritative notice of Richard Dabney is the sketch contributed by Lucian Minor of Louisa County, Va., thirty years after the poet's death, to E. A. and G. L. Duyckinck, *Cyclopædia of Am. Lit.* (1856), II, 98-100. On this all subsequent notices have been modeled, without any effort to reveal facts omitted by Minor, or any attempt to corroborate his critical opinions. When it is recalled that Minor was a zealous temperance advocate, it is reasonable to assume that, in his eagerness to point a stronger moral, he may have been led unconsciously to enlarge upon both the poet's intemperance and talents.]

                      A. C. G., Jr.

DABNEY, ROBERT LEWIS (Mar. 5, 1820-Jan. 3, 1898), Presbyterian theologian, teacher, author, son of Charles and Elizabeth R. (Price) Dabney, was born in Louisa County, Va., and died in Victoria, Tex. The Dabneys are believed to have descended from Cornelius Dabney, or d'Aubigné, a French Protestant who came to Virginia in the early eighteenth century, after a considerable residence in England. Robert Dabney's father was a planter in moderate circumstances, and the boy, one of eight children, was educated at such schools as the community afforded. He attended Hampden-Sidney College (1836–37), and after teaching school (1838–39), completed his college work at the University of Virginia (1840–42). He studied at the (Virginia) Union Theological Seminary (1844–46) and, becoming a minister, served first as a rural missionary and later as pastor of the Tinkling Spring Church. He was married on Mar. 28, 1848 to Lavinia Morrison, daughter of the Rev. James Morrison of Rockbridge County. From 1853 to 1883, he taught at the Union Theological Seminary, preached at the local chapel, and from time to time conducted courses at the adjacent Hampden-Sidney College. His prowess as a commentator in church publications made him generally known among Presbyterians, and in 1860 he was twice given opportunity to identify himself with important institutions in the North—as professor at Princeton and as minister of the Fifth Avenue Presbyterian Church in New York. He became a Confederate army chaplain in 1861, and in 1862 he was a major on the staff of his friend and idol, Stonewall Jackson. In 1883, the condition of his health demanding a warmer climate, he became professor of philosophy in the University of Texas, where he remained till 1894. During the late eighties he was instrumental in establishing the Austin School of Theology. He wrote many philosophic books and essays. The most important of these, *Practical Philosophy* (1897), written first as a series of lectures for college students, is Calvinistic in theology and reactionary in politics, based on an assumption that virtue had its origin by divine fiat—literally, as accounted for in the Bible, and that it is for that reason immutable and deserving of all fealty. His best-known work is his *Life and Campaigns of Lieutenant-General Thomas J. Jackson (Stonewall Jackson)*, published in 1866, and his most vivid one, *A Defense of Virginia and the South* (1867). Others were: *The Christian Soldier* (1863); *A Memorial of Lieut.-Col. John T. Thornton* (1864); *Sacred Rhetoric* (1870); *Syllabus and Notes of the Course of Systematic and Polemic Theology* (1871); *Parental Obligation* (1880); *The New South* (1883). Before the Civil War he opposed secession, but once battles were under way he vouched with a progressive assurance for the wickedness of the North and for the purely Christian nature of the conflict as seen from the standpoint of the South. Defeated, he believed these doctrines still, and was unable to think that the mere event of one day at Appomattox could affect principles which he held absolute. He thought that the only way for Southerners to save the true spiritual South, which alone seemed of interest to him, was for them to abandon the conquered geographic South forthwith and completely, and until about 1870 he concerned himself with projects for a grand-scale migration to Australia or perhaps Brazil. The opposition even of Gen. Lee to these plans was to him negligible, the result of military training rather than of a just apprehension of history and human nature. From 1890 till his death he was infirm and totally blind, but he continued active, delivering in the Carolinas as late as the fall of 1897 the two courses of lectures which later appeared in the volume, *Christ Our Penal Substitute* (1898). At these lectures he was a figure not to be observed dispassionately— he was a blind, groping old man, championing with dogmatism a waning creed; but he was none the less majestic—and those who listened to him felt that he embodied learning and benevolence and romantic honor.

[T. C. Johnson, *Life and Letters of Robt. Lewis Dabney* (1903); *In Memoriam, Robt. Lewis Dabney* (1899); W. H. Dabney, *Dabneys of Va.* (1888); J. C. McAllister, "Robt. Lewis Dabney," *Lib. of Southern Lit.* (1907).]   J. D. W.

DABNEY, THOMAS SMITH GREGORY (Jan. 4, 1798–Feb. 28, 1885), planter, was born at "Bellevue," King and Queen County, Va., of well-to-do Huguenot stock, son of Benjamin and Sarah (Smith) Dabney. His father dying early, the boy grew up in New York at the home of his uncle, Dr. John Augustine Smith. After several sessions of boarding-school in New Jersey he entered the College of William and Mary, but soon withdrew to manage the family estate, "Elmington," in Gloucester County, where for fifteen years he raised wheat and tobacco and followed the agreeable existence of the antebellum Virginia gentleman. He married, June 6, 1820, Mary Adelaide, daughter of Samuel Tyler of Williamsburg, who died three years later, and on June 26, 1826, he married Sophia Hill of King and Queen County.

In 1835, to provide more adequately for his growing family and his numerous slaves, he moved to Hinds County, Miss., and turned cotton planter. A diligent and skilled executive, he was successful from the first. Much of his prosperity proceeded from the sense of responsibility which, out of compassion rather than self-interest, he felt toward his negroes: his consideration and affection, and even firmness, they repaid with unvarying devotion. At the same time he managed—more carefully than his own, it was said—four other plantations; was an eager, although personally disinterested, student of public affairs; fished, hunted, and played whist; entertained so open-handedly as to win reputation as an "incomparable host"; and devoted himself to his large family. His Whig principles helped to make him a strong Unionist, and when secession threatened he would have moved to England save for his inability to provide comfortably for his slaves; yet, when war came, he gave unreservedly to the South his crops, his money, and his sons, and fretted because he himself was not in the field.

Peace found him in straitened circumstances. To cap his losses of over a half-million dollars in slaves, livestock, and household goods, the defalcation of a friend caused the sacrifice of his remaining property and saddled him with a debt which took fourteen years of bitterest self-denial to pay. He could have avoided this by declaring himself bankrupt: instead, the hands that had never performed manual labor learned to garden, saw wood, and even—to save his daughters—do the washing. Adversity chastened him, made him tender, more patient, but did not bend him: to his death he remained the patrician, guileless, generous, high-hearted, courageous, tolerant of all save dishonesty or littleness. His actual achievement was slight; his significance was that he symbolized a class, a section, an era. "I never could forget that I was born a gentleman, and incapable, consequently, of a mean action," he wrote, and in living out this creed he embodied the finest traditions of Southern manhood under the institution of slavery. Without aspiring to drive "the horses of the sun," nevertheless he lived greatly, so naturally and unostentatiously filling a long life with honorable deeds that Gladstone, upon reading his biography, was moved to pronounce him "one of the very noblest of human characters."

[The foregoing sketch is based almost entirely on Susan Dabney Smedes, *Memorials of a Southern Planter* (1887), which besides setting forth Dabney's strongly marked individuality is an interesting, though perhaps idealistic, picture of the old régime in the South. There are other biographical touches in the romantic novel, *The Story of Don Miff* (1886), by his son, Virginius Dabney (*q.v.*).]   A. C. G., Jr.

DABNEY, VIRGINIUS (Feb. 15, 1835–June 2, 1894), teacher, author, son of Thomas Smith Gregory and Sophia (Hill) Dabney, was born at his father's plantation, "Elmington," in Gloucester County, Va., and died in New York City. His father [*q.v.*], an exemplar as near as might be of the legendary Southern gentleman, re-moved in 1835 from Virginia to Mississippi, to a plantation in Hinds County, named "Burleigh." Virginius was educated at home by tutors and was later sent to school in Richmond. From eighteen to twenty-three, with the exception of the fourth of these years, when he was traveling in Europe, he studied at the University of Virginia. Then he married Ellen Maria Heath and went to Memphis to practise law. The death of his wife in April 1860 brought him back to Virginia, and the outbreak of the Civil War interrupted his at best half-hearted intention of returning to his office. He entered the Confederate army immediately upon its organization and continued with it till it was disbanded, having the rank of captain when he was mustered out. After the war he established the Loudoun School in Middleburg, Va., and in February 1867 he married Anna Wilson Noland. During 1873–74 he was in charge of a preparatory school at Princeton, and afterward he conducted the New York Latin School in New York City. He was on the editorial staff of the New York *Commercial Advertiser* and he acted as literary adviser to several prominent publishers. In 1886, he published his novel, *The Story of Don Miff,* the proper name being a lisper's version of John Smith. This book, written, according to the title-page, by John Bouche Whacker, and edited by Virginius Dabney, is a record of Virginia from about 1860 to 1865 addressed by one still a bachelor to his supposititious descendant of the year 2200. Regarded at the time of its appearance as exceedingly profound, it in some degree justifies such an estimate. It is conventional at base, but in many important matters its author is revealed as a whimsical, shrewd, and wise critic of the social order he saw making itself paramount in America. He abandoned his school in 1887, and till the fall of 1893, when he became an official in the New York Custom House, devoted himself entirely to literature. His second novel, *Gold that did not Glitter* (1889), omitting the philosophic elements of *Don Miff,* attained neither popularity nor distinction. Circumstance forbade that in its externals his life should be identical with the romantically feudal lives of his father and his grandfather, and he was more sophisticated than they, more tolerant and humorous—but in the essential matter of his high if often unpractical attitude toward life he was never far removed from them.

[V. Dabney, "A Mighty Hunter Before the Lord," in C. King, *Rancho del Muerto* (1894); S. D. Smedes, *Memorials of a Southern Planter* (1887); W. H. Dabney, *Dabneys of Va.* (1888); P. A. Bruce, *Hist. of the Univ. of Va.* (1922); *Richmond Times*, June 3, 1894.]
J. D. W.

DABOLL, NATHAN (Apr. 24, 1750–Mar. 9, 1818), philomath, maker of almanacs, teacher of navigation, was born in Groton, Conn., the son of Nathan and Anna (Lynn) Daboll. The former, as witness to the will of the Rev. Jonathan Owen, spelled his name "Dibbell." Although he received some instruction in the local school and under the village parson, Rev. Jonathan Barber, young Nathan was for the most part self-taught. His tutor thought him dull, probably because he showed little interest in anything but mathematics. For this science, however, he had great natural aptitude, and while, through force of necessity, he worked as a cooper, he mastered the intricacies of its higher branches. In 1770 Timothy Green of New London was publishing a series of almanacs prepared by Clark Elliott. An error in the calculations for that year, perhaps discovered by Daboll, so mortified Elliott that he withdrew his name from subsequent issues, substituting the *nom de plume* of "Edmund Freebetter," and Daboll was employed to revise the calculations. In 1773 Green also published the *New England Almanack by Nathan Daboll, Philomath,* the first of a series which, continued by son, grandson, and great-grandson, has endured to the present time. For some years, however, Daboll's name was not on the title-page. According to James H. Trumbull (*List of Books Printed in Connecticut 1709-1800,* 1904), "Mr. Daboll's name appeared first on the Almanac of 1773, and was continued on those of 1774 and 1775. It was then dropped for that of 'Edmund Freebetter,' whose almanacs had gained a degree of popularity hardly inferior to those published with the name of Ames. In 1793 the New England Almanack, &c., 'by Nathan Daboll' was published, and in announcing it (Oct. 18, 1792) Green states that 'to Mr. Daboll the public have for many years been indebted for the correct calculation of Freebetter's Almanack.'"

Living in a maritime town, and proficient in navigation and nautical astronomy, he also devoted much time to the instruction of seamen. In 1783 he was persuaded to become teacher of mathematics and astronomy in Plainfield (Conn.) Academy, but returned to Groton in 1788, and resumed his work as a nautical instructor. In 1799 he published *Daboll's Complete Schoolmaster's Assistant,* an early and extensively used school arithmetic. Members both of the merchant marine and of the navy were his pupils. In 1811, on the invitation of Commodore Rodgers, he taught a large class in the cabin of the frigate *President.* He also prepared *Daboll's Practical Navigator: Being a concise, easy, and comprehensive system of Navigation,* calculated for the daily use of seamen, and also for an Assistant to the Teacher.... Also a New, Scientific and very short method of Correcting the Dead Reckoning; with rules for keeping a complete Reckoning at Sea applied to Practice, and exemplified in three separate JOURNALS, in which may be seen all the varieties which can possibly happen in a Ship's Reckoning (1820). It was printed and sold by Samuel Green of New London, who states that the sickness and death of the author is responsible for delay in publication. He is described as of medium height, stoutly built, inclining somewhat to corpulency in later life, with massive head, high, broad forehead, and heavy overarching eyebrows. Taciturn and reserved, he mingled little in society. He was twice married: first to a cousin, Elizabeth, daughter of John Daboll 2nd; and after her death to "Widow Elizabeth Brown" of Noank, Conn.

[*The New England Almanac* for 1894; Chas. R. Stark, *Groton, Conn.* (1922); F. M. Caulkins, *Hist. of New London, Conn.* (1852); *Conn. as a Colony and as a State* (1904), vols. II and IV, ed. by Forrest Morgan; Hugh A. Morrison, *Preliminary Check List of Am. Almanacs, 1639-1800* (1907); letters from Ernest C. Daboll, publisher of the *New England Almanac.*]

H. E. S.

DĄBROWSKI, JOSEPH (Jan. 19, 1842–Feb. 15, 1903), Roman Catholic priest, founder of SS. Cyril and Methodius Seminary in Detroit, Mich., was born at Żółtańce in Russian Poland. He received his elementary education from his mother. After graduation from the gymnasium of Lublin he matriculated at the University of Warsaw, where he specialized in mathematics and the natural sciences. When the Polish uprising of 1863 broke out, Dąbrowski promptly joined a regiment of teachers and students and fought under Mierosławski. Among the many engagements in which he took part was that of Krzywosacz from which he barely escaped with his life. After the collapse of the insurrection he returned to Warsaw, but, since the Russian spies were searching for those who bore arms in the revolt, he left Poland rather hurriedly for Dresden. Afterward he went to Lucerne and then to Berne, where he studied mathematics and technology. Subsequently going to Rome, he entered the Polish College conducted by the Fathers of the Congregation of the Resurrection. On the completion of his theological studies, he was ordained a priest on Aug. 1, 1869. Landing in America on Dec. 31, 1869, he resided for a short time at St. Francis Seminary, near Milwaukee. In 1870 he took charge of the Polish congregation at Polonia, Portage County, Wis. Perceiving the need of schools and teachers for the children of the Polish immigrants he persuaded the Felician Sisters of Cracow to come to America. Five of these arrived in Polonia in the autumn of 1874. He had built a home for them here and he aided them in establishing a Mother-house and an orphanage in Detroit. Mich. Ill health obliging him to leave Polonia in 1883, he then became chaplain to the Felician Sisters in Detroit. Since the number of immigrants had increased, American bishops frequently wrote to Cardinal Ledochowski, Prefect of the Propaganda, to send them Polish priests. Being unable to do this, he proposed the founding of a Polish seminary in America. Father Leopold Moczygemba, sent here to gather funds, collected about eight thousand dollars, but felt that owing to his advanced age he could not complete the undertaking. He therefore turned it over to Dąbrowski, who purchased a tract of land on Forest and St. Aubin Avenues in Detroit. A building was begun in 1884, but owing to lack of funds it was not completed until 1887. Dąbrowksi himself labored as a carpenter on the building, assisted by some of the first students, who worked as carpenters and bricklayers for their board and lodging. The school opened on Dec. 15, 1887 with only six students, but at the close of the term had twenty-six. In 1891 Dąbrowski established a weekly paper, *Niedziela,* published by the Seminary. In January 1903, when he was preparing to build an extension, he was obliged to dismiss twenty-nine students for insubordination. This unfortunate incident preyed on his mind and affected his health, already enfeebled by years of privation, worry, and intensive work. Suffering a heart attack on Feb. 9, he died as the result of another six days later. A kindly and self-sacrificing priest, he was deeply mourned by the Poles in America.

[*Historya Seminaryum Polskiego* (Detroit, 1910); Wenceslaus Kruszka, *Historya Polska w Ameryce* (6 vols., Milwaukee, 1905); *Sodalis Maryański* (Orchard Lake, Mich.), Feb. 1928, pp. 242–46; *Nasze Pisemko* (Felician Sisters, Detroit, 1928), vol. V; *Detroit Free Press,* Feb. 16, 1903; *Detroit Tribune,* Feb. 19, 1903; *Cath. Encyc.,* App.]   J.J.R.

DA COSTA, JACOB MENDEZ (Feb. 7, 1833–Sept. 11, 1900), physician, the son of John Mendez Da Costa, was born on the island of St. Thomas in the West Indies. The Da Costa family was of Spanish and Portuguese extraction; some of the members went to England and from this branch Jacob Da Costa was descended. When he was four years of age the family moved to Europe, where he received his early education, largely in Dresden. He acquired a sound knowledge of the classics, learned to speak French and German fluently, and acquired a

reading knowledge of four other languages. His family having suffered financial reverses, he had to give up his plans to follows politics or diplomacy and decided to study medicine, entering the Jefferson Medical College in Philadelphia in 1849 and having Prof. Mütter as a preceptor. He graduated in 1852 and soon after went to Paris for post-graduate study. Of those under whom he studied, Trousseau, whose clinical lectures are among the classics of medicine, probably had the greatest influence on him. This influence is seen in Da Costa's descriptions of disease, the careful choice of words, the orderly arrangement, and the graceful diction of his later productions. From Paris he went to Prague and Vienna, coming under the influence of many of those who were breaking new paths in medicine, among them Oppolzer, Skoda, Rokitansky, and Hebra. He worked particularly in pathology and clinical medicine, and there is much to suggest that he was following out a well-thought plan looking to a career as a teacher and a practitioner of what to-day is termed internal medicine.

In 1853 he returned to Philadelphia and at once became active in teaching. He also gave private classes in his office which became very popular. Probably his special knowledge of the newer methods in physical diagnosis had much to do with the success of these courses. He evidently attracted the attention of the elder Gross, for in 1857 he assisted Gross in the revision of his work on *Elements of Pathological Anatomy.* He was active in the foundation of the Pathological Society of Philadelphia in 1857, serving as its first secretary. In 1865 he was appointed to the staff of the Pennsylvania Hospital, to which he gave freely of his time and energy until his death. In 1872 he was elected professor of medicine in the Jefferson Medical College, and this position he held until 1891. Here his main work was done, with such colleagues as the elder Gross and Pancoast, and here his reputation as a great teacher and clinician was made. A wealth of tradition remains in Philadelphia as to his great ability in both spheres. He was regarded as having an almost uncanny power of diagnosis, which usually means keen powers of observation and an alert mind.

His medical writings were not voluminous, but all were of value and some of outstanding merit. He insisted on the importance of learning and of clear statement and especially on the evil of publishing crude theories and unproved statements. Of his publications, first place belongs to the work on *Medical Diagnosis* (1864). This work may be said to have opened a new era and its influence was wide-spread on teaching and clinical methods. It went through nine editions and was translated into several other languages. In it the problems of the recognition of disease were discussed in a systematic fashion which altered markedly the conception of medical diagnosis and brought order out of what had been too often haphazard guessing. Of his studies on various diseases, that which is best known is his description of the irritable heart in soldiers, in which from his study of soldiers in the Civil War he described a new clinical syndrome (see *Contributions Relating to the Causation and Prevention of Disease, and to Camp Diseases,* edited by Austin Flint and published by the United States Sanitary Commission, 1867). This malady was an important cause of disability in the World War. He also wrote extensively on typhoid fever. His medical papers were of a high standard and he strove for quality rather than quantity in his writings.

Many honors came to him both in an academic way and in medical societies. He was twice president of the College of Physicians of Philadelphia (1884–86 and 1895–98) and took a deep interest in its welfare. He was an original member of the Association of American Physicians and its president in 1897. He was a member of many medical societies and received honorary degrees from several universities. In addition to being physician to the Jefferson and Pennsylvania Hospitals, he held the same position in the Episcopal and Philadelphia General Hospitals. In 1899 he was made a trustee of the University of Pennsylvania. In 1860, he married Sarah Frederica Brinton, the sister of one of his colleagues, Dr. John H. Brinton [*q.v.*]. She died in 1889, leaving one child. For some years Da Costa suffered from angina pectoris, dying in an attack at Villanova, Pa., on Sept. 11, 1900. Admiration for his character seems to have been as great as for his intellectual and professional gifts. He may be regarded as having lived an ideal life for a physician, devoted to the care of the sick, the teaching of students, and the study of disease. Throughout his life the welfare of members of his own profession was always his concern and he has been called "the physician's physician."

[Memoirs by J. C. Wilson, in *Trans. of the Coll. of Physicians of Phila.*, 3 ser., vol. XXIV (1902); and Mary A. Clarke, in *Am. Jour. Medic. Sci.*, CXXV, 318 (1903).]   T. M.

DAFT, LEO (Nov. 13, 1843–Mar. 28, 1922), electrical engineer, inventor, was born in Birmingham, England, the son of Thomas B. and Emma Matilda (Sturges) Daft. His father was a consulting civil engineer specializing in bridge and iron-ship construction. Daft attended the public schools and Liverpool Collegiate until he was fifteen and then entered his father's office as a draftsman. Among his father's friends were Varley and Siemens, pioneers in electricity, and through them young Daft became interested in this subject, devoting much of his spare time for eight years to study and experimental work. In 1866, believing that his best opportunity lay in America, he sailed for New York. For the next five years he was engaged in a variety of occupations while looking for a suitable opportunity in electricity. Finding none, he started a photographic studio in Troy, N. Y., in 1871. Successful in this, he continued it until 1879 when, upon the death of his father, he began his electrical career in earnest. His first connection was with the New York Electric Light Company, which was soon merged into the Daft Electric Company, developing electric-power machinery and building several electric-power plants in Boston, New York, Worcester, and elsewhere. In 1883 Daft began electric-railroad experiments, built an electric locomotive, named "The Ampere," for the Saratoga and Mt. McGregor Railroad, and in the following year installed a short line at Coney Island, N. Y. In 1884 his company supplied the machinery for the New York Power Company's first distributing station of electric power in Gold St., and also manufactured all the electrical apparatus for the Massachusetts Electric Power Company. This was the first instance of a complete central station for the generation and distribution of electricity for power purposes on a commercial scale. In 1885 the company installed its electric railway system in Baltimore on a branch of the Baltimore Union Passenger Railway. This was the first commercially operated electric road in the United States. The Daft system was subsequently used in a number of cities and a Daft locomotive was tried out on the elevated railroad of New York City. Daft's ability not only in electric construction but in distribution attracted universal attention and gave a direct and lasting impulse to the electric motor industry. Until 1890 he was the only inventor who had taken up the problem of the distribution of electric power and worked it out in the same manner as current for electric lighting, perfecting and providing the necessary apparatus throughout. After this, he directed his attention to the electro-chemical field, his chief invention being a process of vulcanizing rubber onto metal, now generally used. Daft was a charter member of the American Institute of Electrical Engineers; a member of the American

Association for the Advancement of Science; and of the Electro-Chemical Society. He never became a citizen of the United States, but married an American woman, Katherine Anna Flansburgh, on Mar. 11, 1871, at Albany, N. Y. With four children she survived him.

[Records Am. Inst. Electrical Engineers; *Cassier's Mag.*, July 1901; *Electrical World*, Mar. 30, 1889; *Jour. Am. Inst. Electrical Engineers*, May 1922; U. S. Nat. Museum correspondence with the Daft family.]

C. W. M.

DAGG, JOHN LEADLEY (Feb. 13, 1794– June 11, 1884), Baptist clergyman, educator, author, was born in a log cabin near Middleburg, Va., eldest of the eight children of Robert and Sarah (Davis) Dagg. His mother was a daughter of Samuel Davis of Pennsylvania and his wife, Sarah Leadley of New Jersey. His paternal grandfather was Thomas, son of John Dagg, who came to Virginia from Bristol, England, soon after 1700. From his youth John Dagg had two controlling and fortunately parallel ambitions, service in the Christian ministry and the promotion of thorough education. Partly because of poverty, however, he had only six or seven years of formal schooling, and this often interrupted, but he began to teach at the age of fourteen, an invitation to take charge of a school having come to him. Entering the Baptist ministry in 1817, he served as pastor, or supply, at Dumfries and other places in Virginia, and for nine years (1825–34) was pastor of the Fifth Baptist Church in Philadelphia. Forced by an affection of the throat to abandon preaching, he became head of the Haddington Institution, near Philadelphia. Chosen principal of the Alabama Female Athenæum in 1836, he became professor of theology at Mercer University, then at Penfield, Ga., in 1843, and president the following year. Finding an institution of a low grade, he left it in 1856 greatly enhanced in prestige. In all this educational work his prime desire was to influence young men to prepare for Christian work.

He left Mercer with the definite idea of still serving in the field of religious leadership by writing books which would aid young men in the service of the Christian ministry. Thus he prepared first a *Manual of Theology* (1857), which was of such significance that it has continued to be published until recently. His *Treatise on Church Order* (1858) has been equally useful. His *Elements of Moral Science* (1859) and his *Evidences of Christianity* (1868), while not popular for so long a period, were widely influential in their respective fields. All this he accomplished in spite of continuous ill health and a defect of eyesight which for many years rendered him nearly blind. When he could no longer see to use a pen he devised a special board which enabled him to write legibly. He was twice married: on Dec. 18, 1817, to Fannie H. Thornton, who died in September, 1823; and in 1831 to Mrs. Mary (Young) Davis, the mother of Noah Knowles Davis [*q.v.*]. He died at Hayneville, Ala.

[See Dagg's very rare *Autobiography* (Rome, Ga., 1886); Hillyer Hawthorne Straton, "John Leadley Dagg" (MS.); *Baptist Argus*, May 7, 1903; Philadelphia *Christian Gazette*, II (1834), 32, and Philadelphia *Nat. Baptist*, 1884, p. 457; all in the library of the Am. Baptist Hist. Soc., Chester, Pa. See also H. Holcombe, *A Hist. of the Rise and Progress of the Baptists in Ala.* (1840); B. F. Riley, *A Memorial Hist. of the Baptists of Ala.* (1923); *Hist. of the Baptist Denomination in Ga.* (1881), compiled for the *Christian Index*; S. G. Hillyer, *Reminiscences of Ga. Baptists* (1902).]

F. G. L.

DAGGETT, DAVID (Dec. 31, 1764–Apr. 12, 1851), lawyer, politician, jurist, born at Attleboro, Mass., was of Puritan descent, the son of Thomas and Sibulah (Stanley) Daggett. After graduating at Yale in 1783, he began the study of law in New Haven, where he maintained his residence throughout the remainder of a long life. Admitted to the bar in 1786, he was recognized from the start as a young man of great promise. An address delivered by him in New Haven as official orator, July 4, 1787, shows that he had already acquired many of the political principles which later made him prominent in the Federalist party, including a generous allowance of that pessimism regarding the future of American institutions which characterized so many of its leaders. Elected in 1791 to the lower branch of the legislature, he served there continuously, the last three years as speaker, until 1797, when he was elected to the Council. This body, under the old charter government prior to 1818, had many of the characteristics of an upper house, and at the same time a share in executive functions, including the patronage, which made its members exceedingly powerful in party affairs. He served here until 1804, when he resigned. He was elected to another term in the lower house in 1805, and in 1809 reëntered the Council where he remained until sent to the United States Senate in 1813.

He had in the meantime acquired a considerable practise and was active in a variety of local business and social affairs. The Jeffersonian Republicans, who became active in Connecticut about 1800, found in him one of their most active opponents. Early in the contest he clashed with Abraham Bishop [*q.v.*], and the two champions belabored each other in a series of pamphlets and newspaper articles. Various pamphlets of Daggett's published in these years, all of considerable literary merit, show his intensely conservative character. In *Count the Cost* (1804) he made an effective presentation of his views on state affairs, defending the church establishment and the retention of the old charter government, and denouncing democracy and universal suffrage. In the Senate he pursued much the same course as the other New England Federalists, who in the space of a dozen years had been transformed by the exigencies of party politics into defenders of state rights. The debates for this period were scantily reported but both of Daggett's recorded speeches, one against the militia bill, Nov. 16, 1814 (*Annals of Congress*, 13 Cong., 3 Sess., pp. 70 ff.), and the other on internal improvements, Feb. 26, 1817 (*Ibid.*, 14 Cong., 2 Sess., p. 165 ff.), are strict-constructionist expositions of the Constitution.

At the close of his term in 1819, he resumed practise in New Haven. In 1826 he began a service of twenty-two years at Yale as Kent Professor of Law, and in the same year was appointed an associate justice of the superior court. He was also mayor of New Haven, 1828–30. In 1832 he became chief justice of the supreme court of errors, serving until Dec. 31, 1834, when he was obliged to retire under the established age limitation. The noted case of Prudence Crandall [*q.v.*] arose (October 1833) during his term as chief justice. This was a prosecution under a Connecticut statute prohibiting the instruction of non-resident colored persons except by permission of the selectmen of the town. Judge Daggett's instructions to the jury, on the basis of which Miss Crandall was convicted, were to the effect that free negroes were not citizens of the United States within the terms of Art. IV, Sec. 2, of the Constitution and that the statute was therefore within the competence of the legislature. This pronouncement has a recognized place in the history of the constitutional status of the American negro. It is less well known, however, than it would have been had the supreme court not reversed the judgment on technical grounds, the chief justice dissenting, and thereby avoided adjudication of the main issue (10 *Conn.* 339). Daggett continued active in the practise and teaching of law for many years after his retirement from the bench. He married, Sept. 10, 1786, Wealthy Ann, daughter of Dr. Eneas Munson of New Haven. Following her death on July 9, 1839, he married, May 4, 1840, Mary, daughter of Capt. Major and Susanna (Mansfield) Lines, who survived him.

[F. B. Dexter, *Biog. Sketches Grads. Yale Coll.*, IV (1907), 260–64, gives a summary of Daggett's career with a bibliography and list of his publications. Dwight Loomis and J. Gilbert Calhoun in *Judicial and Civil Hist. of Conn.* (1895) give a brief sketch. The Yale library has a considerable collection of his papers. An obituary appeared in the *New Haven Jour.*, Apr. 14, 1851.]   W.A.R.

DAGGETT, ELLSWORTH (May 24, 1845– Jan. 5, 1923), metallurgist and mining engineer, was the son of Rev. Oliver and Elizabeth (Watson) Daggett and the grandson of David Daggett [*q.v.*]. Born in Canandaigua, N. Y., where his father happened to be holding a pastorate, he was sent to school in New Haven, Conn. Here he attended Gen. Russell's Military School and graduated in 1864 from the Sheffield Scientific School, thus conforming to the Yale tradition of his family. After he had done postgraduate work at Yale and attained his majority he went to the Gould and Curry mill, at Virginia City, Nev. Here he obtained practical training in mining and formed acquaintanceship with those influential men for whom, in after years, he did large consulting practise from his office in Salt Lake City. In 1870 he entered the United States Geological Survey of the Fortieth Parallel. The plates in volume III of the Survey's report (James D. Hague, *Mining Industry*, 1870) were made from Daggett's field-drawings. In 1872 he became manager of the Winnamuck smelting plant, Bingham Canyon, Utah. The financial organization of this enterprise he himself largely effected through prominent New Haven men. His masterful article, "Economical Results of Smelting in Utah" (*Transactions of the American Institute of Mining Engineers*, vol. II), based on the operations of the Winnamuck smelter, together with his monumental paper, "The Russell Process in its Practical Application and Economic Results" (*Ibid.*, vol. XVI), describing the use of this method of hyposulphite lixiviation of silver ores at Cusihuiriachic, Mexico, are evidence of Daggett's metallurgical ability. He was practically the first manager of an American lead-smelter to appreciate adequately and apply properly a system of metallurgical accounting to smelting operations, while his work with the Russell process ranks him among the earliest of American hydrometallurgists. He spent the year 1874–75 abroad, attending mining lectures at the Bergakademie, Berlin. Later, in his practise as consulting engineer and in his technical contributions for publication he became more identified with mining than metallurgy. He became largely occupied with examination and reports upon mining properties for prospective purchasers, and with testimony as an expert in mining litigation cases. Appointed in 1888 the first United States surveyor-general of Utah, he required that the mineral surveys be referred to true meridian and otherwise improved the accuracy and reliability of the survey. His effective activities in the development of irrigation projects in Utah eventually won for him the distinction of having a county named in his honor. On June 28, 1874, he married June Spencer of Salt Lake City. Their two sons died in childhood.

[*Trans. Am. Inst. Mining & Metallurgical Engineers,* vol. LXIX (1923); *Yale Univ. Obit. Record* (1923); New Haven *Jour.-Courier,* Jan 6, 1923; personal information from relatives.]   R. C. C—y.

DAGGETT, NAPHTALI (Sept. 8, 1727–Nov. 25, 1780), Congregational clergyman, first incumbent of the first professorship in Yale College, and for more than ten years acting president, was born at Attleboro, Mass., the son of Ebenezer and Mary (Blackington) Daggett. He prepared for college with Rev. Solomon Reed of Abington, Mass., and with Rev. James Cogswell, of Plainfield, Conn. Graduating from Yale in 1748, having gained the Berkeley Scholarship, he studied theology, and on Sept. 18, 1751, was ordained first pastor of the Presbyterian Church at Smithtown, Long Island. On Dec. 19, 1753, he married Sarah, daughter of Richard and Anna Smith, of that town. In 1755, although he was but twenty-eight years old, he was nominated by President Clap [*q.v.*] for the professorship of divinity which had been established at Yale, and on Mar. 4, 1756 he was installed. Previous to his installation, in order, if possible, to get back the college congregation, which President Clap had removed, the First Church of New Haven invited Daggett to become colleague-pastor with Rev. Joseph Noyes, but acting no doubt under the president's advice, he declined. It was then proposed that he preach there for at least half the time, and the students were invited to attend without payment for sittings. After six months' trial, the arrangement was abandoned, and when in 1757 the Church of Christ in Yale College was established, he became its pastor. Upon the resignation of President Clap in 1766 he was appointed acting president, and served in that capacity until March 1777. The unsettled state in which President Clap left the college, and the pre-war conditions, made the period one of difficulty and little growth, but according to President Dwight, who was a tutor under him, "he had very just conceptions of the manner in which a College should be governed." The college prospered under him, but he was not always "happy in the mode of administering its discipline." (See Sprague, *post,* p. 483.) In 1776 the students petitioned the corporation for his removal. After his resignation he continued to serve as professor until his death. He is described as of "middle height, strong framed, in-clining to be corpulent, slow in his gait and somewhat clumsy in his movements" (*Ibid.,* p. 480). He was orthodox, uncontroversial, and as a preacher had a drawling, unanimated delivery. He was an ardent supporter of the Revolution and is credited with the authorship of the "Cato Letters" in the *Connecticut Gazette,* which in 1765 inaugurated the attack on Tax-collector Jared Ingersoll (Lawrence H. Gipson, *Jared Ingersoll,* 1920, p. 158). When in 1779 the British invaded New Haven, he went out with those who resisted them, riding on an old black mare, and carrying a long fowling piece. He was captured and subjected to harsh treatment which, it is supposed, hastened his death.

His publications include *The Faithful Serving of God and Our Generation, the Only Way to a Peaceful and Happy Death, A Sermon Occasioned by the Death of Rev. Thomas Clap* (1767); *The Great Importance of Speaking in the Most Intelligible Manner in Christian Churches* (1768), *The Excellency of a Good Name* (1768), *The Great and Tender Concern of Faithful Ministers for the Souls of their People, Should Powerfully Excite Them Also to Labour After Their Own Salvation* (1770); *The Testimony of Conscience, a Most Solid Foundation of Rejoicing* (1773).

[T. Clap, *The Annals or Hist. of Yale Coll.* (1776); E. Baldwin, *Annals of Yale College* (1831); *The Literary Diary of Ezra Stiles* (1902); F. B. Dexter, *Biog. Sketches Grads. Yale College with Annals of the College Hist.,* vol. II (1896), III (1903), IV (1907); Wm. B. Sprague, *Annals Am. Pulpit,* vol. I (1857).]

H. E. S.

DAHL, THEODOR HALVORSON (Apr. 2, 1845–Jan. 18, 1923), Lutheran clergyman, was born at Baastad, Mellem Borgesyssel, Norway, son of Halvor Thoreson Smaadal and his wife Anne Maastad. After attending Gjertsen's Latin School at Christiania for three years, he emigrated to America, where after two years of study at the (Scandinavian) Augustana Theological Seminary, Paxton, Ill., he was ordained a Norwegian Lutheran minister in 1867. Conspicuously successful as a home missionary among the scattered Norwegians in America, he was rapidly transferred from New London, Minn. (1867–68), to a post near Litchfield, Minn. (1868–73), and then to Green Bay, Wis. (1873–81). Eight congregations sprang up in the two latter places. His last pastoral charge was at Stoughton, Wis., where he served (1881–1903) until he was elevated to the full-time presidency of his synod. As a pastor he showed untiring zeal, an unfailingly affable and considerate spirit, and a devout sincerity. As a preacher he had marked mannerisms of voice and gesture, but never failed to draw large and attentive audiences.

His crowning achievement was his active participation in four successful church unions. When he was ordained in 1867 the synod was called the Scandinavian Augustana Synod. In 1870 the Norwegians and Swedes of this body effected an amicable separation into the Swedish and the Norwegian-Danish Augustana Synods. The majority of the latter body in 1870 joined a small group of other pastors and formed the Norwegian Danish Conference. That young Dahl entered actively into these union movements is amply proved by the fact that he was made a visitor of the Conference, 1873–76, and again, 1890–94. In 1876 he became secretary of the Conference and in 1881 its president, serving in the latter capacity until 1886. In 1887 the so-called Anti-Missouri Brotherhood withdrew from the Norwegian Synod, and after due negotiations entered into a union in 1890 with the conference and the latter's twin sister of 1870, the Augustana Synod, thus forming the United Norwegian Lutheran Church of America. In this work of union Dahl was conspicuously active, writing a brochure, *Fred og Strid* (Peace and Strife), in 1894 in defense of the union. From 1894 to 1902 he served as vice-president of the U. C., as it was familiarly called, and from 1902 to 1917 he served as its president. It is fitting that his presidency terminated with the existence of the U. C., this body uniting with the Norwegian Synod and the Hauge Synod to form the Norwegian Lutheran Church of America in 1917. His declining years were spent as rector of the Fairview Lutheran Hospital, Minneapolis, Minn.

Dahl was too busy to write a great deal. He translated *Lys fra Katakomberne* (Light from the Catacombs) in 1876, and in 1890 wrote a brochure, *Saloonforretningen* (The Saloon Business). He also wrote numerous reports as president and secretary. In all his work he was ably seconded by his devoted wife, Rebekka Oline (Gjertsen) whom he married in 1867 and survived.

[Scattered references are found in J. A. Bergh, *Den Norsk Lutherske Kirkes Historie in Amerika* (Minneapolis, 1914); biographies in Jens C. Jenssen (Roseland), *Am. Lutheran Biogs.* (Milwaukee, 1890); O. M. Norlie, *Norsk Lutherske Prester i Amerika 1843–1913* (Minneapolis, 1914), translated and revised by Rasmus Malmin, O. M. Norlie and O. A. Tingelstad as *Who's Who Among Pastors in All the Norwegian Lutheran Synods of America, 1843–1927* (Minneapolis, 1928).]   J. M. R.

DAHLGREN, JOHN ADOLPHUS BERNARD (Nov. 13, 1809–July 12, 1870), naval officer, inventor of ordnance, was born in Philadelphia, Pa. His father, Bernard Ulric Dahlgren, was a graduate of Upsala, a successful merchant well known for his ability and integrity. He was a man of great stature and strength, being over six feet four inches in height, and otherwise of majestic proportions. In 1804 he became involved in an attempt to disseminate republican principles at Gefle, and was obliged to flee from Sweden, and his property was confiscated by the Crown. After extended travel he landed in New York in 1806. The home government having withdrawn its persecution, he was appointed Swedish consul at Philadelphia, which post he held until his death in 1824. John Dahlgren's mother was Martha Rowan, daughter of James Rowan, who had served as an officer in the American Revolution. Dahlgren received his early schooling in a Quaker school in Philadelphia, and was also instructed by his father. When only fifteen years of age he was a good Latin, Spanish, and mathematical scholar. He was continually occupied in study and was particularly interested in the history of ancient Greece and Rome. Born and reared within sight of the river and shipping, the great object of his early ambition was to enter the United States navy. His first application was refused, notwithstanding the fact that he was recommended by many men of influence, including a judge, and members of the state legislature. He then shipped before the mast in the brig *Mary Beckett* bound for Trinidad de Cuba, in order that he might obtain a knowledge of his intended profession. On his return from this cruise, and before he was sixteen years of age, he wrote his first article, entitled "The Fragment," for the *Saturday Evening Post,* in which he described incidents of the voyage.

Appointed acting midshipman in the navy on Feb. 1, 1826, he made his first cruise in the frigate *Macedonian* under the command of Capt. James Barron (1826–28). He was assigned to the brig *Ontario* of the Mediterranean Squadron from 1829 to 1831, and in 1832 was appointed passed midshipman. The following year he was assigned to the United States Naval Station at Philadelphia, and during his leisure time studied law. His health failing, he was granted a leave of absence of several months, and in February 1834, due to his well-known proficiency in mathematics, he was ordered to duty with the Coast Survey, under F. R. Hassler, who was considered one of the foremost mathematicians of his time. Dahlgren was selected to serve in the triangulation of the survey and assist in the astronomical observations, as well as in the measurement of the base on Long Island, the first base line in the United States ever measured scientifically. He was chosen by Hassler to make the counter calculations of the base, to compare with and verify his own, and remained on this duty until 1836 when he was selected to make observations of the solar eclipses of that year. He was detailed from the second triangulation to assist in the first trials of the great theodolite of Houghton, which had just been completed for Hassler, and was made second assistant in the survey and given charge of a party of triangulation. About the time he was ordered to report to the survey for duty, Dahlgren published a series of remarkable papers on naval topics, in the form of open letters, signed "Blue Jacket," in the *National Gazette* of Philadelphia. These letters were addressed to Mr. Southard, chairman of the Naval Committee of the United States Senate, and excited much comment, as they boldly attacked the new regulations for the navy. Efforts were made to find the author, but even the editor of the *Gazette* never discovered the name of his contributor. Dahlgren was promoted lieutenant on Mar. 8, 1837. Due to his work in the Coast Survey, his eyesight became impaired to such an extent that he was threatened with total blindness and was compelled to relinquish work and enter the Naval Hospital. Finding no relief, he was granted leave of absence with permission to visit Paris for the purpose of placing himself under the care of Sichel, the celebrated oculist. After his return to the United States, he was married, Jan. 8, 1839, to Mary C. Bunker, of Philadelphia, and, on the advice of his physician, went to live in the country, where he remained until 1843 when he returned to duty at the Philadelphia Navy Yard, his eyesight fully restored. Later in the same year, he joined the *Cumberland* for a cruise in the Mediterranean, returning to the United States in 1845. While on this cruise he tried out a percussion lock which he had designed in 1835, but which he did not patent until 1847. In the latter year he was ordered to Washington for ordnance duty, and began labors as an ordnance officer which for sixteen years demanded the most extraordinary energy, and which finally made him chief of the Bureau of Ordnance, and gave him world recognition as a man of science and inventive genius.

Dahlgren's initial task was to investigate and introduce into the navy the Hale system of rockets. Coldly received at first by the Commandant, Commodore Warrington, he soon gained the confidence of that distinguished officer, and in August of the same year was placed in charge of all ordnance matter in the Washington Navy Yard. In addition he was professor of gunnery at An-

napolis. At this time there was no ordnance establishment; the fuse stocks, cannon locks, and shells, were made and fitted in the plumber's shop. The only sign of ordnance at the Navy Yard was the laboratory. Dahlgren suggested a plan for an ordnance workshop which was accepted by the Bureau and directed to be carried into effect. This was the beginning of the ordnance establishment which was to become of such importance to the country at the outbreak of the Civil War. Under the sole direction of Dahlgren, the ordnance department at the Washington Yard acquired the most extensive additions, including a foundry for cannon, gun-carriage shops, an experimental battery, and other equipment of various kinds. In 1848 he proposed equipping the Navy with "Boat Howitzers," a type of gun suited to both field and naval service, combining both lightness and accuracy. After much opposition they were adopted by the navy in 1850, and later by many European and South American countries. In 1850 he published a book, *32 Pounder Practise for Ranges,* and also proposed to the Bureau of Ordnance two guns after his own designs, one a 50 pounder and the other a 9-inch shell gun, the former of 8,000, the latter of about 9,000 pounds. The following year he submitted the design of an 11-inch gun which was approved and ordered cast. All these were smoothbores. Called "Dahlgrens," they were of iron, cast solid, and cooled from the exterior. They were distinguished by great thickness at the breech, rapidly diminishing from the trunnions to the muzzle, and were the practical application of results obtained by experimental determination of pressures at different points along the bore. During the year 1851 Dahlgren prepared for publication *The System of Boat Armament in the United States Navy,* published in 1852. In 1853 he was elected a member of the American Association for the Advancement of Science, and that year his book *Naval Percussion Locks and Primers* was published. He was promoted to commander, Oct. 11, 1855. In 1856 the second edition of his *Boat Howitzers* was published, a model of a rifle musket and a knife bayonet submitted, and a book entitled *Shells and Shell Guns* prepared for publication. This work was considered by many students of ordnance as the best ever written on the subject. In order to introduce innovations which completely revolutionized the armament of the navy, and to remove objections to his 11-inch gun, which was then considered too heavy for use at sea, Dahlgren was permitted to arm the sloop-of-war *Plymouth* entirely as he wished, and to take her on a six months' experimental cruise. On his return, he reported the 11-inch gun perfectly manageable at sea. The last vestige of opposition to his system then finally disappeared, and it was soon after adopted in the arming of the national vessels.

Dahlgren was on ordnance duty in 1861 when Franklin Buchanan, captain in command of the Washington Navy Yard, resigned to enter the Confederate service, and while the law required that the command of the Washington Navy Yard be restricted to the command of a captain, President Lincoln refused to place any officer over him, though some of the captains asked for the assignment on the ground that it was not legal for Dahlgren to hold it. The Washington Navy Yard was of the utmost importance to the North, not only because of its naval resources, but also as the key to the defenses of Washington on the left. In July 1862, Dahlgren was appointed chief of the Bureau of Ordnance in addition to his other duties as commandant of the Yard, though holding only the rank of commander. On Aug. 5, 1862, he was promoted captain, his commission being ante-dated to July 16, and in February of the following year was promoted to rear admiral. At the same time he received the thanks of Congress, and ten years additional on the active list of the navy, which, however, he did not live to enjoy. On his request for active service, he was ordered to sea and relieved Du Pont in command of the South Atlantic Blockading Squadron. In the following months he cooperated with the land forces under Gen. Gilmore in a number of attacks on the land defenses of Charleston, and succeeded in silencing the batteries on Morris Island and at Sumter, and in securing a safe anchorage for the monitors inside the bar, which put a stop to blockade-running at that port. His failure to take Charleston provoked some hostile criticism, but his operations had the approval of the Navy Department. He led a successful expedition up the St. John's River in February 1864, to aid in throwing a military force into Florida, cooperated with Gen. Sherman in the capture of Savannah on Dec. 23, and entered Charleston with Gen. Schimmelfennig on its evacuation in February 1865. On July 12, 1865, he relinquished command of the South Atlantic Blockading Squadron and returned to Washington, where, some weeks later (Aug. 2, 1865), he married Mrs. Madeleine Vinton Goddard, daughter of the Hon. S. F. Vinton of Ohio. In 1866 he was assigned to the command of the South Pacific Squadron where he remained until 1868, when he returned to the United States and was again appointed chief of the Bureau of Ordnance. At his own request he was relieved as chief of the Bureau on Aug. 10, 1869, and as-

signed to the command of the Washington Navy Yard where he died July 12, 1870. Dahlgren had seven children by his first marriage and three by his second. After his death, his *Notes on Maritime and International Law* (1877) appeared with a preface by his widow, indicating the plan of an uncompleted work.

[L. R. Hamersly, *Records of Living Officers of the U. S. Navy and Marine Corps* (1870); J. T. Headley, *Our Navy in the Great Rebellion, Heroes and Battles of the War 1861–65* (1891); M. V. Dahlgren, *Memoir of John A. Dahlgren* (1882); Washington *Star*, July 12, 1870.]   C. F. C—y.

DAHLGREN, SARAH MADELEINE VINTON (July 13, 1825–May 28, 1898), author, was born at Gallipolis, Ohio, the daughter of Samuel Finley Vinton, more than twenty years congressman from the district. Her mother was Romaine Madeleine Bureau, daughter of French émigrés settled at Gallipolis. The first American ancestor of the Vintons, who also claimed French descent, was John Vinton, whose name appeared in records of Lynn, Mass., in 1648. When Madeleine was six, her mother died and soon afterward her brother, the only other child. Her father made her his companion and, as soon as she was old enough, his hostess in Washington. She was educated at Monsieur Picot's boarding school in Philadelphia and the Convent of the Visitation, Georgetown, D. C. In June 1846, she was married to Daniel C. Goddard, an Ohio lawyer and an assistant secretary of the newly formed Interior Department. After his death five years later Mrs. Goddard, with her two children, made her home with her father until he died in 1862. On Aug. 2, 1865, she became the second wife of Rear Admiral John Adolphus Dahlgren [*q.v.*], of the United States Navy, and accompanied him on a South American cruise. In 1870, again left a widow, with three small children, she continued to live in her father's Washington home.

Mrs. Dahlgren began to write in 1859 under the pen names "Corinne" and "Cornelia." Her works include: *Idealities* (1859); *Pius IX and France* (1861), translated from Montalembert; *An Essay on Catholicism, Authority and Order* (1862), translated from the Spanish of Don Juan Donoso Cortés; *Thoughts on Female Suffrage* (1871); *Memoir of Ulric Dahlgren* (1872), edited from the work of Admiral Dahlgren; *Etiquette of Social Life in Washington* (1873); *The Executive Power in the United States* (1874), translated from Adolphe de Chambrun; *South Sea Sketches* (1881); *South Mountain Magic* (1882); *Memoir of John A. Dahlgren* (1882); *A Washington Winter* (1883); *The Lost Name* (1886); *Lights and Shadows of a*

Life (1887); *Divorced* (1887); *Chim: his Washington Winter* (1892); *Samuel Finley Vinton* (1895); *The Secret Directory* (1896); *The Woodley Lane Ghost and Other Stories* (1899). Her writings show versatility, the student's aptitude for detail, knowledge of languages, familiarity with Washington life, and certain political and religious prepossessions. Imagination and charm of style are not marked, but in some of her books, for example, *South Mountain Magic,* love of place inspired literary treatment. Mrs. Dahlgren's later life in Washington was concerned with literary and religious activities. She did not believe in women's participation in politics and her pamphlet against woman suffrage was used before committees of Congress by opponents of the cause. She was identified with Catholic missionary work and built near her summer home, "Dahlgren," on South Mountain, Md., a Gothic chapel dedicated to St. Joseph of the Sacred Heart of Jesus. After the death of her eldest son, Vinton Goddard, in 1877, she led a retired life, but her home was something of a salon for a large circle of literary friends. She was a founder of the Washington Literary Society in 1873, and was a vice-president, a frequent hostess, and a contributor of papers and poetry to the programs. She died at her Massachusetts Avenue home in Washington and was buried on South Mountain, Md.

[John Adams Vinton, *The Vinton Memorial, comprising a Genealogy of the Descendants of John Vinton of Lynn, 1648,* etc. (1858); Minutes of the Washington Literary Soc.; obituaries in *Washington Post,* May 29, 1898, and *Evening Star* (Washington), May 30, 1898.]

S. G. B.

DALCHO, FREDERICK (1770–Nov. 24, 1836), physician, Episcopal clergyman, was born in London, England, where his father, a Prussian officer under Frederick the Great, had taken up residence after having been incapacitated by wounds. On the death of his father, Frederick came to live in Baltimore with an uncle who had himself been in America only a few years. There he availed himself of the general education current in his day, studied medicine, and inquired zealously into botany. In April 1792 he became a surgeon's mate in the United States army, and in May 1794 a lieutenant. In June 1799, while stationed at Fort Johnston, he left the army and became a citizen of nearby Charleston (S. C.). Here he followed the practise of medicine, permitting himself for a while no distractions more grave than the organizing of a public botanical garden and the normal votive activities of an enthusiastic Mason. In 1807 he published *Ahiman Rezon,* a handbook for his fellow craftsmen

in Masonry, an earnest, solemn production which has been the foundation for similar efforts dating as late as 1901. The title-page of this book proclaims its author a member not only of the medical societies of South Carolina and of Philadelphia, but also of the Academy of Arts, Sciences, and Belles-Lettres of Marseilles. In 1807 he became one of the two editors of the Federalist *Charleston Courier.* In 1808, or thereabout, he was married to Mary E. Threadcraft. Two or three years later his attention began fixing itself more and more on theology, and after a while he became a lay-reader of the Episcopal Church in St. Paul's Parish, Colleton. In 1814 he was made deacon; in 1818, priest; and in 1819, assistant minister of St. Michael's, Charleston. In addition to publishing his sermons and editing the ecclesiastical *Gospel Messenger,* he wrote *A Letter on Public Baptism* (1817), *An Historical Account of the Protestant Episcopal Church in South Carolina* (1820), and *Evidences of the Divinity of Jesus Christ* (1820). Conventional and decorous, the *Historical Account* serves still as a dependable source-book of history. As a pastor in daily contact with his congregation he was respected and loved. He died in Charleston. His gravestone in St. Michael's Church attests that "Fidelity, industry, and Prudence were the characteristics of his ministry," that he was "Steadfast and uniform in his own peculiar convictions and action," and that "he lived and died 'in perfect charity with all men.'"

[W. B. Sprague, *Annals Am. Pulpit,* vol. V (1859); G. S. Holmes, *A Hist. Sketch of the Parish Church of St. Michael* (1887); C. Jervey, *Inscriptions on the Tablets and Gravestones in St. Michael's Church and Churchyard* (1906); F. B. Heitman, *Hist. Reg. and Dict. of the U. S. Army* (1903); A. G. Mackey, *Ahiman Rezon* (1901); *Charleston Courier,* Nov. 25, 1836.]

J. D. W.

DALE, RICHARD (Nov. 6, 1756–Feb. 26, 1826), naval officer, was born in Norfolk County, Va., of an old and highly respected family. He was the son of Winfield, a shipwright of the parish of Portsmouth, and Ann (Sutherland) Dale. Thrown upon his own resources at an early age, in 1768 he shipped on board a merchantman commanded by an uncle and made a voyage to Liverpool. Two years later he was regularly apprenticed to a Norfolk ship-owner, for whom he made several voyages to the West Indies. By 1775 he had risen to the station of chief mate. His first naval service, early in 1776 as a lieutenant on board one of the light cruisers fitted out by Virginia, was terminated by his capture and confinement on a prison ship. Wavering in his allegiance, the young adventurer joined a

Loyalist schoolmate who commanded a British tender and in an engagement with the Patriots received a severe wound. Still under the influence of the Loyalists, he next sailed for Bermuda and on the return voyage his ship was captured by the American naval brig *Lexington.* On the day of his capture he entered the Continental navy as a midshipman. In later life he was wont to confess the error of his service with his Loyalist friends.

After a voyage to the West Indies in the *Lexington,* he sailed on this ship in February 1777 for France, now being rated as master's mate. The *Lexington* made a successful cruise in European waters, but shortly thereafter was compelled to surrender to a superior force. Her officers and crew were committed to Mill Prison, Plymouth, charged with high treason. Escaping with his captain in February 1778, Dale after a variety of adventures was retaken and again confined in Mill Prison, this time for a period of forty days in the dungeon, familiarly known as the "black hole." A year later he again escaped and succeeded in reaching L'Orient where he joined the *Bon Homme Richard,* then being fitted for sea by Capt. John Paul Jones [*q.v.*]. Selected by that discerning commander as first lieutenant, he took part in the memorable cruise that culminated in the brilliant sea fight off Flamborough Head. Being in charge of the gun-deck and second in command on the *Richard,* he was the first to board the *Serapis* when she struck her flag, and not until after he had taken possession of her did he discover that he had been severely wounded. In 1779–80 he cruised with Jones in the frigate *Alliance* and later returned to America with his commander on the *Ariel,* arriving early in 1781. Again going to sea, this time as the first lieutenant of the frigate *Trumbull,* he was wounded in that ship's engagement with the British naval vessel *Iris.* His last sea service during the Revolution was in 1782–83 on the privateer *Queen of France,* first as mate and afterward as captain.

From 1783 to 1794 he was lucratively employed in the merchant service, chiefly in command of East Indiamen. In the latter year this employment was brought to an end by his appointment by Washington as one of the six captains of the new navy. His first naval duty was the superintending of the construction of a frigate at Norfolk. In 1795 he obtained a furlough from the navy and returned to his former occupation, sailing for Canton, China, in command of the *Ganges.* Three years later, when war with France was threatening, this ship was purchased by the government and Dale made in her the first cruise undertaken by a vessel of the new navy. Differences with Commodore Truxtun over rank caused Dale to leave the naval service and take command of a privateer, in which he sailed for China in 1799. On the settlement of this dispute in his favor, he again returned to the navy and in 1801 was appointed to the command of a fleet of five vessels, of which the frigate *President* flew the broad pennant of the commodore. This squadron of observation was dispatched to the Mediterranean in anticipation of trouble with the Barbary Corsairs. After effectively protecting American commerce in that sea, Dale sailed for home, and in December 1802, as the result of a dispute with the Navy Department, he retired from the navy, ranking then as the third officer in the service.

Having accumulated a comfortable fortune, he established himself permanently in Philadelphia, where on Sept. 15, 1791 he had been married to Dorothea (or Dorothy) Crathorne (1767–1832). For upward of a quarter of a century he enjoyed in that city the tranquil life of a private citizen. Highly esteemed by the Philadelphians, he interested himself in their welfare and was often called upon to take the lead in public enterprises. For several years he was president of the Washington Benevolent Society of Pennsylvania, and during the War of 1812 he served on the general committee charged with the protection of the city. Two of his sons entered the navy, Richard, who was killed in action, and John M., who died in the service.

[*Port Folio,* June 1814; J. F. Cooper, *Lives of Distinguished Am. Naval Officers,* II (1846), 233–64; *Jours. of the Cont. Cong.,* July 7, 17, 20, 1781; C. W. Goldsborough, *The U. S. Naval Chronicle* (1824); G. W. Allen, *Our Naval War with France* (1909), and *Our Navy and the Barbary Corsairs* (1905); *Pa. Mag. of Hist. and Biog.,* IV (1880), 494–500.]   C.O.P.

DALE, SAMUEL (1772–May 24, 1841), pioneer, soldier, was born in Rockbridge County, Va., and died in Lauderdale County, Miss. His parents, of Scotch-Irish descent, were natives of Pennsylvania, but came to the Virginia frontier soon after their marriage. They kept to the border during all of Samuel's boyhood, moving always as it moved, once in 1775, and again in 1783, when they settled in Greene County, Ga. They both died in December 1792, leaving Samuel with the responsibility of their eight younger children. Having the fixed outlook of a frontiersman, he became a government scout in 1793 and served in that capacity till his company was disbanded in 1796. He then became a trader between Savannah and the border settlements to the west, and in 1808, having acquired some land by state lottery, he set up a mill. These activities were remunerative but not exciting, and he soon abandoned them for the business of guiding immigrants through the Indian lands to Mississippi. He was present in October 1812 when Tecumseh, at the instigation of British agents in Detroit, came to Alabama to enlist the Indians against the Americans. During the hostilities which followed, Dale was engaged in countless stirring adventures with the Indians—now friendly, now hostile. Some of these occurred in December 1814, while he was carrying important dispatches from Georgia to Andrew Jackson in New Orleans, a feat accomplished in the phenomenally short time of eight days. He was elected in 1817 to the first General Assembly of Alabama, and he continued in that body with fair regularity till 1829. His position as legislator and distinguished veteran accounted for his appointment as one of five men to receive Lafayette when he visited Alabama in 1821. Ten years later he was charged with the duty of transporting the expelled Choctaw Indians to the territories which had been assigned to them west of the Mississippi. An accidental injury sustained during the early days of the pilgrimage prevented his going the full distance. He remained in Lauderdale County, Miss., and soon, as the first representative of that county, began anew his career as legislator. Some time after the Choctaw expedition he visited Washington, D. C., seeking compensation for corn and other supplies furnished the troops. Alabama had been pleased to name a county for him and to create him brigadier-general of militia. It seemed reasonable to hope that Washington would give him recognition also—less glittering, perhaps, but more substantial. It was a vain hope. Many prominent men were cordial to him, but the "third auditor," to whom his claim was finally referred, proved, as Dale said, "impracticable. . . . I would rather encounter half a dozen Indians . . . he worried me much and I left the matter unsettled" (Claiborne, *Dale*, p. 212).

[The chief source of this article is I. F. H. Claiborne, *Life and Times of Gen. Sam. Dale* (1860). Here Claiborne serves chiefly as editor, reproducing from memory Dale's own reminiscences as imparted to him some years before the book was written. The form is autobiographical, Dale being represented as speaking in the first person. Other contemporary accounts are in A. B. Meek, *Romantic Passages in S. W. Hist.* (1857); A. J. Pickett, *Hist. of Ala.* (1851); Sketches occur in T. M. Owen, *Hist. of Ala. and Dict. of Ala. Biog.* (1921); D. Rowland, *Mississippi* (1907).]   J. D. W.

DALE, Sir THOMAS (d. Aug. 9, 1619), soldier, colonizer, naval commander, enlisted when a youth, about 1588, as a soldier in the service of the Netherlands. Later we find him in Scotland, in the retinue of Prince Henry, to whom he became deeply attached. He returned about 1603 to the Netherlands, where his bravery and the favor of King James won him advancement to a captaincy. On June 19, 1606, he was knighted at Richmond, as Sir Thomas Dale of Surrey, after which he returned to his company. His reputation as a disciplinarian influenced the London Company to appoint him marshal of Virginia, since the disorders and misfortunes of the colony convinced them that stern repression was needed. In January 1611, the States General granted him leave for three years. Before departing for Virginia he married Elizabeth, daughter of Sir Thomas Throckmorton. On Mar. 27, 1611, he set sail with the *Starr, Prosperous,* and *Elizabeth,* carrying settlers, stores, and live stock, and eight weeks later cast anchor off Point Comfort. In the absence of the governor, Lord De la Warr, Dale ruled the colony until August, when he was relieved by Sir Thomas Gates. Gates left in March 1614, and Dale again assumed control. Finding the colony suffering from insubordination, epidemics, Indian attacks, and famines, he was instrumental in surmounting all these evils. Publishing certain martial laws, he enforced them with great severity. This won him the approbation of the London Company, for it restored order to the colony, but brought upon him the execration of the settlers. The Assembly of 1624 said that in defiance of their charter rights he had subjected the people to a cruel tyranny. Men had been hanged, tortured, broken upon the wheel. "One for stealing two or three pints of oatmeal had a bodkin thrust through his tongue and was tied with a chain to a tree until he starved" (Tragical Relation of Virginia Assembly, 1624, Library of Congress). By founding a new settlement near the falls of the James, Dale checked the epidemics of malaria. In a sweeping bend of the river, far from the mosquito-infested marshes of Jamestown, he built Henrico, enclosed a large tract of land with palisades, and laid out fields of corn. Peace with the Indians came when he sanctioned the marriage of John Rolfe with Pocahontas, the captive daughter of the chieftain Powhatan. When Dale returned to England in 1616 he could boast that he had left the colony tranquil and prosperous. On Nov. 28, 1617, he was appointed commander of a London East India Company fleet, and on Feb. 26, 1618, sailed for the East Indies. At this time the rivalry between the English and the Dutch for the eastern trade was intense, and on Dec. 23, Dale fought with a Dutch fleet "a cruel, bloody fight," which ended in a draw. On July 19, 1619, his fleet arrived at Masulipatam, India, and there he died "after twenty days of languishing sickness." "His body was enclosed and housed in the form of a tomb," and brought to England for burial.

[Ralph Hamor, *True Discourse of the Present Estate of Va.* (1615); *Abstract of the Proc. of the Va. Co. of London* (2 vols., 1888); *Va. Hist. Soc. Pubs.*; Alexander Brown, *The Genesis of the United States* (2 vols., 1891), *The First Republic in Am.* (1898); John Rolfe, "Virginia," *Va. Hist. Reg.*, vol. I, no. 3 (1848); *Calendar of State Papers,* East Indies; Edward D. Neill, *The Va. Co. of London* (1869); *Dict. of Nat. Biog.*]   T. J. W.

DALL, CAROLINE WELLS HEALEY (June 22, 1822–Dec. 17, 1912), reformer, writer, was born in Boston, Mass., the daughter of Mark and Caroline (Foster) Healey. Her father was a well-to-do merchant and banker. His daughter grew up in an atmosphere of substantial comfort and of genuine though somewhat provincial culture, received her education from tutors and in small private schools, and early showed an inclination toward authorship. When her father's investments in railroads turned out badly, she became a teacher and in 1840 went to Georgetown, D. C., as vice-principal of Miss English's School for Young Ladies. In 1844 she married Charles Henry Appleton Dall, a Unitarian clergyman. She bore him a daughter, Sarah, and a son, William Healey Dall [*q.v.*]. After serving several charges, including one in Toronto, Canada, her husband went to Calcutta in 1855 as the first foreign missionary of the Unitarian Church. He returned to visit his family once every five years and died in Calcutta on July 18, 1886. Reform of every kind was dear to Mrs. Dall's heart, but the cause to which she was especially devoted, and which made her career significant, was the extension of equal educational and economic opportunities to women. On this subject she lectured, preached from such pulpits as were open to her, and wrote indefatigably. She seems to have modeled her life consciously on that of Margaret Fuller, but she lacked Miss Fuller's intellectual keenness and critical sense. Her bias and intellectual immaturity are amusingly revealed in a lecture on *Transcendentalism in New England* (1897), in which she asserts with complete confidence that the movement took its origin in Anne Hutchinson and reached its height in Margaret Fuller. In spite of obvious shortcomings Mrs. Dall did render valuable service to the woman's rights movement in the sixties and seventies. Her publications dealing directly or indirectly with the subject are: *Historical Pictures Retouched* (1860); *Woman's Right to Labor* (1860); *Life of Dr. Marie Zakrzewska* (1860); *Woman's Rights under the Law* (1861); *The College, the Market, and the Court, or Woman's Relation to Education, Labor, and Law* (1867);

and *Life of Dr. Anandabai Joshee* (1888). For a time she was editor in Boston of *Una,* a woman's rights magazine. Her later writings are chiefly on literary subjects but are of little importance. *My First Holiday, or Letters Home from Colorado, Utah, and California* (1881) is valuable as a traveler's unvarnished record and is rendered almost comic by its querulous recital of the innumerable discomforts, annoyances, and impositions of western travel. A more gracious mood is exhibited in *Alongside* (privately printed, 1900), a memoir of her early years in Boston and of her father. Some of her other books are: *Patty Gray's Journey to the Cotton Islands* (1869–70), a heavily didactic juvenile in three volumes; *The Romance of the Association, or, One Last Glimpse of Charlotte Temple and Eliza Wharton* (1875), a study of Mrs. Rowson's long-lived novel; *What We Really Know about Shakespeare* (1885); *Sordello—a History and a Poem* (1886); and *Barbara Fritchie—a Study* (1892). During the latter part of her life she made her home in Washington, D. C., where, having outlived her reputation as a publicist, she died in her ninetieth year.

[*Who's Who in America,* 1908–09; *The Evening Star* (Washington, D. C.), Dec. 18, 1912; F. C. Pierce, *Foster Genealogy* (1899).]   G. H. G.

DALL, WILLIAM HEALEY (Aug. 21, 1845–Mar. 27, 1927), naturalist, was the son of Charles Henry Appleton Dall, a Unitarian minister, and of Caroline Wells (Healey) Dall [*q.v.*] who for a time had some distinction as a publicist. He was born in Boston, Mass., and there he was educated in public schools and the Boston Latin School. An early fondness for natural history led to his meeting Louis Agassiz under whom he studied zoology. He also followed courses in anatomy — under Jeffries Wyman — and other medical subjects in the medical department of Harvard, although he never graduated. The earning of his livelihood being necessary, he found employment in commercial pursuits in Chicago, Ill., where he was able to continue his studies in natural history at night in the Chicago Academy of Sciences under the direction of William Stimpson and Robert Kennicott [*qq.v.*], both of whom became his warm friends. In 1865 the Western Union International Telegraph Expedition was organized to ascertain the possibility of quick communication with Europe by way of Alaska and Bering Strait. Kennicott, who was made leader, invited Dall to become his lieutenant, charged with collecting the scientific data of that territory. On the death of Kennicott, Dall was unanimously chosen to succeed him in command of the expedition and for three years, until 1868, he continued in Alaska, accumulating valuable collections in natural history, chiefly of mollusks in which he had already begun to specialize. With the success of the Atlantic cable came the abandonment of the expedition, but Dall, appreciating the value of the information he had acquired, promptly gave to the world in 1870 his famous volume, *Alaska and its Resources,* of which several editions were published, one bearing the date of 1897. For many years it was the accepted authority on Alaska.

In 1871, through the influence of Spencer F. Baird [*q.v.*], he was appointed to the United States Coast Survey, with which service he continued until 1884. During these years he was in charge of a scientific survey of the Aleutian Islands and adjacent coasts, the results of which were published in his useful volumes, *Pacific Coast Pilot: Coast and Islands of Alaska; Appendix I, Meteorology* (1879) and *Pacific Coast Pilot: Alaska* (1883), issued by the Coast Survey. In 1880 he was made honorary curator of mollusks in the United States National Museum, and in 1884 love of his specialty led him to accept a transfer from the Coast Survey to the Geological Survey, in which he was given the rank of paleontologist. Working facilities and a room in which to store his collections were found for him in the north tower of the Smithsonian Institution, and there, surrounded by his private library (which he later gave to the Museum), he prepared hundreds of papers and monographs on mollusks, chiefly of the West Coast. In 1909 the Division of Mollusks was moved to the new Natural History Building and he was assigned larger quarters. Although retired in 1923, he persisted in his work and almost daily was in his office.

In addition to his services for the government he also held the chair of invertebrate paleontology in the Wagner Institute of Science in Philadelphia and periodically delivered a course of lectures, receiving in 1889 the gold medal of the Institute. During 1899–1915 he was an honorary curator of the Bishop Museum in Hawaii. In the latter year he published *Spencer Fullerton Baird: A Biography.* He was honored at home and abroad by elections to scientific societies; in the United States he was a fellow of the American Academy of Arts and Sciences, and in 1897 was elected to the National Academy of Sciences. In recognition of the character of the man and of the value of his work authors in various branches of botany and zoology have conferred his name on varied organisms. In this way a monument to his memory has been raised

in the literature of science. He was survived by his widow, Annette Whitney, whom he had married on Mar. 3, 1880, by two sons and one daughter.

[C. Hart Merriam, "Wm. Healey Dall," in *Science,* Apr. 8, 1927; data furnished by Dall himself for articles published during his lifetime; G. H. Parker, in *Proc. Am. Acad. Arts and Sci.,* 1926–27; *Annual Report, Board of Regents Smithsonian Inst.,* 1927; *Who's Who in America,* 1926-27; personal acquaintance of forty years.]
M. B.

DALLAS, ALEXANDER JAMES (June 21, 1759–Jan. 16, 1817), lawyer, secretary of the treasury, was born on the Island of Jamaica, the third son of Robert Dallas and his second wife Sarah (Cormack) Hewett Dallas. His father, son of James and Barbara (Cockburn) Dallas of St. Martin's, Scotland, emigrated from that country and practised medicine with considerable success in the West Indies. After a few years the family returned to the British Isles where Alexander James attended Kensington School and Edinburgh University; at the former place his scholastic merit attracted the attention of two visitors of the school, Benjamin Franklin and Dr. Samuel Johnson. After financial reverses, his father died, and shortly afterward his mother married Capt. Sutherland of the British navy. As the children were encouraged to look to other sources for support, Alexander in his fifteenth year determined to study law, but postponed this ambition to become a merchant clerk and accountant for his uncle, Mr. Gray. After two years in the latter's business house he returned to Devonshire and resumed academic studies, applying himself under the guidance of a tutor to ancient and modern literature.

On Sept. 4, 1780, he married Arabella Maria Smith, daughter of Maj. George Smith of the British army, who was stationed in Jamaica. The young couple soon quitted England and joined their families in the West Indies. Dallas was there admitted to the bar and appointed a Master in Chancery by Gov. Dalling. Promotion seemed imminent, but his wife's health necessitated a different climate. While contemplating a return to England, and inclined to devote his life to the church, he met the actor, Lewis Hallam, Jr., who had lived several years in the American colonies prior to the Revolution and during their struggle for independence. His description of conditions in the United States influenced Dallas to seek citizenship there. Resolutely he and his wife assembled their meager possessions, secured letters of introduction to William Bingham and Robert Morris, and on Apr. 10, 1783, embarked for the new country. Arriving in New York City on June 7, they proceeded to Philadelphia where Dallas signed citizenship papers ten days later.

A serious and annoying obstacle developed when Dallas found that a newly established requirement of two years' residence in the state must be met before he could satisfy his cherished desire to practise law. By chance he had taken lodgings near the offices of Jonathan Burrall, commissioner for settling the accounts of the commissary and quartermaster's departments of the Revolutionary army. Acquaintance was established, and Dallas was invited to a desk in Burrall's office, where he remained until he opened his own office before the end of 1783. On July 13, 1785, he was admitted as counselor in the supreme court of Pennsylvania. On the return of Hallam from Jamaica in the spring of 1784, he and Dallas attempted the introduction of the regular drama into Philadelphia. Not only did Dallas draw up a memorial to the local legislature in an attempt to allay the common prejudice against the theatre, but even turned his pen to dramatic plots. He also contributed to local papers many articles on pressing political questions and items of literary interest, and in 1787 he served as editor of the *Columbian Magazine,* a monthly miscellany. It was during this period that he edited the first reports of the United States Supreme Court.

Dallas's first political appointment came on Jan. 19, 1791, when he was chosen secretary of the Commonwealth of Pennsylvania by Gov. Thomas Mifflin. He remained with Mifflin through two reappointments, and received one appointment from Gov. McKean. He was a member of the committee of correspondence that organized, on July 4, 1793, the first Democratic society in the United States. Early in March 1805 he aided in the establishment of the Constitutional Republican party, which supported the judiciary of Pennsylvania against the assaults of the extreme Democratic faction, and at various other times devoted himself to political activity. In 1794, at the time of the Whiskey Rebellion, he was appointed aide-de-camp to the governor and as paymaster-general with the military forces he was brought into personal contact with Washington and Alexander Hamilton. His second public appointment came on Mar. 10, 1801, when he was commissioned United States district attorney for the Eastern District of Pennsylvania by President Jefferson. During Dallas's thirteen years in this office he handled many cases with ability and skill, including the Olmstead case in 1809, which, due to the ill-defined and conflicting jurisdiction of local and national authorities, aroused consider-

able controversy. While holding the office he was maligned by political enemies, and from one editor, John Ward Fenno, recovered $2,500 for libel.

Albert Gallatin, a close personal friend of Dallas, left the United States Treasury in May 1813 to promote the mediation of Russia in the War of 1812. President Madison had wished to appoint Dallas to succeed him, but the opposition of the radical Pennsylvania senators, Michael Leib and Abner Lacock, precluded that choice. George W. Campbell was appointed, but his efforts to prevent the suspension of specie payments and provide suitable funds to prosecute the war were weak and fruitless. When he resigned in despair on Sept. 26, 1814, the situation was so desperate that, on Oct. 6, almost as a last resort, Dallas was commissioned secretary of the treasury. He entered office with a bankrupt treasury; the official stoppage of interest payments on the debt was announced in a letter of Nov. 17. His first formal act was an immediate message on Oct. 17 to the Committee on Ways and Means in which he insisted upon a permanent annual revenue of twenty-one million dollars from taxes and duties, a yearly war revenue of like amount to be raised by doubling the direct tax and rate of postage, and a national bank to provide a circulating medium and facilitate exchange (George M. Dallas, *post,* pp. 236–37). This report had a far-reaching psychological effect, and did much to restore confidence. Interest-bearing treasury notes of small denomination were issued in discreet quantities to furnish momentary relief. After some scattered opposition in Congress, his measures for the heaviest taxation hitherto levied by the national government were adopted. The charter of the Bank of the United States had expired in 1811, but Dallas recognized that a national banking institution was the only efficient remedy for the disordered condition of the circulating medium. But after his plan for a bank emerged from the opposition and wrangling of Congress it was so altered that, upon his advice, Madison vetoed the bill. This blighting of prospects was somewhat alleviated by the cessation of war toward the end of 1814. The lack of regulation of state banks and the general financial confusion having forced the Republican leaders to revise their former stand, Calhoun, on Jan. 8, 1816, introduced a bank bill modeled closely on a plan recommended by Dallas. On Apr. 10 it became law. American shipping had been ruined by the war, and manufacturing industries developed with the advent of peace. In his report of Feb. 12, 1816, Dallas made recommendations in regard to a protective tariff that were largely adopted, and thus furnished the basis of a system for the following thirty years. The illness of Monroe caused Dallas to take upon himself, in addition, the duties of acting secretary of war on Mar. 14, 1815. Carrying them until Aug. 8, he organized the army upon a peace establishment of ten thousand men. Although he gave notice in April 1816 of his intended resignation, he was persuaded to remain until the new bank was organized and definite provision made for the resumption of specie payments. On Oct. 20, 1816, these conditions practically accomplished, he formally quit the treasury, leaving with Madison a highly creditable report. Treasury receipts had far exceeded the estimates.

Dallas returned to the practise of law in Philadelphia in an effort to recoup his private fortunes, but scarcely three months later while attending a case in Trenton, N. J., he was seized with what doctors pronounced to be "gout in the stomach." He was immediately taken home, and a few hours later he died. One of his sons, George Mifflin Dallas [q.v.], became vice-president. In physical appearance Alexander James Dallas was commanding. In dress he was meticulous, and his powdered hair, the wearing of which was a rapidly disappearing custom, added a formal touch not inconsistent with his highly polished manners. A prodigious worker, he had the faculty of unbending readily from toil to ease and vivacity, and specially excelled in conversation.

Included among his publications were: *Features of Mr. Jay's Treaty* (1795); *Laws of the Commonwealth of Pa.* (4 vols., 1793–1801); *Address of the Society of Constitutional Republicans* (1805); *Reports of Cases Ruled and Adjudged in the Several Courts of the United States and of Pennsylvania, etc.* (4 vols., 1790–1807); *Treasury Reports; An Exposition of the Causes and Character of the War* (1815). He left incomplete and unpublished a history of Pennsylvania.

[Geo. M. Dallas, *The Life and Writings of A. J. Dallas* (1871); Jas. Dallas, *The Hist. of the Family of Dallas* (1921); Madison Papers, Lib. of Cong.; Dallas Letters, and Simon Gratz Coll., Hist. Soc. of Pa.]
J. H. E.—s.

DALLAS, GEORGE MIFFLIN (July 10, 1792–Dec. 31, 1864), vice-president, diplomat, was born in Philadelphia and bore the indelible stamp of his social environment. The city took its tone in the early days of the republic from a prosperous group, shrewd in business, conservative in politics, and manifesting a genteel interest in culture and the refinements of life. His father, Alexander James Dallas [q.v.], was a

successful man of affairs, and his mother, Arabella Maria Smith, was an Englishwoman, with a tradition of gentility. Under the tutelage of local masters such as Robert Andrews, the boy was prepared for Princeton, from which he graduated in 1810. In his father's law office the Princetonian began his legal preparation. Shortly came the War of 1812 but, though he joined a military company, a career of arms was not to be his. In 1813 he was made secretary to Albert Gallatin [q.v.], then about to set out for Russia on a peace mission. Though not quite of age, Dallas was admitted to the bar and set out for Europe. After visiting Russia, he proceeded to Belgium and England and was about to go to Italy when the peace commissioners received the British terms. They quickly decided to send these to America by Dallas, and in October 1814 he arrived at home. Shortly thereafter he joined his father, who was then secretary of the treasury, as a clerk in his department. The year 1816 found him back in Philadelphia, where he tried his first case in April and on May 23 married Sophia Nicklin. He had planned to practise law with his father but the latter, just retired, died in 1817. Alexander Dallas had been one of the chief sponsors of the newly formed second Bank of the United States, and soon his son became one of its counsel. But politics was in his blood. He was an active Republican, and when the new partisanship of the twenties began to take shape he became a follower of Calhoun and supported his candidacy for the presidency in 1824. Jackson, however, was to be the man of the hour, and Dallas entered his camp. He held numerous offices, deputy attorney-general for the city and county of Philadelphia, mayor, and, when Jackson became president, district attorney, 1829–31. Then came an appointment to fill out a term in the Senate.

In Washington he spent two active years (1831–33), while the Bank and the tariff were the leading political issues. As a close friend of the Bank he was in a difficult position when Jackson made war on it. He presented a memorial for the re-chartering of the Bank and, instructed by the legislature, supported it, though not actively. Protectionist in his views upon the tariff, he supported Jackson in his controversy with South Carolina. As he could not afford further absence from his profession, he retired at the end of his term. Appointed attorney-general of Pennsylvania by Gov. Wolf in the fall of 1833, he held the office until his party lost power in 1835. President Van Buren appointed him minister to Russia in 1837 but there were few questions save trade in the Pacific to occupy his attention. After two years of social gayety, he was recalled at his own request.

The next few years were spent in law and politics. As a lawyer he prospered but as a politician he was barely able to hold his own against James Buchanan. With him, Dallas had an early misunderstanding and, though they patched it up in 1837, they were never very friendly. When Buchanan refused the federal attorney-generalship in 1840, it was offered to Dallas, who in turn declined it. The rivalry between these two men pursued its uneven way through the mazes of Pennsylvania politics until the national convention of 1844. Here Van Buren, Cass, and Buchanan were outdistanced by Polk, and after Silas Wright had declined the vice-presidential nomination it was given to Dallas. The ticket was successful and the new vice-president presided over the Senate through the troubled days of the Mexican War and the debate on the Wilmot Proviso. The question, however, that troubled him most was the tariff. A Pennsylvanian, he was alive to the needs of the protected interests, while his party was pledged to revision downward. In 1846 he labored strenuously for a compromise which would provide more protection than the Walker Bill offered, but when the vote on the latter measure resulted in a tie he voted for it, making it law, on the ground that as a national officer he must obey the national platform of his party. He retired with Polk, and though occasionally talked of for president by the opponents of Buchanan he did not again figure conspicuously in public life until Pierce appointed him minister to Great Britain, upon the resignation of Buchanan from that post in 1856.

He arrived at London at a critical moment. President Pierce had demanded the recall of Crampton, the British minister at Washington, for violating American neutrality by his activities in enlisting men in the United States for the British army. Great Britain refused to comply with the demand and Crampton was dismissed in May 1856. Would the dismissal of Dallas follow? Fortunately the British ministry refrained from that step, and Dallas could turn his attention to the vexatious dispute over the Clayton-Bulwer Treaty. The United States had demanded that Great Britain abandon the so-called protectorate over the Mosquito Indians in Nicaragua, cease interference in a dispute between Nicaragua and Costa Rica, and withdraw from the Bay Islands off the coast of Honduras—all, it was alleged, in violation of the Clayton-Bulwer Treaty. Buchanan had been unable to obtain much satisfaction from the British

ministry, but Dallas and Lord Clarendon after a summer's work signed the Dallas-Clarendon convention, Oct. 17, 1856. The independence of the Mosquito Indians was recognized but they were to be permitted to become a part of Nicaragua by treaty. The boundary dispute between the latter country and Costa Rica was to be arbitrated by the United States and Great Britain. The Bay Islands were to be recognized as a free territory belonging to Honduras in accordance with a treaty just negotiated between that country and Great Britain. Indorsement of the latter treaty was stricken out by the Senate and the Dallas-Clarendon Treaty was then ratified by a close vote. When the British refused to accept it in this form, claiming that it would tempt Honduras to reject the British treaty, Dallas and Clarendon tried an alternative wording, but Buchanan felt that this restored the objectionable feature and did not send the treaty to the Senate. President Buchanan kept Dallas in London during his entire term but conducted the further Central-American negotiations at Washington. The two other matters of diplomatic importance were the right of search in connection with the joint agreement for suppressing the slave-trade, and the clash on San Juan Island over the northwest boundary of the United States. In regard to the latter, Buchanan conducted the negotiations in Washington but Dallas, to his great satisfaction, succeeded in obtaining from the foreign secretary, Lord Malmesbury, a disavowal of the long-disputed right of search. This he felt to be his great diplomatic achievement.

The Civil War closed his career as it did those of so many Democrats. Succeeded by Charles Francis Adams in May 1861, he came home to a distracted country. He had hated abolition and secession both, as he hated all extremes, and though he condemned the South for seceding, he voted the Democratic ticket throughout the war, the end of which he failed to see. He was a striking figure with his shock of prematurely white hair, his strong face, and his distinguished manners. Conservative and cosmopolitan, precise and dignified, he may well be characterized as the gentleman in politics.

[A Series of Letters from London Written During the Years 1856, '57, '58, '59, and '60 (1869), ed. by Julia Dallas; Diary of George Mifflin Dallas while U. S. Minister to Russia, 1837–39, and to England, 1856–61 (1892), ed. by Susan Dallas; Chas. J. Biddle, A Eulogy upon the Hon. George Mifflin Dallas (1865); letters of Dallas scattered through Pa. Hist. Soc. Colls.; Mary W. Williams, Anglo-Am. Isthmian Diplomacy, 1815–1915 (1916); H. B. Learned, "William L. Marcy," and Lewis Einstein, "Lewis Cass," in The Am. Secretaries of State and their Diplomacy, ed. by S. F. Bemis, vol. VI (1928).]   R. F. N.

D'ALOES, CLAUDE JEAN [See Allouez, Claude Jean, 1622–1689.]

DALTON, JOHN CALL (Feb. 2, 1825–Feb. 12, 1889), physiologist, was born in Chelmsford, Mass. The son of Dr. John Call Dalton and Julia Ann (Spalding), the former a representative of a notable medical ancestry, he was apparently predestined for the medical profession. Graduating from Harvard College in 1844 and from the Harvard Medical School in 1847, he went to Paris where he came under the influence of the renowned physiologist, Claude Bernard, and was at once impressed with the great value of experimental work in medicine, particularly in physiology. This is significant, because Dalton was the first physician in the United States to devote his life to the pursuit of experimental physiology and the sciences related thereto. He put aside all thought of medical practise, and began his work as a teacher, opening a new era in the teaching of physiology in America. Before his time the didactic lecture and the textbook were the sole methods of instruction; he introduced the experimental method, illustrating the processes of life with living animals, which the action of ether, just then discovered, made it possible to do without pain. From 1851 to 1854 he was professor of physiology at the University of Buffalo; 1854–56 at the University of Vermont; 1855–83 at the College of Physicians and Surgeons, New York. From 1859 to 1861 he was also connected with the Long Island College Hospital. During the period of the Civil War he served as surgeon in the medical corps of the volunteer army, with the rank of brigadier-general. Such work, however, was not congenial to him; he was better fitted for the experimentation of the laboratory, where, with his logical mind and skilful manipulation, he made clear the functioning of the vital mechanisms of the body. His writings were notable because what he wrote was based largely upon what he had actually seen experimentally. They included a *Treatise on Human Physiology* issued in 1859, which in 1882 had reached the seventh edition; *A Treatise on Physiology and Hygiene* (1868); *Experimentation on Animals as a Means of Knowledge in Physiology, Pathology, and Practical Medicine* (1875); *The Experimental Method in Medical Science* (1882); *Doctrines of the Circulation* (1884). Especially noteworthy was his morphological work, *Topographical Anatomy of the Brain* (1885), for which it is said he prepared with his own hands all the specimens, photographs of which made up a large part of the book. His most important physiological research was on the subject, "Sugar Formation in the Liver" (*Transactions of the New York Academy of Medicine,* 1871); it confirmed the results and views of Claude Bernard which had been discredited by several English physiologists. For years he had to fight against interference by individuals and societies of anti-vivisectionists, who with misdirected zeal sought by legislative action to prevent all experimentation upon living animals, but with his firm conviction of the value to humanity of the knowledge to be gained by such methods of experimentation he used all his powers to contest these efforts and to lead the public to a better understanding of the matter. During the later years of his life he served (1884–89) as president of the College of Physicians and Surgeons, bringing to that office his great breadth of knowledge and critical judgment, combined with administrative powers of a high order which were freely used for the advancement of the college. He lived a simple, unpretentious life, a bachelor, a quiet scholar, devoted to his studies; a deep thinker whose greatest happiness was found in his study and in the laboratory. In the last year of his life he wrote down for his family some reminiscences of his Civil War service. These, still uncompleted, were privately printed in 1892 under the title, *John Call Dalton, M.D., U. S. V.* He was a member of many national and European societies and in 1864 was elected a member of the National Academy of Sciences. He died unmarried.

[Memoir by S. Weir Mitchell published in the *Biog. Memoirs Nat. Acad. Sci.,* III (1895), 177–85; S. J. Spalding, *Spalding Memorial* (1872), p. 84; *The Coll. of Physicians and Surgeons, N. Y.* (n.d.), ed. by John Schrady; for dates of professorships, *Harvard Quinquennial Cat.,* 1915.]   R. H. C.

DALTON, ROBERT (1867–Oct. 5, 1892), desperado, was born probably in Cass County, Mo. His father, Louis Dalton, was of Irish stock, and his mother, Adaline Lee (Younger) Dalton, is said to have been a half-sister of Col. H. W. Younger, the father of the noted bandits. The family, then consisting of the parents, seven boys and one girl, moved to the Indian Territory and about 1882 to Coffeyville, Kan. In the fall of 1888 Robert was appointed a deputy United States marshal, for service in the Indian Territory, but after a short time gave up the place or was discharged. His criminal career began with the killing of a rival in a love affair. With his brothers Grattan and Emmet he soon afterward organized a band of horse-thieves, which operated around Baxter Springs, Kan. Toward the end of 1890 the three brothers went to California, where in the following February they held up a train on the Southern Pacific railroad at Alila, Tulare County. Grattan was captured and sentenced to twenty years' confinement, but on the way to the penitentiary jumped from a moving train and escaped.

Back in their old range, now Oklahoma Territory, Robert, Emmet, and a recruit, Charley Bryant, robbed a train at Wharton, in May 1891. This daring exploit by three men brought to the authorities the realization that an exceptionally capable bandit leader was in the field, and a relentless pursuit was ordered. Bryant was captured and in an attempted escape was killed. The Daltons, however, could not be found, and for more than a year thereafter remained inactive. In June 1892, Robert, Grattan, and Emmet Dalton, "Bill" Doolin (later to be the leader of a band of his own), and two others robbed a train at Red Rock, Okla. Terr., only twenty-six miles from the scene of the Wharton crime, and six weeks later a train at Adair, Okla. Terr. Prompted partly by vainglory, in the hope of outdoing the record of the James brothers, and partly by the hope of a haul which would enable the band to disperse with a competence for each, Robert now directed a raid on the two banks at Coffeyville. The attempt was made by five men on the morning of Oct. 5. In a pitched battle with the townfolk Robert and Grattan Dalton and two others were killed and Emmet Dalton severely wounded and captured. The last-named served a long term in the penitentiary, and on his release became a law-abiding citizen. Like most of the noted Western outlaws, Robert was of fair complexion, with blue eyes. He is described as "romantic looking" and much given to big boots and revolvers prominently displayed. In personal habits he was temperate. He was an outlaw of desperate and reckless will, who knew no fear and never hesitated to shoot, and the record of his band for daring criminality in so short a time is perhaps unequaled.

[E. de Valcour-Vermont, *The Dalton Brothers* (pamph., 1892); *Kan. City Star*, Oct. 5–8, 1892; L. W. Duncan, pub., *Hist. of Montgomery County, Kan.* (1903); incidental references in A. B. Macdonald, *Hands Up!* (1927).]   W. J. G.

DALY, ARNOLD [See DALY, PETER CHRISTOPHER ARNOLD, 1875–1927.]

DALY, AUGUSTIN [See DALY, JOHN AUGUSTIN, 1838–99.]

DALY, CHARLES PATRICK (Oct. 31, 1816–Sept. 19, 1899), jurist, author, was of pure Irish descent, his parents having emigrated from Galway in 1814 and settled in New York City,

where he was born. They were poor, his early education was scanty, and when his father died he had to leave school and earn his own living. He obtained a clerkship in Savannah, Ga., but ran away and shipped as cabin boy on a trading vessel. He spent three years at sea before the mast, being present at Algiers in 1830 when the French captured that town. He then returned to New York City and was apprenticed to a master carpenter. Studying at night in an effort to make good his deficiencies in education, he also joined a literary society, where his abilities attracted attention and subsequently led to his entering a law office in 1836. In 1839 he was admitted to the bar, the seven-year term of studentship being waived in his case on account of his brilliant showing, and he at once commenced practise in New York City. He had already interested himself in politics as an adherent of the Democratic party, was known as an effective platform speaker, and in a short time acquired a reputation as a successful advocate and sound lawyer. In 1843 he was elected to the New York Assembly and here distinguished himself by his able handling of the legislation dealing with the escheat of the Leake and Watts asylum trust. He was then offered the party nomination for Congress but declined, preferring law to politics. Immediately afterward, he was appointed a judge of the court of common pleas of the City of New York, and took his seat on the bench May 4, 1844, being then twenty-eight years old. Though his appointment did not please Tammany Hall, he remained a member of the court for nearly forty-two years, being chosen for four consecutive terms after the position was made elective. For the last twenty-seven years of this period he was chief justice. From the outset he displayed a high conception of the responsibilities of his office, and an implacable determination to follow the course which his instinct convinced him was dictated by principle, totally regardless of public opinion or party sympathies. A notable instance of these characteristics occurred in 1849, after the Astor Place Riots, when seven persons were indicted for complicity in the rioting. Public sentiment was strong in their favor, the prevailing opinion being that occasional riots were safety valves and that a conviction for rioting was impossible. Daly presided at the trial, laid down the law applicable to riots in firm, unmistakable language, and upon the jury rendering a verdict of guilty, imposed heavy sentences, totally oblivious to popular clamor and hostile demonstrations.

During the Civil War, though a Democrat, he supported the administration whole-heartedly, and was consulted on a number of occasions by

President Lincoln and his cabinet. Two important decisions taken in the course of the war were directly due to his advice. In 1861, when members of the crew of the Confederate privateer *Jefferson Davis* were tried, convicted and sentenced to be hanged as pirates, he pointed out the inadvisability of such a course in view of inevitable retaliation, and urged that they be treated as prisoners of war—which was subsequently done. His intervention in the case of Mason and Slidell was, from the international standpoint, of outstanding importance. He advised Secretary Seward that in view of a decision of Chief Justice Marshall's, the seizure of the Confederate envoys could not possibly be justified, and recommended their surrender. William M. Evarts did not agree with him, but the government followed his advice. He exhibited the same sanity and detachment from predilection or prejudice throughout his judicial career, his opinions were invariably developed with the utmost care and based upon exhaustive study of the ultimate sources of the law and displayed an erudition which was astonishing in view of his early lack of education. An example of this occurred in *Re John Snook* (2 *Hilt*. 566) where he had occasion to consider the origin of proper names and exhaustively examined the law and usage respecting them. His opinions are contained in *Reports of Cases Argued and Determined in the Court of Common Pleas for the City and County of New York* (16 vols., 1866–92), covering the period 1859–91, which were prepared by him and are generally known as "Daly's Cases." As a judge he was distinguished by one peculiar failing. When presiding at trials or hearing motions he was a most patient and attentive listener, saying little, but in the appellate branch of the court it was impossible to make a continuous and connected argument before him because of his talkativeness. On appeal he apparently believed "that the colloquial style of argument was the most effective" (*post,* p. 134). He retired from the bench by reason of the age limitation, on Dec. 31, 1885, and though he subsequently opened a law office in New York City, did little afterward except in the capacity of advising counsel. His last years were spent principally in study and writing. He died at North Haven, Sag Harbor, L. I., Sept. 19, 1899. In 1856 he married Maria Lydig of New York City.

After his elevation to the bench he seldom participated in public affairs, the principal exception being in 1867 when he was a delegate to the New York constitutional convention of that year. However, he did not take a very prominent part in the discussions. From his seafaring days

he had evinced intense interest in the science of geography and for more than thirty-five years was president of the American Geographical Society, contributing to its Proceedings valuable papers of which the following were published: "On the Early History of Cartography . . . before the time of Mercator" (*Journal,* vol. II, 1869, p. 1), "Recent Geographical Work of the World" (*Bulletin,* vol. XX, 1888, p. 1), and "On the History of Physical Geography" (*Ibid.,* vol. XXII, 1890, p. 1). In addition, he was an enthusiastic student of the drama, and his library contained a remarkable collection of works on Shakespeare and other dramatic literature.

He wrote voluminously, more particularly on the historical aspects of law and judicial institutions, wherein his extensive research and powers of exposition were displayed to great advantage. He was the author of, *inter alia,* "A History of the Court of Common Pleas," etc. (1855), prefixed to vol. I of E. D. Smith's Common Pleas Reports; *The Nature, Extent and History of the Jurisdiction of the Surrogates' Courts of the State of New York* (1863); *Gulian C. Verplanck; His Ancestry, Life, and Character* (1870); *Life and Services of Dr. David Livingstone* (1871); *Barratry: its Origin, History and Meaning in the Maritime Laws* (1872); *In Memory of Henry Peters Gray* (1878); *The Settlement of Jews in North America* (1893); *The Common Law, its Origin, Sources, Nature and Development and what the State of New York has done to Improve it* (1894); *First Theatre in America: When was the Drama first Introduced in America?* (1896); *Is the Monroe Doctrine Involved in the Controversy between Venezuela and Great Britain?* (1896); and *Birthday Verses* (1897). He also wrote the article on Naturalization in the *New American Cyclopædia.*

[*Legal and Judicial Hist. of N. Y.* (1911), ed. by Alden Chester, I, 395; Theron G. Strong, *Landmarks of a Lawyer's Lifetime* (1914), p. 133; Max J. Kohler, *Chas. P. Daly; a Tribute to his Memory* (1899); *Green Bag,* Nov. 1894; *Am. Law Rev.,* XXXIII (1899), 907; *N. Y. Times,* Nov. 15, 1885; obituaries in *Bull. Am. Geog. Soc.,* XXXI (1899), 398; *N. Y. Times,* Sept. 20, 1899.]   H. W. H. K.

DALY, JOHN AUGUSTIN (July 20, 1838–June 7, 1899), playwright and producer, was born in Plymouth, N. C., the son of Capt. Denis Daly, a ship-owner, and Elizabeth (Duffey) Daly, the daughter of a lieutenant in the British army. Early left a widow with two boys, his mother came to New York City, where Augustin grew up with a passion for the theatre. He belonged to amateur organizations like the Murdoch and Burton Associations, corresponding to the Little Theatre groups of a later time, and he caught the inspiration of the great romantic actors and the sterling romantic plays which were America's contribution to the mid-century theatre and drama. He rarely acted, for his interest lay from the first in the construction and direction of plays. As early as 1856, he rented a hall in Brooklyn and produced without a cent of capital an entertainment, varying from *Toodles* to *Macbeth*. The details of this performance, related in the biography of Daly by his brother, who was his constant companion, are an epitome of his later career of alternate success and failure, met with courage, resourcefulness, and unquenchable confidence. Ten years spent as a dramatic critic on the weekly *Sunday Courier*, during which time he also wrote for the *Sun*, the *Times*, the *Express* and the *Citizen*, gave him a valuable experience, and he began his play-writing while his critical work was in progress.

After the usual rejections, came his first success, *Leah the Forsaken*, a free adaptation from the German play, *Deborah*, by S. H. von Mosenthal. *Leah* was first played at the Howard Athenæum in Boston, Dec. 8, 1862, and Kate Bateman [*q.v.*] carried the leading rôle into favor at home and abroad. During the sixties, Daly experimented in adaptations from the French and German and in dramatizations of novels like *Griffith Gaunt* and *Pickwick Papers*. *Under the Gaslight*, his first surviving original play, which was also the occasion of his first independent production, was performed at the New York Theatre, Aug. 12, 1867. A melodrama of New York life, with realistic settings in the police courts and on the wharves of the North River, it introduced to the American stage the rescue, by the heroine, of a person bound to a railroad track in the path of an onrushing train. It proved to be one of the most popular of melodramas, and when played in London in 1868, inspired Dion Boucicault to his imitation of this sensation, in *After Dark*. Subsequent litigation established the exclusive right of Daly to this theatrical property in the United States. Another vigorous melodrama, *A Flash of Lightning*, produced at the Broadway Theatre, June 10, 1868, revealed in its burning of a Hudson River steamboat a source of danger in the construction of real boats. *The Red Scarf*, played first at Conway's Park Theatre in Brooklyn, in 1869, contained the same element of suspense as *Under the Gaslight*, the hero in this case being bound on a log about to be sawed in two.

On Jan. 9, 1869, Daly married Mary Duff, daughter of John A. Duff, owner of the Olympic Theatre. In August of that year, having leased the Fifth Avenue Theatre, he began to establish his own company, including Fanny Davenport [*q.v.*], Mrs. Gilbert, and James Lewis. Here he produced the best of the older English comedies of manners and laid the foundations for his superb productions of Shakespeare. Of even more significance, Daly gave Bronson Howard [*q.v.*] his first opportunity and produced *Saratoga* in 1870, thus aiding the establishment of the profession of play-writing in America, at a time when managers were looking almost exclusively to foreign sources for their plays. It was not at his own theatre, however, but at the Olympic that his best play, *Horizon*, was performed, Mar. 21, 1871. In this drama of Western American life, with its clear-cut characters and natural language, Daly may justly be regarded as the first of the realists, in the modern sense, among American playwrights. He next attacked a growing social problem in *Divorce*, one of the great successes of the Fifth Avenue Theatre, where it began its run of two hundred nights on Sept. 5, 1871. Here Daly adapted certain ideas from an English novel, Trollope's *He Knew He Was Right*, while changing them so as to apply to native conditions.

On Jan. 1, 1873 the Fifth Avenue Theatre burned. Daly, undaunted, leased the old New York Theatre, and in three weeks opened it as Daly's Fifth Avenue Theatre. In the same year he formed the first organization among the producing managers of New York, to avoid cutthroat competition and to provide for the loaning of players to each other. Booth, Wallack, Fechter, Palmer, and Jarrett were members with him. For a time Daly conducted the Grand Opera House and when the New Fifth Avenue Theatre was built for him on Twenty-eighth St. near Broadway, and opened on Dec. 3, 1873, he found the burden of three theatres too great. He therefore confined his efforts to the new house, which he conducted until 1877. *Roughing It*, an amusing travesty on the life described by Bret Harte and Mark Twain, was put on at the Grand Opera House, Feb. 18, 1873, and *Pique*, one of his most successful plays, was produced at the New Fifth Avenue Theatre, Dec. 14, 1875. To a theme derived from Florence Maryatt's novel, *Her Lord and Master*, that of a woman marrying out of pique because her lover is faithless, Daly added that of the search among the purlieus of the city for a stolen child, probably based upon the famous abduction of Charley Ross. The last of his original plays, *The Dark City*, produced Sept. 10, 1877, a melodrama from which he hoped great results, failed, and the consequent financial loss forced him to give up his theatre. After his visit to England in 1878–79, where he established relations with managers and actors that laid the foundations of his future successes, he turned the Old Broadway Theatre into Daly's Theatre. This was long to be the home of the remarkable company he assembled, including John Drew, Ada Rehan [*qq.v.*], and Otis Skinner. With the opening of the new theatre on Sept. 18, 1879 Daly ceased writing original plays and devoted his talents to the adaptation of French and German drama. His energies were spent largely, too, in the direction of the numerous plays with which he sought to give variety to his audiences. His correspondence reveals his efforts to procure the works of native playwrights like Bronson Howard, whose adaptation from Molière, under the title of *Wives,* was one of the first successes of the theatre. But more and more he grew to depend upon his own adaptations, many of which were radical alterations of the originals. Among the French playwrights, Sardou and Dumas were his favorites and with one exception, *Delmonico's; or Larks up the Hudson* (1871), he preserved the French scene when he dealt with the works of these two dramatists. About 1880 he began to transfer the scenes and characters to American conditions, perhaps because he was dealing with the work of less well-known playwrights. Probably his greatest successes were *Hazardous Ground* (1867) from Sardou's *Nos Bons Villageois; Monsieur Alphonse* (1874) from Dumas (*fils*); *Frou Frou* (1870) from Henri Meilhac and Ludovic Halévy; and *The Lottery of Love* (1888) from *Les Surprises du Divorce* by Alexandre Bisson and Antony Mars. In his adaptations from the German, Daly usually changed the scene to America. In *The Passing Regiment* (1881) hardly a trace of the German flavor of *Krieg im Frieden,* by Von Moser and Franz Von Schönthan, is noticeable, and when Daly adapted the latter's sequel, *Reif von Reiflingen,* it became *Our English Friend,* with an Englishman for a hero. His adaptations of German comedy were almost invariably successful, among the most popular being *Seven-Twenty-Eight; or, Casting the Boomerang* (1883), from *Der Schwabenstreich,* of Franz Von Schönthan; *A Night Off* (1885), from *Der Raub der Sabinerrinnen,* by the Von Schönthan brothers; *The Countess Gucki* (1896) by F. Von Schönthan, which was written for Ada Rehan and is unique among the comedies from the German in that it preserves the foreign atmosphere.

Daly took his company to London in 1884, playing at Toole's Theatre and being especially successful with his representation of Colley Cibber's *She Would and She Would Not.* In 1886, after again visiting London, he invaded the Continent, taking to Germany the first English-speaking company of any importance for nearly three hundred years. His reception in Berlin and Paris was only moderately enthusiastic. On a third foreign trip, in 1888, the most significant event was the production of *The Taming of the Shrew,* probably the first time a comedy of Shakespeare had been produced in Europe by an American company. Paris was not captured by this performance, but in 1891 *As You Like It* and *The School for Scandal* were received there with greater enthusiasm. The position which Daly had achieved by 1891 is evidenced by Tennyson's choice of him to adapt his dramatic poem, *The Foresters,* for the stage. It was a thing of beauty when produced at Daly's Theatre, Mar. 17, 1892, especially noteworthy being the performance of Ada Rehan as Maid Marian. On June 27, 1893, Daly opened his own theatre in London and, after varying fortunes, produced *Twelfth Night* for one hundred nights. He continued his productions of Shakespeare after his return to America, *The Tempest* in 1897 being especially effective. Difficulties arising with the lessor of his theatre in London, he made a business trip abroad in the course of which he died in Paris on June 7, 1899.

Daly was tall, handsome, and his flashing eyes and dominating personality reflected his seafaring and military ancestry. A martinet in his theatre, he demanded of his company the loyalty he gave them. Discriminating in his judgments of actors, he developed many who in their opinion outgrew the position he allowed them and passed from his control. Of those who remained he made probably the finest and most complete interpretative instrument for the drama that America has seen. He built up a clientele which was confident that at Daly's Theatre there would be a play worth seeing, and he achieved an identification of manager, playwright, director, company, and theatre, unique in our stage history. The result was a standard which helped to raise the general level of taste, and his productions of Shakespeare alone would render his position secure. But he was more than an interpreter, he was a creative artist. His place in American dramatic history has suffered from his unwillingness to publish his plays. He wrote, altered, or adapted about ninety plays that were produced on the stage. Many of them were privately printed, but those which were published, *Under the Gaslight* (1867), *Griffith Gaunt* (1868), *Frou Frou* (1870), *Seven-Twenty-Eight* (1897), and *A Night Off* (1897), do not represent him at his best. In *Horizon, Divorce, Pique,* and in his more delicate interpretations of foreign comedy, he proved himself a skilled dramatist. How hard he worked on his adaptations is attested by Otis Skinner (*Footlights and Spotlights*, 1924, p. 146) who tells us that when Pinero's *Lords and Commons* was failing, Daly spent his nights adapting *Love on Crutches*, from Heinrich Stobitzer's *Ihre Ideale*, in order to save the season. Daly's biography, *Woffington, A Tribute to the Actress and the Woman* (1888), reveals him in another aspect of his writing. How thoroughly he knew the dramatic past of America and how he scorned the critical stupidity which demands that American drama shall limit itself to the parochial, is revealed in his article "The American Dramatist" (*North American Review*, May 1886, pp. 485–92).

[The authoritative biography is Jos. F. Daly, *The Life of Augustin Daly* (1917). Of some value are two articles under the general heading, "An American School of Dramatic Art," J. R. Towse, "A Critical Review of Daly's Theatre," and G. P. Lathrop, "The Inside Working of the Theatre," *Century*, June 1898; E. A. Ditmar, *Memories of One Theatre with Passing Recollections of Many Others* (1891), and an informal *Diary of a Daly Débutante* (1910), published anonymously but known to be by Dora Knowlton, one of Daly's company. For criticism of the plays, see A. H. Quinn, *Hist. of the Am. Drama from the Civil War to the Present Day* (1927), I, 1–38, with play list, II, 278–84. The prompt-books of several of Daly's plays and a large collection of his scrap-books are in the N. Y. Pub. Lib. The MSS. are in possession of Samuel French.]

A. H. Q.

DALY, MARCUS (Dec. 5, 1841–Nov. 12, 1900), miner and capitalist, was born in Ireland. His parents, Luke and Mary Daly, were very poor and he grew up with little opportunity for education. At the age of fifteen he came to America. He worked for a while around New York, then went to California where he became a miner. Employed as a pick and shovel man, he soon became an expert on mining. After a time he entered the service of Fair and Mackay in Nevada where he displayed ability enough to attract the attention of Walker Brothers, and in 1876 they sent him to Butte, Mont. There he purchased the Alice Silver Mine in partnership with them, but soon sold his interest for $30,000. Geologists had declared the Butte mines to be of little value. Daly, however, believed that the unusual formation of the country concealed rich beds of ore. He went to California to seek aid from some old friends there. He persuaded George Hearst and others to share his convictions and they bought the Anaconda Silver Mine. It was not long before the silver gave out, but beneath it was a rich vein of copper. Daly closed the mine and quietly bought up others in the neighborhood and then started the great copper-mining operations that were to make Butte and the Anaconda Copper Mining Company famous.

He mined the coal for his furnaces and acquired huge tracts of timber where he cut the wood for his mines. He built a railway from Butte to Anaconda. He established banks, built power plants and irrigation systems, and encouraged other enterprises. In twenty years he built up a fortune of many million dollars.

His feud with William A. Clark [q.v.] dominated Montana society and politics from 1888 to 1900. Daly and Clark had been friends, but their struggle for control of the copper mines of Butte had made them bitter enemies. Clark had control of the Butte reduction plants and Daly built Anaconda with its huge smelter a few miles away. Both men had business and political interest in Missoula, but when Clark gained an advantage, Daly built Hamilton, fifty miles up the Bitter Root, and projected a railroad from Butte and Anaconda, through this town, to the Pacific, with the idea of making it the commercial center of western Montana. He established the *Anaconda Standard* and made it the best paper in the state. Both men were Democrats, and both built up machines of their employees and of business men who were dependent upon them. Daly's genial and generous disposition, combined with a reputation for courage and loyalty, gave him popular favor over the reserved and elegant Clark, who was accused of timidity and a willingness to throw over his friends when they were no longer useful. Daly would never seek office for himself, but he loved to exert influence in politics and for ten years he endeavored to thwart Clark's ambition. In 1888 his followers brought about Clark's defeat as candidate for territorial delegate; in 1893 they prevented his election as senator; and when Clark finally secured his election as senator in 1899, Daly gave $25,000 to carry the fight to the Senate Committee on Elections whose adverse report forced Clark's resignation.

Daly gave lavishly for any cause he favored. He started the first state Democratic campaign with a donation of $40,000, and followed this with more. He apparently spent more than a half million dollars to make Anaconda the state capital. In 1896 he gave $50,000 to the Bryan Campaign fund, out of a total of $350,000 from all sources (statement of J. M. Dixon of a conversation with Senator J. K. Jones, Bryan's campaign manager).

Daly was married in 1872 to Margaret Evans. He built a house in the upper Bitter Root Valley, where he developed one of the finest ranches in the West. There he planted orchards and gave a start to fruit-growing in the valley. His pet extravagance was fast horses. Some of these were among the fastest in the world and he showed great pride in their triumphs on the track. He kept in close touch with the men with whom he had worked as a miner, and brought many of them to Butte and gave them a start to wealth. He was interested in his employees and gave higher wages than were current. His last achievement was the combination of a number of mining and lumber companies into the Amalgamated Copper Company with a capitalization of $75,000,000.

[The sources for the life of Daly are very unsatisfactory. There is a laudatory sketch of him in *Progressive Men of Mont.* (1901), and C. P. Connolly, "Story of Mont.," *McClure's Mag.,* Aug.–Dec. 1906, is partisan in his behalf. S. E. Moffett, "Marcus Daly, Empire Builder," *Rev. of Revs.* (N. Y.), Dec. 1900, is of little value. The files of the *Anaconda Standard,* especially Nov. 3, 1895, express Daly's views and reflect his character; there is a good obituary, *Ibid.,* Nov. 13, 1900. There is also a sketch of Daly in *Harper's Weekly,* Nov. 24, 1900.]

P. C. P.

DALY, PETER CHRISTOPHER ARNOLD (Oct. 22, 1875–Jan. 13, 1927), actor, was born in Brooklyn, N. Y., the son of Joseph J. and Mary (Arnold) Daly, both natives of Ireland. He was christened Peter Christopher, but later took his mother's maiden name and dropped the others. He was educated in parochial schools, after being ejected, so he later declared, from four public schools for opposing rules which he considered "an insult to his intelligence." He became a call boy at the Lyceum Theatre, New York, and his first successful impersonation was that of Chambers, in Frank Mayo's production of *Puddn'head Wilson* in the early nineties. In the next few years he had considerable experience there and in London, acting especially well the crazed lover in Miss Marlowe's production of Clyde Fitch's *Barbara Frietchie* and Imp in the London production of *When We Were Twentyone.* It was while he was with Miss Marlowe that he first conceived the idea of producing G. B. Shaw's *Candida,* a play which Richard Mansfield had put in rehearsal but abandoned. He could not secure, however, the needed support. After Mansfield's tour in 1897–98 with Shaw's *The Devil's Disciple,* no Shaw play had been seen in America. At last, on Dec. 9, 1903, Daly succeeded in making a single matinée production of *Candida,* at the Princess Theatre, New York, with Dorothy Donnelly in the title part and himself as Marchbanks. It was so successful that in partnership with Winchell Smith he rented the Berkeley Lyceum and played *Candida* for 150 performances. This was the real start of the Shaw vogue in America. Thereafter Daly mounted several other Shaw plays—*How He Lied to Her Husband* (written for him), *The Man of*

Destiny, You Never Can Tell (Garrick Theatre, New York, January 1905), *John Bull's Other Island* (Garrick, Oct. 10, 1905), and finally *Mrs. Warren's Profession* (Garrick, Oct. 30, 1905). Before the New York opening of this last play, Anthony Comstock sounded a warning, and after one try-out performance in New Haven the police stopped it there. At the New York première, seats were selling on the sidewalk for $25, and Police Commissioner McAdoo was in the audience. The next morning McAdoo announced that further performances would be a violation of the law. None was given, but Daly and his leading lady, Mary Shaw, were arrested, tried in Special Sessions, and acquitted. Except for John Corbin of the *Sun,* all the newspaper critics called the play indecent, and Shaw was provoked to write a now highly prized pamphlet on the subject. The outbreak of Comstockery cost Daly much money and a quarrel with his managers. After reviving *Arms and the Man* at the Lyric Theatre, he again rented the Berkeley Lyceum, and attempted to conduct that tiny house as "a theatre of ideas," during the season of 1907–08. He gave several bills of one-act plays, revived several Shaw successes, refused to advertise in the newspapers, and denied free seats to their critics. But the venture was not successful. He found himself in serious financial difficulties. The Shaw plays passed into other hands, and he never regained the place he had briefly held as a fighting leader of modernism on the American stage. He thereafter alternated engagements in vaudeville with such parts as he could secure, his better known later appearances being with Madame Simone in *The Return from Jerusalem,* in the title rôle of *General John Regan,* in *The Tavern* (produced by G. M. Cohan), in the title rôle of *Voltaire,* and in the Theatre Guild's production of *Juarez and Maximilian,* in October 1926. On the morning of Jan. 12, 1927, he perished in a fire which swept the house in New York where he had an apartment. His body was found seated in a chair, as if he had been caught asleep. Daly was married, on July 1, 1900, to Mary Blythe, an actress. They had one child, Blythe Daly, who eventually went on the stage. They were divorced in 1903 and were later reunited, only to separate again, Mrs. Daly becoming Mrs. Frank Craven.

Arnold Daly was a victim of tempermental excesses, which manifested themselves in violent quarrels, egotistical outbursts, and lack of co-operative spirit. But he had a genuine appreciation of modernism in drama before most of his fellows, he was ready to fight for it and to sacrifice for it, and as an actor he possessed a nervous sensibility which made him, when willing to submit to a director's control, an extremely vivid and effective player, particularly in such parts as Marchbanks. There can be no question but that his production of *Candida* and other Shaw plays, from 1903 through 1905, marked an important step forward in our theatre, and had it not been for the disastrous interference of Comstockery and his subsequent bankruptcy and intensified truculence, his later influence might have equaled that of his early years. He was a double victim of himself and Mrs. Grundy.

[B. H. Goldsmith, *Arnold Daly* (1927); *Who's Who on the Stage* (1906); Arnold Daly Scrap-Book, Locke Collection, N. Y. Pub. Lib.]   W. P. E.

DALZELL, JOHN (Apr. 19, 1845–Oct. 2, 1927), congressman, parliamentarian, was born in New York City, of Scotch-Irish parents. Samuel Dalzell, a shoemaker, and his wife Mary (McDonnell) had come from County Down in 1840. When John was two, their pioneer urge pushed them farther across the mountains to Pittsburgh. At sixteen, John became discontented with the educational opportunities offered him at the Western University of Pennsylvania, and found his way to Yale. Entering heartily into the social, athletic, literary, and debating activities there, he succeeded in developing leadership and securing recognition. Upon graduation (A.B., 1865), he was desirous of following his natural bent, the law, in his home community. Two years of study there under John H. Hampton led to a partnership with him.

Twenty years of arduous, successful work as a corporation attorney ensued. The firm became counsel for all the western lines of the Pennsylvania Railroad from the time of their amalgamation, for the Westinghouse industries, and for others of more local significance. After the death of Hampton in 1887 the name of the firm was changed to Dalzell, Scott & Gordon, and Dalzell worked actively in it until 1895. In the midst of his labors in behalf of industrial amalgamation and railroad expansion, his friends persuaded him, somewhat against his will, to go to Congress. In this project they were aided and abetted by his wife. Mary Louise Duff, to whom he was married Sept. 26, 1867, was exceptionally well-fitted to be the helpmate of a congressman. Relieving her husband of many of the burdens which constituents place upon their representatives, she also unobtrusively engineered campaign contacts, quietly supervising that meticulous reëlection detail which is the bane of a congressman's existence, a work which Dalzell abhorred and in which he practically refused to engage. Under such favorable auspices, there

began a congressional career which was to last through twenty-six consecutive years.

From 1887 to 1889 and from 1891 to 1895 Dalzell was a member of the minority. He proved himself unwaveringly loyal to Pittsburgh's industries, and although a railroad attorney contributed powerfully to the development of Pittsburgh's waterways. His period of national significance commenced in 1895, when the Republicans gained control of the House; then began a sequence of fourteen years of House leadership, jointly exercised with Reed, Dingley, Payne, and Cannon. From their councils emanated highly developed forms of the special rule, devised to expedite legislation. Already a member of the Ways and Means Committee, Dalzell now went on the Rules Committee, of which he ultimately became ranking member. In this key-position he reported an immense number of the special rules by which much of the important legislation has been since enacted in the House of Representatives. One of the most important of these was that of Mar. 1, 1901, providing for consideration of a conference report without reference to the usual committee, and providing in detail for the previous question thereon.

Dalzell being a thoroughgoing conservative, the La Follette insurgents had him to reckon with from the start. He cornered them many times; as on Mar. 1, 1909, when he proposed Calendar Wednesday in such manner as to put them on record against it; and Apr. 10 and July 31 of that year, when special rules sent the tariff to conference without debate on separate amendments, and provided that the conference report should not be subject to a point of order. Dalzell failed to defeat the Norris resolution abolishing the old Rules Committee; but when the Republicans, debarring from their caucus the insurgents, came to nominate for the new committee, he was named for the ranking position; and when the committee organized he was named chairman. From this new-old vantage, Dalzell reported, June 17, 1910, the first discharge rule of the House, that rule which James R. Mann murdered six months later.

The Senate remained out of Dalzell's reach, Matthew S. Quay [*q.v.*] defeating him in 1899, and again in 1901. For the speakership, he lost in 1902 to Joseph G. Cannon [*q.v.*], the more picturesque Mid-Western candidate. The death of Mrs. Dalzell in 1909 broke the mainspring of his political existence. In 1912 he suffered defeat with Taft, and thereafter steadfastly refused to reënter politics. He chose to remain in retirement in Washington until, two years before his death, he removed to Altadena, Cal.

[*Cong. Record*, Mar. 18, 1906; A. C. McCown, *The Cong. Conference Committee* (1927); P. D. Hasbrouck, *Party Government in the House of Representatives* (1927); G. R. Brown, *The Leadership of Congress* (1922); C. R. Atkinson, *The Committee on Rules and the Overthrow of Speaker Cannon* (1911); W. C. Duyckinck, *Summary of Class Meetings and the Biog. Record of the Class of 1865, Yale Coll.* (1910); *Yale Univ. Obit. Record* (1928); *Pittsburgh Post-Gazette*, Oct. 4, 1927; Dalzell MSS., Lib. of Cong.]   J. P. N.

DALZELL, ROBERT M. (1793–Jan. 19, 1873), millwright, inventor, was born in County Down, near Belfast, Ireland. He was the son of John Dalzell, the last of an old family of Scotch Covenanters that had established itself in Ireland and become a family of influence and character, with large property. When Robert was five years old the Rebellion of 1798 began and his father, one of the recognized leaders, was sought for by British soldiers. He escaped to sea in an open boat and was picked up by the crew of a passing ship and carried to New York. Three years later his wife and children came to New York as immigrants to join him. They established themselves on a small farm at Vernon, Oneida County, N. Y., and began life anew under the most adverse, poverty-stricken conditions. Young Dalzell was given all of the educational advantages that the local country school afforded, after which he was apprenticed to a millwright from whom he learned his trade. Following his apprenticeship he worked locally as a millwright until he was thirty-three years of age, when he moved to Rochester to engage in his chosen occupation. It was about this time that the potential water power of the Genesee River and its falls at Rochester began to be recognized. Among the first enterprises utilizing this power were flour-mills, and in their construction Dalzell, as a millwright, found immediate employment. His mechanical ingenuity combined with his skill in mill construction was quickly recognized and for the succeeding twenty-five years or more his services were in great demand. In fact, practically all of the flour-mills in Rochester, which came to be known as the "Flour City," were designed by him and built under his supervision. In the course of this work he perfected and introduced the elevator system for storing grain and meal which is now universally used in all large ocean and inland ports, but he never patented the system. His refusal to do so was probably due to his conscientious scruples against the accumulation of wealth by an individual; it is said that in all of his private transactions, both when he was in active work and after his retirement, he could never under any form or guise be persuaded to take more than seven per cent interest or discount. For the last twenty-five

years of his life he lived more or less in retirement, his activities centering about his church. He died in Rochester, N. Y., being survived by his widow, Lucy S. Dalzell, and two children.

[*Ann. Cyc.*, 1873; W. F. Peck, *Semi-Centennial Hist. of the City of Rochester* (1884); obituary in Rochester *Democrat and Chronicle*, Jan. 20, 1873; correspondence with N. Y. State Lib. and Rochester Pub. Lib., Division of Local History.]   C. W. M.

DAMROSCH, LEOPOLD (Oct. 22, 1832–Feb. 15, 1885), conductor, composer, violinist, was born in Posen. Like many other musically gifted persons, he encountered paternal opposition as soon as he took steps to follow professionally the art to which he had been inclined since childhood. After graduating from the Breslau Gymnasium, he matriculated as a student of medicine at the University of Berlin in 1854. This, however, was his last concession to his parents' wishes regarding his career; for, once his degree of doctor of medicine was acquired, he abandoned medicine in favor of music, continued his study of the violin with Ries, Dehn, and Böhmer, and soon as a solo artist, and later as a conductor, appeared with success in various minor German towns and cities. In 1857 "he became concert master at the Grand Ducal Opera at Weimar under the direction of Franz Liszt whom he adored and whose music, together with that of Wagner and Berlioz, he promulgated during the rest of his life" (letter from Walter Damrosch). At Weimar he married the talented German *Lieder* singer, Helena von Heimburg, with whom he returned to Breslau in 1858, immediately after his marriage. There he took the position of conductor of the Breslau Philharmonic Orchestra, only to resign it in order to accompany the pianists Von Bülow and Tausig on various concert tours. In 1862, again in Breslau, he organized the Breslau Orchestra Society, a choral society, and a string quartet; and for two years conducted the concerts of the Society for Classical Music and the orchestra of the Breslau Stadttheater, besides appearing as a solo violinist.

With his musical reputation now firmly established, though his financial status was far from good, it was natural that Damrosch, in 1871, should have accepted with pleasure an invitation to come to America, as the conductor of the Arion Society of New York. As his son declared: "My father had become more and more discontented with musical, social and political conditions in Breslau. He was really a republican at heart and the Prussian bureaucracy, which had become more and more accentuated by the war (1870–71) irked and angered him. With the greatest difficulty he could make a bare living for his family, and he found the population of Breslau, except a small band of devoted followers, steeped in materialism and not particularly sympathetic toward art, especially the modern German composers."

On May 6, 1871 Damrosch made his New York *début* in the triple capacity of conductor, composer, and violinist, and found little difficulty in soon winning appreciation for the newer German school of composition represented by Wagner, Liszt, and Schumann. His executive capacity was shown by bringing the Arion Society to the highest point of musical efficiency, by the foundation of the New York Oratorio Society in 1873, and, in 1878, of the New York Symphony Society, which succeeded the Thomas Orchestra at the Steinway Hall concerts. In 1880, Columbia University made the German doctor of medicine an American doctor of music, and the following year he conducted New York's first great music festival. In the old Seventh Regiment Armory, with an audience of ten thousand people for each performance, Berlioz's *Requiem,* with the four orchestras and sixteen kettle-drums in the *Tuba Mirum,* Rubinstein's *Tower of Babel,* Händel's *Messiah,* and Beethoven's *Ninth Symphony* were presented by 250 musicians and 1,200 singers. In 1883 Damrosch made a successful tour with his orchestra in the West. His greatest triumph was his last. In 1884–85, the directors of the Metropolitan Opera House, at the suggestion of James Roosevelt, gave a season of German opera, at which he conducted *Tannhäuser, Lohengrin, Die Walküre,* and other noted operas. In achieving this "final triumph of Wagner's art in the new world," at a time when Italian opera still claimed supremacy, the veteran conductor who was attending rehearsals of the Symphony and Oratorio Societies in the meantime, so overworked himself that he fell an easy victim to pneumonia. Leopold Damrosch exerted a great influence in raising the standard of musical taste and appreciation in America during the past half-century; and in infusing the mechanistic excellence of orchestra and oratorio performance which he found on his arrival in the United States with musical soul and spirit. His own compositions include seven cantatas, orchestral numbers, songs, choruses, and three violin concertos.

[Walter Damrosch, *My Musical Life* (1923); H. C. Colles, ed., *Grove's Dict. of Music and Musicians,* vol. II (1927); J. G. Huneker, *Steeplejack* (1920), II, 36; Alfred Remy, ed., *Baker's Biog. Dict. of Musicians* (3rd ed., 1919).]   F. H. M.

DANA, CHARLES ANDERSON (Aug. 8, 1819–Oct. 17, 1897), newspaper editor, was born at Hinsdale, N. H., a descendant of Jacob, eldest son of Richard Dana who in 1640 was a resident of Cambridge, Mass. He had few early advantages beyond the good blood of Puritan ancestors. His father, Anderson Dana, a country storekeeper, failed in business and removed to upper New York, where he became a farmer; his mother, Ann Denison, died when he was nine. Sent to Buffalo at the age of twelve to clerk in the general store of an uncle, he was thrown entirely upon his own resources at eighteen, when the panic of 1837 ruined his employer. While a boy on the farm he had studied Latin on his own initiative; he used his evenings in Buffalo to read widely, become familiar with the Latin classics, and begin the study of Greek. He joined a literary society there called the Coffee Club, and delivered before it a youthful lecture on early English poetry which was much admired. Thus prepared by his own efforts, he was able to matriculate at Harvard without conditions in the fall of 1839, and took high rank in his first college term. Despite one long absence for teaching school he had begun his junior year in 1841, when his eyesight became impaired by overstudy and he returned to Buffalo. Twenty years later he received from Harvard an honorary A.B., as of the class of 1843. About the time he left college, George Ripley [*q.v.*] was launching the Brook Farm enterprise, which Dana, with an idealistic enthusiasm then characteristic of him, hastened to join. He was engaged to teach German, Greek, or anything else, and to work on the Farm, while in view of his storekeeping experience he was made one of the managing trustees. For the next five years he remained at Brook Farm, placing in it what slender capital he could, and proselytizing earnestly for it. With characteristic energy he taught, sang bass in the choir, wrote essays and poems for the *Dial* and the *Harbinger,* and delivered lectures. According to T. W. Higginson, he was the best all-round man at the Farm. He opposed its conversion into a "Phalanx" as demanded by Fourierist ideas, but after this was effected he remained stanchly loyal to the organization (Lindsay Swift, *Brook Farm,* 1900). In a lecture of 1895 at the University of Michigan he paid a warm tribute to the charm of life at the Farm, and the value of his association there with Ripley, Hawthorne, George W. Curtis, Margaret Fuller, and others.

Dana's writings for the *Harbinger* had so fixed his attention upon journalism that when a disastrous fire terminated the Brook Farm experiment in 1864 he naturally turned to that field. A slight previous connection with the Boston *Daily Chronotype* enabled him at once to become its assistant editor. The paper was too poor to pay much, and its strong Congregationalism repelled Dana, who had now progressed far in Unitarian liberalism. In the absence of the editor he made the *Chronotype* come out "mighty strong against hell," so that his superior later had to write a letter of explanation to every Congregational minister in the state. Within the year Dana used his acquaintance with Greeley to obtain the city editorship of the *New York Tribune,* at the munificent wage of first ten and later fourteen dollars a week. For the next fifteen years he devoted himself to the paper, and soon stood second in its office to Greeley alone. Outwardly this period of subeditorship was uneventful. Its first years were broken by a long trip (1848–9) to Europe, where Dana supported himself by contributing no fewer than five letters a week to as many journals in New York, Boston, and Philadelphia. He could not have gone abroad at a more instructive moment, for he witnessed the uprisings in Paris and Berlin at close range. His experiences did more than acquaint him with European affairs. They swept away many of his idealistic illusions, gave him an insight into the selfishness and chicanery of politicians, and helped lay the foundation for his subsequent cynicism. Later, as managing editor, he had little time for travel, but found leisure to edit an American edition of H. J. Meyer's *Universum* (1852), and to compile *The Household Book of Poetry* (1857), which in successive editions commanded an enormous sale. A trip which Dana made with W. H. Appleton to the opening of the Chicago & Rock Island Railroad resulted in plans for an American Cyclopædia in sixteen volumes under the editorship of himself and George Ripley. The first volume appeared in 1858, and despite the interruption of the war, the work was completed in six years. Two editions of it sold more than three million copies (Grant Overton, *Portrait of a Publisher,* 1925, p. 45).

Dana's years on the *Tribune* gave him experience in two directions. As a writer he became the master of a compressed, sententious style, sometimes epigrammatic, and increasingly tinged by cynicism. His principles were largely, though by no means completely, liberal. He took up Kossuth's cause with ardor, advocated a railway to the Pacific, and ably seconded Greeley's opposition to the expansion of slavery, though he had little use for the Abolitionists. He believed in a high protective tariff, and op-

posed labor unions formed to conduct strikes, arguing that the workers' true remedy for unfair industrial conditions lay in a cooperative industrial effort. His hostility to militant labor persisted throughout his life, and gave many of his utterances on industrial questions an illiberal and even reactionary tendency. In editorial management Dana soon made himself an expert. Frequently, as during Greeley's European trips in 1851 and 1855–56, he was in sole charge. He then decided the entire contents of the paper; edited everything, even Greeley's contributions, with iron hand; and took the initiative in important business changes.

In the events leading up to the Civil War Dana and Greeley acted with substantial harmony, and there is no question that Dana acquiesced in Greeley's willingness to let the erring sisters depart in peace. But, though the words were written by a subordinate, Dana was responsible for the *Tribune's* disastrous warcry, "Forward to Richmond!" which Greeley opposed. This was the first serious token of a divergence in views and temper which rapidly became intolerable. Dana was too aggressive and positive in dealing with both civil and military policy to suit Greeley. The result was that, after Greeley had acted rather shiftily, Dana's resignation was demanded and accepted (Mar. 28, 1862), with a promise of six months' salary. This virtual dismissal was a blessing in disguise. After declining the suggestion that he take a diplomatic post or a place with the Treasury (Wilson, pp. 182–83), he at once entered the service of the War Department, where Secretary Stanton was eager to repay him for editorial support.

The best part of Dana's war service was performed as a special commissioner at Grant's headquarters, nominally to investigate the payservice, but actually to report daily on military operations and thus enable the Administration to measure accurately Grant's capacities. During the Vicksburg campaign his observations were equally valuable to the Washington officials and to Grant himself. Dana instantly perceived the general's high qualities, he increased Lincoln's faith in him, set Stanton right regarding the jealous McClernand, and by his daily dispatches relieved Grant of much irksome letter-writing. Of Sherman's military genius Dana also formed a high opinion. Made assistant secretary of war after the fall of Vicksburg, he was sent to report upon the movements of Rosecrans against Bragg. His judgment was not in all regards unerring, but he was right in urging the removal of Rosecrans. Later with

Grant and Sherman at Chattanooga, Lookout Mountain, and Missionary Ridge, he again proved an excellent advocate for these men. During 1864 he alternated desk service in Washington with field service in Virginia, and formed impressions of Lincoln, the cabinet members, and some leading congressmen which enabled him long afterward to give pungent sketches of them in his *Recollections of the Civil War* (1898). On July 1, 1865, he resigned and immediately left the capital.

Dana's acquisition of the New York *Sun*, which marked the opening of the most significant part of his career, occurred at the close of 1867. It was preceded by an abortive journalistic venture in Chicago, where he became editor of an unsuccessful paper called the *Republican* (*Recollections*, p. 290). When this sheet began to fail, he secured capital for the founding of a newspaper in New York, his associates including W. M. Evarts, Roscoe Conkling, Alonzo Cornell, Cyrus W. Field and A. A. Low. A fortunate chance enabling him to purchase the *Sun* for $175,000, he assumed its editorship on Jan. 25, 1868, with an announcement of policy which has become a journalistic classic. After declaring that the *Sun* would be independent of party, would advocate the speedy restoration of the South, and would support Grant for the presidency, he summed up its new spirit in a single sentence: "It will study condensation, clearness, point, and will endeavor to present its daily photograph of the whole world's doings in the most luminous and lively manner." Imbued with this spirit, the *Sun* at once achieved a new success.

In his capacity as leader of public opinion, Dana was frequently perverse, cynical, and reactionary, and more than once affected by personal resentments. He broke sharply with Grant, and after 1869 attacked his administration more fiercely than did any other New York daily. Yet in 1872, while making the cry "Turn the rascals out" ring through the country and assailing Grant almost scurrilously, he gave only a cynical quasi-support to the Liberal Republican party, whose candidate he contemptuously called "Dr. Greeley." In 1876 the *Sun* opposed Hayes, whom it later branded as a receiver of stolen goods and a fraudulent president. Four years later it relentlessly attacked Garfield, whom it described as a participant in the Crédit Mobilier frauds, the Boss Shepherd thefts, and the back-pay grab; yet at the same time it treated Hancock with ill-veiled condescension, speaking of him as "a good man, weighing two hundred and fifty pounds." The

most remarkable exhibition of Dana's political perversity was his unremitting enmity to Cleveland, which grew out of an unworthy bit of personal pique, the failure of Cleveland to keep a supposed promise to appoint Franklin Bartlett, son of Dana's friend W. O. Bartlett, to a post connected with the state judiciary. Dana at the same time declared that sooner than join in making Blaine president, he would quit work and burn his pen. The consequence was that in 1884 he had to support B. F. Butler and his Greenback ticket, which polled a farcically small vote in New York. In his social and economic opinions of these years Dana showed the same perversity, accompanied sometimes by an impudent levity. He denounced the reformed civil service as "a German bureaucratic system," advocated the annexation of Cuba, Santo Domingo, and if possible Canada, and abused Cleveland for his conciliatory foreign policy, demanding the resignation of Secretary Bayard for negotiating the fisheries treaty with England. He declared that the McKinley Act was the most scientific and valuable tariff the country ever had. Dana's hostility toward labor unions cropped out in the great railway strike of 1878; and later he urged that labor organizations be placed under precisely as stringent governmental regulation as affected the trusts. In New York City the *Sun* supported some of the worst figures in Tammany, and opposed some of the best reform movements.

As a news editor, however, Dana at once took a very high place. The Civil War had tended to exalt news at the expense of editorials. Dana approved of this, declaring that "if the newspaper has not the news, it may have everything else, yet it will be comparatively unsuccessful." Under him the *Sun's* news-pages were characterized by conciseness, cleverness, and sparkle of style. Discarding conventional standards of news importance and emphasizing human interest, he taught the staff that a good story on the Sunday crowd at Coney Island might be worth more space than a column on the Carlist War or a lecture by Huxley. The *Sun* gave prominence to crime in its "daily photograph," and specialized in eye-catching headlines. The enterprise of the reporters obtained many scoops, and the foreign and domestic correspondence of the paper attained such excellence that when in 1897 a long-standing quarrel with the Associated Press came to a head, Dana's managing editor, Chester S. Lord, was able to organize over-night a comprehensive news service of his own. Though sternly excluding fine writing, the *Sun* insisted upon vividness, and made generous room for clever brief essays. The paper was at all costs bright, witty, and enjoyable. As a result it became the "newspaper man's newspaper," and attracted to its staff a singularly brilliant roster of writers. Indeed, one of Dana's titles to fame as an editor is that he gave opportunity and advancement to such editorial writers as E. P. Mitchell, and such news writers as Julian Ralph, David Graham Phillips, Jacob Riis, and Richard Harding Davis. He mingled constantly with the staff, encouraging, suggesting, and praising frequently, while chiding rarely and gently.

Dana was a man of wide intellectual and esthetic interests, which in later life he had leisure and money to indulge. He took quiet pride in learning the chief European tongues, living and dead, his last two trips abroad being for the purpose of perfecting his Russian. He liked to conduct private classes in Dante or Icelandic; he had a valuable collection of Chinese porcelains; and at his home on Dosoris Island in Long Island Sound he grew a remarkable variety of foreign trees, shrubs, and flowers. He prided himself on being a connoisseur of wines, though he seldom did more than taste them. Though much interested in politics, he preferred to make his friends among literary people, musicians, and artists. Married, Mar. 2, 1846, to Eunice Macdaniel, he was devoted to wife and children. He had the faculty of endearing himself to close newspaper associates, but he never forgave a grudge or a slight.

[Jas. H. Wilson, *Life of Chas. A. Dana* (1907), is uncritically eulogistic and emphasizes his war services. Chas. A. Dana, *Recollections of the Civil War* (1898), a graphic and honest work, throwing some light on his years upon the *Tribune,* should be supplemented by *The Art of Newspaper Making* (1895), and *Eastern Journeys* (1898). See also Frank M. O'Brien, *The Story of the Sun* (1918); Edw. P. Mitchell, *Memoirs of an Editor* (1924); Chester S. Lord, *The Young Men and Journalism* (1922); Willard G. Bleyer, *Main Currents in the Hist. of Am. Journalism* (1927); Henry Watterson, *Marse Henry: An Autobiography* (1919); Oswald G. Villard, *Some Newspapers and Newspapermen* (1923); J. J. Dana, *Memoranda of Some of the Descendants of Richard Dana* (1865); and biographies of Greeley. The *Sun* published no obituary. Magazine material is voluminous, but must be used with care.]
A. N.

DANA, FRANCIS (June 13, 1743–Apr. 25, 1811), diplomat, jurist, was born in Charlestown, Mass., the son of Richard [*q.v.*] and Lydia (Trowbridge) Dana. Graduating from Harvard in 1762, he received the degree of A.M. in 1765. After studying law for five years under the direction of his mother's brother, Judge Edmund Trowbridge [*q.v.*], one of the ablest lawyers in the colony, he was admitted to the bar in 1767. Six years later he married Elizabeth Ellery of Newport, R. I., daughter of William

Ellery [*q.v.*]. One of their sons was Richard Henry Dana [*q.v.*], and a daughter, Martha, became the wife of Washington Allston [*q.v.*]. From his father he acquired an interest in politics, as well as the means to indulge it. His fortune, described as competent by one of his descendants, was invested largely in land. Although not a radical by temperament, he found fault with the colonial policy of the British government, and became identified with the Sons of Liberty. In spite of this connection, however, he held no public office during the early years of the Revolutionary movement, but devoted himself primarily to his law practise.

In the fall and winter of 1774–75, while Samuel Adams and his followers wanted independence, another group, including Dana and some other Sons of Liberty, urged reconciliation with Great Britain. Although chosen in September 1774 as one of the Cambridge delegates to the first provincial Congress of Massachusetts, Dana did not take his seat in that body. Instead he undertook an interesting diplomatic venture, half private and half public in character, in the interests of Anglo-American harmony. Carrying letters from Quincy, Warren, and other deaders, he went to England to represent the Patriot cause among the English friends of the colonies, and to discover what the situation actually was in that country. His brother Edmund had gone to live in England, and had married there a daughter of Lord Kinnaird; through her relatives Dana had access to numerous political leaders. Remaining in England for a year and a half, he returned to his home in Cambridge in April 1776 convinced that reconciliation was out of the question and that independence alone would put an end to the controversy over colonial rights and British power. Prepared to devote his whole efforts to the American cause, he was at first undecided whether to take a political or a military part in the war. His constituents may have settled the matter for him; at all events they elected him a member of the Massachusetts Council in 1776, and regularly thereafter until 1780. In December 1776 the legislature made him one of the delegates to the Continental Congress, which apparently he did not attend until Nov. 17, 1777. Four days later he was nominated, though not elected, to succeed Silas Deane as commissioner to France. In 1778 as chairman of a congressional committee on the army he went to Valley Forge to cooperate with Washington in making plans for a general reorganization of the American forces. This work, which took five months, met with the approval of Congress.

In the same year Dana was one of a committee of three appointed to examine the conciliatory proposals of Lord North, the rejection of which was recommended by the committee and unanimously agreed to by Congress. In 1779, when John Adams was appointed minister plenipotentiary to negotiate peace with England, Dana was sent to France with him as secretary of the legation. The two men, who had formerly been associated in their legal work in Boston, reached Paris in February 1780. Finding little opportunity there even to talk peace, Adams went to Holland for the purpose of negotiating a loan, and if possible a treaty. In June, Congress sent Dana a supplementary commission, authorizing him, in the event of the possible disability of Adams, to continue negotiations for loans.

At this time, under the guidance of the Empress Catherine of Russia, the neutral maritime governments of northern Europe joined forces in what was known as the armed neutrality, to prevent the British navy from interfering with their shipping. In order to transform this feeling into actual help for the American cause if possible, Congress determined to send a regularly accredited minister to Russia, and chose Dana for this diplomatic venture. His commission, approved by Congress on Dec. 19, 1780, authorized him to accede to any regulations in harmony with the original declaration which might be adopted by the powers of the armed neutrality, and to sign any treaty embodying the principles of that declaration and at the same time consistent with the dignity and sovereignty of the United States as a free and independent nation. He was also instructed to propose a treaty of amity and commerce between the United States and Russia, "on principles of equality and reciprocity, and for the mutual advantage of both nations."

Before setting out for St. Petersburg, he consulted his American friends in Europe, particularly John Adams, whose youthful son, John Quincy, he took with him as secretary, and also Vergennes, the French minister for foreign affairs, with reference to his proper course in Russia. It was generally agreed that it would be unwise for him to inform the Russian representatives in western Europe of his mission, as Catherine, unwilling openly to offend Great Britain, evidently would not give official consent to the coming of a minister from the United States. It seemed best for him to go to Russia as a private citizen, interested in the country merely out of curiosity. It was apparent that his coming and his real status would be reported to Catherine by her representatives abroad, and probably by Vergennes himself. This situation freed both parties from embarrassment, and at the same time left the way open at any moment for the establishment of official relations.

Dana's stay in St. Petersburg, lasting from August 1781 to September 1783, was by all odds the most dramatic and colorful episode in his whole life, and at the same time probably the least satisfactory to him. For a year and a half after his arrival he found no opportunity whatever to present his credentials and ask for an official interview. By indirect means, however, he did succeed in laying before the Russian foreign office certain arguments in favor of a commercial alliance with his government. Late in December 1782, when he learned of the signing of the preliminary treaty of peace between Great Britain and the United States, he felt that the time had at last come to ask that he be accorded an interview as minister. After receiving unofficial assurance, which seemed dependable, that it would be proper to do so he presented his credentials on Mar. 7, 1783. But the Russian government had not the slightest intention of recognizing him or his country. On Apr. 25 this information was imparted to him orally by Ostermann, the vice-chancellor in charge of foreign relations, not in so many words, but in the form of subterfuges and evasions. Dana asked Ostermann to put his explanations in writing so that he could transmit them to Congress as a reply to his advances. This the wily Russian refused to do. Peace with England, however, had made recognition of the United States by Russia a matter of little importance. Dana was consequently instructed to go no farther with his negotiations, unless they were on the verge of completion. Since they had not really begun and he was anxious to return home, he left for the United States at the earliest opportunity, arriving in Boston in December 1783.

In 1784 Dana was again sent to Congress, but his service with that body was comparatively short. In 1785 Gov. Hancock appointed him one of the associate justices of the supreme court of Massachusetts; from that time until his retirement from public life his career was primarily that of a jurist. In 1787 he was chosen a delegate to the Federal Convention, but poor health prevented him from attending its sessions. In the Massachusetts convention of 1788, however, he was one of the conspicuous advocates of ratification of the Constitution. In 1797 he was asked by his old friend, President John Adams, to serve with Pinckney and Marshall as envoy to France, but again because of ill health was compelled to decline the mission. From 1791 to his resignation in 1806 he was chief justice of the supreme court of Massachusetts. Like many who had been associated with him in the Revolution, he became in his later years a thoroughgoing conservative. His state of mind was shown particularly in his charges to grand juries. A true Federalist, he was seriously disturbed by the growing tendency to find fault with public officials, and looked upon the outspoken Jeffersonians as a menace to the nation. In 1798, not long after the adoption of the Alien and Sedition Acts, the supreme court opened at Salem. Dana, giving the grand jury a longer charge than usual, defined treason and misprision of treason, passed "to a vindication of the Sedition and Alien Bills and then to the negotiation of the United States with France. The necessity of the Sedition Bill he argued from a Liberty Poll [pole] & Inscription at Dedham." He also found an opportunity on this occasion to castigate Talleyrand (*The Diary of William Bentley,* Nov. 13, 1798, II, 289). On Feb. 18, 1799, the Boston *Independent Chronicle,* a Republican newspaper, published a brief commentary on the position of the state, as defined in its constitution. After Dana had laid the matter before the grand jury the next day, the editors of the paper were indicted for the commission of an offense against the peace and dignity of the state. Again in 1800, in another charge to the grand jury, Dana "took notice . . . of the restless aliens who are spreading their disorganizing principles." His views were those of the great majority of the substantial citizens of his community, whose respect and admiration he retained to the end of his life. He was also one of the few leaders of his day looked upon with real affection by John and John Quincy Adams.

[There are two short sketches of Dana's life by R. H. Dana: one, an address published on the occasion of the one hundredth anniversary of Dana, Mass. (1901); the other an address delivered before the Cambridge Hist. Soc., printed in its *Pubs.,* III (1908), 57–78. For his diplomatic career, see Francis Wharton, *The Revolutionary Diplomatic Correspondence of the U. S.* (6 vols., 1884); and F. P. Renaut, *Les Relations Diplomatiques entre la Russie et les États Unis: La Mission Dana* (1923). W. P. Cresson has in preparation a study, "Francis Dana at the Court of Catherine the Great."]

R. V. H.

DANA, JAMES (1735–Aug. 18, 1812), Congregational clergyman, third in descent from Richard Dana who came from England to America about 1640, and son of Caleb, a tanner, and Phœbe (Chandler) Dana, was born in Cambridge, Mass. His father was a brother of Richard Dana [*q.v.*], leader of the Boston bar. The vital records of the town state that James was

baptized May 18, 1735, but the date of his birth is not given. At the age of eighteen he graduated from Harvard; then for some time continued his studies there. In 1758 he was called to the church in Wallingford, Conn., which had been without a pastor since the death of Rev. Samuel Whittelsey in 1752, and a council was summoned to ordain him. There followed the "Wallingford Controversy," a noted incident in the ecclesiastical history of the state. Coming from Massachusetts, Dana was suspected of unorthodoxy, and known to be of the "Old Light" party. Some of the church, instigated, it is said, by "New Light" ministers, determined to prevent his ordination by bringing complaint before the consociation of the county. Ordaining council and consociation met on the same day. Haled before the latter, Dana and his church protested its jurisdiction over them in such a case, and the council, though forbidden by the consociation, proceeded to ordain. Later that body, augmented by the Hartford consociation, declared the pastoral relation between Dana and the church dissolved, and since both ignored the action, it finally passed sentence of non-communion upon them and those who sat in the ordaining council. (For list of pamphlets evoked by the controversy, see Leonard Bacon, *Thirteen Historical Discourses,* 1839, pp. 268 f.) On May 8, 1759 he married Catherine Whittelsey, the daughter of his predecessor at Wallingford, and a granddaughter of President Chauncy of Harvard.

Despite its inauspicious opening, Dana's career in Connecticut was long and distinguished. His learning, sturdy conscientiousness, and good judgment came to be generally respected among the clergy. He won favor with many, also, by taking an early and decided stand for national independence, and whenever the General Assembly met in New Haven, its members expected the pastor of the First Church, Dana's brother-in-law, Chauncey Whittelsey, to exchange with him. Of this church he himself was installed pastor, Apr. 29, 1789, the council being made memorable by a theological tilt between Dana and Jonathan Edwards, the younger. In the controversy between the "Old Divinity" and the "New" he became a strong defender of the former as against the opinions of Drs. Bellamy, Hopkins, West, and Edwards. (For doctrines he assailed, see Bacon's *Discourses,* p. 273.) In 1770 he published anonymously *An Examination of the Late Reverend President Edwards's 'Enquiry on Freedom of Will,'* and in 1773, under his name, *The "Examination . . ." Continued.* Captivated by the preaching of Moses Stuart who supplied the church during the pastor's illness, the Society voted in 1805 that "Dr. Dana retire from his pastoral labors." In December he was dismissed by council, but continued to reside in New Haven until his death. Among his published sermons are *The Intent of Capital Punishment, a Discourse Delivered in the City of New Haven, Oct. 20, 1790. Being the Day of the Execution of Joseph Mountain for a Rape* (1790); *The African Slave Trade* (1791); *The Heavenly Mansions, a Sermon Preached . . . at the Interment of the Reverend Ezra Stiles, D. D., President of Yale-College* (1795); *Two Discourses, I. On the Commencement of a New Year; II. On the Completion of the Eighteenth Century* (1801). Physically he was the mere shadow of a man, tall, slender, and with a sharp, thin face. He is described by those who knew him as kindly and companionable, an interesting conversationalist, and everywhere at ease. The University of Edinburgh honored him with the degree of D.D. in 1768. His first wife died Aug. 18, 1795, and on July 10 of the following year he married Mrs. Abigail (Porter) Belden, daughter of Dr. Ezekiel Porter. She died Mar. 17, 1798, and on Sept. 14, he married Mrs. Mary (Miles) Rice. Samuel Whittelsey Dana [*q.v.*], lawyer, and United States senator, was his son.

[Besides authorities cited, see references in *The Literary Diary of Ezra Stiles* (1901), and *Extracts From the Itineraries and Other Miscellanies of Ezra Stiles* (1916), both edited by F. B. Dexter; Benj. Trumbull, *A Complete Hist. of Conn.* (1818); C. H. S. Davis, *Hist. of Wallingford, Conn.* (1870); W. B. Sprague, *Annals of the Am. Pulpit,* vol. I (1857); John J. Dana, *Memoranda of Some of the Descendants of Richard Dana* (1865); *Vital Records of Cambridge, Mass., to the Year 1850* (1914), vol. I.]   H. E. S.

DANA, JAMES DWIGHT (Feb. 12, 1813–Apr. 14, 1895), geologist, zoologist, the eldest of ten children of James and Harriet (Dwight) Dana was born and passed his boyhood in Utica, N. Y. His father was of New England stock, a nephew of Rev. James Dana [*q.v.*], and a descendant of Richard Dana who came from England in 1640 and settled in Cambridge, Mass. The boy's early training was acquired in Charles Bartlett's academy at Utica where he displayed a markedly studious disposition with strong tendencies toward the sciences. He entered Yale College as a sophomore in 1830, but left it in 1833 in advance of graduation to avail himself of an appointment as instructor in the navy, which involved, incidentally, a cruise in the Mediterranean, on the ship *Delaware*. Returning in 1836, he was for a short period an assistant to Prof. Benjamin Silliman. When the United States exploring expedition to the South Seas under Capt. Wilkes was organized in 1837, he

was appointed geologist and mineralogist. The expedition sailed from New York in August 1838. Off the coast of Oregon his vessel, the *Peacock,* was wrecked near the mouth of the Columbia River, and he and his party made their way overland to San Francisco where they were taken aboard one of the companion ships, the *Vincennes,* and returned home by way of the Cape of Good Hope, reaching New York June 10, 1842. For thirteen years following his return Dana was engaged in writing up his reports in Washington. In 1840 he had been made editor of the *American Journal of Science,* or "Silliman's Journal" as it was commonly known, and on the retirement of Silliman in 1849 was appointed professor of natural history in Yale College, though he did not take up his duties until six years later. In 1864 the title of the professorship was changed to that of geology and mineralogy. This position he retained until he resigned from active duties in 1890.

Dana's industry and productivity under conditions of health that to a less virile man would have been insurmountable were without counterpart in American geological history. His first geological paper was in the form of a letter to Prof. Silliman, descriptive of a visit to the volcano of Vesuvius. This appeared in the *American Journal of Science* for 1835. The first of his reports from the Wilkes Expedition was a quarto volume of 741 pages on *Zoophytes,* with folio atlas of sixty-one plates (1846); the second, on *Geology,* a quarto volume of 756 pages, with atlas of twenty-one plates (1849), and the third, two quarto volumes on *Crustacea,* aggregating 1,620 pages (1852–54), followed by an atlas of ninety-six plates.

While assistant to Prof. Silliman, Dana wrote his *System of Mineralogy,* published in 1837. A *Manual of Geology* followed in 1862 and two years later his smaller *Textbook of Geology.* All these were standard works and passed through several editions, the fourth and the last of the *Manuals* being completed after he had reached his eighty-second year. In 1872 appeared his work on *Corals and Coral Islands* and in 1890, after a second visit to the Hawaiian Islands, a companion volume on *Characteristics of Volcanoes.* In 1859 Dana suffered a serious nervous breakdown, from which he never completely recovered, and through the remainder of his life it was only by husbanding his strength in the most careful manner that he was able to carry on his work. It was during the period of his convalescence that he made his single trip to Europe, barring the one to the Mediterranean in 1833. Another illness followed in 1880 and in 1890 the most serious of all. Thenceforth his periods of labor were limited to but three hours a day at the most. Notwithstanding these difficulties, Dana throughout the entire active period stood head and shoulders above his contemporaries. He had a mental capacity for large problems, though their solution involved the marshaling of infinite details. His interest never flagged; no problem was too large for him to grasp; no detail too small for his consideration.

As a teacher, Dana won the respect and regard of all with whom he came in contact, and left on the minds of his students a lasting and favorable impression. Though he was an attractive lecturer, he was in no sense a popular writer or speaker. In 1872 he was awarded the Wollaston medal by the Geological Society of London, and in 1877 the Copley medal by the Royal Society of the same city. In 1892, the Boston Society of Natural History conferred upon him the Walker prize of $1,000. In 1854 he was made president of the American Association for the Advancement of Science. He received many honorary degrees. He was a member of many scientific societies, including the Royal Society of London, the Royal Academies of Berlin, Vienna, and St. Petersburg, and an original member of the National Academy of Sciences. On June 5, 1844 he married Henrietta Frances Silliman, third daughter of Benjamin Silliman. Four children were born to them, one of whom, Edward S. Dana, became America's leading mineralogist.

[D. C. Gilman, *The Life of James Dwight Dana* (1899); "James Dwight Dana," by his son, E. S. Dana, *Am. Jour. Sci.*, vol. XLIX (1895), containing full bibliography; C. E. Beecher, "James Dwight Dana," in *Am. Geologist*, vol. XVII (1896); addresses at the Dana Centenary, Dec. 29, 1912, by A. T. Hadley, Wm. N. Rice, E. O. Hovey and Geo. P. Merrill (*Bull. Geol. Soc. Am.*, XXIV, 1913).]   G. P. M.

DANA, JAMES FREEMAN (Sept. 23, 1793–Apr. 14, 1827), chemist, was descended in the fourth generation from Benjamin, son of Richard Dana who settled at Cambridge, Mass., in 1640. He was born at Amherst, N. H., the son of Luther and Lucy (Giddings) Dana, and the brother of Samuel Luther Dana [*q.v.*]. First named Jonathan, he became James in 1820 by a legislative act. In 1804 the family moved to Exeter, N. H., where the sons attended Phillips Exeter Academy. Both entered Harvard College in 1809 and graduated in 1813 with the A.B. degree. In college both spent their leisure time in studying natural science. James organized among the students the Hermetic Society, for informal scientific study. He took all the courses in chemistry offered by Prof. John Gor-

ham, and toward the close of the college course took care of the chemical lecture-room and prepared lecture experiments. While an undergraduate he received the Boylston prize for a paper on "Tests for Arsenic." After graduation he continued his work in chemistry and geology, though most of his time was devoted to medical studies, in which he was assisted personally by Prof. Gorham. Selected by the Corporation of Harvard in 1815 to go to England and purchase new equipment for the chemical department, he took lessons in London from Friedrich Accum, the best teacher of experimental chemistry in Europe. On the return voyage he wrote a paper on the "Composition of Oxymuriatic Acid" for which he received in 1817 the Boylston prize a second time. He supervised the installation of the new equipment in both laboratory and lecture-room. Soon appointed assistant to the professor of chemistry, he was really the instructor in experimental chemistry, and at the same time he pursued his medical studies. In 1817 he received the M.D. degree, and immediately began to practise in Cambridge. In the fall he was appointed lecturer on chemistry to medical students at Dartmouth College. Since Cambridge did not offer him much opportunity as a surgeon, he resigned from the faculty of Harvard in 1820, giving up his practise, and moved to Hanover, N. H., where as professor of chemistry and mineralogy at Dartmouth he remained till 1826. He retained his interest in geology and medicine, and in 1818 with his brother Samuel published *Outlines of Mineralogy and Geology of Boston and its Vicinity,* which was one of the first scientific interpretations of this complicated area. He also published the following papers: "On a New Form of Electric Battery," "On the Effect of Vapor on Flame," "On the Theory of the Action of Nitrous Gas in Eudiometry," "Preparation of Euchlorine Gas." In 1825 he published *Epitome of Chymical Philosophy,* which was a summary of his lectures on general chemistry, though some space in it was devoted to chemical theory. His connection with Dartmouth College ended in 1826, when he was appointed professor of chemistry in the College of Physicians and Surgeons at New York. His work was suddenly terminated by his death in the following year. He married in 1818 Matilda, daughter of Rev. Samuel Webber, president of Harvard.

[*N. H. Hist. Soc. Colls.*, vol. II; a short account of his work in *American Chemist*, vol. V, nos. 2, 3, 6, reprinted in Benj. Silliman, *Am. Contributions to Chemistry* (1875); J. J. Dana, *Memoranda of Some of the Descendants of Richard Dana* (1865).] L. C. N.

DANA, JOHN COTTON (Aug. 19, 1856–July 21, 1929), librarian, museum director, author, printer, was born in Woodstock, Vt., the fourth of the six children of Charles and Charitie Scott (Loomis) Dana. He was of New England English lineage, sixth in descent from Richard Dana, who settled at Cambridge, Mass., in 1640, eighth from Joseph Loomis, who settled at Windsor, Conn., in 1639. His father was a first cousin of James Dwight Dana [q.v.]. John Cotton Dana and his immediate forebears were rooted in the soil of Woodstock: he returned there summer after summer to rest and there he was buried. It was eleven years after his graduation from Dartmouth College in 1878 before he found his work. He studied law in Woodstock 1878–80, shattered his health by too sedulous application and was compelled to seek a higher altitude and a drier air, became a surveyor in Colorado and was a member of a party that discovered ruins of the cliff dwellers on the Mesa River in 1881. He resumed the study of law in New York in the office of Bristow, Peet, and Opdyke and was admitted to the New York bar in 1883, but was again threatened with tuberculosis. He engaged in newspaper work for a short time at Ashby, Minn., found a position with a coal and coke company at Glenwood Springs, Colo., in 1884, worked for a year as a civil engineer, was married Nov. 15, 1888, to Adine Rowena Wagener of Russellville, Ky., and in 1889 was appointed librarian of the Denver Public Library and secretary of the board of education. He had had no specific training for librarianship and needed none. During the eight years of his administration the Library grew from 2,000 to 40,000 volumes, readers were given access to the stacks, and a children's department was organized. In 1898 he went to Springfield, Mass., as librarian of the City Library, which had an excellent collection of 100,000 volumes. "The worth of a book is in its use" was one of Dana's favorite precepts, and he proceeded to make the books in the City Library useful. In four years' time its home circulation increased forty-five per cent. On Jan. 15, 1902, Dana became librarian of the Public Library of Newark, N. J.

In Newark he made the Public Library the most effective institution of its kind in the United States. During his administration the number of its books increased from 79,000 to 392,000, the number of its borrowers from 19,-000 to 75,000, the yearly home circulation from 314,000 to nearly 2,000,000—figures far in excess of the proportionate growth of the city. Branch libraries were opened in various parts of the city, including a school library in the Barringer High School and, in 1904, the famous Business Branch, located in the heart of the fi-

nancial and commercial district, which was soon rendering service to users throughout the United States and even abroad. The popularity of the Library was due chiefly to Dana's skilful use of publicity and to his revolutionary changes in library management and policy. He helped to found the Newark Museum Association in 1909 (see article on William Stephen Disbrow) and was director of its museum until his death. He made the Newark Museum in its sphere as popular as the Library; by changing exhibits frequently he coaxed the public into visiting it often; by stressing the industrial arts and the work of contemporary artists he tried to show that art is something living and attainable. "Beauty has no relation to price, rarity, or age" was a legend that met the eye of every visitor to the Museum and that many of the exhibits strikingly exemplified. Dana himself was especially interested in printing; he and his brother had their own Elm Tree Press at Woodstock and produced work of unusual beauty and character. He contributed frequently to magazines and periodicals and published numerous pamphlets and broadsides. His *Library Primer* (1896; numerous later editions) has been a standard text-book since its first appearance. As an author he is best represented, however, by *Libraries: Addresses and Essays* (1916). His style is spare and pungent; he had a knack for aphorism and for making old truths sound startling and portentous. He took delight in deflating sentimental altruisms and in "stirring up the animals," as in his presidential address, "Hear the Other Side," to the American Library Association in 1896. On everything he touched he left the stamp of a unique personality.

Though known as the "first citizen of Newark" he shunned publicity, declined honorary degrees from Dartmouth, Rutgers, and Princeton, and cultivated few close friendships. The honors that he seemed to prize most were a directorship in the Deutscher Werkbund and honorary membership in the Chinese Library Association. For the last five years of his life he was in precarious health. He died in St. Vincent's Hospital in New York. His death was the occasion for editorial comment throughout the United States. Though it is still too early to measure his influence on American culture, it is already clear that he was one of the significant men of his generation.

[J. J. Dana, *Memoranda of Some of the Descendants of Richard Dana* (privately printed, 1865) ; Elias Loomis and Elisha S. Loomis, *Descendants of Joseph Loomis in America* (privately printed, 1908), p. 320 ; H. S. Dana, *Hist. of Woodstock, Vt.* (1889) ; *Gen. Cat. Dartmouth Coll. 1769–1910* (1910–11) ; *Who's Who in America*, 1928–29 ; *Libraries*, Oct. 1929 ; *Nation* (N.

Y.), July 31, 1929 (editorial) ; N. Y. *World*, July 23, 1929 (editorial) ; *Newark Evening News*, July 22, 23, 24, 29, Aug. 1, 1929.]   G. H. G.

DANA, NAPOLEON JACKSON TECUM-SEH (Apr. 15, 1822–July 15, 1905), soldier and business executive, was born at the military post of Fort Sullivan, Eastport, Me. His father, Nathaniel Giddings Dana, brother of James Freeman and Samuel Luther Dana [*qq.v.*], was an army officer, and his grandfather, Luther Dana, had been an officer in the navy during the Revolution. On the side of his mother, Mary Langdon Harris, he was descended from Woodbury Langdon, a member of the Continental Congress and brother of John Langdon. Graduating from West Point in 1842, he was commissioned in the 7th Infantry. In 1844 he married Sue Lewis Martin Sandford, at St. Louis. He served in the military occupation of Texas and in the Mexican War, taking part in the defense of Fort Brown, the battle of Monterey, the siege of Vera Cruz, and the battle of Cerro Gordo, where he was severely wounded at the storming of Telegraph Hill, and left on the field as dead until picked up by a burying party thirty-six hours later. He had been promoted to first lieutenant early in 1847, and in 1848 was appointed a captain and assistant quartermaster. He was stationed in Minnesota, became familiar with business conditions there, and in 1855 resigned from the army, establishing a banking business in St. Paul, as a member of the firm of Dana & Borup. He was brigadier-general in the Minnesota militia from 1857 to 1861. He entered the volunteer army as colonel of the 1st Minnesota Infantry, Oct. 2, 1861, and within a few days took it into action at Ball's Bluff. The regiment, composed in large part of lumbermen, was called upon after the battle to bring off the defeated troops to the Maryland shore of the Potomac, a task reminiscent of Glover's, with his Marblehead men, after the battle of Long Island. Dana was appointed brigadier-general of volunteers, Feb. 3, 1862, and commanded a brigade of the II Corps in the Peninsular campaign and at Antietam, where he was again badly wounded. He was disabled for many months, but was meanwhile appointed major-general of volunteers, Nov. 29, 1862. After his return to duty he had no considerable field service, but commanded successively the defenses of Philadelphia, the expedition which secured a lodgment on the Texas coast late in 1863, and districts along the Mississippi River, no longer the theatre of active operations. He resigned from the army, May 27, 1865. For five years he was general agent of the American-Russia Commercial Company of Alaska, and thereafter an executive officer of several railroads, notably the Chicago, Burlington & Quincy. Under authority of a special act of Congress passed in 1894, he was appointed captain—the rank he had formerly held in the regular army—and placed on the retired list. He was deputy commissioner of pensions from 1895 to 1897. He died at Portsmouth, N. H.

[J. J. Dana, *Memoranda of Some of the Descendants of Richard Dana* (1865) ; G. W. Cullum, *Biog. Reg.* (3rd ed., 1891), II, 135–36, IV, 59, V, 56 ; *Bull Asso. Grads. U. S. Mil. Acad.*, 1907, pp. 30–36 ; *Official Records*, ser. I, vols. V, XI (pts. 1, 2), XIX (pt. 1), XXVI (pt. 1), XXVII (pt. 3), XXXIV (pt. 2), XXXIX (pts. 1, 2, 3), XLI (pts. 3, 4), XLV (pt. 2), XLVIII (pts. 1, 2).]   T. M. S.

DANA, RICHARD (June 26, 1700–May 17, 1772), lawyer, was of the third generation of Danas in America. The European origins of the family are involved in uncertainty but in 1640 Richard Dana was a well-to-do resident of Cambridge, Mass. His son, Daniel Dana, who also lived at Cambridge and was tithingman and selectman, married Naomi Croswell of Charlestown, Mass., and their third son, Richard Dana, was born at Cambridge. No details of his boyhood or early education have survived, but he entered Harvard College and graduated there in 1718. On leaving college he taught school for a time but subsequently studied law at Marblehead and was admitted to the Suffolk County bar. He then commenced practise at Marblehead, but moved to Charlestown, and shortly afterward settled in Boston, with which city he thereafter became permanently associated. Though little or no information is available as to his professional work, contemporary sources testify to his early attainment of a prominent position at the Boston bar, of which in his later years he was described as the leader. He was retained as counsel on behalf of the city in much of its litigation, and acquired great influence in public affairs, though he steadfastly declined all offers of political or municipal office. In the early stages of the growing controversy between the province of Massachusetts and Great Britain he unhesitatingly identified himself with the Colonial cause, and was a prominent figure in all the popular movements in opposition to the various steps taken by the administration to enforce the authority of the home government. From 1763 onward he took a leading part in the town meetings at the Old South Church and Faneuil Hall, frequently acting as chairman, and as a member of the numerous committees through which the wishes of the townspeople were expressed during the preliminary steps of the Revolution, his advice on legal and constitutional points was invaluable. An original member of the Sons of Liberty, he instigated the measures which were taken in 1765 to defeat the enforcement of the Stamp Act, and it was before him as a magistrate that Andrew Oliver, the commissioner, was dragged Dec. 17, 1765 and compelled to swear that he would take no further steps to carry out the provisions of the Act. He was a member of the committee which investigated the circumstances of the Boston Massacre in 1770, and almost the last occasion upon which he appeared in public was the meeting in Faneuil Hall, Mar. 5, 1772 in commemoration of that event, at which he officiated as moderator. His death in Boston some two months later, was at the time regarded as a severe if not irreparable loss to the Colonial cause.

Of unimpeachable integrity, unswerving principles and a fanatic in his devotion to duty as he saw it, his was a strong and impressive but unattractive personality. Austere to the point of parsimony, "he was exemplary in Carefulness, Diligence, and Frugality, whereby he has left to his Widow . . . and to his Children . . . a handsome Fortune. . . . A very steady and strenuous, and it must be confessed, many Times a passionate Opposer of all those . . . who, in his Judgment were Enemies to the Civil and Religious Rights of his Country; and he very well understood what those Rights were" (*Boston Gazette,* June 1, 1772). On May 31, 1737, Dana married Lydia, daughter of Thomas Trowbridge and sister of Judge Edmund Trowbridge; Francis Dana [*q.v.*] was their son.

[*Hist. Families of America* (1907), ed. by W. W. Spooner, p. 47; R. Frothingham, *Life and Times of Jos. Warren* (1865), p. 195; *Proc. Mass. Hist. Soc.,* 1 ser. XII (1873), 246 f.; Alden Bradford, *Biog. Notices of Distinguished Men in New England* (1842).]
H.W.H.K.

DANA, RICHARD HENRY (Nov. 15, 1787–Feb. 2, 1879), poet, essayist, came of distinguished ancestry. His father was Francis Dana [*q.v.*], Revolutionary patriot, and his mother was Elizabeth Ellery, daughter of William Ellery [*q.v.*], a signer of the Declaration of Independence. There were seven children of this marriage, an elder sister becoming the wife of Washington Allston. Richard Henry Dana was born in Cambridge, and almost all his life was passed within the borders of his native Massachusetts. Entering Harvard College in 1804, he was not graduated in regular course, being implicated in the "rotten cabbage" rebellion of the classes in 1807. Many years later he received his degree as of 1808. His studies of law in Boston, Newport, and Baltimore were interspersed

with wide readings in English literature, and on returning to Boston he was admitted to the bar in 1811 and later represented Cambridge in the Massachusetts legislature. Neither the law, nor politics, nor any form of public affairs, attracted him permanently, and before he was twenty-five years of age he had abandoned them wholly for literature, thus forsaking the profession which so many of his forebears had adorned. For some years after the establishment of the *North American Review* in 1815, he was associated with its editorial direction and contributed to it reviews and essays on literary subjects. In 1821 he began the publication of a periodical called *The Idle Man,* modeled upon Washington Irving's *Salmagundi,* continued it for about six months with no financial success, and wrote some of his earliest fiction, including two novels, "Tom Thornton" and "Paul Felton," for its pages. He also wrote for and contributed some of his first poetry to the *New York Review*—edited by his warm friend William Cullen Bryant—the *American Quarterly Observer, The Biblical Repository, The Literary and Theological Review,* and other periodical publications. In 1827 his first book of poetry, *The Buccaneer and Other Poems,* was published, followed in 1833 by his *Poems and Prose Writings,* which seventeen years later was brought out in a new and extended edition. A reviewer in *Blackwood's Magazine* described "The Buccaneer" as "by far the most powerful and original of American poetical compositions," and added that, although Dana was "no servile follower of those great masters," his style showed the influence of Crabbe, Wordsworth, and Coleridge. The supernatural is one of its dominant elements, and for it he may have derived some inspiration from "The Ancient Mariner." Some of his poems appear in anthologies and school books on literature. During the great controversy in 1825–35 which resulted in the schism between the Trinitarians and the Unitarians in the Congregational Church, he took active part with the former, and later in life became affiliated with the Protestant Episcopal Church. Although his reputation survived through his entire lifetime, his active career practically ended by the time he was forty. He had acquired no popularity, none of his writings appealing to the general public, and he did not seek it. As a writer he had little sympathy with or interest in the affairs of the world, or with social and personal progress in politics, art, science, or literature, tendencies which were foremost in the son who bore his name. His view was academic, and he looked upon mankind and the world from the library and the scholar's cloister. The influence of Dana on the literary development of the country came from the vigorous thought, simplicity, and directness of expression which marked his work, in contrast to the sentimental and florid style which characterized most writings of his time. Perhaps his most conspicuous appearance in public was in 1839–40, when he delivered a course of eight lectures on Shakespeare, in Boston, New York, Philadelphia, and other cities, contending that Shakespeare was the greatest poet of the English language, and not Pope, as was then claimed by many authorities. During more than half his years he lived in a quiet and dignified retirement, writing, studying, reading, in Cambridge in early life, later in Boston, and during the summer on the shores of Cape Ann, where his son Richard Henry [q.v.] bought an estate for him in 1845. Although he had been a delicate child, he lived to reach his ninety-second year, during which he died at his home in Boston. He was a notable personality and a man of physical and mental distinction. He married Ruth Charlotte, daughter of John Wilson Smith, of Taunton, Mass., in 1813, and they had four children.

[S. A. Allibone, *Critical Dict. of Eng. Literature and British and Am. Authors* (1858); article by Richard Henry Stoddard, *Harper's Mag.*, Apr. 1879; sketch in *The Later Years of the Saturday Club* (1927), ed. by M. A. De Wolfe Howe; obituaries in *Boston Transcript*, *Boston Post*, Feb. 3, 1879, and *Boston Herald*, Feb. 4, 1879; Chas. Francis Adams, *Richard Henry Dana, a Biography* (2 vols., 1890); valuable information from members of the family.]   E. F. E.

DANA, RICHARD HENRY (Aug. 1, 1815– Jan. 6, 1882), author, lawyer, the son of Richard Henry Dana [q.v.] and Ruth Charlotte (Smith) Dana, was born in Cambridge, Mass. Solely as the writer of a remarkable first-hand account of sea adventure he has a permanent place in American literature; he was also one of the most active and influential lawyers of his day. Entering Harvard College in 1831, he gave up his studies two years later because of eye trouble resulting from measles, and on Aug. 14, 1834 set sail on a voyage around Cape Horn to California as a common sailor on the brig *Pilgrim*. Two years later, a robust young man of twenty-one, he reached Boston on the ship *Alert*. Joining the senior class at Harvard in December 1836, he was graduated the following June, ranking at the head of his class for that year. He became instructor in elocution at Harvard in 1839–40, under Edward T. Channing, and in 1866–68 he was a lecturer in the Harvard Law School. His *Two Years Before the Mast* (1840), published the year of his admission to the bar,

was written from notes made during his voyage, and is a lively, fresh, and unconventional narrative. His definite and successful purpose in it was to give an account of sea life from the point of view of the forecastle, and to secure justice for the sailor. "In it," he wrote, "I have adhered closely to fact in every particular, and endeavored to give everything its true character." The book immediately became popular both in this country and in England, and has since been reprinted in many editions, including one in French attributed to James Fenimore Cooper.

His youthful taste of the salt of the sea had given him a liking for the law of the sea, and he immediately began to specialize in admiralty cases. His manual, *The Seaman's Friend* (1841), became at once a standard work on maritime law, being reprinted in England as *The Seaman's Manual*. Early becoming interested in both the political and social aspects of slavery, he was one of the founders of the Free-Soil party, was a delegate to the convention at Buffalo in 1848, and took personal part in its campaigns, as he did also in the later campaigns of the Republican party. In 1853 he was a member of the convention for the revision of the constitution of Massachusetts, taking a leading part in the debates. Although he did not become an Abolitionist, his political and legal activities involved him deeply in the anti-slavery movement. He was attorney for the defense of the persons involved in the rescue of the negro Shadrach in Boston in 1851, and in the Anthony Burns rendition case in 1854. Serving for five years, from April 1861 to September 1866, as United States attorney for the district of Massachusetts, he succeeded in persuading the Democratic Supreme Court of the United States to sustain the power of blockade and the taking of neutral vessels as prizes during the blockade by the Federal government. In 1867–68, with William M. Evarts, he was counsel for the United States in the proceedings against Jefferson Davis for treason. In 1877 he was senior counsel for the United States before the Fisheries Commission at Halifax. In his many years of practise he was always the advocate, working mainly in the courts and paying little attention to the business of the office, which he disliked and left largely to his partner. He laboriously prepared all his cases himself with indefatigable zeal.

Possibly because of Dana's inability to mingle with the throng and his unwillingness to descend to machine politics, he did not realize upon his political ambitions. Among the disappointments he suffered were his defeat by Benjamin F. Butler in a contest for a seat in Congress in 1868, and his failure to be confirmed by the Senate when he was appointed minister to England in 1876 by President Grant, who had named him without consulting the leaders of his party. Failing to attain high public office, he determined to give his later years to the intensive study of his favorite subject, international law, and to the preparation of an authoritative work upon it. As early as 1866, his edition of Henry Wheaton's *Elements of International Law* was accepted as an authority. An enthusiastic traveler, he visited England in 1856 and 1866, and met the great political and social leaders of the kingdom. The literary result of one of his trips was a book entitled *To Cuba and Back* (1859). He made a journey round the world in 1859–60, and in 1878 he went to Europe for rest, pleasure, and further study of the problems of international law. While in Rome, before he had written his projected work, he died suddenly of pneumonia, and was buried in the Protestant Cemetery, where lie the remains of Keats and Shelley. He married Sarah Watson of Hartford, Conn., Aug. 25, 1841, and was survived by her and their six children, in whose religious and literary education he had taken great interest. He was a man of distinguished and dignified manner, with a certain formality that did not encourage intimacy.

[Chas. Francis Adams, *Richard Henry Dana, A Biography*, 2 vols. (1890); E. W. Emerson. *The Early Years of the Saturday Club* (1918); tribute of the bar, *Am. Law Rev.*, XVI (1882), 253; remarks by Rt. Rev. Wm. Lawrence, Bliss Perry, Moorfield Storey, and Joseph H. Choate, *Cambridge Hist. Soc. Pubs.*, no. X (1917); valuable information from the family.]   E. F. E.

DANA, SAMUEL LUTHER (July 11, 1795–Mar. 11, 1868), chemist, born at Amherst, N. H., was the son of Luther and Lucy (Giddings) Dana and the brother of James Freeman Dana [*q.v.*]. Entering Harvard College in 1809, he graduated in 1813. Immediately after graduation, he joined the army and served till the end of the War of 1812. He then resumed his studies, specializing in medicine, and received the M.D. degree in 1818. He at once began to practise at Waltham, Mass., and continued there until 1826. Realizing the need of solving the chemical problems of the manufacturers of cotton goods in Massachusetts, he gave up medicine and devoted his time to applied chemistry. In 1826 he built a small plant in Waltham for the manufacture of sulphuric acid and bleaching substances. This was soon merged with the Newton Chemical Company, of which he was the superintendent and chemist till 1833. On his return from a professional visit to Europe, he became chemist at the Merrimac Print Works, Lowell, Mass., where he remained till his death. The results of one of his early investigations concerning the bleaching of cotton cloth led to the adoption throughout the United States of what became known as the "American system of bleaching." Another investigation, concerning calico-printing, resulted in the improvement in the minor details which gave the goods printed in Lowell a high reputation. A special result related to the use of cow-dung in calico printing. Dana showed that the action of this animal material was largely due to the sodium phosphate in it. Immediate improvements in calico-printing were made in the United States by the substitution of sodium phosphate, made from bones, for the bulky, undesirable animal excrement. This work naturally led Dana to study the nature of manures. In 1842 he published *A Muck Manual for Farmers*, a work dealing with the chemistry of soils and manures and one of the first scientific treatises on agriculture written by an American and published in the United States. It attracted immediate attention 'and went through several editions. Later he wrote *An Essay on Manures* (1850), which was widely used as a rural handbook and for which the author was awarded a prize by the Massachusetts Society for Promoting Agriculture. About 1848 he investigated the cause of the bright inner surface of lead service-pipes in Lowell, and found the corrosion was due to the chemical action of gases in the water obtained from driven wells. He presented to the local authorities a report in which he pronounced the water unfit for drinking owing to the danger of lead-poisoning. This report was soon followed by his translation from the French of L. Tanquerel Des Planches, of a work which he published under the title, *Lead Diseases* (1848). In 1851 he became interested in the manufacture of oil from rosin and within the next few years he made many improvements in this industry. Much of his time in latter years was spent on a farm, where his views on agriculture were tested. He was twice married, first, on June 5, 1820, to Ann Theodora, daughter of Joseph Willard, a president of Harvard, and subsequently to Augusta, her older sister.

[Obituary notice in *Am. Jour. of Sci.*, May 1868, pp. 424–25; short account of his work in *Am. Chemist*, vol. V, nos. 2, 3, 6, reprinted in Benjamin Silliman, *Am. Contributions to Chemistry* (1875); W. J. Youmans, *Pioneers of Science in America* (1896); J. J. Dana, *Memoranda of Some of the Descendants of Richard Dana* (1865).]   L. C. N.

DANA, SAMUEL WHITTELSEY (Feb. 13, 1760–July 21, 1830), lawyer, statesman, was born in Wallingford, Conn., the elder son of James Dana [*q.v.*], Congregational minister at Wallingford, by his first wife, Catherine Whittelsey. He graduated from Yale in the class of 1775 with high honors. Three years later he was appointed to deliver a congratulatory oration in Latin on behalf of the student body upon the occasion of the inauguration of President Ezra Stiles. He studied law at Middletown, Conn., under Judge J. T. Hosmer and was admitted to the bar in 1778. He interested himself in the Connecticut militia and in 1790 was commissioned brigadier-general. From 1789 to 1796 he served as member of the General Assembly of Connecticut. In January 1797 he took his seat in the lower house of Congress and held this office until he was transferred to the Senate in May 1810, upon the resignation of James Hillhouse. His career in national politics ended with the expiration of his term on Mar. 3, 1821, his defeat being due to the political overturn in Connecticut in 1818. Returning from Washington to Middletown he resumed the practise of law. In 1822, however, he returned to public life as the mayor of Middletown, and held this post almost to the time of his death. From 1825 until his death he was also chief judge of the Middlesex country court. He died as the result of a cerebral hemorrhage. His estate was insolvent, but his contemporaries were agreed that he could have amassed a considerable fortune had he devoted himself continuously to the practise of his profession.

In Congress he belonged to the Federalist group, although he was not a leader. He voted for the Sedition Act of 1798, and in the same year introduced a resolution to abrogate the treaty of 1778 with France. He opposed the acquisition of Louisiana, the Embargo and Non-Intercourse Acts, and also the impeachment of Justice Chase. He consistently supported a navy of frigates and expressed his contempt for those "aquatico-terrene vehicles denominated gun boats." He favored the bill of 1816 increasing congressional salaries and opposed the measure of the same year chartering the second Bank of the United States. He opposed slavery and objected to the Missouri Compromise on the ground that the admission of a state should be considered on its individual merits. In his actions, Dana followed his own judgment and convictions rather than the lead of his party. His speeches were for the most part arguments on legal points raised by pending legislation. His best effort was inspired by a proposed resolution of censure of the actions of the British minister, Francis J. Jackson (*Annals of Con-*

gress, 11 Cong., 2 Sess., pp. 762–83). Dana made clear his complete disapproval of Jackson and of British policy with respect to the United States and then proceeded to discuss in an impressive manner the problems of international law which were involved not only in the pending resolution but in the policy of the Madison administration toward Jackson. The speech was the work of a careful student of political science who was familiar not only with Grotius, but with Martens, Vattel, and Wicquefort.

Dana followed John Adams in distinguishing between the interests of the aristocratic "few" and the "many," and his belief that the system of checks and balances in a republican government was the proper means for the protection of both classes. He broke with Adams on the supreme necessity for the protection of property and did not share in the distrust of the masses which characterized the thinking of Hamilton and Fisher Ames. In his system Dana combined the best thought of the Federalists and the Jeffersonians. His philosophy explains why he shared in neither the plots of Harrison Gray Otis nor the despair of Fisher Ames at the growth of democracy. Two years after the revolution of 1818 in Connecticut had doomed his party in that state, Dana exclaimed: "Look at the young empire in the New World! See the American States advancing in the ascent of glory" (*Observations on Public Principles and Characters,* pamphlet, November 1820). He married on July 13, 1821, Mary Wyllys Pomeroy, widow of Richard Alsop, the poet.

[F. B. Dexter, *Biog. Sketches Grads. Yale Coll.,* III (1903), 558; MSS. (a few letters and an unpublished essay on government) in Yale Library; D. D. Field, *Centennial Address with Hist. Sketches of Cromwell, Portland, Chatham, Middle-Haddam, Middletown and its Parishes* (1853); A. A. Pomeroy, *Hist. and Geneal. of the Pomeroy Family* (1912), I, 352; *Biog. Dir. of the Am. Congress, 1774–1927* (1928); *Middletown Gazette,* July 28, 1830.]   R. H. G.

DANCEL, CHRISTIAN (Feb. 14, 1847–Oct. 13, 1898), inventor, was born in Cassel, Germany. He was educated in the graded and polytechnic schools there and completed the mechanical engineering course, after which he learned the machinist's trade. When a little over eighteen years of age, he emigrated to the United States and settled in New York City. Working for the next two years as a practical machinist in different shops about New York, Dancel during this time devised a machine for sewing shoes. Soon after this, Charles Goodyear, Jr., who was engaged in the manufacture of shoe-machinery in New York, bought Dancel's device and engaged him as superintendent of his factory. The latter first undertook improvements on his own and other inventions and built the first practical machines for sewing turned shoes. About 1870, he turned his attention to making machines for sewing shoe-welts and stitching the out-soles. Using one of the turned-shoe machines as a foundation, he first altered it into a "stitcher," fifty models of which were made and sold to different manufacturers. He then devised and patented a welt-guide, and by adding it to the same machine, produced in 1874 one which would sew both turns and welts. This machine, which Goodyear began manufacturing in 1875, is still used, with minor improvements, in shoe manufacture. In 1876 Dancel opened a machine-shop of his own and patented a number of small machines used in the finishing of shoes, which because of their value to the trade he had no difficulty in selling. While so engaged, he was again called upon by the Goodyear Company to undertake the perfection of a machine to sew the outer sole and the upper of a shoe while the shoe was on the last. He worked constantly on this problem for almost eight years and delivered in 1885 a complete machine, which used a curved needle and sewed a lock-stitch. This was followed by a straight-needle machine, patented Sept. 8, 1891 and delivered in 1892. About 1895 he organized the Dancel Machine Company in Brooklyn, and before he died built a curved-needle machine to sew welts on the shoe with a lock-stitch while the shoe was on the last, the welt, upper, and in-sole being caught by one stroke of the needle. It was Dancel's solution of the stitch-forming problems that made the Goodyear Welt System, now so widely used, a success. Incorporated in each one of his finished products were many devices for which patents were granted to him. Besides his shoe-machine inventions, Dancel was co-patentee in machines for making barbed-wire fence, for skiving leather, for gaging and marking leather, for making leather buttonholes, for rubbing type, and for removing bristles from sealskins. He died in Brooklyn, as a result of a fall, at the age of fifty-two, survived by his widow and two children.

[W. T. Davis, *Professional and Indust. Hist. of Suffolk County, Mass.* (3 vols., 1894); *Shoe and Leather Reporter*, 1898, vol. LXVI, no. 16; Waldemar Kaempffert, *A Popular Hist. of Am. Invention* (1924); obituary in *Brooklyn Daily Eagle*, Oct. 14, 1898; Patent Office records.]   C. W. M.

DANE, NATHAN (Dec. 29, 1752–Feb. 15, 1835), lawyer, statesman, was a descendant of John Dane of Berkhamstead and Bishop's Stortford, Hertfordshire, England, who settled at Ipswich, Mass., in 1638 and subsequently became a freeman of Roxbury. Fourth in the direct line from him, Daniel Dane, a farmer, married Abigail Burnham and resided at Ipswich, where their son, Nathan, was born. His life, until he was twenty, was spent on the farm, his education being obtained at the common schools. In 1772, however, he determined to attempt a college course, and having prepared himself privately in eight months, entered Harvard College in 1774, where he graduated in 1778 with high honors. He then read law in the office of Judge William Wetmore of Salem, at the same time teaching school at Beverly, Mass. In November 1779 he was married to Mrs. Mary Brown. On his admission to the bar in 1782 he commenced practise at Beverly, being in the same year elected a representative of that town in the General Court of Massachusetts. His ability was early recognized; he was reëlected in three successive years, and in 1785 was elected a delegate from Massachusetts to the Continental Congress. In the proceedings of this body he took an active part, serving on important committees and displaying great assiduity in the performance of his duties. He was reëlected in 1786 and 1787. In the latter year the chief subject for consideration before the Congress was the organization and government of the territory lying northwest of the Ohio River, respecting which he took a memorable part. He assisted in drafting the Ordinance for the Government of the Northwest Territory, and, after reporting it to Congress, on his own initiative prepared and moved the addition of an article reading "There shall be neither slavery nor involuntary servitude in the said territory" (*Indiana Historical Society Publications*, no. 1, 1897, p. 69). The Ordinance as thus amended was adopted without further change. He opposed the new Federal Constitution as finally drafted, and at the ensuing election for the state convention to consider its ratification, was an unsuccessful candidate. On retiring from Congress he resumed his law practise at Beverly, but in 1790 was elected to the Massachusetts Senate. He was reëlected in 1793, being the same year appointed a judge of the court of common pleas for Essex County, which position he resigned without taking his seat on the bench. In 1795 he was appointed a commissioner to revise the laws of the Commonwealth. He was reëlected annually to the Massachusetts Senate from 1793 to 1798 (*Fleet's Register and Pocket Almanac*, 1794–99), but the last mentioned year was the last occasion upon which he was a member of the legislature, an increasing deafness rendering it difficult for him to participate in public assemblages. He continued, however, to assist in the work of statute revision and, in 1812, with Prescott and Story, composed the commission appointed to revise and publish the Massachusetts Colonial and Provincial laws. He was also in that year presidential elector, and in 1814 made his last public appearance, at the Hartford Convention, though subsequently he was chosen as delegate from Beverly to the constitutional convention of 1820, it being known at the time that he would be unable to attend. He had now become almost entirely deaf, and, withdrawing from practise, devoted his time to completing two works upon which he had been engaged continuously for upward of thirty years. One of these, "A Moral and Political Survey of America," composed of a lengthy series of essays, was never published. The other, a *General Abridgment and Digest of American Law, with Occasional Notes and Comments,* was published in eight volumes in 1823, a supplementary volume appearing in 1829. This work was important as being the first comprehensive compendium of law to be prepared and printed on this continent, and displayed not only his great legal attainments but a meticulous attention to detail and a methodical labor which was characteristic of everything which he undertook. His outstanding characteristics were industry, directness and simplicity. "He was uniformly prompt, punctual and systematic. He had a particular time and a particular way for doing everything." Always a student, during the last twenty years of his life he never spent less than twelve and often fourteen hours a day in his library. He possessed a singularly well-balanced judgment, a great forethought, and was totally devoid of temperament. Of his powers as a speaker, there is little information, but it may be confidently surmised that his extraordinary influence with his contemporaries was due more to the matter than the manner of his utterances, and that his intellectual endowments more than compensated for his lack of popular attributes. He was a benefactor of Harvard Law School, to which he gave in his lifetime $15,000, the fruits of which were the establishment of the Dane Professorship of Law and the founding of Dane Hall. He died at Beverly, in his eighty-third year.

[Details of Dane's ancestry are contained in J. W. Dean, "A Pedigree of the Dane Family," published in John Dane, *A Declaration of Remarkable Providences in the Course of My Life* (1854). Much the best review of his life and achievements appeared in *Green Bag*, III, 548. See also A. P. Peabody, *Harvard Grads. Whom I Have Known* (1890), p. 12; E. M. Stone, *Hist. of Beverly* (1843), p. 135; *Proc. Mass.*

Hist. Soc., X (1869), 475; *Pa. Mag. of Hist. and Biog.,* XIII (1889), 309; J. A. Barrett, *Evolution of the Ordinance of 1787* (1891). Date of birth given in tombstone inscription published in Stone's *Hist. of Beverly* is Dec. 27, 1752; most accounts, however, including that by Stone, give Dec. 29.]   H. W. H. K.

DANENHOWER, JOHN WILSON (Sept. 30, 1849–Apr. 20, 1887), Arctic explorer, was born in Chicago, Ill., the son of William W. Danenhower. He attended the public schools of his native city until he was seventeen when he secured an appointment to the United States Naval Academy. Upon his graduation in 1870, he was ordered to the European Squadron where he served on both the *Plymouth* and the *Juniata.* His next assignment was with the Portsmouth surveying party in the North Pacific; and in 1875, he was sent to the Naval Observatory for signal duty. He attained the rank of master in 1873 and was commissioned a lieutenant in 1879. In 1878, he showed signs of an unbalanced mind and was confined to an insane asylum for two months. At the end of this period, he had recovered sufficiently to return to active duty and was assigned to the *Vandalia* which was sent to the Mediterranean with Gen. Grant's cruise. While at Smyrna, he heard of the proposed *Jeannette* Arctic expedition and at once offered his services. He was accepted and joined Capt. G. W. De Long [*q.v.*] at Havre, France, just before the *Jeannette* sailed for San Francisco. On this voyage, he acted as executive officer. Upon the arrival at the Mare Island Navy Yard, the *Jeannette* was made ready for the northward voyage. These preparations, which were in charge of Danenhower and Lieut. Chipp, were finally completed and the trip to the Arctic via Bering Strait began on July 8, 1879. On the voyage north De Long studied his crew, and of Danenhower he wrote, in a letter to Mrs. De Long, "He is a hard worker, always writing the log or figuring over his navigation or provision account" (Emma De Long, *Voyage of the Jeannette,* I, 91). A little later, when the ship became wedged in the ice pack, this desire to be always busy led him to start a school of navigation for the crew; but on Dec. 22, 1879, he was rendered unfit for duty by an inflammation in his left eye, which constantly grew worse in spite of dark room treatments and many operations. Throughout the weary months of waiting Danenhower, practically lost to the expedition, bore his troubles bravely.

On June 12, 1881 the *Jeannette* was crushed in the ice in latitude 77°15' north, longitude 155° east; and from this point the party, dragging its boats and provisions over the ice, retreated toward the Asia mainland. On this stage of the journey, which lasted over two months, Danenhower, although handicapped by having one eye bandaged and the other covered with a dark goggle, trudged along resolutely. At last open water was reached and the party set out for the Lena Delta in three boats which on Sept 12 became separated in a gale. The boat to which Danenhower was assigned under the command of Engineer George W. Melville [*q.v.*] weathered the storm and reached the eastern Lena Delta five days later (G. W. Melville, *In the Lena Delta,* 1885). Here its crew was rescued by friendly natives and Danenhower started for the United States, where he arrived May 28, 1882. His book, *Lieutenant Danenhower's Narrative of the Jeannette,* which gives a graphic account of his experiences, was published this same year.

For the next few years, although in bad health, he acted as assistant commander of cadets at Annapolis. On Apr. 11, 1887 he went to Norfolk to assume command of the *Constellation;* but the vessel grounded in going out of harbor; and Danenhower, much disturbed, returned to the Academy. There on Apr. 20, while brooding over this mishap, he committed suicide. His widow and two children survived him.

[Besides the authorities cited above, the following are important: R. W. Bliss, *Our Lost Explorers: the Narrative of the Jeannette Arctic Expedition* (1882) ; H. L. Williams, *Hist. of the Adventurous Voyage and Terrible Shipwreck of the U. S. Steamer Jeannette in the Polar Seas* (1882) ; Record of the proceedings of a Court of Inquiry to investigate the loss of the steamer *Jeannette, House Exec. Doc. 108,* 47 Cong., 2 Sess.; *Jeannette Inquiry, House Miscel. Doc. 66,* 48 Cong., 1 Sess. Obituary notices appeared in the Washington *Evening Star,* in the *Washington Post,* and in the *N. Y. Times* for Apr. 21, 1887.]   G. H. B.

DANFORTH, CHARLES (Aug. 30, 1797–Mar. 22, 1876), inventor, manufacturer, was born at Norton, Mass., the fifth child of Thomas and Betsey (Haskins) Danforth. He was a descendant in the seventh generation from Nicholas and Elizabeth Danforth of Framlingham, England, who came to America in 1634 and settled in Cambridge, Mass. Charles's father was a farmer and clothier as his father and grandfather had been before him; he served in the Revolution as fife-major, and was with Washington on Long Island and at New York. From early boyhood young Danforth showed a decided inclination to the mechanical arts, and after attending school until he was fourteen years old he entered a cotton-mill at Norton as a throttle-piercer. With the outbreak of the War of 1812, he joined the army, first as a substitute and later on his own account, and after the war went to sea for several voyages as a common sailor. Then taking up school-teaching, he was given charge of a district school near Rochester, N. Y., but he soon returned to the cotton-manufacturing business, this time as foreman of a factory in Matteawan, N. Y. When twenty-eight years old he moved with his family to Sloatsburg, N. Y., on the Ramapo River, where he worked in a cotton factory as a carder and setter-up of machinery. While engaged in this latter occupation he designed and patented, on Sept 2, 1828, an important improvement in spinning frames known as the cap spinner. This contrivance, which improved the spinning of weft before the self-acting mule was devised, was immediately in great demand. The idea was appropriated by others, with the result that Danforth received very little profit from it. Armed with his patent, however, he moved to Paterson, N. J., obtained a machinist's job with the firm of Godwin, Rogers & Clark, and after explaining his patent, prevailed upon them to manufacture his spinner. Within a comparatively short time he was offered and accepted Rogers's place in the firm, but continued in the machine-shop and designed and patented at least five definite improvements on the original cap spinner. In 1840 he purchased the machine-shop branch of the company's operations and two years later bought the cotton-mill as well, and immediately undertook the expansion of the business to include the making of machine tools. Remarkably successful in this, and wishing to add a locomotive shop to his works, in 1852 he prevailed upon John Cooke, a foreman in the Rogers Locomotive Works, to join him. Within two years the company, then known as Danforth, Cooke & Company, received a large order for locomotives from the Delaware, Lackawanna & Western Railroad which brought them so much celebrity that their good name was firmly established and their locomotives were sold throughout the world. In 1865 the Danforth Locomotive and Machine Company was incorporated, Danforth retaining the presidency until 1871 when he retired and was succeeded by John Cooke. Cooke died in 1882, but his sons carried on the business until 1901 when the works were sold to the International Power Company, who in turn sold them to the American Locomotive Company. Danforth married Mary, daughter of Thomas and Sarah Willett of Matteawan, N. Y., on Oct. 18, 1823. Although averse to public life, he accepted the presidency of the Paterson City Council for one term. He died in Paterson, at the age of seventy-nine, survived by his wife and daughters.

[Wm. Nelson and C. A. Shriner, *Hist. of Paterson and Its Environs*, vol. I (1920); John Joseph May, *Danforth Genealogy* (1902); *N. Y. Tribune*, Mar. 23, 1876; Patent Office records.]   C. W. M.

DANFORTH, MOSELEY ISAAC (Dec. 11, 1800–Jan. 19, 1862), engraver, painter, was born in Hartford, Conn., the son of Edward and Jerusha (Moseley) Danforth. In 1818 he began the study of engraving under Asaph Willard of the Hartford Graphic Company, and in 1821 established himself in New Haven, where his work soon gained him a wide reputation. Later he moved to New York and became one of the founders of the National Academy of Design. In 1827 he went to London to study at the Royal Academy; there he found that he was already favorably known for his full-length portrait of Lafayette. For ten years he remained in London, associating with Sir Thomas Lawrence, Gilbert Stuart Newton, Washington Irving, and other men of note, and upholding an excellent reputation as an engraver and water-colorist. Perhaps his best-known work was his engraving of Leslie's painting, "The Sentry Box"; but his original water-colors were very popular and brought high prices, and his copies of Titian and Veronese were much admired. His drawings from the Elgin Marbles are to-day considered remarkable. Danforth returned to New York in 1837. In 1843 he married Mrs. Hannah B. Duryee Kennedy, daughter of Abraham Duryee of Harlem, and after a few years in Hartford, made his permanent home in New York. During these years he became interested in the engraving of banknotes, and his work in this department was characterized by great finish and delicacy. About 1850 he formed the firm of Danforth, Underwood & Company, which about 1858 was merged with the American Bank Note Company, of which he was vice-president at the time of his death. Judged by his few paintings now in this country, Danforth had great ability in portraiture. The following are some of his best-known engravings: "Don Quixote"; "Sir Walter Scott," of which 14,000 prints were sold; "Lord Holland's Daughter"; "Washington Irving"; "Andrew Jackson"; "Alexander Pope"; "Landing of Columbus"; "Landing at Jamestown"; "Chaldean Shepherd"; "Forsaken"; "Lady Arabella Johnson"; "The Token"; "Red Jacket"; and portraits of many early preachers. Danforth was fond of music and played the flute. His was a lovable personality, deeply religious, loyal in friendship, and of great modesty; he was "a man whose good qualities cannot be too highly estimated, an honor to art and society" (French, p. 65).

[W. Dunlap, *Hist. of the Rise and Progress of the Arts of Design in the United States* (1918), III, 164; H. W. French, *Art and Artists in Conn.* (1879); D. M. Stauffer, *Am. Engravers upon Copper and Steel* (1907), pt. I, p. 58 and pt. II, p. 75; W. S. Baker, *Am. Engravers and their Works* (1875), p. 37; Manuscript genealogy, letters, and papers in possession of family. Collections of Danforth's work are in the Nat. Acad. of Design, the Metropolitan Museum of Art, and the Pub. Lib. in N. Y. City; the Wadsworth Atheneum and Morgan Memorial in Hartford, Conn.; the U. S. Nat. Museum in Washington, D. C.; and the Pub. Lib. in Newark, N. J.]   M. D. D.

DANFORTH, THOMAS (November 1623–Nov. 5, 1699), deputy-governor of Massachusetts, was born at Framlingham, Suffolk, England, and baptized there Nov. 20, 1623. He was the eldest son of Nicholas and Elizabeth Danforth, whose family name was spelled in eleven different ways in the parish registers. The father was evidently a man of considerable property, and after the death of his wife emigrated to Massachusetts (*c.* 1634), taking his children with him. He was elected to various political offices in the colony, and his son Thomas was admitted as a freeman May 10, 1643, soon becoming a man of note. In 1650 he was named as treasurer of Harvard College in the charter granted to the institution in May of that year, although he does not appear to have assumed the duties of office until 1654, from which time he performed them until 1669. In that year he became steward, serving until 1682. He was also chosen clerk of the Overseers in 1654. His interest in the college was deep and continuing, and its historian, Josiah Quincy, speaks of him as among "the earliest, most steadfast, and faithful of its friends."

He was also distinguished on the small stage of the colony's political life. With the organization of Middlesex County he was elected recorder of deeds (1652) and held the office until 1686. He represented Cambridge, in which town he lived, as deputy in the General Court in 1657 and 1658 and was chosen an Assistant for twenty successive years beginning with 1659. From May 28, 1679 until the dissolution of the government in May 1686, he was associated with Simon Bradstreet [*q.v.*] as deputy-governor. He was appointed president of the Province of Maine, Feb. 4, 1680, and held that office until dropped by the Dudley administration, May 29, 1686. He also for many years served his town in the offices of selectman and town clerk, and at times was head of the Commissioners of the United Colonies. He was an acknowledged leader of the popular as opposed to the prerogative party, was an enemy of Joseph Dudley [*q.v.*], and in 1682 was one of the committee entrusted with the task of drawing up instructions for the colony's agents. Owing to his political opinions, he was naturally not in office during the Andros régime. On Apr. 18, 1689, he was one of those who signed the demand upon Andros [*q.v.*] to surrender the government and after the fall of the governor, he was again annually elected to his former offices until the grant of the new charter in 1692. In December of that year, however, he was chosen an associate judge of the superior court and held that office until his death.

He was a man of strong character and, although willing to go to almost any length in opposing the Laws of Trade and the demands of the British government, he was far from being as narrow-minded as most of his party. In the public excitement attending the Indian war of 1675 he joined Daniel Gookin and John Eliot [*qq.v.*] in defending the "Praying Indians," incurring so much obloquy by so doing that his life was threatened. Again he showed his ability to rise above the mob by his condemnation of the witchcraft trials in 1692. He appears to have had ample means and lived on what is now Kirkland St., Cambridge, owning, besides other property, ten thousand acres at Framingham, in which town he bequeathed three valuable leases to Harvard. In February 1644 he married Mary, daughter of Henry Withington of Dorchester, by whom he had twelve children. She died Mar. 26, 1697.

[J. J. May, *Danforth Geneal.* (1902); Wm. Thaddeus Harris, "Notes on the Danforth Family," *New Eng.-Hist. and Geneal. Reg.*, VII (1853), 315–21; Josiah Quincy, *Hist. of Harvard Univ.* (2 vols., 1840); *Me. Hist. Soc. Colls.*, all three series, *passim.*]

J. T. A.

DANFORTH, THOMAS (May 22, 1703–*c.* 1786), pewterer, was born in Taunton, Mass., the ninth of fourteen children of Samuel Danforth, who was born in 1666, graduated from Harvard in 1683, and entered the ministry. His grandfather, Samuel, a graduate of Harvard in 1643, was ordained in 1650, and became a coworker with John Eliot, missionary to the Indians. Nicholas, the first colonial Danforth, left England in 1634 and settled in Cambridge, Mass. Thomas learned the pewterer's and brazier's trade, and became the ancestor of the two largest pewtering families in America, the Danforths and the Boardmans. Moving to Norwich in 1733 he there opened a pewter and copper shop. In 1730 he had married Sarah Leonard, who bore him five children; four months after her death in 1742 he wed Hannah Hall, who became the mother of nine. Thomas engaged actively in the pewterer's trade until 1773, and from then on intermittently until his death. His output of pewter was large and diverse, the metal was of good quality, the workmanship conscientious, and the feeling for form sympathetic and intelligent. He was what is known as an "eight inch plate man," and was one of six contemporaries who adhered to the English style of marks. His products included plates, platters, trenchers, porringers, flagons, mugs, basins, salts, spoons, buttons, alphabet stamps, and various molds. Two sons, Thomas and John, learned the pewterer's trade. The latter was the only native craftsman who used a date in his touch mark. A grandson —also a Thomas—opened a branch in Philadelphia, 1807–13, and his son Thomas fashioned pewter in Philadelphia and Augusta, Ga. Sarah, probably the grand-daughter of the first Thomas, married Oliver Boardman of Hartford, Conn., in 1781, and their son, Thomas Danforth Boardman, was the first pewterer of the Danforth-Boardman group.

[J. B. Kerfoot, *American Pewter* (1924); Louis G. Myers, *Some Notes on American Pewterers* (1926); J. J. May, *Danforth Genealogy* (1902).]   R. M. K.

DANIEL, JOHN MONCURE (Oct. 24, 1825–Mar. 30, 1865), journalist, diplomat, son of John Moncure and Elizabeth (Mitchell) Daniel, was born in Stafford County and died in Richmond, Va. His rearing as well as his actual schooling was conducted almost exclusively by his father, a country doctor. At fifteen, he went to Richmond to live with his father's uncle, Judge Peter V. Daniel [*q.v.*]. After several years he went to Fredericksburg to study law in the office of an attorney held in esteem by his family, but in 1845 the death of his father and his own indifference to law resulted in his coming back to Richmond. At a salary of $100 a year he became librarian of the Patrick Henry Society, a body of aspiring young gentlemen interested in reading and debating. Soon he became editor of the *Southern Planter,* and a little later (1847) of the new *Richmond Examiner*. His quick, sharp intelligence and his slashing literary style were both dominated by a superb journalistic instinct, practical enough to earn him wealth. His paper was irresistibly interesting, and its name and power soon went far beyond Virginia. In 1853, in recognition of certain political exertions, President Franklin Pierce made him representative of the United States at the Court of Sardinia. As a diplomat his independent conduct and frank speech often involved him in difficulties with the magnificos of Turin, but he was sufficiently discreet to refuse a request made of him by Garibaldi that he take over Nice as an American protectorate. On learning of the secession of South Carolina, he hurried home and reassumed the editorship of the *Examiner*. Still under middle age, handsome, dark, slight of build, his body padded with luxurious clothing, he was a romantic figure and conscious of the fact. His likes and dislikes among men were fast and furious. He entertained frequently in his rooms, amusing his guests at times by provoking battle between his two dogs, by displaying his books, or, mounted on a kind of throne, by discoursing endlessly with recurrent gusts of dogmatism. As for women, he was contemptuous of them: he had loved one only—her he would not name—and he would love no other, for there were no others worthy. Solitary, misanthropic, cloudy in his opinions as to the deity, he was none the less severe in his demand for the most punctilious niceties of social convention. His political opinions were unmistakable. He thought that secession was the only course left open to the Southern states, and he fiercely urged in his editorials that that inescapable action be taken promptly. He advocated the adoption of military conscription, over the protest of Jefferson Davis, and, as the war advanced, he became almost frantic in his distrust of the Davis administration. He served two brief terms in the army, once in 1861 and again in 1862. The military life was, he admitted, indeed horrible, but he softened his own excursions into it as best he could by taking with him two slaves and other elaborate provisions for his comfort, and he was anxious for an honorable scar to show (Bagby, *post*, p. 10). Wounded in his right arm in the summer of 1862, he usually thereafter thought of himself as incapacitated for further service at the front. In 1864, he was wounded again, this time in a duel with the Confederate secretary of the treasury. For many months before the war ended he favored peace by negotiation. The dream he had for the future was to buy the family estate in Stafford County, retire thither, and, as soon as he could provide all the feudal equipment which he held necessary, set himself up as a pattern for Virginians. Then, he confided to a friend, "I shall teach these people what they never knew—how to live like a gentleman" (*Ibid.*, p. 36). But disease laid hold of him, and then he died, and a few days afterward, in the great fire which marked the Confederate abandonment of Richmond, the plant of the *Examiner* perished utterly.

[*Richmond Examiner During the War: or Writings of John M. Daniel with Memoir of his Life by his Brother, Frederick S. Daniel* (1868); G. W. Bagby, *John M. Daniel's Latch-key* (1868); R. W. Hughes, *Editors of the Past* (1897); *Richmond Examiner*, Mar. 31, 1865; *The South in the Building of the Nation*, vol. XI (1909); L. G. Tyler, *Encyc. of Va. Biog.*, vol. III (1915).]

                                J. D. W.

DANIEL, JOHN WARWICK (Sept. 5, 1842–June 29, 1910), senator from Virginia, was born in Lynchburg, Va., the only son of William and Sarah Anne (Warwick) Daniel. From Gessner Harrison's classical school the handsome, high-minded, and ambitious lad went into the Confederate army as a private in May 1861. At twenty he was major and chief of Early's staff, but a wound in the battle of the Wilderness (May 1864) ended his military career and put him on crutches for life. After a year at the University of Virginia (1865–66) the young major began the practise of law with his father in Lynchburg. In 1869 he married his neighbor, Julia E. Munnell. Slowly, against keen competition, he won a remunerative practise. He was peculiarly good at oral argument before the state supreme court. Slowly and laboriously, too, he brought to publication *A Treatise on the Law of Negotiable Instruments* (1876). Meanwhile he had entered politics. In the House of Delegates he spoke out boldly against the passage of the debt-funding act in 1871; but as state senator (1875–79), believing that the honor of Virginia was involved, he worked for its support through measures of Spartan economy. On this issue he stumped the state in 1879 against the Readjusters. Meanwhile he had twice unavailingly sought the Democratic nomination for Congress and once (1877) for governor. When, in 1881, he gained the gubernatorial nomination, he was decisively defeated by a coalition of Readjusters and Republicans. Elected to Congress, however, in 1884, and a year later to the United States Senate for the term beginning Mar. 4, 1887, he represented his state continuously, and was a member of every Democratic national convention, until his death.

As a party leader his chief concern was the solidarity of the whites. "I am a Democrat," he said in 1881, "because I am a white man"; and in 1902 he forced through the constitutional convention of Virginia suffrage provisions which still substantially secure his great objective (*Report of the Proceedings and Debates*, 1906, pp. 2943 ff.; W. A. Watson, *Notes on Southside Virginia*, 1925). His political method was direct appeal to the masses. His Roman face, his lameness converted into grace and ever recalling his war service, his courtliness of manner, his sonorous voice and solemn rolling phrases, all combined to hypnotize them. To them he was the "Lame Lion," and though he was no special pleader for the "forgotten man," he doubtless deemed himself their tribune. Hence, though associated with the Democratic machine, he was never a part of it (*Richmond Times,* December 1893, *passim*); and he virtually spurned the powerful and politically inclined Anti-Saloon League (*Civic Sentinel,* January 1905). In 1896, as temporary chairman, he organized the Democratic convention for Free Silver and delivered the key-note address; in 1900 and in 1904, as a faithful friend of Bryan, he headed the convention's Committee on Resolutions (*Review of Reviews,* New York, August 1896, August 1900, August 1904). In the Senate, despite his excellent committee assignments, he initiated no important legislation. His colleagues, however, noted that he was dignified, courteous, sincere, that he spoke infrequently but showed that "he had thought much and independently." As an occasional orator he was much sought after. His style was "copious, ornate, solemn, touched always with emotion, appealing at once to the head and to the heart." He felt that fighting the Civil War to the last ditch not only "gave finality to its results and well-nigh extinguished its embers with its flames" but also preserved to Southerners "their title to respect . . . and their incentive to noble and unselfish deeds." To his personal friends alone, however, were known his open-heartedness, his loyalty, and his brave fight against unceasing pain.

[See Lyon G. Tyler, *Men of Mark in Va.* (1906); *Memorial Addresses of Cong.,* "*Senator Daniel*" (1911); Wm. M. Thornton, *John Warwick Daniel* (1915); E. M. Daniel, ed., *Speeches and Orations of John Warwick Daniel* (1911). C. C. Pearson, *The Readjuster Movement in Va.* (1927), gives the setting down to 1888.]   C. C. P.

DANIEL, PETER VIVIAN (Apr. 24, 1784– May 31, 1860), jurist, was a member of a family whose connection with Virginia dated from the early days of the colony. His grandfather, Peter Daniel, was one of the pioneer settlers in Stafford County and a justice of the peace. His father, Travers Daniel, married Frances, daughter of Rev. John Moncure, and resided at "Crows Nest," Stafford County, where he owned an extensive estate. Peter Vivian Daniel was born at "Crows Nest." Receiving his early education at home from private tutors, he subsequently proceeded to the College of New Jersey (Princeton), but did not complete his academic course. He took up the study of law in the Richmond office of Edmund Randolph, attorney-general and later secretary of state in Washington's cabinet, and was admitted to the Virginia bar in 1808. The same year he fought a duel with Capt. John Seddon, father of J. A. Seddon, Confederate

secretary of war, in which he wounded his adversary. Following the traditions of his family, the members of which had always taken a prominent share in provincial affairs, he entered the Virginia legislature in 1809, when only twenty-five years of age. In 1812 he was elected a member of the Privy Council of Virginia, and on the adoption of the new constitution, whereby the membership of that body was reduced from eight to three, he was again elected, continuing as such until 1835. He was lieutenant-governor of the state and *ex officio* chairman of the Council during the latter years of his tenure of office. In 1834 President Jackson had tendered him the position of attorney-general of the United States in succession to Roger B. Taney, but he declined. In 1836, on the elevation of Judge P. P. Barbour to the Supreme Court bench, he was appointed by President Jackson judge of the United States district court of Virginia. Four years later, following the death of Judge Barbour, he was nominated by President Van Buren associate justice of the Supreme Court of the United States. The appointment was confirmed Mar. 3, 1841, and he continued a member of the Court until his death at Richmond, Va., May 31, 1860. As a judge he was neither learned nor profound, but he displayed great care and industry in the study of all causes which came before him, overlooking nothing and weighing the arguments with the utmost solicitude and detachment. A man of wide culture and considerable scholarship, his opinions were distinguished by their fine literary style as well as by their clarity.

The year after his admission to the bar he had married Lucy Nelson, daughter of his legal mentor, Edmund Randolph. Late in life (1853) he married, as his second wife, Mary, daughter of Dr. Thomas Harris. In politics a steadfast Democrat, his absolute rectitude of character, unswerving adherence to his principles and code of conduct, and conscientious dedication to the calls of public duty, rendered him a much respected figure in Washington and Richmond.

[A good account of Daniel's life and career appeared in H. E. Hayden, *Va. Genealogies* (1891), p. 309, which also contains a careful survey of his ancestry. See also 24 *Howard,* iii; and obituary in *Richmond Enquirer,* June 1, 1860.]   H. W. H. K.

DANIELS, FRED HARRIS (June 16, 1853– Aug. 30, 1913), engineer, metallurgist, inventor, born in Hanover Center, N. H., was one of the five children of William Pomeroy and H. Ann (Stark) Daniels. He was a lineal descendant of Robert Daniel who came from England in 1636 and settled in Watertown, Mass., and of Thomas Harris who accompanied Roger Williams to

America from Bristol, England. When he was a year old his parents moved to Worcester, Mass., where he lived for the rest of his life. At the age of twenty, immediately after receiving the degree of M.E. from Worcester Polytechnic Institute, he entered the employ of the Washburn & Moen Manufacturing Company at Worcester, makers of steel rod and wire products, where he continued for a little over a year. Upon the opening of the college term of 1874, he entered Lafayette College at Easton, Pa., as an assistant in chemistry, and also took a special course in chemistry under the head of the department, Dr. Thomas M. Drown. Employed for a summer at the close of the school term by the Glendon Iron Works at Easton, completing the plans of their blast furnaces, he then returned to Worcester to resume his connection with the Washburn & Moen Manufacturing Company as mechanical engineer and chemist. His greatest pleasure was derived from experimental work in the laboratory, and as early as 1878, when but twenty-five years of age, he had made some remarkable inventions relating principally to the manufacture of steel rods and wire. These earlier inventions were patented jointly with Charles H. Morgan who was his senior by twenty-one years and an engineer of wide reputation. In Daniels, however, Morgan found a worthy associate, and for years worked with him on rolling-mill problems. As his special abilities in iron and steel working developed, Daniels was sent several times to Europe in the interests of his company for the particular purpose of studying methods, especially in Sweden. Between 1880 and 1909, upwards of one hundred patents were granted to him, all relating to the manufacture of steel rods and wire. Twenty-five of these were of the greatest economic importance inasmuch as they greatly improved the quality of the finished product, tremendously increased the speed of production, and materially lowered the cost of production of the finished rods. During this period, too, Daniels advanced through the position of chief engineer and when but thirty-six years of age was made general superintendent and chief engineer of all of the company's properties. Ten years later (1899), when the Washburn & Moen Manufacturing Company was purchased by the American Steel & Wire Company, he was made chief engineer of the thirty-two wire plants which came into the ownership of that corporation, and in 1902 he became a director of the company. Finally, when the American Steel & Wire Company became the property of the United States Steel Corporation, he was ap-

pointed chairman of the board of engineers of the latter, and for the last six years of his life he served as president of the Worcester plants of the American Steel & Wire Company.

Daniels was an honored member of the American Institute of Mining and Metallurgical Engineers, the American Society of Mechanical Engineers; the American Society for Testing Materials, and the British Iron and Steel Institute. The Paris Exposition of 1900 awarded him the Grand Prize and gold medal for his meritorious achievements in the development of the steel rod and wire industry, and William Garrett, famous as the inventor and builder of rolling-mills, said of him in 1901: "No one has done more than he to perfect wire drawing in all its phases." Daniels was an ardent sportsman, particularly in the hunting of big game, and a prominent clubman. He was married on May 17, 1883, to Sarah Lydia White, of Worcester, Mass.

[Ellery B. Crane, *Geneal. and Personal Memoirs of Worcester County* (1907), vol. II; *Who's Who in America*, 1914–15; Chas. G. Washburn, *Industrial Worcester* (1917); Correspondence with secretary, Industrial Museum Committee, Am. Steel and Wire Co., Worcester; Patent Office records.]   C. W. M.

DANNREUTHER, GUSTAV (July 21, 1853–Dec. 19, 1923), violinist, conductor, teacher, was the son of Abraham and Sophie (Fishbacher) Dannreuther, who came from Strasbourg to Cincinnati in 1849. There Gustav was born four years later. After studying the violin with Henry Eich, of Cincinnati, he was sent, in 1871, to the Berlin Hochschule, which had been reorganized by Joseph Joachim only a few years before, and there he studied the violin with Heinrich DeAhna, the eminent solo violinist and quartet player, who had joined the faculty of the Hochschule, and with Joachim himself; besides taking theory courses with Heitel. Leaving the Hochschule in 1874, he spent six months in Paris, and then passed to London, where he taught and played in public until 1877. He then returned to the United States and became a member of the Mendelssohn Quintet Club of Boston, with which he traveled through the United States, as well as in Canada and Newfoundland, until 1880. It was a period favorable toward a string organization devoted to high ideals. The severe industrial depression of 1873 had abated; the South was emerging from the era of the carpet baggers with Reconstruction well under way; in the West the age of the mining camp was merging in that of the railroad town. Musicians of merit devoted to the ensemble could win an appreciation once only accorded to the virtuoso; and the services of

Dannreuther

Gustav Dannreuther and his associates in this field played their part in laying a foundation for the present widespread cult of chamber music in the United States. In 1880, the year of Garfield's election to the presidency, Dannreuther established himself in Boston; and the year following he became a member of the Boston Symphony Orchestra called into existence by the liberality of Col. Henry Lee Higginson, and played in its first concert in the old Music Hall, Oct. 22, 1881. As soon as a favorable opportunity offered, however, he felt himself unable to refuse a call to return to the chamber music ensemble, and from 1882 to 1884 was active as the conductor of the Buffalo Philharmonic Society, an organization which gave some sixty concerts of chamber music during the time he had it in charge. In 1882, in Buffalo, he married Nellie M. Taylor of that city. In 1884 he realized a long-cherished ambition and formed a string quartet of his own, which antedated by two years the founding of the Kneisel Quartet. The Beethoven String Quartet, renamed the Dannreuther Quartet on the tenth anniversary of its existence, was composed of Dannreuther himself (first violin), E. Schenck ('cello), O. Schill and later F. L. Smith (second violin), and I. Kovarik (viola). For a time it was the oldest in the United States, and its cultural achievement during its more than thirty years of existence under the direction of its founder represents the latter's greatest contribution to the cause of better music in America. While prior to 1899 he was for three years the leader of the New York Symphony and Oratorio Societies under Walter Damrosch, after that date he devoted himself altogether to chamber music and to teaching, in which he was notably successful. He became an instructor in music at Vassar College in 1907. His activities as a teacher (in which connection he wrote a set of *Chord and Scale Studies for Young Players*) are cast in the shade, however, by his service in arousing appreciation for the classic literature of the string quartet, presented with meticulous beauty and reverence by the organization which bore his name. For years the three concerts given annually in New York by the quartet, assisted by distinguished artists, were regarded by the cognoscenti as events of the musical season, and while at the time the Dannreuther Quartet played, composers such as Debussy, Stravinsky, Goossens, Bloch, Malipiero and others had not yet introduced new harmonic factors of color and atmosphere in string quartet literature, the Quartet established, for the older literature, the standard the Kneisels maintained.

Da Ponte

[*The Dannreuther Quartet; A Sketch of Its Hist.* (1904), issued in commemoration of the organization's twentieth anniversary, gives a survey of its work. See also "The Dannreuther Quartet" in *Musical America,* Dec. 9, 1905. An obituary notice of Dannreuther may be found in *Musical America,* Jan. 5, 1924; and a reliable sketch of his life in *The Metronome,* Nov. 1903.]   F. H. M.

DA PONTE, LORENZO (Mar. 10, 1749– Aug. 17, 1838), poet, librettist, and founder of Italian culture in America, was born in the Ghetto at Ceneda, near Venice. The son of a Jewish tanner named Geremia Conegliano and his wife Rachele Pinerchele, Lorenzo was originally named Emanuele. At the age of fourteen, together with his father and two brothers, he turned to the Christian faith and was baptized by Monsignor Lorenzo Da Ponte, bishop of Ceneda; and following the custom of the time he took the distinguished name of his spiritual father. Placed through the bishop's influence in the seminary of Ceneda and later in that of Portogruaro, Lorenzo acquitted himself so well that in 1770 he was made tutor in the latter school and in 1771 became its vice-rector, having meanwhile taken ecclesiastical orders. In 1773, however, under the delusion of persecution that was to torment his entire life, he resigned this office and went to Venice, where he spent a year in idleness and dissipation. Then followed two years of teaching in the seminary at Treviso, a pleasant post in which his stay was cut short by certain ill-considered utterances in verse, the *Accademia Poetica,* which led to his expulsion. Returning to his former profligacy in Venice, he was by 1779 so variously involved in personal delinquencies and public scandals that he was banished from Venetian territory for fifteen years and threatened with imprisonment for seven in case of his return. He escaped into Austria.

Circumstances now forced him to seek a living by his pen. After drifting from Gorizia to Dresden and thence to Vienna, he was fortunate enough to secure appointment in the Austrian capital as "Poet to the Italian Theatre." This stroke of fortune converted him overnight from a struggling adventurer into a man of letters and of fashion, whose librettos were sought by the foremost operatic composers of Europe. It was at this time that he wrote *Il Ricco d'un Giorno, Il Burbero di Buon Cuore,* and *Il Finto Cieco;* but only after his collaboration with Mozart was he recognized as the foremost living librettist. Their first opera, *Le Nozze di Figaro,* was successfully produced in 1786, and was followed by *Don Giovanni* (1787) and *Cosi Fan Tutte* (1790). Meanwhile he continued to write for the score of Salieri, Martini, Righini, and Storace, and to this period belong such pieces as *Gli Equivoci, Una Cosa Rara, Il Filosofo Punito, Bertoldo, L'Arbore di Diana, Il Pastor Fido, La Cifra,* and *Axur, Re d'Ormus.* After the death of Joseph II in 1790 the poet's customary indiscretions led to another disgrace, and he was ordered to quit Vienna. For a year he lived in Trieste, where he married Ann Celestine Ernestine ("Nancy") Grahl, the English daughter of a German merchant in the city; and after another year or so of travel, during which he visited Prague and his old friend Casanova, settled in London late in 1793.

The rest of his long career is mainly a story of disappointment and misfortune ameliorated by the loyalty and sound sense of his wife. Continuing his career as librettist he wrote, among other things, *La Capricciosa Corretta, L'Isola del Piacere,* and *La Scuola de Maritati* for production at Drury Lane. But his genius for falling out with his associates led to his discharge from the theatre about the end of 1799. He had previously set up a small printing-shop and after his dismissal opened a bookstore. In 1803 he was recalled to the theatre for a time and wrote *Castore e Polluce* and *Il Ratto di Prosperina;* but ill-advised speculation brought him to bankruptcy and in 1805 he set sail for America. Faced in late middle life with the task of providing for a family of small children in a strange land, he opened a grocery business in New York, and later, in Elizabethtown, N. J., following this by a variety of similar ventures at Sunbury, Pa. All ended in failure. He was more successful, however, with a class of pupils in Italian in New York, where he gathered so large and aristocratic a following that in 1825 he was appointed professor of Italian literature in Columbia College. Charm of personality and an extensive learning enabled him to give the initial impetus to the spread of Italian culture in this country, and particularly to the study of Dante. Though now advanced in years he established a business for importing Italian books and undertook the furthering of Italian opera in America. By 1833 he had raised sufficient capital to build an Italian opera house. But this venture also failed. He died a poor man five years later. In 1823 he had published his *Memorie* in Italian, an interesting but unreliable autobiography.

[J. L. Russo, *Lorenzo Da Ponte, Poet and Adventurer* (1922), gives a full account and exhaustive bibliography; a revised and enlarged edition of the *Memorie* was published 1829-30, and two English translations in 1929, one by L. A. Sheppard, with an introduction and notes, and one by Elisabeth Abbott edited and annotated by Arthur Livingston.] E. H. W.

DARBY, JOHN (Sept 27, 1804–Sept. 1, 1877), educator, author, was born at North Adams, Mass. One of several children of poor parents, Joseph and Farrand Darby, he was left fatherless at ten years of age and had to bear his share of the support of the family. Apprenticed to a fuller, he had few opportunities for schooling but worked at his books while at his machine in the mill. Thus learning the subjects required for entrance to college, he entered Williams when he was twenty-three. Following graduation in 1831 he taught in the Williamstown Academy but, forced to leave New England for the sake of his health, he accepted a position in the Barhamville Seminary for young ladies near Columbia, S. C. Devoted to the study of science, he published in 1841 *A Botany of the Southern States* as a text-book for the schools of the South. This, improved and enlarged in subsequent editions, became the authoritative manual for the flora of this part of the country. In 1842 he was made professor of natural science in Wesleyan Female College, Macon, Ga. His health failing after several years of teaching here, he returned to Williamstown, where he was appointed professor of mathematics in Williams College. After a year, however, the state of his health again compelled him to go to a warmer climate and for two years he taught again at Barhamville Seminary. Assuming then the direction of Sigourney Institute at Culloden, Ga., he continued at that school for six years and he is credited with having contributed largely to the renown it gained (Knight, *post*). In 1855 he accepted the headship of Auburn (Ala.) Masonic Female College which he relinquished after a year to become professor of natural science in the East Alabama Male College, also located at Auburn and just established under the auspices of the Methodist church. Of this he was one of the trustees whose names appear in the Act of Incorporation. Here he remained till the Civil War caused a suspension of college activities. In 1860 he published a text-book on chemistry which was widely used thereafter. Accepting in 1869 the professorship of science in Kentucky Wesleyan College at Millersburg, he remained there as professor and president till his resignation in 1876. On Aug. 20, 1833, he married a fellow teacher of his in the Barhamville Seminary, Julia P. Sheldon, daughter of Calvin Sheldon of Manchester, Vt. She died in 1875. There were several children, with whom in New York City the last few years of his life were spent. He was active and prominent in the Methodist church and a frequent contributor to the religious press. He won from his students both high respect for his scholarship and their regard because of his character as a man and inspirational power as a teacher.

[The chief source of information about John Darby is the *Obituary Record of Grads. of Williams Coll. deceased during the Academical Year ending June 15, 1878*, ser. 2, no. 3. See also L. I. Knight, *Georgia's Landmarks, Memorials and Legends* (1913–14). A sketch of his life appeared in the *N. Y. Tribune*, Sept. 21, 1877.]

W. J. C.

DARBY, WILLIAM (Aug. 14, 1775–Oct. 9, 1854), geographer, was born in Hanover Township, Lancaster (now Dauphin) County, Pa., the eldest son of Patrick and Mary (Rice) Darby. Both parents were Irish, and settled in Pennsylvania a few years prior to the Revolution. In 1781 they migrated to the Ohio country, where William's youth was spent. Without means of securing an education, he read assiduously, and at the age of eighteen began teaching school. After the death of his father in June 1799 he went to Natchez, where he became a cotton-planter. He suffered heavy losses by fire in 1804 and during the next five years was deputy surveyor for the United States. Conceiving the plan of a map and statistical account of Louisiana, he found government surveys inadequate and began a series of extensive explorations at his own expense. Interrupted by the British invasion, he acted as one of Jackson's topographical staff in the campaign of 1814–15. He returned to Pennsylvania in 1815, after having failed to secure aid from Louisiana officials in publishing his surveys. In Philadelphia, John Melish [*q.v.*] agreed to publish Darby's *A Geographical Description of the State of Louisiana . . . Being an Accompaniment to the Map of Louisiana* (1816, 2nd edition, 1817). Using Darby's statistical account and map, which Jackson and members of his staff considered accurate and valuable, the publisher compiled the Melish map of the United States, which was used as the basis for boundary delineation in the treaty of 1819 between the United States and Spain. This map, which brought profit and prestige to Melish, left the explorer "to mourn for non-requited toil and mis-directed credit" until Congress appropriated (Aug. 1, 1854) $1,500 as partial compensation (*U. S. Statutes at Large*, 33 Cong., 1 Sess., ch. 170). In 1818 Darby was one of the surveyors engaged in running the boundary between the United States and Canada, made the trip to the Michigan territory described in *A Tour from the City of New-York to Detroit*

(1819) and wrote, for Kirk & Mercein, *The Emigrant's Guide to the Western and Southwestern States and Territories* (1818), valuable for its information upon French and Spanish land titles. During the next thirty-five years he lived in Harrisburg, Pa., on a farm near Sandy Spring, Montgomery County, Md., and in Washington, D. C., where he was for some years a government clerk. He lectured widely, wrote and compiled much, and for a quarter of a century was one of the leading American geographers. He compiled three editions (1823, 1827 and 1843) of Richard Brookes's ever popular *General Gazetteer or Compendious Geographical Dictionary* (London, 1762). Brookes's work he found defective and he substituted his own so freely that *Darby's Edition* bears little resemblance to the original. He wrote most of the geographical articles in Vols. XIII to XVIII of the first American edition (Philadelphia, 1832) of Sir David Brewster's *Edinburgh Encyclopædia*. In 1833 he and Theodore Dwight, Jr., prepared *A New Gazetteer of the United States of America* (2nd edition 1835). He contributed a long series of border tales under the signature of Mark Bancroft to Samuel C. Atkinson's *The Casket*, a Philadelphia monthly magazine, and wrote upon public affairs under the pseudonym Tacitus for the *Daily National Intelligencer* (Washington, D. C.). He also published a *Plan of Pittsburgh and Vicinity* (1817), *Memoir on the Geography and Natural and Civil History of Florida, Attended by a Map of that Country* (1821), *Lectures on the Discovery of America and Colonization of North America by the English* (1828), *View of the United States, Historical, Geographical and Statistical* (1828), *Mnemonika, or, the Tablet of Memory* (1829), and *The Northern Nations of Europe, Russia and Poland* (1841). He was twice married: first, at Natchez, to Mrs. Boardman, a widow with a family of children "and quite handsome property"; she died Oct. 23, 1814, and in February 1816 he married Elizabeth Tanner, sister of Benjamin and Henry S. Tanner [*qq.v.*].

[Autobiographical letters written by Darby in 1834 to Dr. M. L. Dixon, of Winchester, Tenn., printed in Wm. H. Egle's *Dixons of Dixon's Ford* (pub. in 1878 by the Dauphin County Hist. Soc.) and in *Notes and Queries* (Harrisburg, 1894); *Senate Report No. 236*, 30 Cong., 1 Sess.; *Senate Report No. 222*, 33 Cong., 1 Sess.; *Hist. Mag.*, Oct. 1867; G. D. Harris and A. C. Veatch, *A Preliminary Report on the Geology of La.* (1899); *Daily Globe* and *Daily National Intelligencer* (both Washington, D. C.), Oct. 10, 1854.]

F. E. R.

DARE, VIRGINIA (b. Aug. 18, 1587) was the first English child born in America. On July 22, 1587, Gov. John White with 150 householders landed at Hatteras, on his way to plant a colony on the Chesapeake. It was decided to remain and settle at Roanoke. That summer, on Aug. 18, Gov. White's daughter, Ellinor, or Elyoner, wife of Ananias Dare, gave birth to a daughter, who was christened Virginia. On Aug. 27, Gov. White sailed to England to obtain help and supplies for the colony, but the Spanish War interfered and it was not until 1591 that help came. No trace could be found of the colonists and their fate has remained a complete mystery. Unless absorbed by some Indian tribes, they must all have perished. Virginia's known life is thus limited to nine days, and she is perhaps the youngest person to appear in any biographical dictionary as the subject of a separate article.

[For the history of the colony, see Alexander Brown, *The Genesis of the U. S.* (1891), I, 14–21. Virginia is mentioned in the few contemporary accounts of the settlement, *e.g.*, John Smith's *Travels and Works* (Arber, ed. 1910), I, 328, but there is no information beyond that noted above.]   J. T. A.

DARGAN, EDMUND STROTHER (Apr. 15, 1805–Nov. 24, 1879), jurist, the son of a Baptist minister of Irish descent who married a Miss Lilly, of English parentage, was born in Montgomery County, N. C. His father died when he was young, and he was compelled to earn his living by farm labor. Though practically self-educated, he acquired a fair knowledge of the classics and in 1828 entered a law office at Wadesboro, N. C. The following year he went to Alabama, walking the entire distance to Washington, Autauga County, where he was admitted to the bar and commenced practise, at the same time teaching school. He was elected a justice of the peace, but there was little scope for a lawyer in that district and in 1833 he moved to Montgomery, opened a law office, and in a short time, despite certain peculiarities of habit and temperament, obtained a good connection. Defeated for the state legislature in 1840, he was the following year elected by the General Assembly judge of the circuit court for the district of Mobile and took up his residence in that town, but resigned in 1842 in order to resume practise. He had now commenced to take an active interest in public affairs, and in 1844 became mayor of Mobile, in the same year serving as a member of the state Senate. In 1845 he went to the Twenty-ninth Congress as a Democrat, and took a prominent part in the House discussions on the Oregon question. It was he who, in the course of debate, suggested the compromise settlement which was ultimately adopted. Declining a renomination at the end of his term, he was elected by the General Assembly a judge of the supreme court of Alabama, Dec. 16, 1847, becoming chief justice on July 1, 1849. On the bench he displayed a judicial ability which his somewhat erratic temperament had ill prepared the public to expect. His opinions were characterized by an originality which did not detract from their soundness, and his resignation, Dec. 6, 1852, deprived the court of the most picturesque figure in its history. He resumed practise in Mobile, abstaining from active politics until the crisis which induced the constitutional convention of 1861, in which, as a delegate from Mobile, he voted for the ordinance of secession. His district also elected him to the Confederate Congress of 1862, but he declined reëlection in 1864, and thereafter took no part in public affairs. He died at Mobile. His wife was Roxana Brack of Montgomery.

"In person, Judge Dargan has a dull and unattractive look, as if he was always drowsy, and dissatisfied with things about him. His conversation is sluggish, and he appears to be in a reverie most of his time, when he is without a law-book in his hand, and when not engaged in Court. *There,* he wakes up . . . a transformation comes over him and the purest logic and the boldest grasp of thought comes to his aid as if by intuition . . . his face is luminous with intellectual life until he closes his argument, and then he looks sleepy again." (W. Garrett, *post.*) His eccentricity in dress and habits was a source of many anecdotes, and his general views upon current events indicated a train of thought that was independent of environment or precedent.

[Vivid contemporary appreciations appeared in Wm. Garrett, *Reminiscences of Public Men in Ala.* (1872), p. 385, and in W. Brewer, *Alabama: Her Hist., Resources, War Record and Public Men* (1872), p. 411. See also *Memorial Record of Ala.* (1893), II, 152; B. F. Riley, *Makers and Romance of Ala. Hist.* (n.d.), p. 176; and *Southern Law Jour. and Reporter*, I, 64 (Dec. 1879).]   H. W. H. K.

DARKE, WILLIAM (May 6, 1736–Nov. 26, 1801), soldier, son of Joseph Darke, was descended through his paternal grandmother from John Rush, one of Cromwell's commanders who became a Quaker and emigrated in 1683 to Pennsylvania. When William was only a few years old, his parents moved to Virginia, settling near Shepherdstown (now W. Va.). His military career began when he served as corporal in the Rutherford Rangers for a brief period (1758–59) during the French and Indian War. There appears to be no proof of the assertion that he shared in Braddock's defeat. After about fifteen years on the Virginia frontier, as soldier-farmer, he received at the outbreak of the Revolution a commission as captain of a company raised among his neighbors and friends. Captured at the battle of Germantown in October 1777, he was confined on board a prison-ship at New York until November 1780, when he was exchanged. In the spring of 1781 he recruited the Berkeley and Hampshire regiment, which rendered effective service at the siege of Yorktown. Some of these troops were discharged a few days before the surrender of Cornwallis, but there is evidence which suggests Darke's presence on that historic occasion. He retired from the Revolution with the rank of lieutenant-colonel as the reward of distinguished service.

Darke was one of a distinguished group of officers sent to the Virginia convention of 1788 to ratify the Federal Constitution. Though he served on no committees and made no speeches, the records show that he voted for ratification. He was a member of the Virginia legislature in the session of 1791–92, but apparently served only three days (*Journal of the House of Delegates,* 1791, p. 6), resigning to accept a military commission from the United States in order to fight the Miami Indians in the Ohio Territory with Gen. St. Clair. He commanded the left wing of the army at the defeat of Nov. 4, 1791, where he saw his youngest son, Capt. Joseph Darke, fall mortally wounded and he himself sustained a severe wound. He was rewarded for his services by being given the rank of brigadier-general and a generous grant of nearly 8,000 acres of public land (L. A. Burgess, *Virginia Soldiers of 1776,* 1927, I, 79). He spent the last decade of his life on his estate near Charles Town (now in West Virginia), serving at one time as justice of the peace. Darke, with his herculean frame, was a striking figure; his manners were rough; his disposition was frank and fearless. Notwithstanding a fiery temper, he was loved as well as respected by his officers and neighbors. His wife was a widow named Sarah Delayea. She bore him three sons, all of whom died in early manhood, and a daughter who has left descendants.

[F. V. Aler, *Aler's Hist. of Martinsburg and Berkeley County, W. Va.* (1888); Danske Dandridge, *Historic Shepherdstown* (1910); F. B. Heitman, *Hist. Reg. of Officers of the Continental Army during the War of the Revolution* (1914); V. A. Lewis, *Hist. of W. Va.* (1889); J. E. Norris, *Hist. of the Lower Shenandoah Valley* (1890); L. G. Tyler, *Encyc. of Virginian Biog.,* vol. II (1915); *Pa. Mag. of Hist. and Biog.,* XVII (1893), 330.]   E. L.

DARLEY, FELIX OCTAVIUS CARR (June 23, 1822–Mar. 27, 1888), illustrator, was the son of John Darley, a comedian, and his wife, Eleonora Westray, at one time a popular actress. Though both were natives of England they were married in the United States in 1800, while John Darley was serving as lieutenant of United States marines (*Polyanthos,* October 1806). Of their children, older than Felix, one became a teacher of music and another a portrait-painter. Felix was born in Philadelphia, where his parents had settled, and at fourteen was an apprentice in a mercantile house there. In 1842 some of his sketches of Philadelphia street characters were brought to the attention of Thomas Dunn English [*q.v.*] and shortly reached the editor of the *Saturday Museum,* who published them. Others appeared in *Godey's Magazine* and the *Democratic Review.* In 1843 J. R. Colon published in six monthly numbers a series, *Scenes in Indian Life,* by Darley, in outline, etched on stone. About the same time the young artist was commissioned by Carey & Hart to make illustrations for their series, the Library of American Humorous Works. His facility in caricature lent itself readily to the interpretation of the American humor of the forties. There was in him, however, a more serious vein, already suggested by the *Scenes in Indian Life,* which showed itself in sketches made for his own pleasure to illustrate Sylvester Judd's *Margaret.* These drawings, not published until later, were shown to the managers of the American Art Union and so pleased them that after Darley's removal to New York in 1848 they commissioned him to illustrate Irving's *Rip Van Winkle* and *Legend of Sleepy Hollow.* The illustrations of these two tales appeared in 1849 and 1850 respectively. He also illustrated several of Irving's works for G. P. Putnam with considerable success, Irving later saying to his nephew, "Jarvis tried, but failed to embody my conception of Diedrich Knickerbocker, Leslie also. Darley hit it in the illustrated History of New York" (P. M. Irving, *Life and Letters of Washington Irving,* vol. IV, 1864, p. 242; the edition referred to was published in 1850). Elected to the National Academy of Design in 1852, Darley was thenceforth regularly represented at its annual exhibitions. "Illustrated by Darley" became a potent phrase in new-book advertisements. His notable productions during the early fifties include illustrations for "Ik Marvel's" *Lorgnette* (1851) and the title-page of a comic periodical, *The Lantern* (1852). The thirty *Compositions in Outline from Judd's Margaret,* etched on stone like the *Scenes in Indian Life, Rip Van Winkle,* and *Sleepy Hollow,* were published in 1856. In these he "invited comparison with Moritz Retzsch, master of outline. He showed much of the grace of that German artist and vigor of characterization to which the other one does not quite attain" (Weitenkampf, "Illustrated by Darley," *International Studio,* March 1925, p. 49). In the same year he was commissioned to illustrate Cooper's works for James G. Gregory. The illustrations, reproduced on steel by bank-note engravers, were also published as *The Cooper Vignettes* (1862), in a large folio volume of India proofs. After his marriage, in 1859, to Jane, daughter of Warren Colburn the arithmetician, he established his home at Claymont, Del. He drew regularly for *Appletons'* and *Harper's,* continued his book illustrations, made vignettes for bank-notes, and drawings for large framing prints. Among these, "On the March to the Sea," engraved by A. H. Ritchie, was perhaps the best known. In 1868, after a visit to Europe, he published *Sketches Abroad With Pen and Pencil.* Other outstanding work included illustrations of Longfellow, notably *Evangeline,* Dickens, and Shakespeare, the latter with Alonzo Chappell (1886). Perhaps the most distinguished product of his later years was the series, *Compositions in Outline from Hawthorne's Scarlet Letter* (1879), which he dedicated to Longfellow.

Prolific and versatile as he was, he apparently did not permit the quantity of his production to mar its quality. He was always a good draftsman, and had a keen appreciation of the picturesque and the dramatic. His genius was essentially American; he was at his best in the reflection of American humor, the characterization of American types, the illustration of American scenes. His work attracted favorable attention at the Paris Exhibition of 1867 and at the Centennial Exhibition in Philadelphia in 1876.

[The best recent criticisms of Darley are those by Frank Weitenkampf, in *American Graphic Art* (1912), *passim,* and "Illustrated by Darley," *International Studio,* Mar. 1925, pp. 445–49. See also R. H. Stoddard in *Nat. Mag.,* Sept. 1856; H. T. Tuckerman, *Book of the Artists* (1867), pp. 471–76; obituary in Phil. *Telegraph,* repr. in *Am. Architect and Building News,* Apr. 14, 1888; Appletons' *Ann. Cyc.,* 1888; *N. Y. Times, N. Y. Tribune,* and *Evening Post* (N. Y.), Mar. 28, 1888.]   E. R. D.

DARLING, FLORA ADAMS (July 25, 1840– Jan. 6, 1910), author, founder of patriotic organizations, descendant in the seventh generation of Henry Adams who settled in Braintree, Mass., in 1636, was born in Lancaster, N. H., the daughter of Harvey and Nancy (Rowell) Adams. Her father, to whom she was devoted, was a Democrat and she shared his views of his-

tory and politics, subjects in which she was interested from childhood. On Mar. 12, 1860, she was married to Col. Edward Irving Darling, twenty-two years older than herself, and went with him to his Louisiana home just before the outbreak of the Civil War. Throughout that struggle her sympathies were divided between North and South, and as a Yankee Protestant her life was not altogether easy in a family of Southern Catholics. Going to England with her husband in January 1861, she tried to keep him there when the Civil War began, but he hastened home and joined the Confederate army. Before the birth of her son in October 1862, she returned to her father's New England home, intending to remain there until the war was over, but her husband's serious illness from a wound caused her to join him at Richmond in February 1863, after much difficulty in securing permission to cross the lines. Her husband, wounded at Franklin, Tenn., died Dec. 2, 1863. Under suspicion because she had taken the oath of allegiance to the Confederacy, she was arrested in New Orleans by Union officials and on her release found that her securities and jewelry had been stolen from her trunks. This loss occasioned a prolonged claim case before Congress. Illnesses from malarial and typhoid fever in the South injured her health, and a recurrence of malaria in 1876 resulted in the loss of her hearing and the impairment of her sight. After the war, she was for a time employed in a government department in Washington, where most of her remaining life was passed.

In September 1890, Mrs. Darling asked Mrs. Mary S. Lockwood to join her in organizing a patriotic society, which became the Daughters of the American Revolution, formally founded Oct. 11, 1890. She was the second signer, was elected vice-president in charge of the organization of chapters, and became editor of the official organ, the *Adams Magazine.* Friction shortly arose between her and the National Board of the D. A. R. because she opposed eligibility to membership through the maternal side and because of her alleged refusal to recognize the authority of the Board. By a resolution of the Board, July 1, 1891, she was removed from office and on Aug. 7, 1891, she resigned her life membership and severed all connection with the organization. The Darling Chapter of New York, named for her, also withdrew and became the parent of the Daughters of the Revolution, founded by Mrs. Darling Aug. 20, 1891, on the basis of lineal descent only. On Jan. 8, 1892, she founded the Daughters of the United States of the War of 1812, of which she became the first president-general. Mrs. Darling was the author of several books, most of them autobiographical: *Mrs. Darling's Letters, or Memories of the Civil War* (1883); *A Winning, Wayward Woman* (1889); *A Social Diplomat* (1889); *Was It a Just Verdict?* (1890); *Memories of Virginia* (1907); *The Senator's Daughter* (1907). Her writing is emotional, very personal in point of view, and reveals her as opinionated and given to controversy. Late in life she organized the Edward Irving Darling Musical Society in memory of her son, a composer. She died at the home of her brother, John Quincy Adams, in New York City.

[Flora Adams Darling, *Founding and Organization of the D. A. R. and D. R., with an App., The Adams Ancestry in Europe and America* (1901); Mrs. Adlai E. Stevenson, *A Brief History of the D. A. R.* (1913); Mary S. Lockwood and Emily Lee Sherwood, *Story of the Records, D. A. R.* (1906); *Who's Who in America*, 1908–09; obituary in Washington *Evening Star*, Jan 6, 1910, and *Washington Post*, Jan. 7, 1910.]   S. G. B.

DARLING, HENRY (Dec. 27, 1823–Apr. 20, 1891), Presbyterian clergyman, eighth president of Hamilton College, was born at Reading, Pa., the son of Judge William Darling, a native of Maine, and Margaretta Vaughn Smith. Graduating at nineteen from Amherst College, he declined an appointment as instructor to take training for the ministry. Since his religious connections were with the New School Presbyterian Church, he entered Union Theological Seminary. Desire for preparation for missionary work in the West led him a year later to Auburn Seminary, where he graduated in 1845. After a year in charge of the Presbyterian Church at Vernon, N. Y., near Utica, he became pastor of the Presbyterian Church of Hudson. Thence in 1853 he went to the Clinton Street Church of Philadelphia, succeeding Joel Parker. During his eight successful years in this pastorate he began his long activity in general ecclesiastical affairs. For nine years from 1854 he was permanent clerk of the General Assembly, and he served in the church's missionary and educational organizations. Compelled by illness in 1861 to resign his pastorate, he lived for three years in Germantown. During this time he wrote: *The Closer Walk* (1862), a devotional book which attained considerable fame, being republished in England and translated for use in India; "Worship as an Element of Sanctuary Service" (*Presbyterian Quarterly Review,* April 1862), an article which marked him as a pioneer in the movement among non-liturgical churches for betterment of worship; and *Slavery and the War* (1863), which was widely circulated as a pamphlet.

His best years were the seventeen spent in the pastorate of the Fourth Presbyterian Church of Albany, N. Y., beginning in 1864. The church, which had had conspicuous ministers, flourished more than ever under his leadership, and exerted a powerful influence in the city. Competent in all phases of church work, he was preeminently a pastor, and was warmly regarded for constant personal ministry. He was active in the reunion of the New School and Old School Presbyterian churches in 1869, and in efforts for the union of the Presbyterian Church in the United States of America with the Reformed (Dutch) Church and the Presbyterian Church in the United States (Southern). In 1881 he was elected moderator of the General Assembly. The same year he became president of Hamilton College, being also professor of Christian evidences and pastor of the college church. While his ten years of service saw a measure of advance in teaching and in buildings and funds, his chief contribution to the life of the college lay in the strengthening of religious influences and in friendly relations with students. He was remembered for establishing a "more wholesome confidence and sympathy" between students and faculty. He died in the midst of his work at Hamilton.

Darling was married in 1846 to Julia Strong of Fayetteville, N. Y., who died in 1851, and in 1853 to Ophelia Wells of Hudson. His publications, besides the book mentioned, were contributions to the *Presbyterian Quarterly Review* and other periodicals, and sermons.

[Richard W. Darling, *Memorial of Pres. Henry Darling* (1893), containing valuable address by A. S. Hoyt, newspaper articles at time of death, resolutions of ecclesiastical bodies, etc.; Minutes Gen. Assembly Presbyt. Ch. New School and Presbyt. Ch. reunited, *passim*; H. C. Stanton, *Origin and Growth of Presbyterianism in Albany* (1886); C. E. Allison, *Hist. Sketch of Hamilton Coll.* (1889); *Biog. Record of Alumni of Amherst Coll., 1821–71* (1883); general biographical catalogues of Union and Auburn seminaries; *Hamilton Coll. Alumni Reg., 1812–1922* (1922).]   R. H. N.

DARLING, SAMUEL TAYLOR (Apr. 6, 1872–May 20, 1925), pathologist and authority on tropical medicine, the son of Edmund Adams Darling by his wife, Sarah Ann Patterson, was born in Harrison, N. J. He passed his early life at Pawtucket, R. I., where he attended public schools and later became a druggist. His interest was thus aroused in medicine, the study of which he began rather late in life at the College of Physicians and Surgeons in Baltimore. He received the M.D. degree from that institution in 1903 and served there during the next two years as instructor in histology and pathology, being at the same time pathologist to the Baltimore City Hospital. In 1906 he joined the Isthmian Canal Commission under Gen. W. C. Gorgas [q.v.], and held the post of chief of laboratories at the Panama Canal Zone until 1915. During 1913–14, however, he went in company with Gorgas to investigate the sanitary conditions of the Rand Mines in Rhodesia. He received appointment in 1915 to the staff of the International Health Board, and during the next three years carried out investigations on the cause of anemia common among the people of Fiji, Java, and Malaya. Having completed this work, he accepted in 1918 the post of professor of hygiene and director of laboratories of hygiene at the medical school of Sao Paulo, Brazil. He returned to the School of Public Health at Baltimore in 1921, and in the following year became director of the field laboratory for research in malaria under the International Health Board of the Rockefeller Foundation. He went accordingly to Leesburg, Ga., where the chief laboratory was located, and continued to work there until his death.

Through his study of sanitation, Darling was one of those who made possible the construction of the Panama Canal. During his stay in the Canal Zone he identified the organism, *trypanosoma hippicum* (Darling), which was responsible for a fatal epidemic among mules and work horses, discovered its mode of transmission, and checked the epidemic which threatened to delay operations. While at Leesburg he made valuable additions to the knowledge of malaria, his emphasis upon the diagnostic value of splenic enlargement in early and in chronic cases being of particular value since it often disclosed unsuspected carriers ("The Spleen Index in Malaria," *Southern Medical Journal*, 1924, XVII, 590–6). His last published work was an article entitled "Comparative Helminthology as an Aid in the Solution of Ethnological Problems" (*American Journal of Tropical Medicine*, 1925, V, 323–37). He was a leading authority on the bionomics of the hookworm, introducing important measures for control of hookworm disease. He shared with Gorgas the distinction of being elected an honorary fellow of the Royal Society of Tropical Medicine and Hygiene in London, no other Americans being so honored. In March 1925, he left America to join the Malaria Commission of the Health Section of the League of Nations, of which he had recently been appointed corresponding member, to assist in a survey of the malaria conditions of Syria, Palestine, and Sicily. On May 20, he and another member of the commission

were killed near Beirut, Syria, in a motor accident. He was married on Feb. 18, 1905, to Nannyrle Llewellyn.

[*Amer. Jour. Tropical Medicine*, 1925, V, 319–21; *Lancet*, London, 1925, I, 320–21; M. C. D. Gorgas and B. J. Hendrick, *William Crawford Gorgas, His Life and Work* (1924); *Who's Who in America*, 1924–25.]   J.F.F.

DARLINGTON, WILLIAM (Apr. 28, 1782–Apr. 23, 1863), botanist, the son of Edward and Hannah (Townsend) Darlington, was born at Dilworthtown, Chester County, Pa. His early life was that of the hardy farm boy, and like John Bartram, his great neighbor of an earlier generation, he was observant at his plow of every weed and sapling. His early education was obtained under John Forsythe, one of the best teachers in the locality, and later he studied medicine under Dr. John Vaughan of Wilmington, Del. In 1804 he received the degree of M.D. from the University of Pennsylvania where he received splendid training in medical botany from Dr. B. S. Barton. In 1806 he was appointed surgeon on a ship clearing for Calcutta, and soon after his return, in June 1808, he married Catherine, daughter of Gen. John Lacey of New Jersey. When the War of 1812 sounded the call to arms, Darlington was appointed a major in the "American Grays," a unit of state volunteers, but did not see active service. During the remainder of his life he practised medicine, engaged in politics and finance, and gave himself to the avocation of botany, the one field in which his name will be long commemorated. His political services were of a minor sort; he was elected representative from his district to the Fourteenth, Sixteenth, and Seventeenth Congresses, and spoke against the extension of slave territory when the admission of Missouri was under discussion. In 1830 he was elected president of the Bank of Chester County, and for some years he was prothonotary and clerk of the courts. He served on the Canal Commission with Gallatin, being also a trustee of the Westchester Academy and an organizer of the Chester County Cabinet of Natural Sciences and of the Medical Society of Chester County. He enjoyed membership in forty learned societies.

Darlington's contributions to science were perhaps more highly esteemed in his day than the same works would be if produced at present. His *Florula Cestrica* (1826) and *Flora Cestrica* (1837) were models of careful natural history studies of a local nature, and were received with marked respect. More important at the present time are reckoned his *Reliquiae Baldwinianae* (1843), an excellent biography and collection of the works of William Baldwin the naturalist, and his *Memorials of John Bartram and Humphry Marshall* (1849), which, though the biographies are imperfect, constitute valuable collections of historical material relating to early botany in America. His *Agricultural Botany* (1847) was useful in its day and still, from an historical point of view, makes interesting reading. In 1859 he published *American Weeds and Useful Plants*. The impress which he made upon his science is not clearly seen in his works, and is only implied in the writings of his contemporaries. His fresh enthusiasm for his subject, his wide correspondence and friendship with naturalists throughout the country, made him a personal force and inspiration in his day. In his old age he was called by Asa Gray, "the Nestor of American botany," and there is no doubt that if he was not precisely the leader of American botany at any time, he enjoyed a position of unusual respect and affection. The inscription upon his tomb, composed by himself, conveys rather poignantly his love of the placid charm of the flora of his native county: *Plantae Cestrienses quas dilexit atque illustravit super tumulum eius semper floreant.*

[Washington Townsend, *Memorial of Wm. Darlington* (privately printed, Chester, Pa., 1863); T. P. James in *Proc. Am. Phil. Soc.*, IX, 330–43 (1863–64); *Bull. Chester County Hist. Soc.*, Sept. 1913; J. W. Harshberger, *Botanists of Phila.* (1899).]   D. C. P.

DAVEIS, CHARLES STEWART (May 10, 1788–Mar. 29, 1865), lawyer, was born in Portland, Me. Ebenezer Davis of Haverhill, Mass., probably a descendant of an Amesbury family, had fought throughout the Revolutionary War and at its close settled in Portland, marrying Mehitabel, daughter of Deacon Ebenezer Griffin of Bradford, Mass. Charles, their only child, received his early education at the common schools in Portland. When his father died in 1799 the family was left in straitened circumstances, but his mother, a woman of strong character, was able to send him in 1802 to Phillips Academy at Andover, and in 1803 he entered Bowdoin College, which had been founded only the previous year. While there he read extensively and was known as "Grecian Daveis." He graduated in 1807 at the head of his class, and in the same year took up the study of law with Nicholas Emory of Portland. On his admission to the bar in 1810 he commenced practise in Portland, with which city he remained associated throughout his life. Though possessing no local influence he was energetic, of untiring industry, and a close student; and gradually acquired a good practise, specializing in Admiralty law, a department wherein it was said later that he had no equal in the state. His legal reading had been of wide scope, embracing both common law and the English equity jurisprudence, and when in 1821 the state legislature extended the equitable jurisdiction of the supreme court he secured a large proportion of the new Chancery business. In 1827 the long-drawn-out dispute with Great Britain over the northeastern boundary of Maine as delimited in the Treaty of 1783 came to a head, a United States citizen being arrested on his own land within the disputed area by the New Brunswick authorities, and Daveis was retained by the governor of Maine—a personal friend of his—to proceed to Fredericton, N. B., with instructions to demand the release of the prisoner and at the same time to procure all information possible as to the British encroachments. His mission failed, since the lieutenant-governor of New Brunswick refused to treat officially with an agent of the State of Maine, but on his return in January 1828 he presented to the Executive a long report embodying the information he had collected (*Maine Legislature, Jan. Sess., 1828, Document No. 18*). Shortly afterward the controversy was submitted to the arbitration of the King of the Netherlands, and, at the request of the United States minister to The Hague, Daveis was appointed special agent of the United States government to receive the evidence and present it to the arbitrator. He left New York, Jan. 11, 1830, and proceeded to The Hague, where he remained for a month, after which he traveled through England and Scotland, returning to Boston, Aug. 26, 1830. He at once resumed practise at Portland, declining a professorship at the Harvard Law School which was tendered him a short time afterward. In 1838 he was again retained by the State of Maine in connection with the boundary question. The award under the submission to arbitration had been unsatisfactory; nothing had been done by either government to adjust the controversy; and he was sent by the governor of Maine to Washington to urge the claims of the state. For two months he was engaged at the Capital, but only partially accomplished his objects. The following year, however, he was called to Washington by the federal secretary of state for a conference on the subject. In 1840 he was elected to the state Senate from Cumberland County, having been defeated the previous year, and as chairman of the joint special committee on the northeastern boundary prepared the able and exhaustive report of Mar. 30, 1841, embodying the claims of Maine (*Senate Report 19, 21*

Leg.). In 1842 the Ashburton Treaty finally terminated the controversy to which he had practically devoted fifteen years of his life. The ability which he had displayed throughout was warmly recognized by both state and federal authorities. He retired from active practise in 1850, and died at Portland, Mar. 29, 1865. On June 1, 1815, he had married Elizabeth Taylor, daughter of John Taylor Gilman, governor of New Hampshire.

In politics a Whig, Daveis had no desire for public office, and was never a partisan, though in 1848 he actively supported Taylor for the presidency. He frequently wrote for the current magazines on various subjects, but his only permanent contributions to literature were his extremely able reports on the boundary question.

[The chief authority on Daveis's life and career is the excellent biography by D. G. Haskins in *New-Eng. Hist. and Geneal. Reg.,* LI (1897), 141. See also W. Willis, *Hist. of the Law, the Courts and the Lawyers of Maine* (1863), p. 577; N. Cleaveland, *Hist. of Bowdoin Coll.* (1882), p. 153; *The Letters of John Fairfield* (1922), ed. by A. G. Staples, App. 1; and H. S. Burrage, *Maine in the Northeastern Boundary Controversy* (1919).]   H. W. H. K.

DAVEISS, JOSEPH HAMILTON (Mar. 4, 1774–Nov. 8, 1811), lawyer, was the son of Joseph Daveiss, of Irish descent, and Jean (Hamilton) Daveiss, of Scotch ancestry. His parents were both born in Virginia and resided in Bedford County, from which they removed in 1779 and settled near Danville, Ky. Young Daveiss had no formal instruction until his twelfth year, when for some time he attended private schools in the vicinity of Harrodsburg. Here he made rapid progress in the classics and in natural science, largely impelled, it seems, by an ambition for distinction rather than a zeal for scholarship. Already skilful in fighting Indians, he took part in a campaign north of the Ohio at the age of eighteen. On his return he studied law under George Nicholas, and at twenty-one began at Danville the practise of his profession. In the winter of 1801–02 he argued the celebrated land case of *Mason* vs. *Wilson* before the Supreme Court of the United States (1 *Cranch,* 45). His associates were at first inclined to sneer at the uncouth backwoods lawyer, but he presented his argument so as to gain their respect and win the admiration of Chief Justice Marshall. His marriage in 1803 to the latter's sister, Ann, confirmed him in his Federalist leanings. In 1800 Adams had made him district attorney for Kentucky.

Early in 1806, shortly after Aaron Burr [*q.v.*] made his first visit to the western country, Daveiss called Jefferson's attention to his movements. Daveiss claimed that those who formerly had been concerned in the "Spanish Conspiracy," including Gen. James Wilkinson [*q.v.*], were reviving that project, and that Burr's activities had some relation to their machinations. His first warning was followed by other reports, and he became increasingly bitter in his charges against contemporary officials. Failing to arouse the administration to take the action which he regarded as necessary, he attempted to organize public opinion against the supposed peril by joining Humphrey Marshall and others in publishing the *Western World,* a sheet that bitterly attacked the alleged conspirators. Moreover, when Burr crossed the mountains a second time and visited Kentucky, Daveiss made complaint against him in the federal district court and tried to procure his indictment by a grand jury. In the course of two hearings Daveiss failed to establish the charge of conspiracy against the United States to separate the western states from the Union, or to lead an expedition against Mexico. Removed from office by President Jefferson after this failure, he vented his resentment in a pamphlet (*post*), which bitterly criticized the latter's conduct. If he and his associates had hoped to discredit the administration and build up a Federalist following in the West, their attempt was an utter failure. Shortly after this, he removed to Lexington, where he continued the practise of law. In the campaign against the Indians under Gen. Harrison he served as volunteer with the rank of major, was wounded in the battle of Tippecanoe, and died the next day. In addition to the pamphlet to which reference has been made, he also prepared an *Address to Congress* describing a proposed system for organizing the militia of the country.

[The pamphlet of Daveiss, *View of the President's Conduct Concerning the Conspiracy of 1806* (Frankfort, 1807), is a biased narrative of the events described, but affords an insight into the temper of the author. It may be supplemented by the manuscript autobiography of Jas. Taylor, Durrett Papers, Univ. of Chicago; and the letters of Taylor to Madison and Jefferson, in Madison MSS. and Jefferson MSS., Lib. of Cong. See also Maria T. Daveiss, *A Hist. of Mercer and Boyle Counties* (1885); Mann Butler, *A Hist. of the Commonwealth of Ky.* (1834), ch. 18; Chas. Warren, *The Supreme Court in U. S. Hist.,* vol. I (1922); *Quart. Publication Hist. and Philos. Soc. of Ohio,* vol. XI (1917); L. J. Bigelow, *Bench and Bar* (1857); *Harper's Weekly,* Apr. 27, 1867; Alfred Pirtle, "The Battle of Tippecanoe," Filson Club *Pubs.,* no. 15 (1900). The name is also spelled "Daviess" and occasionally appears in contemporary print as "Davis."]
    I. J. C.

DAVENPORT, EDWARD LOOMIS (Nov. 15, 1815–Sept. 1, 1877), actor, was born in Boston, the son of an inn-keeper, Asher Davenport, and his wife, Demis Loomis. In his youth he drifted from one commercial position to another, nursing an increasing desire to go on the stage. In spite of his father's aversion to such a career, he made his theatrical début, under the transparent name of "Mr. Dee" (Davenport), at the old Lion Theatre, or Brick Circus, in Providence, playing Parson Willdo in *A New Way to Pay Old Debts* to Junius Brutus Booth's Sir Giles Overreach. His first ten years in the theatre were devoted to playing every variety of character in the exhaustive and exhausting routine of the stock companies, and at the end of that decade he emerged a finished actor, in a position among the foremost young leading men of his time. He had headed companies in Boston, Philadelphia, and New York, and had toured with success throughout the country. His versatility was such that he had as yet made no particular rôle or type of rôle his own. In 1847 he went to England as leading man for Anna Cora Mowatt, with whom he played Claude Melnotte in *The Lady of Lyons*, Clifford in *The Hunchback*, Benedick in *Much Ado About Nothing*, and other standard rôles. When Gustavus Brooke joined the company, Shakespeare's *Othello* was revived, and Davenport and Brooke alternated in the rôles of Othello and Iago. Brooke, whose style was somewhat robust, had two years before made something of a sensation for himself as Othello, yet one critic, in writing of Mrs. Mowatt's revival, said that "when he [Davenport] plays Iago to Mr. Brooke's Othello, Iago is the ruling spirit of the piece; but when the cast is reversed Iago sinks to the level of a truculent ruffian, and Othello rises into the dignity of a brave, honorable and injured man." There were other comments in favor of "the American actor's superior discrimination, intelligence and good taste" (Edgett, *post*, p. 25). During his six years in England, Davenport added Shylock, Virginius, Hamlet, Richelieu, Wolsey, Brutus, Ingomar, and King Lear to his English repertoire, and, in spite of his many comedy and romantic characters, he became known as "the American tragedian." One of his successful comedy impersonations was William, in Douglas Jerrold's *Black Eyed Susan*, sacred in London's esteem to their popular comedian, T. P. Cooke. In this rôle he followed Macready's season at the Haymarket Theatre, with a first night's audience which included Charles Dickens, William M. Thackeray, Mark Lemon, and the author, Douglas Jerrold, himself. The performance was acclaimed with the same enthusiasm as London had already shown for his tragic characterizations. Davenport returned to America in 1854 and for twenty years thereafter sustained his position as one of America's leading contemporary actors. His health began to fail about 1874, and during the ensuing three years he acted infrequently, spending most of his time at his home in Canton, Pa., where he died. He was buried in Forest Hills Cemetery, Boston. Temperamentally Davenport had a natural dignity without austere reserve and was known for a genial, courteous disposition. Though his early education was limited he later in life became distinguished as "a scholarly actor." His wide versatility made it difficult to define his manner of acting, but he was acclaimed for his penetration and force in tragedy, his vigorous impulsive style in romantic rôles, and his intelligence in acting every character that he attempted. From the long list of rôles associated with his career those which emerged finally as the favorites were Shakespeare's Brutus and Sir Giles Overreach in Massinger's *A New Way to Pay Old Debts*.

While in England, in 1849, Davenport married Fanny Elisabeth Vining (Mrs. Charles Gill), a popular English actress. She was the daughter of Frederick Vining who, at the time of her birth (in July 1829), was the manager of the Haymarket Theatre, London. Her mother was the daughter of the Irish comedian, John Johnstone, and was a first cousin to Lester Wallack. Fanny Vining was carried on the stage as a baby in arms; she made her début at the Haymarket Theatre in 1847, as Juliet to the Romeo of Gustavus Brooke. After her marriage to E. L. Davenport, she acted with her husband as long as he acted, always in America after her début in New York, Mar. 2, 1855. Her last appearance was made at the Globe Theatre, Boston, Apr. 7, 1890, as Lady Macbeth. She died at her home, Canton, Pa., July 20, 1891 (see obituary in *New York Times*, July 22, 1891). The Davenports had nine children, seven of whom lived to grow up and adopt the stage as a profession. Of these, Fanny Lily Gypsy Davenport [*q.v.*] was the eldest and became the most celebrated.

[*Edward Loomis Davenport*, ed. by E. F. Edgett (Dunlap Soc., 1901); Anna Cora Mowatt, *The Autobiography of an Actress* (1854); *Actors and Actresses of Gt. Britain and the U. S.* (1886), ed. by Brander Matthews and Laurence Hutton; Lewis Strang, *Players and Plays of the Last Quarter Century* (1902); Montrose J. Moses, *Famous Actor-Families in America* (1906), which contains a Davenport bibliography; Eugene Tompkins, *Hist. of the Boston Theatre* (1908); Mary Caroline Crawford, *The Romance of the Am. Theatre* (1913); John Ranken Towse, *Sixty Years of the Theatre* (1916), esp. ch. XVI; Arthur Hornblow, *Hist. of the Theatre in America* (1919); H. P. Goddard, "Recollections of E. L. Davenport," in *Lippincott's Mag.*, Apr. 1878; E. S. Loomis, *Descendants of Joseph Loomis in America* (1908).]
P. W.

DAVENPORT, FANNY LILY GYPSY (Apr. 10, 1850–Sept. 26, 1898), actress, was a real child of the theatre. She was the daughter of E. L. Davenport [*q.v.*], one of America's leading actors during the nineteenth century, and Fanny (Vining) Davenport, daughter of an English actor and manager and herself an actress all her life. The eldest of seven brothers and sisters who all adopted the theatre as a profession, Fanny Davenport was born in London, in a house opposite the British Museum, while her father was in the midst of six years in the English theatre. Her parents brought her with them to America in 1854, and she went to school in Boston where the family made their home. "I cannot remember when I did not love the theatre," she wrote in *Lippincott's Magazine,* in October 1888; "and a passion for acting seemed born in me. When but ten years old I was constantly engaged in writing scenes (which my younger sisters would never study, much to my annoyance), arranging climaxes for acts, and planning all sorts of things to perform." She made her first public appearance as the child in *Metamora,* with her father's company at the Howard Athenæum, Boston, and thereafter she accompanied her parents on tour, whenever a child was needed being chosen to play the part. She spoke her first lines on the stage of Burton's Theatre, in New York City, Feb. 23, 1857. In these earlier appearances she was billed as "Miss Fanny." Always rather robust than petite, she was often cast for boy parts and actually made her début in an adult rôle as King Charles of Spain, in *Faint Heart Never Won Fair Lady,* with her parents, at Niblo's Garden, New York City, Feb. 14, 1862. Soon after this she left her father's company and began an independent career, acting first in the Louisville Theatre company as Carline in *The Black Crook,* and later in Mrs. Drew's company at the Arch Street Theatre, Philadelphia, where she attracted the attention of Augustin Daly [*q.v.*], who engaged her for his old Fifth Avenue Theatre in West Twenty-fourth St. She made her first appearance there as Lady Gay Spanker, in *London Assurance,* and met with immediate success. So began the second phase of her career. Here, and later at Daly's Globe and new Fifth Avenue theatres, she acted a wide variety of leading rôles in revivals of Shakespearian and other old English comedies as well as in new comedies. As she matured in this experience she developed a capacity for more emotional and dramatic rôles. Her success in W. S. Gilbert's *Charity* induced Daly to write *Pique,* in which she created the part of Mabel Renfrew, Dec. 14, 1876. The play

ran for 238 consecutive performances. After this run she entered upon the third phase of her career by purchasing *Pique* and in it beginning a tour at the head of her own company. Gradually she accumulated a repertoire of Shakespearian and modern French works covering a wide range, though eventually she forsook her earlier comedy rôles for more emotional and tragic parts. In 1882 she attempted to establish herself on the English stage, and chose *Pique* for her London début, but met with little success. At that moment Sarah Bernhardt's performance of Sardou's *Fédora* had carried both actress and playwright to the zenith of their careers. With the American rights to this play, Fanny Davenport returned to New York, where she produced it with such success that she continued to act it profitably for five consecutive seasons. Thereafter, as long as she acted (with the exception of a brief ill-fated effort in a play on Joan of Arc), she played only Sardou's *La Tosca, Cleopatra,* and *Gismonda.* On July 30, 1879, she married Edwin H. Price, an actor in her company. They were divorced in 1888, and on May 19, 1889, she married Melbourne MacDowell, also an actor in her company, who became her leading man. He survived her. She was of a full-blown, buxom type, and strikingly handsome. There is no question of her wide popularity or of the eminence of the position she reached and maintained in her profession. Of her acting there is a variety of opinions, though all seem to agree in choosing Nancy Sykes in *Oliver Twist,* Fédora, and La Tosca as her best rôles. She died at her summer home at South Duxbury, Mass.

[Jay B. Benton in F. E. McKay and C. E. L. Wingate, *Famous Am. Actors of To-day* (1896); M. J. Moses, *Famous Actor-Families in America* (1906); M. C. Crawford, *Romance of the Am. Theatre* (1913); Arthur Hornblow, *A Hist. of the Theatre in America* (1919); obituaries in *N. Y. Clipper* and *N. Y. Dramatic Mirror* for Oct. 8, 1898. Fanny Davenport is best studied in the dramatic criticisms of the daily papers of her time. References are made to her in the published reminiscences of contemporary players, especially in those of Clara Morris, Mrs. Gilbert, John Drew, and Otis Skinner. There is an extended, but discursive and verbose, sketch of her in Lillie W. Brown ("Amy Leslie"), *Some Players* (1899). Some account of her childhood, over her own signature, appeared in *Lippincott's Mag.,* Oct. 1888.]   P. W.

DAVENPORT, GEORGE (1783–July 4, 1845), soldier, trader, one of the founders of Davenport, Iowa, was born in Lincolnshire, England. As a boy he followed the sea, and came as a member of a ship's crew to New York in 1804. While his vessel lay in the harbor, he broke his leg in attempting to save a fellow sailor from drowning. This accident rendered him unfit for duty, and he was left at that city in the hospital. Soon after his recovery he enlisted in the United

States army, receiving an appointment as a sergeant. In the spring of 1806 his regiment was ordered to New Orleans where it was placed under the command of Gen. James Wilkinson. Davenport served as a soldier in the regular army for ten years, participating with distinction in expeditions into the Indian country and in the War of 1812. After his discharge from the army he was employed by Col. William Morrison of Kentucky, a government contractor, as his agent to supply troops with provisions. In the spring of 1816 he accompanied a body of troops from St. Louis to Rock Island, where Fort Armstrong was erected. Soon after his arrival at Rock Island he began trading with the Indians both in that part of Illinois and in the Iowa country, and in a short time built up an extensive and profitable business. In 1825 a post office was established at Rock Island and Davenport received the appointment as postmaster. In the fall of 1826 he quit independent trading with the Indians and became a member of the American Fur Company, having charge of the trade from the mouth of the Iowa River north to the Turkey River. He took an active part in the Black Hawk War, receiving an appointment from Gov. John Reynolds of Illinois as acting quartermaster-general with the rank of colonel. In 1833 he built the fine residence on Rock Island which is still preserved as one of the historic spots in this part of the Mississippi Valley. In 1835, he and a company of associates purchased a tract of land in Iowa opposite Rock Island. The new owners laid out a town which was called Davenport out of respect for their friend and associate. His influence with the Indians, particularly the Sauk and Foxes, was great. In 1837, he accompanied a delegation of Sauk and Fox chiefs to Washington and assisted in negotiating the second Black Hawk Purchase. Again in 1842 he was of considerable assistance to Gov. John Chambers in shaping the treaty by which the Sauk and Foxes surrendered the remainder of their land in Iowa. On the fourth of July 1845, while his family was absent attending a celebration, he was brutally murdered by a band of ruffians who planned to rob him. He was a man of a free, generous, and open-hearted disposition, pleasing in conversation, and full of wit and humor. He delighted to recount anecdotes connected with his wild and adventurous life.

[Franc B. Wilkie, *Davenport Past and Present* (1858), pp. 145–66; *Annals of Iowa*, 1 ser., VIII, 305–09; A. P. Richter, *Geschichte der Stadt Davenport und des County Scott* (1917); Davenport Collection, in Historical, Memorial and Art Building at Des Moines, containing valuable records of his activities as a fur-trader.]   B. E. M.

DAVENPORT, HOMER CALVIN (Mar. 8, 1867–May 2, 1912), cartoonist, was born at Silverton, Marion County, Ore., the son of Timothy Woodbridge Davenport, a politically minded farmer, and his wife Florinda Geer, daughter of R. C. Geer of Waldo Hills, Ore. Homer's mother died when he was but three and a half years old. The farm home was the scene of his early childhood. After various unsuccessful attempts to enter the business world, he finally obtained a position on the Portland *Oregonian* and, in 1892, on the San Francisco *Examiner*. In 1895, after three very successful years on the latter paper, he was brought by William Randolph Hearst to New York where his cartoons for the *New York Evening Journal* won for him an international reputation and caused him to become one of the highest-salaried men in the profession. As a cartoonist for the *Journal* he greatly influenced public opinion during the free-silver campaign of 1896, the Spanish-American War, and the second McKinley campaign of 1900. With the *New York Evening Mail* during the Roosevelt campaign of 1904, Davenport drew the noted "He's Good Enough for Me" cartoon, of which millions of copies were printed. His work was responsible for the attempt to pass an anti-cartoon bill in the New York legislature.

Certain of his creations, notably Mark Hanna's dollar-marked suit of clothes and the Trust figure—brutal, unintelligent, lawless, relentless —have been accepted as permanent contributions to the symbolism of his craft. His Uncle Sam also was one of the best conceived by any cartoonist. Despite the lack of formal education and technical training in art, Davenport made steady progress because of his ability to express his ideas with clarity and force, and to use the satirical touch skilfully. His first work of wide significance was the creation of C. P. Huntington as a comic character. He excelled as an advocate of municipal reform and is said to have done for San Francisco what Thomas Nast did for New York during the Tweed scandal. His picture, "The Boss" (Sam Rainey), duplicated the success of Nast's famous "What Are You Going To Do About It?" When Admiral Dewey was being criticized for presenting to his wife the house given him by admiring friends, Davenport's cartoon depicting his victory in Manila Bay and bearing the significant caption "Lest We Forget," brought about a change of public sentiment which earned for Davenport the Admiral's lasting gratitude. Davenport attended the Dreyfus trial, making studies of the principal characters connected with it. He also caricatured prominent English statesmen. Returning to the

Hearst press, he joined the staff of the *New York American,* occasionally lecturing on the influence and work of the cartoonist. In 1898 he published *Cartoons,* with an introduction by John J. Ingalls. Other published works include: *The Bell of Silverton* (1899); *Other Stories of Oregon* (1900); *The Dollar or the Man?* (1900); *My Quest of the Arab Horse* (1909); *The Country Boy* (1910). As an avocation he raised horses, and he longed for an Arabian steed. Through a letter from Theodore Roosevelt to the Sultan of Turkey, he finally obtained twenty-seven Arabian horses for his farm at Morristown, N. J. On Sept. 7, 1893, he married in Chicago, Daisy, daughter of Robert A. Moore of San Francisco.

[*Overland Monthly,* Aug. 1912; *Who's Who in America,* 1910–11; *Rev. of Revs.* (N. Y.), June 1912; *Chicago Tribune,* Sept. 6, 1893 (marriage license recorded); *N. Y. Tribune,* May 4, 1912; Walter Geer, *The Geer Geneal.* (1923).]   J.M.H.

DAVENPORT, IRA ERASTUS (Sept. 17, 1839–July 8, 1911), medium, was the son of Ira and Virtue (Honeysett) Davenport, and was the elder brother of William Henry Harrison Davenport, who was born Feb. 1, 1841. During the excitement caused in 1848 by the so-called "spirit rappings" of Margaret [*q.v.*] and Kate Fox, a number of children became the flattered objects of attention of parents alert for supernatural phenomena. Among these were the Davenport boys, in Buffalo. While tied with heavy sash-ropes in intricate knots—known later as the "Davenport ties"—they could produce sounds from musical instruments hung near them in a darkened room. Their reputation spread and they were brought to New York in 1855 but were soon exposed as mere sleight-of-hand performers and sent home. They then worked out a more elaborate program in which they were tied hand and foot at opposite ends of a large boxlike affair with doors. When the doors were closed, instruments hung in the cabinet were played, bells sounded, and "spirit hands" appeared in the small opening in one of the doors. The brothers were immediately successful in attracting public interest and in 1864 went to Europe where they became the center of excited controversy in which many prominent people took part. William M. Fay acted as their manager and sometimes substituted for William whose health was poor. J. B. Fergeson joined them as a lecturer, and later his place was taken by T. L. Nichols, both firm believers in the supernatural character of the Davenports' performance. At one time Harry Kellar traveled with them. During their stay in Paris, apparently in the spring of 1866, Ira married his second wife, Louise Toulet, hav-

ing previously been married in February 1862 to Augusta Green who died soon after. The next year William was married, according to his father, to Matilda May in Königsberg, and, according to Houdini, to Adah Isaacs Menken, "the Bengal Tiger Woman," in Paris. The first tour abroad lasted four years. The brothers then toured America until 1874 when they started on a world tour that ended with the death of William in Australia, July 1, 1877. Ira was much broken by the death of his brother and retired to a farm near Mayville, N. Y. He made one brief attempt to "come back" with Fay in 1895, but it was without success and he returned to Mayville, where he died July 8, 1911.

The brothers, who looked much alike, were handsome men of medium height, with mustaches and goatees. Their cabinets and rope-ties were the fathers of many vaudeville acts thereafter. In a letter to Houdini in 1909 Ira wrote, "We never in public affirmed our belief in spiritualism, that we regarded as no business of the public, nor did we offer our entertainments as the results of sleight of hand, nor on the other hand as spiritualism, we let our friends and foes settle that as best they could between themselves." No such statements, however, have shaken the faith of certain groups who still consider the Davenports to have been possessed of supernatural powers.

[The fullest and most accurate account of the career of the Davenports is found in the letters written by the older brother to Harry Houdini, which are now in the possession of Mrs. Houdini. A brief account of the brothers and the Houdini-Davenport relationship can be found in Houdini's *A Magician Among the Spirits* (1924). See also *The Davenport Brothers* (1869), by Ira Davenport, father of the brothers, an amusing but not always accurate account; *A Biography of the Brothers Davenport* (London, 1864), by Thos. L. Nichols; *Spiritual Experiences, Including Seven Months With the Brothers Davenport* (1867), by Robt. Cooper.]   K.H.A.

DAVENPORT, JAMES (1716–1757), clergyman, was born in Stamford, Conn., the son of Rev. John Davenport, great-grandson of the celebrated minister of New Haven, and Elizabeth (Morris) Maltby Davenport. He graduated from Yale College in 1732, one of the youngest men who ever took her degree. Remaining in New Haven to study theology, he was licensed to preach on Oct. 8, 1735, and three years later was ordained minister of the church in Southold, Long Island. Coming under the powerful influence of George Whitefield, he resolved to become an itinerant preacher. Calling his people together, he addressed them for twenty-four hours, and as a result was confined to his room for several days. He journeyed through New York and New Jersey, traveling part of the time with the great evangelist himself. The latter afterward said of him, "that he never knew one keep so close a walk with God." In 1741 Davenport conducted vigorous revivals in Connecticut in the settlements between Stonington and New Haven. Immersed in the spirit of the Great Awakening, he embodied the zeal, many of the virtues, and most of the unsafe extravagances of that revival. A man of considerable eloquence, he was a leader of those who claimed a special illumination of the Spirit and who trusted to impulses and impressions to guide their conduct. He denounced as unconverted the ministers who were opposed to emotional extravagances and urged their parishioners to withdraw from their unregenerating ministrations. In New Haven his influence was such that many members left the historic First Church and formed a new organization known as the North Church.

So intense was the excitement and so pronounced were the abuses connected with this revival that the General Assembly of Connecticut in 1742 passed an "Act for regulating Abuses and correcting Disorders in Ecclesiastical Affairs," treating as vagrants those who preached in a parish without the consent of the minister, or a majority of the church. A month later two inhabitants of Stratford entered a complaint against Davenport for disturbing the peace of that town. Brought before the Assembly at Hartford, he was judged not fully sane and sent back to Southold. Before the end of the month he was once more on his travels. On his arrival in Boston the ministers of that town interviewed him, and, being dissatisfied with his answers, declared against him. Davenport preached in the streets with such violent condemnation of the clergy that he was imprisoned by the authorities, adjudged insane, and sent back to his home. At the call of his church in Southold, a council of ministers met to consider his frequent absences from his church and his unusual behavior, and passed a vote of censure, but not of dismission. In March 1743 he went to New London, Conn., to organize a company of his converts into a church. To cure them of idolatrous pride in the things of this world he compelled them to bring their ornaments and fine clothes to be burned. Books whose teachings did not meet with his approval, by such men as Increase Mather, Colman, and Sewall, were also cast into the flames, the smoke reminding Davenport of the eternal torment which their authors must suffer in hell. This fanaticism led to earnest expostulations on the part of his friends, which, aided by a protracted illness, so sobered him that he wrote his *Confession and Retractions* (1744). In this he humbly confessed that he was led by a "false spirit" in severely judging his fellow ministers, in advising separations, in following "impulses," in encouraging private persons to exhort, and in his practise of singing in the streets. Dismissed from his church in Southold in 1743, he served various churches in the presbyteries of New Brunswick and New York, and was finally installed as pastor in Hopewell, N. J. This relationship being not altogether satisfactory, a petition was presented to the presbytery in 1757 for his removal. Before action was taken his stormy career came to a close.

[F. B. Dexter, *Biog. Sketches Grads. Yale Coll., 1701–45* (1885) ; A. B. Davenport, *A Supp. to the Hist. and Geneal. of the Davenport Family* (1876) ; A. E. Dunning, *Congregationalists in America* (1894) ; Leonard Bacon, *Thirteen Hist. Discourses on the Completion of Two Hundred Years*, etc. (1839) ; letters in Yale Lib.]   C. A. D.

DAVENPORT, JOHN (1597–March 1669/70), clergyman, author, was born at Coventry, England, and was baptized there in the Church of the Holy Trinity, Apr. 9, 1597, presumably a few days after his birth, the exact date of which is unknown. He was the fifth son of Henry Davenport who was mayor of Coventry, Warwickshire, in 1613, after having been chamberlain and sheriff, and who had married, as his first wife, Winifred, daughter of Richard Barnabit. The American compiler of the Davenport genealogy traces the family back in the direct line to Ormus de Dauneporte who was born in 1086. In any case the line was an ancient and honorable one.

As a boy Davenport attended the Free Grammar School of Coventry, at the age of sixteen going up to Oxford, where he apparently became a member of Merton College in 1613. (Mather says Brazenose in 1611 and there is some doubt.) After two years he transferred to Magdalen but left without taking his degree because he did not have sufficient money to continue. In 1615 he was preaching in the private chapel of Hilton Castle, near Durham, probably as chaplain to the Hilton family. He was there until at least March 1616 but after that the record is blank until June 1619 when we find him chosen curate of the Church of St. Lawrence Jewry in London. Here he became acquainted with members of the growing Puritan party and with some noble families, notably the Veres. In 1624 he was elected to the vicarage of St. Stephen's in Coleman Street, the adjoining parish, and one of the rare ones in which the parishioners had the right of electing their own vicar. The election met with much ecclesiastical opposition, and in a series of letters Davenport disclaimed any Puritan leanings and professed complete conformity. He was finally allowed to enter upon his work and in 1625 returned to Magdalen for a short time where he took his degree as Bachelor of Divinity. He appears to have been a faithful vicar to his flock, rendering particularly notable service when he remained at his post in London throughout the great plague of 1625.

It is impossible to say how early Davenport may have turned to the Puritan wing of the church but about this time we find him becoming closely associated with it. He appears to have become the spiritual adviser of that stanch Puritan, Lady Mary Vere, and in 1629 he was deeply interested in the procuring of the charter for the Massachusetts Company. Although not named as an incorporator, he contributed £50 and attended several meetings of the corporation. He became an object of suspicion to Laud from having been one of a group who had formed a plan of buying up certain lay impropriations in order to elect and provide ministers for such parts of England as most needed them. Innocent and even admirable as the plan was, its possibilities of erecting a sort of minor ecclesiastical organization within the larger one of the Church of England were obvious and it was impossible that it should escape the condemnation of the higher powers. The leaders were proceeded against, and the considerable amount of money already spent in the purchase of the impropriations was confiscated to the Crown, although personal criminal proceedings were dropped.

By 1632 Davenport seems to have definitely become a non-conformist, though still hoping that he might continue within the Church. He entertained John Cotton while in London on his flight to America, and talked over the problems of the times with him, but it was not until it was definitely known that Laud was to become archbishop that Davenport himself decided to flee the country. He resigned his cure and on Aug. 5, 1633 escaped from London into the country, crossing to Holland about three months later. Arrived at Haarlem he was invited to become the assistant in the Rev. John Paget's English church; but he objected to the baptism of children whose parents were not themselves leading Christian lives, came into conflict with the Dutch Classis, and was obliged to stop preaching within six months of his arrival. As usual, a printed controversy started, and Davenport, who had entered the lists before leaving England, published several pamphlets. Since he was unable to preach either in England or Holland, his thoughts now naturally turned to New England. His friend John Cotton had written to him of conditions there. Moreover the closest friend of his

entire life from boyhood on, Theophilus Eaton the London merchant, had also been much interested in the founding of the Massachusetts colony. Davenport therefore returned to England, probably early in 1637, for the purpose of emigrating to America. Eaton decided to go also and as joint leaders of a new expedition the two set sail with their company, arriving at Boston in the *Hector* and another vessel, June 26, 1637. Meanwhile Davenport had married Elizabeth Wolley and had had a son John, born, it is said without proof, in London in 1635. The child was left in England and did not arrive at New Haven until 1639.

On arrival, the party remained in Boston about nine months, having reached the little town in the midst of the exciting Antinomian controversy, in which Davenport took part. For a number of reasons, they decided not to remain but to establish an independent colony, and in April 1638 settled at the present New Haven in Connecticut. Eaton became governor and Davenport pastor of the church in the new colony. Church and state were closely united and a New England clergyman was almost of necessity a politician, but, although never shirking his duties in that regard, Davenport seems to have been rather less aggressively political than most of the cloth. Throughout his life his biography is largely that of the colony, but he found time also to publish many tracts and small volumes on religious topics.

In 1661 the somewhat even tenor of his life was punctuated by a dramatic incident—the coming to the colony of the regicide judges Whalley and Goffe. Pursued by the vengeance of the returned Stuarts, the two proscribed men had landed at Boston and after a time, deeming it safer, had retreated farther into the wilderness. Davenport had generously paved the way for them at New Haven by a series of sermons and there they found refuge temporarily while the royal officers searched for them. It is said that for a month they remained hid in Davenport's own house. He, however, disclaimed all knowledge of their whereabouts in a letter which one of his Connecticut biographers says he wishes "for his sake were blotted out." About this time he also took part in the controversy which was rending New England and which resulted in the adoption of the "Half Way Covenant" to which he was strenuously opposed.

When Connecticut was applying for a new charter and it became evident that New Haven might be absorbed by its largest neighbor, Davenport began to take a more active and leading part in politics. On Oct. 17, 1662, he was one of the ten signers of a letter to the General Court of Connecticut asking for delay and that New Haven might remain a distinct colony until more definite news came from Winthrop. He spoke a number of times in meetings of the New Haven Freemen, strongly denouncing the proposed union, denying that they could be legally annexed or that they should ever voluntarily give up their independence. With Nicholas Street he was appointed to draw up the pamphlet called *New Haven's Case Stated*. [Reprinted as Appendix VII in Atwater's *History of New Haven*, 1881, pp. 566–95.] When the union was finally consummated he felt that Christ's interest was "miserably lost."

This failure of his life's work, as he felt it, was perhaps influential in his acceptance of a call which came to him, in 1667, to the pastorate of the First Church in Boston, following the death of John Wilson. The church in New Haven was opposed to his dismission. According to the prevailing ideas of the times, a church had almost a vested interest in its pastor, and without proper dismission officially from one church, he could not accept a call to another. Whatever his reasons may have been, Davenport evidently wished to go to Boston. The church there was divided on the question of the call, a considerable body opposing it, in part because of Davenport's position on the Half Way Covenant. Certain of the elders in favor of Davenport felt that the two letters sent him by his former congregation would not be considered adequate as dismission in Boston, and, with his knowledge, these were suppressed and a portion only of the second one was read to the Boston church. The true state of affairs was finally revealed and resulted in a great scandal. Davenport claimed, incorrectly, a certain amount of ignorance but defended the three elders and his own son, who he said had written the abstract of the letter. This episode was the most disastrous in Davenport's life, which it probably shortened. It had, as all religious matters then had, its political repercussions and, combined with the feeling over the Half Way Covenant, resulted in a split in the First Church and the founding of the Third. It was an example, and not the first, in Davenport's life, of his acceptance of the doctrine that the end justifies the means. The letters, however, from the New Haven church indicated a deep love and reverence for their pastor. He lived in Boston only a few months, dying on Mar. 11, 15 or 16, according to varying accounts, in the year 1669/70. He was buried in King's Chapel Burying Ground.

[There is no full biography of Davenport. There is a sketch of his life by Cotton Mather in his *Magnalia Christi Americana* (ed. 1853), I, 321–31. Leonard Bacon in his *Thirteen Historical Discourses* (1839) devotes considerable space to him in the naturally laudatory fashion of a fellow Congregational divine. A somewhat more scholarly account, with a bibliography, is given by Franklin B. Dexter in his "Life and Writings of John Davenport" in the *New Haven Colony Hist. Soc. Papers*, vol. II (1877). Many of the earlier accounts are conflicting, and Wood's life in *Athenæ Oxonienses* (ed. 1817) is inaccurate, as is also the genealogy in the *New-Eng. Hist. and Geneal. Reg.*, vol. IX. The descent of the family has been worked out by A. B. Davenport in *Hist. and Geneal. of the Davenport Family* (1851) and *Supplement to the History* (1876) which include a number of documents and letters. The letter written by Davenport and Eaton relative to planting the colony in New Haven, addressed to the Mass. General Court, has been reprinted many times, e. g., see *Mass. Hist. Soc. Colls.*, 3 ser. III, 165–67. For the incident of the suppressed letters and the call to the Boston church see H. A. Hill, *Hist. of the Old South Church* (1890), I, 12 ff., and *Proc. Am. Antiquarian Soc.*, n. s., VIII, 9–13. See also the general histories of New Haven.] J.T.A.

DAVENPORT, THOMAS (July 9, 1802– July 6, 1851), inventor of the electric motor, was born on his father's farm in Williamstown, Orange County, Vt., the eighth in the family of eleven children of Daniel and Hannah (Rice) Davenport. He had attended school but a few years when his father died, and he was forced to assist in the support of the family. When fourteen years old he was apprenticed to the local blacksmith with whom he remained for seven years. Immediately after the close of his apprenticeship, in 1823, he moved to Brandon, Vt., where he opened a blacksmith shop and prospered, as indicated by the fact that shortly after his marriage to Emily Goss of Brandon on Feb. 14, 1827, he "built a commodious brick house." The topic of conversation around Brandon in 1831 was a mysterious magnet (a Henry electro-magnet) used at the Penfield Iron Works at Crown Point, N. Y. When Davenport saw the magnet, he was overcome with the desire to possess one like it. Trading his brother's horse for a poorer one (without his brother's knowledge) to gain the necessary cash, he purchased an extra magnet which the iron works had for sale instead of the iron for which he had gone to Crown Point. He afterward made a larger one, his wife sharing his enthusiasm to the point of tearing up her silk wedding dress to insulate the wires. For some unaccountable reason he saw in the device a possible source of power, and with the help of a friend "handy with tools," by July 1834 he had built a little machine composed of four electro-magnets, two arranged as opposite spokes in a horizontally revolving wheel and two fixed, and the four connected up through a crude commutator to an electric battery. When current was applied the wheel revolved at a high rate of speed. This machine unquestionably constituted a complete embodiment of the principles of the modern electric motor. Upon the advice of a college professor of Middlebury, Vt., Davenport, with the financial assistance of friends, for he had totally abandoned his regular business during the preceding two years, went to Washington in 1835 to have his machine patented. By the time he reached there, having stopped at various cities to show his device to prominent individuals, his money was gone, and he made his way back to Brandon totally discouraged. Amos Eaton [q.v.] of Rensselaer Polytechnic Institute prevailed upon him, however, to demonstrate his motor at Troy, N. Y., that autumn, and as a result he secured some additional financial assistance. In the hope of obtaining sufficient funds to patent the motor and go into manufacture, Davenport spent the year of 1836 building and exhibiting a number of miniature machines, including one which is now recognized as the embyro of the electric trolley car. With the money thus raised, he applied for a patent, sending in a model, but all was lost in the Patent Office fire on Dec. 15, 1836. A second application and model were immediately submitted and Davenport received letters patent on Feb. 25, 1837. For the next six years he endeavored in various ways to establish a market, but never succeeded. He organized a workshop and laboratory in New York City where he was constantly engaged in improving and enlarging his machine, but one after another of his supporters deserted him. He undertook to publish a technical journal called the *Electro-Magnet and Mechanics Intelligencer,* for which an electric motor of his own design operated the printing press, but after a few issues this was abandoned. Finally, about 1843, he broke down physically, returned to Brandon, and three years later retired to a small farm in Salisbury, Vt. Here in the last year of his life he undertook successful experiments with an electro-magnetic player piano, but his death at the early age of forty-nine brought an end to this work. He was survived by two sons.

[F. L. Pope in *The Electrical Engineer,* Jan. 7 to Feb. 4, 1891; Waldemar Kaempffert, *A Popular Hist. of Am. Invention* (1924); D. B. E. Kent in *Proc. Vt. Hist. Soc.,* 1926–27–28; Patent Office records; U. S. Nat. Museum records.]   C. W. M.

DAVENPORT, WILLIAM H. (1841–1877) [See Davenport, Ira Erastus 1839–1911.]

DAVEY, JOHN (June 6, 1846–Nov. 8, 1923), known as "the father of tree surgery in America," was born in Somersetshire, England, the son of Samuel and Ann (Shopland) Davey.

From his father, who had charge of a large farm, he learned much in his boyhood days about elementary agriculture. Indeed, the farm was his school, for no formal educational opportunities were offered him. At eight years of age he began working ten hours a day, but instead of permitting his tasks to become drudgery he made them aids to learning and to physical and mental discipline. At eighteen a foreman superintending an estate, he could neither read nor write, but his own application soon remedied the lack. In 1866 he went to Torquay to make himself more proficient in horticulture and landscape gardening. After serving an apprenticeship of six years in those branches, he emigrated to the United States. Friends having preceded him to Warren, Ohio, he made that place his destination. For several years after his arrival there the country was in a period of financial depression. Davey's attempt to conduct a greenhouse and landscape-gardening business was unsuccessful, but after his removal to Kent, Ohio, he enjoyed steady prosperity for many years.

Davey was past fifty before he really struck his stride. His unusual knowledge of the vegetable world, acquired as a youth in England and continually broadened and amplified after he came to America, was gradually brought to the notice of estate-owners and others who needed his counsel. In regard to shade and ornamental trees, especially, he possessed a stock of information that seemed almost uncanny. It was the result of years of research and experiment. Once having grasped the importance of a better understanding of the care and culture of trees in America, he set out on a one-man campaign to advance the cause. In his early efforts to spread the gospel of tree surgery, he expended thousands of dollars. Bringing out his first book, *The Tree Doctor* (1902), put him in debt, and years elapsed before the practise of his new profession was in itself remunerative. After his service came widely into demand it was necessary to start at Kent an institute for the training of helpers. Later a research department was organized. This was intended to test proposed improvements in tree surgery and to furnish free information about the care of trees. Although two-thirds of Davey's lifetime was spent in preparation for his actual career, the progress made in the last twenty years was significant. At his death in 1923, he left a business of $750,000 a year. His methods of tree surgery were everywhere in use and his researches were regarded by scientists with respect. In addition to *The Tree Doctor* he published: *A New Era in Tree Growing* 1905),

Davey's Primer on Trees and Birds (1905), *Instruction Books on Tree Surgery and Fruit Growing* (1914), and various magazine articles on the subject of tree surgery.

On Sept. 21, 1879, he was married to Bertha A. Reeves, of Salem, Ohio. He left two sons, Martin Luther Davey, member of Congress, and Paul H. Davey, who carried on their father's work from the headquarters at Kent.

[Lester S. Ivins and A. E. Winship, *Fifty Famous Farmers* (1924), pp. 199–209; *Who's Who in America*, 1922–23; Mary B. Mullett in *Am. Mag.*, Aug. 1922; *Literary Digest*, Dec. 29, 1923.]   W. B. S.

D'AVEZAC, AUGUSTE GENEVIÈVE VALENTIN (May 1780–Feb. 15, 1851), lawyer, diplomat, was born in Santo Domingo, where his father, Jean Pierre Valentin Joseph D'Avezac de Castera, of French parentage, owned an extensive plantation. His mother, her husband's kinswoman, was Marie Rose Valentine de Maragon D'Avezac de Castera. The family being wealthy, Auguste was sent to Europe for his education and attended the College of La Flèche, France. In 1791 his two older brothers were killed in the Santo Domingo insurrection of that year, his father fled to Virginia, where he died of yellow fever, and the other members of the family escaped to Louisiana. On returning to America Auguste joined his mother and sister Louise in New Orleans, where the latter became, June 3, 1805, the second wife of Edward Livingston [*q.v.*]. He studied law in his brother-in-law's office and on admission to the Lousiana bar commenced practise in New Orleans. His knowledge of law was not profound, but he possessed an intuitive appreciation of the mental processes of the mixed Spanish and French population from whose ranks the average Lousiana juries were drawn, and he soon became known as an exceptionally successful advocate. Following the declaration of war against Great Britain in 1812 he joined the local Committee of Defense organized by Livingston and in December 1814 when Jackson assumed command of the forces in New Orleans he became the latter's personal aide, being also appointed judge advocate. In the subsequent operations his topographical knowledge was of inestimable service to Jackson, who twice specially commended him in dispatches. On the termination of hostilities he resumed practise in New Orleans, serving an extensive if not first class clientele, and was recognized as without a rival in the criminal courts, to which his work was mainly confined. He was constantly retained in homicide cases, where his Gallic eloquence had full scope, and it has

been said that no client of his ever suffered capital punishment. During this period he retained the friendship of Jackson who, on becoming president, appointed him secretary of legation at The Hague, Aug. 11, 1829. Promoted chargé d'affaires to the Netherlands Oct. 15, 1831, he was, Jan. 30, 1833, appointed special diplomatic agent of the Two Sicilies and empowered to negotiate a treaty of general commerce, upon which mission he spent a year in Naples. Upon his retirement from the Netherlands legation, July 15, 1839, he settled in New York City and, becoming actively affiliated with Tammany Hall, was elected to the state legislature in 1843. On the nomination of President Polk he again became chargé d'affaires to the Netherlands, Apr. 19, 1845. Leaving the service Sept. 28, 1850, he returned to New York City, where he died a few months later.

Of outstanding natural ability and charm, enjoying the esteem and confidence of Jackson, and for thirty years closely associated with Livingston, who was his constant mentor and during his early diplomatic career his anxious adviser, he was a striking and distinguished figure in contemporary Lousiana affairs. Yet his career presents somewhat of an enigma. Perhaps because of too volatile a nature, an inconstance of purpose, or lack of high ideals, he never attained the eminence which his intellectual endowments should have assured. He was the author of the anonymous "Fragments of Unpublished Reminiscences of Edward Livingston," which appeared in *The United States Magazine and Democratic Review,* VIII (1840), 366.

[See C. H. Hunt, *Life of Edward Livingston* (1864), *passim;* Louise Livingston Hunt, *Memoir of Mrs. Edward Livingston* (1886); H. S. Foote, *The Bench and Bar of the South and South West* (1876), p. 194; *Louisiana* (1909), ed. by A. Fortier, I, 336; files of Dept. of State, Washington, D. C.; *U. S. Mag. and Democratic Rev.*, Feb. 1845; *N. Y. Herald*, Feb. 16, 1851.]   H.W.H.K.

DAVID, JOHN BAPTIST MARY (June 4, 1761–July 12, 1841), Catholic missionary, theologian, and bishop, was born in Couëron, Brittany, the son of Jean and Jeanne (Audrain) David, humble tillers of the soil. Intended for the church, he was trained by an uncle, a nearby pastor, and entered the College of Nantes conducted by the Oratorians. On receiving his master's degree, he enrolled in the Seminary of Nantes where the notorious Fouché was a fellow student. Serving as a tutor on completion of his training, he joined the Sulpicians and was ordained in 1785. Thereupon, he was appointed lecturer in theology and Scripture in the petit seminary of Angers under Father Benedict Joseph Flaget. His quiet, studious life ended when the seminary was seized by the French Revolutionists. The faculty and students escaped with their lives, David finding a refuge with a courageous family of his acquaintance.

Father David besought Superior-General Emery to send him with the heroic Sulpicians who were embarking for the United States, and Emery gave his consent. David, Flaget, Stephen Badin, and Guy Chabrat arrived in Philadelphia (1792) after a stormy voyage of three months. Proceeding to Baltimore, David was assigned to the missions of Charles County, Md., where his spirituality and untiring labors won the recognition of his charges and also episcopal favor. Within four months, he was preaching in acceptable English. A strongly built man of middle height, full of vigor, active of mind, he made an ideal missionary, able to stand fatigue and buffeting. In 1804, he was called to teach philosophy at Georgetown College. Soon he was transferred to the Sulpician Seminary at Baltimore, from which he attended Charles Carroll's chapel on Doughoregan Manor. In 1806, the bishop wished to send this tried servant to take charge of ecclesiastical affairs in schism-torn New Orleans, but David was without episcopal ambitions and declined the doubtful honor. For a short interval he acted as superior of the spiritual and temporal affairs of Mother Seton's Sisters of Charity who had recently commenced their mother house and St. Joseph's College for girls at Emmitsburg, Md.

In 1811 he accompanied the recently appointed Bishop Flaget to his primitive See of Bardstown, Ky. It was a tortuous journey across the mountains to Pittsburgh and thence by flatboat to Louisville and over the trail to Bardstown, especially as the missionaries were burdened by vestments, religious articles, a library, and a slave-boy. Only men of Gallic blood could visualize a bishop's palace and cathedral in the two-room log cabin. In Kentucky, there were only ten log-chapels, eight priests, and a few hundred communicants of doubtful practise. Growth was relatively rapid as Maryland colonists appeared and as public works brought Irish laborers. David proved a tower of strength to Flaget, as the business head of the diocese. On a donated farm near Bardstown, he and his Sulpician associates erected with their own hands a frame building which served as his seminary. In time this little Seminary of St. Thomas prospered and David's students became ardent frontier missionaries and in several in-

stances renowned bishops. The older students were soon removed to the major seminary at Bardstown where in 1816 the corner stone of the cathedral was laid. A primitive school, nurtured by David, became the College of St. Joseph. He also aided in the foundation of St. Mary's College in Marion County. In the meantime, seeing the need of a teaching order of women he founded the Sisters of Charity of Nazareth with Mother Catherine Spalding as superioress. To the end of his life, he was their guide and benefactor, and it was with pride that he saw their mother house at Nazareth grow strong enough to establish several academies and send out hundreds of nuns as teachers and nurses.

For the diocese of Bardstown, it is well that Father David had successfully plead to Rome and Archbishop Carroll against an appointment to the See of Philadelphia. In 1819, lest he be removed, Flaget had him named coadjutor-bishop. David still continued as an active missionary braving all hardships, even heated religious debates with challenging exhorters. For them the spirited French scholar was a dangerous opponent, since the untutored auditors had a mysterious respect for his erudition and linguistic powers. He won the countryside and the town of Louisville by his sacrifices during the cholera days of 1831 when his priests and nurses aided the stricken, and cared for their orphans in the newly established St. Vincent's Asylum in Louisville. He was more than a missionary and builder, however; he was a writer of religious books and brochures in a region devoid of literary men. He contributed original articles and French translations on theological and philosophical subjects to the Cincinnati *Catholic Telegraph* and to the *Metropolitan*. Some of the writings of Bellarmine and St. Alphonsus Liguori are said to have been first rendered into English by his pen. His *True Piety* (1814) was long used as a prayer book; his compiled *Catechism of Christian Doctrine* (1825) served for a generation; his *Spiritual Retreat for Eight Days* was edited (1864) by his scholarly student Bishop M. J. Spalding; and his *Manual of the Religious Life* outlined the guide of conduct for the Sisters of Nazareth. In addition, he wrote several respectable brochures of a purely controversial and tractarian character. A student of church music, he issued in 1815 *Compilation of Church Music and Hymns*. He humbly resigned his bishopric in 1833, a year after he had succeeded Flaget, and thereafter had more time for study and missionary visitations. He was named representative to the Second Provincial Council of Baltimore (1833) where his views on church administration won general attention. Full of vigor, he continued active until his death.

[Sister Columba Fox, *The Life of the Rt. Rev. J. B. M. David* (U. S. Cath. Hist. Soc. Monographs, IX, 1925); W. J. Howlett, *Hist. Tribute to St. Thomas Seminary* (1906); A. B. McGill, *The Sisters of Charity of Nazareth* (1917); M. J. Spalding, *Sketches of Early Cath. Missions in Ky.* (1844), and *Sketches of the Life, Times and Character of the Rt. Rev. Benedict Joseph Flaget* (1852); P. K. Guilday, *Life and Times of John Carroll* (1922); C. G. Herbermann, *The Sulpicians in the U. S.* (1916); Ben J. Webb, *Centenary of Catholicity in Ky.* (1884); R. H. Clarke, *Lives of the Deceased Bishops of the Cath. Ch. in U. S.* (1872); *Cath. Encyc.,* IX, 387; *Cath. Herald* (Phila.), July 29, 1841.]   R. J. P.

DAVIDGE, JOHN BEALE (1768–Aug. 23, 1829), anatomist and surgeon, founder of the University of Maryland, was born at Annapolis, the son of Capt. Davidge of the British army and Honor Howard of Anne Arundel County, Md. When he was a small boy his father died, and his mother resolved to apprentice him to a cabinetmaker, but his ambition to study medicine was gratified by aid afforded by friends and by the legacy of some slaves on the death of a relative. He entered St. John's College, where he received his M.A. degree in 1789, and shortly afterward began the study of medicine with Drs. James and William Murray of Annapolis. Continuing his education in Edinburgh, he specialized in anatomy, and received the degree of M.D. at Glasgow in 1793. About this time he married Wilhelmina Stuart of the Firth of Solway, several years his senior. For a short time he practised medicine in Birmingham, England, but soon removed to Baltimore. He played a prominent rôle in fighting the great epidemic of yellow fever in Baltimore (1797) and his views and work have been widely quoted (*Transactions of the International Medical Congress,* 1876). At the foundation of the Baltimore General Dispensary (1801) he was one of the attending physicians. From 1802 to 1807 he delivered private courses of medical lectures, and in the latter year he was associated with Drs. James Cocke and John Shaw in obtaining a charter for a medical school, known as the College of Medicine of Maryland. When the charter for the University of Maryland was issued (1813), this school became the medical department, and Davidge occupied the chairs of anatomy and surgery until his death. For a part of this time he was also dean. His first wife dying, he married Mrs. Rebecca Troup Polk, widow of Josiah Polk of Harford County, Md. He died in Baltimore of malignant disease.

His most important writings are his *Treatise on Yellow Fever* (1798), *Nosologia Methodica,* in Latin (1812, 2nd edition 1813); two volumes of *Physical Sketches* (1814 and 1816), *Treatise on Amputation* (1818), and an edition of *Bancroft on Fevers* (1821). He edited the *Baltimore Philosophical Journal and Review,* a quarterly journal of which but a single issue appeared (1823). His name is associated with a number of operations for which he was well known, including shoulder joint amputation (1792), ligation of the gluteal artery for aneurysm (he was the first to ligate this vessel), ligation of the carotid artery for fungus of the antrum, and total extirpation of the parotid gland (1823). His method of amputation became known as the "American." His lectures, said Prof. Lunsford P. Yandell, "were models of simple elegance," but "the moment he took his pen in hand he seemed to forget the English idiom," his style being obscure, stiff, and full of obsolete spellings and expressions (*Ibid.,* 234).

[The foregoing account is based on the several articles contributed to the *Hist. Sketch of the Univ. of Md.* (1891), *Medic. Annals of Md.* (1903), and H. A. Kelly and W. L. Burrage, *Am. Medic. Biogs.* (1920) by Eugene F. Cordell.]   E. E. H.

DAVIDGE, WILLIAM PLEATER (Apr. 17, 1814–Aug. 7, 1888), actor, was born in London, at Ludgate Hill, the son of a merchant. When he was only nine or ten years of age he loitered about the stage doors of theatres in order to catch a glimpse of the actors and actresses, whom he considered more than mortal. When he was about fourteen, some one discovered that he could sing and he was immediately given vocal lessons. He made his stage début in June 1836, at Nottingham, playing Adam Winterton in *The Iron Chest.* Following this he filled engagements at the Queens, Victoria, Olympic, and Drury Lane theatres. In 1845 he gave an entertainment based on the works of Dickens, in whom he was intensely interested. Through mutual friends he later met the author and spent several happy evenings with him. He came to America in 1850 and made his first appearance as Sir Peter Teazle at the Old Broadway Theatre in New York City. During the next five years he supported many of the stage favorites of that time, then went on the road with stock companies and appeared in the leading American cities. From 1860 to 1868 he played again in New York City, appearing at various theatres. He was happiest when playing Shakespearian comedy. He joined Augustin Daly's company in 1869 and remained with him until 1877. Probably his most noted and important rôle was that of Dick Deadeye in the first American presentation of *H. M. S. Pinafore,* at the Standard Theatre in New York. In 1885 he joined the Madison Square Theatre Company and was traveling with them in Wyoming at the time of his death. In addition to playing eleven hundred different rôles during his career, he wrote a play, *The Family Party* (which Daly promised to produce but never did), articles for newspapers, and an autobiographical book, *Footlight Flashes* (1866), which possesses no literary value and contains little information. In 1859 he attracted some attention by a paper, *The Drama Defended,* written in reply to an article by the Rev. Dr. Cuyler attacking theatricals and theatre folk. Davidge was one of the original members of the American Dramatic Fund Association. On Sept. 30, 1842, he was married to Elizabeth Clark. For her and their three children he maintained as a home in Brooklyn a house he had won in a lottery in 1858.

[W. D. Adams, *A Dict. of the Drama* (1904), vol. I; *The Theatre,* Sept. 1888; obituaries in *N. Y. Tribune, Sun* (N. Y.), Aug. 8, *Cheyenne Weekly Leader,* Aug. 9, *N. Y. Clipper,* Aug. 25, 1888.]   M. S.

DAVIDSON, GEORGE (May 9, 1825–Dec. 2, 1911), geodesist, geographer, astronomer, was born in Nottingham, England, the son of Thomas Davidson and Janet Drummond. In 1832 he came to America with his parents, who settled in Pennsylvania. He graduated first in his class, from the Central High School, Philadelphia, and in 1843 was appointed magnetic observer at Girard College, through the influence of Alexander D. Bache [*q.v.*], who had been a member of the High School faculty. His service in the United States Coast Survey began in 1845, when he went to Washington as secretary to Superintendent Bache, and ended with his retirement in 1895. He was sent to California in 1850, at the head of a party entrusted with the task of making an accurate survey of the Pacific Coast to meet the needs of navigation. The rest of his life, with the exception of the years 1860–66, which he spent in the Atlantic Coast service, was passed in the West. The first requirements of the survey were the determination of the latitudes and longitudes of prominent coast features, and the survey of harbors and harbor surroundings. Longitudes of principal stations were determined from observations of the moon's place among the stars and from occultations of stars by the moon; those of secondary stations by the transport of chronometers. Telegraphic communication was at that time not available. Data were so quickly and thoroughly assembled that soon he was able to issue his first "Directory for the Pacific Coast of the United States" for the use of mariners. (Published first as App. 44 of *Senate Executive Document No. 14,* 35 Cong., 2 Sess., it went through many later editions under the title, *Coast*

Pilot of California, Oregon and Washington Territory.) Its great value came from the fact that the compiler had become intimately acquainted with all the natural dangers and possibilities of the coast. His experience enabled him to devise a much improved form of meridian instrument which was generally adopted for use by the Coast Survey. In 1866 he was ordered to make a survey of the coast of Alaska. His official report, first published as an appendix to the report of the superintendent of the Coast Survey (App. 18, *House Executive Document No. 275,* 40 Cong., 2 Sess.), was republished in revised and enlarged form as the *Coast Pilot of Alaska* (1869). In 1869 telegraphic signals were exchanged between Harvard College Observatory and a temporary observatory in San Francisco and the longitudes of Pacific Coast points placed on an accurate basis.

Davidson's work in applied astronomy gave him the incentive to contribute also to pure astronomy, and his reports and writings show that he always had this broader aspect of his work in mind. At various stations he observed several partial eclipses of the sun and, more elaborately, two total eclipses and a transit of Mercury. He was appointed to direct the observations of the transit of Venus, once in Japan (1874) and once in New Mexico (1882). From time to time he published catalogues of star positions. At the San Buena Ventura station, he observed 556 meteors in 1870. At a station in the Sierra Nevada Mountains he tested astronomical conditions and was much impressed by the advantages of a high altitude. This investigation bore important fruit when Davidson adroitly guided and defined the somewhat vague intention of James Lick [*q.v.*] to leave money for a great telescope, although the final selection of the site, on Mount Hamilton instead of in the high Sierras, was somewhat of a disappointment to the former. Before the Lick Observatory was built, Davidson had his own private observatory in LaFayette Park, San Francisco. Erected in 1879 and containing a 6.4-inch Clark telescope, this was the first observatory in California. Here, in 1891–92, he made a long series of observations of latitude pairs as a contribution to the puzzling question of the variation of latitude, and confirmed the results found elsewhere ("On the Variation of Latitude in San Francisco, Cal.," App. 11, *Senate Executive Document No. 19,* pt. 2, 53 Cong., 2 Sess.).

While his chief studies were in astronomy, his help and interest were always available in other departments of science. He was president of the California Academy of Sciences for many years and of the Geographical Society of the Pacific. He was an authority on the early history of the Pacific Coast. He was appointed a member of the Irrigation Commission of California in 1873, and the following year was sent by the federal government to China, India, Egypt, and Europe to examine and report upon irrigation and reclamation work. He served on the Advisory Harbor Improvement Commission for San Francisco, 1873–76, the Mississippi River Commission, 1888, and the United States Assay Commissions of 1872 and 1884. He was elected a Regent of the University of California, serving in 1877–84, and later was appointed honorary professor of geodesy and astronomy in the University. It is said that for sixty years his name was more familiar to the scientifically inclined on the Pacific Coast than that of any other resident. His interest in the concerns of his community was active and his personal charm brought him many friends. In October 1858 he was married to Ellinor Fountleroy of Virginia.

[*Reports Supt. U. S. Coast and Geodetic Survey; Univ. of Cal. Biennial Report of the President, 1896–98 and 1898–1900*; biographical sketches of Davidson by J. J. Gilbert and Wm. Churchill in *Bull. Am. Geog. Soc.*, Jan. 1912; R. S. Holway in *Univ. of Cal. Chronicle and Official Record*, Jan. 1912, and in *Science*, Feb. 16, 1912; Geo. W. Dickie, Ralph Harrison, and Samuel B. Christy in *Proc. Cal. Acad. Sci.*, 1914; W. W. Campbell, in *Pubs. Astronomical Soc. of the Pacific*, Feb. 1914; *San Francisco Chronicle*, Dec. 3, 1911.]

R. S. D.

DAVIDSON, JAMES WOOD (Mar. 9, 1829–*c.* June 15, 1905), author, journalist, was born in Newberry County, S. C., the son of Alexander and Sarah Davidson. His parents were in hard circumstances, but he early developed such a regard for education that he determined to pursue it even though he knew it would be necessary for him to work his way through college. Graduated from the South Carolina College in 1852, he taught Greek in one village or another, in Winnsboro for five years, till 1859, when he went to teach in Columbia. During the Civil War he was adjutant of the 13th Regiment of South Carolina Volunteers, serving in Virginia with the army corps of Stonewall Jackson. After the war he returned to teach in Columbia and to work as a graduate student at his alma mater. As late as 1868 he was still so impoverished that he was wearing his old army uniforms. Later he worked with newspapers, first for two years in Washington and afterward for ten years in New York, where he was on the staff of the *Evening Post*. In 1869 he published *A School History of South Carolina* and *Living Writers of the South*. In the former, while clearly holding orthodox Southern views, he succeeded admirably in the desire expressed in the preface, to be "as little as possible tinged with sectional feelings." *The Living Writers* is made up of specimen pieces from many Southern writers, accompanied by biographical and critical notices. It has been justly characterized as "incondite and curious, but interesting" (Wauchope, *post*), and it is certain that it is highly informative about important matters not to be learned of elsewhere. In 1884 he married Josephine Allen, a widow, and moved from New York to a home near Lake Worth, Fla. Two years later he was a member of the Florida constitutional convention, and in 1887 he was in the state legislature. In 1886 he published *The Correspondent,* a handbook for persons wishing to write conventional letters. Soon after this, he went to live in Washington where for a long time he was a clerk in the Treasury Department. In 1888 he published *The Poetry of the Future,* a critical volume which is undoubtedly his most urbane memorial. Learned without being pedantic, it exhibits remarkable perspicacity in its maintenance of rhythm as perhaps the only technical requirement of verse. His *Florida of Today*, the handbook of a sincere enthusiast, appeared in 1889. From the time of his preparation of the *Living Writers* to the date of his death, he was engaged upon a dictionary of Southern authors which comprised at last, it is said, 4,000 names. This has never been published. He also wrote a long but undistinguished poem, "The Bell of Doom."

[*Who's Who in America*, 1906–07, 1908–09; G. A. Wauchope, *Writers of S. C.* (1910); E. A. Alderman and J. C. Harris, *Lib. of Southern Lit.* (1909), vol. XV; J. C. Yonge, letter, Mar. 2, 1928; E. L. Green, letter, May 24, 1928; Columbia *State*, July 25, 1897, and July 3, 1905.]

J. D. W.

DAVIDSON, JOHN WYNN (Aug. 18, 1823–June 26, 1881), soldier, was born in Fairfax County, Va. His grandfather was a general in the Revolution, and his father, William Benjamin Davidson, served in the Florida wars and died in the service in 1840. After graduating from West Point in 1845, Davidson did frontier duty in Kansas and Wisconsin. Assigned to the Army of the West at the outbreak of the Mexican War, he participated in the battles of San Pasqual, Passage of the San Gabriel River, and the Plains of Mesa. After the war, again on the frontier, he took part in the Indian fights at Clear Lake, Russian River, and Sacramento River. In 1854 he defeated the Jicarilla Apaches at Cieneguilla, N. Mex., where he himself was wounded. In this hard-fought engagement, the American troops surrounded and captured the Indian camp, but while plundering it were in turn surprised by the Indians, who had escaped. Davidson was taken at such a disadvantage that his command narrowly escaped annihilation. He was promoted captain in 1855. At the beginning of the Civil War he was offered a commission in the Confederate service, but, though a Virginian by birth, family ties, and education, remained loyal to the Union. In February 1862 he was appointed brigadier-general, United States Volunteers, and commanded a brigade in the Peninsular campaign, participated in the battles of Gaines's Mill and Golding's Farm, and won the brevets of lieutenant-colonel and colonel for gallant conduct. He took part in the actions at Lee's Mills, Mechanicsville, Savage Station, and Glendale, commanded the St. Louis District in 1862, the Army of Southeast Missouri the following year, the Army of Arkansas in 1863–64, and was chief of cavalry, Division of the West Mississippi, in 1865. He participated in the Little Rock expedition, directed the movement of troops against Pilot Knob, Fredericktown, and Cape Girardeau, drove Marmaduke out of Missouri, commanded in the actions of Bayou Metre and Ashley's Mills, Ark., and received the brevets of brigadier-general and major-general for his services in the capture of Little Rock. On Jan. 15, 1866, he was mustered out of the volunteers and assigned to the 2nd Cavalry. He served in the Inspector-General's Department (1866), was professor of military science and tactics at the Kansas Agricultural College (1868–71), and held various commands in Indian Territory and Texas during the next seven years. On Mar. 20, 1879, he was promoted colonel, 2nd Cavalry, and served in the District of the Yellowstone and at Fort Custer, Mont. At the latter station he received an injury when his horse fell upon him, from the effects of which he died four months later while on sick leave at St. Paul, Minn. Though a strict disciplinarian Davidson was thoughtful and considerate of his men, and a popular commander. He married the daughter of George K. McGunnegle of St. Louis.

[*Asso. Grads. U. S. Mil. Acad., Ann. Reunion, June 12, 1882* (1882); G. W. Cullum, *Biog. Reg.* (3rd ed., 1891); *Battles and Leaders of the Civil War*, II (1887), 206; *Official Records* (Army), ser. 1, vols. I, V, IX, XI, XIII; obituaries in St. Paul *Pioneer Press*, St. Louis *Missouri Republican*, June 27, 1881, and *St. Louis Globe Democrat*, June 30, 1881.] C. F. C—y.

DAVIDSON, LUCRETIA MARIA (Sept. 27, 1808–Aug. 27, 1825) and **MARGARET MILLER** (Mar. 26, 1823–Nov. 25, 1838), poets, were born at Plattsburg, N. Y., the daughters of Oliver and Margaret (Miller) Davidson. Their father, a doctor with cultivated tastes, was barely able to support his family; their mother, who had received the showy, superficial instruction in music, drawing, and belles-lettres then usual among girls of good family, was always in delicate health and was frequently confined to her bed for several months at a time. Seven of her nine children died before her. Lucretia Maria, an intelligent, affectionate, docile child, began to draw and to scribble rhymes in a chirography of her own before she had properly been taught to write. She was covered with shame when her papers were discovered and exclaimed over as evidences of unfolding genius. Her mother encouraged the child to write more and bestowed great pains on her moral, religious, and literary instruction at home. When the mother became seriously ill, Lucretia would act as housekeeper; at other times she read avidly and wrote rapidly, occasionally producing four or five copies of verses in a single day and standing, sometimes, rather than take time to sit down to her work. Finding the child's fondness for versifying was developing into an obsession, Mrs. Davidson forbade her to write altogether. Her daughter quickly grew depressed and nervous, and was allowed to resume her writing. She enjoyed several trips to friends and relatives in Canada; and through the generosity of a family friend, Moss Kent, a brother of James Kent the jurist, she was sent in November 1824 to Mrs. Willard's School at Troy. There she studied feverishly, but was already hopelessly consumptive and neurotic. The school physician attempted to restore her health with emetics and bleeding, and the ordeal of a public examination took what vitality was left. She was taken home sick, but her father, with the advice of another doctor, sent her to a school in Albany, thinking that she would benefit by the "change of air." She died of tuberculosis a month before her seventeenth birthday, her last words being an expression of gratitude to her benefactor, Moss Kent.

Margaret Miller Davidson was brought up to revere the memory of her gifted sister and early began, with her mother's encouragement, to emulate her. Her career closely paralleled Lucretia's, except that she was never sent away to school and that on an extended sojourn in New York she had—what her sister had never experienced—an evening at a theatre. Like her sister she read constantly and almost as constantly wrote verse that is indistinguishable from Lucretia's. She died of tuberculosis at Saratoga in her sixteenth year. The poetical remains of the two children and, even more, the story of their pitiable, exemplary lives made a strong appeal to the religious and moral sentiments of their generation. Distinguished writers were easily induced to furnish biographical introductions to their poems, and critical eyes suffused with sympathetic tears quite naturally mistook precocity for poetic merit. One reader, Caroline Southey, the wife of the Poet Laureate, even went so far as to address Mrs. Davidson in a sonnet that compared the grief of the mother over her two children to the anguish of the Virgin Mary at the crucifixion of the Saviour. As a matter of fact, the work of the Davidson sisters was what precocious verse is almost inevitably—an echo of the conventional poetic language and sentiment of its time. To the social and literary historian their writings and the full accounts preserved of their lives are of considerable value.

[Samuel F. B. Morse, "Biog. Sketch" in L. M. Davidson, *Amir Khan and Other Poems* (1829); Catharine Maria Sedgwick, "A Memoir of L. M. Davidson" in Jared Sparks, ed., *Library of Am. Biog.*, vol. VII (1837) and in various eds. of the *Poetical Remains* (1841, and subsequent eds.); Robt. Southey in *Quart. Rev.*, XLI, 289–301; Washington Irving, *Biog. and Poetical Remains of the Late M. M. Davidson* (1841, 1849, new ed., rev., 1852); *Selections from the Writings of Mrs. Margaret M. Davidson, the Mother of Lucretia Maria and Margaret M. Davidson* (1843); Edgar Allan Poe in *Complete Works of E. A. Poe* (Va. Ed., ed. by J. A. Harrison), X, 174–78 and 221–26 (original reviews in *Graham's Mag.*, Aug. and Dec. 1841); Caroline May, *The American Female Poets with Biog. and Critical Notices* (1848); R. W. Griswold, *The Female Poets of America* (1848, and subsequent eds.); *The Davidson Family* (a pamphlet of unknown source in the Library of Congress).]   G. H. G.

DAVIDSON, ROBERT (1750–Dec. 13, 1812), Presbyterian clergyman, was born at Elkton, Md., and graduated from the University of Pennsylvania in 1771. While a student of divinity he was taken dangerously ill at a farmhouse and was kept alive only by the assiduous care and kind nursing of the farmer's daughter. On his recovery he ascertained that there was only one way to repay his benefactress. "Although she was older than himself, had not the slightest pretension to beauty, and moved in a humble sphere of life," wrote his son by a second marriage, "she made him for upward of thirty years an excellent and devoted wife." In his twenty-third year he was ordained by the Second Presbytery of Philadelphia. Until 1784 he lived in that city, teaching history in the University of Pennsylvania and acting as assistant to Dr. Ewing of the First Presbyterian Church. At the outbreak of the Revolution he spoke so frequently and vigorously in behalf of the revolting patriots that when the British occupied Philadelphia he found it prudent to retire unobtrusively into Delaware. In 1784 first appeared his *Geography Epitomized; or, a Tour round the World: Being a short but comprehensive De-*

scription of the Terraqueous Globe attempted in Verse for the Sake of the Memory: And principally designed for the Use of Schools. Other editions of the pamphlet, with its ingenious rhymes, were published in London in 1787 and at Burlington, N. J., in 1791. In November 1784 he was called to Carlisle, Pa., in the double capacity of professor of history, geography, chronology, rhetoric, and belles-lettres in Dickinson College and of pastor of the Presbyterian Church. There for twenty-eight years he served church, state, and school with his extensive learning and his sterling private character. Acquainted with eight languages, well read in theology and in the sciences he had studied at Franklin's college, he was particularly fond of astronomy. In 1794 with mingled tact and resolution he upheld law and order against the Whiskey Insurrectionists. In 1796 he was chosen moderator of the General Assembly of the Presbyterian Church. From Dr. Nisbet's death in 1804 until 1809 he was president of Dickinson College, resigning to devote his time to his ministerial duties. His second wife, Margaret Montgomery of Carlisle, died in 1809, and on Apr. 17, 1810, he married Jane Harris, who survived him. In 1811 he published *The Christian's A. B. C., or the 119th psalm in metre, each octave commencing with the appropriate letter of the alphabet, with the exception of Q, X, and Z*. In the year of his death appeared a *New Metrical Version of the Psalms*, which his son rates above Sternhold and Hopkins but below Watts. He left behind him twenty manuscript volumes of sermons and scientific lectures, for, strangely diffident of his powers, he always entered pulpit or classroom with his discourse completely written out.

[Article by Davidson's son in W. B. Sprague, *Annals of the Am. Pulpit*, vol. III (1858); *The Centennial Memorial of the Presbytery of Carlisle* (2 vols., 1889); A. Nevin, *Churches of the Valley or an Hist. Sketch of the Old Presbyt. Congregations of Cumberland and Franklin Counties in Pa.* (1852) and *Men of Mark of Cumberland Valley, Pa., 1776–1876* (1876); incidental mention in S. Miller, *Memoir of the Rev. Charles Nisbet, D.D.* (1840), pp. 158, 228, 288–96; *Gen. Alumni Cat. of the Univ. of Pa.* (1917); R. Davidson, *A Sermon on the Freedom and Happiness of the U. S. A., preached in Carlisle on the 5th Oct. 1794 before President Washington, Gov. Mifflin, etc.* (1794); J. C. Fitzpatrick, *The Diaries of Geo. Washington, 1748–99* (1925), IV, 212.]   G. H. G.

DAVIDSON, THOMAS (Oct. 25, 1840–Sept. 14, 1900), philosopher and wandering scholar, was born in the parish of Old Deer in Aberdeenshire, Scotland. He came of very humble antecedents, his father, Thomas Davidson, being a small farmer, and his mother, Mary Warrender, of sturdy peasant stock. She was a stern disciplinarian, and a woman of deep piety and resolute will, qualities which were but intensified in her son Thomas. He was from the first avid of learning and eagerly devoured all the books he could lay hands upon. Games and sports played no part in his life, but Baxter's *Saints' Rest* was his delight. The reading of this book marked an epoch in his life. It gave him a sense of religious exaltation and illumination that transformed his world, and left an indelible impression of the sublimity of human life and its infinite possibilities for weal or woe. At the same time his never-failing and contagious good humor made him a general favorite with his companions, old and young. He was prepared for college by Robert Wilson, the parish schoolmaster of Old Deer, who, discovering the making of a scholar in him, took him into his home and treated him as a son, helping him in his studies every evening in return for his assistance during the day in teaching the junior classes in school. At the age of sixteen he entered King's College, Aberdeen, having won a four-year scholarship in the Bursary Competition. Here he acquired, as a second nature, the habit of exact and thorough scholarship. He distinguished himself especially in the classics, carrying off the highest honors in Greek, the Simpson prize, on his graduation in 1860. After serving for three years as rector of the Old Aberdeen Grammar School, he went to England and taught Latin and Greek, first at Tunbridge Wells and later at Wimbledon. In 1866 he moved to Canada where he taught for a year in the Collegiate Institute of London, Ontario. He then came to the United States, and, after a short stay in Boston, where he fell among the radicals, with whom he cordially sympathized, he accepted a position in the public schools of St. Louis, where he was soon promoted to the principalship of a branch high school. Here he made the acquaintance of that famous group of enthusiastic Hegelian philosophers whose leader, W. T. Harris [*q.v.*], became his intimate and life-long friend. The influence of this group was profound and lasting, although Davidson himself could never find anything in Hegel. They convinced him of the shallowness of positivism, which had all but caught him in the stormy years of doubt that had followed his college career; sent him back to the study of German thought, and through that to the deeper study of Plato and especially of Aristotle who remained for him to the end "the master of those who know"; and they gave him a better appreciation of the educational value of art and literature when interpreted philosophically.

But Davidson was a radical individualist and a born dissenter, and could not and would not fit into any niche. He chafed under all restraint, and was not entirely contented until, after removing to Boston in 1875, he found his liberty in the life of a free lance and wandering scholar, gaining a modest livelihood by teaching private classes, tutoring, lecturing, writing, while holding himself responsible to himself alone. His mode of life gave him six months of every year for leisurely study and frequent opportunities for long visits to Europe. He took extended walking tours through Greece where he gained a vivid appreciation and a thorough and intimate knowledge of ancient Hellenic art and culture. From 1878 to 1884 most of his time was spent in Domo d' Ossola, Italy, in close contact with the members of the Rosminian order. Here he lived the life of a hermit, devoting himself to the study of the writings of Rosmini, in which he felt that he had at last found the philosophy that all his life he had been seeking, one that justified the claims of the intellect and provided an adequate ground for a spiritual, religious interpretation of life. At the same time he carried further his researches into the whole period of scholastic philosophy. His own philosophy underwent further development in later years, but never wholly lost the Rosminian stamp. If it must be described in a word it might be said to be a form of pluralistic idealism (apeirotheism, he sometimes called it), coupled with a stern ethical rigorism,—but all labels are misleading.

While studying in Italy he seriously contemplated joining the Catholic Church, but he could not bring himself to accept the dogmas. Nevertheless the practical activities of his later life were given direction by this experience. Their common purpose was the organization of the spiritual life, but on the basis of philosophical insight rather than of dogma. During a brief sojourn in London in 1883, he founded the Fellowship of the New Life, of which the Fabian Society was an offshoot. Later he established a branch of the Fellowship in New York, and a Summer School for the Culture Sciences, held first at St. Cloud, N. J., then at Farmington, Conn., and finally on a farm that he had bought in the Adirondacks near the village of Keene, N. Y. None of these undertakings proved entirely satisfactory and it was only toward the end of his life that he stumbled, almost by chance, upon the opportunity to carry out his ideal in a way that seemed to him altogether encouraging. In association with the People's Institute and the Educational Alliance of New York he gathered together a group of eager, earnest young men and women from the lower East Side and organized a Bread-Winners' College inspired by the idea of helping the wage-earners to share in the best culture of the ages and to rise to a higher level of mental and spiritual power.

Davidson had a prodigious memory; he seemed never to forget anything he had ever read. He spoke nearly all the languages of Europe except Slavic with fluency, including Latin and modern Greek. The range of his learning was vast, and his scholarship accurate and thorough. Yet he carried this load lightly, and with all modesty, and prized it only for its value in pointing the way to a nobler life for himself and for others, to whom he was ever ready to give himself without stint. It is perhaps chiefly as a great personal force that his influence has been manifest. He had a vivid and exuberant personality and a genius for friendship, and he carried with him an air of elevation which came from his constant association with the saints and seers of all times.

Davidson was a frequent contributor to philosophical periodicals, especially the *Journal of Speculative Philosophy,* and also wrote for the *Radical* (Boston), the *Round Table* (New York), and the *Western Educational Review* (St. Louis), of which for a time he was editor. His published works include : *The Philosophical System of Antonio Rosmini-Serbati,* with a sketch of Rosmini's life(1882) ; *The Parthenon Frieze and Other Essays* (1882) ; *Scartazzini's Handbook to Dante,* with notes and additions (1887) ; *Prolegomena to In Memoriam* (1889) ; *Aristotle and Ancient Educational Ideals* (1892) ; *Education of the Greek People, and its Influence on Civilization* (1894) ; *Rousseau and Education According to Nature* (1898) ; *A History of Education* (1900) ; translation of Rosmini's *Psychology* (1883).

[Wm. A. Knight, *Some Nineteenth Century Scotsmen; Being Personal Recollections* (1902), and *Memorials of Thos. Davidson* (1907) ; Wm. James, art. on Davidson in *Memories and Studies* (1911) ; Morris R. Cohen, in *A Cyc. of Education,* vol. II (1911) ; personal recollections, and unpublished letters and MSS.]

C. M. B.

DAVIDSON, WILLIAM LEE (1746–Feb. 1, 1781), Revolutionary soldier, was born in Lancaster County, Pa., the son of George Davidson, who, in 1750, settled in Rowan (now Iredell) County, N. C. He was educated in the rural schools and then attended Queen's Museum College in Charlotte. He married in early life Mary Brevard, the sister of Dr. Ephraim Brevard, reputed author of the Mecklenburg Declaration of 1775. After serving on the Rowan County Committee of Safety, he was appointed major of the 4th North Carolina Regiment (1776) and marched north under Gen. Francis Nash to join Washington's army in New Jersey. For gallant conduct in the battle of Germantown he was promoted to lieutenant-colonel (1777). In November 1779 the North Carolina line was detached and ordered to reinforce the southern army. Davidson stopped in North Carolina to visit his family and upon his arrival at Charleston found the city so closely invested that he was unable to rejoin his regiment. After the surrender of Gen. Lincoln he returned to Mecklenburg, where he commanded the local militia in its efforts to subdue uprisings of the Loyalists, who were much encouraged by the success of the British in the South. While proceeding vigorously in this service he was severely wounded in an engagement at Coulson's Mill on the Yadkin in the summer of 1780. He was then promoted to brigadier-general of militia, in command of the Salisbury district. After defeating Tarleton at the battle of Cowpens, Gen. Morgan began retreating northward with great celerity, pursued by Cornwallis. Davidson, commanding the hastily assembled local militia, called by Cornwallis "Gang of Plunderers," was ordered by Greene to guard the fords of the Catawba, after Morgan's passage. Early on the morning of Feb. 1, 1781, Cornwallis crossed the river at Cowan's (or McCowan's) Ford, in spite of a "galling and constant fire" from the Americans. Davidson, with the majority of his forces, was some distance away, and arrived too late to prevent the passage of the British. He was killed and his troops were dispersed. Gen. Henry Lee wrote that the loss of Davidson was "particularly detrimental" at that time, "as he was the chief instrument relied upon by Greene for the assemblage of the militia" (*Memoirs,* I, 398). A monument to his memory was voted by the Continental Congress (Sept. 20, 1781) but the money was not appropriated by Congress until 1903. The monument has since been erected on the Guilford Court House battle-field. His name is also perpetuated in Davidson College in his adopted state, and in counties in North Carolina and Tennessee.

[*Jours. of the Continental Cong.,* Sept. 20, 1781; *N. C. State Records* (1895) ; Banastre Tarleton, *Hist. of the Campaigns of 1780 and 1781 in the Southern Provinces of North America* (1787) ; Chas. Stedman, *Hist. of the Origin, Progress and Termination of the Am. War* (1794) ; Henry Lee, *Memoirs of the War in the Southern Dept. of the U. S.* (1812) ; Wm. Johnson, *Sketches of the Life and Correspondence of Nathanael Greene* (1822) ; J. H. Wheeler, *Hist. Sketches of N. C.* (1851) ; Jas. Graham, *Life of Gen. Daniel Morgan of the Va. Line* (1856) ; C. L. Hunter, *Sketches of Western N. C., Hist. and Biog.* (1877) ; Robt. Henry, *Narrative of the Battle of Cowan's Ford* (1891) ; F. B. Heitman, *Hist. Reg. of Officers of the*

Continental Army (1893); Wm. A. Graham, *Gen. Jos. Graham and His Papers on N. C. Revolutionary Hist.* (1904); S. A. Ashe, *Biog. Hist. of N. C.*, vol. IV (1906).]　　　　　　　　　　　F. E. R.

DAVIE, WILLIAM RICHARDSON (June 20, 1756–Nov. 29, 1820), Revolutionary soldier, governor of North Carolina, was born at Egremont, Cumberlandshire, England. Taken by his father, Archibald Davie, to the Waxhaw settlement, S. C., in 1763, he was there adopted by his maternal uncle, William Richardson, a Presbyterian clergyman. He attended Queen's Museum College, Charlotte, N. C., and Princeton, where, after about four years of study and a bit of military service in New York, he graduated with first honors in 1776. Though he at once began to study law at Salisbury, N. C., and was licensed to practise in 1780, he chiefly pursued war during the next seven years. After three months' service under Gen. Allen Jones in the Camden region during 1777–78, he helped raise a troop of cavalry near Salisbury and received successive commissions as lieutenant, captain, and major. Joining Pulaski's division, he was seriously wounded on June 20, 1779, while leading a charge at Stono, near Charleston. After a slow recovery he raised another troop early in the next year, equipping it partly from a bequest from his uncle. Operating north of Waxhaw Creek, independently or with Sumter, he kept the Patriot cause alive in western North Carolina despite Tarleton and the numerous Loyalists. When Gates fled from Camden, Davie, now a colonel, acting contrary to that general's orders, thrust his little command to the rear, saved valuable equipment, fought a reckless but brilliant rear-guard action at Charlotte on Sept. 26, 1780, and continued to harass Cornwallis until the latter retreated into South Carolina in October. Having in these glorious six months proved himself not only a daring and skilful individual fighter but also an alert and resourceful commander, Davie was seeking a separate command when Gen. Greene enlisted him as commissary-general for the Carolina campaign and procured his appointment in a similar capacity by the North Carolina Board of War on Jan. 16, 1781. Though almost without funds, he succeeded in feeding Greene's army and the state militia to the satisfaction of that general, who liked him and kept him with him from Guilford Court House to Ninety-six (March–May 1781). Davie detested his work and resented bitterly the inevitable criticism, but persisted in the office until it was discontinued and his voluminous accounts were fully made up.

Settling at Halifax, N. C., in 1782, he married Sarah Jones, daughter of his old commander and niece of Willie Jones, who brought him a fine farm and eventually bore him six children. For the next fifteen years he rode the circuits of the state, save the westernmost, as a lawyer. Soon he was appearing in all the important civil cases, and for the defense in every capital case. Men ranked him with Alfred Moore as first of an able bar. Since he liked to argue broad principles rather than precedents, he was helpful in the necessary adjustment of the old law to the new situation. With the instinct of a military man he found the strong points in the case, and brought to bear on them a studied oratory. Tall, elegant, and commanding, he had a mellow and flexible voice and a "lofty and flowing" style which became him well and "astounded and enraptured" his audiences (Hubbard, *post,* p. 83). Representing the borough of Halifax in the legislature of North Carolina almost continuously from 1786 to 1798, he more than any one else was responsible for the action of that body in ordering the revision and codification of the laws, the sending of representatives to the constitutional conventions at Annapolis and Philadelphia, the cession of Tennessee to the Union, and endeavoring to fix disputed state boundaries. He was chiefly responsible for the establishment, location, building, and endowment of the University of North Carolina, selected its instructors and planned for it an elastic curriculum that included literary and social studies as well as the familiar mathematics and classics. As Grand Master of the Masons he laid the cornerstone of its first two buildings. The University, in turn, awarded him its first honorary degree and dubbed him "father," years before Jefferson's intellectual child, the University of Virginia, was born. The state made him commander of its troops in 1797, chairman of its boundary commissions, and governor in 1798.

These honors and achievements can by no means be ascribed to politics; for North Carolina was thoroughly Democratic and Davis was not. In the Federal Convention, though he represented a large state, he swung his delegation to the "Connecticut Compromise," lest the movement for stronger government fail. He there favored election of senators and later of presidential electors by the legislature, and strenuously insisted on representation for slave property. In the fight for ratification in North Carolina he was second only to Iredell. While governor he denounced the Virginia and Kentucky Resolutions and accepted appointment from President Adams, first as brigadier-general for the French War, and in 1799 as peace commissioner to France. Returning after an enjoyable year, he advised against Federalist support of Burr as bad policy, but urged the appointment of popular and active men as federal judges since the cause of Federalism depended on their exertions. Under presidential appointment, he negotiated the Tuscarora treaty in 1802 but otherwise waved aside overtures from "that man" Jefferson. His political attitude seems to have been grounded originally on contempt for the war boards, the judges, and the legislators whom democracy thrust up; it was confirmed by the subservience of politicians to Virginia leadership. Refusing either to modify his aristocratic habits or to solicit votes personally, he was eliminated from politics by the Jefferson-Macon machine in the important congressional election of 1803. Disgusted with politics and saddened by the loss of his wife, he retired in 1805 to his plantation, "Tivoli," in Lancaster County, S. C., where he could enjoy farming, friends, horses, and books, and give an occasional bit of advice to his university or make a biting remark about North Carolina politicians. He was the first president of the South Carolina Agricultural Society. Though long an admirer of Madison, he declined appointment as major-general in 1813 and defended the conduct of the New England Federalists during the War of 1812.

[F. W. Hubbard, "Life of W. R. Davie," in Jared Sparks, *The Lib. of Am. Biog.*, ser. 2, vol. XV (1848), an uncritical work but based on papers now lost; sketch by J. G. de R. Hamilton, and letters with notes by Kemp P. Battle in *Jas. Sprunt Hist. Monographs*, No. 7 (1907); Walter Clark in W. J. Peele, *Lives of Distinguished North Carolinians* (1898), for Davie's career as soldier and lawyer; Wm. K. Boyd, *Hist. of N. C., 1783–1860*, vol. II (1919), for his services in the Federal Convention; H. M. Wagstaff, in *Proc. N. C. Lit. and Hist. Asso.*, 1920, for his Federalism; S. A. Ashe, *Biog. Hist. of N. C.*, vol. VI (1905), which should be read in connection with Wm. E. Dodd's sketch of Willis Alston in same work.]   C. C. P.

DAVIES, ARTHUR BOWEN (Sept. 26, 1862–Oct. 24, 1928), painter, was born in Utica, N. Y. His father was a Welsh immigrant, David Thomas Davies, who brought his English wife, Phœbe Loakes, to America, set up a tailor's shop, and interested himself in the Welsh church, and especially in its choir. The marriage was blessed with five children of which Arthur was the fourth. He passed a free and happy boyhood, roving the rich meadows and river terraces of the Mohawk, observing its trees, its windswept vast skies, and the distant rim of its blue hills. He began to draw early, and his parents sympathetically encouraged his bent, putting him under the tutelage of a local painter, Dwight Williams, who, with prophetic intuition of Davies's genius, confined his teaching to sharpening the boy's naturally keen and accurate vi-

sion and inculcating broad principles of composition. Soon the family moved to Chicago, and the youth found casual employment in business with the Board of Trade, working also for a time with an engineering expedition in Mexico. Returning to Chicago after two years in the West, Davies with three young painters undertook and achieved the copying of Munkacsy's gigantic painting of "Christ before Pilate," in the hope that the group might raise money for European study through its exhibition in circuit. The plan failed, but at least it demonstrated that tenacity and athleticism which were no small part of Davies's artistic endowment.

Before and after his two years in Mexico and the West, Davies had studied with Charles Corwin at the Chicago Art Institute. In 1887 he sought new fortunes at New York, pursuing his studies with the Gotham Art Students and at the Art Student's League. Davies's cronies at this time were Robert Henri and George Luks. Falling under the attention of that most open-minded of art editors, Alexander W. Drake of the Century Company, Davies began to draw for *Saint Nicholas*. To the volumes for 1888 and 1889 he was a steady contributor, and thereafter occasionally until 1891. This work, influenced perhaps by the English Pre-Raphaelites, is charming, but it gives little hint of what was to come. Davies was refractory even to the gentlest editorial supervision, and within three years he had abandoned illustration, and a relatively sure success, for poverty and painting. In 1890 he exhibited two small paintings at the National Academy without attracting attention. Marrying Dr. Virginia Merriweather Davis, like himself of Welsh extraction, he retreated to a little farm near the Hudson at Congers, N. Y., where he alternated between tilling the soil and filling his portfolio with sketches of romantic scenery. The Academy continued to accept his small landscapes, and a few were sold. He competed for the decoration of the Appellate Court of New York, and the merits of his design were recognized, but it was feared that a painter barely thirty could not execute the sketch creditably, and the commissions fell to such veterans as Cox, Mowbray, and Simmons.

About 1894 the far-sighted and sympathetic Scotch dealer, William Macbeth, took Davies up, soon gave him a studio over the shop in lower Fifth Avenue, and with the aid of the merchant prince and art collector, Benjamin Altman, sent Davies to Europe. There ensued a sudden and beautiful flowering of his genius. The few canvases of his early days, such as "Along the Erie Canal," in the Phillips Memorial Gallery of

Washington, are notable for their simple composition and fragile harmonies. The pictures were small and invariably idyls. Women and children played, brooded, or merely lived blissfully amid flowers in green paradises embowered with great trees. The pastorals recalled the pensiveness of a Giorgione or a Watteau, but were also oddly near to our common experience. Every posture and gesture had been observed and lived. These denizens of an Arcadia were after all akin to real women and children. One felt that the Arcadia itself was real, and that a sufficiently searching eye might find it round the corner. In short, Davies had created his illusion without much departing from the look of things. One of the richest of these early pictures is the "Fantasy of the Vine," a lovely arrangement of nudes in landscape. There is a hint of Puvis in it, though it is far richer in color. In general it is idle to try to trace influences in Davies. Being of a curious and scholarly disposition, he drew from many sources, but from none overtly or constantly. For the little idyls of the nineties the moment was unpropitious. Conservative taste still favored the artificial polish of the French Institute; radical taste was attached to the various naturalisms of Courbet, Manet, and the Impressionists. In the nineties in New York one could buy the idyls of Monticelli, akin to Davies's, though more flimsy and fantastic, for a matter of twenty-five dollars. Still, under Mr. Macbeth's tactful and convincing championship, Davies became the idol of a cult, whose spokesman in criticism was soon to be the brilliant and enthusiastic James G. Huneker. There ensued a modest prosperity, more frequent trips to Europe, the beginnings of what was to be a notable art collection. To many art-lovers the idyls which Davies produced between his thirtieth and fortieth years are still his best work. They early passed into the hands of discriminating amateurs, and for the most part are now in private collections.

About the turn of the century his style changed. The canvases are somewhat larger, the color is cooler and more limited in range, the scene is vaster, and its denizens are no longer women and children one might see, but abstract figures, frequently nude, symbolizing poetical ideas. The forms are now moderately distorted for the sake of greater compositional coherence. If in the early idyls one thought of Giorgione and Schiavone, now one divined Blake of the prophetic books. The material is less rich, the meaning more various, recondite, and profound. Some of his best pictures are transitional; such as "Four O'Clock Ladies," in the Phillips Memorial Gallery, in which the old idyllic theme of girls at play is treated in the new technique and with the new breadth. The pictures in this second manner have passed into the public galleries. The Phillips Memorial Gallery, which is rich in every phase of Davies's work, has five or six; the Metropolitan has "The Girdle of Ares"; and the Chicago Art Institute, "Leda and the Dioscuri"; but many of the best pictures are in private collections. In this adventure in symbolism and mythology, Davies's work kept its actuality. The forms, whether human figures or the architecture of trees and earth, had been justly observed before their ultimate pictorial transformation. Nothing was flimsy or improvised. He drew incessantly in every medium, and he kept and classified his drawings. They were of every sort, but most were of the nude in every posture and in every scale. Many of the drawings were complete and elaborate compositions. There must be thousands of these studies. No artist of our day has made such rich and intense preparation. It is this element of probity that keeps the sanity and soundness of Davies's art even in its most sublimated flights and even through its not infrequent preciosities. In his last fifteen years he occasionally perpetuated these exercises in admirable lithographs and etchings which are quintessential for his talent and accessible to those who cannot own or see his pictures.

It was inevitable that a man of Davies's mobile yet strenuous intelligence should respond to those modernists who sought a new basis for the arts in an unlimited emotionalism or in an equally unlimited intellectualization. And it was as inevitable that he should find his affinities, not with the Expressionist Left, but with the Intellectualist Right which found expression in that Cubism which in turn stemmed from Cézanne. His own experiments in this direction, dating from about 1914, were moderate enough. In the main he employed geometrical surface patterns, and sought to create a sense of space without evoking a specific place. A large frieze of dancing figures and the decoration of a private music room in New York are the more permanent products of this adventure, which was also very variously pursued in his lithographs and etchings. These experiments may be taken at best as a mere episode in a varied career, or at worst as an interesting aberration of a versatile and distinguished mind.

Davies's single public gesture was made in connection with the modernistic movement. Accepting the presidency of the Society of Independent Artists, he arranged the memorable Armory Show of 1913, in which, beside a full representation of the so-called Post-Impressionists and Cubists and Futurists, was hung a series of fine pictures from a century back. It was an informing and liberating effort, bringing into the art atmosphere of New York, and for that matter of America, which had gone very stale, a salutary whiff of contention and ideas. It was the single public act of a habitual recluse, and a notable one. Davies fought for his privacy, and his personal dignity and reticence served him as a good defense. Of middle stature, black-haired, slight and alert, with gray eyes that would have been sharp except that his gaze seemed directed inward, Davies to a superficial observer might readily have seemed an efficient university professor or an intellectual West Pointer. He never saw you first, but if you addressed him he responded charmingly and with tact. When people began to find and visit his studio, he took a new one. But his seclusion was enriched by strong family ties, by a few firm friendships, by much reading and speculation, and by an incredible amount of work.

It may be doubted whether, following precedent, one should speak of a third manner for Davies. After a trip to California, in 1905, his landscapes inspired by the Sierras are larger; and in his later years the figure composition in his mythologies and abstractions are more dense and elaborate, more closely knit with the lines and forms of the landscape, and tend to assume the form of a frieze. Perhaps the most instructive picture of the latest phase is "Movement of Waters," in a private collection. Here the group of nudes in the foreground surges and sinks with the rhythm of the waves behind. It would be easy to find the accord too conscious and farfetched, and difficult to deny its ingenuity and distinction.

Always a devout admirer of Greek art, Davies sought to discover its principles. Thus a few years before his death he worked out the theory that the peculiar vitality of Greek art, its sense of aspiration, lay in its use of the act of inhalation. The figure is caught as it inhales, the stroke is drawn while the artist inhales. The act centralizes, informs, and energizes the posture and the stroke. The theory is developed at length by Davies's friend the archeologist, Dr. Gustavus Eisen (in *Phillips Publications* no. 3). Perhaps this conscious control of the breathing while working may have contributed to that weakness of heart from which Davies died. The warning came in 1923. After a seizure, he lay alone and helpless for many hours in his studio. Travel and apparent convalescence led to even more relentless activity. He practised small sculpture,

prepared for new mural decorations, made tapestry designs which were executed by the Gobelins, did admirable mural decorations, now free from Cubist mannerism, in International House, New York. His fame grew rapidly, and brought unavoidable interruptions. He decided to spend half of every year in Europe. As he was passing from Paris to Florence, amid the mountains of Italy, the fatal attack came. He died in Florence unknown, on Oct. 24, 1928, having just entered his sixty-seventh year. The news did not reach his family in America for six weeks. It was a characteristic end for a spirit which had ever courted solitude. He received few official honors, for the reason that he did not value them, and rarely exhibited where they were awarded. Among them were the silver medal of the Pan-American Exposition, Buffalo, 1901, an honorable mention at the Carnegie Institute, Pittsburgh, and the W. A. Clark Prize and Corcoran gold medal, Washington, 1916.

[Appreciations and some biographical material may be found in "Arthur B. Davies: Essays on the Man and his Art" in *Phillips Pubs.* no. 3 (1924), and in F. Newlin Price, *Etchings and Lithographs by Arthur B. Davies* (1929). The earliest substantial critical recognition of Davies was that by Samuel Isham in his *Hist. of Am. Painting* (1905). Jas. G. Huneker was thereafter Davies's constant champion in the N. Y. *Sun.* See also Huneker's *The Pathos of Distance* (1913); *Art in America*, Oct. 1918, Aug. 1929; *Art Digest*, Jan. 1929; *Am. Mag. of Art*, Feb. 1929; *Art News*, Apr. 27, 1929; *Art and Archæology*, Sept. 1916; *International Studio*, Feb. 1921, June 1922, June 1923.] F. J. M., Jr.

DAVIES, HENRY EUGENE (July 2, 1836–Sept. 6, 1894), Union soldier, was born in New York City, the son of Henry Ebenezer and Rebecca Waldo (Tappan) Davies. His original immigrant ancestor was John Davies, who came from Herefordshire to Litchfield, Conn., in 1735. After spending a year at Harvard and a year at Williams, Henry graduated at Columbia in 1857, studied law, was admitted to the bar, and began to practise. On Aug. 10, 1858, he married Julia daughter of John T. Rich. His first military service was as captain in the 5th New York Infantry (mustered in May 9, 1861), but he was appointed major, Aug. 1, 1861, in the 2nd New York Cavalry (called the Harris Light Cavalry), and remained in the mounted service for the rest of the war. As it was a part of McDowell's corps, his regiment remained near Washington when the army moved in the spring of 1862, and so did not participate in the Peninsular campaign. Under Judson Kilpatrick, who was its lieutenant-colonel and later its colonel, it had some experience in skirmishes, and saw its first hard fighting at the second battle of Bull Run. From that time it served with the Army of the Potomac, but took no part in the battle of Gettysburg, being at Westminster, Md., with the rest of the brigade. Until he was advanced to higher command, Davies served with it constantly, being promoted lieutenant-colonel, Dec. 6, 1862, and colonel, June 16, 1863. He was appointed brigadier-general of volunteers, Sept. 16, 1863, and commanded brigades in the second and third divisions of the Cavalry Corps until after Appomattox, occasionally holding temporary command of a division. He took part in the great raids toward Richmond in 1864, and in the cavalry operations which immediately preceded Lee's surrender. He was appointed major-general of volunteers, May 4, 1865, and resigned from the army, Jan. 1, 1866. After the war he returned to the practise of law in New York, was for a time public administrator for the city, and was later assistant district-attorney for the southern district of New York. In the latter part of his life he made his home at Fishkill. He published *Ten Days on the Plains* (1871); a genealogical work, the *Davies Memoir* (1895); and a biography, *General Sheridan* (1895). He died at Middleboro, Mass. Though without early military training, he was a cavalryman by instinct, and quickly learned his trade. His rise was steady and was well earned. Gen. Rodenbough describes him as "unpolished, genial, gallant" (*Battles and Leaders of the Civil War*, 1887–88, IV, 188.)

[*Davies Memoir* (1895); F. B. Heitman, *Hist. Reg. and Dict. U. S. Army* (1903), I, 356; *Official Records* (*Army*), ser. 1, vols. XII (pt. 1), XXIX (pt. 1), XXXIII, XXXVI (pt. 1), XL (pt. 1), XLII (pts. 1, 2, 3), XLVI (pts. 1, 2, 3).]   T. M. S.

DAVIES, SAMUEL (Nov. 3, 1723–Feb. 4, 1761), fourth president of the College of New Jersey, now Princeton, was born in New Castle County, Del. He was the son of David and Martha (Thomas) Davies, both of Welsh extraction. His mother early determined that the boy should be trained for the ministry, and with that end in view he was enrolled in the famous school of Samuel Blair at Fagg's Manor, Pa. He was licensed to preach by the Presbytery of New Castle on July 30, 1746, and on Oct. 23 of that year married Sarah Kirkpatrick. Ordained as an evangelist on Feb. 19, 1747, he was forthwith sent to Virginia on evangelical service. His first wife having died, on Oct. 4, 1748, he was married to Jean, daughter of John Holt of Hanover County, Va.

In Virginia dissenters were frowned upon, and the activities of their preachers were made the subject of strict surveillance. When Davies settled in Hanover County there were many suits in court against Presbyterians for holding forbidden assemblies and preaching without license from the General Court. He made the cause of the non-conformists his own, and was soon regarded as the advocate and defender of their civil rights and liberties. Though always in feeble health he spared neither his body nor his time in his proselytizing efforts. Almost single-handed he built up a strong Presbyterian membership in Virginia. He conducted services in seven houses of worship scattered through five counties; and in addition traveled over the whole state organizing revival meetings. He was "the animating soul of the whole dissenting interest in Virginia and North Carolina" (Collins, *post,* 59).

In 1753, with Gilbert Tennant, he was commissioned by the Synod of New York to go to the British Isles and endeavor to raise funds for the College of New Jersey, which since its inception in 1747 had been in straitened circumstances. The envoys were eminently successful. Over £3,000 were raised; the larger portion among loyal Presbyterians of Scotland. To Davies, despite his youth, for he was but thirty, came renown. In England and Scotland he delivered some sixty sermons, many of which were distributed and widely read. As a result of his work for the college he became intimately associated with Jonathan Edwards, Aaron Burr, Sr., and others of its supporters. Immediately after his journey he returned to Virginia, where in the latter part of 1755, largely through his instrumentality, the Presbytery of Hanover, the first presbytery in Viginia, was founded.

Two years later occurred the death of President Burr of the College of New Jersey, and within a few weeks that of his successor, Jonathan Edwards. The trustees, after a considerable delay, elected Samuel Davies to the presidency. He felt constrained for a time to reject the offer, since faction was rife among the trustees, but finally, yielding to their importunities, he took office on July 26, 1759. On Feb. 4, 1761, he died of pneumonia. During his brief régime, however, he inaugurated several important changes. The standard for the bachelor's degree was raised and the requirements for admission were strengthened. Plans for a more suitable library were made, but these were interrupted by his death. Although his career was short, Davies left behind an enviable record. Lacking the educational background of his predecessors, he had attained the presidency of the College of New Jersey. He had also achieved the reputation of being the greatest pulpit orator of his generation. For fifty years after his death, his sermons were more widely read than those of any of his contemporaries.

[See John Maclean, *Hist. of the Coll. of N. J.* (1877); V. L. Collins, *Princeton* (1914); J. DeWitt,

Planting of Princeton Coll. (1897) ; J. F. Hageman, *Hist. of Princeton and its Institutions* (1879) ; J. W. Wilson, *An Hist. Sketch of the Coll. of N. J.* (1859) ; W. B. Sprague, *Annals Am. Pulpit*, vol. III (1858) ; H. A. Davis, *The Davis Family* (1927). Davies's writings, largely addresses and sermons, are listed in Maclean, vol. I, 245. A complete collection is in the Princeton Univ. Library.]   J. E. P.

DAVIESS, JOSEPH HAMILTON [See DAVEISS, JOSEPH HAMILTON, 1774–1811.]

DAVIESS, MARIA THOMPSON (Nov. 25, 1872–Sept. 3, 1924), painter, author, daughter of John Burton Thompson and Leonora (Hamilton) Daviess, was born in Harrodsburg, Ky., and died in New York City. Her father belonged to a family long prominent in Kentucky, and his mother, whose full name he gave to his daughter, was a woman of considerable literary interests and performance. He died early and his widow with her children took up residence at her family home, Nashville, Tenn. There, except for long visits to her father's relatives in Kentucky, Maria spent all of her childhood. After attending the Nashville Young Ladies' College and the Hill School in Shelbyville, Ky., she entered Wellesley, where she remained (1891–92) until her mother's ill health necessitated her being at home. She studied in the (Nashville) Peabody Art School, and, after her mother's death, spent two years (1902–04) in various schools of art in Paris. In 1904–05 specimens of her painting were exhibited in the Paris Salon. Returning to Nashville in the summer of 1904, she taught art, and during the next few years maintained a studio of photography, miniature painting, jewelry design—and general discussion for the local illuminati. Almost by accident she discovered that she could write stories acceptable to the juvenile readers of Sunday-school magazines, and in 1909 her *Miss Selina Lue and the Soapbox Babies* made it evident that she could please also many persons of more advanced years. By 1920 she had published thirteen other books, romances for the most part, all thin and sentimental, but all popular, inspired by a quick, ebullient, amiably disposed mind. Her best-known work, *The Melting of Molly* (1912), attained the distinction of being rendered into drama and motion picture. Some of her other books had distinct and aggressive aims: *The Tinderbox* (1913), to advance the cause of woman suffrage; *Over Paradise Ridge* (1915), to check the flow of population from farm to city; *The Heart's Kingdom* (1917), to solve religious difficulties; and *The Matrix* (1920), to emphasize the extent of the nation's indebtedness to Lincoln's mother. Most of these purposes were restated along with many convictions of hers in her autobiography, *Seven Times Seven,* presented in seven "reels," as she named her chapters, during 1924. As soon as the income from her books warranted her doing so she bought a farm near Nashville and lived on it when she was not more attracted to New York. During the World War in 1917–18 she was commissioned by the government to go about making speeches to show the importance of food conservation. For the last five years of her life she suffered pitiably from articular rheumatism.

[Sources not already mentioned: *Who's Who in America*, 1924–25 ; *N. Y. Times*, Sept. 4, 1924 ; *Nashville Banner*, Sept. 4, 1924.]   J. D. W.

DAVIS, ALEXANDER JACKSON (July 24, 1803–Jan. 14, 1892), architect, was born in New York City, the son of Cornelius Davis, editor of the *New York Theological Magazine,* bookseller and publisher of religious books, and of Julia Jackson, his second wife. As a boy he showed marked talent for drawing, and at the age of seventeen he was, according to Dunlap (*post*), a compositor in a printer's shop in Florida, N. Y. When twenty years old, he was again in New York City and a member of the "Antique School" which met in the rooms of the Philosophical Society. He early began a series of views of important buildings in New York and was soon busy with other illustration work in the course of which he made two trips to New England, in 1827 and 1828. These produced a famous view of the State House in Boston, drawn directly on stone, the best example of architectural lithography produced up to that time in America. During his early twenties Davis was also working, probably as an apprentice, with J. C. Brady, an architect in New York City, under whom he made an intensive study of Greek detail. He was later employed as draftsman by Ithiel Town [*q.v.*], who had just come to New York from New Haven, for whom Davis made such a beautiful elevation of his Connecticut capitol design at New Haven, that Town took him in as an associate and on Feb. 1, 1829, they opened an office together. Their first important work was the New York Customs House in 1832 (still standing on the northeast corner of Wall and Nassau streets, although the interior was never completed according to their wishes). From this time on, the firm of Town & Davis was continuously busy with a large amount of work, some of it of great importance. After 1843 Davis practised by himself for over thirty years. The complete list of the buildings designed by him, and by the firm of Town & Davis, includes outstanding examples of every style fashionable in America from 1820 to 1880.

The high reputation of the firm is witnessed by the four state capitols entrusted to it: Indiana (1832–35); North Carolina (1831), in association with David Paton; Illinois (1837, altered and enlarged from Davis's designs, 1866–67); and Ohio (1839), where Davis acted as expert and produced a design in association with Thomas U. Walter, Martin E. Thompson, and Thomas Cole. In addition, Davis was the designer of the Patent Office, Washington, D. C. (1832); the Pauper Lunatic Asylum, Blackwell's Island, New York City (1834); the Wadsworth Atheneum, Hartford (1842); the assembly hall of the University of North Carolina (1844); buildings for the Virginia Military Institute (1852, 1859); Alumni Hall at Yale (1852), destroyed to make way for Wright Hall; the North Carolina Hospital for the Insane (1852); and Davidson College, North Carolina (1858). Besides all this public work, Davis designed many churches, commercial buildings, and private houses in New York and in the country, and after his retirement, he claimed to have designed more buildings than any other living American architect. In addition, he made many studies for buildings executed by others, e.g., Haviland's Egyptian design for the Tombs, New York City, which Davis maintained was adapted from one of his unexecuted sketches, this claim being borne out by a drawing in the Metropolitan Museum.

The chief characteristic of Davis as designer and draftsman is his meticulous care. This appears even in drawings of his student days, which are frequently rendered with painstaking beauty and exquisite finish. It is this quality which sets his lithographs of the America of 1820 apart from so many of the engravings and drawings of the time. Their accuracy is unimpeachable, and by their quality they give perfectly the atmosphere of the place and period. It is this same quality which gives such soundness to his Greek Revival work, as in the New York Customs House and the Patent Office at Washington. Alert to the intellectual movement of the day, he frequently anticipated popular taste. His Gilmer house in Baltimore (1832) and the buildings for the University of Michigan (1838) are remarkably advanced examples of Gothic for their period. Yet he was not tied to any current style, for the Stevens "palace" in New York (1845), perhaps his finest work, returns to the Greek Revival for its details, although it is freely composed. Davis's drawings (preserved in the Metropolitan Museum and the New York Historical Society) comprise dozens of schemes for museums, libraries, and public buildings of all kinds, which show not only a consistent feeling for logical planning, but also an inventive mind, continually irked by the limitations of his period. Despite Davis's training in the strict use of Greek forms, and later in the romanticism of the Victorian Gothic, he was not blind to the architectural possibilities of metal. Town & Davis were responsible for the first iron shop-front in New York (for the Lyceum of Natural History in 1835), and in an undated drawing for a building at 751 Broadway (New York Historical Society) there is an amazingly modern expression of vertical lines, the front consisting merely of slim vertical marble shafts, the spaces between entirely filled with glass and bronze. One of many sketches for the New York Post Office (1867–68, Metropolitan Museum) shows a huge circular building with a central circular tower, running up several stories, whose windows are treated in the same way, with metal panels between them, so that the masonry piers run through unbroken.

From the beginning of his professional career, Davis was in the center of the artistic life of New York. Dunlap remarks that the great architectural library of Ithiel Town was a center of interest in his day, and Davis's wide acquaintance among those interested in the arts is evidenced by his membership in numerous societies. He was one of a committee of three appointed by a group of architects who had met in New York to arrange and issue the call for the first meeting of the American Institute of Architects in Philadelphia, in May 1837. Although thus a founder of the A. I. A., he fell out of sympathy with it in his later life, and, despite many efforts on its part to renew his membership, he consistently refused to return. He was the author of Views of the Public Buildings in the City of New York (published without date, probably prior to 1830); and Rural Residences, Consisting of Designs Original and Selected for Cottages, Farmhouses, Villas and Village Churches (1837). On July 14, 1853, he married Margaret Beale, at Florida, N. Y. Instrumental in 1857 in the founding of Llewellyn Park, West Orange, N. J., he spent his later years near there, at his home, "Wildmont," where he died.

[Wm. Dunlap, Hist. of the Rise and Progress of the Arts of Design in the U. S. (new ed., 1918, III, 210) has an account of Davis's work up to the date of its first edition, 1834. S. A. Ashe, in an address reprinted in the N. C. Hist. Commission Pubs. (Bull. No. 4, Mar. 12, 1909) gives almost entire credit for the N. C. capitol to Paton, but this is not borne out by original drawings in the Metropolitan Museum and the N. Y. Hist. Soc. See also: manuscript papers of the A. A. F. A. in the N. Y. Hist. Soc.; "An Architect of the Romantic Era," by Richard H. Platt in House and Garden, Oct. 1927 (LII, 122); N. Y. Herald and N. Y. Tribune, Jan. 17, 1892; Appletons' Annual Cyc., 1892, p. 543.] T. F. H.

DAVIS, ANDREW JACKSON (Aug. 11, 1826–Jan. 13, 1910), spiritualist, the son of Samuel Davis, was born in Blooming Grove, Orange County, N. Y. His father, a stern, poverty-stricken shoemaker, given to drink, was totally uneducated, as was also his mother, a woman with a weak body but with strong visionary powers. They moved frequently from one small New York town to another without seeming to better themselves. Some time prior to 1842 they finally settled in Poughkeepsie, N. Y., whence Davis later received his name of "the Poughkeepsie Seer." His academic education consisted of a total of five months' schooling acquired at different periods of a few weeks each. He declares in his autobiography (written about 1857) that he had read only one book, but this statement was probably not literally true. At the age of fifteen he was apprenticed to a shoemaker and when he seemed incapable of learning the trade was employed by a merchant in a general store; but he was a failure at this latter occupation as well. In 1843 at the age of seventeen, he allowed a Profesor Grimes, who visited Poughkeepsie and performed mesmeric miracles at the town hall, to attempt to hypnotize him. The attempt was unsuccessful, but a few weeks later William Levingston, a local tailor and amateur mesmeric philosopher, succeeded in "magnetizing" him. The result was such a "rare clairvoyance" that Levingston gave up his own business and devoted his whole time to Davis and to using his "clairvoyant" powers for the cure of disease. After two years during which Davis was subject to the will and hypnotism of Levingston, he had his first "psychic flight through space" in January 1844. Davis supposed himself influenced while in the trance state by a number of persons and particularly by Swedenborg whom he believed to have guided his steps personally from the time he was twenty-one. A "clairvoyant clinic" which he opened at Poughkeepsie and which extended to Bridgeport had but indifferent success. By 1845 he felt the urge to turn from healing to writing. He selected as magnetizer, Dr. S. S. Lyon, a Bridgeport physician, and as reporter and scribe, the Rev. William Fishbough. From Nov. 28, 1845, to Jan. 25, 1847, he delivered in Manhattan, while in a state of trance, one hundred and fifty-seven lectures. These, copied down verbatim by the Rev. Fishbough, constituted his *Principles of Nature, Her Divine Revelations, and a Voice to Mankind,* published in 1847. In this strange mélange of occult history, mysticism, philosophy, and science, critics have discerned likenesses to the works of Swedenborg and Brisbane. Next came *The Great Harmonia* (1850–

52) and from 1851 to 1885 a long succession of twenty-six works in all, of which perhaps the most important, aside from two autobiographical works, were *The Philosophy of Spiritual Intercourse* (1856), *The Penetralia* (1856), *A Stellar Key to the Summer Land* (1867), *Views of our Heavenly Home* (1878), and *The Children's Progressive Lyceum* (1893). *The Great Harmonia* and all subsequent publications were written without the assistance of magnetism; thus marking Davis's transition from mesmerism to spiritualism. Davis was best known for his "clairvoyant" prescriptions for disease and for his idea of the Children's Lyceum or Spiritualist Sunday School. He was twice married. His first wife died Nov. 2, 1853. Two years later he married Mrs. Mary (Robinson) Love, who, like his first wife, was a divorcée.

Davis belongs to the interregnum between mesmerism and spiritualism; he practised both but was wholly identified with neither. In common with transcendentalism and the idealistic socialism of his day, he preached social reconstruction as going hand in hand with spiritual regeneration. He gave modern spiritualism much of its phraseology and first formulated its underlying principles.

[*The Magic Staff* (1857), an autobiography of Davis, and its sequel, *Beyond the Valley* (1885); E. C. Hartmann, *Who's Who in Occultism* (1927); G. B. Butt in the *Occult Rev.*, Mar. 1925; W. B. Pickens and W. H. Evans, articles on Davis in *Light* for 1925 and 1926; Frank Podmore, *Modern Spiritualism*, vol. I (1902).]

H. W. S.
R. R.

DAVIS, ANDREW McFARLAND (Dec. 30, 1833–Mar. 29, 1920), author, antiquarian, was born at Worcester, Mass., youngest son of John Davis, governor of Massachusetts, and a descendant of Dolor Davis, who came to America in 1634. His mother was Eliza Bancroft, sister of George Bancroft [*q.v.*], the historian. He was educated at the public schools of Worcester, with the intention of entering Harvard College; but his uncle secured for him an appointment to the Naval Academy at Annapolis, and for three years he remained in service, being attached to the Mediterranean Squadron. He then entered the Lawrence Scientific School of Harvard College, receiving the degree of B.S. in 1854. For a brief period he was employed on railroads in the Southern and Middle states. Within a few years he returned to Worcester, studied law, and was admitted to the bar in 1859. He entered the office of his brother, John C. B. Davis [*q.v.*], in New York, counsel of the Erie Railroad, and was employed by that company as general freight agent. When Gould and Fisk obtained control of the Erie, he resigned and moved with his family to San Francisco, where he joined his brother Horace [q.v.], already engaged in flour milling. For a time he served as president of the board of education of San Francisco. In 1882 he returned to Cambridge, Mass., where he henceforth made his home. He abandoned active business pursuits, and devoted his leisure time to research, particularly in the field of American colonial history. Among his earliest contributions, in 1887, were chapters in Justin Winsor's *Narrative and Critical History of America*: "Canada and Louisiana" (vol. V, pp. 1–63) and "The Indians and the Border Warfare in the Revolution" (vol. VI, pp. 605–47). His antiquarian interest soon centered upon the history of currency and banking experiments in the colony of Massachusetts; on these topics he wrote many papers and monographs which showed exhaustive research in original documents, diaries, and account books. He was a member of the American Antiquarian Society, Massachusetts Historical Society, Colonial Society of Massachusetts, New-England Historic Genealogical Society, and Fellow of the American Academy of Arts and Sciences. The results of his studies were first presented before these societies, and in printed form are to be found scattered in their proceedings. The studies dealing with colonial currency were incorporated into an extended treatise, "Currency and Banking in the Province of the Massachusetts Bay," which appeared in *Publications of the American Economic Association* (Pt. I, "Currency," ser. 3, vol. I, December 1900, pp. 692–1173; Pt. II, "Banking," ser. 3, vol. II, May 1901, pp. 293–632). He performed a useful and lasting service in editing reprints of pamphlets which appeared in the early eighteenth century in Massachusetts in connection with the currency controversy. These appeared as: *Tracts Relating to the Currency of the Massachusetts Bay, 1682–1720* (1902); and *The Colonial Currency Reprints, 1682–1751,* four volumes in Publications of the Prince Society (Boston, 1910–11). In this latter collection there are fifty-eight reprints, to which Davis added many notes. He also prepared a monograph for the National Monetary Commission on "The Origin of the National Banking System" (published as *Senate Document No. 582,* 61 Cong. 2 Sess., 1910), and "Certain Old Chinese Notes or Chinese Paper Money" (*Proceedings of the American Academy of Arts and Sciences* for June 1915, vol. L, pp. 245–86).

Davis had a strong, alert personality, and impressed some as brusque. His friends, however, found him sympathetic and warm-hearted. The brief tribute of the Council of the Colonial Society of Massachusetts summed up his characteristics as: "Blunt, witty, sagacious, generous, tender-hearted, and dependable." He married Henrietta Parker Whitney Oct. 23, 1862, and had four children.

[H. H. Edes in *Proc. Mass. Hist. Soc.,* LIII (1920), 141–45, and "Memoir" by Wm. Roscoe Thayer, in *Proc. Mass. Hist. Soc.,* LIV (1922), 204–11.]

D. R. D.

DAVIS, CHARLES HENRY (Jan. 16, 1807–Feb. 18, 1877), naval officer, born in Boston, youngest of the thirteen children of Daniel Davis, solicitor general of Massachusetts, and Lois (Freeman) Davis, came of pure New England stock. He was accurately described by his friend, Admiral Samuel F. Du Pont, as "a man of science and a practical officer, keeping the love of science subordinate to the regular duties of his profession." After preparation in the Boston Latin School and two years at Harvard, he was appointed midshipman, and sailed in January 1824 in the frigate *United States* for the west coast of South America. There transferred to the schooner *Dolphin,* he had the novel experience of a year's cruise in the South Seas. After his return in 1827 he took his examination for lieutenant, standing sixth of the thirty-nine who passed, and was then in the Mediterranean in the *Ontario,* 1829–32, flag lieutenant in the *Vincennes,* 1833–35, and in the *Independence* on a voyage to Russia and thence to Brazil, 1837–41. Between cruises he studied mathematics at Harvard, and after this last cruise took his degree. He was married in 1842 to Harriette Blake Mills, daughter of Elijah Hunt Mills, and maintained his home at Cambridge, Mass., until after the Civil War.

The next fifteen years were taken up with scientific work connected with the navy. In charge of the coast survey from Rhode Island north, Davis made the first thorough study of the dangerous waters around Nantucket; served on numerous harbor commissions; and published two notable scientific articles, "A Memoir upon the Geological Action of the Tidal and Other Currents of the Ocean" (*Memoirs American Academy,* vol. IV, n.s. 1849), and "The Law of Deposit of the Flood Tide" (*Smithsonian Contributions to Knowledge,* vol. III, 1852). He was a prime mover in establishing the *American Ephemeris and Nautical Almanac* in 1849, and supervised its publication at Cambridge until 1855 and again 1859–62. Enlisting the aid of scientific leaders in this work, he brought the navy into profitable cooperation with scientific progress. He was one of the founders of the National Academy of Sciences in 1863. Promoted to commander in 1854, he resumed sea duty in command of the *St. Mary's* in the Pacific, 1856–59, during which service he secured the release of the filibuster William Walker and his followers besieged at Rivas, Nicaragua.

At the outbreak of the Civil War he became practically executive head of the new Bureau of Detail for selecting and assigning officers; and his alert mind, facility in writing, and great capacity for work led to his appointment on several important commissions engaged in planning and organizing the naval war. The active board for consideration of measures for effectually blockading the South Atlantic Coast, of which he was a member and secretary, planned the expeditions against Hatteras Inlet and Port Royal and was in no small measure responsible for the earlier naval strategy of the war. Appointed Du Pont's fleet captain in the latter expedition, Davis organized the immense flotilla, took charge of sounding and buoying Port Royal Channel, and, with Du Pont, should be given considerable credit for the admirable plan of attack (Nov. 7, 1861), which was later imitated by Dewey at Manila. Recalled to Washington in February 1862, Davis in May assumed command of the Upper Mississippi gunboat flotilla above Fort Pillow. His position was singularly difficult and required generosity and tact as well as leadership, for Foote, on sick leave, was left in titular command until June 17, and the rams under Ellet, though operating with Davis, were under the War Department and outside his control. On May 10, the day after his arrival, the Confederate flotilla delivered a sharp attack which was repulsed, several vessels on both sides being disabled. When the Confederate army evacuated Fort Pillow, Davis moved down to Memphis, where on June 6 his five gunboats, with Ellet's rams, destroyed or captured seven of the eight Confederate vessels. He now joined Farragut before Vicksburg. In discussing plans for destroying the ram *Arkansas,* which had run through the whole Union fleet and taken refuge under the guns of Vicksburg, Davis's judgment came in sharp though friendly conflict with the impetuosity of Farragut. This spirit of discretion, remarked upon by Secretary Welles (*Diary of Gideon Welles,* 1911, I, 158) as a reason for the later appointment of Porter to the flotilla, was perhaps a weakness in Davis since recklessness was warranted by the Northern superiority of means; and, rightly or wrongly, it operated against his selection for high sea-command later in the war. Commissioned chief of the Bureau of Navigation in July 1862, Davis did not turn over his

command until September. In his Washington post, which included the old Bureau of Detail and supervision of all scientific activities of the navy, he did important administrative work until 1865. Thereafter he was superintendent of the Naval Observatory for two years, and following command on the Brazilian station, 1867–69, and at the Norfolk Navy Yard, 1870–73, was again at the Observatory until his death. Of his three sons, Charles Henry [*q.v.*] became a rear admiral, the others dying young; of his three daughters, one married Brooks Adams and another, Henry Cabot Lodge. Senator Lodge (*Early Memories,* 1913, p. 195) describes his father-in-law as a most charming and lovable man, "handsome and distinguished looking," with perfect manners. This glowing tribute is borne out by the admiral's popularity in the service. A lover of literature as well as science, he combined intellectual distinction with well-proved capacity for active administration and command.

[In addition to the excellent *Life of Chas. Henry Davis, Rear Admiral, 1807–1877* (1899), by Chas. H. Davis, there is a brief sketch by the same author in *Biog. Memoirs, Nat. Acad. Sci.,* vol. IV. See also Hiram Paulding, *Jour. of a Cruise of the U. S. Schooner Dolphin,* etc. (1831), and the various Civil War records.]

A. W.

DAVIS, CHARLES HENRY (Aug. 28, 1845–Dec. 27, 1921), naval officer, son of Charles Henry Davis [*q.v.*] and Harriette Blake (Mills) Davis, was born and brought up in Cambridge, Mass. Though without similar opportunities for wartime distinction, his career followed closely that of his father, whom he resembled in scientific bent and versatility of mind. At sixteen he entered the Naval Academy, then at Newport, graduating in November 1864. The following winter he was in the receiving ship at New York, and during the next two years, when he was attached to the *Colorado* in European waters, we catch glimpses of him at Paris with his elder brother, an art student, and his future brother-in-law, Henry Cabot Lodge (Lodge, *Early Memories,* p. 159). After ten years of routine assignments, Davis spent two years in astronomical and geodetic work at the Naval Observatory. He then engaged in a series of expeditions (1877–85) in the North Atlantic, Far East, and on the west coast of South America, for fixing exact longitude by use of submarine cables, the results of which he published in three volumes, each prepared in collaboration with another officer, on *Telegraphic Determination of Longitudes* (1880, 1883, 1885). He also published in 1877 a treatise, *Chronometer Rates as Affected by Changes of Tempera-*

ture and Other Causes (*Navy Scientific Papers*, no. 6). He was promoted to commander in 1885, and his special qualifications were recognized by his appointment, in intervals between sea commands, as chief intelligence officer (1889–92), and superintendent of the Naval Observatory (1897–1902). This last duty was interrupted by the Spanish-American War, during which he commanded the auxiliary cruiser *Dixie* in Cuban waters and was in charge of the division which, on July 27, 1898, forced the surrender of Ponce, Porto Rico, preparatory to its occupation by the army. He was made a rear admiral in August 1904, and thereafter commanded a division and then a squadron of the Atlantic Fleet.

Davis's range of interests and attractive personal qualities led to his selection for various special duties, notably as representative of the president at the reception of the Infanta Eulalie on her visit to the United States in 1893, as a member of the joint army and navy board that reported favorably on the Langley flying machine in 1898, of the international commission that met in Paris in 1904–05 to investigate the Dogger Bank dispute between England and Russia, and of the Perry's Victory Centennial Committee in 1912. On Mar. 31, 1875, he married Louisa, daughter of Dr. John Quackenbush of Albany, N. Y. His elder son, Charles Henry Davis, entered the navy prior to his father's retirement, so that in 1928 there had been one of that name in the navy continuously for 105 years. In later years Davis found his chief recreation in water-color painting, to which he devoted himself with notable success, selling many pictures and giving exhibitions in Newport, Boston, and Washington. Nervous, irritable, and whimsical at times—his barred cabin had to be entered once through a port-hole to apprise him of an admiral's call—he was enthusiastic in his pleasures, a delightful companion, thoroughly democratic, and had an extraordinary store of general information. On shipboard he was a strict but just disciplinarian, and drew his men to him by personal affection.

[Some information regarding his early life may be drawn from his *Life of Chas. Henry Davis, Rear Admiral, 1807–1877* (1899). See also *Army and Navy Reg.*, Dec. 31, 1921; *Science*, Feb. 24, 1922; *Boston Transcript*, Dec. 28, 1921; *Who's Who in America*, 1920–21.]   A. W.

DAVIS, CHARLES HENRY STANLEY Mar. 2, 1840–Nov. 7, 1917), physician, philologist, Orientalist, was born at Goshen, Conn., the son of Timothy Fisher Davis, also a physician, and Moriva (Hatch) Davis. He was educated in the public school of Meriden, Conn., and then

by a private tutor. Beginning the study of medicine at the University of Maryland about 1864, he took his medical degree at the University of the City of New York in 1866. He then did some post-graduate work at Boston and began the publication of the *Boston Medical Register* which he conducted for its first year. He pursued further medical study at New York, London, and Paris; married Caroline Elizabeth Harris, Sept. 23, 1869; and settled in Meriden, Conn., where he was to remain for the rest of his life. In addition to his professional activities he took a lively interest in local history and politics. In 1870 his *History of Wallingford, Conn., . . . including Meriden* appeared, and in 1873 he was elected to the legislature, serving again in 1885 and 1886. His first effort in philology was in 1878, when he published his *Grammar of the Old Persian Language*. In the same year he began an *Index of Periodical Literature* which was maintained for the period 1878–81. He was active professionally in, and from 1870 until 1917 was clerk of, the local medical society. Among the subjects of his interest was child welfare: in 1879 he published an account of the epidemic of diphtheria which had prevailed in Meriden during 1875–76, while in 1883 appeared his booklet *Classification, Education and Training of Feeble-Minded, Imbecile and Idiotic Children*. In 1886 he was appointed physician to the Curtis Home for Orphans, which position he retained until 1898; in 1895 he began to serve as physician to the State School for Boys, resigning in 1900. During 1887–88 he was mayor of Meriden and from 1898 to 1908 he was president of its board of education. In addition to the medical publications already mentioned he was the author of *The Voice as a Musical Instrument* (1879, reprinted 1907); *The Self-Cure of Consumption without Medicine* (1904), and *How To Be Successful as a Physician* (1905).

His career as an antiquarian appears to have begun in earnest in 1887 when he took over the editorship of *Biblia,* a journal of Oriental archeology, which in 1906 was merged in the *American Antiquarian and Oriental Journal*. He published two volumes on Egypt, the *History of Egypt in the Light of Modern Discoveries* (1896) and *The Egyptian Book of the Dead* (1894). In 1909 he returned to philology in the publication of his *Grammar of the Modern Irish Language*. Finally he was the author of two philosophical works, *Greek and Roman Stoicism* (1903) and *Some of Life's Problems* (1914), his last literary effort. His death took place at the Connecticut State Hospital from a perforated duodenal ulcer.

[Wm. B. Atkinson, *The Physicians and Surgeons of the U. S.* (1878); *Commemorative Biog. Record of New Haven County, Conn.* (1902); *Jour. Am. Medic. Asso.*, Nov. 24, 1917; *Who's Who in America*, 1916–17.]   E. P–e.

DAVIS, CUSHMAN KELLOGG (June 16, 1838–Nov. 27, 1900), lawyer, governor of Minnesota, United States senator, was born at Henderson, N. Y., the eldest of eight children. His father, Maj. Horatio Davis, a pioneer settler there, was of Puritan stock, while his mother, Clarissa F. (Cushman) Davis, was a direct descendant of Thomas and Mary (Allerton) Cushman, both of whom came early to Plymouth. Visiting New England only late in life, Davis "took great delight in his descent from the early settlers of Plymouth, and valued exceedingly the good-will of the people of Massachusetts" (Hoar, *post*). He received his formal education at Carroll College, an academy at Waukesha, Wis., and the University of Michigan, from which he was graduated in 1857. He was admitted to the bar and practised in Waukesha until he enlisted in 1862 as first lieutenant of Company B, 28th Wisconsin Infantry. Frequently serving as judge-advocate, he was for a time adjutant-general on the staff of Gen. Gorman. He resigned his commission in 1864 and returned to Waukesha, where he married Laura Bowman. Subsequently a divorce by agreement was obtained, and in 1880 he married Anna Malcolm Agnew of St. Paul, Minn. Moving to St. Paul, he joined his former commanding officer in the legal firm of Gorman & Davis. Adding politics to law, he was elected to the legislature in 1867, and was United States district attorney from 1868 to 1873. He was interested in the Granger Movement and his speech on "Modern Feudalism," an attack on railroads, was delivered before many audiences and even, by invitation, before the state legislature. Made available by his anti-railroad stand, and brought forward as a result of internal faction in the Republican party, Davis was nominated for governor in 1873 and elected by a narrow majority. By preventing a bolt of Granger Republicans to the Anti-Monopoly-Democratic fusion ticket, he had accomplished the purpose of his backers (William W. Folwell, *A History of Minnesota*, 1926, III, 81–85). "But the anti-monopolists were inevitably disappointed. They did not realize that the rhetoric of a lecturer could never be the policy of a governor" (St. Paul *Pioneer Press*, Nov. 28, 1900). He did not seek a renomination in 1875, but was brought forward to contest the senatorial seat of the veteran Alexander Ramsey; the ensuing deadlock resulted in the choice of a third man. For eleven years Davis, inactive in politics, devoted himself to his profession. His firm, Davis, [F. B.] Kellogg & [C. A.] Severance, was one of the strongest in the Northwest, while Davis himself was regarded as a particularly outstanding member of the bar in his state. The ex-governor found an avocation in the study of Shakespeare, publishing a volume on *The Law in Shakespeare* (1884), and on the life of Napoleon. He had not forsaken his political career, but awaited a favorable time for resuming it. Elected United States senator in 1887, he was reëlected in 1893 by a close vote, and again in 1899 with no serious opposition.

As senator, Davis rarely participated in formal debates on the floor, but concentrated his efforts on committee work, especially in the Committee on Pensions, of which he was chairman from 1887 to 1893. He was particularly instrumental in pushing through the Dependent Pension Bill in 1890. Whatever interest he had in the tariff, trust legislation, monetary questions, and the like, was manifested only by a rare remark, or by his vote. He supported Cleveland in sending federal troops to Chicago in 1894, in the face of considerable Minnesota sentiment against this action, and thus strengthened his position with the upholders of law and order. In 1891 he became a member of the Committee on Foreign Relations and here, throughout the remainder of his life, he found the most congenial part of his public work. He strenuously opposed President Cleveland's foreign policy ("Two Years of Democratic Diplomacy," *North American Review*, March 1895); advocated the annexation of the Hawaiian Islands (speech of Jan. 10, 11, 1894, *Congressional Record*, 53 Cong., 2 Sess., 621–28, 694–702); and opposed the Chinese Exclusion Act of 1892 which he characterized as "flagitious and ferocious legislation" (*Ibid.*, 53 Cong., 1 Sess., 1893, pp. 3080–85). In bringing before the Senate the joint resolution evoked by Cleveland's Venezuelan message, he reaffirmed adherence to the Monroe Doctrine but maintained that throughout the controversy there had been no danger of war between Great Britain and the United States, for interests of both countries "in the great and common cause of civilization" were "too enormous and too vital to each of them to bring about such a consummation" (*Ibid.*, 54 Cong., 1 Sess., pp. 1786–92). Nevertheless he was "among the first senators clearly to perceive and to explain the hidden pitfalls of the proposed arbitration treaty between Great Britain and the United States" (St. Paul *Pioneer Press*, Nov. 28, 1900).

In 1897, when Sherman became secretary of

state, Davis as chairman of the Committee on Foreign Relations was brought into intimate contact with the renewed project of Hawaiian annexation, advocated the ratification of the treaty of 1897, and, when that failed, led the fight to push through the joint resolution in the face of a determined filibuster (*Congressional Record*, 55 Cong., 2 Sess., pp. 6140–6403 *passim*). On the Cuban issue, Davis was in close touch with the administration throughout. He introduced in the Senate the joint resolution authorizing the President to intervene in Cuba and led in opposing a minority which would recognize the independence of Cuba, maintaining that such action would infringe upon executive prerogative (*Ibid.*, 55 Cong., 2 Sess., pp. 3827 ff.). He was convinced that the "Spanish war was a just and necessary war" (speech before the Union Club of Chicago, Feb. 2, 1899). As one of the Paris peace commissioners, he joined with Reid and Frye in believing that some of the Philippines should be retained by the United States, but, according to Reid, was not at first insistent on retaining all (Royal Cortissoz, *The Life of Whitelaw Reid*, 1921, II, 247). Once committed to the idea of retention, he even objected to paying the twenty millions to Spain (letters quoted in Folwell, *History of Minnesota*, III, 238 n.). The Philippines and Hawaii, he believed, would protect the western coast of the United States from an inundation of Chinese (Union League Club speech, Feb. 2, 1899). He was, however, opposed to tariff barriers between the United States and the new dependencies (*Congressional Record*, 56 Cong., 1 Sess., 1900, p. 2648). The situation arising from the Boxer Rebellion in China filled him with alarm lest it might lead to a general war (Cortissoz, *Reid*, II, 258). His career, which some thought might bring him to the presidency, was suddenly terminated while he was participating in the campaign of 1900. His *Treatise on International Law, including American Diplomacy* (1901), was published posthumously.

[Biographical sketches of Davis by Geo. F. Hoar in *Proc. Am. Antiq. Soc.*, n.s., XIV (1901), reprinted in Hoar, *Autobiog. of Seventy Years* (1903); Samuel G. Smith in *Rev. of Revs.* (N. Y.), Jan. 1901; Samuel H. Church in the *Century Mag.*, May 1901; Jas. H. Baker in *Minn. Hist. Soc. Colls.*, vol. XIII (1908); *Western Mag.*, Aug. 1918; *Outlook*, Dec. 8, 1900; memorial addresses in both Houses of Congress reprinted from the *Cong. Record* as *Sen. Doc. No. 230*, 56 Cong., 2 Sess.]
L. B. S.

DAVIS, DAVID (Mar. 9, 1815–June 26, 1886), jurist, born in Cecil County, Md., the son of Dr. David Davis, came of Welsh ancestry. He was the cousin of Henry Winter Davis. At seventeen he had completed an academic course at Kenyon College, Gambier, Ohio, after which he studied law in the office of Judge Henry W. Bishop of Lenox, Mass., and later in the Yale Law School, from which he graduated in 1835. In the same year he settled as a practising lawyer at Pekin, Ill., but finding the river town unhealthful he moved in 1836 to Bloomington, Ill., which remained thereafter his home. From the commonplace activities of a struggling lawyer in a pioneer town he turned to politics and was elected as a Whig to the state legislature in 1844. He was an active member of the state constitutional convention of 1847, devoting special attention to the judiciary. Despite the heavy circuit duties and traveling expenses of the state judges, he urged for the judicial office the low salary of $600, which was not adopted; and he advocated popular election of judges, contending that he would rather see them become "the weather-cocks of public sentiment" than the tools of the legislature or the governor.

For fourteen picturesque years (1848–62) he presided over the noted eighth judicial circuit in Illinois, his popularity being demonstrated in three elections as judge. Many lawyers of distinction, including Lincoln, Orville H. Browning, Douglas, Leonard Swett, S. T. Logan, and Lyman Trumbull, practised before him. An intimate friendship with Lincoln was formed during this period; Davis has even been referred to as "Lincoln's closest friend" (*Chicago Tribune*, June 27, 1886). Lincoln at times presided over Davis's court when the Judge was pressed with private business. In the Republican convention at Chicago in 1860, Davis was the acknowledged leader of the Lincoln forces. "To Judge Davis," wrote a contemporary, "more than to any other man, . . . is the American people indebted for . . . the nomination . . . of Abraham Lincoln" (letter of Jesse W. Fell, quoted in *Chicago Tribune*, June 27, 1886, p. 11). Having assisted in opening the Lincoln headquarters at the Tremont House prior to the convention, he labored tirelessly for his friend's success; and after the nomination he was active in promoting the Lincoln campaign. In February 1861 he accompanied Lincoln from Springfield to Washington, his great bulk and white hat being no less conspicuous than the rugged form of the president-elect. Lincoln further showed his confidence by appointing him in 1861 to investigate claims in Frémont's Missouri department. By request of the family he became administrator of Lincoln's estate.

Davis's eagerness for an appointment to the supreme bench was no secret to his friends; and one of them, Leonard Swett, claims the credit for persuading Lincoln to name him at a time when many regarded the choice of Orville H. Browning as a foregone conclusion. Swett is not inclined as others are to attribute Lincoln's action to the motive of rewarding a friend for having promoted his nomination; and it should be noted that Lincoln had appointed two supreme justices, Swayne and Miller, before choosing Davis. Davis remained a member of the Supreme Court for over fourteen years (1862–77), during which time he supported the prevailing nationalistic tendency in judicial interpretation. He delivered the opinion in the Milligan case (4 *Wallace*, 107), holding the trial of citizens by military commission in areas not within the theatre of military operations to be unlawful, though conducted in war time. For this he was abused by the Republican press but commended by Democratic papers; and his fondness for the Democratic party now becomes increasingly noticeable. When the constitutionality of the Legal Tender Act of 1862 was denied in *Hepburn* vs. *Griswold* (8 *Wallace,* 603), he dissented; and he stood with the majority of the Court when this decision was reversed (Legal Tender Cases, 12 *Wallace,* 457). While he was a member of the Supreme Court his circuit covered Illinois, Indiana, and Wisconsin; and he is said to have remarked that his heavy judicial duties shortened his life.

His judicial office had not caused him to avoid politics; and in 1872 his friends made a vigorous effort to obtain for him the Liberal Republican nomination. Having become known for certain "radical" views, he was nominated for the presidency by the Labor Reform Convention at Columbus, Ohio, in February 1872. This convention denounced monopolies and advocated paper-money legislation, the payment of the national debt in paper, a low tariff, general amnesty, and the collection of the cost of future wars from the wealth of the country. The wealthy Davis, however, was far from the typical labor reformer; and it was generally supposed that he associated himself with the movement not for itself, but as a preliminary to the coming Liberal Republican and Democratic nominations. When the Republican liberals met in convention at Cincinnati in 1872, Davis was reckoned one of the foremost contenders for the nomination. He was widely indorsed by Democratic conventions in the Middle West; and, despite the vigorous candidacy of Trumbull, he commanded great strength among the Liberal Republicans of Illinois. A number of factors, however, worked against him: his monetary policies, his judicial office, his alliance with Labor, division within the Illinois forces, influential newspaper opposition, and, perhaps chiefly, the overactivity of his friends. Though he received 92½ votes on the first ballot, Davis's strength soon dwindled; and the net result of his candidacy was the diminution of the chances of such men as Trumbull or Charles Francis Adams whom many earnest liberals regarded as preferable to Greeley, the convention's choice. The inference that his place on the Columbus ticket had been intended as a stepping-stone to the Cincinnati nomination was strengthened when, after failing at Cincinnati, he withdrew as Labor nominee.

In 1877 Davis passed from the Supreme Court to the United States Senate under circumstances that produced wide-spread comment. In the presidential contest between Hayes and Tilden the Democrats in Congress would probably never have supported the Electoral Commission Bill, had they not expected that Davis would serve as the fifth justice—the all-important "fifteenth member"—whose vote they hoped would turn the scale for Tilden. With a strange fatuity, however, the Democrats of the Illinois legislature, after a protracted contest, joined with the Independents to elect Davis to the United States Senate. His acceptance of the office, affecting as it did the presidential controversy, brought down on his head a storm of abusive epithets. As the wits remarked, he was transferred "from the bench to the fence," for in an evenly divided Senate his wavering vote turned the scale now to the Republicans and now to the Democrats. When Vice-President Arthur became president, Davis, as presiding officer of the Senate, still wielded the balance of power; and as he came more and more to support the Republican administration, he was denounced as a betrayer of the Democrats to whom he owed his senatorship. As a member of the Judiciary Committee of the Senate he made certain proposals in regard to federal appellate jurisdiction which were later adopted. His support of Hancock in 1880 and of Blaine in 1884 emphasized his lack of party regularity.

Davis was twice married. His first wife, Sarah Woodruff, daughter of Judge William Walker of Lenox, Mass., whom he married Oct. 30, 1838, when a young lawyer at Bloomington, died in 1879; and on Mar. 14, 1883, he married Adeline Burr of Fayetteville, N. C. Two children of the first marriage survived him. A man of great physical bulk who, as some wit remarked, had to be "surveyed" for a pair of trousers, he was practical rather than brilliant in his mental operations. He had a talent for party organization and combined in his person the dissimilar qualities of jurist and politician. His peculiar aptitude seems to have been for the work of circuit judge in pioneer Illinois, where he commanded such confidence that many cases were submitted to him without a jury. His decisions in this period were rarely appealed and seldom reversed. By making systematic investments in real estate, buying in farms at tax sales, foreclosing mortgages, and the like, he accumulated immense wealth, which he guarded with rigid economy and augmented by the vigorous collection of all claims due him. It was estimated that his estate at the time of his death was worth two million dollars. After his retirement from the Senate in March 1883, he spent his remaining years at Bloomington, where he died.

[H. E. Pratt, "David Davis" (MS. dissertation, Univ of Ill., 1930); J. M. Palmer, ed., *The Bench and Bar of Ill.* (1899), I, 154, 541–49; H. C. Whitney, *Life on the Circuit with Lincoln* (1892), ch. iii; *Memoirs of Gustave Koerner, 1809–1896* (1909), II, 539 ff.; *Chicago Times*, Mar. 20, 1880; *Chicago Tribune*, June 27, 1886; Thomas Dent, "David Davis of Illinois: A Sketch," *Am. Law Rev.*, July–Aug., 1919; Leonard Swett, "Memorial Address," etc., *Proc. Ill. State Bar Asso.*, 1887.]　　　　　J. G. R.

DAVIS, EDMUND JACKSON (Oct. 2, 1827–Feb. 7, 1883), governor of Texas, was born in St. Augustine, Fla., but moved to Texas with his widowed mother in 1838, settling at Galveston. He studied law in Corpus Christi and practised his profession in Brownsville, Laredo, and Corpus Christi. He was deputy collector of customs under the Fillmore administration, was elected district attorney for the Rio Grande Valley district in 1853, and became judge of that district in 1854, serving until 1861. Alienated from the Confederate cause by his defeat in the race for delegate to the Secession Convention, he organized a regiment of Texas Unionists in Mexico. While recruiting near Matamoras he was captured by Confederates and narrowly escaped hanging. He led the unsuccessful Union attack on Laredo in 1864, but his regiment spent most of the war period in Louisiana. Davis was made a brigadier-general after the battle of Mansfield. He declined Gen. Sheridan's appointment as chief justice of the Texas state supreme court in 1865.

As a delegate to the constitutional convention of 1866 and as president of the Reconstruction convention of 1868–69 he advocated disfranchisement of ex-Confederates, unrestricted negro suffrage, and other radical measures of his party; in the latter convention he advocated dividing Texas into three states. In an election held by the military commander in 1869 he was elected governor of Texas over A. J. Hamilton, Democrat and Union army officer. His majority was less than one thousand, but he was the state's dictator for the next four years. He supported measures which, passed by the subservient Radical legislature, gave unusual power into the hands of the governor and alienated all but his own political partisans. The governor was empowered to appoint more than eight thousand state, county, and local officials, leaving a very small percentage of the state's employees to be elected by the voters.

The verdict of the people was that almost all of the Davis appointees were either incapable or dishonest. Although Richard Coke [*q.v.*] polled a majority of more than 40,000 in the election for governor in 1873, Davis declared the election law unconstitutional and refused to give up his office. He appealed to President Grant to order troops to Austin to sustain him in his claim. While Gov. Coke and the Democratic legislature organized the new administration on the second floor of the Capitol, Davis and the old legislature continued to maintain their positions on the first floor, guarded by a company of negro troops. After several days of dual government, during which time an armed clash was constantly expected, President Grant wired Davis that he declined to intervene, and Davis retired from office.

He continued to make his home in Austin, practised law, and was the Republican leader in the state until his death. He ran for governor against O. M. Roberts in 1880, but was defeated by a hundred thousand votes. He was warmly supported by a strong faction for a place in the cabinet of President Arthur, and was defeated for Congress in the Austin district in 1882. Even his most bitter opponents believed that he was personally honest (*Dallas Herald*, Feb. 8, 1883). He was the "ablest and most influential" Texas Republican of the Reconstruction period, and had the power of a czar within his own party. His domestic and social life was above reproach, and he was a man of unusual culture and refinement. At Corpus Christi in 1858 he had married Anne Britton, daughter of Maj. Forbes Britton, Texas officer in the Mexican War. Although her twin brother and other relatives were Confederates and Democrats, Mrs. Davis remained loyal to her husband throughout the period of the war and Reconstruction.

[Newspaper files in the Univ. of Texas Lib.; *Senate and House Jours.*, 1866–74; *Constitutional Convention Jours.*, 1866, 1869, and 1875; Executive Correspondence, Davis, File Boxes 206–20, in Secretary of State's office, Austin, Texas; S. S. McKay, "Texas During the E. J. Davis Régime" (MS., Austin, 1919); S. S. McKay, *Making the Texas Constitution of 1876* (1924); C. W. Ramsdell, *Reconstruction in Texas* (1910); F. W. Johnson, *A Hist. of Texas and Texans* (1914), I, 563; *Daily Statesman* (Austin), and *Galveston News*, of Feb. 8, 1883; *Weekly Democrat Statesman* (Austin), Feb. 15, 1883. Date of birth from tombstone erected by Davis's brother in the State Cemetery, Austin.]   S. S. M.

DAVIS, EDWIN HAMILTON (Jan. 22, 1811–May 15, 1888), archeologist, physician, a son of Henry Davis and Avis (Slocum) Davis, was born at Hillsboro in southern Ohio. This locality is celebrated for the number of circular, square, and octagonal earthworks of the Mound Builders, and as a youth Davis became attracted to the question of their origin. Archeology at that time being a science offering little sustenance to its followers, the young man was bent toward medicine, yet he kept up the exploration of the mounds while studying at Kenyon College where he graduated in 1833. His address on the subject at the college commencement interested Daniel Webster, then traveling in the West, and the latter's encouragement stimulated Davis in his determination to continue the researches at the first opportunity. Graduating at Cincinnati Medical College in 1837 or 1838, he began to practise in Chillicothe, Ohio, where he was to remain until 1850. His profession keeping him occupied, he joined hands with E. G. Squier, an ambitious archeologist, talented but without means, and thus at his own expense prosecuted the survey of one hundred mounds. The results of this collaboration were published as the first work issued by the newly founded Smithsonian Institution: *Ancient Monuments of the Mississippi Valley* (Smithsonian Contributions to Knowledge, no. 1, 1847, by E. G. Squier and E. H. Davis). This large memoir, well presented and illustrated, and embodying the surveys and descriptions of the more important works of the Mound Builders, being based on facts, has lost none of its value to archeologists. As a historical record of the ancient works of the Indians, especially since many of the monuments have disappeared under the plow and the encroachment of habitations, it is of summary value. A. Morlot, the Swiss archeologist, declared it to be as "glorious a monument of American science, as Bunker's Hill is of American bravery" (*American Philosophical Society Proceedings*, November 1862). During his stay in Ohio, Davis gathered a collection of cultural objects of the Mound Builders which was remarkable in revealing the surprising advance these Indians had made in art. The larger collection was acquired by the Blackmore Museum at Salisbury, England, where it has been for many decades an object of pilgrimage of American archeologists. A smaller collection by Davis is in the American Museum of Natural History of New York City.

Called to the chair of materia medica and therapeutics in the New York Medical College in 1850, Davis taught there till 1860. As might be suspected, he managed to interest some members of his classes in his hobby, for he refers to specimens "sent by my former students from Central and South America" (*Smithsonian Report*, 1866, p. 370). Addressing Prof. Joseph Henry, secretary of the Smithsonian, in 1866, he broached a project for correlating specimens with tribes on which he had been engaged, using the ethnological map of Waitz and taking in the results of Gallatin, Ludwig, Gibbs, and Morgan. In making this map, which did not become a reality for many years, he suggested the use of physical measurements on the skeleton and sent Prof. Henry the scheme of Scherzer and Schwarz for use of the Institution (*Smithsonian Report*, 1866, p. 371). In 1854 he delivered a course of lectures on archeology before the Lowell Institute of Boston and later repeated these lectures to societies in New York City and Brooklyn. He was tall, and distinguished by a highly refined, intellectual countenance. Kindly, a gentleman in temperament, he was learned in medical science, but easily imposed upon with regard to fees. He was married on Nov. 9, 1841, to Lucy Woodbridge who bore him nine children, among them John Woodbridge Davis, a well-known civil engineer.

[*N. Y. Times, N. Y. Tribune*, May 16, 1888; *Appletons' Annual Cyc.*, 1888; John Woodbridge, *The Woodbridge Record* (1883); information from Dr. Marcus Benjamin.]   W. H.

DAVIS, GARRET (Sept. 10, 1801–Sept. 22, 1872), lawyer, congressman and senator from Kentucky, was born in Mount Sterling, Ky., the son of Jeremiah Davis and his wife, a Miss Garret before marriage, who were both natives of Maryland. His father, though a blacksmith, was a leader in his community, serving for a time in the Kentucky legislature. Garret's brother, Amos, was a member of Congress from 1833 until his death in 1835. After attending the common schools, Garret studied Latin, Greek, and history without help. He was early led to an interest in law through his services as a deputy in the office of the clerk of the circuit court, first in Mount Sterling and then in Paris, to which town his family had moved. Admitted to the bar in the latter place in 1823, he there began the practise of his profession. Elected to the legislature in 1833, he served three consecutive terms in this body (1833–35). As political disputations were pleasing to him and he desired to continue in the service of his state, he ran for Congress and was elected. Here he served four consecutive terms (1839–47), representing for the last six years

Henry Clay's noted Ashland district, to which Bourbon County had been transferred from the Maysville district. He was an enthusiastic Whig and a close friend of Clay. He refused to break a promise not to run again for Congress in 1847 and declined the nomination for the lieutenant-governorship the next year. Elected to the state constitutional convention in 1849 he participated with great zeal in its debates, but quit the sessions and returned home when his fight against the elective judiciary failed and, in common with the Whigs, opposed the new constitution. Following the trend of a growing opposition to Roman Catholics, he made a bitter speech against them in the convention and shortly went over to the Know-Nothing party. In 1855 he declined the nomination for the governorship, and the following year the Know-Nothing nomination for the presidency.

The approach of the Civil War awakened him to great activity. When most Kentuckians were undecided in their course of action he came out for unswerving and complete adherence to the Union. In April 1861 he talked with Lincoln about Kentucky affairs, and in May supervised the distribution of Federal rifles to Kentucky Unionists throughout the central and eastern parts of the state. As a reward he was elected in December to the United States Senate to the seat vacated by John C. Breckinridge, and now became one of the most radical of the senators in his support of the Union, proposing among other things the confiscation of the property of all who aided the "rebellion" in any way. But it took only three years of war to work a complete revolution in him. In January 1864 he introduced a set of resolutions so astonishingly critical of Lincoln's war policy that he himself escaped expulsion only by explaining them away, and he ever afterward fought with all his powers of oratory and sarcasm against the war party and the radical reconstructionists. He was reëlected in 1867 by the Democrats, whom he had by this time solidly embraced. Davis was regarded as an effective debater and a learned man. He developed a large estate and became a close student of agriculture. He was married in 1825 to a daughter of Robert Trimble, later a justice of the United States Supreme Court. Three years after her death in 1843, he married the widow of Thomas Elliott, a lawyer of Paris, Ky. He successfully lived down his war record and died highly respected by his fellow Kentuckians, whose sympathies were now strongly Southern.

[Sketches of Davis may be found in L. and R. H. Collins, *Hist. of Ky.* (1882), II, 82–83; *Biog. Cyc. of the Commonwealth of Ky.* (1896), pp. 385–86; and *Biog. Encyc. of Ky.* (1878), pp. 413–14. See also: W. H. Perrin, ed., *Hist. of Bourbon, Scott, Harrison and Nicholas Counties, Ky.* (1882). His speeches in Congress are in the *Cong. Globe*. Much concerning his war record may be found in the *Official Records (Army)*, ser. 1, vols. II, IV, XVI, XXXVI, LI, LII.] E. M. C.

DAVIS, GEORGE (Mar. 1, 1820–Feb. 23, 1896), lawyer, attorney-general of the Confederacy, was born at Porter's Neck, New Hanover (now Pender) County, N. C., at the home of his parents, Thomas Frederick and Sarah Isabella (Eagles) Davis. Among his ancestors were Sir John Yeamans and Gen. James Moore of South Carolina and the Lillington and Swann families of the Albemarle Sound region. For nearly a century the Davis family had been living in the Cape Fear district. Graduating from the state university in 1838 at the head of his class, he was admitted to the Wilmington bar and soon gained a flattering reputation as a lawyer and an orator. A sincere and active Whig, he was very nearly named for governor in 1848, though he never sought office and never carried his home county for his party. A strong Union man in 1860, he was sent to the Peace Conference of February 1861; but in a "masterly" address in Wilmington, Mar. 2, he repudiated as dishonorable the recommendations of that body. In the Provisional Congress of the Confederacy he was the lawyer and the literary man, careful of the interests of property and critical of verbosity, as well as the conscientious representative, presenting many petitions. He served in the Confederate Senate from 1862 until he became attorney-general, Jan. 4, 1864 (*Journal of the Congress of the Confederate States of America*, 1904, III, 517). Jefferson Davis found him congenial and valuable, not always agreeing with the president but generally "right at last." On the collapse of the Confederacy, Apr. 26, 1865, having correctly ended his work as attorney-general, he fled the country, desperate but cool, only to meet imprisonment at Fort Hamilton for several months.

Back at the law in Wilmington, he met marked success, notably as leading counsel of the Atlantic Coast Line system during its formative period. Judges listened to him because he was careful, honest, and learned. To the public, however, he was known mainly through the occasional addresses in which for forty years he voiced the opinions of cultured and propertied Wilmingtonians. His "Early Men and Times of the Lower Cape Fear" (*Address before the Literary Societies of the University of North Carolina, Raleigh*, 1855), which is no longer accepted as final, had "brought the most romantic section of North Carolina permanently into history" (Smith, *post*, III, 1229). Fittingly, his last public address was in eulogy of Jefferson Davis (1889). Short, heavy-set, dark, without striking advantage of voice, he was an effective speaker because of his careful preparation, interpretative imagination, and a style "clear, strong, flexible." For his service "in shaping and toning the political ethics of our society" Gov. Vance tendered him in 1878 the chief justiceship, which he declined for pecuniary reasons. The next year Gov. Jarvis, wishing through the sale of the Western North Carolina Railroad to reverse the state's historic policy as to railroads, sought his legal skill and political influence; these he gave, in company with Thomas Ruffin, refusing compensation. He was buried with military honors from St. James's Church, Wilmington. He was twice married: on Nov. 17, 1842, to Mary A. Polk, who died in 1863; and on May 9, 1866, to Monimia Fairfax of Richmond.

[S. A. Ashe, *Geo. Davis, Attorney-General of the Confed. States* (1916); H. G. Connor, *Geo. Davis* (1911); Jas. Sprunt, *Chronicles of the Cape Fear River* (2nd ed., 1916). Selections from Davis's addresses appear in *A Memorial of the Hon. Geo. Davis* (1896) and in E. A. Alderman and J. C. Harris, *Lib. of Southern Lit.*, vol. III (1909), which also contains a sketch by C. Alphonso Smith. The Davis eulogy was published in *Wilmington's Tribute . . . Jefferson Davis* (1890). The *Wilmington Morning Star*, Feb. 25, 1896, and the *Wilmington Weekly Tribune*, Feb. 28, 1896, carried obituaries.]   C.C.P.

DAVIS, GEORGE BRECKENRIDGE (Feb. 13, 1847–Dec. 15, 1914), soldier and judge advocate general, was born at Ware, Mass., where his parents, Solomon B. and Sarah (Dunbar) Davis resided. His education was received at the public schools at Ware and Springfield, immediately upon leaving which in 1863 he enlisted in the 1st Massachusetts Volunteer Cavalry, and served with that regiment till the close of the Civil War, attaining the rank of lieutenant. He then, with a view to a permanent career in the army, entered the Military Academy at West Point as a cadet, July 1, 1867, and graduated June 12, 1871, being assigned to the 5th Cavalry as second lieutenant. On July 6, 1871, he married Ella I. Prince of West Springfield, Mass. For the next two years he saw service in Wyoming and Arizona, but returned to West Point Aug. 30, 1873, as assistant professor of Spanish, later giving instruction also in French, chemistry, mineralogy and geology. Promoted first lieutenant, May 9, 1878, he spent the next five years on service in the West. He was appointed principal assistant professor of history, geography and ethics, and assistant professor of law at West Point on Aug. 28, 1883, and during his tenure of office wrote *Outlines of International Law with an Account of its Origin*

and Sources and of its Historical Development (1887), a work which became popular and passed through several editions. On his promotion to captain, Aug. 21, 1888, he returned to frontier duty, being stationed in Indian Territory. Four months later, however, he was appointed judge advocate with the rank of major, being at first detailed on special duty in the office of the secretary of war, Washington, D. C., and subsequently assuming charge of the publication of the *War of the Rebellion: Official Records of the Union and Confederate Armies.* He began the study of law at Columbian (now George Washington) Law School and graduated in 1891. He was appointed deputy judge advocate general and promoted lieutenant-colonel, Aug. 3, 1896, becoming in addition professor of law and history at West Point. In 1897 he published *The Elements of Law: An Introduction to the Study of the Constitutional and Military Law of the United States,* and under direction of the secretary of war prepared a manual of *The Military Laws of the United States* (War Department Document no. 64, 1897). This was followed by *A Treatise on the Military Law of the United States, Together with the Practice and Procedure of Courts-Martial and other Military Tribunals* (1898), which became the standard work on the subject. At the close of the Spanish-American War he was engaged in the investigation and trial of the so-called "canned beef cases." He relinquished his professorship on appointment as judge advocate general with the rank of brigadier-general and occupied this position for nearly ten years. In 1906 he was United States delegate to the Red Cross Conference at Geneva. In 1907 as United States delegate he attended the second Peace Conference at The Hague. He retired with the rank of major-general, Feb. 13, 1911, and died at Washington, D. C., Dec. 15, 1914.

He contributed a number of articles to military and historical publications, among them being "The Operations of the Cavalry in the Gettysburg Campaign" in *Cavalry Studies from Two Great Wars* (1896), and "The Antietam Campaign," "The Strategy of the Gettysburg Campaign," "From Gettysburg to Williamsport" and "The Bristoe and Mine Run Campaigns" in *Papers of the Military Historical Society of Massachusetts,* vol. III (1903).

[G. W. Cullum, *Biog. Reg.* (3rd ed., 1891); F. B. Heitman, *Hist. Reg. and Dict. of the U. S. Army* (1903), I, 358; obituary in *N. Y. Times,* Dec. 17, 1914; *Who's Who in America,* 1912–13.]   H.W.H.K.

DAVIS, GEORGE WHITEFIELD (July 26, 1839–July 12, 1918), soldier, engineer, was born in Thompson, Windham County, Conn., the son of George and Elizabeth (Grow) Davis, whose ancestors were early settlers in Massachusetts and Rhode Island. He attended district school in his native village and an academy in a neighboring town, and then divided his time between working on his father's farm and teaching school. In 1860 he secured a place as tutor in the family of a Georgian, but the outbreak of the war cut short this employment. In September 1861 he made his escape to the North. His long and difficult journey was interrupted by his arrest in Atlanta, and in its last stages was through the theatre of active operations in Kentucky. Enlisting in the 11th Connecticut Infantry, Nov. 27, 1861, he accompanied his regiment on the North Carolina expedition and after its first engagement, at New Berne, was appointed first lieutenant, Apr. 5, 1862. The regiment was with the Army of the Potomac at South Mountain, Antietam, and Fredericksburg, and was then sent to southeastern Virginia, where it eventually became a part of the Army of the James and participated with it in the final campaign against Richmond. As captain and major, Davis then served as a quartermaster in the XXV Army Corps, which was stationed in Texas in preparation for possible war in Mexico against Maximilian and the French.

He was mustered out of the volunteer service, Apr. 20, 1866, and appointed a captain of infantry in the regular army, Jan. 22, 1867. He served for some years with his regiment in the Southwest, was in charge of building operations at Fort Douglas, Utah, and San Antonio, Tex., and was then selected as assistant engineer on the construction of the Washington Mounment. After the completion of this work he was aide to Gen. Sheridan and later an instructor at the service school at Fort Leavenworth. Though a self-trained engineer, he had acquired so high a reputation that the Nicaragua Canal Construction Company sought his services, and by joint resolution of Congress he was granted indefinite leave of absence without pay that he might accept their offer. He was vice-president and general manager of the company from 1890 to 1893, when financial difficulties caused the suspension of work and his return to military duty. He was promoted major in 1894. In 1895 he became president of the board in charge of the publication of the *Official Records* (of the Civil War), succeeding Maj. George B. Davis, with whom he is constantly confused, and carried on the work until the outbreak of the Spanish-American War. He became lieutenant-colonel on Apr. 26, 1898, and on May 4 he was appointed

brigadier-general of volunteers. He organized and commanded a division of the II Corps, stationed at Camp Alger, Va., and then commanded the department of Pinar del Rio, in Cuba, until recalled to serve on the court of inquiry convened to investigate Gen. Miles's allegations as to the quality of the beef furnished to the troops in the field. He thus played a part in the "embalmed beef" controversy. From April 1899 until December 1900 he held the military governorship of Porto Rico. He was promoted colonel in the regular army in October 1899, retaining his brigadier-generalcy of volunteers until appointed brigadier-general in the regular army, Feb. 2, 1901. From Porto Rico he was sent to the Philippines, where he served as provost-marshal general in Manila for a short time, as commander of the department of Mindanao for fourteen months, and, after his appointment as major-general in July 1902, as commander of the entire Philippine division. He was retired from active service on July 26, 1903, and returned to the United States. In 1904 President Roosevelt appointed him a member of the Isthmian Canal Commission, according to an intention which he had confidentially expressed shortly before Davis's retirement. The latter was also designated as governor of the Canal Zone, where he organized the new government before retiring from office in 1905. He served as chairman of the board of engineers convened to recommend the type of canal to be constructed, his vote being cast in favor of a sea-level canal. His opinion was shared by all the foreign members of the board, but by a minority of the Americans. He resided in Washington for the remainder of his life, but twice went on special diplomatic missions to Guatemala. On Apr. 30, 1870, he married Maria Carmen, daughter of Alexander J. Atocha.

[Brief autobiography filed in the War Dept.; F. B. Heitman, *Hist. Reg. and Dict. of the U. S. Army* (1903), I, 358; G. W. Davis, *John Grow of Ipswich* (1913); *Puerto Rico, embracing the Reports of Brig. Gen. Geo. W. Davis, Mil. Gov.* (War Dept., 1899); G. W. Davis, *Report on the Mil. Govt. of the City of Manila, P. I., from 1898 to 1901*; Jos. B. Bishop, *The Panama Gateway* (1913, 1915). The sketch in *Who's Who in America* is incorrect as to several dates.]

T. M. S.

DAVIS, HENRY (Sept. 15, 1771–Mar. 8, 1852), clergyman, president of two colleges in their formative periods, was born at East Hampton, L. I., the son of John and Mary (Conkling) Davis, who were of Connecticut stock. Graduating from Yale in 1796, he was for a time tutor at Williams and then, from 1798 to 1803, at Yale. During the latter period he studied theology with Rev. Charles Backus of Somers,

Conn. In 1801 he was elected professor of divinity at Yale, but while he was preparing to assume this position the failure of his health caused him to decline it. He was married on Sept. 22, 1801, to Hannah Phoenix, daughter of Thomas Treadwell of Smithtown, L. I., a member of the Continental Congress. Leaving Yale, Davis spent some time in travel for his health, and in 1806 became professor of Greek at Union College. Three years later he became president of Middlebury College, which had been established in 1800. His administration was such that after eight years he was offered in 1817 the presidency of Hamilton College and that of Yale, in succession to Timothy Dwight, both of which he declined. Later in the year, however, he was again elected president of Hamilton and took office. The college was only five years old, and his task in many ways was that of a first president, not a second. Under his direction Hamilton at first prospered, the number of students rising to about a hundred. Before long, however, he and the leading trustees were in disagreement. The country was booming, and the trustees wished the college to boom likewise. They were unacquainted with college management, as they showed by interference in discipline, and were overconfident in their use of funds. Davis was conservative in opinions and temper, and steeped in New England college traditions. While very kindly in spirit and manner, he was undiplomatic, humorless, and unyielding in what he thought his duty. His disapproval of Finney's methods in revivals in neighboring towns increased opposition to him among the trustees. In this discord the college lost most of its faculty, and in 1829 had only nine students. Davis held on in almost impossible circumstances and was ultimately victorious. Having seen the board of trustees and faculty reconstituted and the student body restored, he resigned the presidency in 1832. The rest of his life was spent at the college, in much bodily feebleness. By his character, teaching, and preaching Davis exercised a strong influence over his students. His earnest religious life moved many to enter the ministry, especially through Auburn Theological Seminary, in the establishment and early life of which he took an important part. He published several sermons and addresses and *A Narrative of the Embarrassments and Decline of Hamilton College* (1833), recounting the college troubles in excessive detail.

[Davis's papers and letters in the lib. of Hamilton Coll.; his sermons and addresses; F. B. Dexter, *Biog. Sketches Grads. Yale Coll. 1792–1805* (1911); G. G. Bush, *Hist. of Education in Vt.* (1900); *Documentary*

Hist. of Hamilton Coll. (1922); *A Memorial of the Semi-Centennial Celebration of the Founding of Hamilton Coll.* (1862); J. Q. Adams, *A Hist. of Auburn Theol. Sem., 1818–1918* (1918).]   R. H. N.

DAVIS, HENRY GASSAWAY (Nov. 16, 1823–Mar. 11, 1916), United States senator, railroad builder, the son of Caleb and Louise Warfield (Brown) Davis, was descended from old Maryland families. The third of six children, he was born at Woodstock, Md. From his father's shoulder he witnessed in 1828 the exercises marking the beginning of the construction of America's first railroad, the Baltimore and Ohio, on which his father was later a construction contractor, and of which he himself became a trusted employee. His early schooling was begun by his mother who, after her husband's financial reverses which were soon followed by his death, opened a school for girls to contribute to the support of the family. Entering the service of the Baltimore and Ohio Railroad as a brakeman in 1842, he rose to the position of conductor, and in 1847 became supervisor of the line to Cumberland. He personally installed the first night trains. On Feb. 22, 1853, at Frederick, Md., he married Katharine Anne, daughter of Gideon Bantz. Following his marriage he sought a wider field of action. Accepting the position of station agent at Piedmont, Va. (now W. Va.), he really assumed the duties of a division superintendent because of his responsibility for directing the movement of trains up the long incline to the summit, and over the Appalachian Divide. During the first year he lived in a box car while building a home to which he brought his wife a year later.

A general store which he started at Piedmont in 1854 marked the beginning of his enterprises, which came to include trading with the interior and the opening of timber and coal fields. In 1858 he resigned his railroad position to devote his entire time to his growing business. With profits accumulated during the Civil War from the sale of supplies to the government and of equipment to railroads, he pursued larger plans based on his confidence in the resources of the upper Potomac region and the country beyond on the Cheat River. In 1867 he bought several thousand acres of timber-land on the crest of the Alleghanies, built a home in the woods, began lumbering on a large scale, and soon thereafter laid out the village of Deer Park. By 1870 he was regarded as a man of large wealth. In 1881 he began the construction of the West Virginia Central and Pittsburgh Railway, which was completed through primeval woods to Elkins in 1889, and with a branch extension to Durbin on the Greenbrier in 1904. At Elkins he built a large residence which became his home in 1892. In 1902 he sold the West Virginia Central and began the construction of an important outlet from the upper Monongahela region of Tygart's Valley via the Elk to Charleston, the Coal and Coke Railway which was completed in 1906 and the management of which he supervised until 1912. His success was largely due to business foresight, tenacity and determination, incessant industry, and inflexible and economical business rules, but also in part to social qualities.

In politics he attained prominence. In 1861 he voted against the secession of Virginia, and throughout the Civil War he was a strong Union man. At the close of the war his sympathies were with the Republicans on the questions of a protective tariff and industrial development, but his advocacy of a conciliatory policy toward the Confederates and his opposition to test-oaths and negro suffrage determined his later cooperation with the Democrats. In 1865 he was elected to the West Virginia House of Delegates as a Union-Conservative candidate. In 1868 he was elected, and two years later was reëlected, to the state Senate. For two decades after 1868 he represented his state in the Democratic national conventions. Elected to the United States Senate in January 1871, he was reëlected in 1877, but declined to be a candidate for a third term, chiefly because of the desire to devote himself to his railroad projects. In the Senate he was a useful member of the special committee on transportation routes to the seaboard, and for two years was chairman of the Committee on Appropriations. He was a delegate to the first two International American (Pan-American) Congresses. He was also appointed a member of the Intercontinental Railway Survey Commission which held sessions from 1890 to 1894. In 1904, at the age of eighty-one, he was the Democratic candidate for vice-president. He died in Washington at the home of his daughter, Mrs. Stephen B. Elkins.

[Chas. M. Pepper, *The Life and Times of Henry Gassaway Davis* (1920); Geo. W. Atkinson and Alvaro F. Gibbens, *Prominent Men of W. Va.* (1890); J. M. Callahan, *Hist. of W. Va., Old and New* (1923).]

J. M. C.

DAVIS, HENRY GASSETT (Nov. 4, 1807– Nov. 18, 1896), pioneer orthopedic surgeon, born at Trenton, Me., was the son of Isaac Davis, manufacturer and mechanic, by his wife, Polly Rice, and grandson of Deacon Isaac Davis of Northboro, Mass., who was descended from Dolor Davis, an early settler at Cape Cod (1634). Henry Davis intended to follow his father's trade and was on his way South to set

up an establishment for the manufacture of cotton-bagging when, en route, he stopped to visit a sister who was under treatment for scoliosis. The treatment appeared to him completely to ignore certain elementary mechanical principles, and he forthwith gave up his intended career to begin the study of medicine. He received his M.D. in March 1839 from the Yale Medical School, having obtained the greater part of his clinical training at Bellevue Hospital. He spent the first fifteen years of his medical career practising at Worcester and Millbury, Mass., after which he settled in New York. He gained wide experience as a general practitioner and surgeon, and it was not until his removal to New York that he directed his attention more exclusively to the problems of orthopedics. In so doing he became the founder of the so-called "traction school" of orthopedic surgery. While still in Millbury his interest had been aroused in the treatment of fractures and deformities, and he advocated energetically the use of continuous traction for the correction of deformity and for relief of joint irritation. His first use of weights and pulleys and of other traction devices for treatment of fracture (*American Medical Monthly,* May 1856) preceded those introduced in 1860 by Gurdon Buck [*q.v.*] and met with equal success. His practise eventually grew so large that he opened a private hospital at Thirty-seventh St. and Madison Ave., chiefly to receive patients from abroad. Davis's beliefs, new in their day, concerning the nature and treatment of club foot, congenital dislocation of the hip, chronic diseases of the joints, and the deformities resulting from poliomyelitis, formed the basis for the modern approach to these problems. It is interesting that in dealing with abscesses he recommended opening and evacuation, and subsequent lavage with warm water and a French preparation of chlorine, thus anticipating the Carrel-Dakin therapy used at the present time. He was the first to devise a splint for traction and the protection of the hip joint (Nutt). Davis was also a physician in the broad sense of the term, for in treating the part he did not neglect the whole, and constitutional treatment is not more wisely taught to-day than by him in the middle of the nineteenth century. He influenced younger men who were about him, notably Lewis A. Sayre [*q.v.*], Charles Fayette Taylor [*q.v.*], and, though less directly, Edward Hickling Bradford [*q.v.*], and it was through these followers that the specialty of orthopedic surgery in this country was rapidly developed. His most important work, *Conservative Surgery, as Exhibited in*

Remedying some of the Mechanical Causes that Operate Injuriously both in Health and Disease (1867), is a volume of unusual clarity and literary excellence, and was the first notable textbook in the history of American orthopedic surgery. Several other contributions were important: "On the Effect of Pressure upon Ulcerated Vertebrae" (*New York Journal of Medicine*, 1859), "On the Pathological Basis of the Treatment of Joint Disease" (*American Medical Monthly*, 1862), "The American Method of Treating Joint Diseases and Deformities" (*Transactions of the American Medical Association*, 1863). He was a member of local medical societies in New York and in 1895 was elected an honorary member of the newly formed American Orthopedic Association. At the age of eighty-nine he died at his home in Everett, Mass. He was survived by his widow, Ellen W. Deering, whom he had married in 1856, and by a son and two daughters. He is said to have been the first to suggest to railroad engineers the advantage of elevating the outer rail of the track at curves.

[Two excellent accounts of Davis are available by J. J. Nutt, *Medic. Record*, N. Y., 1905, LXVIII, 298–302; *Ibid.*, 868–69. See also *Trans. Am. Orthop. Asso.*, 1889, II, 7; *Ibid.*, 1897, X, 4; *Bull. N. Y. Acad. Med.*, ser. I, vol. I, 1861; J. D. Estabrook, *Three Generations of Northern Davises 1781–1894* (1908).] J.F.F.

DAVIS, HENRY WINTER (Aug. 16, 1817–Dec. 30, 1865), politician, statesman, was the son of Rev. Henry Lyon Davis, president of St. John's College (Md.), an ardent Federalist and Episcopalian, and Jane (Brown) Winter, a cultured woman with aristocratic connections in the town of Annapolis. During the campaign of 1828 Davis's father was removed from his position by the partisans of Jackson on the board of trustees of the college, and set adrift under circumstances which greatly influenced the career of Henry Winter Davis. After a strenuous course at Kenyon College (Ohio), young Davis procured, after much delay and difficulty, the meager funds necessary to enable him to study law at the University of Virginia. He left the University in June 1840 with some knowledge of law, mainly *Coke on Littleton*, and began his career at Alexandria, Va., a handsome man of twenty-three, six feet tall, and of aristocratic bearing and manner. Here he quickly won an enviable reputation, obtained a good income from his profession, and on Oct. 30, 1845, married Constance C. Gardiner, daughter of a prominent citizen of the town. After her death, he married, on Jan. 26, 1857, Nancy Morris of Baltimore, whither he had moved in 1849.

Attaching himself to the Whig party, Davis appeared on the platform as a speaker with Robert Winthrop and Horace Greeley in the unhappy campaign of Gen. Winfield Scott for the presidency in 1852. In 1855 he was chosen to a seat in Congress where he immediately took a prominent place among the leaders of the Know-Nothing party. The hot disputes about Kansas left him unmoved, nor did the ardent campaign of 1856 budge him from his steady conservatism. He supported Fillmore, and endeavored to hold his neutral position from 1856 to 1860. But the decline of the Know-Nothing party and the break between Douglas and Buchanan compelled him to take sides. On the last day of January 1860, after a deadlock of seven weeks, he cast his vote for William Pennington, Republican candidate for speaker. This enabled the new party to organize the House and to prepare more effectively for the presidential campaign already opened. The decision made Davis a national character, but the legislature of Maryland repudiated his action by a vote of 62 to 1. From that day to his death every public act of Davis was a matter of immediate concern to the country. He was for a moment candidate for the Republican nomination for the vice-presidency, and thought of himself from that time forward as a suitable candidate for the presidency. He was guided by an overweening ambition, but his abilities as a statesman and an orator were acknowledged to be extraordinary. In his district he was both hated and loved beyond all other public men and his campaigns for reëlection were violent and bloody. Notwithstanding his vote for the Republicans in January 1860, he was the guiding spirit of the Bell and Everett party in Maryland; and he procured the nomination of Thomas H. Hicks [q.v.], Unionist, for governor. His purpose was not to defeat the Republican party in Maryland, but the regular Democrats, with Breckinridge as their candidate. Bell and Everett won; Hicks likewise was successful.

Davis, serving the balance of his term in the House of Representatives during the critical winter of 1860–61, keenly desired to sit in the new cabinet. But Montgomery Blair, a member of perhaps the most influential family in the country and the leader of a forlorn hope of Republicans in Maryland, was chosen. Davis was alone and without a party, for the Union party was rapidly disintegrating. On Feb. 7, when the Confederacy was just raising its head in Montgomery and the leading Republicans of the North were acquiescing in the secession movement, Davis in one of the important speeches of his life asserted that in Maryland they did not recognize the right of secession and that they would not be dragged from the Union (*Congressional Globe, Appendix,* 36 Cong., 2 Sess.). But Gov. Hicks and the people of Maryland did recognize the right of Southerners to secede and they seemed about to take legislative action in that direction. Davis said later that but for his activity Lincoln would have been inaugurated in some Pennsylvania village. He wrote a public letter to the *New York Tribune* urging that the Federal forts in Maryland be placed in the hands of Union men. Then he simply announced himself as a candidate for a seat in the House of Representatives. It was the 15th of April. Four days later the 6th Massachusetts Regiment was attacked in Baltimore. One of the most spectacular and bitter of political contests ensued, with Davis everywhere the militant leader of the Unionists. On June 13 his opponent, Henry May, a Southern sympathizer, was elected by a vote of 8,335 to 6,287.

It was a decisive defeat, but Davis became even better known to the country, traveled widely, and spoke often for the Union. However, either his chagrin at the presence of Montgomery Blair in Lincoln's cabinet or the President's open violation of many of the sacred traditions of the country led him into opposition. He could hardly contain himself when he thought of the procedure in the many courts martial of the day, or of the thousands of men in prison without proved offense. To him the *habeas corpus* was sacred beyond a question. Before a very hostile Brooklyn audience, early in November, he bitterly arraigned the President and all about him. There are few instances of a speaker's attaining such complete mastery over his audience as Davis did on that occasion. Nor did he ever cease to oppose most of the President's policies. He was not arrested or imprisoned, however, and in the hotly contested election of 1863 he was returned to the House, where he was at once made chairman of the Committee on Foreign Relations. He then became and remained a close friend and ally of Thaddeus Stevens, chairman of the Committee of Ways and Means. It was at the moment when Lincoln sent to Congress his program of reconstruction, known as the Louisiana Plan. Davis ranged himself at once on the side of the opposition, attacking upon every possible occasion the "usurpations" of the President, and ridiculing unmercifully the foreign policy of Seward, the management of the navy by Gideon Welles, the conduct of Gen. Frank P. Blair as an army commander, and the unrelenting campaign of Montgomery Blair

against himself in Maryland. In a little while the great majority of the House hung upon his words and followed him implicitly. He was more the master of that body than Thaddeus Stevens himself.

The most important of Davis's campaigns in the House of Representatives began early in the session and culminated in a victory over the President in spite of all that Seward, Welles, and the Blairs could do. Instead of reporting a reconstruction bill such as Lincoln suggested, Davis wrote and substituted a measure of his own. The President would leave the reconstructed states to abolish slavery themselves; Davis would compel immediate emancipation. The President would allow ten per cent of the voters to set up a new state government; Davis would require a majority. The President would proscribe only a few of the leading Confederates; Davis would proscribe a vast number. The President said nothing about repudiating Southern debts; Davis would compel repudiation of all Southern war debts, state and Confederate. His was a policy of "thorough," like that of the Cromwellians in England. Davis's principal speech in support of his drastic plan was made on Mar. 22, 1864, when the supporters of the President and the rising radical opposition were engaged in the bitterest warfare. He denied the right of the President to reconstruct a state and considered the Emancipation Proclamation as invalid until approved by Congress. He claimed all power for Congress and wished so to reconstruct the Southern states, when they were completely beaten and utterly helpless, that no court could ever undo the work. The Davis bill passed the House and the Senate by large majorities. When at last, after his renomination and the adjournment of Congress, Lincoln pocket-vetoed the measure, Davis was beside himself with rage. He took the extreme risk of a violent attack upon the nominee of his party at a moment when few thoughtful men had any real hope of complete success in the war. In July, conferences of leading Republicans were held in New York. Davis took part. In the spirit of these troubled men, Davis wrote the famous Wade-Davis manifesto which appeared in the leading papers on Aug. 8, 1864. In this document he reviewed the history of the congressional plan of reconstruction and ridiculed the President's plan in unmerciful language (*Speeches and Addresses of Henry Winter Davis,* pp. 415–426).

It is said that Davis never entered the White House during Lincoln's incumbency and that this manifesto brought the relations of the two men, as well as of the opposing groups in the Republican party, to the necessity of some understanding. The presidential election was pending and the people of the North had plainly lost heart. Davis was in Baltimore waging his campaign for reëlection, while Seward, Weed, Welles, and the rest were fighting in Washington and elsewhere for the success of their chief. On July 1, Chase resigned and gave up his open fight on the President. On Sept. 4, the news of victory at Atlanta reached Washington. Early in September, Montgomery Blair ceased his war upon Davis and offered his resignation. Before the end of September, Davis called at the White House and henceforth made speeches on behalf of the President. Lincoln was reëlected and Chase took his seat as chief justice, but the ambitious chairman of the Committee on Foreign Relations was defeated in his district.

When Congress met, however, in December 1864, Davis, now a "lame duck," was the most popular man in it. He fought through the short session, saw Andrew Johnson inaugurated with more than wonted pleasure, and, after the death of Lincoln, went to Chicago to make another of his great speeches: He attacked Johnson as he had attacked Lincoln, and outlined once more the program of congressional reconstruction which was indorsed by Charles Sumner at Worcester on Sept. 14 and readopted by Congress the next year. Davis, still only forty-eight years old, looked forward to the day when he might sit in the coveted White House, meanwhile impeaching Andrew Johnson, as he must have sought the impeachment of Lincoln if the latter had lived. A private citizen of extraordinary prestige, he returned to Washington in December 1865, and with his mere presence at the door of the House of Representatives broke up the session. Exposed to inclement weather during the holidays, he took cold. This developed into pneumonia and on Dec. 30 he died.

[There has never been an adequate study of Davis's career, though Bernard C. Steiner, *The Life of Henry Winter Davis* (1916), offers a brief review of the main facts and incidents. J. A. J. Creswell's sketch of Davis's life is published as an introduction to *The Speeches and Addresses Delivered in the Cong. of the U. S. and on Several Public Occasions, by Henry Winter Davis* (1867). Gideon Welles and Adam Gurowski make frequent mention of him in their diaries.]

W. E. D.

DAVIS, HORACE (Mar. 16, 1831–July 12, 1916), manufacturer, congressman, was born in Worcester, Mass., the son of "Honest John" Davis [*q.v.*] and Eliza (Bancroft) Davis, sister of George Bancroft, the historian. His brothers were J. C. Bancroft Davis and Andrew McFarland Davis [*qq.v.*]. Upon his graduation from Harvard College in 1849, he entered the Law School, but because of failing eyesight soon withdrew. He thereupon sailed for San Francisco, via Cape Horn. Upon his arrival in California, he started for the gold-mines and for a short time ran, unsuccessfully, a store at Shaw's Flat. Returning to San Francisco, he successively found employment as lumber-surveyor on the water-front, as supercargo on a coasting steamer owned by his cousin, Isaac Davis, and as a purser in the Pacific Mail Steamship Company. In 1852 he was one of a small group who organized the Mercantile Library Association, the oldest public library in California. Since the enterprise was suffering from lack of financial support, he was persuaded to assume the duties of librarian in February 1854. Under his administration popular interest was revived, and the library was soon operating upon a substantial foundation. His duties, however, especially in compiling the first catalogue, strained his eyes and so undermined his health that he resigned in December 1855. He and his brother Andrew had loaned their savings to a miller, and in satisfaction of the unpaid debt were obliged to take over the milling property; in 1860 he established the Golden Gate Flouring Mills, which proved to be highly profitable. He became an accepted authority on wheat and the production of flour; and at his death, was president of the Sperry Flour Company. At the beginning of the Civil War, he was active in the "Home Guard," a secret league formed in San Francisco to insure the loyalty of California to the Lincoln administration. The league helped elect Leland Stanford governor by keeping peace around the polls on election day, and then dissolved. Later Davis was an active member of the Sanitary Commission.

Elected to Congress in 1876, he served two terms there. His most important activity as a member of the House was in connection with the Chinese question. In January 1878, he introduced a bill to restrict immigration from China, and he made his only lengthy speech in Congress, June 8, 1878, in support of it (*Congressional Record*, 45 Cong., 2 Sess., pp. 4328–32). He was president of the Produce Exchange in San Francisco for ten years previous to his election to Congress. After his retirement from that body, he became president of the San Francisco Chamber of Commerce (1883–84), president of the Savings and Loan Society (1885), and member of the Republican National Committee (1880–88). In February 1888 he was elected president of the University of California, but resigned in April 1890. He was also closely associated with Stanford University, having been named by its founder as one of the original trustees, and in his last years served as president of the board. One of his chief interests was the School of Mechanic Arts in San Francisco, established by James Lick [*q.v.*]. He served as president of its board of trustees, and was instrumental in effecting its consolidation with the Wilmerding and Lux schools. A devoted Unitarian, he was deeply interested in the Pacific Unitarian School for the Ministry, to which he contributed generously.

Davis found time to take an active interest in historical and literary studies, and to publish a number of essays. The most important of these was his monograph, "American Constitutions," in which he traced the changes in the relations of the three departments of government "which have been silently going on in the United States for the past century" (*Johns Hopkins University Studies in Historical and Political Science*, I, 1885). He was twice married. His first wife, the daughter of Capt. Macondray, died in 1872 after years of invalidism. Three years later, he married Edith, the daughter of Rev. Thomas Starr King [*q.v.*]. He died at San Francisco at the age of eighty-five, following an operation for appendicitis.

[Newspaper clippings pertaining to Horace Davis's political life, 1876–80, pamphlets on Cal., and "How I Got into the Library Business" (MS. 1916), in the Univ. of Cal. Lib.; "The 'Home Guard' of 1861," reprinted from H. Morse Stephens and H. E. Bolton, *The Pacific Ocean in Hist.* (1917); W. C. Jones, *Illustrated Hist. of the Univ. of Cal.* (1901), pp. 140 ff.; *San Francisco Chronicle*, July 13, 1916; C. A. Murdock, *A Backward Glance at Eighty* (1921), pp. 219–24; *Who's Who in America*, 1916–17.] P.O.R.

DAVIS, JEFF (May 6, 1862–Jan. 3, 1913), governor of Arkansas, United States senator, son of Lewis W. and Elizabeth (Phillips) Davis, was born in Little River County, Ark. He attended the common schools, the preparatory department of the University of Arkansas, and the law school of Vanderbilt University, and received a degree in law from Cumberland University. Admitted to the bar at nineteen, he began practising with his father at Russellville, Ark. Entering public life in 1890, he remained in it most of the time until his death. Prosecuting attorney of the fifth judicial district for four years (1890–94), he became attorney-general of Arkansas in 1899. Shortly after assuming the latter office, he attracted considerable attention by his interpretation of the state anti-trust law, which provided that no corporation belonging to an association for the fixing of prices should be allowed to do business in Arkansas. Davis, holding this to mean any asso-

ciation outside as well as inside the state, secured indictments against numerous corporations, but was overruled by the supreme court. This decision and the building of a new state capitol became the issues on which he was elected governor for three terms (1901–07), breaking all records in the state. His first and second legislatures refused to amend the law, but the third (1905) changed it to meet his wishes. The result was that the insurance companies quit the state. The law soon became a dead letter and part of it was repealed in 1907. He supported the bill to repeal the fellow-servants rule, which it took several years of agitation to enact; and he favored the abolition of the suicide clause in life-insurance policies, more liberal Confederate pensions, and larger appropriations for state charitable institutions. At the close of his last term he juggled the financial statement so as to make it appear that the state was out of debt and had a surplus, and induced the legislature to reduce the taxes,—a policy which caused a deficit and a later bond issue. Following his governorship, he served a term in the United States Senate (1907–13). Two days after being sworn in he introduced a bill to apply his anti-trust law to the nation, and kept it on the calendar for five years. He denounced "gambling in agricultural products" and introduced a bill prohibiting dealing in futures. Another bill proposed to prohibit the sale or gift of intoxicating liquors in prohibition territory. Although he supported the repeal of the fellow-servants rule in Arkansas, he opposed, in Congress, the employers' liability and workmen's compensation bill in 1912. He made little effort to push his own bills, but "occupied himself with looking after the wants of his constituents, answering their letters, . . . sent out all the seeds allotted to him and all he could borrow . . . and kept himself in political condition for the next campaign."

Davis revolutionized Arkansas politics. He was largely instrumental in bringing about the substitution of the general primary for the convention system in nominating officers. Most of those who opposed him he treated as personal as well as political enemies, but he became completely reconciled when they returned to his camp. His unalterable purpose was self-advancement and every one who stood in the way had to pay the penalty. Most of the newspapers opposed him, but Davis capitalized this, telling his "hill-billies" and "red necks" that the newspapers said no one would vote for him "except the fellow who wears patched breeches and one gallus and lives up the forks of the creek, and don't pay anything except his poll tax." He set the country against the town. He never scrupled to repeat stories proved to be false. No one in his day in Arkansas excelled him in ability to appeal to the passions and prejudices of the people. He was fond of fishing, hunting, and baseball. He rarely wore black, his favorite suit being a Prince Albert of Confederate gray. He was a member of the Baptist church, but was turned out for drinking. Thereafter he referred to those who turned him out as "quart" Baptists, himself as a "pint" Baptist. His first wife, Ina McKenzie, whom he married in 1882, bore him twelve children. Of her Senator J. P. Clarke said that she was the only person who could influence Davis against his own convictions. In October 1911 he married Leila Carter.

[Chas. Jacobson, *The Life Story of Jeff Davis* (1925), a well-written, unbiased account by his private secretary, who might have told more; L. S. Dunaway, *Jeff Davis, Governor and U. S. Senator: His Life and Speeches* (1913), made up almost wholly of speeches and Memorial Addresses; *Arkansas Gazette*, Mar. 31, 1912, and Jan. 3, 1913; *Arkansas Democrat*, Jan. 3, 1913; Davis's messages to the legislature, in *House Jour.*, 1901, pp. 42 ff.; 1903, pp. 35 ff.; 1905, pp. 28 ff.; 1907, pp. 43 ff.; *Cong. Record,* 60 Cong., 1 Sess., pp. 136, 634; 2 Sess., pp. 65, 361; 61 Cong., 2 Sess., pp. 76, 5542, 8455–57; 62 Cong., 2 Sess., pp. 616, 617, 5810–11; Memorial Addresses in *Cong. Record,* 62 Cong., 3 Sess., pp. 4389–93.]   D. Y. T.

DAVIS, JEFFERSON (June 3, 1808–Dec. 6, 1889), president of the Confederate States of America, was born in Christian (now Todd) County, Ky., the tenth child of Samuel and Jane (Cook) Davis, who had moved westward from Georgia. Samuel Davis commanded a troop of irregular horse in the Revolutionary War. His father, Evan Davis, was a Welsh emigrant who had entered America through Philadelphia and had followed the drift of emigration southward into the new lands of Georgia. In Kentucky, the Davis family do not appear to have thrived. When Jefferson was a mere child they wandered on to Mississippi, where they found their anchorage on a small plantation near Woodville, Wilkinson County. Though Samuel Davis does not appear to have done much by way of lifting his middle-class family in the social scale, that result was achieved by his eldest son, Joseph Emory Davis, who rapidly acquired a fortune, an education, and a prominent position in the new community of the Southwest. While Samuel Davis lapses into the background of the picture, Joseph becomes the real head of the family and the patron of his younger brother, many years his junior. Eventually Joseph Davis was considered one of the wealthiest men in the South.

Jefferson Davis was an extremely sensitive, a highly imaginative child and boy. At the age of seven he rode northward, nearly a thousand miles, to become a pupil of the Roman Catholic Seminary, St. Thomas's College, in Washington County, Ky. What induced his Baptist parents to place him there is not known. They very nearly had a reward that doubtless would have appalled them. The impressionable lad became so fond of the priests who were his teachers that he wished for a time to adopt their religion (Davis, *Memoir, post,* I, 13–14). The incident in its fullness has a reminder of Henry Esmond and Father Holt. Indeed, one may find a sort of clue to Davis, to his strength and his weakness, his loftiness, his sensibility, his egoism and his illusions, in Thackeray's famous character. Nothing came of the juvenile Roman enthusiasm, and at nine he was back in Mississippi. After several years in local schools he was entered at Transylvania University, in 1821. Very little is known of his college life. The early records of Transylvania have been destroyed and the traditions are few. Davis himself has said, "There I completed my studies in Greek and Latin, and learned a little of algebra, geometry, trigonometry, surveying, profane and sacred history, and natural philosophy" (*Memoir,* I, 27). He did not finish the course at Transylvania. A Mississippi congressman nominated him to West Point. It is safe to attribute this to the growing influence, social and political, of his brother Joseph. On Sept. 1, 1824, Jefferson Davis matriculated at West Point. In 1828 he was graduated and became a second lieutenant in the United States army. Among the other distinguished Southerners who were cadets when he was, and who were destined to have fateful relations with him in after time, were both the Johnstons and Robert E. Lee. Of the youth of Davis anecdote has preserved a good deal and if most of it may be trusted, we may think of him as a very engaging young man, fearless, generous, modest, with personal charm, and in friendship rashly loyal.

His military apprenticeship of nearly seven years was spent in Wisconsin and in the unsettled portions of Illinois, in little, remote posts, garrisoned by mere handfuls of men, in as lonely regions as the world possessed. The Black Hawk Indian war in 1832 was like a brief interlude of relieving storm that blew across this dreary period. Nobody did anything distinguished in that war. But both Jefferson Davis, as a minor officer of the regular army, and Abraham Lincoln, as an inconspicuous officer of volunteers, took part in it. They did not meet. In 1833 Lieut. Davis was stationed much of the time at Fort Crawford, Wis., where the commandant was Col. Zachary Taylor. He had a daughter, Sarah Knox. The young people fell in love. Col. Taylor disapproved. But they would have their way. Davis resigned June 30, 1835; Miss Taylor sought a friendly aunt in Kentucky; Davis followed; they were speedily married and set out for Mississippi.

During the next ten years, 1835–45, from the age of twenty-seven to the age of thirty-seven, he was a planter, absorbing the mental atmosphere of the distinctive new state, which had been peopled by emigrants from so many regions and where his family was now entering the upper rank. The outward story of these years was lacking in drama except for one event. His early romance closed suddenly, tragically within three months of his marriage. Mrs. Davis died of malarial fever Sept. 15, 1835. Except for a little travel in Cuba while convalescing from the same malady that had killed his wife, followed by a brief visit to New York and Washington, where he made a short sojourn among important politicians at a senatorial boarding-house, the remainder of the ten years was spent quietly on his plantation or at near-by cities. The period closed with two events which took place close together, his election to the national House of Representatives and his second marriage. Varina Howell, who on Feb. 26, 1845, became the second Mrs. Davis [q.v.] was a local beauty, a member of the upmost social rank, a high-spirited and accomplished woman. This marriage identified him conclusively with the local aristocracy.

It was during these long quiet years as a country gentleman that Davis's mind was formed politically. His father who had died several years before had bequeathed him a little money. His brother Joseph added to it. Not far from Joseph's plantation, "Hurricane," the plantation "Brierfield" became the seat of the younger brother. It was rough new land overlooking the Mississippi. Much of it was "cleared" for the first time by its new owner. He was a hard worker, taking the most intense interest in his estate, and often sharing field work with his slaves. Nevertheless, he now became an extensive, even omnivorous, reader especially in the fields of politics and history. Joseph was also a natural student. He had been bred to the law and never lost his delight in close argument. Frequently the brothers would spend the night at the same plantation and there would be long evenings of discussion of books and politics. Hitherto the younger Davis had lived since childhood away from home; he had been a student or a soldier in distant lands; he had lacked the sense of soil. This he now acquired. He was permeated by that peculiar atmosphere which belonged to the Mississippi environment. Like those others whom it had drawn to itself from such great distances he became devoted to its social system.

The quietude of life at Brierfield in the late thirties was a sharp contrast with the stormy life of the nation at large. The Abolitionists had begun their crusade. The country rang with their denunciation of the Southern social system. As was often pointed out, they made no distinction between slavery and slaveholders, cursing both in the same breath. The relation of Davis to his slaves was peculiarly gentle and patriarchal. He resented bitterly the Abolitionist attack, and, like practically all the members of the planter class, met it with state-rights arguments. These were destined to be turned against him when he was chief executive of the Confederacy.

It is more than likely that a temperamental influence throughout these quiet years was his deep-seated love of the army and of the military life. He had renounced it for sentimental reasons; he was destined to renounce it twice again for other reasons; but he never lost his zeal for it. Nor did he ever lose his faith in himself as a soldier. A rooted egoism was thus revealed. Though he never did anything of first importance in a military way he was capable, in the heat of the Civil War, of regarding himself as the equal of the greatest generals of the time. Another quality of his mind, his lack of humor, was brought out eventually by this invincible delusion. Mrs. Davis, with Olympian indiscretion, has preserved one of the most unfortunate of the slips in speech that have been made by men of genius. In the darkest hour of the Confederacy, Davis said to his wife, "If I could take one wing and Lee the other, I think we could between us wrest a victory from those people" (*Memoir*, II, 392).

This extraordinary self-confidence rested on nothing but a brief, creditable service in the year 1846, and on one very gallant action in the year 1847. He had gone to Congress as a Democrat in December 1845; the outbreak of the Mexican War was the cause of his resignation the following June. He accepted command of a volunteer regiment known as the "Mississippi Rifles," swiftly whipped it into shape, and joined Gen. Taylor [q.v.] in time to participate in the attack upon Monterey. What had passed between himself and his former father-in-law since the death of his first wife is not known, but apparently they were again friends. Taylor appointed him one of the commissioners to negotiate the surrender of Monterey. The next year, in the strangely jumbled battle of Buena Vista, Davis won his reputation as a soldier. Very probably the stand made by the Mississippi Rifles at a crucial moment saved Taylor from defeat. The action was praised extravagantly, far and wide. There came a time when the effect of its applause upon Davis's mind formed the basis of sneers. Long afterward, a Confederate newspaper, bitter against Davis's military policy, alluded to the form in which he disposed his men at Buena Vista, and said "If the Confederacy perishes, it will have died of a V."

The course of the authorities at Washington caused Davis's second renunciation of the military life. Taylor was side-tracked in favor of Scott, and the Mississippi Rifles were left with the minor force that plainly was to have no more chances. The "Rifles" had enlisted for a short period. At its expiration in the summer of 1847 Davis withdrew from the army. Mississippi made him a national senator. He took his seat in December 1847. He was a conspicuous figure; in the popular eye, he was a "hero" of Buena Vista. But popular heroes are not always the heroes of the Senate. His first period as a senator, closing with his resignation in the autumn of 1851, lasted nearly three years, and while it gave him for the first time a national reputation politically, it ended without his having attained a commanding position in his party. In 1848 he steadily supported President Polk and opposed Calhoun, approving the great seizure of Mexican territory on which the President had set his heart. He went so far as to advocate the occupation of Yucatan by the United States, expressing the fear that otherwise it might be taken by Great Britain (*Congressional Globe,* 30 Cong., 1 Sess., p. 729, May 5, 1848). When it was proposed to organize the territory of Oregon without provision for slavery he "denied that there was any power in Congress or in the people of the Territory to interrupt the slave system" by forbidding a slaveholder to take his slaves thither (*Ibid.,* 30 Cong., 1 Sess., p. 927, July 12, 1848). In the debate over the admission of California he reiterated this position but was willing to compromise on the extension of the line of the Missouri Compromise to the Pacific (*Ibid.,* 31 Cong., 1 Sess., App., p. 286, Mar. 8, 1850). He was one of ten senators who opposed to the last the admission of California and who signed a "Protest against the California Bill."

In his course with regard to California, Davis was opposed by his colleague from Mississippi, Senator Henry S. Foote [*q.v.*], a politician of great boldness. Though the legislature of Mississippi passed resolutions instructing their sena-

tors to resist the admission of California "by all honorable and constitutional means," Foote refused to be bound by them. It turned out that he had gauged the conditions at home with deep shrewdness. He was nominated for governor on a "Union" ticket, supported by Whigs and dissatisfied Democrats, and in September 1851, seemed about to carry the election. The political situation in the South in 1851 was extremely complex and Davis's relation to it is not altogether clear. The struggle against the admission of California and the failure to extend the Missouri Compromise line had produced a general movement for secession. A convention of the whole South which held two meetings at Nashville, one in June 1850, the other in November, had secession in view. The desire to secede was practically universal, but there were two policies on the subject. Extreme state-rights men such as R. B. Rhett [*q.v.*] of South Carolina and W. L. Yancey [*q.v.*] of Alabama wanted their states to rush ahead irrespective of what other states might do. The course followed by another group revealed a point of view that may be labeled Southern nationalism. Between the first and second meetings of the Nashville convention these others concluded that it was impossible to effect an immediate secession of the whole South. Thereupon they threw themselves into an attempt to arrest the secession movement, to postpone it until the whole South could be persuaded to leave the Union together. Rhett, who refused to accept this view, was eventually defeated in a popular campaign, on the issue of secession, by the South Carolina "cooperationists."

A third Southern party was for accepting the compromise measures of 1850 as the start of a satisfactory new chapter in the history of the Union. With this group Foote was associated. His opponent was Gen. John A. Quitman [*q.v.*], who was in Mississippi pretty much what Rhett was in South Carolina. By September 1851 it was plain that the tide had turned. The genuine Unionists and the "cooperationists" between them were going to prevent an immediate movement for secession. The Democratic leaders in Mississippi appear to have concluded that the game was up. They looked around for a way out. Quitman was persuaded to resign; Davis was persuaded to leave the Senate and take his place. Though there is no positive evidence upon his motives a safe guess would fix upon two. He was instinctively a party man; all his military predisposition, his *esprit de corps,* tended that way. The desire to save the party, to perform a strategic retreat with as much credit as possible, must have influenced him. But it is fair to assume a deeper motive. In him, even more thoroughly than in the anti-Rhett men of South Carolina, the vision of the South as a nation was a real thing. We may conclude that Davis took the place of the secessionist Quitman with a view to relieving his party of its hasty commitment to immediate secession and for the purpose of aligning it, tacitly at least, with "cooperation." His strategic retreat was a success. A vote for a convention that was to decide the issue of secession or "submission" had given Foote a majority of 8,000, but when the vote was cast for governor, his majority was less than 1,000.

Davis resumed his life as a planter, only to reënter politics on Mar. 7, 1853, when he became secretary of war in the cabinet of his friend Franklin Pierce. His tenure of the war office was perhaps the peak of his career; certainly no chapter of his life was more to his taste. His health, which both before and after was delicate, was during most of this period robust. The Davises were the center of a delightful coterie in Washington; Mrs. Davis, witty and charming, drew all sorts of people into her drawing-room. Despite political differences, men as unlike her husband as Seward were his close personal friends. The most brilliant portrait of him is contained in a passage from Carl Schurz: "I had in my imagination formed a high idea of what a grand personage the War Minister of this great Republic must be. I was not disappointed. He received me graciously. His slender, tall, and erect figure, his spare face, keen eyes, and fine forehead, not broad, but high and well-shaped, presented the well-known strong American type. There was in his bearing a dignity which seemed entirely natural and unaffected—that kind of dignity which does not invite familiar approach, but will not render one uneasy by lofty assumption. His courtesy was without any condescending air. . . . His conversation ran in easy . . . well-chosen and sometimes even elegant phrase, and the timbre of his voice had something peculiarly agreeable. . . . I heard him deliver a speech in the Senate, and again I was struck by the dignity of his bearing, the grace of his diction, and the rare charm of his voice—things which greatly distinguished him from many of his colleagues" (*The Reminiscences of Carl Schurz*, II, 1907, p. 21).

Apparently, the idea of secession was allowed to lapse in Davis's mind during several years. But the idea of the South as a social and economic unit, a nation within the Union, was constant. His policies were governed by the steadfast hope of so enlarging the South territorially and of so developing it economically that it would prove the equal in political power of the opposite section. Consequently he was eager for expansion southward, and was frequently in opposition to the secretary of state, William L. Marcy [*q.v.*], whose eyes were on the Northern, not the Southern, wing of the party. In their general attitudes toward Spain and Mexico, Davis may be described as belligerent, Marcy as conciliatory. In the case of the ship *Black Warrior* seized by the Spanish authorities at Havana on a legal technicality, and in connection with the Ostend Manifesto issued by three American ambassadors as a statement of our Spanish policy Davis failed to control the foreign policy of the administration. With all the more zeal he turned to the advancement of Southern economic interests at home. Asia had become of first importance in the minds of most Americans who thought about trade. To obtain a window upon the Pacific was a great part of the inspiration of the Southern nationalists in 1850. Davis, still hoping for Southern expansion to the Pacific, took the liveliest interest in promoting a great scheme for a transcontinental railway that should be close to the Mexican border and terminate in that part of California which the Southerners in 1850 had attempted to obtain. To make such a railroad possible he induced Pierce and Marcy to acquire from Mexico the region now known as the Gadsden Purchase. To demonstrate the practicability of such a road he dispatched an expedition comprising engineers, artists, and scientists who prepared a monumental report on the Southwest which the government published in ten large volumes.

The close of his term as secretary of war (1857) was followed immediately by his reëntry into the Senate. During the period in which he had been withdrawn from obvious participation in congressional politics one main chapter in American history had closed, and another had opened. He had had a part in the conclave of party leaders that met at the White House on Sunday, Jan. 22, 1854, from which emerged the Kansas-Nebraska Bill. Just how much he contributed to this epoch-making bill must remain a matter of conjecture. Promptly after his return to the Senate he became again a conspicuous defender of the South. During the three years and more of his second period as senator his arguments are much the same as in the first period; but they are presented with more heat. He defends slavery because it "bears to capital as kind a relation as can exist between them anywhere" and assures the South that the election of an Abolitionist as president "would be a species of revolution by which the purposes of the Government would be destroyed and the observance of its mere forms entitled to no respect" (Speech before the Mississippi Legislature, Nov. 16, 1858; Rowland, *post,* III, 356). It seems probable that he had already passed the summit of his career both mentally and physically. The splendid manifestation of energy that so impressed Schurz is now pathetically absent from the picture. Ill health returned. He suffered intensely from neuralgia, from nervous indigestion, and from a very painful disease of the eyes that came near wrecking his sight. The frequency of the heated tone in his speeches may be a significant symptom. Intellectually, he does not stand forth from the group of Southerners who opposed a firm but desperate front to the growing power of the North. He had a place in their first rank and in all their councils but his contribution to their battle was mainly oratorical and emotional. He was still a brilliant figure in the public eye, and the intensity of his convictions, the patent honesty of his purpose, gave great weight to all his utterances.

In the bitterly furious internal history of the Democratic party from the day of the Dred Scott decision of 1857, to the breakup of the Charleston convention in 1860, Davis and Douglas fought each other to the death. Ostensibly the issue was between "popular sovereignty" defended by Douglas, and the doctrine of the Dred Scott decision which affirmed Davis's constant position that neither Congress nor local law could interfere with slavery in a territory. Behind this ostensible issue was something else that is not quite apparent. Davis joined with Yancey and Rhett in their successful effort to prevent the nomination of Douglas at Charleston, and therefore it has been assumed rashly that he shared their hope for secession as a result of the events of 1860. On the other hand, when the party had been split in two and both Douglas and Breckinridge were "Democratic" nominees, Davis, though a supporter of Breckinridge, wrote to Rhett discouraging secession and reviving exactly the "cooperationist" reasoning of 1851. Perhaps one may assume that what Davis really wanted was a confessed duality within the Union —the South to have substantially what was afterward known as "dominion status," like that of Canada or Ireland in the British Empire today—and that he did not share Rhett's enthusiasm for secession in itself.

He was relatively passive during the anxious weeks that followed the election of Lincoln. The one issue of the moment which seemed to him vital was whether the South was to continue to have an open frontier with the possibility to expand. Lincoln settled this by his declaration that while he would concede almost every other point at issue between the sections, there should be no more slave states. Thereafter Davis's course was predestined. When Mississippi seceded he acquiesced. In one of his most noted speeches he announced to the Senate the secession of his state and himself formally withdrew, Jan. 21, 1861.

Unlike most of the Southern leaders, Davis expected war. There can be no doubt that he hoped to be the chief commander of the Southern armies. Mississippi promptly appointed him major-general of the state troops. Meanwhile, a general convention of the seceding states had made one of those compromise choices so common in American conventions, and had agreed upon a provisional President of the Confederacy who was nobody's first choice. It was Davis. "The messenger with the notification . . . found him in our garden [at Brierfield] assisting to make rose cuttings; when reading the telegram he looked so grieved that I feared some evil had befallen our family" (*Memoir,* II, 18). It was the summons of circumstance to make the third, the final renunciation of his own unconquerable ambition, the desire for military fame. He accepted his destiny. On Feb. 18, 1861, at Montgomery, he was inaugurated president.

A tired man in very delicate health attempted an almost impossible task. The South was unprepared for war, and based its hopes of independence mainly upon the idea that "Cotton was King." Foreign affairs at once became the master key to the situation. But neither Davis nor his successive secretaries of state were able to exert much influence upon the policies of Europe. Those were determined by circumstances beyond their control which are part of Federal rather than Confederate history. The successful blockade of the Confederate coast quickly shut off the outflow of cotton and also prevented the inflow of munitions.

Davis found himself unable to control the course of events except in two respects, both of which brought into clear view convictions and qualities of mind that had been taking form during many years. First of all he kept a close hand upon the management of the army. In doing so he gave rein to his delusion that he was the equal of any one as a strategist. To Lee, alone, does he appear to have conceded preëminence. With other generals, he permitted his egoism and his irritability frequently to assert themselves. He was not always wise in his choice of men to trust. He would not listen to any one who belittled either Gen. Braxton Bragg [*q.v.*] or that brilliant but unpopular Jew who served both as secretary of war and as secretary of state, Judah P. Benjamin [q.v.]. He did not hesitate to set public opinion at defiance. When Congress was about to vote a condemnation of Benjamin because of the disaster of Roanoke Island in 1862, Davis showed his haughty contempt for it by promoting Benjamin from the War Department to the State Department. His animosities were as uncompromising as his friendships. He had a relentless quarrel with Joseph Johnston [q.v.], whom he removed from command in Georgia at a critical moment in 1864. When Congress compelled the reinstatement of Johnston in high command Davis evaded making the necessary appointment and contrived to have it made by Lee. Another assertion of his autocratic will was the letter he wrote to J. A. Seddon [q.v.], secretary of war, deploring the resignation that had been wrung from him by the hostility of Congress.

His imperious temper aggravated by ill health —his wife speaks of his coming home from his office, "fasting, a mere mass of throbbing nerves" —did not help him in the difficult political problems which rapidly developed. As soon as it became apparent that Davis's loyalty was given to the South as a whole, that he would sacrifice the interest of any Southern state if thus he could create a Southern nation committed to the preservation of the Southern social order, excessively theoretical advocates of state rights like Rhett and Yancey became his bitter political enemies. An anti-Davis party was quickly formed which was rallied, ostensibly at least, around the central idea of state sovereignty. Gov. Brown of Georgia and such powerful politicians as Robert Toombs [q.v.] and Alexander H. Stephens [q.v.] were drawn into the opposition. It controlled some of the most influential Southern newspapers including the most influential of all, the *Richmond Examiner*. The *Charleston Mercury,* owned by the Rhett family, was Davis's uncompromising enemy throughout the war (see Owsley, *post*).

The active beginning of opposition to his government very nearly coincided with his formal inauguration as regular president. He had been elected in October 1861, and was inaugurated Feb. 22, 1862. Even before this he had stirred antagonism by his veto of a bill that would have permitted the officering of a Texas regiment by the governor of the state. The *Mercury* was very sharp in its comments on this veto. Within a month of the inauguration he had defied Congress by transferring Benjamin to the State Department. About the same time he proposed a general conscription law which, though enacted,

was at once taken up by the state-rights apologists and denounced as unconstitutional. This was the beginning of a desultory quarrel between state and Confederate authorities over control of enlistments that did not cease until the Confederacy collapsed (see Moore, *post*). Incidental to this controversy were the repeated attempts of the administration party to vest in the President large powers through the suspension of the writ of *habeas corpus*. Though, of course, the usual complex of political interests informed the two parties, it is fair to impute to them a real antagonism over ideas—centralization upon the one hand, local autonomy upon the other. The controversy was quieted briefly by the brilliant military events of 1862, but broke out with renewed vigor after the failure of the great triple offensive—in Maryland, in Kentucky, in Mississippi—of the autumn of that year.

Among the tremendous military events of the following year the political issues seem almost to escape from view, but, in fact, the hostility of the two parties raged with increasing violence. Confederate money had ceased to have value worth talking about. Financial taxation was an unreality. To meet this difficult situation the government revived the ancient system of tithes through a statute known as the Tax in Kind. Being all but unable to support itself, the government was also empowered, by means of an Impressment Act, to seize supplies and to pay for them at prices fixed by official commissioners. A third measure inspired the *Mercury* to publish an attack upon the government entitled "A Despotism over the Confederate States Proposed in Congress." It referred to a renewed attempt to suspend the writ of *habeas corpus*. The argument in favor of suspension was chiefly the flagrant obstruction of the conscription acts, connived at, if not encouraged, by many state officials, especially in North Carolina and Georgia. The leader of the opposition in Congress was the same Henry S. Foote who had defeated Davis for governor in 1851. His furious denunciations of the administration ended in the defeat of the bill.

Despite a great deal of spasmodic opposition, the administration had been able on most questions to obtain adequate support hitherto in Congress. The general elections of the autumn of 1863 made a change. The resulting Congress was composed very largely of men who were new to legislation; and it contained a majority hostile to Davis. The constitutional issue had melted into a less definite but even more dangerous one. There was a real though vague belief widely spread that the President was a despot, that some sort of *coup d'état* might be expected at any moment. An atmosphere of dread, created by unlimited denunciation of Davis's motives, was darkened by a series of difficulties with regard to labor. Early in the war it was tacitly agreed that the government should not be allowed to own slaves. The imaginary vision of a government owning an army of obedient barbarians—a hundred thousand, two hundred thousand—gave point to the cries against despotism and a *coup d'état*. The government had to rent slaves from their owners and used them as army laborers. At the same time it exempted one white man for every plantation of fifteen slaves or more to serve as overseer. This "Fifteen Slave Law" produced envy in men of small property. They were further embittered by a law which permitted the hiring of substitutes by men drafted for the army. They vented their anger in the saying that the Confederacy was waging "a rich man's war and a poor man's fight." There was no end of complaint against impressment commissioners; also charges of profiteering by government officials, some of which seem to have been justified.

Against this background of discontent three passages in Davis's annual message, November 1864, took on, in the popular mind, menacing significance. He urged Congress to authorize the government to purchase outright 40,000 slaves. He suggested that when the government was through with them these slaves should be set free. He recognized the existence of a disturbing popular controversy by saying that he dissented "from those who advise a general levy and arming of the slaves for the duty of soldiers" (*Journal, post,* IV, 258; Rowland, *post,* VI, 396). This was the beginning of the last important controversy of Confederate history. The army, worn and wasted by three and a half years of dreary valor, had to be reinforced. Negroes were the only remaining source of supply. The message was doubtless a "feeler" to take the sense of the country upon a policy which originated probably with Secretary Benjamin. Incidentally it carried with it the policy of emancipation. The administration party at once introduced both subjects into Congressional debate. During the terrible winter of 1864–65, while the military power of the Confederacy was visibly crumbling on every hand, the fanatical slaveholders in Congress kept the discussion in suspense. Eventually a bill was passed permitting a fresh levy of 300,-000 men, but making no mention of emancipation, and providing that these new troops were "to be raised from such classes of the population irrespective of color, in each State as the proper authorities thereof may determine" (*Journal,*

VII, 611–12). Virtually, it was a defeat for the administration. But Davis refused to admit that it was a defeat. He had become infatuated with the idea of emancipation as the last trump in his hand. He believed that by means of it he could yet win over the British government, induce it to enter the war, and at the eleventh hour save the Confederacy. A secret agent, Duncan F. Kenner, was sent to London only to be told that the offer came too late.

The frame of mind of Davis this concluding winter was strangely deluded. He appears to have had no doubt of a successful outcome of the war. In the preceding autumn with Sherman entrenched at Atlanta he had gone South on a tour of inspiration. His aim was to stir up a "people's war" by giving to popular audiences a true picture of the soldier's task. But he was not happy in his way of doing it. In describing Gen. Beauregard whom he had placed in command in Georgia, he attempted to give an impression of soldierly self-effacement. He said that this brave general would do whatever the President told him to do. His enemies seized upon the words. Here was further evidence that he was planning a *coup d'état*. Davis's last effective reinforcement of the army was accomplished by a general order this autumn revoking all exemptions, stripping the plantations of the overseers, and calling to the colors all soldiers furloughed or in hospital "except those unable to travel." Davis returned to Richmond, and Sherman began his march to the sea. While a wide swath of desolation was sweeping over the lower South, Davis confronted a crisis, the seriousness of which he did not in the least appreciate. There were "peace movements" agitating the South, and here and there something like a clamor for negotiations with Washington. The advocates of these movements had no clear notion of what they were trying to do, and had they not inspired overtures from the North would have little historical significance. They contributed indirectly to bring about a series of attempts to negotiate. In the summer of 1864 two Northerners came to Richmond unofficially for the purpose of catching Davis in a trap. They believed that he would refuse to treat for peace on any terms except the recognition of Southern independence, and they wanted to use the fact to hearten the North for the reëlection of Lincoln. As they had no official credentials Davis refused to discuss public affairs with them (Rowland, X, 32). A notable, but informal attempt to induce Davis to consent to reunion was made by Francis P. Blair [*q.v.*] in January 1865. Napoleon III, defying the Monroe Doctrine, had recently established Maximilian as Emperor of Mexico. Blair proposed to Davis a plan of reconciliation involving the complete abandonment of slavery, the reunion of all the states, and an expedition against Mexico in which Davis was to play the leading rôle. Davis cautiously refrained from committing himself, though he gave Blair a letter in which he expressed his willingness to enter into negotiations for peace between "the two countries." The visit of Blair gave new impetus to the peace movements. The Committee on Foreign Affairs of the Confederate House reported resolutions favoring an attempt to negotiate with the United States so as to "bring into view" the possibility of cooperation between the United States and the Confederacy to maintain the Monroe Doctrine. Before the end of the month Davis appointed commissioners to confer with the Northern authorities with regard to peace. There followed the famous Hampton Roads Conference, Feb. 3, 1865, at which Lincoln was present and Stephens was the chief spokesman for the Confederacy. Whether it is true, as tradition has it, that Lincoln told Stephens to write Union at the top of a page and anything he pleased under it, there is no doubt that the tradition fairly represents the situation of the moment. But Davis, though now committed in his own mind to emancipation, was determined to accept nothing short of independence. His delusion of power could not be shaken. Three days after the conference he made his last public oration as President of the Confederacy. He spoke in the precincts of the African Church in Richmond. Snow lay thick on the ground. A man in a dream, he talked with the passion of a seer and for the moment swept his audience before him. "Let us then unite our hands and our hearts, lock our shields together, and we may well believe that before another summer solstice falls upon us, it will be the enemy who will be asking us for conferences and occasions in which to make known our demands" (see Dodd, *post*, p. 353). Two months later Richmond had fallen and Davis was a fugitive.

The President's party left the city on Apr. 3. The next day he was at Danville where he waited five days. On Apr. 4 he issued his last proclamation calling on his people to resist to the last and promising them that Richmond would soon be recovered. The news of Lee's surrender caused him to turn southward. At Greensboro, Apr. 12, a cabinet council was held which Johnston and Beauregard attended. Reluctantly, Davis gave Johnston permission to negotiate for the surrender of his army to Sherman. Twelve days later, at Charlotte, Davis held his last council with his cabinet, approved Johnston's surrender,

and finally admitted that the Confederacy had been overthrown. The party broke up. Davis continued southward hoping to escape out of the country. At Irwinville, Ga., he was captured by Federal cavalry, May 10.

During two years he was a state prisoner in Fortress Monroe. The commandant, Gen. Nelson A. Miles [*q.v.*], acting upon instructions from Gen. Halleck and Assistant Secretary of War Charles A. Dana, ordered him put in irons (*A Statement of the Facts concerning the Imprisonment and Treatment of Jefferson Davis*, etc., 1902). He was later accorded different treatment. His health failed. At length he was assigned comfortable quarters which his family were permitted to share. He was never brought to trial. The lawyers of the government saw technical danger in every charge that was suggested. He was released on bond, May 13, 1867 (Nichols, *post*). Greeley and Gerrit Smith [*qq.v.*], once the bitter enemies of everything Southern, were among his bondsmen.

He was not yet an old man, and twenty-two years of life remained to him. They were valiant but sad years. His fortune was wrecked, his home a ruin, and his health impaired. Though these years, with the exception of three, contain no remarkable achievement they have a moral distinction second to nothing in his career. Health was recovered gradually, partly through European travel but more through sheer resolution and strength of will. In his seventieth year Davis was probably a more vigorous man than at any time since the great days when he was secretary of war. He embarked in a succession of business ventures but as he had no predilection for business and no business experience, they were all unsuccessful. Though a portion of the Brierfield estate was saved he was in his later years a poor man. A home was provided for his old age through the bequest of Mrs. Sarah A. Dorsey, a friend of Mrs. Davis. This was "Beauvoir" on the Gulf of Mexico. There he prepared his own version of his stormy career by writing *The Rise and Fall of the Confederate Government*, devoting to it the three years, 1878–81. Though Mississippi would have sent him to the Senate, he refused to ask for the Federal pardon without which it was impossible for him to take his seat. He died at New Orleans in his eighty-second year.

[The most important biography is Wm. E. Dodd, *Jefferson Davis* (1907). *Jefferson Davis, Ex-President of the Confederate States of America: a Memoir,* by his wife (2 vols., 1890), is an invaluable but rambling and fragmentary collection of details. *Jefferson Davis, Constitutionalist, His Letters, Papers, and Speeches* (10 vols., 1923), ed. by Dunbar Rowland, though voluminous, does not contain all the known private letters, omits all the dispatches in the *Official Records,* and is not complete in its selections from the *Cong. Globe.* For the mind of Davis, previous to secession, the *Globe,* after all, is the true record. His own apologia is *The Rise and Fall of the Confed. Govt.* (2 vols., 1881). J. P. Richardson, *A Compilation of the Messages and Papers of the Confederacy* (2 vols., 1905), contains some of the state papers; others are embedded in *Jour. of the Cong. of the Confed. States of America* (7 vols., 1904–05), being *Sen. Doc. No. 234,* 58 Cong., 2 Sess., and in the Fourth Series of the *Official Records.* Three newspapers may be regarded as government organs: the *Richmond Enquirer,* the Richmond *Sentinel* and the *Charleston Courier.* The official gazette of the government abroad was the *Index* published in London. As Davis was engaged in many controversies, all the writings of Confederate leaders contain Davis matter, but as a rule it is sharply partisan. Important recent studies are: A. B. Moore, *Conscription and Conflict in the Confederacy* (1924); F. L. Owsley, *State Rights in the Confederacy* (1925); R. F. Nichols, "United States vs. Jefferson Davis," *Am. Hist. Rev.,* XXXI, 266–84 (Jan. 1926). A number of excellent essays on Davis have been written by Walter L. Fleming, but have not been collected. For his military career, see G. W. Cullum, *Biog. Reg. Officers and Grads. U. S. Mil. Acad.* (3rd ed., 1891), I, 416.]

N. W. S.

DAVIS, JEFFERSON COLUMBUS (Mar. 2, 1828–Nov. 30, 1879), soldier, the son of William and Mary (Drummond) Davis, was born on a farm in Clark County, Ind., whither his family had come from Kentucky. He had a year's service in the Mexican War as an enlisted man in the 3rd Indiana Regiment, and fought at Buena Vista. Appointed a second lieutenant in the 1st Artillery in 1848, he was promoted first lieutenant in 1852 and captain in 1861. He was in garrison at Fort Sumter at the time of the bombardment. In August 1861 he was appointed colonel of the 22nd Indiana Infantry, and in December was made brigadier-general of volunteers. He commanded a division at the battle of Pea Ridge and at the siege of Corinth. He seemed to have a brilliant future before him when he stained his reputation with a crime which is often remembered when his military services are forgotten. Brooding over a severe rebuke received some days before from Gen. William Nelson, his commanding officer, he sought out Nelson (Sept. 29, 1862) in the lobby of a Louisville hotel with the evident purpose of forcing a quarrel upon him. After high words, Davis crumpled up a card and threw it in Nelson's face, and Nelson retaliated with a slap. Davis then left him, but returning a few minutes later with a revolver shot him as he passed through the hall, inflicting a mortal wound. Partly on account of his military abilities, but more, it is surmised, because of the exertion of strong political influence—especially through his friend, Gov. Oliver P. Morton, who accompanied him when he quarreled with Nelson—Davis went wholly unpunished and after a short time was restored to duty. He commanded a division at Murfreesboro and Chickamauga and

in the Atlantic campaign, and a corps on the march to the sea and in the campaign of the Carolinas. He received, however, no further promotion, although Rosecrans, and later Grant, recommended that he be made a major-general. Perhaps the administration felt about him as Dr. Johnson did about the American colonists, that he "ought to be thankful for anything . . . short of hanging." He was mustered out of the volunteer service in 1866, and appointed colonel of the 23rd Infantry. He served for a considerable time in Alaska, and took part in the Modoc War which followed the murder of Gen. Canby in 1873. He died in Chicago. Gen. Fry describes him as "brave, quiet, obliging, humorous in disposition and full of ambition, daring, endurance and self-confidence." It is said that he never regretted killing Nelson, but that he bitterly resented his failure to receive a major-generalcy of volunteers and a brigadier-generalcy in the regular army. He was married to Mariette Woodson Athon of Indianapolis.

[Jas. B. Fry, *Mil. Miscellanies* (1889), pp. 486–505, gives a full account of the murder of Nelson, which is also described in *Battles and Leaders of the Civil War* (1887), III, 43–44, 60–61. See also: F. B. Heitman, *Hist. Reg. and Dict. of the U. S. Army* (1903), I, pp. 358–59; Jacob B. Dunn, *Ind. and Indianans* (1919), IV, pp. 1563–64; *Official Records* (*Army*), ser. 1, I, III, VIII, XVI (pt. 2), XX (pts. 1, 2), XXIII (pts. 1, 2), XXX (pts. 1, 3, 4), XXXI (pts. 2, 3), XXXII (pt. 1), XXXVIII (pts. 1, 2, 3, 4, 5), XXXIX (pts. 1, 3), XLIV, XLVII (pts. 1, 2, 3), LII (pt. 1).]

T. M. S.

DAVIS, JEROME DEAN (Jan. 17, 1838–Nov. 4, 1910), Congregational clergyman and missionary, was born in Groton, N. Y., one of the seven children of Hope and Brooksy (Woodbury) Davis. The ancestors of both his parents came from England to Massachusetts, John Woodbury to Salem about 1623, and Isaac Davis to Cape Cod about 1690. When Jerome was fourteen or so, his father, a rigid, righteous combination of farmer and country school-teacher, took his family with him to live at Dundee, Ill. Shortly before, the boy had been converted, and when he was sixteen he took part as church clerk in the trial of a minister suspected of Unitarianism. With little or no encouragement from any one, he studied what books he could lay hold of, and by the time he was twenty was head teacher in a school at Carpentersville. As soon as he was twenty-one and was no longer bound to help his father, he began to follow definitely his plans for an education. He attended Lawrence University at Appleton, Wis., decided to become a minister, and during 1860 and 1861 was a sophomore and junior in Beloit College. He entered the Union army as a private in September 1861, and rose in rank till at the close of the war he was a lieutenant-colonel. Among the soldiers he was drastic in his attacks on liquor—rearing empty whiskey bottles on poles with the legend "Death to the Bottle"—and whenever possible he went about distributing Bibles. He was severely wounded at the battle of Shiloh and he conducted himself with bravery and shrewdness on his long march with Sherman to the sea. During 1865–66 he completed his course at Beloit College; and in 1869, he was graduated from the Chicago Theological Seminary, married to Sophia D. Strong, and sent by the Congregational Home Missionary Society to Cheyenne, Wyo. Financial support of his activities was not liberal, and other considerations persuaded him that his true work was in Japan. He left San Francisco in November 1871 as a missionary of the American Board. Arriving at Kobe several weeks afterward, he settled there, and by his teaching formed the nucleus of what became Kobe College. Later, in association with his friend, the American-educated Joseph Hardy Neesima, he helped found and in the most intimate fashion helped shape the Doshisha University in Kyoto. His wife died in 1886 and two years later he was married in Kyoto to Frances Hooper. Practically throughout the nineties, there was controversy both in America and Japan between persons who wished the Doshisha to be Christian pervadingly and by constant implication, and those who wished it to be so pointedly and aggressively. The former of these positions seeming to Davis to be spineless pacifism, he became chief, in a sense, of those who agreed with him, and in the end had the satisfaction of seeing his view adopted in the official policy of the school. He was a prolific writer on subjects of a theological and historical nature. In English, his most important work is perhaps his biography of his friend, *A Maker of New Japan: Rev. Joseph Hardy Neesima* (1890), and in Japanese, the thousand-page *Great Principles of Theology* (1893). For all his virility and the glamour of his Civil War recollections, he counseled his student son at the time of the Spanish-American War to keep out of the army; leave soldiering, he said, in so far as you can, to others —"War is hell on earth—keep out of it" (J. M. Davis, *post*, p. 331). He was a delegate to the World Missionary Conference in Edinburgh in the summer of 1910, and on his way back to Japan he stopped at Oberlin, Ohio. Illness overtook him and it became apparent that he was dying. Some one asked him if he would leave a message to his children. "My life," he said. He had three daughters and one son, all of whom were foreign missionaries.

[J. M. Davis, *Davis: Soldier Missionary* (1916); Beloit Coll. Cat. 1860–62, 1865–66; *Congreg. and Christian World*, Nov. 12, 1910; letter from Beloit Alumni League, Apr. 13, 1928.]   J. D. W.

DAVIS, JOHN (Jan. 25, 1761–Jan. 14, 1847), jurist, was born at Plymouth, Mass. He was the fourth child of Thomas Davis, a native of England who came to Plymouth in 1737, became a prosperous merchant of that town, and married in 1753 Mercy, daughter of Barnabas Hedge, a descendant of Gov. William Bradford. Being a delicate child, John received his early education privately, and was prepared for college by Rev. Ezra Sampson of Plympton. He entered Harvard College in 1777, where he distinguished himself in science as well as the classics, and attended Prof. Samuel Williams on the latter's journey in October 1780 to Penobscot Bay, to take observation of a solar eclipse. After graduating in 1781, he conducted a private school in Plymouth, becoming later tutor in the family of Gen. Otis at Barnstable. He then studied law in the office of Oakes Angier, at Bridgewater, and on being admitted to the bar in 1786, commenced practise at Plymouth. He rapidly came to the front and two years later was chosen delegate from Plymouth to the state convention which was called to consider the adoption of the Federal Constitution—being the youngest member thereof. Taking an active part in public matters, he was three times elected to the state House of Representatives, and in 1795 became state senator for Plymouth County, but in the same year was tendered by Washington the office of comptroller of the treasury of the United States, which he accepted. He held the position for only a year, however, his resignation being prompted by the inadequacy of his salary, and on retiring was appointed by Washington United States attorney for the district of Massachusetts. He thereupon removed to Boston, which became his permanent home. In 1801 he was appointed by President Adams judge of the United States district court for the district of Massachusetts—a position which he occupied for forty years. His judicial career was characterized by patience, urbanity, and sound discretion, and his exploration of the then almost untrodden paths of admiralty and maritime jurisdiction laid the legal profession under lasting obligations to him. Perhaps his outstanding achievement was his wise and firm attitude during the period of commercial embarrassment in New England caused by the Embargo and the War of 1812, when, unaffected by the ill-concealed hostility of the exasperated mercantile interests, he steadily maintained the supremacy of the law, and by so doing ultimately acquired the respect and confidence of the community. He resigned from the bench July 9, 1841, in his eighty-first year, upon which occasion the bar paid him a remarkable tribute. The remainder of his days were spent in retirement in Boston, where he died. In June 1786 he married Ellen, daughter of W. Watson of Plymouth.

Throughout his life he maintained his interest in scientific phenomena, and was deeply versed in the history and antiquities of New England, being president of the Massachusetts Historical Society from 1818 to 1835. He is said to have been the first to use the word "pilgrim" as applicable to the Plymouth colonists, in his ode written for the anniversary celebration in 1794. In addition to a number of addresses and papers contributed to learned societies he edited *Two Lectures on Comets by Professor Winthrop, Also an Essay on Comets by A. Oliver, Jr. Esq.* (1811), with biographies and supplementary matter, and a fifth edition of Morton's *New England's Memorial* (1826), with large additions in marginal notes and an appendix. He was a fellow of the American Academy of Arts and Sciences. A devoted supporter of Harvard, he actively shared in its administration, being successively Fellow in 1803, treasurer in 1810, and member of the board of overseers in 1827, which latter office he retained for ten years.

[Davis's ancestry is traced in W. T. Davis, *Ancient Landmarks of Plymouth* (2nd ed. 1899), pt. 11, p. 82. A detailed and authoritative account of his career entitled "Memoir of Hon. John Davis, LL.D.," by Convers Francis appeared in *Mass. Hist. Soc. Colls.*, ser. 3, vol. X, and was subsequently published in pamphlet form in 1848. See also W. T. Davis, *Professional and Industrial Hist. of Suffolk County, Mass.* (1894), I, 149; *Law Reporter*, IV, 159 and IX, 521.]
H. W. H. K.

DAVIS, JOHN (*c.* 1780–*c.* 1838), operatic and theatrical manager, despite his English name was a French refugee from Santo Domingo. He is said to have come to New Orleans in 1811, though it is possible that he may have appeared some years before, with that "company . . . of half a dozen actors and actresses, formerly attached to the theatre of Cape Français in the isle of San Domingo," mentioned by Berquin-Duvallon (*Vue de la colonie espagnole du Mississippi,* etc., Paris, 1803, p. 30). In 1813 he erected in New Orleans the first Théâtre d'Orléans, where opera was given three evenings a week, and comedy, drama, and vaudeville on the remaining nights. When it was burned to the ground four years later, he rebuilt it with, for that day, unexampled magnificence; so that when it entered upon its first

season (Nov. 20, 1819), it deserved its reputation of being "the grandest" opera-house then existing on the continent. Under Davis's management (he was its owner as well as manager) the Théâtre d'Orléans, provided with all the scenic and mechanical appliances then known to the best European houses, was the musical focus of cultured Creole society, and its winter seasons were a magnet for the wealthy planters along the Mississippi, who came to town with their wives and families to attend the opera. To the theatre proper its owner later added a great separate dancing hall, where the famous New Orleans Quadroon Balls were given and which, when the parquette floor of the opera was boarded over, constituted together with it one immense ballroom. To the dancing hall he adjoined a gambling house and a restaurant, which was a favorite haunt of the gilded youth of New Orleans; and the fortune derived from his gaming-tables, his restaurant, and his dance hall supplied John Davis with the capital for his theatrical ventures. The operas and ballets given in Paris found their way to the Théâtre d'Orléans, where French grand opera was given in the best style by French opera singers, and French actors and dancers appeared in comedy and ballet.

In spite of Davis's local prominence in New Orleans during the first quarter of the nineteenth century, we catch only occasional glimpses of him in the records of his day. It would seem that he enjoyed general respect, however, for we find that when, during Count de Roffigran's mayoralty, the famous old State House was burned, the ballroom of the Théâtre d'Orléans was offered for temporary use "by that good citizen . . . John Davis" (G. King, *Creole Families of New Orleans,* 1912, p. 438). And when Gen. Lafayette was entertained in New Orleans in 1825, and had spent an evening at the Théâtre d'Orléans, he extended his thanks to John Davis and the actors (J. G. de Baroncelli, *Le Théâtre-Français à la Nlle. Orleans, Essai Historique,* 1906, p. 34). It was largely due to Davis that New Orleans became the first American city to have an annual opera season. In his musical and dramatic activities he stressed the French cultural note which still lends a distinctly Latin tone to the modern city.

[The best account of Davis is that given in H. Righter's *Standard Hist. of New Orleans* (1900), p. 467. See also F. L. Ritter, *Music in America* (1890); H. C. Lahee, *Grand Opera in America* (1902), p. 27; W. D. Darby, *Music in America* (1916), p. 115.] F. H. M.

DAVIS, JOHN (Jan. 13, 1787–Apr. 19, 1854), lawyer, statesman, was born in Northboro, Worcester County, Mass., the fifth and youngest son of Isaac and Anna (Brigham) Davis. Preparing at Leicester Academy, he graduated from Yale College in 1812 with high honors, studied law with Francis Blake of Worcester, was admitted to the bar in 1815, and after practising at Spencer, Mass., settled in Worcester. There he rapidly made a reputation as a forceful advocate in the court-room, being recognized as a redoubtable antagonist by even such lawyers as Choate, Mason, and Webster. Elected to Congress in 1824 as a supporter of John Quincy Adams for the presidency, he served four consecutive terms. In 1833, he was the National Republican candidate for governor of Massachusetts, and received a plurality of votes over Adams (Anti-Mason) and Morton (Democrat). Because the law required a majority, the election was thrown into the legislature, where, after Adams had withdrawn, Davis was chosen over Morton. A year later he again defeated Morton, this time by a popular majority of 8,000.

Elected by the General Court as United States senator to succeed Nathaniel Silsbee, Davis took his seat, Dec. 7, 1835, as a member of the newly formed Whig party. At the insistence of the state Whig organization, he resigned in 1840 in order to run for governor against his old rival, Marcus Morton, over whom he was again victorious by a considerable majority. In 1841, he once more won over Morton, but in 1842 the election was thrown into the legislature, where Davis was beaten. He then returned to his law practise, but when Isaac C. Bates, who had succeeded him in the Senate, died (Mar. 16, 1845), Davis was again sent to the Senate, and in 1847 was elected for the full term. He retired on Mar. 3, 1853, after more than twenty-five years of public service in state and nation.

In Congress, first as a Federalist and later as a National Republican and a Whig, he held conservative views on most controversial questions. He became a spokesman for those New England interests which demanded a protective tariff, and consequently opposed Clay's compromise tariff act of 1833. He made some widely circulated replies to the free-trade arguments of Southern statesmen. A consistent opponent of President Jackson and all his works, he protested when, in 1837, the Senate expunged from its records the well-known resolution censuring the Executive. He was against any further spread of slavery in the states or territories, and was one of two senators to vote against the declaration of war with Mexico. It seemed for a time that he would be Clay's running mate on the Whig ticket in 1844, but his uncompromising position with regard to slavery prevented his

nomination. It is probable that if Clay had been elected Davis would have been appointed secretary of the treasury. His speech of Aug. 12, 1846, caused the Senate session to end without a vote on the Wilmot Proviso and led to criticism of his "unseasonable loquacity." He was opposed to the compromise measures of 1850, and exerted all his influence in the campaign of 1852 for the success of the Whig candidate, Gen. Scott.

Although he had little grace of manner and, because of his shaggy locks, reminded people of "a great white bear," Davis possessed a kind of awkward dignity which was impressive. Without being showy or brilliant, he was convincing because of his sincerity and earned the nickname of "Honest John." Though temperamentally cautious, he did not lack courage in a crisis. A man of judgment rather than of imagination, he enjoyed the respect and confidence of his constituents. He married, on Mar. 28, 1822, Eliza Bancroft, daughter of Rev. Aaron Bancroft and sister of George Bancroft. Three of their sons, John Chandler Bancroft, Horace, and Andrew McFarland [qq.v.], had distinguished careers. Davis was president of the American Antiquarian Society and received many honors. He died in Worcester at the age of sixty-seven.

[*Proc. Am. Antiq. Soc.*, Apr. 1854, Oct. 1893; *Trans. and Colls. Am. Antiq. Soc.*, vols. III (1857), VIII (1901); *Memorial Biogs. of the New-Eng. Hist. Geneal. Soc.*, vol. II (1881); F. B. Dexter, *Biog. Sketches Grads. Yale Coll.*, vol. VI (1912); Geo. Watterson, *Gallery of Am. Portraits* (1830); *Memoirs of John Quincy Adams*, vol. IX (1876); *Reminiscences of the Rev. Geo. Allen of Worcester* (1883); *The Diary of Jas. K. Polk* (1910); Wm. Lincoln, *Hist. of Worcester, Mass.* (1837); H. Davis, *Ancestry of John Davis* (1897); J. D. Estabrook, *Three Generations of Northboro Davises* (1908); Geo. F. Hoar, *Autobiog. of Seventy Years* (1903).]   C. M. F.

DAVIS, JOHN CHANDLER BANCROFT (Dec. 29, 1822–Dec. 27, 1907), diplomatist, was born in Worcester, Mass., the son of John Davis [q.v.] and Eliza (Bancroft) Davis, a sister of George Bancroft. He was usually known as Bancroft Davis. After attending the Worcester public schools, he entered Harvard College with the class of 1840. Unjustly suspended in his senior year, he did not return, but was given the A.B. degree in 1847. He studied law, was admitted to the Massachusetts bar in 1844, and then opened an office in New York City. On Aug. 31, 1849, he succeeded John R. Brodhead as secretary of the American legation in Great Britain, acting as chargé d'affaires for several months during the absence of the newly appointed minister, Abbott Lawrence. Resigning on Nov. 30, 1852, he returned to his profession in New York, entering the firm of Kent, Eaton & Kent, which afterward became Kent, Eaton & Davis. From 1854 to 1861 he was American correspondent of the London *Times*. He married (Nov. 19, 1857) Frederica Gore, daughter of James Gore King and grand-daughter of Rufus King. They had no children. Because of ill health he retired from practise in 1862, and after two years abroad settled on a farm in Orange County, N. Y.

Having regained his vigor, Davis was elected to the New York legislature in 1868, and on Mar. 25, 1869, accepted an appointment as assistant secretary of state, a post for which he had exceptional qualifications. He was an arbitrator in a dispute between Portugal and Great Britain regarding their African possessions. When, in 1871, a Joint High Commission was appointed to arrange a settlement of the dispute between the United States and Great Britain arising out of the depredations of the *Alabama* and other cruisers during the Civil War, he was made secretary of the commission on the part of the United States. After the signing of the Treaty of Washington (May 8, 1871) providing for a Tribunal of Arbitration to meet at Geneva, Davis, who had the full confidence of Secretary Fish and was familiar with all the details of the prolonged controversy, was designated as American agent.

He personally prepared "The Case of the United States" (*Senate Executive Document No. 31*, 42 Cong., 2 Sess.; Moore, *post*, I, 591 n.), an imposing book of nearly 500 pages in which American grievances were fully stated. The sixth chapter, which contained the formal statement of claims, was not submitted in advance by Davis for American criticism, as the other chapters had been. In it compensation was demanded not only for losses directly due to the activities of the Confederate cruisers, but also for general injuries to United States commerce, for enhanced insurance rates, and for the expenditures necessitated by the prolongation of the war. Opinions differ as to the merits of Davis's presentation, and particularly as to the wisdom of incorporating the latter claims, termed "national" or "indirect," which aroused bitter British protests (Rhodes, *post*, VI, 364 ff.; Cushing, *post*, p. 31; Moore, *post*, I, 628 ff.). Whether or not his advocacy of American claims was marked by undue assertiveness, it was at least spirited. The case was presented to the Tribunal on Dec. 16, 1871. Meanwhile Davis had sailed for Europe, reaching Havre in November and proceeding to Geneva. Here he set to work preparing the "Counter Case of the United States" (*Senate Executive Document No. 67*, 42 Cong., 2 Sess.), which was delivered on Apr. 15. When the matter of the indirect claims seemed likely to disrupt the Tribunal, Davis's friendly relations with the British agent, Lord Tenterden, enabled him, with the assistance of Caleb Cushing, to devise a plan by which the arbitrators declared themselves in an extra-judicial announcement as not favoring the American demands. After the award, giving the United States a lump sum of $15,500,000 in gold for direct damages, had been announced (Sept. 14, 1872), Davis sailed for home and made a formal report to the Department of State. On Jan. 24, 1873, he was reappointed assistant secretary of state, but resigned in July 1874, to become minister to Germany, in succession to his uncle, George Bancroft. He spent the next three years in Berlin, with occasional intervals of travel in the Mediterranean countries.

After the inauguration of President Hayes, Davis resigned, only to be appointed judge of the United States Court of Claims, on which he served from January 1878 until December 1881. Then, at President Arthur's request, he accepted an assignment as assistant secretary of state, on special duty. At the expiration of six months, he was reappointed to the Court of Claims. Retaining this position until Nov. 5, 1883, he then accepted an appointment as reporter of the United States Supreme Court, editing in this capacity Volumes 108–186 of the *United States Reports*. He retired after nineteen years and spent his last days in Washington. Among his publications were: *The Massachusetts Justice* (1847); a revision of "Treaties and Conventions Concluded between the United States of America and other Powers," etc. (*Senate Executive Document No. 36*, 41 Cong., 3 Sess.); *Mr. Fish and the Alabama Claims* (1893), and a pamphlet on the *Origin of the Book of Common Prayer of the Protestant Episcopal Church in the United States of America* (1897). He was recognized as an authority on historical data relating to the judicial functions of the United States government.

[While at Geneva, Davis kept a diary, which is now preserved in the archives of the Dept. of State. See also H. Davis, *Ancestry of John Davis* (1897); *Harvard Grads. Mag.*, Mar. 1908; *Proc. Am. Antiq. Soc.*, Apr. 1908; *Proc. upon the Occasion of Presenting to the Court of Claims of the U. S. a Portr. of John Chandler Bancroft Davis* (1912); John Bassett Moore, *Hist. and Digest of the International Arbitrations to which the U. S. has been a Party*, I (1898, 495–678); F. W. Hackett, *Reminiscences of the Geneva Tribunal of Arbitration* (1911); Caleb Cushing, *The Treaty of Washington: Its Negotiation, Execution and the Discussions Relating Thereto* (1873); J. F. Rhodes, *Hist. of the U. S.*, vol. VI (1906); *Nation* (N. Y.), Jan. 31,

1907; *Evening Post* (N. Y.), *N. Y. Tribune,* and *Washington Post,* all Dec. 28, 1907.]   C.M.F.

DAVIS, JOHN LEE (Sept. 3, 1825–Mar. 12, 1889), naval officer, was the first child of the young physician—later prominent Democratic political leader—John Wesley Davis [*q.v.*] and Ann Hoover, born shortly after their removal from southeastern Pennsylvania to Carlisle, Sullivan County, Ind. He went to school in Carlisle, and through his father, then a congressman, was appointed a midshipman, Jan. 9, 1841. From then until the Civil War, except for a year at the new Naval Academy, 1846–47, and two tours of duty in the Coast Survey, 1851–52, 1855–57, he was almost constantly in sea service, in the Far East, on the African Coast, in the Pacific, and elsewhere. He had blockade duty in the Mexican War; and in November 1849, while acting lieutenant in the *Preble,* he led a boat party of seventeen which captured a Chinese junk engaged in piracy off Macao, killing three of the crew and wounding many others. In the Civil War he was among the younger ship commanders who won distinction for energy and reliability. As executive officer of the *Water Witch* he was in the sharp engagement with the *Manassas* and other Confederate vessels in the mouth of the Mississippi, Oct. 12, 1861. Declining command of the *Water Witch* in deference to officers senior to him, he was promoted in July following to lieutenant commander. In command of the gunboat *Wissahickon* he took part in an attack on enemy batteries below Fort McAllister, Nov. 19, 1862, in which his vessel was pierced below the waterline, but was run aground and successfully patched at low tide. The *Wissahickon* was in subsequent attacks on the fort on Jan. 27 and Feb. 1 and 28. On Mar. 19, 1863, his vessel sank the valuable blockade-runner *Georgiana* entering Charleston harbor. Transferred in August to command of the monitor *Montauk,* he took active part in the bombardments of the Charleston forts, September–November 1863. In the *Sassacus,* 1864–65, he was engaged in the attacks on Fort Fisher in December 1864, and January 1865, and in subsequent operations in the Cape Fear River. Admiral Du Pont (*Official Records of the Union and Confederate Navies,* XIII, 697) commended Davis's "extreme vigilance and spirit" in blockade work, and the latter was among the officers recommended by Porter for promotion after the capture of Fort Fisher. Advanced to commander, 1866, to captain, 1873, to commodore, 1882, and to rear admiral, 1885, he had shore duty at various times on the Lighthouse, Retirement, and Inspection Boards; commanded the *Trenton,*

flagship of the European Squadron, 1877–78; and was in command of the Asiatic Squadron, 1883–86. He was retired Sept. 3, 1887.

Davis was of erect, handsome figure, with curly reddish brown hair, moustache, and goatee, which turned white in later years. He was strict and sharp in discipline—a "sun-downer" in the naval phrase—but withal respected as a brave, upright officer and expert seaman, the last borne out by the anecdote of the old tar of the eighties who said there were only three sailors left in the Navy, "me, and John Lee Davis, and Stephen B. Luce" (Albert Gleaves, *Life and Letters of Rear Admiral Stephen B. Luce,* 1925, p. 307). Somewhat enfeebled by his Asiatic service, he died of pneumonia at the Ebbitt House, Washington, where he had made his home after the war, and was buried in Rock Creek Cemetery. He was survived by his wife, Frances Latta Robinson, whom he married Dec. 12, 1855, and by one daughter.

[Lewis R. Hamersly, *Records of Living Officers of the U. S. Navy and Marine Corps* (3rd ed., 1878) gives Davis's complete service record to that date. Some comment on his character and his last cruise appears in Rear Admiral A. S. Barker, *Everyday Life in the Navy* (1928), pp. 147–83. See also *Washington Post,* Mar. 13, 1889, and *Army and Navy Jour.,* Mar. 16, 1889.]
           A.W.

DAVIS, JOHN WESLEY (Apr. 16, 1799–Aug. 22, 1859), congressman, the son of Rev. John Davis and ——— (Jones) Davis, was born at New Holland, Lancaster County, Pa. He studied medicine at the University of Maryland, graduating in 1821. Two years later, with his wife, Ann Hoover, he moved to Carlisle, Ind., traveling in a cart and arriving, as he afterward related, with three cents in his pocket. He practised his profession for some years, but yielding to the lure of politics he ran for the state Senate in 1828 and was beaten. His magnanimous opponent, however, aided him to secure the appointment as sergeant-at-arms of that body. In 1829 he was elected probate judge of Sullivan County and soon passed from that post into the state House of Representatives, of which he was six times a member in the course of his career, being three times elected speaker. In politics he was so ardent a Democrat that in a speech made near the close of his career he declared, in reply to a heckler: "I will say now that I endorse everything the Democratic party ever has done, and everything that it ever will do" (Wolfe, *post,* pp. 48–9). Elected in 1835 to the Twenty-fourth Congress, he subsequently served in the Twenty-sixth, Twenty-eighth, and Twenty-ninth. Though not an orator, he wielded much influence and in 1845 was elevated to the speakership, presiding over the House during the first part of the Mexican War. Sent early in 1848 as commissioner to China, he returned home in 1850. He was repeatedly a delegate to Democratic national conventions and presided over the convention of 1852 that nominated Pierce. Upon the return of his party to power in 1853 he was appointed governor of Oregon Territory but resigned the next year. In 1856 he was again elected to the state legislature. Three years later he died at his home in Carlisle. Though he was a strong partisan, no one ever questioned his integrity, and he died a poor man. His oldest son, John Lee Davis [q.v.], rendered distinguished service as a naval officer.

[Thos. J. Wolfe, *A Hist. of Sullivan County, Ind.* (2 vols., 1909) ; W. W. Woolen, *Biog. and Hist. Sketches of Early Ind.* (1883), containing an account of Davis based mainly on an autobiographical sketch by him near the end of his life; a master's thesis on Davis's career by Hope Bedford, Butler Univ. Lib.]   P.L.H.

DAVIS, JOSEPH ROBERT (Jan. 12, 1825–Sept. 15, 1896), Confederate soldier, was a son of Isaac Davis, and a nephew of Jefferson Davis [q.v.]. Isaac Davis, after serving in the War of 1812 as a private and later as an officer in the regiment of Lieut.-Col. Thomas Hinds in the army led by Andrew Jackson, married in 1822 Susan Garthy, a native Mississippian of Irish parentage. Joseph, their second child, was born at Woodville, Wilkinson County, Miss. Educational advantages were meager about his father's plantations in Wilkinson and Warren counties, so as a boy Joseph was sent to Nashville, Tenn., for his preliminary training. The law seemed to afford the best opportunity for the advancement of an aspiring youth, and Joseph's father accordingly sent him to Miami University, Oxford, Ohio, where he was graduated. After thoroughly fitting himself for the profession of law, he entered upon its practise, which he continued in Madison County, Miss., until 1860. In that year he was elected to the Mississippi state Senate, but after his state's ordinance of secession he resigned from the legislature and enthusiastically entered the service of the Confederacy. He was quickly elected captain of a company from the county where he had recently made his home, Madison. In April 1861 he was made lieutenant-colonel in the 10th Mississippi Regiment at Pensacola, Fla. Some four months later, his uncle, the president of the Confederacy, offered "Joe," as Jefferson Davis called his nephew, a commission as colonel on the president's staff. The colonel performed inspection duty in various parts of the South until 1862, when he was assigned to the command of a brigade of Mississippi troops, in the Army of Northern Virginia, with rank of brigadier-general. His brigade was engaged in some of the most bitter battles of the Civil War, including the Wilderness, Cold Harbor, and the siege of Petersburg. At the very beginning of the battle of Gettysburg, the brigade of Davis clashed with Buford's dismounted cavalry, and was much engaged until the third day of the battle, when the entire brigade was in Pickett's charge, conducting itself most gallantly. After Davis had surrendered with Lee at Appomattox, he returned to Mississippi and resumed the practise of law, spending most of the remainder of his life at Biloxi. He was married twice: in 1848 to a Miss Peyton, and in 1879 to Margaret Cary Green, who was the mother of his two daughters and one son, Jefferson. According to Goodspeed's *Biographical and Historical Memoirs of Mississippi* (1891) he was a "logical reasoner, decisive in statement, and possessed of sufficient eloquence to render his declamation vigorous and of the most convincing order."

[Dunbar Rowland in his *Jefferson Davis, Constitutionalist* (1923) refers in several volumes to Jos. R. Davis, prints a number of letters between him and the members of his family, and gives a short biography (V, 346). *The Davis Family in Wales and America* (1927), by Harry A. Davis, is perhaps the best reference for genealogy. *Miss. Hist. Soc. Pubs.*, vol. IX, refers to Davis repeatedly. A short sketch of his life appears in Dunbar Rowland's *Mississippi* (1907), I, 632, and his military career is treated somewhat fully in the same author's *Miss. the Heart of the South* (1925), II, 53–78.]   L.T.L.

DAVIS, MARY EVELYN MOORE (Apr. 12, 1852–Jan. 1, 1909), author, was born in Talladega, Ala., and died in New Orleans. Her mother, Marian Lucy Crutchfield, whose family had migrated from Virginia to Chattanooga, had two brothers who were colonels in the Civil War, one Unionist, the other Confederate. Her father, John Moore, was born and educated as a physician in Massachusetts. He went to Alabama to practise medicine, but as early as 1848 he was interesting himself there in the commercial possibilities of iron deposits. A few years before the Civil War he removed with his family to "La Rose Blanche," a cotton plantation in Texas. Here Mary—Mollie she was called—grew up, educated by private tutors. She was a precocious child, and many of her fervent war poems appeared in Southern newspapers in 1861–65. A collected edition of her verse, *Minding the Gap*, was published in Houston in 1867. She was married on Oct. 20, 1874, to Thomas Edward Davis, who, after serving during the Civil War as major in the Virginia cavalry, had become editor of the *Houston Telegraph*. He was called to New Orleans in 1879 to become associated with the *Daily Picayune*, and he and his wife took up residence in the old French quarter in a house once occupied by Edward Livingston and visited by Andrew Jackson. In this house Mrs. Davis developed and maintained for many years a gathering place for those about her who prized subtlety of talk and thought. She was gentle, humorous, and wise, and many competent witnesses bore testimony to the spell of her presence. This presence and the just scale of values which by direction and indirection she helped to establish constitute her chief claim upon enduring memory. She was among the first to exploit negro dialect for literary purposes, but her writings do not keep their vitality. *Under Six Flags, the Story of Texas* (1897) is of slight permanent value; *In War Times at La Rose Blanche* (1888) and *Jaconetta* (1901) have some autobiographical interest. The little plays in *A Bunch of Roses* (1903)—the poems in *A Christmas Masque* (1896)—the stories in *An Elephant's Track* (1897)—and the novel, *The Little Chevalier* (1903)—though all conscientiously executed, often thrust her into comparison with either Uncle Remus or Dr. Sevier, and the result is not flattering to her. Even local patriotism recognized at the time of her death the discrepancy between the force of her actual self, and the rating which it already seemed would at last be given to her work. She had no children, but she adopted a niece whom she reared as her own daughter. The last years of her life were spent in pain which she bore with fortitude.

[There is a biographical note in the posthumous *Selected Poems* (1927). See also W. B. Smith, "Mary Evelyn Moore Davis," *Lib. of Southern Lit.*, vol. III (1909); J. W. Davidson, *Living Writers of the South* (1869); T. McA. Owen, *Hist. of Ala. and Dict. of Ala. Biog.* (1921), vol. III; *Who's Who in America*, 1908–09; *Daily Picayune* (New Orleans), Jan. 2, 1909.]

J. D. W.

DAVIS, MATTHEW LIVINGSTON (Oct. 28, 1773–June 21, 1850), politician, journalist, born presumably in New York, the son of Matthew and Phebe (Wells) Davis, is remembered for his forty years' association with Aaron Burr, of whom he was an adoring friend, a zealous henchman, and an unwise biographer. His life was passed amid the rough-and-tumble of partisan politics and partisan journalism. Starting as a printer, he edited the short-lived *Evening Post* in 1794, collaborated with Philip Freneau on the *Time Piece and Literary Companion*, 1797–98, and was Burr's indefatigable lieutenant in the New York political campaign of 1800. How much he then contributed to the vote-getting technique of the Tammany Society is a matter of conjecture, but tirelessly active and enthusiastic in the cause he certainly was. By way of reward Burr, with Gallatin's support,

tried to have Davis made naval officer of the port; Jefferson hesitated, and Davis bolted down to Monticello in a tactless, futile effort to secure action. Jefferson's refusal to give Davis an office was a serious affront to the Vice-President, and had its consequences. On July 11, 1804, Davis accompanied his chief across the Hudson to the dueling ground at Weehawken, and subsequently went to jail rather than give incriminating testimony against his friend. Sometime before the War of 1812 he was a member of the trading firm of Davis & Strong, which prospered in South-American ventures, Davis' own profits, later lost, amounting to about $50,000. He was accused of smuggling flour out of the country during the Embargo, which officially he was supporting. In 1814 and 1815 he was Grand Sachem of the Tammany Society, and was a Sachem for some years thereafter. While Grand Sachem he is said, by Myers, to have cleared $80,000 on a government contract. On Sept. 15, 1826, with several others he was indicted for swindles aggregating several million dollars. The first jury disagreeing, they were convicted on a second trial; a third trial was procured for Davis, who was at last acquitted. To Burr he was faithful to the end; he inherited Burr's papers, and after his death (Sept. 14, 1836) published *Memoirs of Aaron Burr* (1836–37) and *The Private Journal of Aaron Burr during his Residence of Four Years in Europe* (1838). For Davis as biographer and as custodian of Burr's papers scholars have shown a good deal of scorn. He destroyed the greater part of Burr's correspondence, gave away letters for their autographs, and displayed scant knowledge of historical methods. In his later years he was Washington correspondent of the London *Times* ("The Genevese Traveller") and of the *Morning Courier and New York Enquirer* ("The Spy in Washington"). In the capital he was known as "the Old Boy in Specs," was reputed to have been a duelist, and was esteemed for his fund of anecdote and reminiscence. After a paralytic stroke in 1848 he gave up writing. Holding a minor political sinecure, he died at his son's home at Manhattanville, N. Y., and was laid to rest in Trinity Cemetery.

[H. Adams, *Hist. of the U. S.*, vol. I (1889, 1898); H. Adams, *Life of Albert Gallatin* (1879); H. Adams, ed., *Writings of Albert Gallatin*, vol. I (1879); W. C. Ford, *Some Papers of Aaron Burr* (1920); F. Hudson, *Journalism in the U. S. from 1690 to 1872* (1873); G. Myers, *Hist. of Tammany Hall* (1901); M. R. Werner, *Tammany Hall* (1928); S. H. Wandell and M. Minnigerode, *Aaron Burr* (1925), portrait of Davis, after original in possession of N. Y. Hist. Soc., in vol. I; obituaries in *Littell's Liv. Age*, Aug. 3, 1850, and in N. Y. newspapers, June 24, 1850; E. A. and G. L.

Duyckinck, *Cyc. of Am. Lit.* (1875); F. L. Pattee, ed., *The Poems of Philip Freneau* (1902), vol. I, p. lxxv; J. Parton, *Life and Times of Aaron Burr* (1892); H. S. Randall, *Life of Thos. Jefferson* (1857).]

G. H. G.

DAVIS, NATHAN SMITH (Jan. 9, 1817–June 16, 1904), "father of the American Medical Association," was born to Dow Davis and Eleanor Smith, both of English descent, in a farmhouse at Greene, Chenango County, N. Y. Here he spent his first sixteen years, attending district school in the winters with one six months' session at Cazenovia Seminary, in Madison County. In 1834 he commenced the study of medicine under Dr. Daniel Clark in the near-by village of Smithville Flats. After three courses of medical lectures at the College of Physicians and Surgeons of the Western District of New York at Fairfield, he was graduated in January 1837. He began practise in Vienna, N. Y., where he married Anna Maria Parker on Mar. 5, 1838, but during the latter year he moved to Binghamton, N. Y., where he remained nine years. There he soon became prominent in medical affairs. He was secretary of the Broome County Medical Society from 1841 to 1843, and from 1843 to 1846 he represented the county society at meetings of the Medical Society of the State of New York. At the session of 1843 he presented a resolution upon the elevation of standards of medical education, which led to the organization of the American Medical Association.

He moved to New York City in 1847, where he took charge of the dissecting room of the College of Physicians and Surgeons, lectured on medical jurisprudence, and assumed editorial charge of the *Annalist,* a semi-monthly medical journal. In 1849 he went to Chicago to fill the professorship of physiology and pathology at Rush Medical College, and in 1850 was given the chair of principles and practise of medicine and of clinical medicine. During the latter year he headed a movement for the introduction of a sewage system and an adequate water supply for the city, then of 27,000 inhabitants, and for the establishment of a public hospital. Through his efforts, funds were raised to furnish twelve beds, the nucleus for Mercy Hospital, the oldest and now one of the largest hospitals in Chicago. In 1859, a group from the faculty of Rush Medical College, including Davis, founded the medical department of Lind University, which later became the Chicago Medical College and still later the medical department of Northwestern University. Upon this faculty Davis was professor of principles and practise of medicine and later emeritus professor until his death. He was dean of the faculty during his entire active association

with the school, and was able to put into practise his advanced ideas on medical education.

Davis was among the small group that organized the Illinois Medical Society and the Chicago Medical Society. He was one of the founders of Northwestern University, of the Chicago Academy of Science, the Chicago Historical Society, the Union College of Law and the Washingtonian Home. He was honorary member of many medical and scientific societies in this country and abroad, and held official positions in most of the societies to which he belonged. He was editor of the *Chicago Medical Journal* from 1855 to 1859. In 1860 he founded the *Chicago Medical Examiner,* which he edited until its merger with the *Chicago Medical Journal* in 1873. He was editor of the *Journal of the American Medical Association* for the first six years after its establishment in 1883. At different times he was also editor of the *Northwestern Medical and Surgical Journal,* of the *Eclectic Journal of Education and Literary Review,* and of the *American Medical Temperance Quarterly.* Besides editorials and journal articles he wrote: *A Text Book on Agriculture* (1848); *History of Medical Education and Institutions in the United States* (1851); *History of the American Medical Association* (1855); *Clinical Lectures on Various Important Diseases* (1873), which went through two editions; *Lectures on the Principles and Practice of Medicine* (1884); and *History of Medicine, with the Code of Medical Ethics* (1903). One of his chief interests was the temperance cause, which he supported actively with tongue and pen. Possessed of a dynamic presence and a fiery eloquence, as a lecturer he has had few equals in American medicine. To his apparently frail body was united a tireless energy and an intense intellectuality. His head was disproportionately large, with a high and broad forehead. His portrait taken in his later years shows the face of a zealot, long, thin, and smooth shaven, with flaming eyes and a ruff of neck whiskers.

[I. N. Danforth, *Life of Nathan Smith Davis* (1907) and a memoir in the *Quart. Bull. of Northwestern Univ. Medic. School,* Dec. 1908; R. O. Beard, in the *Bull. Asso. Am. Medic. Colleges,* I (1892), 32; J. H. Hollister, in the *Ill. Medic. Jour.,* July 1904; F. S. Johnson, in *Science,* Aug. 19, 1904; E. C. Dudley, in the *St. Paul Medic. Jour.,* May 1905; V. Robinson, in the *Medic. Rev. of Revs.,* Aug. 1917; H. O. Marcy, in *Am. Medicine,* July 1919; N. J. Medic. Reporter, VIII (1855), 248; *New Eng. Medic. Monthly,* II (1882–83), 421; *Jour. Am. Medic. Asso.,* June 3, 1899, June 25, 1904; *Medic. Record* and *N. Y. Medic. Jour.,* both June 25, 1904; *Medic. Standard* and *Chicago Medic. Recorder,* both July 1904; *Boston Medic. and Surgic. Jour.,* June 30, 1904, and a memoir by H. T. Byford in the same magazine for June 19, 1919, reprinted in H. A. Kelly and W. L. Burrage, *Am. Medic. Biogs.* (1920).]

J. M. P.

DAVIS, NOAH (Sept. 10, 1818–Mar. 20, 1902), jurist, was born at Haverhill, N. H., but the greater part of his youth was spent at Albion, N. Y., to which place his parents moved in 1825. They were poor, and his only education was obtained at the public schools. Later, by copying deeds in the evening for the deputy clerk, S. E. Church, he earned money which enabled him to attend Lima Seminary in the daytime. Subsequently he studied law at Lewiston, Niagara County, and was admitted to the bar in 1841. Practising first at Gaines, and then at Buffalo, N. Y., he met with no success and returned in 1844 to Albion, where the deputy clerk—now a lawyer—took him into partnership. Under the firm name of Church & Davis they rapidly acquired an extensive practise and became one of the best-known firms in western New York. In March 1857 he was appointed a justice for the 8th division of the supreme court of New York, to fill a vacancy, and when his term expired, November 1857, was elected for the succeeding term. He had always taken an active interest in political affairs, being a strong Republican, and in 1868 he was elected to Congress from Orleans and Monroe counties and resigned from the bench. He did not complete his term, however, as President Grant in July 1870 appointed him United States district attorney for southern New York. It was a critical period in the history of New York City, the contest between the Reform party and the adherents of William M. Tweed being at its bitterest, but his firm and vigorous administration of the duties of his office defeated the endeavors of the "Tweed Ring" to influence the municipal elections, and the Reform party triumphed over bribery and intimidation. The judiciary also needed to be delivered from the Tweed influence, so in 1872 he was nominated by the Republican party, indorsed by the Reform "Committee of Seventy," and elected a justice of the supreme court for the 1st judicial district. The first trial of Tweed took place before Davis in January 1873 and was abortive, owing to disagreement of the jury. A retrial was held in November, its opening being signalized by a unique incident, all the defense counsel signing and presenting to Davis a written protest against his again officiating as trial judge, on the ground that he was prejudiced and had expressed unfavorable opinions respecting the defendant. The second trial resulted in a conviction on twelve counts, and, feeling that to treat the verdict as if rendered upon a single misdemeanor would result in an entirely inadequate punishment, Davis imposed a cumulative sentence upon Tweed of twelve years' imprison-

ment and $3,000 fine. He also treated as a contempt of court the protest of the defense counsel, fining three of them $250 each. Subsequently the court of appeals set aside the cumulative sentence on purely legal grounds. In 1874 he was appointed presiding justice of the General Term, and retained this position until his retirement Dec. 31, 1886, thus completing a service of more than twenty-five years upon the bench. Among other celebrated trials over which he presided were those of Edward S. Stokes for the murder of "Jim" Fisk, Jr., and of Chancellor Wallworth's son for the murder of his father. A great deal of the litigation in which the City of New York was involved through the operations of the Tweed Ring also came before him. On leaving the bench he resumed practise in New York City, and for a time was active in local political circles, but retired from public life in 1901, and died in New York City, Mar. 20, 1902.

As a judge he was an outstanding figure. He "brought to the bench wide experience, broad and comprehensive knowledge of the law, and a dignified and forceful personality which made him the strongest and most eminent of our judges during his entire term of service" (Theron G. Strong, *post*, p. 78). By nature a man of strong convictions and prejudices, he found it difficult to conceal his feelings on all occasions, and his austere demeanor procured for him a reputation for severity which his scrupulous fairness, patient attention, and the care which he bestowed upon all matters before him, did not always dispel. His attitude in the Tweed case, though subjected to strong criticism from some quarters, met with emphatic popular approval. As a public speaker he was in the front rank and his jury charges were masterpieces of exposition. Throughout his life he was a close student of public affairs. An intimate friend of Gen. Grant, he often acted as his personal counsel. His only contribution to literature was a small book, *Intemperance and Crime* (1883).

[An extended sketch of Davis's career appeared in the *Albany Law Jour.*, Nov. 1904, and Theron G. Strong in *Landmarks of a Lawyer's Lifetime* (1914), p. 78, makes a valuable contribution from personal knowledge to an appreciation of his character and services. See also *Hist. of the Bench and Bar of N. Y.*, ed. by D. McAdam and others, II (1899), 123; *Hist. Album of Orleans County, N. Y.* (1879), p. 116; *Green Bag*, Jan. 1897; *N. Y. Times*, Mar. 21, 1902.]

H. W. H. K.

DAVIS, NOAH KNOWLES (May 15, 1830–May 3, 1910), teacher, author, was the son of Noah Davis of Maryland and Mary (Young) Davis of Alexandria, Va. He was born in Philadelphia, where his father, a minister still under thirty, was in charge of the recently formed

Baptist Tract Society. In July 1830, his father died, and a few years later his mother was married to John L. Dagg [*q.v.*], like herself a Virginian, and like her former husband a Baptist ecclesiastic. The Dagg family removed to the far south, and in 1849, during his step-father's term as its president, Noah Davis was graduated from the sectarian Mercer College, then located in Penfield, Ga. Soon afterward he went to Philadelphia and studied chemistry, and later he was for about twenty years connected with the faculties of various Baptist colleges. From 1852 to 1865 he was in Alabama, for seven years as teacher of natural science in Howard College, and for the remaining six as head of the Judson Female Institute. From 1868 to 1873 he was president of Bethel College, in Kentucky. He was married in 1856 (or 1857) to Ella Hunt of Albany, Ga. From 1873 to 1906 he was professor of moral philosophy in the University of Virginia. He was an effective teacher, learned, diligent, and sincere. His writings were largely of the kind used as text-books. His *Theory of Thought* (1880) was followed by his series: *Elements of Psychology* (1892), *Elements of Deductive Logic* (1893), *Elements of Inductive Logic* (1895), and *Elements of Ethics* (1900) —a group employed, it is said, in more than fifty schools and colleges, and so highly regarded as to be "analyzed" in a volume specially devoted to the purpose by his one-time student, the Methodist bishop, Collins Denny. These books, gracefully written and cogently built up, did not neglect the uses and even claims of deterministic scrutiny, but their author kept himself free to abandon all these uses and claims when he believed that more valid considerations presented themselves. He did not hesitate, for example, to condemn a speculation as in essence illusory if, put into practise, it would befog what he considered the ideal goal of mankind, nor did he hesitate to assume the existence of a thing if its existence had been wished for by many good men for many generations. He adhered, in short, to the age-old concepts of virtue by which he was dominated, and by which he was exalted into something approaching greatness. For if he was a metaphysician pondering on Reality in the abstract, he was as well a conforming Baptist whose experience on the Southern frontier had made plain for him other realities which he could never quite disregard. In the early eighties he inaugurated his custom of delivering a religious discourse every Sunday. These lectures were popular in the university community, and the substance of them was made available to a wider audience in his three religious volumes, *Juda's Jewels, a Study of the Hebrew Lyrics* (1895), *Synopsis of Events in the Life of Jesus of Nazareth* (1900), and *The Story of the Nazarene in Annotated Paraphrase* (1903). He was a large man, stooped, bearded, deliberate, garbed in baggy black, crowned with a high silk hat—eccentric to look upon, eccentric too, in many of his opinions—openly, a little boisterously, irreverent of much knowledge usually held sacrosanct. The last four years of his life were spent in retirement in Charlottesville.

[C. Denny, *Analysis of Noah K. Davis's Elements of Deductive Logic and of his Elements of Psychology* (1916); "Noah Knowles Davis," *Lib. of Southern Lit.*, vol. III (1909); W. B. Sprague, *Annals Am. Pulpit*, vol. VI (1860); *Who's Who in America*, 1910–11; P. A. Bruce, *Hist. of the Univ. of Va.* (1921); L. G. Tyler, *Men of Mark in Va.*, vol. V (1909); *The South in the Building of the Nation*, vol. XI (1909); Catalogues of Howard Coll. 1918, Bethel Coll. 1917–18, Mercer Univ. 1902–03; *Richmond Times Despatch*, May 4, 1910.]   J.D.W.

DAVIS, PAULINA KELLOGG WRIGHT (Aug. 7, 1813–Aug. 24, 1876), editor, suffragist, was born in Bloomfield, N. Y., daughter of Capt. Ebenezer and Polly (Saxton) Kellogg. Both parents were very conservative in their views and their associates. When Paulina was seven years old she was left an orphan and was subsequently adopted by an aunt in Le Roy, N. Y., where she received her education. Her aunt was an unyielding Puritan and the child was under constant restraint, which probably accounts for her later advocacy of freedom and personal rights. Religion was part of her daily routine, and upon leaving school she decided to become a missionary to the Sandwich Islands. This idea was abandoned in 1833 when she married Francis Wright, a merchant of wealth and position in Utica, N. Y. The Wrights took an active part in the anti-slavery convention held in Utica in 1835. Mr. Wright died during that year. Mrs. Wright had spent much of her leisure time in studying anatomy and physiology, and in 1844 she began lecturing on the subject to groups of women. She imported from Paris the first known *femme modèle* in this country. Its use in her lectures brought much unfavorable comment. Her early efforts, however, helped to open the medical profession to women. She contributed many articles to the *Woman's Advocate* and *McDowell's Journal*. In 1849 she married Thomas Davis of Providence, R. I. When he was elected to Congress in 1853, she went with him to Washington. There she was badly received by the women, who considered her knowledge and work unbecoming to her sex. In February 1853, she established the *Una*, the first distinctively woman's rights paper published in this country, which she continued for nearly three years at her own expense. The paper expressed the broadest view of individual freedom. In 1859 she visited Europe and spent a year in travel, giving her leisure time to picture galleries and the study of art. On her return she continued her activities in behalf of woman suffrage. She took charge of the arrangements for the meeting of the National Woman Suffrage Movement held in New York in 1870. At the opening session she gave a report of the history and progress of the movement during the preceding twenty years (published as *A History of the National Woman's Rights Movement*, 1871). In 1871, with her niece and an adopted daughter, she visited Europe, where she took up seriously the study of art, under the direction of Carl Marko, of Florence, Italy. In 1874 her health failed and she returned to the United States. Most of her remaining time was spent as an invalid at her home in Providence, R. I., where she died in 1876.

[An obituary of Paulina Davis appears in the *Woman's Jour.*, Sept. 2, 1876. See also Elizabeth Cady Stanton and others, *Hist. of Woman Suffrage* (1881), I, 283–89; Timothy Hopkins, *The Kelloggs in the Old World and the New* (1903).]   M.S.

DAVIS, PHINEAS (1800–Sept. 27, 1835), inventor, the son of Nathan and Mary Davis, was born on his father's farm in Grafton County, N. H. He attended the common schools near his home during the winter months and displayed at an early age an unusual amount of mechanical ingenuity. The farm yielded few opportunities in this field and at the age of fifteen Davis left home. Some months later he arrived in York, Pa., alone and unknown. He soon found employment, however, with the local clock- and watch-maker, Jonathan Jessup, with whom he remained for six years, gaining a local reputation for his inventive skill, reliability, and ambition. In 1821 he met and formed a partnership with Israel Gardner, the proprietor of an iron foundry and machine-shop for the manufacture of steam-engines. After making a few stationary engines of Davis's design the partners began work on an iron-clad steamboat. In this undertaking they called in to assist them a local boat-builder and a fourth helper. Several years were required to complete the boat, but on Nov. 22, 1825, the *Codorus* was launched at York on the Susquehanna River and made one or two voyages to its headwaters. Small as was its draft, the boat, which was sixty feet long and sheathed with sheet iron, was unsuited at certain seasons for the shallows of the river and was abandoned. The engine, designed by Davis, was of the high-pressure type, working under a pressure of one hundred pounds per square inch. In January 1831 when the Baltimore & Ohio Railroad Company issued an advertisement offering $4,000 for the best locomotive delivered on or before June 1, 1831, Davis entered the competition. The requirements were that the locomotive must burn coal or coke, consume its own smoke, and draw fifteen tons' weight at fifteen miles an hour. Davis delivered his locomotive, "York," on time, transporting it by wagon to Baltimore, and won the prize against four competitors. Shortly thereafter the railroad company offered him, and he accepted, the managership of its mechanical shops. Moving to Baltimore with his family early in 1832, he continued to design locomotives and locomotive parts. Under his superintendence the first steel springs were installed on the "York" in 1832, and that year he and Gardner placed in service the "Atlantic," first of the "Grasshopper" engines which were the standard type for many years on the railroad. Davis made a close study of all improvements through actual trial on the company's road between Baltimore and Washington. When he was returning to Baltimore on one of these trial trips, a misplaced rail threw the engine off the track and Davis, who was on the tender, was crushed to death between the engine and the trailing cars, though no one else on board was injured. He had married Hannah Taylor of York on Nov. 15, 1826.

[John C. Jordan, *An Hist. Citizen, Career of Phineas Davis* (1904); Angus Sinclair, *Development of the Locomotive Engine* (1907); W. Kaempffert, *A Popular Hist. of Am. Invention* (1924); Edw. Hungerford, *The Story of the B. & O. R. R.* (1928); *Baltimore American*, Jan. 4, July 13, 1831.]   C.W.M.

DAVIS, RAYMOND CAZALLIS (June 23, 1836–June 10, 1919), librarian, was born in Cushing, Knox County, Me., the son of George and Katharine (Young) Davis, of English and Welsh descent through his father, and Scotch and Irish on his mother's side. His father had had long experience on the sea, and eked out the meager returns from his sea-coast farm by commanding tramp sailing vessels. In September 1849, after the death of his wife, he started for California as captain of the ship *Hampton*, taking with him his two sons, the younger of whom, Raymond, although but little over thirteen years of age, was already nearly six feet in height. This trip was continued for two years till the circuit of the globe had been completed, and Raymond had become a proficient sailor. On his return to America he prepared for college, and in 1855 entered the University of Michigan at Ann Arbor. In 1857 he was obliged to give up his studies on account of ill health, and for some years he engaged in the coasting trade. But his heart clung to schools and schooling, and in 1868 he secured the position of assistant librarian in the University of Michigan. This work with the books was suited to his ideals and ambitions, and he retained the position for four years, during which time he published *Reminiscences of a Voyage Around the World* (1869). Without prospect of advancement, except by displacement of the incumbent librarian, he resigned in 1872, and returned to follow the sea for five years.

In 1877, the office of librarian of the University of Michigan having become vacant, Davis was appointed to that position, which he retained with marked success for twenty-eight years. During his administration, from 1877 to 1905, the library grew from 23,909 volumes to 194,672, becoming one of the important libraries of the country. To help freshmen in the use of books and in the library, he started, in 1879, a short course of lectures, to which was added in 1881 a course in bibliography, for which university credit was allowed. This course he described in a paper read at the Milwaukee Conference of the American Library Association in 1886 (*Papers and Proceedings*, 1886, pp. 91–96). In 1887 he was called to give lectures on bibliography in the newly established Library School in Columbia University. These courses were probably the beginning of the instruction in library economy and the use of books which is now becoming common in many educational institutions. On July 6, 1880, he was married to Ellen Regal, daughter of the Rev. Eli Regal, a minister of the Disciples of Christ. In the following year the Regents of the University of Michigan conferred upon him the honorary degree of A.M. Davis had a keen sense of humor, which induced him to write some short stories and sea-yarns which delighted his friends. Several of these appeared in *Fore and Aft* and other magazines. After his retirement as librarian in 1905 he continued his lectures on bibliography until 1914, when he dropped the lectureship, and was made beneficiary of the Williams Emeritus Professorship Fund. He died in Ann Arbor in 1919, survived by his wife and leaving his impress as one of the pioneers of the library movement in America.

[In addition to the references above, see *Who's Who in America*, 1918–19; Davis's own comments on "The Function of a Librarian" in the *Mich. Alumnus*, Mar. 1906; his annual reports, 1878–1905; W. W. Bishop, "In Memoriam, Raymond C. Davis" (with portr.) in *Mich. Alumnus*, Oct. 1919; C. B. Grant, *Ibid.*, Dec., 1919; Memorial adopted by the University Senate, *Ibid.*, June 1920; B. A. Finney, "As it Was in the Beginning: Raymond C. Davis" (with portr.) in *Public Libraries* (Chicago), Oct. 1924; Elizabeth M. Farrand, *Hist of the Univ. of Mich.* (1885); B. A. Hinsdale, *Hist. of the Univ. of Mich.* (1906); Wilfred B. Shaw, *The Univ. of Mich.* (1920).]   B.A.F.

DAVIS, REBECCA BLAINE HARDING (June 24, 1831–Sept. 29, 1910), novelist, daughter of Richard Harding and Rachel Leet Wilson who was of old Virginia descent, was born in Washington, Pa. In her early childhood her parents removed to Alabama and shortly afterward to Wheeling, then in Virginia, where she lived until her marriage. She was very largely self-educated. Attracted to literature by the phenomenal success of the feminine writers of the fifties —Mrs. Stowe, the Warner sisters, Maria Cummins, and others—but without guidance or knowledge of literary art save as she had gained it from voluminous reading, she began early to write fiction, some of which was accepted by the periodicals of the day. She was thirty, however, before she gained anything like real recognition. In April 1861, Lowell published in the *Atlantic*, at the time the leading magazine in America, her short story "Life in the Iron Mills," following it in October with the beginning of her serial "A Short Story of To-day," later issued as *Margaret Howth* (1862). She quickly found herself famous. Though often crude and amateurish in workmanship, these stories were nevertheless remarkable productions, distinct landmarks in the evolution of American fiction. Written when the American novel was in all its areas ultra-romantic and over-sentimental, they are Russian-like in their grim and sordid realism. That she was doing pioneer work she seems fully to have realized. "You want something," she said, "to lift you out of this crowded, tobacco-stained commonplace; to kindle and chafe and glow in you. I want you to dig into this commonplace, this vulgar life, and see what is in it. Sometimes I think it has a new and awful significance that we do not see."

On Mar. 4, 1863, she was married to L. Clarke Davis, later a prominent figure in Pennsylvania journalism, and for the rest of her life made her home in Philadelphia. With a growing family she did not cease from literary activity. In 1869 she became a member of the editorial staff of the *New York Tribune* retaining the position for several years. She was a constant contributor to the magazines and until late in life continued to produce popular fiction. Her leading titles are, *Dallas Galbraith* (1868); *Waiting for the Verdict* (1868); *Berrytown* (1872); *John Andross* (1874); *A Law unto Herself* (1878); *Natasqua* (1886); *Silhouettes of American Life* (1892); *Kent Hampden* (1892); *Doctor Warrick's Daughters* (1896); *Frances Waldeaux*

(1897). None of her later works, however, fulfilled the promise of her first *Atlantic* stories. With achieved reputation she allowed herself to drift into the prevailing fictional conventions and sentimentality. Practically none of her work has been republished. She died at Mount Kisco, N. Y., Sept. 29, 1910. Two sons, Richard Harding Davis [*q.v.*] and Charles Belmont Davis, both writers of distinction, survived her.

[In 1904 Mrs. Davis published an autobiographical volume entitled *Bits of Gossip*. See also a biographical sketch by Dalton Dorr in the *American*, III, 328, Mar. 4, 1882; *N. Y. Times*, Sept. 30, 1910; *Who's Who in America*, 1910–11.] F. L. P—e.

DAVIS, REUBEN (Jan. 18, 1813–Oct. 14, 1890), lawyer, was the youngest of the twelve children of the Rev. John Davis, a Baptist minister who had gone to Tennessee, settling near Winchester. About five years after the birth of Reuben the family removed to northern Alabama. Here Reuben spent much time with the Indians, though he attended the public school about three months each year. Disregarding the boy's early inclination to the law, his father, who thought that "lawyers were wholly given up to the Devil even in this world" and that "it was impossible for any one of them ever to enter the kingdom of heaven," persuaded Reuben, then about sixteen years old, to "read medicine" with his brother-in-law, Dr. George Higgason, in Monroe County, Miss. But a brief experience of the medical profession was sufficient to confirm Davis's original preference for the law (*Recollections*, pp. 2–9). Meanwhile, in 1831, he was married to Mary Halbert. In 1832 he opened a law office in Athens, Monroe County, but later moved to Aberdeen. From the beginning, his success as a lawyer was remarkable. At the age of twenty-two, he was elected district attorney of the 6th Mississippi judicial district. At twenty-six, he had saved $20,000 from his earnings. Defeated for Congress on the Whig ticket in 1838, he was, in 1842, appointed judge of the Mississippi high court of appeals, but resigned after four months on the bench. When the Mexican War broke out, he was elected colonel of the 2nd Mississippi Volunteers. This organization reached the mouth of the Rio Grande the day of the battle of Buena Vista; but Davis, whose health was poor, saw no actual fighting, returning home in June of the same year. After serving a term as a member of the state legislature (1855–57), he was elected to Congress, as a Democrat, and served two terms (1857–61). He believed that war between the North and the South was inevitable, and so strongly defended the Southern position that his opponents called him a fire-eater. After

his resignation from the Federal Congress in 1861, he became major-general of Mississippi troops, commanding a brigade for a short time; but was soon elected to the Confederate Congress, and was present at the Richmond inauguration of President Davis. He served in the Confederate legislative body till 1864, when he resigned because of his inability to work harmoniously with President Davis, to whom, incidentally, he was not related. His criticism of the Confederate war policy probably caused his defeat by Gen. Charles Clark for the governorship of Mississippi in 1863. During the Reconstruction period, Davis belonged to the group who believed in controlling the negro by threats of force. (See G. J. Leftwich, "Reconstruction in Monroe County," *Publications of the Mississippi Historical Society*, IX, 76.) He was defeated for Congress in 1878 as a candidate of the Greenback party. During most of the last quarter-century of his life he devoted his energies to the practise of criminal law. He defended more than two hundred clients accused of murder, not one of whom went to the gallows. His principal literary work is his book, *Recollections of Mississippi and Mississippians,* published in 1889. He died the following year in Huntsville, Ala.

[Reuben Davis's *Recollections of Mississippi and Mississippians* (1889) is virtually his autobiography. The *Miss. Hist. Soc. Pubs.* refer to him frequently, especially volumes II, V, IX, X, and XIV. The Goodspeed Publishing Company's *Biog. and Hist. Memoirs of Mississippi* (1891), I, 632–34, contains a considerable sketch of his life. Dunbar Rowland's *Mississippi* (1907), I, 632, tells of the career of Davis, and the same author's *Hist. of Mississippi: the Heart of the South* (1925), vols. I and II, refers to him many times. See also obituary in the *Daily Picayune* (New Orleans), Oct. 15, 1890.] L. T. L.

DAVIS, RICHARD HARDING (Apr. 18, 1864–Apr. 11, 1916), journalist, author, was born in Philadelphia, the son of L. Clarke and Rebecca (Harding) Davis [*q.v.*]. His surroundings were literary from his childhood. His father was editor of the Philadelphia *Public Ledger,* and his mother was one of the prominent feminine novelists of her generation. Reared in the city of his birth, he attended the Episcopal Academy at Swarthmore, Pa., Ulrich's Preparatory School at Bethlehem, Pa., Lehigh University, where he spent three years, and finally Johns Hopkins. In 1886 he entered actively upon the newspaper career that was to make him the most widely known reporter of his generation. After employment by the *Philadelphia Record* for a brief time, he went to the *Press,* for which he reported the Johnstown flood disaster. Later he was sent by the *Telegraph* to England with the cricket team, and in

Davis

September 1889 he joined the staff of the New York *Sun.* His stories and "specials" in this paper and his articles in *Scribner's Magazine* attracted wide attention. Leaving the *Sun* in 1890, he became managing editor of *Harper's Weekly* and for this journal made a tour of the West, the literary result of which appeared in 1892 under the title, *The West from a Car Window.* During the next year he spent several months making a comprehensive tour of the Mediterranean for *Harper's Weekly,* his letters appearing in book form in 1894 with the title, *The Rulers of the Mediterranean.* Other journalistic tours during this period he recorded in *Our English Cousins* (1894), and *About Paris* (1895). Next sent to report on conditions in the regions bordering the Canal Zone, he wrote *Three Gringos in Venezuela and Central America* (1896). In a single year he witnessed the coronation of the Czar, the millennial celebration at Budapest, and the Queen's Jubilee in London. It was his fortune to report for prominent New York and London papers six notable wars: the Spanish War in Cuba, the Greco-Turkish, the Spanish-American, the Boer War, the Russo-Japanese, and finally the World War. Seven volumes record his observations: *Cuba in War Time* (1897); *A Year from a Reporter's Note Book* (1898); *The Cuban and Porto Rican Campaigns* (1898); *With Both Armies in South Africa* (1900); *Notes of a War Correspondent* (1910); *With the Allies* (1914); *With the French in France and Salonika* (1916). Only one other of his many assignments need be recorded, his trip to Central Africa in 1907 for *Collier's Weekly* to investigate the reported atrocities, the resulting book being *The Congo and the Coasts of Africa* (1907). As a correspondent Davis was quick to see the picturesque, and unerring in his selection of the features having news value. A tendency, however, to the sensational and startlingly dramatic is to be found in all his journalistic work.

Davis was equally successful in the field of popular fiction. His short story "Gallegher," first published in *Scribner's Magazine* in August 1890, and used a year later as the title number of a collection of tales, attracted wide attention. Following it at varied intervals came eleven other collections aggregating upward of eighty stories with widely varied backgrounds and technique: *Van Bibber and Others* (1892); *The Exiles and Other Stories* (1892); *The Lion and the Unicorn* (1899); *Ranson's Folly* (1902); *The Scarlet Car* (1907); *Once Upon a Time* (1910); *The Man Who Could Not Lose* (1911); *The Red Cross Girl* (1912); *The Lost Road*

(1913); *The Boy Scout* (1917). In addition, he produced no less than seven popular novels, some of them among the best sellers of their period: *Soldiers of Fortune* (1897); *The King's Jackal* (1898); *Captain Macklin* (1902); *The Bar Sinister* (1903); *Vera the Medium* (1908); *The White Mice* (1909). In all his fiction Davis was essentially a journalist, quick to sense the demands of the larger public and working in the fashions of the hour. Most of his critics agree that while he was always vivid in his descriptive passages, often picturesque, and easily readable, he dealt mainly with the surface of life, and that even his best work will not long endure. He was too facile, too headlong, too obsessed with contemporaneousness, and he unquestionably published too much.

It was but natural that the lure of dramatic composition should have worked its spell upon him. From his pen came first and last no less than twenty-five dramatic pieces, some of them highly successful on the stage. *Ranson's Folly* had a long run at the Hudson Theatre in 1904; *The Dictator* was presented by Charles Frohman at the Criterion Theatre the same year; *Miss Civilization,* with Ethel Barrymore, as star, was the attraction of the Broadway Theatre in 1906; *The Seventh Daughter* ran for a month at the Cort Theatre in Chicago in 1910; and *The Girl from Home,* a musical comedy, was an attraction in New York as late as 1920. He added, however, nothing permanent to American drama. He was twice married: first, on May 4, 1899, to Cecil Clark of Chicago, who divorced him in 1910; second, on July 8, 1912, to Elizabeth G. McEvoy (Bessie McCoy), who survived him. He died suddenly at his home at Mount Kisco, N. Y.

[Four sets of his writings have been published: first collected edition (8 vols., 1898); second collected edition (6 vols., 1899); third collected edition (6 vols., 1903); and the Cross Roads edition (12 vols., 1916). See also Chas. Belmont Davis, ed., *Adventures and Letters of Richard Harding Davis* (1917); Henry C. Quimby, *Richard Harding Davis, a Bibliography* (1924); and, for criticism of his fiction, Blanche C. Williams, *Our Short Story Writers* (1920).]

F. L. P—e.

DAVIS, VARINA ANNE JEFFERSON (June 27, 1864–Sept. 18, 1898), daughter of Jefferson and Varina (Howell) Davis [*qq.v.*] was born at Richmond during the darkest days of the Confederacy. With her mother she spent some time in Fortress Monroe while her father was a prisoner there. At an early age she showed a remarkable love for books, and at twelve could repeat many passages from Shakespeare. At the age of thirteen she was taken abroad by her parents, and left in a boarding-school at Karlsruhe, Germany, where she remained five years. In 1882 she went to Paris, and on her return spoke French and German more fluently than she did English. At "Beauvoir," now the family home, she was her father's constant companion, and she frequently accompanied him on his trips through the South. On one of these occasions Gov. Gordon of Georgia presented "Winnie" Davis to an enthusiastic crowd as the "Daughter of the Confederacy," a title which she valued and by which she has ever since been known. Adopted, idolized, idealized by the veterans, she became one of the cherished symbols of the "Lost Cause." Beginning her writing before her father's death, she continued it as a means of support when she and her mother went to New York to live. Her published works include: *An Irish Knight of the Nineteenth Century: Sketch of the Life of Robert Emmet* (1888); *The Veiled Doctor; A Novel* (1895); *A Romance of Summer Seas; A Novel* (1899). She died at Narragansett Pier and was buried in Richmond.

[An essay by C. C. Ferrell, "'The Daughter of the Confederacy,'—her Life, Character and Writings," *Miss. Hist. Soc. Pubs.*, II (1899), 69–84; articles in *N. Y. Times*, New Orleans *Picayune*, *Atlanta Jour.*, Sept. 19, 1898, and in other newspapers; incidental references in the writings of her mother.]   M. T. S.

DAVIS, VARINA HOWELL (May 7, 1826–Oct. 16, 1906), wife of Jefferson Davis [*q.v.*], president of the Confederacy, was born at "The Briers," near Natchez, Miss. Her father was William Burr, son of Richard Howell, Revolutionary governor of New Jersey; her mother was Margaret Louisa, daughter of James Kempe, a Virginian of Irish descent. Her girlhood was spent chiefly on the plantation or at Natchez. Much of her early education was received from a devoted tutor, a friend of her father's, Judge George Winchester, whom she affectionately called "Great Heart." Later she spent two years at Madame Greenland's school at Philadelphia. On Feb. 26, 1845 she married Jefferson Davis who that year entered Congress. Mrs. Davis lived in close intellectual companionship with her husband. Though brought up a Whig, she eventually accepted his politics, became jealously watchful of his reputation, and was keenly sensitive to any criticism of his political theories. While her husband was at the front in the Mexican War, she took sole charge of their plantation, "Brierfield." In 1847 he was sent to the Senate. Though Mrs. Davis felt regret at leaving "Brierfield," this was overcome by her pride in her husband's elevation. Being of an ambitious nature, she was gratified by her social success at Washington. While her husband was

a senator, and later when he was secretary of war, the drawing room of their house was the scene of many distinguished gatherings. The hostess was a brilliant and vivacious talker, often witty.

Very different was her life a few years later as the wife of the president of the Confederacy. Conditions at Richmond were hard and there was much captious criticism. If she entertained, there was an outcry that the "White House" was indifferent to the sufferings of the people; if she lived simply, her critics complained that she was not keeping up the dignity of her position. Her Northern antecedents made her an object of suspicion, but there was no doubt of her sympathy with the Southern cause. With her husband she had great influence, which her enemies believed to be far from beneficial, especially in the matter of appointments.

The whole of her later life was filled with bitter trials in which she was sustained by her deeply religious nature. The flight from Richmond with her husband and four children was followed by his capture and imprisonment, which for a time she was allowed to share. She made long and untiring efforts for his release, and was at last successful. At "Beauvoir," which they purchased soon after, she was his amanuensis while he wrote *The Rise and Fall of the Confederate Government* (1881). Here, after his death, she wrote her one important literary work: *Jefferson Davis, Ex-President of the Confederate States of America: A Memoir* (2 vols., 1890). Giving "Beauvoir" to the state of Mississippi as a home for Confederate soldiers, Mrs. Davis with her daughter "Winnie" (see article on Varina Anne Jefferson Davis) went to New York, where she wrote articles for periodicals and magazines as a means of support. She survived all but one of her six children.

[The only biography is Eron (Mrs. Dunbar) Rowland, *Varina Howell, Wife of Jefferson Davis* (1927), which contains many reminiscences. The *Memoir* of her husband contains a tolerably full narrative of her personal life. A sympathetic character study is in Gamaliel Bradford, *Wives* (1925). There is a large amount of disjointed information about her scattered through the Southern newspapers of the war period.]
M. T. S.

DAVIS, WILLIAM AUGUSTINE (Sept. 21, 1809–Jan. 15, 1875), postmaster, inventor, was born in Barren County, Ky., the son of Hardin and Elizabeth (Wynne) Davis and a descendant of Nathaniel Davis who came from England about 1690 and settled in Virginia. He attended the district schools in winter and helped with the farm work until he was fourteen, and was then sent alone on horseback over the mountains to Charlottesville, Va., to live with a relative and attend private school there. His uncle was postmaster at Charlottesville and in his spare time while at school, and later while at the University of Virginia, young Davis helped in the post-office and became thoroughly acquainted with mail distribution methods. At the age of twenty-one and before completing his University work he accepted a position in the Richmond, Va., post-office. Here he remained for twenty-five years, serving several terms as postmaster. In the spring of 1855 he resigned his position and moved with his family to St. Joseph, Mo., where on Oct. 19, 1855 he was commissioned postmaster. Within a year this position was made a presidential one and he was recommissioned, serving until 1861, when a Republican was appointed, and after that continuing as assistant. The St. Joseph post-office was at that time the point where all western mails were transferred from railroad cars to overland stage-coaches. To make their journeys the stage-coaches had to leave promptly and although there was a three-hour interval in which to sort the mail between the scheduled train arrival and stage-coach departure, the irregularity in arrival of the former rarely permitted sufficient time for this work to be completed, so that the stage-coaches often departed without their consignment of mail. To alleviate this condition, Davis, in the spring of 1862, suggested that the distribution of mail for the West be made on the railroad cars before they reached St. Joseph. With his recommendation he submitted drawings and sketches of his proposed arrangement of cars for the purpose. As a result and with the approval of the Post Office Department, in July 1862 a railroad post-office was successfully inaugurated on the Hannibal & Saint Joseph Railroad (Quincy, Ill., to St. Joseph, Mo.) with Davis in charge of the undertaking. In the *History of the Railway Mail Service,* published by order of Congress in 1885, appears the following: "There seems to be no doubt that Mr. Davis was the first to distribute through mails in the United States, and the first to have cars prepared for that purpose, as was done by the Hannibal and Saint Joseph Railroad for the transportation of the over-land mails" (p. 81). He operated the system until by the extension of railroads westward to connect with the Union Pacific Railroad, the distribution of overland mails was changed. On June 25, 1843, he married Anne Hopkins of Richmond, Va., by whom he had four sons and four daughters, all of whom with his wife survived him at the time of his death in St. Joseph.

[*Hist. of Eminent Men,* pub. by Jas. T. White; *Ry.*

Postoffice, n.s., vol. VII, no. 12; *Hist. of the Railway Mail Service,* cited above; original correspondence and documents.]   C. W. M.

DAVIS, WILLIAM THOMAS (Mar. 3, 1822–Dec. 3, 1907), lawyer, author, was descended from Thomas Davis who, settling in Plymouth, Mass., in 1737, engaged in the shipping business and foreign trade. The latter's grandson, William Davis, also of Plymouth, married Joanna, daughter of Capt. Gideon White, and their youngest son, William Thomas Davis, was born there. His early education having been received in private schools, he entered the high school in Plymouth in 1832, proceeding thence to Harvard College, graduating in 1842. He then studied medicine for a short time and in 1846 went to Europe, spending some months in Paris and London. Returning to the United States in 1847, he entered his brother's law office in Boston, and was called to the Suffolk County bar on Nov. 9, 1849. Ten days later he married Abby Burr, daughter of Thomas Hedge of Plymouth. He practised his profession in Boston for four years, but had no great inclination for law, and in 1853 returned to Plymouth, where he entered into business, and remained closely identified with that town during the remainder of his life. He devoted much of his time to investigating the pioneer records of the Plymouth settlement and until 1892—a period of thirty-eight years—there was not a year when he did not hold municipal office. In 1858 and 1859 he represented his district in the state Senate, and in 1876 served as a delegate to the Republican National Convention at Cincinnati. He was also prominent in the Pilgrim Society of which he became president. He embodied the results of his researches into the early history of his neighborhood in two authoritative volumes, *Ancient Landmarks of Plymouth* (1883) and *History of the Town of Plymouth* (1885), which were distinguished for their erudition and attractive style, and also contributed a number of historical articles to the *History of Plymouth County, Mass.* (1884), edited by D. H. Hurd. Thereafter he was constantly engaged in literary production, much of which maintained the high standard attained by his first works. He edited *Records of the Town of Plymouth,* volumes I to III (1889–1903), *The Professional and Industrial History of Suffolk County, Massachusetts* (1894), and *The New England States* (1897), a history in four volumes, contributing himself a number of the articles which appeared in the two last named. He wrote a *History of the Judiciary of Massachusetts* (1900), and in 1906 published *Plymouth Memories of an Octogenarian,* containing much autobiographical material. His last undertaking was the editing of *Bradford's History of Plymouth Plantation 1606–1646* for Scribner's series, Original Narratives of Early American History, to which he contributed a valuable introduction. He died at Plymouth Dec. 3, 1907, while the volume was in the press.

[Davis's ancestry is traced in his *Ancient Landmarks of Plymouth,* pt. 2, pp. 82–83, and a biographical sketch appears in the *Professional and Industrial Hist. of Suffolk County,* vol. I, p. 150. His *Plymouth Memories* contains much personal matter not to be found elsewhere. There is an obituary notice in the *Boston Transcript,* Dec. 4, 1907.]   H. W. H. K.

DAVIS, WINNIE [See DAVIS, VARINA ANNE JEFFERSON, 1864–1898.]

DAVISON, HENRY POMEROY (June 13, 1867–May 6, 1922), banker, head of the Red Cross War Council 1917–19, the son of George B. and Henrietta (Pomeroy) Davison, was born at Troy, Bradford County, Pa., where he received his schooling up to his fifteenth year. During the ensuing five years he attended Greylock Institute at South Williamstown, Mass. He began teaching in the Troy school in which he had been a pupil, as early as his seventeenth year, and returned to it at intervals for three years. His first work after leaving the academy was in the bank at Troy owned by brothers of his mother. There he began at the bottom and as he worked up became restless and eager to find a wider horizon than the Pennsylvania town afforded. At twenty-one he applied for a job in a New York City bank, but failed to get it. For the next three years he was employed by a bank at Bridgeport, Conn., rising step by step to a receiving tellership. In 1891 a new bank, the Astor Place (later absorbed by the Corn Exchange), opened its doors in New York. Davison obtained personal interviews with the cashier, was twice told that his application would have to be declined because of his limited city acquaintance, but at the third interview was given the position. He quickly made friends and easily held them. Near the end of the third year of his service there as paying teller a mentally deranged man approached the teller's window, pointed a revolver at Davison, and presented a check calling for the payment of $1,000,-000 "to the Almighty." Davison was alone in the teller's cage. As calmly as if the demand were an every-day business detail he remarked, in a slightly raised voice so as to attract the attention of his associates, "A million dollars for the Almighty—how will you have it?" and proceeded to count out bills of small denomination. The bank detective heard the words, sensed the

situation, and quickly seized and disarmed the would-be payee. The afternoon papers of that day, carrying the story, reached the board-room of a downtown New York bank at the moment when the directors were planning to fill the post of assistant cashier. Davison was already known to one of them, who soon convinced his colleagues that the courage, resourcefulness, and steadiness of nerve displayed in the Astor Place incident would be useful in the position under consideration. Davison thus became assistant cashier of the Liberty National Bank in 1894, and within five years he was president of the institution. It was then that he conceived the plan which resulted in the formation of the Bankers' Trust Company, intended to serve as a depository for the funds of national banks and insurance companies. In 1902 George F. Baker and Francis L. Hine of the First National Bank invited him to become vice-president and director. There he soon won recognition from J. Pierpont Morgan, Sr., who frequently consulted him, especially in the monetary crisis of 1907, when Davison had an important part in determining the action of New York banks. During the next year he joined the Monetary Commission headed by Senator Aldrich and in the capacity of banking expert with that commission he visited France, Germany, and England. He then acquainted himself with the prevailing European idea of a flexible national currency. In association with Senator Aldrich, Paul M. Warburg, Frank A. Vanderlip, and A. Piatt Andrew, he took part in drawing up the "Jekyl Island" report that led to the crystallization of sentiment resulting in the creation of the Federal Reserve System. Having become a partner in J. P. Morgan & Company, he served with distinction in 1910 as chairman of the Six-Power Chinese Loan Conference at Paris. He was now one of the small group of Americans whose names were recognized at the counsel board of international finance.

When the United States entered the World War it was clearly foreseen that great responsibilities would devolve upon the head of the Red Cross War Council. The appointment of Davison by President Wilson as Chairman of the Council was hailed as one of the most important steps taken by the government at Washington in the first stages of the war. He accepted the appointment on the condition that the proposed solicitation of a $15,000,000 fund for the American Red Cross be abandoned and that plans be made at once for a national drive to raise $100,-000,000. In the outcome $115,000,000 was secured at a time when the war demands in every city and village of the country were exceeding anything ever before dreamed of; but the second drive, in 1918, had even greater results, reaching the unparalleled total of $170,000,000 for the Red Cross war chest. The handling of these great sums in time of war called for administrative talent of the highest order. Having the vision and the knowledge of war-time conditions that enabled him to understand more clearly than most of his contemporaries in America the true magnitude of the war effort required of the United States, he saw that only the most generous support of the Red Cross could make that effort successful. He refused to think of the organization as merely incidental to military and naval operations, insisting that it was a vital and essential part of the government's war machinery. He impressed this conception upon his aides, chosen with fine discrimination, many of whom, like himself, were men of wealth giving their services without pay and in not a few instances meeting their own expenses. After the Armistice in 1918, Davison, in cooperation with the Red Cross officers of the Allied nations, planned an International League of Red Cross Societies intended to function somewhat as the League of Nations. In 1922 he died as the result of an operation for tumor on the brain. He had married Kate Trubee, of Bridgeport, Conn., on Apr. 13, 1893. She, with two sons and two daughters, survived him. In the last year of the war he received decorations and honors from all the Allied nations.

[In 1919 Davison published *The Am. Red Cross in the Great War*. See also *Who's Who in America*, 1922–23; articles in the *N. Y. Times* for May 7, 8, 9, 10, 15, and 29, 1922; article in *Everybody's Mag.*, Nov. 1917.]
                                            W. B. S.

DAWES, HENRY LAURENS (Oct. 30, 1816–Feb. 5, 1903), congressman, senator, was born in Cummington, Hampshire County, Mass., the son of Mitchell and Mercy (Burgess) Dawes. After graduating from Yale College in 1839, he taught school for a few months, gaining meanwhile some newspaper experience writing editorials for the Greenfield *Gazette and Courier* and the North Adams *Transcript*. Admitted to the bar in 1842, he opened an office in North Adams, but moved later to Pittsfield, where, in 1848, he began his long political career by being chosen to the Massachusetts lower house, of which he was a member in 1848, 1849, and 1852. He sat for one term (1850) in the state Senate, and he was an active participant in the Massachusetts constitutional convention of 1853. For some years (1853–57) he was United States attorney for the western district of Massachusetts.

He married, on May 1, 1844, Electa Allen Sanderson (1822–1901), daughter of Chester Sanderson, of Ashfield, Mass.

Dawes came into national prominence in 1857, when he was elected to the Thirty-fifth Congress from the Berkshire district of Massachusetts; and he sat in the House of Representatives term after term until 1875, growing steadily in influence until he was recognized as perhaps its most useful and reliable member. His colleague, George F. Hoar, wrote of Dawes, "There has never been, within my experience, a greater power than his on the floor of the House" (*Autobiography*, I, 203). At first appointed only to the Committee on Revolutionary Claims, he became chairman in succession of the two most important House committees, Appropriations (1869) and Ways and Means (1871). He was also for ten years chairman of the Committee on Elections. There was very little law-making of this period in which he was not consulted. He was a consistent advocate of a protectionist policy and was himself the author of important tariff measures, including the wool and woolen tariff of 1868 which he wrote conjointly with Bingham of Ohio. Manufacturers of textiles in New England depended upon him as their champion when legislation affecting them was introduced. He was responsible for the establishment of the Fish Commission, and, in 1869, at the suggestion of Prof. Cleveland Abbe [*q.v.*], he initiated a plan for a daily weather bulletin, which was to collect and compare weather reports from all sections of the country, and which soon became the United States Weather Bureau. He was chairman, in 1872, of a House committee for investigating the so-called "Sanborn Contracts." In 1869 he was a candidate for speaker, but was defeated by James G. Blaine.

In 1875 Dawes was elected to succeed William B. Washburn as United States senator from Massachusetts and served three consecutive terms, retiring in 1892. As a member of the Committee on Buildings and Grounds, he proposed and carried through a bill under which the Washington Monument, left unfinished since 1856 because of lack of funds, was finally completed and dedicated in 1885. His most enduring work, however, was accomplished as chairman of the Committee on Indian Affairs. A faithful and intelligent friend of the red men, he did his utmost to make their lot a happy one, and Edward Everett Hale said of him, "While he held the reins, nobody talked of dishonor in our dealings with the Indians." He was the author of the Dawes Act of 1887, which conferred United States citizenship upon every civilized Indian, and granted homesteads of 160 acres to heads of families and smaller parcels to others. It was his influence which created a system of Indian education and placed the Indians under the protection of the federal criminal laws. After his retirement from the Senate, he visited Indian Territory in 1895, as the head of the Commission to the Five Civilized Tribes, designated by Congress to secure the voluntary consent of the Indians to the abandonment of tribal relations. His report was widely discussed.

Senator Hoar once declared that Dawes had "proved himself fit for every position in our Republican army except that of trumpeter." In appearance, he was a shrewd-looking Yankee, with high cheek-bones and a gray beard. He was a man of simple tastes, without any showy qualities, and he never sought popular applause. Without any gift of eloquent speech, he confined himself always to a dignified and lucid presentation of his case; but he worked more often in the committee rooms than on the floor of the House or the Senate. Although he influenced legislation upon which millions of dollars depended, he never accumulated a fortune, and his probity was unquestioned. During his last months in the Senate, Dawes was troubled by an increasing deafness, which prevented him from seeking another term. Upon his formal retirement, after thirty-six years of continuous service in Congress, he was tendered a farewell banquet by his associates. In his old age, he became the "Sage of Pittsfield," where he died in his eighty-seventh year.

[There is no extended biography of Dawes, but ample material upon him is to be found in newspapers and magazines of the period. See G. F. Hoar, *Autobiog. of Seventy Years* (2 vols., 1903); *Biog. Dir. Am. Congress, 1774–1927* (1928); *Obit. Record Grads. Yale Univ.* (1910); *Outlook,* Feb. 14, 1903; *Boston Transcript,* Feb. 5, 1903.]

C. M. F.

DAWES, WILLIAM (Apr. 6, 1745–Feb. 25, 1799), one of the "warners" of the 18th of April 1775, the descendant of a William Dawes who was born in Sudbury, England, in 1620 and emigrated to Massachusetts in 1635, was the second of the nine children of William and Lydia (Boone) Dawes of Boston. His father was tailor, grocer, and goldsmith by turns, and owing to the fact that he survived his son the latter was always referred to as "Junior." He learned the tanner's trade and had a tan-yard for some years. On May 3, 1768, he married Mehitable May, by whom he had seven children. Tradesmen had been active in the Revolutionary movement and in some way he had been brought to the attention of its leaders. He was one of the two men chosen to spread the alarm if the British troops should

attempt a raid on the countryside. Such an occasion occurred on Apr. 18, 1775. It had been thought possible that a messenger might not be able to get out of Boston, so Paul Revere was staying on the mainland side of the Charles River and the well-known signal displayed from the North Church tower was for him. As soon as it became necessary to arouse the country, however, Joseph Warren sent for Dawes and started him by way of Brighton Bridge and the Cambridge Road. He slipped through the British lines and met Revere at Parson Clark's at Lexington where Hancock and Samuel Adams were staying. Having warned the two leaders and made a short stop for refreshments, Revere, Dawes, and a new recruit, Dr. Prescott, went on toward Concord, rousing the men at all the houses on the way. Revere was captured and never reached Concord but either Prescott or Dawes, it is not known which, got through and gave the alarm. After the siege of Boston began, Dawes joined the Continental Army and is thought to have fought at Bunker Hill. Before long, however, he moved his family to Worcester, where he was appointed by Congress a commissary to the army. While there he became a partner of his brother-in-law Coolidge in the grocery business, and when he returned to Boston after the war, he continued in the same business. His first wife died on Oct. 28, 1793, and on Nov. 18, 1795, he was married to Lydia Gendall.

[The best account is H. W. Holland, *Wm. Dawes and his Ride with Paul Revere* (privately printed 1878). See also E. H. Goss, *The Life of Col. Paul Revere* (2 vols., 1891); R. Frothingham, *The Alarm on the Night of April 18, 1775* (pamphlet, 1876), and *Hist. of the Siege of Boston* (1851).]

J. T. A.

DAWKINS, HENRY (fl. 1753–1780), was one of the earliest engravers to work upon copper in America, and although even the years of his birth and death are unknown, much apocryphal information has been printed about him. He learned to engrave upon metals in London, and about the year 1753 settled in New York City. He is said by Dunlap to have been originally an engraver of buttons and shop bills, but after coming to this country he became a general practitioner of the art, finding the field open. His book plates, of which about twenty have been identified, are poor copies of the Chippendale style. The earliest example of his work in America is the book plate for John Burnet of New York, which bears the date 1754. In 1757 he was in Philadelphia as assistant to James Turner, engraver, and in the following year he began business for himself. In the *Pennsylvania Journal,* July 19, 1758, in an advertisement, he described himself as engraver from London, who lately wrought with Mr. James Turner," and stated that "he engraves all sort of maps, shopkeepers bills, bills of parcel, coats of arms for gentlemen's books, coats of arms, cyphers, and other devices on plate; likewise seals, and mourning rings cut after the neatest manner and at the most reasonable rates." He married Priscilla Wood, Oct. 2, 1757, in Philadelphia, and there his seven children were born. Two of them were buried in that city, the second being Capt. John Dawkins, a mariner, who died in 1804. Dawkins was notorious for his poor equipment for the higher forms of engraving which he essayed. He cut caricatures, notably one picturing an incident in Philadelphia in 1764, at the time of the Paxton Boys excitement. While in Philadelphia he became a member of the Grand Lodge of Masons, and in 1764 was elected junior warden of his lodge. Two of his engravings illustrate the first volume of the *Transactions of the American Philosophical Society,* 1771; one of these is a plate to illustrate the paper by Rittenhouse on the Transit of Venus, 1769. During the Revolution (May 1776) he was arrested in New York on suspicion of counterfeiting Continental and Provincial currency. In October 1776, he petitioned the New York Committee of Safety "for a termination of his sorrows by a death." The history of the Grand Lodge of Pennsylvania (*Philadelphia Devizes Lodge No. 1, Pennsylvania,* vol. II, 1899) states that Dawkins was probably hanged for counterfeiting. That this view is erroneous is proved by the *Journals of the Continental Congress* (XVIII, 922), where it is recorded that on Oct. 13, 1780, a warrant to Henry Dawkins was issued on the treasurer for fifteen hundred dollars "on account for engraving and altering the border and back pieces for striking the bills of credit of the United States." After this date he disappears from view.

[Records of Christ Church, Phila. (MS.) ; *Jours. of the Provincial Cong. . . . of the State of N. Y.* (2 vols., 1842) ; Wm. Dunlap, *Hist. of the Rise and Progress of the Arts of Design in the U. S.* (1834) ; *Am. Archives,* ser. 5, vol. III ; D. M. Stauffer, *Am. Engravers upon Copper and Steel* (1907) ; Chas. Dexter Allen, *Am. Book Plates* (1905) ; *Jours. of the Continental Cong.,* vol. XVIII.]   J. J.

DAWSON, FRANCIS WARRINGTON (May 17, 1840–Mar. 12, 1889), journalist, who, on coming to manhood, changed his name from Reeks, was born and educated in London. His parents were Austin and Mary Perkins Reeks. After completing his schooling, he promptly began literary work; four or five comedies from his pen were acted at the city theatres. As a result of his studies and because of his romantic

nature, he became an ardent partisan of the Southern States, and when Fort Sumter fell determined to enlist in their armed service. The Confederate cruiser *Nashville* having run the blockade from Charleston and arrived at Southampton Nov. 21, 1861, he hastened from London to present himself to its commander, Capt. Pegram, but this officer in view of Dawson's youth refused to take him on board. A few days before the ship sailed, however, Dawson, this time dressed as a sailor, succeeded in enlisting on her in Pegram's absence. For his service on the voyage home he was made master's mate in the Confederate navy. After serving at Norfolk and in the James River, wishing more action he resigned his commission in the navy and enlisted as a private in Purcell's battery, Hill's division, Army of Northern Virginia, in June 1862. He was promoted for valiant action at Mechanicsville, and after serving as ordnance officer with Longstreet's Corps received his captaincy in April 1864, becoming ordnance officer of Fitzhugh Lee's division. He fought in a dozen battles, was three times wounded, and suffered imprisonment at Fort Delaware. After the surrender, he had only a three-cent postage stamp in the pocket of his uniform. Going to Richmond in July 1865, he planned to start a small weekly newspaper with a friend. The plant was seized by the military forces before the first issue appeared, and, after brief service as a bookkeeper in Petersburg, Dawson worked on the *Richmond Examiner* and later the *Richmond Dispatch* until September of the next year. He then became route agent for the National Express and Transportation Company, but this project soon failed. Through B. R. Riordan, whom he had known on the *Examiner* and who had gone to the *Charleston Courier,* Dawson was engaged for the *Charleston Mercury,* where he began work Nov. 10, 1866. A year later, with Riordan and Henry Evans he purchased the *Charleston News.* Acquiring the much older *Courier* in April 1873, they combined the two papers as the *News and Courier,* of which Dawson became editor.

Dawson was quick of perception, sudden to anger and as sudden in forgiveness. He was thoroughly democratic and made loyal friends, but his imperiousness and persistence in his decisions made him bitter enemies. He was an accurate observer, had an unusual memory for scenes and conversations, and wrote with ease, interest, and vigor. At a time when it was dangerous in South Carolina to counsel moderation and advocate compromise, he favored the placing of negroes on the Democratic ticket for municipal office in Charleston. When Chamberlain, the Radical governor whom he at first opposed, proved a good executive, he supported him against the popular idol, Wade Hampton. His most important service was in advocating economic measures for the rebuilding of the state and section after the war. In this work he was original, resourceful, successful. He is the first conspicuous figure in the post-bellum movement to "bring the cotton mills to the cotton fields." He urged agricultural diversification, particularly through the introduction of tobacco culture in South Carolina. He wanted Southern farmers to grow their own meat instead of depending so heavily upon the West. Immigration of European farmers and artisans and of workers from the North was constantly espoused by Dawson. He was largely responsible for the South Carolina statute against dueling, and for this service was made a Knight of the Order of St. Gregory the Great by Pope Leo XIII in 1888. He was a devoted Catholic. He first married Virginia Fourgeaud of Charleston, daughter of a French family, in 1867. In January 1874 he married Sarah, daughter of Judge Thomas Gibbes Morgan of Louisiana, who with two children survived him. Dawson was shot and killed by Dr. T. B. McDow in the latter's office whither he had gone resentful of an affront to the Swiss governess of his children. McDow was acquitted, many believed through corrupt means, but some years later died under circumstances pointing to suicide.

[Dawson's partial but spirited autobiography, *Reminiscences of Confed. Service* (Charleston, 1882; only a few copies distributed); *Centennial Edition, The News and Courier* (1903); sketch in Abbeville, S. C., *Medium*, Feb. 9, 1876, and a brief paraphrase of this in J. T. Scharf, *Hist. of the Confed. States Navy* (1887), p. 712; files of the *Charleston News* 1867–73, and of the *News and Courier* 1873–89; Sarah Morgan Dawson, *A Confed. Girl's Diary* (1913), ed. by Warrington Dawson, a lively recital of the early life of his second wife; private information.]   B. M—l.

DAWSON, HENRY BARTON (June 8, 1821–May 23, 1889), editor, historian, came with his parents, Abraham and Mary (Barton) Dawson, from his birthplace at Gosberton, Lincolnshire, to New York City in 1834. His formal education, begun in England and continued in the public schools of New York, ended in March 1836. His natural interest in books was undoubtedly enhanced by a short but agreeable term of service in a publishing and book-selling house in Ithaca, N. Y., whither the family had moved in 1837. From 1839 to 1856 he was engaged in business in New York City. For a few months in 1847, he was the editor and proprietor of the financially unsuccessful *Crystal Fount and Rechabite Recorder*, a temperance paper. He was

associated with several pre-Republican party movements (*Historical Magazine,* ser. 3, II, 329–33), including the Free-Soil party, for whose first New York City meeting he issued the call, and of which he was elected secretary. Later, thinking that he had discovered in the Republican party a tendency to a centralization which he considered unconstitutional, he retired from politics.

The publication of Dawson's article, "The Park and its Vicinity" (in Valentine's *Manual of the Corporation of the City of New York,* 1855), and several valuable historical papers which followed, established his reputation and enlarged his circle of friends. He gained wide recognition from his *Battles of the United States by Sea and Land* (2 vols., 1858). His strictures therein on the military conduct of Gen. Israel Putnam led to bitter controversy in the columns of the *Hartford Daily Post* (reprinted as *Gleanings from the Harvest-field of American History,* Part VI, 1860). His excellent edition of *The Fœderalist* (1863), of which but one volume appeared, resulted in controversy with James A. Hamilton and with John Jay (*Current Fictions Tested by Uncurrent Facts, No. I,* 1864). After a year as editor of the *Yonkers Gazette,* he purchased the *Historical Magazine,* which he edited from July 1866 to its discontinuance for financial reasons in April 1876. His frequent contributions to this magazine, including hundreds of book-notices, show, as do his other writings, critical ability, accuracy, keen analysis, great industry, and trenchancy of style. These characteristics, combined with his "revisionist" tendencies, were bound to provoke controversy and hostility among local patriots and filio-pietistic zealots. His natural pugnacity was undoubtedly increased by his ill health, which, proceeding from an attack of malaria in 1868, prostrated him completely from 1876 to 1884. He recovered sufficiently to write what is perhaps his ablest work, "Westchester County, New York, during the American Revolution" (in J. T. Scharf, *History of Westchester County,* 1886). During his life many historical societies honored him with membership. He died at Tarrytown, leaving his wife, Catherine (Martling) Dawson, whom he had married May 28, 1845, and several children.

[See C. C. Dawson, *A Collection of Family Records with Biog. Sketches* (1874); a memoir of Dawson by John A. Todd in the *New-England Hist. and Geneal. Reg.,* XLIV (1890), 233–48; and a nearly complete bibliography in the sale catalogue, *The Lib. of the Late Henry B. Dawson, LL.D.* (1890), pt. I, pp. 33–37, 77–78; pt. III, pp. 26–27.]   R. E. M.

DAWSON, JOHN (1762–Mar. 30, 1814), statesman, was a son of the Rev. Musgrave Dawson and nephew of the Revs. William and Thomas Dawson, both of whom were presidents of William and Mary College. Musgrave Dawson was a bachelor of arts of Queen's College, Oxford (1747), who later came to Virginia where he served Raleigh parish, Amelia County, and St. Mary's parish, Caroline County. In 1757 he married Mary Waugh, who became the mother of John Dawson. The latter, "Beau" as he was called because of his immaculate dress and courtly manners (H. A. Garland, *Life of John Randolph,* 1851, II, 92; *William and Mary College Quarterly,* XVII, 141, 251), graduated from Harvard at the age of twenty, and four years later was already representing Spotsylvania County in the House of Delegates (1786–87, 1787–88, and 1789). He also represented, with James Monroe, the same county in the Virginia convention on ratification of the Federal Constitution. Here he was considered by Madison one of the leading opponents of the Federal Constitution (*Letters and Other Writings of James Madison,* congressional edition, 1865, I, 387). He made only one speech, in which he admitted serious defects in the Articles of Confederation and likewise the high motives of the members of the Philadelphia convention, but agreed that "by the adoption . . . [of the Constitution] as it now stands, the liberties of America in general, the property of Virginia in particular, would be endangered." He believed in a "firm, federal, energetic government," but feared a "consolidated" government. He further feared a union of executive and legislative departments, the probable high cost of running the government, the extent of the president's treaty-making power, and the absence of a declaration of rights. Finally he feared the establishment of an army "whose only occupation would be idleness; whose only effort the introduction of vice and dissipation; and who would, at some future day, deprive us of our liberties . . . by the introduction of some military despot" (J. Elliott, *Debates in the Several State Conventions on the Adoption of the Federal Constitution,* 1854, III, 604–13). Nevertheless, he later referred to the Constitution as "the greatest of all good," and to the wilful violator of it, as "the greatest of all traitors." Dawson was also a member of the Executive Council of Virginia (*National Intelligencer,* Apr. 2, 1814), presidential elector in 1793 (C. C. Dawson, *A Collection of Family Records,* 1874, p. 315), and bearer of the ratified convention of 1800 to France (*Annual Report of the American Historical Association,* 1912, pp. 697–99). He was a member of Congress continuously from 1797 to 1814. As a Jeffersonian

he opposed the Alien and Sedition Acts (*Annals of Congress,* 6 Cong., pp. 1048–49), favored the amendment of the Federalist Judiciary Act of 1801 (*Ibid.,* 7 Cong., 1 Sess., pp. 762–67), proposed an amendment providing for the separate election of the president and vice-president (*Ibid.,* 8 Cong., 1 Sess., p. 374), and for several years before the War of 1812 advocated "the adoption of every measure, the object of which was to place our country in a complete state of defence" (T. H. Benton, *Abridgment of the Debates of Congress,* 1860, IV, 452–53). During the war, as a voluntary aide to Gen. Jacob Brown, he made a trip to the Great Lakes that led to an illness developing into tuberculosis, from which he died on Mar. 30, 1814. He was a bachelor and owned a home in Fredericksburg. The personal property and land-tax books of Spotsylvania County (manuscript in the Virginia State Library) indicate that in 1810 he owned no slaves. His total tax bill on personalty and real estate was $2.07.

[In addition to the references above, see *Wm. and Mary College Quart.,* II, 51–52, V, 211; *Biog. Dir. Am. Cong.* (1928); S. J. Quinn, *Hist. of the City of Fredericksburg, Va.* (1908).]   E.L.F.

DAWSON, THOMAS CLELAND (July 30, 1865–May 1, 1912), diplomat, was born in Hudson, Wis., the son of Allan and Anna (Cleland) Dawson. He graduated at Hanover College, Indiana, in 1883, studied at Harvard during 1884 and 1885 and received the degree of LL.B. from the Cincinnati Law School in 1886. He practised law in Des Moines, 1886–89 and in Council Bluffs, Iowa, 1891–97; was assistant attorney-general of Iowa, 1891–94; and during these years was active in state and national politics in connection with the Republican party. After 1897 he was in the diplomatic service beginning his career as secretary of the United States legation in Brazil. He remained at that post for nearly seven years and it was during this period that he wrote his two-volume history, *The South American Republics,* published in 1903–04. During this period also he was married to Luiza Guerra Duval, of Porto Alegre, Brazil, the ceremony taking place in London, Apr. 5, 1900. In 1904 he became minister resident and consul general to the Dominican Republic. He entered upon his duties at the time when the government was practically bankrupt and European creditors were pressing for payment. On Dec. 30 Dawson was directed to suggest to the Dominican government that it request the United States to take charge of its customs. He negotiated a convention, signed early in 1905, providing that the United States should conduct the custom houses of the Republic, administer its finances, and settle its financial obligations. The Senate failed to ratify the agreement, but under a *modus vivendi* a receiver of customs was appointed who administered affairs under the protection of the United States navy. Later the Senate decided to give a legal status to the collection of revenue and ratified a new convention negotiated by Dawson. During the entire time he was in Santo Domingo the internal political conditions were in a very turbulent state and foreign affairs were scarcely less disturbed. The situation made the work of the American representative very difficult.

Late in 1907 Dawson became envoy extraordinary and minister plenipotentiary to Colombia, where he remained until April 1909, when he was transferred to Chile. His service in that country was brief, for with the establishment of divisions in the State Department he was, on Aug. 31, 1909, appointed chief of the division of Latin-American affairs—the first to hold the position. In 1910 he was appointed to represent the United States in Panama. He had scarcely entered upon his duties, when he was instructed to go to Nicaragua, where there had been a successful revolution, to arrange a settlement of the differences between the United States and the new government. An agreement was signed early in November 1910. On June 27, 1911, Dawson was appointed resident diplomatic officer in the Department of State, an office which he held until his death on May 1, 1912.

At the time of his death he was referred to as "the foremost Latin-American diplomat of the government." He was personally familiar with every Latin-American country and had served in many of them. In this service he injured his health and his early death was primarily due to this cause. The New York *Evening Post* declared that "the fairness, the fearlessness and the plain American sense of this diplomat made him a traveling specialist who triumphed wherever he was sent." He was famous for his skill in handling difficult problems. Many times his work was done at the risk of his life. He knew how it felt to look into the muzzle of a revolver in the hands of a fanatic whose pet project he was thwarting. He had sat quietly in his home when it was besieged by furious mobs. He had addressed hostile crowds in Santo Domingo and Colombia when he fully expected that the reply to his arguments would be a shower of bullets. But he was no boaster and he was seldom willing to describe his adventures.

[J. E. Briggs, "Iowa and the Diplomatic Service," *Iowa Jour. of Hist. and Politics*, XIX, 360–65 (July 1921); *Rev. of Revs.* (N. Y.), May 1905 (portr.); *Bull. Pan American Union*, XXXIV, 579 (portr.); *Register and Leader* (Des Moines), May 2, 5, 1912;
John H. Latané, *America as a World Power* (1907), pp. 278–81; N. Y. *Evening Post*, May 1, 1912; *Washington Post*, May 2, 1912; Washington *Evening Star*, May 1, 1912; *Who's Who in America*, 1912–13.]

F. E. H.

DAWSON, WILLIAM CROSBY (Jan. 4, 1798–May 5, 1856), senator, a son of George and Ruth (Skidmore) Dawson, was born in Greene County, Ga., where his father was a farmer. Greene County was then on the extreme western frontier of Georgia and the Dawsons were among the earliest settlers. The future senator was not a member of one of the aristocratic families that controled state politics, though his associations in after life were largely with that group. He received the best educational advantages available, in the academy of Greensboro, at the University of Georgia, graduating in 1816, and at the Litchfield Law School in Connecticut. Returning to Georgia after completing his law course, he set up as a lawyer in Greensboro and was soon regarded as an able advocate. In 1828 he was appointed by the legislature to compile the statutes of Georgia, and the well-known *Compilation of the Laws of the State of Georgia* (1831) was the result of his labors. After serving a political apprenticeship in the Georgia House of Representatives and Senate, he was elected to Congress in 1836 as a Whig. In his first election he was the only Whig who defeated his Democratic opponent. After three years in the House, he resigned and resumed the practise of law at Greensboro. Four years later he was appointed judge of the Ocmulgee circuit. As a judge he made an excellent record, though he remained on the bench less than a year, and then went back to the practise of his profession.

His reputation as a politician was made in the United States Senate. He took his seat in 1849, having defeated a strong Democratic opponent, Walter T. Colquitt [*q.v.*]. His senatorial colleague in the Thirty-first and Thirty-second Congresses was John MacPherson Berrien, and in the Thirty-third, Robert Toombs, both Whigs. In the House in the same period were Alexander H. Stephens, Howell Cobb, and Alfred H. Colquitt. Dawson was on intimate terms with Webster and Clay. With Toombs, Stephens, and Cobb he championed Clay's compromise measures in 1850 and is said to have been instrumental in bringing Webster to their support (Cole, *post*, p. 165 n.). He was a leading member of the Georgia convention in 1850 which adopted the "Georgia Platform," committing the state to the compromise measures, and he was one of the originators of the Union party which supported Howell Cobb for governor on a compromise platform (1851). He also supported the Kansas-Nebraska Act of 1854.

At the close of the Thirty-third Congress, Dawson did not offer for reëlection. He retired to his home in Greensboro, where he died suddenly the following year. He was married, first, in 1819, to Henrietta Wingfield, by whom he had seven children, and who died in 1850, and, second, in 1854, to Mrs. Eliza M. Williams. He is described as above medium height, well knit and strong; his voice powerful, his walk elastic and his carriage erect; his gray eyes "quick, vigilant and hilarious."

[S. F. Miller, *Bench and Bar of Ga.* (1858), vol. I, containing a long account of Dawson's career, the last part of which is a sketch prepared by Judge Eugenius A. Nisbet immediately after Dawson's death; G. C. Cole, *The Whig Party in the South* (1913); R. H. Shryock, *Ga. and the Union of 1850* (1926); C. C. Dawson, *A Collection of Family Records* (1874).]

R. P. B.

DAY, BENJAMIN HENRY (Apr. 10, 1810–Dec. 21, 1889), printer, journalist, was sixth in descent from Robert Day, who came from England with his wife Mary in the *Elizabeth* in 1634 and settled at Cambridge, Mass., to become, two years later, one of the original settlers of Hartford, Conn. Robert's son Thomas established himself in West Springfield, Mass., where this branch of the family lived for two centuries. Benjamin H. Day was the son of Henry Day and Mary Ely, his mother being a descendant of Elder William Brewster, fourth signer of the *Mayflower* compact. He entered the office of the *Springfield Republican* as an apprentice soon after it was founded by Samuel Bowles [q.v.] in 1824. When he was twenty years old and a first-class compositor, he went to New York City and worked at the case in the offices of the *Evening Post,* the *Commercial Advertiser* and the *Journal of Commerce.* On Sept. 13, 1831, he married Eveline Shepard and a year later, with savings from his wages, set up as a job printer. In 1833 the business depression, caused by the faulty banking system and the visitation of cholera on the city, made Day's business so poor that in desperation he started a newspaper. It was based on the obsession of Dave Ramsey, a compositor with whom he worked on the *Journal of Commerce* in 1830, that a one-cent daily, to be called the *Sun,* would be successful. The "penny paper" was not a new idea. The *Cent* in Philadelphia, the *Bostonian* in Boston, and the *Morning Post* in New York City had tried and failed. The solemn "six-penny" papers held the New York field. Day got out the first number of the *Sun* on Sept. 3, 1833, practically single-handed, in a 12 x 16 room at 222

William St., setting the type, rewriting news from other papers, and "lifting" advertisements to make a show of prosperity. There were four pages, each 11¼ x 8 inches. The *Sun* announced that its object was "to lay before the public, at a price within the means of everyone, all the news of the day." Day engaged a reporter, George W. Wisner, at four dollars a week and hired newsboys to hawk the *Sun*—an innovation in journalism. In four months the paper had a circulation of 4,000, almost equaling that of the *Morning Courier and New York Enquirer.* In April 1834, the *Sun* sold 8,000 copies daily. In the summer of 1835 Wisner left the *Sun,* and his place was taken by Richard Adams Locke [q.v.], who wrote for the *Sun* the Moon Hoax, a fabrication which made the circulation (*Sun,* Aug. 28, 1835) the highest in the world. Day boasted that with 19,360 copies daily he had surpassed the 17,000 circulation of the London *Times.* In that year he used steam power for printing—its first trial in America. "From the epoch of the hoax," wrote Edgar Allan Poe (*The Literati,* 1850, p. 126) "'The Sun' shone with unmitigated splendor. The start thus given the paper insured it a triumph. . . . Its success firmly established 'the penny system' throughout the country." On New Year's Day 1836, when the size of the *Sun's* page was increased to 14 x 20 inches, Day boasted that his paper had a circulation "double that of all the six-penny respectables combined." Of all his rivals who had rushed in to compete with the *Sun* in the popular field, only James Gordon Bennett's *Herald* had survived; Horace Greeley's *Tribune* was not founded until 1841.

Day sold the *Sun* to his brother-in-law and mechanical superintendent, Moses Yale Beach [q.v.], in 1838, for $40,000. The price was low, considering that Day had made in some years $20,000 profit. "The silliest thing I ever did in my life," he said in his old age, "was to sell that paper" (interview with Day written by Edward Page Mitchell and printed in the *Sun* on Sept. 3, 1883). In 1840 Day established another penny paper called the *True Sun,* which he sold after a few months. In 1842, with James Wilson, he founded *Brother Jonathan,* a monthly which republished English novels. This afterward became the first American illustrated weekly, with Nathaniel P. Willis [q.v.] as one of its editors. Day retired from business in 1862, when the Civil War caused a paper famine, and he spent the remainder of his life at ease. He died in New York City. He was a man of industry and determination. His portraits show an intellectual forehead and an aggressive jaw.

He was inclined to be professionally belligerent, as is indicated by his journalistic assaults on J. Watson Webb of the *Courier and Enquirer* and Bennett of the *Herald*. He was not a great editor, but he proved that newspapers at a popular price could be successful. "More by accident than design," as he said at a dinner to Robert Hoe in 1851, he "remade American journalism."

[The important facts are taken from the files of the *Sun* and particularly from the issue of Sept. 3, 1883. See also F. M. O'Brien, *The Story of the Sun* (1918); G. E. Day, *A Geneal. Reg. of the Descendants . . . of Robert Day, of Hartford, Conn.* (2nd ed., 1913); *Am. Year Book,* 1889, which gives Apr. 11 as day of birth.]   F. M.O'B.

DAY, DAVID ALEXANDER (Feb. 17, 1851–Dec. 17, 1897), Lutheran missionary to West Africa, was born out of wedlock in Adams County, Pa., on a farm near Dillsburg. His childhood was one of poverty and hardship. His early schooling was meager. At the age of twelve he became a hostler in the government stables at Harrisburg, and he relates that in his sense of utter loneliness he often cried himself to sleep on his bed of straw. When not yet fourteen he enlisted in Company D, 78th Pennsylvania Volunteers, and served for eight months. Returning to the farm in Pennsylvania, he professed conversion the next year at a revival meeting held in the school-house near his home. He became an ardent and active Christian and his thought soon turned to the gospel ministry. He had shown much aptitude in study, and after teaching one winter term in the country school, in the fall of 1869 he entered Missionary Institute (now Susquehanna University) at Selinsgrove, Pa., to prepare for the Lutheran ministry. After a year and a half in the classical department and three years in the theological department of the Institute, he was ordained as a minister (May 1874) and sent as a missionary to the Muhlenberg Mission in Liberia, Africa. In this field he spent the remaining twenty-three and a half years of his life with the exception of two short furloughs, one in 1883 and the other in 1893. The inroads of the African fever upon his robust frame finally compelled him to leave the Mission for America, but he died on board the Cunard liner *Lucania,* the day before landing in New York. He was buried at Selinsgrove.

Those who knew Day were impressed with his manliness, his strong will, his great courage, his sound judgment, his child-like faith, and his utter unselfishness. All these varied talents were devoted without reserve to the cause that was single and supreme in his affections, the Christian Mission in Liberia. Flattering offers from Church and State failed to tempt him away from that work. His many-sided nature led him to expand his work of the Mission so that it included not only the preaching of the gospel but also the founding of schools and the organizing of industrial operations such as farming, carpentering, and blacksmithing. This enlargement of program, together with Day's tenacity of purpose and his ability to interest the people at home, assured the permanence of the missionary undertaking that the Lutheran Church had begun in Liberia in 1860.

Day was married twice. In May 1874, before sailing for Africa, he married Emily V. Winegarden of Selinsgrove. Their three children all died in Africa, two in infancy, the third at the age of nine. Mrs. Day died in America in 1895. On Dec. 6, 1896, Day married Anna E. Whitfield of Dundas, Ontario, who also was a missionary on the west coast of Africa.

[L. B. Wolf, *Missionary Heroes of the Lutheran Ch.* (1911), ch. ix, by Geo. Scholl; *Lutheran Observer,* Jan. 21, 1898; *Reports of Lutheran Foreign Mission Board,* 1875–98.]   A. R. W.

DAY, DAVID TALBOT (Sept. 10, 1859–Apr. 15, 1925), chemist, statistician, geologist, was born in East Rockport (Lakewood), Ohio, near Cleveland, son of Willard Gibson and Caroline (Cathcart) Day. In 1881 he received the degree of A.B. from Johns Hopkins University, and in 1884 that of Ph.D. He served for a year as demonstrator in chemistry at the University of Maryland, and made a connection with the United States Geological Survey. In 1886, when he was twenty-seven, he married Elizabeth Eliot Keeler of Mayport, Fla., and in the same year became chief of the Mineral Resources Division of the Geological Survey, a position which he held until 1907 when he undertook petroleum investigations for the Survey. As chief of the Division of Mineral Resources he instituted the direct collection of data from the producers of minerals and advocated personal contact between them and members of the Survey. Previously such statistics had been obtained from secondary sources and were of doubtful value. He was called the father of the Mineral Resources Division. From September 1901 to October 1902 he edited the *Engineering & Mining Journal,* a task for which he was not particularly well-fitted. While making petroleum investigations for the Survey from 1907 to 1914, he joined with others in recommending the creation of reserves of western lands containing petroleum and oil shales, and out of these reserves the present Naval Reserves eventually grew. The problem of the oil shales interested him in particular and it was largely through his interest and enthusiasm that the modern researches that have led to such wide-spread recognition of the potential value of this resource were inaugurated. For several years he continued his oil-shale studies and investigated cracking processes for increasing the yield of light distillates from petroleum. Several patents for such processes were granted to him and to him and his nephew, Roland B. Day, in conjunction. In 1914 he became consulting chemist for the Bureau of Mines, continuing in that capacity until 1920 and at the same time carrying on private practise as a petroleum chemist. Upon his retirement to private work he moved to Santa Maria, Cal., in order to be near the oil fields and the shale lands, and there he made extensive experiments on the treatment of oil shale in a special plant. Perhaps his most widely known work was the voluminous *Handbook of the Petroleum Industry,* compiled by himself as editor and published in 1922, a book of timely interest at that period. During his long official career in government work in Washington, he served in many temporary and honorary capacities, such as director of mining and oil exhibits at national and international expositions, commissioner on petroleum tests, and member of committees of adjudication. He gave much time to the Geological Society of America, but he was really a chemist rather than a geologist, although he figured in the public eye as a geological authority. Day was essentially one of the types of scientist that have built up the government's technical bureaus at Washington, and the period when he was there was a formative one in the history of those bureaus. He died in Washington, in his sixty-sixth year.

[*Who's Who in America,* 1924–25; obituaries in *Engineering & Mining Jour.-Press,* Apr. 25, 1925; *Mining & Metallurgy,* June 1925 (by M. R. Campbell); *Trans. Am. Inst. Mining and Metallurgical Engineers,* LXXI (1925), 1371; *Evening Star* (Washington), Apr. 16, 1925.]   P. B. M.

DAY, FRANK MILES (Apr. 5, 1861–June 15, 1918), architect, was born in Philadelphia. His father, Charles, came from Kent, England, in 1842; his mother, Anna R. Miles, was a member of one of the earliest Welsh families to settle in Pennsylvania and was also a descendant of early Swedish settlers on Tinicum Island in the Delaware. Day was educated at Rittenhouse Academy and at the department of architecture of the University of Pennsylvania where he graduated as valedictorian in 1883. He traveled extensively in France, Italy, and England, residing abroad for three years and continuing his studies at the Royal Academy, the South

Kensington Museum, and in the office of the London architect, Basil Champneys. Returning to Philadelphia in 1886, he opened his own office on Oct. 10, 1887, with the Philadelphia Art Club as his first large commission. This building, begun in that year, was a most original composition in the then fashionable Francis I style. On Feb. 1, 1892, he formed a partnership with his brother, H. Kent Day, as Frank Miles Day & Brother, and on Jan. 1, 1911, Charles Z. Klauder was added to the partnership, then known as Day Brothers & Klauder. H. Kent Day retired at the end of 1912 and the firm name continued as Day & Klauder until Frank Miles Day's death.

Day established practise at a period of popular bad taste, but to it he never succumbed. Although some of his initial work is obviously of that period, all of it is refined, careful, and inventive. As time went on he showed increasing mastery of form. His early work was of a varied character, comprising the office building of the American Baptist Publishing Society in Philadelphia, an interesting tower-like treatment of a building of great height (twelve stories) for its date; residences in New York and Philadelphia; and hospital buildings in Philadelphia and Washington. Of these, a residence on Locust St., Philadelphia, is the most interesting. The sureness of the design shows how fitted was its Tudor style to express those special qualities of good taste, quietness, and freedom which characterized Day's work.

But it was in educational architecture that he found his most creative and congenial expression. His Gymnasium at the University of Pennsylvania is a quiet but forceful composition in a free collegiate Gothic; its plan is direct and simple. He was supervising architect at Yale, Johns Hopkins, Delaware College, New York University, Pennsylvania State College, and the University of Colorado; he also supervised portions of the Wellesley College group. Besides buildings designed for these colleges, the firm did much educational work elsewhere. Prudence Risley Hall at Cornell shows immense skill in adapting the informality of the collegiate style to hilly sites, and in producing groups full of charm and picturesque character derived absolutely from the demands of the problem. The greatest work of the firm is undoubtedly the freshman dormitory and dining hall group at Princeton, known as "Holder and the Halls" (1909). Here with a more ample site, units are larger, lower, simpler; the plan economical, and with that simplicity which only painstaking study can give; the details in the great tower and dining halls, both inside and out, of exquisite richness and delicacy.

Day was never a stylist, though so much of his work was in the collegiate Gothic. Sensitive to the colonial tradition so strong in Philadelphia, his firm aimed to adapt local materials and traditions to the work in hand. This accounts for the direct forcefulness of the colonial designs for the dormitory group at Delaware College and the much simplified southern renaissance of the Liberal Arts building and women's dormitory at the University of Colorado. It also shows in the Gothic of the Liberal Arts building at Wellesley, which differs greatly in character from much of Day's other collegiate work. Constant familiarity with the use of brick and stone in the Philadelphia colonial work also accounted for much of his skill in holding true the balance between brick and stone, or between rubble walling and cut stone in his own designs. Even his collegiate Gothic work is never strictly archeological, but shows a continually growing creative freedom and inventiveness. Day's interests outside of his office were wide; he was a lecturer at Harvard and the University of Pennsylvania and a professor of perspective at the Pennsylvania Academy of the Fine Arts. He was deeply interested in the legal and professional aspects of architecture and at the time of his death was engaged in work on a book on professional practise.

He was the author of *Suggestions in Brickwork* (1895); *The Existing and Proposed Outer Park Systems of American Cities* (1905), with A. W. Crawford; and the preface of *American Country Houses of To-day* (1912). He died of apoplexy at his home, Mount Airy, Philadelphia. He was married on Nov. 5, 1896, to Anna Blanchard Blakiston, daughter of Presley Blakiston, a publisher.

[Sketch in *Brickbuilder*, Dec. 1915; tribute by Dean West of Princeton and an extended obituary in the *Jour. Am. Inst. Architects*, Aug. 1918; the *Architectural Record*, May 1904, containing an enlightening critical study by Ralph Adams Cram.]   T. F. H.

DAY, HENRY NOBLE (Aug. 4, 1808–Jan. 12, 1890), Congregational clergyman, educator, was born in New Preston, Conn., the son of Noble and Elizabeth (Jones) Day. Almost from the cradle to the grave his life lay within the influence of Yale College. After obtaining his first instruction in the local academy and in a family school, he was sent for three years to the Hopkins Grammar School at Hartford, where he had Solomon Stoddard (Yale 1820) and Edward Beecher (Yale 1822) for preceptors. He proceeded as by a law of nature to Yale College, where during both undergraduate and postgraduate days he lived with his uncle, President Jeremiah Day [*q.v.*], whose second wife was a sister of Henry's mother. Following his graduation in 1828 he taught for one year in John Gummere's seminary at Burlington, N. J., studied law in Philadelphia with Charles Chauncey (Yale 1792), was tutor at Yale 1831–34, traveled for a year in Europe, and on Apr. 27, 1836, married Jane Louisa Marble of New Haven, who outlived him. On Nov. 9 of the same year he was ordained and installed as pastor of the First Church of Waterbury, Conn. In 1840 he went to Hudson, Ohio, as one of the professors of theology in Western Reserve College, where he remained till 1858, laboring with his colleagues to make the institution even in matters of architecture an exact duplicate of Yale. After 1852, however, his connection with the institution was nominal, the theological department having disappeared during the troubles that beset the administration of President George E. Pierce. For a while Day edited the *Ohio Observer* and dabbled in railroading as a director of the former Cleveland & Pittsburgh Railroad, and as president for a few months of a branch road connecting Hudson with Akron. He is also said to have conceived grandiose plans for an East and West trunk system. From 1858 till 1864 he was president of Ohio Female College at College Hill, on the outskirts of Cincinnati. The college did not prosper and at last its trustees transformed it into a sanitarium. Day returned to New Haven, where he remained for the rest of his life, and devoted himself to writing text-books, of which he produced almost twenty in all. He began with bookkeeping, grammar, and rhetoric but later turned to the group of subjects then known as the "mental sciences." In rhetoric he claimed some originality in emphasizing content more than expression; his books on esthetics, ethics, psychology, and philosophy all belong to the period when these subjects, in American education, were still the handmaidens of theology; and since his style lacks animation his books are now of interest only to historians of education. In their generation, however, they filled a worthy place. The most important of them are: *Elements of the Art of Rhetoric* (1850); *The Systematic Accountant: the Art of Book-Keeping Methodically Unfolded* (1861); *Rhetorical Praxis* (1861); *Elements of Logic* (1867); *The Art of Discourse* (1867); *Grammatical Synthesis: the Art of English Composition* (1867); *An Introduction to the Study of English Literature* (1869); *The Science of Æsthetics* (1872);

The Science of Ethics (1876); *Logical Praxis* (1876); *Elements of Psychology* (1876); *Outlines of Ontological Science* (1878); *Elements of Mental Science* (1886); *The Science of Thought* (1886); and *The Science of Education* (1889).

[*Biog. Sketches of the Class of 1828 in Yale Coll.* (1898); *A Geneal. Reg. of the Descendants in the Male Line of Robert Day* (2nd ed., Northampton, Mass., 1848); *The Family of the Rev. Jeremiah Day of New Preston* (1900); E. L. Clarke, *Remarks at the Funeral Services of H. N. Day* (n.d.); C. Cutler, *Hist. of Western Reserve Coll.* (1876), pp. 36, 51, and 58.]
G. H. G.

DAY, HORACE H. (July 10, 1813–Aug. 23, 1878), manufacturer of rubber fabrics, was born at Great Barrington, Mass. He was a son of William and Mary (Pixley) Day, in the seventh generation of the family in America. As a lad he went to live with an uncle, Samuel H. Day, at New Brunswick, N. J. When only fourteen or fifteen years old he experimented in processes for manufacturing India rubber, but it is not known that he achieved any practical results until 1839, in which year, with the financial aid of friends and neighbors of his uncle, he opened a small factory at New Brunswick for the production of rubber fabrics. At that time all rubber manufacturers were seeking a process that would enable the fabric to retain its texture when subjected to heat. Charles Goodyear and Nathaniel Hayward [*qq.v.*] had introduced sulphur in the treatment of molten rubber, at first without complete success. Goodyear, by accident, hit on the practical process of vulcanization, but it was not until 1844 that he could secure a patent. In the meantime Day, through several of his employees, had obtained patents on different branches of rubber manufacture. The personal interests of Day and Goodyear soon clashed. Each claimed violation of his rights and brought suit in the United States circuit court. In the manufacture of shirred goods Day's process and machinery were generally preferred and adopted by other manufacturers, several of whom combined to resist his monopoly. After jury disagreements in the first cases, Goodyear pressed new suits against Day and his agents and customers in Massachusetts, Pennsylvania, New Jersey, Maryland, and New York. There is no question that Day's processes in making shirred goods were being used by the men who were combining to fight him, under Goodyear's banner, but how far there was actual infringement of patents is still a matter of doubt. At any rate there was enough merit in his claims to cause Goodyear to sign an agreement with Day in 1846 by the terms of which the latter was to discontinue the manu-

facture of all but shirred goods, while the former was to put an end to violations of the Day patents. Almost immediately there were complaints of the breaking of this contract by the "Shoe Associates," a group of manufacturers allied with the Goodyear interests. Day charged that these men were still using his processes for shirred goods. In 1848, he repudiated his agreement with Goodyear and began making all kinds of rubber fabrics. About the same time he bought the rights, for the United States, under an English patent for making car springs. His New Brunswick factory yielded a profit of $50,000 a year, but this was practically all spent in litigation which came to a climax in March 1852 in equity suits brought in the federal circuit court at Trenton, N. J., by Goodyear to obtain a permanent injunction against Day. In point of money interests involved the case was one of the most important ever brought, up to that time, in an American court. Daniel Webster was retained by Goodyear and Rufus Choate by Day. Thus two of the ablest lawyers in the country were pitted against each other. The arguments on both sides were highly praised by members of the bar, but only that of Webster has been preserved. He upheld Goodyear's claims as a pioneer in the vulcanizing process, and his reasoning convinced the court. The injunction was issued, and Day was never able to reinstate his business. In 1860 he took over the completion of the power canal at Niagara Falls, but several years passed before any use was made of this canal by factories, and he seems never to have been repaid for his investment. In 1870 he planned the utilization of the power in the form of compressed air, promising to deliver 6,000 horse-power at Buffalo, twenty miles distant. His experiments in that direction were approved by competent engineering authority, but the project failed to command sufficient capital and was not carried through. On Apr. 25, 1838, Day married Sarah Wykoff from whom he was divorced six years later (*Divorce Case: Mrs. Sarah Day and Horace H. Day*, 1844); and on Sept. 14, 1844, he married Catherine Alice Day, his cousin. He died at Manchester, N. H.

[Geo. E. Day, *A Geneal. Reg. of the Descendants in the Male Line of Robert Day of Hartford* (1848); *Decision in the Great India Rubber Case of Charles Goodyear vs. Horace H. Day* (1852); *Speech of Daniel Webster in the Great India Rubber Suit at Trenton, N. J., March 1852 . . . Goodyear vs. Day,* reported by Arthur Cannon; J. W. Wallace, reporter, *Cases in the Circuit Court of the U. S. for the Third Circuit,* vol. II (1854); "The Great India-Rubber Litigation" in *Hunt's Merchant's Mag.,* Mar. 1856; obituaries in *N. Y. Tribune, N. Y. Times, N. Y. Herald,* Aug. 27, 1878.] W. B. S.

DAY, JAMES GAMBLE (June 28, 1832–May 1, 1898), jurist, was of English descent. His father, George Day, was a farmer in Jefferson County, Ohio; his mother, Sarah (Gamble), was a sister of Judge John A. Gamble of the Pennsylvania court of common pleas. His youth was spent upon his father's farm, his early education being obtained in the public schools. In 1850 he entered Richmond College, Ohio, and after spending two years there became a school-teacher, reading law in his spare hours. Three years later he entered the Cincinnati Law School where he graduated in 1857. That same year he went West, and opened a law office in Afton, Union County, Iowa, becoming prosecuting attorney. In 1860 he removed to Sidney, Fremont County, which continued to be his home for the ensuing twenty-three years. On the outbreak of the Civil War he enlisted in the 15th Iowa Infantry which was organized at Keokuk, November 1861. Commissioned first lieutenant, he took part in much heavy fighting in the West, was promoted captain, and at the battle of Shiloh, Apr. 6, 1862, was so severely wounded as to be incapacitated for further service. While yet with the army he had been nominated by the Republican judicial convention for judge of the 3rd judicial district of Iowa, and elected. He took his seat on the bench Jan. 1, 1863, and was reëlected in 1867. In August 1870 he was appointed by Gov. Merrill a judge of the supreme court of Iowa to fill a vacancy. By subsequent election and reëlection he retained this position till Jan. 1, 1884, being chief justice in 1871, 1877, and 1883. As supreme court judge he enhanced his already considerable judicial reputation. "He was . . . one of the very best judges that ever sat upon that bench. His learning was mature, his judicial temperament perfect, his opinions models of good reasoning, clearness and force" (Stiles, *post*). In addition he displayed a boldness and independence of thought which ultimately brought him into collision with public sentiment. In 1882 an amendment to the Iowa constitution prohibiting the manufacture and sale of intoxicating liquors within the state had been adopted by a large majority, but in the opinion of the state supreme court the procedure had not complied with constitutional requirements. The public displeasure at this decision prompted a petition for a rehearing, and the case was reargued; but the court, ignoring the popular feeling, adhered to its previous holding. Day, who was at the time chief justice, embodied his reasons in a masterly opinion, in the course of which he said: "If courts could be coerced by popular majorities into a disregard of their provisions [*i. e.*, of constitutions], constitutions would become mere 'ropes of sand,' and there would be an

end of social security and of constitutional freedom. The cause of temperance can sustain no injury from the loss of this amendment, which would be at all comparable to the injury to republican institutions which a violation of the constitution would inflict" (*Koehler et al.* vs. *Hill*, 60 *Iowa*, 543 at p. 646). Although a candidate for reëlection in the following year, he was refused the Republican nomination on account of his stand, as were also his three concurring colleagues. Speaking later of his decision in this case he said that it was "one which I could not have refused to make without a surrender of manhood." On relinquishing office he removed to Des Moines, where he resumed practise, but abstained from further participation in public life. He died at Des Moines. On Dec. 1, 1857, he had married Minerva C. Manley of Steubenville, Ohio. He was of powerful physique, nearly six feet in height, and broad in proportion. In disposition singularly equable, with his feelings invariably under control, and his natural dignity never ruffled, he was extremely popular with all classes, and quickly lived down the unreasoning resentment which his opinion on the prohibition amendment had provoked.

[An excellent account of Day's career appeared in E. H. Stiles, *Recollections and Sketches of Notable Lawyers and Public Men of Early Iowa* (1916), p. 595, the author being a contemporary court reporter. See also *Am. Bar Asso. Report*, 1898, p. 661; *Hist. of Fremont County, Iowa* (1881); obituary in *Iowa State Register*, May 2, 1898.]   H. W. H. K.

DAY, JAMES ROSCOE (Oct. 17, 1845–Mar. 13, 1923), Methodist clergyman, educator, was born in Whitneyville, Me., the son of Thomas and Mary Plummer (Hillman) Day. His mother was a daughter of Samuel Hillman, a Vineyardman six feet six inches tall, who got religion in the depths of the Maine woods and became an old-time Methodist preacher, earnest, untaught, bold of speech, and unabashed in his habit of mixing politics with religion. In mind and body Day closely resembled this burly grandfather. With his father, who was a lumberman, he went by sea in 1860 to the Pacific Northwest, where for about five years he worked as a steamboat roustabout, stage-driver, and cattle herder. "I have been through the whole gamut of the workingman," he wrote late in life, "omitting the saloon and its kindred precincts." Somewhere in the course of his rovings he acquired a glass eye that added not a little to his picturesqueness of figure and deportment. On his return to Maine he went through the experience known as conversion and determined to be a minister. After studying for a while at Kent's Hill Seminary he was assigned to a charge in Auburn. While in

Auburn, 1871–72, he attended the scientific course in Bowdoin College, being rated as a sophomore, presumably because of his earlier studies for the ministry. His college course did not extend beyond this single year. In 1872 he was ordained and on July 14, 1873, married Anna E. Richards of Auburn, who survived him. He quickly became the most popular Methodist preacher in the state. His pastorates were: Bath, 1872–74; Biddeford, 1874–76; Portland, 1876–79; Nashua, N. H., 1879–81; First Church, Boston, 1881–82; St. Paul's, New York City, 1883–85; Trinity, Newburgh, N. Y., 1885–89; and Calvary, New York City, 1889–94. Even after leaving the active ministry he continued to be one of the dominating forces in the Methodist Church. At the General Conference of 1900 he got 199 votes for bishop, and in 1904 he was actually elected after a hot fight during which he himself took the floor and denied that he had ever knocked down a brother clergyman for impugning his attitude toward the higher criticism. Two days later he resigned the episcopal office, explaining that he felt that his real work lay in education. Such was indeed the fact. While pastor of the wealthy St. Paul's congregation in New York he had had John D. Archbold [q.v.] as one of his pewholders, the two men became friends, and when Syracuse University needed a new chancellor Archbold, as chairman of the board of trustees, secured Day's election to the vacancy. Under Day's energetic, optimistic, paternalistic management Syracuse grew like corn under an August sun. In 1894 it was a drooping denominational institution with three departments, some 750 students, and property worth about $1,780,000. In 1922, when he became chancellor emeritus, it was a flourishing university with eight colleges, eight schools, a stadium officially described as "somewhat larger than the Colosseum at Rome," and an enrolment of more than five thousand students. Approximately ten million dollars had flowed into the treasury. But although Syracuse was rich in grounds and buildings it had no adequate budget system nor provision for the future, its teachers were overworked and underpaid, the yearly deficit was dangerously large, and murmurs against some of Day's mannerisms and policies at times became distinctly audible. The chancellor resigned soon after an attempt to raise an endowment fund had been abandoned for lack of support. To a public that cared little about his other activities Day was known as a publicist. From the time when, in 1907, he engaged in a personal controversy with President Roosevelt over the merits of large corporate enterprises in general and of

the Standard Oil Company in particular, his frequent, and often picturesque, utterances on questions of politics, economics, and morals were regarded by the newspapers as good copy. He published two books: *The Raid on Prosperity* (1907) and *My Neighbor the Workingman* (1920). The second is a remarkable revelation of the after-war state of mind. He died while on a vacation at Atlantic City.

[*Gen. Cat. Bowdoin Coll. 1794–1912* (1912); letter from G. G. Wilder, librarian of Bowdoin Coll., to editor, Jan. 28, 1928; *The Golden Jubilee of Syracuse Univ. 1870–1920* (n.d.); obituaries in *Christian Advocate*, Mar. 22, 1923, in *Zion's Herald*, Mar. 21, 1923, and in various newspapers, Mar. 14 and 15, 1923; R. F. Dibble, "The Hammer of Heretics" in *Am. Mercury*, Nov. 1924; S. Allen and W. H. Pillsbury, *Methodism in Maine* (1887). Numerous references to Day may be located through the *N. Y. Times Index* from June 1914 till his death.] G. H. G.

DAY, JEREMIAH (Aug. 3, 1773–Aug. 22, 1867), educator, for twenty-nine years president of Yale College, was the son of Rev. Jeremiah and Abigail (Noble) Osborn Day, and a descendant of Robert Day who came from Ipswich, England, in 1634, settled in Newtown (Cambridge), Mass., and later became one of the original proprietors of Hartford, Conn. He was born in the parish of New Preston, Conn., then a part of New Milford, but since 1779, of Washington, where his father was pastor of the Congregational church. (For biography of Jeremiah Day, Sr., see W. B. Sprague's *Annals of the American Pulpit*, 1857, I, 688.) One of the latter's theological pupils, David Hale, brother of Nathan, first instructed him, and later he continued his preparation for college under John Kingsbury of Waterbury, Conn. He entered Yale in 1789, left because of pulmonary trouble in 1791, reëntered in 1793, having taught school in the meantime, and graduated in 1795. He then succeeded Timothy Dwight [q.v.], as principal of the academy which the latter had established at Greenfield Hill, Conn., but soon left there to become tutor at Williams College. Two years later he accepted a similar position at Yale. On June 3, 1800, he was licensed to preach by the New Haven West Association of Ministers. During all this time he had been suffering from tuberculosis, and in July 1801 a hemorrhage brought on by the exertion of preaching caused him to go to Bermuda where he spent nearly a year. Upon his return he went to his father's home with little expectation of recovery, but life among the Connecticut hills arrested the disease, and in the summer of 1803 he undertook the duties of the professorship of mathematics and natural philosophy at Yale to which he had been elected shortly after his departure for Bermuda. On Jan. 14, 1805, he married Martha, daughter of the

Hon. Roger Sherman and Rebecca Prescott, who died in 1806; and on Sept. 24, 1811, Olivia, daughter of Major Daniel and Olive (Tinker) Jones of Hartford, Conn.

For sixty-nine years he was officially connected with Yale College. On Apr. 22, 1817, he was appointed president, succeeding Timothy Dwight, and was both installed and ordained to the ministry on July 23. In his seventy-fourth year he insisted on resigning, but was immediately elected a member of the Corporation, in which office he served until a month before his death, which occurred just after the completion of his ninety-fourth year. In 1835 he had been urged to become head of Andover Theological Seminary, but had declined. Never strong, and after 1836 subject to attacks of angina pectoris, he prolonged his life by self-knowledge and moderation in all things. He was a man of dignity and extreme reserve. Although, as described by Timothy Dwight, the younger (*post*, p. 42), "he was a wise disciplinarian, a judicious governor, a thorough and accurate scholar, a valuable teacher, and a man of intelligent and penetrative mind," his influence was due chiefly to his goodness and his reputation for deep wisdom. He combined serenity, self-control, modesty, and unselfishness in such a degree that all of the 2,500 students who had been under him, according to President Woolsey, would have unquestionably declared him the best man they had ever known. As president he built slowly on the foundation laid by his predecessor. Stability, conservatism, and great caution were his conspicuous characteristics. Improvements that were made were generally suggested by others. Outside of Connecticut he was known principally through his text-books. In 1814 he published *An Introduction to Algebra,* which went through many editions. This was followed by works on trigonometry, geometry, and the mathematical principles of navigation and surveying. After 1820 he taught mental and moral philosophy, and in 1838 published *An Inquiry Respecting the Self-determining Power of the Will*; and in 1841 *An Examination of President Edwards's Inquiry on the Freedom of the Will.* He also contributed numerous articles to periodicals, and published a few sermons.

[Full and discriminating accounts of Day's character and work are given in the funeral address by President T. D. Woolsey, printed in the *New Englander*, Oct. 1867; and by Timothy Dwight in *Memories of Yale Life and Men* (1903). See also Geo. E. Day, *A Geneal. Reg. of the Descendants in the Male Line of Robt. Day of Hartford, Conn.* (1848); Thos. Day Seymour, *The Family of the Rev. Jeremiah Day of New Preston* (1900); Ellen D. Putnam, *Some Chronicles of the Day Family* (1893); F. B. Dexter, *Biog. Sketches Grads. Yale Coll. with Annals of the Coll. Hist.*, vol. V (1911).

A portrait painted by S. F. B. Morse is the property of Yale Univ.]   H. E. S.

DAY, LUTHER (July 9, 1813–Mar. 8, 1885), jurist, was born at Granville, Washington County, N. Y., the son of David and Rhoda (Wheelock) Day. His father was a farmer and sawmill proprietor in a small way, and he barely obtained the rudiments of an education, being required to assist on the farm at the age of twelve years. In 1826 his father was accidentally killed and he was compelled to devote himself entirely to the task of operating the farm and mill in order to save a home for his mother. This he had accomplished by 1833, when he proceeded to remedy his educational deficiencies and in 1835 entered Middlebury Academy, Vt., where he was able to spend two years by teaching and doing other odd work in his spare time. In 1838 he went to Ravenna, Portage County, Ohio, and entered the law office of R. P. Spalding, defraying his expenses by undertaking clerical work for the clerk of the common pleas of Portage County. On his admission to the bar he rapidly acquired a reputation for competence and reliability. In 1843 he was elected prosecuting attorney for Portage County and, with an intermission of one year which he spent at Akron, held that position till 1851. In the election of 1850 he was unsuccessful Democratic candidate for the representation of the district in Congress, but in 1851 he was elected judge of the common pleas for the united counties of Portage, Trumbull, and Mahoning, and remained on the bench for six years. He was a stanch supporter of the Lincoln administration in the pre-war period and on the outbreak of the conflict left the Democratic party. For a short time in 1862 he acted as judge advocate general on Gov. Tod's staff, with the rank of colonel. The following year he was elected as a Republican to the state Senate, but resigned on being elected a judge of the supreme court of Ohio in 1864. On the supreme court bench, if not brilliant, he was efficient. A sound lawyer, familiar with Western customs of life and business, and exercising great care in the consideration of all cases which were brought before him, he procured the confidence of the bar and the public alike. Reëlected in 1869, he was for four years acting chief justice, but in the elections of 1874 he met defeat, the Democratic ticket sweeping the state. On his retirement in 1875 he was appointed by Gov. Allen a member of the commission to revise and codify the state statutes, but resigned in February 1876, having been appointed by Gov. Hayes to the first supreme court commission, a position which he occupied for three years, during one of which he was chief justice. He died at Ravenna, Ohio. He was married on July 24, 1845, to Emily Spalding, daughter of his old principal, R. P. Spalding, and after her death, was married in April 1854 to Ellen Barnes. William Rufus Day [q.v.] was his son by his first wife.

["In Memoriam Luther Day," 42 *Ohio*, xi; *Bench and Bar of Ohio* (1897), ed. by G. I. Reed, I, 29; *Green Bag*, VII, 278; *Hist. of Portage County, Ohio* (1885), p. 818; obituary in *Cincinnati Enquirer*, Mar. 9, 1885.]   H.W.H.K.

DAY, STEPHEN (c. 1594–Dec. 22, 1668), first printer in British America, was born in England about 1594. He was a locksmith in Cambridge, England, in 1618, when he married Rebecca, widow of Andrew Bordman, a baker of that town. In the summer of 1638, with his wife, two boys, and stepson, he emigrated to New England in the ship *John* of London, under contract to work two years for the Rev. Josse Glover of Sutton, Surrey. Glover brought with him a printing-press which cost £20, a font of type, and £60 worth of paper, but died on the voyage to Boston. Mrs. Glover settled in Cambridge, and purchased a house for the Days, on the present Holyoke St. There the press was probably set up. The first imprint, a single sheet reproducing the Freeman's Oath of the colony, was issued within six months. There are known to have been twenty-two imprints made by the Cambridge press before 1649, when Samuel Green became the printer: the Freeman's Oath; ten annual almanacs; five Harvard commencement broadsides; the Capital Laws, 1642; *The Book of General the Lawes and Libertyes,* 1648; the Bay Psalm Book, 1640; a spelling book, 1643; Winthrop's *Declaration of . . . the Narrowgansets,* 1645; and Norris's Catechism, 1648. Copies of only nine of the twenty-two are known to be extant.

Stephen Day's relationship to the Cambridge press during this period is a matter of conjecture. The General Court made him a land grant on Dec. 10, 1641, as "the first that set upon printing" (*Records of the Governor and Company of the Massachusetts Bay in New England,* 1853–54, I, 344), but his name does not appear on any existing imprint. There is no evidence that he knew anything about printing before coming to America; and his letters are those of an uneducated, almost illiterate, man. As a locksmith he undoubtedly set up the press, and managed it for Mrs. Glover. She married, on June 21, 1641, Henry Dunster [q.v.], to whose house, on the site of Massachusetts Hall, the press was soon removed. When Mrs. Dunster died in 1643, Stephen Day, who disliked President Dunster, may then have left the management of the press

to his son Matthew, who had probably been apprenticed to the printing trade in England, and whose name appears on the title-page of the Almanac for 1647. Mr. Wilberforce Eames, however, believes that the press remained under the nominal if not actual management of Stephen until 1649, and that he should be credited with all previous imprints. Stephen Day had acquired considerable land by 1642, when he became active as a mining prospector in the wilderness for the Winthrops and as a promoter of ironworks at the plantation of Nashaway (Lancaster), of which he was an "undertaker." Committed by a local court "for his defrauding several men" in 1643, he was released two days later by the General Court (*Ibid.*, II, 47). About 1655 Day forfeited his rights in Nashaway for non-residence, settled down to his old trade in Cambridge, joined the church, married a second time in 1664, and died Dec. 22, 1668, leaving a small property, including gunsmith's and locksmith's tools. His name is spelled *Day* in most contemporary documents, and in the greater part of his surviving signatures; in the others it is spelled *Daye*.

[Samuel A. Green, *Ten Fac-Simile Reproductions Relating to New England* (Boston, 1902); George E. Littlefield, *The Early Massachusetts Press* (Boston, Club of Odd Volumes, 1907, vol. I), a work to be used with caution; A. McF. Davis, "The Cambridge Press," *Proc. Am. Antiq. Soc.*, n.s., V, 295–302 (1888); Dunster MSS., Harvard University Archives. The above list of imprints of the Cambridge Press, 1639–48, represents Mr. Eames's opinion of what actually was printed; other conjectural items are in Evans's *American Bibliography*.]   S. E. M.

DAY, WILLIAM RUFUS (Apr. 17, 1849–July 9, 1923), secretary of state, justice of the Supreme Court, was born at Ravenna, Ohio, the son of Luther and Emily (Spalding) Day. His ancestry ran back to sound New England stock. In his maternal line was found the name of Zephaniah Swift, at one time chief justice of Connecticut, while both his father, Luther Day, and his maternal grandfather, Rufus P. Spalding, had been judges of the Ohio supreme court. He was educated at the University of Michigan, where he graduated in 1870. He then read law for a time at Ravenna, spent another year at the University, and was admitted to the bar in 1872. He began practise at Canton, where he soon made the acquaintance of William McKinley, who was at that time county prosecutor.

Successful at the bar, Day won the respect and esteem of the people of his county to such a degree that he was elected judge of the court of common pleas in 1886 upon the nomination of both political parties. In 1889 he was appointed, by President Harrison, United States district judge for the northern district of Ohio, but because of ill health resigned before taking office.

The intimacy already formed with McKinley made him the latter's legal and political adviser during McKinley's service as member of Congress and governor of Ohio. Once more Day refused high office when McKinley as president offered him the attorney-generalship. It was only when Secretary of State Sherman's physical condition made the choice of an able lieutenant a matter of necessity that the President, in March 1897, was successful in persuading Day to accept the post of first assistant, on the plea of personal loyalty. Acceptance, it is said, cost Day the sacrifice of a $15,000 income as practitioner for a salary of $4,500 (H. H. Kohlsaat, *From McKinley to Harding,* 1923, p. 65). In April 1898, a serious lapse of memory on Sherman's part, during a conversation with the Austrian minister, led to Day's appointment as secretary of state; but he did not desire the appointment, and it is probable that the President was already turning his thoughts toward John Hay. On Aug. 13, he notified Hay of his desire to have him assume the secretaryship not later than Sept. 1, as Day would resign to serve with the United States Commission appointed to make peace with Spain.

Soon after the completion of the last-named task, Day was appointed (1899) to succeed William H. Taft as judge of the United States court of appeals for the sixth circuit. In January 1903, as chairman of a memorial meeting at Canton, held on the anniversary of McKinley's birth, he introduced President Roosevelt as the speaker of the day; and Roosevelt, by addressing him as "Mr. Justice Day," announced his intention of elevating him to the Supreme Bench, an intention carried out in the ensuing month. Day served nearly twenty years as associate justice of the Supreme Court, resigning late in 1922 to become umpire in the Mixed Claims Commission chosen to pass upon the claims of American citizens against Germany. In spite of a winter in Georgia, however, failing health compelled him, in May 1923, to resign this position also. In June he went, as had been his custom for forty years, to his summer home on Mackinac Island, where death overtook him a few weeks later. An attack of pneumonia in 1920 had left his left lung seriously impaired, and as his physician said, he had "lived on his nerve," during his last years. His wife, who died in 1912, was Mary Elizabeth Schaefer, whom he had married in 1875. She came of an old Southern family, members of which had fought under Marion during the Revolution.

In the State Department, on the Paris Commission, and as associate justice, Day rendered signal service. In diplomacy he had had no training, but he was acquainted with international law, and his tact, discretion, and ability to make use of trained subordinates enabled him to perform his duties as secretary with more than ordinary success. During the period of negotiation with Spain over Cuba he secured the recall of Weyler and the promise of reforms; and when war came, after the blowing up of the *Maine,* he succeeded in the difficult task of securing the neutrality, if not the good will, of the powers of western Europe. "Judge Day made one of the greatest reputations of the Spanish-American War," wrote the editor of the *World's Work* (September 1923). "Day," said President McKinley, "never made a single mistake."

When in the summer of 1898 M. Cambon proposed a cessation of hostilities between Spain and the United States, the protocol was prepared under Day's direction. On the question of the Philippines cabinet opinion was divided, Day desiring to relinquish everything except a naval station—which called forth McKinley's humorous comment, "Judge Day wants only a hitching-post." It was in relation to the Philippine problem that Day made his chief contribution to the work of the United States Commission. His associates, Reid (former ambassador to France), Davis, and Frye (Republican senators), desired to require the cession of the entire archipelago, while Gray (Democratic senator) opposed the acquisition of any portion of it. Day took an intermediate position. In the spirit of fairness which characterized him, he urged that the United States had made no conquest which justified a demand for the cession, and questioned the ethics of acquisition of territory by conquest. Writing to the President on Nov. 2, he said that, since there had been no conquest which could give ground for demanding the cession, it was unnecessary to "consider how far the United States, as the leading Christian nation of the world, in a war unselfishly waged in the interest of humanity, would permit itself to stand upon the ancient practise of holding territory taken from an enemy in course of war, without compensation or other reason for permanent acquisition than military occupation" (Olcott, *post,* II, 115). Thus he paved the way for the treaty provision under which the United States paid Spain $20,000,000 for the islands.

Despite some differences of opinion, the members of the Commission esteemed Day highly. Writing to McKinley near the end of the negotiations, Reid said: "Judge Day, in particular, has shown great clearness, precision of view, and well-balanced judgment" (*Ibid.,* 127). Gray, although of the opposite party faith, declared:

"No State in this Union could have contributed to that function . . . a mind and a character more equipoised, settled, clear and strong than was contributed by Ohio when she sent that quiet, sensible, strong statesman, William R. Day, to Paris to conclude the treaty of peace" (quoted in *New York Times,* editorial, July 10, 1923).

As a lawyer, Day had won a reputation for fluent and effective oratory. As associate justice he was highly regarded for his learning, and was chosen by the Court to deliver some important decisions. These concerned chiefly questions affecting interstate commerce, bankruptcy, patents, corporate rights, contracts, and court procedure. The following may be noted: *Dorr* vs. *U. S.* (1903), 195 *U. S.* 138; *Hammer* vs. *Dagenhart* (1917), 247 *U. S.* 251; *U. S.* vs. *Doremus* (1918), 249 *U. S.* 86; *Hawke* vs. *Smith* (1919), 253 *U. S.* 221; *Green* vs. *Frazier* (1919), 253 *U. S.* 233. He also concurred in the dissenting opinion of Justice Harlan in the famous case of *Lochner* vs. *New York* (1905), 198 *U. S.* 45. His language was always chaste and elegant, and his opinions are models of concise judicial expression.

Judge Day was a slight man, who through life was hampered by ill health. He never participated in sports of any kind, although he was an ardent baseball "fan." Highly endowed with intellect and purpose, he was singularly modest, and never sought office. Reserved and dignified, he nevertheless was the soul of tact and courtesy, and was much beloved by those who knew him. He was never more happy than when in private life in his unostentatious Canton home, amid his books and friends. As the *Ohio State Journal* commented at the time of his death, "He represented the type of American citizen, contented at home, but ready for high service if the call came."

[Some data concerning Judge Day's ancestry may be found in *Biog. Cyc. and Portrait Gallery, with an Hist. Sketch of the State of Ohio* (1895), VI, 1359; also in the *Hist. of Portage County* (1885), p. 818. The main facts relating to his service in the State Department and on the Peace Commission are given in T. E. Burton, *John Sherman* (1906), C. S. Olcott, *The Life of William McKinley* (1916), and W. R. Thayer, *The Life and Letters of John Hay* (1915). See also F. E. Chadwick, *Relations of the U. S. and Spain* (1911), and J. F. Rhodes, *McKinley and Roosevelt Administrations* (1922). The chief available source of biographical information, however, consists of the sketches and notices which appeared in newspapers and other periodicals at the time of Day's death. See *Outlook,* July 18; *World's Work,* September; *N. Y. Times,* July 10, 11; *Ohio State Jour.,* July 10, 13; *Evening Repository* (Canton), July 9–12, 1923.]

H. C. H.

DAYTON, ELIAS (May 1, 1737–Oct. 22, 1807), soldier, was the son of Jonathan Dayton, a militia captain, Presbyterian church trustee, and leading citizen of Elizabeth-Town (now Elizabeth), N. J. He was descended from Ralph Dayton who left England for Boston, Mass., about 1638, later founding East Hampton, L. I. Apprenticed as a mechanic, Elias became lieutenant of militia Mar. 19, 1756, and captain Mar. 19, 1760, serving under Wolfe at Quebec and against Pontiac near Detroit. Later opening a general store on the town square across from church and court-house, he acquired an independent competency and was chosen alderman before the Revolution. He was a member of the local committee of thirty-one, appointed Dec. 6, 1774, to enforce measures recommended by the Continental Congress, and on Oct. 26, 1775, became one of the four Essex County muster-masters. He was commissioned colonel of the 3rd Battalion, New Jersey Line, on Jan. 10, 1776, and on the 22nd of that month led seventy-seven volunteers in three shallops to capture the British supply-ship *Blue Mountain Valley,* for which exploit Lord Stirling got the credit (*American Archives,* ser. 4, IV, 987–89). His son Jonathan [*q.v.*] served under him from Feb. 9, 1776, first as paymaster and later as captain. His regiment was at Albany in May 1776; it built Fort Schuyler, and Fort Dayton (at Herkimer), and warded off Indian raids from Johnstown and German Flats, returning to Morristown, N. J., in March 1777.

Dayton saw service at Bound Brook, Staten Island, and Brandywine, and spent the winter of 1777–78 at Valley Forge. He had horses shot under him at Germantown, Springfield, and Crosswicks. After harassing Clinton's march and fighting at Monmouth, his regiment guarded New Jersey against British raids from Staten Island until ordered on Sullivan's campaign of reprisals against the Indians of northern New York (May 11–Oct. 9, 1779). Dayton destroyed Runonvea, near Big Flats (Stryker, *post,* p. 25), but neither Dayton nor his son signed the semi-political indorsement which Sullivan secured from his officers (Botta, *post,* II, 196).

Declining election to Congress, Dayton led in foiling Knyphausen's and Clinton's sallies against the Continental Army at Morristown, for this service winning the comment "Colonel Dayton merits particular thanks" (Washington's General Orders, June 1780; Maj.-Gen. Greene's orders also; see *New Jersey Archives,* ser. 2, IV, 460). Leading his brigade of 1,328 men to Yorktown, he was in active service until the discharge of the New Jersey Line on Nov. 3, 1783. On Jan. 8, 1783, in response to Washington's insistence, he had been promoted brigadier-general, the resolution being in Hamilton's handwriting (*Journals of the Continental Congress,* XXIV, 38).

After the war he returned to Elizabeth and to the general store of Elias Dayton & Son. A leading citizen of his town and state, he served as major-general of militia; trustee of the Presbyterian church; member of Congress, 1787–88; recorder of Elizabeth, 1789; member of the New Jersey Assembly 1791–92 and 1794–96; and president of the New Jersey Society of the Cincinnati. He died of "gout in the stomach" in his seventy-first year. By his wife, a Miss Rolfe, he left eight children. He is described as open, generous, and sincere, ardent in friendship, scrupulously upright; and in appearance is said to have resembled Washington.

[N. Murray, *Notes, Hist. and Biog. Concerning Elizabeth-Town* (1844); E. F. Hatfield, *Hist. of Elizabeth, N. J.* (1868); *Revolutionary Hist. of Elizabeth, N. J.* (1926), prepared by the Sesquicentennial Committee; W. W. Clayton, *Hist. of Union and Middlesex Counties, N. J.* (1882); W. S. Stryker, *Gen. Maxwell's Brigade of the N. J. Continental Line in the Expedition against the Indians in the Year 1779* (1885); Chas. Botta, *Hist. of the War of the Independence of the U. S. A.* (3rd ed., 1834).]   W.L.W—y.

DAYTON, JONATHAN (Oct. 16, 1760–Oct. 9, 1824), soldier, congressman, son of Elias Dayton [*q.v.*], was born in Elizabeth-Town, N. J. He graduated from the College of New Jersey in 1776, served with his father through much of the Revolution, and was a captain at Yorktown. After the war he studied law and was admitted to the bar. He sat in the New Jersey Assembly 1786–87, and at the age of twenty-seven in the Federal Convention, his father having declined an appointment in his favor. He was the youngest member of the Convention. William Pierce, an army comrade, described him as "of Talents, with ambition to exert them. . . . There is an impetuosity in his temper that is injurious to him, but there is an honest rectitude about him that makes him a valuable Member of Society" (Farrand, *post*, III, 90). Dayton attended the convention from June 21 to the end, spoke frequently, and while opposing some features finally signed the Constitution.

On Nov. 25, 1788, he was chosen to the First Congress under the Constitution, but declined to serve. He served, however, in the New Jersey Council in 1789, and in the following year in the Assembly, of which he was speaker. He was chosen for the Second, Third, and Fourth Congresses, and served as speaker in the Fifth Congress. He argued in favor of having the secretaries of the treasury and of war appear in the House, and for a larger regular army, rather than militia. With Elias Boudinot he

voted five times (Mar. 1, 1793) to uphold Hamilton's financial policy against the Giles-Madison assaults. His first speech was on his own motion to sequester British debts. He took a leading part in the debate of Nov. 24, 1794, supporting the administration in its report on the Whiskey Insurrection. As speaker of the House he is described as of ordinary ability, "of commanding mediocrity" (H. B. Fuller, *The Speakers of the House,* 1909, p. 30), yet his "personal popularity" is said to have been of "vast importance to the nation . . . in tempering the bellicose attitude of the House" toward the Jay Treaty (*Ibid.,* pp. 26–27). Dayton served also as a member of the Senate for one term (1799–1805). Here he voted against the repeal of the Judiciary Act of 1801. After a visit to New Orleans in July 1803, he favored the purchase of Louisiana. He opposed the Twelfth Amendment, but his remarks did not prevent its adoption. In the impeachment of Justice Chase his vote on all eight counts was "not guilty."

Dayton was interested in the projected canal around the Ohio Falls and held title to some 250,000 acres between the Big and Little Miami rivers. Dayton, Ohio, was subsequently named for him. He played some part in his friend Burr's adventure, but probably from ill health he did not accompany Burr's expedition down the Ohio. He was indicted for high treason and misdemeanor June 25, 1807, but a *nolle prosequi* was entered Sept. 1, 1807 (David Robertson, *Aaron Burr. Trial for Treason,* etc., 1808, I, 330, II, 448). His political career was now ended, though he held local office and served two terms in the New Jersey Assembly (1814–15). He was visited by Lafayette at Elizabeth in 1824, and "such were his exertions to honor his guest and gratify the numbers of people to see him that he . . . expired a few days later" (D. L. Pierson, *Narratives of Newark,* 1917, p. 261).

[References occur in *The Records of the Federal Convention of 1787* (3 vols., 1927), ed. by Max Farrand; T. H. Benton's *Abridgment of the Debates of Congress* (1861), and in local histories, especially E. F. Hatfield, *Hist. of Elizabeth, N. J.* (1868); W. W. Clayton, *Hist. of Union and Middlesex Counties, N. J.* (1882). W.F.McCaleb, *The Aaron Burr Conspiracy* (1903), and Henry Adams, *Hist. of the U. S.,* vol. III (1890), have minor references. These authorities, Channing, and McMaster also, are not exempt from mistakes of fact as to Dayton. The usual historical treatments of him entirely divorce his career prior to Mar. 4, 1805, from what took place later.]   W.L.W—y.

DAYTON, WILLIAM LEWIS (Feb. 17, 1807–Dec. 1, 1864), lawyer, politician, diplomat, great-grandson of Elias Dayton [*q.v.*], was born at Baskingridge, N. J., his father, Joel, being a mechanic who educated two sons to law and one to medicine. His mother, Nancy, daughter of Edward and Nancy (Crowell) Lewis, was a grand-daughter of Edward Lewis, a commissary of Washington's army. After finishing at the local academy under Dr. Brownlee, he was graduated from Princeton in 1825, taught school at Pluckemin, and read law with Peter D. Vroom at Somerville, being admitted to the bar in May term 1830. Despite feeble health and slowly maturing powers, his "large mind and strong common sense" (J. P. Bradley, *post,* 75) made Dayton a master of common law. Settling at Freehold, N. J., he attracted attention in November 1833 by persuading the court to quash certain indictments (L. Q. C. Elmer, *post,* 375), and became the leading lawyer there. Elected to the legislative council in 1837, as a Whig, he was chosen one of two new associate justices of the state supreme court on Feb. 28, 1838. He decided the important case of *Freeholders* vs. *Strader* (3 *Harrison,* 110) but resigned in 1841, against friendly protests, to practise law in Trenton, the salary of a justice ($2,000) being too small to support his growing family. On July 2, 1842, Gov. William Pennington appointed him United States senator for the unexpired term of S. L. Southard, and the legislature chose him for the full term to Mar. 4, 1851. He resolutely defended his right to independence of action in the face of legislative instructions, insisting (December 1843) that, "if the legislature of New Jersey go further than to advise me of their wishes . . . they usurp a power which does not belong to them" (Bradley, *post,* p. 85).

An independent Whig, he urged protection for home markets and industrial independence (speech of April 1844), and opposed the tariff of 1846. Favoring arbitration of the Northwestern claims, he thought statehood for Oregon undesirable and improbable. He voted against the treaty for the annexation of Texas (June 8, 1844), warning his Newark constituents that the annexation would mean the repeal of a protective tariff and four more slave states (speech of Feb. 24, 1845). Although he protested against the Mexican War, "he invariably voted the necessary measures to sustain the executive in its prosecution" (Bradley, p. 99). He opposed the extension of slavery but voted for the ratification of the Mexican Treaty.

Following the policy of the new administration he opposed the compromise measures of 1850, especially the Fugitive-Slave Act, and lost his seat in the Senate to Commodore Robert Field Stockton, Democrat. Resuming law practise at Trenton, he was "almost invariably employed on one side or the other of every impor-

tant cause" (Bradley, *post,* 114). With Chancellor Green, S. G. Potts, and P. D. Vroom he had compiled the New Jersey revised statutes of 1847. He served as attorney-general of New Jersey 1857–61, and as such acted as prosecutor in the famous Donnelly murder case (2 *Dutcher,* 463, 601). His speech at the "Fusion Convention" in Trenton, May 28, 1856, resulted in his being nominated for vice-president on the ticket with Frémont, though many of his friends desired him to have first place, and in the Republican convention of 1860 his state supported him, on the first three ballots, for the presidential nomination (C. M. Knapp, *New Jersey Politics During the Period of the Civil War and Reconstruction,* 1924). In 1861 he was appointed minister to France. Not knowing French, quite unversed in diplomacy, he yet established the best of relations with Louis Napoleon's government, with diplomatic colleagues, and with the press. He wore court dress since "he had not come to France to make a point with the government about buttons" (Elmer, *post,* p. 391) and gained the entire confidence of the Emperor whom he had "frequently met during his residence in New Jersey" (Galignani's *Messenger,* Paris, Dec. 5, 1864). Keeping both governments advised on innumerable topics, he was able to avert French intervention, to stop Confederate use of French ports, to prevent construction of six Southern war vessels, to intern the *Rappahannock,* and to force the *Alabama* out to meet the *Kearsarge.* His long letter on the war, Nov. 16, 1862, to Drouyn de l'Huys, produced gratifying results (Seward to Dayton, Jan. 9, 1863, see *Executive Document No. 38,* 37 Cong., 3 Sess.). Seward came to have much confidence in him, and referred to his "approved discretion" (Seward to Dayton, Feb. 8, 1864). Dayton died abruptly at 9 p. m., Dec. 1, 1864, of apoplexy, leaving an estate of over $100,000. His wife, Margaret Elmendorf Van Der Veer, whom he married May 22, 1833, bore him five sons and two daughters. Their married life was entirely happy. He had no enemies. At his funeral John Bigelow said of Dayton, "He could not act falsely."

[J. P. Bradley, "A Memoir of the Life and Character of Hon. Wm. L. Dayton," in *Proc. N. J. Hist. Soc.,* ser. 23, IV, 69–118; L. Q. C. Elmer, *The Constitution and Govt. of the Province and State of N. J. . . . with Reminiscences of the Bench and Bar* (1872), pp. 372–96; genealogy in *Lewis Letter* (Lisle, N. Y.), Nov.–Dec. 1889, pp. 135, 138; obituaries in many newspapers.]   W. L. W—y.

DEADY, MATTHEW PAUL (May 12, 1824–Mar. 24, 1893), jurist, son of Daniel and Mary Ann (McSweeney) Deady, was born near

Easton, Talbot County, Md. His father and his mother's father came from County Cork, Ireland. Matthew acquired a taste for good literature by access to his father's well-stocked library, where as a boy he read such books as Pope's *Iliad* and *Odyssey* and Hume's *History of England.* He attended schools taught by his father until he was twelve years of age, spent four years on the latter's farm in Ohio, and left home at the age of sixteen to attend the Barnesville (Ohio) Academy. At the same time he was apprenticed to the blacksmith's trade for four years. He then taught school and studied law until admitted to the Ohio bar in 1847. Two years later he worked his way to Oregon, taught school at Lafayette during the winter that followed, and began the practise of law at the same place the next spring. He was elected to the territorial House of Representatives in 1850, and in 1851 was elected a member of the Council, over which he presided during the session of 1852–53. On June 24, 1852, he was married to Lucy A. Henderson. In 1853 he was appointed an associate justice of the territorial supreme court. As his circuit was made up of the five southern counties, he made the Umpqua Valley his home until 1860. He presided over the convention assembled in 1857 to form a state constitution and exercised a conservative influence over that body. He suggested the provision prescribing six-year terms for judges, and supported those providing biennial sessions of the legislature and four-year terms for state officers, all of which were incorporated in the fundamental law. He favored the *viva voce* method of voting, unsuccessfully opposed a provision giving married women exclusive control of their own property, and succeeded in having struck out a provision for a state university on the ground that "experience had demonstrated it to be of little use to anybody." Elected a justice of the state supreme court, he accepted, instead, in 1859, appointment as United States district judge for Oregon. Portland, the seat of his court, thenceforth became his home until his death.

Some three hundred and fifty of Judge Deady's decisions, prepared by him for publication, show that he gave most exhaustive study to every issue that came before his court. While generally reverential toward the common law and established precedent, he dared at times, when moved by a strong common sense, a spirit of justice, or conceptions of a sound morality, to make new rules of interpretation. He was lawgiver as well as judge. He drew up codes of civil and criminal procedure, a penal code, and a code of procedure and practise for justices of the peace which were

enacted into law by the state legislature, and which, but slightly amended, are still in force. He twice, 1864 and 1872, codified all the general laws of the state. He often acted, in his own words, as "judge and advocate" for the judicial committees of both houses of the legislature and drafted much important legislation; such as the corporation act of 1862 and the Portland charter act of 1864, a measure that became the model for other city charters. His salary as judge, paid in paper currency and at times worth as little as $800 in coin and never much in excess of $3,000, proved inadequate to the needs of a growing family. He wrote weekly letters for the *San Francisco Bulletin,* accepted fees for drawing legal papers or for opinions given clients, received pay from the state for making codes and compilations ($2,500 for the four years ending with 1864), and in other ways supplemented a meager salary.

Deady contributed much to the cultural progress of his community and the state. He was founder of the Multnomah County Library and long its managing director, raising its endowment and selecting its books; he wrote editorials for the *Oregonian;* he was much in demand as a public speaker and delivered lectures on a variety of subjects that show study and erudition; he was a devoted churchman; and, having modified his earlier opinion, for twenty years as president of the board of regents of the State University (during its formative period, 1873–93), he dominated its policies, secured for it necessary financial support, and was the most important single influence in assuring its survival and progress. He was Oregon's "first citizen" in his day and, probably, more than any other single individual gave form to its political, cultural, and legal institutions.

[Deady's diaries and letters, in possession of the Ore. Hist. Soc., are the best source of information. The life in H. H. Bancroft, *Chronicles of the Builders of the Commonwealth,* II (1892), 465–515, is an autobiography. *Great Am. Lawyers,* ed. by W. D. Lewis, VII (1909), 357–92, contains an appreciative sketch by H. G. Platt.]   R.C.C—k.

DEAN, AMOS (Jan. 16, 1803–Jan. 26, 1868), lawyer, educator, the son of Nathaniel and Rhoda (Hammond) Dean, was born at Barnard, Vt., where his father, originally from Hardwick, Mass., had a farm. He attended public school during the winters, working on the farm in the summers, and saved sufficient money to enable him to enter the academy at Randolph, Vt., whence he proceeded to Union College, Schenectady where he graduated with honors in 1826. He then studied law with his maternal uncle, J. D. Hammond, at Albany, N. Y., and in May

1829 was admitted to the bar. He commenced practise by himself at Albany but in 1833 entered into partnership with Azor Taber, who was at the time one of the leading lawyers in that part of the state. Having no aptitude for court work he confined himself to consultation and the preparation of documents, and was frequently employed as a referee. He took a keen interest in the well-being of the youth of the city, and in December 1833 organized "The Young Men's Association of Albany" for the purpose of mutual improvement and education—the first of its kind. So successful was the venture that it was taken as a model for similar associations which were gradually established throughout the country. In 1838 he was active in the organization of the Albany Medical College, and became, as professor of medical jurisprudence, a member of its original faculty—a position which he held for over twenty years. On Sept. 14, 1842, he married Eliza Joanna Davis of Uxbridge, Mass. In 1851 he procured the establishment of the Department of Law (unofficially known as the "Albany Law School") of the University of Albany, joined its faculty, and became its active manager. Lecturing regularly, he set a high standard for the students and laid the foundation for the ultimate complete success of the undertaking. He retired from active practise in 1854. When the University of Iowa was chartered in 1855 he was elected its chancellor and professor of history and for three summers resided in Iowa City, devoting his energies to establishing the university upon a firm and broad basis, but he did not enter on the more special duties of his office (A. H. Dean, *post*). In 1860 he resigned, and returned to Albany. Resuming his position on the faculty of the Law School, he thenceforth devoted himself to his professorial duties and literary pursuits. He died at Albany, Jan. 26, 1868.

A man of wide sympathies, high ideals, and great driving force, he was yet never in the front rank as a lawyer. As a professor, he was more a source of inspiration than of knowledge, though his lectures were clear, accurate, and interesting. As a promoter of educational interests, however, he was in advance of his times, and his uniform success in this connection is his chief claim upon posterity. He shunned public life and was not interested in politics, though his sympathies were with the Whigs. He was a wide reader, not only in law but in history, medicine, and general literature, as is evidenced by the catalogue of his library containing 1,893 items, which was printed for the sale which took place after his death.

He was a voluminous writer on many subjects, and left a large mass of manuscripts, a great por-

tion of which was in a completed state. During his lifetime he published: *Lectures on Phrenology* (1834); *A Manual of Law for the Use of Business Men* (1838); *The Philosophy of Human Life* (1839); *Eulogy on the Life and Character of the Late Judge Jesse Buel* (1840); *Principles of Medical Jurisprudence, a Course of Lectures* (1850), and *Bryant & Stratton's Commercial Law for Business Men* (1863). After his death the following selections from his unpublished works were printed: *The History of Civilization* (1868–69) in seven volumes; *History of European Art* (1876); *History of Religion and Government in Europe* (1876); *The British Constitution* (1883). He was also the author of numerous addresses on social and historical subjects.

[A well-balanced review of Dean's career appeared in the *Am. Law Reg.*, Mar. 1868, and a long biographical sketch in vol. I (1868), of his *Hist. of Civilization.* For details of his academic life and activities, see Andrew V. Raymond, *Union University* (1907), and A. H. Dean, "Amos Dean" in *Iowa Hist. Record*, Apr. 1895. See also Joel Munsell, *The Annals of Albany*, vols. IX (1858), X (1859), and *Colls. on the Hist. of Albany*, vol. II (1867); *Albany Evening Jour.*, Jan. 27, 1868; *New-Eng. Hist. and Geneal. Reg.*, July 1868; Roland Hammond, *A Hist. and Geneal. of the Descendants of Wm. Hammond* (1894).]   H. W. H. K.

DEAN, BASHFORD (Oct. 28, 1867–Dec. 6, 1928), zoologist, armor expert, was the son of a wealthy New York lawyer of a Tarrytown family, William Dean, and of Emma (Bashford) Dean of Yonkers. His ancestry was Puritan with Dutch and Huguenot strains. The major interests of his life—ichthyology and armor—rooted themselves in childhood. At five he was fascinated by a Gothic helmet; he bid in his first piece of ancient arms before he was ten. Prof. Edward Morse, of Salem, introduced him at the age of seven to the charms of fishes. Apparently so diverse, these interests were made to dovetail harmoniously throughout his career. His education was scientific. At nineteen he graduated from the College of the City of New York, where he began his teaching as tutor in natural history. Meanwhile he attended Columbia College where he won his A.M. in 1889, his doctorate in 1890, studying American paleozoic fishes under John S. Newberry. After study in Munich and Naples, he joined the Columbia faculty as instructor in 1891, becoming full professor of vertebrate zoology in 1904, a post which he held until his death. As early as 1889 he was elected fellow of the New York Academy of Sciences on the strength of his published researches. His summers he devoted to investigating oyster-culture in England, France, Belgium, Spain, Portugal, Italy, and later Japan, for the United States Fish Commission. At twenty-three he was made director of the Biological Laboratory at Cold Spring Harbor, L. I. He married in 1893 Mary Alice Dyckman, of an old Manhattan family. He edited Newberry's memoirs on Devonian fishes and undertook a remarkable series of restorations based on Newberry's collection which, according to Osborn, established his fame as an ichthyologist (*post,* p. 102). In search of early developmental stages of hag-fish and sharks he made explorations in Japan, California, and Puget Sound. Between 1891 and 1909 he published a long series of important papers on paleichthyology and the embryology of fishes. "A thorough fusion of zoological and paleontological concepts . . . characterized all his work" (Gregory, *post,* p. 635).

Always an avid collector and student of ancient arms and armor, Dean seized opportunities offered by his scientific quests to study foreign museum and private collections and to explore remote castles where armor could be studied in its original setting. Pursuit of primitive fish-forms in Oriental waters led to his acquiring a notable collection of Japanese armor. His interest in both subjects was developmental. A student of Devonian armored-fishes he was, wrote one of his students, "quick to perceive the striking analogies in the evolution of human armor," the study of which "was to him almost a branch of zoology" (*Ibid.,* p. 637).

In 1903 he became curator of reptiles and fishes at the American Museum of Natural History. Here during seven years of active service, he planned and directed the installation of the synoptic exhibit of fishes, a series of habitat groups, and the collection of fossil fishes. He outlined plans for a new Hall of Fishes which, after years of disappointment and delay, was dedicated shortly before his death. In 1906 he began his curatorship of arms and armor at the Metropolitan Museum of Art, where, before his retirement in 1927 he had built up a collection ranking easily first in America and perhaps fourth among armor-museums of the world. Himself a large donor, he secured important gifts and made important discoveries during arduous armor-hunts abroad. "Not a nook or corner of Europe or Asia escaped his search. He even excavated wells in Crusaders' castles in Palestine. He probably knew the location of every potentially purchasable piece of armor in existence" (*Bulletin of the Metropolitan Museum,* January 1929, p. 5). His growing absorption in this work caused him in 1910 to resign his post at the American Museum where he was made honorary curator. During the World War, as major of ordnance, he used his technical knowledge in designing special helmets and body-armor for trench and aerial warfare.

He had considerable skill as an artist, and illustrated his work with minutely finished drawings and lithographic engravings. Of his many publications over two hundred are on fishes, and a hundred or more on ancient and modern armor. The monumental *Bibliography of Fishes* (3 vols., 1916–23), one of the great enterprises of his life, catalogues details relating to fishes from remote classical times to the present, indexing 50,000 titles. For this he was awarded in 1923 the Elliot medal of the National Academy of Sciences. A similar bibliography of armor, completed before his death, awaits publication by the Metropolitan Museum. He carried on these multiform activities, together with the organization of his private armor-collection at his home at Riverdale, despite physical handicaps which would have quenched a lesser man. On his retirement from the curatorship of arms and armor in the Metropolitan Museum he was made a trustee of that institution. His death occurred in Battle Creek, Mich.

[W. K. Gregory in *Science,* Dec. 28, 1928; H. F. Osborn in *Natural Hist.,* Jan.–Feb. 1929; *Nature* (London), Jan. 19, 1929; *N. Y. Times,* Dec. 8, 1928; *N. Y. Herald-Tribune,* Jan. 26, 1929; L. Hussakof, *Bibliog. of Bashford Dean, 1887–1910* (1910).]   M. B. H.

DEAN, JULIA (July 22, 1830–Mar. 6, 1868), one of the most beloved actresses in the theatrical annals of the country, was the daughter of an actor named Edwin Dean and Julia Drake, the second daughter of "Old Sam" Drake, the pioneer Kentucky theatre-manager. She was born in Pleasant Valley, N. Y., and after her mother's death two years later, was brought up there by her father's Quaker parents. When she was about eleven, Dean took her from her grandparents and carried her about with him, using her as a drudge in a boarding-house kept by him and his wife and in small rôles in the various theatres with which he was connected. In 1844–45 the three Deans were members of the Ludlow and Smith company in Mobile, and there Julia served a rather trying apprenticeship. In 1845, she went North with her father and, the following year, appearing on short notice as Lady Ellen in *The Lady of the Lake,* scored her first success. Dean promptly took her to New York, where on May 18, 1846, she played Julia in *The Hunchback* at the Bowery Theatre. So great was her success that for a time she made this favorite tragic rôle almost her own. She was, according to Laurence Hutton, "the *Julia* of *Julias,*" for "quiet effect and subdued intensity" excelling in his opinion all others. The next few years saw her rise to the highest place in her profession and to a popularity which few, if any, have since achieved. Her success was short-lived, however. In 1855 she married Dr. Arthur Hayne, son of Senator Robert Hayne of South Carolina, and from that day her fortunes declined. The marriage proved wretchedly unhappy, and the public for some reason turned away from its favorite. The next year, the Haynes went to California, with which state the greater part of her subsequent career was identified. In San Francisco she became again a popular idol, and she traveled about the state playing in small towns and even acting as joint proprietress of a theatre in Sacramento. In 1865 she toured the Rocky Mountain states, ending up at Salt Lake City late in July. She remained in the Mormon capital till the following June when she returned to San Francisco. There she at last divorced her husband, and set out once more for New York, which she had not visited for several years and where she tried again, but in vain, to win back her former place. Hardship and distress had broken her, and her acting had lost the simple naturalness which had constituted its charm. In 1867 she married James G. Cooper, but died suddenly in childbirth, on Mar. 6, 1868, five months after her last appearance on the stage. That Julia Dean was a great actress is certainly to be questioned, but she was undoubtedly a talented one, and the beauty of her gentle personality as well as the loveliness of her face won her way to the hearts of the public, who saw in her their ideal of American girlhood.

[See J. N. Ireland, *Records of the N. Y. Stage* (2 vols., 1866–67); N. M. Ludlow, *Dramatic Life as I Found It* (1880); *The Autobiog. of Joseph Jefferson* (1889); Francis Wilson, *Joseph Jefferson* (1906); Constance Rourke, *Troupers of the Gold Coast* (1928); Geo. D. Pyper, *The Romance of an Old Playhouse* (1928); Laurence Hutton, *Plays and Players* (1875). The many biographical sketches published in the various New York papers after Julia Dean's death, should be read with caution.]   W. G. B. C.

DEAN, SIDNEY (Nov. 16, 1818–Oct. 29, 1901), Methodist clergyman, Congressman, author, was the second of seven sons of Amos Dean, a silk and woolen manufacturer of Glastonbury, Conn., and his wife, Nancy Robinson Kempton. His father was descended from Walter Dean of Taunton, a colonel of the Massachusetts train bands, and his mother from Manasseh Kempton who came to Plymouth in the ship *Anne* in 1623. Sidney learned his trade in his father's mill at Glastonbury and at twenty entered the employ of the Du Ponts in Delaware. Deciding to enter the ministry he studied at the academies at Wilbraham, Mass., and Suffield, Conn., and began preaching in the latter state in 1843. His first charge was the Lyme, Saybrook and Haddam circuit. This was followed by an appointment at Woodstock and next at Putnam where ill health compelled him to abandon the ministry for business. His strong anti-slavery interest which was aroused by his experience in Delaware, led him into politics. He was a member of the Connecticut legislature from Putnam in 1854, and in 1855 was elected to Congress on the American ticket. Two years later he was reëlected as a Republican. During both terms he served on important committees and was the Washington correspondent of the New York *Independent*. He was an outspoken Abolitionist, a member of the Underground Railroad, and had a price set on his head in two Southern states.

Declining renomination, he spent a year in travel and then resumed the work of the ministry. He served in Pawtucket, R. I., from 1859 to 1861, at the Mathewson Street Church in Providence from 1861 to 1863, and at Warren, R. I., from 1863 to 1865. From 1865 to 1880 he was editor and publishing manager of the *Providence Evening Press*, the *Providence Morning Star*, and a weekly, the *Rhode Island Press*. In addition to his editorial work he preached and lectured extensively during this period. In 1870 he was a member of the Rhode Island Senate. Retiring from journalism in 1880 but continuing to live in Warren, he devoted himself to writing and published *A History of Banking and Banks from the Bank of Venice to the Year 1883* (1884). The last ten years of his life were spent in retirement in Brookline, Mass., where he died.

Dean was of robust stature, and had the orator's power of winning a hostile audience. He was a man of strong convictions, a strenuous opponent of slavery and the liquor traffic, and a militant upholder of public morals. In the early days of the Prohibition party in Rhode Island he was prominent in its councils and was once its candidate for the United States Senate. In 1884 he became a Cleveland Democrat and remained such till 1896 when he returned to the Republican party. He was prominent in Masonry and Odd Fellowship. His tastes were refined and his home contained a valuable collection of books and art treasures. In 1839 he married Martha A. Hollister of South Glastonbury, Conn., who died in 1841. In 1865 he married Annie Eddy of Warren. His children were a son and a daughter by the first marriage and three sons by the second.

[*Boston Transcript, Providence Jour.*, Oct. 30, 1901; *Biog. Dir. Am. Cong., 1774–1927* (1928); information from Dean's son concerning his father's career and personal characteristics.]   F. T. P.

DEANE, CHARLES (Nov. 10, 1813–Nov. 13, 1889), merchant, historian, was the son of

Dr. Ezra Deane of Connecticut who settled at Biddeford, Me., where he engaged in the practise of medicine and there married his second wife, a daughter of the Rev. Silas Moody of Kennebunkport, the mother of Charles. The boy went to the public school at Biddeford, then to the Academy at Saco, and a private school. It was intended that he should enter Bowdoin, but the death of a brother prevented and at fifteen he went to work in a store at Kennebunkport where he remained a year and a half. After spending a couple of years in a store at Saco he went to Boston and found a position with the well-known dry-goods house of Waterston, Pray & Company. In 1840 he became a partner; a year later married Helen, the eldest daughter of Mr. Waterston; and in 1864 retired with an ample fortune. After that he devoted himself almost wholly to research work in American colonial history. Even while still in business it had been his avocation and in recognition of his work he had been made a member of the Massachusetts Historical Society in 1849, of the American Antiquarian Society in 1851, and had received the honorary degree of A.M. from Harvard in 1856. Eleven volumes of the *Proceedings* of the Massachusetts Historical Society were issued under his supervision, to all of which he contributed important articles. He had secured a copy of the supposedly long-lost *History of Plymouth Plantation* by Gov. Bradford from England, and in 1856 edited it with copious and scholarly notes. This is the most important single piece of work which he did. In 1865 he gave standing to the newly started series of publications of the Prince Society by editing the first of them, Wood's *New England Prospect*. The following year he was one of the three delegates elected to represent the American Antiquarian Society at the Archeological Congress to be held at Antwerp. In 1878 he was elected a member of the London Society of Antiquaries. Deane in the opinion of such contemporaries as Justin Winsor was "almost peerless" as an American historical scholar although he had no long-sustained historical work to his credit as author. His special field was early Virginia and New England including certain earlier special topics such as the Cabot voyages and the Cabot *mappe-monde* of 1544. He was unbiased, judicial, tireless in minute research. He was friend and counselor of most of the leading historians of his time. So much of his work was devoted to the correction and elucidation of minor points that, invaluable as it was, he is considered rather an antiquarian than a historian. He set a most useful and scholarly standard in the editing of documents.

[The best account of Deane is the memorial by Justin Winsor in the *Proc. Mass. Hist. Soc.*, ser. 2, VII (1892), 45–89. There are also appreciations of him at the time of his death in the same series vol. V (1890), pp. 116–41, and a fairly complete bibliography of his writings in vol. VI (1891), pp. 224–28.]   J. T. A.

DEANE, SAMUEL (July 10, 1733–Nov. 12, 1814), Congregational clergyman and agricultural writer, was a descendant of Walter Deane of Chard, England, who emigrated to Boston in 1636. The son of Samuel and Rachel (Dwight) Deane, he was born in Dedham, Mass., where from 1732 to 1745 his father was a blacksmith and keeper of the inn. The younger Samuel was educated at Harvard College, graduating in 1760. He was an excellent scholar, fond of the classics, and had some ability as a poet. He contributed an English poem of twelve six-line verses to a collection of congratulatory addresses to George III on his accession to the throne, included with thirty others in a small volume, *Pietas et Gratulatio Collegii Cantabrigiensis apud Novanglos, Bostoni, Massachusettsium* (1761). From the time of his graduation till 1763 he was tutor and librarian at the College. In 1764 he was called to the first parish in Portland (Me.), then included in the Town of Falmouth, as a colleague of its pastor, Rev. Thomas Smith, and was ordained Oct. 17, 1764. He remained connected with the church as colleague and pastor for fifty years. In October 1775 a British fleet bombarded and burned the larger part of the village of Portland. The church was hit though not seriously damaged, but its members became scattered, poverty-stricken, and discontented as a result of the war. In November Deane moved to a farm in Gorham, built a house at "Pitchwood Hill," and lived there some six years. During this period, though he went frequently to Portland to preach, he was much engaged in farming operations and experiments, and probably in the preparation of his best-known work, announced in 1787 and published in 1790 with the title, *The New England Farmer or Georgical Dictionary, Containing a Compendious Account of the Ways and Methods in which the Most Important Art of Husbandry in all its Various Branches is or may be Practiced to the Greatest Advantage in this Country. By a Fellow of the American Academy of Arts and Sciences*. A second edition was printed at Worcester in 1797 and a revised edition was printed much later (1822) by Fessenden. This encyclopedic work, the first of the kind in this country, contains the results of his own experience and reveals wide acquaintance with the observations and experimental work of other American authors. Deane also published an oration, July 4, 1793, several sermons, short verses in periodicals, and a long poem, "Pitchwood Hill," written in hexameters and published without his consent in the *Cumberland Gazette,* Mar. 5, 1795, and later in pamphlet form. Returning to Portland, in March 1782, he remained there till his death; until 1795 as the colleague of the Rev. Thomas Smith who died in that year, and then as pastor of the church. In 1809 the Rev. Mr. Nichols was chosen his colleague. In the sharp religious controversies of that day Deane occupied a middle ground betwen the strict Calvinists and the Unitarians. He denied Calvin's views of the Trinity and the Atonement, nor did he fully accord with the views of the Unitarians. His catholicity of spirit is indicated by the fact that while firm in his own convictions he was in friendly relation with the representatives of both factions. He was vice-president and a trustee of Bowdoin College from 1794 to 1813. From Harvard College he received the degree of M.A. and from Brown University the degree of D.D. in 1790.

On Apr. 3, 1776, he married Eunice Pearson, who died Oct. 14, 1812, aged eighty-five. They had no children. Deane was of commanding presence, tall, erect, and portly, with grave and dignified carriage and deportment and keen wit. His ministry began in a time of controversy and church factions, his church was demoralized by the war, but he brought strength to it and lived to see his parish on a firm foundation. He died in the eighty-second year of his age and the fifty-first of his ministry.

[*Jours. of the Rev. Thomas Smith and the Rev. Samuel Deane, Pastors of the First Church in Portland* (2nd ed., 1849), ed. by Wm. Willis; B. W. Dwight, *Hist. of the Descendants of John Dwight of Dedham, Mass.* (1874); Wm. Willis, *The Hist. of Portland, 1632–1864* (1865); Wm. Goold, *Portland in the Past* (1886); H. D. McLellan, *Hist. of Gorham, Me.* (1903); *Gen. Cat. Bowdoin Coll., 1794–1902.*]   E.H.J.

DEANE, SILAS (Dec. 24, 1737–Sept. 23, 1789), member of the Continental Congress, diplomat, was born in Groton, Conn., the son of Silas Deane, blacksmith, and his wife, Sarah Barker of Marshfield, Mass. After his graduation from Yale in 1758 (A.M. 1763) he taught school and studied law. In 1761 he was admitted to the bar, and in the following year he opened a law office in the thriving town of Wethersfield, Conn. His first wife, Mehitabel Webb, whom he married in 1763, was possessed of such resources as to give her husband a substantial start toward worldly success. A widow, she brought him, along with six children, a prosperous store. After her death in 1767, Deane married Elizabeth Saltonstall of Norwich, grand-daughter of a former governor of the colony; by this step he

strengthened his connections with the Connecticut aristocracy. These highly satisfactory alliances made it unnecessary for him to undergo the training in adversity which often comes to a young man in his profession. On the contrary, he rose almost at once to a position of comparative affluence, as well as of social prestige, and for eleven years after his first marriage he lived as a prosperous lawyer and merchant in Wethersfield.

Even had he desired to do so, a man of his prominence and connections would have found it difficult to keep clear of politics, and Deane had no such desire. In 1769 his fellow townsmen made him chairman of a local committee to enforce a non-consumption agreement, to help defeat the Townshend Acts. Three years later he became a member of the General Assembly. In May 1773 he held the post of secretary of the newly appointed legislative committee of correspondence. During these years he became one of the recognized leaders of the Revolutionary movement in his colony, not in the capacity of mere agitator, but rather as a substantial man of affairs, prepared to sacrifice his own comfort and well-being in behalf of a cause he believed to be right. In 1774 the Connecticut Committee of Correspondence, under the authorization of the legislature, sent him as one of the three delegates to represent the colony in the first Continental Congress; the next year he was appointed to the second Congress. Just before leaving for Philadelphia in 1775 Deane, with S. H. Parsons and S. Wyllys, assumed the responsibility of sending the force which resulted in the capture of Fort Ticonderoga. As a member of the second Congress, he of necessity had an active connection with the various preparations for war. He served on committees appointed to formulate rules for the new Continental navy, to purchase ships for the service, and to secure arms and ammunition. For some reason which is not entirely clear, the Connecticut Assembly refused to give him an appointment for a third year in Congress, and in January 1776 he withdrew from that body.

If Deane's talents and services to the American cause were lost upon his constituents in Connecticut, they were fully apparent to his colleagues in Congress; these men had no intention of allowing him to resume his former comfortable place in private life. In March 1776 he was selected to go to France—the first American to represent the united colonies abroad. Marking as it did the climax of his life and the end of his official career—of his private fortune, health, and peace of mind too, for that matter—this mission deserves special notice. He derived his authority from two separate committees of Congress, both secret, one commercial, the other diplomatic in character. The commercial committee, on behalf of Congress, entered into a formal contract with five merchants, of whom Deane was one. These merchants were authorized to buy colonial produce, with money furnished by Congress; to ship commodities so purchased abroad, sell them there, and invest the proceeds in supplies needed by the colonies. Deane was specifically named to handle the European end of these commercial transactions, for a consideration named in the contract. The other committee, the "Committee of Secret Correspondence" instructed Deane to go to France for the purpose of buying clothing and arms for 25,000 men, also munitions and artillery. These he was to secure on credit if possible, otherwise by direct purchase. In addition to this, he was ordered to sound the French foreign office on the subject of American independence, and to find out whether an American ambassador would be received and whether the French government would be willing to enter into treaties of alliance and commerce with the colonies. According to the instructions, Holland and even England were included within the scope of his activities. With the help of one of those extraordinary characters who sometimes appear in public life, Caron de Beaumarchais, Deane succeeded in securing eight shiploads of military supplies. These reached the colonies in time to be of material, perhaps decisive, help in the Saratoga campaign in 1777. Besides sending these supplies Deane commissioned and sent over a large number of European military officers, some of whom, especially Lafayette, De Kalb, Steuben, and Pulaski, gave valuable help to the American cause. Along with these he sent many more of the merest soldiers of fortune, whose coming proved an embarrassment to Congress and a liability to the country.

In September 1776 Congress decided to strengthen its connection with France, and for that purpose it appointed a commission of three: Deane, Benjamin Franklin, and Arthur Lee. The work originally undertaken by Deane alone was continued so successfully that in February 1778, the commissioners signed two treaties with the French government, one of commerce, the other providing for an offensive and defensive alliance. This was Deane's last work as diplomatic representative. Shortly after the treaties were signed he learned that Congress had ordered him home, ostensibly to give information concerning the state of affairs in Europe. The real reason for his recall, as he himself suspected, lay in certain insinuations made against him by Arthur Lee. This erratic personage professed to believe that all the supplies which Deane had secured in France were intended as gifts by the French government to the Americans, and that Deane and Beaumarchais, in asking Congress to pay for them, were planning merely to line their own pockets. Some members of Congress found it easy to believe these libels on Deane's character; others found fault with him because he had shown poor judgment in sending over so many military adventurers.

Deane had responded so promptly to the order for his recall that before he left Europe he could not secure proper vouchers covering his financial transactions. Without these it was impossible to effect a settlement with Congress. After waiting for two years, he returned to Europe, of course as a private citizen, hoping to speed up the auditing of his accounts there. Still finding it impossible to secure a settlement, smarting under a sense of injustice, and worn down by ill health, he lost confidence in the American cause. In 1781 he was so indiscreet as to embody his pessimistic views in letters to friends in America, advising them to drop the war for independence, and to work for a reconciliation with England. These were private letters, but unfortunately for Deane they were intercepted by the British, and published by a Loyalist press in New York. This evidence seemed to prove that he was a traitor, as well as a rascal. After the war he lived as an exile, financially bankrupt and broken in health, for a short time in Ghent, and for a few years in England. He died on shipboard, just outside Deal, England, as he was starting on a voyage to Canada.

Deane's services to the American cause were substantial, and his own losses were heavy. For all this he was rewarded with suspicion, calumny, and ill will. In 1842 Congress made partial restitution to his heirs, voting them the sum of $37,000. At this time the original audit of his accounts, the one made under Lee's direction, was characterized as *"ex parte*, erroneous, and a gross injustice to Silas Deane."

[The best biography of Silas Deane is G. L. Clark, *Silas Deane* (1913). His papers have been published in the *N. Y. Hist. Soc. Coll.*, vols. XIX–XXIII. *Paris Papers; or Mr. Silas Deane's Late Intercepted Letters* was published in New York in 1782. Additional material is contained in Francis Wharton, *The Revolutionary Diplomatic Correspondence of the U. S.* (1889). See also F. B. Dexter, *Biog. Sketches Grads. Yale Coll.*, vol. II (1896).]   R. V. H.

DEARBORN, HENRY (Feb. 23, 1751–June 6, 1829), soldier, secretary of war, and congressman from Massachusetts, was born at Hampton, N. H., the son of Simon Dearborn and his wife

Sarah Marston. He was descended from Godfrey Dearborn, a native of Exeter, England, who in 1639 came to America, settling first at Exeter, N. H., and subsequently at Hampton, with which place four successive generations of his descendants were connected. Henry attended the local district school and studied medicine under Dr. Hall Jackson of Portsmouth. In 1772 he began practise as a physician at Nottingham Square, N. H. As trouble with England approached, young Dearborn undertook the organization of a militia company and was elected captain. Upon receiving the news of the fighting at Lexington and Concord, he led his sixty men with celerity to Cambridge. His company was incorporated in the regiment of Col. John Stark and took part in the battle of Bunker Hill, June 17, 1775. In September 1775 Dearborn volunteered for service in Benedict Arnold's expedition to Quebec. In that trying and hazardous march through the Maine woods, in which he commanded one of the companies of musketmen, he kept a journal which is an important source of information for the campaign. On the latter part of the march he became seriously ill and had to be left behind in a cottage on the Chaudiere River, but rejoined the army in time to take part in the assault on Quebec by the combined forces of Arnold and Gen. Richard Montgomery, Dec. 31, 1775. In the battle, in which Montgomery was killed and Arnold seriously wounded, Dearborn was taken prisoner and confined for a time at Quebec. In May 1776, he was released on parole, but was not exchanged until March 1777. He was then (Mar. 19) appointed major of the 3rd New Hampshire Regiment, commanded by Col. Alexander Scammell. In September 1777 he was transferred to the 1st New Hampshire Regiment, Col. Joseph Cilley. He took part in the campaign against Burgoyne, being in the fighting at Ticonderoga and Freeman's Farm. He passed the winter of 1777–78 at Valley Forge, and at the battle of Monmouth in the following June the conduct of his regiment won commendation from Gen. Washington. In the summer of 1779 his regiment formed a part of Gen. John Sullivan's army in the campaign from the Wyoming Valley against the Six Nations, which laid waste the Genesee Valley and the region of the Finger Lakes in central New York. He later joined Washington's staff and served at the siege of Yorktown. In June 1783 he received his discharge from the army and settled in Kennebec County, Me., then a district of Massachusetts. He became a brigadier-general and later a major-general of militia, and in 1790 was appointed United States marshal for the District of Maine. He represented this district of Massachusetts as a Republican in the Third and Fourth Congresses (1793–97) but was not prominent there. When Jefferson became president, Dearborn was appointed secretary of war, and in this position he served through Jefferson's eight years of office. As secretary of war he helped form the plan for the removal of the Indians beyond the Mississippi (*Annual Report of the American Historical Association*, 1906, I, 253–54). In March 1809 he resigned his position in the cabinet and became collector for the port of Boston. In January 1812, President Madison made him the senior major-general in the United States army and placed him in command of what was expected to be the most important theatre of war—the northeast sector from the Niagara River to the New England coast. Dearborn, like William Hull [*q.v.*], had exhibited excellent military qualities as a young officer in the Revolution, but, as with Hull, those qualities appeared to have evaporated with age and long disuse. Dearborn prepared a plan of campaign which called for simultaneous attacks upon the British at Montreal, Kingston, Niagara, and Detroit, but showed neither energy nor speed in preparing for its execution. After establishing headquarters at Albany he went to Boston to superintend recruiting and coast-defense. His stay here was prolonged for weeks beyond the declaration of war, with the result that no preparations were made for attacking the British at any point east of Detroit. Consequently, Gen. Brock was enabled to throw his whole force against Hull at Detroit and compel his surrender. The year ended with another American defeat at Queenston on the Niagara River and a futile march to the Canadian border and back again by the troops at Plattsburgh under Dearborn's direct command. The campaign of the following spring (1813) gave further proof of Dearborn's incompetence. John Armstrong [*q.v.*], now secretary of war, gave orders for an attack on Kingston at the eastern end of Lake Ontario. Dearborn, greatly overestimating the British strength at Kingston, secured Armstrong's consent for an attack upon the western end instead. He captured York (Toronto), Apr. 27, 1813, but with heavy losses and no corresponding advantage. He also took Fort George at the mouth of Niagara River (May 27), but the British army escaped and inflicted severe defeats upon two detachments sent in pursuit. Dearborn was taken ill, and the active command devolved upon Gen. Morgan Lewis. Meanwhile Sackett's Harbor, the American base at the east end of the lake, had been left exposed to the

British fleet and army at Kingston, which in a surprise attack, May 28, barely failed in their effort to capture it, and retired only after inflicting considerable damage. The entire campaign had been so seriously mismanaged that the demand for Dearborn's removal was imperative. A letter from Armstrong, July 6, 1813, relieved him of command on the frontier. Dearborn's request for a court of inquiry went unheeded, but he was given command of New York City and was later appointed president of the court martial which tried and condemned Gen. Hull—a most improper appointment, since Dearborn's negligence had contributed to bring about Hull's defeat. Dearborn was honorably discharged from the army on June 15, 1815. Madison had nominated him in March for secretary of war, but the nomination called forth such strong remonstrance that Madison withdrew it. The Senate had meanwhile rejected his name, but consented to erase the record from its journal. In 1822 Monroe sent him as minister to Portugal, a post which he held two years. He returned at his own request and retired to Roxbury, Mass. Dearborn was thrice married: to Mary Bartlett in 1771; to Dorcas (Osgood) Marble in 1780; and to Sarah Bowdoin, widow of James Bowdoin, in 1813. Henry Alexander Scammell Dearborn [q.v.] was his son by his second wife.

[Dearborn's "Journal while on Arnold's Expedition to Quebec" mentioned above, journals which he kept at various times from July 1776 to March 1783, are published in *Proc. Mass. Hist. Soc.*, ser. 2, vol. III (1886–87). Another portion of his journals is included in *Jours. of the Military Expedition of Maj.-Gen. John Sullivan against the Six Nations of Indians in 1779* (1887), ed. by Frederick Cook, pp. 62–80. For other accounts of the march to Quebec consult Justin H. Smith, *Arnold's March from Cambridge to Quebec* (1903) and *The Struggle for the Fourteenth Colony* (2 vols., 1907). Of Dearborn's performances in the War of 1812 the best account is in Henry Adams, *Hist. of the U. S.*, vols. VI and VII (1890–91). Dearborn's side of the case was presented by his son, Gen. H. A. S. Dearborn, in *Defence of Gen. Henry Dearborn against the Attack of Gen. William Hull* (1824). See also Jos. Dow, "The Dearborns of Hampton, N. H.," in *The Hist. of Hampton, N. H.* (1893).]   J. W. P.

DEARBORN, HENRY ALEXANDER SCAMMELL (Mar. 3, 1783–July 29, 1851), politician, author, was the son of Henry Dearborn [q.v.] and his second wife Dorcas, daughter of Col. John Osgood of Andover, Mass., and widow of Isaac Marble. He was born at Exeter, N. H. After a boyhood spent on a farm in Maine, he attended Williams College, Mass., but, on his father becoming secretary of war and moving to Washington, D. C., in 1801, he entered the College of William and Mary, Williamsburg, Va., where he graduated in 1803. For a time he studied law in the office of Wil-

liam Wirt, at Washington, D. C., then completed his course with Judge Story at Salem, Mass., and was admitted to the Massachusetts bar. Having conceived a distaste for law he then applied for a foreign diplomatic station, but, under the advice of President Jefferson, relinquished the idea and commenced to practise at Salem. In 1806, however, he was appointed to superintend the erection of the new forts in Portland harbor. On the completion of these works, he became an officer in the customhouse at Boston, of which port his father had been appointed collector. In 1812, on Gen. Dearborn's assumption of the command of the Northern army, he was appointed collector in his father's stead, becoming also brigadier-general of militia in charge of the defenses of the port. He resided at Roxbury, Mass., and on the termination of the war, took an active interest in local affairs. At the same time he devoted a portion of his leisure to literary pursuits, writing a *Memoir on the Commerce and Navigation of the Black Sea and the Trade and Maritime Geography of Turkey and Egypt* (1819), in two volumes with an additional volume of charts. Retaining his position as collector throughout the administrations of Madison, Monroe, and John Quincy Adams, he was removed by President Jackson in 1829. In that year he was elected representative for Roxbury in the Massachusetts legislature, becoming shortly afterward a member of the Governor's Council. In 1830 he was a delegate to the state constitutional convention, being also elected state senator for Norfolk County. The following year he was elected representative from Roxbury in the federal House, but served only one term. In 1835 he received the appointment of adjutant-general of Massachusetts, and held this position for eight years. He was Massachusetts commissioner, or "Superintendent of Massachusetts" for the sale of the Seneca Indian lands in 1838–39. In 1843, in the absence of the governor, he loaned the state arms to the government of Rhode Island for the purpose of suppressing the "Dorr Rebellion" then in progress, and was dismissed from office in consequence. In 1847 he was elected mayor of Roxbury, and continued to hold that position until his death which occurred at Portland, Me., July 29, 1851.

In addition to his work on the Black Sea he was the author of: *Defence of Gen. Henry Dearborn against the Attack of Gen. William Hull* (1824); a translation from the French of *Monography of the Genus Camellia* (1838), by the Abbé Lorenzo Berlese; *Letters on the Internal Improvements and Commerce of the West*

(1839); *A Sketch of the Life of the Apostle Eliot* (1850), and a large number of papers and addresses on various subjects, particularly horticulture, in which he was deeply interested. Many of his writings, left in manuscript at the time of his death, have never been published.

His career was one of ceaseless activity and his interests were very diverse. As a public officer he was efficient without being brilliant, and his integrity and devotion to duty were unquestioned. He was keenly alive to the necessity of public improvements, particularly lines of internal communication, and vigorously supported the project of the Hoosac Tunnel. The Massachusetts Horticultural Society largely owed its success to his efforts in its behalf. His personality was attractive. Tall and of fine physique, the essence of dignity, at the same time he kept in touch with all classes of the community, and was extremely hospitable, maintaining open house at Roxbury. When Collector he "usually drove to the Custom House in a stately carriage drawn by a double span of horses with postillions, and his elegant turnout was the envy of all" (F. S. Drake, *post*).

[Daniel Goodwin, Jr., *The Dearborns* (1884); Geo. Putnam, *Address Delivered Before the City Government and Citizens of Roxbury on The Life and Character of the Late Henry A. S. Dearborn* (1851), containing intimate details of Dearborn's life by a close associate; Francis S. Drake, *The Town of Roxbury* (1878); H. A. Homes, *An Account of the MSS. of Gen. Dearborn as Mass. Commissioner in 1838 and 1839* (1881); Dearborn's Journals, 1838–39, printed in *Buffalo Hist. Soc. Pubs.*, vol. VII (1904), which also contains a sketch of Dearborn by F. H. Severance; *Salem Register*, July 31, 1851, reprinted in the *Portland Daily Advertiser*, Aug. 2, 1851; *Boston Daily Advertiser*, July 31, 1851; *Norfolk County Jour.* (Roxbury), Aug. 9, 1851.]   H. W. H. K.

DEARING, JOHN LINCOLN (Dec. 10, 1858–Dec. 20, 1916), missionary, for twenty-eight years associated with the Christian movement in Japan, was born in Webster, Me., the son of Joseph Henry and Susan Vinton (Adams) Dearing. A farmer's boy, eager for an education, he prepared for Colby College from which, having supported himself throughout his course, he graduated in 1884. For the next two years he was superintendent of schools in Deep River, Conn. He then entered Newton Theological Institution, graduating in 1889. The call to missionary service had come to him in 1888 at a Student Volunteer Convention, and, soon after his graduation, having first been ordained to the Baptist ministry, he sailed for Japan under appointment by the American Baptist Missionary Union. Returning in 1891, he married, July 27, Mary Lyon Hinckley of Lynn, Mass., daughter of Rev. Henry L. Hinckley.

During his entire missionary career his home was at Yokohama. The first years were spent in acquiring the language and in general evangelical work. He was essentially an administrator, however, and in 1894 he became president of Yokohama Baptist Theological Seminary, and professor of theology and ethics. This office he held for fourteen years, during which time the institution improved greatly in both buildings and equipment as well as in the character of its instruction. He also prepared and published in Japanese, *Outline of Theology* (1895). His advanced ideas regarding missionary organization and administration, moreover, had a marked influence on Baptist activities throughout the empire. From 1908 to 1911 he was general missionary superintendent of the American Baptist Missionary Union for Japan, China, and the Philippines. When this plan of field administration was discontinued he instituted at Yokohama a work for Japanese business and professional men, centering in a night school and dormitory combined. During the last years of his life he was prominent in the advancement of union missionary enterprises, serving them in various capacities, notably as secretary of Federated Missions in Japan and as editor of its annual publication, *The Christian Movement in the Japanese Empire*, both of which offices he held at his death. Returning to America on a furlough in May 1916, he was conducting the annual course of lectures on Missions at Colgate Theological Seminary when, in November, he suffered an attack of spinal meningitis from which he died at the Clifton Springs Sanitarium on the 20th of the following month.

[*Third General Catalogue of Colby College, . . . 1820–1908* (1909); *Who's Who in America*, 1916–17; Jas. H. Franklin, "John Lincoln Dearing," in the *Watchman-Examiner*, Jan. 4, 1917; Shailer Mathews, "John L. Dearing: An Appreciation," in the *Standard*, Jan. 20, 1917; *One-Hundred-Third Ann. Report, Am. Baptist Foreign Mission Soc.* (1917); *The Christian Movement in the Japanese Empire*, 1917.]   H. E. S.

DEARTH, HENRY GOLDEN (Apr. 22, 1864–Mar. 27, 1918), painter, was born at Bristol, R. I., the son of John Willis and Ruth (Marshall) Dearth. His early instruction was received from Horace Johnson, a portrait-painter of Providence, with whom he began work on the figure. Later, at the École des Beaux-Arts, in Paris, he studied under Hébert and Aimé Morot. The charm of the Normandy coast turned his attention to landscapes and in 1893 he was awarded the Webb Landscape Prize by the Society of American Artists, of which he was a member.

His earlier work reflected the influence of

picturesque France. He was a fine draftsman and a colorist of unusual ability; his work is characterized by a directness and simplicity indicating close sympathy with his theme, and by an appreciation of values—a skilful subordination of mass and group and tones to achieve their proper relations. By a hint here and there, a graceful suggestion of thought that the imagination may carry further at will, he used detail to complete his idea. This characteristic is especially noticeable in "A Sunset in Normandy," with its delightful arrangement of trees, earth, and sky, and a few brush strokes indicating the cattle which complete the scene. About 1912, a distinct change was apparent in his technique, and his paintings, including both portraits and genre subjects, became brilliant interpretations in broken colors, the pigment being thickly applied. Noteworthy canvases of this period included pictures of the rock pools of Brittany, done with a fine, imaginative touch. Entirely different characteristics marked the later period of his art. Many of his still-life groups were from treasures in his own remarkable collection; frequently there is an Oriental touch in the backgrounds of Chinese carving and similar details. A high note of estheticism and idealism is apparent in all these later paintings.

Dearth received a bronze medal at the Paris Exposition of 1900, a silver medal at Buffalo in 1901, a medal at Charleston in 1902, and one at St. Louis; was made an associate of the National Academy of Design in 1902 and an academician in 1906.

He spent his winters in New York, his summers in Normandy, and a few months of each year in his studio at Montreuil-sur-Mer in the Pas-de-Calais by the English Channel. On Feb. 26, 1896, he married Cornelia Van Rensselaer Vail of New York. At the age of fifty-four, he died of heart disease, survived by his wife and their daughter. He was a member of the Fencers', Lotos, and Century clubs.

[*Century Mag.*, May 1905, p. 157; *Who's Who in America*, 1916–17; sketch by Cornelia B. Sage-Quinton, Art Director, Albright Art Gallery, Buffalo Fine Arts Academy, in the *Catalogue*, 1918–19, no. 7; obituary in *N. Y. Times*, Mar. 28, 1918.]   J. M. H.

DEAS, ZACHARIAH CANTEY (Oct. 25, 1819–Mar. 6, 1882), commission merchant, Confederate soldier, was the son of Col. James Sutherland Deas and Margaret Chesnut of Camden, S. C. His mother was a sister of James Chesnut, Jr. [*q.v.*], United States senator from S. C. He was educated in Columbia, S. C., and at Caudebec, France. He moved with his parents from Charleston to Mobile, Ala., in 1835 when the "flush times" spirit in the state was rife. Great developments were in prospect and with certain transportation improvements Mobilians expected to see Mobile become the commercial exchange for a vast hinterland, including all of Alabama and portions of Mississippi, Tennessee, Georgia, North Carolina, and Virginia. Thus Mobile seemed an ideal place for one who was interested in commercial pursuits. Deas became a cotton broker and acquired considerable wealth. He married on May 16, 1853, Helen Gaines Lyon, the daughter of Francis Strother Lyon [*q.v.*], one of the state's most favorably known citizens who had distinguished himself by saving the state from financial bankruptcy and discredit after the collapse of the state bank.

Deas had seen service in the Mexican War, and when the Civil War began he promptly enlisted with the Alabama volunteers. He fought in some of the most stubborn engagements of the war and was wounded several times. His first duty was that of aide-de-camp to Gen. J. E. Johnston. In the fall of 1861 he was commissioned colonel and with the assistance of Maj. Robert B. Armistead recruited the 22nd Alabama Infantry which he equipped with Enfield rifles at a cost to himself of $28,000 in gold. He was reimbursed by the government in Confederate bonds. At Shiloh (Apr. 6–7, 1862) he commanded his brigade after his superior officers had fallen, was badly wounded himself, but recovered in time to lead his regiment through Kentucky with Gen. Bragg. Commissioned brigadier-general on Dec. 13, 1862, in the battle of Murfreesboro (Dec. 31, 1862–Jan. 3, 1863), he superseded Gen. Gardner. He led his brigade in the battles of Chickamauga (Sept. 19–20, 1863) and Missionary Ridge (Nov. 25, 1863), and in the battles and skirmishes against Gen. Sherman from Dalton to Atlanta and Jonesboro. He returned to Nashville with Gen. Hood and took a conspicuous part in the battles of Franklin and Nashville (Nov. 30 and Dec. 15–16, 1864). After the latter engagement he was transferred to the East to assist in the opposition to Sherman's march through the Carolinas. At Raleigh he became ill and turned his command over to Col. H. T. Toulmin. After the war he removed to New York City and reëntered the cotton trade. He became a cotton broker again and a prominent member of the stock exchange, but in New York, as formerly in Mobile, he lived the life of "a quiet and modest citizen."

[W. Brewer, *Alabama* (1872); T. M. Owen, *Hist. of Ala. and Dict. of Ala. Biog.*, vol. III (1921); *Confed. Mil. Hist.*, VII (1899), 401 ff.; *Daily Reg.* (Mobile, Ala.), *N. Y. Tribune*, Mar. 7, 1882.]   A. B. M.

DE BARDELEBEN, HENRY FAIRCHILD (July 22, 1840–Dec. 6, 1910), Alabama industrialist, was the descendant of a Hessian captain who landed in South Carolina during the Revolution to serve against the colonies. De Bardeleben's father, Henry, had migrated to Alabama where he married Jennie Fairchild of New York. He died when his son was ten years of age. The mother subsequently moved to Montgomery where the boy secured work in a grocery. When he was sixteen he became the ward of Daniel Pratt [q.v.], the first great industrial magnate of Alabama, whose plants were at Prattville, a few miles from Montgomery. Young De Bardeleben lived in the Pratt mansion and attended school. He was made "boss" of the teamsters and foreman of the lumber-yard, and later superintendent of the gin factory. Upon the outbreak of the Civil War he joined the Prattville Dragoons in the Confederate service, serving at Pensacola and in the Shiloh campaign. On Feb. 4, 1863, he married Pratt's second daughter, Ellen.

In 1872, when Pratt, the wealthiest man in the state, turned his attention toward the district surrounding Birmingham—which town had been founded in the previous year—bought a controlling interest in the Red Mountain Iron & Coal Company, and undertook the reconstruction of the Oxmoor furnaces and the development of the Helena mines, he made De Bardeleben manager, although the latter stated frankly that he knew nothing of making iron. The panic of 1873 temporarily closed the works. This same year Pratt died, leaving his son-in-law the richest man in the district. In 1877 J. W. Sloss [q.v.] and T. H. Aldrich interested him in the great Browne seam of coal west of Birmingham. He joined them in the Eureka Coal Company, doubling the capital. The name of the seam was changed to that of "Pratt" in honor of Daniel Pratt. "De Bardeleben," said his partner, T. H. Aldrich, "put the whole power of his fortune, his credit, and his tremendous vitality into the advancement of the company." A year later the company was reorganized as the Pratt Coal & Coke Company, with De Bardeleben as president. With T. T. Hillman [q.v.] he built the Alice furnaces in 1879–81, naming them in honor of his eldest daughter.

Fearing that he was developing tuberculosis, in 1881 he sold his holdings and went to Mexico, but was sufficiently recovered to return to Birmingham the next year, when, with W. T. Underwood, he built the Mary Pratt furnace and named it for his second daughter. Illness again attacked him and he went to Texas. Whenever he traveled away from home his personality attracted men of means and enterprise who followed him to Birmingham. Thus David Roberts joined him in 1886, and together they formed the De Bardeleben Coal & Iron Company. He also organized the Pinckard & De Bardeleben Land Company. These interests, with a capital of $2,500,000, founded the town of Bessemer, ten miles west of Birmingham, and near the great Red Mountain iron seam. Here four furnaces and an iron mill were erected. The firm held 150,000 acres of mineral lands. The venture was the greatest up to that time in the South. All of this property in 1887 was formed into the De Bardeleben Coal & Iron Company, capitalized at $13,000,000. In 1891 it was taken over by the Tennessee Coal, Iron & Railroad Company, of which De Bardeleben was made vice-president. After three years of virtual retirement his restlessness tempted him to go to New York and make the attempt to obtain control of the company. In this effort he failed, however, losing, it is said, his entire fortune save a forgotten bank deposit of $75,000. Indomitable in the face of ill fortune, with his sons Henry and Charles De Bardeleben, he explored new fields and started mining at Margaret in St. Claire County, Ala., and in the Acton Basin southeast of Birmingham.

De Bardeleben's Red Mountain seam, with his Pratt coal seam, was the basis for the development of industrial Birmingham. He was the first to succeed in making pig iron in Birmingham cheaper than it could be made elsewhere. He built the first coal road in Alabama, and aided T. H. Aldrich in exploring and in exploiting the Montevallo coal fields. He contributed to the development of his region not only through the enterprises with which he was directly connected but also by attracting to Birmingham moneyed men of ambition who established others. President M. H. Smith of the Louisville & Nashville stated that De Bardeleben persuaded him to build the Mineral Railroad and invest in all thirty millions of the company's funds in the district. He was "always talking steel"; in fact he talked of it long before it was made in the Birmingham district. Through him the Caldwell interests were led to build the first rolling-mill in Birmingham. He induced J. W. Sloss to build furnaces and joined T. T. Hillman in building others. "The King of the Southern Iron World" as he was called, he was the most spectacular figure in Alabama's industrial growth. After the death of his first wife, De Bardeleben married a sister of Judge W. P. McCroffin.

[De Bardeleben's early life is mentioned by Mrs. S. F. H. Tarrant in *The Honorable Daniel Pratt* (1894). There are many references to him in Ethel Armes, *The Story of Coal and Iron in Ala.* (1910), B. F. Riley, *Makers and Romance of Ala. Hist.* (1914), and G. W. Cruikshank, *Hist. of Birmingham and Its Environs* (1920). See also the obituary in *Birmingham Age Herald*, Dec. 7, 1910. Valuable scrapbooks on his career are in the possession of his son Chas. F. De Bardeleben of Birmingham.]   H. A. T.

DE BERDT, DENNYS (*c.* 1694–Apr. 11, 1770), colonial agent, was a member of a family which emigrated from Ypres in Flanders to England to escape religious persecution under the Duke of Alva. They had a good estate on the continent but took with them only money and jewels. After reaching England some of the family left off the "De" and others spelled the name Bert. At first they settled at Colchester but John De Berdt, the father of Dennys, was apprenticed to a cousin who was a merchant in London. Dennys was born in or about 1694 and the *Gentleman's Magazine,* August 1731, records the death of a John De Berdt "of Battersea, Esq.; Grandson to the late Sir John Fleet," who was probably his father. Dennys was of a very devout religious temper and a pronounced Dissenter. Of his earlier interest in America or his connections with the Massachusetts leaders we know almost nothing. In 1758 the Rev. Samuel Davies preached a sermon in Virginia called "The Curse of Cowardice" and sent a manuscript copy to De Berdt who, the same year, published it in London with a dedication, favorable to the colonies, to the Earl of Halifax. Again in 1766, in one of the numerous pamphlets relating to the founding of the Rev. Eleazar Wheelock's Indian School, the forerunner of Dartmouth College, it was stated that English donations might be left with Dennys De Berdt, "Merchant, in Artillery-Court, Chiswell-street." On Nov. 5, 1765, the lower house of the General Court at Boston, considering the nomination of an agent for the colony in London, agreed on the name of De Berdt, who was then seventy years old. The house, in their notification of his election, said that since they were informed of his "Ability and Inclination to serve the Province" his election had been soon determined by a very large majority. The first letter from Samuel Dexter to De Berdt in his official capacity says that for some years De Berdt had been known as a "sincere friend of the American colonies."

It has been stated that he was agent for New York also but this is an error. He was, however, agent for Delaware as well as Massachusetts, and the former colony sent him a piece of silver plate for his services in securing the repeal of the Stamp Act. Massachusetts frugally contented herself with a vote of thanks on the same occasion, and finally settled the arrears of salary due him with his son Dennis after his death. Years afterward the state accepted the gift from his friend, Richard Cary, of his portrait which now hangs in the State House. He left a considerable estate and his will mentions his wife Martha as residuary legatee. Besides the son, Dennis, he had a daughter, Esther, who married the American Joseph Reed [*q.v.*] in London. As agent he seems to have been assiduous and faithful in a very trying period in spite of his advanced age.

[There is no biography of De Berdt and the contemporary references to him are scanty except for the official votes and letters in connection with his agencies. The only account of him, drawn upon for this article, is that by Albert Mathews in the *Mass. Colonial Soc. Pubs.,* XIII (1912), 294–307, forming an introduction to the reprint of his Letter-Book, the original of which is in the Lib. of Cong. A few other letters not in that are appended.]   J. T. A.

DE BOW, JAMES DUNWOODY BROWNSON (July 10, 1820–Feb. 27, 1867), editor, statistician, was born in Charleston, S. C. His father was Garret De Bow, a native of New Jersey, once a prosperous merchant, but ruined shortly before his death. His mother was a Miss Norton. De Bow was left an orphan when still a lad, and used his tiny patrimony to enter a mercantile house in Charleston. Here he saved his money with Spartan self-denial for seven years in order to attend the Cokesbury Institute, Abbeville District. He entered the College of Charleston, and resorted to many shifts to maintain himself. In his last year he was in particularly desperate straits, his friends scarcely knowing how he lived. He graduated in 1843 at the head of his class, and, still existing on a crust, devoted an arduous year to the reading of law, after which he was admitted to the bar. He soon saw that he would not succeed in this profession; he was a poor speaker, and his emaciated appearance was against him. The *Southern Quarterly Review,* published in Charleston, offered an escape. He began contributing philosophical and political essays to its columns, and soon became its editor. His most notable article, "Oregon and the Oregon Question," appeared in July 1845; in this he discountenanced the claims of France to the northwest country, but saw much in those of Britain, toward which country he counseled, against the popular clamor, moderation and a spirit of compromise. This article attracted notice abroad, being debated in the French Chamber of Deputies. At the Memphis Convention, held the same year, De Bow was one of the secretaries. The convention considered principally projects of internal improvement in the South, and the extent to which the federal government should be expected to aid in their construction. This discussion of economic questions decided young De Bow to found a monthly magazine devoted to social and business matters, so, after Calhoun, Poinsett, and others had encouraged the venture, he left Charleston with "a diminutive capital and a very slender baggage" for New Orleans as a more bustling commercial center. The South had supported literary journals poorly, and economic ones not at all, but De Bow believed he could succeed because the interests of the southern frontier were practical. Accordingly he issued, in January 1846, the first number of the *Commercial Review of the South and Southwest*. He had difficulty in getting contributors, there were almost no subscribers, and in a few months his capital was exhausted and the *Review* suspended (August 1847). Then matters began to mend. He came to the notice of Maunsel White, who, from a poor Irish immigrant, had risen in sugar planting and merchandise to wealth. He admired the young editor and loaned him money to resume publication, promising more should it be needed. For a time De Bow and his assistant endured a struggle which only youth could have survived. After working till far into the night, they slept on a mattress on the floor of a room given them by J. C. Morgan, the bookseller. De Bow said afterward that they rarely spent more than ten cents each for a day's food. Within two years, however, they had the largest circulation of any magazine published in the South; De Bow had paid his debts, moved his office to better quarters, and was able to eat steak and chops for the first time in his life. He soon had money enough to make a trip through New England, which resulted in added information for the *Review*.

When the University of Louisiana was organized at New Orleans, he advocated inclusion of a comprehensive course of economic and commercial instruction in its curriculum, outlined the subjects to be treated (recommending the works of Henry C. Carey [*q.v.*] with those of the English classical school) and persuaded his friend Maunsel White to subsidize the professorship of political economy. De Bow was promptly appointed (1848) to the chair (probably the first of its kind in this country), but it was an empty honor, for he had no students and few listeners at his public lectures. Soon afterward he was made head of the new Louisiana Bureau of Statistics, and within a year compiled and presented to the legislature a report made up from returns to a brave questionnaire. The bureau went out of existence when the legislature failed to make

further appropriation. De Bow, bound to have the South systematic, was one of the founders of the Louisiana Historical Society, which dragged out a sickly life until merged with the Academy of Sciences. Greater opportunity opened to him when he was appointed by President Pierce superintendent of the United States Census. He issued the seventh census, of 1850, and in 1854 the Senate printed his *Statistical View of the United States*, a compendium of the larger work. De Bow in an introductory essay made important suggestions for the improvement of the census, particularly through appointment of a permanent superintendent who should maintain a staff between decennial periods. While bringing out the report of the census he continued to publish his *Review*, and when he quitted his government post in 1855 took to public lecturing. He presided at the commercial convention at Knoxville in 1857, and wrote on American subjects for the *Encyclopædia Britannica*.

He will be longest remembered for *De Bow's Review*, which occupied in the South and Southwest a place similar to that of *Hunt's Merchants' Magazine* in the country at large. The journal was always influential, and had a part in bringing on the Civil War. His own articles appeared regularly, and were marked by serious, if somewhat lengthy, deliberation. Beginning with the resolve not to engage in debate on the matters threatening to divide North and South ("We have the broadest notions of our country; we cherish Maine and Louisiana as sisters; we have no jealousies of the North") he became, little by little, an outspoken and violent partisan. This was a natural consequence of his abiding admiration for Calhoun. More interested than Calhoun in economic prosperity, however, he retained a measure of the nationalism which his preceptor abandoned. He was influenced by the writings of the Careys, felt that protective tariffs were often desirable, and did not wish to contract the field of federal operation in internal improvements. He believed that "the negro was created essentially to be a slave, and finds his highest development and destiny in that condition." He worked for industry in the South, but expected to see agriculture remain predominant in that section. He contributed importantly to the policies of the series of commercial conventions held in the South prior to the Civil War, particularly with respect to a transcontinental railroad through the South, direct trade between the South and Europe, and a canal through Central America. His economic advocacies, where practical and untinged with political pique, had little constructive issue. In the main he was a very vocal drifter with the tide which set toward secession.

During the Civil War the Confederate government made him its chief agent for the purchase and sale of cotton. In the false flush of prosperity that came to the Southern commercial cities immediately after the war, he revived the *Review,* and at the same time was president of the Tennessee Pacific Railroad Company, a paper project which seemed to embody his old ambition of a transcontinental line through the South. He died of pleurisy, at Elizabeth, N. J., after a short illness contracted on a journey to the bedside of his dying brother and co-worker, B. F. De Bow. De Bow was ugly, with a great shock of hair standing in every direction, and a heavy moustache and beard. His nose was prominent, he had a long lower lip and an obstinate chin. Though in his writings he took himself very seriously, he was genial in personal contacts. He married in 1854 Caroline Poe, of Georgetown, D. C., and in 1860 Martha E. Johns, who with three children survived him.

[For biographical sketches see *De Bow's Review,* post-war series, Apr. and May 1867, pp. 480–81 ; June 1867, pp. 497–506 (with a rare portrait) ; July and Aug. 1867, pp. 1–10. *De Bow's Review,* with differing titles, was published in New Orleans, Columbia, or Nashville, with longer or shorter suspensions, from Jan. 1846 to June 1880. De Bow's *Industrial Resources of the Southern and Western States* (3 vols., 1853), contains the more important articles published in the *Review* up to that time.]   B. M—l.

DE BRAHM, WILLIAM GERARD (1717–c. 1799), surveyor general of the Southern District, first used the given name of John Gerar William. A Dutch Protestant who had received competent training as a military engineer, he was also the founder of a prosperous colony in Georgia, a surveyor of that province, surveyor general for the Southern District, a geographer, climatologist, naturalist, meteorologist, navigator, and the author of navigation tables, pilot guides, and treatises on barometric hypsometry, the apparition of eternity, and the everlasting Gospel. He prefaced his reports on his surveys of South Carolina, Georgia, and East Florida with summaries of the early history of those provinces. His reports fill four folio volumes, are copiously illustrated with local and general maps, and contain his observations on practicable inlets and rivers, their surroundings, his directions for mariners, his notes on soils, useful trees and shrubs, game, fish, Indians, Spaniards, etc. These volumes show an excellent command of the English language, some classical knowledge, and much special and technical information.

De Brahm's young manhood fell in the period of the scientific renaissance in Europe, when science began to be applied to the affairs of life. It was also a time of political readjustment and colonial expansion. After serving in the army of Emperor Charles VI as a captain of engineers, De Brahm proceeded in 1751 with 160 Protestant Salzburgers by way of England to Georgia, where he founded Bethany. Before the end of another year the town's population was increased by about thirteen hundred relatives and acquaintances of the first settlers. Their progress during the next two decades in agriculture and horticulture was notable among the many German communities of the Georgian coast and Savannah River. When, in August 1754, the king appointed the officials of Georgia, De Brahm was made a surveyor at a salary of £50 per annum. Three years later he planned the town of Ebenezer on the Savannah, erected its fort, and took up lands there on both sides of the river. At that time also he drew the first map of Georgia and South Carolina. In 1755 he rebuilt the curtain line around the battery at Charleston, extending it to Vanderhorst Creek. Six years later he constructed Fort George on Cockspur Island in the Savannah, and in 1762 fortified the town of Savannah against the Indians. After ten years of valuable service, in June 1764, he was appointed by the king surveyor general for the Southern District, at a salary of £150, and was given £30 more for his deputy, Bernard Romans [*q.v.*]. Early in January 1765 he set out from Savannah in the schooner *Augustine* with three boats and other equipment for an eighteen weeks' cruise to survey the coast from St. Augustine to the Cape of Florida. Meantime, he had been named one of the commissioners to mark the northern boundary of New Jersey from the Hudson to the Delaware. Besides sounding and mapping the inlets along the Florida coast, he platted the land along the rivers flowing into them. He also conducted inland surveys, marking out lands for settlement and locating town sites with their church and school lands. In November 1766 he announced in the *South Carolina Gazette,* of Charleston, the building of a galley on St. John's River with which to continue his survey down to the promontory and his wish to employ a master acquainted with the Keys and qualified in theoretical and practical navigation, also a geometrician versed in navigation. During this period his residence was at St. Augustine and he acquired a grant of 10,000 acres in the province of Florida.

On Oct. 4, 1770, Gov. James Grant suspended De Brahm from the provincial surveyorship for incivilities, overcharges, and obstructing applicants for lands. He appointed De Brahm's son-in-law, Capt. Frederick George Mulcaster, as his successor; but the Surveyor General continued to perform his duties until he sailed for England. There he produced a map of the Atlantic Ocean for his mariners' guide, *The Atlantic Pilot,* published in London in 1772. He also delivered his general map of East Florida to the plantation office, submitted his elaborate report, and sought reinstatement, presenting a memorial to that end in 1774. In the same year he published two volumes, *The Levelling Balance and Counter-Balance; or, The Method of Observing, by the Weight and Height of Mercury* and *De Brahm's Zonical Tables for the Twenty-Five Northern and Southern Climates.* Early in July he sailed with Mrs. De Brahm for Charleston in an armed vessel placed at his disposal by the Privy Council. They arrived on Sept. 7, and the next day Mrs. De Brahm died. Nearly two months later the Lords of the Treasury wrote to the Council of East Florida that in their opinion the Surveyor should be reinstated. Thereafter De Brahm seems to have divided his time between St. Augustine and Charleston. On Feb. 18, 1776, he was married to Mary, daughter of Thomas Drayton and widow of Edward Fenwick. Late in the course of the Revolution he wrote to London begging not to be superseded. He was left unprovided for from 1783 to the end of his life, except that he was awarded £1,138 6s 8d for his property losses in Florida by the British commissioners on East Florida claims. During this period he lived in Philadelphia, where he published several small works, including *Time an Apparition of Eternity* (1791) and *Apocalyptic Gnomon Points Out Eternity's Divisibility,* etc. (1795). His will, dated July 11, 1796, was proved July 3, 1799.

[De Brahm's Report to the King as surveyor general for the Southern District of North America, 4 vols. (MS.) in Brit. Museum; copies of Vols. I and II in Harvard Coll. Lib.; part of Report in P. C. J. Weston, *Docs. Connected with the Hist. of S. C.* (London, 1856); also in De Brahm, *Hist. of the Province of Ga.* (1849), ed. by G. Wymberly-Jones; *Acts of the Privy Council, Colonial Ser., 1745-1766,* p. 647; *Ibid., 1766-1783,* pp. 394, 592; Colonial Office 5/571, Minutes of Council of E. Florida, Apr. 6 and Oct. 4, 1770; *Am. Archives,* ser. 4, III, 835, 837; W. H. Siebert, *Loyalists in E. Florida, 1774-85,* being *Fla. State Hist. Soc. Pubs.,* No. 9 (2 vols., 1929), II, 337-38; P. L. Phillips, *Notes on the Life and Works of Bernard Romans,* pp. 16, 29, being No. 2 of the same series; *S. C. Hist. and Geneal. Mag.,* XI (1910), 160, and XIV (1918), 7-9; C. C. Jones, *Hist. of Ga.* (1883), I, 212, 374, 460-62, 505; information from Ernest Spofford, Esq., librarian of the Hist. Soc. of Pa.]   W. H. S.

DEBS, EUGENE VICTOR (Nov. 5, 1855–Oct. 20, 1926), Socialist advocate, was one of the ten children of Jean Daniel and Marguerite Marie (Bettrich) Debs and was born in Terre Haute, Ind. The parents, who were married in New York City on Sept. 13, 1849, were both natives of Colmar, Alsace, and had come to America in that year. After some wandering they settled in Terre Haute in the fall of 1854. Young Debs attended school until the middle of his fifteenth year, when he went to work in the shops of the Terre Haute and Indianapolis Railway, later becoming a locomotive fireman. Four years later (1874) he quit his fireman's job and took a clerkship in a wholesale grocery house. In February of the following year he participated in the organization in his city of a lodge of the Brotherhood of Locomotive Firemen, of which he was made secretary, and in 1878 he was appointed associate editor of the *Firemen's Magazine.* He continued with the grocery firm (doing his work for the labor-union at night) until September 1879, when he was elected city clerk. In 1880 he was appointed (and later in the year elected) national secretary and treasurer of the Brotherhood and editor of its magazine. By working incredibly long hours he contrived to fill all three offices until the close of his term as city clerk in 1883, thereafter for ten years giving most of his time to his union. On June 9, 1885, he was married to Katherine Metzel of Pittsburgh, and in the fall of the year was elected to the lower house of the Indiana legislature. In 1892 he resigned his offices in the union, but against his protest was unanimously reëlected.

From an early day he was an opponent of the organization of labor by crafts and an advocate of organization by industries. In June 1893, he took part in the formation of a labor society of the "industrial" type, the American Railway Union, of which he was chosen president. In several minor contests with employers the new union won considerable prestige, and it came into nation-wide prominence through the strike for higher wages (Apr. 13, 1894) against the Great Northern Railroad. Eighteen days later the employees returned to work with most of their demands granted. In June the employees of the Pullman Company, at South Chicago, went out, and an appeal was made to the A. R. U. to aid them by a sympathetic strike. Debs opposed the move as inexpedient, but at a hastily called convention of the union a boycott on the moving of Pullman cars was ordered, and he at once took energetic charge of the campaign. Against the protest of Gov. Altgeld, President Cleveland ordered federal troops to Chicago; Judges Grosscup and Woods issued a sweeping injunction against the strikers, and on July 10 a federal grand jury, charging conspiracy to obstruct the mails, indicted Debs and three others, who were immediately arrested, and were again arrested on July 17 for contempt of court in violating the injunction. The trial before Judge Grosscup, Feb. 6–12, 1895, resulted in a discontinuance because of the illness of a juror, but on the charge of contempt Debs and six others were sentenced by Judge Woods to six months in the McHenry County jail at Woodstock. Here Debs spent much of his time in reading, with the result that he avowed himself a convert to Socialism. Released on Nov. 22, he returned to Chicago, where he was accorded one of the most remarkable demonstrations in the history of the city, and thence to Terre Haute.

In 1896 he campaigned for Bryan, but, in June 1897, brought about the transformation of what was left of the A. R. U. into the Social Democratic Party of America. Three years later a tentative combination was made with the faction of the Socialist Labor party that had seceded in 1899, and Debs, as the fusion candidate for president, polled 96,116 votes. In the following year the two wings were formally united under the name of the Socialist Party of America, and in 1904 Debs was again nominated for president, polling 402,321 votes. About this time he became associate editor of the Socialist weekly, the *Appeal to Reason,* of Girard, Kan., and for five or six years gave his time to editorial work and to lecture tours in behalf of the *Appeal* and the Socialist party. At Chicago, June 27–July 8, 1905, he aided in founding the Industrial Workers of the World, but after a time became dissatisfied with the organization and withdrew, though frequently thereafter defending its members from charges he deemed unjust. In 1908 he was again the Socialist candidate, and in a train known as the "Red Special" made a speaking canvass of the entire country; but though he drew large crowds, his vote (420,973) showed only a slight gain over that of 1904. In 1912 he was nominated for the fourth time, and he again made a general canvass. The year was one of an unparalleled social ferment; and though the liberal platform of Wilson and the specifically progressive platform of Roosevelt were expected to diminish the Socialist vote, it increased to 901,062, or nearly six per cent of the total. In 1916 Debs declined to be a candidate.

The manifesto of the St. Louis convention of the party (April 1917), denouncing the war and counseling party members to oppose it by all means in their power, was warmly approved by Debs, though later in the year he favored some modification of the language and of the party's policy. But in the following year, stirred no doubt by resentment over the many convictions for sedition, he took more extreme ground. At the Socialist state convention in Canton, Ohio, June 16, 1918, he delivered a speech in which he bitterly assailed the administration for its prosecution of persons charged with sedition. Four days later, at Cleveland, he was indicted by a federal grand jury for a violation of the Espionage Act, and on Sept. 14, after a four-days trial, was sentenced to ten years' imprisonment on each of two accounts, the sentences to run concurrently. Appeal was taken to the federal Supreme Court, which on Mar. 10, 1919, upheld the verdict. On Apr. 13 Debs was taken to the penitentiary at Moundsville, W. Va., and on June 13–14 was transferred to the penitentiary at Atlanta. In the following year, while still a prisoner, he was nominated for the fifth time as his party's candidate for president, and polled 919,799 votes, a figure exceeding that of 1912 though representing but little more than half its proportion of the total. On Christmas Day, 1921, by order of President Harding, he was released, though without restoration of his citizenship.

He returned to his home, but in the following year spent several months in the Lindlahr Sanitarium, at Elmhurst, near Chicago. During this period he prepared for a newspaper syndicate a series of articles on prison conditions, which, in 1927, with additions, were published in book form with the title *Walls and Bars.* In 1924 the Socialist party, with Debs's approval, joined with the La Follette forces. In the following year it established in Chicago a national weekly organ, the *American Appeal,* of which Debs was made editor. His health declining, early in 1926 he went to Bermuda. In April he returned home, but in September again became an inmate of the sanitarium at Lindlahr, where a month later he died. Funeral services, attended by 10,000 persons, were held in his home city on Oct. 23. The body was cremated at Indianapolis, and the ashes were buried in Terre Haute.

Though the standard-bearer of his party, Debs was at no time its intellectual leader. He was not a student or a reasoner, but a passionate advocate, and his words and acts were impulsive. He initiated none of the policies of the party, and he formulated none of its programs. Even his place as standard-bearer was anomalous; for though the fundamental tactic of the party was to seek a close affiliation with the trade-unions, Debs was their steadfast opponent, and in his prime there was perhaps no man in the labor movement whom the union leaders regarded as a greater menace. He had promoted the organization of two rival bodies (the A. R. U. and the I. W. W.), and he might at any time, it was feared, break bounds and join in some further action deemed disruptive. This anomaly was not unrecognized by thoughtful members of the party; but the sterling character of the man, his moral earnestness, his personal popularity, and his energy as a campaigner combined to override all opposition within the ranks.

Everywhere he drew large and responsive audiences. His manner as an orator was impressive; and his diction, if not always eloquent, was fluent and forceful. Tall, lean, and supple, his eager countenance aflame, he bent far forward over the edge of the platform and with right arm extended and long forefinger pointing from place to place at his audience, he thundered out his invectives against the capitalist system and sought to bring home to each of his hearers a guilty sense of responsibility for its continuance. Each of his addresses was, from the standpoint of its immediate influence over his hearers, a personal triumph, and he was greeted with every demonstration of approval. But though the common people heard him gladly, most of them voted against him. They learned to respect and love the man, but his message did not convert them.

His language, both of denunciation and of praise, was often extreme. His social philosophy was naïve and all-embracing; capitalism, with all its works, was an unqualified evil, and Socialism, with all its promises, a panacea. He had neither time nor thought for any modification of this simple creed; what was not white was black, and he spoke his convictions with a positiveness that revealed a mind untroubled with doubts. He was often inconsistent. Though he opposed repression and violence, he could find palliation for either provided it was employed in behalf of "the cause." To a friendly interviewer who talked with him in the Atlanta penitentiary he asserted (*Appeal to Reason*, Apr. 17, 1920) that because the Russian revolution was "a forward step" it was right for the Soviet Government to suppress free speech and a free press, whereas it was wrong to deny free speech in his own case because American participation in the war was "a reactionary step." He denounced the assassination of the Czar and his family, and on July 26, 1922, protested to Lenin by cable against the probable execution of twenty-two Social Revolutionists then on trial; but in a long manifesto issued on the following Oct. 8 indulged in a sweeping defense of the Soviet Government in spite of its imprisonment and execution of dissentients.

His personal character won tributes from all who knew him. His home life was happy; not often is there revealed to the world a family such as his, so closely bound by affection and community of interest and belief, and to one of its members, his brother Theodore, for many years his constant companion and auxiliary, must be credited no small part of his achievement. Debs's rectitude, his genial and unaffected friendliness, his sympathy and his open-handed generosity were widely recognized, and nowhere was he held in greater regard than in his home city. "While the overwhelming majority of the people here are opposed to the social and economic theories of Mr. Debs," wrote Mayor James Lyons in 1907 to an inquirer, "there is not perhaps a single man in this city who enjoys to a greater degree than Mr. Debs the affection, love and profound respect of the entire community."

[*Debs: His Life, Writings and Speeches, with a Department of Appreciations* (1908), ed. by Stephen Marion Reynolds; David Karsner, *Debs: His Authorized Life and Letters* (1919), and *Talks with Debs in Terre Haute* (1922); E. V. Debs, *Walls and Bars* (1927); *Speeches of Eugene V. Debs* (1929), ed. with a critical introduction by Alexander Trachtenberg; *Debs and the Poets* (1920), ed. by Ruth Le Prade; files of the *Firemen's Mag.*, later the *Brotherhood of Locomotive Firemen's Mag.*, and still later *The Brotherhood of Locomotive Firemen and Enginemen's Mag.*; Grover Cleveland, "The Government in the Chicago Strikes of 1894," *McClure's Mag.*, July 1904; Debs's reply in the *Appeal to Reason*, Aug. 27, 1904; *N. Y. Times*, Oct. 21–25, Nov. 7, and Dec. 22, 1926; information as to specific facts from Theodore Debs; notes and recollections of the writer.]   W. J. G.

DE CAMP, JOSEPH RODEFER (Nov. 5, 1858–Feb. 11, 1923), painter, was born at Cincinnati, Ohio, the son of Lambert and Lydia (Garwood) De Camp. He received his early training in the Cincinnati School of Design, under Frank Duveneck [*q.v.*], and continued his studies later in the Royal Academy at Munich. He was a member of the group of art students who accompanied Duveneck to Munich, Florence, and Venice, in 1878. In the company were Alexander, Twachtman, Chase, Vinton, MacEwen, Rolshoven, Currier, Grover, Bacher, and others. This band of students attained a certain celebrity; they figured in fiction as "the Inglehart boys" in William Dean Howells's *Indian Summer* (1885). There can be no doubt as to the marked influence of Duveneck's personality and principles on all the young men. Though few of them remained as consistent adherents of the Munich methods as their leader, none of them failed to make his mark in his own way. De Camp returned to America in 1880 and settled in Boston, where he was soon recognized as a sound and capable portrait-painter and an efficient teacher. He was for many years instructor in the Massachusetts Normal Art School. He held to the fundamental essentials of his art, especially good drawing and firm construction. In September 1891 he married Edith F. Baker, daughter of Joseph E. Baker, lithographer, a colleague of Winslow Homer in Bufford's shop, Boston, 1855–57. De Camp's home was in Medford, and his studio was in Boston. His vacations were spent on an island in Penobscot Bay, where his occupations included designing and building boats, piers, cottages; gardening, fishing, golfing. His friend George R. Agassiz spoke of his courage, honesty, and humanity; "under a somewhat rugged exterior lay the simplicity and tender-heartedness of a child." His death occurred at Bocagrande, Fla.

Many of De Camp's best paintings were first shown at the St. Botolph Club, of which he was a member. In 1911 he exhibited seventeen pictures there, including his full-length portrait of Theodore Roosevelt, presented by his classmates to the Harvard Union; a portrait of Frank Duveneck; a self-portrait; and likenesses of Sally and Polly, the artist's daughters. He was also a regular exhibitor at the Guild of Boston Artists, the annual exhibitions of the Ten Americans, and the Pennsylvania Academy. His best-known figure pieces are: "The Pink Feather," "The Guitar Player," "The Fur Jacket," "The New Gown," "The Blue Cup," "The Window," "La Penserosa." Ten of his works were in the retrospective exhibition of the Ten Americans, 1908. His works may be seen in the permanent collections of the Cincinnati Museum, the Boston Art Museum, the Worcester Art Museum, the Pennsylvania Academy of the Fine Arts, the Wilstach collection, Memorial Hall, Philadelphia, and the Boston Art Club. Among his last works were his portraits of Prime Minister Borden of Canada and Gen. Currie, commander of the Canadian forces in France (1919); also a noteworthy picture of the elderly negro chef of the Porcellian Club, Harvard University, in the act of bringing to the table a roast suckling pig.

De Camp was a member of the National Institute of Arts and Letters, the Portrait Painters, the Ten Americans, associate member of the National Academy of Design, member of the Philadelphia Art Club, the St. Botolph Club, and the Guild of Boston Artists. Among the honors conferred on him were three prizes from the Pennsylvania Academy of the Fine Arts, viz.: the Temple gold medal, the Beck medal, and the Lippincott prize; the gold medal of the Louisiana Purchase exposition; the gold medal of the Philadelphia Art Club; the second Clark prize of the Corcoran Gallery, Washington; and the first prize in the Philadelphia City Hall decorative competition.

[*Jos. De Camp: an Appreciation* (1924), edited by Lee W. Court, and published by the Student Asso. of the Mass. Normal Art School, contains tributes and reminiscences by Geo. R. Agassiz, Geo. H. Bartlett, and Rose V. S. Berry; a portrait of the artist, and reproductions of seven of his pictures. See also Wm. H. Downes, "Jos. De Camp and His Work," *Art and Progress*, Apr. 1913; Arthur Hoeber, "De Camp, a Master of Technique," *Arts and Decoration*, Apr. 1911; *Am. Mag. of Art*, Apr. 1923; *Art News*, Feb. 17, 1923; *Boston Herald* and *Boston Transcript*, Feb. 12, 1923.]

W. H. D.

DECATUR, STEPHEN (1752–Nov. 14, 1808), naval officer, was the son of a French seaman of the same name, who according to family tradition was a lieutenant in the French navy. Of a seafaring family originally Dutch (de Kater) but settled for a century in La Rochelle, France, the father came to Newport, R. I., about 1750 and was married there in Trinity Church, Sept. 26, 1751, to Priscilla Hill. According to the records of this church their son Stephen was baptized June 7, 1752. The family soon moved to Philadelphia, where the father died in straitened circumstances. The boy Stephen followed his father's calling and in 1774 was master of the sloop *Peggy*. He was married, Dec. 20, 1774, at the home of Capt. Moore, her guardian, to Ann Pine, of Scotch-Irish descent, daughter of John and Nancy Pine (daughter of James Bruce of Edinburgh). During the Revolution he engaged in privateering, commanding in succession, 1779–81, the galley *Retaliation*, sloop *Comet*, brig *Fair American*, and ships *Royal Louis* and *Rising Sun*. All these were Pennsylvania vessels (*Naval Records of the American Revolution*, 1906). In 1781, before his cruise to Teneriffe in the last-named vessel, he was for some months imprisoned in New York (Scharf and Westcott, *History of Philadelphia*, 1884, I, 423). Later, with the Philadelphia merchants Gurney & Smith, he was commander and part owner of the ships *Pennsylvania* and *Ariel*, taking his son Stephen, aged eight, on one voyage to Bordeaux. Commissioned captain in the United States navy, May 11, 1798, at the outbreak of hostilities with France, he put to sea in the *Delaware*, and in July captured the French privateer *Le Croyable*, renamed *Retaliation*, the first prize of the war and of the new American navy. In the *Delaware*, with two smaller vessels, he was senior officer during the winter of 1798–99 off northern Cuba. In May 1800, he arrived on the Guadeloupe station in the new frigate *Philadelphia*, and was senior officer of the squadron there until August. The *Philadelphia* captured five prizes, returning home in March 1801. Honorably discharged at the close of hostilities, and after some further connection with Gurney & Smith in Philadelphia, Decatur purchased an estate, "Millsdale," near Frankford, Pa., where he established a gunpowder works. His portrait, an apparently excellent likeness of this later period by St. Memin, pictures a frank, open-faced seaman, rougher and heavier of feature than his famous son. Four children lived to maturity: Ann, who married Lieut. James McKnight of the Marine Corps; Stephen [q.v.]; James, killed before Tripoli; and John Pine, who retired after three years' naval service in 1810. At a dinner in Philadelphia in honor of his son Stephen after the Tripolitan War, the father with mingled pride and grief responded to a toast with the words, "Our children are the property of their country." He died at "Millsdale," and, with his wife, who died four years later, lies buried in St. Peter's churchyard, Philadelphia.

[In addition to references cited, see A. S. Mackenzie, *Life of Stephen Decatur* (1846); Wm. Decatur Parsons, *The Decatur Geneal.* (1921); G. W. Allen, *Our Naval War with France* (1909).]   A. W.

DECATUR, STEPHEN (Jan. 5, 1779–Mar. 22, 1820), naval officer, came of seafaring stock, his father Stephen [q.v.] having risen to prosperity by commerce and privateering. Stephen, Jr., was born in a log cabin at Sinepuxent on the Eastern Shore of Maryland, where his mother had gone during the British occupation of Philadelphia. Brought soon afterward to the family home on South Front St., he grew up in the pleasant companionship of his elder sister Ann and his younger brothers. From childhood he was daring and a bit belligerent, if we accept stories of his dives from the tips of jib-booms and defense of his mother against a drunken ruffian at fourteen. He attended the Episcopal Academy and was for over a year at the University of Pennsylvania. Impatient of studies, he entered the employ of Gurney & Smith, a shipping firm in Philadelphia. At the outbreak of the naval war with France he was commissioned midshipman, Apr. 30, 1798, and sailed in July in the *United States,* Commodore Barry, for the West Indies, and on a second cruise in November. Aptitude and advanced age gained him quick promotion on this cruise to acting lieutenant, his commission dating May 21, 1799. Five feet ten, erect and athletic, with handsome aquiline features, large eyes, and waving brown hair, he is described by a younger officer as even then a man "more highly endowed than any other I ever knew" (Mackenzie, *post,* p. 35). During the summer of 1799, in a quarrel arising from recruiting duty in Philadelphia, he fought with the mate of a merchant vessel the first of the two duels in which he was a principal, wound-

ing his opponent in the hip. In the winter he sailed in the *United States* with the peace commissioners for France: then, after a short cruise in the *Norfolk,* he was again in the *United States* on the Guadeloupe station until the close of hostilities. There is general testimony that in these early years Decatur won the hearts of his men and maintained excellent discipline. After but three years' service, he was appointed first lieutenant of the *Essex* in Commodore Dale's squadron to Tripoli (May 1801–July 1802), and, in August 1802, to the same responsible position in the *New York,* Capt. James Barron, in the second squadron which sailed in September. On this last cruise, acting as second for Midshipman Joseph Bainbridge in a duel with the secretary to the governor of Malta, Decatur protected his principal against an expert opponent by insisting on a distance of but four paces. The secretary was killed, and the American participants were sent home (March 1803). In November 1803, Decatur was again in the Mediterranean in his first command, the *Argus,* shifting at Gibraltar to the schooner *Enterprise* (12 guns).

This was the year of action in the Tripolitan War under Commodore Preble, and of Decatur's rise to fame. Off Tripoli he captured the ketch *Mastico* (4 guns), renamed *Intrepid,* and proposed to Preble her use for destruction of the frigate *Philadelphia,* which had stranded and fallen into the hands of the Tripolitans. This exploit, in words ascribed to Nelson "the most bold and daring act of the age," was carried out on the evening of Feb. 16, 1804. With her Mediterranean rig, the ketch approached within 200 yards of the *Philadelphia* before she was hailed. A request from the Maltese pilot Catalano to moor alongside was granted, and in a moment the Americans, eighty-one all told (G. R. Clark, and others, *A Short History of the United States Navy,* 1911, p. 76), were leaping aboard the frigate. Completely surprised, the Tripolitan crew were for the most part swept overboard. Combustibles were placed and fired, and in twenty minutes the boarders, with but one man wounded, were back in the *Intrepid* and leaving the harbor, lighted by the burning frigate and under fire from shore batteries. For this daring and effective blow Decatur was promoted to post captain, his commission arriving six months later. Meantime, in the first bombardment of Tripoli on Aug. 3, 1804, with six gunboats procured from Naples, he commanded one of the two divisions. In this hard-fought action Decatur with twenty-three men boarded and cleared the decks of an enemy craft with a crew estimated at thirty-six. Learning, as he towed out his prize, that his younger brother James, in command of another boat, had been treacherously killed, he reëntered the enemy line and with but ten followers leaped aboard a second vessel. In the fierce fight that followed, Decatur, armed with a cutlass, attacked the Tripolitan leader, a huge man wielding a boarding pike. The two grappled and fell. A blow directed at Decatur by another Tripolitan was foiled by a devoted sailor, Daniel Frazier (for identity see "Reuben James or Daniel Frazier," by C. L. Lewis, *Maryland Historical Magazine,* March 1924), who received the blow on his own head and was severely wounded. Decatur finally killed his opponent with a pistol, fired from his pocket, just as the Tripolitan, who was uppermost, was aiming a blow with his knife.

These feats of dashing leadership and personal prowess made Decatur the most striking figure of the war. He commanded a division in the second bombardment on Aug. 7, 1804, and in subsequent attacks. In September, after receipt of his captain's commission, he was given command of the *Constitution,* then overhauling at Malta, but in November was shifted to the *Congress.* After peace with Tripoli in the next spring, the *Congress* was stationed for a time off Tunis, Decatur going ashore to negotiate with the Bey, and then, in September 1805, returning to America with the Tunisian envoy. Upon his arrival at Norfolk he first met his future wife, Susan, daughter of Luke Wheeler, a wealthy merchant and mayor of the city, to whom he was married Mar. 8, 1806. At this time he commanded the gunboat flotilla in the Chesapeake, and during the next winter he was head of the Norfolk Navy Yard. In 1808 he was given charge of naval forces on the southeastern coast, hoisting his flag in the *Chesapeake* and later (1810) in the *United States.* He was a member of the court martial that suspended Capt. James Barron [*q.v.*] in 1808 after the *Chesapeake-Leopard* encounter, and president of the court of inquiry in 1811 after the *President–Little Belt* affair.

Still in the United States at the outbreak of the War of 1812, Decatur joined his squadron of three vessels with those of his senior Rodgers in New York, sailing thence on June 21 for a cruise which netted only seven prizes. Again with Rodgers he left Boston Oct. 8, but this time separated from the other vessels, following his preference for independent cruising, and on the 25th, near Madeira, fought the *Macedonian,* gaining the second of the three famous frigate victories in the first year of the war. Having a slower ship but fifty per cent superiority in artillery, Decatur maneuvered with wariness and great skill, using his longer-range guns when the *Macedonian* held off to windward, and upon her final approach shooting away all three of her topmasts, with but slight injuries to his own vessel. The casualties were 104 British to 12 American. The *United States* with her prize entered New London Dec. 4, and thence proceeded to New York, where a series of festivities celebrated the victory. Attempting to get to sea through the Sound at the close of the following May, the two ships were driven by the blockading force into New London, remaining there till the close of the war. In May 1814, Decatur, taking along his devoted ship's company, was transferred to the *President* in New York, where during the summer and autumn he had charge also of the naval defenses of the port. In a heavy northeaster, on the night of Jan. 14, 1815, the *President* attempted escape to sea, but grounded for two hours on the bar with injuries which cut down her speed, and next morning off Long Island ran into the British blockading force—the razee *Majestic* (56 guns) and frigates *Endymion* (40), *Pomone* (38), and *Tenedos* (38). The chase continued till nightfall, when all the pursuers had been thrown off save the *Endymion.* With four to three superiority of broadside (Mahan, *post,* II, 401), Decatur now turned on the *Endymion* and in two hours left her stripped of sails, though meantime the *President's* crew had suffered severely from the enemy fire directed at her decks. Unfortunately at eleven P.M. the *President* again came in contact with the pursuers, and now surrendered without further firing, "with one-fifth of my crew killed and wounded, my ship crippled, and a more than four-fold force opposed to me" (Decatur's report). Only the *Pomone* seems to have been in actual range at the time, and Mahan (*post,* p. 403) remarks truly that the defense should not be called "desperate" or "heroic." Decatur himself was painfully though not seriously wounded, and the constant strain of the preceding twenty-four hours, together perhaps with a recognition that the war was virtually over (the treaty had been signed at Ghent Dec. 24), influenced his decision to avoid further bloodshed. After weathering a severe gale the prize was taken to Bermuda. Efforts to attribute the victory to the *Endymion* alone were hotly resented by the Americans, who found comfort however in Admiral Cochrane's comment, "She [the *President*] was completely mobbed." Decatur was soon paroled, landing in New London on Feb. 22. The court of inquiry ascribed his capture to injuries in crossing the

Decatur

bar, credited him with a victory over the *Endymion,* and gave him the highest praise.

Offered by the secretary almost his own choice of future duties, he selected command of the first squadron of nine ships which sailed from New York, May 20, 1815, to settle with Algiers for injuries which had persisted since 1812. After an extraordinarily fast passage, the squadron reached Gibraltar June 15. On the 17th it captured the Algerian flagship *Mashuda,* on the 19th drove another enemy vessel ashore, and on the 28th was off the port of Algiers. Decatur sent officers ashore giving the Dey choice of war or peace on American terms. Two days later, aboard the flagship *Guerrière,* a treaty was negotiated, ending tribute and requiring full payment for injuries to Americans. This was sent ashore for the Dey's signature. No truce was granted, and when in the interval an Algerian vessel approached the harbor Decatur was prevented from attack only by the hasty appearance of a boat with a white flag, the pre-arranged signal that the treaty was signed. On this occasion the Commodore wore full uniform, his "splendid figure" enhanced by "laced coat and hat, tight cassimere pantaloons, and long boots . . . bound at the top with gold lace and having tassels of gold in front" (Mackenzie, p. 267). This is the costume of the Sully portrait in the New York City Hall. The squadron proceeded to Tunis and then to Tripoli, exacting payment for injuries suffered during the British war. When Bainbridge arrived with a second squadron the work was already done, a result in large measure due to Decatur's energy and prestige with the Barbary powers. Fêtes and dinners again greeted his return. It was to a toast at one of these dinners in Norfolk that Decatur made his familiar response: "Our country! In her intercourse with foreign nations may she always be in the right; but our country, right or wrong."

From November 1815 until his death Decatur served with Rodgers and Porter on the Board of Navy Commissioners. In this administrative work, Porter (*Memoir,* p. 277) declares he was "arbitrary" and "interfering," but he could ably defend his views, as evidenced by his well-argued report favoring Norfolk as chief base in the Chesapeake (Mackenzie, Appendix, p. 386). On Oct. 10, 1818, he was second to his close friend Perry in a duel with a marine officer at Weehawken. Prize money had brought him considerable wealth, which he invested largely in Washington realty (*Records of the Columbia Historical Society,* XXVIII, 4), building his own home on President's (now Lafayette) Square. The Decaturs were prominent in Wash-

ington society. Childless themselves, they were devoted to the daughters of Decatur's widowed sister, Mrs. McKnight. Decatur's death was an aftermath of the suspension of Capt. Barron. As Navy Commissioner he vigorously opposed Barron's efforts to secure reinstatement, on the ground that Barron had not made proper efforts to reënter the service in 1812. A heated correspondence, in which Decatur was correct though not conciliatory, led to Barron's challenge. The meeting was at Bladensburg, near Washington. Decatur in deference to his opponent's faulty eyesight selected the shortest distance, eight paces, and stated privately that he would aim low to avoid mortal injury. At the first exchange both fell, Barron wounded in the thigh and Decatur shot through the body. The intense feeling of the time was expressed in the words of the *National Intelligencer,* "Mourn Columbia! for one of thy brightest stars has set, a son without fear and without reproach." All official Washington attended the stately funeral on Mar. 24. The body was placed in a vault on the Joel Barlow estate near Washington, but in 1846 was removed to St. Peter's churchyard, Philadelphia, and placed beside the bodies of Decatur's parents.

Decatur's attractive personal qualities are best seen in the devotion of his crews, and in his genial relations with fellow officers. Not a student or reader, he had a mechanical bent, shown in experiments with shells and in the invention of a device for making horseshoes, and a lively, intelligent mind in conversation, as suggested by the poet Coleridge's citation of a remark of Decatur's—on the danger to national unity in the rapid expansion of his country—made years before in Malta. A stickler for honor, passionate for glory, he was neither braggart nor bully. Commanding only in single-ship actions, he attained not quite the first rank among American naval leaders, but has remained a popular favorite through his stainless character, winning personality, and the brilliant exploits of Tripolitan days.

[The biographies by Benj. Folsom (*A Compilation of Biog. Sketches of Distinguished Officers of the Am. Navy,* 1814), and S. Putnam Waldo (*The Life and Character of Stephen Decatur,* 1821) were superseded by Capt. A. S. Mackenzie's *Life of Stephen Decatur* (1846), which has remained standard, more trustworthy than the shorter life, *Stephen Decatur* (1900), by C. T. Brady. Aside from naval histories, especially G. W. Allen, *Our Navy and the Barbary Corsairs* (1905), A. T. Mahan, *Sea Power in its Relations to the War of 1812* (1905), and Theodore Roosevelt, *The Naval War of 1812* (1882) and sources there cited, material on special points may be found in *Correspondence between . . . Decatur and . . . Barron* (Washington, 1820), *Docs. Relative to the Claims of Mrs. Decatur* (for *Philadelphia* prize money) (Georgetown, 1826); *Memoir of Commodore D. Porter* (Albany, 1875), pp. 416–18 (on Decatur-Barron duel); and "De-

189

catur and Coleridge," by C. G. Calkins, *Proc. U. S. Naval Inst.,* XXXIV (1908), 917.]   A. W.

DE COPPET, EDWARD J. (May 28, 1855–Apr. 30, 1916), banker, patron of music, was the son of Louis de Coppet, a Swiss who came to America in 1828, and married Juliet Minerva Weston of Connecticut. Edward was educated in Switzerland, and on his return to America as a young man succeeded his father as a banker in New York, eventually founding the Stock Exchange house of De Coppet & Doremus. So passionately was he devoted to the art of tone in one of its noblest manifestations, the chamber ensemble, that finance might be called his avocation and music his profession. A cultivated Mæcenas in the highest sense of the word, his devotion to music was shared by his wife, an excellent pianist; and it was in the sympathetic atmosphere of a home where the cult of the string ensemble (as of the piano trio, quartet, and quintet) was supreme, that the central interest of his life took form, which always will be associated with his name. His fine impersonal desire to advance the art he loved raised his efforts above the status of a mere personal amusement. It is only just to regard him as an artist whose masterpiece was the Flonzaley Quartet. As Daniel Gregory Mason has said, "He never supposed that, as do those who aspire to be patrons of art less for the sake of the art than for that of patronage, that he could create what he was after by the simple process of signing checks. His method was that of all genuine art: indefatigable experiment . . . extending through a long series of years." The books in which are recorded the programs, participants, and guests of all his musical gatherings for thirty years, from Oct. 21, 1886, to Apr. 21, 1916, record one thousand and fifty-four meetings for chamber music in his home. The Flonzaley Quartet which, though long self-supporting, was Edward de Coppet's great achievement, was founded in 1904. It represented an attempt to weld four artists of superior merit into a homogeneous artistic whole, by making it financially possible for them to devote their entire time and effort to the development of a perfect string ensemble. The members of the original Quartet (Messrs. Betti, Pochon, Ara, and Archambeau) entered with zeal into the spirit of the esthetic adventure. It took the name of the "Flonzaley Quartet" from the Villa Flonzaley, near Vevey, on Lake Geneva, the De Coppet summer home in Switzerland; and passed in time from playing for the private entertainment of its patron and guests, and in public concerts made possible by his generosity, to independent existence as a self-supporting musical organiza-

tion whose primacy in its particular field was still generally acknowledged after a quarter of a century. To thousands of American music-lovers it has revealed at their best the choicest works of ancient and modern string quartet literature. Edward de Coppet died a few hours after listening to the ensemble he had created play one of the later Beethoven quartets. In an "Appreciation" written by his friend Ara, the latter said: "Sustained by Beethoven's sublime thought, whose beauties he had lucidly analyzed an hour before his death, he passed suddenly and painlessly away . . . and this death, so serene and simple, seemed the inevitable epilogue of a life like his, altogether expended in the pursuit of goodness and the love of beauty."

[Of modest and retiring disposition Edward de Coppet was averse to publicity. The best idea of the man and his work is given by Daniel Gregory Mason, "Edward J. de Coppet," *Musical Quart.,* Oct. 1916; *Musical America,* May 6, 1916, the *Bull. of New Music,* Oct. 1916, and the *N. Y. Times,* May 2, 1916, contain obituaries.]   F. H. M.

DE COSTA, BENJAMIN FRANKLIN (July 10, 1831–Nov. 4, 1904), clergyman and writer, was born in Charlestown, Mass. The surname was brought to Boston from England in 1699 by Isaac De Costa, a Huguenot of Portuguese ancestry who had been driven from France by the revocation of the Edict of Nantes. Beginning with Isaac, the Massachusetts line found wives in New England families of English descent. Ezekiel Carver De Costa, fourth generation from Isaac, married Elizabeth Jackson, and Benjamin Franklin De Costa was the fifth of their six children. In 1856 he graduated from the Biblical Institute at Concord, N. H. In 1857 he entered the Episcopal ministry and served for three years as rector in Massachusetts, one year in North Adams, and two years in Newton Lower Falls. From 1861 to 1863 he was chaplain of Massachusetts troops in the Civil War, and special correspondent of the Charlestown *Advertiser.* He also wrote some letters for other newspapers. Leaving the army, he settled in New York and engaged in editorial and historical work. The *Christian Times* (New York) carried his name as editor from Dec. 22, 1864, to Mar. 29, 1866, and he seems to have served for about nine months afterward its continuator, the *Episcopalian* (New York and Philadelphia). Fruits of historical research began to appear in 1864, and eventually reached about fifty titles. He was married in 1866 to Harriet Cooper Spencer, and with her traveled extensively (especially after 1873), lingering with special interest in places where he might collect historical material and crossing the ocean twenty-two times (*New York Tribune,* Aug. 24, 1899).

His historical publications relate chiefly to early American discovery and exploration, including cartology, and most of them are brief, ranging from eight to twenty-five pages. A considerable number consist of documents with editorial introductions and notes. His *Pre-Columbian Discovery of America by the Northmen* (1868, revised in 1890 and again in 1901) presented in this way the case for the Northmen and brought together the largest collection of sagas available in English before the appearance of Reeves's *Finding of Wineland the Good* (1890). A better piece of editing, however, is found in his edition of Bishop William White's *Memoirs of the Protestant Episcopal Church* (1880). Several of his works show an amiable weakness for rescuing characters and events from the neglect or disparagement of historians. The service performed for the Northmen was extended to Verrazano, Champdoré, John Walker, and others, and to Welsh and Irish discoverers of America.

In 1881 De Costa became rector of the Church of St. John the Evangelist in New York City. The duties of his office were arduous and were made more so by his activity in social-uplift movements. He organized the first American branch of the White Cross and wrote a history of the movement (*The White Cross: Its Origin and Progress,* 1887). He frequently addressed working men, and was a member of the Knights of Labor. He was one of the charter members and first president of a church association for the advancement of labor. He was one of the organizers, and for years secretary, of the Church Temperance Society. He still, however, found time for historical work; in 1881 he went as a delegate to the International Congress of Americanists at Madrid; he was for a time (1882–83) editor of the *Magazine of American History*; he contributed to Justin Winsor's *Narrative and Critical History of America* two chapters, including the critical essays on the sources—the chapter on "Norumbega and its English Explorers" in vol. III (1885), and the chapter on "Jacques Cartier and his Successors" in vol. IV (1885). In 1899 he became involved in the controversy over the ordination of Prof. C. A. Briggs [*q.v.*], late of Union Theological Seminary, as a priest in the Episcopal Church. De Costa, taking strong ground against the higher criticism of the Bible, led the opposition. Briggs was ordained in May. In August De Costa offered his resignation as rector. In October he withdrew from the Episcopal ministry and was deposed by Bishop Potter. In December he became a member of the Roman Catholic Church. The death of his wife in 1901 invited a further step; he prepared for the priesthood, and in November 1903 was ordained in Italy by the Bishop of Fiesole.

[For genealogy see *De Costa Family Chart* (1876), and references in De Costa's memorial sketches of Wm. Hickling De Costa (1878), Elizabeth De Costa (1880), and Mary Rebecca De Costa (1896). For his travels, see his memorial sketch, *In Memoriam: Harriet Cooper Spencer De Costa* (1901); for activities after 1864, the files of the *New-Eng. Hist. and Geneal. Reg.*; for his change of faith, the *N. Y. Tribune,* May 22, Aug. 24, Oct. 10–23, 1899, and Nov. 30, 1903; further clues are found in his article, "The Bible in the Life, Thought, and Homes of the People," *Catholic World,* Sept. 1900, and in his *Whither Goest Thou?* (1902). In 1899 he published a bibliography of his writings, *The Titles of 55 Separately Printed Works, with some other Matters, Covering a Half Century.*]

H. J.

DEEMER, HORACE EMERSON (Sept. 24, 1858–Feb. 26, 1917), Iowa jurist, was born in Bourbon, Ind., the eldest son of John A. and Elizabeth (Erwin) Deemer. His paternal ancestors emigrated from Holland to Pennsylvania after the Thirty Years' War, and his mother's family were Scotch-Irish. On both sides his ancestors were opponents of slavery. His early church associations were with the Friends and Baptists. The family moved from Indiana to a farm near West Liberty, Iowa in 1866. The son attended the public schools and was a member of the first class graduating from the local high school. Later he entered the State University and graduated from the law school in June 1879. He is said to have been the first college baseball pitcher to use the curved ball, having developed the method from reading accounts of big league players. During all the time that he was getting his education, he paid his own way. Then, for a while, he worked with his father in the lumber business, and, incidentally, learned the carpenter's trade.

After his admission to the bar, he entered a law office in Lincoln, Nebr. He remained there only a few months and, on his return to Iowa, he formed a partnership with a classmate, Joseph M. Junkin of Red Oak. The firm was successful from the beginning and it continued until his elevation to the bench in 1886, when he was still only twenty-eight years old. Four years earlier he had married Jeannette Gibson of Red Oak, July 12, 1882. He served very successfully as district judge for more than seven years, until he was appointed to the supreme court in 1894. He remained on the bench of the highest state court up to the time of his death in 1917. His service of twenty-three years constituted the longest continuous tenure of any judge in that court. By rotation he was chief justice in 1898, 1904, 1910, and 1915. His opinions numbered about two thousand. Many of them were in cases involving the construction of anti-trust statutes; others involved problems of constitutionality, such as the constitutionality of the mulct law, of the party-wall statute, of damages in delayed death messages, of the anti-cigarette act, and of various police measures, including the regulation of the use of oleomargarine. His decisions gave ample evidence of his legal knowledge, his sense of justice, and his ability as a writer. He was twice considered for appointment to the Supreme Court of the United States, and he received the indorsement of the lawyers of his own state and of the whole country.

Besides his legal decisions, which comprise his most important work, Deemer probably gave most time and thought to his duties as trustee of the State Library, of the governing board of which he was *ex officio* a member. For many years he was chairman of the book committee, and under his guidance a great reference library was developed. With Judge Kinne he had an important part in the establishment of traveling libraries. From 1895 to 1904 he was a lecturer in the law department of the state university. His work on *Iowa Pleading and Practice, Law and Equity with Forms* was published in three volumes in 1914, and a revised edition in two volumes was issued in 1927. In 1911 he received votes as a successor to Jonathan P. Dolliver in the United States Senate. He consented to be a candidate only on the understanding that it would help to "adjust serious differences within the Republican party." Johnson Brigham, librarian of the Iowa State Library, in a tribute to Deemer after his death, described him as "a man of rare capacity and unbounded desire for service. He had a genius for friendship and yet was wholly free from the petty arts of a 'jollier.' Absolutely honest himself, he could brook no dishonesty in others."

[*Proc. Iowa State Bar Asso.* (1917), XXIII, 116–22; *Iowa Jour. of Hist. and Politics,* XV, 319–20; E. H. Stiles, *Recollections and Sketches of Notable Lawyers and Public Men of Early Iowa* (1916), pp. 953–54; *Des Moines Reg.,* Feb. 27, 28, 1917; B. F. Gue, *Hist. of Iowa* (1903), IV, 70 (portrait).]

F. E. H.

DEEMS, CHARLES FORCE (Dec. 4, 1820–Nov. 18, 1893), clergyman, author, son of George W. and Mary (Roberts) Deems, was born in Baltimore and died in New York City. His father, whose ancestral name was De Heems, was of Dutch extraction; his mother was the daughter of Zachary Roberts, a Methodist minister. Both were extremely pious. Their son, a melancholy boy, oppressed by the

sinful state of man, was at about thirteen soundly converted—not, however, without striving, for he had made "temperance" lectures repeatedly to that end, and had prayed out of doors before spectators in front of a little altar improvised of stones. His mother died in 1834, and he was sent under the suzerainty of a maiden aunt to the Methodist Dickinson College, to study law. He soon determined to enter the ministry. Following his graduation in 1839, he preached in New York, at some of "the most aristocratic worshiping places of Methodism" (Deems, *Autobiography,* p. 61), but he was soon "located" in Asbury, N. J. Here he renewed his acquaintance with Annie Disosway, whom he had met in New York, and whom, on June 20, 1843, he married. In 1840 he went to North Carolina as an agent for the American Bible Society. From 1842 to 1848 he was professor of humanistic studies in the University of North Carolina, and during 1849 of natural sciences in Randolph-Macon College, Va. During 1850–54 he was president of the Greensboro (N. C.) Woman's College. From 1854 to 1859 he was actively engaged in the ministry, busying himself—after his life-long habit—not only with the routine duties of his profession but with the editing of many theological and semi-theological pronouncements. During 1859–60 he was in charge of a boarding-school at Wilson, N. C. He believed that secession was inexpedient, but once the Civil War began, he conducted himself as a loyal Carolinian—to the point of losing his eldest son in battle on the Southern side. Late in 1865 he changed his residence to New York, at first to edit a paper which he called *The Watchman,* but soon to begin preaching—independently—in an auditorium hired by himself. As late as 1866 he was mentioned in connection with a bishopric in the Southern Methodist Church, but in spite of his own persistent orthodoxy, the ecclesiastical body of which he was head—The Church of the Strangers—had no ties with any recognized religious denomination. His reputation as a preacher and author, reënforced by his intimacy with people of wealth and influence, soon made him one of the conspicuous men of his environment. Among his many books, the ponderous biography, *Jesus* (1872), was perhaps the one to cost him most effort in the writing, but the *Scotch Verdict in re Evolution* (1885) was probably most widely read. It was for him that Cornelius Vanderbilt first violated his resolve against philanthropy by presenting him with a church (1870) and it seems that it was somewhat through his influence that a group of Southerners—with whom he always retained a kind of sentimental identity—procured the million dollars which enabled them (1873) to establish Vanderbilt University. In 1880 he visited Europe and Palestine. On his way home, at a meeting of the Victoria Institute in London, he conceived the idea of organizing an American Institute of Christian Philosophy. This was accomplished in 1881, and the Institute continued in operation till two years after the death of the founder. Then its resources were combined to create the Deems Lectureship of Philosophy in the University of the City of New York. Except for his final year, when he was incapacitated by illness, he spent the last part of his life in the zealous pursuit of his ministry.

[Sources not already mentioned: C. F. Deems, *Autobiog. and Memoir by his Sons* (1897); *Dr. Deems' Sermons* (1885); K. P. Battle, *Hist. of the Univ. of N. C.* (1907); R. Irby, *Hist. of Randolph-Macon Coll.* (1898); C. F. Himes, *Dickinson Coll.* (1879); *Cat. Officers and Students Dickinson Coll.*, 1840; *Appletons' Annual Cyc.* (1893); *N. Y. Times*, Nov. 19, 1893; A. D. H. Smith, *Commodore Vanderbilt* (1927).]

J. D. W.

DEERE, JOHN (Feb. 7, 1804–May 17, 1886), manufacturer, was born at Rutland, Vt., the third son of William Rinold and Sarah (Yates) Deere. His father was a native of England, while his mother was born in Connecticut, the daughter of a British army officer who served through the entire Revolutionary War and subsequently settled in Connecticut. John had the usual country boy's experiences, attending the common schools of his native town and acquiring an ordinary education. At the age of seventeen he started to learn the blacksmith's trade, beginning as an apprentice to Capt. Benjamin Lawrence of Middlebury, Vt. This apprenticeship required four full years but at the end of that time Deere had fully mastered his trade, proving it during the succeeding twelve years by the admirable work which he did in various towns of his native state. In 1837, when thirty-three years old, he went West, taking his tool kit with him. He headed for Illinois and eventually settled at Grand Detour in that state, where he immediately opened a blacksmith shop, sending back for his wife and children in the following year. His skill was quickly recognized and the pioneer farmers about him kept him and his forge busy hammering out lap rings for chains, welding clevises, and laying their plowshares. His contacts with the farmers early revealed the fact that the plow brought from the East was most unsatisfactory for working the prairie soil of the new West, and Deere immediately began experimenting on plow improvements. Within a year three new plows were made by Deere and his partner, Maj.

Andrus. These plows had a wrought-iron landside and standard, and for the former wooden mouldboard there were substituted a mouldboard and share of sheet steel cut from an old sawmill saw and bent to shape over a log shaped for the purpose, and with the beam and handles of white oak rails. While the excellent work which these three plows did aroused considerable interest and they were readily sold by Andrus and Deere, the latter continued experimenting, particularly in an effort to determine the curvature of the steel mouldboard that would be most efficacious for scouring not only new land but old and sticky bottom land as well. Ten improved plows were made in 1839, and in 1840 a second anvil was added to the shop and forty plows were produced. The business continued to develop until, in 1846, the annual output had been increased to approximately a thousand plows. About this time Deere became convinced that Grand Detour was poorly situated in regard to transportation and sources of power and raw materials, so he sold out his interest to Andrus and moved to Moline, Ill., where he organized a new company. He had concluded, too, that the greatest obstacle to further plow improvements was the quality of the steel plates then available. He knew the kind of steel he needed, but found that it could be obtained only in England. Accordingly he ordered a quantity of English steel sufficient for fifty plows which he made in his new plant in 1847 and distributed throughout the country in order to test out his theories. The experiment proved entirely successful, whereupon he opened negotiations in Pittsburgh for the manufacture of steel plate and brought about the first manufacture of plow steel in the United States. In J. M. Swank's *History of the Manufacture of Iron in All Ages* (1884, p. 297) is written, "The first slab of cast plow steel ever rolled in the United States was rolled by William Woods, at the steel works of Jones & Quigg, in 1846, and shipped to John Deere of Moline, Ill." There is some question about Swank's date, but the event undoubtedly occurred *circa* 1846 or 1847, and by 1857 Deere's annual output of plows had risen to 10,000. In 1858 he took his son Charles into partnership, and five years later, his son-in-law Stephen H. Velie, and in 1868 the firm was incorporated under the name of Deere & Company, with John Deere president; his son, vice-president and general manager; and Velie, secretary, the business having by that time expanded to include the manufacture of cultivators and other allied products known as "plow goods." Deere continued as active president until his last illness, when his son succeeded him. He was twice married: first, on Jan. 28, 1827, to Damaris Lamb of Granville, Vt., who died at Moline Feb. 17, 1865; and second, in 1867, to Lucinda Lamb, a younger sister of his first wife.

[R. L. Ardrey, *Am. Ag. Implements* (1894); Newton Bateman and Paul Selby, *Hist. Encyc. of Ill. and Hist. of Rock Island County* (2 vols., 1914); U. S. Nat. Museum correspondence with Deere & Co.] C. W. M.

DEERFOOT (1828–Jan. 18, 1897), Indian runner, was born on the Cattaragus Reservation, Erie County, N. Y., and died on the same reservation. A Seneca of the Snipe Clan, his real Indian name was Ha-ga-sa-do-ni, and his English name, Lewis Bennett. The name "Deerfoot" was assumed for professional purposes. Under the old Indian system of training, he early developed extraordinary ability as a distance runner. He competed successfully in many races in western New York and Pennsylvania, but he was most remarkable for his endurance. According to the testimony of several old Indians he could run so long a time that he frequently exhausted horses, and it is tradition that one of them died after having followed him for thirty or forty miles. Attracting the attention of promoters of pedestrianism, Bennett was taken to England in the summer of 1861 and matched, under the name "Deerfoot" against the leading English distance runners. Among these were such famous champions as John White, "the Gateshead Clipper," Edward Mills of East London, and W. Lang of Middlesbrough. By sporting experts the Indian was conceded little chance. But though Deerfoot lost his first race, he soon turned the tables and in a series of stirring contests, defeated practically every notable British distance runner (*The Times,* London, Sept. 24, 1861, p. 10; Oct. 3, 1861, p. 7; Oct. 15, 1861, p. 12 and *passim*). His strongest rival was Mills, with whom in an eight-mile match for £200 at Hackney-Wick, he ran a dead heat (*Ibid.,* Dec. 17, 1861, p. 4). During 1862–63 he continued his English career. His greatest single achievement was the record for twelve miles, made in a race at the Crystal Palace on Apr. 3, 1863, when he ran the distance in one hour, two minutes, and two and a half seconds, though he lost the race by a half yard to Lang who had a handicap of 100 yards (*New York Clipper Almanac,* 1876, p. 53). He made other records of ten miles in fifty-one minutes, twenty-nine seconds; of twelve miles in one hour, five minutes, and six seconds; and of eleven and a half miles in one hour less six seconds. Considering the relatively crude condition of tracks

in his day these were unusual performances, but the Senecas have always insisted that Deerfoot while at home, under the strict conditions of Indian training, had far surpassed these exploits. He was a remarkably handsome Indian, standing five feet, eleven and a half inches and weighing 160 pounds. He usually appeared on the track clad in a wolfskin with feathers in his head-band and tinkling bells around his waist (*The Times,* London, Oct. 3, 1861, p. 7). English critics were astonished at the curious loping stride of the Indian runner in contrast with the fine track "style" of their own distance men, but Deerfoot finished most of his races quite fresh. He enjoyed unbounded popularity in the British Isles, being greeted by great crowds at railway stations and receiving ovations on the track. After one of his races the Prince of Wales shook hands with him and gave him a purse. He sometimes capitalized the fact that he was an Indian by curious actions like giving two huge leaps in the air after winning a ten-mile race at Portsmouth and uttering a war-whoop to frighten from the track Irish spectators who had invaded the course before the finish. His career would no doubt have attracted more attention in the United States had it not come at the time of the Civil War.

[Printed sources of information are scanty. Deerfoot's races in England can be followed in the London *Times.* Comment is also given in the contemporary New York sporting paper, *Wilkes' Spirit of the Times.* The recollection of Deerfoot among the Seneca Indians has been furnished the writer by Arthur C. Parker, Director of the Rochester Municipal Museum, himself a Seneca.] E. P. T.

DEERING, NATHANIEL (June 25, 1791–Mar. 25, 1881), author, editor, and dramatist, was the son of James Deering (1766–1850), and the grandson of Nathaniel Deering (1737–1795), an influential merchant, shipbuilder, landowner, and man of affairs during the formative days of Portland, Me., where the younger Nathaniel was born. He was a descendant in the eighth generation from George Deering, who emigrated from England to Maine in the early part of the seventeenth century. His mother was Almira, daughter of Enoch Ilsley, at one time a selectman and town treasurer of Portland. After studying first at a private school in Portland, and following a course at Phillips Academy in Exeter, N. H., he went to Harvard College, from which he was graduated in 1810, the fourteenth in a class of sixty-three. Upon his graduation he entered a counting-house in Portland with the intention of becoming a merchant, but after a short experience in business, and in compliance with the wish of his father, he studied law and was admitted to the bar in 1815. For a time he practised his profession in Skowhegan. Returning to Portland, where his beginnings in authorship and journalism were made as a member of a literary club and as editor of a manuscript paper, he gradually turned his professional interests toward books and writing, eventually becoming editor of the *Independent Statesman,* a political paper which supported the candidacy of Henry Clay for the presidency. At one time he was in popular demand as a Fourth of July orator. During the greater part of his life he was an assiduous contributor of prose and verse, usually unsigned, to newspapers and other publications in Portland and elsewhere. Attracting the attention of William Cullen Bryant, he was offered a position on the staff of the New York *Evening Post,* but declined it. He wrote several plays, among them, *Carabasset, or the Last of the Norridgewocks,* a tragedy in five acts dealing with the incidents of the massacre of the Rasle and the Norridgewock Indians by the British in 1720; *The Clairvoyant,* a comedy which was acted in Boston and Portland; and *Bozzaris,* another tragedy, which was published in 1851. He had a little musical talent; wrote ballads and political songs, and composed some church music. In October 1824 he married Anna Margaret Holwell, a daughter of Maj. John Z. Holwell of the British Army. They had nine children, four sons and five daughters. Deering's last years were spent in retirement on the family estate of two hundred acres on the outskirts of Portland. He was the last survivor of a large family of brothers and sisters, the youngest of the latter being the wife of William Pitt Fessenden [*q.v.*].

[H. C. Williams, *Biog. Encyc. of Me.* (1885); *Biog. Rev. Cumberland County, Me.* (1896); brief obituary in *Daily Eastern Argus* (Portland, Me.), Mar. 26, 1881.]   E. F. E.

DEERING, WILLIAM (Apr. 25, 1826–Dec. 9, 1913), manufacturer, the son of James and Eliza (Moore) Deering, both of Puritan descent, was born in South Paris, Me., where his father was engaged in woolen cloth manufacture. He was educated in the public schools and later attended Readfield Seminary, from which he graduated in 1844. He then began the study of medicine with Dr. Barrows of Fryeburg, Me., but his father persuaded him to enter his manufacturing company in which for several years he acted as manager. On Oct. 31, 1849, he was married to Abby Reed Barbour, daughter of Charles and Joanna (Cobb) Barbour. During the next few years he was interested in western farming lands, but, on the death of his wife

in 1856, he returned to South Paris, where he opened a dry-goods store. He was married to Clara Hamilton, on Dec. 15, 1856. After a number of years he organized a wholesale commission dry-goods house under the firm name of Deering, Milliken & Company in 1865 with headquarters at Portland, Me., and offices in New York City. He continued as its directing head for five years acquiring in the interval the executive ability and foresight which enabled him subsequently to take a leading part in the development of America's agricultural machinery business. In the meantime one of his old Maine friends, a Methodist preacher named Elijah H. Gammon, who had been for many years in Illinois, became interested in the manufacture of agricultural machinery, particularly in the hand-binding harvester of the brothers Charles W. and William W. Marsh. Gammon purchased the rights to manufacture the Marsh harvester and aroused Deering's interest in the project to such an extent that he gave up his wholesale business and went to Plano, Ill., to join Gammon as a partner. Deering invested $40,000 in the company, and, owing to his persistent and tireless management, the harvester trade was pushed out into channels that it had hitherto been unable to reach. A year later the manufacture of the Gordon wire binder was undertaken much against the advice of his partner, but Deering seemed to see more clearly than any one else the demand for a harvesting machine with automatic binding. Again, in 1879, when he became sole owner of the business, Deering made another bold move by beginning the manufacture of a twine binder after the invention of John F. Appleby, and with the jeers of his competitors ringing in his ears he built and moved to a new and larger establishment at Chicago. The venture almost failed, because of the difficulty of finding a twine adapted for use on the binder. Deering at last persuaded Edwin H. Fitler, a large Philadelphia rope manufacturer, to undertake experiments for him, and Fitler eventually produced a single strand manila twine that made the binder successful. From 1880 the business progressed steadily. Year after year the shops were enlarged and new departments added until it became the largest agricultural-implement factory in the world, employing in the neighborhood of 9,000 operatives. Deering had the business incorporated in 1883 under the name William Deering & Company, having taken into the organization in 1880 his two sons, Charles W. and James E., and, subsequently, his son-in-law, Richard F. Howe. Later the name was changed to the Deering Manfacturing Company. In 1901 Deering retired and in 1902 the corporation was merged with the International Harvester Company of Chicago.

Although his knowledge of public affairs was recognized, Deering's only public service was in the councils of Governors Chamberlain and Perham of Maine in 1870–73. He was a director of the Metropolitan National Bank of Chicago and president of the board of trustees of Northwestern University at the time of his death. His gifts to educational and charitable institutions were many, especially to Northwestern University, the Garrett Biblical Institute, and Wesley Hospital, all of Chicago. He also built and endowed the Deering School at Lake Bluff, near Chicago, for the accommodation of the orphanage there. He died at his winter home at Cocoanut Grove, Fla., survived by his wife and two sons.

[*Wm. Deering* (Chicago, privately printed, 1914); *Wm. Deering* (n.d.); E. L. Barker, *Creeds of Great Business Men* (1913); Robt. L. Ardrey, *Am. Agric. Implements* (1894); *Chicago Evening Post, Chicago American,* and the *Portland Evening Express and Daily Advertiser,* all Dec. 10, 1913; *Chicago Daily Tribune, Daily Inter Ocean* (Chicago), and *Farm Implement News* (Chicago), all Dec. 11, 1913; *Implement Age* (Springfield, Ohio), Dec. 20, 1913; *Custer County Chief* (Broken Bow, Nebr.), Dec. 26, 1913.] C.W.M.

DE FONTAINE, FELIX GREGORY (1834–Dec. 11, 1896), journalist, author, was born in Boston, Mass., and died in Columbia, S. C. His father, Louis Antoine De Fontaine, a French nobleman attached to the court of Charles X, accompanied that monarch into exile in Edinburgh. In the latter part of 1830 he came to America, and about two years later he was married to a woman whose surname was Allen, said to have been of the family of Ethan Allen. Their son Felix was educated by private tutors. He was in Washington in 1859, acting as reporter in the notorious trial of a congressman for shooting a district attorney. About 1860, he married Georgia Vigneron Moore, daughter of the Rev. George W. Moore of Charleston, S. C. At about this time he founded in Columbia the *Daily South Carolinian.* In February 1861, the *New York Herald* published his discussion of anti-slavery agitation and of conditions then obtaining in the South. These articles, completely Southern in view-point, soon appeared in a booklet, *A History of American Abolitionism together with a History of the Southern Confederacy* (1861). At the bombardment of Fort Sumter, his friendship with Gen. Beauregard resulted in his being able to send out to the *Herald* the first account of that event to appear in the Northern press. In May 1861, as a military correspondent with the rank of major, he

went to the front with the first South Carolina regiment. He continued in this capacity throughout the war, signing all that he wrote, "Personne." In 1864, he published under this name his *Marginalia,* a reprint of newspaper clippings selected from various sources, with the one fervent purpose of exalting the South and debasing the North. His press was burned in the fire that occurred when Sherman entered Columbia. In November 1867 he was secretary of a convention in Columbia, held to consider the abuses of carpet-bag rule. Soon afterward he went to live in New York. For three years he was managing editor of the *Telegram,* and for the remainder of his active life he was the financial editor and later the dramatic and art editor of the *Herald.* He did a considerable amount of writing aside from his routine work for his paper. "Shoulder to Shoulder, Reminiscences of Confederate Camps and Fields" appeared in the (Charleston) *XIX Century,* June 1869–January 1870. In 1873 he published his ponderous *Cyclopedia of the Best Thoughts of Charles Dickens.* A second edition, called *The Fireside Dickens,* appeared in 1883. In 1886 he published *De Fontaine's Condensed Long-Hand and Rapid-Writer's Companion.* At the time of his death, he was preparing from documents which fell into his hands early in 1865 a book on the missing records of the Confederate cabinet.

[F. G. De Fontaine, *Trial of the Hon. Daniel E. Sickles* (1859); W. H. De Fontaine, letter to the writer, Jan. 30, 1928; Y. Snowden, *Hist. of S. C.* (1920), II, 884; *Appletons' Annual Cyc.,* 1896; *Charleston News and Courier,* Dec. 12, 1896.] J.D.W.

DE FOREST, DAVID CURTIS (Jan. 10, 1774–Feb. 22, 1825), merchant and Argentine consul, was born at Huntington, Conn., the eldest son of Benjamin and Mehitable (Curtis) De Forest. His father, a prosperous farmer, came of a Walloon Protestant family, whose founder in this country, Isaac, emigrated from Amsterdam to New York in 1636. David was a robust and adventurous boy who ran away from home and followed the sea until 1795, when he invested his small patrimony in business at Bridgeport. In the following year his store was robbed and the firm failed. From March 1799 to June 1800 he was a lieutenant in the army which the United States raised when war with France impended. He then returned to the sea as officer on a vessel which he quitted on the coast of Patagonia late in 1801. Thence he went to Brazil, and by land back to the La Plata River, studying carefully commercial possibilities and languages. Settling at Buenos Aires, he established there the first permanent American commercial house. Despite British attacks and generally unsettled political conditions, his business so prospered that by 1809 he was wealthy. A change of viceroys in that year drove him into an exile which he improved by returning to Huntington and marrying on Oct. 6, 1811, Julia Wooster, a blonde beauty less than sixteen years of age. Permitted in 1812 to return to Buenos Aires, he had hardly reopened his establishment when the war with England forced him to close it again. By the autumn of 1814 he was once more extremely active in commerce. Dispensing open-handed hospitality, he played the part of merchant prince and through a friend who was secretary of the treasury he obtained much government business. When Buenos Aires revolted against Spain in 1815, he received letters of marque for privateers from the revolutionary authorities. These he gave to American shipowners in return for a commission on prizes and cleared over one hundred thousand dollars. In April 1817 he sent his family home and a year later followed them, after presenting his large ranch to the new republic. With him he brought a fortune and a commission as consul general to the United States from the nascent Argentine Republic. Building a large mansion at New Haven, he lived on a generous scale and devoted his time to the interests of his adopted country. On May 7, 1818, he interviewed Secretary of State John Quincy Adams, asking for an exequatur as consul general. This was refused, as it implied official recognition of Argentine independence at a time when Adams was negotiating with Spain for the cession of Florida. Undismayed by the secretary's frigid attitude, De Forest continued to importune both Adams and President Monroe for recognition, presenting "cunning and deceptive" (Adams, *Memoirs,* IV, 223) notes which provided Henry Clay with ammunition against the administration when referred to Congress in January 1819. His activities in Washington earned him a reputation as "one of the most troublesome of the South American agents" (Adams, *Ibid.,* IV, 472), while his lavish annual celebration in New Haven of the Argentine Independence Day kept his mission well advertised. Though the recognition of the new South American nations was decided in March 1822, he was refused an exequatur a month later on the ground that a new commission was necessary, while his claim to be received as diplomatic representative was denied because he was an American citizen. But his task was over, and he resigned his official position. In 1823 he endowed at Yale College the De Forest scholarships and a prize in English. During the following year he was much annoyed by suits for dam-

ages arising out of the illegal activities of privateers which had operated under his guarantee, but he died before the cases were decided. A man of swarthy complexion, powerful physique, and haughty manner, his generosity was almost unlimited, while in business and diplomacy he was enterprising to the point of temerity.

[J. W. De Forest, *The De Forests of Avesnes* (1900); C. F. Adams, ed., *Memoirs of John Quincy Adams* (1875), vols. IV and V; Henry Hill, *Recollections of an Octogenarian* (1884); *Am. State Papers, Foreign Relations,* IV, 412–18.]   W.L.W—t.,Jr.

DE FOREST, ERASTUS LYMAN (June 27, 1834–June 6, 1888), mathematician, was descended from an old Walloon family, and was the only son of Dr. John and Lucy Starr (Lyman) De Forest, and the last of the male line of Benjamin De Forest of Watertown, Conn. Entering Yale at the age of sixteen, he was graduated in 1854 with the degree of B.A. He then pursued his scholastic work in the engineering department of the Sheffield Scientific School (Yale), where he was graduated two years later with the degree of Ph.B. In 1867 he received the degree of M.A. Although he inherited sufficient means from his grandfather to provide for his modest needs, he determined to show his independence of such assistance. The gold fever of 1849 had not yet subsided when he left Sheffield, and a year later he went to California where for a time he worked in the mines. Inspired no doubt by the love of travel, he next went to Australia and became a tutor in the University of Melbourne. After this venture he traveled in the East and in Europe, finally returning to America to the enjoyment of a more quiet life, devoting the rest of his years to mathematical research in a field at that time but little cultivated in the United States. In 1886 he gave $4,000 to Yale to increase the fund established by his father in 1855—still the source of the De Forest Mathematical Prizes. Just before his death (1888) he gave $10,000 toward the endowment of a chair of mathematics in that university. He was never married.

His scientific work related chiefly to the theory of probability and errors and has come to be looked upon in late years as showing unusual ability. His first paper appeared in the *American Journal of Science* (XLI, 371–79) in 1866, and from that time until his death he published on an average approximately a paper a year, all in the same general field. Most of these papers appeared in the journal mentioned, in *The Analyst,* or in the Smithsonian *Reports.* Being of a technical nature, they failed to attract popular attention and, indeed, were hardly appreciated during his lifetime by scientists in his particular line of interest. Hugh H. Wolfenden, however, called the attention of a mathematical congress at Toronto, in 1924, to the notable work done by De Forest. In the paper there presented it was shown that his contribution to the development of formulas for graduation by linear compounding (a subject of great importance in actuarial work), "in a most invaluable series of papers which appeared in the Smithsonian *Reports* of 1871 and 1873, a pamphlet, *Interpolation and Adjustment of Series* (1876), and *The Analyst* (Des Moines), 1877–80," was one of the most important of its kind ever made by an American scholar.

[For a complete list of De Forest's papers and for a study of his scientific work, see the article by Hugh H. Wolfenden in the *Trans. Actuarial Soc. of America,* May 1925, XXVI, 81–121. There is a brief biographical sketch on p. 121 of the same article, together with a bibliography relating to the De Forest family.]   D.E.S.

DE FOREST, JOHN KINNE HYDE (June 25, 1844–May 8, 1911), missionary to Japan, was the son of the Rev. William Albert and Martha (Sackett) Hyde, being the fifth of their eight children. He was born at Westbrook, Conn. When he was ten years of age, his father moved to a parish in Greenwich, Conn. John's earliest education was obtained in the public schools of Westbrook and Greenwich. He afterward spent a year and a half in Phillips Academy, Andover, Mass., and graduated in 1862, ranking fifth in a class of forty-five. He served in the Civil War for nine months during 1862–63 in Company B, 28th Connecticut Volunteers, and entered Yale College in the fall of 1863. For want of funds he had to withdraw shortly and take a position as teacher in a boys' school at Irvington-on-Hudson, N. Y. After a few months at Irvington he learned that the income from a De Forest Fund at Yale would be available to him on condition that he assume the name of De Forest. With this aid and other sums loaned by friends, he spent the years 1864–68 in Yale, graduating with honors in 1868. The next three years were spent in Yale Divinity School from which he received the degree of B.D., in 1871. In the same year he was ordained to the ministry, assumed the pastorate of the Congregational church in Mt. Carmel, Conn., and married, on June 5, 1871, Sarah C. Conklin of New Haven. The death of his wife and their baby the following spring was so great a shock to him that he was given leave from his parish for several months for recovery. On Sept. 23, 1874, he married Sarah Elizabeth Starr of Guilford, Conn., and almost immediately sailed with her from San Francisco to Yokohama for service in Japan under the American

Board. The edicts against Christianity had been removed the previous year by the Japanese Emperor. After a brief stay in Yokohama, the De Forests went on to Kobe, and thence to Osaka, spending the winter with Dr. and Mrs. M. L. Gordon of that station. On the arrival of their possessions, they went to a home of their own. For twelve years De Forest was officially stationed at Osaka. He devoted himself seriously to a mastery of the spoken Japanese and in due time gave his earnest attention to the written language, attaining ultimately a remarkable command of Japanese. He preached frequently and gave much time to translation. In September 1886 with Mrs. De Forest and their four children he removed to Sendai, where, in the following March a church—one of the first Kumi-ai or independent churches—was organized. In June 1887 he opened there the Tokwa School for boys. After 1889 the Sendai station suffered much opposition from Japanese nationalists, and the Tokwa School was closed in 1892. The church continued and from 1897 had its own Japanese pastor. De Forest was from the first among those who advocated Japanese responsibility and independence in Christian affairs in Japan, and he proved an acceptable co-worker toward these ends. He made five trips to America. On his return to Japan from his furlough in 1895 he left his children in America. He traveled in Manchuria in 1905, spent the summer of 1909 in China, and in 1910 made a tour of Korea on behalf of Japanese Christians there. On his return from Korea he fell ill from heart disease to which, after five months, pneumonia was added. He was taken to St. Luke's Hospital in Tokyo, and died there. He was buried in Sendai, where the De Forest Memorial Church now stands. In November 1908, the Emperor of Japan had conferred upon him the Fourth Order of the Rising Sun in recognition of his work among Japanese troops in the Russo-Japanese War, and for his part in famine relief in the Sendai area in 1905–06. De Forest wrote often for the *Missionary Herald,* the *Religious Herald,* the *Congregationalist,* and the Japanese press, and for many years was a regular correspondent of the *Independent.* He was the author of "The Ethics of Confucius as Seen in Japan" (*Andover Review,* May 1893, reprinted in Tokyo); *Mixed Residence* (Yokohama, 1898); *Sunrise in the Sunrise Kingdom* (1904, revised in 1908); *Sketch of the Japan Mission of the American Board, 1869–1904* (1904); and the article on Shintoism in *Religions of Mission Fields* (1905).

[*Annual Reports, Am. Board of Commissioners for Foreign Missions,* 1875–1911; *Missionary Herald,* 1875–

1911; C. B. De Forest, *The Evolution of a Missionary: A Biog. of John Hyde De Forest* (1914); S. L. Gulick, *John Hyde De Forest* (1914); *Outlook*, May 27, 1911; *Congregationalist*, May 20, 1911; *Japan Evangelist*, June 1911; H. P. Wright, *Hist. of the Class of 1868, Yale Coll., 1864–1914* (1914); *Obit. Record Grads. Yale Univ.* (1911).]

J.C.A.

DE FOREST, JOHN WILLIAM (May 31, 1826–July 17, 1906), author, was born in Humphreysville, now Seymour, Conn., the son of John Hancock De Forest, a successful merchant and cotton manufacturer, and Dotha Woodward, daughter of Elijah Woodward of Watertown, Conn. The De Forests came from Avesnes in French Hainaut, the first to settle in this country being Isaac, son of Jesse, who sailed for New Netherland in the fall of 1636, on a ship owned jointly by the De Forest and Van Rensselaer families. Here he became a great burgher, a schepen, and a member of the Nine Men. His son, David, settled in Stratford, Conn. The parents of John expected to send him to Yale, but the death of his father when the boy was thirteen years old, and a serious illness, deprived him of a college education, although in 1859 Amherst College awarded him an honorary A.M. He had a decided taste for study and writing, however, and as early as 1851, after a careful investigation of available sources, he published under the patronage of the Connecticut Historical Society a *History of the Indians of Connecticut*. He spent several years abroad, chiefly in Syria, where at Beirut his brother, Rev. Dr. Henry A. De Forest, conducted a girls' school, and in Florence and Paris. Returning to this country, he married in New Haven, Conn., June 5, 1856, Harriet Silliman Shepard, daughter of Charles Upham Shepard [*q.v.*], considered in her day an exceptional classical scholar, and the center of a brilliant group of university people. The literary fruits of his life abroad were *Oriental Acquaintance* (1856), and *European Acquaintance* (1858), pleasantly written books descriptive of persons and scenes encountered in his travels. In *Witching Times* (1856), and *Seacliff* (1859) he also made a successful beginning as a novelist. He was again in Europe when the Civil War broke out, but hastening back he recruited a company in New Haven which was mustered into the service as Company I, 12th Connecticut Volunteers, of which he became captain. He served under Generals Weitzel and Banks in the Southwestern states, and under Gen. Sheridan in the Shenandoah Valley. He also acted as inspector general of the 1st Division of the XIX Corps, and as aide on the staff of that corps. He was brevetted major, Mar. 13, 1865. After the war he was commissioned as captain in the Veteran

Reserve Corps, detailed as captain of Company I, 14th Regiment, and assigned to duty as acting assistant adjutant-general. For a period he was in command of a district of the Freedman's Bureau, with headquarters at Greenville, S. C. He was mustered out of the service Jan. 1, 1868.

The rest of his life was spent for the most part in New Haven. His military service had not altogether interrupted his literary work, for he had written for *Harper's Monthly* some vivid descriptions of battle scenes, and in 1867 he published a novel dealing with the war and its results, *Miss Ravenel's Conversion from Secession to Loyalty*. Another novel, *Kate Beaumont*, a notable portrayal of certain aspects of Southern life, appeared in 1872. Other short stories and novels followed, among the latter: *The Wetherel Affair* (1873), *Honest John Vane* (1875), *Justine's Lovers* (1875), *Playing the Mischief* (1876), *Irene the Missionary* (1879), *The Bloody Chasm or Oddest of Courtships* (1881), *A Lover's Revolt* (1898). Critics agree that these novels with their vigorous realism and skilful character portrayal deserve more appreciation than they have received. Their excellences and limitations have been pointed out by W. D. Howells (*Harper's Bazar*, XXXV, 538–44, October 1901), who attributes their failure to achieve a longer popularity to a "sort of disdainful honesty to the effects of art," and to "a certain scornful bluntness in dealing with the disguises in which women's natures reveal themselves," because of which they failed to gain feminine approval. In his later years De Forest published two volumes of verse, *The Downing Legends* (1901) and *Poems: Medley and Palestina* (1902). He was also the author of *The De Forests of Avesnes (and of New Netherland) a Huguenot Thread in American Colonial History* (1900).

[Main facts of career furnished by a grandson, L. Effingham de Forest. See *Who's Who in America*, 1906–07; *New Haven Evening Register*, July 18, 1906.]

H.E.S.

DE GRAFFENRIED, CHRISTOPHER [See GRAFFENRIED, CHRISTOPHER, BARON DE, 1661–1743.]

DE HAAS, JOHN PHILIP (c. 1735–June 3, 1786), Revolutionary soldier, was born in Holland, the son of John Nicholas De Haas, a descendant of Baron Charles De Haas of Brandenburg, Prussia, and later of Strasbourg, Alsace, who is said to have received the family arms—those of the city of Florence—from Emperor Rudolph as a reward for services in the conquest of Italy. The parents of John Philip emigrated to America about 1737 and settled in

Lancaster County, Pa. Practically nothing is known of his early life prior to his entry into the military service other than that he had married Eleanor Bingham. He was commissioned ensign of the Provincial Battalion of Pennsylvania in December 1757, and was stationed at Fort Augusta on the Susquehanna River. In 1758 he participated in the Forbes expedition against the French at Fort Duquesne, and from then on to the close of the war he served continuously, his last campaign being with Col. Henry Bouquet [q.v.] on the western frontier. From 1765 until 1779 he was a local magistrate in Lancaster County and was engaged in the iron industry of that place. On the outbreak of the Revolution, without waiting for a commission, he raised a company of militia on his own responsibility. The Continental Congress appointed him colonel of the 1st Pennsylvania Battalion on Jan. 22, 1776 (*Journals of the Continental Congress,* vol. IV, 1906, p. 78). By that time his regiment was already on its way to join Gen. Benedict Arnold on his ill-fated Canadian expedition. He joined his regiment and rendered valuable service, saving Arnold from possible capture by the British commander Forster at Lachine, by arriving with four companies and forcing Forster to retire to Fort Allen, at the head of Montreal Island. During June 1776 Arnold kept De Haas's detachment "dancing between Sorel and Montreal," and soon thereafter the invading army, defeated and thinned by desertion, fell back on Fort Ticonderoga. The troops of the 1st Pennsylvania Battalion reached their homes in December, and afterward formed the nucleus for the 2nd Pennsylvania Regiment, Continental Line. De Haas was commissioned brigadier-general of the Continental Line, Feb. 21, 1777, but at the close of that year he suddenly resigned his commission and returned to Lancaster County. His resignation has never been fully explained. He seems to have been a strict disciplinarian and hence made enemies in the service; but Washington believed him to be a capable officer and regretted his loss. In 1778 De Haas offered his services to the board of war to lead an expedition against the Indians who had raided the Wyoming Valley. He collected some local militia and marched to the scene, but Gen. Arnold sent Col. Hartley with a detachment of regular troops and orders to take command. The next year De Haas moved to Philadelphia where he remained until his death.

[Abram Hess, "The Life and Services of Gen. John Philip de Haas," in *Lebanon Hist. Soc. Papers,* vol. VII, no. 2 (1916) ; Washington Papers (Lib. of Cong.), Correspondence with the Military, BII, pt. 2, 257; *Pa. Archives,* ser. 1 and 2, *passim*; *Pa. Mag. Hist. and Biog.,* vols. II (1878) and V (1881).]   T.D.M.

DE HAVEN, EDWIN JESSE (May 7, 1816–May 1, 1865), naval officer, was the son of William and Maria (McKeever) De Haven of Philadelphia. He was a descendant of Evert in den Hofen who in 1690 emigrated to Philadelphia (now Montgomery) County, Pa., from Mülheim on the Ruhr, Germany (H. D. H. Ross, *History of the De Haven Family,* 1st ed., 1894, App.). Entering the navy on Oct. 2, 1829, as a midshipman, he made his first cruise on the *Natchez* in the West Indies. In 1832–35 he was with the Brazil Squadron, first on the *Lexington* and later on the *Natchez,* being advanced in the latter year to the grade of passed midshipman. In 1837 he went to sea on the *Falmouth* and saw service in the Pacific. Two years later at Callao he joined the *Vincennes,* the flagship of the Wilkes exploring expedition, receiving the rating of acting master, and during the next three years visited the Antarctic continent, many of the islands of the Pacific, and the west coast of North America. When the sloop *Peacock,* one of the vessels of this expedition, was wrecked at the mouth of the Columbia River, De Haven saved the lives of a boat's crew and received the thanks of the Navy Department for his bravery. He was commissioned lieutenant on Sept. 21, 1841, taking rank from Sept. 8. After serving on several vessels of the Home Squadron, in 1847–48 he was attached to the steamer *Mississippi* and took part in the Mexican War. He next was employed at the Naval Observatory in Washington under Lieut. Matthew F. Maury [q.v.], the noted meteorologist.

Early in 1850 the federal government, in coöperation with Henry Grinnell, a wealthy New York merchant, decided to send an expedition in search of Sir John Franklin and his companions who disappeared in the Arctic region in 1845 while on a voyage of discovery. Having had experience in polar exploration and having acquired a reputation as a scientific officer, De Haven was chosen to command the expedition. Most of the month of April 1850 he spent in New York preparing his fleet for sea. It consisted of two small brigs, the *Advance* and the *Rescue,* with a complement of thirty-three officers and seamen. According to his instructions, the chief object of the expedition was to search for Franklin and his companions and relieve them if found, and the secondary object was to acquire scientific information. On May 22 he sailed from New York and two months later to the westward of Greenland began his search for the missing Englishmen. In September the vessels were caught and frozen in the ice and for nine months were confined in this perilous situation, drifting to and fro more than a thousand miles. De Haven discovered and named Grinnell Land, but failed to find Franklin. He arrived at New York on Sept. 30, 1851.

In 1853–57 he was employed with the Coast Survey in making deep-sea soundings off the Southern coast and in other work of that service. He never went to sea after 1857, as his eyesight was affected and his health impaired by his Arctic experiences. In 1862 he was placed on the retired list, the first in the grade of lieutenant. He is buried in Old Christ Church graveyard, Philadelphia. On May 7, 1844, he was married to Mary Norris Da Costa.

[Record of Officers, Bureau of Navigation, 1830–66; Letters to Officers Ships of War, vol. XLIV, and Officers' Letters, Apr. and May 1850, and Oct. 1851, Navy Dept.; U. S. Navy Registers, 1830–66; *Report of Sec. of Navy*, 1850 and 1851; E. K. Kane, *The U. S. Grinnell Expedition* (1854); A. Gleaves, "The De Haven Arctic Expedition" (*U. S. Naval Inst. Proc.*, LIV, 1928, 579–91); Letters of Mrs. Kate DaC. (De Haven) Rolfe to the writer, Jan. 1929; note of death in *Pub. Ledger* (Phila.), May 3, 1865.]   C.O.P.

DEINDÖRFER, JOHANNES (July 28, 1828–May 14, 1907), Lutheran clergyman, was born in Bavaria at Ross-stall near Nürnberg, the son of Georg Heinrich and Anna Eva (Leupold) Deindörfer. His father was a farmer and basket maker. In pursuance of his desire to become a minister Deindörfer studied theology 1847–51 in Nürnberg and Neuendettelsau under Friedrich Bauer and Wilhelm Löhe. In those years Löhe was giving much of his time to preparing missionaries for work among the German Lutherans in the western United States and recently had founded three Lutheran colonies—Frankenmuth, Frankentrost, Frankenlust—in Saginaw County, Mich. At Löhe's suggestion Deindörfer accepted the pastorship of a fourth colony, Frankenhilf, which was to be comprised chiefly of young couples who were unable to obtain legal permission to marry in Bavaria because of their poverty. He was ordained at Hamburg Sept. 14, 1851, by the Rev. J. Meinel and preached his first sermon at Frankenhilf on the second Sunday in Advent. On Oct. 18, 1852, he married Katharina Elisabeth Weege, by whom he had nine children. The other German Lutheran pastors in the country round about were members of the Missouri Synod, with the exception of his friend Georg Martin Grossmann [q.v.]; and when the rupture over the doctrine of the ministry came between Löhe and the Synod, Grossmann and Deindörfer, for failing to agree with the Missourians, found themselves in a serious position. It was soon clear that they must either move further west to territory unoccupied by the Missouri Synod or else prepare to endure ceaseless petty persecution. In July and August 1853, therefore, Deindörfer and the one man of property among his parishioners, Gottlob Amman, visited northeastern Iowa on a tour of inspection, and that autumn they and Grossmann with their families settled there. Grossmann took up his work in Dubuque, while Deindörfer made his headquarters in Clayton County at a spot that he piously named St. Sebald, in honor of the saint who first brought the evangel to the vicinity of Nürnberg. The hardships of pioneer life told heavily on Deindörfer: during the first winter he and his family suffered severely from cold and were compelled to take refuge at last in Amman's log cabin; a little later Deindörfer almost succumbed to typhoid fever. On Aug. 24, 1854, in Deindörfer's cabin at St. Sebald, he, Grossmann, Conrad Sigmund Fritschel [q.v.], and Michael Schüller organized the German Lutheran Synod of Iowa. Deindörfer was vice-president of the Synod 1854–93, meanwhile serving as pastor at St. Sebald 1853–56; Madison, Wis., 1856–60; West Union and Waucoma, Iowa, 1860–65; Toledo, Ohio, 1865–70; Defiance, Ohio, 1870–89; and Ripon, Wis., 1889–93. For sixteen years he was president of the Eastern District. He was president of the Synod from 1893 to 1904 and editor of its *Kirchenblatt*, with a few interruptions, from 1878 to 1904. It was characteristic of him that when he accepted the presidency he stipulated that his salary should be but $800 a year, since he had found that he could live sufficiently on that sum. He was a good student and had a distinct literary gift. He published *Denkschriften* commemorating the tenth, twenty-fifth, and fiftieth anniversaries of the founding of the Synod and in 1897 an excellent *Geschichte der Evangel.-Luth. Synode von Iowa*. His simplicity, kindliness, and strength of character made him generally beloved. He died at Waverly, Iowa.

[G. J. Fritschel, ed., *Quellen und Dokumente zur Geschichte und Lehrstellung der ev.-luth. Synode von Iowa* (Chicago, n.d.); obituary notice in *Dubuque Times-Jour.*, May 15, 1907; additional information, derived from Deindörfer's MS. autobiography and other papers, through the courtesy of Prof. Geo. J. Fritschel of Wartburg Theological Seminary.]   G.H.G.

DEITZLER, GEORGE WASHINGTON (Nov. 30, 1826–Apr. 10, 1884), anti-slavery leader in Kansas, the son of Jacob and Maria Deitzler, was born at Pine Grove, Pa. There he grew to manhood with only a common-school education—"very common" he once said. While still a young man he emigrated to the new West. After a short residence in Illinois and in California he went in March 1855 to Lawrence, Kan., where he engaged in farming and real-estate dealing. He soon took an active part in politics, so that when the plan to organize a free-state government, in opposition to the pro-slavery territorial government, was set on foot he was sent to Boston to see Amos Lawrence and other friends of the cause. He at once received an order for one hundred Sharps rifles which were very soon on their way to Kansas in boxes marked "books." Other shipments of "books" followed. Military companies armed with these new weapons were formed among the free-state men. In the so-called Wakarusa War in November 1855, Deitzler was aide-de-camp to the commander of the free-state forces and during part of the time was in full command. A few months later, when the territorial judiciary began to function, Chief Justice Lecompte instructed a grand jury sitting at Lecompton that levying war on the authorities of the territory was treason against the federal government. Deitzler and several other free-state leaders were promptly indicted on a charge of treason. They were immediately arrested and kept in a prison tent at Lecompton for about four months. In September 1856 they were freed on bail. Later their cases were nolle-prossed.

Deitzler's activities in behalf of the free-state cause were incessant. He served on committees, attended meetings and conventions, of which there were many, counseled with other leaders, and wrote for the press. He was elected a member of the free-state territorial legislature of 1857–58 and was chosen speaker of the House of Representatives. He was also a member of the Kansas Senate under the Topeka constitution. In 1860 he became mayor of Lawrence and in 1866 treasurer of the University of Kansas. When the Civil War began he was active in organizing the first regiment of Kansas Volunteer Infantry and was appointed its colonel. In August 1861 his regiment took a prominent part in the battle of Wilson's Creek where he was severely wounded. Promoted to the rank of brigadier-general in November 1862, he served under Grant until October 1863 and then resigned on account of impaired health caused by his former wound. During all of these years he had remained a bachelor. His home was at the Eldridge House in Lawrence. In September 1864 he was married to Anna McNeil of Lexington, Mo. A month later Gen. Price led an invading Confederate army into Missouri and eastern Kansas. The entire militia of the latter state were called out—about 20,000 in number—and Deitzler was placed in chief command with the rank of major-general. He directed the movements against the Confederates in the successful campaign that followed. Various enterprises engaged his attention after the return of peace. He promoted the Emporia Town Company and was a director in the new Leavenworth, Lawrence & Fort Gibson Railroad Company. In 1872 he removed with his family to California. While in southern Arizona in the spring of 1884 he was thrown from a buggy and killed.

[The main facts of Deitzler's career are presented in his brief autobiography, now in the archives of the Kan. State Hist. Soc. Secondary sources are: D. W. Wilder, *Annals of Kan.* (1875); G. T. Andreas, *Hist. of the State of Kan.* (1883); L. W. Spring, *Kansas* (1885); F. W. Blackmar, *Life of Chas. Robinson* (1902); *Trans. Kan. Hist. Soc.*, IV (1886–88); V (1891–96); VI (1897–1900); VIII (1903–04); X (1907–08); XIII (1913–14). The date of his death is sometimes given as Apr. 11, although the Leavenworth *Evening Standard*, Apr. 11, 1884, states that he died Apr. 10.]   T. L. H.

DE KAY, GEORGE COLMAN (Mar. 5, 1802–Jan. 31, 1849), sea fighter in the service of the Argentine Republic, was born in or near New York City, the second son of George and Catherine (Colman) De Kay, and younger brother of James E. De Kay [*q.v.*]. During George's infancy his father died. The lad was placed for a time in a private school in Connecticut, but eluded his guardian and shipped before the mast on a merchantman. At twenty he was captain of a ship and at home in many foreign ports. Arriving at Buenos Aires in 1826, while Brazil was blockading the port as an incident to the dispute with the Argentine Republic over the province that later became the Republic of Uruguay, he offered his services to the Argentine navy, and was intrusted by Admiral Brown with the command of the *Brandzen,* a brig of eight guns with a motley crew of Americans, Irish, Scotch, and a few South Americans. Having run the blockade of the Rio de la Plata, he engaged two Brazilian men-of-war and captured one of them. In the following summer (1827) he took three Brazilian ships and fought the *Cacique* (18 guns) off Pernambuco, boarding her and accepting surrender from Capt. Manson, in spite of the fact that his crew was outnumbered three to one by that of the *Cacique*. His success was attributed to his skill in maneuvering his ship rather than to any superiority in gunnery. The Brazilian fleet, with which he had to contend, was manned and commanded, for the most part, by Englishmen. Taking command of the *Cacique* and hoisting the Argentine colors, De Kay sailed past Rio de Janeiro, northward through the Carribbean Sea, and as far up the North American coast as New York. He had been made a captain and after his victories was made a lieutenant-colonel—a rank that nearly corresponded with the then existing naval grade of commodore in the United States navy. From the date of this promotion he was known in the United States as Commodore De Kay. In the following year while returning to Buenos Aires, the *Brandzen* was surrounded and overpowered in the Rio de la Plata by Brazilian ships. De Kay scuttled her and, taking off the crew, proceeded by land to Buenos Aires. Peace was declared and, shortly, relieved of active duty, he returned to the United States, promising to rejoin Argentine service whenever he should be recalled. After his return to New York he was associated, as he had been earlier, with Henry Eckford [*q.v.*], the ship-builder. In 1831 he sailed a corvette, or sloop-of-war, built by Eckford for the Sultan of Turkey, to Constantinople. With him on the voyage went his brother, James E. De Kay, and Eckford himself. While in Turkey during the following year Eckford died and De Kay returned to America with the body. His marriage in 1833 to Janet Halleck Drake, a grand-daughter of Henry Eckford, and the only child of the poet, Joseph Rodman Drake, continued and cemented his early alliance with the ship-builder's family and the group of writers with whom he had been associated from boyhood days. His placid life as a family man in the Palisades region of New Jersey for several years was in sharp contrast with the adventurings of his youth. From this peaceful existence he was summoned during the Irish famine of 1847 to take leadership in an international enterprise of succor and good will which was a forerunner of the great Red Cross and other emergency relief efforts of the present century. He prevailed upon Congress to grant the use of the federal war-ship *Macedonian* for transporting goods from New York to Ireland. Although the United States was engaged in war with Mexico at the time, the appeal in behalf of the Irish famine-sufferers met with a quick response. A cargo of corn meal, Indian meal, rice, beans, and clothing, valued at over $60,000, was promptly secured and the cost of the expedition (amounting to $15,000) was voted by public meetings. De Kay took the responsibility of sailing the ship to Cork. This novel use of a war vessel on an errand of mercy caught the British imagination for the moment, but the well-intentioned enterprise suffered disastrously from lack of organization. The pledges made in public meetings remained unfulfilled. De Kay was compelled to advance from his own pocket the principal cost of the voyage and to look to Congress for reimbursement (R. B. Forbes, *Personal Reminiscences,* 1876). He died suddenly at Washington, where he had just purchased a house, survived by his wife and seven children.

[Chas. De Kay, the youngest son of Geo. Colman De Kay, published in the *National Marine* for Apr. 1918 extracts from the log of the *Brandzen* in 1827 and in the same article he supplied information about his father's early life. See also J. E. De Kay, "The Book of the Children of De Kay" (MS.) in Lib. of Cong.; obituary notice in *Nat. Intelligencer* (Washington), Feb. 3, 1849.]   W.B.S.

DE KAY, JAMES ELLSWORTH (Oct. 12, 1792–Nov. 21, 1851), naturalist, author, was the eldest son of George and Catherine (Colman) De Kay and brother of Commodore George Colman De Kay [*q.v.*]. His birthplace was probably Lisbon, Portugal, where his father, an American sea captain, had lived for many years, and had married a girl of Irish parentage. George De Kay took his family to New York in 1794, died when James was ten years old, and was survived only four years by his widow. The senior member of an orphaned family, the boy grew up in and near New York City. Most of his formal schooling was obtained in Connecticut, but the name and location of the school have not been preserved. De Kay early showed bookish proclivities and was also a keen observer and student of nature. At nineteen he was a medical student, spending at least one summer at Guilford, Conn., in reading to fit himself for that profession. Botany and zoology attracted him more than medicine, however, while in his early twenties he became closely associated with a group of young writers in New York. Throughout his life his relationships with literary men seem to have been more intimate than those with physicians or scientists. It was he who brought together Fitz-Greene Halleck and Joseph Rodman Drake. He was one of the five men to whom was entrusted the secret of the Drake-Halleck authorship of the papers of "Croaker & Co." in the *Evening Post*. He stood with Halleck at Drake's death-bed and was probably among the first to read, in manuscript, the lines beginning, "Green be the turf above thee"—long regarded as one of the most exquisite epitaphs in the language. De Kay went to Europe in the spring of 1818 and for a year was in attendance as a student of medicine at the University of Edinburgh, where he received the degree of M.D. in 1819. Returning to New York, he interested himself in the activities of the Lyceum of Natural History, which had been recently organized by Samuel Latham Mitchill and others and was known as the fourth institution of its kind to be founded in the United States. De Kay served the Lyceum in various capacities. He edited the first two volumes of its transactions, acted as librarian, building up a collection of scientific works that was remarkable for its day, and helped in assembling a museum.

While thus employed De Kay was married, on July 31, 1821, to Janet Eckford, one of the daughters of Henry Eckford [q.v.] and sister of the widow of Joseph Rodman Drake [q.v.]. For several years he seems to have toyed with the thought of a writer's career. Henry Eckford at one time had a controlling interest in a New York political journal, the *National Advocate,* and proposed to install De Kay as editor, but nothing came of the suggestion. Later De Kay himself offered to start a literary magazine, with Halleck as editor. This dream also failed to materialize. After his father-in-law had sustained severe business losses and had been commissioned by the Sultan of Turkey to take charge of the Turkish navy yard, De Kay sailed with him to Constantinople in a corvette built by Eckford for the Sultan and temporarily commanded by Commodore George C. De Kay. The group remained in Turkey for several months in 1831–32. Eckford died there. On returning to the United States, De Kay published anonymously *Sketches of Turkey by an American* (1833), his impressions of Turkey and the Turks. So far as these were favorable to the Turkish people, they were displeasing to the strong pro-Greek partisans who had sympathized with the recent revolution; but they undoubtedly were in accord with the matured opinions of such American observers as Dr. William Goodell, the missionary, and Commodore David Porter, then serving as United States Minister to the Porte, with both of whom De Kay had conversed.

While in Turkey De Kay had made a special study of the Asiatic cholera, about which little was known in America. After his return to New York the research was continued and in epidemics that later swept large regions in this country De Kay did what he could as a physician to stem their ravages. But, like several of his contemporaries among the scientific men of New York who had been educated in medicine, much of the time he took only a

secondary interest in his profession. There was pioneer work to be done in natural science and he was always eager to have a part in it. An unexampled opportunity came to him in the form of a commission from the State of New York to prepare the zoological section of the elaborate Natural History Survey to be published by that state. This undertaking occupied him for nearly eight years, and resulted in the *Zoology of New York* (6 pts. in 5 vols., 1842–44). He described 1,600 species of animal life, including mammals, birds, reptiles, amphibians, fishes, molluscans, and crustaceans. As the work was intended for popular use, he introduced the common names of species so far as possible. His researches demanded much travel and personal investigation. The remainder of his life was passed at Oyster Bay, Long Island, where he died on Nov. 21, 1851, about two months after the death of James Fenimore Cooper, his friend of many years' standing.

[A typewritten copy of a manuscript entitled "The Book of the Children of De Kay" prepared by Jas. E. De Kay, and annotated by Gen. A. W. Greely, is in the Lib. of Cong. This traces the De Kay genealogy to Holland and, ultimately, Franche-Comté. Letters to and from De Kay are to be found in *Correspondence of Jas. Fenimore Cooper* (1922); these are dated, for the most part, in the decade of the forties; the intimacy of the two men seems to have antedated Cooper's long residence in Europe. See also H. L. Fairchild, *Hist. N. Y. Acad. Sci.* (1877); Jas. Grant Wilson, *Life and Letters of Fitz-Greene Halleck* (1869); E. D. G. Prime, *Forty Years in the Turkish Empire; or Memoirs of Rev. Wm. Goodell* (1876), pp. 120–21; *Am. Jour. Sci.,* 2 ser., XIII (1852), 300–01; *N. Y. Herald,* Nov. 23, 1851.]   W. B. S.

DE KOVEN, HENRY LOUIS REGINALD (Apr. 3, 1859–Jan. 16, 1920), composer, was the son of Dr. Henry de Koven of Middletown, Conn., who was a brother of the Rev. James de Koven [q.v.]. His mother was Charlotte Le Roy of New York. Reginald de Koven was born in Middletown, but at the age of eleven accompanied his father to England where he remained until he took his degree at St. John's College, Oxford, in 1879, with intermittent periods at Stuttgart, where he studied the piano with Speidel. After his graduation he spent a year in Stuttgart, studying piano with Lebert and harmony with Pruckner. These studies were supplemented by a six months' course in composition with Hauff (Frankfort), by a vocal course with Vannuccini (Florence), and the study of operatic composition under Genée (Vienna, 1888) and Delibes (Paris, 1889). On May 1, 1884, he married Anna Farwell of Chicago. During the winter of 1887 his first comic opera, *The Begum,* was produced. It was followed by *Don Quixote* (Boston, 1889). On June 9, 1890, in Chicago, his one outstanding score, the romantic comic opera *Robin Hood,* was first heard; it was produced in London on Jan. 5 of the following year under the title *Maid Marian.* In *Robin Hood* he achieved a score to Harry Smith's libretto which "is analogous in its melodic fertility to Sullivan." It had more than 3,000 successive performances after its initial success in Chicago. As his wife has said in her memoirs, "in the forty-one productions which succeeded this opera he wrote music quite as melodic, and often more mature, but for freshness and gayety, and for uninterrupted flow of happy inspiration, 'Robin Hood' is unquestionably preëminent" (*A Musician and his Wife,* p. 134). Similarly, the composer's best-known and most popular song remains his "O Promise Me," interpolated in this score, and which for a number of years has been widely used as an organ number at weddings. *Robin Hood* at once established De Koven's reputation, and in rapid succession a number of light, melodious comic opera scores flowed from his facile pen. They included: *The Fencing Master* (Boston, 1892), *The Algerian* (Philadelphia, 1893), *Rob Roy* (Detroit, 1894), *The Tzigane* (New York, 1895), *The Mandarin* (Cleveland, 1896), *The Paris Doll* (Hartford, 1897), *The Highwayman* (New Haven, 1897), and *The Three Dragoons* (New York, 1899). In addition he was music-critic for the *Chicago Evening Post* from 1889 to 1890, and for the New York *World* from 1892 to 1897. In the latter year the De Koven family transferred its residence from New York to Washington, D. C., and there, in 1902, the composer organized the Washington Philharmonic Orchestra, which he conducted for three seasons. During this time De Koven was the music-critic for the *New York Journal* (1898–1900). After his return to New York, he again became the music-critic of the New York *World* (1907–12), and produced *Red Feather* (New York, 1903), *Happy Land* (New York, 1905), *Student King* (New York, 1906), *The Golden Butterfly* (New York, 1907), *The Beauty Spot* (New York, 1909), *The Wedding Trip* (New York, 1911), and *Her Little Highness* (New York, 1913). His grand opera, *The Canterbury Pilgrims* (New York, Mar. 7, 1917), with book by Percy Mackaye, was composed in Switzerland, in the first year of the World War. At the time, his wife wrote later, "we sometimes even heard the echo of the guns over the Lake of Geneva." It was a departure from his accustomed field, and achieved a *succès d'estime.* His last opera, *Rip Van Winkle,* which he

wrote with the same librettist, was an essay in what he termed "folk-opera," developing an American subject. It was given for the first time in Chicago, Jan. 2, 1920, and was favorably received. On the evening of Jan. 16, the day on which he had received word that the house had been "sold out" for the third performance of *Rip Van Winkle,* De Koven was stricken with apoplexy at a supper party given in his honor, and died in ten minutes without regaining consciousness. Aside from his twenty comic operas (his "grand" and his "folk" operas may be regarded as endeavors to adapt his natural gifts in the field of light music to types alien to them), he wrote some 120 songs and a number of piano pieces of the salon variety. Among the individual songs, the setting of Kipling's "Recessional" is probably the best-known. The originality of his melodies, in various instances, has been questioned; but though he did not create a distinctive type of operetta, like Sullivan, his *Robin Hood* is regarded as a classic of its kind; and his service in a legitimate musical cause will make him long remembered. As a critic and writer on musical subjects, he was consistently committed to a recognition of American composers and artists equaling that accorded foreigners.

[Summary biographies are found in *Grove's Dict. of Music and Musicians* (3rd ed., 1919), rev. by Alfred Remy; A. Eaglefield-Hull, *A Dict. of Music and Musicians* (1924); *Who's Who in America,* 1920–21; Helen Beach, *The Descendants of Jacob Sebor, 1709–93, of Middletown, Conn.* (1923). An obituary sketch and a good editorial summary of achievement will be found in *Musical America* (Jan. 24, 1920). The most detailed account of his life and work, however, is contained in *A Musician and his Wife* (1926), by Mrs. Reginald de Koven.]　　　　　　　F. H. M.

DE KOVEN, JAMES (Sept. 19, 1831–Mar. 19, 1879), Episcopal clergyman, became the leader of the so-called "ritualistic group" in the Protestant Episcopal Church during the factious period following the Civil War. He was born in Middletown, Conn., and was the son of Henry Louis and Margaret (Sebor) de Koven. Graduating from Columbia College in 1851, second in his class, he attended the General Theological Seminary, was graduated in 1854, and was immediately ordained deacon. The Protestant Episcopal Church in America had reflected the Oxford disputes during the forties and the Home-Mission group had associated itself at that time with the high-church party, toward which De Koven was inclined. Quite naturally, therefore, he chose the Home Mission field for his labors. In 1855 Bishop Kemper, who was still missionary bishop of the Northwest, ordained him to the priesthood.

His life in the West began strenuously. During his first year he became assistant rector of a church at Delafield, Wis., and professor of ecclesiastical history at Nashotah Theological Seminary, and was also placed in charge of St. John's Hall, a preparatory school for Nashotah. Bishop Kemper transferred him in 1859 to Racine College where he was made rector, or warden. Racine developed greatly under his charge—not in size only, but in definiteness of policy as well. It was but natural that a man of his convictions should feel that the greatest problem in education lay in the misguiding influence of science and the weakening of faith. He discussed this problem in 1874 in a general report on the educational needs of the times. Inevitably, the strict ceremonial observed at Racine aroused adverse criticism, and many disquieting rumors—mostly false—in regard to the "papal abominations" encouraged at that institution disturbed the bosoms of low churchmen.

From 1868 to the end of his life, De Koven represented his diocese in the General Convention. His gifts as a debater, his incisive wit, and his thorough knowledge of ecclesiastical history made him feared as well as admired in the lower house. His greatest contribution to the Church was, perhaps, his opposition to the low-church effort to dictate ritualistic uniformity. From 1871 to 1874 he fought this attempt with ardor and ability, and he won his cause. The great speech of his life was delivered upon this subject in 1874. In it he movingly explained the attitude of the sincere ritualist and refuted all charges of Romanism.

Church partisanship was particularly acrimonious in the seventies. De Koven was attacked in religious papers and in the secular press. In 1871 Rev. James Craik of Louisville, Ky., even accused the rector of Racine of idolatrous views and practises. De Koven was not the man to sit silent under such an onslaught, and replied in the *Church Journal and Gospel Messenger* (see correspondence beginning Nov. 21, 1871). His published works are mostly sermons, tracts, and letters regarding religious controversies. Some of his papers were included in an undated collection, covering the years 1870–75, which was published under the title, *Tracts by Dr. De Koven and Others*. The year after his death *Sermons Preached on Various Occasions* was published, with a preface by Morgan Dix.

The diocese of Massachusetts failed to elect him bishop in 1873 by a few votes only. On the death of Bishop Kemper in 1874, he lost the election of Wisconsin by his failure to command the lay vote. On this occasion a series of garbled and misleading allegations concerning candles on the altar, incense during ceremonies, and auricular confession assumed great importance. In 1875 he was elected Bishop of Illinois but the Standing Committee of the General Convention refused to accept his election because of his opinions on the Eucharist, and he withdrew his acceptance. Trinity Church of New York City and St. Mark's in Philadelphia both called him to their parishes, but he declined these invitations and remained at Racine, where he died in March 1879. He left his property, including his library and all his papers, to Racine College.

[The preface by Morgan Dix in De Koven's *Sermons Preached on Various Occasions* (1880) is almost a memoir. See also: *Hist. of Racine and Kenosha Counties, Wis.* (1879), pp. 404–14; Helen Beach, *The Descendants of Jacob Sebor, 1709–93, of Middletown, Conn.* (1923), pp. 21–22; *Jours. of the P. E. Ch. in Wis., 1854–79*; *Jours. of the Gen. Convention of the P. E. Ch. in America*; catalogues of Racine Coll.]

K. J. G.

DE LACY, WALTER WASHINGTON (Feb. 22, 1819–May 13, 1892), soldier, engineer, was born at Petersburg, Va. His father, William De Lacy, was of distinguished Irish family, claiming descent from Hugh de Lacy, one of the conquerors of Ireland in the twelfth century. His mother, Eliza, was the daughter of William Charles Lee, long British vice-consul at Oporto, Portugal. Walter De Lacy's parents died when he was quite young and he was brought up and given his early education by two maiden aunts. In 1834 they sent him to St. Mary's Catholic College in northern Maryland where he remained four years, engaged chiefly in the study of mathematics and languages. During this time he secured the promise of an appointment at West Point, but in some way the promise failed of fulfilment. There was at West Point an eminent mathematician and engineer, Prof. Mahan, who felt under obligations to De Lacy's family, and he offered to give Walter private lessons in mathematics and engineering free of charge. After a year there, De Lacy began work as a construction engineer for the Illinois Central and Iron Mountain railways. In 1840 he became assistant professor of French at West Point and later taught foreign languages to midshipmen in the navy. In 1846 he was employed by a syndicate to search for abandoned mines in Texas. While he was there the Mexican War broke out, and he volunteered and served throughout the war. Afterward, he was engaged in railroad work, helping survey the thirty-second parallel from San Antonio to San Diego. In 1855 he was in the Puget Sound country and served with distinction in the Nez Percé War.

In 1858 De Lacy joined the party of Lieut. John Mullan, who was building the "Mullan Road" from Fort Benton to Walla Walla. He was placed in charge of construction from Sohon Pass to the Bitterroot River. He was also directed to make a map and report of the Bitterroot country. In 1860 he had finished this task and in 1861 became a prospector for gold in what is now Montana. He did not have much success and engaged for a time in packing from Walla Walla to the gold-mines. In 1863 he led a gold-seeking party into the Snake River country and discovered Shoshone Lake and the Lower Geyser Basin of the Yellowstone Park. The first legislature of Montana (1864–65) employed him to make the first map of Montana; and it long remained the best. From then on, he was engaged in surveying. He located the initial point for public surveys in Montana and did much work in surveying and locating the line of the Northern Pacific. The last few years of his life he was employed in the surveyor general's office in Helena, Mont.

"Col. De Lacy," as he was popularly called, always remained a bachelor. He was regarded as a genial and charming companion and had many friends. He was a brilliant talker and a noted teller of humorous stories and tales of adventure. He was one of the founders of the Montana Society of Engineers and of the Montana Historical Society.

[There are brief sketches of De Lacy in: *Contribs. Hist. Soc. Mont.*, vol. II (1896); *Quart. Jour. Mont. Soc. Engineers* (Jan. 1916); *Jour. Asso. Engineering Socs.* (June 1897). His own account, *A Trip up the South Snake River in 1863* is in *Contribs. Hist. Soc. Mont.*, vol. I (1876).]

P. C. P.

DELAFIELD, EDWARD (May 7, 1794– Feb. 13, 1875), ophthalmologist and surgeon, third son among the eleven children of John Delafield [*q.v.*], an English merchant who had emigrated to America, by his wife, Ann Hallett of New York. He received his primary education first under a tutor named Adam Smith, and later at the Union Hall Academy under L. E. A. Eigenbrodt who gave him a good foundation in mathematics and the languages. He graduated from Yale with the degree of A.B. in 1812, after which he became a pupil to Dr. Samuel Borrowe of New York, under whose tutelage he obtained, in 1816, the degree of Doctor of Medicine from the College of Physicians and Surgeons, New York, for which he wrote *An Inaugural Dissertation on Pulmonary Consumption* (1816).

After receiving his degree, Delafield went to Europe with John Kearny Rodgers where he had a year (1817) in the clinics of England, Scotland, Holland, and France. On returning to New York, though he continued in general surgery and obstetrics, his attention was directed chiefly to the diseases of the eye. He edited in 1825 an American edition (based on the third London edition) of Benjamin Travers's *Synopsis of the Diseases of the Eye, and Their Treatment,* with notes and additions, and he later made important contributions to ophthalmological journals. He was thus one of the first in the United States to devote himself to ophthalmology. In 1818 he formulated a plan for establishing the New York Eye Infirmary modeled after the London Infirmary in which he had studied, and succeeded in carrying it out in association with Kearny Rodgers in 1820; two rooms were opened (No. 45 Chatham St.), and during the first seven months 436 patients were treated. Later, largely through Delafield's influence, more ample accommodations were secured. Between 1820 and 1906 over a million patients were treated. In 1824 the Massachusetts Charitable Eye and Ear Infirmary was founded in Boston by Edward Reynolds and John Jeffries [*q.v.*], who had received their stimulus from New York. Delafield was one of the founders and the first president of the American Ophthalmological Society (1864), an organization which immediately flourished and is still in existence. He was also largely responsible for founding a society in 1842 for the relief of the widows and orphans of medical men, which also was based upon a similar society then existing in London. In addition to his labors at the Eye and Ear Infirmary, he occupied from 1825 until 1838 the chair of obstetrics and diseases of women and children at the College of Physicians and Surgeons of New York, and from 1858 to 1875 he was president of the College. As a practitioner he was unusually successful and is said to have possessed to a remarkable degree the power of inspiring the confidence of his patients. He was a genial and kindly man, and owing to his long gray beard and sideburns was rather striking in personal appearance. In October 1821 he married Elina E. Langdon Elwyn, grand-daughter of John Langdon, governor of New Hampshire and president *pro tempore* of the Senate in the First Congress of the United States. There were six children, all of whom died before their father. In January 1839 he married his second wife, Julia Floyd, grand-daughter of William Floyd, signer of the Declaration of Independence; she became the mother of Francis Delafield [*q.v.*], the pathologist.

[S. W. Francis, *Medic. and Surgic. Reporter,* XV (1866), 509–15; *Medic. Record,* N. Y., X (1875), 135; *Trans. Am. Ophthalm. Soc.,* II (1876), 275, 339–41; A. A. Hubbell, *The Development of Ophthalmology in America 1800–1870* (1908).]   J.F.F.

DELAFIELD, FRANCIS (Aug. 3, 1841– July 17, 1915), pathologist and physician, was the son of Edward Delafield [*q.v.*] and his wife, Julia Floyd. After receiving the degree of A.B. from Yale in 1860 he entered the College of Physicians and Surgeons in New York and there received his medical degree in 1863. On graduation he went immediately to Europe where he continued his medical work in London, Berlin, and Paris, taking full advantage of the opportunities then being offered for detailed postmortem study. The influence of Rudolf Virchow was at that time beginning to be felt strongly in medical science, and Delafield became an ardent follower. He returned to America firmly convinced that pathological anatomy was the *sine qua non* of scientific medicine, and he accordingly passed the greater part of his time during the next thirty years in the post-mortem room making detailed studies of pathological tissues, meticulously correlating his findings with clinical features observed before death. He was soon recognized as a leading authority in pathology and clinical diagnosis. In 1866 he became curator at Bellevue Hospital, in 1871 pathologist at the Roosevelt Hospital, and in 1875 visiting physician in the Bellevue Hospital. In the following year he was made adjunct professor of pathology and the practise of medicine at the College of Physicians and Surgeons, New York, and in 1882 was made full professor in the place of Alonzo Clark [*q.v.*]. In 1886, in company with William Osler, James Tyson [*qq.v.*], James E. Graham, and William Pepper [*q.v.*], he founded and became president of the Association of American Physicians, which was to have a profound influence upon the development of medicine. The first meeting of this organization was picturesquely referred to by Osler as "the coming-of-age party of internal medicine in America" (*International Clinics,* Philadelphia, 1915, IV, 1).

Delafield was a remarkably effective teacher. It is said that his lectures were particularly attractive because of his simple, forceful delivery and the fact that the information which they contained was based wholly on first-hand experience. By nature he was somewhat austere and little given to amusements or levity, but to his students he was stimulating and always sympathetic. In accordance with a decision made early in life, he retired from professional and hospital duties at the age of sixty, though he was then at the height of his physical and mental vigor. He continued in practise as a consultant until shortly before his death, which resulted from apoplexy, at Noroton, near Stamford, Conn.

Delafield made contributions of first importance to pathology, especially of nephritis and of the diseases of the colon. He was also among the first to insist upon the difference between acute lobar pneumonia and bronchopneumonia (1882). His scientific papers number nearly a hundred, and his influence and teachings were widely felt through an unusually successful textbook, *A Handbook of Post Mortem Examinations and of Morbid Anatomy,* first published in 1872, and revised and enlarged, in collaboration with T. Mitchell Prudden, in 1885. The twelfth edition appeared in 1922. In 1878 Delafield issued with Charles F. Stillman a *Manual of Physical Diagnosis.* His fame as a pathologist was greatly enhanced through the publication of his *Studies in Pathological Anatomy,* an elaborately illustrated pathological atlas which appeared in parts between 1878 and 1891. He also contributed chapters to many medical and surgical treatises, such as his "Pyæmia and Allied Conditions" in *The International Encyclopedia of Surgery* (1881) and his "Diseases of the Kidneys" in *Twentieth Century Practice* (1895). On Jan. 17, 1870, Delafield married Katherine Van Rensselaer of New York.

[T. C. Janeway, *Medic. Record,* 1915, LXXXVIII, 929; *N. Y. Medic. Jour.,* 1915, CII, 202; *Am. Medicine,* 1915, X, 522; *Boston Medic. and Surgic. Jour.,* 1915, CLXXIII, 186; *Jour. Am. Medic. Asso.,* 1915, LXV, 349; *Who's Who in America,* 1914–15.]
     J.F.F.

DELAFIELD, JOHN (Mar. 16, 1748–July 3, 1824), merchant, son of John and Martha (Dell) Delafield, was among the first men of English birth to establish themselves in America after the close of the Revolution. His family had lived in England since the Norman Conquest, having been, as the name suggests, of French origin. His father was a prosperous dealer in cheese. One of his sisters married William Arnold, customs collector on the Isle of Wight, and was the mother of Dr. Thomas Arnold of Rugby, while another sister became the teacher of the six-year-old boy Thomas after the death of his father. John Delafield as a young man had accumulated property and at thirty-five was prepared to emigrate to the United States and cast his lot with the new Republic. The manner of his coming had in it something of the spice of adventure. He took passage on a British ship that carried letters of marque; during the voyage a French merchantman was seized and Delafield received £100 as his share of the prize money. He arrived at New York, which was still held by British troops, in the spring of 1783, bringing with him the first copy of the provisional treaty of peace between the United States and Great Britain to reach America. Shortly after the British evacuation of New York, Delafield went into trade and conducted his affairs so shrewdly that within fifteen years he became one of the wealthiest men in the city. He married Ann, the daughter of Joseph Hallett, a Revolutionary officer. They had eleven children. His home on Long Island, just across the East River from New York, was among the best-known mansions of its period. He was one of the original directors of the Mutual Assurance Company of New York, organized in 1787 by Alexander Hamilton and others. In 1798 he retired from mercantile business, but later became president of the United Insurance Company. During the War of 1812, when American merchantmen were at the mercy of both British and French war vessels he shared the fate of all American underwriters who had offered marine insurance; to meet the losses he was compelled to sacrifice his property. Stripped of his wealth, Delafield found himself far less favorably situated than when he landed at New York thirty years before. At this time his oldest son John Delafield [*q.v.*], while technically a prisoner in London because of his American citizenship, was permitted to engage in banking. Thus in a few years the family fortunes were measurably retrieved. Delafield was the founder of a line that was notable in New York to the second and third generation, in commerce, in finance, in the army, and in the medical profession. His personal example in assuming obligations that were not legally his as to the payment of losses to policy-holders in his insurance companies was of great value in the early days of American underwriting practise. It was the irony of fate that he, a man of English birth and antecedents, should suffer in America from British depredations on American shipping, although he retained strong family ties and associations with the mother country.

[*The Pedigree of Delafield* (Extract from the Records of the College of Arms, London); *Matthews American Armory and Blue Book* (1901), ed. by John Matthews; M. A. Hamm, *Famous Families of N. Y.* (1902), I, 79; S. H. Weston, *Memorial Sermon on the Brothers Delafield* (1875).]   W.B.S.

DELAFIELD, JOHN (Jan. 22, 1786–Oct. 22, 1853), banker and farmer, was the eldest son of John [*q.v.*] and Ann (Hallett) Delafield. He was born in New York City three years after his father's arrival from England. The elder Delafield had become a citizen of a country that as yet had no established national government. He soon prospered in business and gave his son as good a schooling as the New York of that period afforded. The boy was graduated from Columbia College at sixteen. Then going as supercargo on merchant ships he made several voyages from the port of New York and after a few years became himself the owner of vessels. It was in the course of a voyage on one of his own ships that he witnessed the siege of Corunna, Spain, by the French. When the shipping in the harbor was fired he escaped, with several members of the Spanish nobility who took refuge on his ship and sailed to England. In London he engaged in banking and for some years prospered in that undertaking. During the War of 1812 his American citizenship caused him to be technically held as a prisoner of war, but influential family friends obtained for him unusual liberties, including permission to continue his business unmolested, so long as he kept within the limits of a certain area, having its center in London. After the war he continued for a time to accumulate wealth, but serious reverses came in 1819 through the failure of some of his investments. It was then that Washington Irving, who had become his intimate friend, wrote for the *Sketch Book* the story of Delafield's experiences in the chapter entitled "The Wife" (Delafield had married his English cousin, Mary Roberts of Whitechurch, Buckshire), alluding to the courageous and sweet-tempered spirit in which the bride faced the loss of home and comforts. In the following year Delafield returned to America after a twelve years' absence, taking the cashiership and later the presidency of one of the New York banks, which he held for eighteen years, in the meantime becoming interested in various enterprises outside his business. He was a prominent member of the New York Philharmonic Society, was active in raising funds for the University of the City of New York at the time of its founding, and took part in the revival of the New York Historical Society. In 1838 he became president of the New York Banking Company, which had only a brief career, suffering heavy losses through the failure of Western institutions. For the second time Delafield's fortune was wiped out. He left the city and engaged in farming in Seneca County, N. Y. Within a few years his had become one of the model farms of the state (*Transactions of the New York State Agricultural Society*, 1847, p. 200). He gave his attention to the practical problems of drainage, soil analysis, and rotation of crops. In these matters he was far in advance of his times. Chosen president of the State Agricultural Society, he exerted much influence in his later years in behalf of progressive and scientific farming. Two books seem to have been erroneously attributed to him—*A Brief Topographical Description of the County of Washington, Ohio* (1834), and *Inquiry into the Origin of the Antiquities of America* (Cincinnati, 1839). There is evidence that both were written by his son, John Delafield, Jr., a graduate of Columbia College, who lived in Ohio in 1831 and for many years thereafter (Wilson Waters, *The History of Saint Luke's Church, Marietta, Ohio,* Marietta, 1884, pp. 39–40). His second wife was Harriet Wadsworth Tallmadge. He died at Geneva, N. Y.

[*The Pedigree of Delafield* (Extract from the Records of the College of Arms, London); John Matthews, ed., *Matthews Am. Armory and Blue Book* (1901); M. A. Hamm, *Famous Families of N. Y.* (1902), I, 790; *N. Y. Times,* Oct. 25, 1853; *N. Y. Herald,* Oct. 26, 1853.]   W.B.S.

DELAFIELD, RICHARD (Sept. 1, 1798–Nov. 5, 1873), military engineer, was the son of John Delafield [*q.v.*] of London, who came to America in 1783, married Ann, the daughter of Joseph Hallett, and founded one of the well-known families of New York. The Delafield family (of noble French descent) held rich possessions in Alsace, and John brought wealth with him to the New World. He became one of the richest merchants of New York City and has often been called "one of the fathers of Wall Street." His son Richard was born in New York City and entered West Point Military Academy at the age of sixteen. He was graduated and commissioned a second lieutenant in July 1818. He was twice married: first, to Helen Summers and, after her death, to Harriet, the daughter of Gen. E. M. Covington.

In forty-eight years of continuous service in the United States army, Richard Delafield rose from a second lieutenancy to the rank of major-general. He served twice—from 1838 to 1845, and again from 1856 to 1861—as superintendent of the United States Military Academy at West Point. At the outbreak of the Civil War, at the age of sixty-three, he was appointed to the staff of Gen. Morgan, in which position he helped to organize and equip New York state forces for the field, and to supply ordnance stores for the Atlantic and Lake defenses. Part of this time he was superintending engineer of the defenses for The Narrows in New York harbor, of the fortifications of Governors Island, and of the fort at Sandy Hook. Then, on Apr. 22, 1864, he was made brigadier-general and chief of engineers, United States army, and until his retirement in August 1866 was in command of the Corps of Engineers and in charge of the Engineer Bureau in Washington. In 1865 he was brevetted major-general "for faithful, meritorious and distinguished services in the Engineer Department during the Rebellion."

In his earlier years of service Delafield was engineer on the construction of fortifications and defenses at Hampton Roads, Va., 1819–24; at the Plaquemine Bend on the Mississippi River, 1824–32; and on the Atlantic Coast defenses, 1845–55. Many of his plans, drawings, and studies were preserved and treasured because they so admirably combined an artistic value with a strict scientific accuracy. He was appointed in 1855 to act as a member of the Military Commission to the Crimea and the theatre of the war in Europe, and his report and observations, entitled "Report on the Art of War in Europe in 1854–56" was published by order of Congress in 1860. He lived for seven years after his retirement from active army service and during part of that time served as a member of a commission for the improvement of the Boston harbor and as a regent for the Smithsonian Institution.

[Material for this sketch has been found in *Professional Memoirs, Corps of Engineers, and Engineer Dept. at Large, U. S. Army* (1911), III, p. 416; Richard Delafield, *The Pedigree of Delafield* (1925); "Famous N. Y. Families—The Delafields," in *N. Y. Evening Post,* June 1, 1901.]   E.Y.

DE LAMAR, JOSEPH RAPHAEL (Sept. 2, 1843–Dec. 1, 1918), capitalist, son of Maximilian and Johanna (Teune) De Lamar, was born in Amsterdam, Holland, and died in New York City. He was privately educated. While he was still young he went to sea. Once when he was on a voyage, the captain of the ship died, and he—though only twenty-three years old—was put into control. Soon after this he came to America and settled at Vineyard Haven, Mass., as a ship-contractor. Perhaps his most notable achievement in this connection occurred in 1872 when he raised the submerged transatlantic liner, *Charlotte.* The excitement over gold discoveries in Colorado tempted him West in the late seventies. He secured certain tracts of land near Leadville, and then returned to Chicago where he studied chemistry and metallurgy. After about two years he sold his mining property to a London organization for two million dollars. In 1884 he was a member of the territorial Senate of Idaho, but he soon abandoned politics, and though his mining interests in the West were in a sense personally maintained till 1891, he spent most of his time after 1888 in New York

City. He married Nellie Sands, the daughter of a New York druggist, and the two went to live in Paris. They were later divorced. He was back in New York by 1902. He became a director in many rich corporations, and for a long time he was vice-president of the International Nickel Company. In his business relationships he was extremely taciturn and aloof, but he belonged to numerous clubs and he entertained lavishly at his expensive residences in the city and at Glen Cove, L. I. He was an accomplished organist. When he died, half of his estate of twenty million dollars was left to his daughter, Alice Antoinette, and the other half was divided between the medical schools of Columbia, Harvard, and Johns Hopkins Universities.

[Who's Who in America, 1916–17; H. T. French, *Hist. of Idaho* (1914); *N. Y. Times,* Dec. 2, 10, 1918.]

J. D. W.

DELAMATER, CORNELIUS HENRY (Aug. 30, 1821–Feb. 7, 1889), mechanical engineer, was born at Rhinebeck, Dutchess County, N. Y., the only child of William and Eliza (Douglass) Delamater. When he was three years of age his parents took him to New York City and there he received a common-school education. He had neither profession nor trade, but being studious and very fond of reading, he acquired more than most boys who had only his advantages. At the age of fourteen he left school to become an errand boy in the hardware store of Schuyler & Swords, where he remained for two years. At sixteen he entered the office of James Cunningham who had established the Phœnix Foundry on West St., New York City, and who had as his associates Peter Hogg, an engineer and draftsman, and Cornelius's father, William Delamater, as cashier and confidential adviser. Cornelius started as a clerk but he made himself so useful and gained such an insight into the work that Cunningham, desiring to retire, offered the business to him and his cousin, Peter Hogg. The offer was very promptly accepted and the two young men found themselves at the head of a fairly prosperous business, doing repair work and building boilers and engines for side-wheel steamers. Their capital was small but their friends were many and warm and they prospered.

When in 1839 John Ericsson [*q.v.*] settled in New York he was persuaded by Samuel Risley of Greenwich Village to give his work to the Phœnix Foundry. There he met Cornelius Delamater and a friendship was formed which was to be life-long. Rarely thereafter did either of them enter upon a business venture without consulting the other. Delamater's foundry built, after designs developed by Ericsson, the first iron boats and the first steam fire-engines used here. The 36-inch cast-iron pipe used for the Croton Aqueduct was made at the Phœnix Foundry and before the end of 1840 over fifty propeller steamers were also constructed. At the end of eight years when the lease on the foundry expired, Hogg and Delamater bought property at the foot of West Thirteenth St., on the North River, and in 1850 they built the large establishment in which they conducted their business until 1856, when Hogg retired from the firm. Delamater continued alone with the business for many years, the firm thereafter being known as the Delamater Iron Works.

Upon the outbreak of the Civil War, the firm entered upon a new and interesting chapter of its history. When in August 1861 the government, in response to the news that the Confederates were building the *Merrimac,* advertised for proposals to build iron-clad vessels, Delamater at once called upon Ericsson to determine a method of approaching the government with the latter's plans for an armed iron-clad turreted steamer. The contract on the basis of Ericsson's plans was received in October 1861, the keel of the *Monitor* was laid the same day at the Continental Iron Works in Greenpoint, L. I. (now Brooklyn, N. Y.), and the engines were built at the Delamater Iron Works. The *Monitor* left New York harbor on Mar. 6, 1862, and three days later engaged in the famous battle with the *Merrimac.* The men who actually operated the boilers and engines of the *Monitor* on that occasion were workmen from the Delamater Iron Works.

In 1869 the Delamater Works constructed thirty gunboats, each armed with a 100-pound bow-chaser, for the Spanish government. The firm was notable too for its propellers; for the manufacture of air compressors; and for constructing in 1881 John P. Holland's first successful submarine torpedo-boat. In fact a complete enumeration of the important productions at these Works would prove that they were a veritable school of invention, contributing greatly to the history of the country. Delamater, the guiding genius, was a man of deep, kindly, tolerant sympathies, well-known for his genial disposition, and his warm and lasting friendships. He believed in human nature and as an employer invested in it. At one time in his career he became bankrupt through no fault of his own, but his creditors had such faith in him that they helped him to continue the Works. In later years he invited them all to a banquet at which each of them found under his plate a check with compound interest for what was owed him. He was one of the original members of the American Society of Mechanical Engineers. Early in life he was married to Ruth O. Caller of Poughkeepsie, N. Y., who with five daughters and one son survived him. He died suddenly of pneumonia after an illness of eight days, and was buried in Woodlawn Cemetery.

[Files of the Am. Soc. Mech. Engineers, and *Trans. Soc. Mech. Engineers*, X (1889), 836–38; account of the Delamater-Ericsson Commemoration in New York City (privately printed, 1920); H. F. J. Porter, "The Delamater Iron Works—The Cradle of the Modern Navy," *Trans. Soc. Naval Architects and Marine Engineers*, vol. XXVI (1919); Wm. C. Church, *The Life of John Ericsson* (2 vols., 1890), *passim*; obituary notices in *Engineering News*, Feb. 16, 1889; and *Am. Machinist*, Feb. 14, 1889, as well as in many other trade and technical papers and in all of the leading newspapers of New York City.]   K. W. C.

DE LANCEY, JAMES (Nov. 27, 1703–July 30, 1760), chief justice and lieutenant-governor of colonial New York, political leader, was the eldest son of Stephen De Lancey and Anne van Cortlandt. His father, a refugee from France after the revocation of the Edict of Nantes, came to New York in 1686, having first obtained letters of denization in England. By virtue of his success in business, his marriage into the Van Cortlandt family, and the vigorous part which he took in the politics of the city and province, he came to occupy a place in the provincial aristocracy. James, his eldest son, was sent to England for his education, and was a fellow commoner at Corpus Christi College, Cambridge, later reading law in the Inner Temple. During his period of residence in England he made personal acquaintances and connections which were of great importance in his subsequent career. Returning to New York in 1725, he was shortly afterward admitted to the bar, was called to the Council on Jan. 26, 1729, and not long before this was married to Anne, elder daughter of Hon. Caleb Heathcote, receiver general of customs of North America, who brought him additional wealth. With advantages afforded by social position enhanced by his considerable gifts he began his career in New York politics.

At first he threw in his fortunes with the group who supported the governor and the official class, and in June 1731 received an appointment as second judge of the supreme court. During the administration of William Cosby [*q.v.*], from 1732 to 1736, a period when the violence of factional passion and popular excitement reached dangerous heights, De Lancey was promoted to be chief justice (1733), the governor thus brusquely dismissing the veteran Lewis Morris [*q.v.*] from that office. De Lancey now engaged without reserve in the defense of Cosby and the supreme court against their opponents who, through the use of the press, a weapon then first becoming effective in provincial politics, were making dangerous headway. In the government prosecution of Peter Zenger [*q.v.*] for libel, the passionate boldness of both sides led the youthful chief justice to disbar James Alexander and William Smith [*qq.v.*], the two leaders of his profession in the province, for a plea which in his judgment called in question the very existence of his court. From his part in the Zenger trial, which the eloquence of Andrew Hamilton [*q.v.*] turned into a triumph for the freedom of the press, De Lancey reaped much unpopularity. But, considering the circumstances and standards of the time, his conduct professionally seems to have been altogether reputable and what would naturally be expected from his training.

During the administration of George Clarke, [*q.v.*], from 1736 to 1743, he figured less conspicuously, though he was an active and increasingly influential member of the Council. It was at this period that the Assembly became the dominant element of the provincial government, attaining at last the key position of complete financial control. With the accession of George Clinton [*q.v.*] to the governorship, however, especially after his grant (Sept. 14, 1744) to the Chief Justice of a commission for his office for good behavior instead of during pleasure, De Lancey completely reversed his political rôle. Undeterred by any scruples touching the nonpartisanship of the judicial office, he developed with great energy and success a system of control of both Council and Assembly which effectually blocked all the governor's efforts to lead New York's participation in the third intercolonial war with the vigor desired by other colonies and by the Home Government. Clinton's "interest" at Whitehall proved inferior in effectiveness to that of De Lancey, reinforced as the latter was by the prestige of his brother-in-law, Sir Peter Warren. At Clinton's departure in 1753 he was obliged to deliver to De Lancey a commission for the lieutenant-governorship which he had kept suppressed for six years.

The immediate exercise of this commission came unexpectedly as a result of the suicide of the new governor, Sir Danvers Osborne. De Lancey was thus put in an extremely delicate position, for Gov. Osborne's instructions required an enforcement upon the Assembly of a complete surrender of those features of legislative "encroachment" upon prerogative which had been developed out of their financial control under the leadership of De Lancey himself. By the exercise of great political dexterity, and undoubtedly favored by the emergency conditions imposed by the fourth intercolonial war, he succeeded in keeping both of his great offices and at the same time in preserving for the Assembly the essential features of the position of dominance in the provincial government which were retained until the Revolutionary period. In 1754 he presided over the Albany convention and in the following year attended the conference of governors with Gen. Braddock at Alexandria, Va. He signed the charter for King's College in 1754, thus helping to fix the charge of "Episcopalianism" upon "the De Lancey party," and raising a Presbyterian opposition under William Livingston which soon came to be known as "the Livingston party." These issues, groupings, and names survived for long after De Lancey's death. He remained the leading figure in New York during the term of Gov. Hardy, 1755–57, and again, as lieutenant-governor, administered the affairs of the province in 1757–60. He died suddenly on July 30 of the latter year, being succeeded in the lieutenant-governorship by his political opponent, Cadwallader Colden [q.v.], president of the Council.

[The most accessible sources are to be found in the *Docs. Relative to the Colonial Hist. of the State of N. Y.*, vols. VI and VII (1855–56). There is a memoir by E. F. De Lancey in E. B. O'Callaghan, *Doc. Hist. of the State of N. Y.*, vol. IV, quarto ed. (1851). William Smith, *Hist. of N. Y.* (Albany, 1814), covers the whole period. For the Zenger trial see Livingston Rutherfurd: *John Peter Zenger* (1904); H. L. Osgood, *Hist. of the American Colonies in the Eighteenth Century*, vol. II (1924), ch. v; and J. G. Wilson, *Memorial Hist. of the City of N. Y.* (1892–93), vol. II, ch. vii. On the Clinton administration, see Osgood, vol. IV, ch. x, and Wilson, vol. II, ch. viii. For date of birth see Thos. Jones, *Hist. of N. Y. during the Revolutionary War* (1879), I, 650.]   C. W. S.

DE LANCEY, JAMES (1732–1800), colonial politician, turfman, was the eldest son of Lieutenant-Governor James De Lancey [q.v.] and Anne Heathcote. Born in New York City, in a house built by his grandfather, Stephen De Lancey, which later became famous as Fraunce's Tavern, he was educated at Eton and Cambridge, and on leaving the University entered the army, reaching the rank of captain. He is said to have served as aide to Abercrombie in the Lake George campaign of 1758, and was certainly with Prideaux and Johnson at the capture of Fort Niagara in 1759. His military activities, however, were brought to a close by the sudden death of his father, in 1760, which left him, before his thirtieth year, with the responsibilities of the headship of one of the wealthiest and most powerful families of the provincial aristocracy.

During his young manhood in England he had acquired the sporting tastes of the period. Soon after he came into his great property he imported what are believed to have been the first English race-horses, or thoroughbreds, ever brought to New York, and in a few years assembled the largest and most select stud and stable of running horses in the Colony if not in the whole country. Cadwallader R. Colden, historian of the early racing, called him "the Father of the New York Turf." His chief opponent in racing and in politics was Lewis Morris, Jr., later a signer of the Declaration of Independence. From Wildair, Lath, and the Cub Mare, imported by De Lancey, were descended most of the great race-horses of America prior to the Civil War period, while True Briton, another of his horses, was, according to the Morgan Horse Register, the progenitor of that famous breed of early American road and carriage horses.

His responsibilities as head of the family comprehended not only the development of the extensive De Lancey estates and the conduct of the family mercantile business, but also the continuation of the political influence of the "De Lancey interest." At first, under the leadership of the son, who lacked his father's dominant official position in the province, and his powerful influence in London, the political fortunes of the family suffered a decline. At the Assembly elections in 1761 held in consequence of the demise of the Crown, the Livingston party scored a triumph. But the next seven years offered abundant opportunity for the younger De Lancey to exercise a gift for dexterous management which came to be recognized as not inferior to that of his father. Provincial resistance to the policies of the British government in these exciting days was a matter in which the aristocratic De Lancey faction and the Livingston "Whigs" could and did combine with great effect. Into this contest, however, an element new to the political life of the province, the unfranchised classes, ready for radical and dangerous extremes of action, had begun to force its way. Taking advantage of the reaction against this encroachment of the masses, the De Lancey merchant ticket won the city delegation in the elections of 1768 over the "Whig lawyers," and again in 1769 the Tory-Episcopalian De Lancey combination obtained control of the Assembly. At this time "Captain James" was offered and refused a seat at the Council. In the proceedings of this last Assembly of New York's provincial period, which were in line with its traditional policy of over half a century, he took a leading part. At its last session, beginning in

January 1775, his hand is to be traced in the papers addressed to King, Lords and Commons, strongly resisting the ministerial policy but as carefully refraining from commitments to revolutionary activity. His was one of the eleven negative votes—to ten in favor—upon the resolution to approve the proceedings of the First Continental Congress. Shortly thereafter he sold out his stud and racing stable and, taking his family with him, retired to England. He was included with his uncle Oliver and his cousin James [*qq.v.*] in the Confiscation Act of 1777 and the Act of Attainder of 1779, and thus the famous "De Lancey interest" became a casualty of the American Revolution.

On the conclusion of peace De Lancey became very active in proceedings for compensating the Loyalists. He and his uncle Oliver were among those who suffered the heaviest losses by the American success. In dealing with the commissioners appointed by Parliament the claimants acted through a board of Agents, and in this organization James De Lancey represented New York, served as vice-president of the Board, and, next to Sir William Pepperell, was the most active member. He claimed a loss of $284,000 and was allowed $160,000, an amount of grant in this connection exceeded only by those to Frederick Phillipse and Sir John Johnson. His holdings of New York City real estate, situated on what is now the lower East Side, brought at the sale of forfeited estates shortly after 1783 something over $234,000, a figure which bears a quaint ratio to its present-day valuation. De Lancey's death at Bath, England, is recorded in the *Gentleman's Magazine* for April 1800. As his children died without issue the eldest male De Lancey line became extinct. His wife, whom he had married in 1771, was Margaret Allen of Philadelphia, daughter of William Allen [*q.v.*], chief justice of Pennsylvania, and grand-daughter of Andrew Hamilton [*q.v.*], of Zenger trial fame.

[C. L. Becker, *The Hist. of Political Parties in the Province of N. Y. 1760–76* (1909) ; A. C. Flick, *Loyalism in N. Y.* (1901) ; J. H. Wallace, *The Am. Horse* (1897) ; information as to his sporting interest from Gurney C. Gue, Esq., Merrick, N. Y. See also bibliographies of others of the De Lancey family.]
C. W. S.

DE LANCEY, JAMES (1746–May 2, 1804), Loyalist, leader of partisan troops, was the fourth son of Peter De Lancey and Elizabeth, eldest daughter of Cadwallader Colden [*q.v.*], lieutenant-governor of New York just before the Revolution. Peter De Lancey, "Peter of the Mills," was a brother of James De Lancey [*q.v.*], chief justice and lieutenant-governor of the province, and was the second son of Stephen, the

founder of the family in America. Presumably he bore his share in the family politics, though his alliance with the Colden family must have created awkward personal situations. He represented the Borough of Westchester in the Assembly from 1750 to 1768. His son, "Colonel James," held the office of sheriff of Westchester from 1770 to 1776. From the occupation of New York City by Howe in the autumn of the latter year to the close of hostilities, "The Neutral Ground," a belt some twenty miles in width between the northern end of Manhattan Island and a line from the mouth of the Croton River to the Sound, was the scene of irregular partisan warfare, full of exciting incidents of the most destructive and demoralizing character, pictured later by J. Fenimore Cooper in his story of *The Spy*. Amid these activities "De Lancey's Horse" became a household word of terror, for in 1777 he had become captain of a troop of fifty men, selected from the Westchester militia by Gov. Tryon. They had soon gained the nickname of "Cowboys" from their success as cattle-raiders. In 1781 their leader signed himself as "Colonel, Westchester Refugees." "The Outlaw of the Bronx" was one of his soubriquets.

He was proscribed by the New York Act of Attainder of 1779, and in 1782 removed with his family to Nova Scotia, where he settled at Annapolis on a farm a part of which is still held by his descendants. He became a member of the Assembly of the province and in 1794 was appointed to the Council. His wife, by whom he had six sons and four daughters, was Martha Tippetts, of the family which until the Revolution held Tippetts' Hill, immediately north of Spuyten Duyvil Creek.

[T. Jones, *The Hist. of N. Y. During the Revolutionary War* (N. Y. Hist. Soc., 1879) ; Carl L. Becker, *The Hist. of Political Parties in the Province of N. Y. 1760–76* (1909) ; A. C. Flick, *Loyalism in N. Y.* (1901), in Columbia Univ. Studies in Hist., etc. ; R. Bolton, *The Hist. of the Several Towns . . . of the County of Westchester* (1881) ; J. T. Scharf, *Hist. of Westchester County, N. Y.* (1886) ; O. Hufeland, "Westchester County During the Am. Rev.," *Westchester Hist. Soc. Pubs.,* 1926.]
C. W. S.

DE LANCEY, OLIVER (Sept. 16, 1718– Oct. 27, 1785), colonial politician, Loyalist soldier, was the youngest son of Stephen De Lancey and Anne van Cortlandt. Like the other members of his family he was a successful merchant. For a time he was associated in business with his brother-in-law, John Watts. It was Oliver De Lancey's fate to cooperate with his brother James [*q.v.*], the chief justice and lieutenant-governor, in erecting the De Lancey party into a powerful position in New York provincial politics, to survive his brother into a period of entirely new conditions in contest with which the family "interest" was utterly wrecked, and finally himself to die in exile. He lacked entirely the far-sighted astuteness, the capacity for persistent pursuit of objects by indirect methods, and the urbanity of demeanor which characterized his leader-brother. His contribution was made by vigor in action and in exploiting the prestige and formidable power of the family interest. The violence of his language and conduct in behalf of the faction opposed to Gov. Clinton was frequently referred to in the latter's dispatches to England, with particular emphasis laid on the difficulty in finding lawyers willing to appear in court to prosecute for his words a person so nearly related to the chief justice of the province. These circumstances were mentioned in the famous Representation by the Lords of Trade to the Privy Council in the affairs of New York in 1751. Oliver De Lancey was prominent in New York's participation in the fourth intercolonial war, raising troops and commanding the provincial contingent in the Ticonderoga campaign of 1758. For such services he twice received votes of thanks from the Assembly of the province. He served as an alderman for the Out Ward from 1754 to 1757 and was a member of the city delegation to the Assembly elected in 1759. At the close of 1760 he took his seat in the Council by virtue of a *mandamus* dated two years earlier, and was a member of that body until the end of the provincial period. He was appointed receiver general in 1763, and in 1773 was colonel-in-chief of the Southern Military District. The notable contribution of his military career was in raising a brigade of fifteen hundred Loyalists "for the defense of Long Island and for other exigencies." Of these "De Lancey's Battalions," two afterward took a brilliant part in the British campaigns in the south, while the third remained in Queens County during the whole period of hostilities. De Lancey himself, in chief command of this force as brigadier-general, remained in New York, and was the senior Loyalist officer in the British army in America. Patriot notice of his zeal was effectively shown by the sacking of his mansion at Bloomingdale in 1777 and by his inclusion in the New York Act of Attainder of 1779, by which his property was confiscated. On the other hand, Lord George Germain in a dispatch in 1780 commented on the satisfaction it must afford De Lancey "to know that his services are approved by His Majesty" (*Documents*, VIII, 790).

After the war, in the proceedings in England for the benefit of the Loyalists, he received $125,000 on a claim of $390,000 loss. Two years

after leaving New York he died, in 1785, at Beverley, England, and was buried in the cathedral church of that town. His wife was Phila, daughter of Jacob Franks of Philadelphia. Of their children, two sons attained high office, one as chief justice of the Bahamas and governor of Tobago, and the other as adjutant general of the British army.

[*Orderly Book of the Three Battalions of Loyalists Commanded by Brig. Gen. Oliver De Lancey 1776–78* (N. Y. Hist. Soc., 1917); Thos. Jones, *Hist. of N. Y. During the Revolutionary War* (1879), ed. by E. F. De Lancey; A. C. Flick, *Loyalism in N. Y.* (1901); *Docs. Relative to the Colonial Hist. of the State of N. Y.*, esp. vol. VIII (1857); references in bibliographies of other members of the family.]   C. W. S.

DE LANCEY, WILLIAM HEATHCOTE (Oct. 8, 1797–Apr. 5, 1865), Episcopal bishop, was the third son of John Peter De Lancey of Mamaroneck, N. Y., and Elizabeth Floyd of Mastic, N. Y. His father was the fourth son of Lieutenant-Governor James De Lancey [*q.v.*]. In spite of his service in the British army and as major in a Pennsylvania corps of Loyalists, John Peter De Lancey seems to have succeeded in escaping the vengeful notice of New York politicians, and in 1789 settled on the Heathcote property in Mamaroneck. His son William was graduated at Yale in 1817, and until Mar. 6, 1822, when he received priest's orders in the Protestant Episcopal Church, was occupied in studies with Bishop Hobart and with services in Trinity and Grace churches in New York City and at St. Thomas's in Mamaroneck. The next fifteen years constituted a period of apprenticeship which, as it turned out, was of especial serviceability for his later episcopal career. His position as one of the assistant ministers of the united parishes of Christ's, St. Peter's, and St. James's in Philadelphia brought him into close intimacy with Bishop White of Pennsylvania. He served as secretary of that diocese for seven years, and as secretary of the House of Bishops of the General Convention in 1823 and in 1826. From 1828 to 1833 he was Provost of the University of Pennsylvania and had very considerable success in checking a decline into which that institution had fallen.

By 1838 a division of the original diocese of New York had become imperative. The territory west of Utica was set off as the diocese of western New York and De Lancey was elected as its first bishop, being consecrated at Auburn, May 9, 1839, and thereafter making Geneva his residence. Of decided opinions, expressed with moderation and unfailing courtesy of demeanor, he carried much before him by sheer weight of personality. "He was the most *impressive* man I have ever seen," wrote Andrew D. White. "I have stood in the presence of many prelates in my day, from Pope Pius IX down; but no one of them has ever so awed me as this Bishop of western New York. His entry into a church chancel was an event; no music could be finer than his reading of the service; his confirmation prayer still dwells in my memory as the most perfect petition I have ever heard, and his simple, earnest sermons took strong hold of me" (*Autobiography*, 1905, II, 524). In the administration of his extensive charge De Lancey succeeded in laying foundations of orderly management and steady ecclesiastical progress which earned for it the reputation of "the model diocese." Regarded at the time of his election as a "High Church" man, he was able in the reverberations in America of the controversy over the Oxford Movement to preserve a remarkable degree of unity in the affairs of his diocese. He took great interest in denominational institutions of education, and the continuation of Hobart College and the founding of De Veaux College at Niagara Falls have been ascribed to his exertions. In respect to church affairs on a national scale, he was the first to suggest officially a plan of provincial organization, though the proposal did not bear fruit till a much later date. His appointment by the General Convention to represent the American Church in 1852 at London, at the third jubilee of the Society for the Propagation of the Gospel was peculiarly appropriate in view of the substantial labors in behalf of the work of the Venerable Society in America accomplished by one of his great-grandfathers, Caleb Heathcote [*q.v.*]. Upon this visit to England the Bishop received the degree of D.C.L. from Oxford; he had already received that of D.D. from Yale in 1827. He was married, Nov. 22, 1820, to Frances, second daughter of Peter Jay Munro of Mamaroneck. Of their eight children, Edward Floyd De Lancey is especially remembered as the editor of Judge Thomas Jones's *History of New York During the Revolutionary War* (1879), the manuscript of which had been confided to the Bishop in 1835.

[C. W. Hayes, *The Diocese of Western N. Y.* (1904); *Jour. Proc. Twenty-eighth Ann. Convention Protestant Episc. Ch. in the Diocese of Western N. Y.* (1865); H. G. Batterson, *A Sketch-Book of the Am. Episcopate* (1878); W. S. Perry, *The Episcopate in America* (1895); J. V. Van Ingen, *An Address . . . at the Funeral of the Rt. Rev. Wm. H. De Lancey* (1865); *Am. Ann. Cyc.,* 1865; J. T. Scharf, *Hist. of Westchester County, N. Y.* (1886).] C.W.S.

DE LANGLADE, CHARLES MICHEL (May 1729–c. 1801), was a remarkable French half-breed of the West. His father, Augustin Mouet de Langlade, was a scion of nobility from Guienne, and his mother (baptized Domitelle) was an Ottawa Indian, daughter and sister of the chiefs Nis-so-wa-quet or La Fourche. Charles, born at Mackinac, was their only child, but by his mother's previous marriage to a trader named Villeneuve, he had several half brothers and sisters. He was educated by the Jesuit priests of the post where he lived, wrote a good hand, and was everywhere received as a gentleman. The first event of his career occurred when at the age of ten he accompanied his Indian uncles on a war expedition down the Mississippi. Thither a considerable French army came from New Orleans, and built a post near Memphis and there passed a winter preparing for a campaign against the rebellious Chickasaw. Young De Langlade became enamored of military life and learned much of its details from French officers. Before 1750 he had been enrolled as a cadet in the colonial troops, in 1755 was ensign, and in 1760 lieutenant. His first expedition was that of 1752, when he drove the British traders from the post of Pickawillany and killed the Miami chief "Old Britain."

During all the French and Indian War De Langlade was actively employed as a leader of Indian auxiliaries; he was credited by his contemporaries with the victory over Braddock; he defeated Rogers's Rangers in 1757 on Lake Champlain; he aided in the attack on Fort William Henry; and served in the Quebec campaign of 1759. The next year he left Montreal before its capitulation to Amherst, and brought to Mackinac the news of the French downfall. Upon the desertion of that post by the commandant, De Langlade as second in command delivered it to the English, and soon thereafter transferred his allegiance and became a loyal British subject. In Pontiac's conspiracy he was instrumental in saving the lives of several British soldiers; soon thereafter he removed his home to Green Bay, where he and his father had long had a trading-post. There as the chief settler he became known as the "Father of Wisconsin." His services for the British during the American Revolution were considerable; he had the rank of captain in the Indian department and sent Indian auxiliaries to Carleton and Burgoyne. In the West he parried the efforts of George Rogers Clark, and opposed both American and Spanish partisans. The King granted him lands in Canada for his services. In 1754 he was married at Mackinac to Charlotte Bourassa, and left numerous descendants chiefly in the Grignon line. He lived at Green Bay in patriarchal fashion and there died in the midst of his descendants and retainers.

Essentially military in his characteristics,

known to the western tribesmen as Akewaugeke-tauso, a soldier chief, he was in his home a kind and devoted father and master, was deeply loved by the Indians, and maintained under three flags his integrity and honor.

[De Langlade's life is narrated by his grandson in *Wis. Hist. Soc. Colls.*, III (1857), 195–295 ; a sketch by Tassé is translated in *Ibid.*, VII (1876), 123–88. Documentary evidence corrected these earlier sketches and is the basis of a sketch in *Ibid.* (1908), XVIII, 130–32. See also Jos. Tassé, *Les Canadiens de l'Ouest* (Montreal, 1878) ; *Ontario Hist. Soc. Papers and Records*, III (1901), 147–49 ; "Langlade Papers, 1737–1800" in *Wis. Hist. Soc. Colls.*, VIII (1879), 209–23.]

L. P. K.

DELANO, AMASSA (Feb. 21, 1763–Apr. 21, 1823), ship-captain, author, son of Samuel and Abigail (Drew) Delano, was born in Duxbury and died in Boston, Mass. The founder of the Delano family in America, Philippe de La Noye, was a Huguenot who affiliated himself with the English Puritans while they were in Holland, and came with them to America in 1621. Samuel Delano, after serving in the French and Indian War, returned to his work of ship-building in Duxbury, and with the exception of two years spent in Braintree continued there till the time of the Revolution. Amassa was a vigorous youngster too absorbed in sports to give much time to books. In later life he recognized his "want of an early and academic education," but added, "I have always seized every possible opportunity during my whole life for the improvement of my mind in the knowledge of useful literature and those sciences that are immediately concerned with the pursuits to which I have been professionally devoted" (Delano, *Narrative of Voyages*, p. 17). Upon the outbreak of the Revolution, Amassa's father entered the Colonial army, but he was soon taken prisoner and confined on the British ship *Rainbow*. Amassa, aged fourteen, also went into the army, and remained in it intermittently till 1779, when he was for some months on board the privateer *Mars*. Afterward he was engaged off and on in shipping between various American ports and the West Indies. This was a stirring life, involving for some years ceaseless vigilance in the direction of the British, and sometimes actual fighting. In the spring of 1787, he took command of a ship bound for Portugal. In returning he was wrecked off Cape Cod, and he came home to find himself in a tangle of difficulties. Notes which he had been obliged to draw on the ship's owner had not been honored, and he was out of acceptable work. His financial state was acute, and he seized as a kind of bonanza an opportunity to become second officer of the *Massachusetts*, a 900-ton ship newly built in Quincy, expressly for the Canton trade. The years of his life from 1790 to 1810 were spent almost wholly at sea, first in one trading-ship, then in another, the most notable of them being perhaps *The Perseverance* and *The Pilgrim*. His experiences during this time, and his meticulous, sometimes naïve, observations are set forth in his book, *Narrative of Voyages and Travels in the Northern and Southern Hemispheres, Comprising Three Voyages Round the World* (1817). In general he writes without digression, but sometimes he turns philosopher—"virtue and vice, happiness and misery," he once pronounces, "are much more equally distributed to nations than those are permitted to suppose who have never been from home, and who believe, like the Chinese, that their residence is the center of the world, of light, of privilege, and of enjoyment" (*Ibid., Voyages*, p. 256). The last years of his life were spent in obscurity. A contemporary account refers to "his recent misfortunes and embarrassments," and the assurance felt by his friends that though he had sometimes erred in judgment, he was "not capable of designing to do wrong to others" (*Ibid.*, p. 593). He was married in Boston to a widow, Hannah Appleton. They had no children.

[J. A. Delano, *Geneal. Hist. and Alliances of the Am. House of Delano 1621 to 1899* (1899) ; D. H. Hurd, *Hist. of Plymouth County* (1884) ; L. V. Briggs, *Hist. of Shipbuilding on North River* (1889) ; S. E. Morison, *Maritime Hist. of Mass.* (1921) ; F. S. Drake, *Dict. Am. Biog.* (1879) ; H. H. Scudder, "Melville's Benito Cereno and Capt. Delano's Voyages" in *Mod. Lang. Asso. Pubs.*, XLIII (1928), 502–32, with portrait.]

J. D. W.

DELANO, COLUMBUS (June 5, 1809–Oct. 23, 1896), congressman from Ohio, secretary of the interior, was born at Shoreham, Vt. He was the son of James and Elizabeth (Bateman) Delano, and was descended from a French Huguenot, baptized at Leyden, Holland, as Philippe de la Noye, who came to America on the ship *Fortune*, arriving in Plymouth Harbor in November 1621 (Joel A. Delano, *The Genealogy, History and Alliances of the American House of Delano*, 1899, p. 311). His father died when Columbus was six years old, and two years later, in 1817, the boy's mother moved with him to Mount Vernon, Ohio. His education was the meager schooling of a poor boy in a frontier village. After the manner of the time he read law for a year in a law office and in 1831 secured his license to practise. Three years later, on July 13, 1834, he married Elizabeth Leavenworth of Mount Vernon. For several years, he was prosecuting attorney of Knox County. In 1844 he was elected to Congress, serving one term, 1845–47. He was a Whig and like the other members of his party regarded the Mexican War as a

Southern conspiracy for the extension of slave territory, an offensive war of the United States, with a wicked purpose (*Congressional Globe,* 29 Cong., 2 Sess., App., pp. 278–82). On the Oregon question he supported Polk's boundary compromise at the 49th parallel. In 1847 he tried without success to be the nominee of his party for governor of Ohio. Soon after retiring from Congress he moved to New York City, where he became a member of the banking firm of Delano, Dunlevy & Company (1850–55). He has left no account of this chapter in his life. On his return to Ohio he established his home on the outskirts of Mount Vernon, and gave his attention chiefly to agriculture, sheep raising in particular, but he retained an active interest in party politics. In 1860 and again in 1864 he was delegate to the Republican National Convention. During the Civil War he was for a short time commissary general of Ohio, and for one term a member of the state House of Representatives. From 1865 to 1869 he again represented his district in the national House of Representatives. Though at first inclined to the support of the presidential reconstruction policy, he was among the radical congressmen in 1867, convinced that the South required military government. He was one of the most effective advocates of protective duties for wool and a supporter of the Wool and Woolens Act of 1867 (Delano's speech, July 10, 1866, *Congressional Globe,* 39 Cong., 1 Sess., App., p. 258). In debate, according to Rutherford B. Hayes, one of his associates in Congress (see *Diary and Letters,* vol. III, 1924, pp. 7, 10), Delano was "clear and correct . . . a good specimen of the lively, earnest style of Western talkers." In 1869 President Grant appointed him commissioner of Internal Revenue. Under his administration the whiskey revenue frauds, already notorious when he took office, continued to blacken the record of the national government. In 1870 he succeeded Gen. J. D. Cox as secretary of the interior, and during his five-year tenure serious charges of frauds in the Bureau of Indian Affairs came to a head. Congressional committees of investigation and a special commission appointed by the President, partisan bodies, found evidence of neglect and incompetency within the Indian Bureau, but refused to throw the blame upon the officials at the head (*House Report No. 98,* 42 Cong., 3 Sess., *No. 778,* 43 Cong., 1 Sess.). In order to escape the persecution that newspaper critics visited upon his conduct of public affairs, Delano resigned. It is impossible to avoid the conclusion that though he was probably personally honest he was woefully lacking in high ideals of public service or an appreciation

of the responsibility of a department chief (J. F. Rhodes, *History of the United States,* vol. VII, 1906, p. 182 n.; E. P. Oberholtzer, *A History of the United States Since the Civil War,* vol. III, 1926, p. 168; *Report of the Special Commission Appointed to Investigate the Affairs of the Red Cloud Indian Agency,* 1875; *House Miscellaneous Document No. 167,* 44 Cong., 1 Sess.). The care of his country place, the presidency of the National Wool Growers' Association, and duties as a trustee of Kenyon College were the interests of his latter years. He gave liberally to the endowment of the college and built for it Delano Hall.

[*Biog. Record of Knox County* (1902), pp. 184–90 (portrait); public documents cited in text. See list in Oberholtzer, III, 167–70; *Cincinnati Commercial Tribune, Cincinnati Enquirer,* and *Cleveland Plain Dealer,* all Oct. 24, 1896; *Nation* (N. Y.), Apr. 29, Aug. 5, 19, Sept. 18, 30, Oct. 14, 28, 1875 and Mar. 16, 1876.]

E.J.B.

DELANO, JANE ARMINDA (Mar. 12, 1862–Apr. 15, 1919), teacher, nurse, descended from New England stock, was born at Townsend, N. Y., the second child of George and Mary Ann (Wright) Delano. After a brief period of teaching she entered the Bellevue Hospital School of Nursing, New York City, in 1884. Those associated with her during this period speak of her as a well-poised, earnest student, so unobtrusive in her work that to few, if any, of her classmates did it occur that she possessed the force and character that would later bring her name and accomplishment before the eyes of the world. In 1887, the year after her graduation, she was superintendent of nurses at a hospital in Jacksonville, Fla., during an epidemic of yellow fever. The following year she gave to pioneer service as a visiting-nurse in a mining camp at Bisbee, Ariz. After a period of private practise she was appointed superintendent of nurses at the University of Pennsylvania Hospital School of Nursing, serving 1891–96. In 1898 she took a course at the New York School of Civics and Philanthropy. She was Director of the Girls' Department, House of Refuge, Randall's Island, New York, in 1900–02; and from May 1902 to October 1906 was Director of the School of Nursing at her alma mater, resigning to take care of her aged mother whose death two years later released her for work destined to be the most important in her career.

During the Spanish-American War she had joined the New York Branch of the American Red Cross and become interested in securing nurses for enrolment in the Red Cross Nursing Service. After the reorganization of the American Red Cross in 1905, the National Nursing Associations secured an affiliation with that organization which placed the enrolment of nurses in the hands of state and local committees of Red Cross nurses supervised by a National Committee, of which, in 1909, Miss Delano, just appointed superintendent of the newly authorized Army Nurse Corps, was made chairman. While occupying this dual position she developed the plan for making the Red Cross Nursing Service the reserve of the Army Nurse Corps. From 1908 to 1911 she was president of the board of directors of the *American Journal of Nursing,* and from 1909 to 1912 she was president of the American Nurses' Association.

She resigned from the Army Nurse Corps in 1911 to devote her entire time to Red Cross organization. A Bureau of Nursing Service was created in 1916 under which was placed the selection and assignment of nurses and organization of all military and other nursing units. The writer, then superintendent of the Bellevue and Allied Hospital Schools of Nursing, was selected for this office, Miss Delano retaining her connection with the service as chairman of the National Committee. The declaration of war in 1917 was quickly followed by a speeding up of all Red Cross activities. The demand for nurses made by the Army, the Navy, and the United States Public Health Service in its work in the extra cantonment zones, as well as for the use of the Red Cross brought such heavy burdens upon both the chairman of the National Committee and the director of the Bureau of Nursing Service that a Department of Nursing was created in 1918 with Miss Delano as director. When the Armistice was signed the Red Cross Nursing Service had assigned 17,931 nurses to the Army; 1,058 to the Navy; 284 to the United States Public Health Service, while 604 were working under the Red Cross with the civilian population in the countries of the Allies. The Nursing Service also supplied 553 Red Cross aides for special work in France, and to the influenza epidemic in 1918, especially to war industries, over 15,000 graduate and practical nurses and volunteer aides.

The war over and the influenza epidemic allayed, Miss Delano sailed on Jan. 2, 1919, for France, on her last tour of inspection. Developing a mastoid, from which she never recovered, she died at Savenay Hospital Center, Apr. 15, 1919. It was characteristic of her devotion to the Red Cross that her last words were, "What about my work? I must get back to my work." It was also characteristic of her that, as a memorial to her mother and father, she should leave a legacy, together with the royalties from the

American Red Cross Textbook on Elementary Hygiene and Home Care of the Sick (1913), which with Isabel McIsaacs she found time to prepare during her busy Red Cross days, and to support one or more visiting nurses in communities where none existed. Many decorations were bestowed upon her by foreign countries; the Distinguished Service Medal of the United States and that of the American Red Cross were posthumously awarded.

[*Hist. of Am. Red Cross Nursing* (1922); *Am. Nat. Red Cross, Ann. Report,* June 30, 1919; H. P. Davison, *The Am. Red Cross in the Great War* (1919); *Red Cross Bulletin,* Apr. 21, May 12, 1919; *N. Y. Times,* Apr. 17, 20, 1919; J. A. and M. Delano, *The Hist. and Geneal. of Delano and Launoy* (1899), p. 522; personal acquaintance.]   C. D. N.

DELANY, MARTIN ROBINSON (May 6, 1812–Jan. 24, 1885), first negro major in the United States army, was born in Charles Town, Va. (now in W. Va.), the son of free negroes, Samuel and Pati Delany. His paternal grandfather, a member of the Golah tribe, once fled to Toronto with his wife and two sons, but was brought back and later lost his life in an encounter with a slaveholder. His maternal grandfather, a prince of the Mandingo tribe, had been captured in the Niger Valley, sold, and brought to America along with his betrothed. As a boy of six Delany received his first instruction from peddlers of books. Because of persecution his people were forced to remove to Chambersburg, Pa., in 1822. In 1831 he went to Pittsburgh, where he found better opportunity for study under Rev. Louis Woodson, who was employed by a society of negroes interested in education. By 1834 he was already showing his interest in organizations for the welfare of the poor people of the city; and within the next two years he began the study of medicine under Dr. Andrew N. McDowell, though his work in this field was soon interrupted. On Mar. 15, 1843, he was married to Kate A. Richards of Pittsburgh, and he became the father of eleven children. In 1843 also he began in Pittsburgh the publication of the *Mystery,* a small paper that somehow attracted a good deal of attention to itself, as when it gave a notable description of the fire in the city in 1844. Sued for libel by a negro who was said to be assisting slave-catchers, he was once fined $200 and costs; but several citizens came to his assistance and the fine was later remitted. During the years 1847–49 he was associated with Frederick Douglass in bringing out the *North Star,* published by that orator at Rochester, N. Y. In July 1848 he was mobbed in northern Ohio. The next year he resumed his studies, being received in the medical department of Harvard College after he had been refused entrance at institutions in Pennsylvania and New York. After leaving Harvard he lectured in the West and served with great efficiency in the cholera epidemic in Pittsburgh in 1854. His little book, *The Condition, Elevation, Emigration, and Destiny of the Colored People of the United States, Politically Considered,* issued in Philadelphia in 1852, was earnest and thoughtful, and anticipated Booker T. Washington in its emphasis on practical education. In 1854 he issued a call for a National Emigration Convention, which met in Cleveland in August. The convention established a permanent board of commissioners, of which Delany was made president. A second convention was held in Cleveland in August 1856, and in this year he removed to Chatham, Ontario, where he engaged in the practise of medicine. Two years later a third convention, held at Chatham, chose Delany as chief commissioner to explore the Valley of the Niger, making inquiries "for the purpose of science and for general information and without any reference to, and with the Board being entirely opposed to, any Emigration there as such" (see *Official Report of the Niger Valley Exploring Party,* 1861, by Delany himself). Accordingly, in May 1859 he sailed from New York in the bark *Mendi,* owned by three African merchants. The next year he visited Liverpool and London. On his return to the United States he assisted Charles L. Remond and Charles H. Langston in recruiting negro soldiers, and he was an acting examining surgeon in Chicago. On Feb. 8, 1865, he received his commission as major and on Apr. 5 was ordered to Charleston. After the war he served for three years in the Freedmen's Bureau, was for several years custom-house inspector in Charleston, also for four years a trial justice in the city. He was a severe critic of the corruption of the Reconstruction period in South Carolina and, with Richard H. Cain [*q.v.*] and Joseph H. Rainey, was a leader of the Honest Government League. He was nominated for lieutenant-governor on the Independent Republican ticket, in 1874, but was defeated. In 1879 he published *Principia of Ethnology: the Origin of Races and Color,* etc. In 1884 he was employed to act as agent for a Boston firm in Central America; but by this time his health was failing. He died the following year at Xenia, Ohio.

[In addition to references given above see A. Rollin, *Life and Public Services of Martin R. Delany* (1868); sketch in Wm. J. Simmons, *Men of Mark* (1887); W. P. and F. J. Garrison, *Wm. Lloyd Garrison* (4 vols., 1885–89); A. A. Taylor, *The Negro in S. C. during the Reconstruction* (1924); *Daily Morning Post* (Pittsburgh), Oct. 18, 1854; *News and Courier* (Charleston, S. C.), Feb. 13, Sept. 2, 15, Oct. 2, 3, 1874; Jas. T. Holly, "In Memoriam," *A. M. E. Church Rev.,* Oct. 1886.]
B. B.

DELANY, PATRICK BERNARD (Jan. 28, 1845–Oct. 19, 1924), electrical engineer, inventor, was born in Killavilla, Kings County, Ireland, the son of James and Margaret Delany. Until he was nine years of age he lived in Ireland and attended private school there, but in 1854 his parents came to the United States with their children and settled in Hartford, Conn. Here Delany continued his education, attending parochial schools for the next five years. He then went to work as an office boy in a telegraph office in Hartford. He had always been greatly interested in electricity and took every opportunity to learn telegraphy. By the time he was sixteen years old he had the reputation of being a good telegraph operator. Making this his chosen profession he progressed rapidly and at eighteen was appointed press telegraph operator at Worcester, Mass. Two years later he was given the position of night telegraph circuit manager at Albany, N. Y., for all wires between New York and Buffalo, and three years later became chief operator of the Franklin Telegraph Company at Philadelphia. About 1870 he left Philadelphia to become assistant general superintendent of the newly organized Southern & Atlantic Telegraph Company at Washington, D. C., whose wires began there and spread out through the Southern states to New Orleans, Memphis, and Louisville. About five years later he resigned this position to accept one of superintendent of the Automatic Telegraph Company, also of Washington. His association during these years with George H. Grace, to whom the success of the Southern & Atlantic Telegraph Company was largely due and who was one of the originators of the American Press Association, influenced Delany to abandon telegraphy about 1876 and become a newspaper correspondent. Subsequently, but only for a short time, he was editor of the *Old Commonwealth,* a newspaper at Harrisonburg, Va., but in 1880 he gave up this work to devote his whole time to electrical invention, particularly telegraphy. In that year he moved North with his family and settled in South Orange, N. J., where he became a neighbor and close friend of Thomas Edison for the rest of his life. All told, in the course of his inventive career Delany received a hundred and fifty or two hundred patents. Of these inventions the most prominent were the anti-Page relay; anti-induction cables; a synchronous, multiplex telegraph by which six messages could be sent simultaneously over a single wire and which was subsequently adopted by the British Post Office Department; a perforator for telegraphic transmitting tapes; telegraphic keyboard apparatus; a sound-reproducing machine; a talking-machine recorder and reproducer; as well as the method for manufacture of a talking-machine, known commercially as Vox Humana. He devoted years to improving cable telegraphy, the reward of which was that his automatic system for cables when put in service showed an increase of thirty per cent in speed over hand signaling. During the World War Delany's experimental work in his laboratory at Nantucket, Mass., was concerned principally with the invention of devices for submarine detection and the general location of submerged metallic objects. With these latter inventions, for which he received patents between 1916 and 1918, and with apparatus based on them, it is said that a valuable shipment of gold bullion sunk with the liner *Laurentic* off the coast of Ireland during the war was recovered for the British government. Credit is also given Delany for the recovery in 1923 of a large quantity of copper buried in nine feet of mud on the floor of New York Harbor. He received the Elliott Cresson gold medal on two separate occasions and also the John Scott legacy medal, both awarded by the Franklin Institute. At both the Buffalo and St. Louis expositions he was awarded gold medals for his inventions. He was charter member of the American Institute of Electrical Engineers, founded in 1884, and was one of its vice-presidents, and was also a member of the American Association for the Advancement of Science. He married Annie M. Ovenshine of Philadelphia on Mar. 31, 1869. He died at South Orange and was buried at Nantucket, Mass. An only son survived him.

[*Jour. Am. Inst. Electrical Engineers,* Nov. 11, 1924; *Telegraph and Telephone Age,* Nov. 1, 1924; Jas. D. Reid, *The Telegraph in America* (1879); *Who's Who in America,* 1922–23; obituary in *N. Y. Times,* Oct. 20, 1924; Patent Office records; U. S. National Museum correspondence.]   C. W. M.

DELAVAN, EDWARD CORNELIUS (1793–Jan. 15, 1871), reformer, publisher, was born in Westchester County, N. Y. Although named Edward Cornelius, he rarely used the "Edward." His father having died, at the age of eight he went to Albany with his mother, a brother, and two sisters. He entered a printing-office in that place at the age of thirteen, worked there for several years, then went into his older brother's hardware store. While in the hardware store he also engaged in selling wine, which proved very successful financially. In 1814 he formed a partnership with his brother and shortly after went to Europe as purchasing agent for the firm. Returning to America in 1816 he settled in New York City where he lived until 1825. He then returned to Albany and dealt in real estate for the next five years. His speculations in that field added greatly to his already ample fortune. By the time he had reached middle age he was convinced of the evils of alcohol and during the remainder of his life spent a considerable fortune for the temperance cause. With Dr. Eliphalet Nott [*q.v.*] he organized the New York State Temperance Society in 1829. The *American Temperance Intelligencer,* and the *Temperance Recorder,* both published at Albany, were virtually under his control, and with his own money he secured a large circulation, thus enabling his two papers to exert more influence than all other temperance journals then published. In 1835 he engaged in a public discussion of the undesirability of alcoholic wines for use in church communion, and his arguments attracted wide attention. In the same year he published an article in the *Albany Evening Journal* stating that the Albany brewers were using filthy water for brewing. He was sued for libel, and other persons, gaining courage from the brewers, sued for contended damage in times past. Delavan won the first case and the others dropped their suits. He had the entire proceedings of the trial printed for use as propaganda. When the American Temperance Union was organized in 1836 he became chairman of the executive committee and donated $10,000 to its funds. In 1840 he secured a collection of drawings of the human stomach showing the evil effects of alcohol. At a personal expense of $7,000 he circulated in the state of New York 150,000 of these colored and engraved plates. In 1841 he began to publish the *Enquirer,* a small temperance journal. In 1843 he collected and edited a group of documents which had appeared in the public papers in relation to the drawings which he had published. In 1858 he presented to Union College, Schenectady, a deed of trust to a collection of shells and minerals valued at $10,000. Later publications of Delavan's include a pamphlet, *Temperance of Wine Countries* (1860), and a collection of articles, published in book form under the title, *Temperance Essays* (1865). Delavan was twice married: first, to Abby Smith of Lyme, Conn., and second, to Harriet Schuyler, daughter of Cornelius Schuyler of Albany. He died at his home in Schenectady, N. Y.

[*Nat. Temperance Advocate,* Feb. 1871; *Standard Encyc. of the Alcohol Problem,* vol. II (1924); G. W. Schuyler, *Colonial N. Y.* (1885), II, 154.]   M. S.

DE LA WARR, THOMAS WEST, Baron (July 9, 1577–June 7, 1618), first governor and captain general of the colony of Virginia, was the son of Thomas West, second or eleventh Baron De La Warr, and Anne, the daughter of Sir Francis Knollys. He was born probably at Wherwell, Hampshire, where he was baptized. He matriculated at Queen's College, Oxford, Mar. 9, 1591/2, but left without having taken a degree. After traveling in Italy, he returned to England in 1596 and on Nov. 25 of that year married Cecilia, the daughter of Sir Thomas Shirley, at St. Dunstan's in the West, London. In the following year he was elected to Parliament for Lymington. After serving with distinction in the army in the Low Countries, he was with his cousin, the Earl of Essex, in Ireland in 1599, and was there knighted by Essex on July 12 (W. A. Shaw, *The Knights of England*, 1906, II, 96). He was implicated in the Essex rebellion, imprisoned in the Counter in Wood St., London, in February 1600/1, and subsequently fined 1,000 marks. West's father died Mar. 24, 1601/2, and he succeeded to the peerage and was named a member of the Privy Council. He was created M.A. of Oxford on Aug. 30, 1605.

De La Warr was named as a grantee in the second charter to the Virginia Company of London. He was a member of the Council of the Company in 1609 and it was planned that he should head a mammoth expedition to Virginia. As an initial step the Company appointed Sir Thomas Gates [*q.v.*] lieutenant-general and Sir George Somers admiral. They sailed from England with eight ships and a pinnace, carrying five hundred colonists, in June 1609. The vessel upon which Gates and Somers embarked was wrecked at Bermuda and they were forced to remain there until two pinnaces had been built to carry them to the mainland. It was not until May 1610 that they reached Virginia, where they found the colonists in a deplorable condition and decided to abandon the colony and take them back to England.

Meanwhile, on Feb. 28, 1609/10, the Company had appointed De La Warr first governor and captain general for life of the Colony of Virginia. He sailed from England at the head of an expedition of three ships and 150 colonists on Apr. 1, 1610, arriving at Cape Henry on June 5, at Point Comfort on the following day, and at Jamestown on June 10 just in time to save the colony, the inhabitants of which Gates had already embarked on vessels for the return voyage to England. De La Warr dispatched Somers to Bermuda for supplies and Gates to England for help. He caused Fort Henry and Fort Charles at the mouth of the river and a third fort at the falls to be erected.

De La Warr had arrived in Virginia in the summer season. The company he brought with him suffered severely from the effects of the heat and he himself became ill. He appointed Capt. George Percy as deputy governor, until Sir Thomas Dale should arrive in the colony, and on Mar. 28, 1611, sailed for the island of "Mevis" [Nevis?] in the West Indies to recuperate, but was driven from his course to the Western Islands, whence, upon his recovery, he returned to England, arriving in June 1611. There he published *The Relation of the Right Honourable the Lord De-la-Warre, Lord Governour and Captaine Generall of the Colonie, planted in Virginea* (London, 1611), and worked to win support for the colony. He was planning a second voyage to Virginia as early as December 1616, but it was not until March 1617/18, that he sailed from England with 200 men. The vessel touched at Terceira in the Azores where De La Warr and his crew were feasted. Immediately afterward they became ill, and it was suspected that they had been poisoned. De La Warr died on June 7, 1618.

Lady De La Warr survived her husband and was named executrix of his will. To provide for her five daughters, she petitioned for and was granted on Sept. 13, 1619, a pension of £500 per annum to be paid by the farmers of the customs of Virginia for thirty-one years. This was renewed in 1634 but lapsed during the period of the Civil Wars, the Commonwealth, and the Protectorate. A new grant of £200 per annum was made to Jane West, a daughter, in 1662. De La Warr left seven children, of whom Henry, born Oct. 3, 1603, succeeded to the title.

[*Calendar of State Papers, Domestic Ser.*; *Calendar of State Papers, Colonial Ser.*; *Acts of the Privy Council*; *Acts of the Privy Council, Colonial Ser.*; Alexander Brown, *The Genesis of the U. S.* (2 vols., 1890); *The Records of the Va. Company of London* (2 vols., 1906), ed. by Susan Myra Kingsbury; E. S. Neill, "Va. Governors under the London Company," in *Macalester College Contribs., Dept of Hist., Lit., and Pol. Sci.*, 1 ser., no. 1 (1889). There is an article in the *Dict. of Nat. Biog.* with further references.]   I. M. C.

DE LEON, DANIEL (Dec. 14, 1852–May 11, 1914), Socialist advocate, was of Jewish stock, the son of Salomon and Sara (Jesurun) De Leon, and was born on the island of Curaçao. His early education was received at home, but was interrupted by the death of his father, a surgeon in the Dutch colonial army, when the boy was twelve years old. In 1866 he was sent to a gymnasium at Hildesheim, Germany, and he afterward studied at Amsterdam. The belief that he was a graduate of the University of Leyden is not borne out by the records of the institution, which do not reveal his name. About 1874 he came to the United States, making his home in New York City, where later his mother rejoined him. For a time he was associate editor of a Spanish paper advocating Cuban liberation and later taught school in Westchester County, N. Y. While thus employed he attended classes in law and political science at Columbia College, in 1878 receiving the degree of LL.B. After practising law for a time in Texas, he returned to New York City and in 1883 won a prize lectureship at Columbia in Latin-American diplomacy, which he retained for two three-year terms, thereafter retiring from the college.

In the meantime he had become deeply interested in social questions. He actively supported the candidacy of Henry George for mayor in 1886; in 1888 he joined the Knights of Labor; about a year later he became affiliated with the Nationalist movement, founded by Edward Bellamy, and in October 1890, he joined the Socialist Labor party. His partisans have always asserted that his retirement from the college was forced by his radical activities, but the statement has been denied by competent authority, and it is evident that his lectureship expired by self-limitation. In 1891 he was appointed national lecturer of the party and later in the year was chosen as its candidate for governor of New York. About the beginning of 1892 he became the editor of its organ, *The People,* a weekly, to which a daily edition was added in 1900 but discontinued in February, 1914. He was again a candidate for governor in 1902 and several times conducted spirited but unsuccessful campaigns for the state Assembly and for Congress.

He early assumed a dominant position in the party, and despite repeated attempts to dislodge him maintained his leadership to the end. He took a strongly antagonistic attitude toward the existing trade-unions, characterizing their leaders as "labor fakers," and demanding the reorganization of the unions on a frankly Socialist basis. In 1895 he led a seceding faction from the Knights of Labor and founded the Socialist Trade and Labor Alliance, and in the following year obtained its indorsement by the national convention of the party. An opposing faction, friendly to the old unions, now began to make headway, and charging De Leon with being a "doctrinaire" and a "dictator," gradually won to its side the greater part of the membership. In July 1899, failing to oust De Leon from his place, this faction withdrew and formed a new organization, which ultimately became the Socialist Party of America. From this loss of members

and prestige his own party never recovered. At Chicago, in June 1905, De Leon took part in the formation of the Industrial Workers of the World, the Socialist Trade and Labor Alliance being immediately merged with it. The new organization, however, soon came under the control of the extreme "direct actionists," who rejected all political effort, and in the convention of 1908 De Leon was refused a seat. A few weeks later, at Paterson, N. J., his partisans organized a rival I. W. W., which subsequently changed its name to that of the Workers' International Industrial Union. To a greatly diminished following he continued during the next six years to expound his conception of Socialism and Socialist tactics and to excoriate those who disagreed with him. In 1913 he moved from New York City to Pleasantville, in Westchester County. He died in a hospital in New York City.

De Leon was twice married—on Aug. 2, 1882, to Sara Lobo (who died in April 1887), and on June 10, 1892, to Bertha Canary, who survived him. His character has been the subject of the most contradictory estimates. His opponents have assailed him as a disruptive fanatic, avid of power and an adept in dissimulation and intrigue. It is certain that in at least one matter he was uncandid, for despite the known facts regarding his ancestry, he professed among his intimates to be a "Venezuelan Catholic," of a wealthy and aristocratic family. His partisans have portrayed him as a man friendly in disposition, genial in temperament, and of incorruptible integrity, content in his single-minded devotion to the cause of the workers to live and die poor. The value of his contribution to social politics is also a matter of dispute. By his opponents he is held to have brought to the social movement nothing but turmoil and dissension. His followers, on the other hand, declare that his concept of a revolutionary working-class organization, formed by industries instead of by crafts, determined to "take and hold" and operate the means of production and distribution, is a prescient foreshadowing of the means by which society is some day to be reconstructed. Lenin, who became acquainted with his writings after the Bolshevik revolution, admired them greatly and declared that they incorporated the germ of the Soviet system. His literary product was mostly propaganda pamphlets such as *Two Pages from Roman History* (1903), *What Means This Strike?* (1898), *Socialist Reconstruction of Society* (1905), but he also translated Marx's *The Eighteenth Brumaire of Louis Napoleon* and seventeen of the nineteen historical romances in Eugène Sue's series, *The*

Mysteries of the People; or History of a Proletarian Family Across the Ages.

[*Who's Who in America*, 1914–15; *Daniel De Leon, The Man and His Work. A Symposium* (1919); Olive M. Johnson, *Daniel De Leon* (pamphlet, 1923); *Annual Registers of Columbia College* (1883–89); records of the University of Leyden; recollections of the writer; information as to certain details from Sol. J. Delvalle of the Congregation Mikve Israel of Curaçao, Solon De Leon (the son of Daniel) and Arnold Petersen of New York City, J. M. L. Maduro of The Hague, and others.]

W.J.G.

DE LEON, THOMAS COOPER (May 21, 1839–Mar. 19, 1914), author, son of Mardici Heinrich and Rebecca (Lopez-y-Nunez) De Leon, was born in Columbia, S. C., and died in Mobile, Ala. The ancestors of both his parents came to this country from the Spanish West Indies before the Revolution. His father was a physician, an intimate friend of Thomas Cooper, president of the University of South Carolina, for whom he named the youngest of his three sons. Of the older sons, David Camden became surgeon-general of the Confederacy, and Edwin, an author and a diplomat in Egypt. Thomas Cooper was educated primarily in Washington at Rugby Academy and at Georgetown University; at the first, he was a fellow student of Henry Watterson, and at the second, of James Ryder Randall. From 1858 to 1861 he was in Washington as a clerk in the bureau of topographical engineers. He was in the Confederate army (1861–65), apparently always on duty at the capital, whether Montgomery or Richmond. His experiences and observations during this period—social as well as political—were recorded later in his graphic and judicious if somewhat journalistic books, *Four Years in Rebel Capitals* (1890) and *Belles Beaux and Brains of the 60's* (1907). He was in Baltimore (1865–66) as editor of the *Cosmopolite Magazine,* and in New York (1866–67) as writer for various newspapers and magazines, and—to the scandal of his friends—as translator of French novels. His anthology, *South Songs* (1866), and his political writings under the name Dunne Browne recommended him favorably to Southern publicists, and in 1868, on the summons of John Forsyth, he removed to Mobile as managing editor, and after 1877 as editor, of the *Mobile Register*. He remained there for the rest of his life, incredibly tireless and versatile—as editor, printer, advocate of free-silver, theatre-manager, director of carnivals both North and South, and society-man agreeably tinged with Bohemianism. In addition, he was a poet, essayist, parodist, novelist, and playwright—in whatever capacity, always keenly sensitive to the shifts of popular taste. Aside from his important books of war reminiscence, the most notable of his writings were perhaps his burlesque play, *Hamlet ye Dismal Prince,* produced in New York in 1870, and said to have been the first American play to run for 100 nights—his two "travesties," *The Rock or the Rye* (1888) parodying Amélie Rives, and *Society as I have Foundered It* (1890) parodying Ward McAllister—and his two local-color novels *Creole and Puritan* (1889) and *Crag-Nest* (1897). Although he was blind for the last eleven years of his life, he remained ceaselessly active. He never married.

[T. McA. Owen, *Hist. of Ala. and Dict. of Ala. Biog.,* III (1921); L. DeV. Chaudron, "Sketch of the Author of Four Years in Rebel Capitals," in T. C. De Leon, *Four Years in Rebel Capitals* (ed. 1892); *Who's Who in America,* 1912–13; *Mobile Reg.,* Mar. 20, 1914.]

J.D.W.

DELÉRY, FRANÇOIS CHARLES (Jan. 28, 1815–June 12, 1880), physician, writer, was a typical Louisiana Creole, born in the Parish of St. Charles, La., of French-Canadian ancestry. His father was Louis Boisclair Deléry; his mother, Marie Corbin Babin. In 1829 he was sent to Paris to complete his classical education and to prepare himself for medicine. His studies successfully ended, his thesis, *Questions sur diverses branches des sciences médicales,* published in Paris in 1842, he returned to Louisiana to exercise his chosen profession and to take an active part in civic affairs. He was for seven years city physician of New Orleans, and president of the board of health for two; he founded *l'Union Médicale* to which he contributed frequently; in 1858 he represented his adopted city at the Quarantine Congress held in Philadelphia. He opposed secession, but when it had occurred his love for Louisiana caused him to espouse the Southern cause and he was one of the first to leave New Orleans after the arrival of Federal troops. He went to Havana, where he wrote in support of the Confederacy. On his return to New Orleans, after the war, he became city coroner.

His chief claims to fame are his writings on the problems of yellow fever: *Précis historique de la fièvre jaune de 1858* (1859), *Réplique au mémoire du Dr. Faget* (1860), *Mémoire sur l'épidémie de fièvre jaune qui a régné à la Nouvelle-Orléans et dans les campagnes* (1867), *Quarantaine* (1878). These reveal sound scientific training, skilful treatment, and a sincere passion for investigation. He studied his subject carefully and thoroughly. He fought quarantine as a preventive of yellow fever, although he attributed the cause of the disease to a germ. With the exception of an unpublished collection of poems written under the influence of the French poet Delavigne, his non-medical writings were educational, philosophical, and patriotic. They include: *Essai sur la liberté* (1847), *Études sur les passions, suivies d'un aperçu sur l'éducation qu'il convient de donner au peuple* (1849), *Quelques mots sur le Nativisme* (1854), *Confédérés et Fédéraux* (1864), *Le dernier chant du guerrier orateur, à la mémoire du lieutenant-colonel C. D. Dreux* (1861), *Le spectre noir ou le radicalisme aux États-Unis* (1868), and a comedy in one act, *l'École du peuple* (1877). All were published in New Orleans and in French; *Black Ghost* was also published in English. Deléry was a man of ideals, devoted to his profession and his state. He had the courage of his convictions and he worked consistently and persistently for what he felt to be right. His last years were spent in the practise of his profession at Bay St. Louis, where he died, survived by his wife Odile, who was also a Deléry.

[Chas. Testut in his *Portraits littéraires* (1850), and J. W. Davidson in *Living Writers of the South* (1869) have both contributed interesting sketches of Deléry. C. P. Dimitry in the *Times-Democrat* (New Orleans), Oct. 9, 16, 1892, and Grace King in *Creole Families of New Orleans* (1921), see "Lafreniere," have given the family background. A good obituary notice is to be found in the *New Orleans Medic. & Surgic. Jour.* for Dec. 1880. See also Bussière Rouen, "Les Poètes Louisianais" in the *Comptes Rendus* of the Athenée Louisianais, Jan.–April 1921, and Ruby Caulfeild, *The French Literature of Louisiana* (1929), pub. by the Inst. of French Studies, Columbia Univ.]   L. C. D.

DEL MAR, ALEXANDER (Aug. 9, 1836–July 1, 1926), mining engineer, economist, historian, was born in New York, the eldest son of Jacques and Belle (Alexander) Del Mar. The former was descended from a Spanish family which settled in Pennsylvania in the seventeenth century and the latter was of British stock. Jacques Del Mar, for many years an official in the Treasury Department, maintained an active interest in his Spanish connections, and his son, receiving his early education in private schools in New York, spent several of his boyhood years in England and Spain. In the latter country he attended the Madrid School of Mines. In London he came under the guidance of his uncle, Manuel Del Mar, an author, and also Sir Arthur Helps. These associations stimulated his interest in history and political economy. Returning to New York in 1854, he found no opening for the active practise of his profession. By nature a student and investigator, at an early age he undertook to prepare a book on the history of precious metals published much later. He also formed editorial connections with *Hunt's Merchants' Magazine, DeBow's Review,* the *Commercial and Financial Chronicle,* and the *Social Science Review,* and contributed to these journals essays dealing for the most part with public finance and monetary problems.

From 1866 to 1869 he was director of the Bureau of Statistics, a new bureau designed to concentrate statistical work previously undertaken by officers in the Treasury and State departments. Unfortunately, he undertook to develop these statistical inquiries on a scale far too extended, and became involved in administrative difficulties with his superiors. In 1871 he moved to Brooklyn, where for a brief period he was engaged in promoting municipal reform and in 1872 joined the Liberal Republican party in support of Greeley. During the same period he rendered a signal service to life insurance companies in predicting, contrary to prevailing opinion, that interest rates would fall and that consequently it would be necessary for these companies to face decreasing earnings (*Proceedings of the Second Session of the National Insurance Convention,* 1872, pp. 188–216). In 1872 also he accepted an invitation from the Russian government to attend the sessions of the International Statistical Congress in St. Petersburg and in 1876 he served as mining engineer of the United States Monetary Commission. After a period in California studying the history of mining in the Western states, in 1878 he returned to the East to serve for a short while as clerk to the committee on naval expenditures of the House of Representatives.

Two years later he published in London *A History of the Precious Metals from the Earliest Times to the Present* (1880; second edition, thoroughly revised, New York, 1901). This supplements William Jacob's *Historical Inquiry into the Production and Consumption of the Precious Metals,* published in 1831. Del Mar's volume contains a series of tables showing the stocks of gold and silver coin in each country over a long series of dates. The influence of new supplies of gold and silver in the progress of civilization had early absorbed his attention; in this book he noted particularly that the search for gold had extended the area and prolonged the establishment of slavery. The cost of production theory as applied to the precious metals in his opinion had no significance. Moreover, he held, the changes in price, due to new supplies of metallic money, were not synchronous, or uniform for all commodities, and speculators were thus enabled to reap large rewards. The *History of the Precious Metals* was followed by a long series of monographs and pamphlets dealing with metallic money, coinage, and the mints, including: *The Science of Money* (1885); *Money and Civilization* (1886); *The History of Money in America from the Earliest Times to the Establishment of the Constitution* (1899). He also published historical and archeological studies, in which he assembled much curious information in regard to the interrelations of the religions of ancient peoples with their economic life. Among these were: *The Worship of Augustus Cæsar* (1900), based upon a study of coins, money, calendars, astronomical and astrological cycles; *The Middle Ages Revisited; or, The Roman Government and Religion and Their Relations to Britain* (1900); *Ancient Britain in the Light of Modern Archeological Discoveries* (1900); and *The Messiah* (1907), developing the history of the Messianic cult. Between 1899 and 1902 he edited the *Cambridge Encyclopædia* of esoteric subjects. In his contributions to the study of money, he accumulated much curious data, but for students of monetary theory his volumes have but a limited value. He was married in 1861, to Emilia José (Emily Joseph), and after her death in 1912, to Alice Demorest who survived him. He died at the home of his daughter, in Little Falls, N. J.

[Most of Del Mar's volumes contain in appendices the long list of the various pamphlets which he issued. See also Hamilton Willcox, *The Life of the Honorable Alexander Del Mar* (1898); *Who's Who in America*, 1924–25; obituary in *N. Y. Times*, July 3, 1926.]

D. R. D.

DELMAS, DELPHIN MICHAEL (Apr. 14, 1844–Aug. 1, 1928), lawyer, the son of Antoine and Coralie Delmas, was born in France, but his father joined the gold rush in 1849, and the family followed to California in 1854, settling at San José in the Santa Clara Valley. The boy's early education was received at home, and in 1858 he entered Santa Clara College, where he graduated with a brilliant record (A.B., 1862, A.M. 1863), and was awarded a gold medal for proficiency in the classics. After a few months in a law office in San Francisco, he entered the Yale Law School (LL.B., 1865), and was admitted to the California bar in February 1866. Opening an office in San José, he made slow progress, and was compelled to add to his means by teaching school. In 1867, however, an eloquent Fourth-of-July address attracted the attention of the local Democrats, who elected him district attorney for Santa Clara County, in which office he displayed marked efficiency. Among his early cases was a series of successful damage suits against the Southern Pacific Railroad in which he exhibited such ability that he was soon enjoying a large and lucrative practise. In February 1883 he removed to San Francisco where he quickly became one of the leaders of the California bar. For the next twenty

years, not confining himself to any special field, he was associated with every outstanding case before the state courts, including *Colton* vs. *Leland Stanford et al.* (82 *Cal.*, 351), by reason of the vast financial interest involved the most important private litigation ever conducted in California; and the spectacular claim of Nettie R. Craven to the Fair estate. A delegate to the Democratic National Convention in 1904, he there nominated William Randolph Hearst for the presidency.

In 1907 he achieved nation-wide notoriety through his conduct of the defense of Harry K. Thaw on the latter's first trial for the murder of Stanford White in New York City. His invocation on Thaw's behalf of a higher and "unwritten" law and a type of insanity which he designated *"dementia Americana"*—stigmatized as "brain storm, the paranoia of the millionaire," by the district attorney, W. T. Jerome—was a contribution of doubtful value to criminal jurisprudence. For a short period thereafter he was engaged professionally in New York City, but ultimately returned to California, practising in San Francisco and later in Los Angeles, up to within a few months of his death, which occurred at Santa Monica. He married, Apr. 7, 1869, Pauline, daughter of Col. J. P. Hoge of San Francisco.

Known as the "Napoleon of the California bar" from his strong facial resemblance to the Emperor, he also possessed the latter's trait of rapid decision and faculty of instinctively finding his opponent's weak spots. An accomplished lawyer, a master of the art of cross-examination, an astute tactician of keen intellect and wide vision, he prepared his briefs with infinite care, leaving no contingency unprovided for. Endowed with unusual fluency and a wide vocabulary, which, aided by his classical education, he assiduously cultivated, he earned the title of the "silver-tongued spell-binder of the Pacific Coast," though he never sacrificed lucidity to mere phrase-making. A book entitled *Speeches and Addresses,* published in 1901 in San Francisco, embodies his outstanding achievements.

[*Who's Who in America*, 1928–29; Santa Clara College catalogues, 1858–63; *Hist. of the Bench and Bar of Cal.* (1901), ed. by Oscar T. Shuck, p. 625; *The Trial of Harry Thaw* (London, 1928), ed. by F. A. Mackenzie; *Hist. of Santa Clara County, Cal.* (1881), p. 707; *The Bay of San Francisco* (1892), II, 453; *Santa Clara County and its Resources* (1895), p. 268. Obituary notices appeared in the San Francisco, Los Angeles, and New York City press of Aug. 2, 1928.]

H. W. H. K.

DELMONICO, LORENZO (Mar. 13, 1813–Sept. 3, 1881), restaurateur, was born at Marengo, at the eastern base of Mount St. Gothard, in the canton of Ticino, Switzerland. His father was a small farmer and Lorenzo's schooling advantages were slight—a deficiency that he sought to remedy in after years. At nineteen he left his native village and migrated to America, landing at New York, whither two uncles, John and Peter Delmonico, had preceded him. John, the elder, had been master of a sailing vessel trading between Cuba and the United States, but in 1825 he had given up the sailor's calling, settled in New York City, and become a dealer in wines. With his brother Peter he had started a small confectionery and catering business. After some hesitation, they took their nephew into partnership, and he soon suggested a departure in their modest business which was destined to make the name Delmonico famous throughout the United States and in every European capital. His idea was that the firm open a restaurant in downtown New York which should provide foods cooked and served in the European manner of the day. As a people Americans had neglected the science of the table. The value of salads was practically unknown. In a land of abundance only the most imperfect use was made of vegetables, many of which could have been provided at a minimum of cost. Lorenzo Delmonico became a teacher of gastronomy, and in a surprisingly short time he won national recognition. Without capital and at first without influential friends, within twenty years he made New York known the world over as a center of good living. From materials that could be had almost for the asking he prepared dishes such as few native New Yorkers had ever tasted. The variety of American game, fish, and meats that appeared on his menus astonished all visitors from the Old World. Yet he was merely making obvious use of what had been largely overlooked by the Americans themselves. He seems to have been guided by his own shrewd divination of New York's culinary needs and the practical means of supplying them. His fame spread so quickly that within a few years experienced cooks from Parisian kitchens were coming to New York and offering Delmonico their services. He was never at a loss for competent help nor for information of the latest developments in European cuisine. The first Delmonico restaurant, on William St., was destroyed in the great fire of 1835. It was succeeded by restaurants at 76 Broad St., and at Beaver and William Sts. About the same time the Delmonicos bought more than 200 acres of land within the limits of what later became the Borough of Brooklyn and began farming operations modeled on those with which they had been familiar in Switzerland. Among their

guests during that period were Louis Napoleon and the Prince de Joinville.

John Delmonico having died in 1842, Lorenzo continued the business with Peter, and in 1848 succeeded to the chief proprietorship of the business. From 1846 to 1856 a Delmonico hotel was conducted at 21–25 Broadway and from 1855 to 1875 the principal restaurant was at Broadway and Chambers St., but one was opened at Fourteenth St. and Fifth Ave., the first year of the Civil War, and in 1876 began the career of the famous Delmonico restaurant at Broadway and Twenty-sixth St. Lorenzo's brother Siro and other members of the family came from Switzerland and took places in the organization, which grew to be one of the greatest of its kind in existence. In 1861, through unfortunate investments in oil stocks, Delmonico lost $500,-000, which was made up within a few years from the profits of the restaurants. In 1856 he had married a widow, Mme. Miège. He founded a public school in his native village and was for years a liberal giver to the Catholic Church in New York. Together with his noteworthy part in bringing about changes in American diet, he was largely responsible, through his success in entertaining the public, for the growth of the restaurant as an institution in American cities. Before his time New York had no restaurants where extensive bills of fare were served, save at particular hours. His restaurants at once sprang into favor. It was said at the time of his death, in 1881, that every president of the United States from Jackson to Garfield had been his guest, while New York, next to Paris, was believed to be better supplied with restaurants than any other city in the world. Delmonico was a quiet, methodical man of business, noted for his thrift; he was an inveterate smoker, often consuming thirty strong Havana cigars in a day. For many years after his restaurant business had become the largest in the city he personally attended to the marketing.

[*N. Y. Times*, Sept. 4, Dec. 20, 1881; Geo. S. Chappell, *Restaurants of N. Y.* (1925), pp. 16–18; Leopold Rimmer, *Hist. of Old N. Y. Life and the House of the Delmonicos* (1898), an employee's recollections.]

W. B. S.

DE LONG, GEORGE WASHINGTON (Aug. 22, 1844–Oct. 30, 1881), Arctic explorer, was born in New York City, the son of Levi and Catherine Greames De Long. His parents moved to Brooklyn when the boy was four years old and there he spent his boyhood, which, because of parental fear of the dangers of the outside world, was one of great seclusion. He attended the public schools of Brooklyn and "was a hard student, thorough in his application to books, and faithful to his school work" (Emma De Long, *post*, I, 2). His ambition was kindled by reading some tales of exploits in the War of 1812, and he resolved to become a naval officer. When he was selected for an appointment to the Naval Academy in 1857, however, his parents refused their permission as they were desirous of having him enter a profession. He finally yielded to his parents' wishes and began the study of law in the office of John Oakey. With the outbreak of the Civil War, Oakey entered the service and De Long begged hard to accompany him but without success. Having been denied a place in the army, the young man again turned his thoughts toward the Naval Academy. After considerable persuasion, he secured the consent of his parents and by sheer determination won an appointment. He applied himself vigorously to his work and was graduated with distinction in 1865.

His first sea duty was a three-year cruise on the *Canandaigua* to the western shores of Europe and Africa and in the Mediterranean. Then followed assignments to several vessels, a period at Washington for signal practise, and work in the equipment division in New York. In 1869 he was commissioned a lieutenant and in 1879 a lieutenant-commander. Early in 1871, he obtained a leave of absence to journey to Havre, France, where, on Mar. 1, he married Emma J. Wotton. One daughter was born to this union.

In 1873, De Long was assigned to the *Juniata* which was soon afterward sent to the Arctic in search of the missing steamer *Polaris*. The adventures of this trip fired his enthusiasm for further Arctic research; and upon his return to New York, he interested James Gordon Bennett in the project. After several years of planning, they secured the Arctic steamer *Pandora,* rechristened her the *Jeannette,* and fitted her out for the dash through Bering Strait to the Pole. With a crew of thirty-three officers and men, the *Jeannette* sailed from San Francisco, July 8, 1879. On Sept. 5, while about twenty-five miles east of Herald Island, the vessel was caught in an ice pack and drifted to the northwest for over twenty-one months, finally reaching latitude 77° 15′ north and longitude 155° east, where on June 12, 1881, she was crushed by the heavy ice floes and sank at four in the morning of the next day. De Long was prepared for this emergency, however, and abandoned the ship in an orderly fashion, salvaging most of the provisions and equipment. The retreat southward toward the Siberian coast commenced on June 18 and for over two months De Long and his men,

hampered by their provisions and boats, fought their way over a frozen sea. At last open water was reached and the party embarked in three boats for the Lena Delta.

During a heavy gale on Sept. 12, the boats became separated; and while the two commanded respectively by De Long and Engineer Melville managed to weather the storm, Lieutenant Chipp's craft was never heard from again. The two surviving boats reached widely separated portions of the delta; Melville's party landed in one of the eastern outlets and was rescued by natives; while De Long's group reached a northern arm of the river and landed in an uninhabited country. With only a few days' provisions, De Long, ever hopeful of rescue, led his men southward, until thoroughly exhausted they could go no farther. Two of the strongest—Nindemann and Noros—were sent ahead to bring assistance but without avail. Finally toward the end of October, the entire command succumbed one by one to starvation and exposure. Their bodies were found the next spring by Melville and were subsequently brought to New York and buried with honors. Melville also recovered the records of the expedition including De Long's journal, which was later published by his widow under the title, *The Voyage of the Jeannette.* Although the *Jeannette* expedition failed in its original purpose, it established the existence of a northwestward polar drift and at the same time changed the map of the Arctic by delimiting the size of Wrangel Island and by discovering the small group of islands now named for its courageous commander.

[*Lieut. Danenhower's Narrative of the Jeannette* (1882); Emma De Long, ed., *The Voyage of the Jeannette* (1883); I. II. De Long, *The Lineage of Malcolm Metzger Parker from Johannes De Lang* (1926); Wm. H. Gilder, *Ice-Pack and Tundra* (1883); G. W. Melville, *In the Lena Delta* (1885); R. W. Bliss, *Our Lost Explorers* (1882); H. M. Prentiss, "The *Jeannette* Search and the Polar Current" in his *Great Polar Current* (1897); Record of the Proceedings of a Court of Inquiry, to investigate the loss of the steamer *Jeannette, House Exec. Doc. No. 108,* 47 Cong., 2 Sess.; *Jeannette Inquiry, House Miscel. Doc. No. 66,* 48 Cong., 1 Sess.]
G. H. B.

DE MÉZIÈRES Y CLUGNY, ATHANASE (c. 1715–Nov. 2, 1779), soldier, explorer, Indian agent, was born in Paris, St. Sulpice Parish, the son of Louis Christophe de Mézières and Marie Antoinette Clugny. His was a distinguished family. One of his sisters, the Marchioness de Montessons, married the Duke of Orleans; two uncles were generals in the French army; a cousin, Minard de Clugny, was minister of state; a nephew, the Marquis de Genlis, was inspector of infantry; a niece was lady-in-waiting to the Duchess of Chartres. De Mézières came to Louisiana about 1733. Ten years later he was a soldier at Natchitoches, where most of his career was spent thereafter. He rose through the ranks of ensign, lieutenant, and captain to that of lieutenant-colonel. On Apr. 18, 1746, he married Marie Petronille Feliciane de St. Denis, daughter of the famous Luis Juchereau de St. Denis. She died in 1748 and some time later he married Dame Pélagie Fazende. In 1756 he was appointed by Gov. Kerlérec on a commission to determine the Texas-Louisiana boundary at the Gulf of Mexico. Besides being a soldier he was a trader and a planter. He was prosperous, and in 1766 he possessed thirty-five slaves and ten thousand pounds of tobacco.

When Louisiana was transferred to Spain he entered the Spanish service, and for ten years he was ruler of Red River Valley. The governor of Texas declared that he had "such knowledge of these provinces of Texas and Louisiana as is possessed by no one else, and likewise of the tribes which surround them." This reputation he sustained until his death.

His most signal service was to supervise the Indian trade, and to win to Spanish allegiance the tribes of Louisiana, Texas, Arkansas, and Oklahoma. To install the new system he held an assembly of chiefs at Natchitoches (Apr. 21, 1770). He issued licenses to traders, cut off illicit traffic, and induced the Indians to deliver up vagabonds or intruding Englishmen. To hold conferences with distant tribes he made extensive explorations, and his well-written diaries and reports give us our first definite information regarding a large part of northern Texas. In 1770 he went to Cadodachos and held a council with several tribes, making eloquent speeches. The fruit of this meeting was a treaty made at Natchitoches in 1771. In the next year he made a long tour to the northwest, visiting Quitseis, Yscanes, Tawakoni, and Wichita villages on the Trinity and Brazos rivers, and conducting seventy chiefs and headmen to San Antonio to see the governor of Texas. On this expedition he had spent eighty-seven days. His report of the journey is a classic. By his persistent efforts of three years having won to Spanish allegiance the "Nations of the North," he now went to France and Spain, "to recuperate his health and settle various matters of private business which he had pending in those realms." While abroad he was promoted by the King of Spain to the rank of lieutenant-colonel (Nov. 8, 1772), and was made a knight of the Order of St. Louis. Back at Natchitoches, he devoted the next five years to extending trade and influence among the new allies. By his energetic fostering of the Louisi-

ana trade he aroused opposition from ambitious San Antonio merchants, but he was vigorously defended by the Baron de Ripperdá, governor of Texas. The reorganization of the northern provinces of New Spain by Teodoro de Croix [q.v.] after 1776 brought De Mézières and his work into greater prominence. Croix made a tour of the frontier, and held councils at Monclova and San Antonio. After long deliberations it was decided to cement the alliance with the Nations of the North and lead them in a grand campaign against the Apaches, farther West. The advice of De Mézières was needed and he was called to San Antonio. The plan which he presented there is a most illuminating document. While Croix and others were considering the proposals, De Mézières made a tour up the Brazos, and to the Taovayas on Red River (1778). On the way he wrote sixteen reports which constitute another historical treasure. At the end of this tour he returned to Natchitoches, but in further preparation for the great war, at the request of Croix he was permanently released from his Louisiana post. On his way to San Antonio he made still another tour among the northern tribes (1779). While en route he received from the King of Spain a letter of thanks for his distinguished services. In September he reported at San Antonio for duty, only to be told, a few days later, that he had been appointed governor of Texas in the place of Cabello. He never entered upon his new office, however, for he died on Nov. 2 from the effects of an accident during his last journey. He was buried at the parish church, now the Cathedral of San Fernando, in San Antonio, where his remains still rest.

De Mézières was cultured and versatile. He wrote letters in French, Spanish, and Latin, and we are told that he was a mathematician of ability. In his day he was a prominent figure on the frontier, and with propriety he can be compared with his contemporaries, Juan Bautista de Anza, Bernardo de Gálvez, and George Rogers Clark [qq.v.].

[The principal sources of information regarding De Mézières are his own letters and reports. These were translated and edited by H. E. Bolton in *Athanase De Mézières and the Louisiana-Texas Frontier, 1768–80* (2 vols., 1914). A summary of his work is contained in H. E. Bolton, *Texas in the Middle Eighteenth Century* (1915).]   H. E. B.

DE MILLE, HENRY CHURCHILL (Sept. 17, 1853–Feb. 10, 1893), playwright, the son of William Edward and Margaret Blount (Hoyt) De Mille, both of Washington, N. C., was born in that place and spent his boyhood on a farm. Going to New York, he became a student in Columbia College, being graduated in 1875 and receiving the degrees of A.B. and A.M. His first intention was to become a clergyman, but he soon changed his mind, and, after teaching at the Columbia Grammar School in New York, he became permanently associated with the theatre, successively as an actor for a short time under A. M. Palmer's management, as an instructor in the American Academy of Dramatic Arts, as a reader of plays at the Madison Square Theatre, and as a writer of plays. A thorough knowledge and understanding of the technique of the stage enabled him to do skilful work in the revising and reshaping of plays by other hands for production at the Madison Square, where he was closely associated with Steele MacKaye and David Belasco. His first original play, *John Delmer's Daughters or Duty,* was produced there on Dec. 10, 1883, but it attracted the public for only one week. After the production, at the Lyceum Theatre, on Sept. 18, 1886, of *The Main Line or Rawson's Y,* a melodrama of Western scenes and incidents written in collaboration with Charles Barnard, he began the partnership with Belasco which resulted in a series of plays that reflected more of the glare of the footlights than of the actual light of day. These were *The Wife,* produced Nov. 1, 1887; *Lord Chumley,* produced Aug. 21, 1888, written especially for E. H. Sothern to give that actor a character somewhat like the Lord Dundreary his father had made famous; and *The Charity Ball,* produced Nov. 19, 1889. They were among the most popular plays of the period and, acted for several successive seasons throughout the country under the management of Daniel Frohman at whose Lyceum Theatre they had first been produced, gave De Mille a national reputation. Since he saw life mainly in terms of the theatre, his plays were artificial in structure, written in the conventional manner of the society drama of the day, with alternate layers of intrigue, drama, farce, and comedy, their only appeal being in their entertaining qualities and in the opportunity they gave for skilful acting by groups of expert players. Except for occasional performances by local stock companies, their popularity did not continue beyond the early years of the twentieth century. Another Belasco–De Mille play, *Men and Women,* produced at Proctor's Twenty-third Street Theatre in New York on Oct. 21, 1890, dealt with the sensations of American business and political life. De Mille's last play, also produced at Proctor's, was *The Lost Paradise,* an English version of the German dramatist Ludwig Fulda's *Das Verlorene Paradies.* He died suddenly of pneumonia at his home in Pompton, N. J. In 1876 he married Mathilde

Beatrice Samuel; of their three children a daughter died in childhood, and two sons, William C. and Cecil B. De Mille, have reached positions of prominence in the motion-picture world.

[M. J. Moses, *The Am. Dramatist* (1917), pp. 237–40; T. A. Brown, *A Hist. of the N.Y. Stage,* III (1903), 421; Wm. Winter, *The Life of David Belasco* (1918); A. H. Quinn, *A Hist. of the Am. Drama from the Civil War to the Present Day* (1923); C. M. S. McLellan in *The Theatre,* Nov. 24, 1888; contemporary articles and newspaper reviews; information from William C. De Mille and Miss Agnes De Mille.]   E.F.E.

DEMING, HENRY CHAMPION (May 23, 1815–Oct. 9, 1872), lawyer, politician, was a member of a family identified throughout with Connecticut. John Deming recorded his homestead at Wethersfield, Conn., in 1641. His descendants settled at Lyme and later at Colchester, and one of them, David Deming, was a prominent merchant of the latter place and a member of the legislature. He married Abigail, daughter of Henry Champion, and their youngest child, Henry Champion Deming, was born at Colchester. His parents were well-to-do, and his early education was of the best, being completed at Yale, where he graduated in 1836. He then entered the law school at Harvard (LL.B., 1839), and on being admitted to the Massachusetts bar moved to New York City, where he opened a law office. His inclinations however were toward literature rather than law, and for a time he was on the editorial staff of the *New World,* a literary monthly. In 1847 he returned to Connecticut and practised law at Hartford for a short time. Possessed of unusual gifts as a public speaker and debater, he entered into local politics. A Democrat of the old school, he was elected as representative of Hartford in the state legislature in 1849, and from that time forward practically relinquished law and devoted himself to public affairs. In 1851 he became a member of the state Senate and in 1854 was elected mayor of Hartford, which office he held for five successive years. In 1859 he became again the city representative in the state legislature, and in 1860 was once more elected mayor. When the Southern states threatened secession he was strongly opposed to the adoption of coercive methods, and after the outbreak of the Civil War, announced that, though he adhered to the Federal government, he would not support a war of aggression or invasion of the seceded states. The subsequent advance of the Confederate forces upon the Federal capital, however, induced him to become a strong Unionist, and the Republican majority elected him speaker *pro tempore* of the state legislature. Late in 1861 the 12th ("Charter-Oak") Connecticut Regiment was raised, in order to participate in the New Orleans expedition, and he was appointed lieutenant-colonel. He took part in all the subsequent operations under Gen. Butler and the regiment under his command was the first body of Federal troops to enter New Orleans. In October 1862 he was detached and appointed provisional mayor of New Orleans, performing his difficult duties with great tact and efficiency. He resigned however in February 1863, returned to Hartford, and was at once elected to the Thirty-eighth Congress by the Republicans. He served two terms in Congress, being placed on the committees on military affairs and on expenditures in the War Department, of which latter he was chairman. In the national House, his oratorical powers, strong character, and practical experience of war conditions combined to assure him an outstanding position. In 1866 he was a delegate to the Loyalists convention at Philadelphia, and in 1869 was appointed United States collector of Internal Revenue for his home district. This latter position he continued to hold till his death, which occurred at Hartford, Oct. 9, 1872. He was married twice: in 1850 to Sarah, daughter of Laurent Clerc of Hartford, and in 1871 to Annie Putnam, daughter of Myron W. Wilson and widow of Sherman L. Jittson.

Holding public office almost uninterruptedly for twenty-three years, prominent alike in federal, state, and municipal politics, his reputation rested principally upon his unusual oratorical powers, though he possessed great administrative ability. Of cultured tastes and widely read, he published translations of Eugène Sue's *Mysteries of Paris* and *The Wandering Jew* (1840), and, in collaboration with G. C. Hebbe, *The Smugglers of the Swedish Coast, or The Rose of Thistle Island* (1844), from the original Swedish of Mrs. E. S. F. Carlén. He also wrote *The Life of Ulysses S. Grant, General, United States Army* (1868).

[J. K. Deming, *Geneal. of the descendants of John Deming of Wethersfield, Conn.* (1904), traces his ancestry and contains a sketch of his life. See also *Annual Cyc.,* 1872, p. 630; *Obit. Record Grads. Yale Coll.,* 1873; *Hist. and Biog. Record of the Class of 1836 in Yale Coll.* (1882); *Hartford Daily Courant,* Oct. 10, 1872.]   H. W. H. K.

DEMING, PHILANDER (Feb. 6, 1829–Feb. 9, 1915), pioneer court stenographer, lawyer, author, was born in Carlisle, Schoharie County, N. Y., the third son of Rev. Rufus Romeo Deming, a minister in Champlain Presbytery, and Julia Ann, daughter of Norman Porter, M.D., of Oneida County. He was descended from Thomas Deming, one of the early settlers of Wethers-

field. The Deming family moved from one charge to another; they lived for a time in Huntingdon, Quebec. From there they moved to Burke, Franklin County, N. Y., where during 1852–54 Philander Deming taught school. In Burke, also, for a number of years he and two of his brothers operated a sawmill which they had built, machinery and all, with their own hands. He prepared for college at Whitestown Seminary, Whitesboro, N. Y.; he was graduated from the University of Vermont in 1861 with the rank of Phi Beta Kappa. In 1864 the University conferred upon him the A.M. degree; in 1881 he gave the oration before the associate alumni, and was president of that body 1891–92 (*General Catalogue of the University of Vermont and State Agricultural College, 1791–1900,* p. 117). In 1872 he was graduated from the Albany Law School, and was admitted to the bar at May sessions the same year.

As a boy he had taught himself shorthand; at the close of his college course he obtained a file of Albany newspapers, and in two months' time he had mastered the technique of legislative reporting. He was legislative reporter for the *Albany Evening Journal* in 1862 and in 1864–65 for the *New York Times.* In 1863–64 he was assistant editor of the *Burlington Free Press.* In November 1865, he demonstrated in an Albany court-room the value of verbatim reporting. Thereafter he was so overwhelmed with court work that he was forced to give up his legislative and newspaper reporting. He was made official stenographer of the supreme court, 3rd Judicial District, New York, and continued in that position until his retirement about 1882. In 1878–79 he was president of the New York Law Stenographers' Association. His handbook, *The Court Stenographer,* was published in 1879.

The *Atlantic Monthly* in 1873 contained the first of Deming's series of short stories or sketches depicting scenes and the life of the people in the Adirondacks and in the Valley of the Hudson. In consequence of this "the reporter learned the pleasant road to Boston, and trod the pathway to the famous banquets to meet the great names he (and all America) had so long honored in the realm of letters" (*Story of a Pathfinder,* p. 55). These sketches were later published in *Adirondack Stories* (1880), followed by *Tompkins and Other Folks* (1885), and *The Story of a Pathfinder* (1907). One and all these grew directly out of Deming's own life and observation, so it is not surprising that they were self-revealing to a marked degree. They give us the reticence, the quiet tastes, the mellowness of a man at once self-possessed, reflective, and shy. One understands why his fellows at college dubbed him "the philosopher," why the people of Burke considered him "odd," even why the pastor of the Albany Congregational Church, of which he had been a member since 1880, found it as difficult as it was rewarding to draw him into conversation. Long before it was customary to take long walks for the fun of it, Deming roamed the country side. He enjoyed fishing, although he outgrew his early zest for hunting because of his distaste for the wantonness of killing. He had a distinct bent for things mechanical, but refused to patent his inventions. In later life he was a striking figure on the streets of Albany, because of his abundant white hair and his deeply lined face. He resembled portraits of Franz Liszt. He was highly esteemed, yet few knew him intimately. He never married. He died at his rooms, 12 Jay St., Albany, and was buried at Burke.

[Pages 3–55 in *The Story of a Pathfinder* are autobiographical; besides these Philander Deming wrote "Growing Old" for *Scribner's Mag.*, Mar. 1915. See also "The Curious Origin of the Court Reporter," by W. H. Brainerd in *Leslie's Weekly*, May 24, 1906. Deming appears in *Who's Who in America*, 1899–1915, and in the *Cat. Alumni Albany Law School*, 1851–1908, pp. 42, 99. The reference librarian of the New York State Library, the minister of the First Congregational Church, Albany, and the town clerk of Burke have furnished data for this sketch compiled from their own knowledge or from that of relatives and friends of Deming. For a critical estimate of Deming's writings see F. L. Pattee, *History of Am. Lit. since 1870* (1915), p. 24; and W. D. Howells, "Recollections of an Atlantic Editorship," *Atlantic Monthly*, Nov. 1907, p. 600.]

L. M. M.

DEMING, WILLIAM [See DENNING, WILLIAM 1736–1830.]

DEMME, CHARLES RUDOLPH (Apr. 10, 1795–Sept. 1, 1863), Lutheran clergyman, was born at Mühlhausen in Thüringen, Germany, the son of Hermann Gottfried and Frederika (König) Demme. His father was an eminent Lutheran divine, Superintendent in Mühlhausen and later General Superintendent in Altenburg. Demme studied at the Gymnasium in Altenburg and at the Universities of Göttingen and Halle. He was wounded in the battle of Waterloo, and a scar across nose and cheek served as a lesser, although life-long, reminder of that 18th of June. His friends in the United States believed that it was his experiences as a soldier that turned his thoughts from the law to the ministry and made him decide to leave Germany for America. Whatever his inner life may have been, the young man who came to Philadelphia in 1818 and sought ordination from the Lutheran Ministerium of Pennsylvania proved to be a sound

scholar, a devoted pastor, and a born leader of men. After ministering for three years to several congregations in Hummelstown, Pa., and its vicinity, he was called in 1822 to the historic St. Michael's and Zion's Church in Philadelphia as assistant to Frederick David Schaeffer [q.v.]. On Oct. 7, 1828, he married Schaeffer's only daughter, Mariana. Of their eleven children only five survived him. After his father-in-law's retirement in 1834 Demme was sole pastor until 1850, when William Julius Mann [q.v.], who in turn was to succeed him, became his assistant. By virtue of his scholarship but still more by virtue of his personality Demme became the most influential man in the Ministerium, and his influence continued even after his own career had ended. His one independent book was *Die Werke des Flavius Josephus* (Phila., 1839), a revision of the German translation by J. F. Cotta and A. F. Gfrörer with variorum notes drawn from many sources, but this was less important than his editorial work on the Lutheran *Liturgie und Kirchenagende* (1842; 2nd ed., 1855) and the *Deutsches Gesangbuch* (1849). The conservative Lutheranism of his theological position did much to arrest the Methodistic tendencies of many Pennsylvania Lutherans, for beginning in 1846 he gave formal instruction in theology to candidates for the ministry. He was a member of the American Philosophical Society, did much work for the American Tract Society, and was untiringly active in his efforts to reclaim criminals in the penitentiaries. He was one of the greatest masters of sacred rhetoric that the United States has ever heard, but since he preached in German, and allowed only a few of his sermons to be printed, his fame is incommensurate with his achievement. His sermons were primarily logical in their appeal, but so charged with emotion was the preacher that at times tears would roll down his cheeks, though his voice never faltered or quavered. He was a close student of Reinhard in German, Bourdaloue in French, and South in English. Overwork brought on a mental breakdown from which he never recovered; he was made pastor emeritus in 1859; and his last years passed in all but complete darkness. To the end he prayed and read in the Bible and would cry softly when he heard the bell of his church on Sunday mornings.

[M. L. Stoever, "Chas. Rudolph Demme, D.D.," in the *Evangelical Quart. Rev.*, XV, 428–48 (1864); W. J. Mann, *Rede über Dr. Demme* (1863); J. G. Morris, *Fifty Years in the Lutheran Ministry* (Baltimore, 1878); *Documentary Hist. of the Ev. Luth. Ministerium of Pa.* (1898); A. Spaeth, "Hist. of the Liturgical Development of the Ministerium of Pa.," in *Luth. Ch. Rev.*, XVII, 93–119 (1898); personal information. A number of Demme's sermons, together with some letters to

Chas. Philip Krauth, are in the library of the Luth. Hist. Soc. at Gettysburg, Pa.]   G.H.G.

DEMPSTER, JOHN (Jan. 2, 1794–Nov. 28, 1863), theologian, pioneer founder of Methodist theological seminaries, was born in Florida, Montgomery County, N. Y. His father, the Rev. James Dempster, a Scotch Presbyterian and a graduate of the University of Edinburgh, came under Methodist influence and was sent by Wesley to America, where he served as a missionary in New York City. Severing his Methodist connection, he became pastor of the Presbyterian church in Florida, N. Y., where he died in 1803. John, the second son of his second wife, grew up after the death of his father a frivolous young man with scarcely the rudiments of a common-school education. At the age of eighteen, while employed as a tin-peddler, he received at a Methodist camp meeting a powerful religious impulse which transformed his life. He at once began a rigorous course of self-education which continued as long as he lived. Almost without instruction he became a proficient scholar in the classics, mathematics, Hebrew, theology, and philosophy, at the same time preaching constantly. In 1816 he began a regular conference ministry and served various charges in New York State with growing power and influence till 1836, when on account of impaired health he went to Buenos Aires where he built a Methodist church, established day and Sunday-schools and had an active ministry among the Protestant population of the city and the surrounding region. Returning to the United States in 1842, he spent the next three years in two Methodist pastorates in New York City.

Early in his ministry he became convinced of the need of theological training for Methodist ministers and zealously advocated it, often in the face of stubborn opposition. Largely as the result of his efforts which were continued by correspondence from South America, the Wesley Theological Institute was founded at Newbury, Vt., in 1845, the first Methodist theological seminary in the United States. It was removed to Concord, N. H., in 1847 and to Boston in 1867, later becoming the Theological School of Boston University. At the close of his New York ministry, Dempster spent several months in the British Isles, making friends and collecting funds for the school, after which he passed seven years as professor of theology at Concord, exerting a strong influence on his pupils and throughout the region. In 1854 he resigned and became one of the founders of the Garrett Biblical Institute in Chicago, taking, when its permanent faculty was formed in 1855, the office of senior professor,

which he held till the close of his life. He died while on a leave of absence for the purpose of founding a theological seminary on the Pacific Coast.

Dempster was of medium size, pale, with bright eyes, deep and penetrating voice, courtly manners and impressive presence. He had a strong will, great originality and an alert and philosophical mind. He was widely read and inspired his pupils with enthusiasm. The only book that bears his name is, *Lectures and Addresses . . . with an Appendix, containing the Funeral Sermon and Memorial Services occasioned by the Death of the Author* (1864), edited by the Rev. Davis W. Clark. He was survived by his wife, one son and three daughters.

[In addition to biographical material already referred to, see *Methodist Quart. Rev.,* July 1864; *Minutes of the Annual Conferences of the M. E. Ch.,* 1864; *Zion's Herald,* Dec. 9, 1863, and Aug. 26, 1896. The latter contains a portrait.]   F.T.P.

DENBY, CHARLES (June 16, 1830–Jan. 13. 1904), lawyer, diplomat, was born at Mount Joy, Botetourt County, Va. His grandfather emigrated from England and settled in Virginia, where his father, Nathaniel Denby, a merchant at Richmond, was born. His mother was Jane Harvey, daughter of Matthew and Magdalen (Hawkins) Harvey, and descendant of Benjamin Burden, an Englishman who brought with him to Virginia a grant of many acres on the Shenandoah and James rivers, known as Burden's Grant. His mother's father served in Lee's legion in the Revolution. From the Tom Fox Academy in Hanover County, Va., he proceeded to Georgetown College, D. C., where he spent three years, taking in 1842 "three medals, more than had ever before been received by any one boy" (*Georgetown College Journal,* vol. XIII, no. 8, p. 93). Among his classmates was Thomas J. Semmes, later a member of the Confederate Senate. While still a youth Denby accompanied his father to Marseilles, France, and attended the Collège Royal in that city, where his father was United States naval agent. On returning to the United States, he entered the Virginia Military Institute at Lexington, Va., from which he was graduated with high honors in 1850. After three years as professor of tactics at the Masonic University, Selma, Ala., he moved to Evansville, Ind., where he was employed by John B. Hall as editor of the Democratic newspaper, *Daily Enquirer,* learning to set type and frequently setting up editorials, while at the same time he studied law in the office of Baker & Garvin. Admitted to the bar in 1855, he began the practise of law the following year in Evansville, in partnership with Judge James Lockhart, and in the same year was elected to represent Vanderburg County in the state legislature. The day after Fort Sumter fell, he abandoned his law practise to raise a regiment for border service. In September 1861 he was appointed by Gov. Morton as lieutenant-colonel of the 42nd Indiana Volunteers, serving in southern Kentucky, first with Crittenden's division from Fort Donelson to Nashville, and thence to Huntsville, Ala., under Gen. Mitchel. Returning with Gen. Buell in the summer of 1862 in pursuit of Bragg, he engaged in the battle of Perryville, Ky., on Oct. 8, 1862, and was severely wounded, his horse being killed under him. Some days later (Oct. 21, 1862) he was appointed colonel of the 80th Indiana Volunteers, but in January 1863 he resigned on a surgeon's certificate of disability, returned to the practise of law in Evansville, and became interested in politics again. In 1876 he was a delegate to the St. Louis Democratic Convention which nominated Tilden and Hendricks and in 1884 to the Chicago Convention which nominated Cleveland and Hendricks. His consistent support of Hendricks of Indiana resulted in his appointment on May 29, 1885, by President Cleveland as minister to China to succeed John Russell Young, and in this position he continued during Harrison's administration and Cleveland's second administration. On July 11, 1898, President McKinley yielded to political pressure and appointed Edwin H. Conger in his place. In his thirteen years in China, Denby came very close to the Chinese statesmen and his efforts in aid of peace with Japan at the time of the Sino-Japanese War put him in high favor in China. His prestige was enhanced by the fact that the Japanese government had entrusted its interests in China to his care. Upon his retirement he received many complimentary resolutions from various missionary boards in the United States and China. In September 1898 President McKinley appointed him a member of the committee which investigated the conduct of the war with Spain, and in the next year appointed him a member of the Philippine Commission. On Apr. 4, 1898, he participated with the other members of the Commission (Jacob Gould Schurman, Dean C. Worcester, Admiral George Dewey, and Gen. Elwell S. Otis) in issuing a proclamation to the effect that, while the supremacy of the United States would be enforced, the Government had in view the welfare and advancement of the people. The *Report of the Philippine Commission to the President* (four volumes) was published in 1900-01, while Denby's "observations, reminiscences and conclusions" as an American diplo-

mat, entitled *China and Her People* (two volumes profusely illustrated with reproductions of photographs collected by the author, with a biographical sketch by the editor), appeared in Boston posthumously in 1906. In September 1858 he had married Martha, elder daughter of Senator Graham Newell Fitch and Harriet S. Fitch of Logansport, Ind. There were eight children born of this union. On Jan. 13, 1904, he was stricken with heart trouble at Jamestown, N. Y., where he had been lecturing, and where he died.

[*Who's Who in America*, 1903-05; *N. Y. Times*, Jan. 14, 1904; *Georgetown Coll. Jour.*, XLVII, 195.]

H.F.W.

DENBY, EDWIN (Feb. 18, 1870–Feb. 8, 1929), secretary of the navy, was born in Evansville, Ind., a son of Charles and Martha (Fitch) Denby, both of whom were of old American stock. After an education in the local schools, he was taken by his parents to China, where his father was minister from the United States. Here he was for ten years employed in the Chinese customs service. Returning to the United States he entered the University of Michigan, acquiring fame as a football player, and a degree of LL.B. in 1896. In the war with Spain he volunteered as a common seaman, and ended as a gunner's mate aboard the *Yosemite*. When the World War came he was overweight and unqualified for active duty, but he accomplished his enlistment in the Marine Corps as a private, and was used in building up the morale of that service. He rose through the non-commissioned grades, and was discharged as a major, with which rank he entered the Officers' Reserve Corps. In the years between the two wars he practised law in Detroit and undertook various enterprises in connection with the automobile trade. In 1903 he was in the Michigan legislature, and two years later he became representative from the first Michigan district in the Fifty-ninth Congress. He was twice reëlected to Congress. The announcement that President Harding had selected him to be secretary of the navy came without warning to the public, and with little to Denby himself.

As secretary of the navy he appears to have had little influence upon naval organization, or upon national naval policy. It has not been shown that his decisions were important in connection with the Washington Conference on Limitation of Armaments, or with the treaties that arose from it. His administration was terminated by a scandal in the handling of the naval oil reserves.

In the autumn of 1923 the Senate Committee on Public Lands and Surveys, engaged in the investigation of the oil reserves, came upon a series of events that endangered the safety of naval reserve No. 1 at Elk Hills, and No. 3 at Teapot Dome. By act of June 25, 1910, various withdrawals of oil lands from public entry, made by President Roosevelt with perhaps incomplete authority, were legalized by Congress; and after long discussion an oil-land leasing act, to be administered by the secretary of the interior, was passed Feb. 25, 1920. By the naval act of June 4, 1920, the reserves that had been set aside for navy use, under the act of 1910, were placed under jurisdiction of the secretary of the navy. They were already coveted by the oil-producing interests, and there was a suggestion that they were in some danger of losing their oil by drainage into adjacent basins not controlled by the government. The administration of the naval oil reserves was transferred to the Department of the Interior by executive order of President Harding, May 31, 1921, upon the theory that the Department of the Interior, having the machinery for controlling leases of other oil lands under the act of 1920, could administer the reserves to better advantage than could the Navy Department. Almost instantly the secretary of the interior, Albert B. Fall, entered into negotiations with the oil interests represented by Edward L. Doheny and Harry Sinclair, and into contracts for taking the oil from the ground, which the lessees insisted must bear the signature of Denby as well as that of Fall. These leases the Supreme Court later declared to have been "consummated by conspiracy, corruption and fraud" (*Pan American Petroleum and Transport Company et al. vs. United States, 273 U. S.,* 509). While executing these contracts Fall was at the same time accepting favors and financial assistance from both Doheny and Sinclair. The testimony as to this sinister relationship became public in the winter of 1923–24. Fall had retired from the cabinet and was beyond reach of impeachment. Denby took "no active part in the negotiations" (*273 U. S.,* 498), and was not seriously charged with corruption. "Stupidity is the high crime and misdemeanor of which the Senate accuses Mr. Denby, and the only one," said the *New York Tribune* (Feb. 12, 1924). The Senate on Feb. 11, 1924, by resolution requested President Coolidge to dismiss Denby from the cabinet. It had already joined the House in asserting a belief that the leases were "executed under circumstances indicating fraud and corruption," and in setting in motion suits for cancellation that resulted in the restoration of the lands to the government. Coolidge declined to dismiss Denby, and the latter continued to insist that the leases were both legal and ex-

pedient (*Leases upon Naval Oil Reserves. Hearing before the Committee on Public Lands and Surveys, United States Senate, on S. Res. 282 and S. Res. 294,* Washington 1923–24, pp. 283, 363, 1283). Denby resigned on Feb. 18, 1924, believing that a further continuance in the cabinet of President Coolidge "would increase your embarrassment" (*New York Tribune,* Feb. 19, 1924); but he made the resignation effective only on Mar. 10, and defied the House of Representatives to initiate impeachment proceedings against him. He returned to Detroit where he enjoyed the personal esteem of his associates until his death. He was survived by his wife, Marion (Thurber) Denby, and two children.

[There is a good obituary in the *New York Times,* Feb. 9, 1929; and a good survey of the Teapot Dome proceedings in the same for Jan. 24, 1927. See also *Who's Who in America,* 1928–29.]   F. L. P—n.

DENNIE, JOSEPH (Aug. 30, 1768–Jan. 7, 1812), essayist and editor, was born in Boston, Mass., the only child of Joseph and Mary (Green) Dennie. His father came of a prosperous family of West-India merchants, but he had hardly established himself in business when his career was cut short by recurring periods of insanity. His mother's family, the Greens, had been for several generations engaged in the printing trade.

The first seven years of Dennie's boyhood were spent in Boston. During the siege of 1775 his parents, who numbered many Loyalists among their kin, removed to Lexington, where the boy was sent to dame school and read largely in his father's library. His precocious literary talent was not encouraged, but after two years in commercial school and counting-house had proved his unfitness for a business career, he was allowed to prepare for Harvard under the care of Rev. Samuel West of Needham. He entered college as a sophomore, and though his course was interrupted by illness and during his senior year by a period of rustication, he was permitted to graduate with his class in 1790. Partly because he smarted under college discipline, partly because he considered the course of study arid, Dennie conceived a petulance against Harvard which occasionally found vent in his later writings. He was noted among his classmates for his elegance and for his unusual acquaintance with polite letters.

After six months' hesitation Dennie selected the law as a means of livelihood. He served a not very assiduous clerkship of three years in the office of Benjamin West, brother of his tutor, at Charlestown, N. H., and was admitted to the bar in March 1794. His practise, however, never became extensive and he soon abandoned it. During his clerkship he had made the acquaintance of several young professional men who acted as volunteer writers for local newspapers and who strongly encouraged his bent for letters. With one of them, Royall Tyler, he now formed a partnership for the production of light literary wares under the firm name of "Colon & Spondee." (Dennie was Colon and sometimes signed his contributions with a C). At about the same time he commenced a series of periodical essays called the "Farrago" in which he sought to revive "the Goldsmith vivacity of thought and the Addisonian sweetness of expression." These essays, in part reprinted from New Hampshire journals, formed the main feature of a weekly paper devoted to belles-lettres, the *Tablet* (May 19–Aug. 11, 1795), which Dennie started in Boston but which was discontinued by the publisher after the thirteenth number. Between 1792 and 1802 he wrote twenty-nine numbers of the "Farrago," but the series was never collected in book form.

Failing to find other employment in Boston, Dennie returned to New Hampshire and settled at Walpole. There he soon became the center of a group of "wags, wits, and literati" from all the surrounding country, who, like the Hartford Wits, were fond of holding convivial meetings for the discussion of literature and politics. They were all strong Federalists. Stimulated by this congenial company, Dennie entered upon his most active period of authorship. For the *Farmer's Weekly Museum* of Walpole, one of the best New England papers of its day, he wrote a new series of miscellaneous essays entitled the "Lay Preacher," in which, by heading his lucubrations with a text and posing as a moralist, he was successful in winning the applause of even puritanical and utilitarian readers. The publishers of the *Farmer's Museum* were not slow to perceive the value of his services. In April 1796, he was appointed editor. He enlisted his literary friends as contributors, gave the previously non-partisan sheet a strong Federalist bias, and within a year and a half could boast that his paper was read in nearly every state in the Union. Its literary success, however, did not bring its financial prosperity. In several successive failures of his publishers Dennie was himself a heavy loser. Though he continued to act as editor at a reduced salary, he was convinced that a literary career could not be pursued in a small town. Philadelphia, as the political and literary centre of the nation, naturally attracted him. His services to the Federalist cause secured him an appointment as per-

sonal secretary to Timothy Pickering, Adams's secretary of state. He also accepted an editorial position on Fenno's *Gazette of the United States,* a semi-official Federalist organ. And a final inducement was an offer from William Cobbett to publish a handsome edition of the "Lay Preacher" and to pay generously for the copyright. With these bright prospects before him, Dennie left Walpole in September 1799, and journeyed leisurely to Philadelphia.

His reception by Philadelphia society was as cordial as he could have wished, but his affairs did not prosper. Pickering was dismissed from the cabinet in May 1800, and Dennie was not retained by John Marshall, the new secretary. His connection with Fenno's *Gazette* ended in December of the same year, soon after Jefferson's election to the presidency had marked the end of Federalist rule. And Cobbett, having been convicted of libel and heavily fined, was obliged to leave the city before the publication of the "Lay Preacher" could be effected. An attempt to publish the work by subscription failed.

Nothing daunted, Dennie persuaded a bookseller named Asbury Dickins to join him in establishing a new magazine. On Jan. 3, 1801, *The Port Folio,* edited by "Oliver Oldschool, Esq.," commenced publication as a weekly devoted to literature and politics and enjoyed from the first a great success. Dennie rallied to its support the brightest talent of Philadelphia, which he organized in the Tuesday Club. During the period of its greatest popularity, from 1802 to 1805, the magazine had a distinguished list of contributors in all parts of the country and even attained the previously unheard of honor of printing from the original manuscripts poems by such English writers as Campbell, Moore, Leigh Hunt, and "Monk" Lewis. Until the *North American Review* was founded in 1815 it remained without a rival. Dennie's own contributions consisted of a large number of "Lay Preacher" essays reprinted from the *Farmer's Museum,* a few new ones, and a considerable body of literary criticism, including notably some early appreciations of *Lyrical Ballads.* But his activities as an editor and man about town, combined with frail health and temperamental indolence, severely limited his output. He was, moreover, in constant financial difficulties, which were greatly increased by the long illness that preceded his death. He was buried in the churchyard of St. Peter's, Philadelphia. *The Port Folio* continued publication in various forms until 1827.

Dennie's reputation as an original writer rests upon his "Lay Preacher" essays (118 numbers, 1795–1808), which unfortunately have never been collected. About forty of the early numbers were issued in a volume printed at Walpole in 1796, and this book, according to the English traveler John Davis, was in 1803 "the most popular work on the American continent." A second selection, edited by J. E. Hall, appeared in Philadelphia in 1817. As an "American Addison" Dennie was soon superseded by Irving; moreover, his failure to get his books published and the neglect of his early biographers have doomed him to an unmerited obscurity. He should rank with Freneau and Charles Brockden Brown as a pioneer American man of letters.

Two portraits and a full-length silhouette of Dennie are extant. Buckingham has preserved an amusing description of his appearance and habits during his residence in Walpole (*Specimens of Newspaper Literature*, II, 196), and Irving, who met Dennie in 1807, used his whimsicalities as the basis for "Launcelot Langstaff" (*Salmagundi*, no. 8. Dennie was slight of build; fastidious to an extreme in dress and speech, mercurial in disposition. The charm of his conversation was widely attested and his love of sound literature was genuine and infectious. Born of the mercantile aristocracy of Boston and nurtured on the English classics of the eighteenth century, he cherished the past, especially the tradition of British gentility, and loathed democratic innovation in any form. In the course of a life of perpetual disappointment he had perhaps his supreme reward when the rising Irish poet Thomas Moore, after his visit to America in 1804, declared that the few agreeable moments which his tour through the United States afforded him were those passed in the society of Dennie and his friends.

[The most complete account of Dennie is by H. M. Ellis, *Joseph Dennie and His Circle* (1915), with portrait, list of Dennie's essays, and full bibliography. Among earlier sources the following are the most valuable: E. P. Oberholtzer, *Lit. Hist. of Phila.* (1906); *The Port Folio*, Feb. 1812 (memorial article, with silhouette); *New Eng. Galaxy*, July 10 and 24, 1818; J. E. Hall, *Phila. Souvenir* (1826); J. T. Buckingham, *Specimens of Newspaper Lit.* (1850); W. W. Clapp, Jr., *Joseph Dennie* (1880), with portrait; G. Aldrich, *Walpole as It Was and as It Is* (1880); A. H. Smyth, *Phila. Mags. and their Contributors* (1892); A. R. Marble, *Heralds of Am. Lit.* (1907). Smyth's assertion that Dennie was the "first American editor of Shakespeare" has been shown to have little foundation.]
G. F. W.

DENNING, WILLIAM (1736–Dec. 19, 1830), maker of cannon for the Revolutionary army, is said to have made the first successful attempt to manufacture cannon of wrought iron. Nothing is known of him until he became an "artificer" for or in the Revolutionary army. He made two small cannon successfully at Middlesex, Pa., and then attempted to make a larger

one at Mount Holly. The latter experiment was a failure, owing, it was said in the obituary written at the time of his death, to the fact that he could get no workmen who could stand the heat which was so great as to melt the lead buttons off their clothes. The cannon were made of wrought-iron staves, hooped with bands of wrought iron, four layers of staves, breaking joints, being finally bound together, and then boxed and breached like other cannon. One of those in use at the battle of Brandywine was captured by the British and placed in the Tower of London where it may still be seen. The British government offered a large sum and an annuity to any one who would instruct them in the manufacture of the cannon, but Denning declined. The United States government, however, gave him no reward until near his death and he passed his later years in poverty. He died in his ninety-fourth year at his home in Mifflin Township, Cumberland County, Pa.

[The main source is the obituary in Samuel Hazard's *Register of Pa.*, Jan 15, 1831. The account in the *Pa. Mag. of Hist. and Biog.*, vol. XXXVIII (1914), p. 459, is wrong in several particulars.]
J. T. A.

DENNIS, GRAHAM BARCLAY (June 1, 1855–Aug. 18, 1923), capitalist, was born in London, England. His father, Mendenhall John Dennis, was a Presbyterian clergyman, educated at Oxford and Heidelberg, and his mother, Sophia (Kiehl) Dennis, was of German ancestry. The family came to America, and Graham lived as a boy in Boston and Cincinnati. He left school at the age of fourteen but took a course four years later at Bethany College (1873–74). He became city editor of the *Dayton Daily Journal*, Dayton, Ohio, in 1875 and, after two years on the city desk, served as business manager for two years. In the next six years, he engaged in various private enterprises in Dayton. He invented an electric postal canceling machine, organized G. B. Dennis & Company, a general brokerage firm, and established and edited an agricultural newspaper, *The Farmer's Home*. Partly on account of poor health, in May 1885 he moved to Spokane, Wash., where he published the *Spokane Miner*, 1885–86, and engaged in real estate and mining operations. The population of Spokane was then only 2,000. The Northern Pacific Railroad had been completed two years before, and the development of the "Inland Empire" was just commencing. The lode mining industry, which was the foundation of the region's prosperity, began in the year Dennis arrived with the discovery of the Old Dominion mine, near Colville. About 1891 or 1892, in association with three Chicago men, Dennis bought the mine. He became its manager, and expended some $550,000 on improvements. One showing of ore which had been picked up seemed so promising that the company was offered $1,000,000 for the property. Dennis wished to sell, but his partners refused, and after a carload or two had been taken from it the new showing was exhausted.

In the nineties Dennis was president or treasurer of eight or ten mines. He organized a company to develop the mica deposits of Idaho, was for many years, from its beginning in 1895, president of the Northwest Mining Association and in 1896 represented it at parliamentary hearings in Victoria, B. C., when the mining interests were successful in opposing a proposed 2 per cent tax on the gross output of the British Columbia mines. In 1897, he assisted in drafting a memorial to Congress regarding revision of the federal mining laws. With his numerous business connections he combined civic interests. He was a member of the Spokane City Council in 1886–88 and was elected to the school board in 1890. In the same year, he organized the Spokane Industrial Exposition and served as its vice-president. He was treasurer of Jenkins University, a pioneer educational experiment. He organized and built the Ross Park Electric Railway, opened in 1889, one of the first electric lines in the West. In 1906, he was the first president of the Pacific Northwest Development League, formed by leading men of the four states.

A nervous breakdown curtailed the activities of his last ten years, and he died of apoplexy on Aug. 18, 1923. He had an attractive personality and was forceful in his business leadership. He won confidence because he believed thoroughly in all his enterprises and put his own money into them. On May 20, 1879, he married Hester L. Bradley of Dayton, Ohio. Besides his widow, living in Spokane, he left three children.

[Jonathan Edwards, *An Illustrated Hist. of Spokane County* (1900), pp. 487–89; N. W. Durham, *Hist. of the City of Spokane and the Spokane Country* (1912), vol. I, ch. xli, and vol. II, p. 5; G. W. Fuller, *The Inland Empire* (1928), III, 67; *Sketches of Washingtonians* (1906); obituary in the *Spokesman-Review* (Spokane), Aug. 19, 1923.]   G. W. F.

DENNIS, JAMES SHEPARD (Dec. 15, 1842–Mar. 21, 1914), missionary in Syria, historian, and statistician of missions, was the son of Alfred Lewis Dennis, an important and wealthy business man of Newark, N. J., and Eliza (Shepard) Dennis. His boyhood was surrounded with influences of culture and earnest religion. He graduated with the degree of B.A. from Princeton in 1863, and after a year's study

of law at Harvard entered Princeton Theological Seminary, graduating in 1867. Ordained in the following year by the Presbytery of Newark, early in 1869 he arrived in Syria as a missionary of the American Board. A year later, when the mission was taken over by the Presbyterian Board of Foreign Missions, he joined the service of this board, with which he was connected all his life. For four years he was a field missionary in Sidon and Zahleh. It is remembered as characteristic that since the sound of his name has an unpleasant sense in Arabic he dropped its first letter, and was called by the Syrians "Ennis," meaning "courteous." He was married in Newark, June 26, 1872, to Mary Elizabeth, daughter of James B. Pinneo. From 1873 to 1891 he was professor in the Presbyterian Theological Seminary in Beirut. His command of Arabic led him into writing texts for missionary teaching, of which the most important were *Evidences of Christianity* (1877), *Biblical Interpretation* (1880), and *Christian Theology* in two volumes (1882–83). These books attained large use in missionary work among Arabic-speaking peoples. Because of business responsibilities and family circumstances in 1892 he resigned his missionary appointment. He had determined to serve the missionary cause by literary work, the way to which was opened by inherited wealth.

Returning to America he lived in New York City and Montclair, N. J. Soon there came to him, in connection with lectures given in Princeton Seminary (published as *Foreign Missions after a Century,* 1893), the idea of a thorough presentation of the social effects of Protestant missions on non-Christian peoples. He sought information on a large scale from over three hundred missionaries in all parts of the field. An immense correspondence resulted, giving him a unique acquaintance with missionaries and their work, and bringing him a flood of material. The issue was three large abundantly documented volumes on *Christian Missions and Social Progress* (1897, 1899, 1906). While this book has defects natural to work which broke much new ground, as a contribution to the science of missions it has not been surpassed in America. In addition to its great value as a storehouse of knowlege of missionary results, it deeply influenced the thinking of the friends of missions. Beside the older individualistic proselytizing conceptions it established the idea of missions as an enterprise releasing transforming forces into the common life of peoples. While the book was in preparation, portions formed the material for lectures at several theological seminaries.

As a "statistical supplement" to this book, Dennis published his *Centennial Survey of Christian Missions* (1902), reporting all Protestant missionary operations which were being maintained at the close of the nineteenth century and exhibiting with descriptions and statistics their conditions and achievements in all forms of work—"the most comprehensive and authoritative collection of missionary statistics which had ever been made" (R. E. Speer). Some of this material was presented by Dennis to the Ecumenical Missionary Conference in New York in 1900. In the preparations for this and also for the World Missionary Conference at Edinburgh in 1910 he took active part. For the Edinburgh Conference he did important work in improving methods of missionary statistics, and was editor of the statistical section of its *Statistical Atlas of Christian Missions*. In the *World Atlas of Christian Missions* (1911), he provided a directory of missionary societies, enrolling all Protestant missionary organizations in the world.

Dennis wrote many articles for missionary periodicals and papers for missionary meetings, of which some were collected in *The New Horoscope of Missions* (1908) and *The Modern Call of Missions* (1913). He spent much money in preparing and publishing his books, and took no financial returns. After his return from Syria he maintained active connection with missionary work, as honorary secretary of the Presbyterian Board, giving large service, and as a member of the Board from 1904 till his death. Seldom making public appearances, he greatly impressed and attracted those who knew him by a singular grace and loftiness of character. He died at Montclair.

[Records of Presbyterian Board of Foreign Missions, containing biographical data supplied by Dennis himself; records of Presbytery of Newark; his books, especially prefaces; general catalogues of Princeton Univ. and Princeton Theol. Sem.; issues of *Men (and Women) of America* and *Who's Who in America*; H. H. Jessup, *Fifty-three Years in Syria* (1910); article by R. E. Speer, in *Missionary Rev. of the World*, June 1914; *Ecumenical Missionary Conference*, N. Y., 1900, vols. I, II; Report of Commission I, *World Missionary Conf.*, 1910; articles in *N. Y. Times* and *Newark Evening News* at time of his death.]   R. H. N.

DENNISON, AARON LUFKIN (Mar. 6, 1812–Jan. 9, 1895), pioneer watch manufacturer, was born at Freeport, Me., the third of ten children of Andrew and Lydia (Lufkin) Dennison. His father, a soldier in the War of 1812 and later a colonel of militia, was a shoemaker by trade who in his later years experimented with the making of paper boxes. At the age of thirteen Aaron was earning his living sawing wood and

at fifteen was learning the cobbler's trade in his father's shop at Brunswick, Me. The boy, having a distinct mechanical bent, took little interest in cobbling, and his father, recognizing the fact, apprenticed him in 1830 to James Carey, a Brunswick watchmaker. Three years later Aaron left for Boston to perfect himself as a journeyman, entering first the employment of Currier & Trott, then of Jones, Low & Ball, and finally setting up for himself. As his skill increased and his knowledge of watches widened he was astonished at the imperfections in even the best of the hand-made products and became convinced that watches could be manufactured by machinery under a system of interchangeable parts. He predicted "in the year 1846 that within twenty years the manufacture of watches would be reduced to as much system and perfection and with the same expedition that firearms were then made in the Springfield armory. He often visited this armory and took great interest in examining the various processes of finishing fire-arms" (Hazlitt, *post*, p. 11). In 1849 Edward Howard, a clock and scale maker of Boston, tried to interest Dennison in the manufacture of locomotives, but instead he was himself persuaded to embark upon the manufacture of watches. Samuel Curtis of Boston invested $20,000 in the project, and while Dennison was on a tour of investigation in Europe, Howard supervised the construction of a factory in Roxbury. Here Dennison designed the first factory-made watches in the world. The business was conducted first under the name of the American Horologue Company and later under that of the Boston Watch Company. Two or three years' experience convinced the management that the atmosphere in Roxbury was too dusty, and a new location was determined upon at Waltham. The expenses of these early years, however, combined with the effect of the panic of 1857, forced the concern into bankruptcy. It was purchased by New York and Philadelphia interests and was continued after Feb. 8, 1859, as the American Watch Company and finally as the American Waltham Watch Company, which developed into the largest watch company in America. Dennison continued as superintendent under the new management until December 1861, while Howard returned to Roxbury and continued the manufacture of watches there.

In 1864 Dennison interested A. O. Bigelow of Boston in the idea of manufacturing medium-priced watches, certain parts of which were to be made in Switzerland, the whole to be assembled in America. As a result the Tremont Watch Company was organized and Dennison went to

Zurich to oversee production of Swiss parts. The company prospered until 1866 when the management decided to manufacture all of the parts in America. Dennison thereupon withdrew, but remained in Switzerland until 1870, having taken a contract to furnish certain material for the firm. The company soon fell into financial difficulties and Dennison returned to America in the hope of reorganizing it. Failing in this, he succeeded in selling the machinery to an English firm. He himself eventually moved to Birmingham, England, where he successfully manufactured watch-cases. Known during his lifetime as the "Father of American Watchmaking," he is believed to have been the first person to have constructed the entire watch under one roof by machinery manufacturing interchangeable parts. An inventor and not a business man, he saw other men grow rich with the tools that he devised, and in the end was forced to earn a living manufacturing merely the shell to surround the delicate mechanism which he knew so well. On Jan. 15, 1840, he was married to Charlotte W. Foster, by whom he had five children.

[G. M. Rogers, *The Dennison Family* (1906), pp. 50–1; G. H. A. Hazlitt ("H. G. Abbott"), *The Watch Factories of America Past and Present* (1888), chs. i and ix; D. H. Hurd, *Hist. of Middlesex County, Mass.* (1890), III, 738–49; *Daily Evening Transcript* (Boston), Jan. 10, 1895; *Springfield Republican*, Jan. 11, 1895.]

H. U. F.

DENNISON, WALTER (Aug. 9, 1869–Mar. 18, 1917), teacher, scholar, was born at Saline, near Ypsilanti, Mich., the son of James L. and Eliza J. (Flowers) Dennison. He received his early education in public schools, entered the University of Michigan, and was graduated in 1893 as bachelor of arts. While an undergraduate he married, Aug. 5, 1891, Anna L. Green of Ypsilanti. Upon graduation he was appointed to a fellowship for two years, the first of which he spent in the Graduate School of the University of Michigan, receiving the degree of M.A. in 1894. The following year he spent in Europe, first at the University of Bonn, then in Italy. When the American School of Classical Studies in Rome was opened in 1895, Dennison received one of the two fellowships established in connection with the School, and his appointment was renewed for the year 1896–97. One of the four papers which resulted from his studies in Rome, "The Epigraphic Sources of Suetonius," was accepted as a thesis by the University of Michigan, which granted him the degree of Ph.D. in 1897. The paper was published in the *American Journal of Archæology* in 1898. He was instructor in Latin in the University of Michigan, 1897–99; professor of Latin and Ro-

man archeology at Oberlin College, 1899–1902; junior professor of Latin at the University of Michigan, 1902–10; and professor of Greek and Latin at Swarthmore College from 1910 until his death. In the year 1908–09 he was annual professor of Latin in the American School of Classical Studies in Rome. He was a member of the American Philological Association and the Archæological Institute of America. For three years, 1913–16, he was secretary of the Philadelphia Society of the Institute, and he was a member of the council of the Institute from 1916 until his death. He was one of the founders, and first president, of the Philadelphia Society for the Promotion of Liberal Studies, and in 1914–15 was president of the Classical Association of the Atlantic States. He was also (1913–17) associate editor of the *Classical Weekly*.

During his earlier stay in Italy Dennison came upon a collection of Latin inscriptions formed by the parish priest of Pozzuoli, De Criscio, which he published under the title, "Some New Inscriptions from Puteoli, Baiae, Misenum, and Cumae," in the *American Journal of Archæology*, in 1898. Eventually he secured the inscriptions themselves for the University of Michigan. During his year as annual professor in the school in Rome he attended an archeological congress at Cairo, and while there learned of the discovery of a gold treasure of the Roman period. This he recommended to the attention of Charles L. Freer of Detroit, who purchased it for his collection of objects of art. Dennison published, in addition to valuable articles, *A Junior Latin Book* (with John C. Rolfe, 1898), an edition of *Livy, Book I and Selections from Books II–X* (1908), revised editions of F. W. Kelsey's *Topical Outline of Latin Literature* (1899) and H. S. Frieze's *Virgil's Æneid* (1902). At the time of his death the final proofs of his scholarly monograph, *A Gold Treasure of the Late Roman Period,* were awaiting his attention. It was published in 1918 as Part II of Volume XII of the University of Michigan Studies, Humanistic Series.

Dennison was above the average height, well formed and of erect carriage. His hair and moustache were dark brown, with a reddish tinge. His habitual expression was kindly, gentle, and thoughtful. He was a very lovable man. As a teacher he impressed his students by the breadth and soundness of his learning, his high ideals of scholarship, his modesty and sincerity. His classes were cheery and pleasant, yet stimulating and thorough. He did not make his students work, but inspired them with the desire to learn. His interest in his pupils was hearty and unaffected. He knew them well, and they talked with him as with a friend. He had a gentle, kindly humor and refrained from all unkindly criticism. His colleagues found in him a friendly and considerate associate. He was an untiring worker, and organized his life so as to enable him to accomplish the tasks which he set out to accomplish. His death came upon him suddenly, as the result of pneumonia, while he was in the midst of the work which he loved and in which he excelled.

[*Who's Who in America*, 1916–17. A privately printed booklet contains a portrait, an appreciation by Spencer Trotter, the main facts of Dennison's life, minutes and resolutions of the faculty, the Phi Beta Kappa chapter, and the Student Government Associations of Swarthmore College, of the Pa. Soc. of the Archæological Inst. of America, and of the Phila. Soc. for the Promotion of Liberal Studies; also a poem, "*Integer Vitae*," by John Russell Hayes, and several photographic illustrations. Obituary notices are published in the *Classical Jour.*, June 1917, pp. 587–88; the *Am. Jour. of Archæol.*, XXI (1917), p. 341 (a summary of the preceding); in *A Gold Treasure of the Late Roman Period*, pp. 167–68 (by F. W. Kelsey), and in *The Phœnix* (Swarthmore Coll. paper), Mar. 20, 1917. The *Phœnix*, Apr. 10, 1917, contains an account of the funeral services.]   H. N. F.

DENNISON, WILLIAM (Nov. 23, 1815–June 15, 1882), governor of Ohio, was the son of William Dennison, who with his New England wife, Mary Carter, about 1805 removed from New Jersey to Cincinnati, and there became a successful business man. The son attended Miami University, where he proved to be a capable student of political science, history, and literature. Graduating in 1835, he read law in the office of Nathaniel G. Pendleton, father of George H. Pendleton [*q.v.*]. He was admitted to the bar in 1840 and practised until 1848, when he was elected to the state Senate as a Whig. After a hot contest, which prevented organization of the Senate for two weeks, he was defeated as his party's candidate for the position of presiding officer.

In 1844, in his maiden speech before the public, Dennison had opposed the admission of Texas and the extension of the area of slavery. The position then taken foreshadowed his course through the next twenty years. As a member of the state Senate, he had a part in the fight for the repeal of the notorious "Black Laws," and while adhering to the Whig party through 1852 he was one of the first of the Ohio party leaders to join the Republican movement. In February 1856 he attended the preliminary convention at Pittsburgh and served as a member of the Committee on Resolutions; and in June he was acting chairman of the Ohio delegation in the Philadelphia Convention, which nominated Frémont. Three years later, as Republican candidate for governor, he defeated Judge Rufus P. Ranney, who ranked as the leader of the state bar, and thus found himself in the executive chair when the Civil War began. He came to the governor's chair with little experience in public affairs. Although he was well regarded by the business men of the capital city, to whom in large part he owed his nomination, he was but little known to the public, and his nomination was thought to be due to a dearth of able rivals. He campaigned with unexpected brilliance in 1859, but his success did not win for him the full confidence of the people, who decided that he was aristocratic and vain. Thus handicapped, he met the war crisis without adequate support in public opinion. Disposed in advance to be discontented, the people of Ohio were unable for a time to appreciate the energy and wisdom with which he performed his duties. Regarding the Ohio River as an unsafe line of defense for his state, Dennison dispatched McClellan with state troops to aid the loyal citizens of western Virginia in driving out the Confederates. He advocated a similar campaign in Kentucky, but the Federal government preferred to respect the state's neutrality. As a means of preventing the transportation of war supplies and war news without his approval, he practically assumed control of the railways, telegraph lines, and express companies at the outset of hostilities; and against the advice of his attorney-general, he used money refunded by the Federal government on account of state military expenditures without turning it into the treasury for reappropriation. Many complaints thus arose, not without some justification, in spite of the fact that he had with extraordinary promptness succeeded in placing in the field more than the state's quota of the troops called for by the Federal government. As a war governor, Dennison proved unpopular, and the party leaders did not venture to renominate him in 1861. Moreover, they felt the necessity of uniting with the War Democrats, and effected this purpose by supporting David Tod. Dennison accepted the situation without any show of personal feeling, and continued to give loyal support to his party. Gov. Tod, in particular, constantly sought his advice and aid.

In 1864, Dennison acted as chairman of the Republican National Convention, and in the same year was appointed postmaster-general by Lincoln, which office he held until 1866, when he resigned it on account of dissatisfaction with President Johnson's course. In 1872 he was mentioned for the vice-presidential nomination, and in 1880 was defeated by Garfield for the Republican nomination as United States senator. In the same year he was chairman of the Sherman Committee in Ohio, and leader of his forces in the national convention. It is thought that had Grant been nominated, Dennison might have won the vice-presidency.

Notwithstanding his prominence in political affairs, Dennison was primarily a business man. Soon after his admission to the bar he had married the daughter of William Neil of Columbus, a promoter of stage transportation, and had settled in that city. In the early fifties he became president of the Exchange Bank, member of the city council, and organizer of the Franklin County Agricultural Society. In the dawning era of the railway, he was a pioneer promoter of the new type of transportation, leading in the organization, especially, of the Hocking Valley and Columbus & Xenia railroads. An enterprise of another type which he was influential in establishing was the Columbus Rolling Mills. By such ventures, notwithstanding heavy losses in the panic of 1873, he acquired a considerable fortune. To the end of his life, mostly on account of his reserved manner, few knew him well. On the street he spoke only to old and intimate friends. Yet no man knew better how to treat his fellows in parlor or office, and never, intentionally, did he mistreat friend or foe (*Cincinnati Enquirer,* June 16, 1882). He died in Columbus after a period of invalidism lasting about eighteen months.

[Most sketches of Dennison are based on Whitelaw Reid, *Ohio in the War* (1868), I, 1017–22, and index. See also E. O. Randall and D. V. Ryan, *Hist. of Ohio* (1912), IV, *passim*; *Ohio Archæol. and Hist. Soc. Pubs.*, I, 123; IV, 444; IX, 149; *Harper's Weekly,* Jan. 28, 1865; *Ohio State Jour.* and *Cincinnati Enquirer,* June 16, 1882. The best source for the years of Dennison's governorship is his message of Jan. 6, 1862, which includes documents.]   H.C.H.

DENT, FREDERICK TRACY (Dec. 17, 1821–Dec. 24, 1892), soldier, was born in St. Louis County, Mo., son of Frederick F. and Ellen (Wrenshall) Dent, and a classmate of Gen. Grant, who married his sister, Julia Dent. He was graduated from the United States Military Academy, July 1, 1843. Promoted brevet second lieutenant of the 6th Infantry, he served on frontier duty at Fort Towson, Indian Territory, at Baton Rouge, La., and through the Mexican War, taking part in the siege of Vera Cruz, the capture of San Antonio, and the battles of Contreras, Churubusco, and Molino del Rey. In the last of these battles he was severely wounded. After the Mexican War he served on the Pacific Railroad Survey, in the removal of the Seminole Indians, and at various frontier posts. He participated in the Yakima Expedition (1856), the Spokane Expedition in Washington Territory,

the combats of Four Lakes, Spokane Plain, Spokane River, and the expedition to Snake River, Ore., to rescue the survivors of the massacre of Salmon Falls. During the Civil War he served in command of a regiment in the Army of the Potomac, and as a member of the military commission for the trial of state prisoners. Upon the appointment of Gen. Grant as lieutenant-general, he was selected by his brother-in-law as one of his aides-de-camp, with the rank of lieutenant-colonel. He served on the staff of Gen. Grant during the Richmond campaign, and upon the fall of the city of Richmond he was made its military governor, and later commanded the garrison of Washington. He was appointed brigadier-general, United States Volunteers, Apr. 5, 1865, and was mustered out of the volunteer service Apr. 30, 1866. On May 3, 1866, he was again appointed aide-de-camp to Gen. Grant, with the rank of lieutenant-colonel, and in July of the same year was promoted colonel. When Gen. Grant became president, Dent accompanied him to the White House as military secretary, and remained in this capacity until May 1873 when he was assigned to the command of Fort Trumbull, Conn. He was brevetted first lieutenant and captain at the battles of Contreras, Churubusco, and Molino del Rey in the Mexican War, and in the Civil War received the brevets of lieutenant-colonel, colonel, and brigadier-general, for his services. He was retired from active service as colonel of the 1st Artillery, Dec. 1, 1883, upon his own application, after more than forty years of service. While Dent was not a brilliant soldier, and owed much to his relationship to Gen. Grant, he was a brave and chivalrous man, kindly, and of unfailing courtesy, who did his duty zealously and well. He was of medium size, pleasant address, and amiable manners.

[G. W. Cullum, *Biog. Reg.* (3rd ed., 1891); *Official Records (Army),* ser. 1, vols. XXXVI and L; *Battles and Leaders of the Civil War,* IV (1889), 736; *Twenty-fourth Annual Reunion Asso. Grads. U. S. Mil. Acad.,* 1893.]   C.F.C—y.

DENVER, JAMES WILLIAM (Oct. 23, 1817–Aug. 9, 1892), lawyer, soldier, was of Irish descent, his grandfather, Patrick Denver, a participant in the Rebellion of '98, having fled to the United States and settled in Virginia. He was born at Winchester, Frederick County, Va., and his youth was spent on his father's farm there, and at Wilmington, Clinton County, Ohio, where his parents, Frederick and Jane (Campbell) Denver, moved with their family in 1830. He was educated in the local schools, studied engineering and land surveying, and in 1841 went to Missouri in the hope of procuring some survey work. This he failed to do, and so took up school-teaching, both there and in Kentucky. In 1842 he determined to become a lawyer, removed to Ohio, entered the Cincinnati Law School, and graduated in 1844. Opening an office in Xenia, Ohio, he commenced practise, also editing *The Thomas Jefferson,* a local Democratic paper, but in a few months returned to Missouri, and finally settled at Platte City. After the outbreak of the war with Mexico, in 1847 he raised a company for the 12th United States Volunteer Infantry, was commissioned captain, joined Gen. Scott's army at Pueblo, and served throughout the subsequent campaign, participating in all the fighting, including the battles of Molino del Rey and Chapultepec. At the close of the war he returned to Platte City, resumed practise, and purchased the *Platte Argus,* which he edited. In the spring of 1850, attracted by the gold discoveries in California, he traveled to Sacramento by way of Salt Lake and engaged in trading. Shortly afterward, without his knowledge or consent, he was elected state senator, and served in that capacity during 1852–53. In 1852 Gov. Bigler placed him in command of the supply trains which had been provided by vote of the legislature for the assistance of the overland immigrants who were pouring over the mountains and meeting with great hardships. This duty he performed with complete success. Bitter criticism of the project by Edward Gilbert, editor in chief of the *Daily Alta California,* resulted in a duel between the latter and Denver, Aug. 2, 1852, in which Gilbert was killed. Public opinion was overwhelmingly with Denver, and no action was ever taken against him in the matter. Early in 1853 he became secretary of state for California, and while holding that office was elected as a Democrat to the Thirty-fourth Congress. He took his seat in December 1855, and at once became a prominent figure, being appointed chairman of the Special Committee on Pacific Railroads. He astonished the House by reporting a bill providing for three transcontinental lines, but the members declined to support even one. At the close of his term in 1857 he was appointed Commissioner of Indian Affairs by President Buchanan, and in that capacity went West to negotiate treaties with the Indians. Kansas at that period was experiencing a wave of lawlessness and chronic disorder which successive governors had failed to cope with, and President Buchanan, seeking a strong man to take charge of the situation, in the autumn of 1857 turned to Denver. He reluctantly consented and became secretary of the Territory of Kansas in December 1857, and governor in May 1858. Acting with great decision and impartiality, and

impervious to threats, in less than a year he had restored law and confidence, and when he resigned in October 1858 violence and intimidation had ceased and the government was functioning normally. The city of Denver was so named in his honor, he having provided the machinery for the civil organization of Arapahoe County, at the time when the town site was laid out. Returning to Washington, he resumed the commissionership of Indian Affairs, assisting also in the separation of Colorado from Kansas, and suggesting the name for the new Territory. He remained commissioner until March 1859. On his retirement, he returned to California, was unsuccessful candidate for a senatorship and, realizing that he had lost touch with that state, went back to Ohio. On the outbreak of the Civil War he was commissioned brigadier-general of volunteers by President Lincoln, and placed in command of the troops in Kansas. He subsequently joined Halleck at Pittsburg Landing, and commanded a brigade in the Army of the Tennessee, taking part in the advance upon Corinth. He resigned his command, however, in the spring of 1863, and saw no further service. At the termination of the war he opened a law office in Washington, D. C. In 1866 he was a delegate to the Soldiers Convention at Cleveland, and four years later was unsuccessful candidate for Congress from Ohio. He continued active in politics, and in 1876 and 1884 his name was mentioned in connection with the Democratic nomination for the presidency. A distorted version of his duel with Gilbert made its appearance on each occasion, much to his disadvantage. He died in Washington, D. C.

Essentially a product of the frontier, he was a man of fine physique, being six feet two inches in height, and broad in proportion. Remarkable for energy, tenacity and far-sightedness, he was an outstanding figure in the West, where his sincerity of purpose and absolute fearlessness in the discharge of his public duties were appreciated to the full. "Genial, dignified and urbane, he possessed peculiarly winning ways, and the faculty of making men his loyal and enduring friends" (Smiley, *post*). In 1856 he had married Louisa C. Rombach, a native of Ohio. Their son Matthew Rombach Denver was a member of Congress from Ohio.

[An excellent sketch of Denver's career appeared in J. C. Smiley, *Hist. of Denver* (1903), p. 216, which also contains details of his connection with the location of that city and the first organization of Colorado. The article "Jas. W. Denver and Edward Gilbert and their fatal duel in 1852," in O. T. Shuck, *Hist. of the Bench and Bar of Cal.* (1901), p. 227, is informative. See also *A Democratic Nomination for 1884, Jas. W. Denver, of Ohio. His Life, his Services and his Availability*

(1884), a political pamphlet, but interesting; *Hist. of Clinton County, Ohio* (1882), p. 854; *Biog. Dir. of the Am. Congress* (1928).]
                   H.W.H.K.

DE PAUW, WASHINGTON CHARLES (Jan. 4, 1822–May 5, 1887), manufacturer, philanthropist, was born in Salem, Washington County, Ind., the second son of John and Elizabeth (Battiste) De Pauw. The name is derived from Pau, the capital of French Navarre, where the family originated, but from which, owing to its Huguenot sympathies, it migrated in the late sixteenth century to French Flanders and the Walloon provinces where the name was modified to its present spelling. Cornelius De Pauw (1737–99) was the private reader of Frederick the Great. Charles, his son, born at Ghent in 1756, was educated in Paris, became imbued with the principles of the American Revolution and came to America with Lafayette in 1776. At the close of the Revolution he married a Virginia lady and settled in the Blue-Grass region of Kentucky. Here John, the father of Washington Charles, was born. In early manhood he settled in Washington County, Ind., where he was made county surveyor; and in 1814 he laid out the town of Salem (Dunn, *post*, I, 299). Later he was admitted to the bar, was a member of the state constitutional convention of 1816, became a judge, was a general of the state militia, and on four different occasions served as a member of the General Assembly.

Washington De Pauw spent his early life in Salem, Ind. Before the age of twenty-one he entered the county clerk's office and at the age of twenty-two was elected to the clerkship. He invested his first savings in a saw and grist-mill, and on retiring from the clerk's office (1853), started a small bank. He later invested in other banks and became one of the leading bankers in the state. At the opening of the Civil War he was employed for a short time in the army-supply department, but soon withdrew, devoting his entire time to banking. He was a large purchaser of government bonds and securities—as a patriotic duty—but he later profited greatly from these investments. Following the war he became interested in manufacturing, and among other ventures established a plate-glass plant in New Albany, Ind., which became one of the largest and most successful of its kind in the country. In 1882 it was estimated that his manufacturing enterprises in New Albany alone represented an investment of $2,000,000 (*History of the Ohio Falls Cities and their Counties*, 1882, II, 230–31).

From early manhood he was interested in religious and educational activities, but he always declined to participate in politics, refusing the Democratic nomination for lieutenant-governor in 1872. For a number of years he was a trustee of Indiana University, and also of Indiana Asbury University. He was a delegate to the General Conference of the Methodist Episcopal Church in 1872 and 1876, and to the Ecumenical Methodist Council in London in 1881. He gave liberally to schools and churches, but his largest benefaction was made to Indiana Asbury University (established 1839) which became De Pauw University in 1884. In 1881 he provided in his will for the founding and endowment of an institution to be known as De Pauw University. At this time Indiana Asbury University was in financial distress, and when it became known to the trustees that De Pauw contemplated the founding of a new institution, they appealed to him to take over Indiana Asbury, the trustees offering to change the name to De Pauw University. The negotiations were successful and the contract was signed Oct. 16, 1882. The contract between De Pauw and the trustees provided for the raising of $150,000 for the purchase of additional grounds and the erection of buildings, De Pauw agreeing to pay two dollars for every one dollar thus raised. Altogether De Pauw gave, during his lifetime, about $300,000 to the University. His sudden death—from the effects of an apoplectic stroke—left his affairs in confusion, and the terms of his will, which had made liberal provision for carrying on the work of the University and for an endowment, were found impossible of fulfilment.

De Pauw was married three times. His first wife, Sarah Malott, whom he married about 1846, died after the birth of their second child. In 1855 he married Katharine, daughter of Dr. Elijah Newland. She bore him three sons, and died while the youngest was an infant. On Jan. 8, 1867, De Pauw married Frances Marion Leyden, by whom he had four daughters, two dying in infancy. He was a broad, solid, and strong man, slightly below the average in height, with a florid, good-humored face. Deeply religious, and generous to every good cause, he abhorred waste and prodigality. His business ethics were far above the average of his time and no man ever had a more sincere desire to serve his fellow men.

[J. C. Ridpath, in *Meth. Rev.*, May 1890; J. P. Dunn, *Indiana and Indianans*, I (1919), 299; *Asbury Mo.*, 1881–84; *De Pauw Mo.*, 1884–89; manuscript minutes of the Board of Trustees Indiana Asbury-De Pauw University; information from Mrs. Florence De Pauw Seaman, a daughter of W. C. and Frances (Leyden) De Pauw.]
                  W.W.S.

DEPEW, CHAUNCEY MITCHELL (Apr. 23, 1834–Apr. 5, 1928), lawyer, wit, railway president, United States senator, was the son of

Isaac and Martha (Mitchell) Depew. His father was of French Huguenot descent and a man of enterprise. His mother came from the line of Roger Sherman, Connecticut statesman and signer of the Declaration of Independence, being a grand-daughter of the latter's brother, Rev. Josiah Sherman. To few men has it been given to live so long and well as did Chauncey M. Depew. His path followed the lines of good fortune and least resistance from his birth in the Hudson River town of Peekskill, Westchester County, N. Y., to his death at 27 West 54th St., New York City. Peekskill had been the home of the Depew family ever since the first of the name arrived along with the Palatines imported by Robert Livingston to clear his land grants on the eastern shore of the lordly river. Isaac Depew took to river transportation before the days of railroads and did well with it. From the start his son had advantages. He began his education with five years in a private school kept by Mrs. Westbrook, wife of the Dutch Reformed pastor in Peekskill, to whose faith his father and mother conformed and which was his own through life. The school was adequate; its course classical. A high-school course at the Peekskill Academy fitted him for Yale, which he entered in 1852. Among his classmates in New Haven were David James Brewer and Henry Billings Brown, who were to become justices of the United States Supreme Court. Fellow students of note and life-long intimacy were Wayne MacVeagh, later attorney-general of the United States, and Andrew D. White, president of Cornell University. Depew was a popular student and a superior scholar. He was one of the Commencement Day orators when graduating in 1856.

Returning to Peekskill he entered the law office of Edward Wells and for two years studied the statutes and the intricacies of justice. In 1858 he was admitted to the bar and began practise in his native village, a risky proceeding which like all else in his lucky life turned out well. The Republican party came into being before young Depew's departure from Yale. Though his family were Democrats the doctrine of free soil appealed to the rising attorney. Upon graduation he joined his fortunes with the new organization locally and made a name for himself when put on the stump by the state committee in the Frémont-Buchanan campaign. He attended the New York Republican state convention in 1858 as a delegate from Peekskill. Won over by Thurlow Weed, he supported for the governorship Edward D. Morgan, a metropolitan merchant, who was nominated, elected, then reëlected for a second term that made him a "war" governor.

When the Civil War began in 1861, Depew was prominent in public counsels. He served in the legislature in the sessions of 1862 and 1863, being Republican nominee for the speakership the latter year. The two parties were tied in the House, though the Republicans controlled the Senate and had a sufficient majority in joint-session to insure the election of their candidate for the United States Senate, Gov. Morgan, if only the House could be organized. After a prolonged deadlock, during which Depew's name was withdrawn and again presented, a deal was finally effected whereby a Democrat, T. C. Callicot, was chosen speaker in return for the assurance of Morgan's election to the Senate. Depew refused to take advantage of the offer of a group of Democrats to give him the speakership if he would oppose this scheme, and relates that he was overwhelmed with compliments on his virtue (Depew, *My Memories of Eighty Years,* pp. 24–6). He could hardly have acted otherwise without affronting the powerful Thurlow Weed, who was managing Morgan's candidacy and was party to the arrangement. Owing to legal action instituted against Callicot by injured Democrats, however, Depew acted as speaker a good part of the session. He was also chairman of the ways and means committee, and floor leader for his party. His activities brought him into contact with Lincoln and made him nationally prominent. Political promotion was easy. In 1863 he was elected secretary of state and in the campaign of 1864 he stumped New York, following and answering Gov. Horatio Seymour who was running for reëlection. After Lincoln's assassination Depew, as secretary of state, received his body in New York and escorted it to Buffalo, on the way to Springfield, Ill., where it was interred.

Appointed in 1866 by Andrew Johnson as the first minister from the United States to Japan, he was duly confirmed by the Senate. The salary —$7,500 a year—looked large in Peekskill, but while Depew was contemplating acceptance Commodore Cornelius Vanderbilt, then head of the Hudson River and Harlem railroad lines, offered him the place of attorney for his roads at a much smaller salary. He hesitated. "Railroads are the career for a young man; there is nothing in politics. Don't be a damned fool," the Commodore is said to have remarked. Depew resigned and entered the service of Vanderbilt interests, which did not take him out of politics. He handled the political contacts of his employer with great tact and skill. At the Commodore's behest Depew joined the Independent Republican movement in 1872, took a hand in securing Horace Greeley's nomination for president and himself ran for lieutenant-governor in New York State on the Greeley ticket. He was beaten but made a good race. It was all in the day's work as Vanderbilt's attorney. Legislation had a considerable share in his duties and he smoothed the way for his client at Albany. The consolidation of the several cross-state lines that became the New York Central was full of complexities, legal and legislative. These he straightened out. Securing Chicago connections was a matter of further importance. In 1874 he became a director in the Vanderbilt system; in 1875 its general counsel; in 1877, a director in the Chicago & Northwestern; in 1882 second vice-president of the New York Central & Hudson River, which had become the designation of the combined railroads; and in 1885, its president. During his term of office, which lasted thirteen years, he brought about the absorption of the rival West Shore system and was for a time its president.

In 1881, following the resignation of the New York senators, Conkling and Platt, Depew was a candidate before the legislature. After prolonged balloting during which he was within ten votes of election, he withdrew his name. In 1885 he was offered the Republican nomination for senator from New York, but declined. In 1888 his party in the state indorsed him for president. He attended the convention at Chicago where he received 99 votes. Railroads were unpopular at the moment and he withdrew in favor of Benjamin Harrison, whom he nominated and whose candidacy he actively supported in the campaign that followed. Harrison tendered him a cabinet position of his own choice but he declined. When James G. Blaine retired as secretary of state in 1892 the President invited Depew to fill out the term but he again refused. In the presidential campaign of that year Depew again took the stump for Harrison. In 1896 he nominated Levi P. Morton for president, but the honor went to McKinley. In 1899 he was elected United States senator from New York and retired from the presidency of the New York Central Railroad but became chairman of the board of directors, a position he retained to the end. He was received in a hostile spirit at Washington as a railway man but preserved his personal popularity. In 1905 he was reëlected and served another full term. That year his name came under a cloud through the revelation made by Charles E. Hughes, counsel for the Armstrong legislative committee when investigating the practises of the great New York life insurance companies, that he had been receiving an annual retainer of $20,000 from the Equitable Life Assurance Company. This he at once gave up. The exposé put him in the background for a time, but the spot in the public heart that had grown cold, warmed up in season and Depew resumed his place in general esteem.

He was a favorite after-dinner speaker and raconteur. "I am known as an after-dinner speaker," he said on his eightieth birthday. "I hope I am also known as the man who works. My dinners have never interfered with my business. They have been my recreation. . . . My digestion might have bothered me if I had not been careful. . . . I soon determined to play with everything, but to eat nothing except the roast and game courses. The trouble with the average man is that he cannot restrain his appetite. But a public banquet, if eaten with thought and care, is no more of a strain than a dinner at home." He was fond of quoting President James A. Garfield to the effect that "he might be president if he did not tell funny stories." He would drink nothing but champagne and that in moderation. With his fortunes well guided by the Vanderbilts he escaped worry, and with his rules of health was able to continue active until past ninety. His only office besides those named was that of Regent of the University of the State of New York, which he held from 1877 to 1904. He was a delegate to every Republican national convention from 1888 to 1924. At eighty-two he calmed the convention of 1916 which almost got out of hand. On the appeal of the chairman, Warren G. Harding, Depew took the floor for forty-five minutes and mastered the disorder. He spoke again at the gathering of 1920. For thirty years he attended an annual birthday celebration given by the Montauk Club of Brooklyn. Yale alumni dinners and the choice affairs of the Lotos Club were occasions upon which he shone conspicuously.

He occupied a large place in directorates, holding membership on the boards of many railroads, chiefly the New York Central and its dependencies, the Western Union Telegraph Company, and various bridge companies. He was a member of the Society of the Cincinnati, and, from 1893 to 1906, of the Yale Corporation. At the time of his death he was the oldest graduate of Yale. He was devoted to the interests of the university and to many benefactions during his lifetime he added by will a million dollars. Depew married Elsie A. Hegeman, Nov. 9, 1871. One son, Chauncey M. Depew, Jr., was born to them. Mrs. Depew died May 7, 1893. On Dec. 27, 1901, at Nice, Depew married May Palmer, who survived him.

[Depew's speeches have been published in a succession of volumes, the most extensive collection being

Orations, Addresses and Speeches, ed. by J. D. Chaplin (8 vols., 1910). His *My Memories of Eighty Years* (1922), and *The Depew Story Book* (1898), ed. by W. M. Clemens, are of interest. See also *Century Mag.*, Aug. 1925; *Literary Digest*, Apr. 28, 1928; *Rev. of Revs.* (N. Y.), May 1928; *Nation* (N. Y.) and *Outlook*, both Apr. 18, 1928; *Current Hist.*, Apr. 1926; W. A. D. Eardeley, *Chronology and Ancestry of Chauncey M. Depew* (1918); F. J. Conkling, "The Family of Dupuis, De Puy, Depew, etc.," *N. Y. Geneal. and Biog. Rec.*, Jan., Apr., July, Oct. 1901; *Yale Univ. Obit. Rec. of Grads.* (1928); obituaries in *N. Y. Times, N. Y. Herald Tribune*, and *World*, Apr. 6, 1928.]
D. C. S.

DE PEYSTER, ABRAHAM (July 8, 1657–Aug. 2, 1728), colonial merchant and public official, was born in New Amsterdam, the son of Johannes and Cornelia (Lubberts) de Peyster. The father was a native of Haarlem and descended from a line of ancestors conspicuous "in goldsmithing industry and in other handicraft arts," of considerable wealth, and for the most part converts to the Protestant faith; he emigrated to New Amsterdam prior to 1649 and was one of the dozen or so most substantial citizens. Abraham enlarged the possessions inherited from his father, became an enterprising merchant, "importing in his own ships," built warehouses near the dock which are mentioned several times in the city records, and acquired a tract of land north of the Wall (the present Wall St.) which was known as the "Great Garden of Col. de Peyster." He built a house near the East River shore in 1695, for years one of the finest residences in the city. In a list of members of the Dutch Church, his name appears as one of six to which the courtesy title "de Heer" is attached, emblematic of influence and wealth. The young city struggling under its financial burdens often looked to him for loans; an entry in the Council Minutes, Apr. 22, 1702, states that "Abr'm de Peyster offers to assist the government in financial difficulties" (*Calendar*). Letters from Gov. Bellomont (in *De Peyster and Watts*, pp. 124–40) reveal the extent to which the Governor relied on De Peyster in connection with supplies of ship timber and wine, and in money matters generally. It is apparent that the latter combined with his affluence and business capacity popularity and good sense, for he was called by his fellow citizens or the provincial authorities to fill almost every public office in municipality or province: alderman (1685), captain of a train band, mayor for four successive terms (1691–94), colonel of the local militia, member of the governor's council (1698–1702, 1709, 1710–22), and as such, in 1701, acting-governor for a short period, deputy auditor-general (1701) and receiver general of the port (1708), justice of the supreme court (1698–1702; he succeeded to the

position of chief-justice on Jan. 21, 1701, holding the office until Aug. 4 of that year), and finally, treasurer of the province (1706–21). As mayor he was instrumental in developing a system for the better care of the city poor. He possessed a decided military instinct and was one of six captains of train bands in 1689, at the time of the Leisler rebellion. He was identified with the Leisler faction although he was one of those who signed a petition of protest (May 19, 1690) to William and Mary against being ruled "by the sword at the sole Will of an Insolent Alien" (*Documents*, III, 748–49). During the years of war which followed between English and French colonists De Peyster (now with the rank of colonel) was active on committees for building or repairing fortifications, and on one occasion, at least, when government funds were lacking he shared with another the entire expense of subsisting "the soldiers in his Majesty's Pay" (*Journal of the Votes and Proceedings of the General Assembly*, Apr. 14, 17 and 18, 1701).

De Peyster went to Holland in 1684 and married Catharine de Peyster, a kinswoman, by whom he had eight sons and five daughters. His son Abraham succeeded him as treasurer of the province in 1721.

[Important contemporary sources include: *Minutes of the Common Council of the City of N. Y. 1675–1776* (8 vols., 1905), vols. I, VIII; *Calendar of Council Minutes, 1668–1783* (N. Y. State Lib. Bull. 58, 1902); *Documents Relative to the Colonial Hist. of the State of N. Y.*, vols. III, IV, V (1853–55); De Peyster Papers (MS.) in N. Y. Hist. Soc., some of which are printed in J. Watts de Peyster, *De Peyster and Watts Geneal. Reference* (1854). "The De Peyster Family in Connection with the Colonial Hist. of N. Y." in Valentine's *Manual of the Corporation of the City of N. Y.*, 1861, pp. 556–76, and W. W. Spooner, *Hist. Families in America*, I, 1–40, are secondary accounts which need to be checked for inaccuracies. See also Frank Allaben, *John Watts de Peyster* (1908), I, 17–19; Jas. G. Wilson, *Memorial Hist. of N. Y.*, esp. vol. I (1892).]
A. E. P.

DE PEYSTER, JOHN WATTS (Mar. 9, 1821–May 4, 1907), author, soldier, the son of Frederic de Peyster and Mary Justina Watts, was born in New York City at the home of his maternal grandfather, John Watts. The De Peysters were of "stout Holland ancestry," descendants of Huguenot refugees, Johannes de Peyster being the first of the family in America. John's paternal grandmother was English, a daughter of Gen. Hake of the British army, while his own mother was of Scotch descent. Philanthropic interests, participation in the civic events of their times, and especially a marked devotion to military pursuits were characteristic of many branches of his family, and he rather faithfully reflected this background, adding to it extended activities as a scholar and writer. Inherited fortunes gave him the leisure and means for the pursuit of his various interests.

His mother died soon after his birth and he was reared in the home of his grandfather Watts, of whom he speaks in terms of affection and esteem. His education was largely tutorial, supplemented by wide reading and European travel. His dedication in his *History of the Life of Leonard Torstenson* pays the following tribute to his father: "Throughout my life, nothing has afforded me such unalloyed pleasure as that taste for the study of history, to which you early ministered by furnishing my book-shelves with sound and instructive publications judiciously selected." His early military interests were quickened by association with his cousin Philip Kearny [*q.v.*], later a famous general. Nearly all their leisure time, he says, was spent managing mimic campaigns involving four to six thousand lead soldiers. At the age of eighteen De Peyster, while in service as foreman of a volunteer fire company, became the victim of a troublesome heart affection from which he suffered throughout his life. He entered Columbia College, but ill health prevented his graduation. A lifetime of self-education was however recognized by various collegiate institutions and he received degrees of M.A., Ph.D., Litt.D., and LL.D.

In 1841 he married Estelle Livingston, daughter of John Swift Livingston. Much of their time was spent at the country estate, Rose Hill, in Dutchess County. In 1845 he joined an infantry brigade of New York militia, drawn from the northern districts of the county, as judge-advocate with rank of major, and the next year he was made colonel of the 111th Regiment of New York State Infantry. Although legislated out of office by change of law in 1849, he was later placed by Gov. Fish in command of the 22nd Regiment in spite of the fact that he was the youngest available colonel; two years later he was ranked as brigadier-general. Gov. Clark chose him for his adjutant-general, but he resigned after a few months of service. Circumstances prevented the acceptance by President Lincoln of three regiments which De Peyster offered to raise at the outbreak of the Civil War, nor was the latter physically able to serve on the field. He contributed three sons to the service, however, and used his influence for the cause whenever possible through the press or otherwise. In 1866, by concurrent action of the legislature of New York, the governor was empowered to confer upon him the brevet rank of major-general in the National Guard for meritorious services.

In 1851, a serious bronchitis threatening to develop into consumption caused his doctor to order him to go abroad. He secured an appointment from Gov. Hunt as military agent and spent the next few years in the study of military affairs and the conduct of fire companies in Europe. The results were embodied in a full report and formed the basis for later improvements in the state troops. He also advocated a paid fire department, steam fire-engines, and fire-escapes, and he was interested in the reorganization of the New York City police force.

As a writer he was exceedingly versatile, his works including drama, historical romance, poetry, genealogical and biographical sketches, miscellaneous articles such as "Did our Savior speak Greek?" "Buddhism and Romanism compared," "Michael Angelo," "Gypsies." His principal works dealt with historical events and characters, representative productions being: *The History of the Life of Leonard Torstenson* (1855), *The Ancient, Medieval and Modern Netherlanders* (1859), *Practical Strategy, as Illustrated by the Life and Achievements of a Master of the Art, the Austrian Field Marshal Traun* (1863), *Secession in Switzerland and in the United States Compared* (1863), *Personal and Military History of Philip Kearny* (1869), *An Inquiry into the Career and Character of Mary Stuart* (1883), *Napoleone di Buonaparte* (1896). He rejoiced in overriding conventionalities and often showed strong bias, particularly in defense of a family connection, but his writings show exceptional knowledge of military history and science. His philanthropies and memberships in clubs and other organizations were nearly as varied and numerous as his writings. Family estrangements embittered his later years, which despite physical frailties extended to the advanced age of eighty-six.

[Frank Allaben, *John Watts de Peyster* (2 vols., 1908), carries a portrait as a frontispiece and ends with an exhaustive fifty-page list of his writings. See also obituaries in *N. Y. Times*, *N. Y. Herald*, and *N. Y. Sun*, issues of May 6, 1907; *Who's Who in America*, 1906–07; J. W. de Peyster, *De Peyster and Watts* (1854).]

A. E. P.

DERBIGNY, PIERRE AUGUSTE CHARLES BOURGUIGNON (1767–Oct. 6, 1829), judge, governor, was born in Laon, France and died in Gretna, La. His parents were Auguste Bourguignon and Louise Angeline Blondel d'Herbigny. As they were of noble family, their son found it expedient, about 1793, to migrate from revolutionary France to Santo Domingo. In the time remaining before 1800, he lived successively in Pennsylvania—where he married Félicité Odile Dehault de Lassus—in

Missouri, in Florida, and in Louisiana, where he soon became a French colonial official. He was secretary of the municipality of New Orleans under French rule, and official interpreter of the American territorial government under Claiborne. In 1804 he delivered in French the first Fourth-of-July oration ever made in New Orleans. In 1805, as one of three commissioners—representing to a degree the longer established elements of the population in Louisiana—he went to Washington to protest against the determination of the federal government to delay the admission of the new territory as a state. The protest was not fruitful. He returned home disgruntled, and after some delay collaborated with others in publishing a statement of grievances. At the organization of the "University of Orleans" in 1805 he was made one of its regents, and later he was clerk of the court of common pleas, secretary of the legislative council, and member of the first state legislature. In 1813 he became a member of the state's first supreme court. As a jurist he was impeccable but not brilliant. It is said that in framing his opinions he labored always under the handicap of being obliged to translate into English, ideas which he had first thought out in a French fashion and in the French tongue. In 1820 he resigned as judge and became a candidate for governor. During the campaign the number of votes cast for him was not so great as the number cast for one of his opponents, T. B. Robertson. The final choice between the two lay with a legislature which, often more Franco-American than Anglo-American in its composition, could with reason be supposed to prefer Derbigny. He repudiated the office in advance, saying that he was too good a democrat to contravene the will of the people, and that he hoped his friends would vote for the majority candidate. As secretary of state (1820–27) he found time, in addition to his other duties and a meticulous devotion to his large family, to interest himself in the operation of the first steam ferry upon the Mississippi River, and also, in company with Edward Livingston and Moreau-Lislet, to revise the Civil Code of Louisiana. Inaugurated governor in 1828, he advocated popular education and did what he could to obliterate the old political cleavage between persons who were in general of French tradition and those who were in general of English tradition. On Oct. 1, 1829, as he was riding near the village of Gretna, his horses, becoming frightened, overturned his carriage, inflicting upon him an injury which proved fatal.

[W. C. C. Claiborne, *Letter Books 1801–1816* (6 vols., 1917); *Louisiana Courier* (New Orleans), Oct. 7, 1829; J. D. B. DeBow, "Louisiana," in *DeBow's Review*, May 1846; C. Gayarré, *Hist. of La.* (4 vols., 1854–66); Marc Villiers du Terrage, *Les Dernières Années de la Louisiane Française* (1904); A. Fortier, *Hist. of La.* (1904), and *Louisiana* (1909); H. P. Dart, "Hist. of the Supreme Court of La.," and W. K. Dart, "Justices of the Supreme Court" in *La. Hist. Quart.*, Jan. 1921; Parish Records of St. Louis Cathedral, New Orleans, examined by Prof. Jas. E. Winston.] J. D. W.

DERBY, ELIAS HASKET (Aug. 16, 1739–Sept. 8, 1799), merchant and ship-owner, was born in Salem, Mass., the son of Richard Derby [*q.v.*] and his first wife, Mary Hodges. His father was a merchant in Salem, who built up a considerable trade with the West Indies and the Spanish Peninsula in the latter part of the Colonial period, and Elias Hasket Derby succeeded to this business at about the outbreak of the Revolution. During the war, in common with other American merchants, he fitted out a number of his ships as privateers and the spoils brought in by these vessels, together with the proceeds of a number of successful trading voyages, made him at the close of the Revolution one of the wealthiest merchants in New England. He did not, however, thereupon retire to a life of ease, but taking advantage of the new circumstances embarked upon an extensive commerce to many parts of the world hitherto unvisited by Americans. In 1784 he dispatched his ship *Light Horse* from Salem to St. Petersburg, Russia, with a cargo of West India sugar. This was the first vessel to display the Stars and Stripes in the Baltic. In 1785 he sent his ship *Grand Turk* on a trading voyage to the Cape of Good Hope and the next year dispatched her to the Isle of France in the Indian Ocean. From there she proceeded to Canton, China, being the first New England ship to reach the Orient. Encouraged by these pioneer voyages, Derby's vessels found their way to such distant ports as Manila, Batavia, Rangoon, Calcutta, Bombay, and Canton. But while he traded with all these ports and with the ports of Europe and the West Indies as well, his most lucrative trade was with the Isle of France, or Mauritius as it is now called, a small island in the Indian Ocean, where he exchanged the humble products of the New England farms for the exotic commodities of the East. Toward the end of his career, he profited greatly through the situation created by the Napoleonic Wars, when neutral ships were in demand for the carrying trade.

His success lay partly in his far-seeing initiative as a trader—he had the courage to embark in new fields of commerce and was ever ready to take advantage of changing conditions—and partly in the superior type of men which he employed as captains and supercargoes of his ships.

As the vessels were often gone a year or more without their owner hearing from them, responsibility for the outcome of the voyage rested largely in the hands of the captain or supercargo. These men were therefore encouraged by Derby with large shares in the profits, and as a result many of them became wealthy. In fact, some of the principal family fortunes of New England were founded by men who sailed in Derby ships. Derby himself never went to sea, but he had, nevertheless, a thorough knowledge of ships and most of his fleet was built under his own supervision. Of all the vessels he dispatched to the ends of the earth, only one was lost.

Although Derby was one of the leading citizens of Salem and took an active interest in the welfare of the town, he never held political office. During the Revolution he gave freely of guns, ammunition, and supplies for the use of the Continental Army, and after the war he took an active interest in the original tariff acts. It was largely through his advice that the bonded warehouse system was adopted by the Government.

He devoted practically his entire time to his business and the little relaxation which he allowed himself was principally of a domestic nature. As he began to prosper he purchased a large farm on the outskirts of Salem where he experimented with many new plants brought by his ships from abroad. Although for the greater part of his life he lived in a house of modest proportions, in 1797 he built a magnificent mansion, the finest in Salem. The plans were drawn by McIntyre, the noted American architect of the period, and many of the elaborate furnishings for the house were brought from Europe and China; it was surrounded by stables and gardens. The owner, however, lived to enjoy it but two years. In September 1799, while still at the height of his career, he died, leaving one of the largest fortunes amassed in America up to that time. On Apr. 23, 1761, he had married Elizabeth Crowninshield, thus uniting two of the leading merchant houses of Salem. Four sons and three daughters survived him. The eldest, Elias Hasket Derby, Jr. [q.v.], carried on the great business until the adverse period of the Embargo, when the Derby flag disappeared from the high seas. The trade, however, which the elder Elias Hasket Derby established to China, India, the East Indies, and the Baltic laid the foundations of American commerce with those distant parts of the world.

[Derby business papers, in Essex Inst., Salem, Mass.; E. H. Derby, "Memoir of E. H. Derby," in *Hunt's Merchants' Mag.*, XXXVI (1857), 147–88;
Robt. E. Peabody, *Merchant Venturers of Old Salem* (1912); Perley Derby, "Geneal. of the Derby Family," *Essex Inst. Hist. Colls.*, III (1861), 154–67, 201–07.]

R. E. P.

DERBY, ELIAS HASKET (Jan. 10, 1766–Sept. 16, 1826), merchant, was born in Salem, Mass., the third child and eldest son of Elias Hasket Derby [q.v.], the famous Salem merchant, by his wife, Elizabeth Crowninshield. A year or two at Harvard was the least part of his education, which in other respects was the counterpart of that given to all the Derby apprentices: several years in the counting-house, thorough instruction in navigation under old Capt. Jonathan Archer, several voyages as captain's clerk, and finally a voyage to the West Indies as supercargo of the brig *Rose*. In November 1787 he sailed in the *Grand Turk* for the Isle of France (Mauritius), which had been opened to American commerce in 1784, and did not get back to Salem until Dec. 31, 1790. During these three years he also visited Bombay, Madras, and Calcutta and established the Derby firm as the dominant American commercial house on the Isle of France. These activities are said to have added $100,000—a large sum for the time—to the Derby fortune. On July 14, 1799, he sailed from Salem in the *Mount Vernon,* a new ship of 355 tons and armed with twenty guns, for the Mediterranean. The Napoleonic Wars made the certain hazards and the possible profits of this voyage triply great. The *Mount Vernon* had several brushes with the French but was able either to outsail or to outshoot them. She captured a large latineer off Algeciras Point but was unable to bring her to port. At Naples Derby was entertained by Lord Nelson and Lady Hamilton. This voyage added another $100,000 to the Derby fortune, but before Elias Hasket Derby, Jr., reached Salem, July 7, 1800, the head of the house was dead.

The rest of his career was an anti-climax. In recognition of his extraordinary services, the elder Derby in his will left his son an equal share in the estate, although he had already received his portion. As a result a family quarrel arose; once Derby and his brother-in-law, Nathaniel West, came to blows on the Derby wharf (Bentley, II, 353); and the once proud family became a subject of gossip and scandal. Derby, too, cut a somewhat ridiculous figure as a brigadier-general of militia; he was embroiled in the violent politics of Salem; and his reduced income did not suffice to maintain the Derby mansion, which had been built to satisfy the extravagance and vanity of his mother. In 1809, in an effort to retrieve his fortune, he made a voyage to Rio de Janeiro and London in the *Mount Hope,* but this venture was a failure. He then moved to Londonderry, N. H. He was the first to bring merino sheep to America in any number. During the War of 1812 he manufactured broadcloth. He died at Londonderry of gout. His wife, Lucy Brown, who had borne him four daughters and five sons, survived him.

[Perley Derby, "Geneal. of the Derby Family," in *Essex Inst. Hist. Colls.,* III (1861), 154–67, 201–07, 283–89; E. H. Derby, "Memoir of E. H. Derby, Merchant of Salem, Mass.," in *Hunt's Merchants' Mag.,* XXXVI (1857), 147–88; *The Diary of Wm. Bentley, D.D.* (Salem, 1905–14); Fiske Kimball, "The E. H. Derby Mansion in Salem," in *Essex Inst. Hist. Colls.,* LX (1924), 273–92; Robt. E. Peabody, *Merchant Venturers of Old Salem* (1912); *Essex Register* (Salem, Mass.), Sept. 18, 21, 1826.]   G. H. G.

DERBY, ELIAS HASKET (Sept. 24, 1803–Mar. 31, 1880), lawyer, was born in Salem, Mass., the son of Elias Hasket Derby, second [*q.v.*], and Lucy (Brown) Derby. He was a twin, and the fourth son to be named for the father and grandfather. He received his preparatory schooling at Dr. Stearns's academy in Medford, Pinkerton Academy in Londonderry, N. H., and the Boston Latin School. After graduating in 1824 from Harvard College, he read law in the office of Daniel Webster and was admitted to the bar of the court of common pleas in Suffolk County in October 1827 and of the supreme court in October 1829. He soon won distinction at the bar, especially in railway cases. He acquired an extensive knowledge of railroading, was president for some years of the Old Colony Railroad and a director of several others, worked indefatigably to extend various lines, and was instrumental in securing the completion of the Hoosac Tunnel. Much of his work brought him into close relations with public men and public affairs; he was sometimes consulted by high officers of the government on matters of difficulty and contributed not a little toward shaping their opinions and determining their policy. His most notable services of this nature were his *Preliminary Report on the Treaty of Reciprocity with Great Britain to Regulate the Trade between the United States and the Provinces of British North America* (1866), prepared for Secretary of the Treasury Hugh M'Culloch, and his *Letter to the Hon. William H. Seward . . . [on] the Relations of the United States with the British Provinces and the Actual Condition of the Question of the Fisheries* (1867). He wrote much for the press on a wide range of business and economic subjects, so that his favorite signature, "Massachusetts," was long familiar to readers in the neighborhood of Boston. He also contributed to the *Atlantic Monthly,* the *Edin-*

burgh Review, and other periodicals. His few independent publications were of little importance, though they now possess some interest for a curious reader. *Two Months Abroad; or, A Trip to England, France, Baden, Prussia, and Belgium* (1844) and *The Overland Route to the Pacific: A Report on the . . . Union Pacific and Central Pacific Railways* (1869) are fairly well described by their titles. In both of them the serious student of railways and the business man alert for more business are much in evidence. Another side of Derby's character is revealed in *The Catholic: Letters Addressed by a Jurist to a Young Kinsman Proposing to Join the Church of Rome* (1856). The young kinsman, the preface announces with modest pride, was dissuaded. Derby died in Boston at his home on Charles St. He was survived by his wife, Eloise Lloyd Strong, daughter of George W. Strong of St. George's Manor, L. I., whom he had married on Sept. 4, 1834, and by five of his seven children. He had amassed what was for the times a considerable fortune and was known for his generosity to his less fortunate relatives.

[Perley Derby, "Geneal. of the Derby Family" in *Essex Inst. Hist. Colls.,* III (1861), 154–07, 201–07, 283–89; *Mem. Biogs. of the New-Eng. Hist. Geneal. Soc.,* vol. VII (1907); H. F. Jenks, *Cat. of the Boston Public Latin School* (1886); *Harvard Quinquennial Cat. 1636–1915* (1915); W. T. Davis, *Bench and Bar of the Commonwealth of Mass.,* vol. I (1895); Abner Forbes, *Rich Men of Mass.* (2nd ed., 1852); *Boston Transcript,* Apr. 1, 1880.]   G. H. G.

DERBY, GEORGE HORATIO (Apr. 3, 1823–May 15, 1861), humorist, although notable for his development of the boisterous "Western" style of humor, was born in Dedham, Mass., the son of John Barton and Mary (Townsend) Derby, and the descendant of a long line of New England ancestors. His father was known for his oddity of character and his literary bent, both of which he transmitted to his son. The latter attended school at Dedham, and then lived for a time at Concord, Mass., working in a store, reading voraciously, and already displaying his eccentric qualities. Entering the United States Military Academy on July 1, 1842, he graduated four years later, standing seventh in a class of fifty-nine. At the Academy he established a reputation as a wit and notorious practical joker which remained with him throughout life. He was first appointed brevet second lieutenant of ordnance, but was almost immediately transferred to the Topographical Engineers, with which corps he served thenceforth.

After a brief period spent in the survey of New Bedford Harbor, the outbreak of the Mexican War gave him a taste of active campaigning. He served at the siege of Vera Cruz, and with distinction at Cerro Gordo, where he was severely wounded. For gallant and meritorious conduct in that battle he was brevetted first lieutenant. After recovering from his wound he served in the Topographical Bureau (1847–48), and on exploring expeditions in Minnesota Territory (1848–49). Early in 1849 he was sent to California. According to a tradition, which has at least the value of illustrating his character, his transfer to the Pacific Coast was a kind of banishment resulting from too great flippancy in a report addressed to the secretary of war. Except for a brief term of duty in Texas (1852), he remained on the Pacific Coast until 1856. He conducted three exploring expeditions in California (in the gold country, in the San Joaquin Valley, along the Colorado River), and wrote the official reports describing them, managing to enliven even such dry-as-dust material with sudden outbursts of his burlesque humor.

Since 1850 he had been writing sketches; in 1853 he was sent to San Diego, and there almost by accident became famous. His friend, J. J. Ames, editor of the *San Diego Herald,* left town temporarily, putting Derby in unofficial charge of the paper. In the course of a few issues the latter transformed a sober, Democratic, small-town weekly into a riotous conglomeration of wit, burlesque, and satire, devoted to the Whig party. All California laughed, and Derby's outbursts were even reprinted in the East. He became immediately the state wit, and humorous stories without number were credited to him. The founders of *The Pioneer; or California Monthly Magazine* (San Francisco, 1854) solicited his aid, and introduced him to their readers as one "whom not to know argues oneself unknown." Much of his best work appeared in this short-lived monthly. In 1855 Ames, with consent of the author, selected some of the sketches, and the next year published *Phœnixiana; or Sketches and Burlesques,* a volume which became immediately, and remained for a generation, immensely popular. The pseudonym, John Phœnix, was in this case an advertisement rather than a disguise, since Derby was commonly known by that appellation or by his nickname, "Squibob."

Derby continued in the army, regarding writing only as an avocation. While in California he married Mary Ann Coons of St. Louis. In 1856 he was transferred to the East, and there wrote other humorous sketches, some of which were published in book form as *The Squibob Papers* (1859). He was promoted to the rank of captain on July 1, 1860. In the previous year, while working as light-house engineer in Florida he had suffered a sunstroke which, reacting upon his already eccentric personality, deranged his mind. After Dec. 20, 1859, he was on sick leave, and a year and a half later he died in New York City.

Derby's writings are important as representing one of the earliest developments of the so-called American, or Western, style of humor. As a master of puns, grotesque exaggeration, ridiculous understatement, pseudo-serious irony, and robustious burlesque, he is scarcely excelled. His influence can be seen in many subsequent writers of whom Mark Twain is the most noteworthy. As a personality he was unusually interesting; his hoaxes, and his ready wit under cover of extreme gravity were for many years the subject of reminiscences in California, and in the army.

[See preface to an edition of *Phœnixiana* edited by John Vance Cheney and published in 1897; G. W. Cullum, *Biog. Reg. U. S. Mil. Acad.* (3rd ed., 1891); C. Johnston, "The First Jester in California," *Harper's Weekly,* May 17, 1913; W. P. Trent, "A Retrospect of Am. Humor" in *Century Mag.,* Nov. 1901. One of Derby's reports is contained in P. T. Tyson, *Geology and Industrial Resources of California* (1851).]

G.R.S., Jr.

DERBY, RICHARD (Sept. 16, 1712–Nov. 9, 1783), was a leading New England ship-owner and merchant of the Colonial and Revolutionary periods. Born in Salem, Mass., the son of Richard and Martha (Hasket) Derby, he went to sea at an early age and when only twenty-four became captain of the sloop *Ranger* trading between Salem and ports in Spain and the West Indies. After sailing for a number of years in the employ of several Salem merchants, he acquired a vessel of his own, and by means of successful trading was enabled at the age of forty-five to retire from the sea and set up for himself as a merchant in Salem. He then began to build up a thriving commerce with Spain, and at the same time he sent his vessels on voyages through the West Indies exchanging New England fish, lumber, and farm products for rum and sugar. In those days England was almost continually at war with France and Spain, but Derby and other New England merchants, in spite of being British Colonials, continued to trade with Spain and the French islands in the West Indies. Derby's ships were, therefore, subject to capture not only by French and Spanish men-of-war as natural enemies, but by British men-of-war on account of trading with the enemy. Under these circumstances it was inevitable that several of his ships should be captured; but so great were the profits made by those which successfully evaded seizure that he began to amass a considerable fortune. To take care of his increasing business, he built Derby Wharf in Salem harbor and soon he became recognized as one of the most substantial men of the community.

In 1735 he married Mary Hodges of Salem. The family, including three sons and three daughters, lived in a fine brick mansion near the head of Derby Wharf. In 1770 Mrs. Derby died and in 1771 Derby married Mrs. Sarah (Langley) Hersey of Hingham.

The various British Acts of Trade and Navigation which gave rise to the Revolution so greatly hampered Derby's business that it was only natural for him to take an active part in the cause of the Colonies. When in February 1775 a detachment of British troops was sent to Salem to seize some cannon and ammunition concealed there, Derby headed the band of determined citizens which met the troops at the entrance to the town. On the commander demanding that the guns be given up, Derby is said to have replied, "Find them if you can, take them if you can, they will never be surrendered." Whereupon the British commander, evidently fearing to provoke an engagement, hastily withdrew. Two months later, however, actual hostilities began with the battles of Lexington and Concord and shortly thereafter, in order to enlist the sympathy of the British people, the Provincial Congress decided to send a fast vessel to England with affidavits showing that the British troops began the affair and that the Colonists acted only in self-defense. Derby immediately placed his schooner, *Quero*, at the disposal of the Congress for this service. The little vessel, commanded by his son John, reached England two weeks ahead of the ship bearing the British general's dispatches, and caused a great sensation in London. By this time Derby had begun to withdraw from the active management of the business, turning his affairs over to his second son, Elias Hasket Derby [q.v.], and a few years later, in 1783, the old merchant died.

[Jas. D. Phillips, *The Life and Times of Richard Derby, Merchant of Salem* (1929); Robt. E. Peabody, *Merchant Venturers of Old Salem* (1912); Perley Derby, "Geneal. of the Derby Family," in *Essex Inst. Hist. Colls.*, III (1861), 154–67.]   R.E.P.

DE ROSSET, MOSES JOHN (July 4, 1838–May 1, 1881), physician, came from a family of distinguished medical ancestry, François Rosset (1590) having been known as a medical writer. Moses, born at Wilmington, N. C., was the fifth child of Dr. Armand John De Rosset (b. 1807) of that city and Eliza Jane Lord, his wife, and grandson of Dr. Armand John De Rosset (1767–1859). At the age of sixteen he was placed in Diedrich's Academy at Geneva, Switzerland, where he remained as a student for three years, thereafter spending a year at Cologne to acquire German. He returned to America in 1857 and

began the study of medicine with Dr. Gunning S. Bedford of New York, and graduated at the Medical Department of the University of the City of New York in 1860. As a result of a competitive examination he was appointed a resident physician at Bellevue Hospital, New York, in the same year, and there remained until the outbreak of the Civil War, when he returned to North Carolina and was commissioned assistant surgeon in the Confederate army (1861). He served as surgeon of Marye's battery of artillery through Gen. Jackson's campaign in the Valley of Virginia. On his promotion to surgeon (1863) he was placed in charge of General Hospital No. 4 (officers' hospital) in Richmond and later was inspector of hospitals for the Department of Henrico. At the close of the war he moved to Baltimore (1865), where he was soon made adjunct professor and later professor of chemistry both at the medical department of the University of Maryland and the Baltimore Dental College. In Baltimore he became interested in diseases of the eye and ear and devoted himself thenceforth to this field. In 1873 he returned to Wilmington, there continuing his specialty until 1878, when he removed to New York where, after three years, his brilliant career was cut short by death. He was buried in the Oakdale Cemetery at Wilmington. He was married, on Oct. 13, 1863, to Adelaide Savage Meares (b. 1839) of Wilmington, N. C., who bore him seven children.

De Rosset was not only skilled in his own branch of medicine but had an extensive knowledge of general science. In addition to many papers on ophthalmology and otology and the physiology of vision and audition, he issued a translation of *Bouchardat's Annuaire* entitled *Annual Abstract of Therapeutics, Materia Medica, Pharmacy and Toxicology for 1867 by A. Bouchardat*, but the work was a financial failure, on account, it was said, of the decline in interest in French therapeutics. He was known as an independent thinker, a teacher and practitioner who accepted no theories without confirmation and demonstration. For a time he was editor of the *North Carolina Medical Journal*.

[*N. C. Medic. Jour.*, VII (1881), 309; *Medic. Record of N. Y.*, XIX (1881), 586 f.; family documents printed in Jas. Sprunt, *Hist. Monograph No. 4* (1904); D. C. Meares, *Annals of the De Rosset Family* (1906); manuscript memoranda of Louis Henry (brother of Moses John) De Rosset, in the possession of the family.]   E.E.H.

DE SAUSSURE, HENRY WILLIAM (Aug. 16, 1763–Mar. 29, 1839), lawyer, director of the United States Mint, chancellor of South Carolina, was born at Pocotaligo, Prince William's Parish, S. C., descendant in the eighth generation of Antoine, Sieur de Dommartin in Lorraine, who, having adopted the Protestant religion, emigrated to Switzerland, where he became a citizen of Lausanne in 1556. He was the grandson of Henry (d. 1761), the founder of the De Saussure family in America, who came to South Carolina about the year 1730 and settled near Coosawhatchie, Beaufort District, and the eldest child and only son of Daniel and Mary (McPherson) De Saussure. Daniel (1735–1798), the father, was a successful merchant, first at Beaufort and later at Charleston, who served the state in important civil and military capacities during the Revolution and was for a number of years after the war a member of the state Senate. Henry William's education, promisingly begun in private schools of Beaufort and Charleston, was interrupted when at the age of sixteen he volunteered for service during the siege of the latter place. Being made a prisoner on the fall of the city, he was first paroled, then confined on a prison ship in the harbor, and finally (1781) sent to Philadelphia for exchange. There he was reunited with his father who had been held a prisoner at St. Augustine, and his mother and sisters, who had been forced by the British to leave their home (E. McCrady, *The History of South Carolina in the Revolution 1780–1783*, 1902, p. 378). In Philadelphia he entered the law office of Jared Ingersoll and attended lectures on moral and natural philosophy and mathematics at "the university of the city." He was admitted to the bar of Philadelphia in 1784 and, having returned to Charleston shortly afterward, to that of South Carolina in 1785. In the latter year he married Eliza Ford, daughter of Col. Jacob Ford of Morristown, N. J. His political career began when he sat for his constituency in the state constitutional convention of 1790. From time to time during the next eighteen years he was a member of the lower house of the General Assembly (1790–94, 1796–98, 1800–02, 1807?, and 1808). His chief concern as legislator was the conflict between up-country and low-country over the apportionment of representation in the legislature. He defended the disproportion then apparently existing in favor of the low-country chiefly on the ground that property as well as population was entitled to representation (see his *Letters on the Questions of the Justice and Expediency of Going into Alterations of the Representation in the Legislature of South Carolina. By Phocion,* 1795). Realizing, however, that the low-country could not permanently retain its leadership, he advocated a programme of gradual concessions to the up-country. In 1801 he took an active part in the establishment

of the state university at Columbia in order that the up-country might have trained leaders, and in 1808 he supported a reapportionment measure which partially redressed the balance between the two sections. During one of the intervals in his attendance upon the legislature while seeking "the restoration of his health at the North," De Saussure was appointed (1795) director of the United States Mint. His administration, especially his success in bringing about the first coinage of gold, won the approbation of Washington, but, eager to return home, he resigned before the year was out (Washington to De Saussure, MS. in the possession of the De Saussure family). During another interval he served as intendant of the city of Charleston (1797–98). In 1808 he was elected to the chancery bench, a position which he occupied for the next twenty-nine years. In this capacity he performed his principal public service. "To him," says Judge J. B. O'Neall, "the system of equity owes its shape, *form and existence.* He was to South Carolina what Kent was to New York" (*post,* I, 245). This reputation rests not only upon his decrees but also upon his work of compiling and publishing four volumes of Chancery Reports (1817–19) covering the years from the Revolution to 1817.

[Four years before his death De Saussure prepared a "Memoir of the American Branch of the De Saussure Family" in which he gave the main facts of his own career. This was later supplemented by a genealogy compiled by Col. Jas. D. Blanding. Both of these MSS. are now in the possession of descendants living in Charleston, S. C. Other sources of information about him are: Wm. Harper, *Memoir of the Life, Character and Public Services of the Late Hon. Henry Wm. De Saussure* (1841); J. B. O'Neall, *Biog. Sketches of the Bench and Bar of S. C.* (1859), I, 243–52; *Eminent and Representative Men of the Carolinas* (1892), I, 59–60; and obituary in the *Charleston Courier,* Apr. 1, 1839. For a careful study of his part in the reapportionment of representation in 1808 the writer is indebted to Miss Louisa E. Gaillard, a student in his historical seminar in the Coll. of Charleston.]   J.H.E—y.

DE SCHWEINITZ, EDMUND ALEXANDER. [See SCHWEINITZ, EDMUND ALEXANDER DE, 1825–1887.]

DESHA, JOSEPH (Dec. 9, 1768–Oct. 12, 1842), congressman, governor of Kentucky, was born in Monroe County, Pa., of French Huguenot ancestry. In 1781 his parents became a part of the great western migration then beginning, and settled in Kentucky, where they remained only a year before going on to the Cumberland district in Tennessee. Here Desha grew into young manhood, spending more time fighting the Indians than seeking an education. In these skirmishes he acquired his first taste for military activities, a taste bred more by his hatred of the Indians for killing his two brothers than by any innate liking for war. When twenty-one years old he married Peggy Bledsoe, a daughter of Col. Jesse Bledsoe, a prominent Tennessee pioneer, and three years later returned to Kentucky, settling in Mason County. In 1794 he joined Gen. Anthony Wayne's forces against the Indians north of the Ohio River and rendered valuable service in the campaign which ended with the Treaty of Greenville in 1795. He soon developed political ambitions, and with the military record he had acquired he found little trouble in winning election to the state House of Representatives five times before 1802, at which time he was elected to the state Senate, where he remained until he was elected to Congress in 1807. He was constantly returned to Congress until 1819, serving in all six consecutive terms.

Desha's congressional career was characterized by rather ornate oratory, and an extreme patriotism. He did not speak, however, as often as did some other congressmen who were less able than he, as he held it to be the part of wisdom "to think much and speak but little." In 1807 he called for an adequate army to protect American territory—especially to prevent any disaffection in New Orleans. He supported Jefferson on the Embargo measures and refused to abandon these laws until a substitute could be found. During this period he showed bitter hatred of England and France, and in January 1810, he was one of the most intensely warlike of all the lesser War Hawks. During the conflict he argued for larger armies and longer terms of service, and in 1813 he left the halls of Congress long enough to accept a major-generalship of Kentucky volunteers and to command a division in the battle of the Thames. With the coming of peace he opposed a large standing army. He was also opposed to re-chartering the United States Bank and to increasing the pay of congressmen. Desha was essentially a man of the people with all the rugged honesty and mistaken zeal that often went with being such a representative. At no time did these qualities show more clearly than in his term as governor of Kentucky. He was elected to this position in 1824 by a majority of more than 8,000 on the issues of relief and replevin laws and hostility to the federal judiciary and to the two Kentucky branches of the second United States Bank. When balked by the Kentucky court of appeals he led the fight for setting up the new court. As governor he stood for internal improvements, for common schools, and against the aristocratic Transylvania University. While governor he brought down upon himself much criticism by pardoning his son Isaac B. Desha, who had been

convicted of murder. He retired from the governorship in 1828 to his farm in Harrison County and twelve years later died at Georgetown in Scott County.

[Lewis and Richard H. Collins, *Hist. of Ky.* (Covington, 1882), I, 32, 33, 538, II, 547, 705, 706; W. E. Connelley and E. M. Coulter, *Hist. of Ky.* (1922), vol. II, chs. xlix, l, li; *Biog. Encyc. Ky.* (Cincinnati, 1878), p. 37; *Biog. Cyc. Commonwealth of Ky.* (Cincinnati, 1896), p. 389; *Niles' Reg.*, XXIX, 221; *Proc. Ky. State Bar Asso.*, 1915, pp. 48, 49; *Annals of Congress* from 1807 to 1819.]   E.M.C.

DE SMET, PIERRE-JEAN (Jan. 30, 1801–May 23, 1873), Jesuit missionary, was born at Termonde, Belgium, the son of Josse-Arnaud De Smet and Marie-Jeanne Buydens De Smet. He was educated at the seminary of Malines, where he distinguished himself both in his studies and in what was the contemporary equivalent of athletic sports. His physical strength and prowess were remarkable and go far to explain the wonderful endurance with which he bore the almost inconceivable toils incident to his later missionary labors. His youthful friends called him "Samson." In stature he was medium, about five feet six inches, stockily built, muscular, and resilient. His countenance was oval, regular in outline, exceedingly handsome and benignant; the eyes were peculiarly luminous, expressing both shrewdness and spirituality. His weight tended to be excessive, around two hundred and ten pounds, which caused him at times to employ drastic reducing methods in order to keep fit for his taxing physical labors. He once fasted thirty days, thereby losing thirty-five pounds. His appearance and bearing were so friendly, his actions so frank and trust-inspiring, that red men of all tribes and whites of every nationality instinctively confided in him.

De Smet came to America in July 1821 and entered the novitiate of the Jesuit order established near Baltimore (at Whitemarsh) ten years earlier. In 1823 he was chosen for the new novitiate, the second in the United States, which was founded at Florissant near St. Louis and which became the Catholic University of St. Louis. He was ordained in 1827 and after devoting somewhat more than a decade to a round of priestly service, including several years spent in Europe to solicit reinforcements and supplies for his order in America, he entered in 1838 upon his distinctive career as missionary to the Indians. His first mission was St. Joseph at the site of the later Council Bluffs, among the Potawatomi. In 1840 he was commissioned to survey the possibilities for Catholic missions in the Oregon country. From that time the scope of his activities widened to include the Pacific Northwest as well as the great plains; for all of which work he sought support in the eastern cities, in New Orleans, in Ireland, England, Holland, Belgium, France, and Italy. In carrying out his great projects he traveled 180,000 miles. He crossed the Atlantic sixteen times, and once he sailed from Europe around Cape Horn and up the Pacific coast to Oregon. He aided the Catholic mission established in the Willamette Valley by Canadian priests—Fathers Blanchet and Demers; he founded, in September 1841, St. Mary's Mission among the Flatheads; also the Mission of St. Ignatius among the Kalispels; later he planted the Sacred Heart Mission of the Cœur d'Alenes; he touched with his unique regenerative influence nearly all the native populations of the Columbia Valley. This work was accomplished mainly between the years 1840 and 1846.

In his travels to the far West, Father De Smet made the acquaintance also of the Sioux, the Blackfeet, and other tribes east of the Rockies, all of whom held "Blackrobe" in highest esteem. Accordingly, when troubles arose among rival tribes, he was the one man who could hope to bring peace. Also, when the Indians, goaded by ill treatment at the hands of Indian agents or of traders, actually broke bonds and went on the war-path against the whites, Father De Smet was the final resource as mediator. In 1851 he attended the great council held near Fort Laramie, and aided powerfully to bring about a general understanding among the tribes who had become restive under the flood of emigration through their country. He mediated also in the "Mormon War" and in the Yakima Indian War of 1858–59. But his most notable achievement in Indian diplomacy was in June 1868 when he visited in the Bighorn Valley the camp of Sitting Bull's hostiles who had sworn to take the life of the first white man to show himself among them. There, again, as the reverend missionary who always held the scales even between the two races, he succeeded in paving the way for a conference and eventual peace. De Smet's service in this supreme instance was performed quite independently of the government; the Indians, who were intent on attacking the American flag, yielding to the magic of his priestly emblem.

Father De Smet was a zealous churchman, devoted to the promotion of the faith as he understood it. In practical matters he was efficient and business-like; in social intercourse cheerful, of charming address, fond of genial conversation, and full of a simple delightful humor. His kindly tolerance extended to all except religionists of non-Catholic persuasion. He was quite as unable to see the merit of the work done by Prot-

estant missionaries as they were to appreciate the value of Catholic missionary effort. Yet he was the personal friend of all whom he met. And to the Indians of the great West he was the ambassador of Heaven—he was "Blackrobe."

[*Life, Letters and Travels of Father Pierre-Jean De Smet,* ed. by H. M. Chittenden and Alfred Talbot Richardson (1905), is the best source of information. In it are assembled most of the materials published during the missionary's lifetime, some of which were printed in several languages, also his detailed journals and many letters not published previously. English translations are given in all cases. Additional references are E. Laveille, *Life of Father De Smet* (1915); J. D. Shea, *Hist. of the Cath. Missions Among the Indian Tribes of the U. S.* (1855); L. B. Palladino, *Indian and White in the Northwest* (1922).] J.S—r.

DE SOTO, HERNANDO (*c.* 1500–May 21, 1542), discoverer of the Mississippi River, was born at Barcarrota, Spain, of an impoverished but noble family. His education was obtained through the generosity of Pedrarias Dávila, who is said to have sent his protégé to the University of Salamanca. When the youth was about nineteen he followed Pedrarias to Central America, serving as captain in that cruel governor's conquests; and he married his patron's daughter Isabel, thus becoming brother-in-law to Vasco Núñez de Balboa. After earning a reputation for valor in Central America, he sailed in 1532 to serve Francisco Pizarro and Diego Almagro in the conquest of Peru, arriving in time to be the first European to salute the Inca Atahualpa, whom he met at Caxamarca. The Inca admired the doughty conqueror for his horsemanship and soldierly qualities, and Soto was one of the few Spaniards who condemned Pizarro for executing Atahualpa, though Soto himself had led the van in the Inca's capture. Following the sack of Cuzco and the development of the Pizarro-Almagro feud over possession of that city, Soto astutely withdrew from Peru, leaving behind him his mistress, the princess Curicuillar, and their daughter, and carrying to Spain a share of Inca booty amounting to 180,000 *cruzadas*. With this fortune, a pleasing manner and handsome face, and deserved reputation as a vigorous but not needlessly bloodthirsty *conquistador,* he won the favor of Charles V, and at Valladolid on Apr. 20, 1537, obtained from the monarch a contract to conquer Florida. His reward was to be a marquisate and twelve square leagues of land; he was also made governor of Cuba, which island he used as the base of his expedition. His small army was composed of Spanish and Portuguese Estremadurans, and numbered nearly one thousand men. Alvar Núñez Cabeza de Vaca, then returning to Spain after crossing North America with three survivors of the Florida expedition of Pánfilo de Narváez, declined to join

Soto, having hoped for this new commission himself.

Soto's fleet sailed from San Lucar on Apr. 6, 1538, reaching Cuba in May. After replenishing his equipment, he left the island in charge of his wife, and sailed from Havana on May 18, 1539. He landed on the Florida coast on May 30, near the village of Ucita on Charlotte Bay, not at Tampa, as has sometimes been stated.

Here began that warfare with the Indians which continued with brief interludes through three years. Soto's method was to capture the chiefs he visited, compelling each in turn to guide the Spaniards through his territory. For interpreter he had Juan Ortiz, a rescued Spaniard who had been twelve years among the Indians. Leaving four ships under guard, he marched his army north through Florida, entering successively Georgia, North and South Carolina, Tennessee, Alabama, Mississippi, Arkansas, Oklahoma, and Texas; detachments may have entered Missouri and Louisiana. The quest, like those of Coronado in New Mexico and Narváez in Florida, was for another Mexico or Peru; failing to find such a Golden Chersonese, he would tarry nowhere, though his followers were several times ready to plant colonies.

After approaching the Carolina border, he returned south and west to Apalache. Wintering here, the Spaniards discovered on Horse Bay, now called Ocklockonee, remnants of the outfitting of the makeshift ships of the unfortunate Narváez. From here Juan de Añasco, Soto's readiest navigator, went to bring forward the people from Charlotte Harbor, and another subordinate, Francisco Maldonado, sailed west along the Gulf to find a better port. Maldonado located Achusi (Pensacola) sixty leagues away, and then went to Cuba, with orders to return the next season. Breaking camp on Mar. 3, 1540, the gold-hunters crossed the Flint and other rivers, reaching the Savannah at Cutifachiqui, some miles below Silver Bluff. The unnamed queen of this realm graciously presented them with many pearls, and they found relics of the Lucas Vásquez de Ayllón expedition to the nearby Atlantic coast, but there was no gold, and Soto marched north to Xualla province, around the headwaters of Broad River, North Carolina. Crossing the Blue Ridge into northeastern Georgia, the adventurers rested in Guaxule province, where they feasted on "dogs," praising the flavor of what may have been opossum. In near-by Chiaha they heard of gold in Chisca, thirty leagues away, but it proved to be only copper, and the march was resumed from what is now Loudon County, Tenn., southward through Coste, just above Chattanooga, to Cosa in Talladega County, Ala. Here was a chief of sumptuous ménage who urged the strangers to tarry and colonize his opulent land, but Soto, unimpressed, and anxious now for word and supplies from Cuba, hurried along the Alabama to Mauvila, between the Alabama and the Tombigbee. In October the Mauvilians trapped and defeated him, killing many soldiers and horses. Mortified at the reverse, Soto nevertheless concealed the fact that Maldonado was waiting at Achusi, and again led his ragged army north, to winter at Chicaça, in Pontotoc County, Miss., where new Indian attacks added numerous losses to other miseries.

April 1541 found the dogged explorers floundering through swamps to the Mississippi, which the most recent authoritative opinion thinks to have been crossed from Tunica County below Memphis. It was the first conscious discovery of the great river by white men; Narváez had passed the mouth unknowingly, and Cabeza de Vaca had landed to the west of it. Fortune now beckoned Soto's men into St. Francis and Mississippi counties, Ark. At Pacaha, their farthest north, the undaunted treasure-hunters swung west to Quiguate, perhaps in Lee, or St. Francis County, and thence through Woodruff and Cleburne counties into Oklahoma on Grand River. A final bitter winter was spent in "Autiamque" beyond Fort Smith.

Another April arriving, the now disillusioned *conquistadores* turned homeward. Crossing the Arkansas near Pine Bluff, they struggled on to Guachoya, probably near Arkansas City, reaching the Mississippi on Apr. 16; but lack of vessels and Indian hostility rendered futile all efforts to cross. Balked thus, the tireless leader was forced to bed, death at hand. Taking leave of his companions, and naming Luis de Moscoso [*q.v.*] his successor, the warrior died. Buried first within the camp to conceal his death from the enemy, his body was soon disinterred for the same purpose, and ceremoniously consigned to the river.

[The sources on Soto are: *The True Relation* of the Gentleman of Elvas, the Narrative of Luis Hernández de Biedma, an account by Rodrigo Rangel, Soto's secretary, found in Oviedo's *Historia general*, and the memoirs of participants used by Garcilaso de la Vega in *La Florida del Inca*. All are available in English in E. G. Bourne, *Narratives of the Career of Hernando de Soto* (2 vols., 1904). There are also several Soto letters; and in the Archivo de Indias is a map, 148-7-8, reproduced in Henry Harrisse, *The Discovery of America* (1892). It is also reproduced by T. H. Lewis, *Spanish Explorers in the Southern United States* (1907) and the findings of that investigation are followed in this article. J. G. Shea, "Ancient Florida," in Justin Winsor, *Narr. and Crit. Hist. of America*, vol. II (1886), gives ample bibliography, and locates Soto's letters. W. Lowery in *The Spanish Settlements within the Present Limits of the U. S.* (1905), reviews anterior commentators, subordinates itineraries to human interest, but errs in places and distances. R. B. Cunninghame Graham, *Hernando de Soto* (1924), draws largely for story and style from Garcilaso. Dunbar Rowland and A. C. Sanders have "A Symposium on the Place of Discovery of the Mississippi River by Hernando de Soto" in *Miss. Hist. Soc. Special Bulletin No. 1* (1927), which reviews the controversy over the spot of the crossing. See also John Preston Young, *De Soto at Chickasaw Bluffs* (1918).]   H. I. P.

DETMOLD, CHRISTIAN EDWARD (Feb. 2, 1810–July 2, 1887), civil engineer, writer, was born in Hanover, Germany, the son of Johann Detmold, a practising physician. He was educated at a military academy in Hanover and at the age of sixteen came to the United States on his way to Brazil to enter the army there. Unsettled conditions in Brazil at that time, however, deterred him, and he remained in the United States. Shortly after his arrival he went to Charleston, S. C., and established himself as a surveyor. His first major work was in making the surveys for the projected railroad of the newly organized Charleston & Hamburg Railroad & Canal Company. Upon completing this in 1830, he competed for and won a five hundred dollar prize offered by the railroad company for the best locomotive operated by horse-power. Detmold's mechanism, consisting of a horse treadmill mounted on a four-wheel car, carried twelve passengers at a speed of twelve miles an hour. After remaining in Charleston a few years longer, Detmold in 1833–34 was in the employ of the United States War Department and superintended the laying of the foundation of Fort Sumter. During the succeeding ten years he was engaged in railroad survey work on various projected roads in the East, after which he became interested in the manufacture of iron and from 1845 to 1852 was engaged in this business in Maryland. The success of the great industrial exposition held in London in 1851 brought about the agitation for a similar exposition to be held in New York. As a result, on Jan. 3, 1852, the municipal authorities of New York granted a site for a building to be erected on Reservoir Square at Sixth Ave., between Forty-first and Forty-second Sts., and two months later the state legislature granted a charter for the "Exhibition of the Industry of All Nations." In granting the lease the authorities stipulated that the building should be constructed of iron and glass. Because of his interest in the project and his reputation as an engineer, Detmold was made supervising architect and engineer and he, in turn, appointed as consulting engineer Horatio Allen, with whom he had been associated on the Charleston Railroad. The opening of the great

Crystal Palace of New York City took place on July 14, 1853, the opening address being made by President Pierce. Following this work Detmold spent a number of years traveling in Europe and upon his return to the United States became interested to a considerable extent in various manufactories. Failing health, however, compelled him to return to Europe where he remained, residing in Paris, until a few years before his death when he again returned to New York where he died. Detmold was a lover of literature and art and possessed a fine collection of paintings. He spent a number of his last years in the translation of Machiavelli's writings. These were published in Boston in 1882 in four volumes, under the title, *"The Historical, Political and Diplomatic Writings of Niccolo Machiavelli; Translation from the Italian."* Detmold married Phœbe Crary who with two daughters survived him.

[*First Semi-Annual Reports . . . of the S. C. Canal and Railroad Co.,* 1828–30; *Cat. Mechanical Engineering Coll. in the U. S. Nat. Museum* (1922), by Carl W. Mitman; *N. Y. Tribune,* July 6. 1887; *N. Y. Times,* July 5, 1887.]   C. W. M.

DE TROBRIAND, RÉGIS DENIS DE KEREDERN (June 4, 1816–July 15, 1897), soldier, author, son of Joseph, Baron de Trobriand and Rochine Hachin de Courbeville, was born at his father's château near Tours, France, and died in Bayport, L. I. The history of his family has been traced to Irish warriors who settled on the continent of Europe early enough to accompany William on his conquest of England. They returned thereafter to France, and their descendants were in 1426 made French nobles. Joseph de Trobriand, a student in Paris at the outbreak of the French Revolution, became a soldier in Royalist forces outside France, but after 1806 he served as an officer under successive French governments till 1830. Then—relentlessly hostile to Louis Philippe—he resigned his commission as general, and left the army. In 1825 his son Régis was sent to school in Paris, but was driven away for exposing a priest—as he thought—in a betrayal of the confessional (*Post. De Trobriand,* p. 50). He was graduated in 1834 from the Collège de Tours, and in law (1837) from Poitiers. He engaged in duels, wrote poetry, and published a novel, *Les Gentils-hommes de l'Ouest* (1840). In 1841, on something resembling a dare, he came to America. He made the customary tour of the country, wrote a story, "Le Rebelle: Histoire Canadienne" which was published in the *Courrier des États-Unis,* became acquainted with prominent people, and betrothed himself in New York to the heiress, Mary Mason Jones. These two were married in Paris in January 1843. After a year spent in touring Europe, they settled in Venice, where they associated intimately with all the available royalty and nobility—exiled and otherwise. In 1847 they returned to New York. There De Trobriand became a member of the facile literary group adorned by N. P. Willis and George P. Morris. He was a rich man accustomed to making voyages to Europe, he was editor of the *Revue du Nouveau Monde* (1849–50), and he was a regular contributor, commenting with a wealth of allusion on opera and whatnot, to *Le Courrier des États-Unis*. In the summer of 1861, on being elected colonel of the "Gardes Lafayette" of the New York militia, he became an American citizen, and set out to help subdue the Confederacy. He was a valiant and sagacious officer throughout the war, and in April 1865 he was made by brevet a major-general of volunteers. In July 1866 he was commissioned colonel in the regular army, but he was in France when this news reached him, and he continued there on leave till June 1867 in order that he might complete his reminiscent *Quatre Ans de Campagnes à l'Armée du Potomac* (2 vols., 1867–68). This book, highly praised at the time of its publication, and translated, before long, into English, assumes a philosophy of the war which is often not valid. Returning to America, he was on duty with the army—between his numerous trips to France—in Dakota, in Montana, in Utah, and in Wyoming. In 1874, on the death of a cousin, he succeeded to the title of count. In January 1875, as the federal officer charged with upholding an alien government in Louisiana, he performed his work with a tact which won the regard even of his opponents. Upon his retirement from the army in March 1879, he made his residence in New Orleans. He read much, cultivated his roses, visited in France, and spent the summers with his daughter on Long Island. This was his routine until he died.

[M. C. de T. Post, *Post Family* (1905), *Life and Memoirs of Comte Régis de Trobriand* (1910); F. B. Heitman, *Hist. Reg. and Dict. of the U. S. Army* (1903); *New Orleans Daily Picayune*, July 17, 1897.]
J. D. W.

DEUTSCH, GOTTHARD (Jan. 31, 1859–Oct. 14, 1921), educator, son of Bernhard L. and Elise (Wiener) Deutsch, was born in Kanitz, Austria. He received his elementary and secondary education in the schools of his birthplace and of Nikolsburg from whose gymnasium he graduated at the age of seventeen. Shortly thereafter, on Oct. 6, 1876, he entered the famous rabbinical seminary at Breslau, Germany. While pursuing his Jewish studies at this seminary he attended also afternoon classes at the university of that city. Foremost among the professors at the rabbinical seminary was Heinrich Graetz, the famous historian whose *History of the Jews,* has long been recognized as the *magnum opus* in the field of Jewish history. Graetz exerted so decisive an influence on the young student that he was chiefly instrumental in determining the bent of his studies. At the close of a three years' term, the "academic triennium," at Breslau Deutsch went to Vienna with the purpose of matriculating at the university. He began his studies there in the fall of 1879, specializing in the history and literature of the Jews. The two leading Jewish scholars in the Austrian capital at this time were Isaac Hirsch Weiss, an encyclopedic Talmudic scholar, and Adolf Jellinek, famed not only as a great preacher but as an authority in the province of midrashic research. These two men were inspiring influences in the formative student years of young Deutsch. After a stay of two years at the university he received the degree of Ph.D. He also passed the required examination for a teacher's diploma in history. At about the same time he received his rabbinical diploma from Isaac Hirsch Weiss.

His first position after graduation was in the religious school of the Jewish congregation at Brünn, the Moravian capital. In 1882 he was appointed teacher of religion in the German high school of that city. He had chosen the teaching profession rather than the rabbinate but owing to the governmental discrimination against Jewish teachers he was led to change his purpose and in 1887 accepted the call extended to him by the congregation of Brüx to become its rabbi. He served there for four years, resigning in 1891 to accept the position of professor of history and philosophy of religion at the Hebrew Union College, the rabbinical seminary of liberal Judaism at Cincinnati, Ohio, upon which post he entered on Dec. 2 of that year and which he filled with distinction until his death. He served as acting president of the institution for six months from February until October 1903. While still at Brüx he had married Hermine Bacher in 1888.

During his residence of three decades in the United States, Deutsch occupied a distinguished position in the Jewish world. He played an active rôle in many Jewish movements. He wrote extensively, both on historical themes and on subjects of current Jewish interest. He was a constant contributor not only to the well-known Cincinnati Jewish journals, the *American Israelite* and its German supplement, *Die Deborah,* but likewise to Jewish newspapers in Europe and throughout the United States. Shortly after his removal to Cincinnati he contributed to the *Allge-meine Zeitung des Judenthums,* the foremost Jewish newspaper of Germany if not of the European continent, a series of sketches on American-Jewish life that created somewhat of a sensation at the time. As one of the editors of the *Jewish Encyclopedia* and the head of its historical department he contributed many articles to this publication. Possibly the most important of these contributions is his lengthy article on Anti-Semitism in which he traced the origin and history of this movement. He was a very prolific writer. Besides the hundreds of newspaper and magazine articles which flowed from his facile pen he published the following books: *Para-digmen—Tafeln zur hebräischen Grammatik* (Brünn, 1886); *Die Symbolik in Cultus und Dichtung bei den Hebräern* (Brünn, 1886); *Philosophy of Jewish History* (Cincinnati, 1897); *Andere Zeiten, eine Erzählung aus dem jüdischen Leben der jüngsten Vergangenheit* (Berlin, 1898); *Unlösbare Fesseln, eine Erzählung aus dem jüdischen Leben der Gegenwart* (Frankfurt-a.-M., 1903); *Memorable Dates of Jewish History* (1904); *Four Epochs of Jewish History* (1905); *Israel Bruna, An Historical Tragedy* (1908); *The History of the Jews* (1910); *Der Glaube an Hobelspäne* (1915), a survey of modern Judaism; *Scrolls* (2 vols., 1917, 3rd vol., 1919), studies in Jewish history, literature, etc.; *Jew and Gentile* (1920).

[*Year-Book Central Conference Am. Rabbis,* XXXII, 145–50; *Hebrew Union Coll. Mo.,* vol. VIII, no. 5; obituaries in Cincinnati newspapers, Oct. 15, 1921; Adolph S. Oko, *Selected List of the Writings of Gotthard Deutsch* (1916).]   D. P.

DE VARGAS ZAPATA Y LUJAN PONCE DE LEON, DIEGO (*c.* 1650–Apr. 4, 1704), Marqués de la Nava de Braziñas, Spanish governor of New Mexico, was born in Madrid, Spain, the son of the *maestro de campo,* Alonso de Vargas Zapata y Lujan, chevalier of the order of Santiago, and Maria Margarita de Contréras, both of whom were natives of Madrid. De Vargas belonged to the Spanish-born governing class of New Spain. The events of his life prior to his appointment as governor and captain-general of New Mexico (June 18, 1688) are not known. At that time he was holding the office of chief magistrate of the Real de Minas de Talpugajua in Mexico; he had reached his early forties and had had some military training and experience. On Aug. 14, 1690, a power of attorney was executed in Madrid which gave his wife, Juana de Vargas Ponce de Leon, control over extensive property rights in Spain and Mexico. In 1692 he made a military reconquest of the upper Rio Grande Val-

ley, out of which the Spanish settlers had been driven in 1680 by the Pueblo Indians. In the following summer (1693) he led the settlers northward to their former homes. He quelled several uprisings of the Pueblos between 1693 and 1697.

Having succeeded where others had failed, namely, in the reconquest of New Mexico, he was reappointed to his office by the viceroy of New Spain, Feb. 22, 1696, but the king had already selected his successor, Pedro Rodríguez Cubero [*q.v.*], who arrived at the capital, Santa Fé, July 2, 1697. De Vargas was thrown into prison on charges brought against him by the *cabildo* (town council) of Santa Fé. He and his friends made a concerted effort to obtain what they deemed to be justice, and their activities bore fruit. A short time before the close of Cubero's governorship De Vargas was appointed by the king for a second term as governor and captain-general of New Mexico. In recognition of his services to the Crown of Spain in bringing about the reconquest of New Mexico he was made Marqués de la Nava de Braziñas. His second administration was cut short by his death. He assumed office on Nov. 10, 1703, and died Apr. 4, 1704, while conducting a campaign in the Sandia mountains against the Faraon Apache who had been making attacks upon the Indian pueblos and the Spanish haciendas in the Rio Grande Valley between Bernalillo and Belen.

De Vargas was a man of courage, military skill, and administrative ability. His will leads one to believe that he liked fine articles of clothing, silverware, and jewelry; and that he was considerate of his family, servants, and debtors. His successful reconquest of New Mexico in 1693 and the reëstablishment of the Spanish settlements, which were never again destroyed, gives to him a prominent place in the history of the Southwest.

[R. E. Twitchell, *Old Santa Fé* (1925), pp. 87–150, and "The Pueblo Revolt of 1696," in *Old Santa Fé,* III (1916), 27–34; extracts from the journal of De Vargas were published under the titles: "The Last Campaign of Gen. De Vargas," in *Old Santa Fé,* II (1914–15), 66–72, and "The Reconquest of New Mexico, 1692," *Old Santa Fé,* I (1913–14), 288–307, 402–35; C. F. Coan, *A Hist. of New Mexico* (1925), I, 214–28; F. V. Scholes, "Documents from the Archives of Mexico City," in manuscript.]   C.F.C—n.

DEVENS, CHARLES (Apr. 4, 1820–Jan. 7, 1891), soldier, jurist, cabinet officer, was born in Charlestown, Mass., the son of Charles and Mary (Lithgow) Devens, and the grandson of Richard Devens, a Revolutionary patriot. After preparing at the Boston Latin School, he graduated from Harvard in 1838, studied at the Harvard Law School, and was admitted to the bar in 1840. He then established himself as a lawyer, first in Northfield and later in Greenfield, Franklin County, Mass. He sat for two terms in the Massachusetts Senate (1848–49), and held for four years (1849–53) the office of United States marshal for the district of Massachusetts. On Apr. 3, 1851, the Boston police arrested Thomas Sims, a negro slave who had escaped from his Georgia owner. The United States commissioner under the Fugitive-Slave Act heard the case, decided it in favor of the master, and directed Devens, as marshal, to escort the prisoner to the vessel on which he was to be carried back to Savannah. Although this legal duty was repugnant to Devens, he performed it. Later, however, in 1855, he tried to obtain the freedom of Sims, offering to pay whatever sum was necessary for the purpose, but he was unsuccessful. During the Civil War Sims was liberated, and Devens was able eventually to secure for him a government position.

Devens resumed the practise of law in 1854, settling in Worcester, Mass., and forming a partnership with George F. Hoar and J. Henry Hill. He acted as city solicitor for three years (1856–58) and quickly made a reputation as an advocate and a public speaker. Having early displayed a keen interest in military matters, he was steadily promoted in the state militia until he reached the rank of brigadier-general. When the news of Lincoln's call for 75,000 volunteers arrived in Worcester, Devens immediately turned over his affairs to another lawyer, offered his services to the Government, was chosen major of the 3rd Battalion of Massachusetts Rifles, was commissioned on the next day (Apr. 16, 1861), and departed for the front on Apr. 20. He was shortly (July 24, 1861) appointed colonel of the 15th Massachusetts Regiment. At Ball's Bluff (Oct. 21, 1861) he was struck by a musket ball which would have pierced his heart if it had not hit a metallic button. On Apr. 15, 1862, he was made a brigadier-general of volunteers and assigned to Couch's Division of the IV Corps, being in action during the Peninsular campaign. Severely wounded at Fair Oaks (May 31, 1862), he would not leave the field of battle until evening; but he recovered in season to participate at Fredericksburg (Dec. 13, 1862), where he commanded the advance guard. At Chancellorsville (May 3, 1863), he was wounded in the foot early in the day, while leading a division of the XI Corps. He took part in the battle of Cold Harbor (June 3, 1864), while he was so crippled with inflammatory rheumatism that he had to be carried along the line on a stretcher. On Apr. 3, 1865, he led the advance on Richmond and was brevetted a major-general. For a year after hos-

tilities were over, he remained in service, being assigned as second in command to Gen. Sickles in charge of the Southeastern Department. He was mustered out in June 1866, after a military career covering five years and three months.

During his absence in the field, Devens was nominated in 1862 for governor of Massachusetts by the so-called "People's Party." Although he took no part in the campaign, he received the support of the Democrats and of some moderate Republicans. He was defeated by John A. Andrew, the Republican candidate, whose majority was 20,000. After the war he attempted to resume his practise. In April 1867 he was appointed, by Gov. Bullock, as a justice of the superior court, and, in 1873, was named by Gov. Washburn as judge of the supreme court of Massachusetts. President Hayes offered him a place in his cabinet as secretary of war, but he declined it, only to accept a nomination as attorney-general (Mar. 10, 1877). At the expiration of his term in the cabinet, he was appointed by Gov. Long to his former position as judge of the supreme court and held his seat on the bench until his death.

As a lawyer, Devens was distinguished by his thoroughness in research, his fidelity to his clients, and his skill in pleading. He was a handsome man, with a commanding presence, and his native gifts as an orator were great. He delivered several notable addresses, among them a speech at Bunker Hill on the occasion of the Centennial of 1875, an oration before the Army of the Potomac at New Haven in commemoration of Gettysburg, and a eulogy on Gen. Grant spoken at Worcester. He received the degree of Doctor of Laws from Harvard (1877), and, as President of the Harvard Alumni Association, presided in 1886 at the observance of the 250th anniversary of the founding of the college. As a judge, he was distinguished by his perfect impartiality, his abundant learning, and his scrupulous integrity. In his capacity as attorney-general, he was recognized as one of the strongest members of a strong cabinet. He had a wide acquaintance, and his urbane and kindly nature made him a social favorite. He never married.

It was, however, as a soldier that he was best known. He was for years Commander of the Military Order, Loyal Legion, in Massachusetts, and he was elected National Commander of the Grand Army of the Republic in 1874 to succeed Gen. Burnside. When he died in Boston, at the age of seventy-one, he was buried from Trinity Church, with military honors. In 1894 the Massachusetts legislature appropriated $15,000 for a bronze statue of him in uniform by Olin H. Warner, and this was erected on the State House grounds, where it now stands. During the World War, in 1917, the New England army camp, established at Ayer, Mass., was named Camp Devens, in his honor. A volume of *Orations and Addresses,* edited by A. L. Devens, was published in 1891.

[See John C. Ropes, "Memoir of Chas. Devens," in *Procs. Mass. Hist. Soc.,* 2 ser., VII (1891–92), 104; *Biog. Encyc. of Mass.,* vol. II (1883); W. R. Cutter & W. G. Adams, *Genealogical and Personal Memoirs,* vol. IV (1910).]   C.M.F.

DE VERE, MAXIMILIAN SCHELE [See Schele, Maximilian De Vere, 1820–1898.]

DEVEREUX, JOHN HENRY (Apr. 5, 1832–Mar. 17, 1886), civil engineer, railroad executive, came from an adventurous stock. A remote ancestor was a Robert d'Evreux of the Norman conquerors of England. Another was among the founders of Marblehead, Mass. (*The Probate Records of Essex County, Mass.,* I, 60). John Henry's father was Capt. John Devereux, a well-known Marblehead and Boston sea captain (B. J. Lindsey, *Old Marblehead Sea Captains, and the Ships in Which They Sailed,* 1915, p. 41). The son's life was that of a pioneer among the builders of the modern American railroad system, an adventurer in capitalism. Only fragments of information of his early life have survived. He attended an academy in Portsmouth, N. H., for a time. At sixteen, the age his father went to sea, young Devereux left his home to begin life in Cleveland, Ohio. His arrival in Cleveland (1848) was at the beginning of its railroad era. Capitalists had been slow to invest in the new means of transportation. Cleveland found the solution in municipal aid, voting to the Cleveland, Columbus & Cincinnati Railway Company $200,000 for a line to Columbus and to the Cleveland & Pittsburgh $100,000 for one to Pittsburgh. Construction work on these lines gave the newcomer his opportunity, and a short apprenticeship in an engineering corps made him a railway engineer. In 1851 he married Antoinette, the daughter of L. A. Kelsey (mayor of Cleveland, 1848). The following year his profession led him to Nashville, Tenn., also a center of western railroad building. On the outbreak of the Civil War he returned to Ohio. When the Federal government took over the operation of the border railroads for military purposes, Devereux offered his services. In 1862 he became superintendent of the railroads centering at Alexandria, Va. The *Official Records* bear frequent testimony to his share in maintaining an efficient railroad service back of the Army of the Poto-

mac (1 ser., vol. XII, pt. 3, pp. 634, 636; vol. XIX, pt. 2, pp. 559, 564).

At the beginning of 1864 Devereux withdrew from government service to become general superintendent and shortly vice-president of the Cleveland & Pittsburgh Railroad (leased in 1871 by the Pennsylvania Railroad). In 1868 he resigned in order to accept a place as vice-president and general manager of the Lake Shore & Michigan Southern. Five years later (1873) he became president of the Big Four (Cleveland, Columbus, Cincinnati, & Indianapolis), an office he held until his death. From 1874 to 1880 he was also receiver of the Atlantic & Great Western (later incorporated in the Erie System), and in 1881 its president. During his connection with the Atlantic & Great Western, entrances into Pittsburgh and Chicago were acquired. During the same period the Big Four was extended to St. Louis. His administration of these railroads fell across the hard times of the seventies and the severe railroad competition of the eighties. He sought to maintain a profitable business through pooling and consolidations. Attempts to combine the Big Four with the Atlantic & Great Western and later with the Cincinnati, Hamilton & Dayton were frustrated by the courts of Ohio. Under Devereux's régime extensions were financed by bond issues. Fierce competition brought down rates. Before the two attacks on profits—increasing fixed charges and declining rates—dividends on Big Four stock vanished. Devereux was ready for government control, that is, government intervention as a protection for railway investments. As a witness before the Cullom Interstate Commerce Committee in St. Louis in June 1885 he advocated the punishment of railway officials giving secret rebates, legalization of pooling, publicity of rates, and, if constitutional, an interstate commerce commission with power to maintain fair rates (*Senate Report,* 49 Cong., 1 Sess., vol. III, no. 46, pt. 2, pp. 816–39). His professional life was also intimately connected with the New York Central. He was William K. Vanderbilt's agent in the negotiations by which the New York Central acquired the New York, Chicago & St. Louis Railroad (the Nickel Plate). On the whole his achievements were to the advantage of his section, as well as to his personal fortunes. He was a man of large physique and great energy. Those who knew him said his most marked characteristic was a genial magnetic personality. His interests reached far beyond his business activities. He was one of the incorporators of the Case School of Applied Science, a member of the Cleveland Humane Society, and a life member of the American Association for the Advancement of Science.

[J. H. Kennedy, "Gen. J. H. Devereux," in *Mag. of Western Hist.*, IV (1886), 217–29; *Cleveland Plain Dealer,* Mar. 18, 1886; *Railroad Gazette,* Mar. 26, 1886.]

E.J.B.

DEVIN, THOMAS CASIMER (Dec. 10, 1822–Apr. 4, 1878), soldier, was born in the city of New York, and except for five years spent in Missouri passed his entire early life there. He was educated in the common schools, and became a painter by trade. Entering the New York militia, he rose to the rank of lieutenant-colonel before the outbreak of the Civil War. Organizing a company of men selected from his militia regiment for the three months' service, he was mustered in, July 19, 1861, as captain in the 1st New York Cavalry, which was stationed in the vicinity of Washington. A month after this organization was mustered out, he returned to the army, Nov. 18, 1861, as colonel of the 6th New York Cavalry (called the 2nd Ira Harris Guards). After some months spent in camps in Pennsylvania and Maryland, the regiment joined the army at Washington, and during Pope's Bull Run campaign of 1862 was employed in observing the country south of the Rapidan. South Mountain was its first real battle, followed immediately by Antietam, and thereafter the regiment was actively employed until Lee's surrender. After the battle of Fredericksburg, Devin succeeded to the command of a brigade, of which the 6th New York was a part, in Pleasanton's cavalry division. Within the next few months Pleasanton repeatedly and unsuccessfully urged his appointment as brigadier-general. Devin's brigade fought at Chancellorsville and Beverly Ford, and as a part of Buford's command, fighting on foot, met the Confederate advance west of Gettysburg at daybreak on July 1, 1863, and helped to hold it back until the infantry arrived on the field. Still with the Army of the Potomac, it went through the Wilderness campaign of 1864, and took part in Sheridan's great raid around Richmond. Early in August it moved to the Shenandoah Valley, for service in Sheridan's campaign against Early. In the action at Crooked Run (Aug. 16) Devin was slightly wounded; he continued in the saddle during the fight, but was absent from the army, recuperating, for the next month. He returned to duty in time to take part in the battles of Winchester, Fisher's Hill, and Cedar Creek, and was at last appointed brigadier-general of volunteers (Mar. 13, 1865, to date from Oct. 19, 1864). He commanded a division of the Cavalry Corps at Five Forks, Sailor's Creek, and Appomattox. After his muster out

of the volunteer service he was appointed lieutenant-colonel of the 8th Cavalry, July 28, 1866, and became colonel of the 3rd Cavalry, June 25, 1877. Long service on the frontier, following the strenuous campaigning of the Civil War, undermined his health, and he was absent from his regiment, on account of sickness, for nearly a year in 1873–74. In 1878, following another breakdown in his health, he returned to his home in New York, where he died. Much older than most of the cavalry leaders of the Civil War, many of whom were little more than boys, the "Old War Horse" was one of the best.

[*Hist. of the 6th N. Y. Cavalry* (1908), pp. 417–30; *The Union Army* (Madison, Wis., 1908), VIII, 73–74; *N. Y. Herald* of Apr. 5, 1878; *Official Records (Army),* ser. I, vols. XXV (pt. 1), XXVII (pts. 1, 3), XXIX (pts. 1, 2), XXXIII, XXXVI (pt. 1), XLIII (pts. 1, 2), XLVI (pts. 1, 2, 3); unpublished records in the War Dept.]

T.M.S.

DE VINNE, THEODORE LOW (Dec. 25, 1828–Feb. 16, 1914), printer, the son of Daniel and Joanna Augusta (Low) De Vinne, was born in Stamford, Conn. Instruction from his father (including Latin), and the village schools of Amenia and White Plains, N. Y., gave him his early education. At fourteen he was apprenticed to the printer's trade in the office of the Newburgh *Gazette.* He went to New York City in 1848, and, after working in various printing-offices, entered the employ of Francis Hart. In the same year, 1850, he married Grace Brockbank of New York City. He soon became foreman of the composing-room, and in 1858 he was made a junior partner. On the death of Hart in 1877, De Vinne became, under the terms of the will, possessed of the business. The firm name was changed to Theo. L. De Vinne & Company, his son Theodore B. becoming associated with his father. In 1908 the business was incorporated as The De Vinne Press, De Vinne retiring from active management but taking the office of president.

As a printer, De Vinne was the most learned man of his time in the history of the art and in its practise. His printing-office became prominent through the work which it did on *Scribner's Monthly, St. Nicholas,* and especially the *Century Magazine.* The publishers of the latter demanded a degree of excellence in its printing which was then unknown, and through cooperation of the publishers with De Vinne, and the latter's installation of heavier presses, the use of hard packing, and the invention of coated paper (by S. D. Warren & Company of Boston, largely at De Vinne's instigation), fine-line wood-engravings and later half-tone plates were printed with a brilliance never before achieved. De Vinne was a meticulous workman in all the technical minutiæ of printing. He printed most of the early books for the Grolier Club (of which he was a founder and president), thereby setting a high standard; the Book of Common Prayer and the "Jade" book are two of his fine productions; while the *Century Dictionary* is considered by many critics as his finest achievement.

As an employer he was active in the affairs of employers' organizations, being one of the founders of the Typothetæ of the City of New York and of the United Typothetæ of America, serving as secretary and president of these organizations. In and out of these groups he worked for years to make printing a profitable craft, and to make the relations of masters and men as harmonious as the changing industrial conditions would allow. In his own office he was a kindly employer whose one insistent demand was first quality work. His almost exclusive devotion to his calling gave him an insight into its problems which was unusual and always at the service of his fellow employers and workmen.

De Vinne's name is likely to live longest in connection with his writings. His major published works include: *The Printers' Price List* (1869); *The Invention of Printing* (1876), the standard work on the subject in English, used as the text for George Bruce's Sons & Company's type specimen books of 1878 and 1882; *Historic Printing Types* (1886); *Christopher Plantin* (1888); *The Practice of Typography* (four volumes, 1900, 1901, 1902, 1904); *Title-Pages as Seen by a Printer* (1901); *Notable Printers of Italy During the Fifteenth Century* (1910). He also contributed prefaces and notes to Moxon's *Mechanick Exercises,* printed by him and issued by the Typothetæ of the City of New York in 1896, and a preface to *A Decree of Star Chamber Concerning Printing,* the first publication of the Grolier Club (1884). The printer's specimen books of the De Vinne Press also contain much historical information from his pen.

De Vinne's contribution to the progress of printing in America consisted in his codification of the practises of the craft as they obtained in his lifetime, of historical writings relating to the history of printing, and more especially, as a master printer, of successful working out of details of composition and presswork as effected by photo-mechanical processes of reproduction and the type-setting machine. The types he used and the way he used them are not now esteemed as highly as in his day, which is to say that his taste in typographic design suffered from the general low state of printing in the nineteenth century; his zeal for perfection, however, set new stand-

ards which were a fitting and necessary prelude to the work of present-day American printers.

[*Catalogue of Work of The De Vinne Press* (1929), pub. by the Grolier Club and containing addresses by Ira H. Brainerd and others; *Theodore Low De Vinne, Printer* (privately printed, 1915); *Literary Review of the N. Y. Evening Post,* Jan. 20, 1923; *Century Mag.,* Nov. 1910, Nov. 1911; *Inland Printer,* July 1922, p. 515; *N. Y. Herald, N. Y. Times, N. Y. Tribune,* Feb. 17, 1914.]
C.P.R.

DEVOY, JOHN (Sept. 3, 1842–Sept. 29, 1928), journalist and Fenian leader, born at Kill, County Kildare, Ireland, was the son of a farmer, actively interested in the Young Ireland movement and in Catholic Emancipation. His mother was Elizabeth Dunne Devoy. The Devoy household was a small debating club and local political center; here and in the schools of Dublin, whither the family had moved, Devoy received his early education; he later attended evening classes at the Catholic University. In 1861 he joined the Irish Republican Brotherhood and, to obtain military experience, he served a year with the French Foreign Legion in Algeria. Returning to Ireland in 1862, Devoy, a born conspirator, became conspicuous in the Republican movement. Because of his notorious organizing of Fenians within the British army the government attempted to arrest him in September 1865, but it was not until he had assisted in the escape of James Stephens from a Dublin jail, that he was finally apprehended in February 1866. Judged guilty of treason he was sentenced to fifteen years' penal servitude, but was released with four other Fenian prisoners in 1871 on the understanding that they would not return to the United Kingdom until after the expiration of their sentences. They arrived in New York in February 1871, where they were received with honors by the Irish population. Devoy joined the staff of the *New York Herald* as a reporter; he became telegraph editor and later was in charge of the foreign desk. After eight years he was dismissed by James Gordon Bennett [*q.v.*] because of his support of Charles Stewart Parnell, whom Bennett opposed. Before he established his weekly newspaper, the *Irish Nation,* in New York in 1881, he was connected with various newspapers: the *Daily Telegraph* and the *Morning Journal* of New York and the *Herald* and the *Evening Post* of Chicago. From the time of his arrival in New York his efforts toward Irish freedom were more vigorous and fruitful. He organized the famous "Catalpa" rescue of Irish prisoners from Australia in 1875–76; he was later instrumental in securing funds for the submarine experiments of John P. Holland [*q.v.*] that they might aid in the destruction of the British navy. The moral and financial support that Devoy secured from the Clan-na-Gael in America and the Irish Republican Brotherhood contributed greatly to the success of the Land League movement under Parnell. The *Irish Nation* had been forced to cease publication in 1885; in 1903 Devoy founded in New York the weekly *Gaelic American* to combat British propaganda and to disseminate the principles of the Fenians and the Clan-na-Gael, who had withdrawn their support from the Irish parliamentarian movement. He edited the *Gaelic American* until his death in 1928. During the World War he was closely associated with German agents in America and was responsible for much of the financial support given the Irish insurgents in the Dublin Easter Week Rebellion of 1916. He was later conspicuous in organizing Irish opinion in America against the League of Nations and the World Court, which he considered to be entangling alliances dangerous to American freedom. He was associated with De Valera until the latter advocated an English protectorate for Ireland; he supported the treaty under which the Irish Free State was established and aided successfully in floating its first bonds in America. He had completed his *Recollections of an Irish Rebel*, a substantial contribution to the history of Fenianism, when he died in Atlantic City in his eighty-sixth year. Devoy, the last great Fenian leader, was characterized by English opinion as "the most bitter and persistent, as well as the most dangerous enemy of this country which Ireland has produced since Wolfe Tone" (*Times,* London, Oct. 1, 1928), and in that statement Devoy would have found ample satisfaction.

[John Devoy, *Recollections of an Irish Rebel* (1929); *N. Y. Times,* Sept. 30, 1928; *Manchester Guardian* and *Times* (London), Oct. 1, 1928; *Gaelic Am.* (N. Y.), Oct. 6, 13, 20, 27 and Nov. 3, 10, 1928; private information.]

F. M.

DE VRIES, DAVID PIETERSEN (fl. 1618–1655), merchant skipper and colonizer of New Netherland, was born in 1592 or 1593 at La Rochelle, France, where his father, a native of Hoorn, North Holland, had resided at different times since 1584. His mother was of Amsterdam. After his fourth year he lived mostly in Holland, being from his youth well trained in merchandising, both there and in France. In 1618–19, as owner and commander of a new ship of 400 tons burden, mounting eight guns, he made a voyage to the Mediterranean. The next year he sailed to Newfoundland to procure a cargo of codfish, which he sold in Spanish ports. In the course of this voyage he won a notable fight against pirates off Cartagena, and at Toulon was engaged by the Duc de Guise to serve

with his ship against the Turks. When shortly afterward the Duke sought to change his contract and to employ him against the Huguenots at La Rochelle, De Vries refused to comply with his request, sold his ship, and returned overland to Holland. In 1624 he made preparations to go to Canada for furs, but his plans were frustrated by the Dutch West India Company and he sailed to La Rochelle instead. In 1627–30 he made a voyage to the Dutch East Indies. Shortly after his return from this voyage he entered into partnership with Samuel Godyn and other directors of the West India Company to plant a colony on the Delaware. An expedition sent out by them in 1631 founded a small settlement, called Swanendael, on the west side of Delaware Bay, near the present town of Lewes, which was soon after destroyed by the Indians. Thereafter De Vries made three voyages to America: May 24, 1632–July 24, 1633, under a contract with his former partners, in command of a ship and a yacht, to Delaware, Virginia, and New Amsterdam; July 10, 1634–October 1636, in the interest of another group of merchants, who wished to plant a colony on the coast of Guiana, to that coast, the West Indies, and New Netherland; and Sept. 25, 1638–June 21, 1644, in partnership with Frederick de Vries, secretary of the city of Amsterdam, to plant a colony on Staten Island. Shortly after his return from his second voyage, on Dec. 8, 1636, he made application to the West India Company to be sent to New Netherland as director, in the place of Wouter van Twiller [*q.v.*], who was about to be recalled, but his petition was rejected with the statement that "a more capable person is needed." In addition to the small settlement on Staten Island established during his last voyage he planted a colony near Tappan, which he called Vriessendael. Both colonies were destroyed in the disastrous Indian war of 1643. Discouraged in his undertakings, he returned to Holland and settled at Hoorn, where some ten years later he wrote an interesting account of his travels, printed at Alckmaer in 1655 under the title: *Korte Historiael, ende Journaels aenteyckeninge Van verscheyden Voyagiens in de vier deelen des Wereldts-Ronde, als Europa, Africa, Asia, ende Amerika gedaen.* Of this little book, which contains a portrait of the author, dated 1653, on which his age is given as sixty years, but a few copies are known to be in existence. Written in a plain but vivid style, the book contains many picturesque descriptions of events in New Netherland that are not known from official documents, so that it forms a valuable source for the history of the colony. On the title-page De Vries is called Artillery Master of the Deputy States of West-Vrieslandt and the Noorder-Quartier, or northern quarter of the province of North Holland. Little is known of his later life, and the date of his death is uncertain.

[The chief source of information about De Vries is his above mentioned *Korte Historiael*. A complete reprint of this book, edited by Dr. H. T. Colenbrander, with portrait, two maps and eighteen plates, was published at 's-Gravenhage in 1911 as volume III of the *Werken* issued by the Linschoten-Vereeniging. All the parts of De Vries's book relating to Newfoundland, New Netherland and Virginia are presented, in translation by Henry C. Murphy, in the *N. Y. Hist. Soc. Colls.*, 2 ser., III, 1–129, and were separately printed in 1853 by James Lenox. A revised translation of the parts relating to New Netherland is included in the *Narratives of New Netherland, 1609–1664* (1909), ed. by J. F. Jameson, pp. 181–234.]   A. J. F. v—L.

DEW, THOMAS RODERICK (Dec. 5, 1802– Aug. 6, 1846), economist, was the son of Thomas Dew, who was born in Maryland in 1753 of an old family of that state. The latter moved to King and Queen County, Va., when a young man, and soon, by successful farming and money lending, came to own the plantation called "Dewsville." He married Lucy E. Gatewood, a native of the county, and they had ten children, several of whom came to some distinction. Thomas Dew served for a time in the Revolutionary army, was a captain in the War of 1812, and died the leading figure in his community. His son, Thomas R. Dew, attended the College of William and Mary, probably entering in the grammar school, and graduating with the degree of A.B. in 1820. He traveled two years in Europe, and in 1827 was appointed to one of the six chairs in the College as professor of political law, his assignment including "History, Metaphysics, Natural and National Law, Government and Political Economy." Political economy was probably taught at William and Mary as early as 1798, Smith's *Wealth of Nations* being the text, and it is certain that in 1801 this college gave the earliest instruction in the subject as a science. Political economy was given separate recognition when Dew became professor; indeed, he came very near being described as "Professor of Political Economy." His salary was $1,000, and he probably lived with the other bachelors in the college building. He published his *Lectures on the Restrictive System* ("delivered to the senior political class of William and Mary College"), in 1829, a compact volume of 196 pages. In this he upheld the free-trade argument, relying upon the Physiocrats and Smith and Say. Though he declared his intention "to avoid mingling in the politics of the day," his lectures came squarely into collision with the heated assertions of the protectionist

school, then being cemented under the advocacy of Mathew Carey [*q.v.*] and the Philadelphia Society for the Promotion of National Industry. The Virginian, in an economic environment of a staple agriculture, foretold that disunion would follow if protection were pressed by the industrial North, and from his cloister he resented the imputation of men of affairs that sound practise gave the lie to current economic theory. It has been thought by some that his work influenced the subsequent reduction in the tariffs. In 1832 he published in Richmond his *Review of the Debate* [on the Abolition of Slavery] *in the Virginia Legislature of 1831 and 1832*. (This became better known after it was incorporated in a volume of Southern essays under the title *The Pro-Slavery Argument*, 1852, second edition, 1853.) George Wythe and St. George Tucker [*qq.v.*], Dew's predecessors in the faculty of the College, had been anti-slavery men. But now Dew's pro-slavery opinion reflected what appeared to be the economic interest of the dominant tide-water counties. His argument was inclusive, careful and ingenious, but proved too much. The state was still in the custom of looking to the College for guidance, and his pronouncement undoubtedly exercised a wide influence. J. D. B. De Bow [*q.v.*], as might have been expected, said of Dew that his "able essay on the institution of slavery entitles him to the lasting gratitude of the whole South." Dew's *Digest of the Laws, Customs, Manners, and Institutions of the Ancient and Modern Nations*, an outline printed first for the use of his students, and after his death published (1853) in New York, shows, as Herbert B. Adams has said, that Dew's teaching of history exhibited a lively appreciation of human institutions at a time when contemporaries were following dull chronology. While he accepted scriptural authority on antediluvian history without question, he had his own views on after developments. In 1836 he became president of the College, succeeding Rev. Adam P. Empie. Since the Revolution, due largely to the cession of Virginia's claims to public lands, the loss of royal favor, and the removal of the capital to Richmond, the College had declined in wealth and in students, those in attendance sometimes numbering as low as twenty. Dew, by "tact at management, great zeal, and unwearied assiduity," in the words of Bishop Meade, brought the number of students to 140, and made the institution almost as prosperous as ever before. He was a tall, angular man, awkward in movement, but amiable in his manners. He married Natilia Hay, daughter of a physician of Clarke County, Va., in 1845, and died on his wedding trip, in Paris, probably of pleurisy or pneumonia.

[Herbert B. Adams, *The Coll. of Wm. and Mary* (1887), containing an excellent bibliography of the history of the college, useful in connection with Dew's life; Wm. Meade, *Old Churches, Ministers and Families of Va.* (1857), I, 177 f.; E. R. A. Seligman, in *Economic Essays Contributed in Honor of John Bates Clark* (1927), ed. by J. H. Hollander; *Wm. and Mary Coll. Quart.*, VI (1897), 186, XIV (1906), 81 ff., XXVII (1920), 135; *Southern Lit. Messenger*, Oct. 1856.]   B. M—l.

DEWEES, WILLIAM POTTS (May 5, 1768–May 20, 1841), physician, obstetrician, was born near Pottstown, Pa., founded by his maternal grandfather, Thomas Potts. On his father's side he was of Swedish descent. He apparently had only a moderate amount of school education, seems to have made an early decision to study medicine, and was placed in the office of a Dr. Phyle who was a practising apothecary. Later he was placed with Dr. William Smith, a practitioner of medicine, and attended classes at the University of Pennsylvania from 1787 to 1789. There is some doubt as to whether he took the degree of M.B. at that time. In any event it was not until 1806 that he received the degree of Doctor of Medicine from the University of Pennsylvania. His thesis was entitled *An Essay on the Means of Lessening Pain and Facilitating certain cases of Difficult Parturition* (1806). He began practise at Abington, Pa., and in December 1793 he moved to Philadelphia, it is said with the encouragement and patronage of Dr. Benjamin Rush.

At this time the subject of obstetrics received little attention from the profession in general and the great majority of deliveries were in the hands of midwives. There was no proper teaching of the subject and no formal instruction was given in the University of Pennsylvania. There was still a strong prejudice against men engaging in obstetrics. The "man midwife" was an object of derision well exemplified in the character which Laurence Sterne drew of Dr. Slop in *Tristram Shandy*. It must have required a good deal of courage to take up this specialty. Dewees devoted himself not only to the practise of obstetrics but to teaching it and was soon giving instruction to classes in his office. He became a very successful practitioner and it is said that he delivered over ten thousand women.

About this time there was strong pressure brought to bear on the authorities of the University of Pennsylvania to establish a chair of obstetrics and after much pleading this was done in 1810, but with the handicap that attendance on the lectures was not necessary for graduation. There was a keen struggle for the appointment

and Dewees saw it given to a rival, Dr. Thomas C. James. Other disappointments came as his health failed and he developed pulmonary tuberculosis. On this account he was compelled to give up the practise of medicine for a time and went to Phillipsburgh, where he took up farming. He lost money in this venture but regained his health so that in 1817 he was able to return to Philadelphia and resume practise. He became associated with the Medical Institute and resumed teaching. Soon afterward he was made a member of the American Philosophical Society. As the health of Dr. James had been such that he was unable to carry on the duties of his chair, Dewees was appointed adjunct professor of obstetrics in the University of Pennsylvania in 1825 and did most of the work of the department for nine years. He succeeded James in 1834 when he was appointed professor of obstetrics. Misfortune continued to follow him, as in 1835 he had what was probably a cerebral hemorrhage and was compelled to resign his professorship. It was a tragedy that when he had reached the height of his ambition, sickness so soon compelled him to give up active work. Afterward he lived in Mobile, Ala., for four years, later returning to Philadelphia where he died in 1841.

Dewees did much to advance the art of obstetrics by his skill but more by his teaching and writings. His chief work was *A Compendious System of Midwifery* (1852), which went through twelve editions. It must be regarded as the first authoritative work in America on the subject. In it Dewees followed the ideas of the French School to a considerable extent but introduced his own ideas and showed much original thought. He also published volumes on the diseases of women and children and went farther afield in a work on the practise of medicine. This last was evidently written hurriedly and did not add to his reputation. He is described as having been a good speaker and teacher but caustic in his criticism. He was married twice: first, to Martha Rogers, a daughter of a Dr. Rogers of New England, and second, to Mary Lorrain of Philadelphia (1802).

[S. W. Williams, *Am. Medic. Biog.* (1845); Jos. Carson, *Hist. of the Medic. Dept. Univ. Pa.* (1869); *Autobiography of S. D. Gross* (1887); F. P. Henry, *Standard Hist. of the Medic. Profession of Phila.* (1897); A. L. Kelly and W. L. Burrage, *Am. Medic. Biogs.* (1920).]   T. M.

DEWEY, CHESTER (Oct. 25, 1784–Dec. 15, 1867), Congregational clergyman, educator, pioneer scientist, was born in Sheffield, Mass., the son of Stephen Dewey and Elizabeth Owen, and a descendant of Thomas Dewey, one of the first settlers of Dorchester, Mass. His boyhood was spent on a farm where he acquired the vigorous constitution and sound health which he enjoyed throughout life. Here, too, was probably awakened that compelling interest in plants, minerals, and the weather which determined the trend of his scientific studies. After a common-school education he prepared to enter Williams College and was admitted at the age of eighteen. Graduating in 1806, he followed a strong religious bent and studied for the ministry. A year later he was licensed to preach by the Berkshire Congregationalist Association. After a brief pastorate at West Stockbridge and Tyringham, Mass., he returned to Williams College as a tutor. From 1810 to 1827 he served as professor of mathematics and natural philosophy during which period he devoted much time to the development of work in physics and chemistry on the laboratory side and to the collection of museum specimens of geology and botany. Most of these he gathered by personal effort, others he obtained by exchange with collectors in this country and abroad, thus making the start for the fine museum now owned by the Institution. In 1823 he organized among the students the first antislavery society in Massachusetts. He served as principal of the Berkshire Gymnasium, at Pittsfield, Mass., 1827–36, and of the High School, afterward known as the Collegiate Institute at Rochester, N. Y., 1836–50. At the founding of the University of Rochester in the latter year he was elected the first professor of chemistry and natural sciences, which position he held until his retirement in 1861 as emeritus professor. From 1837 until within a week of his death, he made daily observations on the weather conditions of Rochester. He also lectured for many years, beginning in 1822, on chemistry and medical botany in the Berkshire Medical Institution, and in the Medical School at Woodstock, Vt., from 1842 to 1849. He was a born teacher and acquired knowledge, seemingly, chiefly for the purpose of communicating it to others. He was a leaven of intellectual activity in whatever community he resided.

His scientific observations covered a wide range. To the first volume (1819) of the *American Journal of Science* he contributed a "Sketch of the Mineralogy and Geology of the Vicinity of Williams' College," and fifty-three later volumes contain papers by him. Between 1824 and 1866 he contributed a long series on the sedges entitled "Caricography." These were never collected into a single volume but were characterized by Asa Gray as an "elaborate monograph patiently prosecuted through more than forty years." He further classed Dewey with Schweinitz and Torrey, two of the foremost students of North American plants, saying that they "laid the foundation and insured the popularity of the study of Sedges in this country." Dewey also prepared a *Report on the Herbaceous Plants and on the Quadrupeds of Massachusetts,* published by the state in 1840, and the section on the *carices* or sedges in Alphonso Wood's *Class-Book of Botany* (1845), the work being dedicated to him. His service to botany has been recognized in the name of the genus *Deweya,* umbelliferous plants of California. In the line of ethnology his writings include two critical reviews of Agassiz's *Essay on Classification* (*Princeton Review,* 1863), and one entitled "Examination of Some Reasonings Against the Unity of Mankind" (*Ibid.,* July 1862). Although familiar with the teachings of Lamarck and Darwin regarding evolution his acceptance of them was apparently prevented by his theological beliefs.

Dewey was married twice: in 1810 to Sarah Dewey, and in 1825 to Olivia Hart Pomeroy of Pittsfield, Mass. There were five children by the first marriage and ten by the second.

[Obituary by Asa Gray in *Am. Jour. Sci.,* 2 ser., XLV (1868); Martin B. Anderson, "Sketch of the Life of Prof. Chester Dewey" in *Smithsonian Inst. Ann. Report,* 1870; Chas. W. Seelye, "A Memorial Sketch of Chester Dewey, M.D., D.D.," in *Proc. Rochester Acad. Sci.,* vol. III; Florence Beckwith, "Early Botanists of Rochester," in *Ibid.,* vol. V (1912); and the sketch in H. A. Kelly and W. L. Burrage, *Am. Medic. Biogs.* (1920); L. W. Spring, *Hist. of Wms. College* (1917); W. F. Peck, *Hist. of Rochester, Monroe County, N. Y.* (1908); family records, including a four-page sketch by Dewey's son, prepared for the Rochester Hist. Soc. Obituaries appeared in newspapers all over the country; see especially *Rochester Express* and *Rochester Daily Democrat* for Dec. 16, 1867.]

C. W. D.

DEWEY, GEORGE (Dec. 26, 1837–Jan. 16, 1917), naval officer, was born at Montpelier, Vt. Among his ancestors were Douai, a Huguenot, who settled in Kent, England, the latter half of the sixteenth century; Thomas Duee of Sandwich, Kent, who emigrated to Dorchester, Mass., in 1634, changing his name to Dewey; Josiah Dewey his son, who had the rank of sergeant in King Philip's War; William Dewey, great-grandfather of the admiral, one of the volunteers at the battle of Lexington. George was the youngest of three sons, children of Dr. Julius Yemans Dewey and Mary Perrin. His mother died when he was five years old, but his father, whom his son characterizes as "a natural leader," with "ideas of right and wrong . . . very fixed, in keeping with his deep religious principles," gave himself without stint to the bringing up of his boys. "To my father's influence in my early training I owe, primarily, all that I have accomplished in the world," Dewey later wrote. When he was between sixteen and seventeen he was appointed a midshipman at the United States Naval Academy at Annapolis. The class numbered sixty on entrance, and the modesty of Dewey's beginning is shown by the fact that out of thirty-five surviving at the end of the first year he stood number thirty-three. At the close of the four-year course in June 1858, fifteen graduated, and Dewey had now risen in standing to five. This he further improved on the final examination after two years at sea. He was third in his class to receive his commission, and plainly had found a serious interest in his profession.

On leaving Annapolis he had been assigned to the steam-frigate *Wabash,* which sailed for the Mediterranean. During the next year he visited such historic cities as Constantinople, Beirut, Jerusalem, and Alexandria. In April 1861, he was commissioned lieutenant, and a few months later in spite of his youthful age, he was made executive officer of the *Mississippi,* a side-wheeler, one of the largest and most heavily armed ships in the Union navy. The *Mississippi* was assigned to Farragut's fleet about to begin operations against New Orleans; and as the Union ships advanced to take that city, passing Forts Jackson and St. Philip in the battle of Apr. 24, 1862, she occupied an important position in the first division. Her commanding officer, Capt. Melancthon Smith, mistrusting his ability to direct the ship in the darkness, assigned that duty to Dewey, with his "younger eyes," while he himself took charge of the battery. Dewey, his post on the hurricane deck, succeeded in passing the forts without running the ship aground, and also had a sharp encounter with the Confederate ram *Manassas,* which in the end was compelled to make for the shore, where she was set on fire. Two years later when Farragut made a similar move against Port Hudson, the *Mississippi* was again in the thick of the fight. Though an experienced river pilot was in charge of the ship, he ran her hard aground, where, being at the mercy of the Confederate batteries, she caught fire. Officers and crew worked desperately to save her, but in vain. Dewey's coolness and efficiency were commended in the official report. Later he was made the executive officer of the *Monongahela,* which Farragut used as his flagship when he supervised operations on the lower Mississippi. This gave opportunity for an intimate acquaintance with the first admiral of the United States navy. "Valuable as the training of Annapolis was, it was poor schooling beside that of serving under Farragut in time of war" (*Autobiography,* p. 50). After a brief period of service on the James River, Dewey was made executive officer of the heavy steam-frigate *Colorado;* he brought an undisciplined crew under control, and his ship was one of Porter's fleet that participated in the attack on Fort Fisher. After nine years at sea, Dewey was ordered to the Naval Academy for his first shore duty. The same year, on Oct. 24, 1867, he was married to Susan Boardman Goodwin, daughter of ex-Governor Goodwin of New Hampshire. She died in 1872, five days after the birth of a son, George Goodwin Dewey.

Dewey's first command was the sloop-of-war *Narragansett.* When the *Virginius* affair was arousing the country, the *Narragansett* was engaged in surveying the Gulf of California. Wardroom officers were gloomy, for if a conflict with Spain were to follow they "would be entirely out of it." In the light of later events Dewey's reply is interesting: "On the contrary, we shall be very much in it. If war with Spain is declared, the *Narragansett* will take Manila." Dewey had read a few books about the Philippines, and saw that they would be a logical point of attack. Further tours of duty, of minor importance, followed: first, as light-house inspector for the Second District, with headquarters in Boston; second, as naval secretary of the Light-house Board, which brought him to Washington, with a round of dinners and the opportunity of meeting prominent officials; and, third, as commanding officer of the sloop *Juniata,* ordered to the Mediterranean. The last duty was cut short by a severe illness, a complication of typhoid fever and abscess of the liver. Dewey was taken to the British naval hospital at Malta, where only the skill and personal care of the head surgeon saved him. At the age of forty-seven he was promoted to the rank of captain. Then followed another cruise in command of the *Pensacola,* of no significance save for the many agreeable meetings with men of distinction in northern and southern Europe. In July 1889, he was made chief of the Bureau of Equipment, Navy Department, Washington. This was a fortunate assignment. Recently authorized cruisers were being completed and the first battleships were being planned. Not less important as leading to his great achievement of 1898 was his assignment in October 1895, as president of the Board of Inspection and Survey. Several battleships were then approaching completion, and it was the Board's duty to pass on them, making sure that construction was sound and conforming to specifications. Presiding at the trials of the *Texas, Maine, Iowa, Indiana,* and *Massachusetts,* and also of several of the cruisers and torpedo-boats, Dewey gained an intimate and detailed knowledge of the "New Navy."

In November 1897, he was ordered to take command of the Asiatic Squadron. Relations with Spain were strained, but conservative Americans did not believe that war was probable. Dewey, however, resolved to take every precaution. Before sailing he began an intensive study of the Philippine Islands. Inquiring into the supply of ammunition in his new command, he learned that the ships had not even a peace allowance; further, that the cruiser which was scheduled to take the ammunition to them was under repair and not likely to be in commission for six months. By insistence and personal application, he succeeded in getting one-half of the necessary stores loaded at once on the little *Concord,* with the assurance that the rest should be expedited to Honolulu where it would be forwarded by the cruiser *Baltimore.* As it happened, the latter ship reached him only forty-eight hours before the message that war had been declared.

He took over his new command in the harbor of Nagasaki, Jan. 3, 1898. For two years he had held the rank of commodore. In February the ships proceeded to Hongkong, nearer to their possible objective, and from then until April there was constant drilling of the crews, as well as docking and overhauling of ships and machinery. Knowing that the British in case of war would, with strict neutrality, grant no harbor facilities, Dewey quietly improvised a base at Mirs Bay, purchased two supply ships, and contracted with the Chinese for the delivery of coal, provisions, and general stores, as needed. In Washington he had applied at the Office of Naval Intelligence for information relating to Manila, but as our warships had not visited the latter for years, none was to be had. While at Hongkong, however, Dewey kept closely in touch with O. F. Williams, the American consul at Manila, who sent valuable reports. It was seemingly hazardous to operate against an enemy fleet in a harbor that had great defensive possibilities, supported by an army with land batteries, an arsenal, and a large city. The British in Hongkong, though friendly to the American forces, were frankly doubtful of the outcome, and at the clubs betting odds heavily favored the Spanish. Dewey, however, had made every preparation, and when, on Apr. 26, he received a cablegram that war had been declared he waited only that Williams might arrive and then set his course for Manila Bay, six hundred miles distant.

When near his destination he reconnoitered Subig Bay, where the Spanish Squadron had made a brief visit a few days before. Finding that they were not there, he steamed on to Manila Bay reducing his speed so that he might not enter until about midnight. He had heard from both the consul-general of Singapore and Williams that Boca Grande (the main entrance) had been mined. Although on the American ships there were fifty-three guns above four-inch caliber to the Spaniards' thirty-one, and 1,743 men to their 1,134, in the Spanish land batteries there were thirty-nine heavy guns, the largest of greater caliber than any in the American Squadron. These, the ships being unarmored, might if properly handled have been the decisive factor. A defeat or even a serious check to the American forces, with the nearest navy-yard 7,000 miles away, would have been fatal. Dewey afterward related that his mind went back to the advance on the forts below New Orleans thirty-six years before. Asking himself the question "What would Farragut do?" he drew strength from the conviction that he was doing precisely what the great leader would have done. The entrance into the bay was executed without a hitch. Not a mine exploded. Only a few shots were fired from the land batteries, and these fell harmlessly as the rear of the column was passing. The squadron then steamed slowly on toward Manila, twenty-five miles distant. When the mist of tropical dawn cleared away, the Spanish ships were discovered at anchor in front of Cavite, "formed in an irregular crescent" protected on the west by Cavite peninsula and the battery at Sangley Point, and on the east by the shoals off Las Pinas. The American column, consisting of the *Olympia* (flagship), the *Baltimore,* the *Raleigh,* the *Petrel,* the *Concord,* and the *Boston,* headed south toward the Spanish Squadron. At 5:30 A.M., May 1, Dewey gave the word to begin firing, and an eight-inch shell from the *Olympia* was the signal to the squadron for battle. They had been approaching on a converging course, and as they reached the five-fathom curve near Cavite they turned westward and ran in the general direction of the Spanish line, using their port broadside. Reaching its extremity, with helm to port, they "countermarched" and brought the opposite batteries to bear. In this way they traversed the course three times to the west and two times to the east, the range varying from 5,000 to 2,000 yards. The fire from the land batteries, as was soon evident, could be for the most part ignored. And though the Spanish ships fought with spirit, the inaccuracy of their fire showed that the rapid shots of the American Squadron and the changing range had proved utterly confusing. At 7:35, when the battle had been in progress about two hours, and the Spanish Squadron, as far as could be seen, was still intact, Dewey withdrew. He had received a disturbing report that ammunition was near to exhaustion. The report proved to be erroneous, but the interruption served to disclose the effectiveness of the American gunnery. Of the Spanish Squadron, the *Castilla* burst into flames and the *Reina Cristina* (flagship) blew up. The smaller vessels fled for refuge behind the arsenal at Cavite, and only the *Don Antonio de Ulloa* kept her ensign flying and held to her original position beside the battery on Sangley Point. At 11:16 Dewey again led his ships into action, and soon the *Ulloa* went down. In the afternoon the little *Petrel* took or destroyed the small ships, tugs, and launches concealed in the harbor of Cavite. The entry in Dewey's diary written that evening reads: "Reached Manila at daylight. Immediately engaged the Spanish ships and batteries at Cavite. Destroyed eight of the former, including the *Reina Cristina* and *Castilla*. Anchored at noon off Manila." (*Autobiography*, p. 223). Rarely has there been such disproportion in losses. The *Olympia* was hulled five times and her rigging cut, the *Baltimore* was hit five times, and the *Boston* and the *Petrel* received some unimportant hits; but the total American casualties amounted to only eight wounded. On the other hand, the Spaniards, besides losing all their ships, had one hundred and sixty-seven killed and two hundred and fourteen wounded (Chadwick, p. 205).

The victory at once made the United States one of the principal powers in the East, and was of influence with the American people in that it showed the quality of the "New Navy," in which some had not felt any too great confidence. Following his victory Dewey had a problem to face much like that of Farragut immediately after the battle of New Orleans; he had a large enemy city at his mercy, but no army with which to occupy it. Informing Washington of his victory by cable from Hongkong, he told of his need, and then waited for reënforcements. Meanwhile circumstances developed which caused anxiety. Spain at the beginning of the war had fitted out a fleet for the West Indies, and now giving her attention to the East organized another fleet under Admiral Camara, which in tonnage, type of ship, and guns was superior to Dewey's squadron. When this started for the Orient, going by the short route through Suez, it had a chance of reaching the Philippines before the arrival of additional American ships. Meanwhile Great Britain, France, Germany, and Japan were hurrying certain of their ships already in the East to Manila. Furthermore, Filipino insurgents swarmed about Manila and Cavite in increasing numbers.

The batteries at Manila had been silenced by the threat of a bombardment of the city. Mindful of the Spanish forces there and what they might do with torpedoes, Dewey employed, especially at night, every means to safeguard his ships. He had established a blockade, but permitted warships of neutral powers to enter and leave the bay as they pleased, subject to the commonly recognized rules of blockaded waters. The British, French, and Japanese reported their arrival and asked where they should anchor. But the Germans came in with little or no formality, choosing their own anchorage. Altogether, there appeared five of their warships under Vice-Admiral von Diederichs—a force out of all proportion to the limited German interests in the Islands. Their officers were guilty of visiting Spanish posts and of ignoring the blockade in other particulars. But Dewey, taking a firm stand and receiving the moral support of Capt. Chichester, the senior British officer, maintained control in important affairs and avoided a rupture. Meanwhile the Filipino leader, Aguinaldo, had, with Dewey's encouragement, organized native forces and invested the city on the land side. (It is difficult to determine just how far Dewey may also have encouraged Aguinaldo's aspirations for the independence of the Islands. Dewey's extensive testimony before the Senate Committee in 1902 was exceedingly confused. See *Senate Document No. 311, Pt. III, 57 Cong., 1 Sess*). Finally, Major-General Merritt arrived with the necessary troops. The army and the navy joined in attacking Manila, Aug. 13, and, after a few shots from Dewey's guns, the city surrendered.

Dewey's duty in the East lasted for a year after the battle of Manila Bay. Meanwhile enthusiasm at home knew no bounds, and a grateful Congress had created for him the rank of Admiral of the Navy, with the provision that he should not be placed on the retired list except by his own application. On his return he received an ovation of unprecedented brilliance in New York and elsewhere, and was presented a home in Washington by the American people. He was married on Nov. 9, 1899, to his second wife, Mrs. Mildred McLean Hazen. An unfortunate incident followed when he deeded to her the home that had been the gift of the nation, the incident calling forth much adverse criticism. Yielding to numerous suggestions that he become a candidate for the presidency of the United States, he gave out a public interview on Apr. 4, 1900, in which he said, "If the American people want me for this high office, I shall be only too willing to serve them . . . Since studying this subject I am convinced that the office of President is not such a very difficult one to fill." Popular support of his candidacy failed to develop, however, and his name was not brought up at either of the party conventions. Dewey was made president of the General Board of the Navy Department in 1900 on its inception, and held this office until his death seventeen years later. By his keen interest in its problems and by his prestige he gave power to that body such as otherwise it would not likely have had during the years following the Spanish-American War. His career "ran in full current to the end." He served in the navy, including the period at the Naval Academy, for over sixty-two years. Proud, especially in his old age, of his physical vigor he kept the existence of disease (arteriosclerosis) a secret even from close friends until a week from the end when, on Jan. 16, 1917, he died in Washington.

[*Autobiog. of Geo. Dewey* (1913); French Ensor Chadwick, *Relations of the U. S. and Spain* (1911), vol. I; *Official Records* (*Navy*), vol. XVIII (for New Orleans) and vol. XIX (for Port Hudson); "Appendix to the Report of the Chief of the Bureau of Navigation, 1897–98," *House Doc. No. 3,* 55 Cong., 3 Sess. (for Manila Bay); R. F. Dibble, *Strenuous Americans* (1923); Mark Sullivan, *Our Times* (1926), vol. I.]
C.S.A.

DEWEY, ORVILLE (Mar. 28, 1794–Mar. 21, 1882), clergyman, author, was a son of Silas and Polly (Root) Dewey of Sheffield, Berkshire County, Mass. His boyhood was spent on his father's farm and at the district school. At sixteen he began to prepare for college under William H. Maynard and Elisha Lee of Sheffield, entered Williams College in the third term of sophomore year, and graduated with the valedictory in 1814. The next two years were spent in teaching at Sheffield and in business in New York. He graduated from Andover Seminary in 1819, spent eight months as agent for the American Education Society, and a year as pastor of the Congregational church at Gloucester, Mass. While a student at Andover he began to question the doctrine of the Trinity and during his Gloucester pastorate he became a Unitarian. His Unitarian pastorates were as follows: from 1821 to 1823 he was associated with Dr. Channing at the Federal Street Church in Boston; from 1823 to 1833, First Church, New Bedford, Mass.; from 1835 to 1848, Second Congregational Church (later Church of the Messiah), New York; from 1857 to 1861, New South Church, Church Green, Bos-

ton. He supplied Unitarian churches two winters each in Washington and in Albany and preached and lectured extensively. After his retirement from his New York pastorate, he lived mostly at his Sheffield home, where he died. He was the fourth president of the American Unitarian Association, serving from 1845 to 1847. Harvard gave him the degree of D.D. in 1839. He made several trips to Europe, and spent nearly two years there with his family, October 1841–August 1843. His Lowell lectures in 1851 on "The Problem of Human Destiny" (published under the same title in 1864) were given in various places and were afterward repeated in Boston at Lowell's request. He gave a second Lowell course in 1855 on the "Education of the Human race." His publications include: *Discourses on Various Subjects* (1835); *The Old World and the New* (1836), the fruit of his first trip to Europe; *The Works of Orville Dewey* (1844, republished in 3 volumes, 1847) and numerous sermons and addresses. He was the first clerical member of the Artists' Club of New York, was deeply interested in social questions, and was a founder of the Employment Society which first put poor relief in that city on an organized basis. He was an opponent both of slavery and of abolitionism, thus subjecting himself to criticism in both North and South. After an attack of measles while in college, his eyesight was always defective and his work was several times interrupted by ill health.

He had a natural eloquence and preached on the great subjects with extraordinary insight and ability. He was an unusual interpreter of religious life, and has been characterized as "a man of unique power in the pulpit . . . in whom thought was more intimately blended with emotion than in any other great preacher we can bring to mind" (J. H. Allen, *The Unitarians,* American Church History Series, 1894). He retained his youthful spirit to an advanced age, and was a vivacious and charming companion. He was married, Dec. 26, 1820, to Louisa Farnham of Boston.

[*Autobiography and Letters of Orville Dewey,* ed. by his daughter, Mary E. Dewey (1883); J. H. Allen, *Hist. Sketch of the Unitarian Movement Since the Reformation* (Am. Ch. Hist. Ser., vol. X, 1894); W. H. Fowler, *The Am. Pulpit* (1856); Calvin Durfee, *Williams Biographical Annals* (1871).]
F.T.P.

DEWING, FRANCIS (fl. 1716–1722), was the first important engraver on copper in America. He sailed from London in the *Jollif Galley* commanded by Capt. John Aram and arrived in Boston on July 12, 1716. On July 30 he advertised in a local newspaper: "Lately arrived from London, Francis Dewing who Engraveth and Printeth Copper Plates, Likewise Coats of Arms and cyphers in Silver Plate. He Likewise Cuts Neatly in wood and Printeth Callicoes, etc. Lodging at Mrs. Hawksworths against the Bunch of Grapes in King Street." He executed the repeating designs which were cut upon heavy blocks of pear-wood and were used in printing cotton cloth. His engraving coats of arms would imply that he also engraved bookplates. When the Massachusetts Bay Colony first issued a paper currency in 1690 it was counterfeited so quickly and successfully that the treasury officials had difficulty in identifying their own currency: all engravers were suspect. The Town Clerk had carefully noted Dewing's arrival. On July 9, 1718, Gov. Shute issued a warrant for his arrest as Francis Doing, for "being suspected to be concerned in Counterfeiting the Bills of Credit of this Province, and searching his chamber and seizing any tools and materials that probably have been employed." He was probably cleared of the charge and on the following Jan. 7 Sheriff Edward Winslow was paid £4–10–0 for his expenses in making the arrest. Dewing married Katherin Hart on Dec. 8, 1719 (*Boston Marriages*, 1898, p. 98). He engraved Southack's "Sea Coast of English America and the French New Settlements" in 1716, Southack's "Canso Harbour" and his "Casco Bay" in 1720, and possibly the first issue of his "New York to Cape Breton" in the same year. His most important work was Capt. John Bonner's "The Town of Boston," which he engraved on copper in 1722. Authorities have thought that Dewing either died of the smallpox in Boston in 1723 or that he emigrated to St. Lucia in that year. In 1745, however, he was again in England and engraved a view of the East front of the New Organ in Salisbury Cathedral (Thomas Dodd, Memoirs of English Engravers, in British Museum).

[Justin Winsor, *Memorial Hist. of Boston*, vol. II (1881); Wm. Dunlap, *Hist. of the Rise and Progress of the Arts of Design in the U. S.*, vol. III (ed. 1918); David McNeely Stauffer, *Am. Engravers upon Copper and Steel*, vol. I (1907); Brit. Mus. Add. MSS. 33,400; information from A. E. Popham of Brit. Mus. and C. S. Brigham of the Am. Antiquarian Soc.] F.M.

DEWING, MARIA RICHARDS OAKEY (Oct. 27, 1845–Dec. 13, 1927), painter, the daughter of William Francis and Sally (Sullivan) Oakey, was born in New York City. After a period of study at the National Academy of Design and under John La Farge and Dr. Rimmer, in 1876 she went to London, Italy, and France, while in Paris being a pupil of Thomas Couture. Returning to the United States she published *From Attic to Cellar: A Book for Young Housekeepers* (1879), which was followed by *Beauty in Dress* (1881) and *Beauty in the Household* (1882). She also contributed to magazines. On Apr. 18, 1881, she was married to Thomas Wilmer Dewing, an American painter who during the previous year had opened a studio in New York City.

For some years Mrs. Dewing devoted her efforts chiefly to painting flowers out-of-doors, in the garden of her summer home in Cornish, N. H. In later years she painted both figures and portraits in her New York studio. Because of her long residence in New York, she had a wide circle of friends and in her professional contacts met practically all the foremost artists of her time. Her work was delicate and refined, yet vigorous. In referring appreciatively to the salient features of her art, Royal Cortissoz has emphasized her deep feeling for beauty and intensely individual touch; her rare ability to interpret the soul, the genius of a flower, with marked originality of vision. She will be gratefully remembered for her inspiring contribution to the dignity of flower painting in which she was rivaled only by La Farge in America and Fantin-Latour in France (*New York Herald Tribune*, Dec. 18, 1927). Her life-size "Mother and Child" exhibited at the 1927 Winter Academy Exhibit, is full of delicacy, charm and sentiment, strengthened by a fine harmony of color. It represents another phase of her versatility and evoked warm tribute as showing an art of profound distinction (*New York Times*, Dec. 4, 1927). She was awarded a bronze medal at the Columbian Exposition, Chicago, 1893, and also at the Pan-American Exposition, Buffalo, 1901.

Notable flower pictures painted out-of-doors were: "Poppies and Italian Mignonette," "Rose Garden, Roses with Border of White Carnations," "In the Springtime, Persian Lilacs, Narcissus Poeticus, Flowering Almond," "White Mountain Roses," "Iris at Dawn," "Marigold and Ribbon Grass." Among her flower pictures painted in the studio were "The Cabbage Rose," also called "Provence and Centifolia," "Carnations in Japanese Vase," "Carnations in a Satsuma Vase," "Souvenir de Mal Maison Roses," painted in extreme youth, "Roses Against Antique Brocade," "An Oak Wreath," "Marigolds in a Glass," "The Peacock Fan with Roses," "Heliotrope and Daphne Odorata," "Annual Phlox." Figure pictures were "The Mother," "The Prelude," "The Rose," "In Italy," "Child with Doll," "Elizabeth Dewing at the Age of Six Months," "Sketch for Portrait of My Father, William Francis Oakey." Taken together, these pictures enumerated are representative of the work of Maria Dewing in its various phases.

She died in her New York studio, survived by her husband and a daughter.

[Pa. Acad. of the Fine Arts, *An Exhibition of Paintings of Maria Oakey Dewing* (Mar. 1–23, 1907); B. F. Dewing, *Descendants of Andrew Dewing of Dedham, Mass.* (1904), p. 108; Mich. State Lib., *Biog. Sketches of Am. Artists* (1912), p. 96; *Who's Who in America, 1924–25*; *Am. Art Annual*, XXIV (1917), 540; J. D. Champlin, Jr., *Cyc. of Painters and Painting* (1886), I, 401; family data; date of birth verified by Mr. Thomas Wilmer Dewing.]   J. M. H.

DeWITT, SIMEON (Dec. 25, 1756–Dec. 3, 1834), surveyor-general of New York, was born at Wawarsing, Ulster County, N. Y., the son of Dr. Andries and Jannetje (Vernooy) DeWitt. After having received such an English education as a colonial rural community could afford, he was placed with the Rev. Dr. Romeyn of Schenectady to prepare for college, and in due time entered Queen's (now Rutgers) College in New Jersey. His course, however, was sadly interrupted by the Revolution, for the British burned the college buildings and dispersed the students. In spite of this break, he was awarded the bachelor's degree in 1776 and twelve years later received from the same institution the master's degree. With the closing of the college, he returned to his home and pursued his studies as he found opportunity; but when the whole state rose in arms to repel Burgoyne's invasion, he joined a battalion being formed in Ulster County and was given the rank of adjutant. Upon reaching the scene of action, this unit was absorbed into another regiment and DeWitt, deprived of his command, became a private, and in this capacity participated in the battles that led up to Burgoyne's surrender. This emergency over, he again went home and continued his mathematical studies, combining with these an attention to the practical business of surveying which served him in good stead when Gen. Washington wrote to his uncle, Gen. James Clinton, inquiring if he knew of any person qualified to act as geographer to the army. DeWitt was immediately recommended and in 1778 was appointed as assistant to Col. Robert Erskine, then geographer-in-chief. Upon the death of Col. Erskine in 1780, DeWitt became the head of the department. Ordered to headquarters by Gen. Washington in December of that year, he remained attached to the main army until the end of the campaign. This led him to Yorktown where he witnessed the surrender of Cornwallis. Besides making the necessary surveys and maps for the conduct of military operations, he prepared an interesting series of maps showing the course of the war. This he tried to induce Congress to publish but the state of the public finances forbade it.

At the close of the Revolution, he planned to go on with his surveying work, and, on May 13, 1784, upon the resignation of Gen. Philip Schuyler as surveyor-general for New York State, he was appointed to the office. For over fifty years he served the state in this capacity. In 1786–87 he was one of the commissioners actively engaged in delineating the boundary between New York and Pennsylvania and during this same period began work upon a map of New York which was finally published in 1802. This map is an index even to this day of what the state was at that time. Offered the position of surveyor-general to the United States by Washington in 1796, he reluctantly declined the honor and remained with his work in New York. When the state adopted its canal policy, the surveyor-general was naturally chosen one of the commissioners for "exploring the whole route, examining the present condition of . . . navigation, and considering what further improvement ought to be made therein" (Whitford, *post*, p. 63).

Although busy with these regular duties, he found time to engage in educational and scientific matters. He served the University of the State of New York from 1798 until his death, first as a regent, then as vice-chancellor, and finally, after 1829, as chancellor. In this latter office, he originated the taking of meteorological observations by every academy under the board. As early as 1790 he was a member of the American Philosophical Society, and he contributed to the sixth volume of its *Transactions* (1809), a communication entitled "Observations on the Eclipse of the Sun, June 16, 1806, at Albany." He was also one of the charter members of the Society for the Promotion of Agriculture, Arts and Manufactures, founded in New York in 1793, and in 1813 became its second president. Upon the establishment of the state Board of Agriculture, the Society was merged with the Lyceum of Natural History as Albany Institute, and for many years DeWitt served this body as vice-president. To the older organization he contributed two papers: one "On a Plan of a Meteorological Chart," and the other on "Establishment of a Meridian Line in the City of Albany," while his writings for the *Transactions* of Albany Institute were "A Table of Variations of the Magnetic Needle," "Observations on the Functions of the Moon, Deduced from the Eclipse of 1806," and "A Description of a New Form of Rain Gauge." In *American Journal of Science* he discussed the theory of meteors; and in 1813 his writings upon drawing and perspective were published in book form under the title, *The Elements of Perspective*.

DeWitt married three times. His first wife

was Elizabeth Lynott, whom he married on Oct. 12, 1789. Her death occurred in 1793 and he later married Jane Varick Hardenberg, by whom he had six children. After the latter's death, he married, on Oct. 29, 1810, Susan Linn, daughter of the Rev. William Linn. DeWitt died at Ithaca, N. Y., on Dec. 3, 1834.

[T. Romeyn Beck, *Eulogium on Life and Services of Simeon DeWitt* (1835); B. J. Lossing, *The Empire State* (1887); Cuyler Reynolds, *Hudson-Mohawk Geneal. and Family Memoirs* (1911), I, 364–66; N. E. Whitford, "Hist. of the Canal System of the State of N. Y.," *Ann. Report of* (N. Y.) *State Engineer and Surveyor*, Supp., 1905; Jas. G. Wilson, *Memorial Hist. of the City of N. Y.*, vols. III and IV, *passim*; Thos. G. Evans, *The DeWitt family of Ulster County, N. Y.* (1886).]

G. H. B.

DE WOLF, JAMES (Mar. 18, 1764–Dec. 21, 1837), slave-trader, manufacturer, senator, was born in Bristol County, R. I., and was the seventh son of Mark A. and Abigail (Potter) De Wolf. Both his father and his uncle Simeon Potter were seafaring men, and had been interested in slave-trading in French Guinea. The family was poor and the boys hoed corn on their father's farm until, throwing down their hoes, they walked to Providence and sailed upon one of Potter's privateers. This was during the Revolutionary War and the sea was infested with private pirates who increased in audacity and lucrative gain after the French Revolution. James De Wolf went through wild experiences. He fought in many naval battles, was captured twice by the enemy, and once was imprisoned. The result of this cruelty and hardship made him a man of force and indomitable energy with no nice ethical distinctions. Before his twentieth birthday he was master of a ship and before he was twenty-five he had accumulated wealth enough to make him independent for the rest of his life.

His earliest voyages were made to Africa where he seized and transported Africans as slaves to the West Indies. Providence merchants of highest commercial and social standing backed him in this trade. Apparently he had no qualms of conscience, and often went to Southern ports personally to supervise the sale of his captives. He was careful to follow the lines of largest profit. As long as the slave-trade was flourishing after the Revolutionary War, his ships were in it. Later some of them turned to the furs of the northwest coast, then to whale-fishing, and finally even went to China. His principal trade, however, was always in the West Indies, and when, in 1804, South Carolina threw open her ports to the importation of slaves because of the threatened national prohibition, De Wolf leaped to aid, and ten of the 202 vessels that entered Charleston between 1804 and 1808 belonged to him.

The attitude of England during the Napoleonic Wars greatly angered and embarrassed De Wolf and he sustained heavy losses through the impressment of seamen. He was a strong advocate of war with England and eleven days after the declaration of the War of 1812, he offered the government at his own expense "an armed Brig (one of the most suitable in this country for a Privateer), of one hundred and sixty tons burthen, mounting eighteen guns and carries one hundred and twenty men, called the *Yankee,* commanded by Oliver Wilson." The *Yankee* was immensely successful. It made six cruises in less than three years and captured more than five million dollars' worth of British property.

After the close of the war, De Wolf sensed the coming development of manufactures in the United States. Gradually he withdrew his capital from shipping and he had already built one of the earliest cotton-mills in the United States, at Coventry, R. I., in 1812. He sensed, too, that the new industry needed political influence. For thirty years he represented the town of Bristol in the Rhode Island legislature, becoming finally speaker of the House. In 1821 he was elected to the United States Senate. Here he was a strong advocate of protection for the new young industries and he opposed the extension of slavery to Missouri and the West. His interest now was no longer in the African slave but in the white mill laborer. He did not like the atmosphere of Washington and resigned his seat in the Senate in 1825 and returned to the legislature of Rhode Island. He made the town of Bristol his especial care. Here on a great estate of one thousand acres, he built himself a stately mansion, and devised many schemes for the advancement of the town and its industries. De Wolf was tall and commanding in person and very careful about his dress. He married Nancy Bradford, a daughter of William Bradford, and died in New York City.

[W. H. Munro, *Hist. of Bristol, R. I.* (1880), and *Tales of an Old Sea Port* (1917); C. B. Perry, *Charles D'Wolf of Guadaloupe, His Ancestors and Descendants* (1902); G. M. Fessenden, *Geneal. Memoir of the Descendants of Wm. Bradford* (1850).]

W. E. B. D.

DEXTER, FRANKLIN (Nov. 5, 1793–Aug. 14, 1857), lawyer, the son of Samuel Dexter [*q.v.*] and of his wife Catherine (Gordon) Dexter, was born in Charlestown, Mass. He received his early education in the public schools, and, proceeding to Harvard College, graduated there in 1812. He then read law with Samuel Hubbard and was admitted to practise in the court of common pleas, Suffolk County, September 1815, and in the supreme judicial court, December 1818. On Sept. 28, 1819, he was married to Catherine Elizabeth, daughter of Judge William Prescott of Boston. He commenced practise in Boston and from the first evinced great interest in public affairs. In 1825 he was elected representative from Boston in the Massachusetts House of Representatives, in the same year also becoming a member of the Common Council of Boston. The first occasion upon which he came prominently before the public was the trial of Theodore Lyman for a criminal libel upon Daniel Webster in the *Jackson Republican*, Oct. 29, 1828. He was retained for the defense, which he conducted with great ability, and the jury were unable to agree, a nolle prosequi being subsequently entered on behalf of the Commonwealth (12 *American State Trials*, 327). This case attracted national attention owing to its political attributes. In 1830 as counsel for defense of the two Knapps in connection with the murder of Joseph White at Salem he at once stepped into the foremost rank as an advocate. The Commonwealth had retained Daniel Webster on the trial of John Francis Knapp who was charged with murder, and after a ten days' hearing, the jury disagreed, but at the new trial the accused was found guilty, as was also Joseph Jenkins Knapp, Jr., who was charged as an accessory (7 *American State Trials*, 395). Though both prisoners were hanged, Dexter's conduct of the defense was considered masterly. In 1835 he was elected state senator and in 1836 again became representative from Boston in the legislature, serving on this occasion as a member of the Select Committee on Revision of Statutes. In 1840 he was associated with another Boston *cause célèbre*, the trial, of Mrs. Kenney for the murder of her husband, appearing for the defense and securing an acquittal. In 1841 he was appointed by President Harrison United States district attorney for Massachusetts and retained this position for four years exhibiting "the most exact appreciation of the duties of his station and every qualification for their performance" (*Monthly Law Reporter*, X, 316). In 1848–49 he was a lecturer at Harvard Law School. He was reappointed district attorney by President Taylor in 1849, but held office only a short time. He had practically retired from professional work at this period, and devoted the remainder of his life to travel and literary study. He died at Beverly, Mass.

Although he was conspicuous among his contemporaries for his sound legal knowledge, possessing outstanding ability as an advocate and equipped with every qualification for public life, Dexter's achievements fell far short of his intellectual promise. The possession of independent means obviated the necessity of continuous and sustained effort to put forth his best, and posterity can only judge him by his record in the three great cases with which his name is associated.

[See O. P. Dexter, *Dexter Geneal.* (1904), p. 136; W. T. Davis, *Professional and Industrial Hist. of Suffolk County, Mass.* (1894), I, 568; *Proc. Mass. Hist. Soc.*, XIX (1881–82); Jos. Palmer, in *Boston Daily Advertiser*, July 21, 1858, reprinted in Palmer's *Necrology of Alumni of Harvard Coll.* (1864). For the memorial meetings of the supreme judicial court and the Suffolk bar, see the *Boston Daily Advertiser*, Sept. 9, 1857.]   H. W. H. K.

DEXTER, FRANKLIN BOWDITCH (Sept. 11, 1842–Aug. 13, 1920), antiquarian and historian, was born in Fairhaven, Mass., where his father, Rodolphus Williams Dexter—a direct descendant of the Puritan Thomas Dexter of Bristol, England, who in 1630 was settled at Lynn, Mass.—was engaged in business. His mother, Mary Hathaway Taber, was also of old New England stock. He prepared for college at a typical New England school, Williston Seminary, and entered Yale with the class of 1861. He proved himself a painstaking and competent, rather than brilliant, scholar, graduating with membership in Phi Beta Kappa. For two years after graduation he taught Greek in Gen. Russell's "Collegiate and Commercial Institute" in New Haven, and then (in 1863) entered the service of Yale University, holding in turn the following positions: librarian of the Linonian Society (1863); tutor in Yale College, first in mathematics, later in Greek (1864–67); assistant in the College Library (1867–68); assistant in the Treasurer's office (1868–69); assistant librarian of the College (1869–1912); registrar of the College Faculty (1869–92); secretary of the Yale Corporation (1869–99); Larned Professor of American History (1877–88); assistant librarian emeritus (1912–20).

His entire life, from 1857, when he entered Yale College, until his death sixty-three years later, was spent in New Haven, and except for the two years of his school-teaching he gave his time almost exclusively to the interests of the University. His gifts were not those of an administrator or of a teacher. His mind was mainly concerned with ascertaining historical facts regarding Yale College, its graduates, and its city, and in publishing them with extraordinary accuracy and completeness. He was happy if he could run down information hitherto not generally known and was content to state it succinctly in volumes that were extremely well arranged, well annotated, and well indexed, and that showed throughout that capacity for meticulous research characteristic of great antiquarians. Of the philosophy of history and of the interpretation of events, there was practically none.

In addition to more or less routine University publications, all of which he greatly improved, and three editions of the new *Acts of the General Assembly of the State of Connecticut with other Permanent Documents respecting Yale College* (1871, 1878, 1889), he published: *Roll of Honor* (1866), a roll of the alumni of Yale in the United States service 1861–65, reprinted with additions in Kingsley's *Yale College, a Sketch of its History* (1879); *The College Hymnal for Divine Service in the Battell Chapel* (1876); *Sketch of the History of Yale University* (1887); *A Catalogue, with Descriptive Notices, of the Portraits, Busts, etc. belonging to Yale University* (1892); *Diary of David McClure, Doctor of Divinity, 1748–1820* (1899); *Literary Diary of Ezra Stiles, D.D., LL.D.* (1901), in three volumes, a work of special value to every student of New England history because of its thorough editing and full notes; *Biographical Notices of Graduates of Yale College, including those graduated in classes later than 1815, who are not Commemorated in the Annual Obituary Records* (Supplement to *Obituary Record*, 1913); *Documentary History of Yale University, 1701–1745* (1916); *Extracts from the Itineraries and other Miscellanies of Ezra Stiles, 1755–1794* (1916); *Jared Ingersoll Papers* (1918). New Haven as the home of Yale College and as the home of his wife's Davenport ancestors also greatly interested him. Among his publications in this congenial field of research were: *The First Public Library in New Haven* (1900); *Historical Catalogue of the Members of the First Church of Christ in New Haven . . . 1639–1914* (1914); and *New Haven Town Records, 1649–1662 and 1662–1684,* two volumes (1917, 1919).

The most important of his literary labors is his *Biographical Sketches of the Graduates of Yale College with Annals of the College History,* commonly referred to by its cover title of *Yale Biographies and Annals.* This includes the classes from 1701 to 1815, after which date competent class records began to be published, and is contained in six volumes published from 1885 to 1912. The work, suggested by Sibley's *Biographical Sketches of Graduates of Harvard University* (1873–85), contains the College Annals for each year, followed by the biographies of all men graduating in that year. It is a monumental work of reference, devoid of any attempt at literary charm, but so accurate and exhaustive that although new editions may be called for, it will never be superseded. Among his other writ-

ings two may be mentioned as of specially broad interest and value: *The Influence of the English Universities in the Development of New England* (1880) and *Estimates of Population in the American Colonies* (1887). These are both included in *A Selection from the Miscellaneous Historical Papers of Fifty Years* (1919). For forty years, from 1867 to 1907, he was directly responsible for the catalogue of the University Library, which increased in this period from about 50,000 to nearly 400,000 books, writing in his own hand tens of thousands of library cards. He also prepared and published *A Catalogue of the Linonian and Brothers Library* (1873), and was engaged in his seventy-seventh year, just prior to his death, in preparing an "author list" of the manuscripts in the Library.

His industry was as prodigious as his scholarship was exact, and his loyalty to Yale unbounded. He was over six feet tall, and of slender build, and had a quick, nervous manner and walk. He was shy and reserved, playing no part in public life and little part in social life, except for attending the fortnightly meetings of "The Club"—a dining club made up mostly of older members of the Faculty. He was a member of the Massachusetts Historical Society, and foreign secretary and a member of the Council of the American Antiquarian Society. He was a Congregationalist, attending regularly the College Church Sunday mornings, until late in life when he transferred his membership to the Center Church. His wife, who survived him, was Theodosia Mary Wheeler, daughter of Russell Wheeler of New York City.

[In addition to Dexter's writings, and personal acquaintance over a period of twenty-five years, the principal authorities for the above sketch have been the *Yale Univ. Obit. Record* for 1921–22; the various *Records* of the Class of 1861, Yale College; resolutions of the Yale Corporation, Sept. 11, 1920; and a sketch of his life under the title "The Annalist of Yale" in the *Yale Alumni Weekly,* Oct. 15, 1920. His portrait, painted in 1913 by Paul K. M. Thomas, is in the Yale Library. An earlier picture is reproduced in Kingsley's *Yale College.*]

                              A. P. S.

DEXTER, HENRY (Oct. 11, 1806–June 23, 1876), sculptor, son of Smith and Clarasa (Dexter) Dexter, was born in grim poverty on a wilderness-surrounded farm in Nelson, N. Y., where his parents had settled the year before. He could trace his ancestry through eight generations to the Rev. Gregory Dexter of Olney, England, called the first educated printer in New England, who in London in 1643 printed for Roger Williams a dictionary of the Indian language and in the following year accompanied Williams to Providence. Henry's childish impulse toward art was inborn. Having neither canvas, colors, nor the money with which to buy them, he painted on scraps of cloth with the juice of red and green berries. His efforts met reproof as signs of sinfulness. When he was eleven years old, his father disappeared. His mother was from Connecticut, and returning thither, placed the boy on a Connecticut farm, where he worked industriously three years. He was kindly treated, went to school in winter, and stood at the head of his class. At sixteen, much against his secret hope for an artist's career, he was apprenticed to a blacksmith. In 1828, having mastered his craft, he married Calista Kelley, daughter of Ebenezer Kelley and niece of the enterprising portrait-painter, Francis Alexander [q.v.], a man but six years Dexter's senior. Alexander dissuaded him from trying to make likenesses for a living, and induced him to work at his trade seven years longer. At last, in the spring of 1836, Dexter went to Providence, R. I., where he opened a studio, and for some months painted likenesses, first at five, then at ten, then at fifteen, and finally at twenty dollars apiece, Alexander giving him friendly counsel. That autumn, he moved to Boston, where, acting on a chance suggestion to make use of some clay left by the sculptor Greenough, he attempted the modeling of portrait-busts. Having completed in marble (1838) the portrait of Samuel A. Eliot, mayor of Boston, he presently received commissions for busts of other distinguished men. Among his sitters were Longfellow, Agassiz, Henry Wilson, Anson Burlingame, Prof. C. C. Felton of Harvard, and Charles Dickens. While the novelist was sitting, Dexter's studio was a rendezvous for the élite of Boston. Both Dickens and his wife expressed pleasure in the portrait when completed.

Dexter's success in portrait-busts (he is said to have made nearly two hundred) shows what could be done by a self-taught pioneer, inventive, industrious, and agreeable, working in a circle of intelligent and even intellectual persons, at a time when knowledge of the art of sculpture was extremely limited in the United States. Undoubtedly his training as a blacksmith was of service, not only because of the skill of hand gained thereby, but because of the ability it gave him to make and keep in condition the tools necessary in marble cutting. Also, he had a gift for "catching the likeness," and this was mainly what his sitters wanted. In 1857 his wife died, and two years later he married Mrs. Martha Billings of Millbury, Mass. He had just formed an interesting project of making portrait-busts of all the governors in the United States. As a prelude, taking with him a letter from Edward Everett, he went to Washington, where he was favorably received by President Buchanan, whose bust he made. He thereupon began his tour as itinerant sculptor of governors, visiting every state but California and Oregon. In 1860 he returned to Boston with his plaster casts of thirty-one portraits, exhibiting these casts in the State House rotunda, and preparing to immortalize their subjects in marble. Unfortunately the Civil War defeated this ambition; only four of the portraits were made permanent. The collection was largely dispersed, history, if not art, losing thereby. Dexter's eight marble statues, ranging from the "Binney Child," Mt. Auburn Cemetery (1839), to the "Gen. Warren," Charlestown (1857), appear to-day of little importance, however remarkable they may be as the work of a self-taught artist, who before his own attempts had never seen any one model in clay or carve in marble. Dexter's nature was at once sensitive and energetic. He enjoyed music and poetry, and wrote interestingly of his experiences. He died in Boston at the age of seventy, honored and beloved.

[John Albee, *Henry Dexter* (privately printed, 1898); Lorado Taft, *Hist. of Am. Sculpture* (1903); S. C. Newman, *Dexter Genealogy* (1859).]   A. A.

DEXTER, HENRY (Mar. 14, 1813–July 11, 1910), business man, the son of Jonathan Marsh and Elizabeth (Balch) Dexter, and a descendant of Richard Dexter, who was admitted freeman of Boston in 1642, was born at West Cambridge, Mass. He was educated in public and private schools. Beginning in his fourteenth year he served a three-year apprenticeship in a Boston printing office. Although he never attended Harvard College as he had desired to do at one time, that institution contributed greatly to his education through opportunities offered him during three years which he spent as second foreman in the printing office of the college. He went to New York in 1836 and six years later bought an interest in the firm of Dexter & Tuttle, dealers in books, periodicals, and daily newspapers, having had, meanwhile, several years of business experience including employment in a hardware store conducted by the Whittemores, inventors of the carding machine. The firm of Dexter & Tuttle later became Dexter & Brother, then Henry Dexter & Company, and still later H. Dexter, Hamilton & Company. Dexter's greatest achievement was a consolidation of leading newspaper dealers which developed into the present American News Company of which he was president for many years until 1896. He organized a similar London corporation, the International News Company.

On Oct. 11, 1853, he was married to Lucretia Marquand Perry. He was greatly interested in civic projects. He gave liberally to the Metropolitan Museum of Art at the time of its founding and contributed approximately $225,000 toward the building of the present home of the New York Historical Society. A dispute arose over this gift. On the day the building was opened Dexter caused pamphlets to be distributed to the guests stating that he had erected it in memory of his only son, Orrando Perry Dexter. Trustees of the society stopped distribution of the pamphlets, claiming that Dexter did not have a right to claim the building as his own since the society had put some $171,000 into its construction in addition to his gift and had supplied the valuable site for the building. One room of the New York Historical Society building is known as Henry Dexter Hall and an ornamental doorway leading into the lecture hall memorializes his son.

The extent of Dexter's interest in reform movements and in philanthropy is indicated by the long list of organizations with which he was connected. He was vice-president of the Protestant Episcopal Church Missionary Society for Seamen, trustee of the Midnight Mission, life director of the American Bible Society and American Tract Society, and member of the New York Society for the Prevention of Cruelty to Children, St. Luke's Hospital Society, the Children's Aid Society, the Home for Incurables, the Charity Organization Society, the New York Association for Improving the Condition of the Poor, and the Home for Aged Married Couples. Not long before his death, he published a collection of his letters written to newspapers on various topics between his nineteenth and ninety-fourth birthdays.

[*Who's Who in New York City and State,* 1907; *N. Y. Times,* July 12, 1910; Orrando Perry Dexter, *Dexter Geneal. 1642–1904* (1904), pp. 160–63; Moses King, *Notable New Yorkers 1896–99* (1899), p. 315.]

D. W. M.

DEXTER, HENRY MARTYN (Aug. 13, 1821–Nov. 13, 1890), Congregational clergyman, was born at Plympton, Plymouth County, Mass. He was the son of the Rev. Elijah and Mary (Morton) Dexter, and sixth in descent from Thomas Dexter, who was a prominent colonist of Lynn by 1630. Elijah Dexter was a graduate of Brown University and for more than forty-two years pastor of the Congregational Church at Plympton. In 1836, at the age of fifteen, Henry entered Brown, changing in his sophomore year to Yale, where he graduated in 1840, having partially supported himself by teaching summers during his college course. On graduation he became principal of the Academy at Rochester, Mass., for a year, after which he attended Andover Theological Seminary, graduating in 1844. On Nov. 6 of that year he was ordained pastor of the newly organized church in Manchester, N. H., where he remained for four and a half years. He was married to Emeline Augusta Palmer, daughter of Simeon Palmer of Boston on Nov. 19, 1844. On Apr. 18, 1849, he became pastor of the Pine Street Church in Boston and continued there for eighteen years in spite of internal troubles in the church which were not of his own making. A few months after his move to Boston he became a special contributor to the newly established *Congregationalist,* and for some years was special correspondent of the New York *Independent.* In October 1851 he became a member of the editorial staff of the *Congregationalist,* a post he retained, with an interval of a year, until his death. From 1856 he was editor-in-chief. In 1854 he took the leadership of the New England clergy in drawing up resolutions opposing the Nebraska Bill, going to Washington to present the protest personally to Congress. In the same year he moved to Roxbury. In 1858 he helped to found the *Congregational Quarterly.* In 1867 he had a call, which had been made previously also, to a church in California, and was about to accept when he was offered the editorship and partial ownership of the combined *Congregationalist* and *Boston Recorder.* He resigned his pastorate and from that time devoted himself to editorial and historical work, from 1873 making his home in New Bedford.

Dexter's passion for the advancement of Congregationalism was life-long. He wrote much on that topic and also on early New England history. Among his more important books may be mentioned: *Congregationalism* (1865); *The Church Policy of the Pilgrims* (1870); *As to Roger Williams* (1876); *The Congregationalism of the Last 300 Years* (1880); *A Handbook of Congregationalism* (1880). His writings for the periodical press were voluminous, and his editorial contribution of considerable value, in the case of such works as *Mourt's Relation* and Church's *King Philip's War.* Much of his writing was special pleading and marred by his strong bias in favor of the Puritans and Congregationalists, but it was accurate in detail. He was a member of many historical societies, including the Massachusetts Historical and the American Antiquarian. He was chairman of the committee appointed to erect in Leyden a memorial to John Robinson. He was an indefatigable worker, a competent scholar, and in constant demand as preacher and lecturer. He took an active part in the ecclesiastical affairs and controversies of his day. In 1890 he was chosen one of the representatives of American Congregationalism at the Conference held in London, but was found dead in his bed on Nov. 13 of that year.

[Wm. A. Warden and Robt. L. Dexter, *Geneal. of the Dexter Family in America* (1905); *Proc. Mass. Hist. Soc.*, 2 ser. VI (1891); sketch by John E. Sanford, *Ibid.*, VII (1892), 90–103, with a bibliography of Dexter's more important writings.]   J.T.A.

DEXTER, SAMUEL (Mar. 16, 1726–June 10, 1810), merchant, was descended from Richard Dexter, a native of County Meath, Ireland, who was admitted a townsman of Boston, Mass., in 1642 and settled at Malden. His great-grandson, the Rev. Samuel Dexter, married Catherina Mears, and their eldest son, Samuel, was born at Dedham, Mass., where his father was minister of the First Church. He was apprenticed to a merchant in Boston and later built up a prosperous business of his own in that town. He married Hannah, daughter of Andrew Sigourney, and when thirty-six years of age retired to Dedham with a modest fortune. In the troublous years 1764–68 he represented his native town in the General Court (Herman Mann, *Historical Annals of Dedham*, 1847, p. 106) and from 1768 to 1774 he was a member of the Council (*Monthly Anthology*, IX, 5). In 1774 his election to the Council was negatived by Gov. Gage because of Dexter's political sentiments. In the first Provincial Congress he was one of the delegates from Dedham (*Journals of Each Provincial Congress of Massachusetts*, 1838, p. 7) and was placed on the committee to provide for the public defense; subsequently he was one of the committee for the support of the army besieging Boston. He differed with his associates in regard to the conduct of the war, believing that better results could be accomplished by withdrawing the army from the siege and training it efficiently for a vigorous campaign. In July 1775 he retired to private life. This induced a popular suspicion that he had become a lukewarm patriot. Dexter disdained to justify his action, left Dedham, and established himself in Woodstock, Conn., where he resided about ten years. He appears to have returned to Dedham in or before 1785, for in that year he was a representative from that town in the General Court. In 1786 he moved to Weston, Mass., and made his home there till 1800. The closing years of his life were spent in Mendon, Mass. Samuel Dexter [*q.v.*], born in 1761, was his youngest child.

By his will Dexter bequeathed $5,000 to Harvard College to promote critical study of the Bible. This bequest reflected his profound interest in the Scriptures and his longing for the truth. His benevolence expressed itself throughout his life in unostentatious generosity to the poor and by contributions to educational and charitable institutions. One of the provisions of his will stipulated that he was to be buried in a certain field in Woodstock, Conn., in such manner that his grave might not be visible after the earth had settled; no monument should mark where his body lay. A pamphlet of sixty pages entitled *Thoughts Upon Several Passages of Scripture, Both in the Old and New Testament, Relative to Jacob and Esau with Incidental Excursions* (Worcester, 1791) is probably the only one of his writings which he printed. This he issued under the pseudonym "Philotheorus." In it he defends Esau, expresses doubt as to his eternal damnation, and suggests that a more careful study of the original text would sustain this view. Dexter's belief in a just God was stronger than his belief in orthodox Calvinism.

[The most comprehensive account of Dexter's life is in Clarence Winthrop Bowen's admirable *Hist. of Woodstock, Conn.* (1926), pp. 179–95. It is the result of long, careful study, abounds in helpful references, and includes a portrait by Maj. John Johnston. A sketch by C. A. Staples, *Samuel Dexter,* containing a portrait and other illustrations, was printed in *Dedham Hist. Reg.*, Apr. 1892, and was also published (1892) in pamphlet form. Glimpses of Dexter are given in Sidney Willard, *Memories of Youth and Manhood* (1855), II, 68–72; and in Herman Mann, *Hist. Annals of Dedham* (1847); and the family genealogy in O. P. Dexter, *Dexter Geneal.* (1904). A number of Dexter's letters are preserved in the library of the Mass. Hist. Soc. An excellent obituary by Samuel Dexter, Jr., is in *Monthly Anthology*, IX, 3–7 (July 1810).]   L.S.M.

DEXTER, SAMUEL (May 14, 1761–May 4, 1816), lawyer, was born at Boston, Mass., the youngest child of Samuel [*q.v.*] and Hannah (Sigourney) Dexter. Brought up with great care, he received a thorough classical education at the hands of the Rev. Aaron Putnam of Pomfret, and entered Harvard College in 1777 where he graduated in 1781 with highest honors. He then studied law at Worcester, Mass., with Levi Lincoln and was admitted to the Worcester County bar in 1784. He commenced practise in Lunenberg in 1786, but moved to Chelmsford and later to Billerica, finally establishing himself at Charlestown in 1788. He was in the same year elected a member of the state House of Representatives from Charlestown, and during his two years in that body acquired a wide reputation for sound judgment, and exercised great influence over its deliberations. In 1792 he was elected Federalist representative of Middlesex, Mass., in the Third Congress and served as such till Mar. 3, 1795. Four years later he was elected United States senator from Massachusetts, occupying that position from Dec. 2, 1799 till June

1800, when he resigned in order to enter the cabinet of President Adams as secretary of war, to which office he had been appointed on May 13. He remained head of the War Department until Dec. 31 of that year, when he became secretary of the treasury. His temperament and intellectual endowment ill suited him for that minute diligence and attention to intricate details which the departments of War and Finance impose on incumbents of office, but his application was intense and his success undoubted (Story, *post*). For a short period he, in addition, executed the office of secretary of state in order to administer the oath of office to John Marshall on the latter's appointment as chief justice of the United States. Shortly before the termination of the Adams administration the President offered him a foreign embassy but he declined and remained in office till after the accession of Jefferson, when Gallatin succeeded him on Jan. 26, 1802. He then moved to Roxbury, Mass., and resumed the practise of law. Partially withdrawing from political activities, he devoted himself to his profession, and in a short time attained a commanding position at the bar, being constantly retained in the higher state courts and particularly in the Supreme Court of the United States. In 1807 he appeared as leading counsel for the defense of Thomas O. Selfridge, charged with the murder of Charles Austin, a Harvard student. The prominent position of all the participants caused intense interest to be taken in the proceedings, which resulted in a verdict of acquittal (2 *American State Trials*, 544). In his address to the jury Dexter is said to have "combined the closest reasoning with the most finished eloquence" (Davis, *post*). He had always manifested considerable independence of thought, invariably approaching both political and legal problems in his own way, and his attitude in the matter of the War of 1812 was thoroughly characteristic. He believed that the war was a just one and, declining to follow the Federalists, actively supported the policy of the government in that respect, but was vehemently opposed to the Embargo and non-intercourse policy, and unsuccessfully contested its constitutionality. In 1815 he was offered an extraordinary mission to the Court of Spain by President Madison, which he declined. In 1814 and 1815 he was an unsuccessful candidate for governor of Massachusetts, disclaiming all sympathy with Madison's policy apart from his attitude toward Great Britain. He died at Athens, N. Y. On Mar. 7, 1786, he married Catherine, daughter of William Gordon of Charlestown, and Franklin Dexter [*q.v.*] was their son.

Dexter was inclined to be reserved, precise, and formal in manner, and his appearance on public occasions was not impressive. He had a strong dislike for mass meetings at which he never appeared to advantage. Possessed of rare intellectual gifts, however, he enjoyed a prestige both in Congress and the courts of last resort which placed him in the first rank of contemporary public men. At the same time it is doubtful whether he was profoundly learned. One who knew him well says that the impression was that he read few professional books (Sargent, *post*), and Story bears testimony to the fact that he referred to "black lettered law" as "the scholastic refinements of monkish ages." A poem, *The Progress of Science* (1780), and a biographical notice of his father in the *Monthly Anthology and Boston Review*, July 10, 1810, are the most noteworthy of his published writings.

[Dexter's ancestry is traced in O. P. Dexter, *Dexter Genealogy 1642–1904* (1904), which also contains (p. 86) a short biography. Judge Story's "Sketch of the life and character of the Hon. Samuel Dexter" in 1 *Mason, 523*, and *Reminiscences of Samuel Dexter* (1857), by Lucius Manlius Sargent under the pseudonym "Sigma," are authoritative surveys of his life and career. See also C. W. Bowen, *Hist. of Woodstock, Conn.* (1926), pp. 190 ff., and "Samuel Dexter, Councilor, and his son, Hon. Samuel Dexter, Secretary of War, and Secretary of the Treasury," *Proc. Am. Antiq. Soc.*, n.s., XXXV, 23 (Apr. 8, 1825); W. T. Davis, *Hist. of the Bench and Bar of Suffolk County, Mass.* (1894); *Memoir of Theophilus Parsons* (1859), by his son, T. Parsons, p. 180; and Charles Warren, *Hist. of the Am. Bar* (1911), p. 309.]   H. W. H. K.

DEXTER, TIMOTHY (Jan. 22, 1747–Oct. 23, 1806), merchant, was born in Malden, Mass., where his ancestor, Richard Dexter of County Meath, Ireland, had settled some hundred years before. His parents, Nathan and Esther (Brintnall) Dexter, were indigent and inconspicuous. He had little schooling and throughout his life ignored the conventional rules of spelling and punctuation. At the age of nine he was placed on a farm, but, after nearly seven years of service, went to Charlestown, where he "stayed Leven months at Dressin of skins for briches & gloves." Having earned his freedom from apprenticeship, he arrived in Newburyport in 1769, with a "bondel" and "Eight Dolors & 20 sents" in cash.

In May 1770, having set up as a leather dresser, he married Elizabeth (Lord) Frothingham, a widow with four children and a small property. The couple had two children,—Samuel, born in 1772, and Nancy, born in 1776. With his wife's money and what he himself was able to accumulate, he shrewdly bought up depreciated Continental currency during and after the Revolution at a fraction of its face value; and, when Hamilton's policy of funding and assumption was adopted in 1791, he suddenly found himself a wealthy man. With prosperity, he indulged his vanity and a natural inclination toward eccentricity. Although he soon became an inveterate sot, he transacted his business in the morning when he was comparatively sober, and he engaged in enterprises which have become legendary. According to his own statements, he sent 42,000 warming pans to Cuba, where they passed as cooking utensils; he cornered the market in whalebone, disposing of 342 tons at a large profit; and he bought 21,000 Bibles, which he sold in the "west inges" at an advance of one hundred per cent. Some of these wild stories may have a basis of fact. It is certain that he owned two vessels, that he was the largest stockholder in the Deer Island Bridge across the Merrimac (opened in 1793), and that he achieved notoriety as a cunning speculator.

In 1791 he bought the splendid house of Patrick Tracy, one of Newburyport's broken-down merchant princes, furnished it luxuriously, and emerged in the rôle of gentleman. In 1796, annoyed by some practical jokers, he moved to Chester, N. H., but returned in a few months to Newburyport, now styling himself "Lord" Timothy Dexter, with a title "made by the voice of hamsher state," and purchased the mansion of Jonathan Jackson, on High St. He engaged Joseph Wilson, a ship carver, to make more than forty life-sized wooden statues, painted in colors, of great personages, including Presidents Washington, Adams, and Jefferson, three of the apostles,—St. Paul, St. John, and St. Peter,—Adam and Eve, Benjamin Franklin, John Jay, Louis XIV, Lord Nelson, and others. These were arranged on the grounds so that they could easily be seen from the street. Most striking of all was an image of himself on a pedestal near the front fence bearing the inscription, "I am first in the East." He subsidized a laureate, Jonathan Plummer, formerly a fish peddler, who composed odes in his honor, and appeared as an author himself in a pamphlet entitled *A Pickle for the Knowing Ones,* filling twenty-four small pages and privately printed in 1802. The first edition had no marks of punctuation whatever, but at the end of the second Dexter added a whole page of "stops," telling his readers to "peper and solt it as they plese."

In his old age he was a quaint figure in a wide cocked hat and long blue coat, who strolled aimlessly about his estate, carrying a gold-headed cane and followed by a porcine dog. His eccentricity displayed itself in startling ways, as, for instance, when he had his coffin made and kept

on exhibition in his parlor and actually held a mock funeral, after which he beat his wife because of her failure to shed tears. With an insatiable mania for publicity, he offered a market house to Newburyport on condition that it be called Dexter Hall and agreed to repave High St. if it could be named after him; but the town refused his proposals. He did, however, make gifts to various institutions, including a bell to the Second Presbyterian Church; and, of the $35,000 which he left at his death, $2,000 was bequeathed to Newburyport, the income of which is still used for the benefit of the poor. Many of his images were blown down in the great tempest of 1815, but the three presidents still kept their places on the entrance arch until 1850. The house is still standing (1930), with Dexter's gilded eagle shining on the roof.

[The best book on Dexter is John P. Marquand's *Lord Timothy Dexter* (1925), which deals with him in a delightfully ironic manner. There are two excellent essays on him by W. C. Todd in his *Biog. and Other Articles* (1901). An early biography was written by S. L. Knapp, a resident of Newburyport (*Life of Timothy Dexter,* 1838), but it is unreliable. Dexter's *A Pickle for the Knowing Ones, or Plain Truths in a Homespun Dress* is printed in full in Marquand's biography. See also *Births, Marriages and Deaths in the Town of Malden, Mass., 1649–1850* (1903), pp. 21, 126, and O. P. Dexter, *Dexter Geneal.* (1904).]   C.M.F.

DEXTER, WIRT (Oct. 25, 1832–May 17, 1890), lawyer, was a grandson of Samuel Dexter [1761–1816, *q.v.*], and son of Samuel William Dexter and his third wife Millisent Bond. His father, a native of Boston, and a brother of Franklin Dexter [*q.v.*], moved West, became a county judge in Wisconsin, and subsequently practised law at Dexter, Wis., a town which he had founded and where his son Wirt was born. Having obtained his early education in the local schools, the latter went to Ann Arbor, Mich., where he studied for a time, later attending Cazenovia Seminary in New York State. On his return to Michigan he entered the lumber business, in which his father was largely interested. This involved the management of saw-mills, the marketing of the output, and the organization of logging camps, all the details of which he mastered. The life, however, had no attractions for him, and in 1853 he moved to Chicago, read law, and was admitted to the bar. Opening an office there, he soon obtained a good practise, particularly in commercial cases, his previous experience in business standing him in good stead. His successful defense of Devine, a foundryman, who had shot an employee during a quarrel, first attracted public attention to his abilities. The case was one of more than ordinary local interest and his speech to the jury was remarkable for its force and effect. From that time forward, he was in constant request, and soon became one of the leading counsel in Chicago. He did not specialize, and the wide range of cases in which he was briefed testified as much to his versatility as to his legal attainments. In *Pullman Palace Car Company* vs. *Smith* (73 *Ill.*, 360), appearing on behalf of the company, he successfully established that the liability of his clients for property lost or stolen from passengers while riding in Pullman cars was neither that of an innkeeper nor a common carrier. His argument in *Blatchford et al.* vs. *Newberry et al.* (99 *Ill.*, 11), involving the construction of a will and the application of the doctrine of acceleration of remainders, was masterly, and, though unsuccessful, was concurred in by Judge Dickey, who contributed a dissenting opinion fifty-five pages in length. This case was unique in legal experience, owing to one of the appellate judges' changing his opinion after the decision had been rendered. He was retained in [Northwestern] *University* vs. *People* (99 *U. S.*, 309) on behalf of the University in the Supreme Court of the United States, where he obtained a reversal of the opinion of the Illinois court to the effect that the University was liable for taxes on land owned by it but not in its immediate use. For a number of years prior to his death he was general counsel and member of the executive committee of the Board of Directors of the Chicago, Burlington & Quincy Railroad Company and represented it throughout the "Granger" litigation. He took intense interest in all movements for the advancement of the interests of Chicago, and was one of the founders of the Chicago Relief and Aid Society, being chairman of its executive committee in 1871 when the Chicago fire occurred, and to him was confided the work of administering the $5,000,000 contributed from all over the world for the purposes of relief. He at once gave up all professional work and for a year devoted himself solely to the task of evoking order out of chaos and distributing relief. In this work his services were invaluable and crowned with complete success. He was not interested in political matters, and never held or aspired to public office. Normally a Republican, he declined to follow his party in its nomination of Blaine for the presidency, and in local contests invariably supported whomsoever he considered the better man, irrespective of politics.

For years prior to his death he was admittedly the leader of the bar in Chicago. Both in consultation and in court he was distinguished for an intuitive common sense which dominated all his utterances. A fluent speaker, methodical, always thoroughly prepared, and impressive in his earnestness, he was extremely effective with a jury, and his legal acumen and power of analysis always carried great weight with the bench. He was tall, with an athletic frame, and an air of dignity and refinement, "genial and affable, . . . luxurious in his habits and artistic in his tastes" (F. B. Wilkie, *post*). He was married twice : on June 15, 1858, to Kate Augusta Dusenberry of Marshall, Mich., who died in 1864, and on Dec. 18, 1866, to Josephine Moore. He died suddenly in Chicago in his fifty-eighth year.

[O. P. Dexter, *Dexter Geneal.* (1904), p. 194 ; F. H. Head in *Great Am. Lawyers*, vol. VIII (1909), ed. by W. D. Lewis ; J. M. Palmer, *The Bench and Bar of Ill.* (1899), II, 659 ; F. B. Wilkie, *Sketches and Notices of the Chicago Bar* (1871), p. 42 ; *Daily Inter Ocean* (Chicago), May 19, 1890.]   H.W.H.K.

DE YOUNG, MICHEL HARRY (Sept. 30, 1849–Feb. 15, 1925), editor and publisher, was born in St. Louis, Mo., the son of Michel H. and Amelia (Morange) de Young. At the age of five he went with his family to a California mining town and later to San Francisco, then a village. He was educated in the public schools of that town, and spent his life as one of its citizens, taking an active part in its civic and political affairs. When he was a boy in his teens, San Francisco had a theatrical activity equaled in only a few Eastern cities, and his entry into newspaper publishing came via the *Daily Dramatic Chronicle*, which he and his brother Charles founded in January 1865 when M. H. de Young was sixteen and his brother two years older. At first, the paper was little more than a theatre program, filled with advertising and circulated free. It had a crisp, snappy manner of presenting and commenting upon news which attracted readers, and it soon became a full-fledged newspaper, paralleling in its rapid growth the expansion of the city. The position of the new daily surprised and alarmed its competitors as it soon grew to have the largest circulation on the Coast. Among its early contributors, before any of them had achieved fame, were Mark Twain, Bret Harte, Prentice Mulford, and Charles Warren Stoddard. The word "dramatic" was dropped from the title, Sept. 1, 1868, the paper then appearing as the *Daily Morning Chronicle,* and later as the *San Francisco Chronicle.* In 1872, it began an agitation against land monopoly which led to the exposure of several federal officials, bringing about the retirement of a group of politicians. One of the results was the establishment of a bank commission for the state. In 1879 the *Chronicle* successfully fought for a new state constitution.

On the death of his brother Charles in 1880, M. H. de Young became owner and editor-in-chief. Personally and through the paper he exerted a powerful influence on the Pacific Coast. He was thoroughly identified with the Republican party, acting as delegate to three national conventions, those of 1888, 1892, and 1908, and serving on the National Committee for eight years, and as its vice-chairman for four years. In 1892 he was an unsuccessful candidate for the United States Senate to succeed George Hearst, throwing his votes to Charles N. Felton to break a deadlock. He was named commissioner from California to the Paris Exposition in 1889; three years later he was selected as commissioner and as vice-president of the World's Columbian Exposition; in 1898 he was commissioner-general from California to the Trans-Mississippi Exposition at Omaha; he attended the Paris Exposition in 1900 as president of the United States Commission; and in 1915 he was vice-president of the Panama-Pacific Exposition. For twenty-five years he was a director of the Associated Press, and for a short time he served as president of the International League of Press Clubs. Following the San Francisco fire he served on the executive committee of the Red Cross directing relief work. In spite of many political and civic connections and frequent trips to the East and abroad, he never lost close touch with the *Chronicle*. He continued to define its policies and watch their execution carefully. It is said that until his final and extremely brief illness those in his employ regularly awaited the kindly, constructive comments on the handling of news and editorials which it was his practise to make daily.

[Information from Mrs. Marjorie D. Brown, librarian of the *San Francisco Chronicle*; issues of that paper for Feb. 16–19, 1925; *N. Y. Times*, Feb. 16, 1925; *New International Year Book*, 1925; John P. Young, *Journalism in Cal.* (Chronicle Publishing Co., San Francisco, 1915); *Who's Who in America*, 1899–1925. M. H. de Young apparently preferred to use only his initials. His name is sometimes given as Michael Henry, and in *Who's Who in America*, 1924–25, appears as Meichel Harry; the form adopted above is that used in *Who's Who in America* from 1899 till 1923. The date of his birth is given as Oct. 1 in *Who's Who in America*, but as Sept. 30 in a biographical article said to have been dictated by De Young shortly before his death and used in the *Chronicle*, Feb. 16, 1925.]

J.M.L.
H.J.S.M.

DIAZ, ABBY MORTON (1821–Apr. 1, 1904), author, was born in Plymouth, Mass., the only girl among the six children of Ichabod and Patty (Weston) Morton. Her father was described by Emerson as "a plain man who formerly engaged in the fisheries with success" (Swift, *Brook Farm*, p. 120). It was said of him that he was a Puritan divested of all the Puritan's superstition and bigotry (Swift, *Brook Farm*, p. 79), and it

seems sure that as concerned organized religion both he and his daughter were at the opposite extreme from dogmatism. Once while he was in Boston he saw by a supernatural light which flooded his room a vision of a world governed by the principles of human brotherhood. He determined to help make this vision a reality, and to that end became a temperance worker and later the pioneer abolitionist of Plymouth. Abby was still a child but she quickly made the slaves' cause her own, and became secretary of a juvenile abolitionist society (see "Anti-slavery Times in Plymouth," *New England Magazine*, April 1899). Later, when her father's interest shifted to the Brook Farm activities—he was a trustee December 1842–April 1843—she and two of her brothers were sent there to live. The entire family joined them in the spring of 1843. After two weeks, persuaded that sentiment rather than sound judgment was ruling the community, Ichabod abandoned the house he had built, and went home. Abby remained longer, a teacher in the infant school. Later she was married to Emanuel Diaz, but after a brief married life which left her with the care of two sons, she began teaching school in Plymouth. It was her habit to write verse for use in local festivities, and in May 1861, the *Atlantic Monthly* published her "Pink and Blue," a prose story of "how I won my wife." Upon this she determined to devote her life to writing, and from then till the close of the century she published books at a rate of considerably more than one every two years. She was most widely known by her humorous and homely stories for children—the series beginning with *The William Henry Letters* (1870) having become within five years so popular that they were turned into drama. In 1878, with N. A. Calkins, she published a natural history series, setting forth in six booklets the family history of creatures ranging from cow to condor. She was also active as an emancipator of women, "slaves," as she expressed it, "of the rolling-pin" (Diaz, *Domestic Problems*, 1884, p. 123). Her concern was to explain "how woman may enjoy the delights of culture and at the same time fulfil her duties to family and household" (*Ibid.*, p. 7). She discussed this subject in four books, the most vigorous, perhaps, *Only a Flock of Women* (1893). As early as 1876 she published *Neighborhood Talks* on arbitration versus war, and as years went on she interested herself in questions of always greater magnitude and vagueness. She contributed articles to the *Metaphysical Magazine* (New York), wrote four papers on the "Science of Human Beings," and from December 1901 to September 1902, published in the magazine *Mind* (New York) a long sequence of articles called "Hindrances to World Betterment." After about 1880, she lived in Belmont, Mass. At the time of her death she was collecting extracts from her past writings with the view of putting them together in a kind of anthology.

[L. Swift, *Brook Farm* (1900); *Who's Who in America*, 1903–05; W. T. Davis, *Plymouth Memories of an Octogenarian* (1906); *Boston Transcript*, Apr. 1–2, 1904.]   J.D.W.

DIBBLE, ROY FLOYD (Mar. 12, 1887–Dec. 3, 1929), author, was born in Portland, Chautauqua County, N. Y., the son of George E. Dibble, a farmer, and Miriam H. (Quilliam) Dibble. His life until he became of age was spent almost entirely in his native county, where he grew up on his father's farm and attended the local schools at Elm Flats and Westfield. Graduating from the Westfield high school in 1906, he was prevented from proceeding directly to college by the necessity of caring for a sick brother. This and farming for his father were his occupations for the next two years; though it was at this time also that the reading he had done in Shakespeare inspired him to write a lengthy and resounding series of sonnets on the themes of love and poetry. In 1908 he entered Allegheny College in Pennsylvania, but at the end of the first term he went on to Clark University, where he graduated in 1912. After a summer's walking tour in France and the British Isles he commenced a career as teacher at the Sanford School for boys, Redding Ridge, Conn.

The reading he had done in college, however, together with his own natural bent determined that he should pursue the study of literature in a larger place, and in 1914 he entered the Graduate School of Columbia University. The next year he was made a University Fellow in English, and in the year following he was given the position of instructor in English in Columbia College. The remainder of his life was to be spent in New York, though an operation he was forced to undergo in the summer of 1916 led him to believe that less life remained for him than actually did. The surgeon who removed a tubercular kidney from his body told him that he had Addison's Disease and had only three years to live. The general effect of this sentence was to dull the edge of his ambition, and to confirm in him a quietism which had always been present in his character but which had been encouraged for a number of years by annual readings of Thoreau's *Walden,* which he often called his "bible." As a teacher at Columbia he made a greater impression upon his students, who found him contagiously enthusiastic about the authors he taught, than upon his colleagues, who found him singularly uninterested in himself. His life proceeded uneventfully; the summers were spent either in Europe or on the farm near Westfield; the winters passed in teaching; his spare time was given to a dissertation for the Ph.D. degree, a life of Albion W. Tourgée, which was published in 1921.

Meanwhile the business of teaching "war aims" at Columbia in 1918 had stirred him to make an examination of his ideas; the result was a sudden access of energy which at first expressed itself in terms of the prevailing radicalism, but which a little later found definite expression in a desire to write iconoclastic biographies in the manner of Lytton Strachey, whose *Eminent Victorians,* appearing in America, created a whole school of "new" biographers. Dibble set to work upon a series of biographical essays which he published in 1923 under the title *Strenuous Americans* and with a dedication, somewhat less cryptic perhaps than he thought it, "To the Greatest Living Biographer." The subjects treated were Jesse James, Admiral Dewey, Brigham Young, Frances E. Willard, James J. Hill, P. T. Barnum, and Mark Hanna; the treatment was remarkable for its gusto, its narrative power, its pervasive though not always subtle irony, and its orotund, decorated, yet rapid style. Encouraged by the success of this book, Dibble resigned his position at Columbia in order that he might devote all of his time to authorship. His next work was *John L. Sullivan: An Intimate Narrative* (1925), a rollicking and rather Rabelaisian life of still another strenuous American. This was followed in 1926 by *Mohammed,* wherein he went far afield in search of picturesque and violent material. His interest thus aroused in religious leaders, he wrote a life of Martin Luther, but this volume failed to find a publisher; and in 1927 he resumed his teaching, becoming associate professor of English at Hunter College, New York City. At the time of his death he had in hand a second collection of biographical essays, which he had contributed to various magazines. For the *Dictionary of American Biography* he wrote the article on Robert Prometheus Fitzsimmons. He died when his disease passed at last into an acute stage, probably in consequence of depression over unfortunate investments. In appearance he was short, stout, fair, and phlegmatic; he always lived alone; and though he had many friends, few of them ever got beyond the well-armed exterior to the sensitive man within.

[*Who's Who in America,* 1928–29; obituary in *N. Y. Times,* Dec. 5, 1929; personal acquaintance 1915–29.]   M. V–D.

DIBRELL, GEORGE GIBBS (Apr. 12, 1822–May 6, 1888), merchant, planter, politician, soldier, industrialist, was descended from Dr. Christopher Du Brey, a French Huguenot, who settled with a colony of refugees on the James River in Virginia fifteen years after the revocation of the Edict of Nantes. His son Charles was a patriot soldier in the American Revolution, and the son of this Charles, whose name was Anthony, migrated from Virginia to Kentucky where he married Mildred Carter, who was also from Virginia. In the meantime, the name Du Brey had been changed to DeBrill and finally to Dibrell. In 1811 Anthony moved his family to White County, Tenn., and settled in the little town of Sparta, where he became successful as a merchant and presently rose to be a man of some political importance. Here his son George Gibbs was born. The boy helped his father on the farm and attended the local school. When he was fifteen years old he drove a herd of cattle to market in Virginia, a difficult and responsible job for a lad of his age. During the next year he went for one term to the East Tennessee College at Knoxville. The following year his father was a candidate for Congress and George managed the farm during his absence. The elder Dibrell about this time lost much of his property by indorsing notes for friends, and it became necessary for his son to shift for himself. His career began in 1840 when, at the age of eighteen, he was elected clerk of the branch of the Bank of Tennessee which had been established at Sparta. He served in this capacity until 1846, and later acted for some years as clerk of the court of White County.

In 1842, at the age of twenty, he married Mary E. Leftwich, whose father also was a merchant of Sparta and a native of Virginia. Four years later, he severed his connection with the Bank of Tennessee and went into business as a merchant. His first venture proved decidedly profitable, and from this time until the outbreak of the Civil War he continued in business on his own account. He followed his father in his loyalty to the Whig party, and followed his party in its opposition to secession. He let it be known, however, that, in case of a conflict, his sympathies were with the South. Accordingly upon the outbreak of hostilities, he volunteered as a private in the Confederate service, and on Aug. 10, 1861, he was elected lieutenant-colonel of his regiment. He served in Tennessee and Kentucky under Gen. Zollicoffer, but when the army was reorganized at Corinth he was not reëlected as lieutenant-colonel. He thereupon repaired to Richmond to obtain authority to raise a body of cavalry. Re-

turning to his home at Sparta, he organized the 8th Tennessee Cavalry Regiment, behind the Federal lines, as a body of independent partisan rangers; but he joined Gen. Forrest at Murfreesboro and his troops were mustered into the service as regular cavalry, with Dibrell as colonel of the regiment. After this time he saw much service under Forrest. On the death of Col. Starnes, he was given command (July 1, 1863) of Forrest's "Old Brigade" and continued in command of that organization until the end of the war, being raised to the rank of brigadier-general in July 1864. After having taken part in the battle of Chickamauga, this brigade was detached from Forrest's command and ordered to join Joseph E. Johnston at Dalton, Ga. It took part in the retreat to Atlanta, and later in the retreat through South and North Carolina. On reaching Raleigh, it was ordered to join Jefferson Davis at Greensboro, from which point it accompanied him to Washington, Ga., where the military force was disbanded. Dibrell's Tennessee regiment marched home in a body. Debts and desolation awaited them, but Dibrell himself soon restored his fortunes. In 1865 he again embarked in the mercantile business. His friends aided him, and he prospered as before the war. In 1870 he took part in the convention which drew up the new constitution of the state, and in 1874 he was elected to Congress. For ten years he served diligently in the House of Representatives, and retired voluntarily in 1884.

In the meantime, he had ceased to be a merchant and had become a financier. In 1866 the legislature revived the charter of the Southwestern Railroad, which was to connect Sparta with the Nashville-Chattanooga road at Tullahoma (*Acts of the State of Tennessee*, 1865–66, p. 295). He was immediately made a director of this company, and in 1869 he became its president. The road was completed under his direction and a branch was built to the Bon Air coal mines, where fifteen thousand acres of his land had served as the nucleus around which he had organized a successful mining company (Scrapbook, clippings on county history, sketch of White County, in Tennessee State Library). His last years were spent in the quiet of his Sparta home, where he died in 1888.

[The best account is that in *Sketches of Prominent Tennesseans* (1888), ed. by W. S. Speer; another is in the Goodspeed Publishing Company's *Hist. of Tenn.*, White County Suppl. (1887). All other sketches appear to be based upon these two. There is a detailed account of the operations of the 8th Tenn. Cavalry written by Dibrell himself and published in J. B. Lindsley, *The Military Annals of Tenn., Confederate* (1886).] T.P.A.

DICK, ELISHA CULLEN (Mar. 15, 1762–Sept. 22, 1825), physician, the son of Archibald and Mary (Barnard) Dick, was born near Marcus Hook, Pa. His father was a Pennsylvania farmer of means, a horse-breeder and a publicist. Elisha was sent to an academy in Philadelphia, then to the "Pequa Academy." He returned to his father's house at the age of sixteen and there continued his studies under Rev. Samuel Armor. In 1780 he began the study of medicine under Dr. Benjamin Rush, but the following year he entered the office of Dr. William Shippen. He graduated from the University of Pennsylvania as bachelor of medicine in March 1782, and settled in Alexandria, Va., where he became successful professionally and prominent socially. In October 1783 he married Hannah Harman of Darby, Pa. He was one of the organizers of the Masonic Lodge at Alexandria and served as its Worshipful Master both before and after George Washington's tenure of the office. In 1794 he commanded a troop of cavalry in the Whiskey Rebellion in Pennsylvania. For years he was colonel of the cavalry regiment in Alexandria, and in 1804 he was chosen mayor of the city.

For many years Washington's friend, he was also one of the two physicians called in consultation by Dr. James Craik [q.v.] at the time of Washington's last illness, and with Craik he signed the account of the illness and death which was published in *The Times* of Alexandria on Dec. 19, 1799. He likewise conducted the Masonic services at Washington's funeral. He published in the *Medical Repository* (Second Hexade, vol. I, p. 190, 1804) an article on "Yellow Fever at Alexandria," describing an epidemic of some two hundred cases, which he attributed to the stench of decomposing oysters and shells which were treated in a brick-kiln for the purpose of making quicklime. This is on a par with Benjamin Rush's attribution of the Philadelphia epidemic to decomposing coffee. In 1808 he wrote on "Facts and Observations Relative to the Disease Cynanche Trachealis, or Croup" (*Philadelphia Medical and Physical Journal*, 1806, p. 2). This disease was assigned by Craik and Dick as the cause of Washington's death. Most of such cases are nowadays shown to be diphtheria, and that appears to have been what Dick was discussing, as the term *angina membranosa* is used as a synonym, some cases of tracheotomy are reported, and Washington's case is discussed. The disease was then epidemic in and about Alexandria, and three adults had suffered attacks before Washington became sick. Dick had advocated tracheotomy in Washington's case. The treatment used in the case, repeated blood lettings, administration of calomel and tartar emetic, and application of blisters, was that advocated by medical leaders of the day.

An accomplished musician and in early life a believer in and attendant at duels, Dick later changed his church affiliation from Episcopalian to Presbyterian and then to Quaker, threw his dueling pistols into the river, destroyed as a useless vanity an organ which he had built, and otherwise took a more serious view of life and eternity. He was described as being five feet ten inches tall, weighing 175 pounds, and, before he became a Quaker, addicted to ruffles, wearing his hair in a queue or tied with a ribbon. He had a fine and attractive sickroom presence and courtly manners. He died at Alexandria.

[*Va. Herald*, Sept. 28, 1825; W. A. Wells, "Last Illness and Death of Washington," *Va. Medic. Monthly*, Jan. 1927; J. M. Toner, "A Sketch of the Life of Elisha Cullen Dick," *Trans. Medic. Soc. of Va.*, 1885; date of birth and name of wife from a grand-daughter, Miss Ethelinde Crisfield of Washington, D. C.]   P.M.A.

DICK, ROBERT PAINE (Oct. 5, 1823–Sept. 12, 1898), jurist, was born in Greensboro, N. C. His father, John McClintock Dick, was an able and respected judge; his mother, Parthenia P. Williamson, came of a prominent family of Person County. After attending Caldwell Institute, young Dick entered the University of North Carolina and graduated in 1843. He read law, was admitted to the bar in 1845, practised at Wentworth but returned to Greensboro. Immediately after he began practise he married Mary Eloise, the daughter of George Adams of Pittsylvania County, Va. Active in Democratic politics, and a delegate to the Baltimore convention of 1852, he was made federal district attorney in 1853 and served to 1861. In 1860 he supported Douglas, with whom he was on terms of close friendship, in the Charleston convention. Later at Baltimore he was the one North Carolina delegate who refused to secede, and, after voting for Douglas, he returned to North Carolina and, securing the nomination of a Douglas electoral ticket, made a tireless campaign for it; he pleaded for his election as the sole hope of preserving the Union, and was one of the Spartan band of 1,500 who voted for him. With the call for troops he gave up the fight, and was a member of the secession convention where, after voting for the Badger ordinance of revolution, he voted for the ordinance of secession. In 1862 the legislature elected him to the council of state, and in 1864 he supported Holden for governor and was himself elected as a peace candidate to the state Senate, At the close of the war President Johnson summoned him to Washington for advice as to restoration, and, without success, Dick urged him to undertake it on the basis of the Sherman-Johnson agreement and to proclaim a general amnesty. Johnson declined to follow his advice, but appointed him federal judge for North Carolina. In spite of the attorney-general's ruling that he was eligible, Dick felt unable to take the "iron-clad" oath, and declined. He was active in the "Johnson" convention of 1865–66, and, conservative, he seemed inclined to part from his late political associates, but in 1866 he advocated the Fourteenth Amendment and, gradually aligning himself with the radicals, supported Congressional Reconstruction and participated in organizing the Republican party in North Carolina. Under the new constitution he was elected an associate justice of the supreme court, serving from 1868 until 1872 when he was appointed federal district judge.

On the supreme bench of the state he took an important part in deciding the many difficult questions growing out of the new constitution and the system of jurisprudence ushered in by the code of civil procedure. His opinions are clear, brief, and direct. He was, perhaps, a better trial than appellate judge. A hard and consistent student, he grew steadily and tempered knowledge with understanding, common sense, and humanity. As the passions of reconstruction cooled, he won a wide and deserved popularity. For many years, with John H. Dillard, he conducted a private law school which won reputation for the legal training it gave.

[B. D. Caldwell, *Founders and Builders of Greensboro* (1925); *Cyc. of Eminent and Representative Men of the Carolinas of the Nineteenth Century* (1892), II, 633; J. Dowd, *Sketches of Prominent Living North Carolinians* (1888); 63–66 *N. C. Reports*; *Who's Who in America,* 1899–1900.]   J.G.deR.H.

DICKERSON, EDWARD NICOLL (Feb. 11, 1824–Dec. 12, 1889), lawyer, son of Philemon [*q.v.*] and Sidney (Stotesbury) Dickerson and nephew of Mahlon Dickerson [*q.v.*], was born at Paterson, N. J. Entering the College of New Jersey (Princeton) at an early age, he there met Joseph Henry of the Smithsonian Institution, who induced him to take an interest in science and mechanics which gradually developed into an absorbing study and had a permanent effect upon his professional career. Leaving college without graduating, he read law with his father, and was admitted to the New Jersey bar at Paterson in 1845. For a short time thereafter he officiated as clerk of the federal district court, of which his father was judge, and then commenced practise for himself. By this time he had become an expert mechanical engineer; he ran the first locomotive that was used on the railroad between Paterson and Jersey City. His earliest case of first-class importance was *Colt* vs. *Mas-*

sachusetts Arms Company (*Fed. Cas.* no. 3030), a suit brought to establish the validity of Samuel Colt's patent for fire arms. Dickerson represented the plaintiff throughout and at the trial, which took place at Boston and extended over three weeks, won a decisive victory, despite the fact that Rufus Choate was his opponent. In 1852 he moved his office to New York City, and at once assumed a leading position at the bar there, specializing in patent law. During this period his outstanding case was *Goodyear* vs. *Day* (*Fed. Cas.* no. 5569), involving the validity of Charles Goodyear's patent for vulcanized India rubber, in which he was associated with J. T. Brady and Daniel Webster for the plaintiff, Rufus Choate being for the defense. The heavy work in connection with the vital scientific details of the case was all performed by him and resulted in a complete triumph. He was now recognized as the outstanding authority on patent law in the United States. He was an incessant worker and, despite his weighty professional engagements, which of their very nature invariably involved intense technical attention, continued to enlarge the scope of his investigations in the field of mechanical engineering, more particularly as regards marine propulsion. This gave rise eventually to his connection with the "expansion" and "non-expansion" controversy, at the commencement of the Civil War. Acting upon a theory of the chief engineer of the navy that James Watt had made a serious error in maintaining that steam produced more power when worked expansively than otherwise, Secretary Gideon Welles had ordered engines of the non-expansion type for the new naval vessels. Dickerson promptly protested, in letters to the secretary and in communications to Congress which attracted wide attention, and, though his efforts were fruitless at the time, experience subsequently demonstrated the correctness of his views.

At the height of his reputation he retired temporarily from practise in order to undertake an extensive program of foreign travel, in the course of which he spent considerable time in Europe, and also visited Central America. In 1873, however, he returned to the bar, and thenceforth was constantly engaged, the great majority of his retainers being in patent matters. He appeared for the defense in the suits arising out of the disaster to the Staten Island ferry boat *Westfield* involving the loss of many lives, and gained a verdict in each case. The last years of his life were occupied chiefly in the suits involving the electrical patents of Thomas A. Edison, and the rights of the Western Union Telegraph Company and the American Bell Telephone Company. He acted as counsel for the latter company throughout its protracted litigation, and made the final successful argument in the Supreme Court of the United States (126 *U. S. Reports*). As an advocate in his own sphere he was supreme, his profound knowledge of scientific technique combining with a facility of lucid explanation and intense industry in mastering every detail of his cases to make him equally formidable on trial or in appeal. He did not, however, possess a judicial mind, his greatest fault being his inability to see more than one side of a case.

Apart from law and science, his only interest was sailing; he maintained and himself sailed a splendidly equipped yacht. Politically he was "a Democrat of the Jackson school of Democracy" (George Ticknor Curtis, *post*), though he never took a prominent part in public affairs. During the Civil War he was a War Democrat and was outspoken in support of the reëlection of Lincoln. Later he disapproved of the free-trade policy of his party under Cleveland. His appearance was impressive. He was six feet three inches in height, of massive frame, always erect, firm of step and dignified in manner. He died at "Wave Crest" near Far Rockaway, L. I.

[Dickerson's ancestry is traced in C. J. Werner, *Geneals. of Long Island Families* (1919), pp. 1–19. A careful summary of his career appeared in *N. Y. State Bar Asso. Report*, 1890, p. 123; and the authoritative obituary notice by George Ticknor Curtis in the *Sun* (N. Y.), Dec. 13, 1889. See also *N. Y. Times* and *N. Y. Tribune* of same date, and *Ann. Cyc.*, 1889, p. 628.]

H.W.H.K.

DICKERSON, MAHLON (Apr. 17, 1770–Oct. 5, 1853), governor of New Jersey, senator, secretary of the navy, brother of Philemon Dickerson [*q.v.*], was descended from Philemon Dickerson who emigrated from England on the *Mary Anne* of Yarmouth in 1637, became a freeholder of Salem, Mass., in 1638, and later purchased a tract of land at Southold, L. I., where he died. Philemon's grandson, Peter Dickerson, removed in 1741 to Morris County, N. J., becoming an extensive landowner. His son Jonathan married Mary, daughter of Thomas Coe of Queens, L. I., and their son Mahlon was born at Hanover Neck (Morris Plains?), N. J. Graduating at Princeton in 1789, he engaged in the study of law and was licensed as an attorney in 1793. Following a brief military experience in the expedition which suppressed the "Whiskey Rebellion," he settled with two of his brothers in Philadelphia. His active political career began in 1802 with his election to the Philadelphia Common Council. In 1805 Gov. M'Kean appointed him adjutant-general of Pennsylvania, which office he resigned in 1808 to become recorder of the city. His fa-

ther died two years later, leaving an extensive estate to be settled and a large iron business to be carried on. Mahlon, having purchased the claims of the other heirs, transferred his residence to Succasunna, N. J., and took over the management of the famous iron works of that name. This change from a professional to a business life colored his subsequent political career. Though a Democrat, being a manufacturer he became, for the remainder of his public career, an uncompromising advocate of a protective tariff; his reputation among his contemporaries was summed up by President Van Buren who referred to him as "that ultra-protectionist," and he may rightly be regarded as one of those who established the policy of protection.

In 1811 and 1812 he was elected a member of the Assembly from Morris County, and while serving in that body was chosen a justice of the state supreme court, which position he held until elected governor (and chancellor by virtue of that office) in 1815. Reëlected the following year, he resigned when elected to the United States Senate, serving in that body from 1817 to 1833. His career in the Senate was noteworthy for his able support of two policies, one of which originated with him. Fearing that the treasury surplus expended under the "general welfare" clause would result in a centralization of governmental power, he advocated the division of the surplus each year to the states, prorating it according to the ratio of direct taxation (speech in United States Senate, Feb. 1, 1827, *Register of Debates in Congress*, pp. 209–22); and President Jackson paid him the compliment of adopting this proposal in a message to Congress. The other policy which received his able support was that of a protective tariff. As chairman of the Committee of Manufacturers in the Senate, he was in a strategic position to war against free trade which he denounced as "a system as visionary and impracticable as the everlasting and universal pacification of the world." In 1832 he was a prominent candidate for the vice-presidential nomination after Calhoun's retirement from the Democratic party, but gave way to his friend, Van Buren. In May 1834 he declined the post of minister to Russia, remaining at home to promote Van Buren's aspiration for the presidency. He was soon after appointed secretary of the navy, taking office June 30, and serving until ill health forced his resignation in 1838. Retiring to private life he soon regained his health, rescuing as well his business, threatened by the depression following the panic of 1837.

In 1844 he was a prominent and useful member of the constitutional convention which revised the fundamental law of New Jersey. Meeting at the same time in Baltimore, the Democratic Convention nominated Polk. This was so bitter a disappointment to Dickerson who had supported Gen. Cass, that he took no part in the campaign. He could never excuse the nomination of Polk by that "horrible Democratic Convention" and worked vigorously during the ensuing four years to prevent his renomination and to secure that prize for Cass. In this he was successful, but the disappointment of Gen. Taylor's election was overwhelming to him and marked the end of his active participation in politics. He was then seventy-eight years of age and retired permanently to his estate, "Ferrommonte," where he died five years later. He was unmarried.

[J. C. Pumpelly, "Mahlon Dickerson," in *Proc. N. J. Hist. Soc.,* 2 ser., XI, 133–56; obituary notice in *Daily True American* (Trenton), Oct. 8, 1853; G. B. Lee, ed., *Geneal. and Memorial Hist. of the State of N. J.* (1910), III, 1074; "Autobiography of Martin Van Buren," ed. by J. C. Fitzpatrick in *Ann. Report Am. Hist. Asso. for the Year 1918* (1920); L. Q. C. Elmer in *N. J. Hist. Soc. Colls.,* VII, 168–73; C. G. Bowers, *Party Battles of the Jackson Period* (1922).]   C. R. E., Jr.

DICKERSON, PHILEMON (June 26, 1788– Dec. 10, 1862), jurist, was born at Succasunna, N. J., a son of Jonathan and Mary (Coe) Dickerson, and a younger brother of Mahlon Dickerson [*q.v.*]. Much of his youth was passed in Philadelphia, where he attended the public schools, subsequently passing to the University of Pennsylvania and graduating there in 1808. He then took up the study of law and in 1813, on being licensed as an attorney, opened an office in Philadelphia. In 1816 he removed to Paterson, N. J., which thenceforth remained his home. In 1817 he was admitted a counselor-at-law and, devoting himself steadily to his profession, gradually acquired an extensive practise. He was a member of the state Assembly in 1821–22. In 1834 he became a sergeant-at-law, being the last to hold that dignity in New Jersey. A Jacksonian Democrat, he was elected a representative from New Jersey in the Twenty-third Congress, and was reëlected to the Twenty-fourth, serving from 1833 to Nov. 3, 1836, when he resigned, having been elected governor of New Jersey and chancellor by the state legislature. He held this office for only one year, being defeated on seeking reëlection in 1837. In 1839 the "Great Seal War" occurred. He was again the Democratic nominee for Congress, and the election returns showed that he had been elected together with four other Democrats and one Whig. The balance of parties was such that the control of the House depended upon the complexion of the New Jersey delegation. Charges of fraud were made,

and the Whig governor, on counting up the votes, rejected returns from two townships, and affixed the Great Seal of the State of New Jersey to certificates of election of the six Whig candidates. This action transferred the dispute to Washington, where a bitter discussion took place, though ultimately by vote, Feb. 28, 1840, the five Democrats were declared to be members of the House. On the expiration of his term in Congress, Dickerson was appointed by President Van Buren United States judge for the district of New Jersey. At that period and for a number of years thereafter, the business of the court was small in volume, and in the performance of his judicial duties, which were not onerous, he gave general satisfaction. The outbreak of the Civil War caused a large accession of work, litigation in all the federal courts becoming heavy, and his health broke down under the sudden strain, but he remained on the bench till his death at Paterson, Dec. 10, 1862.

As judge he had little opportunity of showing his qualifications for judicial office. A few of his opinions delivered during the year in which he was chancellor are reported in Green's *Chancery Reports,* vol. III, but no cases of any major importance came before him when on the district court bench. However, though he had no pretense to being a learned lawyer, he was energetic, impartial, and dignified. For a number of years he was a leader of the Democratic party in the state, and possessed great influence in its counsels. He was instrumental in procuring for Paterson its city charter, Mar. 19, 1851, and was the author of *The City of Paterson, its Past, Present and Future* (1856). His wife was Sidney, the daughter of Col. John Stotesbury of New York. His second son, Edward Nicoll Dickerson [*q.v.*], became a leading member of the New York bar.

[C. J. Werner, *Geneal. of Long Island Families* (1919), p. 11; E. Q. Keasbey, *The Courts and Lawyers of N. J.* (1912), II, 672, 801; F. B. Lee, *N. J. as a Colony and as a State* (1902), III, 327–44; *Biog. Dir. Am. Congress, 1774–1927* (1928).]   H. W. H. K.

DICKEY, THEOPHILUS LYLE (Oct. 2, 1811–July 22, 1885), jurist, soldier, was descended from John Dickey, a native of northern Ireland, who, early in the eighteenth century, emigrated to Virginia and settled in North Carolina. John Dickey's grandson, James Henry Dickey, a Presbyterian minister, married Polly De Pew of Halifax County, Va., and their son, Theophilus Lyle Dickey, was born at Paris, Bourbon County, Ky. The family moved to Ohio in 1814, and Dickey's early education was received in the country schools there and in Kentucky. In 1826 he entered Ohio University at

Athens where he spent four years, proceeding thence to Miami University at Oxford, Ohio, and graduating there with honors in 1831. He then taught school in Ohio and Kentucky for two years. In 1834 he removed to Macomb, McDonough County, Ill., and studied law, being admitted to the bar in 1835. For a short time he practised law at Macomb, but in 1836 went to Rushville, where, in addition to his legal work, he edited a newspaper and became largely interested in real estate. The following year, owing to a financial panic, he lost everything, in addition to being saddled with a heavy debt which embarrassed him for many years, but which he finally paid in full. In 1839 he moved to Ottawa, Ill., which became his permanent home. Here he built up a large practise, acquiring a wide reputation as a skilful advocate and sound lawyer. At the outbreak of the war with Mexico he raised a company for the 1st Illinois Infantry, was commissioned captain, and saw service in Mexico, but was compelled to retire on account of ill health, whereupon he resumed practise in Ottawa. In 1848 he was elected judge of the circuit court for his district, and remained on the bench four years, resigning in 1852, and opening an office in Chicago in 1854. In the latter year he was a delegate to the first Republican state convention at Bloomington, and in 1856 was an Independent candidate for Congress, but withdrew. During this period he retained his residence in Ottawa, and resumed practise there in 1858, having finally paid off his old debts. In 1858 and 1860 he was an ardent supporter of Stephen A. Douglas against Lincoln, speaking throughout the state on behalf of the former. In 1861 when the Civil War broke out, he raised the 4th Illinois Cavalry and became its colonel. Joining Grant at Cairo in December, he took part in the capture of Fort Henry, led the advance at Fort Donelson, and was present at Shiloh. In 1862 he became a member of Grant's staff and was placed in command at Memphis, Tenn., subsequently becoming commander of Grant's cavalry division. He suggested and organized Grierson's Raid in 1863, but in the latter part of that year resigned his command and returned to Ottawa. In 1866 he was nominated for congressman-at-large for Illinois against Gen. Logan. In 1868 he became assistant attorney-general of the United States, having the conduct of all suits in the Court of Claims, and in the course of his duties appeared frequently in the United States Supreme Court. In this capacity he displayed great ability and efficiency, but was compelled to resign in 1870 owing to ill health. He thereupon resumed practise at Ottawa but in 1873 moved again to Chicago, where he was in August 1874 appointed corporation counsel. In December 1875 he was elected a judge of the supreme court of Illinois to fill a vacancy and in 1879 was reëlected as an Independent, remaining on the bench till his death, which occurred at Atlantic City, N. J. He was married twice: first, on Dec. 6, 1831, to Juliet Evans of Hillsboro, Ohio, who died on Dec. 31, 1854; and second, in the summer of 1870, to Mrs. Beulah Hirst.

A contemporary describes him as "a man of very superior legal ability, without very great learning, but who is a natural lawyer" (F. B. Wilkie, *Sketches and Notices of the Chicago Bar,* 1871). A brilliant advocate, he achieved his success by means of a singular forcefulness and simplicity of appeal, never attempting oratory. He possessed a remarkably retentive memory and great resource. On the bench he exhibited clearness of perception and an independence of thought which did not detract from the soundness of his opinions—very few of them being reversed on appeal. Possessing great charm of manner, kindly, considerate and generous to a fault, he was extremely popular with all classes.

[See *Proc. Ill. State Bar Asso.,* 1886, p. 62; 121 *Ill.,* p. 9; *Bench and Bar of Chicago* (1883); J. D. Caton, *Early Bench and Bar of Ill.* (1893), p. 147; John M. Palmer, ed., *Bench and Bar of Ill.* (1899), I, 61; *Jour. Ill. State Hist. Soc.,* Jan. 1911; *Daily Inter Ocean* (Chicago), July 23, 1885; *Official Records (Army)*; J. Dickey Templeton, *Dickey Genealogy* (1918).]

H. W. H. K.

DICKIE, GEORGE WILLIAM (July 17, 1844–Aug. 17, 1918), engineer and ship-builder, was born in Arbroath, Scotland, the son of William and Margaret (Watson) Dickie. In earlier years at Perth, Scotland, and subsequently on a strip of land bordering the Tay at Arbroath which is still known as Dickies Beach, at least five generations of Dickies had built wooden ships after the practise of the day. Dickie's education, aside from what he received at home, comprised three years in the parochial school, under an Oxford graduate who not only took care of the stated curriculum but who acted as town clerk and city engineer as well, and held evening classes in navigation. From him the boy acquired a love for study which continued throughout life, and through him he met Dr. Thomas Dick, the author of several works on science and philosophy which had great vogue in the middle decades of the nineteenth century. The latter gave Dickie an opportunity to meet Michael Faraday and Sir David Brewster, a meeting which awakened the youth's ambition and was an inspiration to him in later years. Dick also planted in him his life-long interest in astronomy.

The trend toward the use of iron and steel for shipbuilding, which developed in the late sixties, forced upon many wooden-ship builders a competition difficult to meet, and the Dickie family came to the United States and to San Francisco late in 1869. There Dickie first found employment with the Pacific Gas Company in the design, construction, and erection of a gas plant; then, in the employ of the Risdon Iron Works, he was engaged in other important engineering undertakings of an ever widening scope. He was interested in pioneer enterprises and in new and bold projects. It is claimed that he designed the first successful triple-expansion engine built in the United States, and the first Scotch marine boiler built on the Pacific Coast. He was also a successful designer of marine compound engines for steamers navigating Pacific waters. These achievements in the field of marine design brought him into contact with Irving M. Scott of the Union Iron Works; he became a member of that organization, and was its general manager from 1883 to 1905. During that time he was responsible for the construction of some eleven vessels of the then new steel navy—most notable among them being the battleship *Oregon* which made a name for itself by its record voyage around Cape Horn at the beginning of the Spanish-American War, and the cruiser *Olympia* which served as Dewey's flagship at Manila Bay. He was also responsible for the design and construction of many ships for the merchant marine and for a wide variety of other engineering work carried on by his company, including the dome of the Lick Observatory, designed and built under his direction. With the entrance of the United States into the World War in 1917, he offered his services to the government and was appointed chief inspector at the Moore & Scott Yards in Oakland, Cal., in which position he was active up to the time of his death.

He was a prolific writer on engineering subjects, especially in the field of marine construction. He took an active part in the organization of the American Society of Naval Architects and Marine Engineers and was a frequent contributor to its *Transactions* and a regular attendant at its annual meetings. He was also a member of the American Society of Mechanical Engineers and served a term as vice-president of that organization. His special contribution to his day and age is to be found in the example which he set of high standards of life both professionally and personally and more directly in the pioneer work which he did in many fields of engineering design and construction. Through work of this character carried out to practical and useful application and often discussed and presented in the form of papers before the societies of which he was a member, he made a deep and lasting impression on engineering art and practise, especially on the Pacific Coast. He was a man of wide vision and of many interests outside that of his profession. Most notable perhaps were his interest in astronomy already referred to, and his interest as a bibliophile in the collection of books and of rare and beautiful bindings. One of the tragedies of his life was the loss of his library of rare and precious bindings and of rare first editions in the San Francisco fire of 1906. He was a man of deep and lasting friendships, kindly and sympathetic in his relations to those with whom he came in contact, but not sparing in helpful and searching criticism where he judged such to be called for. On Aug. 5, 1873, he married Anna Jack, born in Denny, Scotland, on her mother's side coming from a long line of Presbyterian preachers. After her death, he was married a second time, in 1901, to Louise Barney. He died as he would have wished, in harness, active to the last, and left an enduring record both as an engineer and as a good citizen and a kind friend.

[*Trans. Am. Soc. Mech. Engineers,* XL (1919), 1152; *Trans. Soc. Naval Architects and Marine Engineers,* vol. XXVI (1918); C. E. Grunsky in *Pacific Marine Rev.,* Sept. 1918, and in *Jour. Am. Soc. Mech. Engineers,* Oct. 1918; *Who's Who in America,* 1918–19; *San Francisco Chronicle,* Aug. 18, 1918; information as to certain facts, including names of Dickie's parents, from a son, A. J. Dickie of San Francisco; personal acquaintance.]   W. F. D.

DICKINS, JOHN (c. Aug. 24, 1747–Sept. 27, 1798), clergyman of the Methodist Episcopal Church, and prominent among those who laid its foundations in this country, was born in London, received a good education, and came to America some years before the Revolution. He was converted in 1774, began evangelistic work in Virginia, and was admitted to the itinerant ministry on trial at the Conference of 1777, bringing to the Methodist movement an intellectual equipment, an interest in literature and learning, and an administrative wisdom, which few of his contemporaries possessed. He traveled extensively in North Carolina and Virginia until 1781, when the Conference Minutes list him among those "who desist from travelling." On Apr. 5, 1783, Asbury, then in North Carolina, records: "This day I prevailed with Brother Dickens to go to New-York, where I expect him to be far more useful than in his present station" (*Journal of Rev. Francis Asbury,* 1852, I, 458). Here, with the exception of 1785, he labored until 1789, rehabilitating John Street Church, cradle of Methodism in America, which the removal of Loyalists, and other war conditions, had weakened. He became an intimate friend and counselor of Asbury. They were "like unto Jonathan and David, . . . one in hand, mind, and mutual affection" (Ezekiel Cooper, *A Funeral Discourse, on the Death of that Eminent Man, the Late Reverend John Dickens*, 1799). He was the first to meet and advise with Dr. Coke when the latter arrived as Wesley's emissary in 1784. At the "Christmas Conference" held the same year, he was one of the leading spirits, offering the resolution which constituted the Methodist Episcopal Church in America, the name of which he himself had suggested. At this Conference he was ordained deacon, but was not made elder until Sept. 16, 1786 (Asbury's *Journal*, I, 518). He was one of the few married men in the itinerancy, having married Elizabeth Yancey of North Carolina (John Lednum, *A History of the Rise of Methodism in America*, 1859, p. 198); and the text of Asbury's ordination sermon included the admonition: "Even so must their (the deacons') wives be grave, not slanderers, sober, faithful in all things." With Thomas Morrell he was delegated by the Conference of 1789 to wait on President Washington with a copy of the bishops' congratulatory address. He also accompanied them when the President received them and made his reply.

Perhaps Dickins's most important contribution to Methodism was his work in behalf of education. He was associated with Asbury and Coke in the founding of Cokesbury College, and when the Conference of 1789 established the Methodist Book Concern, he offered the loan of all his savings, £120, about $600, to finance it. He was appointed Book Steward, being then pastor of the church in Philadelphia, St. George's. During the nine years of his management, which included the superintendency of printing, binding, and distribution, he made the Book Concern a permanent and increasingly valuable institution. Besides issuing more than one hundred and fourteen thousand copies of books and pamphlets, he published the *Arminian Magazine* (1789–90) and the *Methodist Magazine* (January 1797– August 1798). Although urged to seek safety, he continued at his work during the yellow fever epidemic of 1798, and died of that disease. "What I have greatly feared for years," Asbury wrote, "hath now taken place. Dickins, the generous, the just, the faithful, skillful Dickins, is dead!"

[Besides references above and general histories of Methodism, see S. A. Seaman, *Annals of N. Y. Methodism* (1892); W. F. Whitlock, *The Story of the Book Concerns* (1903); H. C. Jennings, *The Methodist Book Concern* (1924); W. B. Sprague, *Annals Am. Pulpit*, vol. VII (1859); *Beams of Light on Early Methodism in America* (1887), comp. by G. A. Phoebus; J. B. Wakeley, *Lost Chapters Recovered from the Early Hist. of Am. Methodism* (1858); G. W. Archer, *An Authentic Hist. of Cokesbury Coll.* (1894).] H. E. S.

DICKINSON, ANSON (Apr. 19, 1779–Mar. 9, 1852), portrait-painter in miniature and oils, was born in Milton, Litchfield County, Conn. He was the eldest son of Oliver Dickinson, Jr. (1757–1847), who is known to have painted a few portraits in oils. Oliver's wife was Anna Landon of Long Island. Of their ten children, Anson and his brother Daniel who was born in 1795, seem to have carried on the artistic tradition of the family. Anson was apprenticed to a silversmith and worked at that craft until, toward the turn of the century, he began to interest himself in painting. Of his early work in oils little is known. About 1804 he commenced painting portraits in miniature. At this time he was living in New York City, and had come under the influence of Edward Malbone, to whom he sat for a portrait in 1804. The story is told that during one of the sittings the funeral of Alexander Hamilton passed the house. Dickinson would have gone to the window to look out, but Malbone was too intent on his work to allow his sitter even this respite. In 1805 Dickinson went to Albany, where he remained until 1810. It was during this time that William Dunlap met him and perceived his work to be "indicative of talent." By 1811 Dickinson had returned to New York and was established as a leader in his profession there. In 1818 he visited Canada where he met and married Sarah B——, a woman of French descent. They had no children of their own, but later, while living in New York, adopted two children whose father was an Englishman named Walker. From 1818 to 1840 Dickinson seems to have wandered a good deal, working for a time in Boston. After 1840 he lived first in New Haven and later in Hartford. He died in 1852 at his birthplace, Milton.

Among the most noteworthy of Dickinson's patrons and sitters was Gilbert Stuart, of whom three miniatures by Dickinson are in existence (one in the possession of the New York Historical Society). Other prominent persons who sat to him were Robert Fulton, Archbishop Du Bois, Gov. Oliver Wolcott, Chancellor Livingston, the Seymours of Litchfield, and Gov. Sam Houston of Texas. Other portraits now in existence include those of Robert Dorlon, Dr. Jonathan Hall, J. W. Gale, and Mrs. Robert Watts (the last two now in the Metropolitan Museum of Art in New York City). At its best Dickinson's work is characterized by capable draftsmanship, as in the miniature of Dorlon, which is now in the Dupuy collection. His accomplishment was very uneven, however, and it is chiefly as a colorist, and, especially in this aspect of his work, as a follower and imitator of Malbone, that he is distinguished.

[William Dunlap, *Hist. of the Rise and Progress of the Arts of Design in the U. S.* (1834; new ed., 1918); H. W. French, *Art and Artists in Conn.* (1879); T. Bolton, *Early Am. Portrait Painters in Miniature* (1921); H. B. Wehle and T. Bolton, *Am. Miniature* (1927), containing a colored reproduction of a miniature by Dickinson; A. T. Gesner, *The Dickinson Family of Milton and Litchfield* (1913); *History of the Dickinson Family* (Amherst, 1884); Metropolitan Mus., *Cat. of an Exhibition of Miniatures Painted in America 1720–1850* (1927).]   L. T. B.

DICKINSON, CHARLES MONROE (Nov. 15, 1842–July 3, 1924), newspaperman, diplomat, the son of Richard and Bessie (Rea) Dickinson, was born on a farm near Lowville, N. Y. The only educational advantages he had as a youth were afforded by the public schools, Fairfield Seminary, and Lowville Academy. By his fifteenth year he was doing a man's work assisting his father who was a farmer and miller. A tenth of the first year's wages which he earned in this way was invested in a copy of Webster's *Unabridged Dictionary*. His diligent study of this volume was an important factor in preparation for his literary work. For two years after leaving Lowville Academy he taught at Haverstraw-on-the-Hudson, where, in 1863, he composed "The Children," a poem which became widely popular and is included in most collections of American verse.

He began the study of law in the office of the distinguished Daniel S. Dickinson [q.v.] at Binghamton, N. Y., in 1864. The following year he was admitted to the bar and practised in Cameron County, Pa. Returning to Binghamton, he began law practise with Giles W. Hotchkiss, whose daughter, Bessie Virginia, he married on Mar. 24, 1867. His advancement in the law was rapid, resulting in the establishment of his office in New York City where he conducted a large practise until 1877 when the great volume of his work broke his health and compelled him to abandon his profession. Retiring to Binghamton, he lived an outdoor life while improving the estate which he purchased there. In 1878 he resumed his public career by acquiring a controlling interest in the *Binghamton Republican*, which continued under his management until 1911. As a newspaperman he took a prominent part in bringing about the organization of the present Associated Press. Appointed consul general to Turkey by President McKinley in 1897, in 1901 he received an additional appointment as diplomatic agent to Bulgaria. In that capacity, he obtained the release of Ellen M. Stone [q.v.], American missionary, whose kidnapping by Bulgarian brigands was one of the most widely discussed events of the time. He was appointed consul general at large with jurisdiction over consulates of the entire Middle East in 1906, and in the same year was appointed on the board to draft regulations for the entire consular service. He retired from public service in 1908 because of the illness of his wife, who died in that year. On Feb. 2, 1910, he married Alice Bond Minard of Poughkeepsie. The closing years of his life were spent in Binghamton where he devoted himself to business and literary interests. His literary work includes: *History of the Dickinson Family* (1885); *The Children and Other Verses* (1889); *Political History of New York State—Cleveland to Hughes* (1911); *Political History of New York State—From the Colonial Period* (1914); *The Children After Fifty Years in Little Verses and Big Names* (1915); "The Greatest Miracle," in *Liber Scriptorum* of the Authors Club, 1921.

[The best account of Dickinson's life is to be found in the *Binghamton Press*, June 5, 1920. Additional information is available in accounts of his funeral in the *Binghamton Press and Leader* and *Binghamton Sun*, July 7, 1924. A partial record is included in *Biographical Review . . . of Broome County, N. Y.* (1894). A portrait and complete account of his activities are available in W. F. Seward, ed., *Binghamton and Broome County, N. Y., A History*, vol. III (1924). E. C. Stedman's *Lib. of Am. Lit.* includes a reprint of "The Children" (vol. X, 1889, p. 129) and a brief biographical sketch (vol. XI, 1890, p. 502). See also *Who's Who in America*, 1899–1925.]   D. W. M.

DICKINSON, DANIEL STEVENS (Sept. 11, 1800–Apr. 12, 1866), lawyer, politician, was born at Goshen, Conn., the fourth of eight children of Daniel T. and Mary (Caulkins) Dickinson. Both parents were natives of Connecticut and of English descent, the father being a farmer in moderate circumstances. They moved in 1806 to Chenango County, N. Y., settling at the present Guilford. There young Daniel did the usual boy's work on the farm and attended the local public schools. While apprenticed to a clothier he managed to study (alone) Latin, mathematics, and more or less of general science. For five years he taught in public and private schools, studying law and surveying at the same time. Continuing his legal studies in the office of Clark & Clapp, at the county seat, Norwich, he was admitted to the bar in 1828 and began practise at Guilford, where he was postmaster. Three years later he moved to Binghamton, where he soon acquired a good practise and became prominent in the Democratic party. When Binghamton was incorporated (1834) Dickinson was elected its first president. The next year he was a member of the national convention which nominated Van Buren and Johnson. From 1837 to 1841 he was one of the Democratic leaders in the state Senate, taking much interest in such matters as banking reform, railroads, and canals. Defeated for lieutenant-governor in 1840, he declined to be a candidate in 1842 yet was nominated and elected. Besides presiding over the Senate this office entailed the presidency of the court of errors and membership on the canal board, to both of which Dickinson rendered valuable service. By this time he was recognized as one of the leading conservative Democrats of New York, along with Silas Wright, Horatio Seymour, and the like. At the national convention of 1844 he cast the vote of New York for Polk. When the state convention nominated Silas Wright over Gov. W. C. Bouck, Dickinson refused the nomination for lieutenant-governor, despite Wright's urging. Upon the resignation of United States Senator N. P. Tallmadge (December 1844), Gov. Bouck appointed Dickinson for the rest of the term. The legislature promptly confirmed this nomination and elected him for the ensuing term (1845–51). For much of this time he was chairman of the finance committee, being recognized as one of the leading Democrats in the Senate. He spoke upon the annexation of Texas, the occupation of Oregon, the Mexican War, the Wilmot Proviso (which he opposed), and the Clayton-Bulwer Treaty. As a member of the Committee of Thirteen he did such valiant service for the compromise measures of 1850 as to evoke the praises of both Clay and Webster. In December 1847 he introduced some resolutions which practically embodied the doctrine of "squatter sovereignty." He was a member of the national Democratic conventions of 1848 and 1852. After leaving the Senate, he devoted himself to the law, occasionally delivering addresses at fairs, centennials, corner-stone and dedication ceremonies, and before temperance and literary societies. In the campaigns of 1852 and 1856 he took the stump for the Democratic ticket. President Pierce nominated him as collector of the port of New York (1853), and the Senate confirmed him without reference, but he declined the position. He hoped to receive the nomination for president in 1860, but never got over sixteen votes in the convention. After the secession of South Carolina he strove for reconciliation with the South, holding the North responsible for secession, but after the firing on Fort Sumter he vigorously supported the government, making hundreds of speeches in Pennsylvania, New York, and New England and doing much to stimulate enlistment in

his own district. Both the 89th New York Infantry and the battery recruited at Binghamton were named for him. His earnest support of the government procured him the nomination and triumphant election as attorney-general on the "Union" ticket in 1861. The next year he sought in vain the Republican nomination for United States senator. Appointed and confirmed on the Northwest Boundary Commission in 1863, he declined this office as well as Gov. Fenton's proffer of a seat on the state court of appeals. He was a delegate to the Union convention of 1864, where, though he would have preferred another candidate to Lincoln, he supported the latter loyally. On the first ballot for vice-president Dickinson received 108 votes. In 1865 he was appointed federal district attorney for the southern district of New York, and served until his death the following year in New York City. He was married in 1822 to Lydia, the daughter of Colby Knapp, a physician of Chenango County. Dickinson was not only an able lawyer—as president of the court of errors he wrote some able opinions—but a skilful debater; clear, forceful, at times scathingly sarcastic.

[*Speeches and Correspondence, etc. of the Late Daniel S. Dickinson of N. Y.* (1867), ed. by his brother, John R. Dickinson, contains a biographical sketch. Besides the newspapers of the period, E. H. Roberts, *New York* (1887), and D. S. Alexander, *A Political Hist. of the State of N. Y.*, vols. II (1906) and III (1909), should be consulted.]   M. L. B., Jr.

DICKINSON, DONALD McDONALD (Jan. 17, 1846–Oct. 15, 1917), lawyer, postmaster-general, was born at Port Ontario, Oswego County, N. Y., the son of Col. Asa C. and Minerva (Holmes) Dickinson. One of his boasts was that his paternal grandfather and great-grandfather and his maternal grandfather and great-grandfather were all natives of American soil. His ancestors had an enviable record of service in the Revolutionary army and in the formation of the federal government. His father, as a young man, explored the shores of Lakes Erie, Huron, and Michigan in a birch-bark canoe and was greatly impressed with the future of the country. In 1848 he moved with his family to Michigan, settling on an island in the St. Clair River. Four years later he removed to Detroit. Don M. Dickinson attended the public schools of Detroit but was prepared for college under the instruction of private tutors. He entered the Law School of the University of Michigan at Ann Arbor and was graduated with the class of 1867. Admitted to the bar in the same year, he entered at once upon a brilliant and successful career. He gained a reputation as one of the leading lawyers of the Middle West and was frequently called upon to argue important cases before the Supreme Court of the United States. Worthy of particular mention in this connection are the Telephone Appeals case, in which his argument for Drawbaugh is printed in full in the stenographic record (126 *U. S.,* 329–73), and the Homestead cases (155 *U. S.,* 356–88). In the latter cases he successfully defended the rights of homesteaders upon lands covered by unearned public grants to railroads, thereby securing to many poor farmers their homes and lands.

He was the second Michigan Democrat—the first being Lewis Cass—to rise to a position of national political importance. His political career began in 1872, when he was chosen to serve as secretary of the Democratic state central committee in the Greeley campaign. Attributing the overwhelming defeat of Greeley to the Democratic party, he wrote to Dr. Foster Pratt, chairman of the state committee, declaring that Greeley's defeat broke any link which might have bound the progressive men of the party to it, that he would never vote or act with the party again, but would await the new party which should carry forward the living principles of the dead leader, Greeley. However, he did not carry his threat into execution. The leadership of Gov. Tilden of New York quickened the party into new life, and the campaign of 1876 found Dickinson in the position of chairman of the Democratic state central committee. In 1880 he was chosen a member of the Democratic national committee for Michigan and served in that capacity until 1885. He had early formed a high opinion of Grover Cleveland, and his support of Cleveland for the presidency marked the definite beginning of a close and enduring political and personal friendship between the two men. After Cleveland's election, there being no Democratic senator from Michigan, the President recognized Dickinson as the titular head of the party in that state and consulted him on all appointments to office affecting Michigan men. Dickinson did not desire a political office for himself, but when William F. Vilas was transferred from the position of postmaster-general to that of secretary of the interior, he accepted the postmaster-generalship upon the urgent request of President Cleveland. He was nominated for the office Dec. 6, 1887, was confirmed and commissioned Jan. 16, 1888, and entered upon his duties the next day (*Executive Register of the United States,* 1903, p. 250). He served until the close of the administration in 1889. In his honor the Democratic legislature of Michigan in 1891 organized a new county in the Upper Peninsula and named it

Dickinson County (*Public Acts,* 1891, pp. 98 ff.). In 1892 he took a leading part in the campaign which elected Cleveland to the presidency for the second time. He declined an unsolicited offer of a cabinet position, preferring to devote himself to the profession of law and to private life. During Cleveland's second administration and in his opposition to the free-silver wing of the party, Dickinson gave him unfailing support. He opposed the nomination of Bryan in 1896, and in 1900, when Bryan was again nominated, advocated the reëlection of President McKinley. In 1912 he again showed his independence in politics by sending a telegram to Roosevelt, dated Oct. 16, pledging to him his unqualified support "because of the reactionary teachings of the two old parties" (Fitzgibbon, *post*).

Twice in his later years he was called to the service of the government in his legal capacity. In 1896 he was senior counsel for the United States before the international high commission on the Bering Sea claims (*Bering Sea. Fur Seal Arbitration,* etc., 1897). He was the member for the United States of the court of arbitration formed in 1902 to adjust a controversy between the United States and the Republic of Salvador, arising from a claim against Salvador presented by an American company which had a concession for the collection of port duties at the port of El Triunfo. The majority of the commission, Dickinson and Sir Henry Strong, chief justice of the Dominion of Canada, decided against Salvador. Señor Don José Rosa Pacas, the representative of Salvador, declined to sign the award (see *Papers Relating to the Foreign Relations of the United States, 1902,* pp. 838–73). For several years prior to his death at his home in Trenton, Mich., Dickinson lived in retirement. He was a man of exalted character, loyal to friends or to a cause, and always ready to fight for what he deemed to be right (Reed, *post,* p. 142). On June 15, 1869, he was married to Frances Platt, daughter of Dr. Alonzo Platt of Grand Rapids, Mich.

[See *Who's Who in America,* 1899–1917; *Am. Biog. Hist.* (Mich. Vol., 1878), pp. 42–43; C. M. Burton, *The City of Detroit, Mich.* (1922), IV, 6–9; *Chronography of Notable Events in the Hist. of the Northwest Territory and Wayne County* (1890), comp. by Fred Carlisle, pp. 357–62; Silas Farmer, *Hist. of Detroit and Wayne County* (1890), II, 1114–19; Chas. Moore, *Hist. of Mich.* (1915), II, 668–69; *Bench and Bar of Mich.* (1897), ed. by G. I. Reed, pp. 138–42. The most comprehensive account of Dickinson's political activities is given by John Fitzgibbon. "Don M. Dickinson One of the State's Two Great Democrats," *Detroit News,* Oct. 17, 1917. His papers are in the possession of his family in Detroit. His letters to Cleveland were sent to Princeton for use in R. McElroy's *Grover Cleveland* (1923), and several were printed in the second volume of that work. For his suggestions concerning the P. O.

Dept., see his article, "Progress and the Post," *North Am. Rev.*, Oct. 1889.]   E. S. B—n.

DICKINSON, EMILY ELIZABETH (Dec. 10, 1830–May 15, 1886), poet, was born, lived, and died in Amherst, Mass. Her father, Edward Dickinson, was a leading lawyer of Amherst, a member at various times of the state legislature and of Congress, and treasurer of Amherst College. In this last office he was succeeded by his son, William Austin, who in 1856 married Susan Gilbert and occupied a house built for him next door to his father's. Emily's mother, who was Emily Norcross of Monson, and younger sister, Lavinia, completed the family circle. Edward Dickinson, though austere in his domestic manners, demanded that his children remain about him. Neither daughter married, and the fact that the family circle was not broken until her father's death in 1874 made it possible for Emily to protract her childhood relation to her parents almost to the end of her own life.

She received rather more than the normal education of a New England girl of good family at that time, in the public schools, at Amherst Academy, where the encouragement given her by the young principal, Leonard Humphrey, strongly affected her awakening mind, and for one year, 1847–48, at Mount Holyoke Female Seminary in the neighboring village of South Hadley. Among her schoolmates were several girls of marked individuality, including her life-long friend Helen Fiske, later Helen Hunt Jackson. Emily Dickinson was noted for her wit and love of drollery, which found expression in comic valentines sent to members of her brother's college circle and in humorous squibs contributed to a manuscript magazine circulated at the Academy. She was fond of music, of country walks, and of gardening, joined a Shakespeare club, and attended dancing parties surreptitiously organized by the girls of the village. In her own home and in the homes of various college dignitaries she met preachers, missionaries, men of affairs, and writers. Among these last, Samuel Bowles, the proprietor and editor of the *Springfield Republican,* and his wife, and Dr. and Mrs. Josiah Gilbert Holland were intimate friends of the family. In the social life of the village, then devoid of standardized amusements except for the annual college commencements and the autumn cattle shows, Emily took part freely until her middle twenties. Gradually, however, as her individuality asserted itself, she became increasingly impatient of all formal occasions.

During the spring of 1854, Emily with her mother and sister spent a few weeks in Washington, where her father was attending Congress, and on the return journey stopped to visit a friend in Philadelphia. It is supposed that at this time she met the man to whom her love poems were later addressed, but the circumstances of this episode are still far from clear. According to her niece and biographer, Mme. Bianchi, she fell in love with a young preacher and awakened in him an answering passion that made him reckless of his ties of family and profession. Upon learning that he was a married man, she fled to Amherst and finally refused his proposal to elope (*Life and Letters,* pp. 45 ff.; *Further Poems,* pp. xvi–xx). Miss Josephine Pollitt (*post*), offers the inherently improbable suggestion that Emily's lover was Lieut. Edward Bissell Hunt, the husband of her friend Helen Fiske. Local tradition perpetuates the story that Emily wished to marry an eligible young man, but refused him because of her father's opposition to the match (Clara B. Green, *Bookman,* November 1924).

For the rest of her life she lived quietly at home, never leaving Amherst except to go to Boston for the care of her eyes in 1864 and again in the following year. However important the frustration of her love may be as a background for her poetry, it should not be thought of as wrecking her life or even as the direct cause of her preference for solitude. "She lived in seclusion from no love-disappointment" is the categorical statement of Mrs. Todd, her ablest editor (*Poems,* Second Series, p. 8). Most of her early friends had married and left town. Imperceptibly she drifted into a habit of seclusion, finding her satisfactions in the hills and sunsets, her garden, the companionship of her dog, and "the little toil of love" of her household routine. Her retirement may in part be explained by her increasing preoccupation with poetry, which she says in a letter to her literary mentor, Thomas Wentworth Higginson, began in the winter of 1861–62. Her desire for "polar privacy," indulged by a brother and sister who in their own ways were no respecters of convention, deepened as the years passed. After the shock of her father's death, which was followed a year later by the invalidism of her mother, she immured herself in the house and showed a morbid dread of being seen by strangers. But until she was stricken by illness two years before her death, she continued to perform her part in the exacting duties of her New England housekeeping. She has described herself in a letter to Higginson: "I . . . am small, like the wren; and my hair is bold, like the chestnut burr; and my eyes, like the sherry in the glass that the guest leaves."

Emily Dickinson, like Emerson, belonged to

the generation when the frost was coming out of the Puritan soil. Her intense inner life recognized no law save that of her own nature. Though her days to outward seeming were utterly eventless, her brief, breathless poems, written in the solitude of her room and guarded like a secret journal, show that her mind was filled with events, with tiny ecstasies set in motion by home and garden incidents, with deep and candid intuitions of her own states of consciousness, with speculations on the timeless mysteries of love and death suggested by her reading, by her quick imaginative sympathy, and by her piercing memories.

Only two of her poems were printed during her lifetime, neither with her consent. One was sent to the *Springfield Republican* (Feb. 14, 1866) by her sister-in-law. Mrs. Jackson was responsible for the inclusion of the other, without signature, in G. P. Lathrop's *A Masque of Poets* (1878). After her death her poems were found among her papers and by a fortunate decision of her sister Lavinia were preserved and published in three series: *Poems* (1890), *Poems* (1891), *Poems* (1896). A fourth volume, *The Single Hound* (1914), contains the messages in swift, spontaneous verse that she was in the habit of sending across the lawn to her sister-in-law, and a fifth, *Further Poems* (1929), includes a series of love poems reflecting her frustrated attachment. The first four are reprinted in *Complete Poems of Emily Dickinson* (1924).

[The prefaces to the several volumes of poems listed above contain some biographical information. The *Letters of Emily Dickinson*, published in 1894 by Mrs. Mabel Loomis Todd and preceded by Col. Higginson's "Emily Dickinson's Letters," *Atlantic Monthly*, Oct. 1891, have been supplemented by Mme. Bianchi's "Selections from the Unpublished Letters of Emily Dickinson," *Atlantic Monthly*, Jan. 1915, and M. H. Barney's "Fragments from Emily Dickinson to her Brother's Family," *Atlantic Monthly*, June 1927. Martha Dickinson Bianchi's *Life and Letters of Emily Dickinson* (1924) reprints material given in the earlier collection with some additions and many omissions; the early printings of this book (1924–29) are marred by gross inaccuracies. Josephine Pollitt's *Emily Dickinson: The Human Background of her Poetry* (1930) is fully documented. Manuscript letters and poems of Emily Dickinson, some unpublished, are in the Galatea Collection of the Boston Public Library. Important studies of her character have been written by Gamaliel Bradford, *Portraits of Am. Women* (1919), Conrad Aiken, preface to his *Selected Poems of Emily Dickinson* (1924), and Katherine Bregy, *Catholic World*, Dec. 1924.]   G.F.W.

DICKINSON, JACOB McGAVOCK (Jan. 30, 1851–Dec. 13, 1928), lawyer, secretary of war, son of Henry and Anna (McGavock) Dickinson, was born in Columbus, Miss. His father was long a chancery judge (a vice chancellor, 1843–54) of the state; his mother's grandfather was Felix Grundy [*q.v.*]. When only fourteen

years of age Dickinson served as a private in the Confederate cavalry. After the war his parents moved to Nashville, Tenn., the home of his mother's family. He took a college course, graduating with distinction, in the University of Nashville (A.B. 1871, A.M. 1872), briefly studied law at Columbia College and then continued his studies abroad—chiefly in law—in Leipzig and in Paris. To the end of his life he retained a fair command of the classics. He spoke German easily, and French and German books were conspicuous in his library. After admission to the Tennessee bar, in 1874, he made his home in Nashville until 1899, when he moved to Chicago. In his profession he attained a standing that was very high, and of stainless repute. His most striking characteristics in the preparation and argument of cases were a strict attention to details and to truth. He scorned resort to a specious argument. Perhaps not unnaturally, therefore, although he was of commanding physique and of distinguished bearing and manners, he was not particularly notable as a jury lawyer. The presidency of the Bar Association of Tennessee (1889–90), four appointments for temporary service as a member of the supreme court of the state (1891, 1892, 1893), and two years of service as an assistant attorney-general of the United States (1895–97), marked the high regard which he enjoyed among his fellows. In the early years of practise he gained as a client the Louisville & Nashville Railroad, of which he ultimately became the general attorney (1897–99); passing from its service to that of the Illinois Central, as general solicitor (1899–1901) and general counsel (1901–09). He was not, however, a mere specialist in railroad law, but a general practitioner of notable all-round ability. In 1907–08 he was president of the American Bar Association. Public life called him briefly in 1903, when he served with distinction as one of counsel (making the closing argument) for the United States before the Alaskan Boundary Tribunal; and his continued interest, thereafter, in international problems was manifested in his participation in the organization, in 1906, of the American Society of International Law, which he served as a member of the Executive Council (1907–10) and as a vice-president (1910 onward). In 1909 he became secretary of war (March 1909–May 1911) in the cabinet of his old-time friend and professional associate, President Taft. This office was abandoned when his family suffered financial reverses. Later, he served the government as a special assistant attorney-general in the prosecution of the United States Steel Corporation (1913), and in important labor cases (1922); and from 1915 to 1917 was receiver of the Rock Island Lines, and markedly successful. After this he gradually abandoned practise. In 1927–28 he was president of the Izaak Walton League at a critical moment in its history. A life-time devotion to fishing and hunting had made him appreciative of the need, and sympathetic to the conservation purposes, of that organization. His services to it illustrated as well as any task of his life his wisdom, force, and winning personality. He owned and gave much time to a plantation, and a stock farm of national repute.

Dickinson belonged by family tradition in the Democratic party, and long served it actively; but voted, apparently, more often as a Republican than a Democrat after the Bryan campaign of 1896. He was devoted and ever loyal to friends; notably sociable, fond of converse and companionship, though not of conventional sports and amusements; devoted to reading, and widely informed. Rather than compete with friends he rejected what was at least a probability of appointment to the federal bench. High spirits, a keen humor, great stores of anecdotes, and varied knowledge made him a prized companion. Temperance characterized his personal habits; tolerance, his opinions—except of intolerance, as in some forms of social legislation. He was married (on Apr. 20, 1876) to Martha Overton who bore him three sons, two of whom survived him. Before his burial, in Nashville, his body lay in state in the capitol.

[Blewett Lee, "Jacob McGavock Dickinson: 1851–1928," *Jour. Am. Bar. Asso.*, Feb. 1929, pp. 69–71; *N. Y. Times*, Dec. 14, 1928, p. 29; editorial (by C. N. Burch) in *Commercial Appeal* (Memphis), Dec. 15, 1928.]   F.S.P.

DICKINSON, JOHN (Nov. 8, 1732–Feb. 14, 1808), statesman, was the second son of Samuel Dickinson of Talbot County, Md., and his second wife, Mary Cadwalader of Philadelphia. In his boyhood, the family moved to a new estate near Dover, Del. There were a number of children and they were educated at home by a tutor. In 1750 John became a student in the law office of John Moland, one of the leading members of the Philadelphia bar. Three years later he went to London to continue his studies in the Middle Temple, remaining there until 1757 when he returned to Philadelphia and at once began the practise of law. Within five years he had risen to eminence and was arguing cases before the colonial supreme court. His interests, however, were historical and political rather than legal, and after the beginning of the Revolution he left the bar completely. In October 1760 he was

elected to the Assembly of the Lower Counties (Delaware), and became speaker. Two years later he was elected representative from Philadelphia to the Pennsylvania legislature. The questions of the proprietary government, taxation, military service, representation, and the frontier were then being discussed with the greatest bitterness, and Dickinson and Franklin were opposing leaders. The former, who was always intensely conservative, adopted the unpopular side. In the great debate of 1764 he admitted all the evils of the proprietary system but feared that any change might bring worse, and that any royal government granted by a British ministry of that day would be still more dangerous. As a result, he lost his seat in the Assembly and was not re-elected until 1770.

In 1765 he published a pamphlet, *The Late Regulations Respecting the British Colonies ... Considered.* He believed that the only way to secure the repeal of the Sugar and Stamp acts was to enlist the English merchants on the American side by economic interest, and his argument was therefore devoted to showing the injury that would be done to the British mercantile interests by attempting to enforce the acts. His opposition to these acts and his knowledge of the subject resulted in his appointment by the legislature, October 1765, as one of the Pennsylvania delegates to the Stamp Act Congress at New York, and he was there called on to draft the resolution (Stillé, *post,* pp. 339–40). Although one of the leaders of the opposition to the Stamp Act, he had also opposed all violent resistance, including even the non-use of stamps by lawyers.

Owing to the continued crisis between England and the colonies, the Non-Importation agreement was proposed in Boston in 1767. In December of that year, Dickinson began publishing anonymously in the *Pennsylvania Chronicle* the series later known in pamphlet form as *Letters from a Farmer in Pennsylvania to the Inhabitants of the British Colonies* (1768). In these he pointed out the evils of the British policy, suggested force as an ultimate remedy, but stated a belief that conciliation was possible. The *Letters,* although very pacific in tone, showed wide knowledge both of the practical economics of the situation and of the broad legal principles underlying English liberty and created a deep impression here and abroad. He was thanked at a public meeting in Boston, given the degree of LL.D. by Princeton, and received other honors. In April 1768 he addressed a great meeting in Philadelphia and strongly urged the adoption of the Non-Importation and Non-Exportation agreement. In 1771, as a member of the legislature, he drafted the Petition to the King which was unanimously adopted. He was opposed, however, to the resort to force and because he condemned the more violent opinions and actions in New England he lost most of his popularity and influence there. In 1774, when Boston asked aid from the other colonies after her actions had precipitated a crisis, Dickinson refused to sanction anything other than friendly expressions of sympathy, as he felt she had destroyed the hope of conciliation. He became, however, chairman of the Philadelphia Committee of Correspondence. At the conference held in July to discuss the situation and consider appointing delegates to a Continental Congress, Dickinson drew up three papers which were unanimously adopted. They consisted of a series of resolutions stating the principles upon which the colonies based their claim to redress; instructions to the Congressional delegates to be chosen by the Assembly; and a treatise on the constitutional power of Great Britain to tax the colonies. These papers expressed the views of the more conservative patriots up to the time when all was thrown over on the adoption of the Declaration of Independence.

In October 1774 Dickinson was a member of the Continental Congress, although for a week only, he believing he had been excluded up to that time by Galloway's influence. It was Dickinson, however, who drew up the Petition to the King, and the address to the people of Canada. On June 23, 1775, he was made chairman of a committee of safety and defense and held the post for a year, and he became colonel of the first battalion raised in Philadelphia. At the second Continental Congress, 1775, he still wished to adopt peaceful methods of settlement if possible and wrote the second Petition to the King, although he was engaged at the same time in strengthening the military resources of the colony. His action in drawing up the petition greatly angered the New England members. He also wrote the great part, if not all, of the "Declaration of the Causes of taking up Arms." In the Assembly, November 1775, he drafted the resolutions instructing the delegates to the Congress to meet in 1776, which asked them to use every possible means to gain redress of grievances but to countenance no measures looking toward separation. The general feeling in the country was changing and by the beginning of 1776 many began to believe separation the only solution of the problem. Dickinson and some of the other leaders still clung to conciliation.

In Congress, desirous of making one more peaceful effort and fearful of the results of a civil war without foreign allies and with no federal government binding the colonies together, he cast his vote against the Declaration of Independence. It should be noted that although he did what he believed to be his duty in this voting, yet when it came to fighting he and McKean were the only two members of Congress who took up arms in defense of the measures they had been advocating. He at once went with his regiment, as ordered, to Elizabethtown, but shortly afterward, when new members of Congress were elected and his name was rejected, he resigned his commission. Soon, for other causes, he resigned from the Assembly. In November he was elected to Congress from Delaware but declined to serve. In December, when the British neared Philadelphia, he retired to his estate in Delaware. Temporarily he appears to have served as a private in a special force raised in that colony which took part in the battle of Brandywine. In 1779 he was again elected to Congress from Delaware and took his seat. In the autumn he resigned but in 1781 was elected president of the Supreme Executive Council of Delaware. Returning to live in Philadelphia he was elected to the same office in Pennsylvania. At this time he was scurrilously attacked in a series of articles signed "Valerius," which he answered in his "Vindication," published in the Philadelphia *Freeman's Journal*, January–February 1783. In 1787 as a delegate from Delaware he became a member of the convention to frame the Federal Constitution, and took an active and useful part in its proceedings. In a series of letters signed "Fabius" he strongly urged the adoption of the new instrument. For the seventeen years which he lived afterward he held no public office, but continued an active interest in public affairs. In 1801 he published two volumes of his writings under the title, *The Political Writings of John Dickinson, Esq., Late President of the State of Delaware and of the Commonwealth of Pennsylvania*. These were republished in 1814. In 1895 P. L. Ford edited the first of what was to be a complete set, in three volumes, and it was published in that year as Vol. XIV of the Memoirs of the Historical Society of Pennsylvania, with the title, *The Writings of John Dickinson, vol. I, Political Writings 1764–74*. The others have not appeared. Dickinson was married on July 19, 1770, to Mary Norris, daughter of Isaac Norris of Philadelphia. He died at Wilmington.

[The standard biography is that by C. J. Stillé, *The Life and Times of John Dickinson* (1891), being vol. XIII of the Memoirs of the Hist. Soc. of Pa. In 1882 G. H. Moore prepared a paper for the N. Y. Hist. Soc. Pubs., as *John Dickinson, the Author of the Declaration on Taking up Arms in 1775* (1890), to prove that Dickinson wrote the whole of that Declaration, a part of which has been attributed to Jefferson.]   J.T.A.

DICKINSON, JOHN WOODBRIDGE (Oct. 12, 1825–Feb. 16, 1901), educator, was born to William Dickinson and his wife, Elizabeth (Worthington) Dickinson, in Chester, Mass., the youngest but one of nine children. His boyhood was spent at South Williamstown in the Berkshires where his early scanty schooling consisted of a few weeks each winter at the district school. This he later supplemented by attendance at the Greylock Institute, South Williamstown, and Williston Seminary at East Hampton. In 1848 he entered Williams College, graduating in 1852 with classical honors and local renown as a logician. That year he became instructor in the Westfield (Mass.) State Normal School, and held that position till in 1857 he became its principal. In this office he remained for twenty years, and his leadership gained for the school a national reputation. Memory of his service to it is preserved there by Dickinson Hall, erected in 1903 and named in his honor. In 1869 he spent six months in Germany, making an intensive study of the school systems there. During his principalship at Westfield he was regularly a speaker at the teachers' institutes held annually throughout the state, and came to be recognized as one of the foremost educators of New England. In 1877 he was chosen secretary of the Board of Education of Massachusetts and held this office till his resignation, Dec. 31, 1893. In this position he originated and promoted measures that proved of lasting value to the schools of the state and enhanced his distinction as an educational leader. Among these measures were the abolishing of old district systems and the substitution of town control; the instituting of free text-books and school supplies; the establishing in nearly every county of parental schools for truant children; the expansion of the normal-school system by the addition of four new normal schools; the strengthening and reorganizing of teachers' institutes; and the introduction of the new practise of holding institutes (in sixteen districts) for school committees and superintendents (*Annual Report* of the Board of Education, 1899–1900, p. 253). Probably his chief service in this office was the originating and carrying out of the plan by which the smaller and poorer towns were given improved schools through a co-partnership system of employing school superintendents. Towns unable alone to buy expert supervision thus got it through co-operation. (*Springfield Weekly Republican,* Feb. 22, 1901.) His name appeared frequently in the list of those chosen to address the gatherings of

the National Education Association. From 1886 to 1890 he was a trustee of Williams College. During the last years of his life he held an instructorship in the Emerson School of Oratory in Boston. Besides his official reports, public addresses and contributions to the educational magazines, he published the following: *The Limits of Oral Training* (1890), *Brief Descriptive Sketch of the Massachusetts Public School System* (1893), *Principles and Method of Teaching, Derived from a Knowledge of the Mind* (1899), *Rhetoric and Principles of Written Composition* (1901), and in collaboration with M. B. C. True, *Our Republic* (1888).

He was of tall and graceful figure, dignified, quiet, unassuming, scholarly. Yet physical, mental, and moral virility was characteristic of him; his views were positive, clearly defined, effectively expressed. Throughout his adult life he was actively connected with the Congregational Church. In 1857 he was married to Arexene G. Parsons of North Yarmouth, Me. His residence from 1877 was at Newton, Mass., where for several terms he was a member of the city school board. Of a son and daughter, the latter alone survived him.

[The chief sources of information about him are the *Sixty-Fourth Ann. Report of the Board of Educ. of Mass.,* 1899–1900, p. 253; *Education,* Oct. 1901, p. 65; *Springfield* (Mass.) *Weekly Republican,* Feb. 22, 1901; *Sunday Herald* (Boston), Feb. 17, 1901; *Boston Daily Globe,* Feb. 17, 1901; information as to certain facts from Dickinson's daughter.]   W.J.C.

DICKINSON, JONATHAN (Apr. 22, 1688–Oct. 7, 1747), first president of the College of New Jersey (now Princeton), was born in Hatfield, Mass. His parents, Hezekiah and Abigail, came of pioneer Connecticut Valley stock. Jonathan was graduated from Yale College in 1706 and forthwith turned to the study of theology. He was ordained pastor of the church at Elizabeth Town, N. J., in September 1709. Shortly before, he had married Joanna Melyen, the sister of his predecessor. The Elizabeth Town charge like many early New Jersey churches was Congregational and did not share its pastor's admiration for the Presbyterian organization. Not until 1717 was Dickinson able to persuade his congregation to join the presbytery of Philadelphia. Though the youngest of the members of the synod, he was soon regarded as one of the ablest. Twice he was elected moderator of that body, in 1721 and 1742. For nearly forty years he labored in behalf of the church, earning the reputation of being "one of the greatest and safest men of his age" (Hatfield, *post,* 354). Within the synod faction was rife; many desired to enforce a rigid and narrow view of Presbyterianism. On several occasions, for example, it was proposed to compel the clergy to subscribe to the Westminster Confessions and Catechisms. Dickinson, in keeping with his Congregational heritage, opposed such measures on the ground that the rights of the clergy would be infringed. For many years by the exercise of rare judgment he was able to compose the differences between the factions. At the same time he defended Presbyterianism with great vigor against external criticism. His pen was active in all the religious controversies of his day, and indeed his ability to define authoritatively such a variety of theological issues led Dr. Erskine of Edinburgh to remark that the British Isles had produced no such critics on Divinity in the eighteenth century as Dickinson and Edwards (Sprague, *post*, p. 17). Particularly bitter were the assaults made upon the actions and sermons of George Whitefield, the evangelist. Dickinson not only defended the revival in the synod but repelled the attacks of those outside the church who dared question the sincerity of the mission. He was impatient of the erratic movements of the day, particularly Deism and Arminianism. "It may be doubted whether, with the exception of the elder Edwards, Calvinism has ever found an abler or more efficient champion in this country, than Jonathan Dickinson" (*Ibid.*, p. 16).

The need of a school to train young men for the ministry had become pressing. At Neshaminy the Rev. William Tennant had founded a school which its opponents had derisively dubbed the "Log College." In 1738, however, the synod decreed that no one without a degree from Harvard, Yale, or a European institution might be ordained without its consent. This ruling outraged the feelings of the Log College adherents and finally led, among other differences, to the "great schism." The dissatisfied presbyteries of New Brunswick and New York met at Elizabeth Town in 1745 and organized the Synod of New York, with Dickinson as moderator. Dickinson clearly realized the need of an institution of higher learning in the Middle Colonies, not only to train men for the ministry but to serve in a broad sense the whole community. He was not satisfied with the Log College. With a larger purpose in view he approached the Anglican Gov. Morris of New Jersey, but his application for a charter was refused. Shortly after, on Oct. 22, 1746, Acting-Governor Hamilton, though also an Anglican, was prevailed upon to grant the first charter of the College of New Jersey. The college was formally opened in May of 1747 at Elizabeth Town and Dickinson was elected its first president. Great must have been his joy

when it was learned that the new governor, Jonathan Belcher, not only approved the undertaking but was willing to cooperate in obtaining a more secure charter. Plans were made to remove the college to Princeton, more centrally situated. Before these changes could be consummated Dickinson died suddenly, on Oct. 7, 1747, from an attack of pleurisy. He was survived by his second wife, Mary Crane Dickinson, whom he had married in April 1747.

[A. Alexander, *Biog. Sketches of the Founder . . . of the Log Coll.* (1851); H. C. Cameron, *Jonathan Dickinson and the Coll. of N. J.* (1880); V. L. Collins, *Princeton* (1914); F. B. Dexter, *Biog. Sketches Grads. Yale Coll.*, vol. I (1885), which includes a list of Dickinson's publications; J. DeWitt, *Planting of Princeton Coll.* (1897); J. F. Hageman, *Hist. of Princeton and its Institutions* (1879), vol. II; E. F. Hatfield, *Hist. of Elizabeth, N. J.* (1868); J. Maclean, *Hist. of the Coll. of N. J.* (1877); W. B. Sprague, *Annals Am. Pulpit*, vol. III (1859).]
J. E. P.

DICKINSON, PHILEMON (Apr. 5, 1739–Feb. 4, 1809), Revolutionary soldier, congressman, was the son of Judge Samuel and Mary (Cadwalader) Dickinson, and the brother of John Dickinson [*q.v.*]. His birthplace was probably Croisia-doré, Talbot County, Md., though it is sometimes given as somewhere near Dover, Kent County, Del. His education began under the tutorship of William Killen afterward chancellor of Delaware, at that time a law student in Judge Dickinson's office. He then entered the College of Philadelphia (now the University of Pennsylvania), from which he was graduated in 1759. For some time prior to his father's death in 1760 he managed the latter's enormous estates in Kent County, Del., and in Talbot, Dorchester, and Queen Anne counties, Md. He then settled in Philadelphia, where he read law with his brother John, whom he later joined in signing the non-importation agreement of November 1765. When New Jersey voted to raise ten battalions of infantry in 1775, Philemon, who had an estate near Trenton, was appointed colonel of the Hunterdon County Battalion, and in October was commissioned brigadier-general of New Jersey militia. The following year he was elected to the Provincial Congress of New Jersey, but he was not a member, as is alleged, of the committee that drafted the New Jersey constitution of 1776 (*Journal . . . of the Convention of New Jersey*, 1776). In January 1777 Dickinson, with 400 raw militia, defeated a foraging expedition sent out by Cornwallis to capture flour stored in a mill near Somerset Court House on the Millstone River, and captured forty wagons and a hundred draft horses. In reporting the engagement to the president of Congress Washington warmly commended Dickinson. In June, Gov.

William Livingston appointed him major-general and commander-in-chief of the New Jersey militia. In November Dickinson suggested that he himself descend upon Staten Island while Gates and Putnam attack Long Island and New York. Washington disapproved the proposed attack on Long Island, but thought the general plan "of counteracting the intended reinforcements for Mr. Howe's army, by a demonstration of designs upon New York . . . an exceedingly good one." Dickinson accordingly landed on Staten Island, which was occupied by the Loyalist regiments of Gen. Cortland Skinner and the Waldeckers of Gen. Campbell, both of whom, warned of Dickinson's plans, narrowly escaped. In the spring of 1778 Clinton, having evacuated Philadelphia, began retreating across the Jerseys toward New York. Dickinson and Gen. William Maxwell, having been ordered by Washington to obstruct the roads and harass the British, "destroyed every bridge on the road," as Clinton reported, in a country abounding in small streams and marshes. The delay enabled the Continental Army to come up with the British. Then came the battle of Monmouth, following which victory Washington, in his order to the troops, thanked Dickinson and the New Jersey militia. In July Dickinson acted as second to Gen. John Cadwalader [q.v.] in his duel with Thomas Conway [q.v.]. He was for a short time chief signal officer of the middle department (1778–79). For his "spirited attack" at the battle of Springfield in June 1780 he received the praise of Gen. Greene.

Defeated for governor by William Livingston [q.v.] in 1778, 1779, and 1780, he was appointed in 1781 commissioner of the newly created state loan office, and the following year was elected to Congress from Delaware, where he was a property owner. In Congress he was chairman of the committee that was appointed to consider what powers were to be vested in the secretary at war. Elected to the New Jersey Council, he served two terms as vice-president of that body (1783–84). In 1785 Congress appointed him, Robert Morris, and Philip Schuyler commissioners to select a site for a Federal capital. The question was not settled, however, until the adoption of the Constitution. Defeated for United States senator by William Paterson [q.v.], Dickinson was later elected to fill Paterson's unexpired term (1790–93) when the latter succeeded Livingston as governor. Dickinson was married twice: on July 14, 1767, to Mary Cadwalader, daughter of his uncle, Dr. Thomas Cadwalader [q.v.], and, after her death, to her sister Rebecca.

[Papers of the Cont. Cong., in the Lib. of Cong.; Jours. of Cong.; Proc. of a Gen. Court Martial, Held . . . for the Trial of Maj. Gen. Lee (1778); Docs. Relating to the Revolutionary Hist. of the State of N. J.; Jared Sparks, ed., Writings of Geo. Washington (1834–37) and Corr. of the Am. Revolution (1853); biog. sketch by Wharton Dickinson, in the Mag. of Am. Hist., Dec. 1881; Pa. Mag. of Hist. and Biog., vol. V (1881); Chas. P. Keith, Provincial Councillors of Pa. (1883); Wm. S. Stryker, Battle of Monmouth (1927); W. J. Mills, Hist. Houses of N. J. (1902); Trenton Federalist, Feb. 6, 1809.]   F. E. R.

DICKMAN, JOSEPH THEODORE (Oct. 6, 1857–Oct. 23, 1927), soldier, was born at Dayton, Ohio, the son of Theodore and Mary (Weinmar) Dickman. He graduated from the U. S. Military Academy in 1881, and was commissioned second lieutenant in the 3rd Cavalry. On Sept. 26, 1882, he married Mary Rector of Fort Smith, Ark. Until the war with Spain his service was chiefly in the West, where he participated in the campaign against Geronimo and aided in suppressing disturbances along the Mexican border. He was an honor graduate of the Infantry and Cavalry School at Fort Leavenworth in 1883, and was an instructor there from 1895 to 1898. He was promoted to first lieutenant, Jan. 18, 1886, and to captain, May 27, 1898. As a staff officer of Wheeler's cavalry division, he took part in the Santiago campaign, and as major and lieutenant-colonel of a volunteer infantry regiment, in operations against Filipino insurgents in the island of Panay. He was chief of staff of the American forces in China, after the taking of Peking, and was discharged from his volunteer commission, May 13, 1901. When the General Staff of the army was organized in 1903, he was selected as one of its original members, serving for three years. In due course he was promoted to major in 1906, lieutenant-colonel in 1912, and colonel in 1914, serving meanwhile with his regiment and for a time as an inspector-general. He was appointed brigadier-general in the regular army May 15, 1917, and major-general in the emergency forces, Aug. 5, 1917. He first commanded the 85th Division at Camp Custer, Mich., and later the 3rd Division at Camp Greene, N. C., and in France. With the latter he went into the battle sector on the south bank of the Marne, June 2, 1918, and commanded it in battle on July 15 and 16, in the repulse of the last great German offensive. He commanded the IV Corps from Aug. 18 to Oct. 12, and the I Corps from then until after the Armistice, assisting in the reduction of the Saint Mihiel salient and the Meuse-Argonne operations. On Nov. 15 he was assigned to the command of the III Army, organized it for the occupation of Germany, and remained with it until Apr. 28, 1919. Decorations for his services in the war were conferred on him by the United States, Great Britain, France, Italy, Belgium, and Panama. He was made major-general in the regular army, Jan. 9, 1919, and retired, Oct. 6, 1921. He died at Washington. It is still too early to pass final judgment on the leaders in the World War, but Dickman must be ranked among the ablest of the American generals in France. His somewhat heavy and unexpressive features masked a shrewd and active mind whose qualities had already been tested in duties of widely varying character. His narrative of the World War, *The Great Crusade* (1927), is not such a rhetorical effusion as its title might suggest, but a simple straightforward account of military operations, clearly and entertainingly written.

[Dickman's military record is given in G. W. Cullum, *Biog. Reg.* (3rd ed., 1891), III, 349–50; IV, 345–46; V, 322; VI A, 319–20. *General Orders No. 17, War Dept.*, 1927, summarizes his career. For his services in the World War, consult *The Great Crusade*. See also Washington *Evening Star* and *Washington Post*, Oct. 24, 1927.]   T. M. S.

DICKSON, DAVID (July 6, 1809–Feb. 18, 1885), farmer and agricultural writer, was of English descent. His father, Thomas Dickson, was a Virginian who served in the Revolutionary War and soon after moved to Hancock County, Ga., where his son David was born. The latter had limited educational advantages, but his natural mental ability and the best use of all his opportunities for reading, study, and thought equipped him well for his future labors and achievements. With a small patrimony he began as a country trader. In 1835 he entered a partnership and opened a store in Sparta, Ga., which was very successful financially. When he was thirty-seven he closed this business and invested all his capital in land, slaves, live stock, and tools at and near his father's homestead. In his boyhood and youth spent on the farm he had recognized defects in the system of management and now had the desired opportunity to experiment in its improvement. From the first he was successful, and land which he bought for one or two dollars an acre under his management increased to many times its original value. His success in securing abundant crops was due to his skill as an organizer, to his improved methods of tillage, of cultivating and harvesting his crops and of increasing the efficiency of his labor. This last point he emphasizes. "I have, in five minutes, taught a hand to pick 100 pounds more of cotton per day than he had picked on the previous day," so that he would pick three bales a week. He taught his workmen similar efficiency in handling the plow, the hoe, and the axe; "with more ease and less of sweat and muscle."

His methods of plowing, planting, and cultivating were quite original and most of his writing on these matters is as valid to-day as it was before the Civil War.

He never had a crop failure even in the driest season, and his crop yields were phenomenal. When the Civil War broke out his property was valued at $500,000. After the first year of the war he abandoned cotton, raising only provisions for the Confederate army, for most of which he received no pay, even in Confederate money. Much of his property was swept away in Sherman's march to the sea, and he lost his 250 slaves, specially trained and valuable laborers. After the war he became prosperous again and at the time of his death he owned a plantation of some 15,000 acres in Hancock and Washington counties and another tract of 13,000 acres in Texas, managing the farm land on the tenant system. He bred a variety of cotton called "Dickson's Select" which, at the time, "outlived every other in productiveness and popularity."

Dickson was the first to introduce the use of Peruvian guano as a fertilizer in the cotton states (1846). He is significant, however, not only because he was the most successful farmer in Georgia and probably in the whole South, but chiefly because his careful study and observation, set forth in voluminous private correspondence and in letters to agricultural journals, led to great improvements in the farm practise of the cotton-growing states. He explained clearly and fully his theory and practise. He gave instruction in seed selection, the management of cattle, and the handling of various crops, indicating that he practised mixed farming, not confining himself to a one-crop system. He emphasized the proper handling of the soil, shallow cultivation, the proper distance of planting, the use of commercial fertilizers, instruction of farm hands in all labor-saving devices, etc. In 1870 his writings were collected in a volume edited by J. Dickson Smith and published under the title, *A Treatise on Agriculture, to which is Added the Author's Published Letters, by David Dickson.* Dickson was above medium height, stout and robust, with a fair ruddy face, in manner serious, thoughtful, and benevolent, with a vein of quiet humor. Quite unpretentious, he nevertheless spoke his mind frankly and with very decided views on matters of general interest as well as on his special business. He died on his plantation on the Little Ogoochee River, in Hancock County, Ga.

[The volume, *A Treatise on Agriculture*, mentioned above, contains a sketch of Dickson; the contents of this volume, considerably abridged, were republished by the Cultivator Publishing Company of Atlanta as *David*

Dickson's System of Farming (1906) and *David Dickson's and Jas. M. Smith's Farming* (1908, 1910). See also the *Rural Carolinian* (Charleston, S. C.), Oct. 1869; the *Atlanta Constitution*, Feb. 19, 1885.]

E. H. J.

DICKSON, ROBERT (*c.* 1765–June 20, 1823), fur-trader, was the son of John Dickson, a merchant of Dumfries, Scotland. As a young man he migrated to Canada about the close of the American Revolution and entered the fur trade. In 1787 he was employed as interpreter and storekeeper of government goods at a great Indian council held at Michilimackinac. As a result of this council he began trading operations among the Sioux. About the year 1797 he took as his wife To-to-win, the sister of an influential Sioux chief. Apparently his position and influence were recognized, for in 1803 the governor of Indiana Territory, which included part of Dickson's trading area, appointed him a justice of the peace for St. Clair County. By 1805 he was one of the chief traders of the region bounded by the upper Mississippi, the James, and the Des Moines rivers. In that year a firm known as Robert Dickson & Company was formed, with headquarters at Michilimackinac. Two years later this firm became a member of the recently organized Michilimackinac Company.

When the War of 1812 broke, Dickson's position became a matter of significance on both sides: the American leaders took steps to prevent him from bringing his Indians to the aid of the British; and Gov. Brock of Upper Canada selected him as his agent to keep the Indians of the Northwest friendly and to lead them to Canada to join the British forces. In the capture of Michilimackinac he and his Indians played a significant rôle and thus aided indirectly, also, in the capture of Detroit. In January 1813 his services and influence were recognized by a commission from Governor-General Prevost making him agent for the Indians west of Lake Huron, with extensive authority. Later he was made superintendent of Indian affairs for these tribes. His power, however, awoke the jealousy of military men in the Northwest and led to his arrest at the close of the war and to his dismissal from the service in 1815. He claimed and secured from the British government a hearing in London which not only cleared his name but recognized his services to the extent of awarding him the title of lieutenant-colonel and a retirement pension of £300 a year. At the close of the war he made arrangements with Lord Selkirk to carry on his business within the supposed limits of the latter's colony on the Red River, close to Dickson's former post. A part of his plan seems to have been an agricultural and industrial settlement of Indians and traders on the site of Grand Forks, N. Dak. In the midst of his plans, however, Lord Selkirk died, and shortly thereafter Dickson himself died suddenly at Drummond Island.

[L. A. Tohill, *Robt. Dickson, British Fur Trader on the Upper Miss.* (1927); Helen D. Weaver, "Life of Robt. Dickson" (M.A. thesis, Iowa, 1924); Selkirk papers in the Canadian archives; papers of John J. Astor, Harvard Univ.; E. A. Cruikshank, "Robt. Dickson, the Indian Trader" in *Wis. State Hist. Soc. Colls.*, vol. XII; manuscript letter-book of Thomas Blackwood, in McGill Univ. Lib.; archives of the War Dept., and Indian Office.]

G. L. N.

DICKSON, SAMUEL HENRY (Sept. 20, 1798–Mar. 31, 1872), physician, second son of Samuel and Mary (Neilson) Dickson, was born in Charleston, S. C. Both parents were Presbyterians of Scottish descent who had emigrated from Belfast, Ireland, before the Revolution. After study with his father, who was a schoolmaster, and with Dr. Mackay of Charleston, he entered the sophomore class at Yale at the age of thirteen, graduating (B.A.) in 1814. He returned to his home and began the study of medicine in the office of Dr. Philip Gendron Prioleau and, under his guidance, practised during the epidemic of yellow fever in 1817. In the two succeeding winters he attended the University of Pennsylvania (M.D., 1819). His practise continued at Charleston where he devoted the greater part of his time to the yellow fever sufferers in the Marine and Yellow Fever Hospitals. Though he was only twenty-one years of age, circumstances gave him entire charge of both institutions. While endeavoring to found a medical school he gave free lectures on physiology, and in 1824 a Medical College came into being as a result of the efforts of Dickson and his colleagues. He was made professor of the institutes and practise of medicine. In 1832 he resigned, in consequence of a controversy with the medical society, and in 1833 founded the Medical College of South Carolina which became entirely successful. He held the new chair until 1847 when he accepted a call to the professorship of the practise of medicine at the University of the City of New York. Here he remained for three years but upon urgent invitation and partly for reasons of health, he returned to his former position at Charleston. In 1858 he accepted a call to fill the chair of practise vacated by the death of his warm personal friend, Dr. John K. Mitchell, at the Jefferson Medical College of Philadelphia, and though suffering from a lingering and painful disease, continued to lecture until within a month of his death, which occurred in Philadelphia. He was thrice married: first, to Elizabeth Brownlee Robertson of Charleston, who died in 1832; second, in 1834, to Jane Robertson Robertson (sister of his first wife), who died in 1842; and third, in 1845, to Marie Seabrook DuPré, also of Charleston, who died in 1873.

Dickson was a versatile man, being not only an "attractive Medical stylist and litterateur" (F. H. Garrison, *An Introduction to the History of Medicine,* 3rd ed., 1921, p. 466), but a public speaker of note. He wrote a large number of articles and monographs on medicine, also papers on philosophy, history, and current events. His most important medical works are: *Manual of Pathology and Practice* (1839 with later editions); *Essays on Pathology and Therapeutics* (2 vols., 1845); *Essays on Life, Sleep, Pain, Intellection, and Hygiene* (1852); *Elements of Medicine* (1855); *Studies in Pathology and Therapeutics* (1867). He claimed to have been one of the first to abandon the heroic treatment of fevers in vogue at the time he began practise, and the first in this country to employ stimulants and anodynes in febrile diseases. He was one of the early writers on racial anthropometry (*Charleston Medical Journal,* 1857, p. 607). He delivered one of the first temperance addresses ever heard in the South and is said to have established the first temperance society, directing his attack against the use of distilled liquors, while approving of wines.

[*Charleston Medic. Jour. and Record,* XII, 3 (with portrait); F. B. Dexter, *Biog. Sketches Grads. Yale Coll.,* VI (1912), 641 (with bibliography); *Phila. Medic. Times,* II (1872), 278, 292; *Press* (Phila.), Apr. 2, 1872.]   E. E. H.

DICKSON, THOMAS (Mar. 26, 1824–July 31, 1884), capitalist, the son of James Dickson, a Scottish millwright of Lauder, Berwickshire, and his wife, Elizabeth Linen, was born in Leeds, England, where his parents were living temporarily. When he was eight years old, the family moved to Canada, and two years later to Dundaff in northeastern Pennsylvania. James Dickson, finding little opportunity to follow his trade, attempted farming in what was then a pioneer community. Finding farming distasteful he sought employment elsewhere, leaving the farm and his large family in charge of his wife and Thomas, the oldest son. These early strenuous experiences constituted Dickson's principal preparation for life. Almost immediately after his schooling began it was abruptly ended by a violent quarrel with the village school-teacher. In the meantime his father had secured employment as a millwright with the Delaware & Hudson Canal Company, and the boy's first job after

leaving school was with the same company, guiding a mule in drawing coal from the mines. It happened that this company, with which Dickson's fortunes were so closely interwoven, had been organized in 1824, the year of his birth (Logan, *post,* pp. 6–24). In various minor positions he saved a portion of his wages, and characteristically added to his hoard the money sent by his grandfather to defray the cost of a visit to Scotland. At length he accumulated savings enough for a venture of his own, under the firm name of Dickson & Company, a manufacturing enterprise organized in 1856 at Carbondale, but soon established at Scranton. Scranton was the center of a region with immense possibilities and potential needs in the rapidly developing mining, lumbering, manufacturing, and transport industries. The crudest of methods prevailed, but these were being supplanted, and the extensive foundries and machine-shops built by the Dickson firm for the making of locomotives, engines for mills and mines, and machinery of various kinds, played a vital rôle in the industrializing of the region (*Ibid.,* pp. 39–52).

The basic resources of the region were particularly important in their relation to other regions, and the early tapping of these resources was largely the work of the Delaware & Hudson Canal Company. Dickson's ingenuity and enterprise in furnishing the company with needed equipment led to his being offered, in 1859, the post of superintendent. This he accepted, while retaining for about ten years the headship of his own company. The latter was reorganized in 1862 as the Dickson Manufacturing Company. Under his direction the two companies rapidly developed the anthracite coal industry and other enterprises in the Lackawanna and Wyoming valleys. The expansion of business led to his resignation as head of his own company and to his being made president, in 1869, of the Delaware & Hudson Canal Company. In the meantime he had become associated with a number of other enterprises, including the First National Bank of Scranton (1863), and the Moosic Powder Company (1865), the latter merging later with the Du Pont projects. When Dickson first became interested in the development of Scranton, there was little more than the beginning of a town. By means of his foresight and business acumen he became the principal molder of the city's fortunes. His influence extended beyond the Lackawanna and Wyoming valleys, not only in the direction of New York and Philadelphia, but northward as well. He promoted, for instance, the extension of a railway line to Canada (*Ibid.,* 98–100; Hitchcock, *post,* I, 89, and *passim*). Thus he became one of the outstanding figures in the American industrial revolution.

Outside of his business life, he was a man of limited attainments. Aside from his boyhood migration to America, his travels were very slight until shortly before his death, when he spent almost a year in a tour of the world. He had virtually no formal schooling. He nevertheless accumulated a choice library, established a circulating library, read extensively, and even cherished literary ambitions. He acquired a remarkable knowledge of law. His associations, aside from his numerous business connections, were slight. His principal benevolences were connected with conventional religious and social groups. On Aug. 31, 1846, he was married to Mary Augusta Marvine. His daughter, Elizabeth Linen, became the wife of Henry Martyn Boies [*q.v.*], another Scranton capitalist.

[S. C. Logan, *The Life of Thomas Dickson* (1888); *Henry Martyn Boies* (1904), ed. by J. H. Odell; F. L. Hitchcock, *Hist. of Scranton and Its People* (2 vols., 1914); *Geneal. and Family Hist. of the Wyoming and Lackawanna Valleys, Pa.*, vol. II (1906), ed. by H. E. Hayden; *Portr. and Biog. Record of Wyoming and Lackawanna Counties, Pa.* (1899).]   W. B.

DIDIER, EUGENE LEMOINE (Dec. 22, 1838–Sept. 8, 1913), author, son of Franklin James and Julia (LeMoine) Didier, was born in Baltimore, where he lived all his life. His father was a physician of literary tastes, who in the early twenties published *Letters from Paris and Other Cities of France, Holland &c.* (1821), and *Franklin's Letters to Kinsfolk* (1822), both written between 1816 and 1820, during a residence abroad. Eugene attended Loyola College, and afterward for a brief time engaged in business. During 1867–68 he was one of the three editors of *Southern Society,* a magazine which published the work of the best-known Southern writers of that time. He was an enthusiastic admirer of Poe—as a young man he cultivated the acquaintance of the aged Maria Clemm; by 1874 he was writing articles about Poe for the magazines, and in 1877 he published *The Life and Poems of Edgar Allan Poe,* a carefully written but sentimental sketch of some 30,000 words. It is said to have gone through nineteen editions (Shepherd, p. 160). In 1879 he published as by "Stylus" (a favorite name with Poe), his *American Publishers and English Authors.* The purpose of this slashing little booklet was to show that only by protecting foreign copyrights could America be independent of England culturally as well as politically. In 1879 he published also *The Life and Letters of Madame Bonaparte,* a frankly curious account of her doings. During the early eighties he was interested in editing a

series of *Primers for the People.* Through this channel it was his plan to popularize knowledge of the following subjects, at the rate of ten cents each: Criticism, History, Matrimony, Politeness, Health, Wealth, and Literature. In the first of these *Primers,* written by himself, he essays to reduce to plain chaff the reputation of many of his contemporaries, particularly of Henry James and Howells. In 1884 he issued his mordant *Political Adventures of James G. Blaine.* Throughout his life he seems to have had money to do as he chose. He had an extensive library, and from time to time he traveled through Europe and America, meeting celebrities. His *Poe Cult* (1909) is made up of about twenty articles which appeared over many years in various magazines. It unquestionably contributed some items to the fund of knowledge about Poe, but it is less valuable on that score than it seems to have been considered by the author. False modesty was never one of his vices. Often indeed, and particularly in this last book, he treads so drastically upon nearly everybody except himself and Poe that even the meekest bookworm at last finds himself turning. In 1873 Didier was married to Mary Louisa Innocentia Northrop, daughter of the Confederate general, Lucius Bellinger Northrop. Their only son, J. D'Arcy Didier, died in early manhood.

[A. J. Northrup, *Northrup-Northrop Geneal.* (1908); *Who's Who in America,* 1908–09; H. E. Shepherd, *Representative Authors of Md.* (1911); *Baltimore Evening Sun,* Sept. 9, 1913.]   J. D. W.

DIETRICHSON, JOHANNES WILHELM CHRISTIAN (Apr. 4, or Aug. 23, 1815–Nov. 14, 1883), Lutheran clergyman, was born at Fredrikstad, Norway, son of Capt. Fredrik Batington and Karen Sophie Henriette (Radich) Dietrichson. Stirred by the fervent religious instruction of his pastor, the Rev. J. Tandberg, Wilhelm decided to become a minister of the gospel. In 1837 he graduated from the university at Christiania (now Oslo) with high honors. After spending one year as a tutor at the salt works at Tönsberg, he returned to Christiania and spent the years 1839 to 1843 in study and teaching. In 1841 he lost his wife, Jörgine Laurense Broch, after two years of wedded life, and this bereavement greatly intensified his spiritual life. Thus trained and tested, he did what could least be expected of the aristocratic clergy of Norway at that time. He overcame the hostility of his own social class to emigration to America, and volunteered to embark for the new country when urged to do so by a pious dyer, P. Sörenson. Securing ordination on Feb. 26, 1844, at the hands of Bishop C. Sörenson, he set out for America. He delivered sermons in New York and Buffalo, and on Friday, Aug. 30, 1844, in Amund Endresen Hornefjeld's barn on the Koshkonong Prairies in Wisconsin, preached his first sermon in the American West.

From his one-room log parsonage, he immediately undertook to rule and order the vast, though chaotic, virgin church among the Norwegian Lutherans in America. Stressing his prerogatives as the first Lutheran pastor in America who had been ordained in Norway, he scrutinized carefully the ordinations of Elling Eielsen and Claus Lauritz Clausen [*qq.v.*], both of whom had been ordained in America in 1843, and found Eielsen's ordination faulty, but Clausen's at least passable. Thus were sown the seeds of future controversies. With a keen strategic sense which he had inherited from forebears who had been prominent in church and state, Dietrichson drew up a pledge consisting of four points, and on this basis organized various Norwegian Lutheran congregations in Wisconsin. Each of these congregations was given a constitution, these constitutions revealing such a remarkable insight into American Lutheran congregational needs that they have become the foundation for all subsequent organizational development in this field among Norwegian American Lutherans.

In order to secure pastors for his prolific American field in which new congregations could be organized almost at will, Dietrichson went to Norway in 1845, remaining one year. While there he was married again, this time to Charlotte Mueller. By means of sermons, debates, articles in the newspapers, and, finally, a book, the title of which, in translation reads: *Travels Among the Norwegian Emigrants in "The United North American Free States"* (1846), he sought to interest the young clergy in the new field. In this endeavor he was successful, attracting to the American Lutheran church some of the finest young clergymen that Norway has ever produced. In 1850, feeling that his usefulness in America had come to an end, he issued a farewell sermon which was printed, and returned to Norway, where he held two pastorates, and the office of postmaster at Porsgrund from 1876 to 1882. In that year he suffered a stroke of paralysis which in the following year caused his death. *The Travels* have been an invaluable source of Norwegian American history.

[J. Magnus Rohne, *Norwegian American Lutheranism Up to 1872* (1926); Rasmus B. Anderson, *The First Chapter of Norwegian Immigration (1821–40)* (1896); *Who's Who Among Pastors in All the Norwegian Synods of America 1843–1927* (1928); J. Arndt Bergh, *Den Norsk Lutherske Kirkes Historie i Amerika* (1914); Thrond Bothne, "Kort Udsigt over det Lutherske Kir- kearbeide Blandt Nordmändene i Amerika" in Knut Takla's edition of Hallvard G. Heggtveit, *Illustreret Kirkehistorie* (1898).]   J.M.R.

DIKE, SAMUEL WARREN (Feb. 13, 1839–Dec. 3, 1913), Congregational clergyman, reformer and sociologist, was born in Thompson, Conn. A descendant of Capt. Anthony Dike who came to Plymouth Colony on the ship *Ann* in 1623, he was the son of George Dike, a farmer, and Hannah Waters (Snow) Dike. After preparation at Nichols Academy, he graduated from Williams College with high scholastic honors in 1863. For two years he studied at the Theological Institute of Connecticut, East Windsor Hill (now Hartford Theological Seminary), and for one year at Andover Theological Seminary, from which he graduated in 1866. He was ordained to the Congregational ministry in 1869 at West Randolph, Vt., and served as acting pastor at Pomfret, Conn., 1866–67; as pastor at West Randolph, Vt., 1868–77; and at Royalton, Vt., 1879–82. During his year at Andover Seminary he became interested in the study of social subjects, especially the family. He wrote editorially on this theme in the *Vermont Chronicle* and in 1881 gave one of the Boston Monday Lectures on "Facts as to Divorce in New England." That same day the New England Divorce Reform League was organized. It became the National Divorce Reform League in 1885 and still later the National League for the Protection of the Family. Dike was creator, corresponding secretary, and mainspring of the League from 1881 until his death. He was the pioneer in the study of American family conditions, and the annual reports of the League written by him constitute the history of the movement for the betterment of the family. He brought such pressure to bear on Congress that Carroll D. Wright, United States commissioner of labor, gathered and published a valuable mass of statistics and information in his *Report on Marriage and Divorce in the United Staes, 1867–86* (1889). Dike did an immense amount of research for this publication. Before colleges, theological seminaries, and scientific societies he lectured on the same theme. He wrote extensively for periodicals, including the *Andover Review, Atlantic Monthly, Princeton Review,* and *Political Science Quarterly.* Many of his articles were reissued in pamphlet form. He powerfully influenced legislation for stricter marriage and divorce laws and achieved international reputation as an authority on them. He devised the Home Department of the Sunday-school. With Bishop Potter, Seth Low, Washington Gladden, and others he formed a "Sociological Group" which did much first-hand work in the study of "present-day problems." Dike had a large philosophic grasp of the complicated social problem of the development and changes in the American family. He combined to an unusual degree patience in the quest for facts with a firm grasp of the whole social situation, a combination in which very few of his more distinguished successors have equaled him (Prof. W. F. Willcox). He was clear in his judgments, tenacious of his opinions, firm in his faith, but modest and self-effacing in his disposition and generous in his relations with his colleagues (Francis G. Peabody in *National League for the Protection of the Family, Annual Report for 1913 and 1914*, p. 3). He married Augusta Margaret Smith of Montpelier, Vt., on Oct. 29, 1872. After taking up the work of the League they resided in Royalton, Vt., until 1887 and then in Auburndale, Mass., until his death.

[*Class of Sixty-three, Williams Coll., 40th Year Report* (1903); autobiographical material in *Nat. Reform League Reports* and *Nat. League for the Protection of the Family Ann. Reports*; *Andover Theol. Sem. Necrology, 1911–14* (1914); *Congreg. Year Book*, 1913, and *Who's Who in America*, 1912–13; personal acquaintance of thirty years.]   T.C.R.

DILL, JAMES BROOKS (July 25, 1854–Dec. 2, 1910), jurist, was born in the village of Spencerport, N. Y. He was the eldest son of a Congregational minister, James Horton Dill, a native of Massachusetts, and of Catherine D. Dill, a member of the Brooks family of Connecticut. The Dills moved to Chicago in 1858 and upon the death of the father, killed in battle in 1862, the family moved to New Haven, Conn., where young Dill's schooling was continued. After three years in Oberlin Academy (1868–71) and one year in Oberlin College, he entered Yale in 1872 and, though supporting himself, graduated with honors in 1876. He then taught for a year in a private school in Philadelphia and studied law at night under the direction of a prominent lawyer. He became instructor in Latin and mathematics in Stevens Institute at Hoboken, N. J., and attended the Law School of the University of the City of New York at night where he graduated as salutatorian of the class of 1878. He was admitted to the bar in New York the same year. Entering upon the practise of the law with a capital of forty dollars, he eked out an income by newspaper work on the *Jersey City Evening Journal* and later on the *New York Tribune*. Dill's days of penury were brief, however. In 1879 he won a conspicuous case, largely on a technicality, freeing his client from heavy liability under the New York law as director of an insolvent corporation. This enlarged his practise and directed his interest to the field of cor-

poration law, an interest evidenced by a pamphlet which he wrote on "The Advantages of Business Corporations," which attracted wide attention. He was admitted to the New Jersey bar in 1894. Upon being consulted by the governor of New Jersey as to the best way to increase the financial resources of the state, Dill suggested the liberalizing of the corporation laws. He thereupon drafted the famous New Jersey statute of 1889, legalizing the holding company and allowing incorporation for almost any purpose. It also required a corporation to have an agent in the state upon whom papers could be served, thus excluding the "tramp" corporation, and prescribed "private publicity," or the keeping of adequate records for the protection of stockholders. The rush of business concerns to take advantage of these laws led Dill to organize a corporation to organize other corporations, the Corporation Trust Company of New Jersey. Later he organized other companies to meet similar needs. He aided in the creation of hundreds of corporations, was director of many, and counsel for many more. His practise was lucrative and he amassed a large fortune. He is reputed to have received the largest fee ever paid to an American lawyer ($1,000,000) for his services in healing the breach between Carnegie and Frick in 1900.

Dill wrote extensively and authoritatively on corporation law. His works, *The Statutory and Case Law Applicable to Private Companies Under the General Corporation Act of New Jersey* (1898), *The Laws of New Jersey Relating to Banks and Banking, Trust Companies and Safe Deposit Corporations* (1899), and *Business Corporations* (1910), served as legal guides for the business world, since the author had largely created the law he was expounding. He occasionally gave addresses or wrote articles on subjects relating to business organizations or corporation law ("Trusts: Their Uses and Abuses," an address before the Merchants' Club of Chicago, 1901; "National Incorporation Laws for Trusts," *Yale Law Journal*, XI, 273–95, 1902; "Some Aspects of New Jersey's Corporate Policy," an address before the Pennsylvania Bar Association, *Report of the Ninth Annual Meeting*, 1903, pp. 265–88). In 1899 he served as member of the committee which revised the laws of New Jersey, and later served as counsel to the committee which revised the laws of Canada. In 1905 he was appointed a member of the court of errors and appeals in New Jersey and served in that office until his death. Dill was married in 1880 to Mary W. Hansell of Philadelphia. While he kept his principal office in New York City, he maintained a beautiful home in East Orange,

N. J., where he had a very large private library. He was fond of out-door activity, especially camping and horseback riding. He was a genial and sociable man with a very large circle of friends.

[*National Corporation Reporter*, XXV, 486 (1902); *N. J. Law Jour.*, XXXIII, 382 (1910); *World's Work*, III, 1902, p. 1885; *Banking Law Jour.*, X, 375 (1894); *N. Y. Times*, Dec. 3, 1910; *Who's Who in America*, 1903–05.]   R. E. C.

DILLINGHAM, WILLIAM PAUL (Dec. 12, 1843–July 12, 1923), lawyer and statesman, was the son of Paul Dillingham, a lawyer by profession and prominent in the politics of the state, and his second wife, Julia Carpenter. He was born at Waterbury, Vt., whither his grandfather had moved from Massachusetts in 1805, attended the local common schools, Newbury Seminary, and Kimball Union Academy, and then moved to Milwaukee, Wis., where he studied law in the office of his brother-in-law, Matthew H. Carpenter [*q.v.*]. Two years later he returned to Vermont and completed his legal studies under his father, then governor of the state. This circumstance favored young Dillingham's entrance into political life. His first public office was that of secretary of civil and military affairs, to which he was appointed in 1866. In 1872 he was elected state's attorney of Washington County, and was reëlected for a second term. During the period from 1876 to 1884 he served four terms in the state legislature. In 1888 he received the Republican nomination for governor and was elected by the largest plurality ever given to a candidate for that office up to that time. On Oct. 18, 1900, he was elected to the United States Senate to fill the vacancy caused by the death of Justin S. Morrill [*q.v.*], being reëlected by the legislature in 1902 and 1908, and by popular vote in 1914 and 1920.

The phase of Dillingham's career of most historical interest is his long service on the Senate Committee on Immigration and his espousal of the quota principle of immigration restriction. He was elected to this Committee shortly after taking his seat in the Senate, in the place of his colleague, Senator Proctor, who asked to be relieved of his duties on it. At the next session of Congress Dillingham became chairman of the Committee, a position which he held from 1903 to 1911, though he continued to be a member till the time of his death. In 1907 Congress authorized the appointment of a special immigration commission, composed of three members from the Senate, three from the House, and three to be appointed by the President, to make a study of the problem and to submit recommendations concerning it. Dillingham was appointed one of the three members from the Senate, and, when the commission effected its organization, was chosen as its chairman. The commission devoted over two years to a thorough investigation of foreign immigration in all its aspects, and its report extending through forty-one volumes is the most complete and exhaustive survey of the subject ever made.

In June 1913 Dillingham introduced a bill proposing that the annual amount of immigration for each nationality be limited to ten per cent of those of that nationality already in the United States. The adoption of the measure would have marked a departure from the immigration policy of the past. The outbreak of the World War, however, and the almost complete suspension of foreign immigration removed the need of immediate legislation upon the subject. At the end of the war the country was in a mood of intensified nationalism and Congress was more favorably inclined toward the restriction of immigration. A bill introduced by Senator Dillingham in December 1920, embodying the quota principle of restriction, passed Congress but was killed by a pocket veto of President Wilson. At the next session the Senate repassed the bill, but the House, while favoring a policy of immigration restriction, had passed another measure for the total suspension of foreign immigration for one year pending a more thorough study of the problem. The main features of the Dillingham measure were accepted in conference between the two houses, then enacted into law. This act, approved May 19, 1921, and commonly referred to in contemporary discussion as the "Dillingham Bill," limited the amount of annual immigration to three per cent of those of that nationality already in the country. It was avowedly a temporary measure, but its essential features were incorporated into subsequent legislation upon the subject, and it remains the basis of the national immigration policy to the present time (1930). Dillingham was married on Dec. 24, 1874, to Mary Ellen Shipman. He died at Montpelier, Vt., from complications following an operation.

[*The Vermonter* published articles relating to the life and career of Dillingham in the following issues: vol. VI, pp. 51–53 (Nov. 1900), vol. VIII, p. 132 (Nov. 1902), vol. XXIX, pp. 20–23 (Feb. 1924). Considerable material relating to his public career and his candidacy for office is scattered through the files of the *Burlington Free Press,* and the several issues following his death on July 12, 1923, contain considerable biographical material and personal reminiscences. A report of the Senate Committee on Immigration, printed as *Senate Report No. 17, 67* Cong., 1 Sess., gives a full account of the history of the Dillingham immigration bill and the evolution of the policy of immigration restriction which he championed. A speech of Dillingham's published in the *Cong. Record,* 64 Cong., 1 Sess., pp. 12,769–77 is a good source of information for his

Dillon

views regarding immigration. Some information has been supplied by personal friends.] A.M.K.

DILLON, JOHN FORREST (Dec. 25, 1831–May 6, 1914), jurist, was born in Montgomery County, N. Y., to Thomas and Rosannah (Forrest) Dillon, both of Irish descent. In 1838 the family moved to Davenport, Iowa, where young Dillon spent a boyhood of plenty of hard work and little regular schooling. At seventeen he began the study of medicine in the office of a local practitioner, later attended lectures at the medical school at Keokuk, and took the M.D. degree in 1850 at the college of physicians and surgeons at Davenport, a branch of the University of Iowa.

He practised medicine at Farmington, Iowa, but discovered that a hernia from which he suffered made unsafe the horseback riding necessary to medical practise in a pioneer country and compelled a radical change of plans. His friendship for a young lawyer of the community inclined him toward the law, and returning to Davenport, he supported himself by running a drug-store while he engaged in a Lincoln-like struggle for a legal education. With no teacher, no law-school training, and no law-office apprenticeship, he achieved admission to the bar of Scott County in 1852. A few months later he was elected county prosecuting attorney at a salary of $250. He held this office till his election in 1858 as judge of the seventh judicial district of Iowa, to which office he was reëlected. In 1862 he was elected on the Republican ticket to the supreme court of the state. Here he sat for six years during the last two of which he was chief justice. In 1869 President Grant appointed him United States circuit judge for the newly created 8th judicial circuit. For ten years he sat on the federal bench, holding thirteen terms of court annually, and traveling more than ten thousand miles. During most of this period he lectured each winter on medical jurisprudence at the University of Iowa. In 1879 he resigned from the court to accept a professorship of law at Columbia College, teaching real property and equity, and at the same time he opened a law office in New York City. He resigned his chair in 1882 and from that time until his death he engaged in the active practise of law in New York.

Dillon quickly assumed a place of prominence and distinction at the bar, arguing many cases of importance before the United States Supreme Court. He was primarily a corporation lawyer, but he never bound himself to any one corporation. He was counsel for the Union Pacific Railroad, the Missouri Pacific Railroad, the Texas Pacific Railroad, and the Western Union Telegraph Company. He was counsel for the Goulds in connection with all their railroad interests and also for the estate of Jay Gould. His practise was lucrative, he was a shrewd business man, and he left a substantial estate.

His reputation, however, rests upon his contributions to legal scholarship, a reputation, as one writer puts it, "so monumental that promotion to any coveted judicial office would not have added to his fame." While district judge in Iowa he made a *Digest of the Decisions of the Supreme Court of Iowa 1839–1860* (8 vols., 1860). Upon promotion to the federal bench he published a work on *Removal of Causes from State Courts to Federal Courts* (1876), which ran through five editions. But his name will always be associated with his monumental treatise on *Municipal Corporations* (1872), a work which created municipal corporations as a separate field of the law. This appeared as a single volume of 800 pages. It ran through five editions, all edited by the author, and the last of which, in five volumes, he dedicated in 1911 to the American Bar Association of which he had been president in 1891–92. He founded the *Central Law Journal* in 1872 and edited it for a year. He was a steady contributor to magazines and law journals. In 1876 he published a work on *The Law of Municipal Bonds*. In 1891–92 he delivered the Storrs Lectures at Yale which he published in 1894 under the title *The Laws and Jurisprudence of England and America*. In 1903 he edited the three-volume collection of addresses and papers on John Marshall which had grown out of the Marshall centenary celebrations in 1901. After the death of his wife he published privately a substantial memoir of her. He had married Anna Price in 1853 and they had two children, a son and a daughter. His wife and daughter were drowned at sea in 1898. His office was in New York but he had a beautiful home at Far Hills, N. J. He was a companionable man, placid in temperament, courteous and unhurried, and perhaps a little ponderous in speech. He had an absolute honesty of mind and integrity of character and in spite of his wealthy corporation practise his services were never to be had in aid of sharp or questionable practises. He was a Republican in politics and had been an ardent anti-slavery advocate before the Civil War.

[E. E. Stiles, *Annals of Iowa* in Apr., July 1909, and in *Recollections and Sketches of Notable Lawyers and Public Men of Early Iowa* (1916); G. S. Clay, Dillon's law partner, in *Green Bag*, Sept. 1911; H. Hubbard in *Am. Bar Asso. Jour.*, Jan. 1928; *Who's Who in America*, 1914–15; "Judge Dillon's Law Publications" in *Annals of Iowa*, Jan. 1903; obituary in *N. Y. Times*, May 6, 1914.] R.E.C.

DILLON, SIDNEY (May 7, 1812–June 9, 1892), railroad-builder and financier, was born in Northampton, Montgomery County, N. Y., where the family had resided for several generations. He was the son of Timothy Dillon, a farmer. The family was poor, and Sidney received only a meager education. At the age of seven, tiring of farm life, he began work as a "water boy" on the Mohawk & Hudson Railroad from Albany to Schenectady, and when this road was finished he was employed in a similar capacity on the Rensselaer & Saratoga Railroad. Later he acted as an overseer and then foreman on several other railroad construction projects in New England. Finally he decided to enter into business for himself, and although he had but little capital he made a bid for the construction of a short section of what is now the Boston & Albany Railroad. The bid was accepted and the work was satisfactorily completed in 1840. This was the beginning of a contracting career of unusual extent and success; during the next thirty years he built thousands of miles of railroad in all parts of the country, either individually or in association with other contractors. Among the roads partially constructed by him were the Rutland & Burlington Railroad, the Central Railroad of New Jersey, the Philadelphia & Erie Railroad, the Morris & Essex Railroad, the Pennsylvania Railroad, the New Orleans, Mobile & Chattanooga Railroad, and the Canada Southern Railroad. He also built for Cornelius Vanderbilt the tunnel from the Grand Central Station at Forty-second St., New York City, to the Harlem River.

The greatest enterprise of his life was the construction of the Union Pacific Railroad, with which company he became actively associated in 1865 through stock purchase in the Crédit Mobilier. He was one of the principal contractors and the directing authority for subsidiary contractors. During the next four years he took an active part in the construction of the road, frequently traveling backward and forward along the line and aiding the builders out of his abundant experience. He took part in the ceremony of laying the last rail in 1869, and one of the silver spikes with which the road was completed remained in his possession until his death. In 1892 he published an article on the opening of the Union Pacific, with the title "Historic Moments: Driving the Last Spike of the Union Pacific" (*Scribner's Magazine*, August 1892). He was a director of the Union Pacific Railroad Company for twenty-eight years (1864–92) and its president for nearly twelve years (from Mar. 11, 1874, to June 19, 1884, and again from Nov.

26, 1890, to Apr. 27, 1892). At the time of his death he was chairman of the board of directors, having been the first to be elected to that office.

After 1870 he was chiefly known as a financier. He had by then accumulated a large fortune, principally invested in railroad securities because of the fact that he had early adopted the policy of taking as part payment shares of stock of the companies for which he did construction work. The management of these investments gradually occupied a larger part of his time and he became actively associated with Jay Gould in the management of many of the properties controlled by the latter. He also served as a director in the Western Union Telegraph Company, the Manhattan Elevated Railroad Company, the Missouri Pacific Railroad, and several other transportation organizations. On Mar. 26, 1870, he was elected a Fellow of the American Society of Civil Engineers. Over six feet tall, heavily built yet active, and speaking in a direct, incisive manner, he conveyed the impression of a man who knew what to do and how to do it, and was fully able to command others in carrying out his plans. He was unusually careful in negotiating and entering into contracts and obligations, but, when once undertaken, displayed great energy and perseverance in carrying them out. In 1841 he married Hannah Smith of Amherst, Mass., and they had two daughters. He died at his home in New York City after an illness of three months.

[Jas. Parton and others, *Sketches of Men of Progress* (1870–71), pp. 587–93; *Trans. Am. Soc. Civil Engineers*, XXXVI, 603–04, Dec. 1896; H. K. White, *Hist. of the U. P. Ry.* (1895); E. L. Sabin, *Building the Pacific Ry.* (1919); N. Trottman, *Hist. of the Union Pacific* (1923); obituaries in the N. Y. papers of June 10, 1892, in *Harper's Weekly*, June 18, 1892, and in the *Ry. Age and Northwestern Railroader*, June 17, 1892.]

J.H.F.

DIMAN, JEREMIAH LEWIS (May 1, 1831–Feb. 3, 1881), clergyman, educator, was born in Bristol, R. I., where his ancestors had lived for four generations. His father, Byron, a business man of scholarly tastes, governor of his native state in 1846–47, was a descendant of Thomas Dimont, of French extraction, who settled in East Hampton, L. I., about 1656; his mother, Abby Alden Wight, was seventh in descent from John Alden. After attending the public schools of Bristol, J. Lewis, as from boyhood he chose to be called, prepared for college under Rev. James N. Sykes. Before he was sixteen he had written a history of Bristol based on researches in the town records and conversations with old inhabitants, which was published in a weekly newspaper. At Brown University, from which he graduated in 1851, he added to the work required a large amount of reading in history, philosophy, and literature. After studying German, philosophy, and the classics for a year with Rev. Dr. Thayer of Newport, R. I., he entered Andover Theological Seminary. Two years later he went to Germany and attended lectures at Halle, Heidelberg, and Berlin. Returning to America, he graduated from Andover in 1856.

Important churches at once sought to avail themselves of his training, rare gifts, and attractive personality, but he chose finally to settle in Fall River, Mass., where he was ordained as pastor of the First Congregational Church, Dec. 9, 1856. Three years later, January 1860, he resigned, and shortly afterward became pastor of the Harvard Congregational Church, Brookline, Mass. On May 15, 1861, he married Emily G. Stimson, daughter of John J. Stimson of Providence. A brilliant career in the ministry seemed to be before him. Horace Bushnell long and patiently endeavored to secure him as his successor at Hartford. Churches in New York, Philadelphia, and Charleston, S. C., beckoned to him. In spite of his gifts and deeply devotional nature, however, he had characteristics which interfered with his happiness in his calling. He was essentially a student and teacher, historically minded, frank and fearless in stating his views, unwilling to wear denominational chains. He abhorred revivals and all cheap expedients to attract people, was strongly inclined to the Episcopal Church, and sympathetic toward much in Roman Catholicism, while some of his doctrinal views led orthodox Bostonians to accuse him of Unitarian leanings. Accordingly, when in 1864 he was offered the chair of history and political economy at Brown University he accepted it.

Here his lectures—for he soon discarded textbook instruction—rich, penetrating, polished, and enlivened by wit, made him the idol of the students in spite of his high-bred reserve (W. C. Bronson, *The History of Brown University,* 1914, p. 409). His historical addresses on public occasions and his contributions to periodicals were widely read. On three occasions President Eliot tried to persuade him to leave Providence for Cambridge; he was offered professorships at Princeton and Johns Hopkins, and the presidency of the University of Vermont, and of the University of Wisconsin; but he chose to stay at Brown. He became an editorial writer for the *Providence Journal* when it was under the management of his intimate friend, James B. Angell [*q.v.*], and was regarded as one of its ablest contributors until his death. Of his publications in periodicals, "Religion in America," a survey for the century 1776–1876 (*North American Review,* January

1876), attracted wide notice. From 1877 to 1881 he reviewed historical publications for *The Nation.* In 1879 he delivered a notable course of lectures at Johns Hopkins on the "Thirty Years' War," and in 1880 he gave the Lowell Lectures, Boston. The latter were published in 1881 under the title, *The Theistic Argument as Affected by Recent Theories.* His career was suddenly cut short by an attack of malignant erysipelas when he was in his fiftieth year. In such high regard was he held in the state that the Rhode Island House of Representatives adjourned to attend his funeral. After his death a volume of selections from his writings, *Orations and Essays: with Selected Parish Sermons* (1882), including a commemorative discourse by James O. Murray, was published.

[In addition to references above, see Caroline Hazard, *Memoirs of the Rev. J. Lewis Diman, D.D.* (1887), and *A Precious Heritage* (1929); Louise Diman, *Emily Gardner Stimson Diman, A Memorial Sketch* (privately printed, 1902); E. R. Dimond, *The Geneal. of the Dimond or Dimon Family* ... (1891); *Proc. Mass. Hist. Soc.,* 1 ser., vol. XVIII (1880–81); *Nation* (N. Y.), Feb. 10, 1881; *Providence Jour.,* Feb. 4, 1881, and following days.]

H. E. S.

DIMITRY, ALEXANDER (Feb. 7, 1805– Jan. 30, 1883), educator, public official, son of Andrea and Celeste (Dragon) Dimitry, was born in New Orleans, where he also died. His father, a Greek from the island of Hydrea, came to America in the last quarter of the eighteenth century. His mother's father, also a Greek, came to New Orleans soon after 1760, but his mother's mother was of a family long resident in Louisiana, and one of her remote ancestors had taken for wife an Indian. Alexander was sent to school in New Orleans, and in 1820 to Georgetown College in the District of Columbia. Returning to Louisiana, he taught for two years in the Baton Rouge College before becoming the first English editor of the *New Orleans Bee,* a paper edited theretofore in French. During this time (1830–35) he contributed some short stories to "annuals" published in New York and Philadelphia. From 1834 to 1842 he was in Washington as a clerk in the Post Office Department and as active member, for some of that time, of the Union Literary Society. His *Lecture on the Study of History as Applied to the Progress of Civilization* and *Address on July Fourth,* both delivered before that body in 1839, exhibit in rounded oratory the erudition and patriotism characteristic of their time and title. He was married in 1835 to Mary Powell Mills, daughter of Robert Powell Mills of South Carolina, architect of the Washington Monument. Returning to Louisiana in 1842 and establishing a school in St. Charles Parish, he continued as its head till

1847, when he began his three years of valuable service as first superintendent of education in his state. From 1854 to 1859 he was a translator in the State Department in Washington, and from 1859 till he resigned, upon the secession of Louisiana, he was minister to Costa Rica and Nicaragua. During the Civil War he was assistant postmaster-general of the Confederacy. After the war he took up his residence in the vicinity of New York City, to remain there till 1867. From then until his death, with the exception of a brief period spent in teaching at Pass Christian, Miss., he lived in New Orleans. He wrote little but read and talked much. Having as a young man faced and definitely put from him the temptation to write books, he indulged instead throughout his life a taste for buying them—up to the number of 15,000—for his private library, and a taste also for setting forth his conclusions in public discourse, whether upon his literary and philological investigations or upon the state-rights theories which he thought should dominate American politics.

[Alcée Fortier, *Hist. of La.* (1906); *Louisiana* (1909); H. Rightor, *Standard Hist. of New Orleans* (1900); E. W. Fay, *Hist. of Education in La.* (1898); J. G. Shea, *Memorial of the First Centenary of Georgetown Coll.* (1891); *New Orleans Times Democrat,* Jan. 31, 1883.]   J.D.W.

DIMITRY, CHARLES PATTON (July 31, 1837–Nov. 10, 1910), journalist, author, was born in Washington, D. C., and died in New Orleans. His father, Alexander Dimitry [*q.v.*], a citizen of New Orleans who spent much of his life in Washington, was a man of considerable literary distinction, and his mother, Mary Powell Mills, was the daughter of Robert Mills, architect of the Washington Monument. As a boy Charles went to school in Louisiana, and in 1856 he entered Georgetown College, but apparently did not graduate, although he was given the degree of A.M. in 1867. At the beginning of the Civil War he was a clerk in New Orleans. He immediately went into the Confederate army, and remained there, in the Army of Tennessee, till 1865. During 1864 he published serially in Richmond a novel, "Guilty or Not Guilty." At the concluson of the war he went to New York, where till 1874 he was connected at one time or another with the *World, Graphic, News, Star,* and *Brooklyn Union*. In 1868 he published *The House in Balfour Street,* a romance with its scenes laid in a Victorian English village. Here he introduced, in dialects which he fancied appropriate to each, a sort of Brontëan hero, a French roué, several shop-keepers and house-servants, and many country ladies and gentlemen. The story is concerned with the struggle

of the most important of these characters through love and disaster, both of which for a while seem criminal, to final just deserts of happiness. He wrote also, besides many short stories, three other novels, published in periodicals: "Angela's Christmas," "Gold Dust and Diamonds," and "Two Knaves and a Queen"; and he contributed frequently to a number of newspapers, among them, the Alexandria *Commercial Advertiser,* the *New Orleans Bee* and the *Washington Daily Patriot*. He was employed for short periods in journalistic work in Mobile, Richmond, and Baltimore, and at one time in his life was engrossed in inventing and patenting an ink which would not rust pens. After reaching middle age he settled down in New Orleans, where he was connected for a long time with the editorial staff of the *Picayune*. There, writing sometimes as Tobias Guarnerius, Jr., or as Braddock Field, he prepared for various newspapers a number of articles on local history. His wife, Anne Elizabeth Johnson, whom he married in 1871 in Alexandria, Va., died in 1880, after the death of their only child. His last years were spent in comparative solitude, made heavier by poverty and approaching blindness.

[Alcée Fortier, *Louisiana* (1909); Georgetown Univ., *Gen. Reg.* (1916); *Who's Who in America,* 1910–11; *New Orleans Picayune,* Nov. 11, 1910; letter from Jas. M. Dimitry of New Orleans, July 3, 1928.]   J.D.W.

DINGLEY, NELSON (Feb. 15, 1832–Jan. 13, 1899), editor, governor, and congressman from Maine, was born in Durham, Me. The first Dingley came to America from Lynn, England, to settle in Lynn, Mass., as early as 1637, and one of his descendants removed to Maine about 1773. Nelson Dingley, the grandson of this early pioneer, married Jane Lambert, a descendant of Revolutionary stock, whose father had been one of the founders of the first Baptist church in the village of Durham, and Nelson Dingley, Jr., was their son. As a lad he was not brilliant, but industrious, conscientious, careful to read the best books, the sort of boy who would begin a diary at the age of fourteen and continue it to within a month of his death. From his earliest youth he was an advocate of temperance, took a keen interest in debating, attended Sunday-school, taught for two months in a day school at the age of sixteen, joined the church when twenty, and the same year was a delegate to a Whig state convention. He attended Waterville College (now Colby University) for nearly two years, and then transferred to Dartmouth College, from which he graduated sixth in a class of fifty-one in 1855. In college, as before, his interests were serious; books, debating, the temperance cause, religion. His political idol was Daniel Webster.

The turning point in his career came in 1856, when, after being admitted to the bar, he decided not to follow the law but purchased a half interest in the *Lewiston Evening Journal*. From that time on, his main interests were the newspaper, politics, and the advancement of education, religion, and the cause of temperance. Under Dingley's leadership the *Journal* immediately espoused the cause of the newly forming Republican party, and he found himself appointed a member of the Republican committee for the second congressional district. From this time onward his absorption in politics became almost complete. In 1861 he was elected to the state legislature as a Republican; he was reëlected five times, and was twice speaker. At this time he was described as a slight, frail, almost delicate man, industrious, methodical, and painstaking. In January 1874 he became governor of Maine, and served two terms. His first inaugural struck some distinctly modern notes, particularly his care for free public education, his insistence on prohibition and on reform in the taxation of railroads and corporations. "Railroads ... are public works," he asserted, "no matter by whose capital built" (Dingley, *post*, p. 109).

In 1881 he was elected to the United States House of Representatives, serving there without intermission until his death. During this period of about eighteen years—the climax of his career—he retained his boyhood interests, matured and expanded. Quiet, regular in his attendance upon his duties, an effective debater but not an orator, a repository of facts and figures, he was uninterested in the usual routines of society but gave evidence of his keen interest in temperance, education, and religion by constant addresses at conferences and institutions of learning. His thorough knowledge of finance, especially as related to the controversy over silver coinage, and his enthusiastic championship of a protective tariff gave him prominence on the floor of the House. He was a member of the Committee on Ways and Means in 1889, and in 1895 was made chairman. When the election of 1896 resulted in the triumph of President McKinley and a Republican Congress, with the consequent choice of Thomas B. Reed as speaker of the House, and of Dingley again as chairman of the Committee on Ways and Means, the latter undertook the task of preparing a tariff measure to replace the Democratic Wilson-Gorman Act. While Dingley was at work on the bill, he was offered the position of secretary of the treasury by President McKinley. On the grounds that his strength was not

sufficient for the arduous duties of the treasury, and that his inclinations lay in the direction of congressional service, he felt obliged to refuse the offer. The tariff law which finally resulted, commonly known as the Dingley Act, was passed in 1897 and remained in force until 1909. In 1898 Dingley was appointed by President McKinley to serve on the United States and British Joint High Commission for the settlement of points relating to the Alaskan boundary, the Alaskan seal fisheries, and other subjects of dispute, but his death occurred in the following January.

Champ Clark described him as a "pronounced brunette, with a Hebraic cast of features," destitute of humor, but a master of the subjects he discussed, who constituted a constant refutation of the common belief that nobody listens to speeches in Congress, inasmuch as the members always gathered when he took the floor. "Physically, Dingley was small, spare, and frail, with an appearance suggestive of consumption. He had what is called 'the scholar's stoop' in a marked degree. He was a frequent, lucid, and instructive, but not a pleasant speaker; had a weak, rasping voice, a well developed nasal twang, an acquiline nose, and a bald head" (Clark, *My Quarter Century of American Politics*, 1920, II, 11). On June 11, 1857, he was married to Salome McKenney.

[*The Life and Times of Nelson Dingley, Jr.* (1902), by his son E. N. Dingley (Kalamazoo, 1902), in the preparation of which Mr. Dingley's diary was largely used; *Just Maine Folks* (1924), published by the Maine Writers' Research Club; *Lewiston Journal*, immediately following Dingley's death.]   C.R.L.

DINSMOOR, ROBERT (Oct. 7, 1757–Mar. 16, 1836), poet, was the great-grandson of John Dinsmoor, who came from County Antrim, Ireland, in 1723 and settled in Londonderry, N. H., and the son of William and Elizabeth (Cochran) Dinsmoor. He was born in Windham, N. H., grew up on his father's farm, and, whenever he could be spared from work, went to such schools as were available in a frontier town, learning to "read, write and cipher tolerably." In 1775 at the age of eighteen he enlisted with the New Hampshire troops under Gen. John Sullivan and took part in the battle of Saratoga. Thoroughly convinced of the truth of the Longer and Shorter Catechisms, he was chosen deacon of the local Presbyterian church and was clerk of the session. He was twice married: first, to Mary Park, who died leaving him two sons and nine daughters, and afterward to Mary Davidson Anderson. He was of massive build, stronglimbed, broad-shouldered, and about five feet ten inches in height. A man of genial humor, a lover of good food and homely joys, he was widely esteemed for his kindly heart and his unbending integrity. Inheriting a gift of versification from his father, who had written some creditable verses in the Lowland Scotch dialect used in the Londonderry settlement, he cheered his lonely hours by writing about the thoughts and happenings of his daily life in natural, spontaneous melodies. Most of his verses were composed in the Scotch dialect, still spoken among his neighbors, and they won for him much local popularity. An edition of his poems was published in 1828, but it was of unsatisfactory appearance. Seventy years later Leonard Allison Morrison made a new compilation and arrangement in a more creditable form: *Poems of Robert Dinsmoor, the Rustic Bard* (1898). The opening poem is a lengthy narrative of "Jamie Cochran; the Indian Captive." Dinsmoor found his inspiration in the events and traditions of his neighborhood, local genealogists and historians have found much material of value in his writings, but that his name has survived is due largely to Whittier's friendship. The Quaker poet felt that American literature was sadly lacking in the "poetry of home, of nature and the affections," and in this "Rustic Bard" he found one who sensed the poetry of common life and in "home-taught, household melody" gave it genuine, if not very competent, expression. Whittier's essay on "Robert Dinsmore" (thus he spelled the name) in his collection entitled *Old Portraits and Modern Sketches* (1850) is well worth reading as a tribute to a friend, and for its reflections on native American literature.

[Besides the essay by Whittier, above mentioned, see *Poems of Robert Dinsmoor* (1898), which contains introductory recollections by the poet's nephew, Jas. Dinsmoor, letters written by Robert Dinsmoor during his service in the Revolutionary army and afterward, an appendix reprinting a letter establishing what is known of the origin of the Dinsmoor family, a brief genealogy of the McKeen family, and short papers on Gen. John Stark and Gen. John Sullivan under whom the New Hampshire men served.]   C. A. D.

DINWIDDIE, ROBERT (1693–July 27, 1770), colonial administrator, the son of Robert Dinwiddie, was born in 1693 at "Germiston," near Glasgow. His mother, a daughter of Matthew Cumming, is called Elizabeth in one place (genealogical sketch, Dinwiddie *Records*, I, xxii) and Sarah in another (p. viii of the same volume). Robert worked in his father's counting house, and later, apparently, became a merchant. On Dec. 1, 1727, he was made collector of customs for Bermuda. In 1730 he was placed upon the regular establishment, at £30 a year. So satisfactory was his work that on Apr. 11, 1738, he was made surveyor-general for the Southern Part of America, with jurisdiction

over the Carolinas, Virginia, Maryland, Pennsylvania, Bahama Islands, and Jamaica. In the same year he visited Barbados, where he uncovered many frauds in the revenues. On June 29, 1743, he appeared before the Lords of the Treasury to explain a plan for collecting the duty on colonial sugar. Late in the same year he was back in Barbados, where he found the frauds in the customs more glaring than ever. Charging several of the officials with false entries, fraudulent sales, and embezzlement, he dismissed them. These men complained to the Lords of the Treasury, and it is probable that Dinwiddie had to spend much time in London defending himself. While surveyor-general he took up his residence in Virginia. His commission entitled him to membership in the councils of the southern colonies, and in October 1741 he took his seat in the Council of Virginia.

On July 20, 1751, he was appointed lieutenant-governor of Virginia. On Nov. 20 he landed at York, with his wife, Rebecca Affleck, and two daughters, and was escorted to Williamsburg. Despite his acquaintance with Virginia affairs, he made the mistake of provoking a quarrel with the House of Burgesses. It had long been the practise in the colony for those taking up land to secure an order for a certain number of acres, and to occupy them for years before securing a patent. In this way they escaped the payment of quit-rents. Dinwiddie not only ordered all land-holders to take out patents at once, but charged a fee of a pistole for signing the patent and for the use of the seal. To the latter provision the Burgesses objected violently. "The rights of the subjects are so secured by law," they declared, "that they cannot be deprived of the least part of their property but by their own consent." Little dreaming that twenty-two years later the American colonies would rebel against the Crown in support of this principle, Dinwiddie persisted in his course. Thereupon the Burgesses laid the matter before the Board of Trade, through the attorney-general, Peyton Randolph. The Board directed that no fee should be charged for patents on land west of the mountains, or upon lands surveyed before Apr. 22, 1752. This meant victory for the Burgesses, and Dinwiddie reluctantly obeyed. But the dispute was settled only after it had done untold harm by preventing the co-operation of governor and Assembly at a time when the French were threatening the very existence of British America.

Dinwiddie was deeply interested in the Ohio region. Upon his arrival in 1751 he brought with him generous gifts for the Indians, in the hope of binding them to the English interest.

He gave his approval and support to the Ohio Company. With alarm he learned that the French not only claimed the region, but had erected a fort on French Creek. If they succeeded in their designs, the English would be cut off from the entire western country. In 1753 he sent George Washington, then a young officer in the Virginia militia, to warn the French to withdraw. When Washington returned with the report that the French were preparing to descend the Ohio with 220 canoes and 1,500 men, Dinwiddie tried to anticipate them. In February 1754 he sent seventy men to the site of Pittsburgh to erect a fort. A few weeks later he dispatched after them two larger detachments, the more advanced under Washington, at the same time appealing for aid to the neighboring governors and to the Board of Trade. When the French drove away his workmen from the fort, attacked Washington at Fort Necessity, and drove him back over the mountains, the governor made strenuous efforts for a new expedition. But the Assembly failed him, some of his troops deserted, and he was compelled to abandon the plan.

Hope revived when news arrived that two picked regiments under Gen. Edward Braddock had been ordered to Virginia. During the spring of 1755 Dinwiddie was busy gathering stores of food, recruiting the Virginia companies, urging other governors to aid, seeking Indian allies, pleading with the Assembly for funds. When Braddock led his force into the wilderness, Dinwiddie was confident of success. After the crushing defeat at Great Meadows, he criticized the English general for "leaving half his army forty miles behind," and for the "want of scouts to clear the woods." But defeat did not discourage him. The Assembly voted £40,000 and 1,200 men, which with the remnant of Braddock's army under Col. Dunbar he thought sufficient to retrieve the situation. To his dismay, Dunbar marched to Philadelphia, leaving "the fort and frontier to be defended by 400 sick and wounded, and the poor remains of our provincial forces." Hard upon the heels of the British came the Indians, robbing, pillaging, burning, murdering. So Dinwiddie had to face alone the task of defending hundreds of miles of exposed frontier. He sent out companies of rangers, raised a regiment and placed it under Washington, sent for the friendly Indians, and built forts at the points of greatest danger. Despite these efforts it was a time of terror for western Virginia, and more than once Dinwiddie had to order out the militia to meet expected raids. An expedition to the Shawnee country failed because of rain, snow, and swollen rivers. At last, in the spring of 1757, some four hundred Cherokees, Catawbas, Saponies, Tuscaroras, and Nottaways gathered at Winchester, and for the time being the frontier was comparatively safe.

From the outbreak of the war until his return to England Dinwiddie constantly was seeking intercolonial cooperation. Repeatedly he wrote to the governors of Pennsylvania, Maryland, and the Carolinas, urging them to send money and men. In April 1755 he went to Annapolis for a conference of governors, and two years later he met the Earl of Loudoun at Philadelphia, to discuss plans of defense. His discouraging experience with assemblies led him to suggest that Parliament impose upon the colonies a poll tax of a shilling and a land tax of two shillings for each 100 acres, to aid in financing the war. "I know our people will be inflamed if they hear of my making this proposal," he added (Dinwiddie *Records*, II, 341). His constant exertions told upon his health. On Mar. 22, 1757, he wrote Pitt asking for leave of absence to visit Bath. He left Virginia on Jan. 12, 1758, and was succeeded by Francis Fauquier. He died at Clifton, Bristol, on July 27, 1770. His career as colonial administrator was marked by vision, strength, attention to detail, and untiring energy. As the man who precipitated the struggle which brought about the downfall of New France, he is a figure of first importance in the early history of the American continent.

[The chief sources of information are *The Official Records of Robert Dinwiddie* (2 vols., 1883–84), in the Va. Hist. Soc. Colls.; Correspondence of the Board of Trade, in the British Public Record Office; *Calendar of Treasury Books and Papers, 1729–30* (1897), *1735–38* (1900), *1742–45* (1903); *Jours. of the House of Burgesses of Va.* (1909); *Exec. Jours. of the Council of Colonial Va.* (3 vols., 1925–28); and *Va. Mag. of Hist. and Biog.*, Jan. 1906.]

T. J. W.

DISBROW, WILLIAM STEPHEN (Mar. 18, 1861–Dec. 26, 1922), physician, collector, was born in Newark, N. J., the son of Henry G. and Catherine Cline (Clickener) Disbrow. His early life was a struggle for education and professional training, but by dint of hard work in factories and drug stores he paid his way through the New York College of Pharmacy (Ph.G., 1880) and the medical department of the University of the City of New York (M.D., 1887). After a year in North Adams, Mass., as a chemist with the Zylonite Company, he returned in 1888 to his native Newark, married Clara E. Valentine of that city, and spent the remaining thirty-four years of his life in the practise of medicine. Over a long period of years he was a staff physician at St. Barnabas's Hospital and at the City Hospital, a professor in the New Jersey College of Pharmacy, and a member of the

Newark board of health, of which he in time became president. His private practise was large, but since his generosity to needy patients was also large it never became especially lucrative. Though his professional career was unusually successful and beneficent, Disbrow's chief claim to remembrance is as a collector. A burly man with great physical and mental powers and a voracious appetite for knowledge, he threw into his hobbies such energy as few men can devote to the main business of their lives. His principal fields were the natural sciences, medical history, and numismatics, but almost anything that interested him and that he thought might interest some one else he gathered in. Whenever an old family was broken up, an old house abandoned, an old cemetery removed, Disbrow was on hand to inquire whether papers, relics, or inscriptions were to be had. He examined every excavation for a new building lest some deposit of sand or clay or some stratum of rock escape him. He ransacked the old bookstores almost daily and kept his eyes open for objects of interest when visiting factories and the homes of his patients. But if he took a freebooter's joy in collecting stamps, coins, medical medals, plants and flowers, weapons, pottery, Indian curios, rocks, minerals, crystals, shells, gums, seeds, fossils, books, pamphlets, maps, pictures, and portraits of physicians, he was generous in bestowing his finds on institutions and on other private collectors; indeed much of his material came to him from men who wished to make some return for the lavish generosity that he had shown them. He was not, as one might suppose, an indiscriminate collector: the range and exactness of his information were amazing. The chief beneficiaries of his collecting were the Smithsonian Institution, the United States National Museum, and the Surgeon-General's Library in Washington, and the Academy of Medicine of Northern New Jersey, the New Jersey Historical Society, and the Newark Museum Association in Newark, to which he gave his largest collection. This consisted of 74,-000 science specimens, 5,000 scientific books, 10,-000 pamphlets, and 5,000 pictures and maps. Housed during the latter years of Disbrow's life on the fourth floor of the Newark Public Library, where he spent the long hot summer days in classifying and labeling his materials, it became after his death the science collection of the Newark Museum. He died at the height of his powers. He was seized with a cerebral hemorrhage just after finishing Christmas dinner at his son's home in Summit, N. J., and succumbed twelve hours after.

[J. C. Dana, G. P. Merrill, F. Neumann, and others,

A Great Collector: Dr. Wm. S. Disbrow (Newark Museum Asso., 1925); *Gen. Alumni Cat. of N. Y. Univ.: Medical Alumni* (1908); *Newark Evening News,* Dec. 27, 1922; *Newark Sunday Call,* Jan. 1, 1923.] G. H. G.

DISSTON, HENRY (May 23, 1819–Mar. 16, 1878), manufacturer, was born at Tewkesbury, Gloucestershire, England, son of Thomas and Ann (Harrod) Disston. His father, a mechanic experienced in the manufacture of lace-making machinery, brought him and his sister to America when the boy was fourteen years old. Three days after reaching Philadelphia, the port of destination, the father died. Left to his own resources, the young immigrant became a saw maker's apprentice. In 1840 he started a small business of his won, with a capital of $350. He had to overcome many difficulties. The industry was then in the handicraft stage, was dependent on imported steel, and was confronted with the competition of superior English technology. In addition, Disston was unfortunate in his relations with lessors. In 1846, however, he established his factory at Front and Laurel Sts., Philadelphia, where during the next quarter-century his business rapidly increased.

His significance as a manufacturer was twofold. In the first place, he was an innovator in technology. Secondly, he transformed a small and struggling industry into one that outrivaled foreign competitors and conquered world markets. As early as 1844 he made use of steam power in his saw factory. Another early innovation was the conversion of waste steel into ingots in place of its reshipment to England. Out of these early experiments he evolved formulas for the manufacture of the highest grade of crucible steel demanded by the peculiar strains to which saws are subjected, and thus the industry was at length freed from dependence on imported steel. His adaptability was indicated by his transformation of his plant during the Civil War into an establishment for manufacturing war supplies. For the purpose of making metal plates, the importation of which was interrupted by the Southern cruisers, he built a rolling-mill. An experimental sawmill was established for the purpose of determining the types of saws best adapted to various kinds of timber and to the varying needs of woodworkers. Timber was conserved by reducing the thickness of the saws while at the same time greater speed and driving power were made possible by improvements in the quality of steel and in the models of saws. He was unusually gifted as a mechanic and inventor, and made personally a large number of improvements. He encouraged his employees to observe defects and to suggest improvements. The expansion of the business continued until at length the works produced all types of saws from the largest circular saw of the lumbering industry to the minute keyhole saw, and also a great variety of files, knives, screw-drivers, trowels, molders' tools, etc. By establishing agencies in various places, the company contributed to the significant tendency of modern manufacturers to subordinate the mercantile to the industrial group. In 1871 the widely known Disston factory at Tacony, near Philadelphia, was opened. The establishment came to include a tract of several hundred acres, and a factory town rapidly grew up, the houses of the workers being financed in part by the company. The plant attracted the interest of visitors from various parts of the world.

Henry Disston was not prominently connected with organized activities outside of his own business, nor was he a man of particular intellectual or cultural distinction. He contributed liberally to community enterprises, however, building a school for the promotion of industrial and general education, maintaining a dispensary, and supporting the conventional activities. His participation in politics included membership on the Hayes electoral ticket and support of protective tariffs. His first marriage was to Amanda Mulvina Bickley; his second, to Mary Steelman, the mother of his children, some of whom came to be associated with him in the firm of Henry Disston & Sons.

[The most important source is the "Disston History," a two-volume manuscript history in the company's archives, compiled in 1920, the second volume being a history of the Works. Some additional information is in the *Public Ledger* (Phila.), Mar. 18, 1878; *The Manufactories and Manufacturers of Pa.* (1875); and J. T. Scharf and T. Westcott, *Hist. of Phila.* (3 vols., 1884).]
                                                          W. B.

DISTURNELL, JOHN (Oct. 6, 1801–Oct. 1, 1877), compiler of guide-books, was born in Lansingburg, N. Y., and died in New York City. He began work as a printer in Albany, N. Y., but the first available contemporary record of his whereabouts is in the New York Directory of 1830. From then till 1865 he appears in successive issues of the Directory as a book-dealer, and from 1865 to 1870 as librarian of the Cooper Union; he is missing from the Directories of 1870–76, but reappears in 1877. He is in the Philadelphia Directories for the early seventies. In 1836 he published *A Guide to the City of New York,* and in the same year, *The Traveller's Guide through the State of New York.* With the rapid development of means of transportation he became a prolific compiler of railway and steamship guides, one of the earliest being *The Western Traveller; Embracing the Canal and Railroad Routes from Albany to Troy, to Buffalo and Niagara Falls. Also the Steamboat Route, from Buffalo to Detroit and Chicago* (1844). For two or three decades in the middle of the century he issued, in various editions and under various titles, *Disturnell's Railway, Steamship and Telegraph Book.* Quick to anticipate popular demand, in 1849, he published *The Emigrant's Guide to New Mexico, California, and Oregon.* He gave off a constant succession of writings about any region or subject, specific or vague, in America or elsewhere, that interested him or might conceivably interest his "trade." He published handbooks, distance-tables, maps, gazetteers, and censuses too numerous to name, a book on *Springs, Waterfalls, Seabathing Resorts, and Mountain Scenery* (1855), and disquisitions on the *Influence of Climate in a Commercial, Social, Sanitary, and Humanizing Point of View* (1860), and on *Political Economy, or Interest, Usury, and Taxation* (1877). From 1851 to 1877 he compiled yearly *The United States National Register Containing Authentic Political and Statistical Information.* In 1866 he issued *Politician's Manual, The Constitution of the United States of America Together with Amendments and Proposed Amendments.* He was a good salesman—not only industrious and aggressive, but comfortably at one with the opinions and desires of his environment. In 1876 he published *New York as It Was and as It Is.* As late as 1877 he was still promoting travel. He thought that Americans should be thrifty like Europeans, so that they too might patronize the centers of rest and recreation. His *Summer Resorts,* published in that year, deals only with the immediate vicinity of New York; it was not, he said, so full as he had meant it to be—want of time and patronage had persuaded him to issue only a part of what he had planned. He hoped, however, that in 1878 he could "continue this work to completion, hereafter furnishing the public with a complete Guide within a circuit of Fifty Miles around the City of New York."

[Disturnell's own publications; New York and Philadelphia directories; *Appletons' Ann. Cyc.,* 1877; *Evening Post* (N. Y.), Oct. 2, 1877.]   J. D. W.

DITRICHSTEIN, LEO (Jan. 6, 1865–June 28, 1928), actor, dramatist, was one of a considerable number of members of his profession who came to the United States from Europe to make their reputations and to spend the greater part of their lives on the American stage. With him, as with others, English was an acquired tongue, and he always spoke it with a noticeable foreign accent. He was born on the paternal estate at Tamesvar, Hungary, the son of Sigismond Ladislav Ditrichstein, and of Bertha von Eötvös, whose father was the Hungarian novelist, Joseph von Eötvös. His parents had other aims for him, but he insisted upon becoming an actor. After several years' service in the theatres of Vienna, where he had the advantage of training from Adolph Sonnenthal, and in Berlin and other Continental cities, including engagements in light opera, he came to the United States, and at once started upon the career in which he achieved distinction as an actor and as a maker of plays.

His first appearance on the American stage was made at the Amberg Theatre in New York, Mar. 12, 1890, with a company of German actors in a production of Sudermann's play, *Die Ehre*. Not long afterward he had gained sufficient facility in the English language to appear in English-speaking parts, and he soon found himself in demand for the playing of important characters. His first part in English was in a popular farce of that period called *Mr. Wilkinson's Widows*, one of William Gillette's adaptations from the French. When the *Trilby* furore began in 1895, his foreign manner and vocal intonations made him the very actor for the eccentric Zou Zou in the stage version of George Du Maurier's novel made by Paul M. Potter. Thereafter he was continuously active in the American theatre as a writer and adapter of plays, and as an actor. He did little original play-writing, but he had the clever knack, so common with many capable actors, of taking a foreign play and of making it over into other scenes and languages. The greater number of plays that bear his name, nearly forty in all, had their originals in the European drama, and since German was thoroughly familiar to him, he drew them mainly from German dramatists. Occasionally he worked in collaboration with American dramatists, notably with Clyde Fitch, with whom he wrote *Gossip* (1895), *A Superfluous Husband* (1897), and *The Head of the Family* (1898). Two of his most popular farces were *All on Account of Eliza* (1900), and *Are You a Mason?* (1901), one of the most popular plays of its kind for more than twenty years. In 1901 he collaborated with Robert Grant in a dramatization of that author's novel, *Unleavened Bread*, but although it was received with critical favor, it met with scant success from the public. His active service as an actor covered nearly thirty-five years of appearance in plays by many others as well as his own. *The Concert* and *The Phantom Rival*, both from the German, *The King*, from the French, and *The Great Lover*, written in collaboration with Frederic and Fanny Hat-

ton, are especially the plays that brought him deserved fame both as dramatist and actor. He had a liking also for melodrama, and in 1920 he appeared in *The Purple Mask*, turning thereto from the intriguing and passionate lover in chase of the sophisticated woman to the fascinating hero who surmounts all dangers and wins his way by his valor to happiness and love. From the graceful youth of such parts as Zou Zou in *Trilby* the years changed him in physique to a heavier and more imposing type of stage character, but there persisted in all his impersonations the light and airy touch that gave a romantic quality to his entire repertory. He had acted minor parts in Shakespeare's plays during his youth in the European theatres, and during his final years on the stage he had an ambition to make Shakespearian productions and play leading rôles in them, but it was not fulfilled. In 1924, he announced his retirement from all stage work, and went abroad to live in Europe until his death at Auersperg, Jugoslavia. His wife, to whom he was married in 1896, was Josephine Wehrle.

[Interview in the *Christian Science Monitor*, Mar. 16, 1920; *Current Opinion*, Nov. 1917; A. D. Storms, *The Playgoers' Blue Book*, 1901; *Who's Who in America*, 1924–25; John Parker, *Who's Who in the Theatre*, 1925; obituary in *N. Y. Times*, June 30, 1928. The date of Ditrichstein's birth is given variously in the last four sources as Jan. 6, 1864, 1867, and Jan. 6, 1865, respectively, the *N. Y. Times* adopting Parker's date.]

E.F.E.

DITSON, GEORGE LEIGHTON (Aug. 5, 1812–Jan. 29, 1895), author, son of William and Mary (Leighton) Ditson, was born in Westford, Mass., and died in New York City. He went to school at the Westford Academy and later began to study medicine in Boston. Here his health failed, and he was advised to take a sea voyage. He went away and remained for two years, largely in Egypt and India, where he became engrossed in the study of oriental languages. He had scarcely returned home when he set out again, this time with a party intending to make excavations around Carthage. During the forties, under both Tyler and Polk, he was the American consul at Nuevitas, Cuba, and in 1842–43 he taught English in a college in Puerto-Príncipe. By 1847 he was off again for the East, making during that year his seventh crossing of the Atlantic. He had already visited western Europe, and it was at this time, most likely, that he went to Russia and Palestine. In 1850 he published *Circassia, or a Tour of the Caucasus*—loyal to America, to be sure, but suggestive of Cooper in its quarrel with American provincialism, and of Byron in its assumption of a flinty sophistication. *The Para Papers on*

France, Egypt and Ethiopia—"para," it is explained, being one of the smallest of oriental coins—was published in English, and in French. A year later (1859) appeared his voluminous *The Crescent and French Crusaders,* based on a residence in Northern Africa. He wrote two novels, both having to do with love and marriage in Scotland and Italy, *Crimora, or Love's Cross* (1852) and *The Federati of Italy* (1871). In 1860 he married Oralie Bartlett, daughter of a naval officer, Washington Allen Bartlett, and his wife, Ruth Budd Bloom. During 1863 and 1864 he was a student at the University of Vermont, and in the latter year he was given his degree in medicine. During his travels he formed a friendship with Madame Blavatsky [*q.v.*] and became a member of the Adyar branch of the Theosophical Society. His home in Albany, N. Y., which she later visited, was the scene of many psychical investigations, and the meeting-place of any spiritualists, apparently, who were in the neighborhood, or could manage to get there.

[The principal source is a letter from Oralie D. Lodge, Albany, N. Y., Feb. 24, 1928. An obituary of Ditson's wife was published in the *Albany Evening Jour.,* Apr. 9, 1906.]   J. D. W.

DITSON, OLIVER (Oct. 20, 1811–Dec. 21, 1888), music publisher, was descended from Hugh Ditson who settled at Billerica, Mass., in 1685. His father, Joseph Ditson, who married in 1797 Lucy Pierce of Lexington, became a Boston merchant and ship-owner, prosperous for a time but later dependent on Oliver, the fifth of nine children. The boy, born at 74 Prince St., near Copp's Hill, was graduated in 1823 from the Eliot School, leading his class. He entered the store of Col. Samuel H. Parker, bookseller and publisher, a founder of the Handel and Haydn Society, and later apprenticed himself to Isaac Butts, then printer of the *North American Review,* from whom he learned the printing trade thoroughly. His most intimate friend, while he was with Butts, was John Henry Howard Graupner, son of Gottlieb Graupner, the celebrated orchestral conductor. Through the Graupners, Oliver became a competent musician and for a time he was organist at the Bulfinch Street Church. He also saw opportunities in music publishing which induced him in 1835 to start his own business at 107 Washington St. The *Saturday Evening Gazette* said, June 6, 1835: "Mr. Oliver Ditson has just published a new song entitled 'There's not a Leaf within the Bower.'" Thus was initiated a business which became the largest of its kind in North America. Ditson interested his first employer in his ven-

ture and in 1836 the co-partnership was announced of "Parker & Ditson, dealers in Piano Fortes and Sheet Music." In 1840 Ditson bought out his partner, and in 1845 he took into his employ John C. Haynes, then fifteen years old, who became his efficient associate and later, under the name of Oliver Ditson & Company, adopted in 1857, his partner. This firm's business, after the Civil War, reached $2,000,000 annually. Its successor, the Oliver Ditson Company, is still (1930) important in the world's music trade.

The success which Ditson achieved as a music publisher was based on sound business methods, understanding of the public capacity to appreciate music, personal sympathy with the aspirations of composers, and sufficient musical ability of his own to professionalize his commercial instincts. He was methodical and industrious. As church organist and as conductor of the Malibran Glee Club he kept in close touch with his fellow musicians. He cherished his friendships, which were many. He was philanthropic and public-spirited. Banks sought his counsel. He was president for twenty years of the Continental Bank, a trustee of the Franklin Savings Bank of which he was an organizer, and a director of other banks. He was a friend and supporter of Father Taylor in his work among seamen. He helped to found the Home for Aged Men on West Springfield St. He was among the subscribers who made it possible for Dr. Eben Tourjée to buy the Franklin Square House as a home for the New England Conservatory of Music.

Ditson was a good trader as well as a humanitarian. He was quick to see a profit where others had met with a loss and made his money largely by publishing popular music at prices low enough to permit large sales. His firm owed much of its expansion to a policy of buying the plates of publishers who were in difficulty. Allied houses were established in several cities. Oliver Ditson performed a service to musical journalism by publishing for John S. Dwight *Dwight's Journal of Music* from 1858 to 1876. He was one of the guarantors who made up the deficit of $100,000 incurred by the Peace Jubilee at Boston in 1872. His personal activities were closely limited to his native city from which he rarely traveled further than to his summer home at Swampscott. In religion he was a Unitarian, though an attendant in his later years upon Episcopal services. In 1888 he suffered a stroke of paralysis which ended his career after a lingering illness. He was buried from Trinity Church, with Phillips Brooks officiating, and with J. C.

D. Parker, a son of his first employer, at the organ. A contemporary said of him, "He was courteous and kindly in manner and, although of a somewhat reserved and retiring disposition, exceedingly amiable, witty and appreciative." He was married, about 1840, to Catherine Delano, by whom he had five children.

[H. A. Hazen, *Hist. of Billerica* (1883); W. A. Fisher, *Notes on Music in Old Boston* (1918); *A Hundred Years of Music in America* (1889), ed. by W. S. B. Mathews; *Boston Musical Review*, Jan. 1889; *Boston Transcript*, Dec. 22, 1888; obituary notices and other biographical data in scrapbook compiled by Allen A. Brown for the collection bearing his name in the Boston Pub. Lib. The date of Ditson's birth is given variously as Oct. 20, 21, and 30, 1811; the authority for the first of these is the sketch in the *Boston Musical Review*, carefully prepared before Ditson's death, and presumably with the aid of his son.]   F. W. C.

DIVEN, ALEXANDER SAMUEL (Feb. 10, 1809–June 11, 1896), lawyer, soldier, railroad promoter, was the son of John and Eleanor (Means) Diven of the town of Catharine, Tioga County—now Watkins, Schuyler County, N. Y., where he was born. He obtained his education in the local school and Penn Yan and Ovid academies. He then took up the study of law in the office of Judge Gray at Elmira, Chemung County, N. Y., and was admitted to the bar in 1831. Commencing practise in Elmira, he acquired in a short time an extensive connection and there formed the well-known firm of Diven, Hathaway & Woods, which for years enjoyed the largest practise in that part of the state. He did not confine himself to the legal profession, but, becoming interested in internal communications, turned his attention to the railroad projects affecting his district. In 1844 he became a director of the New York & Erie Railroad, which at that time was built only as far as Binghamton. The company's funds were exhausted and at a meeting of the directors that year it was proposed to abandon the enterprise. Diven, however, successfully opposed this move, procured the adoption of a resolution recommending the prosecution of the work, and as attorney for the road took charge of the steps required to implement this decision. For the next six years he devoted his time to the task of rescue, including the raising of large sums of money for construction purposes. He drafted the necessary legislation in aid of the road, the first issues of bonds, and the mortgages by which they were secured, and acted as commissioner of construction through its building. After its completion he continued as its attorney. In 1849 he was chiefly instrumental in organizing the company which built the Binghamton-Corning line, and the Williamsport & Elmira Railroad, being president of the latter throughout its construction, and at a later period taking an active part in the extension of its system to the west under the name of the Pennsylvania Northern Central Railroad. He also contracted, in conjunction with Gen. Price and J. P. Kirkwood, for the construction of the Missouri Pacific Railroad and engaged in the construction of the Southwestern branch of the road. He had from an early age interested himself in public affairs, and was prominent in organizing the Republican party, but, owing to his professional and railroad engagements, was unable to take an active part in politics till 1858 when he represented Chemung County in the state Senate. In 1859 he was the Free-Soil candidate for governor of New York. In 1860 he was elected to the Thirty-seventh Congress, from the 27th Congressional District of New York, and served 1861–63, being a member of the Judiciary Committee and as a strong Unionist giving the administration unstinted support. When, however, the proposition was made to confiscate the property of the "rebels" he denounced it as barbarous in a powerful speech. As an anti-slavery man he supported the bill abolishing slavery in the District of Columbia. He drafted and introduced the first measure authorizing the employment of colored troops in the field. In July 1862 at the request of Secretary Stanton, he went to Elmira where he raised the 107th Regiment of New York Volunteers from Schuyler, Chemung, Steuben, and Allegany counties, being commissioned lieutenant-colonel. Joining the 5th Brigade of Whipple's division in the Reserve Corps, his regiment received its baptism of fire at Antietam, after which battle he was promoted colonel (Oct. 21, 1862), and as such was in the thick of the fight at Chancellorsville. In May 1863 he was appointed assistant adjutant-general and assumed command of the troop depot at Elmira. Breveted brigadier-general, Aug. 30, 1864, he acted as assistant provost-marshal-general for the Western District of New York, becoming later commander of the Northern and Western districts, and continuing as such until the close of hostilities, when he returned to Elmira and resumed his law practise. In 1865 he was elected vice-president of the New York & Erie Railroad and held the office for three years. His last public service was as mayor of Elmira, and he retired from active business in 1879. His first wife, Amanda Beers, whom he married in 1835, died in 1875, and in 1876 he married Maria Joy. In character extremely modest and unassuming, he was very methodical in his habits and an incessant worker. As lawyer, soldier, railroad magnate, and politician he was equally successful.

For years he was looked upon as the foremost citizen of Elmira, and his devotion to the city's interests induced the unbounded respect and confidence of his townsfolk.

[H. P. Peirce and D. H. Hurd, *Hist. of Tioga, Chemung, Tompkins and Schuyler Counties, N. Y.* (1879), p. 281; J. L. Sexton, *An Outline Hist. of Tioga and Bradford Counties in Pa., Chemung . . . in N. Y.* (1885), p. 130; F. B. Heitman, *Hist. Reg. and Dict. U. S. Army* (1903); *Biog. Dir. Am. Cong.* (1928).]

H. W. H. K.

DIX, DOROTHEA LYNDE (Apr. 4, 1802–July 17, 1887), humanitarian, of New England ancestry, was born at Hampden, Me. Her parents were Joseph and Mary (Bigelow) Dix. Dorothea (she was christened Dorothy) probably inherited her traits of energy, public-spiritedness, and disregard for popularity from her grandfather, Dr. Elijah Dix, a Boston physician. Her father was a feeble character and religious fanatic. On her own initiative, at ten years old, she left her home, which had been so unhappy that she would never speak of it in detail, to seek with her grandmother, in Boston, stable conditions for an education. "I never knew childhood," she said in later life. At fourteen she was teaching school in Worcester, Mass., and soon after she established in the Dix Mansion in Boston a school for young girls which, with intervals of ill health, she conducted until her thirty-third year. The school mirrored herself. An unusual emphasis was put on the natural sciences, in which she was always keenly interested, but the dominant note was stress on moral character. She taught the children of the Rev. William Ellery Channing [*q.v.*] and traveled to the West Indies with his family. A Unitarian, she was a member of Dr. Channing's congregation. During these years, in addition to her teaching, she produced a number of long-since forgotten books: *Conversations on Common Things* (1824, 60th edition, 1869); *Evening Hours* (1825); *Meditations For Private Hours* (1828, many times reprinted); *The Garland of Flora* (1829); *The Pearl, or Affection's Gift; a Christmas and New Year's Present* (1829); *Ten Short Stories For Children* (1827–28; republished as *American Moral Tales For Young Persons*, 1832); *Hymns for Children, Selected and Altered* (1825; rearranged, 1833). She was, however, nervous, overstrained, and delicate, with incipient lung trouble. Obliged to give up her school, she spent eighteen months with the William Rathbones, friends of Dr. Channing's, at Greenbank, outside Liverpool, England. She returned to Boston in 1838, still an invalid. If she had died then, she would be remembered, if at all, only as one of numberless conscientious, self-sacrificing teachers of youth. But for fifty years she was to be an agent of change, and at her death the attitude of mind toward insanity and the treatment of the insane were to be different over the whole United States because she had lived.

The medieval conception of insanity as a possession by devils had gradually changed to one as cruel in effect, that of nature depraved and fallen to the brute and treated as a beast. In 1840 there were only eight insane asylums in the United States. Devoted and high-principled doctors were there practising the enlightened ideas of Philippe Pinel of France and William Tuke of England, but their efforts made only a flicker of light in the darkness where cruelty, callous indifference, and self-interest created misery unnoticed and unchallenged. An apostle was needed to bring the evil to public attention. On Mar. 28, 1841, Dorothea Dix undertook a Sunday-school class in the East Cambridge (Mass.) House of Correction. Visiting the jail, she found insane persons in an unheated room. After vain protest, she brought the matter to the East Cambridge court, with success. Aroused by the distress she had observed, she spent two years in a quiet, unobserved, thorough investigation of the condition of the insane, in jails, almshouses, and houses of correction, throughout Massachusetts. With incontrovertible evidence in hand, she chose influential men to present a memorial to the state legislature, calling attention to "the *present* state of Insane Persons confined within this Commonwealth, in *cages, closets, cellars, stalls, pens! Chained, naked, beaten with rods, and lashed* into obedience!" (*Memorial to the Legislature of Massachusetts*, 1843, p. 4). By letters to the press, she aroused public opinion. Over indignant protest and disbelief, the bill was carried for the enlargement of the Worcester insane asylum. Miss Dix soon saw the inadequacy of demanding intelligence and humanity from the keepers of almshouses and jails, and that asylums, with intelligent personnel, supported by state taxation, were necessary. Her work became national in scope. Five years later, in her first petition to Congress, she could write: "I have myself seen *more than nine thousand idiots, epileptics, and insane in these United States, destitute of appropriate care and protection*; and of this vast and most miserable company, sought out in *jails,* in *poorhouses,* and in *private dwellings,* there have been hundreds, nay, rather thousands, —bound with galling chains, bowed beneath fetters and heavy iron balls attached to drag chains, lacerated with ropes, scourged with rods, and terrified beneath storms of profane execrations and cruel blows; now subject to gibes and scorn and torturing tricks, now abandoned to the most loathsome necessities, or subject to the vilest and most outrageous violations. These are strong terms, but language fails to convey the astonishing truths. I proceed to verify this assertion, beginning with the State of Maine" (*Senate Miscellaneous Documents No. 150*, 30 Cong., 1 Sess.).

She followed her Massachusetts procedure in each state—a thorough, independent research; wise choice of spokesmen; influence of the press. She never appeared in public. A sweet, low voice, a gentle manner, quiet dignity turned aside hostile comment, while her persistence, driven by the white heat of compassion, was always based on self-observed facts. She had prejudice, as well as ignorance and self-interest, to combat. At this time for a woman to undertake public work was considered unfeminine. At times she hesitated. "I am naturally timid and diffident, like all my sex," she wrote to a friend. The force that carried her over all obstacles was due to three characteristics. First: independence of spirit, "The feeling, right or wrong, that aloneness is my proper position"; second, the emotional intensity of her compassion, "I have no particular love for my species, but own to an exhaustless fund of compassion"; third, the profound influence of Dr. Channing, whose insistence on the presence in every human being, however degraded, of the possibility of endless spiritual development was the heart of her religious belief and gave the driving power to her pity.

Travel was by infrequent railroad, steamboat, a few lines of coaches, and small vehicles; over rough roads, through deep mud, by fords; subject to discomfort, accident, and exposure. In 1845 she wrote, "I have travelled over more than ten thousand miles in the last three years. Have visited eighteen state penitentiaries, three hundred county jails and houses of correction, more than five hundred almshouses and other institutions, besides hospitals and houses of refuge" (Tiffany, *post*, p. 132). She was now middle-aged, with persistent lung trouble and susceptible to malaria, but no difficulty could check her.

Between 1841 and 1845, three hospitals for the insane were enlarged or re-founded (Worcester, Mass.; Butler, at Providence, R. I.; Utica, N. Y.) and three new hospitals founded (Trenton, N. J.; Harrisburg, Pa.; Toronto, Canada). Between 1845 and 1852, she carried the legislatures of Indiana, Illinois, Kentucky, Tennessee, Missouri, Mississippi, Louisiana, Alabama, South Carolina, North Carolina and Maryland, for state hospitals and caused the founding of the hospital at Halifax, N. S. But her great effort for the passage of a twelve-million-dollar bill for land, to be set aside for taxation toward the care of the insane, met defeat in 1854 by President Pierce's veto, after the bill had passed the houses of Congress.

Between 1854 and 1857, she traveled in England and on the Continent, investigating the care of the insane. Queen Victoria's order for a Royal Commission to investigate the condition of the insane in Scotland, the founding of a hospital on the Island of Jersey, and that of a hospital in Rome, were results of this journey. From 1857 to 1861 she was constantly active, raising money, advising on hospital buildings, and choosing hospital personnel. Illustrative of her many other activities, outside her main work, is her accomplishment at Sable Island. In 1853, while working for the hospital at St. John's, Newfoundland, she heard of the dangerous shores of Sable Island, where there was only a small life-saving station with inadequate apparatus, and where, for lack of a lighthouse, there was a succession of wrecks. She went to the island, undertaking the risk of the exposed landing, and herself made an examination of conditions. She then applied to merchants of Boston, New York, and Philadelphia for funds and sent four life-saving boats to the station. Within a week of their arrival a ship carrying 168 persons was thereby saved.

On Apr. 19, 1861, three hours after the 6th Massachusetts Regiment had been fired upon in Baltimore, she passed through that city on her way to Washington to offer her services to the surgeon-general. She was appointed, June 10, 1861, "Superintendent of Women Nurses, to select and assign women nurses to general or permanent military hospitals, they not to be employed in such hospitals without her sanction and approval, except in cases of urgent need." On July 14, 1862, Circular Number 7, issued by William Hammond, surgeon-general, repeated the authorization of selection and assignment of women nurses, now specified as one woman to each two men nurses, and gave her oversight, but put "control and direction" under the "medical officer in charge." General Orders No. 357, Oct. 27, 1863, restated this. Behind these orders are visible the autocratic action of a powerful personality, used to independence, in power over the incompetence, venality, and cruelty inevitable in crises impossible to anticipate, and the jealousy, thwarted ambition, and hurt pride of small natures. Miss Dix's biographer, Dr. Tiffany, considers her war work an episode, not equal in quality to her life-work. It is true that it differs in quality. This was not creative pioneer work. Judged, however, by the unfailing support of Stanton, secretary of war, by the comments of nurses under her personal attention, and seen in the light of nursing experience in the World War, it seems probable that these four years of war work deserve more credit than has been given them.

With the coming of peace, she resumed service in behalf of her hospitals, inspecting, advising, and giving them support. Again she traveled, investigated, and created new hospitals. In her eightieth year, she retired to the home gratefully offered her by her "first child," the hospital at Trenton, N. J. Here she died on July 17, 1887. To the last she longed to serve, saying, "I think even lying in my bed I can still do something."

[Francis Tiffany, *Life of Dorothea Lynde Dix* (1890); Alfred S. Roe, *Dorothea Lynde Dix* (1889); L. P. Brockett and Mary C. Vaughan, *Woman's Work in the Civil War* (1867); *Our Army Nurses* (1895), compiled by Mary A. Gardner Holland; Louisa Alcott, *Hospital Sketches* (1863); Harvey E. Brown, *The Medic. Dept. of the U. S. Army, 1775–1873* (1873); J. S. Woolsey, *Hospital Days* (1870); *Women Nurses with the Union Forces during the Civil War*, reprinted from the *Military Surgeon*, Jan.–Feb. 1928.] C.H.B.

DIX, JOHN ADAMS (July 24, 1798–Apr. 21, 1879), soldier in two wars, cabinet officer, and governor, the son of Col. Timothy and Abigail (Wilkins) Dix, began life in New England with a highly unusual training. This was because his father, a merchant and local leader of Boscawen, N. H., was a man of marked individuality and versatile talents. After giving the boy a good elementary education in the classics, English literature, and public speaking, including a year in Phillips Exeter Academy, and helping personally to instruct him in music and drawing, the father sent him to the College of Montreal, a Catholic institution. This was for tuition in French and contact with a different civilization. After fifteen months here the boy was recalled by the outbreak of the War of 1812, and was sent to a distant relative in Boston who saw that he was privately prepared in Spanish, Latin, mathematics, and elocution. But when he chafed to enter military service, his father, who had become a major of infantry in Baltimore, consented, helped the spirited fourteen-year-old lad to obtain a commission, and was proud to see him participate in the battle of Lundy's Lane as an ensign. Young Dix, large for his years, made an ardent soldier, and at Chrysler's Field wept when ordered to go to the rear with a body of prisoners.

The death of his father in the campaign of 1813 ushered in what Dix called "the most trying period of my life" (*Memoirs*, I, 50). His father's large family, nine children in all, were left in straitened circumstances, and the youth had not only to support himself but to contribute aid to his stepmother. During years "full of anxiety and trial" he remained in the army, gradually rising to the rank of major, and serving for a time in Washington, New York, and elsewhere as traveling aide to Maj.-Gen. Jacob Brown. He read much, was a close student, and improved his social opportunities in the capital, meeting Madison, Randolph, and others of note, and becoming intimate with Calhoun. The belief that he could find a better field than the army was strengthened by the advice of friends, who were struck by his forensic talents, industry, and handsome bearing. He studied law, partly under the direction of Attorney-General William Wirt, and was admitted to the bar in the District of Columbia (1824); while he also did much newspaper writing upon political subjects in the last years of Monroe's administration.

His determination to resign from the army was fixed by his marriage in 1826 to Catharine Morgan, adopted daughter of John J. Morgan, a Representative from New York who owned large areas of land up-state and who offered Dix the position of managing agent at Cooperstown. Settling in this town in 1828, Dix practised law for three years, became county leader of the Jacksonian Democracy, and made himself so prominent that at the end of 1830 Gov. Throop appointed him adjutant-general of the state. The salary was only $800, but Dix seized the place because it carried a seat in the powerful "Albany Regency." From this point his rise in political life was rapid, being checked only by occasional defeats of his party at the hands of the Whigs. He made an especial mark as secretary of state (1833–39) of New York; this position carried with it the superintendency of the public schools, and he did much to improve the training of teachers, while he also took the first steps toward organizing a geological survey of the state. Labors of this nature displayed his scholarly bent to advantage. Following the Harrison victory of 1840, he not only practised law, but established in Albany a literary and scientific journal, the *Northern Light,* which endured for a little more than two years (1841–43). It might have lasted longer but for a breakdown in his wife's health, which took him to Madeira and the Mediterranean, and resulted in a small volume of travel sketches.

Embarkation in national politics came immediately after Dix's return home, when he was elected (1845) to the United States Senate for the five unexpired years of Silas Wright's term. Here he manifested an especial interest in international affairs—he spoke for fixing the Oregon boundary at the 49th parallel, and against the withdrawal of the United States diplomatic agent from the Papal States—while he showed the free-soil sentiments that were ultimately to carry him out of the Democratic party. He was consistently aligned during the Mexican War with the anti-slavery or Barnburner Democrats; he supported the Wilmot Proviso; and in 1848 he was in favor of the separate nomination of Van Buren by the free-soil Democrats, though he opposed any alliance with the free-soil Whigs, and acquiesced very reluctantly in the final free-soil nomination of himself for governor (Alexander, *post,* II, 133). Indeed, his son said that to be associated with Whigs in this campaign was a painful and distressing surprise to him. His last speech in the Senate, in 1849, opposed the admission of New Mexico and California unless the enabling act prohibited slavery in these states.

In the next decade Dix should have been accepted as one of the leaders of Democracy. He was a cultivated writer, a fluent, vigorous speaker, a man of great courage, prompt decision, and proved executive ability. The opposition of the slavery wing of the party was, however, a fatal impediment. Franklin Pierce in 1853 intended to make him secretary of state, but party enemies interfered, and when he was offered the post of minister to France, this also was snatched from him by Southern opposition (James Ford Rhodes, *History of the United States From the Compromise of 1850,* vol. I, 1892, pp. 387, 395). The results were a withdrawal from public life, another trip abroad, a term as president of the Chicago & Rock Island, and the Mississippi & Missouri railroads (1854–57), and practise at the New York City bar. In 1860–61, however, public sentiment in New York City forced his promotion in striking fashion. A disastrous defalcation in the post-office caused his appointment as postmaster by Buchanan to straighten out affairs; and this had no sooner been accomplished than the moneyed interests of the East, in the crisis following the secession of South Carolina, demanded that he be made secretary of the treasury. He took office in January 1861, living at the White House till March.

Dix's chief service to the Union was in his brief period at the head of the treasury. Bankers and financiers had complete confidence in him, and though other states were seceding, he quickly obtained five millions at an average rate of slightly over ten per cent (John Jay Knox, *United States Notes,* 1884, p. 76). Moreover,

one of his dispatches was as a clarion call to the North. On Jan. 29, 1861, he telegraphed a treasury official in New Orleans to take possession of a revenue cutter there, concluding with the words: "If anyone attempts to haul down the American flag, shoot him on the spot" (*Memoirs,* I, 371). In a dark hour this was a heartening vindication of the national honor. He placed the chaotic department in order and handed it over to Chase in excellent condition. Lincoln rewarded him by commissioning him a major-general, and he was ordered to Washington in June to take charge of the Alexandria and Arlington Department. It was believed, however, that at sixty-three he was too old for active service, and political intrigue resulted in changing this assignment to the Department of Maryland. In Baltimore, at Fortress Monroe, and later in New York as commander of the Department of the East, he did useful but never spectacular service. His authority in New York lasted just two years (July 1863–July 1865); arriving just after the end of the draft riots, he took energetic steps to suppress sympathizers with the Confederacy.

Dix's career after the war was that of a distinguished and honored man well past his prime, chosen to public offices with the expectation that he would occupy them with passive dignity. As minister to France for three years, 1866–69, he was popular with the American colony but played no important rôle in diplomacy. Returning to America, he was the recipient in 1872 of an extraordinary compliment. Though still a Democrat, he was nominated for governor by the New York Republicans as the candidate who could best help defeat Horace Greeley in Greeley's own state, and he was elected by a majority of 53,000. Though then in his seventy-fifth year, he was still vigorous, and discharged the routine duties of his office capably. His was not the hand, however, to carry through the great task of cleansing the state's Augean stables, and in 1874 he was defeated for reëlection by Samuel J. Tilden. His last years were spent in peaceful retirement in New York City, with occasional appearances in behalf of civil service reform and other causes dear to him. He left behind him a reputation for loftiness of purpose, serene purity of life, and an amount of learning remarkable in politics. For a number of years he was a vestryman of Trinity Church, New York, of which, in 1862, his son Morgan Dix [*q.v.*] became the rector.

His published works include: *A Winter in Madeira; and a Summer in Spain and Florence* (1850), a popular book which went through five editions; *Speeches and Occasional Addresses* (2 vols., 1864); translations of *Dies Irae* (1863), and *Stabat Mater* (1868), in which he took especial pride.

[The all-sufficient source upon Dix's life is the *Memoirs of John Adams Dix* (2 vols., 1883) compiled by Morgan Dix. This is supplemented by some of his own works, notably the first two mentioned above. Brief characterizations may be found in the *Atlantic Monthly*, Aug. 1883, in D. S. Alexander, *Political History of the State of New York*, II (1906), 2 ff., and in C. C. Coffin, *The Hist. of Boscawen and Webster* (1878), pp. 348–56, with a genealogy of the Dix family on pp. 518–20. See also obituaries in *N. Y. Times*, Apr. 21, 22, 23, 1879, and *N. Y. Herald*, Apr. 22, 23, 1879.]

A. N.

DIX, JOHN HOMER (Sept. 30, 1811–Aug. 25, 1884), ophthalmologist, was born in Boston, Mass., the son of John Dix, a surgeon in the United States Navy, and his wife, Sarah Jaffery Eddy. He was graduated from Harvard College in 1833 and after attending the Harvard Medical School for two years, transferred to the Jefferson Medical College, Philadelphia, where he obtained the degree of M.D. in 1836. The next year he became a member of the Massachusetts Medical Society and began practise in Boston as a specialist in diseases of the eye and ear. On Sept. 9, 1840, he performed one of the first operations in America for congenital strabismus (Dieffenbach operation), reporting his results in a brief letter to the *Boston Medical and Surgical Journal*, Sept. 24, 1840 (1841, XXIII, 128). Further cases were reported the same year (*Ibid.*, 1841, XXIII, 265, also *Medical Examiner*, Philadelphia, 1840, III, 760) and later, in book form (*Treatise on Strabismus, or Squinting, and the New Mode of Treatment*, 1841). In 1846 he went to Europe and studied for a time under Von Graefe. He was one of the early proponents of ophthalmoscopic investigation of the eye and imported various instruments from Europe, including the first ophthalmoscope developed by Helmholtz in 1851. The results of his work were published in four papers in the *Virginia Medical Journal* (1856, VI, 361, 465; 1856, VII, 19, 389). Other papers are concerned with rare diseases of the eye, such as: "On the Sparkling Eye" (*Virginia Medical and Surgical Journal*, 1853, I, 12) and "Dacryocystitis" (*Ibid.*, 1854, III, 279). He was one of the early members of the American Ophthalmological Society.

Dix practised ophthalmology in Boston for nearly fifty years. He was a laborious student, keen to investigate new ideas, especially those from foreign sources, a pioneer and skilful operator on the eye before the days of modern anesthesia, a man of great self-confidence, strict integrity and genial disposition. Much of his fortune was willed to charitable institutions. Besides his contributions to his science, he has been credited with introducing the apartment house into the United States, when, in 1856–57, impressed by dwellings of that type which he had seen in Europe, he built the Hotel Pelham at the corner of Tremont and Boylston Sts., Boston. His wife, whom he married on June 9, 1859, was Helen Perhan Curtis.

[A. A. Hubbell, *The Development of Ophthalmology in America, 1800–1870* (1908); *Jour. Am. Medic. Asso.*, Mar. 24, 1888; *Boston Transcript*, Aug. 26, 1884; J. L. Sibley's Annotated Catalogue of the Early Harvard Graduates (MS.) in Mass. Hist. Soc.]

H. R. V.

DIX, MORGAN (Nov. 1, 1827–Apr. 29, 1908), Episcopal clergyman, for more than half a century connected with the Parish of Trinity Church, New York, and for almost forty-six years its rector, was born in New York; received his higher education there, graduating from Columbia in 1848, and from the General Theological Seminary in 1852; and, after having been long one of its first clergymen and citizens, died and was buried there. He was notably a child, not only of New York, but of Trinity Parish. In one of its chapels, St. John's, his distinguished father, John A. Dix [*q.v.*], had been married to Catharine Morgan, adopted daughter of John Jordan Morgan. The latter was long a vestryman of the parish, and in this office John Dix succeeded him. In St. John's Chapel, Morgan Dix was ordained deacon in 1852, though he was advanced to the priesthood the following year in St. Mark's Church, Philadelphia. Except for a brief term of service as assistant in the latter church, his entire ministry was spent in association with Trinity Parish. He accepted the office of assistant minister in 1855, and in 1859 was elected assistant rector, being recommended by Dr. Berrian, the rector, in preference to older ministers in the parish, because besides being a man of discretion, judgment, unaffected modesty, well regulated temper, and courteous manners, he combined in a rare degree high intellectual gifts with a practical turn of mind, orderly, methodical, business-like habits, and remarkable minuteness and accuracy in all matters of detail. On the evening of Nov. 10, 1862, Dr. Berrian having been buried that afternoon, he was elected rector. Twelve years later, June 3, 1874, he married Emily Woolsey Soutter, daughter of James T. Soutter.

From youth he had all the advantages of wealth, social position, travel, cultivated parents, and inspiring family traditions. Although his father, having rebelled as a boy against the long sermons, bleak theology, barren worship, and intense cold of a New Hampshire meeting-house, had broken the Congregational descent and become an Episcopalian, Morgan Dix was of old Puritan, New England stock, and of a family of fighters as well. Great-grandfather, grandfather, and father all served in the army. Austerity and soldier-like qualities were conspicuous in his character. "You can see in his face," some one said upon meeting him, "that he is determined to keep the devil down." Although rector of the wealthiest and most fashionable parish in the country, he denounced the vices of fashionable society with startling frankness and directness. Pacifism was a doctrine repugnant to him. While the International Arbitration and Peace Conference was being held in New York in 1907, he preached a sermon before the Loyal Legion in which he spoke of the "ancient, honorable, and necessary art of war," and affirmed the dignity of the military profession, and the necessity of an adequate army and navy (*Outlook*, May 9, 1908). He was an able administrator, and during his rectorship the varied religious, educational, and charitable work of the parish had large and wise extension. For years he presided over the House of Deputies of the General Convention, and was influential in the councils of the church. From 1862 to 1908 he was an active trustee of Columbia College. At his death, however, there was unanimous agreement that he was first and foremost a parish priest, concerned primarily with the moral and spiritual needs of his people. He was an active supporter of the Sisterhood of St. Mary, one of the earliest sisterhoods of the Episcopal Church, and long its pastor, preparing for it the *Book of Hours* (1866), and writing the life of its first Mother Superior, *Harriet Starr Cannon* (1896). His liturgical knowledge was extensive, and he did much for the development of church music, especially the choral service. Theologically he was strongly conservative, deploring the exercise of private judgment in matters of religion and worship, and proclaiming the divine institution of the church, priesthood, and sacraments, and the authority of the ancient creeds. Believing that marriage is not merely a civil contract but a holy ordinance, and ought never to be dissolved, he took strong ground against the "divorce abomination." His old-fashioned attitude on the sphere of women, set forth in *Lectures on the Calling of a Christian Woman* (1883), evoked a spirited reply from Lillie Devereux Blake [*q.v.*], entitled *Woman's Place Today* (1883). He had more than average literary ability and his numerous publications include sermons, manuals of religious instruction, aids to worship, lectures on theological subjects, *An Ex-*

position of the Epistle of St. Paul to the Romans, According to the Analogy of the Catholic Faith (1862) and a similar study of Galatians and Colossians (1864); *A History of the Parish of Trinity Church in the City of New York* (4 vols., 1898–1906); and an excellent life of his father, *Memoirs of John Adams Dix* (2 vols., 1883). On Apr. 19, 1908, ten days before his death, he preached the Easter sermon at Trinity Church.

[*Year Book and Register of the Parish of Trinity Church*, 1909; *Columbia Univ. Quarterly*, June 1908; *Who's Who in America*, 1906–07; *The Churchman*, May 9, 1908; *N. Y. Tribune, Times*, and *Evening Post* for Apr. 30, 1908.]   H.E.S.

DIXON, JAMES (Aug. 5, 1814–Mar. 27, 1873), congressman, was born in Enfield, Conn., the son of William and Mary (Field) Dixon. He prepared for college in the neighboring town of Ellington, and entered Williams at the age of sixteen, graduating with the class of 1834. Soon afterward he began the study of law under his father, and on being admitted to the bar, began practise in his home town, Enfield. In 1839 he moved to Hartford, and was taken into partnership with W. W. Ellsworth. On Oct. 1 of the following year Dixon married Elizabeth, daughter of the Rev. Jonathan Cogswell, professor of ecclesiastical history in the Theological Institute at East Windsor, Conn. His political career began in 1837, when at the age of twenty-three he was sent to the state legislature as a representative from Enfield. He was reëlected the following year. After 1839 he became a leader of the Whig party in Hartford. In 1844 he served another term as state legislator. A year later he was sent to Congress, serving until 1849. In Congress he was a conservative Whig. His speeches in the House followed accepted lines of Whig policy. In 1846 he spoke against the reduction of import duties. The point at issue was, he declared, whether this country should employ its own labor to supply its wants, or give occupation to foreign workmen. The laboring classes, he asserted, desired a protective tariff (*Congressional Globe*, 29 Cong., 1 Sess., App., pp. 1061 ff.). He spoke several times on the important question of the Mexican War. In 1847 he energetically supported the Wilmot Proviso (*Ibid.*, 29 Cong., 2 Sess., App., pp. 332 ff.). Later he upheld the Whig point of view that the war had been unnecessarily and unconstitutionally commenced by the president (*Ibid.*, 30 Cong., 1 Sess., pp. 227 ff.). Returning to Hartford from Congress, he resumed law practise, and was also for some years president of the Hartford Life Insurance Company. In 1854 he served a term as senator in the state legislature. Two years later he was elected to the United States Senate, where he remained until 1869, throughout the trying period of the Civil War, and the early years of Reconstruction. In the Senate, in 1859, he made a strong speech against the proposed acquisition of Cuba, on the ground that the matter was a Democratic party scheme for the purpose of furthering slavery interests (*Ibid.,* 35 Cong., 2 Sess., pp. 1335 ff.). Dixon was, of course, a loyal supporter of the Union cause during the Civil War. After the assassination of Lincoln, he became an ardent supporter of President Johnson, partly because of a desire for lenient treatment of the Southern states, and thus incurred the enmity of the radical Republicans. Having, therefore, no chance of receiving the Republican nomination for a third senatorial term, he stood for election in 1868 as a Democrat, but was defeated. In 1869, declining appointment as minister to Russia, he retired to private life, residing in Hartford, and being in rather feeble health until his death in 1873. Mrs. Dixon had died two years previously.

Outside of his political life, Dixon was something of a literary man, with a taste for poetry. He wrote several sonnets, which were published in the *New England Magazine,* and the *Connecticut Courant*. The poems are rather sweet and musical, although very amateurish. In public affairs, his attitude was thoroughly conservative. His political career was guided by ideals of abstract philosophy rather than by considerations of a purely practical, or temporary character. He was survived in 1873 by four children.

[The best source is *The Harvey Book* (1899), a genealogy. Supplementary details may be found in the *Memorial Hist. of Hartford County* (2 vols., 1886), ed. by J. H. Trumbull; *Commemorative Biog. Record of Hartford County, Conn.* (1901); *Biog. Dir. Am. Congress* (1928); and in an obituary notice in the *Hartford Courant*, Mar. 28, 1873. A few of Dixon's poems were published in *The Poets of Connecticut* (1843), by C. W. Everest.]   J.M.M.

DIXON, JOSEPH (Jan. 18, 1799–June 15, 1869), inventor, manufacturer, was the son of Joseph and Elizabeth (Reed) Dixon and was born at Marblehead, Mass., where his father and grandfather before him were born. His education was meager, but he possessed a restless brain and in his early youth displayed remarkable mechanical ingenuity. Before he was of age he had invented a machine for cutting files. He then took up printing, but not having the money to buy metal type, he made type of wood, incidentally becoming a skilled wood-carver and, in turn, mastering wood-engraving and lithography. The desire to possess metal type brought about his invention of a matrix for casting it, and the further necessity of providing a receptacle in which

to melt the type metal caused him to undertake experiments with the mineral graphite. Early in 1820 Dixon was looked upon as a chemist, presumably because of his constant experimental work with crucibles, which he tested with intense fires, and of the then popular conception of an individual so engaged. Besides, he began to study medicine, but he discontinued that because of his lost faith in drugs. He proved to his own satisfaction that graphite was an ideal material to use in crucibles to withstand high temperatures, but he recognized, too, that the market for such a product was extremely limited. In his experiments, however, he had observed a number of other properties of the mineral and he proceeded to devise products for which there was a market, namely, lead pencils and stove-polish. In 1827, therefore, he established at Salem, Mass., a factory for the manufacture of these materials and continued there, it is said, for twenty years. His products were marketed by peddling in which he was helped by Francis Peabody, and supported by the profits, he went on inventing. His interest in lithography led him to devise a photolithographic process; when he found that it afforded a ready means of counterfeiting banknotes, he and Peabody devised and patented, on Apr. 20, 1832, a process in which colored inks could be used to prevent counterfeiting. In the thirties Dixon perfected also a process for making collodion, and as a result of his studies of the work of Daguerre, a camera equipped with a reflector to rectify the position of the image. On Jan. 21, 1845, he was granted a patent for an anti-friction bearing-metal. In the application for this patent, which is a joint one with I. S. Hill of Boston, he gave his address as Taunton, Mass., although his business is supposed to have been at Salem. All this time the pencil and stove-polish business was expanding, and, in order to be nearer the market center, in 1847 Dixon gave up his Salem location and erected a plant in Jersey City, N. J. He apparently decided, too, that the time was ripe to introduce the graphite crucible, and accordingly in March and April 1850, patents No. 7,136 and No. 7,260 were granted him on uses of graphite crucibles in pottery and steel making, respectively. Again, on Nov. 2, 1858, he obtained patent No. 21,948 the title of which is "Improvement in Manufacturing Steel." From this time until his death he was compelled to devote more of his time to the manufacturing end of the business than to research but even so, his mechanical ingenuity was called upon for most of the improvements about the factory. A single instance of this is recorded in patent No. 54,511, granted to him in 1866 for a wood-planing machine for shaping the wood form of pencils. The few spare moments that he had for research were always used to good advantage, evidence of which is his patent of Sept. 2, 1866, No. 57,687, for a galvanic battery. In 1867, realizing that his own strength was failing, he formed the Joseph Dixon Crucible Company, the affairs of which he directed until his death two years later. With his demise the business passed into the hands of men of his own training who retained the original name of the company. Dixon married Hannah Martin of Marblehead on July 28, 1822.

[*Vital Records of Marblehead, Mass.* (1903) ; *New-Eng. Hist. and Geneal. Reg.*, XXIII (1869), 477 ; Elbert Hubbard, *Jos. Dixon* (1912) ; *Am. Ann. Cyc.*, 1869 ; *Biog. Encyc. of N. J. of the Nineteenth Century* (1877) ; *N. Y. Times, N. Y. Herald*, June 16, 1869 ; Patent Office records ; U. S. Nat. Museum correspondence with Jos. Dixon Crucible Co.]   C.W.M.

DIXON, LUTHER SWIFT (June 17, 1825–Dec. 6, 1891), jurist, was born at Underhill, Chittenden County, Vt. He was a descendant of Archibald Dickson of Irvine, Argyleshire, Scotland, who came to Boston in 1719. His father, Col. Luther Dixon, was a Vermont farmer who had commanded a regiment on the northern frontier during the War of 1812. The younger Luther's boyhood was spent on the farm, his early education being obtained at the common schools. He then attended the military academy at Norwich, Vt., for two years, becoming an excellent Latin scholar. Designing to become a lawyer, he taught school for a time in order to defray expenses, studying law at intervals, and, was admitted to the Vermont bar in 1850. In the same year he proceeded West, settled in Portage, Columbia County, Wis., and commenced practise there. In 1851 he was elected district attorney for Columbia County, being reëlected in 1853 and holding the office for four years. In August 1858, Gov. Randall appointed him judge of the 9th judicial circuit of Wisconsin, but he occupied this position for only eight months, being appointed chief justice of the supreme court in April 1859. He was comparatively unknown, and the impression was general that he did not possess the necessary experience. He was almost immediately confronted with the most important judicial question that had ever been brought before the court, arising from a conflict between the state and national governments respecting the enforcement of the Fugitive-Slave Law. The supreme court of Wisconsin had held that law to be unconstitutional, and on a writ of error the Supreme Court of the United States had reversed this decision. The case came before

Dixon at the June term, 1859, upon a motion to file the remittitur, and, despite the strong personal and political influences at work to bring him in alignment with the predominant state-rights supporters, he rendered an opinion upholding the appellate jurisdiction of the Supreme Court (*Ableman* vs. *Booth* and *The United States* vs. *Booth*, 11 *Wis.*, 498). His opinion in this case was masterly from the juridical standpoint and amply vindicated his appointment, but it provoked a political storm. In 1860, however, he was elected to succeed himself as an Independent, having been repudiated by the state Republican party, and, being reëlected three times subsequently, remained on the supreme court bench till 1874, when he resigned because of the inadequacy of his salary. Opening a law office at Milwaukee, he declined an election to the United States Senate, and, devoting himself to his profession, speedily acquired a large practise. During a period of five years he was continuously engaged in heavy litigation, including the "Granger cases," in which he was retained by the state of Wisconsin and successfully upheld the constitutionality of the questioned railroad legislation (*Attorney General* vs. *Chicago & North Western Railroad Company*; *Attorney General* vs. *Chicago, Milwaukee & St. Paul Railroad Company*, 35 *Wis.*, 425). He was counsel for the Atchison, Topeka & Santa Fé Railway Company in the litigation with the Denver & Rio Grande Railroad Company for the right of way through the Royal Gorge of the Arkansas River. In 1879, asthmatic trouble compelled him to seek a higher altitude, and he moved to Colorado, settling at Denver. Here he appeared constantly in the state and national courts of last resort. He died at Milwaukee on Dec. 6, 1891.

Though not brilliant, he was an exceptionally sound judge. He was not a case lawyer, but founded his opinions on established principles, utilizing precedents merely in illustration. His mental processes, singularly clear and invariably logical, were set out in opinions which were distinguished for felicity of style, simplicity of language, and compelling reasoning. In person over six feet in height, broad and athletic, gifted with much charm of manner, he was unobtrusive and retiring by nature. Public life had no attraction for him, and though in principle a Republican, he never appeared as a political speaker.

[*Am. Bar Asso. Report*, 1892, p. 429 ; *Green Bag*, IX, 116 ; *In Memoriam Luther S. Dixon*, 81 *Wis.*, xxxi, 17 *Colo.*, xix ; biographical sketch in *Selected Opinions of Luther S. Dixon and Edward G. Ryan* (1907), ed. by G. E. Roe ; P. M. Reed, *Bench and Bar of Wis.* (1882) ; *Rocky Mountain News* (Denver), Dec. 7 1891.]   H.W.H.K.

DIXON, WILLIAM (Sept. 25, 1850–Mar. 9, 1913), frontiersman, scout, known as "Billy" Dixon, was born in Ohio County, W. Va. His mother dying when he was ten, and his father two years later, he went to live with an uncle in Ray County, Mo. Determined to be a buffalo-hunter and an Indian-fighter, he left home before he was fourteen, and with a boy companion hunted and trapped along the lower Missouri. Early in 1865, despite his youth, he got employment at Fort Leavenworth as a driver in a government mule train, and in this capacity journeyed to such outlying posts as Fort Lyon and Fort Collins, Colo., and Camp Supply, Okla. In the fall of 1869 he left the government service and engaged with a party of hunters and trappers, who in the following year began the hunting of buffaloes for the hides. He bore a distinguished part in the second battle of Adobe Walls, in the present Hutchinson County, Tex., June 27, 1874, when a company of twenty-eight hunters, in an all-day fight, repelled the determined attacks of a force of about 700 Indians led by the Comanche, Quanah. He was one of the party that carried the news to Fort Dodge, where Gen. Miles appointed him a scout, and he returned to the Walls with Lieut. Baldwin's command. The most desperate experience of his career came on Sept. 12, when he and a fellow scout and four enlisted men were suddenly attacked by a band of about 125 Kiowas and Comanches. All six were wounded (one seriously and one mortally) early in the fight. Four took refuge in a buffalo wallow, to which Dixon, under a rain of bullets, carried one of the two badly wounded men; and by keeping up a steady and effective fire the whites forced the savages to withdraw at nightfall, when Dixon brought in the other men. The five survivors received the Congressional medal of honor. The account of this episode in R. I. Dodge, *Our Wild Indians* (1882), is obviously erroneous, and it is generally recognized that Dixon saved the party from annihilation.

Attached to Fort Elliott, which was established in the spring of 1875, he continued as a scout until 1883, when he homesteaded a claim that included Adobe Walls and started a ranch. He was postmaster at Adobe Walls for nearly twenty years, and at various times served as local land commissioner, justice of the peace, and sheriff. On Oct. 18, 1894, he was married to Olive King of Virginia, later to become well-known as a newspaper woman. In 1902 he sold his ranch and moved to the near-by town of Plemons, and about 1906 homesteaded a new claim in the present Cimarron County, Okla. At the solicitation of his wife he began, in the fall of 1912, to dictate to her his reminiscences, which were published in the year after his death.

Dixon was of medium height, strong and rugged, and capable of great endurance. His skill with the rifle was exceptional. He was characterized by W. B. ("Bat") Masterson, who knew him both as a buffalo-hunter and as a scout, as "a typical frontiersman of the highest order," who, though stoical and uncommunicative, was kind-hearted, generous, and hospitable.

[*Life and Adventures of "Billy" Dixon*, etc. (1914), ed. by F. S. Barde, revised edition by Olive K. Dixon (1927); R. I. Dodge, *Our Wild Indians* (1882); J. B. Thoburn, *A Standard Hist. of Okla.* (1916); E. A. Brininstool, "Billy Dixon, A Frontier Hero," *Hunter-Trader-Trapper* (Mar.–Apr. 1925).]   W.J.G.

DIXWELL, JOHN (*c.* 1607–Mar. 18, 1688/9), regicide, was the son of William Dixwell of Coton Hall, near Rugby, Warwickshire, and his wife, Elizabeth Brent. He was the brother of Mark Dixwell of Folkestone, Kent. Upon the death of Mark Dixwell, who had inherited the estates of Sir Basil Dixwell, John Dixwell became the guardian of his brother's children and managed their landed estates in Kent. During the Civil Wars he served on various committees appointed by Parliament to raise forces and to levy assessments in that county. In 1646 he was elected to Parliament from Dover. He was a member of the High Court of Justice erected to try Charles I, was present when sentence was given, and signed the death warrant. On June 27, 1650, he was commissioned colonel of Troop F, in Kent. On Nov. 25, 1651, he was elected a member of the Council of State and served on many committees of the Council. In 1652 he was governor of Dover Castle and, on the outbreak of war with the Dutch, was entrusted to guard the seacoast of Kent. He was a member of Cromwell's Parliaments of 1654 and 1656 (Cobbett, *post*, III, 1429, 1480), and was named a commissioner for Kent in ordinances of Aug. 28, 1654, for ejecting scandalous, ignorant, and indifferent ministers and schoolmasters, and of June 9, 1657, to levy an assessment for three months. On the restoration of the Long Parliament in 1659 Dixwell took his seat for Dover and on May 14 and on Dec. 31, 1659, was again elected a member of the Council of State. Following the Restoration, he was excepted from the Act of Pardon and Oblivion and fled to Hanau, Germany. From Hanau he migrated—just when is not known—to New England. He was first mentioned as being in America in February 1664/5, when he visited his fellow regicides, Edward Whalley and William Goffe [*q.v.*], at Hadley in the Colony of Massachusetts Bay. Soon after this he settled at New Haven, where he assumed the name of

James Davids. He was married twice: to Mrs. Joanna Ling on Nov. 3, 1673, and to Bathsheba Howe on Oct. 23, 1677. From the second marriage there were three children. On Dec. 29, 1685, James Davids, *alias* John Dixwell, was admitted to the church at New Haven (F. B. Dexter, *Historical Catalogue of the Members of the First Church of Christ in New Haven, Conn.,* 1914). On Mar. 18, 1688/9, Dixwell died at New Haven and was there buried. Before his death he had conveyed to his wife and son his estates in Kent, and in September 1693 his widow was taking steps to recover Dixwell's property (James Pierpont to Fitz-John Winthrop, Sept. 6, 1693, in *Massachusetts Historical Society Collections,* 6 ser., III, 266). In 1710 Dixwell's son visited England in an attempt to recover his father's property but was unsuccessful.

[Ivan "Dixwell Papers," ed. by F. B. Dexter, in *New Haven Colony Hist. Soc. Papers,* VI (1900), 337–74; *Calendar of State Papers, Domestic Series;* Jours. *of the House of Commons,* vols. VII, VIII; *Acts and Ordinances of the Interregnum, 1642–60* (3 vols., 1911), ed. by C. H. Firth and R. S. Rait; W. Cobbett, *Parliamentary Hist. of England* (1808), vol. III; John Nalson, *A True Copy of the Jour. of the High Court of Justice for the Trial of Charles I* (1684); *The Memoirs of Edmund Ludlow* (2 vols., 1894), ed. by C. H. Firth; *Vital Records of New Haven* (2 vols., 1917); David Masson, *The Life of John Milton* (7 vols., 1859–94); Mark Noble, *The Lives of the English Regicides* (2 vols., 1798); Ezra Stiles, *A Hist. of Three of the Judges of King Charles I* (1794); Lemuel Aiken Welles, *The Hist. of the Regicides in New England* (1927).]

I. M. C.

DOAK, SAMUEL (August 1749–Dec. 12, 1830), clergyman, educator, was of Scotch-Irish descent, the third son of Samuel and Jane (Mitchaell) Doak, who, in their youth, came to America from the north of Ireland. They were married in Chester County, Pa., and soon after moved to Augusta County, Va. There Samuel was born. He worked on his father's farm until he was sixteen, when he entered a classical school conducted by Robert Alexander and later by John Brown. In order to obtain funds to continue his studies he relinquished his interest in his father's estate, and later earned additional money as assistant teacher in Brown's school. He entered Princeton in 1773, graduated in 1775, and began the study of theology under the Rev. John Blair Smith, at the same time tutoring for Mr. Smith in Prince Edward Academy (later Hampden-Sidney College). On Oct. 31, 1777, he was licensed to preach by the Presbytery of Hanover. He married Esther H. Montgomery, a sister of Rev. John Montgomery of Virginia, by whom he had two sons and two daughters. She died, July 3, 1807. His second wife was Margaretta H. McEwen of Nashville, Tenn.

He began his preaching on the frontier in what is now Sullivan County, Tenn., but soon moved to another settlement, to what is known as the Fork Church (New Bethel) at the fork of the Holston and Watauga rivers. After a year he moved again to a settlement on the Little Limestone, eight miles southwest of the present town of Jonesboro, Tenn., and founded Salem Church and the school which was to become the first institution of higher learning west of the Alleghanies. The founding of Salem Church is said to have come about in the following way: Riding through the woods, seeking a frontier settlement where his services might be of use, his only baggage a sack full of books, he came upon some men felling trees. When they learned that he was a clergyman they asked him to preach for them and his preaching pleased them so much that they asked him to remain. He is described as a man "of powerful frame, medium stature, with a short, thick neck. His hair was sandy, his complexion ruddy and his eyes blue. His demeanor was dignified, his countenance grave. His was a stentorian voice, and he was withal a striking individuality" (S. C. Williams, *post*). His preaching was "original, bold, pungent, and sometimes pathetic." One of the "old side" Presbyterians, he rigidly opposed any innovations in religious tenets. When a schism arose in the Abington Presbytery over the Hopkinsianism taught by one of its members, he was active in the "old side" group opposing the new teaching. His influence in furthering the Presbyterian faith was considerable. In addition to Salem Church, he assisted in organizing churches at New Bethel, Concord, New Providence, and in Carter's Valley (*Pioneer Presbyterianism in Tennessee*).

Active in the affairs of the settlement, he was one of the delegates to the first general convention of representatives from Washington, Sullivan, and Greene counties of North Carolina to consider the formation of a separate state, which movement culminated in the State of Franklin, later a part of Tennessee. Probably his most important work, however, was as an educator. The school which he opened in a log cabin on his farm was, in 1783, chartered by the legislature of North Carolina as Martin Academy, named for the governor of that state. In 1795, when the region had become a territory, it was incorporated as Washington College. "For many years it was the only, and for still more, the principal seat of classical education for the western country" (Ramsey, *post*). Its students were found in all the learned professions in the early days of Tennessee. Especially was it successful in training men for the ministry. Anticipating modern methods, in the early days the pupils were not divided into classes by years, but were allowed to complete the course as swiftly as they could. The nucleus of the college library was a gift of books received by Doak while attending a meeting of the General Assembly in Philadelphia in 1795, and which he had to carry 500 miles on horseback to the settlement. As a teacher his chief interest was philology. Always a student, after he was sixty years old he mastered Hebrew and chemistry sufficiently to teach them. Commencement was his one gala day. "On that occasion he wore his antique wig, his shorts, and his old-fashioned shoes: the muscles of his stern brow were relaxed, and he gave himself up to an unusual urbanity and kindliness of manner" (J. G. M. Ramsey, a former pupil, in Sprague, *post*). In 1818 he resigned the presidency of Washington College and moved to Bethel, Tenn., where he opened Tusculum Academy, later Tusculum College. He died at Bethel in his eighty-first year. Both of his sons were ordained to the ministry, John W. succeeding him in the presidency of Washington College and Samuel W. in that of Tusculum Academy.

[M. L. Morris, *The Irvins, Doaks, Logans and McCampbells of Va. and Ky.* (1916); S. C. Williams, *Hist. of the Lost State of Franklin* (1924); *The Scotch-Irish in America, Proc. and Addresses of the 9th Cong.* (1900); W. B. Sprague, *Annals Am. Pulpit*, vol. III (1858); *Pioneer Presbyterianism in Tenn.* (1898); E. H. Gillett, *Hist. of the Presbyterian Church* (1864); H. A. White, *Southern Presbyterian Leaders* (1911); Alfred Nevin, *Presbyterian Encyc.* (1884); J. Allison, *Dropped Stitches in Tenn. Hist.* (1897); J. T. Moore and A. P. Foster, *Tenn., the Volunteer State 1769–1923* (1923); J. Phelan, *Hist. of Tenn.* (1888); J. G. M. Ramsey, *The Annals of Tenn.* (1853).] B. R.

DOANE, GEORGE WASHINGTON (May 27, 1799–Apr. 27, 1859), second Episcopal bishop of New Jersey, was born in Trenton, N. J., the son of Jonathan and Mary (Higgins) Doane. His father was a contractor and builder. After graduating in 1818 from Union College, Doane read law in the office of Richard Harrison of New York and in 1820 became the sixth student in the General Theological Seminary, which Bishop Hobart was just starting in a room over a saddler's shop. Hobart ordained his pupil a deacon on Apr. 19, 1821, and a priest on Aug. 6, 1823, and kept him as his assistant at Trinity Church until 1825. Doane was professor of rhetoric and belles-lettres in Washington (now Trinity) College at Hartford, Conn., 1825–28, edited for a time the *Episcopal Watchman*, the *Banner of the Church*, and, later, the *Missionary*, was assistant minister and subsequently rector of Trinity Church, Boston, 1828–32. In 1829 he married Eliza Greene (Callahan) Perkins, widow of James Perkins of Boston. On Oct. 31, 1832, in St. Paul's Chapel, New York City, he

was consecrated bishop of New Jersey; since there was no special provision for the support of the bishop, he soon after accepted the rectorship of St. Mary's at Burlington, N. J. Doane was one of the notable bishops of the American Episcopal Church. As a thinker, whether on theological or on other subjects, he does not rank very high, and his want of business acumen brought him to the verge of disaster, but he had other talents that stood him in good stead. He was handsome and magnetic and had a resonant voice and great social gifts. His vitality seemed inexhaustible. On his rector's salary of $700 a year, together with his none too abundant perquisites, he conducted himself successfully in the grand manner of an English prelate, thereby making numerous enemies but also many friends, and building up a strong diocese. He was one of the principal promoters of the missionary movement in the Episcopal Church and of Episcopal schools, founding St. Mary's Hall for girls at Burlington in 1837 and Burlington College for men in 1846. When Parliament repealed the act prohibiting American clergymen from preaching in English churches or taking part in the services, Walter Farquhar Hook, vicar of Leeds, invited him to preach at the consecration of the new parish church in Leeds. Doane's visit to England (1841) did much to bring the English Church into closer relations with its American offshoot. One curious by-product of this visit was the intrusion of three sonnets on "Aspects of Christianity in America" into Wordsworth's *Ecclesiastical Sonnets,* Doane and Henry Reed, Wordsworth's American editor, having besought the poet to recognize the filiation of the American Church. He edited the first American edition (Philadelphia, 1834) of Keble's *Christian Year,* and was himself fond of writing verse. He is, indeed, one of the best American hymn-writers, author of "Softly now the light of day," "Thou art the way, to Thee alone," "Lord, should we leave Thy hallowed feet," "Father of mercies, hear, Thy pardon we implore" [*Audi, benigne Conditor*], "Fling out the banner, let it float," and of several other well-known hymns. Most of these appeared in his *Songs by the Way* (1824). He was the leader of the High Church party in America, having no fellowship either with "dissenters" or with the "Roman intrusion." He was a warm friend of the Tractarian Movement, even going so far as to defend the notorious Tract XC that had brought the Movement to a head. Misfortunes fell upon him in the latter part of his life. In his effort to support his educational institutions at Burlington he finally was forced into bankruptcy

(Mar. 26, 1849). His own diocesan convention exonerated him of any culpability, but a persistent effort was made to bring him to trial before the House of Bishops. To a man of Doane's pride the idea of standing trial was even more humiliating than any imputation of guilt, and he announced that he would "make the trial of a bishop hard." By using every resource at his disposal he managed to block proceedings for almost five years, and eventually the case was dismissed. But a heavier blow awaited him. His elder son, George Hobart Doane, turned Catholic, having come to doubt the efficacy of the ordination received at his father's hands. On Sept. 15, 1855, the Bishop went through the ordeal of deposing his own son. Only four more years were allowed him, but he served his Church and his God indefatigably to the end.

[*The Life and Writings of George Washington Doane, with a Memoir by his son, William Croswell Doane* (4 vols., 1860–61); A. A. Doane, *The Doane Family* (1902); J. Julian, *A Dict. of Hymnology* (rev. ed., 1907); C. C. Tiffany, *A Hist. of the P. E. Church in the U. S. A.* (1895); *Cat. of the Officers and Alumni of Union Coll. 1797–1884* (1884); *Gen. Theol. Sem. Cat.*; G. M. Hills, *Hist. of the Church in Burlington, N. J.* (1876); H. G. Batterson, *A Sketch-Book of the Am. Episcopate . . . 1783–1883* (2nd ed., rev. and enl. 1884); F. C. Morehouse, *Some Am. Churchmen* (1892).]

G. H. G.

DOANE, THOMAS (Sept. 20, 1821–Oct. 22, 1897), mechanical engineer, was descended from Deacon John Doane who came to Plymouth, Mass., on the ship *Fortune*, in 1621. Thomas was born in Orleans, Mass., on Cape Cod, the oldest child of John and Polly (Eldredge) Doane. His father was a lawyer and served for a time in the state Senate. Thomas attended an academy on the Cape and when he was nineteen entered the English Academy at Andover, Mass., spending five terms there. At the conclusion of this period he took advantage of an opportunity to enter the employ of Samuel L. Felton of Charlestown, Mass., a well-known civil engineer. Three years later, having thus served his professional apprenticeship, he accepted his first employment with the Windsor White River Division of the Vermont Central Railroad. He served as resident engineer of the Cheshire Railroad at Walpole, N. H., from 1847 to 1849. In the latter year he began in Charlestown an independent practise as civil engineer and surveyor, which he continued until his death. During his professional career he was associated with practically all of the railroads running out of Boston, but he was more especially known for his connection with the Boston & Maine. Appointed in 1863 chief engineer of the Hoosac Tunnel, on which construction had already been begun, he introduced new engineering methods,

relocated the line of the tunnel, and achieved great accuracy in the meeting of the borings. He was largely responsible for the development, in the United States, of the advanced system of tunneling with machinery and high explosives. He has also been called a pioneer in the use of compressed-air machinery in this country. In 1869 he became chief engineer of the Burlington & Missouri River Railroad in Nebraska, laying down approximately 241 miles of track in about four years. During this period he became much interested in the establishment of a Congregational college at Crete, Nebr., and was instrumental in obtaining for its location a square mile on the Big Blue River near that town. In gratitude for his aid the college was named in his honor and until his death he was one of its trustees. In 1873 he returned to Charlestown where he was again appointed chief engineer of the Hoosac Tunnel. When the tunnel was formally opened, on Feb. 9, 1875, he ran the first engine through it. For two more years he continued in charge of construction. He was actively interested in professional societies, was for over twenty years a member and for nine years president of the Boston Society of Civil Engineers, and joined the American Society of Civil Engineers in 1882. He was active in numerous civic, charitable, and educational enterprises in and around Boston, and was for many years a deacon in his church, the Winthrop Church, at Charlestown. On Nov. 5, 1850, he married Sophia Dennison Clarke, who died in 1868. Later he married Louisa Amelia Barber of Brattleboro, Vt. While on a visit to relatives at West Townsend, Vt., he died of heart-failure, survived by his second wife and four children of his first marriage.

[*Trans. Am. Soc. Civil Engineers*, XXXIX (1898), 690–94, an account prepared by F. W. D. Holbrook, who at intervals for a number of years was Doane's chief assistant; A. A. Doane, *The Doane Family* (1902), pp. 444–47; *Boston Transcript*, Oct. 23, 1897.]

K. W. C.

DOANE, WILLIAM CROSWELL (Mar. 2, 1832–May 17, 1913), first bishop of the Protestant Episcopal diocese of Albany, was one of the most influential leaders of his own communion and an honored figure in American public life. His parents were Rev. George Washington Doane [*q.v.*], afterward Bishop of New Jersey, and his wife, Eliza Greene (Callahan) Perkins, widow of James Perkins. He was born in Boston where his father was at the time Rector of Trinity Church. He graduated at Burlington College, N. J., in 1850, was ordained deacon in 1853 and priest in 1856. Between 1853 and 1869 he was successively rector of St. Mary's Church, Burlington; St. John's, Hartford, Conn., and St.

Peter's, Albany. During the same period he was for six years adjunct professor of literature at Burlington College and for four years lecturer in the same subject at Trinity College. Consecrated bishop on Feb. 2, 1869, he devoted the rest of his long life to the building up of his diocese. He held that no episcopate was complete without its cathedral which should have free seats, frequent services, schools and houses of mercy of all kinds; and the fruition of this idea, All Saints Cathedral of Albany, having in its connection St. Agnes School, the Child's Hospital, St. Margaret's Home, and the Sisterhood of the Holy Child, has been influential in establishing the American ideal of cathedral administration. He was visitor, trustee, and honorary chancellor of Hobart College, and regent and chancellor of the University of the State of New York. At two Lambeth Conferences he was spokesman for the American Episcopate. Indefatigable in his diocesan activities, he was actively interested in the betterment of social and moral conditions, and fearless in expressing his opinion on public questions. He was a stanch upholder of the cause of missions, vigorous in his opposition to divorce and a leader in his church for its suppression. He did much to advance Episcopal legislation in this matter and his influence was also felt in promoting marriage and divorce reform in the civil law. His principal literary work was the biography of his father entitled, *The Life and Writings of George Washington Doane, with a Memoir* (4 vols., 1860–61). His *Rhymes from Time to Time* (1901) show him to have been more than moderately gifted as a poet, and his hymn, "Ancient of Days," has a permanent place in the hymnals of many communions. He was the recipient of honorary degrees from Trinity, Columbia, Hobart, and Union colleges, and from the universities of Oxford, Cambridge, and Dublin.

Doane was a friend and admirer of Dr. Pusey, and in his earlier ministry was looked upon as a high churchman. He was fond of ceremony, wore the dress of an English bishop, and was frequently regarded as aristocratic. While always a pronounced churchman, however, he was really democratic in spirit, and numbered among his friends all sorts and conditions of people. Broadening and mellowing with the years, at his summer chapel at Northeast Harbor, Me., he ministered to and even gave the Communion to members of all denominations. In November 1853 he married Sarah Katharine Condit of Newark, N. J., whom he survived.

[A. A. Doane, *The Doane Family* (1902); *Who's Who in America*, 1912–13; *Outlook*, May 31, 1913;

Rev. of Revs. (N. Y.), July 1913; *Churchman*, and *Living Church*, May 24 and 31, 1913; Jas. Hooper, *A Hist. of St. Peter's Ch. in the City of Albany* (1900); *N. Y. Tribune*, May 18, and *N. Y. Times*, May 19–20, 1913.]

F. T. P.

DOBBIN, JAMES COCHRAN (Jan. 17, 1814–Aug. 4, 1857), secretary of the navy, was a native of Fayetteville, N. C., where his father, John Moore Dobbin, was a prosperous merchant. His mother was Anness, the daughter of James Cochran of Person County, a planter and for several terms a member of Congress. Dobbin's early education was received in Fayetteville and at the Bingham School in Hillsboro. In 1828 he entered the University of North Carolina and was graduated in 1832. For three years he read law, and after his admission to the bar, he settled in Fayetteville. Refusing all requests to engage in politics, he devoted himself to his profession. He had a fine intellect, much charm of personality, and was a spirited and graceful speaker. His tastes were simple, and he led a quiet and dignified life, brightened by much personal friendship. He married Louisa Holmes of Sampson County who died in 1848. In 1845 the Democrats of his district, without his knowledge, nominated him for Congress. He accepted with genuine unwillingness, made a rather brilliant campaign, and serving one term with unusual distinction for a new member, refused reëlection. But in 1848 he was elected to the House of Commons where he won reputation by his efforts in behalf of the charter of the North Carolina Railroad and by the eloquent speech by which, in fulfilment of a promise to his dying wife, he converted the legislature and secured the establishment of a hospital for the insane. He was speaker of the House in the legislature of 1850 and by the close of the session was generally regarded as the leader of his party. Heading the North Carolina delegation in the Baltimore convention of 1852, he made the speech which precipitated the stampede for Pierce, and as candidate for elector at large he made an active campaign for him. He was again elected to the Commons, and was the caucus nominee of his party for United States senator. A deadlock ended in failure to elect any one, but in March 1853 Pierce appointed him secretary of the navy and he accepted.

Like most secretaries of the navy, Dobbin knew little or nothing of naval matters when he was appointed, but he directed his keenly analytical mind to the question, and, by the time he wrote his first report, he had formulated the policy which he successfully carried out. The navy was at a low ebb, with few ships and most of those antiquated, with a large body of officers too old or too incompetent for efficiency, with hopelessness and dissatisfaction general among the officers of lower grades, and with no regularly enlisted body of seamen and a practical impossibility of securing the crews, even for the limited number of ships. To remedy the situation, Dobbin recommended a radical increase in the navy, and, enthusiastic for steam, he urged a minimum of six steam propeller frigates, and, by a later recommendation, of five steam sloops. He suggested the creation of a retired list of officers on half pay, with a naval board to have direction of the system, the institution of a merit system for promotion, and a thorough-going reform of the whole plan of handling seamen. He prevented any restoration of flogging, but secured an effective scheme of punishment to replace it. He further recommended the establishment of a naval apprentice system, the enlistment of seamen for a definite term of years, with better treatment, better provision for their health and comfort, increased pay with adequate rewards for long and meritorious service, and honorable discharge at the end. Bold and aggressive in his attacks upon existing abuses, he secured the passage of the act to increase the efficiency of the navy by which many of them were reformed. No secretary of the navy up to that time so completely won the confidence of the service; and at the same time he secured popular indorsement and approval. Under him the navy was largely remade. He won applause by sending the relief expedition to Dr. E. K. Kane [*q.v.*] and, catching a vision of what cable communication would mean to the world, he performed a valuable service by sending Lieut. Berryman on a naval vessel to make a survey of possible submarine telegraph routes. He was not only a man of vision but an able executive as well; clear-headed, practical, tactful, and possessed of magnetism which, combined with his capacities and the discernible fact that personal considerations carried little weight with him, made him easily the most popular of the Pierce cabinet.

During his service, he was heavily overworked. He was offered a seat in the Senate, but he heeded Pierce's request and as a matter of duty remained at his post. His health, which had never been robust, failed, and he went home from Washington, at the close of the Pierce administration, only to die.

[*North Carolina Booklet*, XVI, no. 1 (1916–17); S. A. Ashe, *Biog. Hist. of N. C.*, vol. VI (1907); *N. C. House Journals*; *Exec. Doc.*, Serial nos. 712, 778, 812, 876; New York and Washington newspapers of the dates of his retirement and death.]   J. G. de R. H.

DOBBS, ARTHUR (Apr. 2, 1689–Mar. 28, 1765), colonial governor of North Carolina, was born at Castle Dobbs, County Antrim, Ireland. His parents were Richard Dobbs of Castletown and Mary, the daughter of Archibald Stewart of Ballintoy. A younger brother was Francis Dobbs, the well-known writer and statesman. Nothing is known of his early life, but it is clear that he was well educated, for he was a man not only of wealth but of broad attainment. In 1711 he succeeded to his father's estate and in 1720 became high sheriff of Antrim. A few years later he published *An Account of Aurora Borealis, Seen in Ireland . . . 1725, with a Solution of the Problem* (see a discussion in *Philosophical Transactions*, 1726). In 1727 he was returned from Carrickfergus to the House of Commons of the Irish Parliament, and while there he gained considerable reputation by his investigations into the trade, agriculture, and political arithmetic of Ireland, the results of which he published in a series of very valuable tracts of which the *Essay on the Trade and Improvement of Ireland* (1729) is best known. In it he advocated an improved system of land tenure and he later pressed the reform in Parliament, declaring that Ireland was suffering "from the Commonalty's having no fixed property in their land." In 1730 Dr. Boulter, Archbishop of Armagh, introduced him to Robert Walpole as "one of the members of our House of Commons, where he on all occasions endeavors to promote his majesty's service. He . . . has for some time applied his thoughts to the trade of Great Britain and Ireland, and to the making of our colonies in America of more advantage than they have hitherto been" (Hugh Boulter, *Letters,* etc., 1770, quoted in J. R. McCulloch, *The Literature of Political Economy,* 1848, p. 46). Walpole at once appointed him engineer-in-chief and surveyor-general of Ireland. In 1732 Dobbs carried through Parliament a bill to encourage the enclosure of waste land and the planting of trees.

About 1730 he became deeply interested in the discovery of a northwest passage to India and was active in promoting the search for it. In 1731 he made abstracts of all the voyages on this quest and after an effort to interest the South Sea Company, laid the matter before the Hudson's Bay Company and the Admiralty. An expedition was sent out under Christopher Middleton who had been recommended by Dobbs, but after his return Dobbs accused him of falsifying his records, and a controversy, lasting some years, followed which drew from Dobbs his *Remarks upon Captain Middleton's Defence* (1744). In the same year he wrote *An Account of the Countries Adjoining to Hudson's Bay,* full of valuable information and advocating the dissolution of the Hudson's Bay Company. A later expedition justified Middleton, and Dobbs, in his *On Bees and the Mode of Gathering Wax and Honey* (see discussion in *Philosophical Transactions,* 1750), made an allusion taking leave of the question.

In 1745 Dobbs with John Selwyn purchased from the McCulloh estate 400,000 acres of land in North Carolina, lying in the present counties of Mecklenburg and Cabarrus, and was thereafter much interested in the affairs of the colony and increasingly dissatisfied with the administration of Gov. Gabriel Johnston. In 1754 he was selected as Johnston's successor and, sailing at once, was sworn in at New Bern on Oct. 31. He was received with great cordiality, and for a time his administration was peaceful. But he was a fanatical Protestant, obsessed by hatred of the French, a zealous servant of the Crown and an opponent of popular government, and very ignorant of conditions in the colony, and quiet could not last. Bent on carrying out his instructions without reference to the will of the people, he was soon in difficulties from which he was never extricated. He urged support of the French and Indian War far beyond the resources of the colony where, indeed, there was small interest in the struggle. At the heart of his North Carolina problems, however, was the question of how far the prerogatives of the Crown, and the governor as its agent, extended, and this question appears in every dispute between the governor and the assembly. Among these disputes were those concerning the appointment of the agent of the colony in London, the appointment of treasurers, the fixing of fees, control of the purse, regulation of the courts, the apportionment of representation, and the support and maintenance of the Church of England. Yet there is abundant evidence to show that Dobbs was eager for the welfare of the people of the colony. Also, he brought North Carolina into the stream of American affairs by his part in the war. But, while he had a quick and vigorous mind, he was impulsive in speech and action, and positive to the point of obstinacy in his own opinions, and his advancing years served only to emphasize these qualities. In 1762, while preparing to go to England, he suffered a stroke of apoplexy and died three years later at his home on Towncreek in Brunswick. He was twice married. His first wife was Anne Norbury of Drogheda, a widow and the daughter and heir of Capt. Osborne of Timahoe, County Kildare. When he was seventy-three years old he married Justina Davis of North Carolina, a girl still in her teens.

[S. A. Ashe, *Biog. Hist. of N. C.,* III (1905), 80; article by H. M. Chichester in *Dict. of Nat. Biog.*; *South Atlantic Quart.,* XVI (1917), 30; *Colonial Records of N. C.,* vols. V and VI (1887, 1888); *Correspondence of Wm. Pitt* (2 vols., 1906), ed. by Gertrude S. Kimball; S. A. Ashe, *Hist. of N. C.,* vol. I, 1908; Connor, *The Colonial Period* (1919).]   J. G. de R. H.

DOCK, CHRISTOPHER (*c.* 1698–1771), Mennonite schoolmaster, came to Pennsylvania between 1710 and 1714, attracted, doubtless, by the freedom accorded there to those of his faith. Reliable information as to his family, early education, and the place and date of his birth is lacking. Possibly in 1714, certainly as early as 1718, he opened a school among the Mennonites on the Skippack, in Montgomery County. After teaching ten years, he devoted his time chiefly to farming till 1738, when, praying that the Lord might "graciously overlook my neglect of youth" for the time past, he returned to the profession of schoolmaster until his death. Two schools, one at Skippack, the other at Salford, now claimed his attention, three days each in turn.

His fame spread, and Christopher Saur of Germantown sought a description of his methods (1749) as a guide for other less skilful teachers. The latter refused, fearing it would appear as an "unsavory monument" to himself and deserve "before God and all pious, Christian people, not honor but rather ridicule and shame." Finally Saur wrote certain questions to a mutual friend, Dielman Kolb, who drew the answers from Dock, the latter stipulating that they should not be published in his lifetime. These answers make up his famous *Schulordnung,* the earliest treatise in America on schoolkeeping thus far discovered. The manuscript was completed on Aug. 8, 1750. Meantime, at the solicitation of Saur, Dock prepared a few articles, in 1764, for the *Geistliches Magazien* and this probably prepared the way for publication of the *Schulordnung* before its author's death. The first and second editions of the latter appeared in 1770, and a third in 1861. The best known of the articles were "A Hundred Necessary Rules of Conduct for Children" and "A Hundred Christian Rules for Children." These rules give an insight into the early German family life much as the *Schulordnung* pictures Dock's school. He also composed a number of hymns, some of which are used to-day.

The fame of the pious schoolmaster rests not wholly upon the early date of his publication on schoolkeeping but upon the modernity of much of his practise. Constructive writing and composition exercises were secured by an interchange of pupils' letters from one school to the other; use of gentle persuasion superseded harsh discipline; rewards were given for good work, social disapproval for the lazy and disobedient; and investigation sought to find the reason for swearing, lying, stealing and quarreling, punishment being varied to suit the individual case. Understanding love was the chief principle of discipline; and simplicity and directness, the chief virtues of his instruction. Each evening, with the roll before him, he prayed that his injustice or neglect of any be forgiven; that on the morrow he might do the best for each and all. Late in 1771 he failed to return from school. There he was found, on his knees, dead.

[The best sources of information are: "Christopher Dock, the Pious Schoolmaster on the Skippack, and his Works," published in S. W. Pennypacker, *Hist. and Biog. Sketches* (1883), and Martin G. Brumbaugh, *The Life and Works of Christopher Dock* (1908).]

T.W.

DOCKSTADER, LEW (Aug. 7, 1856–Oct. 26, 1924), black-face minstrel, vaudeville actor, was one of the most popular comedians of his generation. His trick shoes, voluminous dress suit, engaging smile, and impromptu whimsicalities provoked hearty laughter alike in metropolitan theatres and in remote "opera houses" of provincial towns; his songs—"Oh Mr. Austin"; "Peter, You're in Luck This Morning"; "Everybody Works but Father"; "He Used to Breakfast with Us Every Morning"—were the hits of the day. A diligent student of humorous effects, he became a master at furbishing up old jokes about the Ark, Jonah, Congress, and Hoboken, at convulsing his audiences with unexpected and ingenious "local gags," at mimicking the voice, stride, and gesture of political figures such as Presidents Harrison, Cleveland, and Roosevelt. About all his clowning there was a simplicity and finish that gave it the dignity of art. Among actors he was admired as one of the most versatile and likable men in the profession, and he became the hero of numerous anecdotes. During his fifty years on the stage he is said to have missed only one performance.

His original name was George Alfred Clapp. He was born in Hartford, Conn., the son of Chester and Harriet Gouge (Miller) Clapp. His father kept the bar of the City Hotel, of which an uncle, Caleb Clapp, was the proprietor. From boyhood Clapp seemed cut out for the stage: he was completely at ease before an audience, could play any musical instrument, apparently, that he picked up, and possessed an inexhaustible fund of drollery. He early became the stage manager and end man of an amateur minstrel company and made his professional début, under the name of Lew Clapp, in Hartford in 1873. A few years later he and Charles Dockstader formed an act-

ing partnership and were billed as the Dockstader Brothers, and Clapp was thereafter known as Lew Dockstader. As a member of various minstrel troupes he played in every state in the Union and always cherished an ambition to have a company of his own. He was too generous with his money, however, to be long successful as a manager. His first venture, in New York 1886–89, left him deep in debt and threatened with bankruptcy, but going into vaudeville he soon repaid his creditors in full. In 1898 he returned to minstreldom in partnership with George H. Primrose; and in 1903 he became sole proprietor of the company; but minstrel shows were no longer in favor, and Dockstader had to betake himself again to vaudeville, in which he was highly paid and free from managerial worries. On Jan. 6, 1920, his wife, Lucin, died. In January 1923, at New Brunswick, N. J., he sustained a fall, as a result of which a bone tumor developed in his left leg. In December he had to quit the stage. He died at his daughter's home in New York and was buried at Kensico. His death, as truly as Garrick's, diminished the public stock of harmless pleasure.

[G. W. Russell, ed., *Additional Contributions to the Hist. of Christ Church, Hartford, Conn.*, II, 95 (Hartford, 1908); Ebenezer Clapp, *Record of the Clapp Family in America* (1876), p. 336; *Geer's Hartford City Directory for 1856–57 and for 1860–61*; D. Paskman and S. Spaeth, *"Gentlemen, Be Seated"* (1928); Walt McDougall, *This is the Life!* (1926), p. 213; *N. Y. Times*, Jan. 8, 1920, Oct. 27, 29, Nov. 2 (Pt. VIII), 10, 1924; *N. Y. World*, Oct. 28, 1924 (editorial); *Hartford Daily News, Hartford Courant, N. Y. Herald Tribune*, Oct. 27, 1924.]

G.H.G.

DOD, ALBERT BALDWIN (Mar. 24, 1805–Nov. 19, 1845), Presbyterian minister, college professor, was born in Mendham, N. J., the son of Daniel [*q.v.*] and Nancy (Squier) Dod. His father was a builder of engines, was master of several other trades, read widely in Calvinistic theology, and wrote verse. Proficiency in mathematics was a family trait. From early childhood Albert was quiet and studious, quickly assimilating what the schools of Elizabethtown and Bloomfield, N. J., had to teach him, entering the sophomore class in the College of New Jersey in the spring of 1821, and graduating in the autumn of 1822. At Princeton he came under clerical influences and decided to become a minister. Through Samuel Lewis Southard [*q.v.*], who was a friend of his father's, he secured a place as tutor in a family living near Fredericksburg, Va. After three years in the Old Dominion he studied at the Princeton Theological Seminary 1825–26 and in the following year was made tutor in the College. In 1828 he was licensed to preach by the Presbytery of New York, but although he supplied many pulpits in New York, Philadelphia, and elsewhere, he never felt inclined to abandon teaching for the active ministry. In April 1830 he married Caroline, daughter of Samuel Bayard of Princeton, and in the autumn of that year he was promoted to the professorship of mathematics, which he continued to occupy until his death. His love of mathematics, his zeal for imparting instruction, and his remarkable gift for lucid exposition made him an unusually successful teacher. "There was nothing he could not make plain," said his friend Charles Hodge. He introduced written examinations into the College, and at the suggestion of his colleague, Joseph Henry, gave a course of lectures on architecture. He had a taste for literature and the fine arts, was a laborious student of metaphysics, and from 1835 on contributed able articles to the *Biblical Repertory and Princeton Review*. Of his eight contributions the most interesting are, "Beecher's Views in Theology" (1837), "Transcendentalism" (1839), "Capital Punishment" (1842), and "Vestiges of Creation" (1845). In these articles he displays a real gift for argument, a trenchant style, and a reactionary mind. Hegel, Cousin, and Emerson he lumped together as no better than atheists, thereby winning the commendation of Andrews Norton, who republished one of his reviews in *Two Articles ... Concerning the Transcendental Philosophy* (Cambridge, Mass., 1840). Himself gentle and religiously minded, he believed that God had ordained capital punishment in Genesis IX, 5-6. A committee of the New York legislature agreed with him and adopted his argument as their report. The blunders in Robert Chambers's famous essay, *Vestiges of the Natural History of Creation* (1844), which, though bad science, contained the germ of the Darwinian theory, he exposed scornfully, but failed to appreciate its underlying idea. Among his friends Dod was remembered for his brilliant conversation.

[W. B. Sprague, *Annals Am. Pulpit*, vol. IV (1858); *Gen. Cat. Princeton Univ. 1746–1906* (1908); *Biblical Repertory and Princeton Rev.*, Index Vol. *1825–68* (1871); J. Maclean, *Sermon Preached in the Chapel of the Coll. of N. J., Mar. 1, 1846* (Princeton, 1846), and *Hist. of the Coll. of N. J.* (1877).]   G.H.G.

DOD, DANIEL (Sept. 8, 1778–May 9, 1823), inventor, steam-engine builder, was of the fourth generation descended from Daniel and Mary Dod, natives of England, who emigrated to Branford, Conn., about 1645. His parents were Lebbeus, a brother of Thaddeus Dod [*q.v.*], and Mary (Baldwin) Dod. Daniel was born in northern Virginia whither his father had removed from New Jersey to establish himself as a maker of clocks and watches, but on account of Indian troubles the latter returned north with his family and settled in Mendham, N. J., before the close of the Revolution. Young Dod was trained by his father for the business of clock and watchmaking, mathematical instrument making and surveying. He attended the public schools and also Queen's (now Rutgers) College at New Brunswick. About the time that he became of age, with his two older brothers, he started a manufactory of cotton machinery which developed nicely but failed in the depression following the War of 1812. Just prior to this he had declined the chair of mathematics at Rutgers, and with the collapse of the cotton machinery business he removed with his family to Elizabethtown. For some time he had been interested in steam-engine building, and on Nov. 29, 1811, and May 12, 1812, he was granted United States patents on steam-engines, including boilers and condensers, for use in steamboats as well as mills. These engines operated on the general principle of the Watt engine. In Elizabethtown Dod entered into partnership with the former Governor, Aaron Ogden [*q.v.*], who operated a ferry, to manufacture steam-engines and steamboat machinery. Armed with Dod's patents and the manufacturing rights to John Fitch's steamboat machinery which they had purchased, they began the manufacture of a steam ferryboat and their first product was put in service in 1813. Robert Fulton's steamboat monopoly, which was then in force, prevented, however, Dod and Ogden from continuing to use steam in this ferry service. They continued for five years, making steamboat machinery for boats in other waters: on Lake Ontario; in Philadelphia, Norfolk, Mobile, and New Orleans. Dod's greatest contribution was the machinery for the steamboat *Savannah*, which crossed the Atlantic Ocean in 1819—the first steam-vessel to make this voyage. In 1818 Dod and Ogden dissolved partnership, Dod retaining the manufacturing plant. As a friend he indorsed notes for Ogden who was in need of working capital for his ferry system. Ogden failed, and Dod's works were seized under a mortgage, which loss, together with those on the *Savannah*, forced him in 1819 to pass over all of his property to his creditors. With the help of friends he repurchased all of his tools and in 1820 set up business anew in New York. Three years later, while examining his machinery on board the steamboat *Patent* in the East River, he was so injured by the explosion of the boiler that he died several days later at the age of forty-five. In 1801 he had married Nancy Squier of Caldwell, N. J., who with three daughters and five sons, among them Albert Baldwin Dod [*q.v.*], survived him.

[G. H. Preble, *A Chronological Hist. of the Origin and Development of Steam Navigation* (1883); B. L. Dodd and J. R. Burnet, *Geneals. of the Male Descendants of Daniel Dod* (1864); *Proc. N. J. Hist. Soc.*, vol. IX (1864); H. W. Dickinson, *Robt. Fulton* (1913); *Evening Post* (N. Y.), May 14, 1823.]   C.W.M.

DOD, THADDEUS (Mar. 7, 1740 o.s.–May 20, 1793), pioneer Presbyterian clergyman and educator, was born at Newark, N. J., the second son of Stephen and Deborah (Brown) Dod. The family were of New England Puritan stock, descendants of Daniel Dod, who was born in England and settled about 1645 in Branford, Conn. While Thaddeus was still an infant his parents moved to Mendham, Morris County, N. J., where he was brought up. They were in straitened circumstances, which may account for his lateness in entering college. He graduated from the College of New Jersey in 1773, and began his theological studies. About this time he married Phebe Baldwin, whose sister Mary was the wife of his brother Lebbeus. In 1775 he was licensed and two years later, Oct. 15, 1777, he was ordained *sine titulo* by the Presbytery of New York, for work on the western frontier.

To Lindley's Settlement, an outpost newly established by pioneers from New Jersey, on Ten Mile Creek in the present Washington County, Pa., Dod had made his way that summer, and had there found his future field of work. A week after his ordination he again started westward with his wife and two children; but conditions in western Pennsylvania were unfavorable, and for two years he stayed at Patterson's Creek, Va. In September 1779 he moved with his family to Ten Mile, where he acquired a farm, built a log cabin, and started his pastoral work. The Ten Mile church was formally organized on Aug. 15, 1781. In addition to his ministerial duties there, Dod preached at other settlements where there was no resident pastor. He was one of four clergymen whom the Synod of New York and Philadelphia erected into a separate presbytery in 1781. Their first meeting was not held at the designated place, "as the circumstances of some of the members by reason of the incursions of the savages, rendered it impracticable" (*Minutes Presbytery of Redstone*, p. 3).

In the spring of 1782, in a log cabin near his own home, Dod opened, with thirteen pupils, the first classical school west of the Alleghanies. There he taught English, the classics, and mathematics—this last including surveying. His intellectual attainments were rated highly by those who knew him. He was a good classical scholar, he knew Hebrew (in his extant sermon manu-

scripts the texts are given in the original tongue), he tried his hand at English verse, but his especial interest lay in mathematics. His log cabin academy was closed in the autumn of 1785, when he sold his farm. Two years later he was one of the trustees to whom a charter was granted for Washington Academy; and when the academy was opened on Apr. 1, 1789, Dod was its first principal. He had accepted the position reluctantly and for one year only, though he stayed a few months longer, dividing his time between Washington and Ten Mile. The court-house in which the academy met was burned in the winter of 1790–91, and Dod lost most of his books in the fire. Before the academy reopened, another school was started at Canonsburg, which later became Jefferson College; while Washington Academy became in 1806 Washington College.

As a clergyman, Dod laid his emphasis on personal piety, and he is spoken of as a "son of consolation." Yet he was not superior to the current amenities of theological controversy. "To the witness of Cain," he said in a sermon, "I might add those of Balaam, Saul, Ahab, Judas, Simon the Sorcerer, Julian the Apostate, and John Wesley." He died at Ten Mile on May 20, 1793.

[Jos. Smith, *Old Redstone* (1854), which is the basis of several later accounts; E. C. Wines, *Hist. Discourse* (Pittsburgh, 1859); Jos. Smith, *Hist. of Jefferson Coll.* (1857); *Minutes of the Presbytery of Redstone* (1878); *Centenary Memorial . . . of Presbyterianism in Western Pa.* (1876); B. L. Dodd and J. R. Burnet, *Geneals. of the Male Descendants of Daniel Dod* (1864); "Autobiog. and Memoir of Rev. Thaddeus Dod" in *Presbyterian Mag.*, Aug. and Sept. 1854, with a brief introduction by Dod's son, Cephas Dod; W. B. Sprague, *Annals Am. Pulpit*, III (1858), 356. To Dr. C. T. Dodd of Washington, Pa., and Dr. W. L. Dodd of Amity the writer is indebted for permission to examine MSS. written by Thaddeus Dod.]   A.H.S.

DODD, FRANK HOWARD (Apr. 12, 1844–Jan. 10, 1916), publisher, was born at Bloomfield, N. J., the son of Moses Woodruff and Rachel (Hoe) Dodd. His mother was a member of the Hoe family, long active in the manufacture of printing-presses. His father had been associated with John S. Taylor in publishing religious and theological works at Brick Church Chapel, City Hall Square, New York City; in 1840 he bought out his partner in that business. After the son had been graduated from the Bloomfield Academy (at the age of fifteen), he joined his father in the publishing enterprise, served a ten years' apprenticeship, and in 1870 succeeded to the control of the house, later taking as partners Edward S. Mead, who died in 1894, and B. Van Wagenen, who retired in 1909. The new firm entered the field of popular fiction, bringing out several books that reached a high rank among the "best sellers" of their time. The first pronounced success in that capacity was E. P. Roe's *Barriers Burned Away,* a story deriving its chief incidents from the Chicago fire in 1871. Other popular stories by the same author followed. A score of years passed before the firm published anything comparable in financial returns with the Roe books, although its lists contained many titles of superior literary merit. In 1894, *Beside the Bonnie Brier Bush,* by Ian Maclaren (Dr. John Watson), was brought out in America by Dodd, Mead & Company, and at once achieved a remarkably large sale. Another profitable venture of the house was Paul Leicester Ford's *Janice Meredith* (1899). In the late nineties Dodd and his associates were instrumental in founding and maintaining *The Bookman,* a literary monthly of high quality. In this undertaking they were greatly aided by the cooperation of the London *Bookman.* Dodd at that time formed lasting friendships with several British authors and publishers, among others William Robertson Nicoll and Miss Beatrice Harraden. With the opening of the twentieth century he began to make definite plans for a reference book that should provide for American readers what the German public was then getting from the compilations of Brockhaus and Meyer. The result of his carefully developed project was the *New International Encyclopædia* (1902–04), a work that met with favor because of the convenient arrangement of its material and the compact form of its articles. In 1907 the *New International Year Book* was begun. This annual publication supplemented the information given in the *Encyclopædia* and contained much special material in chronicle form. Before his death the founder saw most of the second edition of the *Encyclopædia* (1914–17) and eight successive issues of the *Year Book* off the press. Dodd had served as president of the American Publishers' Association, had strongly advocated net prices in the book trade, and was always active in promoting the general interests of the craft. He was a leader in accelerating the uptown movement of New York's publishing district. His wife, whom he married in 1868, was Martha Bliss Parker, daughter of President Joel Parker of Union Theological Seminary. His brother, Robert H. Dodd, joined the firm in 1889 and his son, Edward H., in 1903.

[Article in the *New International Year Book,* 1916; *Publisher's Weekly,* Jan. 1916; *Who's Who in America,* 1914–15; *Bookman,* Apr. 1916; Wm. Robertson Nicoll in *British Weekly,* Jan. 20, 1916; B. L. Dodd and J. R. Burnet, *Geneals. of the Male Descendants of Daniel Dod* (1864); *N. Y. Tribune, N. Y. Times,* Jan. 11, 1916.]   W.B.S.

DODD, SAMUEL CALVIN TATE (Feb. 20, 1836–Jan. 30, 1907), lawyer, was born in Franklin, Venango County, Pa., one of the ten children of Levi L. and Julia Parker Dodd. His father was a cabinetmaker and carpenter, a respected citizen, and a stanch Presbyterian. Young Dodd had his early education in the schools of Franklin and worked as errand boy and printer's devil to help finance his college education, which he received in Jefferson College (now Washington and Jefferson), at Canonsburg, Pa., graduating in 1857. He studied law in Franklin for two years and was admitted to the bar of Venango County in 1859, the year in which oil was discovered in western Pennsylvania. His whole career was shaped by this event. A vast influx of capital and business came upon the heels of the great discovery and he found himself immediately involved in the complications and competition growing out of the boom. Unlike most of the lawyers of the community he gave his attention mainly to corporation law and equity, foreseeing that the day of big business was at hand and that the cutthroat competition among the oil producers was wasteful and temporary. The seventies found him fighting the battles of the consumers and the independents against the Rockefeller interests, and he acquired considerable reputation as an anti-rebate lawyer. In 1872–73 he served as a delegate to the Pennsylvania constitutional convention, where he fathered the anti-rebate clause which that body wrote into the new constitution. During this period he served as counsel for numerous oil operators and transportation companies, especially the transportation companies from which the United Pipe Lines were later formed. In 1881 he became general solicitor for the Standard Oil Company and moved to New York. This relationship was in one respect an unusual one. He felt that in order to give the best legal advice he should occupy a detached, almost judicial position, uninfluenced by personal financial interests. Accordingly he refused to allow John D. Rockefeller to place to his credit for gradual payment a block of stock which would have made him many times a millionaire; contrary to popular rumor his salary was never more than $25,000, and he left an estate of less than $300,000. His business relations with the Rockefellers and other Standard Oil magnates were always cordial, but otherwise he stood somewhat aloof, never becoming an intimate friend.

His reputation rests upon his organization in 1882 of the Standard Oil Trust. He is sometimes called the inventor of the trust as a form of business combination. There had, however, been a less comprehensive Standard Oil trust agreement in 1879. The state laws of the period did not afford a way for corporations to combine and what Dodd was seeking was a means of creating a "corporation of corporations." Under the trust agreement which he drew up, the voting stocks of some forty companies were placed in the hands of nine trustees. The change effected was, however, more apparent than real. There had been no competition between the companies thus combined for some time and the nine trustees did in fact own a majority of the stock of the component corporations. The trust agreement was kept secret for six years. It fell to Dodd's lot to officiate not only at its birth but also at its death. In 1892 the Supreme Court of Ohio decided that it was an illegal combination in restraint of trade and also that the Standard Oil Company of Ohio, one of the component companies, had exceeded its lawful corporate powers in entering the agreement. Accordingly, in March of that year Dodd presented the resolutions for the dissolution of the trust. This dissolution did not materially alter the actual conditions of the business. For six years the now dissociated corporations conducted their business under a gentlemen's agreement, and under the shrewd legal guardianship of Dodd who steered them, as one writer puts it, "through the stormy seas of anti-trust agitation," and kept them within the law. In 1899 he drew up the plans for the organization of the great holding company, the Standard Oil Company of New Jersey. He continued as legal adviser until 1905 when he retired from active service on a pension, retaining the title of counsel for the Standard Oil Company.

Dodd was a firm believer in big business lawfully conducted and he bitterly resented the idea that combinations are vicious merely because they are large. Accordingly he criticized the early interpretation of the Sherman Act which penalized all combinations in restraint of trade. He held that only unreasonable combinations should be barred, a view later adopted by the Supreme Court in 1911 (*Standard Oil Company of New Jersey et al.* vs. *United States, 221 U. S., 1*) in dissolving the very holding company which he had organized (see his paper, "Present Legal Status of Trusts," *Harvard Law Review,* Oct. 25, 1893). He was a firm believer in the federal incorporation of business companies and favored a constitutional amendment to make that possible (J. H. Bridge, "Trusts as Their Makers View Them," *World's Work,* November 1902). In politics he was a nominal Democrat, an ad-

mirer of Cleveland, but an independent voter. His published writings include, "Ten Years of the Standard Oil Company" (*Forum,* May 1892); the following pamphlets: *Uses and Abuses of Combinations* (1888); *History of the Standard Oil Company* (1888); *Trusts* (1889); *Aggregated Capital* (1889); and *Trusts* (1900), a collection of addresses.

He married, in 1860, Mary E. Geer of Waterford, Pa., who bore him one son, and died in 1872. On Mar. 8, 1877, he married Melvina E. Smith, who died in 1906. From this marriage there were two children. In private life Dodd was genial, friendly, and generous. He shunned publicity and seldom appeared in court. He lived quietly and modestly with his family, a few congenial friends, and his books. He read deeply in history, economics, and philosophy, and Spencer and Huxley were his gods. Deeply religious, he became in later life a reverent freethinker.

[B. L. Dodd and John R. Burnet, *Genealogies of the Male Descendants of Daniel Dod, of Branford, Conn.* (1864); Paul Latzke, "The Trust Builder," *Nat. Corporation Reporter,* Dec. 4, 1902 (reprinted from *Saturday Evening Post*); "The Master Builder of the Standard Oil Company," *Rev. of Revs.* (N. Y.), Mar. 1908; *Who's Who in America,* 1906–07; obituaries in *N. Y. Times,* Feb. 1, 1907, and *N. Y. Journal of Commerce,* Feb. 1907; information as to certain facts from a son, Mr. Lee Wilson Dodd.]   R.E.C.

DODDRIDGE, JOSEPH (Oct. 14, 1769–Nov. 9, 1826), clergyman, physician, author, and pioneer, was born at Friend's Cove, near Bedford, Pa., eldest son of John and Mary (Wells) Doddridge of Maryland, and brother of Philip Doddridge [*q.v.*]. Four years later his parents removed to Washington County, Pa., then wilderness, so that from childhood he was thrown into intimate association with the Indians and early settlers of the frontier. His powers of observation and his life-long interest in recording historical incident helped him to capitalize this association in his valuable *Notes on the Settlement and Indian Wars of the Western Parts of Virginia and Pennsylvania, from 1763 to 1783 Inclusive* (1824), an accurate account of the country and the life that prevailed there during the days of its colonization.

The elder Doddridge was a devout man who reared his children along strictly pious and moralistic lines, and it was not strange that Joseph at eighteen, with a background of Bible reading, a few sessions of schooling in Maryland, and several years of labor on his father's farm, should have been received as a circuit preacher of the Wesleyan Methodist connection, traveling through western Pennsylvania. The death of his father in 1791 called him from this itinerant ministry, but enabled him to resume his interrupted education. After a year of diligent study at Jefferson Academy, Canonsburg, Pa., he transferred to the Episcopal ministry, received ordination from Bishop White at Philadelphia, and removed temporarily to western Pennsylvania; soon, however, he settled permanently in Charlestown (now Wellsburg, W. Va.), Brooke County, Va. For the remainder of his life he acted as an advance guard of the Protestant Episcopal Church in northwestern Virginia and eastern Ohio, traveling on horseback over an extensive and sparsely settled territory to render truly apostolic service in his effort to keep the church in the van of western progress. After 1800 he extended his missionary operations chiefly into Ohio, and it was owing in great measure to his unselfish and indefatigable exertions that an episcopate was obtained in that state. His never robust physique was undermined by his frequent exposure and constant toil, and his cheerful and hopeful disposition was depressed and turned irritable by a painful asthmatic disease which made his last years burdensome.

About 1795 he married Jemima, daughter of Capt. John Bukey, and soon found it essential that he augment his meager income. He settled upon medicine as a profession compatible with the ministry, completed a course of preparation under Dr. Benjamin Rush of Philadelphia, and thenceforth successfully nurtured the bodily as well as the spiritual wants of his parishioners, winning popularity with his patients at the same time that he won praise from his fellow physicians for his "abilities and scientific skill." He managed also to do a fair amount of writing but beyond the *Notes,* etc., with its wealth of original material, little of it is important. His *Treatise on the Culture of Bees* (1813) reveals one of his especial interests, and his prose drama *Logan* (1823) won him recognition, but its intention to render justice to the famous Indian leader is more apparent than are its dramatic or literary qualities.

[The fullest account of Joseph Doddridge is the Memoir by his daughter Narcissa Doddridge, included in the second (Albany, 1876) and third (Pittsburgh, 1912) editions of the *Notes on the Settlement and Indian Wars.* The edition of 1876 contains likewise a seven-page sketch of him, written in 1855, by Judge Thomas Scott of Chillicothe, Ohio. The latter sketch is quoted in G. W. Peterkin, *Hist. and Record of the Protestant Episcopal Church in the Diocese of W. Va.* (1902), with occasional other references to Doddridge. The index to Vol. II of Perry's *Hist. of the Am. Epis. Church 1587–1883* (1885) may mislead the reader through its confusion of Joseph Doddridge, who did write some unimportant verse, with the English hymn-writer and divine, Philip Doddridge. Most of the *Notes on the Settlement,* etc., has been reprinted in Samuel Kercheval's *Hist. of the Valley of Va.* (1833). See also S. E. Dodderidge, *The Dodderidges of Devon* (1909).]   A.C.G.,Jr.

DODDRIDGE, PHILIP (May 17, 1773–Nov. 19, 1832), lawyer, politician, was the youngest son of John Doddridge, a farmer, and his wife, Mary, daughter of Col. Richard Wells. He was born in Bedford County, Pa., whither his father had removed from Maryland. His youth was spent on the farm and he had little opportunity of acquiring education before he was seventeen, when he went to Charlestown (now Wellsburg, W. Va.), Brooke County, Va., and attended Johnson's private school there. On leaving school he took a trip by flatboat down the Ohio and Mississippi rivers to New Orleans, and upon his return began the study of law. In the spring of 1797 he commenced practise in Wellsburg. Details of his early years at the bar are meager; contemporary testimony agrees, however, that his success was rapid and his powers of speech remarkable. He was appointed state's attorney for Ohio County in 1808, and that his practise was expanding is indicated by the fact that he held briefs in the court of appeals of Virginia and the Supreme Court of the United States. In 1815–16, a period when sectionalism was emerging as a major feature of Virginia politics, he was a member of the House of Delegates, for Brooke County. Under the Virginia constitution of 1776 the basis of representation was such that the legislature was controlled by the "Tidewater" constituencies, despite the rapid settlement of the western counties. Doddridge entered the House as an aggressive western protagonist. His powerful denunciation of existing anomalies made a deep impression, but he could make no progress. He was a member of the legislature again in 1822–23 and 1828, the latter session being of vital importance, inasmuch as a decision had been arrived at to hold a constitutional convention in which any amendments considered should be framed by the legislature. His proposals to make the white population the basis of representation and have a census taken were voted down, but he did not abandon hope. He was delegate from Brooke County to the convention which met at Richmond, Oct. 5, 1829, his eloquence, earnestness, and resource making him the commanding figure there, but again he failed and the amended constitution of 1830 was as unreformed as its predecessor (see J. M. Callahan, *History of West Virginia,* 1923, I, 320–24). His efforts nevertheless paved the way for the creation later of the State of West Virginia.

Doddridge had been an unsuccessful candidate for Congress in 1822 and 1824, but in 1828 was elected and, having been reëlected in 1830, remained a member till his death at Washington, Nov. 19, 1832. On Apr. 30, 1800, he married

Julia Parr Musser of Lancaster, Pa. He was said to have been "not less celebrated on the west side of the Alleghany Mountains for his eloquence and splendid talents, than Patrick Henry was by the men of his day in the eastern portions of Virginia" (*The American Pioneer*, April 1842, p. 135). By the unanimous verdict of his contemporaries he was a lawyer and statesman of the first rank, but since he never became a national figure his brilliant personality was only locally appreciated.

[An excellent review of Doddridge's life and political career appeared in an article, "Hon. Philip Doddridge of Brooke County, Va.," by W. S. Laidley in the *W. Va. Hist. Mag.*, Jan. 1902; see also V. A. Lewis, *Hist. of W. Va.* (1889), p. 685; and W. T. Willey, *A Sketch of the Life of Philip Doddridge* (1875), which though unreliable in the matter of dates gives several of Doddridge's speeches.]   H. W. H. K.

DODGE, AUGUSTUS CÆSAR (Jan. 2, 1812–Nov. 20, 1883), United States senator, diplomat, son of Henry Dodge [*q.v.*] and Christina McDonald, was born at Ste. Genevieve, Mo. At the age of fifteen he removed with his parents to the lead-mines in the southwestern part of what is now Wisconsin. Here he worked with his father at mining and served with him in the Winnebago War of 1827 and in the Black Hawk War in 1832. There was little opportunity for schooling, but on Mar. 19, 1837, he made up for this lack in part, perhaps, by marrying Clara Ann Hertich, the daughter of the Ste. Genevieve schoolmaster. From 1838 to 1840 he was registrar of the public land office at Burlington in the Territory of Iowa. In December of the latter year he entered Congress as delegate for the Territory and for six years held this position, occupying himself largely with the questions of appropriations and boundaries. In 1848 he was chosen as Iowa's first United States senator, after the legislature had been deadlocked over the election for two years. He and his father had been together for four years as delegates from the neighboring territories of Wisconsin and Iowa. Now for a period of over six years they were together in the Senate.

Dodge was a Democrat, warmly attached to the West, and with a sympathy for the South that grew out of his early life in Missouri. He voted for all of the provisions of the compromise measures of 1850. He was outspoken in his opposition to abolitionism and in defense of the Fugitive-Slave Law. In December 1853, he introduced a bill to organize the Territory of Nebraska. This was referred to the committee on territories of which Douglas was chairman. In January a substitute measure was presented providing for the creation of two territories instead of one and applying to this region the principle of popular sovereignty. Dodge supported the Kansas-Nebraska Bill with enthusiasm, characterizing it as "the noblest tribute which has ever yet been offered by the Congress of the United States to the sovereignty of the people." A rising tide of anti-Nebraska sentiment developed, however, in his state, and in January 1855 the legislature chose James Harlan to succeed him in the Senate. President Pierce then appointed him to the post of minister to Spain. One of his first duties in Madrid was the final settlement of the *Black Warrior* affair which had threatened the peaceful relations of the two nations. The particular hope of the administration at this time was to acquire the island of Cuba, and Dodge set himself energetically to the task, but without success. In 1859 he resigned and returned to Iowa, where he was defeated by the Republicans in a race for the governorship in 1859 and, again by James Harlan, in a contest for the United States senatorship in 1860. The remainder of his years, nearly a quarter of a century, he spent in private life in Burlington. He was a representative of the ante bellum Democracy and like his party was unable to adjust himself to the change in sentiment on the slavery question. On issues relating to the West, notably the homestead and Pacific railroad problems, he fought vigorously for measures which the Republican party enacted during its first term of office. He was a man of sincere convictions and aggressive force, consistent in his policies but without great flexibility of mind. He faithfully served his state in the early days when the people of Iowa were largely of Southern origin, but with the influx of Northerners and the growth of Republicanism, his supporters became a minority, with the result that retirement from public life overtook him before he reached the age of sixty.

[Most of Dodge's correspondence was unfortunately destroyed. There exist, however, two letter-books embodying his diplomatic correspondence, and a manuscript containing autobiographical notes. Letters of his contemporaries, newspaper files, and the *Congressional Globe* enable one to follow his public career. An adequate biography is found in Louis Pelzer, *Augustus Cæsar Dodge* (1908). See also William Salter, "Augustus C. Dodge," in the *Iowa Hist. Record*, vol. III, Jan. 1887.]   J. C. P.

DODGE, DAVID LOW (June 14, 1774–Apr. 23, 1852), merchant, founder of the New York Peace Society, was born on a farm in Brooklyn, originally a part of Pomfret, Conn., in the year before the outbreak of the Revolution. His parents were David and Mary (Stuart) Earl Dodge. His father, David Dodge, was of English and Welsh colonial stock, a descendant of Richard Dodge who came to Salem, Mass., from England about 1638; his mother, Mary Stuart, was said to be the daughter of a Scotch nobleman and at the time of her marriage to David Dodge she was the widow of William Earl. The boyhood of David Low Dodge was not without its privations. He was early inclined to reading, but advantages were meager. At the age of six he attended a school kept by a spiritually minded Irish woman, Mary Moxley. From seven to fourteen, except for two months of district school each winter, he was employed on the farm in Hampton, Conn., to which his father had removed. The only books available were the Bible and the school primer, spelling-book, and arithmetic. After his fifteenth year there was little opportunity for schooling; but at nineteen he was a full-fledged schoolmaster, and in that calling he continued successfully for several years, at first in community schools and later in private ventures. On June 7, 1798, he was married to Sarah, daughter of the Rev. Aaron Cleveland [*q.v.*]. His wife's cousins, the Messrs. Higginson of Boston, who were large importers for that day, helped him to inform himself about the dry-goods trade, and in 1802 he began buying stocks of imported wares at Boston, transporting them by wagon to Connecticut, and selling at a good profit. He established a store at Hartford, with a branch at Litchfield. Prospering in this enterprise, in 1807 he started a jobbing business in New York City in co-partnership with the Higginsons, who within a few years suffered serious reverses in the Napoleonic wars. The New York house of Higginson, Dodge & Company was not involved in these losses, but a dissolution of the firm became necessary. In 1813 Dodge became manager of a cotton-mill near Norwich, Conn.

After his removal to New York, he had taken a more and more active part in religious and philanthropic efforts. In 1809 he wrote a pamphlet entitled, *The Mediator's Kingdom not of This World,* containing an argument against the lawfulness of war waged by Christians. He began a vigorous campaign to enlist the so-called evangelical churches of America in his war against war, entering into an extensive correspondence with such contemporary leaders as Lyman Beecher, John B. Romeyn, Walter King, and Aaron Cleveland. In 1812 appeared his second pamphlet, *War Inconsistent with the Religion of Jesus Christ,* and in the same year a group of men in New York, under his leadership, were ready to form a society to promote pacifist principles. They decided on postponement, however, because it was felt that during the war with England the motives of such propaganda might be misunderstood. On Aug. 16, 1815, after the close of the war, the New York Peace Society was launched, with thirty or forty members, representing various religious denominations. It is said to have been the first organization of its kind in the world. Dodge was the first president of the society and took the leading part in shaping its policies. He does not seem to have tried to interest persons outside the membership of churches. His arguments were based on the Scriptures, in the main, and addressed to Christians. His writings indicate, indeed, that he doubted the wisdom of making a more general appeal for the application of peace principles in human governments. He was a thoroughgoing Calvinist and all his pleas were couched in terms familiar to those versed in the precepts of that faith. So far did he carry his disapproval of every form of militarism that he would neither vote nor hold office. In 1827 he retired from business. In the following year the New York Peace Society united with other similar bodies that had been formed since 1815 in creating the American Peace Society. Dodge presided at the organization meeting of the new society, May 8, 1828, and at its first annual meeting, May 13, 1829, was a member of its board of directors, and later became a life director. He was also active in the founding of the New York Bible Society and the New York Tract Society. His son, William Earl Dodge [*q.v.*], and his grandson, of the same name, followed by great-grandsons, continued these and similar activities to the fourth generation.

[Near the close of his life Dodge prepared, at the request of his children, an autobiography. This, with a few selections from his writings, was published for the family at Boston as *Memorial of Mr. David L. Dodge, Consisting of an Autobiography . . . with a Few Selections from his Writings* (1854). Dodge's pamphlet, *War Inconsistent with the Religion of Jesus Christ,* was republished in 1905, with a biographical introduction by Edwin D. Mead. See also E. L. Whitney, *The Am. Peace Soc.: A Centennial Hist.* (1928); *Geneal. of the Dodge Family of Essex County, Mass.* (1894).]

W. B. S.

DODGE, EBENEZER (Apr. 21, 1819–Jan. 5, 1890), clergyman, theologian, educator, was born at Salem, Mass., the son of a sea captain, whose name he bore, and Joanna (Appleton) Dodge. Little is known of his youth save that his early religious influences came from his mother, while his pastor, Rev. Lucius Bolles of the Baptist Church, gave him a broader world horizon which doubtless had been extended by the maritime associations of his boyhood. At the age of seventeen, he entered Brown University from the Salem Latin School, having the legal profession in view; but a religious revival in the college awakened in him a positive conception of the Christian life, so that what he considered his conversion (see *One Honest Effort*, tract issued by the American Tract Society) was almost identical with his call to the ministry. His native scholarly talent was greatly stimulated by Francis Wayland, president of the University, from which he was graduated in 1840. Before proceeding to his theological studies, he served as principal of the academy at Shelburne Falls for two years and then entered Newton Theological Institution, graduating in 1845. Here the influence of Barnas Sears was especially important upon him. After a somewhat unsatisfactory year as teacher in an embryonic theological school at Covington, Ky., he became pastor of the Baptist Church at New Hampton (1846–49) and at New London, N. H. Both were rural fields with educational interests offering incentives to his mental development. In various ways he participated in the broader interests of the churches; in 1848, he made a penetrating report upon some questions at issue connected with the American and Foreign Bible Society.

In November 1853 he was elected professor of Biblical criticism in the Theological Institution at Hamilton, N. Y., and also professor of the evidences of revealed religion in Madison University (now Colgate), beginning his services the following month. Here his career was to continue, though definite calls came later both to Rochester and to Newton. In 1858–59, he spent more than a year in Europe, where he became especially well acquainted with the eminent theologians, Tholuck and Dorner. In 1861, he was transferred to the chair of doctrinal theology in the Seminary and in 1868 he was elected president of Madison University, retaining the professorships he already held, which had come to include psychology and Christian ethics. His administration of the University was marked by substantial progress in the development of the productive assets and by adjustments in the educational program to meet the changing conditions. The secondary and the theological instruction were both separated from the collegiate, the resultant Academy and the relatively more free Seminary being given his sympathetic and honest support. Long after his death, the traditions of his strength of character, his catholicity of feeling and his unselfish disinterestedness were still current on the campus, with many a striking epigram.

His only published book was *The Evidences of Christianity* (1869), but some of his lectures were privately printed for his students' use in his classes, among them a substantial volume entitled *Lectures in Christian Theology*. Dodge was twice married: first, in 1846, to Sarah Abbot Putnam of Salem, who died in 1861; and in 1863, to Eleanor F. Rogers of Providence, R. I., who survived him.

[Biographical sketches by Sylvester Burnham in the memorial number of the *Madisonensis*, Jan. 18, 1890; by Dodge's pastor and successor in the chair of theology, W. N. Clarke, *Baptist Quart. Rev.*, July 1890; a recent tribute by C. H. Dodd, *Crozer Quart.*, July 1925; and J. T. Dodge, *Geneal. of the Dodge Family of Essex County, Mass.* (1894).]

W. H. A.

DODGE, GRACE HOADLEY (May 21, 1856–Dec. 27, 1914), social worker, philanthropist, was born in New York City, eldest of six children of William Earl Dodge, Jr., and Sarah Hoadley. She was a sister of Cleveland H. Dodge and a grand-daughter of William Earl Dodge [*q.v.*]. Her ancestors on both sides for several generations were business men and Grace Dodge had marked business ability. When she was seven, her father built Greyston, in Riverdale, N. J., her much loved summer home throughout life. Her first instruction was from governesses, one of whom taught her the promptness and attention to detail which were always characteristic of her. In 1872 she went to Miss Porter's School in Farmington, Conn., but left in 1874, went abroad with her parents, and on her return became absorbed in social work. Sunday-school and sewing classes and the Children's Aid Society first interested her. Soon she was chairman of the Committee on the Elevation of the Poor in their Homes of the State Charities Aid Association, and helped to initiate the struggle for tenement reform in 1879. Meanwhile she had assisted in the organization of the Kitchen Garden Association, for "the promotion of the Domestic Industrial Arts among the laboring classes" and had founded a working girls' club, from which grew the Associations of Working Girls' Societies. In much of this work she would probably have been more effective had her own education and training been more extended. Perhaps because of a realization of this, she came to believe strongly in education as an all-important social agency. During these early years, her summers at Riverdale were also filled with philanthropic activity. She started a village library, at first housed in her father's greenhouse, a Riverdale woman's club, and a sewing school for girls.

In 1884 the Kitchen Garden Association was dissolved and the Industrial Education Association took its place, with Dr. F. A. P. Barnard [*q.v.*], president of Columbia College, an honorary member. Grace Dodge became vice-president and performed most of the presidential duties. Because of this connection, she was appointed in 1886 a member of the New York City Board of Education. To coordinate home duties with organization business, she equipped an office in the basement of her Madison Avenue home and employed a secretary. She had set herself the task of introducing industrial education into the public schools; the report of a committee of the Board of Education on which she served secured the first experiment in this direction. The Industrial Education Association, with Nicholas Murray Butler as president, was developing in the direction of the training of teachers and in 1889, largely through its influence, the New York College for the Training of Teachers, located at 9 University Place, was provisionally chartered. When, in 1892, a new site was given on Morningside Heights, Grace Dodge became acting treasurer of the College and chairman of the finance committee of the Board of Trustees. In spite of the financial panic of 1893, she succeeded in raising money for completing the main building. Through difficult years, it was, in the words of Dr. James E. Russell, for over twenty-five years dean of Teachers College, "only Miss Dodge's faith that kept Teachers College alive." To her fell the task of raising money for new buildings, mortgage payments, additional professors, and any increases in the budget. Though Teachers College was now her chief interest, her other activities were numerous. In 1896 she resigned the directorship of the Working Girls' Societies, feeling that the movement had developed into an economic struggle, involving legislation and publicity for which she was unsuited. At her home the American Social Hygiene Association was formed, by the merging of five organizations of kindred aims. She was a founder of the New York Travelers Aid Society in 1907, and in her last days was working on plans for a National Travelers Aid Society. She was president of the Board of the Constantinople Woman's College from 1910 and contributed liberally to its needs. The greatest work of her later years was with the Young Women's Christian Associations: first as arbitrator in helping to unite the two overlapping organizations, under the International Board and the American Committee respectively; then, in 1906 as president of the National Board of the united Young Women's Christian Associations of the United States of America. In 1910 she attended the conference of the World's Young Women's Christian Associations in Berlin. She died in New York City, at the height of her many activities.

[Abbie Graham, *Grace H. Dodge; Merchant of Dreams* (1926), is the official biography published by the National Board of the Y. W. C. A. The memorial number of the *Association Monthly* (Y. W. C. A.), Mar. 1915, contains articles by a number of persons associated with her in social work. See also sketch in *Who's Who in America,* 1912–13; obituaries in the *N. Y. Tribune* and *N. Y. Times,* both Dec. 28, 1914.]

S. G. B.

DODGE, GRENVILLE MELLEN (Apr. 12, 1831–Jan. 3, 1916), civil engineer, politician, son of Sylvanus and Julia Theresa (Phillips) Dodge, was born in a farmhouse in Danvers, Mass. He was of English descent—eight generations removed from Richard Dodge who came to Salem, Mass., in 1638, and four generations removed from James Phillips who emigrated to America in 1700. As a boy Grenville M. Dodge was active, robust, and healthy. He drove a butcher's cart, clerked in a store, and worked on Mrs. Edward Lander's celebrated fruit and vegetable farm—where he gained valuable training in business methods—but he was also interested in books, went to school, and prepared for college. During the winter of 1845–46 he attended Durham Academy (N. H.). In 1848 he entered Norwich University (Vt.). He graduated from the scientific department of this institution, and finished at Partridge's private school in July 1851, receiving a diploma as a military and civil engineer. His college days fell in the period of "railroad excitement." Men were dreaming of a transportation system that would stretch from the Atlantic to the Pacific, and even college students were discussing the subject. Dodge became fired with enthusiasm for civil engineering and railroad building, and after graduating he made a beginning in this field at Peru, Ill., where two of his classmates had preceded him. His first job was surveying town lots. Parties, barn-dances, horseback riding, and "girls in flaming calico dresses" interested him. Here he met Anne Brown, and later (May 29, 1854), married her. Together with his classmates, the Ransom boys, he organized an artillery squad, which later saw service in quelling some labor trouble at Vermilionville. In January 1852 he was given a position with an engineering party on the Illinois Central Railroad, and in the autumn of that year he met Peter A. Dey, and was taken into one of his surveying parties. When Dey was selected to make the surveys across Iowa for the Mississippi & Missouri Railroad, he took Dodge with him as his chief assistant and put him in charge of the survey from Davenport to Iowa City (1853). From Iowa City, Dodge pushed on westward with his party and reached the Missouri River near the village of Council Bluffs on Nov. 22, 1853. Here he was to make his permanent home. From 1855 to 1861 he was engaged in railroad construction work in Iowa, and in mercantile business in Council Bluffs, helped to organize a bank, made some reconnaissances and surveys west of the Missouri River under the patronage of Henry Farnham and Thomas C. Durant, traded with the Indians, and did some freighting on the plains between the Missouri River and Denver.

At the outbreak of the Civil War, he tendered his services and the services of the Council Bluffs Guards, a company which he had organized in 1856, to Gov. Kirkwood. Appointed first to a position on the governor's staff, then to the colonelcy of the 4th Iowa Regiment, he saw active service in the field in Missouri, Kentucky, Tennessee, Mississippi, Alabama, and Georgia, and in the end was promoted to the rank of major-general of volunteers. Early in the war he was wounded at the battle of Pea Ridge. On Aug. 19, 1864, in front of Atlanta he was severely wounded in the head and compelled to retire temporarily from active service. He visited Grant's headquarters at City Point upon invitation; and interviewed Lincoln in Washington. Upon his return to the field (Nov. 1, 1864) he saw service in Missouri, and later against the Indians in the country west of the Missouri River. During the war his services both as a soldier and as an engineer were distinguished. In three days he built a bridge 14 feet high and 710 feet long across the Chattahoochee River. For his skill and efficiency in building bridges and reconstructing and equipping railroads for the use of the army, he was highly commended by Gen. Grant.

Relieved of his military command at his own request (May 1866), he immediately entered upon his duties as chief engineer of the Union Pacific Railroad, to which position he had been appointed in January 1866. The first grading on this road had been done in the autumn of 1864; the first rail was laid in July 1865; and the last spike was nailed on May 10, 1869. In one year 568 miles of road were located, built, and equipped. The completion of this stupendous project was the fulfilment of the great ambition of Dodge's life. In January 1870 he resigned as chief engineer. He became chief engineer of the Texas & Pacific Railway in 1871, and upon the failure of that road in the panic of 1873 joined Jay Gould [q.v.] in railroad development in the Southwest. During the ten years of this association he assisted in the building and consolidation of nearly nine thousand miles of road (Perkins, *post*, p. 262). Among the roads in the construction of which he was interested in the later eighties were the Denver, Texas & Fort Worth, and the Denver, Texas & Gulf. He was president of the Union Pacific, Denver & Gulf in

1892, but the road went into the hands of receivers in the following year and he resigned his office. After the war with Spain, in association with Sir William Horne, he organized the Cuba Railroad Company and by 1903 had completed the line from Santa Clara to Santiago. This was his last piece of railroad construction.

Dodge's surveys alone totaled approximately 60,000 miles. For half a century he was active as projector, builder, financier and director of railroads in the West and Southwest and was called by some the ablest railroad lobbyist of his time. His record places him high among the railroad builders of the world. In politics he was a Republican; he attended the national party conventions; took an active part in presidential elections; and always, of course, kept a watchful eye on railroad legislation. In 1866 he was elected to Congress from the 5th Congressional District in Iowa. He declined a renomination in 1868 in order to devote all of his energies to the construction of the Union Pacific. In his later years he was much interested in patriotic organizations such as the Society of the Army of the Tennessee and the Military Order of the Loyal Legion.

[Letters (1856–1916) and an incomplete autobiographical MS. are deposited in the rooms of the Historical, Memorial, and Art Building, Des Moines, Iowa. The best published sources of information are: J. R. Perkins, *Trails, Rails and War—The Life of Gen. G. M. Dodge* (1929); *A Brief Biog. Sketch of the Life of Maj. Gen. Grenville M. Dodge* (1893), comp. from official records by his private secretary, J. T. Granger; and "In Memoriam: Grenville Mellen Dodge," in the *Norwich Univ. Record*, Jan. 29, 1916. See also H. H. Field and J. R. Reed, *Hist. of Pottawattamie County, Iowa* (1907), vol. I; *Who's Who in America*, 1914–15; J. T. Dodge, *Geneal. of the Dodge Family of Essex County, Mass.* (1894).]   B. F. S.

DODGE, HENRY (Oct. 12, 1782–June 19, 1867), soldier, governor, United States senator, was born at Post Vincennes (now Vincennes, Ind.), three years after its capture by George Rogers Clark. His father, Israel Dodge, a Revolutionary soldier, had moved west and married Nancy Ann Hunter, a girl of the Kentucky frontier. After a number of years in the Illinois country and Kentucky, the Dodges crossed the Mississippi and settled in the Ste. Geneviève district of Spanish Louisiana. Here Henry Dodge reached maturity, receiving little formal education but assisting his father in the various frontier occupations of lead mining, farming, brewing and distilling. In 1800 he married Christina McDonald. Five years later he succeeded his father as sheriff of the Ste. Geneviève district, and held this office for sixteen years. From 1813 he served as marshal of the Territory of Missouri, and in the Missouri militia he rose to the grade of major-general.

After the War of 1812, in which he led troops to the relief of the Boone Lick settlement on the Missouri, he returned to lead mining, but the fame of the mineral fields of the Upper Mississippi River caused him to migrate in 1827, settling finally in the region of the present Dodgeville, Wis., then a part of the Territory of Michigan. He commanded a force of mounted volunteers in the Winnebago War of 1827, and took a distinguished part in the Black Hawk War in 1832. His military success led to his appointment by President Jackson as major of a battalion of mounted rangers, recruited to patrol the frontier in the Upper Mississippi Valley. In 1833 this body was replaced by the first regiment of United States dragoons with Dodge as its colonel. Its range of activity is indicated by the march to the Pawnee villages on the upper waters of the Red River in 1834, and the expedition in 1835 to the Rocky Mountains in Colorado.

When the Territory of Michigan was divided in 1836, Dodge was made governor of the Territory of Wisconsin, which comprised the present states of Wisconsin, Minnesota, and Iowa, and parts of the Dakotas. In 1838 the land west of the Mississippi was separately organized as the Territory of Iowa. Dodge continued as governor of the diminished Territory of Wisconsin until 1841 when he was replaced by a Whig. The people, however, at once elected him as their delegate in Congress and in this capacity he served until a Democratic president in 1845 restored him to the office of governor. Three years later Wisconsin was admitted to statehood and Dodge became one of its first United States senators. In 1857 he retired from the Senate and from public life, and died a decade later in his eighty-fifth year.

He was primarily a soldier and a frontiersman. Over six feet in height, erect, aggressive, and courageous, he commanded the respect of his soldiers and of the Indians with whom he waged war and negotiated treaties. His greatest contribution to public life was his service of eight years as governor of a pioneer territory. His varied experiences on the border prepared him for the duties pertaining to the government of settlers and for the associated duties of superintendent of Indian affairs. As delegate to Congress and senator his record is merely that of a conscientious servant of his constituents, whose instructions he sought faithfully to carry out. An interesting instance is his vote against the Kansas-Nebraska Bill which his son and senatorial colleague from Iowa, Augustus Cæsar Dodge [q.v.], was warmly espousing.

[The most important body of original material on Dodge consists of commissions, military order book, and letters in the Hist. Dept. of Iowa at Des Moines. For the history of the dragoons see Louis Pelzer, *The Marches of the Dragoons in the Mississippi Valley* (1917). The best biography of Dodge is Louis Pelzer, *Henry Dodge* (1911). See also William Salter, "Henry Dodge," in the *Iowa Hist. Record,* vols. V and VI (Oct. 1889–Apr. 1890), and Moses M. Strong, *Hist. of the Territory of Wis.* (1885).]　　　　J.C.P.

DODGE, JACOB RICHARDS (Sept. 28, 1823–Oct. 1, 1902), agricultural statistician and journalist, was born at New Boston, N. H., the son of Capt. Jacob D. Dodge and Tryphena (Colburn) Dodge. He was a descendant in the seventh generation of Richard Dodge, who emigrated from Somerset, England, in 1638 and settled in Salem, Mass. At an early age he moved with his family to Nashua, N. H. His education was obtained in common schools and academies. Between 1845 and 1849 he was in charge of an academy in Mississippi. His tastes then led him into journalism. He was editor and publisher of the *Oasis,* Nashua, N. H., from 1850 to 1854, and of the *American Ruralist,* Springfield, Ohio, from 1857 to 1861. He was Senate reporter of the Washington *National Intelligencer* and of the *National Republican* from 1861 to 1862. On the organization of the United States Department of Agriculture in 1862, he entered its employ, becoming editor, and in May 1866, statistician. He continued to serve, however, as editor. The early annual reports of the Department were edited by him as were also the monthly reports of the Division of Statistics. The principal features of the latter were the crop reports, but they also included a large amount of miscellaneous and valuable statistical matter. Dodge soon became eminent among American statisticians and held a foremost place in all statistical matters relating to agriculture. In 1873 he spent the summer in Europe, under a commission from the Department of Agriculture for investigating the statistical methods of European countries, and as one of the commissioners to the Vienna World's Exposition by appointment from the State Department. He resigned his position in the Department of Agriculture in 1878, intending to reënter agricultural journalism, but was induced by the secretary of the treasury to accept a temporary commission for the investigation of commercial agriculture. In 1879 he took charge of the agricultural statistics of the Tenth Census, under Gen. Francis A. Walker, superintendent. Two years later he was recalled to his former position as statistician of the Department of Agriculture. Under a special congressional appropriation he attended the session of the International Statistical Institute in 1887 as a delegate from the Department of Agriculture. He made a more thorough investigation of the statistical bureaus of London, Paris, Rome, Vienna, and Berlin. The Paris Exposition of 1889 awarded him a gold medal for exhibits of graphic illustrations of agricultural statistics. During his more than thirty years of official service he won not only the esteem and confidence of his associates, but recognition by the public at large as a man of rare attainments, broad views, sound judgment, and sterling quality. A study of the history of the Department of Agriculture shows the large part he took in its early development. He finally resigned his position on Mar. 20, 1893, shortly after the change of administration. After his retirement he joined the editorial staff of the *Country Gentleman* as statistical editor, which position he held until his death. Though he was a frequent contributor to magazines, newspapers, and the farm press, and the author of several books, his most voluminous literary work appears in the official monthly, annual, and special reports of the Department of Agriculture from 1862 to 1893. In politics he was a Republican and in his unofficial writings an avowed and ardent protectionist. He was at one time treasurer of the American Protective Association and prepared several brochures on protection for distribution by protectionist organizations. He was married in October 1846, to Frances G. Buxton of Nashua, N. H., by whom he had one child, Charles Richards Dodge. His death occurred in his eightieth year, at Nashua, where he was buried.

[Five scrapbooks of contributions to the agricultural press, in U. S. Dept. of Agric. Library; *Home Market Bull.*, Boston, Apr. 1899; *Country Gentleman*, Oct. 9, 1902; *Experiment Station Record*, Oct. 1902; *Nashua Daily Telegraph*, June 2, 1893, quoted in J. T. Dodge, *Geneal. of the Dodge Family of Essex County, Mass.*, vol. I (1894).]   C. R. B.

DODGE, MARY ABIGAIL (Mar. 31, 1833–Aug. 17, 1896), author, under the pseudonym Gail Hamilton, was born in Hamilton, Mass., the seventh and youngest child of James Brown Dodge and Hannah (Stanwood) Dodge. Her ancestors, of pure English stock, had lived in the same New England county for two hundred years. Very early in childhood she showed evidence of the tremendous vitality and activity that were later to be the recognized qualities of "Gail Hamilton." At two years she not only talked but gave recitations from memory; she is reported to have taken up advanced geography when five years old and to have written creditable essays at six. She received her formal education in Ipswich, Mass., graduating from the Ipswich

Female Seminary in 1850. At the age of twenty-one she became a teacher of English in a high school in Hartford. This position she held until September 1858 when she went to Washington, D. C., to become the governess of the children of Dr. Gamaliel Bailey, the editor of the anti-slavery organ, the *National Era*. Having already, while at Hartford, begun to write for newspapers, as "Gail Hamilton," she now became a regular contributor to the *National Era*. This early work was marked by the same vigorous and rationalistic approach to her subject and the same ready, effervescent wit which caused her later essays to run into edition after edition. Following her two years with the Baileys, she returned to Hamilton to take care of her invalid mother, and remained there until the latter's death in 1868. During these years, she edited, in 1865–67, together with J. T. Trowbridge and Lucy Larcom, *Our Young Folks,* an illustrated magazine for boys and girls which was later merged with *St. Nicholas,* and published somewhat more than a dozen volumes of essays, of which the most notable were *Country Living and Country Thinking* (1862), *A New Atmosphere* (1865), and *Woman's Wrongs: A Counter-Irritant* (1868). All these books had been brought out by Ticknor & Fields, with whom Miss Dodge's relations had been uniformly cordial, but, in 1868, becoming convinced that she had been defrauded in the matter of royalties, she severed connection with the firm, and, in 1870, brought out in *The Battle of the Books,* a veiled account of the whole transaction, written in her usual sprightly, caustic style, but devoid of malice. In January 1871 she moved to Washington which was henceforth to be the center of her activities, varied, however, by frequent trips to Hamilton, a journey across the Continent in 1873, and a trip to Europe in 1887–88. She edited, with S. S. Wood, *Wood's Household Magazine* (1872–73), and continued to produce numerous volumes. Of these the most important were: *Woman's Worth and Worthlessness* (1872), *Our Common School System* (1880), *A Washington Bible Class* (1891), *Biography of James G. Blaine* (1895), and *X Rays* (1896). Owing to her charm of manner, prestige as a writer, and position in Washington—she was a cousin of the wife of James G. Blaine—she is said to have exerted some influence over American politics, in which she was keenly interested throughout her adult life. Such indirect influence she felt to be woman's only proper function in politics, and during a stanch advocacy of other liberal causes she was thoroughly opposed to woman suffrage.

[There is little biographical information beyond that to be found in the carelessly edited *Gail Hamilton's Life in Letters* (2 vols., 1901), and in scatttered notes, of which see especially Wallace Rice in *Dial*, Sept. 16, 1901; *Independent*, Nov. 14, 1901; *Critic*, Aug. 22, 1896; M. B. Thrasher in *Arena*, Dec. 1896.]   G.G.

DODGE, MARY ELIZABETH MAPES (Jan. 26, 1831–Aug. 21, 1905), editor, author, was one of the three daughters of Prof. James Jay Mapes, free-lance scientist and inventor, and Sophia (Furman) Mapes, and a descendant of Gen. Jonas Mapes who served in the Revolution. The Mapes home in New York City, where Mary was born, was frequented by literary and scientific people, among them William Cullen Bryant and Horace Greeley. The Mapes children were educated at home by tutors, and under their father's guidance became familiar with the best in English literature. In 1851 Mary Mapes married William Dodge, New York lawyer, who died in 1858. Under the necessity of supporting her two sons she went to live in her father's home, now near Newark, N. J., and began writing. In a deserted farmhouse near by she fitted up a workshop, decorated with Florida moss and leaves, furnished with cast-off furniture, and warmed by a Franklin stove. Here she worked for regular hours and after work played with her boys and their friends. She was their companion, and tramped, collected specimens, swam, and skated with them. One of the sons died in 1881; the other became an inventor and manufacturer. Her writing was quickly accepted by magazines. Her first volume of children's stories was *Irvington Stories* (1864). *Hans Brinker; or the Silver Skates* (1865), begun as a serial, grew into a book. The idea came from reading Motley's *Rise of the Dutch Republic*, and for years she collected material on Dutch life, though she had never seen Holland. Dutch friends in New York acted as critics. The book had immediate success and has remained her best work and a leading juvenile classic. It was translated into many foreign languages and received a prize from the French Academy. When she afterward visited Holland, *Hans Brinker* was recommended to her son by a Dutch bookseller as the best juvenile story of Dutch life. Her other books are: *A Few Friends and How They Amused Themselves* (1869); *Rhymes and Jingles* (1874); *Theophilus and Others* (1876); *Along the Way* (1879), verse; *Donald and Dorothy* (1883); *When Life is Young* (1894), verse; and *The Land of Pluck* (1894). She wrote frequently for the *Atlantic Monthly*, the *Century*, and *Harper's Magazine*. In 1870 she became associate editor of *Hearth and Home*. The directors of the Century Company, noticing her work here in 1873 secured her as editor for their new juvenile monthly, which she named *St. Nicholas Magazine*. She continued in this position until her death and her sane policy and personal supervision made *St. Nicholas* a leader in its class. She excluded preachiness, sentimentalism, the morbid, and the inartistic. Her acquaintance with authors helped in securing contributions. Her volumes for little children, *Baby Days* (1876) and *Baby World* (1884), were compiled from her contributions to *St. Nicholas*. During this period her home was an apartment near Central Park, New York. In 1888 she purchased "Yarrow Cottage," at Onteora Park in the Catskills. She later added to the cottage, where she always spent as long a summer as possible. There she went in her last illness, hoping for healing among her loved mountains, and there, at the height of summer, she died. The children of the community, all her friends, formed the procession at her funeral. Mrs. Dodge's personality was adapted to both success and friendship. She was brilliant, original, and possessed of discriminating judgment and executive ability. Her sympathy and love of fun never failed. She was a woman of fine appearance, with a full oval face, soft wavy hair, a small nose, and a pouting, childlike mouth. Years drew character lines in her face but made her only more handsome. Her successor as editor of *St. Nicholas* places her, probably with justice, as "the recognized leader in juvenile literature for almost a third of a century." Her stories, wholesome but not "goody-goody," have suggestive atmosphere and truthful characterization. Her verse has humor, quaint turns of thought, and a quality which does not grow old.

["In Memory of Mary Mapes Dodge," by her successor, William Fayal Clarke, in *St. Nicholas*, Oct. 1905; "Mary Mapes Dodge: an Intimate Tribute," by her friend, Sarah S. McEnery, in *The Critic*, Oct. 1905; *Who's Who in America*, 1903–05; Frances E. Willard and Mary A. Livermore, *Am. Women* (1897), vol. I; Lucia Gilbert Runkle, *Our Famous Women* (1884); obituaries in *N. Y. Tribune*, and *N. Y. Times*, Aug. 22, 1905.]   S.G.B.

DODGE, THEODORE AYRAULT (May 28, 1842–Oct. 25, 1909), military historian, son of Nathaniel S. and Emily (Pomeroy) Dodge, was born at Pittsfield, Mass. He was educated abroad, in Berlin, at the University of Heidelberg, and at University College, London. He returned to the United States in July 1861 and at once enlisted in the New York militia. He entered the volunteer army as a first lieutenant, 101st New York Infantry, Feb. 13, 1862, served in the defenses of Washington until May, and then took part in the Peninsular campaign, commanding his company throughout. He was slightly wounded at Chantilly, in the northern Virginia campaign that summer, and immediately after was taken sick with typhoid fever, which kept him from duty until November. He then joined the 119th New York Infantry, to which he had been transferred, and served as its adjutant at Fredericksburg and Chancellorsville. He was wounded on the first day at Gettysburg, and fell into the hands of the Confederates, but was left behind during their retreat after the battle and did not remain a prisoner. His wound required the amputation of his right leg below the knee. Disabled for field service, he was appointed a captain in the Veteran Reserve Corps, Nov. 12, 1863, and assigned to duty in Washington, where he was in charge of the enrolment branch, and later of the deserters' branch, of the Provost Marshal-General's office. He was promoted to major, Aug. 17, 1864, and mustered out of the volunteer service, Dec. 1, 1866. Meanwhile he had taken a bachelor's degree in law at Columbian (now George Washington) University. Appointed captain of infantry in the regular army, July 28, 1866, and later brevetted lieutenant-colonel, he served as superintendent of the War Department buildings until infirmity resulting from his wound caused his retirement from active service, Apr. 28, 1870. He was promoted to major on the retired list in 1904. Upon retirement from military service he made his home at Cambridge, Mass., and entered upon a business career with the purpose of "gathering a fortune which should leave him free for the more congenial pursuit of letters" (Livermore, *post*, p. 211), becoming treasurer and manager of the McKay Sewing Machine Company in 1870. Later, having purchased several patents and become interested in the manufacture of cotton woven hose, he resigned from the McKay Company and in 1880, took the presidency of the Boston Woven Hose Company which became one of the largest manufacturers of rubber, and especially of single-tube tires, in the United States. His business did not absorb all his time, however, some of which he was able to devote to military history. His first studies were concerned with the Civil War, but his books—*The Campaign of Chancellorsville* (1881), and *A Bird's-eye View of Our Civil War* (1883)—were not published until after he had extended his researches to a wider field. In 1877 he went abroad for two years to study European campaigns, and this visit was followed by repeated trips, in the course of which he crossed the ocean over eighty times, until finally, after his retirement from business in 1900, he took up his home in Paris, in order to make use of its library fa-

cilities in studying the career of Napoleon. He planned a history of the art of war, as exemplified in the careers of "great captains." The first work, *Alexander*, appeared in 1890, and was followed by *Hannibal* (1891), *Cæsar* (1892), *Gustavus Adolphus* (1895), and *Napoleon* (4 vols., 1904–07). These are careful studies, based not only on examination of written records but also on personal inspection of the actual battle sites in Europe, Asia, and northern Africa, where he made his own topographical sketches. In the United States there was little appreciation of the practical value of the study of early military history, and at the time of their publication his works attracted the interest of classical scholars rather than of soldiers. The World War has brought about some change in this respect. A series of lectures delivered by Dodge before the Lowell Institute was also published (1889) under the title of *Great Captains*, the name he adopted to designate the series of works already referred to. His literary activity was not confined to military subjects. He wrote numerous essays, reviews, and even verses, and published two books inspired by his interest in horsemanship, *Patroclus and Penelope* (1885), and *Riders of Many Lands* (1894). He was a member of the Massachusetts Historical Society, and a visiting lecturer at Harvard University. He was twice married, first, on Oct. 19, 1865, to Jane Marshall Neil of Columbus, and second, on Oct. 8, 1892, to Clara Isabel Bowden of Boston, who survived him. He died at the Château de Rozières, near Nanteuil-le-Haudouin, in the department of the Oise, and was buried in Arlington National Cemetery.

[This account is based largely on unpublished records in the War Department; F. B. Heitman, *Hist. Reg. and Dict. of the U. S. Army* (1903), I, 377; *Who's Who in America*, 1908–09; memoir by T. L. Livermore in *Proc. Mass. Hist. Soc.*, 1909–10; A. H. Pomeroy, *Hist. and Geneal. of the Pomeroy Family* (1912), pp. 469–71. Dodge's report on the work of his office in 1864–66 is in *Official Records* (*Army*), 3 ser., V, 750–58.]

T.M.S.

DODGE, WILLIAM EARL (Sept. 4, 1805–Feb. 9, 1883), merchant, was born at Hartford, Conn. His father was David Low Dodge [*q.v.*], a school-teacher who became a business man; his mother, Sarah Cleveland. During his boyhood the family, because of changes in the father's business connections, lived for several years in New York City, and New Jersey. William's schooling was obtained in Norwich, Conn., New York City, and Mendham, N. J. He seems to have inherited from his father a certain literary bent, which, however, was never freely followed. When only thirteen years old he began work in a wholesale dry-goods store in New York City. A year later he was employed as a clerk in the country store connected with his father's factory in Connecticut. After the elder Dodge had entered the New York dry-goods trade, in 1825, the son assisted him in the Beekman St. store; but after reaching his majority he went into the wholesale business on his own account. His marriage on June 24, 1828, to Melissa Phelps connected him with a New York family distinguished for its wealth and enterprise in business. His father-in-law had been successful in the metals trade and in 1833 young Dodge retired from dry-goods merchandizing and joined the firm of Phelps, Dodge & Company, which for two generations held a foremost place as dealers in copper and other metals. The firm had an important part in the development of Lake Superior copper and of Pennsylvania iron. Dodge personally made heavy investments outside the metals trade. He bought pine lands extensively in Pennsylvania, Michigan, Wisconsin, and the South. He was also a large stockholder in railroad enterprises—the Erie, Lackawanna, Jersey Central, and Texas Central. He was early interested in religious and philanthropic effort, was one of the organizers and always a stanch supporter of the Young Men's Christian Association in America, and later had a prominent part in the work of the Evangelical Alliance. His public identification with temperance reforms may be dated from the Washingtonian movement of 1840, although as a boy and young man he had been impressed by the evils of alcoholism, and his father had brought about prohibition of the liquor traffic in his Connecticut factory settlement. William supported the work of John B. Gough and Father Mathew as temperance advocates. In 1854 he was one of the leaders in the political campaign that carried New York State for prohibition by a small plurality. From 1865 to his death in 1883, he was president of the National Temperance Society and was characterized by Dr. Theodore L. Cuyler as "the most catholic representative of the temperance reform in all its phases and activities" (*Our Leader and His Life*, 1883, by T. L. Cuyler). He proposed a national commission of inquiry on the liquor traffic. In politics, he escaped many of the bitter antagonisms to which men of prominence were frequently subjected in his day. He was known as an anti-slavery man and yet seems to have retained the respect and good·will of those Southern communities in which he had extensive business interests. He was a member of the unsuccessful Peace Conference held at Washington in February 1861. After the Civil War had

begun he helped to arm and equip Union soldiers in West Virginia and East Tennessee. In 1865 he delivered an address at Baltimore on *The Influence of the War on our National Prosperity*. He was distinctly in advance of his time in pointing out the positive evils and the ultimate futility of war. As a Republican member of Congress from New York City in 1866, he urged moderation in reconstruction measures and maintained an attitude toward the South similar to that which was held ten years later by President Hayes. Dodge was a man of fine physical presence and had a winning manner. He left a son, of the same name, who continued an active interest in the public causes to which his father had been devoted.

[*Memorials of Wm. E. Dodge* (1887), compiled and edited by D. Stuart Dodge; Carlos Martyn, *Wm. E. Dodge: The Christian Merchant* (1890); J. T. Dodge, *Geneal. of the Dodge Family of Essex County, Mass.* (1894).]

W. B. S.

DODS, JOHN BOVEE (1795–Mar. 21, 1872), spiritualist, was born in New York City. He was of a Swiss Huguenot family called Beaufils, but adopted the name Dods from a Dutchman who married his aunt. He preached many years in Levant, Penobscot County, Me., early dabbling in new and strange theories, particularly concerned with psychic phenomena, and continually expounding these theories from the pulpit. In 1836 he moved to Provincetown, Mass., and began to preach universalism. He published a volume entitled *Thirty Short Sermons on Various Important Subjects, Doctrinal and Practical*, in which he defended his universalistic ideas, such as his disbelief in hell, his denial of Christ's divine origin, and his emphasis on the universal Fatherhood of God. He founded a school, called "The Academy," published an English grammar, and devoted much of his time to scholarly pursuits.

His universalism was soon eclipsed by his theories on psychic phenomena. On this subject he published the following works: *Six Lectures on the Philosophy of Mesmerism* (1843); *The Philosophy of Electrical Psychology* (1850); *Immortality Triumphant* (1852); and *Spirit Manifestations Examined and Explained* (1854). Like Dr. Edward Coit Rogers, he at first tried to explain these phenomena neurologically, but whereas Rogers emphasized the action of the cerebrum under the action of a certain "odic force," Dods emphasized the "automatic action of the cerebellum" under some sort of electrical influence. He had vague ideas about the rôle of nerve centers in hypnotism, and several other general theories. The precise mechanisms, however, he failed to understand. Nevertheless he supplemented his philosophical theories and his preaching by continual experiments, demonstrations, and practical lectures.

Hardly had he gotten his cerebellum theory well launched than he abandoned it and joined the spiritualist movement and church. His daughter, Jennie, was a good medium, and with her help Dods soon spread spiritualist practises and teachings. His own interest apparently was chiefly in the medical problems connected with mental disorders. He was commonly called Dr. Dods, though he was merely an amateur physician, practising on his congregations and on his family. He was one of the first to use electricity for therapeutic purposes; he continually carried on experiments in drugs, hypnotism, massage, etc., and gained a sufficient reputation and income from his various devices to enable his widow to build up a practise with them. He was married three times. By his first wife (Mercy Hodgdon), he had three daughters and one son; by his second, one child, and none by the third. He died in Brooklyn, N. Y., Mar. 21, 1872.

[Simeon G. Smith, *Leaves from an Old Church Record Book* (1922); Frank Podmore, *Modern Spiritualism*, vol. I (1902); Emma Hardinge Britten, *Modern Am. Spiritualism* (1870), *Nineteenth Century Minds* (1884).]

H. W. S.
R. R.

DOE, CHARLES (Apr. 11, 1830–Mar. 9, 1896), jurist, was born in Derry, N. H., the youngest child of Joseph Doe, Jr., and Mary Bodwell (Ricker) Doe. He was descended from Nicholas Doe, who, according to family tradition, came from London, England, and who was living at Oyster River, N. H., in 1666. Charles's father, a large landowner and farmer of Somersworth (later Rollinsford), and a member of the legislature, being well off, the boy enjoyed a good education at the academies of South Berwick, Exeter, and Andover, after which he went to Harvard College for a term, and thence to Dartmouth College where he graduated in 1849. He then entered the law office of Daniel M. Christie of Dover, N. H., and subsequently passed some time at the Harvard Law School, but, being offered the post of solicitor for Strafford County, did not complete his course. He accepted the office, was called to the bar in January 1854, and commenced practise at Dover. As county solicitor he had much criminal work, and his family connections assisted him to acquire a good share of the civil business of the neighborhood. He had at an early age taken an active interest in politics on the Democratic side, being assistant clerk of the state Senate in 1853 and 1854 and appearing frequently on the public platform. In 1856 he was, upon an address of the Republican legislature, removed from his office of county solicitor, but three years later he joined the Republican party, being urged thereto by the Democratic attitude toward the growing disaffection in the Southern states and his realization that in this matter there could be no compromise. To the general surprise he was appointed an associate justice of the supreme judicial court of New Hampshire, Sept. 23, 1859. For a considerable time thereafter his position was a difficult one, since politically he was extremely unpopular with a strong element, and in legal circles, owing to his unconventional type of mind and strong reform tendencies, he was unacceptable to the elder generation of judges and practitioners alike. Indifferent however to this under-current of dislike and the more open opposition of personages prominent in public and professional circles, he resolutely adhered to the principles of conduct which he had formulated for himself and declining to modify his views on legal reform, in course of time, earned the respect, if not the assent, of the bar, and impressed the public with his absolute sincerity of purpose. His efficiency and competence were demonstrated from the outset of his judicial career. He never, however, overcame the animosity of his political opponents, and when in 1874 the Democrats obtained control of the legislature, they proceeded to reorganize the state courts, doing away with the supreme judicial court, and substituting a superior court of judicature to which he was not appointed. He did not resume practise, but returned to his home at Rollinsford, and there lived in retirement, declining a proffered nomination for Congress. In 1876, however, the Republican party regained power, created the supreme court of New Hampshire and he was offered and accepted the position of chief justice. Having conceived a distaste for trial work, he made an arrangement with his colleagues in 1878 by which he was relieved of most of the Trial Term business and concentrated his attention on the Law Term. His peculiar genius was afforded full opportunity on the Appeal side of the court, and "for nearly twenty years . . . by the general *concensus* of his contemporaries he was the foremost man of the profession in the state; foremost not merely in name or in official position, but in fact" (Smith, *post*, p. 149). His health now commenced to cause him anxiety, and he experienced recurrent attacks of insomnia. In 1887 he took a vacation in Europe, spending some time in Great Britain and France. On his return he resumed his judicial duties, but never regained his former vigor. His intellect, nevertheless, was unimpaired and he continued to take a dominant part in the administration of justice up to the day of his death, which occurred suddenly at Rollinsford. On Apr. 11, 1865, he married Edith, daughter of George Wallis Haven of Portsmouth, N. H.

The remarkable series of opinions rendered by Doe when chief justice indicate his outstanding legal attainments, and have left an ineffaceable impression upon the law of New Hampshire. Originality marked all his work, and he declined to be bound by precedent, saying, "as there was a time when no precedents existed, everything that can be done with them can be done without them." At the same time, somewhat paradoxically, he delighted in research, frequently investigating legal principles to their foundation, and embodying the result of his labors in opinions which were treatises on the law involved. In *Hale* vs. *Everett* (53 *N.H.*, 8, 133–277), his opinion extended to 144 pages of the report, and it is said that he devoted a whole summer to study of history and theology prior to writing it. His influence was most powerfully exercised, however, in the field of procedure, where he effected a revolution by a radical departure from well-established principles. He held that common law rights existed independently of any particular writ, that a mistake in procedure was formal merely, and not substantive, and therefore that the court had power to effect any necessary amendments independently of the legislature. On this principle, historically untrue, he brought about procedural reforms which were effective, though radical, by means of court decisions and without recourse to legislation. Apart from law his acquaintance with literature was slight, since he never read unless he had some special object in so doing, and it is said that he read only one novel in his life.

In appearance and manner he was plain and unassuming, having a strong aversion to ceremony. He is pictured in middle age as "of medium height, slightly bent, his beard shaggy and grizzled. He might have been a country storekeeper, a farmer, or a lumberman. He wore a sort of brown frock coat, coarse trousers and heavy boots or brogans, which showed no trace of blacking. An old battered straw hat completed the ordinary summer costume of the chief justice of New Hampshire. In winter he frequently wore a dark-blue cloth cap with laps to pull down over the ears; and he wore in court a coarse rug which onlookers insist was a horse-blanket" (Henning, *post*). He was a thorough believer in fresh air and on the coldest days in winter would have all the windows of his court-

room wide open, despite all protest from bar, jury, and public.

[The family antecedents are detailed in *The Descendants of Nicholas Doe* (1918), by Elmer E. Doe. The article "Chas. Doe" by C. D. Henning in *Great Am. Lawyers*, VIII (1909), 241, and "Memoir of Chas. Doe," by Jeremiah Smith in *Proc. Southern N. H. Bar Asso.*, 1897, p. 125, are excellent appreciations of his character and legal achievements. See also *Harvard Law Rev.*, IX, 534; *Am. Law Review*, XXX, 286; *Albany Law Jour.*, LIII, 161, and "Memories of Judge Doe" by Robt. G. Pike in *Proc. of the Bar Asso. of the State of N. H.* (1916).]   H. W. H. K.

DOLAN, THOMAS (Oct. 27, 1834–June 12, 1914), capitalist, was born in Montgomery County, Pa., of obscure ancestry. His formal schooling was limited to a few years in the public schools, his career in business beginning when he became salesman in a store at the age of fifteen. Seven years later his connection with the wholesale knit-goods business began. During the industrial depression of the early Civil War period he successfully reorganized a factory under the firm name of the Keystone Knitting Mills, and maneuvered himself into a position of virtual monopoly in his particular branch of the industry. His business acumen found expression in adaptations not only to war-time conditions but to changes of fashion during the following decades. To meet successive shifts in the demand for fabrics, he reorganized his business for the manufacture, in turn, of knit goods, worsted shawls, and worsted coating goods. His initiative found expression more significantly in important innovations in technology, chiefly the use of electric power in factories. As early as 1882 he became a director of the United Gas Improvement Company of Philadelphia, and he expanded his activities in the fields of public utilities until his interests extended over a large part of the country. In this way he became a national figure in the earlier development of gas and electric lighting and power facilities.

He was made president of the United Gas Improvement Company in 1892, and five years later his company secured a thirty-year lease of the city's gas lighting system, the city retaining the option of resuming operation at the end of ten years. In 1905 the question was reopened. Should the city exercise its option, or continue the existing lease, or negotiate with the company for a new lease? The third course was chosen. The company's operation of the system had been profitable alike to the company and to the city. But on Apr. 20 the Select Council adopted resolutions instructing its finance committee to propose a new lease by which the city would surrender annual payments under the existing lease in return for a cash consideration. The alleged motive was the avoiding of increased taxes and borrowings for needed public improvements. The result was a political storm that attracted nation-wide attention, with Dolan, president of the company, the storm center. It was widely believed that the political organization in control of the city was proposing to mortgage or "rob" the city's future for the sake of ready money for corrupt uses. City officials nevertheless disregarded the storm signals and proceeded to open negotiations for a new lease. As finally adopted in Council, the proposed new lease was to expire in 1980 instead of 1927, and the payments to the city were to amount to $25,000,000 (Philadelphia *Public Ledger,* Apr. 21, 27, May 19, 1905). These actions were accompanied by city-wide organized remonstrances and by threats of violence which went so far as the wearing of buttons bearing a picture of a gallows and the inscription, "No gas steal. The last resort. We mean it" (*Ibid.,* May 3, 1905). Mayor John Weaver was at length induced to veto the Council's bill, and while steps were being taken to pass the bill over the veto, Dolan wrote a letter stating that in view of evidences of opposition his company no longer desired and would not accept the proposed new lease (*Ibid.,* May 28, 1905).

His other business connections were so extensive as to make him a pioneer in the development of modern interlocking directorates. He was one of the organizers and the first president of the Manufacturers' Club of Philadelphia. He was actively connected with many industrial and commercial associations, serving, for instance, as president of the National Association of Manufacturers. Politically, he was prominent in raising funds for a number of presidential campaigns and in bringing personal and group influence to bear on public policies. In 1888 he was organizer and chairman of an advisory committee of the Republican National Committee. He was particularly prominent as an advocate of protective tariffs.

Dolan was often hard and ruthless, and amazing in his display of energy, but he was hardly more than typical of his generation. He was profoundly influenced by the rapid industrial expansion of the North after the Civil War, and by the public and private demoralization of that era. Characteristically, his relations with other business men and with public officials can hardly be described as urbane or even subtle.

[The chief printed sources are the files of the Philadelphia newspapers, particularly the *Public Ledger* and the *North American,* containing extremely detailed accounts especially of the most conspicuous episode in his life (the "gas fight" of April and May 1905). The *Fourth Annual Message* of Mayor Weaver (Phila., 1907) contains numerous letters and annual reports of city officials. Rudolph Blankenburg [*q.v.*], a "reform" mayor of the city, wrote a series of critical articles for the *Arena,* vols. XXXIII and XXXIV (1905, 1906), entitled "Forty Years in the Wilderness," containing illustrations and extracts from documentary sources. The best accounts in local histories are in E. P. Oberholtzer, *Philadelphia* (1912) and J. T. Scharf and T. Westcott, *Hist. of Phila.* (1884) ; The *N. Y. Times* and the Philadelphia papers contained extensive sketches at the time of his death.]

W. B.

DOLD, JACOB (June 25, 1825–Oct. 25, 1909), meat-packer, was born in Tuttlingen, Würtemberg, Germany, where his family had been for generations in the meat business. At ten years of age he was helping his father, John Jacob Dold, in slaughtering and in sausage making; afterward he became apprenticed to the largest butcher in his native town. At sixteen he was given the duties of stock buying. At nineteen he came to the United States and settled in Buffalo, where for two or three years he worked as a butcher for Joshua Barnes, receiving $15 a month and his board. In 1848 he entered business for himself with his savings, at first making sausages in small quantities and peddling them from house to house with a basket on his arm. His trade soon increased to such an extent that he was obliged to buy a horse. In 1852 he sent for his father, mother, brothers, and sisters—six in number—and shortly after they came he built his first slaughter-house, which had a capacity of ten hogs a day. By energy, enterprise, and economy he acquired an extensive trade. His sausages became well known. In 1860 he started a small beef and pork packing plant at the Elk Street Market, putting up a building combining a meat market, dwelling rooms, and an abattoir. With the Civil War, the food resources of the North were taxed to support the needs of the army. Dold received government contracts which gave his business its first real impetus and from that time on his progress was phenomenal. In 1873 he bought ten acres of ground near the Buffalo stock-yards and erected an abattoir which was the nucleus of the present plant. He erected a plant at Kansas City, Mo., in 1880 and five years later, one at Wichita, Kan. In 1888 he incorporated his business into a stock company of which he continued to be the active head for the rest of his life. By 1909 his three plants were killing a million head of live stock annually.

In 1850, or thereabout, Dold was married to Elizabeth Schiesz, and after her death, which occurred in Buffalo some thirty years later, he was married again, to Bertha Bettock who survived him. He was an unostentatious, kindly man, addicted to anonymous charity. On the day of his funeral his family learned for the first time that he had supplied the funds to build the German Lutheran church which he attended. He was succeeded in his business by his son, Jacob C. Dold, as able a man as his father. The latter was instrumental in the establishment of the Institute of American Meat Packers, and was a counsellor of the United States Chamber of Commerce, and of the International Chamber of Commerce. Under his administration the company's activities spread all over the United States and it established selling agencies in many foreign countries. In its subsequent history the traditions and policies of its founder were adhered to, although on the death of Jacob C. Dold in 1924 the financial control of the company passed from the Dold family.

[R. A. Clemen, *The Am. Livestock and Meat Industry* (1923) ; obituaries in the *Nat. Provisioner*, Oct. 30, 1909, and *Buffalo Express*, Oct. 26, 1909 ; obituary of Jacob C. Dold in *Nat. Provisioner*, Sept. 13, 1924 ; letter from E. C. Andrew, president of the Jacob Dold Packing Co., Buffalo ; information as to certain facts from a son, Chas. H. Dold, Esq.]   R. A. C.

DOLE, CHARLES FLETCHER (May 17, 1845–Nov. 27, 1927), Congregational clergyman, was seventh in descent from William Dole of Thornbury, Gloucester County, England, whose son Richard settled in Newburyport, Mass., in 1639. He was born at Brewer, Me., the son of the Rev. Nathan and Caroline (Fletcher) Dole. Nathan Haskell Dole, well known as a translator and author, was his brother. After his father's death at Chelsea, Mass., in 1855, his mother, who died in 1914 at the age of ninety-five, returned with her children to the home of her mother, Sally Ware Fletcher, in Norridgewock, Me. There the boy was reared in an atmosphere of sturdy independence, simplicity, and piety. To the theological dogma of the time and place he was, even as a child, impervious but not recalcitrant. Neither at Harvard College, where he graduated second in the class of 1868, nor at Andover Theological Seminary, where he graduated in 1872, did he gain much from his teachers, though Francis James Child returned his themes "with the most suggestive and useful blue pencilings that I ever had. . . . I owe him thanks to this day for the severe and straightforward style of composition that he set for us," and J. Henry Thayer at Andover impressed him by his unswerving intellectual honesty. Dole was acting professor of Greek at the University of Vermont from January 1873 till the end of the academic year. On Mar. 4, 1873, he married Frances, daughter of the Rev. James and Esther (Swett) Drummond, whom he had known since boyhood. He was pastor of the Plymouth Church, Portland, Me., 1874–76, and of the First Congregational (Unitarian) Society, Jamaica Plain, Mass., for the next forty years, becoming pastor emeritus in 1916. In the summer of 1887 he engaged in missionary work in the Northwest, at Duluth, Superior, and Winona. He visited Europe in 1892, 1896, and 1913, made four trips to Honolulu, where his son, James Drummond Dole, was a pineapple magnate, and traveled somewhat extensively in the South and West. For twenty-three years (1893–1916) he was a trustee of Tuskegee Institute, and he was a constant and devoted supporter, likewise, of Hampton Institute. His political views owed much to E. L. Godkin. A lingering Puritanism made him in time a total abstainer. He was an honest pacifist, and during the Spanish-American War and the European War of 1914–18 he remained honest. For some years he was president of the Association to Abolish War. Fanaticism, however, was utterly alien to his character. He was rich in friends.

In all he published at least thirty books and pamphlets, of which the more significant are: *The Citizen and the Neighbor* (1884) ; *Jesus and the Men About Him* (1888) ; *The Golden Rule in Business* (1895, 1896) ; *The Coming People* (1897) ; *The American Citizen* (1891) ; *The Religion of a Gentleman* (1900) ; *The Smoke and the Flame: A Study in the Development of Religion* (1902) ; *From Agnosticism to Theism* (1903) ; *The Spirit of Democracy* (1906) ; *The Hope of Immortality* (1906, 1908—a Harvard Ingersoll Lecture) ; *What We Know About Jesus* (1908) ; *The Ethics of Progress* (1909) ; *The Coming Religion* (1910) ; *The Burden of Poverty* (1912) ; *The New American Citizen* (1918) ; *A Religion for the New Day* (1920) ; *The Victorious Goodness: An Epic of Spiritual Evolution* (1927) ; and *My Eighty Years* (1927)— the last a summary of his life and opinions. He also wrote for the *Atlantic Monthly* and other magazines.

Neither a popular preacher and leader nor a thinker of striking originality, Dole made little impression on his time. For half a century his quiet voice pleaded for a dogmaless religion of devotion, unselfishness, disinterestedness. A scattered group of intellectuals in America and England, never large but growing with the years, cherished him as one of their most intelligent and persuasive spokesmen.

[*Who's Who in America*, 1926–27 ; *Harvard Coll. Class of 1868 Fortieth Anniversary, 1868–1908* (1909) ; *Harvard Quinquennial Cat. 1636–1915* (1915) ; *Gen. Cat. of the Theol. Sem. Andover, Mass., 1808–1908* (1909) ; *N. Y. Times*, Nov. 28, 1927 ; editorial in *The Southern Workman* (Hampton, Va.), Mar. 1928 ; obituary in *Unitarian Year Book*, 1928–29.]   G. H. G.

DOLE, SANFORD BALLARD (Apr. 23, 1844–June 9, 1926), judge, president of the Republic of Hawaii, first governor of the Territory of Hawaii, was the son of Daniel and Emily (Ballard) Dole. His father, one of the group of New England missionaries who planted and tended Christianity in the Hawaiian Islands, was the first principal of Punahou School (founded by the missionaries). Sanford Dole was born in Honolulu and there and on the outlying island of Kauai he spent his childhood and youth, acquiring a fine physical development, a love of nature and skill in outdoor sports, and a thorough and sympathetic acquaintance with the native Hawaiian people. The main part of his formal education was received in missionary schools in Hawaii, but he spent two years (1866–68) in the United States, attending Williams College and studying law. He was admitted to the bar in Massachusetts and then returned to Honolulu to take up the practise of law. For the next twenty years he devoted his working time to his profession, but not without taking the interest in public affairs which he conceived to be the duty of a citizen. During these years he established himself in the community and won to a remarkable degree the confidence of those with whom he came in contact.

Although thoroughly American in his ideas of government, Dole was not unfriendly to the Hawaiian monarchy, but rather favored it, as being best suited to the native race, and wished it to continue as long as possible. He and many other thoughtful persons observed with deep regret, however, what he called the "retrogressive tendencies" of the monarchy in its later years and "sought through legislative work, the newspapers and by personal appeal and individual influence . . . to avert the catastrophe that seemed inevitable if such tendencies were not restrained" (Dole to Willis, Dec. 23, 1893). In 1880 he had an active share in the movement which compelled the dismissal of an irresponsible adventurer who had been appointed head of the ministry. In 1884 and 1886 he was elected to the legislature by the reform party. He was one of the leaders of the revolution of 1887, which ended the notorious Gibson régime and forced King Kalakaua to grant a new constitution, reducing him to a status somewhat like that of the British sovereign. It was essentially the failure of Kalakaua and his successor, Liliuokalani, to accept in good faith the results of this revolution of 1887 which led to the more thoroughgoing revolution of 1893.

On Dec. 28, 1887, Dole was appointed associate justice of the supreme court, the appoint-

ment being exacted of the king by the reform ministry. He continued in that office until Jan. 17, 1893, when he resigned to become head of the revolutionary Provisional Government. He was not one of the original organizers of the revolution of 1893, and consented to join the movement only after he became satisfied that further continuance of the monarchy was out of the question and that the best interests of all, including the native Hawaiians, demanded its overthrow. He was the more willing to cast in his lot with the revolutionists since their ultimate goal was the annexation of Hawaii to the United States. The immediate object of the revolution— the overthrow of the monarchy—was easily accomplished; but the annexation project was postponed by the opposition of President Cleveland. Dole and his associates believed that Cleveland's Hawaiian policy was originated by Secretary of State Gresham, and that it was based upon a fundamental misapprehension of the facts of the revolution and the character and purpose of the Provisional Government, a misapprehension not removed by the partial and one-sided investigation (so it looked to them) made by Commissioner J. H. Blount [q.v.]. When President Cleveland, speaking through Minister Willis in December 1893, asked the Provisional Government to step down and permit the restoration of Liliuokalani, Dole, as minister of foreign affairs, wrote a reply which is considered one of his ablest and most important state papers, denying the right of the president of the United States to interfere in the internal affairs of Hawaii, setting forth the true causes of the overthrow of the monarchy, and firmly refusing to yield to President Cleveland's demand. At the same time he expressed the conviction that sooner or later the political union of the two countries would be accomplished.

It being evident that annexation could not be expected while Cleveland was president of the United States, a constitutional convention was held and a permanent government, the Republic of Hawaii, was brought into existence on July 4, 1894. By article 23 of the constitution Dole was declared to be the president of the republic, to hold office until the end of 1900. His administration as president was beset with difficulties including a royalist attempt at a counter-revolution in January 1895, dissensions within the ranks of the annexationists, a very serious diplomatic controversy with Japan growing out of the efforts of the Hawaiian government to restrict Japanese immigration. Relations with the government of the United States, while friendly in a formal way during the latter part of

Cleveland's administration, required tact and discretion on the part of the Hawaiian executive; after the inauguration of President McKinley relations were very cordial and a new annexation treaty was negotiated. In January 1898 Dole visited Washington in the interest of the treaty. When the United States became involved in war with Spain, while the annexation treaty still lacked ratification by the United States government, President Dole's view was that Hawaii should shape its policy exactly in accordance with the desires of the American government. After the consummation of annexation in the summer of 1898, he was a member of the commission appointed to recommend to Congress legislation for the future government of the islands, meanwhile continuing as executive head of the existing government; and was then (1900) made first governor of the Territory of Hawaii. He resigned from that office in 1903 to become judge of the United States district court for Hawaii, remaining on the bench until 1915, when he retired to private life.

He was married in 1873 to Anna Cate of Castine, Me., who died in 1918. Dole's interests were many and varied. To the end of his life he kept up his membership in a number of public service societies and semi-public organizations. He contributed a few historical articles to the publications of the Hawaiian Historical Society and to periodicals. Characterized by "quiet modesty . . . calm judgment . . . ready cooperation," he was of a mild and conciliatory disposition where principles were not at stake; but in public matters, having once made up his mind as to the proper course, he followed it with inflexible purpose.

[Public and private papers and official correspondence filed in the Archives of Hawaii and in possession of the Historical Commission of Hawaii; *Who's Who in America,* 1926–27; obituary articles in Honolulu newspapers, among them *Honolulu Star-Bulletin* and *Honolulu Advertiser,* June 10, 1926; Dole's judicial decisions are printed in the reports of the courts over which he presided; part of his state papers are printed in U. S. Congressional documents and Hawaiian government documents. *The Hawaiian Crisis: Correspondence Between President Dole and U. S. Minister Willis, Dec. 1893* was published in Honolulu in 1893.]
R. S. K.

DOLLIVER, JONATHAN PRENTISS (Feb. 6, 1858–Oct. 15, 1910), statesman, was born near Kingwood, Va. (now W. Va.). His father, James J. Dolliver, a camp-meeting convert, was then riding the Preston County circuit with untiring zeal, preaching Methodist salvation and the sin of slaveholding. He and his wife, Elizabeth J. Brown, found shelter for their family at the house of Grandfather Brown, an anti-secession Democrat. Life thereabouts was simple, with food in plenty and money scarce. It was a sturdy, ardent environment. When the time came for Jonathan's advanced schooling, his ambitious parents moved to Morgantown, which had lately become the seat of West Virginia's university. Jonathan helped earn his education in the hard panic years; and the academic episode which made the greatest impression upon him was a suit against the University which unloosed upon the campus a flood of stirring oratory.

At seventeen he found himself a graduate with an urge to explore the world. Toward Illinois he started afoot; then took the stage, and then (he related), "I came to Connellsville in Pennsylvania and saw a railroad train for the first time. I attended Barnum's show in the afternoon, in the evening, full of strange thrills, I started on my journey to the west . . . I said to myself 'This, then, is life, real life'" (J. B. Morrow, *post*). But with his temperament, "life" as a winter-time school-teacher at Sandwich, Ill., and as a summer-time law student in a Morgantown office, seemed dull. He managed to attend the Republican convention of 1876 which, as he recalled, sent him home "full of new joy and fresh noise." At twenty he determined to launch his legal career in Iowa. The career did not immediately eventuate, but Dolliver enjoyed the impecunious interlude, for his warm, friendly nature basked in the personal contacts of the Fort Dodge community, which so delighted in his speeches as to stir him to perfect his epigrammatic style. The easy familiarity of this period took him little further than the office of corporation counsel at $200 yearly (1880–87); but the year 1884 brought a political opportunity. His oratorical prowess had attracted Iowa's Republican vote-getters; and they had him strike the key-note for them at the state convention. Albert Beveridge [*q.v.*], selling books in Des Moines, heard in wonder "this amazing address" (*Palimpsest,* V, 40). To Dolliver's astonishment and delight, he was invited to stump with Blaine, "whom I idolized," he said, "as I have idolized no other man" (Morrow, *post*). Iowa's tenth district began considering him for Congress, tentatively in 1886 and decisively (on the 110th ballot) in 1888.

As a congressman, he subscribed to regular Republican doctrine, especially in regard to protection and soldiers' pensions. He won five reelections, besides obtaining membership on the ways and means committee in 1895. This also was the year of his fortunate marriage with Louise Pearsons. He supported Iowa's favorite son, William Boyd Allison [*q.v.*], for president in 1888 and 1896; but his own candidacy for vice-president, taken seriously by Dawes and others in 1900, neither he nor his wife favored. Allison counseled him in his wonted fatherly manner and Dolliver proved a popular and useful adjunct to the conservative organization. He won his reward when that group chose him—rather than Cummins, who had displeased them—to succeed Senator Gear. Life as a senator proved complicated. Dolliver felt the new spirit expressed by George Roberts in Iowa's tariff plank of 1901, yet the ancient conservative loyalties bound him. He tried to meet Allison's wish that he continue to follow him, but the railroad and tariff issues prevented. Clashes with the Senate's parliamentary leader, Nelson W. Aldrich [q.v.], began in 1903, and grew increasingly significant as Dolliver aligned himself with La Follette, Clapp, and Beveridge. The emotional orator of forty-five with the mid-Western, agricultural constituency, was pitted against the impersonal, silent parliamentarian of sixty-two with the New England manufacturing constituency. As the former turned insurgent, his chances of advancement in the Senate organization inevitably lessened. The year 1906 was most trying. In that year Aldrich thwarted Dolliver's desire to attach his name to the railroad law and Roosevelt abandoned the position on court review of decisions of the Interstate Commerce Commission which Dolliver thought they had agreed upon, thus leaving the latter high and dry in the midst of the controversy. Late the next year there was a burden to shoulder for Allison—to defeat the attempt of Cummins to take the next primary nomination. Dolliver won the nomination for Allison, but the death of the latter in August of 1908 set Dolliver free to cooperate openly with Cummins thenceforward.

He was powerfully energized by his new sense of liberty. Evidence of the change came when, Aldrich refusing him a place on the finance committee, he turned scathingly upon Aldrich's cotton and woolen schedules. Similarly, when with Cummins he mastered the state convention in 1910, he defied the hootings of his former friends among the conservatives with a threat that he would campaign in every district he pleased. Throughout this, his last summer, though wretchedly undermined in health, he immersed himself in plans for the future. He desired to attack Aldrich further, utilizing the rubber schedule. He was complimented by the party harmonizers, when they brought him and Roosevelt together in a love feast at Sioux City and when they demanded Dolliver's skilled services in disaffected Republican districts. In the midst

of these, his days of greatest independence and moral strength, doctors told him his life depended upon complete withdrawal from the political scene, and within a week after their warning he was dead.

[Dolliver gave recollections of his early experiences to Jas. B. Morrow in an interview which the latter copyrighted and syndicated; it can be found entire in the *Dubuque Times-Jour.*, Oct. 16–18, 1910. For Dolliver's political career see *Annals of Iowa* (Iowa State Dept. of Hist., Des Moines), especially 3 ser., vols. IV–VII, IX–X, XIII–XIV; *Palimpsest* (State Hist. Soc. of Iowa, Iowa City), especially Feb. 1924; "Dedication of Dolliver State Park," *Bulletin* (Iowa State Board of Conservation, Des Moines), III, 1–24; Sioux City *Journal*, especially Oct. 16, 1910; *La Follette's Autobiography* (1913); F. E. Haynes, *Third Party Movements* (1916); Champ Clark, *My Quarter Century of Am. Politics* (1920); *Selections from the Correspondence of Theodore Roosevelt and Henry Cabot Lodge 1884–1918* (1925). The best available manuscript collections are W. B. Allison MSS., and G. M. Dodge MSS. (Iowa State Dept. of Hist., Des Moines); W. E. Chandler MSS., and T. Roosevelt MSS. (Lib. of Cong.). For Dolliver's change in attitude toward the tariff, compare his speeches of Mar. 23, 1897, and Aug. 5, 1909 (*Cong. Record*, 55 Cong., 1 Sess., pp. 191–97, and 61 Cong., 1 Sess., pp. 4925–32). For his analysis of the progressive movement, see his "Forward Movement in the Republican Party" (*Outlook*, Sept. 24, 1910). The writer obtained data from many of Dolliver's contemporaries, including the late Senators Beveridge, Clapp, La Follette, ex-Director of the Mint Roberts, and many prominent Iowans.]

J. P. N.

DOLPH, JOSEPH NORTON (Oct. 19, 1835–Mar. 10, 1897), United States senator from Oregon, was born in the village of Dolphsburg, near Watkins, N. Y. He was the son of Chester V. and Eliza (Vanderbilt) Dolph, both of New England ancestry. At sixteen he left the farm to become a lock-tender on the Chemung Canal. Afterward he alternated short terms of attendance at the Genesee Wesleyan Seminary at Lima with the teaching of country schools and the study of law until admitted to the bar at Binghamton in 1861. The next spring he enlisted in a military company bound for Oregon and reached Portland, in October 1862. In October 1864 he was married to Augusta E. Mulkey. Upon settling in Portland he had at once become a law partner of John H. Mitchell, a recent arrival but already a leading attorney of the city and in 1872 elected a United States senator. The commerce and business of Portland were booming at this period as the result of the opening of new mines in the upper Columbia River basin; many business corporations were formed, and the railroad era began. Mitchell & Dolph shared in this prosperity and soon reached a position of leadership in the social, political, and financial life of the city and state. The first great railroad promoter of the state, Ben Holladay [q.v.], became their client and they entered the legislature where they could better serve his interests.

Dolph's rise was rapid; he was city attorney for Portland in 1864, United States district attorney, 1865, chairman of the Republican state committee, 1866, and four times state senator, 1866–76. At the same time he had become a director in and the attorney for the transportation companies organized by Henry Villard and was vice-president of the latter's Northern Pacific Railroad when his turn to be elected United States senator came in 1882 at the end of a session of the legislature and after a long deadlock.

In the Senate his career was creditable though his name is not associated with any legislation of lasting importance. He was an ardent supporter of protection and other party measures, yet generally voted with the more liberal wing of the Republican party on bills that involved a concession to the reform spirit of the time. He voted for the Interstate Commerce Act of 1887 and the Sherman Anti-Trust Act of 1890. He defended the woman's suffrage amendment and spoke in favor of a proposed amendment giving Congress control of marriage and divorce. He voted for the Sherman Silver Purchase Act of 1890, though opposed to free silver, and somewhat inconsistently voted against its repeal when that was called for by President Cleveland. He was reëlected without opposition in 1888, but his stand in opposition to free silver so angered the numerous supporters of that cause in Oregon that he failed of reëlection in 1894. Aside from his being "the only member in Congress from the Pacific Coast who stood unequivocally for the gold standard" (*Morning Oregonian,* Portland, Mar. 11, 1897) his political career was without special distinction. He was an able lawyer, a shrewd political leader, and strong representative of the business interests of his time.

[Oregon newspapers of the period, the journals of the state legislature, and the *Congressional Record* are the available sources for his official career. Biographical sketches are found in H. W. Scott, *Distinguished Am. Lawyers* (1891); *Portrait and Biog. Record of Western Ore.* (1904); *Biog. Dir. Am. Cong.* (1928).]

R.C.C—k.

DOMBROWSKI, JOSEPH. [See DABROWSKI, JOSEPH, 1842–1903.]

DOMINGUEZ, FRANCISCO ATANASIO. [See ESCALANTE, SILVESTRE VELEZ DE, *c.* 1776.]

DONAHOE, PATRICK (Mar. 17, 1811–Mar. 18, 1901), editor, publisher, philanthropist, was in 1872 "the richest and most influential Catholic in New England" (*Pilot,* Boston, Mar. 23, 1901). He was born in Munnery, parish of Kilmore, County Cavan, Ireland, the son of Terrence and Jane (Christy) Donahoe. His mother died when he was an infant. When he was ten years

old he came with his father to Boston, Mass. For one year he attended Adams School where, he said, he was "the only boy of Irish, and perhaps, of alien birth." At fourteen he set out to learn the printing trade in the office of the *Columbian Centinel,* and some time later worked temporarily for the *Boston Transcript* where (he said) he nearly lost his job for "not coming to work on Christmas day." His association with Catholic journalism commenced with *The Jesuit, or Catholic Sentinel,* published after 1829 by George Pepper. When this paper was reorganized (1832), he worked on it with H. L. Devereaux, in company with whom he later began (1836) the publication of the *Pilot.* As owner and editor of the *Pilot,* then perhaps the most influential Catholic weekly newspaper in the United States, as publisher for various Irish-American writers among whom Thomas D'Arcy McGee and Anna H. Dorsey were the best known, and as a merchant and a private banker, he amassed great wealth and influence. Benefactions to the American College in Rome, the Boston Home for Destitute Catholic Children, and the victims of the Irish famine of 1848, together with numerous other gifts to churches and charitable institutions, displayed the readiness with which he placed his means at the service of society. He also supported "Father Mathew" (Rev. Theobald Mathew) in an energetic crusade for temperance reform. The great Boston fire (1872) destroyed his publishing plant and church goods store, plunging him deeply into debt. His bank also failed during the panic that followed. Archbishop Williams purchased the *Pilot,* in 1876, to help pay the bank's depositors, and two years later Donahoe started *Donahoe's Magazine,* a monthly periodical devoted to Catholic and Irish-American interests, which circulated widely and published work by such writers as Ethna Carberry and Louise Imogene Guiney. In 1891, having in the meantime partly restored his banking business, he repurchased the *Pilot,* which he continued to publish until his death. In 1893 the University of Notre Dame conferred on him the Lætare Medal, and in 1894 he was tendered a public banquet by admiring fellow townsfolk. He died in Boston, and his funeral was almost a civic event, the Pope sending his Apostolic Benediction and the Irish, whom he had aided so generously, going in throngs to honor his memory. He was married twice, first, on Nov. 23, 1836, to Kate Griffin, who died in 1852, and second, on Apr. 17, 1853, to Annie E. Davis. As a citizen he was a prominent supporter of the Democratic party; as a patriot, during the Civil War, he was identified with the history of the 9th and 28th Massachusetts regiments, which he helped to organize; as an Irish American, he contributed an incalculable amount to the welfare of his fellow emigrants.

[The chief sources of information regarding Donahoe's personality and career are the *Pilot*, for Mar. 23 and 30, 1901; *Donahoe's Mag.*, Apr. 1901; *Mass. of To-Day* (1892), ed. by Thos. Quinn; and *Catholic Builders of the Nation*, IV (1923), 224. His journalistic and publishing enterprises are dealt with in Paul J. Foik, *Pioneer Efforts of Catholic Journalism in the U. S.* (1912), pp. 174–78, and 261–87; J. M. Finotti, *Bibliographia Catholica Americana* (1872). See also obituary in *Boston Transcript*, Mar. 18, 1901.] G. N. S.

DONAHUE, PETER (Jan. 11, 1822–Nov. 26, 1885), capitalist, founder of the Union Iron Works in San Francisco, was born of Irish parents living in Glasgow. His early life seems to have been one of hardship and little schooling. At the age of nine he was working in a Glasgow factory. When he was eleven his parents emigrated to the United States and settled in Matteawan, N. Y., where he worked first in a factory and then on a farm. About 1837 his parents moved to Paterson, N. J., and there Peter was apprenticed to learn the craft of machinist and millwright. His younger brothers, James and Michael, learned the related trades of boiler-making and molding. Upon returning to New York, in 1845, Peter found employment on the construction of a gunboat for the Peruvian government. He accompanied the completed vessel to Peru as assistant engineer, and remained in that country until 1849, when he embarked for the gold-fields of California. Although detained for some months at Tobago with Isthmus fever, he eventually reached San Francisco on the steamship *Oregon*. En route, the vessel's machinery broke down, but Donahue was able to repair it, and for this service the owners rewarded him with $1,000 and urged him to remain in their employ. At this time the lure of the goldfields still drew him, but after six months in the mines he was back in San Francisco where his two brothers had arrived.

Together they opened a crude blacksmith and boiler-making shop at Montgomery St., near Jackson, the first iron works and machine-shop in California. Later this expanded into the great Union Iron Works, named for the works at Paterson, N. J., where Peter had learned his trade as machinist. The Donahue works, first housed in tents, soon moved to what was then called Happy Valley, between Mission, First, and Frémont Sts. For a furnace they utilized the smokestack of a dismantled steamer, and for a blast used a pair of old-fashioned bellows. Here were made the first castings in the state of California. In a short time they added to their business the

repairing of engines, the construction of quartz mills, mining machinery, mining pumps, and the erection of gas-works.

In 1852 and 1856 Michael and James sold their interests to Peter, who carried on the business in his own name for a time, erecting a large brick building on the site of the roofless shop of 1849. In 1860 he obtained a contract for building a steamer for the United States government, the *Saginaw*, and in 1863 turned out the monitor *Comanche*. These were the first government vessels produced on the Pacific Coast. The first printing-press made in California was also manufactured in his foundry. In 1865 the Union Iron Works finished, for the San Francisco & San Jose Railroad, the first locomotive built in the state. By 1863 Donahue had become so involved in other important enterprises that he was unable to exercise personal supervision over the mechanical branch of the business. He therefore formed a new partnership with H. J. Booth and C. S. Higgins, under the firm name of Donahue, Booth & Company. Two years later he sold his interest to H. J. Booth & Company.

Not only was Peter Donahue the pioneer foundryman of California but he was also a pioneer in the public-utility development of that state. In 1852 he organized the first gas company for street lighting in San Francisco; and for twenty years preceding his death he was president of this highly prosperous concern. He organized (1861) the Omnibus Street Railway, the first street-car line in San Francisco, and for many years was president of the company. In 1860 he was made treasurer of the San Francisco & San Jose Railroad, and, with an associate, soon acquired two-thirds of the stock. In November 1870 they sold the road to the Central Pacific for $3,250,000. In 1862 Donahue became one of the charter members of the Union Pacific Railroad. In 1870 he acquired a controling interest in the San Francisco & Humboldt Railroad, out of which he created the San Francisco & North Pacific Railroad and its branches and extensions lying in Marin, Sonoma, and Mendocino counties. The town of Donahue in this region was named after him. He was also a director of the San Francisco & Colorado River Railroad Company. Although active in support of the Union cause at the opening of the Civil War and interested in civic affairs throughout his life, he would never accept public office. By his industry and business thrift he accumulated great wealth. A contemporary described him as "one of the most charitable of givers, kindest of benefactors, and most generous of friends." He was twice married: his first wife was Mary Jane

Maguire, whom he married in 1852 and by whom he had four children. In 1864 he married Annie Downey, sister of Gov. J. G. Downey, who survived her husband eleven years. He died in San Francisco.

[The main facts in Donahue's life may be gathered from H. H. Bancroft, *Chronicles of the Builders of the Commonwealth* (1891), I, 442–45, and VI, 139, 303; and the same author's *Hist. of Cal.* (1890), VII (see index); Z. S. Eldredge, *Hist. of Cal.* (1915), IV, 269; B. E. Lloyd, *Lights and Shades in San Francisco* (1876), pp. 308–17; O. T. Shuck, *Sketches of Leading and Representative Men of San Francisco* (1875), pp. 855–60; A. Phelps, *Contemporary Biog. of California's Representative Men* (1882), pp. 370–74; *San Francisco Chronicle* and *Morning Call* (San Francisco), Nov. 27, 1885.]   P.O.R.

DONCK, ADRIAEN VAN DER [See Van der Donck, Adriaen, 1620–1655.]

DONELSON, ANDREW JACKSON (Aug. 25, 1799–June 26, 1871), soldier, lawyer, politician, diplomat, was associated from birth with the man for whom he was named. When James Robertson conducted his little band of pioneers through the wilderness to the Cumberland River in the winter of 1779–80, the families and supplies of the party were conveyed by water under the command of Col. John Donelson. After having taken up considerable land in the neighborhood of Nashville, Donelson was killed in the forest, and left his widow with a family which included their children Rachel and Samuel. When Andrew Jackson [*q.v.*] first went to Nashville in 1788, he secured lodging with the widow Donelson, became associated in business with her son Samuel, and married her daughter Rachel. When Samuel eloped with Mary, only daughter of Gen. Daniel Smith, another prominent pioneer, Jackson assisted the young lovers. It was fitting that their son should be named Andrew Jackson. Young Andrew's father died while he was yet a child, and when his mother married a second time, Jackson took his namesake and his wife's nephew to "The Hermitage" and reared him there. He was first sent to Cumberland College in Nashville, and then to the United States Military Academy. On graduating from West Point, where he completed four years' work in three and ranked second in his class, he was appointed aide-de-camp to Gen. Jackson and served with him during the Seminole campaign. Resigning from the army, he now went to Transylvania University at Lexington, Ky., to take up the study of law. In 1823 he was admitted to the bar and began practise in Nashville. In 1824 he married his first cousin, Emily, daughter of Capt. John Donelson, and grand-daughter of Col. John Donelson, the pioneer.

Jackson's first campaign for the presidency was in progress at that time, and Donelson became his confidential secretary. He now made his home at "Tulip Grove," an estate across the way from "The Hermitage," and became once more, in effect, a member of the General's family. During the campaign of 1828, he again served as secretary, and when Jackson was elected, accompanied him to Washington to officiate as private secretary while Emily was to preside as mistress of the White House. Four of their children were thus born in the presidential mansion. When the Eaton storm came up, Emily, like the cabinet ladies, refused to bow to Jackson's mandate that she receive Peggy O'Neill socially, and for this was sent back to Tennessee. Her husband chose to accompany her and they remained in retirement about six months. The General, however, needed Donelson's assistance in getting his state papers into shape, and the family from "Tulip Grove" were presently recalled and restored to favor. Emily died in 1836, and five years later Donelson married another cousin, Mrs. Elizabeth Martin Randolph.

With the end of Jackson's administration, his private secretary returned to Nashville with the General, refusing to take office under the Van Buren administration. Jackson and his friends were not forgotten in Washington, however, and when the question of the annexation of Texas came to a head, President Tyler, hoping to secure Democratic support, appointed Donelson to carry on negotiations with the new republic (J. S. Bassett, *Life of Andrew Jackson,* 1911, II, 742). When Polk came into office, Donelson retained the post, and completed his task in a thoroughly creditable manner (McCormac, *post,* p. 352). His success in this undertaking, as well as his nearness to Jackson, gave him strong claims upon the new administration. Though he was considered for the cabinet, he did not push his claims, and was accredited minister to the Kingdom of Prussia in 1846. This position he retained until 1849, when the Whigs were in power. In 1850 the noted Southern Convention met in Nashville. Donelson took keen interest in the early stages of this movement, but when the second session fell under the influence of the radical Southern element, he withdrew his support (Sioussat, "Tennessee, the Compromise of 1850, and the Nashville Convention," in *Tennessee Historical Magazine,* 1920, IV, 224, 244). In 1851 he succeeded Ritchie as editor of the *Washington Union,* but, not being able to go along with his party in its drift toward sectionalism, he ceased to cooperate with it, and in 1856 accepted the vice-presidential nomination on the

Fillmore ticket. This incident ended his political career.

When Andrew Jackson died, an impoverished old man, he left to his namesake, who had served him so faithfully, his blessing and the sword which his state had presented him. With it he left the injunction that "he fail not to use it when necessary in support . . . of the constitutional rights of our beloved country, should they be assailed by foreign enemies or domestic traitors" (Parton, *post,* III, 651). When the Civil War was precipitated, Donelson was asked to lend his support to the cause of his section, but answered that he could not draw the sword of Jackson against the old flag. Broken by the calamities of the war which he would have done so much to avert, he died at Memphis in 1871.

[The best biographical notices are in J. T. Moore and A. P. Foster, *Tenn., the Volunteer State* (4 vols., 1923), and W. W. Clayton, *Hist. of Davidson County, Tenn.* (1880). Donelson's career, however, is so closely tied up with that of Jackson, that much material on his life is to be found in Jas. Parton, *Life of Andrew Jackson* (3 vols., 1860), E. I. McCormac, *James K. Polk* (1922), and S. G. Heiskell, *Andrew Jackson and Early Tenn. Hist.* (3 vols., 1920–21). A collection of Donelson Papers has been published in the *Tenn. Hist. Mag.,* 1919, III, 51–73 and 134–62. The date of Donelson's birth is recorded in the Donelson family Bible, in the possession of Mrs. Betty Donelson of Nebraska.]   T.P.A.

DONGAN, THOMAS (1634–Dec. 14, 1715), soldier, colonial governor of New York, was born at Castletown, in the county of Kildare, Ireland, being a younger son of Sir John Dongan, Baronet. He adopted the profession of arms and spent some years in France in the service of Louis XIV. He was recalled about 1677 and shortly thereafter received from Charles II an appointment as lieutenant-governor of Tangier, which was then under the English flag. He remained at this post until 1680. His friendship for the Stuarts brought him additional preferment, and by a commission dated Sept. 30, 1682, he was appointed governor of New York by its Roman Catholic proprietor, James, Duke of York. On Aug. 25, 1683, he arrived at his new post.

The territory under his jurisdiction included not only New York itself but also the dependencies of Pemaquid, Martha's Vineyard, and Nantucket. During the five years following his arrival, he governed the province with such ability and energy that he has been referred to by competent authority as "one of the very best of all the colonial governors" (Osgood, *American Colonies in the Seventeenth Century,* II, 131). The Duke's instructions provided for the calling of a representative assembly, and one of the new governor's first acts was to issue writs of election. The body thus chosen met for the first time on Oct. 17, 1683, and its first statute defined more fully the organization and powers of the assembly and came to be known as the "Charter of Liberties." After James's accession to the throne, however, the measure was disallowed, and New York, which had now become a royal province, was again without a representative assembly.

Dongan devoted himself most energetically to the development of the colony. He strengthened the defenses and took steps to determine more definitely the boundaries of the province. He even dreamed of establishing a postal system, to extend from Nova Scotia to the Carolinas, which might serve as a bond of union between the English colonies in America. Though he was himself a Roman Catholic, his administration was marked by a broad tolerance in religious matters. In 1687 he submitted to the home government a report on the state of the province which contains a remarkable description of New York at that time. His greatest service, however, consisted in his early recognition of the growing power of the French to the northward and in his insistence that the home government aid him in checking it. French Jesuits were active among the Iroquois and were using their influence for political ends, while efforts were being made from Quebec to establish something in the nature of a protectorate over those tribes. Dongan protested vigorously to De la Barre, the governor of Canada, and to his successor, the Marquis de Denonville. As early as 1684 he had caused the arms of the Duke of York to be erected in the Iroquois villages, a step which he regarded as equivalent to the establishment of a protectorate. By the winter of 1687–88 an open conflict seemed imminent, and Dongan raised a force for the defense of Albany, superintending the arrangements in person. His vigorous policy, which was undertaken almost solely upon his own responsibility, at length bore fruit when James II rather tardily gave it the sanction of his approval.

In August 1688 Dongan was superseded by Sir Edmund Andros, but instead of returning at once to England, he decided to remain in New York, where he was unfortunate enough to fall a victim to the fanatical anti-Catholic crusade which attended the Revolution of 1689 in the colonies. After some vicissitudes he returned to England in 1691. Upon the death of an elder brother in 1698 he became second Earl of Limerick, a title which he retained until his death. In 1713, twenty-nine years after he had erected the arms of the Duke of York in the Iroquois villages, the French by the Treaty of Utrecht formally recognized the English protectorate over those Indians. By his clearness of vision, no less than by the vigor of his policy, Dongan proved himself one of the race of empire builders.

[Good secondary accounts of Dongan's career as governor are to be found in J. R. Brodhead, *Hist. of the State of N. Y.* (1853–71), vol. II; Francis Parkman, *Count Frontenac and New France Under Louis XIV* (1877); and Herbert Osgood, *The Am. Colonies in the Seventeenth Century* (1904–07), vols. II and III. A wealth of source material is to be found in vols. III and IX of *Docs. Relative to the Colonial Hist. of the State of N. Y.* (1853–87). An interesting sketch is that contained in Franklin M. Danaher, *An Address before the Dongan Club of Albany, N. Y., July 22, 1889* (1889). See also Edward Channing, "Col. Thos. Dongan, Governor of N. Y.," in *Proc. Am. Antiquarian Soc.*, Oct. 16, 1907.]
W.E.S.

DONIPHAN, ALEXANDER WILLIAM (July 9, 1808–Aug. 8, 1887), soldier, statesman, was born near Maysville, Mason County, Ky. His father, Joseph Doniphan of King George County, Va., served in the Revolution and after the war went to Kentucky. He returned to his native state and married Anne Smith of Fauquier County, with her going back to Kentucky in 1790, and settling in Mason County. He died there in March 1813, before his youngest son, Alexander, was five years old. When he was eight, the latter was sent to school at Augusta, Ky., under the tutelage of Richard Keene, and at the age of eighteen he graduated from Augusta College. He studied law in the office of Hon. Martin Marshall, and after two years was admitted to practise in Kentucky and Ohio. Removing to Missouri, on Apr. 19, 1830, he began, at Lexington, a long, brilliant, and successful career in his profession, gaining distinction by his eloquence. Although pitted against many lawyers of ability, his influence over juries was almost infallible, and he was employed in nearly every important case in northwestern Missouri. In one of these he defended the Mormon, Orrin P. Rockwell, who was charged with being party to a conspiracy to murder Gov. McNair. The latter recovered from his wounds, but the excitement incident to the Mormon invasion and the dastardly attack caused the outraged community to demand revenge. Doniphan, however, obtained for his client a sentence of five minutes in jail; virtually an acquittal. In 1833 he moved to Liberty, Mo., which place he thereafter regarded as his home.

His qualities of leadership brought him into prominence in the military movements of his time. He took part in the conflict between the State of Missouri and the Mormons, serving as commander of the 1st Brigade under Gen. Lucas. He refused to shoot down Prophet Smith and several other Mormons after their court-martial, pronouncing the order of Gen. Lucas cold-blood murder. The order was later rescinded. In May 1846, at the request of Gov. Edwards, Doniphan organized the 1st Regiment of Missouri Mounted Volunteers for the Mexican War. This regiment was made up of young men from the best families in the state, and Doniphan, who enlisted as a private, was elected colonel. They marched to the rendezvous at Fort Leavenworth, from there with Kearny's men to Fort Bent, and thence into New Mexico, of which territory Doniphan was placed in command. He was permitted to yield this post to Col. Sterling Price, who came later with a large body of troops. Doniphan then proceeded to the western slope of the Rockies and effected a treaty with the Navajo Indians who had been harassing the whites. Later he went to Chihuahua to form a junction with Gen. Wool, and took possession of the city by right of conquest. On the way, his men defeated the Mexicans in the battles of Brazito and Sacramento. This expedition, which ended by land at Matamoras, is still considered one of the most brilliant long marches ever made; the force, with no quartermaster, paymaster, commissary, uniforms, tents, or even military discipline, covered 3,600 miles by land and 2,000 by water, all in the course of twelve months.

Doniphan's part in civil affairs included election to the legislature in 1836, 1840, and again in 1854. The legislature appointed him delegate to the Peace Conference at Washington in 1861, and after attending the sessions of that body he entertained no hope of avoiding the impending war. During his absence he was elected to the state convention called by the legislature Jan. 21, 1861, to determine whether or not Missouri should secede from the Union. He attended this convention at its sessions in St. Louis, and at the very outset opposed the secession of Missouri. He expressed concern, however, for the rights of the states, believing that the intense feeling of the Union men might lead to the concentration of too much power in the federal government. Doniphan never felt called upon to explain any speech or vote made by him in the convention. He was opposed to invasion by Federal or Confederate forces, favoring neutrality.

In June 1861, Gov. Jackson handed him a commission as major-general in command of the State Guard, which he retained two weeks. His reasons for returning it were the loss of his two sons by accidental death, and the shattered condition of his wife's health. He had married, on Dec. 21, 1837, Elizabeth Jane, daughter of John and Elizabeth (Trigg) Thornton. They had only two children. From 1863 to 1868, Doniphan remained in St. Louis, settling at Richmond, Mo., after quiet was restored. There he stayed nearly twenty-five years, practising law and serving as president of the Ray County Savings Bank. His affection for Clay County, and dislike of being considered a rover, caused him still, however, to claim Liberty as his home, and to look upon Richmond as merely his temporary abiding-place. He died at Richmond, but was buried at Liberty, where a monument marks his grave. The State of Missouri erected a monument to his memory at Richmond in 1918.

[Doniphan letters and autobiography in Mo. Hist. Soc. *Santa Fé Republican*, Sept. 10, 1847; H. L. Conard, *Encyc. of the Hist. of Mo.* (1901), II, 292; W. E. Connelley, *War with Mexico 1846-47* (1907), p. 15; A. J. D. Stewart, *Hist. of the Bench and Bar of Mo.* (1898), 386; W. L. Webb, *Battles and Biog. of Missourians* (1900), pp. 278-80; R. A. Campbell, *Campbell's Gazetteer of Mo.* (Rev. ed., 1875), p. 152; *Hist. of Ray County, Mo.* (1881), p. 498; *Hist. of Caldwell and Livingston Counties, Mo.* (1886), p. 137; *Missouri Republican*, Aug. 9, 1887.]   S.M.D.

DONLEVY, HARRIET FARLEY [See FARLEY, HARRIET, 1817-1907.]

DONN-BYRNE, BRIAN OSWALD (Nov. 20, 1889-June 18, 1928), Irish novelist, the son of Tomas Fearghail and Jane D'Arcy (McParlane) Donn-Byrne of Forkhill, County Armagh, Ireland, was born in New York City, whither his father, interested in bridges, had come on business. At the age of several months he was taken back to Ireland where his childhood was spent in Armagh and in the Glens of Antrim at Cushendun. He matriculated at University College, Dublin, where he acquired fluent command of Gaelic and became deeply interested in the Sinn Fein movement. There too he came under the influence of Douglas Hyde and acquired a wide knowledge of Irish history and literature. After graduation he expected a diplomatic career and studied briefly in Paris at the Sorbonne and at the University of Leipzig. He gave up this expectation and returned to New York City in 1911 in order to join an Irish girl whom he had met in Dublin at University College, Dorthea Mary, the daughter of Anthony Cadogan of Waterford; they were married Dec. 2, 1911. He hoped to become an Irish poet, but was forced to accept less congenial employment on the *New Catholic Encyclopedia,* and later on the *New Standard Dictionary.* Various bits of his verse had been published in obscure periodicals; in 1912 "The Piper" appeared in *Harper's Magazine.* Through the late Joyce Kilmer [*q.v.*], his friend and colleague on the *New Standard Dictionary,* he took up writing seriously. He received fifty dollars for his first short story, "Battle," published in *Smart Set* in February 1914. He did various hack-writing and book-reviewing. He later became a member of the *Century*

Dictionary staff which he left to join the staff of the New York *Sun.* When he was dismissed from the *Sun* because of his "bad English" he accepted a position with the *Brooklyn Eagle.*

Donn-Byrne's short stories found their audience and his contributions to *Smart Set* and to *Harper's Magazine* were numerous. To the direct simplicity of the traditional Irish story-telling he added color and picturesque detail. Although his first novel, *Stranger's Banquet,* was published in 1919, it was not until the publication of his *Messer Marco Polo* in 1921 that he achieved popularity as a novelist. For this narration of Marco Polo's voyage to China as told by a venerable Ulsterman, the most successful and best-known of his books, he drew inspiration from old Irish chronicles and from Coleridge. His *Blind Raftery* (1924) was based upon the story of Raftery, a Gaelic itinerant poet of Cannaugh in the eighteenth century whose songs had been edited by Douglas Hyde. Despite his large payments from the *Pictorial Review,* in which many of his novels ran serially, and the royalties from his many books, he was impecunious. He sold his house at Riverside, Conn., and returned to Ireland where he purchased Coolmain Castle near Bandon, County Cork. There he lived until his sudden death in an automobile accident during June 1928. Donn-Byrne was a typical, romantic, fighting North Irishman. His writings manifest his deep aversion to "progress," his belief in the futility of politics, his love of sport, and his poetic Scots-Irish mysticism. In his work he tried to capture for an instant "a beauty that was dying slowly, imperceptibly, but would soon be gone." And with his feeling for color and his ear for the music of words he succeeded in imparting a mythical and mystical beauty to the Ireland of his imagination.

[Thurston Macauley's *Donn Byrne; Bard of Armagh* (1929), containing bibliographies, is the most complete and satisfactory of existing accounts. See also A. St. John Adcock, *Gods of Modern Grub Street* (1923); *Times* (London), June 20, 1928; *N. Y. Times,* June 20, 1928; Shane Leslie, "A Literary Beau Sabreur," in London *Outlook,* June 23, 1928; Thurston Macauley, "Passport to Tir Nan Og," in *Bookman,* Apr. 1929; Paul Mellon, *Donn-Byrne—His Place in Literature* (N. Y., 1927); *Outlook,* July 4, 1928; private information from Thurston Macauley.]   F.M.

DONNELL, JAMES C. (Apr. 20, 1854-Jan. 10, 1927), producer of crude oil, was born in Ireland. Very little is known about his early life and he seems to have dismissed questions concerning it by declaring that "he was not interested in the past at all" (Smith, *post,* p. 29). His parents, James and Elizabeth (Boyd) Donnell, brought him to the United States as a child of two and at the age of eighteen he was working in the oil-fields of Titusville, Pa., hauling crude oil from field to refinery. Six years later he joined the rush to Bradford Field and took leases in the famous Foster Brook Valley near Red Rock and Derrick City. Here he remained for several years as producer and driller of wells. During this time he also bought land in the Richburg and Allentown Fields of New York state. In 1886 he went to Ohio, attracted by the possibilities of the Lima field, and was one of the few drillers who made a success there. In the following year, when the Standard Oil Company purchased the Ohio Oil Company, he became one of the board of directors and later vice-president. At the same time he served the Standard interests in Indiana where he was in charge of drilling operations. When the Clark County fields were opened in 1905, he took personal charge and, realizing the need for transportation, was instrumental in the building of the Illinois Pipe Line Company. He next spent several months in Roumania representing the Roumanian-American Oil Company and in 1907 he helped form the Standard Oil Company of California. With the dissolution of the Standard Oil Company in 1911, he became the president of the Ohio Oil Company and under his leadership this company enjoyed phenomenal growth, paying entirely out of its earnings for its expansion. This took the form of operations in the new fields of Wyoming and also in Montana, New Mexico, Kansas, Oklahoma, Texas, Arkansas, Kentucky, and Louisiana, as well as in Mexico. In 1916 he made a survey of the Peruvian oil-fields which the Standard interests later took over.

Donnell looked upon his wells as living things, and on oil as something that should be conserved by storage in the ground until needed. During his lifetime he drilled some 42,000 wells, in every oil-producing section of the United States. It has been said that sometimes while inspecting a field, he would take the driller's place so that he could "turn screw" for a while. He was married twice: in 1882 to Sadie Flinn who bore one son, and in 1890 to Elizabeth Meeker. He had banking and railroad interests and served as director of the American Petroleum Institute. During the World War he became a member of the National Petroleum War Service Committee. He did much for his local community and won a popular love greater than that accorded most men.

His death removed the last of the "oil giants" with the exception of the senior Rockefeller, one of his closest friends. He was buried in the Maple Grove Cemetery of Findlay, Ohio. Rockefeller said of him then, "He was a remarkable man and shared our confidence to the fullest extent. He will be greatly missed by a multitude who knew him and who [had] . . . the highest honor and esteem for his noble qualities and charming personality."

[Published accounts are L. E. Smith in *Nat. Petroleum News*, Jan. 12, 1927; portrait and biography in *Oil and Gas Jour.*, Jan. 13, 1927. Special mention must be made of the unique scrap-book patiently compiled by C. L. Fleming, vice-president of the Ohio Oil Co., in Findlay, Ohio,—a photostat copy of which was lent to the writer. This work contains clippings from twenty-two newspapers and magazines.]   A.I.

DONNELL, ROBERT (April 1784–May 24, 1855), was the strongest preacher of the Cumberland Presbyterians in their early days. He was born in Guilford County, N. C., the son of William Donnell and Mary Bell, Scotch-Irish Presbyterians. In his childhood his parents moved to Tennessee, where his father died when Robert was fourteen. The boy's education went little beyond reading the Bible and religious books under his mother's teaching. He was a popular youth, known for height and strength, feats of hunting and rail-splitting, and expertness with tools. At a camp-meeting in the Cumberland revival his religious life was deepened, and in 1801 he determined to preach. Unable to leave farming for the sake of education, he began to hold prayer-meetings and to "exhort." Under the direction of the "Council" formed in 1805 by the workers in the revival, he rode in circuit over a large territory between the Ohio and the Cumberland rivers, and later did pioneer preaching in northern Alabama. From the independent Cumberland Presbytery, organized in 1810 in succession to the Council, he received ordination in 1813. In the growth of this presbytery into the Cumberland Presbyterian Church Donnell was prominent. He was one of the framers of the church's confession, adopted in 1814. With Finis Ewing he wrote in 1813 the article on the Cumberland Presbyterians in Woodward's edition of Charles Buck's *Theological Dictionary* (1814) which brought the sect to general notice. Meanwhile he was always traveling and preaching, much sought after and greatly influential; and also always studying. In 1818 he married Ann, daughter of Col. James W. Smith, who brought him considerable property. Moving to Alabama, he soon had a cotton-farm near Athens, his home for most of his life. In 1832 he was married a second time, to Clarissa, daughter of Rev. Jacob Lindley.

From his home Donnell constantly went out to preach, sometimes being absent for months, working in Alabama, Tennessee, Kentucky, North Carolina, and Pennsylvania. During nearly fifty years he attended, on an average, a camp-meeting every month, and at each preached once or twice a day, in many cases oftener. He planted many churches, especially in northern Alabama. He gave particular attention to the establishment of congregations and the erection of buildings in towns, among them Nashville and Memphis. Contemporary testimony as to the extraordinary power of his preaching, from all sorts of people, is convincing. He had an imposing presence and a great, expressive voice. By vivid imagery, emotional appeal, and singing added to speech, he often produced tears and shouting. Yet he did much expounding of the Cumberland theology, and was specially remembered for persuasive reasoning. He left always a deep impression of religious reality.

Donnell was first president of the first missionary board of his church, in 1837 moderator of its General Assembly, and all his life an acknowledged leader in its affairs, with a great name for peacemaking. Deeply interested in education, particularly ministerial, he was foremost in the establishment of Cumberland University, at Lebanon, Tenn. In 1846 he became pastor there, attracted chiefly by the presence of students. The last six years of his life he spent in Athens, Ala. The volume, *Thoughts on Various Theological Subjects,* issued in 1852, was his only publication.

[D. Lowry, *Life and Labors of Rev. Robt. Donnell* (1867), containing portrait and forty pages of extracts from his *Thoughts*; R. Beard, *Brief Biog. Sketches of Some of the Early Ministers of the Cumberland Presbyt. Ch.* (1867); T. C. Anderson, *Life of Rev. Geo. Donnell* (1858); F. R. Cossitt, *Life and Times of Rev. Finis Ewing* (1853); B. W. McDonnold, *Hist. Cumb. Presbyt. Ch.* (1888); *Semicentennial General Assembly Cumb. Presbyt. Ch.* (1880), ed. by J. Frizzel, containing important extracts from ecclesiastical records; *Cumb. Presbyt. Digest* (1899), ed. by J. V. Stephens; Woodward's Buck's *Theological Dict.* (1814).]

R. H. N.

DONNELLY, CHARLES FRANCIS (Oct. 14, 1836–Jan. 31, 1909), lawyer, was born in Athlone, County Roscommon, Ireland, the son of Hugh Donnelly and his wife, Margaret Conway, the latter of Welsh descent. In 1837 the family removed to Canada, settling at St. John, N. B., and Charles Francis's education was received in the private schools and the Presbyterian Academy there, and continued privately in Yarmouth, N. S., where his parents resided for a short time. In 1848 they moved to Providence, R. I., and he commenced a classical course with a view to the priesthood. Later this idea was abandoned and he went to Boston in 1856 where he read law, entering the Harvard Law School in 1858 and graduating in 1859. He was admitted to the Suffolk County bar and practised in Boston for a few months, during which he

wrote for the local newspapers chiefly upon educational topics. In 1860 he took up his residence in New York City where he remained for two years engaging in literary and journalistic work both there and in Washington, under the pseudonym "Schuyler Conway." In 1862 he returned to Boston and resumed the practise of law. He was early retained on behalf of the Catholic Church in important litigation and his intimacy with the Canon law, to the study of which his previous classical training had directed him, attracted the attention of Bishop Williams of Boston, whose legal adviser he became. For many years he was practically standing counsel to the Catholic Church in Massachusetts and the neighboring states, not only in actual litigation but in numerous questions of a semi-political character involving her constitutional rights and privileges. His handling of matters of this latter nature was particularly successful. He had been instrumental in founding the Home for Destitute Catholic Children, whose fathers had been killed in the Civil War, and thereafter became closely associated with all charitable projects in Boston, in respect to which his kindness "regarded neither race, nor color, nor creed." In 1875 he was appointed chairman of the State Board of Health, Lunacy, and Charity, serving as such for four years and when the legislature in 1879 reorganized the administration of public charities, giving general supervision of the whole system to the Board, he continued a member, devoting much of his time to its work till his retirement in 1907. He took a leading part in the controversy between the Board and Gov. Benjamin F. Butler in 1883. The publication of the correspondence between Donnelly, representing the Board, and the Governor had a marked influence in procuring the defeat of the latter on his seeking reëlection in November of that year. In 1884 he proposed and drafted a bill subjecting dipsomaniacs to the same restraint and treatment as lunatics. Adopted by the General Court in 1885, this act is said to have been the first legislation of its kind in either Europe or America (Conway and Cameron, *post,* pp. 22–23). In 1888 the General Court was the scene of an attempt to pass legislation adverse to separate schools, and Donnelly was retained to represent the Catholic community in opposition. The contest was bitter and prolonged, but he finally convinced the Committee on Education that the Catholics had a right to maintain their own schools under the Bill of Rights and the Constitution, thus winning a notable victory. He displayed marked ability in his conduct of the case, particularly in his handling of the constitutional arguments. He withdrew from active practise in 1900 owing to failing health. He died in Boston, survived by his widow, Amy Francis, daughter of James Collins of Providence, R. I., whom he had married on Sept. 21, 1893.

Politically a Democrat, Donnelly consistently declined public office. Tall, with an erect carriage, clean-cut features, and dignified demeanor, he was an attractive, impressive speaker; and his conscious earnestness invariably induced respect if not conviction. Professionally he stood in the front rank though his practise was circumscribed by the subjects of child welfare, charity, and the interests of the Catholic Church, which absorbed all his best energies. Shortly after his death a volume of his poems, collected by his widow, was printed for private distribution under the title, *Roma and other Poems* (1909). Although he possessed much literary talent, his published work was small.

[See Conrad Reno, *Memoirs of the Judiciary and the Bar of New England* (1901), II, 659; Appletons' *Ann. Cyc. for 1883*, pp. 517, 519; "Foreword" by Mabel Ward Cameron to *Roma and other Poems*; Katherine E. Conway and Mabel Ward Cameron, *Chas. Francis Donnelly, A Memoir, with an Account of the Hearings on a Bill for the Inspection of Private Schools in Mass. in 1888–89* (1909); obituaries in *Boston Post* and *Boston Herald*, Feb. 1, 1909.]   H. W. H. K.

DONNELLY, ELEANOR CECILIA (Sept. 6, 1838–Apr. 30, 1917), author, sixth child of Philip Carroll and Catharine (Gavin) Donnelly, was born in Philadelphia and died in West Chester, Pa. Her father, a physician, died soon after her birth, and her mother found it necessary to earn a livelihood for herself and her children. She personally attended to their education; "with solicitous assiduity she cultivated the talents with which [they] had been so richly endowed" (Walsh, *Records,* September 1917). Besides the training imposed by her mother, Eleanor had the benefit of such counsel in instruction as could be offered by her brother, Ignatius Donnelly [*q.v.*], and by her four sisters, all but one of whom were destined to become school-teachers. It was Ignatius who gave her most encouragement to write poetry. Her first publication, "A Little Girl's Hymn to the Blessed Virgin," appeared when she was nine years old. This was naturally a marvel in her community, and other writings followed. The Catholic clergy in particular valued her art; she was of a nature susceptible to religious influence; and very soon she was helping to edit the *Ave Maria*, an ecclesiastical magazine. She considered becoming a nun, and though she abandoned her inclinations in that direction she always, it seems, looked back upon her decision half regretfully. She was

"above and beyond all . . . Catholic—ultra Catholic" (*Ibid.*), giving nearly all her interest to the Church and its welfare, writing at one moment odes and sonnets to celebrate its festivals, and at another moment historical essays to interpret its progress. Her first book, *Out of Sweet Solitude* (1873), contains some Civil War verse which evidences a passion for social justice, but most of her subsequent books are limited to the mood dominant even in this—one of pious devotion. It was her practise to turn into verse the life of one saint after another, and as soon, apparently, as there were enough of them to group them together, dedicate them to a revered priest of her acquaintance, and publish them. During her seventy years of literary activity she published around fifty volumes, most of them religious poetry, but among them several biographies, and some fiction, all of which is negligible. One of the five Donnelly sisters married young and died soon afterward, but the other four remained spinsters, and, as they grew older, were more and more inseparable. Eleanor, the others were persuaded, was their unique and precious charge, a genius whom they should protect and cherish, one whose least word was to be treasured. They all died several years before her. Her last years were spent chiefly between two convents—St. Benedict's in Washington and Villa Maria in West Chester.

[Introduction by D. I. McDermott to *Poems, by Eleanor C. Donnelly* (1892); H. Walsh, "Eleanor C. Donnelly" in *America*, May 19, 1917, and in *Records of the Am. Catholic Hist. Soc. of Phila.*, Sept. and Dec. 1917, Mar. 1918; *Cath. World*, Mar. 1897; T. M. Schwertner, "Eleanor Donnelly," in *Cath. World*, June 1917; *Who's Who in America*, 1916–17; *Public Ledger* (Phila.), May 1, 1917; *Evening Star* (Washington), May 2, 1917.]   J. D. W.

DONNELLY, IGNATIUS (Nov. 3, 1831–Jan. 1, 1901), politician, reformer, the son of Philip Carroll Donnelly, an Irish physician, and his wife Catharine Frances Gavin, was born in Philadelphia. As a boy he attended the free schools of the Quaker City, and as a young man he read law in the office of Benjamin Harris Brewster, later attorney-general of the United States. A trip to the Northwest in the "boom" period of the fifties, however, led him to abandon his native city and the law to seek wealth through land speculation. With his bride, Katharine McCaffrey, and an abundance of ambition, he removed to Nininger, Minn., fancying himself the founder of a future metropolis (see his *Nininger City*, pamphlet, 1856), but the panic of 1857 killed his town and left him heavily burdened with debts. He turned his lots into wheat-fields, and making his home on the site of his first defeat, he ever thereafter considered himself a farmer. He possessed in exaggerated degree the talent of his race for public speaking, and was thus, inevitably perhaps, drawn into politics during the exciting campaigns that preceded the Civil War. He embraced Republicanism wholeheartedly, spoke effectively for it, and at the age of twenty-eight became lieutenant-governor of his state. It was an easy step to Congress, where he spent three terms, 1863–69, in the lower house. Here he supported the war and reconstruction policies of his party and worked so actively for land grants to railroads in Minnesota and the Northwest that he received a stinging public rebuke from Elihu B. Washburne [*q.v.*], then regarded as the "Watchdog of the Treasury." Donnelly replied in kind, and the quarrel that developed seriously damaged his reputation at home. Local party leaders, already disturbed by Donnelly's ambitions, prevented his return to Congress for a fourth term, and his career as a successful politician ended forever.

His career as a regular Republican also ended. Donnelly now contended that the time had come for men to turn their backs upon the old issues arising out of slavery and the war, in order to face the new issues brought forward by the industrial development of the country. Politics, as he saw it, would in the future be a struggle "between the few who seek to grasp all power and wealth, and the many who seek to preserve their rights as American citizens and freemen." He left the Republican party because it seemed to him eternally wedded to the interests of the few, and in so doing he also abjured its protective tariff and hard-money principles. He became successively Liberal Republican, Granger, and Greenbacker, proclaiming his views not only through his matchless oratory, but also through the columns of the *Anti-Monopolist*, an independent weekly newspaper which he edited from 1874 to 1879. He ran for office repeatedly, and as a member of the state Senate for five consecutive years (1874–78) he worked energetically, although usually unsuccessfully, for reform legislation. As a Greenback-Democrat he was defeated for Congress in 1878 by William D. Washburn [*q.v.*], brother of Elihu B. Washburne, and the contest which he brought before the House after the election was thrown out.

Donnelly now retired to his study to write. He was a great lover of books, had collected an excellent library, and had read more widely than most people would have guessed. In literature as in politics he made it his concern to espouse unusual and unproved theories. His first book, *Atlantis: The Antediluvian World* (1882), purported to demonstrate the truth of Plato's story of an Atlantic island, where, according to Donnelly, original civilization developed and from which it spread to the adjoining continents. His second, *Ragnarok: The Age of Fire and Gravel* (1883), attributed the deposits of clay, gravel, and silt on the earth's surface to contact in some bygone age with a mighty comet. His *magnum opus,* entitled *The Great Cryptogram* (1888), attempted to prove by an ingenious cipher that Francis Bacon wrote the works commonly attributed to Shakespeare. All his books attracted wide attention, and the royalties from the first two—the *Cryptogram* was a financial failure—together with the lecture engagements which, as a noted author, Donnelly was called upon to fill, brought the reformer practically the first comfortable and secure income he had ever known. He made a trip to Europe and came back the better fitted by his observations to play the rôle of "Sage of Nininger," in which his amazed Minnesota friends had decided to cast him. He wrote frequently for such magazines as the *North American Review,* and later he produced several more books, one of which, a novel called *Cæsar's Column; a Story of the Twentieth Century* (1891), invited comparison with Bellamy's *Looking Backward* and was comparable to it also in popularity.

Donnelly never succeeded, however, in retiring from politics for long. He ran for Congress in 1884, and in 1887 he appeared once more in the state legislature, this time as a Farmers' Alliance leader. He soon became president of the state Alliance, and he led it almost to a man into the Populist party, in the formation of which he had an active part. He presided frequently over Populist conventions and assemblies, whose resolutions, also, he was almost invariably called upon to draft. The ringing preamble of the Omaha platform of 1892 was entirely from Donnelly's pen. In this same year he ran for governor of Minnesota on the Populist ticket, but was decisively defeated. In 1896, although he supported Bryan, he was lukewarm as to the wisdom of fusion, and he soon came to regard it as a complete betrayal of the reform movement. Thereafter he figured prominently among the Middle-of-the-Road Populists, whose candidate for vice-president he was in the campaign of 1900, and whose views he proclaimed forcefully in a newspaper, the *Representative,* which he edited in his later years. He also served, less conspicuously than formerly, in the Minnesota state legislature. Survived by his second wife, Marian Hanson, whom he married Feb. 22, 1898, he died on the first day of the twentieth century.

Donnelly was a typical nineteenth-century reformer, advocating always reform only through the ballot-box, and reform measures which a few decades later seemed innocuous enough. In his day, however, these reforms were looked upon as thoroughly radical. He was denounced as a "visionary" and the very "prince of cranks." His disregard of the conventional extended beyond the realm of politics and literature to his personal habits and beliefs. Surrounded by bewhiskered Populists, he was as smooth-shaven as a monk. Born into the Catholic Church, he ever failed to embrace that faith, and in his declining years he lent a receptive ear to spiritualism. Left a widower in his sixties, he took to himself a bride of twenty-one. Nevertheless, in spite of his peculiarities he enjoyed great personal popularity. His unfailing wit and humor made him a favorite as an orator. Let it be noised about that Donnelly was to make a speech in the legislature, and the galleries would be packed. His hospitality was unbounded, and in his well-appointed home at Nininger he was the friendly host of many prominent visitors. He was beloved by his neighbors, and by them he was rarely deserted, even at the polls. As a husband and father he possessed those homely virtues which Americans have ever esteemed highly.

[The Donnelly Papers, including numerous MSS., letter-books, and scrap-books, are in the possession of the Minn. Hist. Soc., and are there available for use. E. W. Fish, *Donnelliana: an Appendix to "Cæsar's Column," Excerpts from the Wit, Wisdom, Poetry and Eloquence of Ignatius Donnelly* (1892), is about what its title would indicate. A preliminary survey of Donnelly's life has been made by J. D. Hicks, "The Political Career of Ignatius Donnelly," in the *Miss. Valley Hist. Rev.*, VIII (1921), 80–132, from which the foregoing summary was reviewed in *Minn. Hist. Bull.*, IV (1922), 157. See also list of biographical sketches in *Minn. Hist. Soc. Colls.*, XIV (1912), 182; R. S. Saby, "R. R. Legislation in Minn.," and H. A. Castle, "Reminiscences of Minn. Politics" in *Minn. Hist. Soc. Colls.*, vol. XV (1915); W. W. Folwell, *A Hist. of Minn.* (4 vols., 1921); obituaries in newspapers of Jan. 2, 1901. The quarrel with Washburne is covered in *Cong. Globe*, 40 Cong., 2 Sess.; pp. 2,355 ff.]   J.D.H.

DONOGHUE, JOHN (1853–July 1, 1903), sculptor, was born in Chicago of parents who had come from western Ireland. As a youth he was clerk in the Recorder's office until a change of administration forced him out. In 1875 he entered the Chicago Academy of Design where he won a scholarship with a bust of a Vestal virgin. After two years he was enabled to go to Paris where he studied under Jouffroy at the École des Beaux-Arts and in 1880 exhibited at the Salon a plaster bust, "Phaedra." The following year he returned to America. He held an exhibition in Horticultural Hall, Boston, and in that city he made his "Boxer," using as a model John L. Sul-

livan, whom he considerably idealized. After reaching Chicago he gained a certain fame from Oscar Wilde's praises, which were also instrumental in enabling him to return to Paris in 1882 or 1883. This time he was under Falguière. To the Salon of 1884 he sent a bronze bas-relief of a seraph, made in Rome. In Rome, likewise, he modeled his best-known work, "Young Sophokles leading the chorus of victory after the battle of Salamis" (1885), a statue suggested by his reading of Plumptre. Of classical statues produced by Americans, it is perhaps the most freshly inspired and pleasing. It was exhibited in the London Royal Academy in 1890. Shortly after the "Young Sophokles" came the "Hunting Nymph," exhibited at the Salon of 1887. To this time also belong some portraits and a statuette, "Hannibal." He returned to America again and to Boston where he did some portrait work. The public library there preserves two bronze busts by him: "Hugh O'Brien" (1888), and "J. B. O'Reilly" (1897). In the late eighties or early nineties he spent about two years in London, exhibiting at the Royal Academy in 1890, besides the "Young Sophokles," a bust of Mrs. Ronalds. He then again went to Rome where he modeled for the Chicago World's Fair a colossal figure called "The Spirit," inspired by Milton. It was so large that he used as a studio the baths of Diocletian. The statue never reached its destination, however. Half of it reached Brooklyn, when the sculptor's funds gave out; this half was finally destroyed and the part left in Rome disappeared. It is said that the Chicago Exposition officials had refused the statue for fear that winds from Lake Michigan might overturn it. It was one of Donoghue's major attempts and its fate was a grievous disappointment to him. He was, however, represented at the Chicago Exposition by the "Young Sophokles," the "Hunting Nymph," and "Kypris." The last-named had figured in the Salon of 1892. Donoghue worked for a time for New York architects in the ornamentation of buildings. The "St. Paul" of the Library of Congress and the "St. Louis of France" for the Appellate Court Building, New York, are due to him. Another recorded work is called "Egyptian Ibis." A second bitter disappointment came when his design for a McKinley memorial for Philadelphia was refused on account of expense.

As a sculptor Donoghue showed much promise though he never reached the first rank. He is now remembered chiefly for his "Young Sophokles." As a man he was tall and handsome, by nature reticent, generous to the point of frequently impoverishing himself, witty, and most winning of manner. Though naturally unaffected he is said to have developed certain eccentricities after meeting and admiring Wilde. Toward the end of his life he became interested in psychical subjects and even contemplated a book on "The New Religion." Worried and oppressed by disappointment and financial difficulties he shot himself. His body was found on the shores of Lake Whitney near New Haven.

[Letter from Mrs. J. J. Schwab, a personal acquaintance; Chas. de Kay in *Art Rev.*, Feb. 1887; W. Lewis Fraser in *Century Mag.*, Apr. 1894; J. C. McCord in *Brush and Pencil*, Aug. 1903; *Am. Art Annual*, 1903; *Illus. Cat. of the Paris Salon*, 1880, 1884, 1887, 1892; *Die Kunst für Alle*, Dec. 15, 1892; Algernon Graves, *The Royal Acad. of Arts* (1905); Lorado Taft, *The Hist. of Am. Sculpture* (1903); *Art World*, Jan. 1917; U. Thieme and F. Becker, *Allgemeines Lexikon der Bildenden Künstler* (1913); *New Haven Evening Leader*, July 2 and 6, 1903; *N. Y. Herald*, July 6, 1903.]

E.G.N.

D'OOGE, MARTIN LUTHER (July 17, 1839–Sept. 12, 1915), Greek scholar, was born at Zonnemaire in the Netherlands. His father, Leonard D'Ooge, was of Huguenot extraction and his mother, Johanna Quintus D'Ooge, came of a Dutch family whose men had for several generations followed the teaching profession. At an early age he came with his parents to Grand Rapids, Mich., where he prepared for college. After receiving the A.B. degree from the University of Michigan in 1862, he was for two years principal of the Ann Arbor High School, resigning that position in 1865 to enter Union Theological Seminary. While still a student at the seminary he accepted in 1867 a call to the University of Michigan as assistant professor of ancient languages. When Prof. Boise resigned his chair in 1868, D'Oooge was made acting professor, and in 1870 professor of the Greek language and literature. He thereupon obtained a two years' leave of absence for study abroad, especially at Berlin and the University of Leipzig, and received his Ph.D. from the latter in 1872. Except for the year 1886–87, when he was on leave as director of the American School of Classical Studies at Athens, and a semester in 1905, when he attended as delegate the International Archæological Congress which met in Greece, he taught continuously at the University of Michigan until his retirement in 1912. In addition to the heavy teaching schedule which he always carried, he served as dean of the College of Literature, Science, and the Arts from 1889 to 1897. The advanced students, to whom he gave his time freely, found him exacting in his standards; he insisted on wide reading and complete mastery of subject matter. While the orators, Homer, and Sophocles appealed to him most strongly, he was keenly interested in every phase of ancient life and thought. In his classroom his pupils felt the great personal charm, vivacity, and unfailing friendliness which made him a popular and well-loved figure in university life. To them, as to his colleagues, his home was always open in the gracious hospitality with which he and Mrs. D'Ooge (*née* Mary Worcester of Auburndale, Mass., whom he married July 31, 1873) delighted to welcome friends of literary and artistic tastes.

His university duties, to which he devoted himself with energy and enthusiastic zeal, left him little time for writing. Besides contributing occasional articles to the *Nation* and various classical journals, he edited *The Oration of Demosthenes on the Crown* in 1875, and the *Antigone* of Sophocles in 1884. His chief work, however, upon which he spent much study and travel, is the scholarly volume *The Acropolis of Athens* (1908). After his retirement he occupied himself with European travel, which always called him insistently, and the translation of the *Arithmetic* of Nicomachus of Gerasa. This was published by his friends and colleagues, Professors Robbins and Karpinski, in 1926 (*Nicomachus of Gerasa, Introduction to Arithmetic*; translated by M. L. D'Ooge with Studies in Greek Arithmetic, by Frank Egleston Robbins and Louis Charles Karpinski. University of Michigan Studies, Humanistic Series, vol. XVI, 1926).

He had only fine scorn for the type of scholar who seeks publicity and preferment. The presidency of the American Philological Association (1883–84) and the other honors which came to him he received with his usual modesty as tributes to his department rather than to himself. He died in Ann Arbor, survived by Mrs. D'Ooge and by his brother, Prof. Benjamin Leonard D'Ooge, the well-known Latinist.

[B. A. Hinsdale and I. N. Demmon, *Hist. of the Univ. of Mich.* (1906); obituary notice by Campbell Bonner in *Classical Philology*, X (1915), 488; appreciation by F. W. Kelsey in *Nation*, Sept. 30, 1915; *Detroit News* and *Detroit Free Press*, Sept. 13, 1915.]

J.G.W.

DOOLITTLE, AMOS (May 18, 1754–Jan. 30, 1832), engraver, was born in Cheshire, Conn., the son of Ambrose and Martha (Munson) Doolittle, being next to the eldest in a family of thirteen. From a craftsman in his native town he began to learn the trade of silversmith, but for some reason turned his attention to engraving on copper. In this he seems to have been his own instructor. While still a young man he left Cheshire, and made his home in New Haven, where he lived the rest of his life. He was one of a number of citizens who memorialized the General Assembly "to construct them a district military company by the name of the Governor's

Second Company of Guards," and thus he became a charter member of that famous organization which is known to-day as the Governor's Foot Guards. When, in the spring of 1775, news came of the battle of Lexington, Doolittle was one of those who under Capt. Benedict Arnold marched to Cambridge. Their services, however, were not needed there at the moment, and they soon returned to New Haven. Doolittle was a practical patriot, and made the expedition serve him to good purpose, for in December of the same year he was advertising in the *Connecticut Journal* four copper plates depicting "the battle of Lexington, Concord," etc., from paintings made by Ralph Earle [*q.v.*]. As representations of what actually took place they can hardly be regarded as of much value. It has been said of them that they are "not to be held amenable to any canons of art, except those formulated and adopted by the artist of his own sweet will" (Andrews, *post*, p. 13). He was an indefatigable worker, turning out from his little shop on the college square a great variety of plates. He seems not to have depended entirely upon the burin for his livelihood, for advertisements in the local papers inform us that he dealt in varnishing, enameling, etc., and that he made silver and metal eagles, and one of his own prints tells us that he had a rolling press. His work as an engraver shows a wide variety of subjects. He furnished numerous portraits and illustrations for books, engraved music, money, and diplomas, and made a number of bookplates. He is said to have assisted Abel Buell [*q.v.*] in engraving the latter's wall map of the territories of the United States according to the Peace of 1783, and he engraved the two maps included in Jedidiah Morse's *Geography Made Easy* (1784). One of Doolittle's principal works, which has received high commendation (Charles Henry Hart, *Catalogue of the Engraved Portraits of Washington*, Grolier Club Publications No. 42, 1904), is his "Display of the United States of America," in which Washington is the central figure surrounded by the coats of arms of the states. There are several variations of this plate. It was followed by a "New Display," in which John Adams was the central figure, and yet again by another "New Display," which carried the portrait of Jefferson. Doolittle was twice married. Regarding his first wife information is lacking, save that her first name was Sally, and that she died Jan. 29, 1797, in her thirty-eighth year (*Connecticut Journal*, Feb. 1, 1797). His second wife was Phebe Tuttle, whom he married on Nov. 8, 1797, and who died in 1825. He died in New Haven and was buried in Grove Street Cemetery.

[Wm. F. Doolittle, *The Doolittle Family in America*, pt. III (1903), pp. 239 ff.; Wm. A. Beardsley, "An Old New Haven Engraver and his Work," published in *Papers of the New Haven Colony Hist. Soc.*, VIII (1914), 132–51, and separately in pamphlet form, with a list (incomplete) of Doolittle's engravings appended; Wm. L. Andrews, *Fragments of Am. Hist. Illustrated Solely by the Works of Those of our own Engravers who Flourished in the XVIIIth Century* (1898); E. G. Porter, *Four Drawings of the Engagement at Lexington and Concord Reproduced from Doolittle's Original Copperplate Engravings with an Explanatory Text* (1883); *Columbian Weekly Register* (New Haven), Feb. 4, 1832. Date of death from tombstone.] W.A.B.

DOOLITTLE, CHARLES LEANDER (Nov. 12, 1843–Mar. 3, 1919), astronomer, was born in Ontario, Ind., the son of Charles and Celia Doolittle. He received his training in astronomy from Prof. J. C. Watson at the University of Michigan. His college course was delayed by his enlistment during the Civil War and later interrupted by service with the United States Northern Boundary Commission along with Lewis Boss, who was in charge of the astronomical observations. Doolittle graduated, however, with the degree C.E., in 1874. Appointed professor of mathematics and astronomy at Lehigh soon after graduation, he remained there until 1895, when he accepted a similar position at the University of Pennsylvania. In 1896 the departments were separated and he became Flower Professor of Astronomy and first director of the Flower Observatory. Here he remained until his retirement in 1912.

Professionally, Doolittle is known chiefly for his researches on the variation of latitude. His observations were begun, before Chandler's investigations of this phenomenon, with a Zenith Telescope which had been discarded by the United States Coast and Geodetic Survey and purchased by Lehigh University for the instruction of engineering classes. The heavy teaching schedule which he was carrying and the small instrumental equipment of the Sayre Observatory set sharp limits to a research program. Ambition, perseverance, and painstaking care, however, achieved results of permanent scientific value even under these conditions. He concluded from his early observations that he had evidence of a variation of latitude. Later, at the Flower Observatory, he came to the conclusion that such a variation could be isolated from sources of systematic error only by making observations under a variety of instrumental conditions. He procured, therefore, a Reflex Zenith Tube. With this instrument and with the Zenith Telescope he continued for many years to make nearly simultaneous observations. The evidence still persisted and the whole series of observations proved a contribution of the highest value in unraveling the tangled mass of evidence. He was the author of: *A Treatise on Practical Astronomy as Applied to Geodesy and Navigation* (1885); *Results of Observations with the Zenith Telescope of the Sayre Observatory from Jan. 19, 1894, to Aug. 19, 1895* (1901); and "Results of Observations with the Wharton Reflex Zenith Tube and the Zenith Telescope of the Flower Astronomical Observatory," in *Publications of the University of Pennsylvania, Astronomical Series* (vol. III, pt. 1, 1908). He was a member of the American Philosophical Society, a Fellow of the American Association for the Advancement of Science, and from 1899 to 1912 treasurer of the American Astronomical Society.

His first wife, whom he married on Sept. 18, 1866, and who died during his first year at Bethlehem, was Martha Cloyes Farrand, also of Ontario, Ind. On May 5, 1882, he married Helen Eugenia Wolle of Bethlehem. His son Eric [*q.v.*] succeeded him as director of the Flower Observatory.

[Obituary by R. H. Tucker in *Pubs. Astronomical Soc. of the Pacific*, XXXI (1919), 103–04; *Who's Who in America*, 1918–19; *Observatory*, XLII, 219–20; *Nature* (London), CIII (1919), 69; *Phila. Press* and *Public Ledger* (Phila.), Mar. 4, 1919.]   R.S.D.

DOOLITTLE, ERIC (July 26, 1869–Sept. 21, 1920), astronomer, was born in Ontario, Ind. Practically his whole life was spent in the atmosphere of an astronomical observatory, for his father, Charles Leander Doolittle [*q.v.*], was appointed director of the Sayre Observatory of Lehigh University in 1875 and Eric became his father's assistant and his successor as director of the Flower Observatory of the University of Pennsylvania. He lost his mother, Martha Cloyes (Farrand) Doolittle, the year the family moved to Bethlehem. He was educated in the public schools of Bethlehem and at the Preparatory School of Lehigh University and graduated from the University in 1891 with the degree of C.E. After spending one year as teacher in the Preparatory School, one as instructor of mathematics in Lehigh University, and two in a similar position in the University of Iowa, he went to the University of Chicago for graduate work in astronomy. He had already advanced himself in mathematics by private study and during his year of graduate work he showed great promise. At the suggestion of his professor, the thesis which he had prepared as a requirement for the master's degree was withheld as sufficiently meritorious for a doctor's thesis. He did not complete the requirements for a doctor's degree, however. Called to the University of Pennsylvania in 1896 as instructor in astronomy, he was placed by his father in charge of

the new eighteen-inch telescope, made by Brashear, and especially suitable, by reason of its great focal length, to micrometric work. He at once threw himself into the observation of double stars. After working all night he often caught but a short nap before it was time to start for his classes at the University, five miles away. He never slighted his class work and was an enthusiastic and inspiring teacher. He accumulated and published a great mass of double-star observations (see *Publications of the University of Pennsylvania, Astronomical Series,* vols. I–IV, 1901–23), and his authority in this field was so well recognized that Burnham of Yerkes Observatory turned over to him the manuscript notes for the extension of the *General Catalogue of Double Stars.* Thenceforth Doolittle entered on cards, without any clerical assistance, all published observations of double stars. He also found time to finish an extensive work of computation, *The Secular Variations of the Elements of the Orbits of the Four Inner Planets* (1912), and to write many popular articles on astronomy.

During the World War, seeking for the most useful thing he could do, he spent much time studying to be a wireless operator until he was called upon to organize the United States Shipping Board Navigation School at Philadelphia. In attempting to teach large numbers of men and to attend to all the details of organization and administration, he broke down. Although he later returned to his regular duties, he never fully recovered. With a strong tendency to overwork and with an unusual ability to use his time profitably, it is a pity that he was given so much to do without liberal clerical and financial assistance. His favorite diversion was reading Dickens. He was a man of extreme modesty and self-effacement. He had a great gift for friendship, firmly based on complete unselfishness and consideration. The appreciations published after his death all show how much his friends loved him. In 1902 he married Sara Bitler Halliwell of Bethlehem. She was in full sympathy with his ideals and willingly endured the great sacrifices she had to make.

[R. G. Aitken in *Pubs. Astronomical Soc. of the Pacific,* XXXII (1920), 322–24; T. J. J. See in *Astronomische Nachrichten,* CCXII, 183–84; S. G. Barton, *Popular Astronomy,* Nov. 1920 and *Science,* Oct. 22, 1920; *Monthly Notices of the Royal Astronomical Soc.* (London), LXXXI (1921), 255–56.]   R.S.D.

DOOLITTLE, JAMES ROOD (Jan. 3, 1815–July 27, 1897), lawyer, statesman, was born in Hampton Township, Washington County, N. Y., the eldest child of Reuben Doolittle of Colonial and English stock and Sarah (Rood) Doolittle. Reared on a farm in western New York, he obtained his preliminary education in the rural school. He graduated from Geneva (now Hobart) College in 1834. In 1837 he was admitted to the bar in Rochester and the same year he married Mary L. Cutting. He began to practise in Rochester, but four years later settled at Warsaw, N. Y., where from 1847 to 1850 he was district attorney of Wyoming County. He also took a prominent part in politics as a Democrat. In 1844 he campaigned extensively for Polk, and at the New York state convention of 1847 he wrote the "corner-stone resolution" in which "the democracy of New York . . . declare . . . their uncompromising hostility to the extension of slavery into territory now free, or which may be hereafter acquired by any action of the government of the United States." This became the essential plank in the Free-Soil platform of 1848 and, in modified phraseology, in the Republican platform of 1856. Doolittle remained a leader of the Barnburner faction of the Democratic party until 1856, except that he supported Van Buren in 1848. Meanwhile (1851) he settled in Racine, Wis., and two years later was elected judge of the first judicial circuit. In 1856 he identified himself with the Republican party.

He was elected, as a Republican, to the United States Senate in 1857 and served till Mar. 4, 1869. His career in politics divides sharply into two periods—before the death of Lincoln and after that event. Although a "state-rights" Republican, prominent in the movement which resulted in Wisconsin's nullification of the Fugitive-Slave Law, he became as senator one of the stanchest and ablest proponents of the doctrine of no compromise with the slave states. Like Carl Schurz, Byron Paine, and other Wisconsin Republicans, he was determined to carry out the party platform, restricting slavery rigorously within the states where it existed under state law. This he believed to be the constitutional method. He was a close personal friend and adviser of Lincoln. Early in 1864 he addressed at Springfield, Ill., a great mass-meeting called to decide whether or not Lincoln must be superseded. In his first dozen words: "I believe in God Almighty! *Under Him I believe in Abraham Lincoln,*" Doolittle aroused such a demonstration for Lincoln that the President's opponents beat a hasty retreat. Johnson's struggle with Congress over reconstruction brought Doolittle into sharp collision with the radical Republicans, who, as he believed, were violating the Constitution in keeping states out of the Union. He ably supported the President, arguing that Johnson was merely carrying into execution Lincoln's policies. On the impeachment question he voted

for acquittal; in the presidential canvass of 1868 he supported Seymour against Grant. The Wisconsin legislature, in 1867, called for Doolittle's resignation, which he refused. In 1869 he retired to make his home in Racine, but opened a law office in Chicago where he practised law extensively almost to the day of his death at the age of eighty-two.

Doolittle was an outstanding personality, physically and mentally. His presence on any platform guaranteed an interested audience. His voice was remarkably fine and so powerful that he could address 20,000 persons with perfect success. He was accounted a great lawyer, was a wide reader and popular lecturer on Bible subjects. He was in great demand for speeches on special occasions and on diverse social, religious, and economic themes. His so-called "betrayal" of the Republican party ended his political career. As a Democrat he was defeated for governor of Wisconsin in 1871, for congressman from his congressional district twice, and once for judge of his judicial circuit. His "Johnsonizing" was bitterly resented, but leading Republicans who had known him long pronounced his motives pure. His nature was strongly emotional and somewhat sentimental. He tended to "fundamentalism" in religion, lecturing on the fulfilment of Bible prophecies. The Constitution he construed with Jeffersonian strictness. In practical politics he was keen, shrewd, masterful, winning the encomium of so skilled a political tactician as E. W. (Boss) Keyes. His personality radiated good will and compelled attention.

[There is a biography in *The Doolittle Family in America*, pt. VII (1908), comp. by Wm. F. Doolittle, pp. 653–710. Collections of pamphlets and clippings; also several hundred letters, manuscript speeches, etc., are in State Hist. Lib., Madison, Wis. See also D. Mowry, "Vice-President Johnson and Senator Doolittle," in *Pubs. Southern Hist. Asso.*, vol. IX, and "Doolittle Correspondence" in the same, vols. IX–XI (1905–07); *Biog. Dir. of the Am. Cong.* (1928); obituary in *Chicago Tribune*, July 28, 1897.]   J. S—r.

DORCHESTER, DANIEL (Mar. 11, 1827– Mar. 13, 1907), Methodist clergyman, superintendent of United States Indian schools, was a writer and preacher of wide influence, an able leader in temperance reform and other movements for social betterment, and the leading religious statistician of his time. He was of pure New England stock, a descendant of Elder Brewster. He was born in Duxbury, Mass., the son of the Rev. Daniel Dorchester, a Methodist clergyman, and his wife Mary Otis. He was educated at Norwich Academy (now the Free Academy) and Wesleyan University, leaving the latter in his junior year, 1847, on account of ill health. Wesleyan granted him the degrees of A.M. in 1856 and D.D. in 1874. After holding various charges in the Providence (now Southern New England) Conference he was in 1855 at the age of twenty-eight elected to the state Senate from Mystic, Conn. Here he served with distinction, being chairman of the Committee on Idiocy, the preparation of its report leading to permanent sociological interest. In 1858 he entered the New England Conference in which he held ten pastorates and served three terms as presiding elder. In 1882 he was elected to the Massachusetts legislature from Natick, where he was chairman of the Constitutional Amendment Committee, at the same time serving as president of the Non-Partisan Temperance League. In 1884 and in 1888 he was a member of the General Conference of the Methodist Church. On Dec. 5, 1889, he was appointed by President Harrison superintendent of Indian Schools of the United States, an office which he held for some four years, traveling over 96,000 miles and visiting 105 reservations. He was instrumental in having government appropriations for sectarian Indian schools withdrawn and increased emphasis placed on industrial education, working in this and other matters in close cooperation with Archbishop Ireland [q.v.]. The reports of his superintendency are published in the reports of the Department of the Interior.

While he was an administrator of marked ability and a preacher of great power, it was with his pen that he exerted his greatest influence. His first book, one that revealed his ability to use statistics, was his *Report of the Commissioners on Idiocy* (1856). His *Problem of Religious Progress* (1881) was a helpful and timely book. But probably his best-known and most influential book is his *History of Christianity in the United States* (1888), a work of immense industry, thoroughness, and impartiality. Other works are: *Concessions of Liberalists to Orthodoxy* (1878); *The Liquor Problem in all Ages* (1884); *The Indictment of the Liquor Traffic* (1885); *The Why of Methodism* (1887); *Romanism versus the Public School System* (1888); *Christianity Vindicated by its Enemies* (1896). In addition he published many sermons and addresses and wrote much for the magazines and reviews.

Dorchester was a tall man of imposing presence, with a winning countenance. His voice was distinct and far-reaching and his manner in the conduct of public services was dignified. On Apr. 12, 1850, he married Mary Payson Davis of Dudley, Mass., who died in 1874. Of this marriage there were seven children, five of whom survived their father. On Oct. 12, 1875, he married Merial A. Whipple of North Charlestown, N. H., who died Apr. 1, 1895.

[*Who's Who in America*, 1906–07; *Zion's Herald*, Mar. 20, 1907; *Christian Advocate*, Mar. 21, 1907; *Minutes of the New England Conference*, 1907; *Boston Herald*, Mar. 13, and *Boston Post*, Mar. 14, 1907; information as to certain facts from Dorchester's son.]

F.T.P.

DOREMUS, ROBERT OGDEN (Jan. 11, 1824–Mar. 22, 1906), chemist, inventor, was born in New York City, the son of Thomas Cornelius and Sarah Platt (Haines) Doremus [q.v.]. He was educated at Columbia College, where he graduated in 1842, and at the University of the City of New York, where he received the degree of M.D. in 1851. He was the first private pupil of John W. Draper [q.v.] and his assistant for seven years, and personally assisted Draper in taking the first photograph ever made of the human face. Before the invention of the dynamo, he perfected for demonstration an arc-light, producing the current for it with a huge battery of Bunsen cells. One unit of these cells is still preserved in the Museum of the Department of Chemistry of the College of the City of New York. In cooperation with Tessie du Motay he perfected the latter's processes for the generation of oxygen and its use in increasing the luminosity of a coal-gas flame. Tradition has it that several blocks of streets in the Twenty-third St. region of New York City were really piped for oxygen transmission and the improved gaslights installed along the lines of the oxygen pipes. In 1848, in association with Charles Townsend Harris [q.v.], Doremus organized a laboratory for investigation and instruction in analytical chemistry, where he lectured to the students of the New York College of Pharmacy. He was elected professor of chemistry at this institution in 1849. In the following year he was prominent among the founders of the New York Medical College. At his own expense, he equipped for it one of the first analytical laboratories connected with any medical college in the United States. He organized a similar laboratory for the Long Island Hospital Medical College in 1859.

Elected professor of natural history in the New York Free Academy (subsequently called the College of the City of New York) in 1852, with the exception of a trip abroad in 1862–64, he remained actively connected with that institution as professor of chemistry and physics and vice-president until his retirement as professor emeritus in 1903.

The general laboratories in the old Free Academy building on Twenty-third St. were among the first college laboratories and were excellent in design and equipment. There Doremus, an impressive personality and inspiring lecturer, awakened in his audiences and pupils an interest in science unusual at that time. His lectures were noted for their scope and vivid demonstrations. Though handicapped by physical deformity, he was a skilful manipulator. The apparatus, often designed by himself, which he used in his classroom and public lectures, was unique in its nature and size. Pieces of it still retained at the City College are so novel as to be really "Museum" specimens. Many of his experiments remain vivid in the minds of his former pupils; his demonstrations of heat reflection, magnetic attraction, heat of hydration of lime, weight of gases, the then entirely novel electric light, primary batteries, oxidation of iron, and dozens of others, were carried through on so large and vivid a scale that one never forgot the phenomenon. He was a dominating figure on the faculty of the college, and his lectures and other outside activities were instrumental in making the college known and in bringing to the public a knowledge of the influence of science on everyday life. He was a prominent member of the Medical Advisory Commission which established the present New York City Department of Health. He greatly influenced medical jurisprudence with his expert investigations in toxicology, and in 1862 he was appointed professor of chemistry, toxicology, and medical jurisprudence in Bellevue Hospital Medical College. Through his efforts, the famous nerve specialist, Brown-Sequard, came to America to lecture at that institution.

In 1862 Doremus made an important visit to Paris at the request of Emperor Napoleon III, spending two years there in perfecting and introducing a compressed granulated gunpowder for firearms. The cartridge which he patented dispensed with the serge envelope previously used in muzzle-loading cannon and thus avoided the necessity of sponging after firing. This invention was adopted by the governments of the United States and France, and was employed in the Civil and Franco-Prussian wars, besides being used extensively in blasting. In 1862, also, he prepared apparatus for generating chlorine gas between decks for use on the steamer which arrived in New York in that year with an epidemic of cholera on board. The process was again used against cholera in 1875 in the hospital wards of New York. This was the first use of chlorine as a disinfectant on so large a scale. He patented several methods of extinguishing fires by chemical action which resulted in the establishment of several chemical industries needed to make the materials. Another important contribution was the preservation of "Cleopatra's Needle" through the use of melted paraffin forced into the porous stone.

Doremus was prominent in social circles and an ardent lover of good music. He was one of the founders of the Philharmonic Society and the first amateur to be made its president. This was the only American orchestra of its kind at that time. He was instrumental in bringing Adelina Patti, Christine Nilsson, and Ole Bull to the United States, and in advancing their public and private performances. Ole Bull was a close personal friend of his, and Doremus took great pride in the possession of a fine watch presented to him by the eminent violinist. He was a Fellow of the Academy of Science of New York, and the American Geographical Society. His wife was Estelle E. Skidmore, daughter of Capt. Hubbard Skidmore.

[Who's Who in America, 1906–07; City College Quart., Dec. 1906; College Mercury (C. C. N. Y.), Apr. 1906; C. F. Chandler in Science, Mar. 30, and Sci. American, Mar. 31, 1906; Medico-Legal Jour., June 1906; N. Y. Times, N. Y. Tribune, Mar. 23, 1906.]

H.R.M.

DOREMUS, SARAH PLATT HAINES (Aug. 3, 1802–Jan. 29, 1877), social worker, one of the daughters of Elias and Mary (Ogden) Haines, was born at Whitehall and South Sts., near Battery Park, New York City. She was a descendant of Robert Ogden of New Jersey. Her brother, Daniel Haines, was twice elected governor of New Jersey (1843 and 1847), and served as a judge on the supreme court bench of that state from 1852 to 1866. Her father was a New York merchant. Sarah Platt Haines had the educational advantages open to girls in the families of well-to-do New Yorkers at the beginning of the nineteenth century. At nineteen she was married to Thomas C. Doremus of New York. Early in life she became intensely interested in various forms of religious and humane effort, and even the demands of bringing up her family of nine children could not keep her from devoting a large measure of her time and strength to such causes. At a time when women rarely assumed leadership in public movements, she was active in a group of women who secured aid for the Greek revolutionists. This was only the first of a series of humanitarian services, continuing for half a century. Throughout her long life she was notable for unusual energy and persistence in pursuing her ends, as well as for serenity and cheerfulness in disposition. She was heartily seconded in her efforts by her husband, who gave liberally of his personal means as the state of his fortune permitted. Although a member of the Reformed Church in New York, she was chiefly interested in work conducted under undenominational or interdenominational auspices. In at least one notable instance—the Baptist Mission of Grand Ligne in Canada, under Madame Feller—she took an active part in promoting an enterprise controlled by a religious body with which she was not affiliated. Her interest in that work began as early as 1835 and continued for many years. In the decade of the forties the neglected condition of the inmates of New York City prisons appealed to her with especial force. Beginning with the effort to maintain religious services in the city prisons, with which she cooperated, she was led to see the importance of aiding discharged convicts and, with a number of other New York women, organized a home that offered temporary shelter to discharged women prisoners. This was later developed into the Isaac T. Hopper Home. During the last ten years of her life, Mrs. Doremus was president of the association that conducted this refuge. Among pioneer efforts to help the women among New York's worthy poor were the House and School of Industry (1850) and the Nursery and Child's Hospital (1854); with both of these she was associated from the first. In 1855, when Dr. J. Marion Sims was seeking support for a hospital to treat the maladies peculiar to women, it was Sarah Platt Doremus who brought about the incorporation of the Woman's Hospital in the State of New York by the legislature and solicited the aid of wealthy women in starting the institution. She was president of its women's supervisory board at the time of her death. Throughout the Civil War she ministered to the sick and wounded of both armies as occasion arose. The famine sufferers in Ireland in 1869 also enjoyed her bounty. Long identified with the promotion of American foreign missions, she was one of the founders, in 1860, of the Woman's Union Missionary Society, through which the Protestant women of America sought to elevate the condition of their sisters in non-Christian lands. Judged by twentieth-century standards of resources and budget, perhaps most of the organizations through which she labored were relatively feeble and ill-equipped, but they were persistent and held their ground, almost without exception. The importance of her leadership lay very largely in her successful attempt to enlist other women of like environment in organized philanthropic effort. In the second and third quarters of the nineteenth century her achievement in that line of effort was outstanding, if not unique. She died as the result of a fall in January 1877. Her only son was Robert Ogden Doremus [q.v.], the distinguished chemist.

[*The Ogden Family in America,* Elizabethtown Branch (1907), comp. by Wm. Ogden Wheeler; the *Missionary Link,* Mar. 1877; annual reports of the Women's Prison Association and the Woman's Hospital; J. Marion Sims, *The Story of My Life* (1884); *N. Y. Times,* Jan. 30, 1877.]   W.B.S.

DORGAN, THOMAS ALOYSIUS (Apr. 29, 1877–May 2, 1929), cartoonist, sports-writer, son of Thomas and Anna (Tobin) Dorgan, was born in the tenement district "south of the slot" in San Francisco, Cal. When he was ten years old his right hand was seriously injured, leaving him only the thumb and first knuckle of his forefinger, unfitting him for manual labor, and permanently affecting his social and psychic attitude. At the age of fourteen he left public school and obtained his first newspaper job in the art department of the San Francisco *Bulletin*. Although untutored in drawing, he soon began to produce stinging cartoons of local events and personalities, which resulted in his employment as the comic artist of the *Bulletin* until 1902. In that year his graphic talents recommended him to William Randolph Hearst who was seeking a political cartoonist of the Nast type to lampoon Tammany Hall in its conduct of New York City politics. Dorgan was called to New York to a place on the staff of the *New York Journal*. In the mayoralty contest of 1905 Hearst ran against George B. McClellan, who was supported by Charles F. Murphy, the Tammany boss. Dorgan's powerful cartoons, depicting Murphy in convict's stripes, nearly swung the election to Hearst, the Tammany candidate finally winning by the narrowest margin in the history of the office.

This was Dorgan's only venture into political cartooning. He turned to sports, became an authority on boxing, and was generally called upon to serve as unofficial referee in no-decision bouts. Thousands of dollars changed hands on his decisions, which were never disputed. Between 1900 and 1920 he was at the ringside of every championship boxing match, and dominated the sporting pages of the country with his syndicated sketches and comments signed "Tad"—the initials of his name. It is said of him that he could sketch from memory any important blow or exchange of blows in the major fights of Corbett, Fitzsimmons, Jeffries, and Johnson. George Bellows once declared that Dorgan was without a rival in reproducing the complex movements of prize-fighters in action.

When Dorgan was thirty years old he took over and developed the comic-strip characters of "Judge Rumhauser" and "Silk Hat Harry."

Despite their external resemblance to dogs they were in reality human beings—all too human, in fact, as Tad delineated their mortal frailties. Mild social satire, directed chiefly at lower middle-class pretenders and petty officials in their pitiful attempts to appear greater than they were, formed the basis of the "Judge Rummy" cartoons and the later series entitled "Indoor Sports." With a sardonic flick of his pen Tad could puncture hypocrisy and pretense, but the necessity of tickling a daily audience, without giving offense, hampered the exercise of his rapier gift. Personally, he was of a misanthropic, anti-social cast; had he taken the button off his foil he could have ranked just below Hogarth and Daumier as a graphic satirist.

His chief contribution to American life was his colorful use of slang, a large part of which he coined or put into circulation. "Yes, we have no bananas," "23, skidoo," "Officer, call a cop," and "Let him up, he's all cut," are a few of the meaningless but irresistible phrases of his invention. "The first hundred years are the hardest," has passed into proverbial usage, while dozens of his shorter expressions have become an integral part of common speech. "Apple-sauce" means obvious flattery; "chin-music" is idle chatter. A hat was a "skimmer," shoes were "dogs," and a stingy person a "nickel-nurser"—first to Tad and afterward to millions of his contemporaries. Probably his best-known simile was "As busy as a one-armed paper-hanger with the hives."

For the last ten years of his life a chronically bad heart kept Dorgan a house-ridden invalid. With a tremendous effort of will, yet with no apparent diminution of power, he continued to turn out his daily copy, keeping in touch with the sporting world by means of radio and the visits of faithful friends. He was two weeks ahead of his publication schedule when he died of heart-failure at his home in Great Neck, L. I.

[The files of current newspapers are the chief written sources of information; see especially F. P. Stockbridge in *N. Y. Times*, May 6, 1929; W. S. Farnsworth and Bill Corum in *N. Y. Evening Jour.*, May 3, 1929; Westbrook Pegler in *Chicago Tribune*, May 3, 1929; Damon Runyon in *N. Y. American*, May 3, 1929; Norman Klein in *N. Y. Evening Post*, May 4, 1929; editorials in *N. Y. Times* and *N. Y. Evening Post*, May 3, 1929; *N. Y. Herald-Tribune*, May 3, 1929. O. O. McIntyre published an article in Hearst's *Cosmopolitan Magazine*, Mar. 1927, repr. in *N. Y. Jour.*, May 3, 1929; *New Republic*, May 15, 1929. H. M. Robinson, "Tad For Short," in *Century Quart.*, fall issue, 1929.]

H. M. R.

DORION, MARIE (*c.* 1791–Sept. 3, 1850), wife of Pierre Dorion, the younger, interpreter of the Astoria land expedition (1811–12), was a member of the Iowa tribe. Her name appears in early Oregon and Washington records as Marie Aioe (sometimes L'Aguivoise, probably an early variant of the name Iowa). Her father-in-law, the elder Pierre Dorion, born of a prominent Quebec family before 1750, made his way to Cahokia, Ill., as early as 1780, lived for a time in St. Louis, and within a year or two established his permanent home with the Yanktons and married a woman of the tribe. In 1804, as an interpreter, he accompanied Lewis and Clark from the vicinity of the present Glasgow, Mo., to the James, where he was authorized to gather a delegation of Sioux chiefs and take them on a visit to Washington. The younger Pierre Dorion, a half-breed, for a time kept a trading-post for Pierre Chouteau among the Yanktons. He had a Yankton wife, Holy Rainbow, whom he seems to have abandoned about 1806 for the Iowa girl. In March 1811, he set out for St. Louis with Wilson Price Hunt's Astorians, taking with him his Iowa wife and two infant sons. On that long and terrible journey, much of the time afoot, Marie showed a patience and fortitude in enduring fatigue, hunger, and hardships unsurpassed by any of the men. On Dec. 30, near the present North Powder, Ore., she gave birth to a child, and in the forenoon of the next day overtook the party "looking as unconcerned as if nothing had happened to her" and ready to continue the march. The child, however, lived but eight days.

In the second summer following the arrival at Astoria, she and the two surviving children accompanied her husband with the John Reed hunting party to the Boise River country. About Jan. 10, 1814, the two sections of this party, widely separated, were attacked by Indians, and all the men were killed. Escaping with her children on a horse, she fled toward the Columbia River, and after nine days' travel, suffering intensely from cold and hunger, found refuge in a lonely spot in the Blue Mountains. Here she put up a rough hut of pine branches, killed her horse for food, and remained for fifty-seven days. After fifteen days' further travel, again enduring extreme privations, she and her children reached the friendly Walla Wallas. Later in the spring, on the Columbia, she met the last party of the returning Astorians and told them the tragic fate of her comrades.

She lived for a time at Fort Okanagon. About 1819 she married a trapper named Venier, of whom nothing seems to be known. In 1823 she formed a union with Jean Baptiste Toupin, interpreter for many years at Fort Walla Walla, who in 1841 took up land in the Willamette Valley, near the present Salem, and settled there. On July 19 of that year her union with Toupin was legalized by a Roman Catholic church ceremony; her two children by Toupin were legitimized, and her son Baptiste Dorion and daughter Marguerite Venier were "acknowledged" by Toupin. Through the publication of Irving's *Astoria* she became famous. Dr. Elijah White, who visited her in the winter of 1842–43, found her living in comfort and was "much impressed with her noble, commanding bearing." She died at her home. Her son Baptiste, who was employed as a guide by the naturalist J. K. Townsend in 1835 and as an interpreter by Dr. White in 1842–43, and who in 1848 was appointed a second lieutenant in the 1st Regiment of Oregon Riflemen, died in 1849. The other son is said to have been the Paul Dorion of Parkman's *The California and Oregon Trail,* though the identification is disputed.

[J. Neilson Barry, "Madame Dorion of the Astorians," in *Ore. Hist. Quart.,* Sept. 1929, and "The First Born on the Oregon Trail," *Ibid.,* June 1911; Washington Irving, *Astoria* (1836); Doane Robinson, "Our First Family," *S. Dak. Hist. Colls.,* vol. XIII (1926); A. J. Allen, *Ten Years in Ore.: Travels and Adventures of Dr. E. White and Lady* (1851); correspondence with C. H. Carey, author of *Hist. of Ore.* (1922). The episode of Marie Dorion's escape is related in Gabriel Franchère's *Relation d'un Voyage à la Côte du Nord-Ouest de l'Amérique Septentrionale* (Montreal, 1820; English translation, 1854); Ross Cox's *Adventures on the Columbia River* (1831); and Alexander Ross's *Adventures of the First Settlers on the Oregon or Columbia River* (1849). The narratives of Franchère and Ross are contained in *Early Western Travels,* ed. by R. G. Thwaites, vols. VI and VII (1904).]   W. J. G.

DORNIN, THOMAS ALOYSIUS (May 1, 1800–Apr. 22, 1874), naval officer, was the son of Bernard and Eliza Dornin. His father, an associate of the Irish patriots who were banished after the rebellion of 1798, settled for a time in Brooklyn, where he became one of the first booksellers to deal almost exclusively in Catholic publications. He soon, however, moved to Baltimore and continued his work there. Thomas Aloysius, born in Ireland, was educated at St. Mary's College, Baltimore, where he was enrolled in 1811 and later years, probably until his entry into the navy on May 2, 1815. Before he was promoted to lieutenant on Jan. 13, 1825, he had served in the Mediterranean on the *Java, Franklin,* and *Peacock,* and seen service under David Porter in the campaign against the West-Indian pirates. In 1826 he cruised in the Pacific on the *Brandywine* and then came home around the world on the *Vincennes.* In 1831–34 he was again in the Pacific on the *Falmouth.* From 1834 to 1836 he was in command of the receiving ship at Philadelphia and was then made commander of the store-ship *Relief,* which was to sail as a part of the Wilkes South Sea Exploring Expedition. He did not, apparently, sail in

her, and the ship herself was soon sent back as unsuitable. In 1837, Dornin married Mrs. James Thorburn (*née* Anne Moore Howison), and he was unemployed most of the time till 1841, when he was promoted to the rank of commander at the same time as was Farragut and sent to the Pacific to command the schooner *Shark.* He returned in charge of the *Dale.* In 1844 he began special work in ordnance while attached to the navy yard in Washington. This tour of duty ended in 1851 after he had served with Farragut for a year and a half on a board detailed to revise the ordnance regulations. In this year he was given command of the *Portsmouth* and sent to the Pacific coast of Mexico, his mission being to keep an eye on William Walker's expedition to Lower California. He hired a passenger steamship, the *Columbus,* and proceeded with it and the slow-sailing *Portsmouth* down the Mexican coast to Ensenada Bay, where Walker [*q.v.*] was encamped with 140 followers. Walker, however, departed with all his unwounded men as soon as Dornin arrived. The latter, before he left the vicinity, rescued some American citizens who had been imprisoned by the Mexicans at Mazatlan on suspicion of their being a reinforcement for Walker. After forcing the Mexican insurgents to allow American ships free access to Acapulco he went to Honolulu, where by his presence he supported the United States consul in blocking British and French moves in the Sandwich Islands. His journals of this cruise mention frequent target practises, an indication that Dornin was ahead of many of his brother officers in foreseeing the value of gunnery. He then returned to the United States (1855), received his promotion to captain's rank, and was put in command of the Norfolk Navy Yard, where he remained till 1859.

In that year he went to the Mediterranean as fleet captain but in 1860 was sent to the coast of Africa in command of the *San Jacinto.* Here during the next year, he seized several slavers, landed the slaves in Liberia, and sent the captured vessels into Norfolk, not knowing that the Civil War had already begun. When he was relieved by Capt. Wilkes in October 1861, he returned to the United States in the *Constellation,* and although retired as a commodore in 1862, commanded the naval station at Baltimore till the end of the war. He spent the next few years in charge of lighthouses in Chesapeake Bay, Pamlico Sound, and on the coast between. He passed the last years of his life in Fredericksburg, Va., and Savannah, Ga. He died in the latter city but was buried in Norfolk. Admiral Ammen (*The Old Navy and the New,* 1891, p.

27), says that in 1837 he "spoke with an Irish brogue, but had a bright, kindly face, and was indeed thoroughly an Irish gentleman."

[Dornin's *Brandywine* and *Portsmouth* journals, and his letters as captain of the *Portsmouth* are in the Navy Dept. Lib. The official record of his naval career can be secured from the Bureau of Navigation, Navy Dept. Most of it, and a fuller sketch of his life, is reprinted in L. R. Hamersly, *Records of Living Officers of the U. S. Navy and Marine Corps,* rev. ed. (1870), p. 65.]

W. B. N.

DORR, JULIA CAROLINE RIPLEY (Feb. 13, 1825–Jan. 18, 1913), author, was born in Charleston, S. C., and died in Rutland, Vt. Her father, William Young Ripley, born in Vermont, was living in Charleston as a merchant when he married Zulma DeLacy Thomas, who, with her parents, natives of France resident in the West Indies, had come to South Carolina to escape negro insurrection. Before Julia, the first child of this marriage, was two years old, her mother's frail health caused her family to remove to Vermont, but the invalid died on the day following her arrival. The child lived with her father here and there in New England and for a while in New York City. Her education was somewhat irregular although she acquired some proficiency in Latin. In 1837, William Ripley took up residence permanently in Rutland, where he operated a lucrative business in marble. There his daughter also spent, but for one interlude, the remainder of her tranquil, comfortable existence. After her marriage in 1847 to Seneca M. Dorr, she lived in Ghent, N. Y., but in 1857 she and her husband went back to Rutland, and her husband became associated in business with her father. From the age of twelve she had written verse, but none of it was made public until her husband soon after their marriage permitted specimens of it without her knowledge to be published in a magazine. Her first three books, *Farmingdale* (1854), *Lanmere* (1856), and *Sybil Huntington* (1869), all novels, were published under the name Caroline Thomas. Among her other novels were, *Expiation* (1873), and *In Kings' Houses* (1898), a story of England under Queen Anne. She wrote also in prose, *Bride and Bridegroom* (1873), a book of sentimental advice to young married couples, and three books of travel, *Bermuda* (1884), *"The Flower of England's Face"* (1895), and *A Cathedral Pilgrimage* (1896). She was most widely known for her verse, however, of which there were published certainly as many as ten volumes, beginning with *Poems* (1872), including *Poems . . . Complete Edition* (1892), and ending with *Last Poems* (1913). As a poet—deliberately shunning, it is said, all expressions which she could not with propriety read to children—she gave utterance in respec-

table but not highly distinguished or passionate phrases to the conventional wisdom of her time and place. Emerson valued her enough to include a poem by her in his anthology, *Parnassus* (1874), and Oliver Wendell Holmes and E. C. Stedman corresponded with her and counted her as a personal friend. She was devotedly attached to her husband, and his death in December 1884 was perhaps the one event of her life which she was not able to explain to herself in terms of what was normally intended.

[H. W. Ripley, *Geneal. of a Part of the Ripley Family* (1867); Hiram Carleton, *Geneal. and Family Hist. of Vt.,* II (1903), 587; W. H. Crockett, *Vermont the Green Mountain State,* vol. V (1921); J. T. Morse, *Life and Letters of O. W. Holmes* (2 vols., 1896); Laura Stedman and G. M. Gould, *Life and Letters of E. C. Stedman* (1910), II, 268, 346; E. C. Stedman and E. M. Hutchinson, *Lib. of Am. Lit.,* vol. XI (1890); *Who's Who in America,* 1912–13; Henry M. Alden in *Harper's Weekly,* Feb. 1, 1913; *Nation* (N. Y.), Jan. 23, 1913; *Rutland Herald,* and *Burlington Free Press,* Jan. 20, 1913.]

J. D. W.

DORR, THOMAS WILSON (Nov. 5, 1805–Dec. 27, 1854), politician and reformer, was born at Providence, R. I., the son of Sullivan and Lydia (Allen) Dorr. His father was a prosperous manufacturer and the family occupied a good social position. Thomas never married, but two of his sisters married prominent men and the son of one of them married the daughter of John Lothrop Motley. Dorr was therefore no plebeian when he led the cause of the unenfranchised classes. As a boy, he attended Phillips Exeter Academy. He graduated from Harvard in 1823, and then went to New York where he studied law under Chancellor Kent and Vice-Chancellor McCoun. He was admitted to the bar in 1827 and returned to Providence to practise. He began his political career as a representative in the Rhode Island Assembly in 1834.

In the half-century following the American Revolution efforts were made nearly everywhere to reap the fruits of that struggle in a wider extension of the limited franchise. In Rhode Island these attempts, made at intervals from 1797 to 1834, had invariably been met by the government with contemptuous obstruction. In 1834 a convention met at Providence to consider the matter again, and Dorr was a member of the committee which drew up an address to the people. All efforts at reform, however, were once more blocked by the legislature. By 1841 Rhode Island was almost the only state which had not adopted practical manhood suffrage. It was also the only state which had not adopted a written constitution, and the old colonial charter, under which the state was ruled, had been outgrown. Under that instrument the original grantees had had the sole right to decide who should have a voice in the management of public affairs, and they had decreed the possession of a moderate landed estate as a qualification for the franchise. By 1840 this obsolete requirement had disfranchised over half the adult male population, and about nineteen towns, having a total population of only 3,500 voters, returned over half the legislature, so that less than 1,800 voters could control the destinies of a state of 108,000 population. Moreover, no person who did not own real estate could bring suit for recovery of debt or obtain redress for personal injury unless a freeholder indorsed his writ.

The situation had become intolerable, and in 1840 the Rhode Island Suffrage Association was formed, and processions and popular meetings held. Dorr took a leading part in the agitation. The legislature refused to remedy such grievances as were in its power, and the old charter did not provide any means of summoning a constitutional convention. A "People's Party," therefore, was formed, which held a convention, adopted a constitution, and submitted it to a vote of the people. There were approximately 14,000 ballots cast in favor of it, and less than 100 cast against it. Of those in favor, over 4,900 were qualified voters so that the proposed constitution was formally approved not only by the majority of the males over twenty-one but, it was alleged, even by a majority of the legal voters. The constitutional question was a delicate one, but the existing government refused to consider any of these acts as legal. It had become sufficiently frightened, however, to call a constitutional convention itself and in turn submit a constitution to the people, though it is difficult to see how these actions were any more legal than those of the People's Party. The government's constitution was defeated by the narrow margin of 676 votes in 16,702. This was the point at which Dorr and his followers may be considered to have made their mistake. The new constitution, though not giving all they had asked, did give them most of the substance. Had they not defeated it they might have had a practical victory. Feeling, however, had become very bitter, and the Dorrites had already put their constitution into effect by electing an entire state ticket with Dorr as governor. In May 1842 there were two governments both claiming the allegiance of the people. The People's Party did not attempt to seize the state house or machinery of government. Both governors issued proclamations, and Gov. King appealed to Washington for federal aid. Dorr then went to Washington to plead his cause before the President. There he received no encouragement, and he returned to Rhode Island.

Meanwhile King had proclaimed martial law, offered $5,000 reward for the capture of Dorr, and made wholesale imprisonments of the latter's followers under the "Algerine Law." Some minor clashes occurred between the Dorrites and the state troops. Many of Dorr's followers deserted him and he voluntarily gave himself up at Providence. King and the old government had lost their heads completely and were ruthless in their revenge. Dorr was tried for treason before the state supreme court and sentenced to solitary confinement at hard labor for life. He was committed June 27, 1844. Public opinion finally made itself felt and in 1845 an Act of General Amnesty was passed and Dorr was released after twelve months of his term. In 1851 he was restored to civil rights, and in January 1854 the legislature passed an act annulling the verdict of the supreme court; but this, of course, the court decided was unconstitutional. Dorr's health had been broken, and after his release he lived in retirement until his death. His work, however, bore fruit, for the old oligarchy had yielded at last, and a third constitution had been drawn up and accepted by the people giving manhood suffrage with trifling qualifications. Dorr, though he showed bad judgment at times, was a genuine reformer and not a self-seeking politician.

[Dan King, *The Life and Times of Thomas Wilson Dorr* (1859), deals almost wholly with the suffrage episode, as does A. M. Mowry, *The Dorr War* (1901). There is much information to be found in "Burke's Report," *House Doc. No. 546*, 28 Cong., 1 Sess. See also *Might and Right by a Rhode Islander* (1844), and Wm. Goodell, *The Rights and Wrongs of R. I.* (1842); sketch by Jos. Palmer, in the *Boston Daily Advertiser*, July 18, 1855, reprinted in Palmer's *Necrology of Alumni of Harvard Coll.* (1864).]   J. T. A.

DORRELL, WILLIAM (Mar. 15, 1752–Aug. 28, 1846), founder of the Dorrellites, a fanatical sect which flourished in Franklin County, Mass., and spread over into Vermont, was born in Yorkshire, England. Perhaps owing to the fact that he himself could neither read nor write, his name appears not only as Dorrell, but as Dorrel, Dorril, Dorriel, and Dorral, the last being the spelling in the record of his intended marriage. As a youth he joined the British army, served through three campaigns in Ireland, and came to America with Gen. Burgoyne. After the latter's surrender in 1777, he was one of those who disappeared from the army and made their home in this country. He lived in Petersham, Mass., Warwick, Northfield, and finally in Leyden. In 1779 he married Molla Chase, daughter of Henry and Abigail Chase of Petersham, the marriage intention being filed Nov. 23 (*Vital Records of Petersham, Mass.,* 1904, p. 88).

Although illiterate, he seems to have had an appearance and natural gifts which enabled him to exert a strong influence upon people. He was over six feet tall, of muscular form, and ruddy countenance. He had a vigorous mind; an exceptional memory, being able to quote copiously from the Bible simply from hearing it read by his wife; and fluency of speech. Professing to have received a "revelation," he began to preach, and by 1794 had a number of followers. As time went on these were joined by others, not only from Leyden, but from surrounding towns, many of them people of respectable standing. Originally his principal doctrine was that man should not eat flesh or cause the death of any living creature. Accordingly his followers abandoned the use of leather, wore wooden shoes, and used rope for harnesses and tow for cloth. As other revelations came to him he declared that each generation has its messiah, and that he was the messiah of his; that he might be worshipped as God united to human flesh; that no human arm could harm him; that the only resurrection is that from a state of sin to the spiritual life; and that those who are so raised are no more responsible to civil law, or bound by the covenant of marriage. (Rev. John Taylor of Deerfield in 1798 secured from Dorrell a detailed "confession of faith" which was published in the *Greenfield Gazette*, Aug. 20, 1798, and is given in Theophilus Packard's *A History of the Churches and Ministers . . . in Franklin County, Mass.*, 1854, pp. 252–58.) Disregard of conventional institutions and the disgraceful behavior of the Dorrellites at their gatherings brought them into disrepute. The death-blow was given the sect when a certain Capt. Ezekiel Foster, hearing Dorrell say at a largely attended meeting of his followers that "no arm of flesh can harm me," proceeded to pummel him till he renounced his doctrines. He continued to live in Leyden for nearly fifty years, falling into the habit of intemperance, and becoming a charge upon the town. He finally starved himself to death in his ninety-fifth year, by refusing to eat, declaring that he had lived long enough, and that if he continued to eat he would never die.

[*Mass. Spy* (Worcester), Sept. 12, 1798; Zadock Thompson, *A Gazetteer of the State of Vt.* (1824), see "Guilford"; *Hist. and Proc. Pocumtuck Valley Memorial Asso.*, vol. II (1898); Lucy C. Kellogg, *Hist. of the Town of Bernardston, Franklin County, Mass., 1736–1900* (1902).]   H. E. S.

DORSCH, EDUARD (Jan. 10, 1822–Jan. 10, 1887), physician, writer of lyrics in German, was born in Würzburg, Bavaria, the son of Francis L. Dorsch (died in 1825), attaché of the Bavarian court, and his wife, Elizabeth. He received his early education in a Catholic institution, entering the University of Munich in his eighteenth year. Medicine was his principal study, subsidiaries were natural sciences, botany, and philosophy. His early lyrics, "Idle Hours of a Munich student," reveal an independent thinker in the oppressive environment of reaction and fundamentalism. After the completion of his work in 1845 he was sent by the Bavarian State to Austria, to supplement his theoretical knowledge with larger practical experience in the hospitals of Vienna. On his return he soon became involved in the liberal movement that fascinated young thinking minds throughout Germany. He served in the capacity of surgeon in the South German revolution, and his active pen incurred the displeasure of the Bavarian government. Escaping capture, he came to America, reaching Detroit in the autumn of 1849. There he heard from his friend Bruckner of a good opportunity for a physician at Monroe, Mich., whither he went with his bride, Sophia Hartung, born in Ingolstadt, Bavaria. Dorsch lived in Monroe the rest of his life. A year after the death of his first wife, he married, in 1885, Augusta (Korte) Uhl.

Though confining himself closely to his profession, Dorsch could not remain aloof from the anti-slavery movement. He became a stanch adherent of the new Republican party, and was presidential elector from the second Michigan district, supporting Abraham Lincoln. He persistently refused all political offices, except the appointment to the Michigan State Board of Education, 1872–78. In the later sixties he accepted the position of examining surgeon of the Pension Office, which he continued to hold until his death. While acting as pension examiner he prepared a draft showing the course and effects of a bullet in the human body, an investigation which was published as authoritative by the Pension Office.

Three volumes of German lyrics represent Dorsch's poetic work. The first, entitled *Kurze Hirtenbriefe an das deutsche Volk diesseits und jenseits des Ozeans* (1851), are the poems of his youth, revolt, and exile. The second, called *Parabasen* (Milwaukee, 1875), is a collection of satires in verse after the manner of the German poets Platen and Prutz. The last volume, *Aus der alten und neuen Welt* (1884), is a selection of the best of his poems from early youth to the date of publication. He was not a poet of passion and genius, but of calm, penetrating reflection, a clear thinker, whose style was correct, smooth, virile. He looked deeply into human life, knew its joys and illusions, and gave them sincere utterance. He had a rich emotional experience to disclose; a lover of liberty, he was expelled from his dearly beloved native land, because he wanted to rid it of princes, priests, and drones. Seeking the land of the free, he found there a trafficking in human flesh and he joined in the fight for the liberation of humanity. Coming with romantic notions of the splendors of the primeval forest, he found it destructive of human life and cultural ideals. Disillusioned in all of his fondest expectations, the poet yet sought happiness in service of the most unselfish kind, that of the frontier surgeon who labors for the sick and suffering, night and day, with meager financial returns and without the glamour of fame. He felt keen satisfaction in never having lost a maternity case, and gloried in the gratitude of the pioneers.

Intimate friends of Dr. Dorsch described him as a man of retiring disposition, a lover of books and the means of culture. He had a large library in his home, paintings, and works of art. His collections of bugs, butterflies, and botanical specimens knew no end. In his garden there was an immense cage containing wild birds and animals, also a pond with blooming lotus plants that he had imported from Egypt, and a well with marble slab and Greek inscription praising the pure water. He bequeathed his books in part to the University of Michigan and in part to the city in which he lived. His second wife left the Dorsch home to the city of Monroe, founding there the Dorsch Memorial Library.

[A collection of papers and MSS. is in the possession of the Lincoln Club of Chicago. Published sources include: *Hist. of Monroe County, Mich.* (1890); ed. by Talcott E. Wing; John M. Bulkley, *Hist. of Monroe County, Mich.* (2 vols., 1913); J. A. Russell, *The Germanic Influence in the Making of Michigan* (1927); *Deutsch-amerikanisches Conversations-Lexicon* (1869–74), ed. by Alex. J. Schem, vol. III; G. A. Zimmermann, *Deutsch in Amerika* (1894), pp. xxxi–xxxii, 51–56 (biographical and critical sketch, and selections from the poems of Eduard Dorsch).] A.B.F.

DORSEY, ANNA HANSON McKENNEY (Dec. 12, 1815–Dec. 25, 1896), author, daughter of William and Chloe Ann (Lanigan) McKenney, was born in Georgetown, D. C., and died in Washington. Her ancestors had been prominent in Maryland for several generations. Her father's people were Quakers, but he himself, after becoming a sort of unattached Methodist preacher, entered the navy as a chaplain. Educated entirely at home, Anna began while still a girl to write verse which proved acceptable to the magazines. She was married in 1837 to Lorenzo Dorsey of Baltimore. They removed after a few years to Washington, where, till his death in 1861, he was connected with the post-office de-

partment of the general government. In 1840 she became a Catholic, as her husband did also at about the same time, both of them influenced by the Catholic revival then current in England. Her first considerable writing, *The Student of Blenheim Forest* (1847), is a novel showing the progress toward Rome of a rich and aristocratic young Virginian who had grown up a Protestant. She was responsible during the next forty years for at least thirty publications, some poetry but mostly prose fiction. Nearly everything she wrote was popular, and all of it—whether like *Woodreve Manor* (1852), touching on slavery and devoted to "the merits and the follies of the times," or, like *Palms* (1887), devoted to the life of ancient Rome—was concerned to display before the world what she held to be the infallible light of her Church. Her hesitancy on moral grounds to depict incidents of unjust suffering (as in *Adrift*, 1887, p. 14) naturally curtailed the power of her work. She shunned personal publicity, and judged herself with modesty—she had not, she said, either "the genius of a Longfellow or the highly attuned talent of a Hemans" (*Flowers of Love and Memory*, 1849, Preface). She was the mother of five children, four of whom lived to maturity—one to be killed in battle during the Civil War. Her patriotic advocacy of the Union cause was expressed in the narrative poem, *"They're Coming, Grandad"* (1865), dedicated to the loyal people of Tennessee. As a widow, she continued to live in Washington, busy with her novels and with her children and grandchildren, comforted from time to time by blessings from the Pope and by praise of her work from the ecclesiastical sources in America.

[Conversation with Miss Ella Loraine Dorsey, Washington, D. C., Jan. 21, 1928; E. C. Donnelly, *Round Table of the Representative Am. Cath. Novelists, with Biog. Sketches* (1897); H. R. Evans, *Geneal. Table . . . Line of Descent . . . from Edward Dorsey* (1898); *Catholic Encyc.*, V (1909); *Ave Maria*, Jan. 16, 1897; *Evening Star* (Washington), Dec. 26, 1896.] J.D.W.

DORSEY, JAMES OWEN (Oct. 31, 1848–Feb. 4, 1895), ethnologist, was a son of Thomas Anderson and Mary Sweetser (Hance) Dorsey of Baltimore, Md. At an early age he showed a tendency toward linguistics, having learned the Hebrew alphabet at six and being able to read the language at ten. His education in the primary schools of Baltimore brought him into the Central High School in 1862. A later period of study in the Protestant Episcopal Theological Seminary at Alexandria, Va., saw him ordained a deacon in 1871. Beginning mission work among the Pawnees of Dakota Territory, he soon acquired ability to speak the language, but, hampered by illness, he returned to Maryland and engaged in parish work in 1880. At this period the newly founded Bureau of American Ethnology under Maj. J. W. Powell [*q.v.*] required his services, and he was sent to study the Omaha Indians, returning later to elaborate his notes. In this way he made a number of trips to the West, collecting linguistic material from various Indian tribes. Brief as was his productive career, he published, besides numerous shorter articles in various publications, a creditable number of major works on a difficult subject. The *Annual Reports of the United States Bureau of American Ethnology* contains most of his larger papers, including: "Omaha Sociology" (*Report* for 1881–82); "Osage Traditions" (*Report* for 1884–85); "A Study of Siouan Cults" (*Report* for 1889–90); "Omaha Dwellings, Furniture and Implements" (*Report* for 1891–92); "Siouan Sociology" (*Report* for 1893–94). In Contributions to North American Ethnology he published *The Cegiha Language* (vol. VI, 1890); and *Dakota Grammar, Texts, and Ethnography by Stephen Return Riggs* (vol. IX, 1893). In various outside media he published: "An Account of the War Customs of the Osages" (*American Naturalist,* vol. XVIII, 1884); and in the same journal: "Mourning and War Customs of the Kansas" (vol. XIX, 1885), and "Migrations of Siouan Tribes" (vol. XX, 1886). One of his early papers was: "Of the Comparative Phonology of Four Siouan Languages" (*Annual Report of the . . . Smithsonian Institution for the Year 1883*). *Omaha and Ponca Letters* appeared in 1891 as Bulletin 11, of the Bureau of American Ethnology, and *A Dictionary of the Biloxi and Ofo Languages,* with J. R. Swanton, as Bulletin 47 in 1912. These studies are of a highly specialized character, requiring trained and expert observation and accurate record. To this work he brought method, rapidity, assiduity, and a keen ear. With these qualifications he accomplished much in a short time. A trained scientist, he bent his energies to recording, holding to facts, and promulgating no theories. On the whole, "in the field of linguistics and sociology Mr. Dorsey collected many facts and much data, which are a permanent addition to our heritage of knowledge" (J. N. B. Hewitt, *American Anthropologist,* April 1895). A delicate constitution, accounting for illnesses which at times slowed up his work, did not prevent Dorsey's being an example of the men whose inner fire drives them on to triumph over adverse circumstances. Always finding time to help others from his store of knowledge, he endeared himself to a large circle of fellow workers. He was honored by various learned societies devoted to ethnology. His active efforts, however, were chiefly devoted to the Anthropological Society of Washington and the American Association for the Advancement of Science, of which he was a Fellow. He gave the impression of distinction, of transparency, and of spirituality. Moving among men as a friend, he was loved and revered by all.

[*American Anthropologist,* Apr. 1895, p. 180; *16th Annual Report of the Bureau of Ethnology, 1894–95* (1897), p. lxxxii; *Evening Star* (Washington), Feb. 5, 1895; personal recollections.]   W. H.

DORSEY, JOHN SYNG (Dec. 23, 1783–Nov. 12, 1818), anatomist, surgeon, came of an old English family, the D'Orseys, who had settled in Maryland. His father, Leonard Dorsey, was a merchant in Philadelphia. Dorsey was born in Philadelphia and received his early education at a school conducted by the Society of Friends. Evidently he made an early decision to study medicine, for at the age of fifteen years he entered the office of his uncle, the celebrated Dr. Philip Syng Physick [*q.v.*]. He graduated in medicine at the University of Pennsylvania in 1802 at the age of nineteen years, his dissertation being *An Essay on the Lithonthriptic Virtues of the Gastric Liquor* published the same year. Soon after his graduation there was an epidemic of yellow fever, which had been prevalent in Philadelphia, and he was appointed a resident physician to the yellow-fever hospital and gained considerable credit by his study of the disease. In 1803 he proceeded to London and Paris for further study, a course which was followed at that time by the majority of those who were able to round out their medical studies by a sojourn abroad. In London he was welcomed by Edward Home, afterward Sir Edward, and seems to have devoted himself principally to the study of anatomy. He also attended lectures on chemistry by Humphry Davy. In Paris he continued his anatomical studies but does not seem to have been much impressed by French surgery and makes little or no mention of some of the great men of the day whom he must have seen. In December 1804, he returned to Philadelphia and began the practise of medicine, in a short time receiving appointments on the staffs of several hospitals. While recognition of his ability came quickly in this form, it apparently came slowly in the form of practise, even with the support of Dr. Physick. On Apr. 30, 1807, he was married to Maria Ralston, daughter of Robert Ralston, a Philadelphia merchant. In the same year he was appointed to the dispensary staff of the Pennsylvania Hospital and elected adjunct professor of surgery in the University of Pennsylvania. In 1810 he was elected a surgeon to the Pennsylvania Hospital, where in 1811 he ligated the external iliac artery, apparently the first time that this operation was done successfully in America. In 1813 he published a work on *The Elements of Surgery,* in two octavo volumes, for which many of the illustrations were prepared by himself. This was very successful and was given considerable recognition abroad, especially in Edinburgh. It is supposed to represent to a considerable degree the views and practise of Dr. Physick. Three editions were published, the last appearing after the death of the author. In 1816, Dorsey was elected to the chair of materia medica, to undergo another translation in 1818 to the chair of anatomy, in which he succeeded Dr. Wistar. His introductory lecture, delivered on Nov. 2, 1818, was described in the accounts of the day as being a most eloquent effort, but on the night of that lecture he was attacked by typhus fever, and he died within a fortnight.

The contemporary accounts of his life lay stress on his remarkable qualities, personal, social, professional, and artistic. He was interested in music and played on several instruments. His skill in drawing was put to practical use in the illustration of his work on surgery. His appointment at an early age to the staff of the Pennsylvania Hospital is evidence of his surgical ability. To have attained the positions which he held at the time of his death, at thirty-five, is evidence of talents of no mean order.

[N. Chapman, in *Phila. Jour. Med. and Phys. Sci.,* 1820, I, 198; *Am. Medic. Recorder,* II (1819), 1; *Freeman's Journal for the Country* and *Democratic Press,* both of Phila., Nov. 13, 1818; *General Advertiser* (Phila.), Nov. 14, 1818; H. Shoemaker in *St. Louis Medic. and Surgic. Jour.,* IX (1851), 297–301; J. J. Janeway, *A Brief Memoir of . . . John Syng Dorsey* (1853); S. D. Gross, *Living Eminent Am. Physicians and Surgeons* (1861); Jos. Carson, *A Hist. of the Medic. Dept. of the Univ. of Pa.* (1869); H. A. Kelly and W. L. Burrage, *Am. Medic. Biogs.* (1920).]   T.M.

DORSEY, SARAH ANNE ELLIS (Feb. 16, 1829–July 4, 1879), author, daughter of Thomas and Mary (Routh) Ellis, was born on her father's plantation near Natchez, Miss., and died in New Orleans. Her education, capped by a tour of Europe, was based chiefly on languages and the fine arts. She was married in 1853 to Samuel W. Dorsey, originally of Maryland, but at the time of his marriage a planter in Tensas Parish, La. A devout woman given to writing, she soon began publishing her pious reflections in the New York *Churchman.* She taught her husband's slaves how to read and write, introduced them to ecclesiastical ritualism, and composed

for their use a series of choral services. Her house was burned during the war, and she was surrounded by armies, but she continued to write for magazines. Removing to Texas for greater tranquillity, she became a nurse in a Confederate hospital. The war injured but did not destroy her husband's considerable property. In 1866 she published her voluble but conscientious *Recollections of Henry Watkins Allen,* Confederate governor of Louisiana. In the preface she stated that if that biography were favorably received she might be encouraged to write others, "to progress still further in this, my labor of love; like Old Mortality, freshening the epitaphs, which are already yielding to the corroding tooth of Time, on the gravestones of Southern Heroes." She progressed instead to fiction, all more or less autobiographical in nature, and written as "Filia"—reminiscent of the name "Filia Ecclesiae" bestowed upon her by the *Churchman.* In *Lucia Dare* (1867), begun as early as 1853— touching, before Hale made him memorable, on the romance of Philip Nolan—she carries the reader from England to Mississippi and through the Civil War. Other novels were: *Agnes Graham* (1869), which appeared first in the *Southern Literary Messenger,* June 1863–March 1864, and *Athalie or a Southern Villeggiatura* (1872), which deals with "country diversions or residence," a kind of belated *Horse-shoe Robinson* of the lower Mississippi. During 1874–75 she prepared a series of papers on philosophy for a learned body in New Orleans, and in 1877 she completed her morbid and sensational *Panola, a Tale of Louisiana.* Her husband died in 1875, and after that time she made her home principally at "Beauvoir," Miss. She had known Mrs. Jefferson Davis since the two were girls, and in the beginning of 1877 Davis himself came to live at her house as a guest. It was her desire to collect and edit his writings and his recollections. She became his amanuensis, and in that capacity—and as his friend—she bent herself to obtain from him the important information which he alone could give. Much of this matter appeared in Davis's *Rise and Fall of the Confederate Government* (1881), but she died before the book was completed. At her death it was disclosed that she had made Davis several valuable bequests, including her home.

[Sources not already mentioned: Varina Howell Davis, *Jefferson Davis* (1890); Dunbar Rowland, *Jefferson Davis* (1923), *Mississippi* (1907); J. W. Davidson, *Living Writers of the South* (1869); I. Raymond, *Southland Writers,* vol. I (1870); M. L. Rutherford, *The South in Hist. and Lit.* (1907); Carl Holliday, *A Hist. of Southern Lit.* (1906); *The South in the Building of the Nation,* vol. XI (1909); *New Orleans Times,* July 5, 1879; *Natchez Democrat,* July 6, 1879; *Vicksburg Commercial,* July 7, 1879.]   J.D.W.

DORSEY, STEPHEN WALLACE (Feb. 28, 1842–Mar. 20, 1916), senator, was born at Benson, Vt., son of John W. and Marie Dorsey. He received an academic education and moved to Ohio while still a boy. At the outbreak of the Civil War he volunteered and served in the Army of the Tennessee and the Army of the Potomac, remaining in active service to the end. He rose to the rank of captain in the 1st Ohio Light Artillery. Returning to Ohio he resumed his place as an employee of the Sandusky Tool Company and was soon elected its president. On the same day he was elected president of the Arkansas Central Railway Company. This was one of the many companies organized to defraud the state under guise of giving state aid to railroads. By the close of 1871 he was interested in three railroad projects. The Helena (Ark.) *World* said of him: "He came here to promote his railroad interests. He obtained state, county, and city aid, under the most solemn pledges. By trickery, hocus-pocus and legerdemain the gauge of the road was changed from standard to narrow gauge, as adopted. To-day we have a wheelbarrow road from Helena westward, costing nothing in comparison with the one he promised to come here to construct" (quoted in Herndon, *post*, I, 307). From the state he secured indorsement of his railroad bonds to the extent of $1,-350,000. Naturally he entered politics and soon after his arrival he became an influential member of the "machine." Here he could look after his railroad interests. The legislature elected him to the Senate and he took his seat Mar. 4, 1873. In his first session he introduced a bill to establish a "National Railroad Bureau for the General Government of the Railroads," but neither he nor any one else ever pushed this move for government control. For several sessions he introduced bills for the organization of Oklahoma territory. Most of his time seems to have been taken up with relief, pension, railroad, District of Columbia and post-office bills, but he exercised very little influence on legislation.

The Democrats having recaptured the state, he did not return to Arkansas. He served as secretary to the Republican National Committee, of which he was a member, though not a resident of Arkansas, and conducted the campaign for Garfield in 1880. In his first Congress he had manifested an interest in the post-office by introducing six bills and four resolutions relating to it. Later in his career he became interested in the Star Routes, and in 1881, along with T. W. Brady [*q.v.*], second assistant postmaster-general, and others, was indicted for conspiring to defraud the government of nearly half a million

dollars. Powerful political and newspaper influences were brought to bear in their behalf, and at the conclusion of the first trial the jury stood ten to two for conviction of Brady and nine to three for conviction of Dorsey, but in the second trial they were both acquitted. M. C. Rerdell, Dorsey's private secretary, pleaded guilty in the second trial. Charges of jury-bribing were brought by both the prosecution and the defense, which led to further indictments and dismissal of officials. Dorsey attributed his prosecution to the hostility of Postmaster-General James, and Attorney-General McVeagh, whose appointment as members of Garfield's cabinet he had opposed. After leaving Washington Dorsey conducted a cattle ranch and was interested in mining in New Mexico until 1892. After that date he devoted his time to mining enterprises and investments. About 1901 he moved to Los Angeles and resided there until his death. He married Helen Mary Wack at Oberlin, Ohio, Nov. 20, 1865. Three children were born of this union. Later he married Laura, daughter of Job B. Bigelow of Washington and London.

[D. T. Herndon, *Centennial Hist. of Ark.* (1922); *Cong. Record*, 1873–79; *Proceedings in the Second Trial of the Case of S. W. Dorsey et al.* (4 vols.), which is indexed so that Dorsey's part can be traced; *Appletons' Ann. Cyc.*, 1882 and 1883; Letter from Dorsey's son, Clayton Chauncey Dorsey, giving family history.]
                                    D.Y.T.

DORSHEIMER, WILLIAM EDWARD (Feb. 5, 1832–Mar. 26, 1888), lawyer, journalist, politician, was the son of Philip and Sarah Dorsheimer. His father came from Germany early in the nineteenth century, settling eventually in Buffalo. William was born at Lyons, Wayne County, N. Y. After preparing at Phillips Andover Academy, he entered Harvard in 1849, but was compelled by ill health to withdraw after two years. Admitted to the bar in 1854, he began practise at Buffalo and soon became active in the Democratic party, although his father was one of the founders of the state Republican party and William Dorsheimer himself supported the Republican ticket in 1856 and 1860. After serving on Frémont's staff in the Missouri campaign of the summer of 1861, he returned to Buffalo and formed a law partnership with Spencer Clifton. President Johnson appointed him federal district attorney for the northern district of New York in 1867. He surrendered this position in 1871 to participate in the movement for the election of Horace Greeley, and was a member of the Liberal Republican convention at Cincinnati in 1872. Returning to the Democratic fold, he was elected lieutenant-governor on the ticket with Samuel J. Tilden in 1874, and reëlected

with L. C. Robinson in 1876. That summer he
was a member of the Democratic convention at
St. Louis which nominated Tilden for the presidency. Dorsheimer reported the platform, which,
as a member of the committee on resolutions, he
had saved from an "inflationist" plank. During the ensuing campaign he made numerous
speeches and wrote for both the newspapers and
magazines in behalf of the Democratic ticket.
He felt that Tilden, through indifference, prevented his being nominated for governor in 1876,
wherefore he supported Kelly, the candidate of
the Tammany wing, instead of Robinson, the
regular nominee. This division within the Democratic ranks insured the election of Cornell, the
Republican candidate. This same year the Democratic delegation in the legislature vainly supported Dorsheimer for United States senator
against Roscoe Conkling. In the next year, Dorsheimer was one of the Kelly delegates to the
Democratic convention at Cincinnati, but the
Tilden wing succeeded in having the whole
Tammany delegation excluded. Dorsheimer was
elected to Congress in 1882. His most important service was on the judiciary committee. He
was also chairman of the House section of the
joint committee which arranged the celebration
upon the completion of the Washington monument. It is alleged that his fellow townsman,
Grover Cleveland, wished Dorsheimer to nominate him at the St. Louis convention in 1884, but
Kelly had prevented Dorsheimer's being chosen
as a delegate, so he attended only as an alternate.
The campaign biography (*Life and Public Services of the Honorable Grover Cleveland*, 1884)
was from Dorsheimer's pen. For this and other
valuable services in the campaign Dorsheimer
was appointed federal district attorney for southern New York in 1885. After about a year he
resigned this position to direct the New York
Star which he had bought and converted into a
daily. This venture did not prove financially successful, and the worries incident thereto probably
increased the illness which took him to Savannah in the winter of 1887, in the vain quest of
health. He died there, Mar. 26, 1888. His wife
was Isabella, daughter of A. D. Patchin of Buffalo. It was said of Dorsheimer that he possessed
"courage, tact, fascination, audacity, rare skill on
the platform, creditable associations and marked
literary attainments." In addition to the campaign biography of Cleveland he wrote reviews
of Parton's lives of Aaron Burr and Thomas Jefferson, in the *Atlantic Monthly* (March and November 1858); a series of articles in the same
periodical for 1862, on "Frémont's Hundred
Days in Missouri"; a sketch, "Buffalo During

the War of 1812" (1863) in the *Publications of
the Buffalo Historical Society* (I, 185). He was
one of the founders of the Buffalo Historical Society and the Academy of Fine Arts in the same
city.

[Besides the sketches in *Appletons' Ann. Cyc.*, 1888,
and the *Encyc. of Contemporary Biog. of N. Y.* (1887),
data concerning Dorsheimer may be found in R. B.
Smith, *Hist. of the State of N. Y.* (vol. III), D. S.
Alexander, *Political Hist. of the State of N. Y.*, vol.
III (1909), the *Pubs. Buffalo Hist. Soc.*, vols. V, XII;
Report of the Harvard Class of 1853 (1913); J. N.
Larned, *Hist. of Buffalo* (1911), vols. I, II; T. C.
White, *Our County and its People, A Descriptive Work
on Erie County, N. Y.* (1898), vol. I.] M. L. B., Jr.

DOS PASSOS, JOHN RANDOLPH (July
31, 1844–Jan. 27, 1917), lawyer, was born in
Philadelphia, the son of Manoel Joquin Dos Passos, of a Portuguese family, and his wife, Lucinda Anne Cattell. Having received his early
education at the public schools in his native city,
he commenced the study of law under private
tutors, and attended law lectures at the University of Pennsylvania. During the Civil War he
enlisted in the Pennsylvania militia, taking part
in the battle of Antietam and the later campaigns. At the close of hostilities he resumed his
law studies and was admitted to the Philadelphia
bar in 1865. He practised there a short time,
but removed in 1867 to New York City, where
he quickly acquired a reputation through his association with the defense in some spectacular
murder trials. Attention was first drawn to him
through his defense of Emil André who killed
his wife in broad daylight on a public street in
New York. Apparently the crime was without
any extenuating circumstances, but Dos Passos
succeeded in inducing the jury to return a verdict of manslaughter, thus saving André's life.
He also assisted in the defense of Edward S.
Stokes when charged with the murder of "Jim"
Fisk, and, on his client's conviction, though not
senior counsel, practically conducted the appeal
which resulted, in June 1873, in the verdict being
set aside. Criminal practise, however, had no
attraction for him, and his natural inclinations
led him to the special study of problems of
finance and exchange. With this object in view
he opened an office in close proximity to the New
York Stock Exchange and soon acquired an extensive connection among brokers and operators
in the financial market. He gradually became
known as an expert on the law of commercial exchange and wrote *A Treatise on the Law of
Stockbrokers and Stock Exchanges* (1882),
which was an immediate success and for a number of years remained the standard text-book on
the subject. Confining himself to corporation
and banking law, he acquired a large practise of

a very responsible and remunerative nature. Possessed of keen business instincts and a natural capacity for delicate diplomacy, he became the confidential adviser of many Wall St. firms. In 1891 he was employed by H. O. Havemeyer [*q.v.*] in the incorporation of the American Sugar Refining Company—the so-called "Sugar Trust"—the legal fee received on account of this work being the largest on record up to that time. For a number of years thereafter he acted as the company's counsel. He also assisted in the formation of other large aggregations, and was a pioneer in the organization and development of the modern trust company. On the subject of trusts he had strong opinions, recognizing as he did both their beneficial and their potentially evil attributes. He believed that the Sherman Anti-Trust Law was "an unnecessary, anomalous and dangerous piece of legislation," and contributed in the public press and through his own publications many suggestions for remedied legislation. He was exceptionally successful in the reconciliation of apparently conflicting interests and the adjustment of disputes in big business. It was mainly owing to his efforts that the reorganizations of the Texas & Pacific, the Reading, and the Erie Railroads were effected. In his later years he took great interest in law reform, some of his views being entirely original and most of them radical in outlook. Shortly before his death he strongly urged in the public press that in a criminal trial the accused should be compelled to testify. He died in New York City, in his seventy-third year. His wife, whom he married on Dec. 17, 1873, was Mary Dyckman Hays.

Although a forceful and impressive speaker, he was prominently in public affairs upon only one occasion, the presidential contest of 1896, during which he undertook a vigorous campaign through Pennsylvania and Virginia on behalf of McKinley, who was a personal friend of his. He was possessed of great physical energy, and when he could get away from his professional employments, devoted himself to open-air pursuits, being a great pedestrian and lover of the country. He was also fond of the sea, and an enthusiastic yachtsman.

He was a constant writer and published, in addition to his book on the stock exchange: *The Interstate Commerce Act: an Analysis of its Provisions* (1867); *A Defence of the McKinley Administration from Attacks of Mr. Carl Schurz and other Anti-Imperialists* (1900); *Commercial Trusts: the Growth and Rights of Aggregated Capital* (1901); *The Anglo-Saxon Century and the Unification of the English Speaking People* (1903); *The American Lawyer* (1907); and *Commercial Mortmain; A Study of the Trust Problem* (1916). He also contributed a number of articles to periodicals and the public press on matters of current interest.

[A competent review of his career, "John R. Dos Passos," by Henry Wollman in *Case and Comment,* July 1917, and extended obituary notices in the *N. Y. Times* and *N. Y. Herald* of Jan. 28, 1917; family names from a son, Louis Hays Dos Passos.]   H.W.H.K.

DOTY, ELIHU (Sept. 20, 1809–Nov. 30, 1864), missionary of the Dutch Reformed Church, was born in Berne, Albany County, N. Y. The son of Stephen Holmes and Phebe (Nelson) Doty, he was a descendant of Edward Doty who came to Plymouth on the *Mayflower,* as a servant to Stephen Hopkins. He graduated from Rutgers College in 1835 and from Rutgers Seminary in 1836, because of his advanced age and mental maturity taking the combined courses in five years. He was ordained at Berne, on May 16, 1836, and on May 30 was commissioned by the American Board of Commissioners for Foreign Missions, with which the Dutch Reformed Church was then affiliated. On June 8 he embarked with Nevius, Youngblood, and Ennis as the first missionary band of the New Brunswick Seminary, and arrived at Batavia, Java, on Sept. 15 (*Centennial of the Theological Seminary of the Reformed Church in America, N. Y.,* 1885, p. 117). There they were delayed and hindered by the jealousy of the Dutch government, but after three years of discouraging labor in Batavia and Singapore, Doty began work on the island of Borneo, in June 1839, devoting himself to the Chinese-speaking portion of the population. While his actual missionary labors were unsuccessful, he made several extensive tours of exploration the valuable results of which are incorporated in his *Narrative of a Tour in Borneo.* The Borneo mission failed and was given up for lack of workers (W. E. Strong, *The Story of the American Board,* 1910), but in 1844 Doty joined the Amoy mission, composed of Dutch Reformed missionaries working under the American Board, and here most of his effective work was accomplished. His connection with the American Board ceased on the final transfer of the Amoy work to the newly organized Dutch Reformed Board, Mar. 23, 1858.

Doty was a member for twenty years of the Amoy mission, where by his character and work he left an enduring impression. He baptized the first Chinese woman to be received into church fellowship, baptized the first children of native Christian parents, and was for a time in charge of the first Chinese day school, in the province (P. W. Pitcher, *In and About Amoy,* 1909). At length he gradually withdrew from the distinctively evangelistic work of the mission and gave himself to literary labors, for which he was well adapted. His principal publications include: *Some Thoughts on the Proper Term for God in the Chinese* (Shanghai, 1850); *Translation of Sacramental and Marriage Forms of the Reformed Protestant Dutch Church into Amoy Colloquial* (1853); *Translation and Revision into the Amoy Dialect of Milner's Thirteen Village Sermons, including Milner's Tract on the Strait Gate* (Amoy, 1854); an Anglo-Chinese *Manual of the Amoy Dialect* (Canton, 1855) which is especially important because it formed the basis of manuals long used by missionaries in this region. Doty was a man of unromantic temperament and not much given to the graces; but he was solid, steadfast, and plodding. He was neither widely read nor a profound scholar, but his accuracy, sound judgment, and freedom from prejudice fitted him admirably for his work. On May 13, 1836, he married Clarissa Dolly Ackley of Washington, Conn., who died at Amoy, Oct. 5, 1845. His second wife, Eleanor Augusta Smith of Parsippany, N. J., whom he married on Feb. 17, 1847, died Feb. 28, 1858, at Amoy.

[Unpublished records of the American Board in Boston; E. T. Corwin, *Manual of the Reformed Church in America* (5th ed. 1922), which contains full bibliography of his works; *Christian Intelligencer*, Mar. 30 and Apr. 6, 1865; J. G. Fagg, *Forty Years in South China* (1894); *Biog. Record Theol. Sem. New Brunswick, 1784–1911* (1912), comp. by J. H. Raven; E. A. Doty, *Doty-Doten Family in America* (1897).]

F.T.P.

DOTY, JAMES DUANE (Nov. 5, 1799–June 13, 1865), politician, speculator, was born in Salem, Washington County, N. Y., of Colonial English stock, the son of Chilius and Sarah (Martin) Doty. He was educated in the common schools of Lewis County, N. Y., and at Lowville Academy, read law, and began practise at Detroit, Michigan Territory, in 1819. He was also clerk of the supreme court of the territory and of the territorial council. Doty accompanied Gen. Lewis Cass [q.v.] as secretary on his tour of the lakes and ascent of the Mississippi in 1820. In 1823 he became judge of the judicial district of Northern Michigan which included a vast territory west of Lake Michigan. In the same year (April 14) he married Sarah Collins at Whitestown, N. Y., and settled at Green Bay in Michigan Territory. His judgeship required him to travel extensively through wilderness regions, and brought him in contact with Indians, rivermen, traders, hunters, soldiers, government agents, and French and American pioneer settlers, creating many difficult situations which his courage, keenness, and ingratiating manners uniformly overcame. He had

many devoted friends and admirers. There is some reason, however, to believe that he diplomatically allied himself with the powerful trading concerns, which alliance may partially explain his facile progress.

Resigning his judgeship, under compulsion, it was said, in 1832, Doty devoted several years to a personal exploration of the West, especially that portion which later became Wisconsin, mapped it, and published a description of the region. One of his objects was to select sites for towns, mills, wharves, etc., for he was an inveterate speculator who was determined, as soon as the lands of Wisconsin were surveyed, to enter a large number of promising tracts scattered through many counties. He was commissioned in 1832 by the War Department to survey the military roads in Wisconsin; he was a member of the legislative council of Michigan from the region west of the lake; he became, in 1839, Wisconsin's delegate in Congress, was reëlected in 1840 and served till 1841 when he became by appointment of President Tyler, governor of the territory. That post he held till 1844, though with one short break during which N. P. Tallmadge was governor.

Doty was the stormy petrel of early Wisconsion politics. He selected the location of the capital, secured its adoption by the territorial council, speculated in lots and became the commissioner to erect the capitol building. These business complications created interests which as governor he sought to protect, thus precipitating an intense struggle with the territorial legislature. While both sides played politics, it is impossible to acquit Doty of actions and intrigues that look grossly irregular. Questions growing out of his action as building commissioner became the subject of congressional discussion, on resolution of his chief rival, Delegate Henry Dodge. It must be said, however, that most of the acts complained of can be explained on the theory that, as a speculator, he was often hardpressed financially. No proof has been found to establish the comprehensive allegations of dishonesty so voluminously uttered by his political enemies, though this fact does not acquit him of the charges. That he became more interested in his own personal affairs than in the public welfare can hardly be denied.

Doty was a prominent member of the first constitutional convention of Wisconsin, and after statehood had been attained, was for two terms, 1849–53, a representative in Congress. In early life he trained with the Democrats, but in 1840 became a Whig, and later a Republican. In 1861 he was appointed superintendent of Indian affairs with headquarters at Salt Lake, and in 1863 was made governor of Utah Territory. He died in Salt Lake City.

Doty possessed the type of mind which marks the acute lawyer. He was a man of culture, had a good library, enjoyed home and friends, loved to hum traditional songs, to surround himself with objects of sentimental interest. His native endowment set him apart from common men. He possessed a great fund of information about the West. His private life was exemplary; had he been able to resist the temptations to speculate, his career, honorable and distinguished in some ways, but badly marred in others, might have been one of outstanding brilliance and conspicuous worth.

[The most comprehensive general account is Albert G. Ellis, "Life and Public Services of J. D. Doty" in *Wis. Hist. Colls.*, V (1868), 369–77. Doty's manuscript journal with synopses of cases tried by him as judge is in State Hist. Lib., Madison, Wis., together with a few other papers by him; some of these were published in *Wis. Hist. Colls.*, XIII (1895), 163–246. *Memories of the Island Loggery*, by Mary Doty Fitzgerald, his daughter, is a reminiscent poem containing many hints about Doty's domestic interests. It is in *Wis. Mag. of Hist.*, June 1927. See also E. A. Doty, *The Doty-Doten Family in America* (1897).]

J. S—r.

DOUBLEDAY, ABNER (June 26, 1819–Jan. 26, 1893), Union soldier, also credited with originating baseball, was of Huguenot descent. The name was originally spelled "Dubaldy." His grandfather, Abner Doubleday, was a soldier in the Revolution, serving at Bunker Hill, Stony Point, and elsewhere, and ending his army career as a prisoner on the *Jersey*. Upon his release he took to the sea, and finished the war as an officer of a privateer. His son, Ulysses Freeman Doubleday, removed from the family home in Lebanon, Conn., to the state of New York, was a newspaper editor for many years at Ballston Spa and Auburn, and sat in Congress, as a Democrat, for four years. He married Hester Donnelly. Of their three sons, two became colonels of volunteers in the Civil War; and the other, Abner, rose to higher rank. He was born at Ballston Spa, attended school at Auburn and Cooperstown, and prepared himself for the profession of civil engineering. While at school in Cooperstown, tradition has it, he created the game of baseball out of the chaos of the popular bat-and-ball games—"one old cat" and its variants. To him is ascribed the adoption of the diamond-shaped field, the assignment of definite playing positions (his teams had eleven players, however), and the selection of the name "baseball" for the game. The essential facts seem fairly well established. A high commission of baseball experts made a formal report, in 1907,

on the origin of the game, after extensive investigation, and declared Doubleday to be its inventor. The original field at Cooperstown is now a public playground, appropriately called Doubleday Field. Doubleday was appointed a cadet at West Point in 1838, graduated in 1842, and was commissioned in the artillery. He was with Taylor's army in Mexico, being engaged in the battle of Monterey, and served against the Seminoles in the hostilities of 1856–58 in Florida. In 1852–53 he was a member of a commission which investigated certain claims for alleged destruction of mines during the Mexican War and pronounced them fraudulent—the "Gardner mine fraud." The remainder of his service before the Civil War was in garrison at posts on the Atlantic Coast. He was promoted to first lieutenant in 1847 and to captain in 1855. In 1852 he married Mary, daughter of Robert M. Hewitt of Baltimore. He was stationed in Charleston harbor in 1860–61, and aimed the first shot fired from Fort Sumter in reply to the Confederate bombardment. His aim was good, but the shot "bounded off from the sloping roof of the [ironclad] battery opposite without producing any apparent effect." In May 1861, he was appointed major of the newly organized 17th Infantry, and served as such in the lower Shenandoah Valley and the defenses of Washington until appointed brigadier-general of volunteers, Feb. 3, 1862. He was assigned to the command of a brigade in McDowell's corps, and took it into action for the first time in a skirmish on the Rappahannock late in August, followed shortly after by the second battle of Bull Run. At the battle of South Mountain, in September, he succeeded to the command of the division, when its chief was wounded, and in that capacity took part in the battles of Antietam and Fredericksburg. He was appointed major-general of volunteers, Nov. 29, 1862. His division was in reserve at Chancellorsville. The battle of Gettysburg brought Doubleday his greatest distinction and his bitterest disappointment. The first day's fight was waged by such Union troops as were within reach, to hold back the Confederate army until the full Union strength could be brought up to the field. Gen. Reynolds was killed, and Doubleday commanded the corps through a day of desperate fighting against heavy odds. He felt that he had fairly earned the permanent command, and when Newton (his classmate at West Point) was assigned that night to take charge of the corps, and he himself was returned to the command of his division, he was deeply humiliated. His resentment toward Gen. Meade, who had made the assignment without full knowledge of the facts, was never appeased. His division was heavily engaged on the second and third days, and took an important part in the repulse of the final great assault. This was his last field service. For the rest of the war he was on duty in Washington. He was mustered out of the volunteer service, Jan. 15, 1866. He had been promoted to lieutenant-colonel in the regular army, Sept. 20, 1863, and on Sept. 15, 1867, he became colonel. While stationed in San Francisco in 1869–71 he obtained the charter for the first cable street railway. He retired from active service, Dec. 11, 1873, and made his home at Mendham, N. J., where he died. He was buried in Arlington National Cemetery.

Doubleday was tall, distinguished in appearance, dignified and courteous in manner. Quiet and cool in times of stress, methodical and deliberate in his ways—he was nicknamed "Forty-eight Hours"—his temperament resembled that of Gen. Thomas. His staff officers have testified to his retentive memory and his faculty for clear statement in giving orders. They noted, too, that he never used a profane word, and that he indulged in neither liquor nor tobacco. He was a man of wide interests and varied attainments. From youth he took pleasure in French and Spanish literature, and in his old age, Cato-like, he studied Sanskrit. He published, in 1876, *Reminiscences of Forts Sumter and Moultrie in 1860–'61*; and in 1882, *Chancellorsville and Gettysburg.*

[The best source of information on Doubleday is a volume published by the state of New York on the occasion of the dedication of monuments at Gettysburg: *In Memoriam, Abner Doubleday 1819–1893 and John Cleveland Robinson 1817–1897* (1918); addresses by staff officers and friends give not only a detailed account of his military career, but also many facts as to his ancestry, early life, and personal characteristics. G. W. Cullum's *Biog. Reg.* (3rd ed., 1891) outlines his military record, II, 132–34. See also *Official Records (Army)*, ser. I, vols. I, II, XII (pt. 2), XIX (pt. 1), XXI, XXV (pts. 1, 2), XXVII (pt. 1), LI. The first day's fighting at Gettysburg is well described by Gen. H. J. Hunt in *Battles and Leaders of the Civil War* (1887–88), III, 255–84. For his connection with baseball, see A. G. Spaulding, *America's National Game* (1911) and F. C. Richter, *Richter's Hist. and Records of Base Ball* (1914).] T. M. S.

DOUBLEDAY, NELTJE DE GRAFF (Oct. 23, 1865–Feb. 21, 1918), naturalist, was born in Chicago, Ill., the daughter of Liverius and Alice (Fair) De Graff. She was educated at St. John's School, New York City, and at the Misses Masters' School at Dobbs Ferry, N. Y. On June 9, 1886, she married Frank Nelson Doubleday at Plainfield, N. J., by whom she had two sons and a daughter. Her husband was at the time of marriage editor of the *Book Buyer* and was subsequently manager of *Scribner's Magazine* and

a member of the Doubleday Publishing Company, so she came into a literary atmosphere, with means of expression ready for her use. But it was not until her youngest child was two years old that she published her first book, *The Piegan Indians* (1894). This was followed by: *Bird Neighbors* (1896), *Birds that Hunt and Are Hunted* (1898), *Nature's Garden* (1900), *How to Attract the Birds* (1902), *Birds that Every Child Should Know* (1907), *The American Flower Garden* (1909), *Birds Worth Knowing* (1917), *Birds* (a selection published posthumously, 1926). It is quite evident from any or all of her work that she became a naturalist because she loved flowers and birds rather than because she loved science. While her writings are always accurate, their charm and the explanation of their popularity lie in the intimate and often homely manner in which she describes the habits and habitats of her subjects. Her volumes—many of them profusely illustrated in colors, and all with topics carefully arranged and classified—are adapted both to interest and to instruct. She also wrote many articles for magazines, especially *Country Life*. Her interests were broad, and her magazine work covered such varied topics as agriculture, antique furniture, and the education of the American Indian, as well as the writing of numerous book reviews. All of her writing was produced under the pen name of Neltje Blanchan. Prominent socially, she yet reserved much of her time and energy for work in charitable organizations. Her vivid personality, quick sympathy, and active temperament admirably fitted her for such work. With these qualifications she had the ability to win easily the confidence of those with whom she came in contact. She was a leading member of the Red Cross Society of Nassau, L. I., and in 1917 was selected by the American Red Cross for a special mission in China. Mr. and Mrs. Doubleday left their home, "Effendi Hill," Oyster Bay, L. I., on Dec. 9, 1917, going first to the Philippines, then to Hong Kong and other Chinese cities, before reaching Canton, from which news of her death was unexpectedly cabled to New York in February.

[*Woman's Who's Who of America*, 1914–15; *Who's Who in America*, 1916–17; *N. Y. Times*, Feb. 23, 1918; personal information from a son, Mr. Nelson Doubleday of New York City.] G. G.

DOUGHTY, THOMAS (July 19, 1793–July 22, 1856), painter, was one of the earliest American landscapists of sufficient merit and originality to attain general recognition. Born in Philadelphia, he began work in the leather business at the age of sixteen, and continued in this occupation for some ten years. Then, at the age of twenty-seven, he resolved to pursue painting as a profession. "My mind," he wrote, "was firmly fixed; I had acquired a love for the art which no circumstance could unsettle." He realized that the financial prospect was anything but bright at the start, but he was buoyed up by the hope that as he acquired skill and knowledge his worldly circumstances would be bettered. He seems to have had little other training than that afforded by a short term of instruction in sepia drawing. Nor was he mistaken in anticipating economic privations. However, his love for the art, which "no circumstance could unsettle," combined with an unquestionable talent and good courage, did at length prevail. His reputation grew, and he was for a time rated as the foremost landscape painter of the famous Hudson River school. This was at the time when the men of 1830 were giving new life to landscape work in France. It is recorded that Doughty worked for a long time in Paris, where he painted some of his best canvases, and he also lived in London for a relatively short period, finding some congenial subjects in the suburbs. The most prosperous years of his career were the early thirties, when, in 1833, in company with Chester Harding, Francis Alexander, and Alvan Fisher, he held an exceptionally successful exhibition in Boston. He had a studio in that city for several years, and was a regular exhibitor in the annual exhibitions of the Athenæum. He also exhibited in the Pennsylvania Academy of the Fine Arts, and National Academy of Design. He produced but few pictures, and these met with ready sale. The British minister to the United States paid him $2,500 for one of his landscapes, a price which was considered notable then. But for some unexplained reason his popularity seems to have waned in his later life, and, toward the end, when he was living in New York, neglect, poverty, and sickness made him very unhappy.

His landscapes are rather small, and are usually in a delicate gray tone, the motives being simple river scenes, with the inevitable woody foreground of the period. The most admirable part of a typical Doughty is the sky, which is more subtly observed and more atmospheric in its values than are those of his American contemporaries. He was felicitous in the rendering of silvery effects of light, somewhat akin to those which are associated with the work of Corot, though far less perfect. He found the majority of his subjects along the banks of the Hudson, the Delaware, the Susquehanna, the Seine, and the Thames, being apparently as devoted to river

scenery as was Daubigny. His works are to be seen in the Metropolitan Museum of Art, New York City; the Pennsylvania Academy of the Fine Arts, Philadelphia; the Brooklyn Institute of Arts and Sciences; the Corcoran Gallery of Art, Washington; and in many private collections. The two landscapes belonging to the Pennsylvania Academy were shown in 1915 at the Panama-Pacific Exposition, San Francisco.

[Original sources of information as to Doughty's life are few in number, and particulars are almost wholly lacking. Wm. Dunlap's *Hist. of the Rise and Progress of the Arts of Design in the U. S.* (1834; rev. ed., 1918) devotes a little over a page to Doughty, but gives only an incomplete outline of his life. H. T. Tuckerman's *Book of the Artists* (1867) contains a brief narrative and appreciation. All of the subsequent accounts in books of reference appear to be derived mainly from the foregoing notices. Brief obituaries appeared in the *N. Y. Times,* July 24, and *Boston Transcript,* July 25, 1856, the latter copied from the N. Y. *Evening Post.*]

W. H. D.

DOUGHTY, WILLIAM HENRY (Feb. 5, 1836–Mar. 27, 1905), physician, son of Ebenezer Wesley and Margaret (Crowell) Doughty, was born in Augusta, Ga., where his father was a successful business man. He received his preliminary education at the Richmond County Academy, a typical school of the ante bellum South, and began the study of medicine with Doctors Dugas, Ford, Eve, and Campbell. He was graduated at the Medical College of Georgia (now Medical Department of the University of Georgia) in 1855 and at once began the practise of his profession in Augusta where, with the exception of the Civil War period, he lived until his death. At the outbreak of the Civil War he was commissioned surgeon in the Confederate army, serving as operating surgeon successively at the Macon Hospital, the Walker Division Hospital at Lauderdale Springs, Miss., and finally at the Second Georgia Hospital at Augusta. After the close of the war he was appointed instructor at the University of Georgia, becoming professor of materia medica and therapeutics in 1868, which position he held until 1875. Thereafter he devoted himself to his practise until his death.

He was one of the highly efficient general practitioners of an earlier generation. Resourceful, conscientious, and a deep thinker, he was beloved for personal as well as professional reasons, and, as so often happened with his type, he disregarded his own health and continued to work even when suffering from a lingering illness. He devoted much of his time to his cherished hobby, climatology, and was a pioneer in this country in the study of climate in its relation to medical science. He early pointed out that Arizona and neighboring regions afford a favorable climate for tubercular patients. Though he never saw the Pacific Ocean or took a sea voyage, he was one of the first to understand the rôle played by the Japan Current in the maintenance of the equable climate of California, and by reasoning and correlating the data obtained by others, he determined what he thought must be the course of the northern and North-American portions of the current, opinions which were later proved correct, as was also his estimation of the northernmost course of the Gulf Stream.

In medicine he wrote many clinical articles, chiefly in the fields of obstetrics and gynecology, though as a physician he is probably best remembered for his method of reducing dislocations of the clavicle. His paper on this subject was "True Method of Treating Dislocations Upwards and Backwards, of the Scapular End of the Clavicle, with Report of a Case Illustrating the Practise Employed" (*Richmond and Louisville Medical Journal,* July 1876). Among other medical writings are: "Atmospheric Distention of the Vagina in the Knee-Chest Posture" (*American Journal of Obstetrics,* October 1876); "The Primary Conversion of Occipito-Posterior into Occipito-Anterior Positions of the Vertex, with Cases Illustrating the Practice" (*Ibid.,* April 1878); and "Dislocations, Upwards and Backwards of the Scapular End of the Clavicle" (*Journal of the American Medical Association,* Aug. 8, 1891). Much of his work, including papers on climatology, was published in the *Southern Medical and Surgical Journal* and the *Southern Journal* of Augusta. He was instrumental in forming the board of health of his state and drafted the act of the legislature calling it into being. He was married on Oct. 11, 1855, to Julia Sarah, daughter of Dr. William L. Felder of Sumter, S. C. His son, William Henry Jr., became a physician of note and was dean and professor of surgery at the University of Georgia.

[W. J. Northen, *Men of Mark in Ga.,* vol. IV (1908); *Who's Who in America,* 1906–07; *Augusta Chronicle,* Mar. 28, 1905; personal data from a grandson, Dr. Roger C. Doughty of Columbia, S. C.]   E. E. H.

DOUGLAS, AMANDA MINNIE (July 14, 1831–July 18, 1916), author, daughter of John N. and Elizabeth (Horton) Douglas, was born in New York City, and obtained her formal education at the City Institute there. In 1853, her family moved to Newark, N. J., where she was to pass the rest of her life. Having early revealed a precocious talent for narration, shown in the telling of long fascinating stories to other children, she studied English and American literature with a private tutor after leaving school and began des-

ultorily to exercise her own pen. At the age of eighteen, however, she was about to take up designing and engraving when illness in the family forced her to stay at home and led her definitely to the pursuit of letters. Before the publication of her first book she contributed numerous stories to the *New York Ledger,* the *Saturday Evening Post,* the *Lady's Friend,* and had already established herself in a literary milieu. She became an important member of the Ray Palmer club— the oldest women's literary organization in the locality—and of the New Jersey Woman's Press Club. Her first book, *In Trust,* appeared in 1866, and from that date until 1913 when her last work, *Red House Children at Grafton,* was brought out, she published one or more volumes every year. In 1893 her novel *Larry* won the $2,000 prize offered by the *Youth's Companion* for the best piece of fiction for young people. Most of her works belonged to three extensive series, the Kathie Series, the Little Girl Series (*A Little Girl in Old New York,* 1896; *A Little Girl in Old Boston,* 1898; *A Little Girl in Old Philadelphia,* 1899, etc.), and the Helen Grant Series. All these were works of fiction intended for young readers. They were loosely constructed domestic chronicles dealing sympathetically with the joys and sorrows of family life, introducing enough of the darker sides of existence to throw into relief the virtues of patience, faith, and honor. Despite the fact that she never married, love of home and children formed the basic theme of all her work. Home in her books is always the haven where sorrows are healed and happiness is found. While her characters exemplify copy-book manners and their geographically informative travels follow guide-book methods and itineraries, there is an undercurrent of warmth and vitality in the work of Miss Douglas that raises her novels somewhat above the level of mere didactic writing. Her clear and simple style, without being brilliant, was well adapted to her audience and subjects. Although she lacked the breadth of interest and humor of her close friend Louisa M. Alcott, her works never rivaling the latter's in popularity, nevertheless during her long life her books circulated widely and even to-day they are in constant demand in public and Sunday-school libraries.

[C. H. J. Douglas, *A Collection of Family Records* (1879); *Woman's Who's Who of America,* 1914–15; *Who's Who in America,* 1916–17; obituaries in *Newark Evening News,* July 18, 1916, and *N. Y. Times,* July 19, 1916. The year of birth is given as 1837 by *Who's Who in America* but as 1831 by the *News* and the genealogy.]   G. G.

DOUGLAS, BENJAMIN (Apr. 3, 1816–June 26, 1894), manufacturer, was born at Northford,

Conn., the eighth and youngest child of Capt. William and Sarah (Kirtland) Douglas. His grandfather, William Douglas [q.v.], had been a colonel in the Revolution and his father a captain of militia in the War of 1812. He was reared on his father's farm, and his education was limited to a few months' attendance at the district school during the winter. At the age of sixteen he was apprenticed to a machinist and in 1836 began work in the shop of Guild & Douglas at Middletown, Conn., a firm established by his brother William in 1832. Benjamin and William in 1839 acquired the entire interest in the business and continued it under the name of W. & B. Douglas. For a time they ran an ordinary foundry and machine-shop, but after the brothers in 1842 invented the famous revolving cistern stand pump, the resources of the foundry were chiefly devoted to the manufacture of pumps. This pump gained recognition slowly, but eventually enjoyed a world market and brought a fortune to the inventors. William, who had been the mechanical genius of the firm, died in 1858 and Benjamin reorganized the concern into a corporation of which he remained president until his death. By the late seventies the company operated the largest foundry in Connecticut, manufacturing 1,200 styles and sizes of pumps.

Douglas for many years was prominent in Connecticut politics. He was a member of the state Assembly in 1854, and Republican lieutenant-governor of the state in 1861. An ardent abolitionist, he had been a founder of the Republican party in Connecticut, being one of the delegates who nominated Frémont in 1856 and one of the presidential electors who cast a vote for Lincoln in 1860. He was instrumental in the formation of one of the companies of the 1st Connecticut Artillery that went from Middletown. His part in the life of Middletown was likewise important. In addition to his service as mayor, 1849–55, he was chiefly responsible for the founding of the First National Bank of which he was president for many years. He was also president of the Farmers' & Mechanics' Savings Bank, and a trustee of the Middlesex Banking Company and of the Asylum Line Railroad. He threw himself into philanthropy and reform with the same enthusiasm that he did into business. A deacon of the Congregational church for thirty years, and for a long period superintendent of the Sunday-school, he acted as president of the Middlesex Branch of the Connecticut Bible Society and president of the Connecticut State Temperance Union. He served as trustee of Wesleyan University, 1862–85, and of the Connecticut State Asylum for the Insane.

He was married on Apr. 3, 1838, to Mary Adaline Parker, daughter of Elias and Grace (Totten) Parker of Middletown, by whom he had six children.

[W. R. Cutter and others, *Geneal. and Family Hist. of the State of Conn.* (1911), I, 293; *Hist. of Middlesex County, Conn.* (1884), 163–64; *Representatives of New England Manufacturers* (1879), I, 194–96; C. H. J. Douglas, *A Coll. of Family Records* (1879); W. F. Moore, *Representative Men of Conn.* (1894), p. 10; J. L. Bishop, *A Hist. of Am. Manufactures* (1866), III, 366, and the *Middletown Penny Press*, June 27, 1894.]   H. U. F.

DOUGLAS, HENRY KYD (Sept. 29, 1838– Dec. 18, 1903), lawyer, soldier, was born at Shepherdstown, near Harper's Ferry, W. Va. His father, Rev. Robert Douglas, was a native of Scotland, who, emigrating to Pennsylvania, married Mary, daughter of Col. John Robertson, and subsequently settled in the Shenandoah Valley. His early education having been obtained privately, Henry Kyd Douglas attended Franklin and Marshall College where he graduated in 1858. He then attended the law school of Judge Brockenbrough at Lexington, Va., obtaining his diploma in 1860, and being admitted to the bar at Charleston, W. Va. Proceeding west he settled in St. Louis, but on the outbreak of the Civil War returned home and enlisted as a private in Company B of the 2nd Virginia Regiment, which formed part of Stonewall Jackson's brigade. He took part in the battle of Bull Run, and rose by successive steps to the rank of captain. In March 1862 he made a spectacular ride, when, selected to convey the order of Stonewall Jackson, then at Mount Jackson, to Gen. Ewell at Brandy Station, he rode 103 miles, crossing the Blue Ridge in a heavy rain-storm, between five in the evening and sunrise the next morning. On his return to his regiment he was appointed inspector-general and aide-de-camp to Jackson. He accompanied the latter throughout the Shenandoah Valley campaigns, the battles of Gaines's Mill, White Oak Swamp, Malvern Hill, and was present when Jackson was killed at Chancellorsville. Promoted major, he was thereafter continually on staff duty till Gettysburg, where he was severely wounded and taken prisoner. Nine months later he was released from hospital and rejoined the Confederate army. In February 1865 he was given command of the Light Brigade in Gen. John B. Gordon's army corps, and after Petersburg his brigade formed the rear guard during the retreat to Appomattox. In the heavy fighting which ensued he was twice wounded, but continued in active command, his brigade firing the last shot and being the last unit of Lee's army to surrender. On being paroled he retired to Shepherdstown, but was arrested for transgressing military regulations and sentenced to three months' imprisonment. A false accusation of association with John Wilkes Booth caused him later to be taken to Washington, but his innocence of this charge was clearly established.

In September 1865 he opened a law office in Winchester, Va., but in November 1867 removed to Hagerstown, Md., where he thereafter made his home. During the labor disturbances of 1877 he commanded the Maryland forces guarding the Baltimore & Ohio and Chesapeake & Ohio railroads, and for some years was lieutenant-colonel of the 1st Maryland National Guard. E. E. Jackson appointed him associate justice of the fourth circuit on Apr. 8, 1891, but he occupied the bench for only seven months, being defeated in the elections of the following November. In 1892 he was appointed adjutant-general of Maryland by Gov. Brown and as such was in command of the state troops during the coal strike in the George's Creek District. He was unmarried.

His brief term on the Maryland bench afforded no opportunity for display of judicial qualities, but he had the reputation of being a sound lawyer, and his fluency of speech enabled him to achieve a measure of success as an advocate. He contributed the articles "Stonewall Jackson's Intentions at Harper's Ferry," and "Stonewall Jackson in Maryland" to *Battles and Leaders of the Civil War* (vol. II, 1887). Not a success as a politician, as a soldier he was in the front rank. Passing through all the grades, at Appomattox he was the youngest brigade commander in either army. He was wounded nine times. Six feet in height, well proportioned, with handsome features and a military bearing which was maintained even in later life, dignified and kindly, he was an outstanding figure in post-war Maryland circles.

[*Franklin and Marshall Coll. Obit. Record*, vol. II, pt. 4, no. 8 (1904); *Portrait and Biog. Record of the 6th Congressional District, Md.* (1898), p. 205; *Who's Who in America*, 1903–05, p. 409; Chas. King, "Long-Distance Riding" in *Cosmopolitan*, Jan. 1894; obituary notices in *The Sun* (Baltimore) and *Baltimore American*, Dec. 19, 1903.]   H. W. H. K.

DOUGLAS, JAMES (Nov. 4, 1837–June 25, 1918), metallurgist, mining engineer, and industrialist, was called by the *Engineering and Mining Journal* "the dean of the mining and metallurgical professions." Yet he began his career with a theological and medical education and was at one time the manager of an insane asylum. His father was a prominent surgeon in the city of Quebec, whence he had come from England, and was a man of philanthropic and cultivated tastes; he introduced the modern treatment of the insane in Canada when he took charge of the Quebec Lunatic Asylum. The father was also named James Douglas; the mother was Elizabeth (Ferguson) Douglas. The son published in 1910 *The Journals and Reminiscences of James Douglas, M. D.*, in memory of his father. The younger James Douglas was born in Quebec. When he was eighteen he went to the University of Edinburgh for two years' study in theology. In 1858 he received an A.B. degree from Queen's University in Kingston, Canada. He then traveled with his father, visiting Europe and Africa. After more study abroad and at home, including some courses in medicine, he was licensed to preach, but not ordained, and served for a time as assistant minister at St. Andrews Presbyterian Church in Quebec. He was married in 1860 in Frankfort, Germany, to Naomi, daughter of Capt. Walter Douglas of Quebec. On the basis of a rather slight instruction in chemistry while studying medicine, he served for several years as professor of chemistry at Morrin College, Quebec. His father had made an unfortunate investment in the Harvey Hill copper mines in Quebec. With Sterry Hunt the son experimented in the extraction of copper from the ores of these mines, and they invented the ingenious Hunt & Douglas process. In later life he paid a tribute to Hunt's influence upon him by writing *A Memoir of Thomas Sterry Hunt, M.D., LL.D.* (1898). At the age of thirty-eight he came to Phoenixville, Pa., to take charge of the copper-extraction plant of the Chemical Copper Company. The plant was not a financial success and was finally destroyed by fire. These were hard years for Douglas and his family. The turning point in his career did not come until he was nearly fifty, but then fortune smiled upon him generously.

In 1880, at the request of the conservative metal-dealers, Phelps, Dodge & Company of New York, he examined some copper claims at Bisbee, Ariz., and on his recommendation these claims were acquired and became the nucleus of the Copper Queen Consolidated Mining Company of which he became president. After several years of seeking an adequate supply of ore, during which his geological insight was of great value, the company began its successful expansion in mining, smelting, and railroading, which helped materially to develop the Southwest, and led to the building in 1886 of the El Paso & Southwestern Railroad. Douglas combined the direction of metallurgical researches and industrial improvements with humanitarian interests. The town of Douglas, Ariz., a smelting center near the Mexican border, was named after him. His policy of publicity for metallurgical improvements helped to dispel secrecy and suspicion in technology in America—an important reform. In 1906 he was awarded the gold medal of the Institution of Mining and Metallurgy (London), and in 1915 the John Fritz Medal for achievement in mining, metallurgy, education, and industrial welfare. He published not only numerous technical papers but also historical books, such as *Canadian Independence, Annexation and British Imperial Federation* (1894), *Old France in the New World* (1905), *New England and New France* (1913). McGill University conferred upon him the honorary degree of doctor of laws, and he later became chancellor of Queen's University. From 1899 to 1901 he was president of the American Institute of Mining Engineers; this institute awards annually the James Douglas gold medal for distinguished achievement in non-ferrous metallurgy. His numerous philanthropies included bequests to educational, medical, and engineering institutions.

His sons, James Stuart and Walter, became prominent in mining and financial circles. Although he lived at Spuyten Duyvil, New York City, and made frequent trips to the Southwest, he did not become a citizen of the United States. In appearance he was spare, bearded, and Scottish-looking. He was a man sincerely loved by many friends, and his personal influence in the mining and metallurgical professions was productive of much good.

[Obituary articles in the *Engineering & Mining Jour.*, July 6, 1918; R. W. Raymond, in *Bull. Am. Inst. Mining Engineers*, Sept. 1918; New York and Montreal newspapers; also an appreciative article by A. R. Ledoux in the *Bull. Am. Inst. Mining Engineers*, Jan. 1916, at the time of the award of the John Fritz medal.]

P. B. M.

DOUGLAS, STEPHEN ARNOLD (Apr. 23, 1813–June 3, 1861), Democratic leader, United States senator, belonged by birth and ancestry to New England but by all the circumstances of his adult life to Illinois and the Mississippi Valley. He was born in Brandon, Vt., and could trace his ancestry through successive generations to William Douglass, a Scotchman who came to Boston about the middle of the seventeenth century. On his mother's side he was related to the Arnolds of Rhode Island. There was, therefore, a strain of Celtic blood in the son of Dr. Stephen A. Douglass and his wife Sarah Fisk. While he was an infant, his father, a young physician, died, leaving the family dependent upon a brother of Mrs. Douglass. To this bachelor uncle Stephen owed his early schooling. For a time he hoped that he might prepare at Brandon Acad-

emy for Middlebury College, but this expectation had to be put aside. Instead he served a short apprenticeship to two cabinetmakers. It was a commonplace boyhood, though it was not without significance for the future politician. Vermont was rich in Revolutionary traditions; it fostered the town-meeting as a democratic institution; and it afforded in its own history a classic example of that popular sovereignty which became a veritable shibboleth in the later speeches of Senator Douglas. On the marriage of his mother to Gehazi Granger and of his sister to Granger's son, he followed them to Ontario County, N. Y., where he entered the Canandaigua Academy and later began the study of law. A certain restlessness took possession of him, however, and in June 1833, against the wishes of his mother, he set out for Cleveland, where he was encouraged to believe that he might be admitted to the bar within a year. He fell ill of typhoid fever, and when he left his bed four months later he was resolved to push farther west. After many wanderings which carried him as far as St. Louis, he finally paused at Jacksonville, Ill., forlorn, weary, and impoverished.

Jacksonville was then little more than a frontier village and just recovering from a scourge of cholera. Opportunities of employment were few, and Douglas was glad enough to move on to Winchester, ten miles away, where he was told a schoolmaster was wanted. There he was encouraged to open a subscription school for three months and eventually enrolled forty pupils. Meantime he boarded with the village storekeeper and read what law he could from borrowed books. In the following spring he returned to Jacksonville, and presented himself before a justice of the supreme court for a license to practise law. He still lacked a month of being twenty-one years of age. Though he opened a law office in the court-house, was elected state's attorney for the first judicial district within a year, and became a judge of the supreme court before he was twenty-eight, there is no reason to suppose that he acquired any profound knowledge of the law; but he was "Judge" Douglas to the end of his days. From the outset law was only the handmaid of his political ambitions. His rise as a politician coincided with that of the Democratic political machine in Illinois, in the making of which, indeed, he had a large part.

With a political wisdom beyond his years he urged upon his Democratic friends the necessity of party discipline if they would win elections. He was a stout champion, in season and out, of the methods he had seen in operation in New York under the Albany Regency. Organization from top to bottom was needed. He was a prime mover in the establishment of county and state nominating conventions, and reaped the reward of his exertions by being nominated and elected as Democratic member of the legislature from Morgan County. The tenth General Assembly which met in December of 1836 contained also Abraham Lincoln as a member of the "Long Nine" from Sangamon County. Soon after the adjournment Douglas accepted the post of register of the land office at Springfield, which this Assembly had decided to make the capital of the state. It was a strategic position and he proceeded to make the most of it. From this time on there was hardly a party maneuver in which he did not have a hand. A congressional district convention at Peoria in 1837 put him in nomination for Congress against the stalwart Maj. John T. Stuart, Whig candidate, much to the amusement of the opposition. It was hard to take this stripling seriously. Yet Douglas took himself seriously enough, campaigned over thirty-four counties, and gave the Whigs a scare that they did not forget for many a day. Douglas lost the election by only thirty-five votes. He now stood high in the party conclaves, and as the presidential election drew near he became the chairman of the Democratic state committee and the virtual manager of the Democratic campaign. It was generally conceded that the victory of the Democratic ticket in Illinois was due in no small measure to his efforts. In the autumn of 1840 Douglas was appointed secretary of state by the Democratic governor whom he had helped to elect. In the following months he took an active part in lobbying for the bill to reorganize the supreme court, and again he had his reward when he was appointed to one of the five new judgeships. While discharging his not very onerous duties Judge Douglas kept in close touch with his Springfield friends, who were bent upon sending him to the United States Senate though he lacked a year of the required age. This time vaulting ambition overleaped itself. He was defeated by five votes. A successful gerrymander by the Democrats, however, had created a promising congressional district which included the most populous counties of his circuit; and on June 5, 1843, a Democratic convention nominated him for Congress. In the exciting contest which followed, he addressed public meetings on forty successive days; and when election day came, he was prostrated by a fever from which he did not recover for months. But he won the election by a majority of 461 votes.

He now entered a larger arena. His personal appearance was not in his favor. An observer wrote of him: "He had a herculean frame, with the exception of his lower limbs, which were short and small, dwarfing what otherwise would have been a conspicuous figure. . . . His large round head surmounted a massive neck, and his features were symmetrical, although his small nose deprived them of dignity." What he lacked in dignity and bearing he made up in self-confidence and audacity. He threw himself into the debate which was raging over the bill to remit the fine imposed upon Gen. Jackson at New Orleans and won not only a hearing—which was as much as he had a right to expect—but enthusiastic applause from the Democratic side of the House. Then he made a plea for the support of Polk as president which delighted the wheelhorses of the party, so that he was asked by the Democratic central committee to take an active part in the campaign in the West. Before the presidential election occurred, he had himself been reëlected by a handsome majority over his Whig opponent.

Douglas was impatient with those who would compromise the claim of the United States to the whole of Oregon, and he was one of that small band of congressmen who shouted for "Fifty-four forty" to the bitter end. It was therefore humiliating to find the new President ready to compromise with Great Britain on the forty-ninth parallel. For a time Douglas sulked in his tent. When the war with Mexico came, however, he sprang to the support of the administration and became one of its most vigorous and successful defenders. A third time he was elected to Congress (1846) by an increased plurality. He seemed likely to be a fixture in the House when the legislature of Illinois elected him to the Senate as the colleague of Sidney Breese. He took his seat in December 1847 and was immediately made chairman of the Committee on Territories. It fell to him, therefore, to deal with the most difficult political problems of the next decade, when the anti-slavery movement reached its greatest momentum. Hitherto he had deplored all agitation against slavery which he regarded solely as a domestic institution wholly within the control of the states which countenanced it. Now he was brought face to face with an active demand on the part of political groups in the Northern states that Congress should exercise its powers at least to prevent the extension of an institution which affronted the moral sense of many citizens. At the same time, he was confronted with an equally insistent demand from Southerners of the Calhoun persuasion that no obstacles should be put in the way of those citizens who desired to take their slaves into territory acquired by their common exertions and now the property of the United States.

At this very time, in his own life, Douglas became acutely conscious of the push and pull of opposing forces. On Apr. 7, 1847, he had married Martha Denny Martin, daughter of Col. Robert Martin, a planter of Rockingham County, N. C., and owner also of a plantation in Mississippi. On the death of her father in the following year, Mrs. Douglas fell heir to his property, including some 150 slaves, which her husband, as a politician with Northern constituents, regarded as a distinct liability. There were always those who persisted—unfairly—in interpreting his subsequent career by this economic interest. Circumstances also drew him in an opposite direction. The center of gravity in Illinois politics was steadily shifting from the southern and central counties, originally settled by people from the Southern states, to the northern counties which were feeling the full force of the "Yankee invasion." In the summer of 1847 Douglas took up his residence in Chicago, invested heavily in real estate, and identified himself with those who had visions of the commercial greatness of the lake city. It was largely through his efforts that the projected Illinois Central Railroad from Galena to Cairo was linked with Chicago at the north and with Mobile at the south, by making common cause with the Mobile and Ohio Company, also a suppliant for congressional aid. Thus amended, the Illinois Central Railroad Bill passed both Houses of Congress just as the last of the compromise measures of 1850 came to a vote.

Meantime Douglas had a not unimportant part in framing two of these compromise measures. The bills providing territorial governments for Utah and New Mexico were drafted by him and Congressman McClernand, after conference with such southern Whigs as Toombs and Stephens, and were eventually adopted in their original form, which left the territorial governments free to enact laws on "all rightful subjects of legislation consistent with the Constitution of the United States" and promised that when the territories should be admitted as states, they should be admitted with or without slavery, as their constitutions should prescribe.

Though Douglas had not voted for the Fugitive-Slave Bill—he was unavoidably absent when the vote was taken—he approved of the Act and at Chicago made one of the best defenses of that much misunderstood measure (Johnson, "The Constitutionality of the Fugitive-Slave Acts," *Yale Law Review*, December 1921). Young men were irresistibly drawn to him by his gener-

osity, his courage, his willingness to assume complete responsibility for his acts even at the cost of popularity. It was this younger element in the party which urged his nomination for president in 1852 and would not be suppressed by their elders, who saw something ridiculous in the pretensions of a man of thirty-five. For a time, as the candidate of "Young America" against "Old Fogyism," he gave the supporters of Cass and Buchanan some concern. By the time the Democratic convention met, however, it was clear that he could not win, though on the thirty-first ballot he received the highest vote of any of the candidates. The success of the Democratic ticket in the election of 1852 assured his reëlection as senator, and he was prepared to assume the leadership of his party in Congress, when the death of his young wife changed the current of his life. When he took his seat in the Senate, his colleagues remarked an unwonted bitterness and acerbity of temper. He grew careless in his personal habits, slovenly in his dress, disregardful of his associates. When Congress adjourned, he sought diversion and rest in travels which took him into Russia and the near East. He returned refreshed in body and mind, if not much wiser by contact with the culture of the Old World.

He now entered upon the most turbulent period of his career. During his absence, events in the Middle West had again brought slavery and the territorial problem to the fore. Nebraska—the great area west of Iowa, Missouri, and Arkansas, which he had repeatedly endeavored to organize as a territory—had become an object of serious concern to Missouri politicians, to settlers lawfully or unlawfully in that region, and to promoters of a Pacific railway. No sooner had Congress met than a bill was introduced by Senator Dodge of Iowa for the organization of the territory, and promptly referred to the Committee on Territories. The chairman was soon made aware of the interests involved. Senator Atchison of Missouri, a friend of Douglas, lost no time in explaining his predicament. Under pressure from Thomas H. Benton, an avowed candidate for his seat, who was advocating the organization of Nebraska and St. Louis as the eastern terminus of a great central railway, he —Atchison—had changed his position and was demanding territorial organization without the slavery restriction (P. O. Ray, *The Repeal of the Missouri Compromise*, 1909, ch. iv). Newspapers in his own state and in the South were suggesting the wisdom of some such settlement as that worked out in the territorial bills of 1850 (*Ibid.*, chs. vi, vii). The urgency of some action was apparent from the presence in the House of two delegates, each claiming to represent a provisional government in Nebraska: one west of Missouri; the other, west of Iowa (*Ibid.*, chs. iii, v). Pacific railway interests also focussed upon the committee room of Senator Douglas. Far-sighted persons in the South, who worked through Secretary of War Davis, had persuaded the administration to open negotiations for a cession of Mexican territory which would make possible a southern route to the Gulf of California. These Southern interests were not averse to dilatory tactics with regard to Nebraska, unless concessions were made to them. All but two Southern senators, it was significant, had opposed the passage of a bill for the organization of Nebraska in the preceding session. Then there were the Chicago constituents of Senator Douglas who had visions of a northern route to the Pacific with the lake city as the eastern terminus. To their representations he could not remain indifferent (F. H. Hodder, *The Genesis of the Kansas-Nebraska Act,* 1913).

Out of the Committee on Territories came finally a new bill with a report, Jan. 4, 1854, which asserted that legal opinion was divided on the constitutionality of the Missouri Compromise, but, avoiding a pronouncement on this legal point, held that the compromise measures of 1850 were designed to establish certain great principles applicable to Nebraska as well as to New Mexico and Utah: to wit, that all questions pertaining to slavery in the territories should be left to the decision of the people residing therein by their appropriate representatives. Cases involving title to slaves were to be referred to the local courts, with right of appeal to the Supreme Court of the United States. An attempt by Southern senators to repeal the Missouri Compromise explicitly by amendment to this bill led to the famous Sunday conference of administration leaders at the White House, on Jan. 22, 1854. Out of this conference emerged the Kansas-Nebraska Bill providing for two territories instead of one and declaring the prohibition of slavery in the Act of 1820 "superseded." A subsequent change, the product of frequent caucuses held by Democratic leaders (Johnson, *Douglas,* pp. 243–45), substituted the phrase "inoperative and void," and added the declaration that the bill did not propose to legislate slavery into or exclude it from any state or territory, but "to leave the people thereof perfectly free to form and regulate their domestic institutions in their own way, subject only to the Constitution of the United States." In the ensuing debates Douglas coined a phrase which became his slogan in after years. This fundamental principle hitherto

dubbed "squatter sovereignty" he now dignified with the name "popular sovereignty," a principle, he averred, as old as the Revolution ("The Genesis of Popular Sovereignty" in *The Iowa Journal of History and Politics,* January 1905).

Meantime the Independent Democrats in Congress had published their "Appeal . . . to the People of the United States," arraigning the bill as "a gross violation of a sacred pledge" and "a criminal betrayal of precious rights" for personal advantage in the presidential game. The insinuation was unfair. Douglas had nothing to gain from subserviency to the South. His best chance of national preferment, if indeed that had been in his thoughts, lay in the opposite course (Johnson, *Douglas,* pp. 205–06). This is not to say that he was not an opportunist, for such he was by nature and political habit. Facing a question that threatened to rend his party, he sought to unite it on what he genuinely believed to be a fundamental principle. By an appeal to an instinct so elemental in American nature as a belief in political self-determination, he expected to offset any reluctance to brush aside a mere legislative fiat on the subject of slavery. What he failed to gauge accurately was the attachment of the Northern Democrats to what Chase called "a compact binding in moral force" for more than thirty years. Nor could he weaken this attachment by the truly statesmanlike assertion that climate, and not any human enactment, dedicated the whole Northwest to freedom (*Washington Union,* Feb. 2, 1854; *Globe,* 33 Cong., 1 Sess., pp. 278–79). Climate seemed a frail reliance where human freedom was at stake.

Though Douglas made two memorable speeches during the debate in the Senate, the real contest was waged in the House. Here Richardson, speaker of the House, and that adroit parliamentarian Alexander H. Stephens, finally secured the passage of the bill by a scant majority of thirteen; but the master mind was Douglas. To him fell "the marshaling and directing of men," and to him belonged the glory—or the blame. As he returned to Chicago, traveling by the light of his burning effigies as he afterward said, he might have doubted—if he had been so inclined— whether he had achieved his objective. Had he united his party on a principle which would be accepted North and South? As events proved, so far from consolidating his own party, it drove Democrats of strong anti-slavery sentiments into temporary fusion with anti-slavery Whigs and Free-Soilers. Another consequence was the contest between pro-slavery and free-state settlers for the control of Kansas. By the spring of 1856, Kansas had two rival governments: a territorial legislature in the control of the pro-slavery elements, and a free-state government at Topeka which had drafted a constitution and applied for admission into the Union.

When Douglas made his report on Mar. 12, 1856, for the Committee on Territories, to which all matters relating to Kansas had been referred, he fixed the responsibility for the breakdown of popular sovereignty upon those who through organizations incorporated in distant states had sought to control the domestic institutions of Kansas. He found a vindication of his principle in the peaceful history of Nebraska, "into which the stream of emigration was permitted to flow in its usual and natural channels." He insisted that the legislature of Kansas was a legal body and proposed a bill to authorize it under certain restrictions to call a convention to frame a constitution; but neither this nor the Toombs Bill which his committee subsequently reported with amendments, came to a vote, for the country was on the eve of a presidential election and politicians were sparring for time.

Douglas had already been indorsed as candidate for the Democratic nomination by several state conventions, but even before the convention met at Cincinnati, a well-organized movement was under way to nominate James Buchanan [q.v.] of Pennsylvania. After the sixteenth ballot, when Buchanan received 168 votes and Douglas 122, Douglas instructed his friends to withdraw his name and to support that candidate who received a majority. On the next ballot Buchanan was unanimously nominated. It was highly creditable to Douglas, under the circumstances, that he put himself unreservedly at the service of the party in the ensuing campaign, speaking in all the doubtful states and contributing liberally out of his own pocket to the party campaign fund. His real-estate ventures in Chicago had proved highly profitable and he was generous to the point of prodigality with his easily acquired wealth.

Soon after the election (Nov. 20, 1856), Douglas married Adèle Cutts, daughter of J. Madison Cutts of Washington and great-niece of Dolly Madison, whom she is said to have resembled in charm of manner. She was indisputably the belle of Washington, beautiful, warm-hearted, and universally loved and admired. It was always a mystery to Washingtonians that she should have chosen to give herself to this unromantic widower, who preferred the society of men, was none too careful in his dress and personal habits, and was convivial beyond even the custom of the day. Yet it proved to be in every respect a happy marriage. She became the de-

voted partner of all his toils and an affectionate mother to his two boys. She brought to him also distinguished social alliances, and at their residence in Washington dispensed a lavish hospitality that was long remembered.

When Douglas returned to Washington in the fall of 1857, a convention at Lecompton, under the control of the pro-slavery elements, had adopted a constitution which in effect guaranteed the right of property in slaves now in the territory, though the fictitious choice was given to the people of Kansas of voting for the constitution with slavery or the constitution with no slavery. Meantime the free-state people, who had unfortunately taken no part in the election of delegates to this convention, had secured control of the territorial legislature. There could be no doubt that in any fair test a pro-slavery constitution would be decisively rejected. Douglas was disturbed by rumors that President Buchanan approved of this constitution and would recommend favorable action by Congress. He immediately sought an interview with the President and found his fears confirmed, whereupon he threw down the gauntlet and declared that he would oppose the policy of the administration to the bitter end. On Dec. 9, he took the irrevocable step and in one of the really great efforts of his career denounced the Lecompton constitution as a travesty on popular sovereignty. The speech made a profound impression, not only upon those who heard it, but on the country, for no one could mistake its import. Douglas had broken with the dominant pro-slavery faction of his party. In the weeks that followed, he was made to pay the price of insurgency. The party press was set upon him; his friends were turned out of office; he was subjected to scurrilous abuse. Nor did he receive much aid and comfort from the ranks of the opposition. Republicans were slow to trust the author of the Kansas-Nebraska Act. His motives were impugned. The weathercock, it was said, had found which way the wind was blowing in Illinois: he was a candidate for re-election. Under these assaults his health broke and for a fortnight he was confined to his bed, rising only by sheer force of will to make an impassioned plea on Mar. 22, 1858, for fair dealing in Kansas and a defense of his own course. Again he spoke to crowded galleries, and to anxious colleagues who saw in his defection a menace to the integrity of the Democratic party.

In the following April the Democratic state convention of Illinois closed the door to reconciliation with the administration by giving Douglas an unqualified indorsement. It was the signal for a bitter and determined effort to prevent his reëlection to the Senate. For a moment it seemed as though he might receive some Republican support. Eastern Republicans who felt that he was now fighting their battles against the administration counseled their Illinois friends not to oppose him; but these Illinois Republicans had minds of their own and nominated Abraham Lincoln as their first and only choice for the United States Senate. Aside from the relentless and often insidious opposition of the administration, Douglas seemed to have every advantage in this interesting contest. He was known everywhere; he was always sure of an audience; he enjoyed the favor of the Illinois Central Railroad which put special trains at his service; he drew liberally upon his own pecuniary resources; he was aided by a gerrymander which gave the Democrats an advantage in electing members of the legislature. He forfeited some of these advantages, however, when he accepted Lincoln's proposal of a series of joint debates, for Lincoln had no such following and could command no such public attention. The picturesque features of these joint debates, in which Lincoln appears for the first time as a national figure, have given them perhaps an undue importance. So far as Douglas was concerned, they only widened the breach between him and the dominant faction of his party by forcing him to deny the full force of the Dred Scott decision as interpreted by friends of the administration. Douglas professed to accept the decision as commonly understood and to Lincoln's insistent demand that he explain how the people of a territory, under the vaunted principle of popular sovereignty, could forbid slavery, when the Supreme Court had declared that Congress had not that power under the Constitution, he replied that the decision of the Court was only *obiter dictum* on that point and that, no matter what the Supreme Court might at some future time decide as to the abstract question, slavery could not exist anywhere without police regulations, which could only be established by the local legislature. If this was not good law, it was a truthful statement of the course of American history whenever federal law has run athwart deep-seated local convictions. The vote throughout the state gave the Republicans a popular majority, but only a minority of seats in the next legislature. When the two Houses met in joint session, Jan. 6, 1859, Douglas received fifty-four and Lincoln forty-six votes for the United States Senate.

Douglas had won a great personal triumph, but he had still to discover that his worst foes were those of his own political household. He was deposed from the chairmanship of the Committee on Territories and regarded with hardly disguised hostility by his Democratic colleagues from the South. He smothered his resentment, however, attended the Democratic caucus, and gave his cordial support to Slidell's bill for the purchase of Cuba, determined to prove his orthodoxy on party policies wherever he could. On Feb. 23, he was drawn into a debate in which, hard pressed by Jefferson Davis and other Southern senators, he declared himself utterly opposed to any active intervention by Congress to protect slave property in the territories. Thenceforth he threw restraint to the winds and lost no opportunity to force the fighting. In letters which he allowed to find their way into the newspapers, he denounced any attempt to revive the African slave-trade or to read into the party creed any such new issues as a congressional slave code for the territories. He prepared an elaborate essay, which was published in *Harper's Magazine,* on "The Dividing Line between Federal and Local Authority," in which he attempted to reconcile popular sovereignty with the Dred Scott decision.

When, then, the Democratic convention met at Charleston in the following April, the lines on which it would divide were already drawn. The majority report of the Committee on Resolutions asserted the right of Congress to intervene in a territory to protect slave property; the minority reports upheld the principle of non-intervention. Both factions agreed to frame a platform before naming candidates; but when one of the minority reports was adopted seven of the Southern delegates protested and withdrew. The rest of the delegations then proceeded to ballot. Douglas led on all fifty-seven ballots but could not command the necessary two-thirds; and on the tenth day the convention adjourned to meet two months later in Baltimore. There, on June 23, after the withdrawal of the other Southern delegations, Douglas was nominated by acclamation, upon receiving all but thirteen votes on the second ballot. The bolters nominated John C. Breckinridge as their candidate. The Democratic party was hopelessly rent in twain. The nomination of Abraham Lincoln by the Republican party and of John Bell by the Constitutional Union party further complicated the political situation.

At the outset of the campaign Douglas believed that he would carry most of the Southern states and enough free states to insure his election, or at least to throw the election into the House of Representatives; but as the summer wore on, he became less confident. His active personal campaign was sharply criticized as a regrettable innovation; but his intimates knew that his designs now went far beyond any personal ambition. By mid-summer he admitted frankly that Lincoln would probably be elected; his own efforts were bent upon reorganizing the Democratic party and quashing the disunion movement in the South. The popular vote in the election of 1860 was a personal triumph for Douglas, for he alone of all the candidates drew votes from every section of the country and his total vote fell only 489,495 short of Lincoln's. Compared with the vote for Breckinridge and for Bell in the South, his vote was negligible, but at the North he ran far ahead of both. It is difficult to escape the conclusion of a shrewd observer that popular sovereignty had a strong hold upon the instincts of nine-tenths of the American people (*New York Times,* June 26, 1860).

In the critical last weeks of the Buchanan administration, Douglas put himself unreservedly at the service of those who feared for the integrity of the Union and who still believed in the efficacy of compromise. He served on the Committee of Thirteen and voted for the ill-fated Crittenden resolutions. As hopes of congressional action faded, he urged upon Lincoln the calling of a national convention to amend the Constitution so as explicitly to forbid the federal government from interfering with the domestic institution of slavery in the states. The insistence of Douglas, supported by Seward, probably led Lincoln to modify his inaugural address at this point (Johnson, *Douglas,* pp. 464-65). Nothing that Douglas ever did was more to his credit than his support of the new president in the early days of his administration. It was not a matter of trifling importance that Senator Douglas purposely made himself conspicuous at the inauguration and courteously held the President's hat while he read his address. Nor was it without significance that Senator and Mrs. Douglas were among the first to call at the White House and to rally Washington society to the support of the plain, homespun couple who seemed so out of place in the presidential mansion (*New York Times,* Mar. 8, 10, 1861).

Immediately after the firing on Fort Sumter, Douglas accompanied George Ashmun to the White House, at the latter's suggestion, to assure the President of his support. He was cordially received and heard the President read a draft of the proclamation calling for 75,000 volunteers to suppress rebellion. His only criticism was: "I would make it 200,000!" Otherwise their accord was complete. In the columns of the newspapers next morning Democrats read the President's proclamation and a dispatch

(written by Douglas) announcing the determination of Senator Douglas fully to sustain the President in the exercise of all his constitutional functions to preserve the Union. From this time on Douglas was in frequent conference with the President. It was on Lincoln's advice that he left the Capital to rouse the people of the Northwest to the seriousness of the crisis. He spoke twice on the way, both times with obvious emotion, deprecating secession and pleading for the support of the government at Washington. On Apr. 25, he made a remarkable speech to his own people in the Capitol at Springfield. Fifty years later, men who had been his political opponents could not speak of it without emotion. "I do not think it is possible," wrote Horace White, "for a human being to produce a more prodigious effect with spoken words" (Herndon-Weik, *Lincoln,* II, 126-27). His great sonorous voice reverberated through the chamber until it seemed to shake the building, stirring men and women to a frenzy of excitement. In a few weeks that great voice was still. Stricken soon after with typhoid fever, he battled resolutely as ever with this last foe, but succumbed on June 3, 1861, his last words a message to his two boys bidding them to obey the laws and support the Constitution.

[Of the first biographies of Douglas published in 1860 for use in the presidential campaign, only that by James W. Sheahan has historical value, but it is both defective and inaccurate for the early part of Douglas's career. A brief sketch was written by W. G. Brown in 1902 for the Riverside Biographical Series, and a *Life* by William Gardner in 1905. Neither was based on intimate study of sources. In 1908 was published Allen Johnson's *Stephen A. Douglas: a Study in American Politics,* the first attempt to use contemporary newspapers to supplement manuscript sources. The footnotes indicate the sources used for it and for the foregoing article. This study was followed by C. E. Carr's *Stephen A. Douglas His Life Public Services, Speeches and Patriotism* (1909), and H. P. Willis's *Stephen A. Douglas* (1910) in the American Crisis Biographies, which contain little new information. In October 1912 the so-called "Autobiography" was first printed in the *Journal of the Illinois State Historical Society,* but it had long been available in manuscript copies. It was hastily written by Douglas in 1838 and never revised, according to Judge Robert M. Douglas. "The Life of Stephen Arnold Douglas" by F. E. Stevens, published in 1924 in the *Journal of the Illinois State Historical Society* (Vol. XVI) contains some fresh information of a personal nature but in general is uncritical and discursive. *Abraham Lincoln 1809-1858* by Albert J. Beveridge (2 vols., 1928), is the only biography of Lincoln which treats Douglas other than as a foil for the hero.]

A. J.

DOUGLAS, WILLIAM (Jan. 27, 1742/3-May 28, 1777), Connecticut sailor and soldier, was born in Plainfield, Conn., the fourth son of John and Olive (Spaulding) Douglas, of a family long prominent in the eastern part of the colony. In 1759, although only sixteen years of age, he enrolled as a clerk in a regiment led by Eleazer Fitch and Israel Putnam in the campaign against Quebec (*Connecticut Historical Society Collections,* vol. X, 1905, p. 170) and served, it is said, as Putnam's orderly sergeant. In early manhood Douglas removed to New Haven, from which port he engaged successfully in the West-Indian trade, building up thereby a modest fortune. On July 5, 1767, he married Hannah Mansfield of New Haven, who bore him four children. He retired from active commercial enterprise about 1774 and established a new home in Northford, about eight miles from New Haven. From the outbreak of the Revolution he was an active supporter of the colonial cause. In April 1775 the Assembly appointed him a major in the militia, but a month later he accepted a captaincy in David Wooster's regiment, raised for service in the Canadian expedition. With this regiment he took part in Gen. Richard Montgomery's advance along Lake Champlain. Because of his nautical experience, Montgomery assigned Douglas to boat service on the lake. He returned to Connecticut in the early winter with his regiment which did not accompany Montgomery down the St. Lawrence to Quebec. During the first three months of 1776 he served as major in a volunteer regiment commanded by Andrew Ward which assisted in preparing the defenses of New York and Brooklyn. At this time the Continental Congress appointed him commodore of the vessels on Lake Champlain in view of his excellent service during the previous year (*Journal of the Continental Congress,* Mar. 26, 1776; American Archives, 4 ser. V, 389, 437–38, 1,378). Douglas declined this command, however, as he preferred to organize and lead a battalion in Gen. James Wadsworth's brigade of Connecticut troops in the New York campaign. Douglas's men were stationed on the extreme right of the American line at the battle of Brooklyn, and he had the mortification of seeing the British in occupation of Fort Sterling, which he had himself helped to erect "in cold, tedious weather." At Kip's Bay, on the Manhattan side of the East River, he commanded a brigade of Connecticut militia on Sept. 15. Under heavy fire from the British war-ships, his raw troops gave way in confusion in spite of strenuous efforts to rally them by Douglas and later by Washington himself. This retreat enabled the British to land on Manhattan, but the incident increased rather than diminished Douglas's reputation for gallantry and coolness under fire. With his battalion he took an active part in the remainder of the autumn campaign, although the necessary hardships and exposure seriously aggravated in him symptoms of tuberculosis which were already well developed. Upon the expiration of the battalion's term of enlistment in December, Douglas at once set about the raising of a new regiment to serve in the Continental Army for the duration of the war, but he was destined never again to take the field. He was elected to the Connecticut Assembly which met on May 12, 1777, but probably was unable to attend since he died at Northford before the month was out. His loss was unfortunate for the Continental Army; he had been unselfishly devoted to the cause and had displayed soldierly qualities of a high order. His portrait shows him to have been tall and slender with an erect carriage and strong features. An older brother, John Douglas (Apr. 12, 1734–Sept. 22, 1809), also served during the Revolution. As lieutenant-colonel and later colonel of Connecticut troops, he took a not very conspicuous part in the siege of Boston and the campaign around New York. From 1777 until the end of the war he held the rank of brigadier-general of militia, in command of the 5th Brigade, but participated personally only in one minor expedition into Rhode Island in the autumn of 1777.

[Some of William Douglas's letters from the field have been printed in Henry P. Johnston, "The Campaign of 1776 around New York and Brooklyn" in *Memoirs of the Long Island Hist. Soc.,* vol. III (1878), and others in the *N. Y. Hist. Soc. Quart. Bull.,* Jan. 1929–Jan. 1930. Information on the military careers of both brothers is to be found in *The Public Records of the Colony of Conn. 1636–1776* (1850–90); *The Public Records of the State of Conn.* (1894–1922), and *Record of Service of Conn. Men in the Revolution.* Genealogical data, portraits of Wm. Douglas and his wife, and a not entirely reliable sketch of his career, are included in Chas. H. J. Douglas, *A Collection of Family Records, with Biog. Sketches, and Other Memoranda of Various Families and Individuals Bearing the Name Douglas* (1879).]

L.W.L.

DOUGLAS, WILLIAM LEWIS (Aug. 22, 1845–Sept. 17, 1924), shoe manufacturer, and governor of Massachusetts, was born at Plymouth, Mass., the son of William and Mary C. (Vaughan) Douglas. His father died when the lad was only five, and the latter's only formal education was secured at brief, irregular intervals in the public schools. In his career he was a fine example of the poor orphan boy made successful and eminent almost entirely by his own industry and enterprise. At the age of seven he was bound out to his uncle, a shoemaker, and set to work pegging shoes when he was so small that he had to stand upon a box to reach the bench. His hours were long, and, besides his routine duties in the shop, he had to gather fuel for two fires. At fifteen he was a full-fledged journeyman shoemaker. He then entered a large cotton-mill at Plymouth, his daily wage being thirty-three cents. During a period when he was on crutches because of a broken leg, he hobbled to school two miles each way. After his recovery, he carried on his trade in Hopkinton, Mass., and later in South Braintree, under Ansel Thayer, a famous bootmaker. At the age of nineteen, he enlisted (Feb. 26, 1864) in Company I, 58th Massachusetts Regiment, but he was wounded in the back at Cold Harbor later in that year and spent many months in army hospitals. Discharged at the close of the war, he went West, settling for a time in Black Hawk, Colo., and later in Golden City in the same state, where he was for a time in the retail shoe trade. He returned East and on Sept. 6, 1868, married N. Augusta Terry, at Plymouth.

From 1870 to 1875 Douglas was a superintendent in the Porter & Southworth factory at North Bridgewater (now Brockton), Mass. In 1876, with a borrowed capital of $875, he began manufacturing for himself in a small room, 30 x 60 feet, with five employees and an output of forty-eight pairs of shoes a day. There were times when Douglas was his own buyer, cutter, and salesman, and even his own expressman, and he often worked eighteen and twenty hours at a stretch. In 1879 he moved into larger quarters, and two years later erected a large three-story factory on Pleasant St. In 1884 he took the unprecedented step of advertising his own shoes; and eventually his own portrait, his first trade-mark, was stamped on the soles of all his products. It was not long before his face, printed constantly in the newspapers to advertise Douglas shoes, became familiar to everybody who had eyes with which to see. In 1892, with the erection of a new and still larger factory at Montello Station, Brockton, the business was incorporated, with a capital of $2,500,000, and was soon employing 4,000 operatives. In 1923, the year before his death, it was manufacturing 17,000 pairs of shoes daily and controlling 117 retail stores scattered throughout the country.

Douglas entered political life in 1884 as a Democratic member of the Massachusetts House of Representatives, and in 1886 he sat for a term in the state Senate. He was a councilman of Brockton, and, in 1890, was chosen mayor of that city. He was a delegate to the National Democratic conventions of 1884, 1892, and 1896, and delegate-at-large in 1904. In the last-named year, he ran for governor, and was elected by a large majority, being, however, the only Democrat on the ticket to be successful. While he was in office (1905–06), the legislature was strongly Republican, and he had little influence on lawmaking. He declined to run for a second term. As governor, he refused to waste time by attending banquets or public functions not associated

with his position, and he enjoyed the respect even of his political opponents.

Douglas was a man of simple and unostentatious tastes, who was never ashamed of his early poverty. He was never talkative, and believed in deeds rather than words. A liberal philanthropist, he gave a complete surgical building to the Brockton Hospital and established the Brockton Day Nursery. As an executive, he was fair and just, and was esteemed highly by labor-unions. His only real recreation was work, though he went South each year for a month in Florida, and he owned a summer home at Monument Beach overlooking Buzzard's Bay. After the death of his first wife, he married on Apr. 10, 1913, Mrs. Alice (Kenniston) Moodie. She and two daughters survived him. He died very suddenly in a hospital after an operation, at the age of eighty, and was buried in the Melrose Cemetery, in Brockton, with many distinguished persons following his body to the grave.

[Much information regarding Douglas may be found in *The Boy Who Pegged Shoes* (n.d.), a little pamphlet published by the W. L. Douglas Shoe Company. See also the *Boston Transcript* for Sept. 17, 1924; *Who's Who in America*, 1922–23.]   C. M. F.

DOUGLASS, DAVID BATES (Mar. 21, 1790–Oct. 21, 1849), engineer, soldier, teacher, was born at Pompton, N. J. A son of Nathaniel and Sarah (Bates) Douglass, he was of Scotch and English ancestry, both the Douglass and Bates families having lived in Morris County, N. J., since the early years of the eighteenth century. The iron-mining region in which he grew up was not well provided with schools, but the boy was well instructed and disciplined by his mother, a woman of unusual intellectual gifts. He was prepared for college by the Rev. Samuel Whelpley, and entered the sophomore class at Yale. He was determined to become an engineer, but at Yale he could do little to prepare himself. At the time of his graduation, in 1813, however, the country was in the midst of its second war with Great Britain; engineer officers were in demand, and careers were open even when training had been deferred. Douglass was accepted and commissioned as second lieutenant of engineers and ordered to West Point where he could train. During 1814 he saw active service on the Niagara frontier. For his gallant conduct in the defense of Fort Erie he was commended in official dispatches by Gen. Gaines, was promoted to a first lieutenancy and brevetted captain. On Jan. 1, 1815, he was assigned, as assistant professor of natural philosophy, to the Military Academy which was under reorganization at West Point. In December of that year he married Ann Eliza, daughter of Andrew

Ellicott, professor of mathematics at West Point. Quickly taking his place as one of the most progressive and efficient among the younger instructors at the post, Douglass was transferred successively to the chairs of mathematics and engineering, bettered his professional standing, and in the meantime received important outside assignments from the government. He served with surveys of the defenses of Long Island Sound, as astronomical surveyor with a commission to determine the Canadian boundary from Niagara to Detroit, and in the exploration of Lake Superior region conducted in 1820 by Gen. Cass. Later he was employed, as consulting engineer or in charge of special projects, by canal and railroad corporations, as well as by the State of Pennsylvania. The number of such engagements led him to resign from the army in 1831.

For nearly three years he had been interested in the Morris and Essex Canal of New Jersey, then under construction, and particularly in the substitution of inclined planes with mechanical lifting power for canal locks. After leaving West Point he directed that work. At the same time (1832–33) he held a professorship of natural philosophy in the University of the City of New York, later becoming professor of civil engineering and architecture with few required duties. He designed the University's building in Washington Square. More noteworthy, however, was his relation to the New York City water supply. Acting as engineer for the commissioners in 1834–36, he selected the Croton water-shed in preference to two other possible sources in Westchester County, located the route of the aqueduct, and determined all the essential features of the system, including the crossing of the Harlem River on a high bridge. With later enlargement this system continued to supply New York with water for seventy-five years. Before the actual building of the Croton Aqueduct had been begun Douglass was superseded as chief engineer, but his plans were followed in the construction, with slight changes. It appeared that incompatibility had developed between him and the chairman of the Board of Commissioners (see *A Memoir of the Construction, Cost, and Capacity of the Croton Aqueduct*, 1843, compiled from official documents by Charles King, pp. 140–43). His next important undertaking was the planning and laying out of Greenwood Cemetery in Brooklyn. This work occupied him until 1840, when at the suggestion of his friend and former pastor, Bishop McIlvaine [q.v.], he was called to the presidency of Kenyon College, then a feeble and struggling institution under

the care of the Protestant Episcopal Diocese of Ohio. The authority committed to Douglass as president was only nominal. The college did not flourish and friction developed with the trustees and with the bishop. Although no charges were preferred against Douglass, in 1844 he was requested by the trustees to resign. On his refusal, he was removed; but the trustees at the same time expressed confidence in him and appreciation of his merits. Returning to his profession, he worked on cemetery projects at Albany, N. Y., and at Quebec for several years, but in 1848 was chosen to the professorship of mathematics and natural philosophy at Geneva (later Hobart) College, Geneva, N. Y. There he died in the following year, as the result of a paralytic stroke.

[C. H. J. Douglas, *Family Records*, etc. (1879); F. B. Dexter, *Biog. Sketches Grads. Yale Coll.*, vol. VI (1912); G. W. Cullum, *Campaigns of the War of 1812–1815 against Great Britain, with Brief Biogs. of the Am. Engineers* (1879), pp. 234–66, and *Biog. Reg. U. S. Mil. Acad.* (3rd ed., 1891); C. B. Stuart, "Maj. David Bates Douglass" in *Van Nostrand's Eclectic Engineering Mag.*, Jan. 1872; N. Cleaveland, *Greenwood Cemetery: a Hist. of the Institution* (1866); *N. Y. Express*, Oct. 25, 1849; *The Kenyon Book* (c. 1890). The Kenyon College controversy is outlined in D. B. Douglass's pamphlet, *A Statement of Facts and Circumstances Connected with the Removal of the Author from the Presidency of Kenyon College* (1844), *Reply of the Trustees of Kenyon College, to the Statement of D. B. Douglass* (1844), and *A Further Statement of Facts in Answer to the Reply of the Trustees* (1845), by D. B. Douglass.] W.B.S.

DOUGLASS, FREDERICK (Feb. 1817?–Feb. 20, 1895), abolitionist, orator, journalist, was named Frederick Augustus Washington Bailey, but assumed the name of Douglass after his escape from slavery. He was born at Tuckahoe near Easton, Talbot County, Md., the son of an unknown white father and Harriet Bailey, a slave who had also some Indian blood. As a child he experienced neglect and cruelty, indulgence and hard work; but particularly the tyranny and circumscription of an ambitious human being who was legally classed as real estate. He turned at last upon his cruelest master, and by fighting back for the first time, realized that resistance paid even in slavery. He was sent to Baltimore as a house servant and learned to read and write with the assistance of his mistress. Soon he conceived the possibility of freedom. The settlement of his dead master's estate sent him back to the country as a field hand. He conspired with a half dozen of his fellows to escape but their plan was betrayed and he was thrown into jail. His master's forbearance secured his return to Baltimore, where he learned the trade of a ship's calker and eventually was permitted to hire his own time. A second attempt to escape, Sept. 3, 1838, was entirely successful. He went to New York City; married Anna Murray, a free colored woman whom he had met in Baltimore, and together they went to New Bedford, where he became a common laborer.

Suddenly a career opened. He had read Garrison's *Liberator,* and in 1841 he attended a convention of the Massachusetts Anti-Slavery Society in Nantucket. An abolitionist who had heard him speak to his colored friends asked him to address the convention. He did so with hesitation and stammering, but with extraordinary effect. Much to his own surprise, he was immediately employed as an agent to the Massachusetts Anti-Slavery Society. He took part in the Rhode Island campaign against the new constitution which proposed the disfranchisement of the blacks; and he became the central figure in the famous "One Hundred Conventions" of the New England Anti-Slavery Society. It was a baptism of fire and brought out the full stature of the man. He was mobbed and mocked, beaten, compelled to ride in "Jim Crow" cars, and refused accommodations; but he carried the programme through to the bitter end.

Physically, Douglass was a commanding person, over six feet in height, with brown skin, frizzly hair, leonine head, strong constitution, and a fine voice. Persons who had heard him on the platform began to doubt his story. They questioned if this man who spoke good English and bore himself with independent self-assertion could ever have been a slave. Thereupon he wrote his *Narrative of the Life of Frederick Douglass* which Wendell Phillips advised him to burn. It was a daring recital of facts and Phillips feared that it might lead to his reënslavement. Douglass published the little book in 1845, however, and then, to avoid possible consequences, visited Great Britain and Ireland. Here he remained two years, meeting nearly all of the English Liberals. For the first time in his life he was treated as a man and an equal. The resultant effect upon his character was tremendous. He began to conceive emancipation not simply as physical freedom; but as social equality and economic and spiritual opportunity.

He returned to the United States in 1847 with money to buy his freedom and to establish a newspaper for his race. Differences immediately arose with his white abolitionist friends. Garrison did not believe such a journal was needed and others, even more radical, thought that the very buying of his freedom was condoning slavery. Differences too arose as to political procedure in the abolition campaign. In all these matters, however, Douglass was eminently practical. With all his intense feeling and his reasons for greater depth of feeling than any white abolitionist, he had a clear head and a steady hand. He allowed his freedom to be bought from his former master; he established the *North Star* and issued it for seventeen years. He lectured, supported woman suffrage, took part in politics, endeavored to help Harriet Beecher Stowe establish an industrial school for colored youth, and counseled with John Brown. When Brown was arrested, the Governor of Virginia tried to apprehend Douglass as a conspirator. Douglass hastily fled to Canada and for six months again lectured in England and Scotland.

With the Civil War came his great opportunity. He thundered against slavery as its real cause; he offered black men as soldiers and pleaded with black men to give their services. He assisted in recruiting the celebrated 54th and 55th Massachusetts colored regiments, giving his own sons as first recruits. Lincoln called him into conference and during Reconstruction, Douglass agitated in support of suffrage and civil rights for the freedmen. His last years were spent in ease and honor. He was successively secretary of the Santo Domingo Commission, marshal and recorder of deeds of the District of Columbia, and finally United States minister to Haiti. His second marriage, in 1884, to Helen Pitts, a white woman, brought a flurry of criticism, but he laughingly remarked that he was quite impartial—his first wife "was the color of my mother, and the second, the color of my father." He was active to the very close of his career, having attended a woman-suffrage convention on the day of his death.

[The chief sources of information about Frederick Douglass are his autobiographies: *The Narrative of the Life of Frederick Douglass, an American Slave* (1845), republished in England and translated into French and German; *My Bondage and My Freedom* (1855); *Life and Times of Frederick Douglass* (1881). The best biographies are: F. M. Holland, *Frederick Douglass, the Colored Orator* (1891); C. W. Chesnutt, *Frederick Douglass* (1899); Booker T. Washington, *Frederick Douglass* (1907). There are numerous references in W. P. and F. J. Garrison, *William Lloyd Garrison 1805–1879* (4 vols., 1885–89), and throughout the literature of the abolition controversy. Many of Douglass's speeches have been published.]   W. E. B. D.

DOUGLASS, WILLIAM (*c.* 1691–Oct. 21, 1752), physician of Boston, the second child of George Douglass, "portioner" of Gifford and factor for the Marquis of Tweeddale, was born in the town of Gifford, Haddington County, Scotland. He apparently received a liberal education, for he was familiar with Greek, Latin, Dutch, French, and English, and was known to have studied medicine at Edinburgh, Leyden, and

Paris. He came under the influence of Pitcairn, the leading physician of Scotland in his day, and was at Leyden during the supremacy of Boerhaave. In his writings (*e.g.,* letter to Cadwallader Colden, Feb. 20, 1721, *Massachusetts Historical Society Collections,* 4 ser., II, 164) he refers to himself as a medical graduate, but whether he received his degree from Edinburgh or Leyden is not known. After a trip to the West Indies, he settled in Boston in 1718. He was first heard of in the colony in connection with the inoculation controversy. Early in the summer of 1721 a severe epidemic of smallpox broke out in Boston, and Zabdiel Boylston [*q.v.*] was prevailed upon by Cotton Mather [*q.v.*] to carry out inoculations for smallpox during the epidemic. Douglass disapproved strongly of the practise and was the more concerned since he had, "sometime before the small-pox arrived, lent to a credulous vain Preacher, Mather, Jr., the *Philosophical Transactions* Nos. 339 and 377 which contain Timonius' and Pylermus' account of Inoculation from the Levant" (*Ibid.*). Douglass held that inoculation might spread smallpox, and he accordingly published a series of four controversial "inoculation" pamphlets, three of which were anonymous. In 1751, when he finally became convinced of the value of the procedure, he wrote, "The novel practice of procuring the small-pox by inoculation, is a very considerable and most beneficial improvement in that article of medical Practice" (*A Summary, Historical and Political,* II, 406). His chief claim to recognition as a physician rests on his masterly description of an epidemic of scarlet fever, *The practical History of a New Epidemical Eruptive Miliary Fever . . . in Boston New England in the Years 1735 and 1736* (1736). From his account it is clear that this was a genuine epidemic of scarlet fever, and is indeed the first adequate clinical description of the disease, for it antedates that of John Fothergill by twelve years. Douglass described fully the eruption and desquamation, and spoke of the greater susceptibility of children and young persons. He moreover carried out necropsies on individuals dead of the disease.

Douglass was versatile and a man of wide interests. He possessed a large library, recorded observations upon the weather and the variations of the needle of the compass, collected plants, and in 1743 published an almanac (*Mercurius Nov-Anglicanus* by "William Nadir"). He also wrote, *A Summary, Historical and Political, of the First Planting, Progressive Improvements and Present State of the British Settlements in North America* (vol. I, 1749; vol. II, 1751; re-

printed in Boston and also in London, 1755; London, 1760), and a treatise on economics entitled, *A Discourse Concerning the Currencies of the British Plantations in America,* etc. (London, 1739; Boston, 1740). The *Summary,* which was written at odd times stolen from his professional work, was often based upon hearsay and tradition since but few documented sources were available to him, and it is therefore marred by many inaccuracies, but it contains a great mass of information on a variety of subjects and is an important source book of early colonial history (Bullock). In his *Discourse* Douglass showed a sound grasp of the principles of exchange, a clear understanding of Gresham's law, and he stated in no uncertain terms that the colony must adhere to the "universal commercial medium" if it is to have dealings with foreign nations. Douglass was highly esteemed in the colony and had a large medical practise. Being a person of strong prejudices he had enemies, but from the records which have come down to us he appears to have been well regarded by all the better educated people of Boston.

[The most authoritative account of Douglass is that of G. H. Weaver, "Life and Writings of Wm. Douglass, M.D., 1691–1752," *Bull. Soc. Medic. Hist. of Chicago,* II, 229–59 (Apr. 1921); see also C. J. Bullock's notes to his reprint of Douglass's *Discourse Concerning the Currencies* in *Am. Econ. Asso., Economic Studies,* II (1897), 265; J. Thacher, *Am. Medic. Biog.* (1828), I, 255; article by Burrage in H. A. Kelly and W. L. Burrage, *Am. Medic. Biogs.* (1920), which gives further references.]   J.F.F.

DOVE, DAVID JAMES (*c.*1696–April 1769), educator, pamphleteer, the son of David and Mary Dove, was born in Portsmouth, England, where his father was a tailor. His early life is obscure. He was a surety in two marriage cases in 1728 in Chichester, where he taught grammar for sixteen years before coming to America. He arrived with his wife in Philadelphia in 1750 and applied for a position in the newly founded Academy. The trustees appointed him English master for one year, beginning Jan. 7, 1751, at a salary of £150. Franklin quickly recognized his unusual abilities. The English school grew in numbers and he was given two assistants. Encouraged by his success he opened in September 1751 an academy for young ladies. He was the first person in Pennsylvania, and perhaps in the colonies, who attempted to supply higher education for women. The trustees of the Academy, however, thought that these new cares caused him to neglect his work in the English school and in February 1753 they reluctantly accepted his resignation which took effect in July. Richard Peters, once a student of Dove's, said that he was a "sarcastic and ill-tempered doggerelizer, who was but ironically *Dove*; for his temper was that of a hawk, and his pen the beak of a falcon pouncing on innocent prey." In 1757 he published *Labour in Vain; or, An Attempt to Wash a Black-Moor White*, a lengthy caricature of Judge William Moore, then under arrest for having libeled the Assembly. His pen turned easily to Hudibrastic verse and the etchings with which he often adorned his broadsides are, despite his lack of formal training, as free and vigorous as any of Gilray or Rowlandson. On the last day of 1758 he issued a pamphlet entitled, *The Lottery. A Dialogue between Mr Thomas Trueman and Mr Humphrey Dupe* and attacking the lotteries then employed by the Academy and other institutions to raise funds as "manifestly no better than public frauds." At this time he conducted a school for both boys and girls in Videll's Alley (now Ionic St.). It was here that Alexander Graydon [*q.v.*] attended school. In his substitution of disgrace for corporal punishment and in other measures Dove showed himself to be well in advance of the pedagogy of his time.

In February 1761 he was unanimously elected to the English mastership of the new Germantown Union School, founded to compete with the Academy in Philadelphia. His tenure began the middle of June, although the Union School was not opened until August. He lodged and boarded twenty of his students in his small quarters at the Union School. To the townspeople who were thus deprived of a source of income this was a genuine grievance; they petitioned the trustees who remonstrated with Dove. The eccentric English master and the trustees were temperamentally incapable of understanding each other; there was bickering and argument. He was meanwhile building his own school alongside the Union School; and when this was completed in the summer of 1763 he resigned and opened his own academy. Under the pseudonym of Philopatrius he published on Feb. 18, 1764, *The Quaker Unmask'd; or, Plain Truth, Humbly Address'd to the Consideration of all the Freemen of Pennsylvania*. This was a defense of the Paxton Boys; in it he suggested that the Quakers were enamored of both Indian squaws and Indian trade and demanded if a Quaker could consistently be the representative of a people who are constantly called upon to make war in their own defense. Noteworthy among the pamphlets and broadsides attacking him was *The Medly* by Isaac Hunt [*q.v.*]. This broadside, containing an etching of Dove probably by Henry Dawkins, accused him of gross immorality. He replied with *The Counter-Medly, being a Proper An-*

swer to all the Dunces of the Medly and their Abettors. He continued his school in Germantown until 1768 when he was again in Philadelphia conducting a school on Front St., near Arch. In the spring of the following year he died and on April 4, 1769, was buried in Christ Church burying ground.

[*Hist. of the Germantown Academy* (1910); T. H. Montgomery, *Hist. of the Univ. of Pa.* (1900); Alexander Graydon, *Memoirs of his own Time*, ed. by John S. Littell (1846); broadsides and pamphlets in libraries of the Hist. Soc. of Pa., and the Philadelphia Library Company; information from Ernest Spofford and Bunford Samuel of Philadelphia.]   F.M.

DOW, HENRY (1634–May 6, 1707), New Hampshire soldier and statesman, the second son of Joan and Henry Dow, was born at Ormsby in Norfolkshire. His father migrated with his family to Watertown in the colony of Massachusetts Bay in 1637, and was there admitted freeman on May 2, 1638. He removed to Hampton in 1644. Henry Dow, Jr., was without formal education but became an important and financially prosperous figure in the town of Hampton and the province of New Hampshire. He was chosen selectman in 1661 and several times reelected to that office. He served as town clerk from 1681 to 1707 (Joseph Dow, *post*, p. 565). He was admitted and sworn as an attorney in 1686 and thereafter represented the town in litigation. He was ensign of the Hampton militia in 1689, captain in 1692, and took part in the first and second intercolonial wars. Dow was sworn in as deputy marshal of the province of New Hampshire in 1680, and was appointed sole marshal of the province at a salary of £5 on Mar. 10, 1681/2 (*Provincial Papers*, XIX, 661, 663, 684). He was appointed justice of the court for New Hampshire under the governments of Joseph Dudley and Edmund Andros, justice of the inferior court of common pleas of the province of New Hampshire in 1695, and senior justice in 1699. He repeatedly represented the town of Hampton in the lower house of the legislature of New Hampshire, serving as clerk and speaker *pro tempore* in 1701 (*Ibid.*, 736). He was treasurer of the province, 1694–95 (*Ibid.*, III, 267, 268), and a member of the Council from 1702 until his death. He was twice married: on June 17, 1659, to Hannah, the daughter of Robert and Lucy Page, and on Nov. 10, 1704, to Mary, the daughter of Capt. Christopher Hussey and widow of Thomas Page and Henry Green. By his first marriage he had four sons.

[R. P. Dow, *The Book of Dow* (1929); Jos. Dow, *Hist. of the Town of Hampton, N. H.* (1893); *Provincial Papers of N. H.*, esp. vols. II, III, XII, XIX, XXXI.]   I.M.C.

DOW, LORENZO (Oct. 16, 1777–Feb. 2, 1834), evangelist, was born in Coventry, Conn., fifth of the six children of Humphrey Dean and Tabitha (Parker) Dow. His parents, natives of Coventry, brought up their children frugally, educating them, as Lorenzo said, "both in religion and common learning" (*Journal*, p. 1). In 1794, he began preaching, making his evangelistic excursions on horseback, and in 1796 he was accepted into a tentative connection with the Methodist ministry—only to be suspended after three months. Then he preached again independently, desperately poor and generally ill, but frequently within one week traveling as much as 150 miles and preaching as often as twenty times. In 1798, readmitted to his former status with the Methodists, he soon afterward, though opposed by his ecclesiastical superiors, set out to carry his gospel into Ireland. After about eighteen turbulent months there, he returned to New York in May 1801, and almost immediately left by sea for Georgia. He preached there for a few months, returned to New York, and in November 1802 again turned southward, this time overland, proclaiming everywhere his threats of hell, and hopes of paradise, bringing in many converts. He visited the Indians, delivered the first Protestant sermon ever listened to in Alabama, talked in Charleston freely enough to be, at a later time, convicted for libel, and turning northward, preached through the Carolinas, Tennessee, and Virginia. Remembering that in Ireland he had seen "the first pair that I thought were happy in marriage" (*Eccentric Preacher*, p. 77), he decided to take a wife, and accordingly on Sept. 3, 1804, in Westernville, N. Y., he was married. The bride, Peggy Holcomb, born in 1780 in Granville, Mass., entered into the union upon the express understanding that she would never hinder him in his roamings. Leaving her the day after the wedding, he began a swing to Mississippi and return, preaching constantly, and jotting down in his diary notes of dreams and of actual occurrences. By April 1805 he was home again; in July he started for the Carolinas; in November, taking Peggy with him, he embarked for England. There Peggy bore a daughter, Letitia, who soon died. They returned to America in June 1807, and together, from Boston to Natchez and Natchez to Boston, they toured the country, he, long-haired and braced in a little leather jacket, calling himself "Cosmopolite," reputedly rich both in money and in the gift of prophecy, and she everywhere and always abetting him. In 1818 he again went to England, but soon after his return in 1820, Peggy died. Three months later he was married to Lucy Dolbeare of

Montville, Conn. From then on, he wrote more and preached less, issuing, after his habit instituted in 1804, a chaotic torrent of egoistic pamphlets, and constantly revising his journals. Living on his farm in Connecticut, he accumulated affidavits about his own good character, compounded medicines recommended for biliousness, quarreled acrimoniously, litigated, to his sorrow, with his neighbors about a mill race, and stormed incessantly against Whigs, anti-Masons, Catholics, and finally against Methodists, who, he said, were badly tainted with popery. Death came to him suddenly in Georgetown, Md.

[*The Dealings of God, Man, and the Devil; as Exemplified in the Life, Experience, and Travels of Lorenzo Dow ... Together with his Polemic and Miscellaneous Writings Complete. To Which is Added The Vicissitudes of Life*, by Peggy Dow (1856); *The Eccentric Preacher; A Sketch of the Life of the Celebrated Lorenzo Dow* (1841); C. C. Sellers, *Lorenzo Dow* (1928); W. J. Townsend, H. B. Workman, G. Eayrs, *A New Hist. of Methodism* (1909); H. Asbury, *A Methodist Saint* (1927).]   J.D.W.

DOW, LORENZO (July 10, 1825–Oct. 12, 1899), inventor, business man, was born in Sumner, Me., the eldest child of Huse and Zilpha (Drake) Dow. He was one of many thousand children named for Lorenzo Dow [*q.v.*], the irregular preacher and inventor of camp-meetings. His father was a Methodist minister and one of the first circuit riders, who died at the age of forty years from overwork and privations. Lorenzo Dow received his primary education in Sumner, prepared for college at the typical "academy," and won the scholarship to Wesleyan University awarded to the oldest son of any Methodist minister. Following his graduation in 1849 he taught school in Vermont and New Jersey for a year and then went "around the Horn" to California where he remained from 1850 to 1853. In the latter year he returned to the East and after teaching school for a few months in Alabama he went to New York and began the study of law. In 1854 he went to Topeka, Kan., completed his law studies in 1857, entered politics, and in 1858 was elected a judge of the supreme court under the Leavenworth Constitution. The following year he was elected mayor of Topeka and also served as editor of the *Kansas Tribune*.

With the outbreak of the Civil War, he turned his attention to improvements in ordnance and on Oct. 1, 1861, obtained his first patent for a waterproof cartridge. The waterproofing substance used was collodion. Upon the adoption of this cartridge by the federal government Dow went to New York and became associated with the Remington Arms Company, in whose plant the cartridges were to be made. Here he continued his experiments and was granted four additional patents on waterproofing cartridges and shells. This work continued except for one interruption of a business trip to Europe in 1862–63, until 1866, when Dow went to South America and took up engineering work and business in Colombia. He cleared the old Spanish dike leading from the Magdalena River to Cartagena and established a steamboat service thereupon to the interior. Upon completing this work in 1870, he moved with his family to Port of Spain, Trinidad, and for the next three years engaged in mining in various parts of Venezuela.

In 1873 he returned to the United States and for nine or ten years engaged in mining work in Colorado, after which he took up his residence in New York City, remaining there for the balance of his life. In 1896 he organized in New York the Dow Composing Machine Company of West Virginia to develop and market the type-distributing and type-setting machines invented by his son Alexander Dow, patents for which were granted Nov. 24, 1896, and Nov. 28, 1899, respectively. Dow continued as president of this company until his death. He was twice married: first on Dec. 25, 1853, to Elizabeth Penfield of Middletown, Conn., and after her death to Mrs. Sabrina (Smith) Anderson, on Oct. 2, 1862. He was survived by a son and a daughter of his second marriage.

[R. P. Dow, *The Book of Dow* (1929), pp. 250–51; *Alumni Record of Wesleyan Univ.* (1911); obituaries in *N. Y. Tribune* and *N. Y. Times*, Oct. 14, 1899; Wesleyan University Records; Patent Office Records.]

C. W. M.

DOW, NEAL (Mar. 20, 1804–Oct. 2, 1897), temperance reformer, the "father of the Maine Law," was born in Portland, Me., the only son of Josiah and Dorcas (Allen) Dow, both parents being of English and Quaker descent. He was early trained in those principles of temperance, industry, and thrift for which the Society of Friends has always stood, and to these principles he remained constant throughout his life, although eventually dismissed from the Society because of his changing views on the use of "carnal weapons." This break was inevitable, for Dow was a man of intense convictions with the moral and physical courage to support them. To these characteristics he added from childhood robust health, and, although a man of medium size and weight, marked physical strength and vitality. He was educated in the schools of Portland, and at the Friends' Academy in New Bedford, Mass., and desired to go on to college and enter the law, but to this his parents objected, and, in consequence, he entered his father's tan-

ning business, eventually becoming a partner. His interest in books continued, however, and at his death he possessed one of the largest and finest private libraries in the state.

On Jan. 20, 1830, he married Maria Cornelia Durant Maynard, by whom he had nine children, four of whom died in infancy. In business he was as successful as his ambition demanded. He was active on the directorates of several manufacturing and other corporations, becoming, in fact, one of Portland's leading men of affairs. After 1857, however, his connection with business became little more than nominal, owing to his increasing participation in the temperance crusade.

The intolerable amount of intemperance prevailing in Maine during his youth, together with his Quaker training and the interest of his parents in temperance reform, constitute the general background of Dow's interest in the temperance movement. Later, his own experiences with the drink evil as an employer of labor, as a member of the Portland fire department, and as an overseer of the poor, definitely convinced him of the serious need of reform, and led to his active interest in furthering it. At the age of twenty-four, when clerk of the Deluge Engine-Company, he made his first temperance address, successfully opposing the presence of liquor at a Company dinner, while about the same time he interested himself in the temperance program of the Maine Charitable Mechanics' Association of which he was a member. In 1834, as a delegate of the Portland Young Men's Temperance Society, he attended the first state temperance convention at Augusta where the Maine State Temperance Society was organized to discountenance the use of ardent spirits. Four years later, he withdrew from this last society to organize, with others, the Maine Temperance Union which was pledged to total abstinence and resolved to consider the expediency of petitioning the legislature for prohibitory legislation. Not until 1845, however, could the Union be committed definitely to the cause of legislative prohibition, and then only following an intensive campaign of popular education on the wisdom of so radical a step. In this task of educating public sentiment Dow was an indefatigable worker, speaking wherever opportunity offered throughout the state. That the reformers were making progress became evident in 1846 when a prohibitory measure based largely upon the report of Gen. James Appleton [*q.v.*], which had been tabled by the legislature nine years before, was finally enacted. This law, however, proved to be unsatisfactory in the provisions for its enforcement, and the campaign for a more severe law continued. In 1851 Dow was elected mayor of Portland, and the city council at once made him chairman of a committee to visit the legislature and urge the passage of a law "stringent in its provisions and summary in its processes" which would make it possible to drive the illegal liquor traffic from the city. Dow drew up the bill he desired, and, May 26, 1851, was given a public hearing at Augusta in the House of Representatives. So convinced was the legislature that Dow had the popular sentiment of the state behind him that his bill promptly passed both houses by large majorities, and, June 2, 1851, was signed by Gov. Hubbard. Backed by this legislation, Dow returned to Portland and summarily cleaned up the city, despite some interesting opposition. With the passage of the "Maine Law" his reputation as a temperance reformer became world-wide. Extensive speaking tours throughout the North followed, and in 1853 he served as president of the World's Temperance Convention in New York City.

Again elected mayor of Portland in 1855, he was scarcely in office when there occurred the "June riot," the work of elements within the city hostile to prohibition. In the reaction which followed this unfortunate affair the "Maine Law" was repealed by the legislature, but the popular sentiment of the state was in favor of prohibition and in 1858 it was again enacted. In 1857, at the request of the United Kingdom Alliance, Dow had visited England and lectured widely on prohibition.

On the outbreak of the Civil War, Dow, whose hostility to slavery had been only less than his opposition to the liquor traffic, offered his services to his state, and in the fall of 1861 became colonel of the 13th Regiment of Maine Volunteers. In February 1862, he joined Gen. Butler's command and went to the Gulf Department, where he was commissioned a brigadier-general of volunteers on Apr. 28, 1862. At the battle of Port Hudson he was twice wounded, and while recuperating in a private home within the Union lines was captured by the enemy and spent eight months as a prisoner in Libby prison, Richmond, and at Mobile. Eventually, Mar. 14, 1864, he was exchanged for Gen. Fitzhugh Lee. Temporarily broken in health he returned to Portland, and resigned from the army on Nov. 30, 1864. Following the war, he wrote and spoke extensively in behalf of prohibition, not only traveling throughout the United States but, in 1866–67 and 1873–75, again visiting Great Britain. In 1880 he ran for president of the United States as the candidate of the Prohibition party, receiving

10,305 votes. Four years later the people approved a prohibitory amendment to the state constitution and in the campaign for this amendment he took an active part, although then eighty years of age. He died in Portland, retaining to the end an active and vigorous interest in the cause he had done so much by his zeal and courage to further.

[Dow's autobiography, *The Reminiscences of Neal Dow, Recollections of Eighty Years* (1898); H. S. Clubb, *The Maine Liquor Law, its Origin, History and Results, including a Life of Hon. Neal Dow* (1856); a campaign biography by T. W. Organ, *Biog. Sketch of Gen. Neal Dow* (1880); A. A. Miner, "Neal Dow and his Life Work," *New England Mag.*, June 1894; Intimate pictures of Dow in his later years by Frances E. Willard, "Neal Dow's Ninetieth Birthday" and Mrs. Jos. Cook, "Neal Dow as Guest and Host," *Our Day*, Jan., Feb. and July, Aug. 1894, respectively.]   W.R.W.

DOWELL, GREENSVILLE (Sept. 1, 1822–June 9, 1881), surgeon, son of James and Frances (Dalton) Dowell, was born in Albemarle County, Va., his parents' home, where he attended the local schools and pursued private study with more than usual success. He attended medical lectures at the University of Louisville (1845–46) and at Jefferson Medical College, receiving the M.D. degree in 1847. He began the practise of his profession at Como, Miss., where on June 29, 1849, he married his first wife, Sarah Zelinda, daughter of John H. White of that place. He practised successively at Memphis, Tenn., and in Gonzales and Brazoria counties, Tex. (1853). In 1863 he entered the Confederate army and served first as surgeon of Cook's Heavy Artillery and later as surgeon-in-chief of the hospital department. After the war he lived at Galveston, Tex., until the end of his life, and in this city acquired a leading professional position. For two years he was professor of anatomy at the Medical Department of Soulé University and he became lecturer in surgery when that institution became the Texas Medical College. He was in charge of the Galveston Hospital for many years, which under government contract cared for marine patients. Though remote from the larger medical centers he managed to publish many papers of worth, and in 1869 founded the *Galveston Medical Journal*. He had charge of the campaign against yellow fever in Vicksburg, Miss., in 1878, being himself immune to the disease from an early attack. In 1868 he married, as his second wife, Mrs. Laura Baker Hutchinson of Galveston.

He is remembered chiefly for his monograph, *Yellow Fever and Malarial Diseases, embracing a History of the Epidemics of Yellow Fever in Texas* (1876), a text which revealed logical application of epidemiological methods as then known and in addition the all-important suggestion that yellow fever is transmitted by mosquitoes. In 1873 he published a short text, *The Radical Cure of Hernia,* in which he described the operation bearing his name. He designed or adapted several surgical appliances, some of which in more or less modified form are still in use, including: a wire speculum, lithotomy instruments, a retention catheter, instruments for extracting bullets and arrow-heads, and a urethrotome. He was original, bold, and resourceful and with better opportunities he might have been a brilliant surgeon. He was noted as a linguist, having knowledge of seven languages.

[*Trans. Am. Medic. Asso.,* XXXIII (1882), 546; W. B. Atkinson, *Physicians and Surgeons of the U. S.* (1878), 199; John F. Y. Paine in H. A. Kelly and W. L. Burrage, *Am. Medic. Biogs.* (1920), p. 327; *Galveston Daily News,* June 10, 1881.]   E.E.H.

DOWIE, JOHN ALEXANDER (May 25, 1847–Mar. 9, 1907), founder of the Christian Catholic Apostolic Church in Zion, was born in Edinburgh. His mother, Ann Macfarlane-Mc-Hardie, was illiterate; his putative father, her second husband, John Murray Dowie, was by vocation a tailor, by avocation a preacher. John Alexander's childhood was passed in poverty, sickness, and precocious piety. At the age of six he took the temperance pledge and early developed a fanatical hatred of alcohol, as well as a life-long conviction of being a peculiar object of God's care. In 1860 his parents moved to Adelaide, South Australia, where he went to work first with an uncle and then with a wholesale drygoods firm of which he later became junior partner. This promising business opportunity he abandoned at the age of twenty in order to study for the ministry. He spent two years at the University of Edinburgh, then returned to Australia, and on May 21, 1870, was ordained pastor of the Congregational Church at Alma. Subsequently he was called to Sydney and then to a larger church in Newton, a suburb of Sydney. In 1878, deciding that it was wrong for a minister to receive a salary, he went into evangelistic work so successfully that in 1882 he was able to build a large independent tabernacle in Melbourne. Hitherto he had devoted himself chiefly to the extermination of liquor and tobacco, defying the laws which prohibited his activities (even serving thirty-four days in jail rather than abandon them); but he now found, or fancied, in himself an ability to heal diseases by means of prayer and such healing was henceforth the major feature of his evangelistic work. During all these years in Australia his sincerity seems to have been unquestioned; his pronounced egotism had not yet passed into megalomania, and his later craving for power, luxury, and notoriety had not yet developed.

He came to San Francisco in June 1888 and remained on the Pacific Coast for two years, meeting, however, with an indifferent response. He then moved to Chicago where for the next six years he carried on services of divine healing with steadily increasing success. In 1895 the clergymen and physicians of Chicago attempted to stop his work through the courts, but although nearly one hundred charges were made against him, Dowie won every case. The ill-advised attempt merely advertised him the more. On Jan. 22, 1896, he called a meeting of those interested in forming a new church under his leadership, and on Feb. 22 the Christian Catholic Church in Zion was definitely organized with Dowie as General Overseer. The church prospered from the outset. Dowie blazed the trail later followed by Billy Sunday: his speeches, adorned with American Billingsgate, vituperative and sensational, easily aroused the passions of his ignorant audiences, while their minds were lulled to sleep by the hypnotic rhythm of his style. His enormous brow, large eyes, and venerable beard gave him an impressive appearance, while his bow-legs were hidden in elaborate flowing robes. His claims to divine inspiration grew ever stronger. In 1899 he identified himself with the Messenger of the Covenant prophesied by Malachi, in 1901 he proclaimed himself to be Elijah the Restorer, and in 1904 he consecrated himself the First Apostle. Meanwhile forty-two miles from Chicago he had built up the most amazing town in America, Zion City, composed of something more than five thousand of his followers exclusively. No theatres, dance halls, secret lodges, drug stores, or physicians' offices were permitted; smoking, drinking, and the eating of pork were penalized; whistles blew for public prayers; while every industry in the town, its bank, and its college were owned and entirely controlled by Dowie. With his accounts unaudited, Dowie's private income became considerable. He now kept two expensive homes, one at Zion City and one near Montague, Mich., and lived with an ostentation unbefitting a second Elijah. His church claimed 50,000 members scattered in various parts of the world; its publications were printed in half a dozen languages; missionaries were beginning to be sent out. In the fall of 1903, however, Dowie met his first check. Having determined upon the conversion of New York City, he and 3,000 followers, on ten special trains, invaded the metropolis, and held meetings during a part of October and November, but without permanent result. New York was at first amused, then disgusted, and finally bored. Insistent upon being a celebrity at all costs, Dowie had given wide publicity to the story that he was really the son of a British nobleman, but even this was of no avail; New York refused to be interested in a problematic scandal fifty years old. The trip had cost $300,000 and there were murmurs in Zion City, but Dowie paid no heed; instead, with a dozen of his officers he went on a "Round the World Visitation." Upon his return, in order to meet the now serious financial situation, he commanded every resident in Zion City, on pain of expulsion, to deposit funds in the Zion City bank; with this accomplished he was off on trips to Mexico in a vain attempt to establish the "Zion Paradise Plantation" there. On Sept. 24, 1905, he suffered a serious paralytic stroke and was taken to Jamaica. As soon as the tyrant was disabled, the slaves rose in revolt. Dowie's most trusted friend, Wilbur Glenn Voliva, to whom he had given full powers of attorney, led a movement which on Apr. 2, 1906, deposed the autocrat, took from him all his Zion City properties, and suspended him from membership in the church on account of "polygamous teaching and other grave charges." Dowie at once returned to Chicago, but broken as he was in health he could not make great headway against the rebellion. Nevertheless he fought on gallantly in the courts until his death less than a year later.

[Rolvix Harlan, *John Alexander Dowie* (1906); *The Personal Letters of John Alexander Dowie,* comp. by Edna Sheldrake (1912); *Zion Banner,* 1901–05; *Leaves of Healing,* I–XX; the *Chicago Tribune,* Mar. 10, 1907.]

E. S. B—s.

DOWNER, ELIPHALET (Apr. 4, 1744–Apr. 3, 1806), "the fighting surgeon of the Revolution," was the ninth child of Joseph and Mary Sawyer Downer. Born in what was then Norwich, but is now Franklin, Conn., he settled in Brookline, Mass., where he married Mary Gardner in 1766 and practised medicine till the Revolution. He was a volunteer fighter against the British on their retreat from Lexington, but later ministered to the wounded Redcoats and even collected wine, linen, and money for their relief. After Lexington he served as surgeon of the 24th Continental Regiment of Foot, and was mentioned by Gen. Heath as active and enterprising. In May 1776, he sailed as surgeon of the privateer sloop *Yankee.* The ship made several rich captures in June, but in July its crew were overpowered by the prisoners aboard and taken first into Dover and then into London. Downer, in a deposition to Franklin, which was sent to the British ambassador in France as a protest against the harsh treatment accorded American prisoners by the British, and which was later circulated in American newspapers, told how the crew were kept in suffocating quarters and were given little attention when sick. Downer himself was confined in various prison ships at London and Sheerness until gangrene set in in one of his legs and he was moved to Haslar Hospital, Gosport. There he recovered, and then escaped to France at some time not later than March 1777 (Stevens Transcripts, No. 670).

From Apr. 16 of that year to about July 6, he served as surgeon of the Continental sloop *Dolphin,* Capt. Samuel Nicholson (Muster Roll of the *Dolphin,* John Paul Jones Papers, vol. I, Library of Congress), which in company with the *Reprisal* and *Lexington,* circled the British Isles and made nineteen captures (Stevens Transcripts, No. 703). In returning to France, however, the *Dolphin* was chased, sprung a mast, and had to throw overboard her guns to get safely into St. Malo. On Sept. 18, 1777, Downer sailed for the United States as a passenger on the *Lexington,* commanded by his former captain of the *Yankee,* Henry Johnson. The next day, however, off Ushant, the ship was captured after a furious engagement of several hours by the British sloop *Alert,* Capt. Bazely, and carried into Dover (Stevens Transcripts, No. 1695). According to his pension claim, Downer volunteered to fight and was severely wounded in the left arm by grape-shot. After confinement in Forton Prison, Portsmouth, from Oct. 13, 1777, to Sept. 6, 1778, he again made his escape to France, this time with fifty-six other Americans, by tunneling under the wall. Downer is said to have been so corpulent that he stuck in the narrow passage until it was enlarged.

When he finally returned to America he was commissioned surgeon-general of the Penobscot Expedition from July to October 1779, and received fifteen dollars in compensation for instruments lost (*Revolutionary Muster Rolls of Massachusetts,* vol. IV, p. 923). After the Revolution he was given a grant of land in the Marietta Reserve, and acted as an agent for the Ohio Company in the sale of land. He died in Brookline, Mass., and is buried in the Walnut Street Cemetery there.

[The fullest accounts of Downer are in S. A. Drake, *Old Landmarks and Historic Fields of Middlesex* (1888) and in D. R. Downer, *The Downers of America* (1900), but their claim that he served on the *Alliance* or with Paul Jones is contradicted by the dates of his imprisonments and of the Penobscot Expedition. His deposition is found in American newspapers of August 1777, *e.g.,* the *Pa. Evening Post* of Aug. 5; his pension claim is in *American State Papers,* Class IX, Claims, vol. I, p. 151. The best account of the cruise of the *Yankee* is in Force, *American Archives,* ser. V, vol. I, cols. 134, 148, 684, 754–55. See also Washington's Regimental Book, MSS. Div., Lib. of Cong.; *Memoirs of Maj.-Gen. Wm. Heath* (1901), pp. 26–27, 184; *New-Eng. Hist. and Geneal. Reg.*, XXXIII, 37, 41 and LXV, 60–62, 143; *Annual Register, 1778*, p. 200; E. E. Hale and E. E. Hale, Jr., *Franklin in France* (1888), I, 122; *Vital Records of Norwich, Conn.* (1913), I, 135; *Vital Records of Brookline, Mass.* (1929), p. 107; *Vital Records of Roxbury, Mass.* (1926), II, 513; *Boston Independent Chronicle*, Apr. 7, 1806.]   W.B.N.

DOWNER, SAMUEL (Mar. 8, 1807–Sept. 20, 1881), manufacturer, was born in Dorchester, Mass., the eldest of the four children of Samuel and Catherine (Ayers) Downer. His grandfather, Eliphalet Downer [*q.v.*], had been a surgeon in the Revolution; his father, Samuel, was a successful merchant and eminent horticulturist who had developed new species of apples, pears, and cherries. The younger Samuel attended the public schools of his native town until the age of fourteen, when he began an apprenticeship with the shipping house of Downer & Baldwin. Upon attaining his majority he joined his father under the firm name of Downer & Son, but after three years associated himself with Silas P. Merriam in the wholesale trade with the West Indies. This partnership was dissolved in 1834, and Samuel joined with his father and Capt. William R. Austin in the manufacture and sale of sperm and whale oils and candles, a business which he directed after the retirement in 1844 of the elder partners.

Downer, like other oil men of his time, was interested in finding a substitute for sperm oil, the only known lubricant for fine machinery, and when his attention was called, about 1854, to hydrocarbon oils, he purchased control of a Waltham concern which had a patent for "Coup oil" and with his assistants, Luther and William Atwood and Joshua Merrill [*q.v.*], commenced a series of experiments which resulted not only in an acceptable hydrocarbon lubricating fluid but in kerosene oil suitable for illumination. Atwood and Merrill, while in Scotland on a commission from Downer, discovered new methods of obtaining oil from coal and of purifying it so that it could be used for lighting. Further experiments upon their return to America led Downer to embark heavily in the manufacture of hydrocarbon illuminating oil distilled from albertite, the bituminous coal obtained from Albert County, New Brunswick. To Downer and his assistants belongs the credit of introducing on a wide scale hydrocarbon lubricating and illuminating oils in America.

The industry was assuming large proportions when it was suddenly disrupted by the discovery of petroleum wells in Pennsylvania. Nothing daunted, Downer founded the Downer Kerosene Oil Company, invested in it most of his fortune, and set out for Pennsylvania to exploit the new discovery. Here he "roughed it" for six years, founded the town of Corry, and established a successful refining business with branches in New York and Boston. Important patents were taken out in the Boston refinery by Merrill, and the products extended to include naphthas, paraffines, and other oil products. It was Downer's technical advisers, the Atwoods and Merrill, who were responsible for the notable improvements in refining processes; his own contribution to the rapid introduction of mineral oil illumination was in the field of promotion and business.

Downer was not only an industrial pioneer but also a political radical. He was an ardent member of the Free-Soil party from its inception and drew up the resolutions at the Dorchester meeting called to choose delegates to the Rochester Convention which nominated Van Buren and Adams. Many years later (Aug. 9, 1877) he held a reunion at his home of some 150 leaders of the 1848 movement, an event which aroused wide interest. Like his father he was interested in horticulture, and developed a beautiful harbor summer resort known as Downer's Landing. He was married, on Oct. 13, 1836, to Nancy Melville, by whom he had eight children.

[D. R. Downer, *The Downers of America* (1900), pp. 83–85; *Biog. Encyc. of Mass. in the Nineteenth Century* (1883), II, 189–96, the best account; J. D. Van Slyck, ed., *New England Manufacturers and Manufactories* (1879), I, 202–04; *Boston Daily Globe*, Aug. 10, 1877, containing an account of the Free-Soil reunion; S. D. Hayes, *On the History and Manufacture of Petroleum Products*, a memoir communicated to the Society of Arts, M. I. T., May 14, 1872; W. D. Orcutt, *Good Old Dorchester* (1893); *Boston Post* and *Boston Transcript*, Sept. 21, 1881.]   H.U.F.

DOWNES, JOHN (Dec. 23, 1784–Aug. 11, 1854), naval officer, was born in Canton, Mass., the son of Jesse and Naomi (Taunt) Downes. His grandfather, Edward Downes, was a lieutenant in the Revolutionary War; and his great-grandfather, of the same name, who emigrated to Canton from Ireland, was a seafaring adventurer. Entering the navy as a waiter to his father, who served as a purser's steward on the *Constitution*, John was in September 1800 appointed acting midshipman; and in June 1802, midshipman. During the war with Tripoli he served in the Mediterranean and in 1803 participated in Lieut. David Porter's attack on the Tripolitans, being commended for his gallantry in that fight. In 1807 he was promoted to a lieutenancy and two years later was ordered to the *Essex*, Capt. David Porter [*q.v.*]. As first lieutenant on that ship he sailed on Oct. 28, 1812, from the Delaware Capes on what proved to be the most memorable cruise of the War of 1812. In April 1813, in the boats of the *Essex,* he captured in the Pacific two British vessels, of one of which, the *Georgiana,* he took command after she had been fitted out as a cruiser. In June near James Island he captured the *Hector,* a privateer of eleven guns, and two other ships. In the meantime Porter had taken the *Atlantic,* renamed the *Essex Junior,* and to her Downes transferred his flag, as she was a larger vessel than the *Georgiana.* On her he cruised for several months, either alone or in company with his commodore. At the island of Nukahiva, one of the Marquesas group, where the fleet was refitted, he had two sharp encounters with natives, when ashore in command of landing parties. In one of these, he suffered a broken leg. In the bloody engagement of the *Essex* and the *Essex Junior* with the *Phœbe* and *Cherub,* Downes, although still suffering from his wound, played a gallant part. He was highly commended by the secretary of the navy for his services in the Pacific. In 1813 he was made a master commandant, and four years later, a captain.

In May 1815, Downes sailed for Algiers as commander of the *Epervier,* one of the vessels of Commodore Decatur's squadron. In the capture of the Algerine frigate *Meshuda* he maneuvered his vessel so skilfully that he received the praise of his commodore and was shortly placed in command of the flagship of the squadron. In 1818 he was ordered to the *Macedonian* and cruised for several years in the Pacific. After a tour of duty on the *Java* of the Mediterranean station, 1828–30, he was given command of the frigate *Potomac* and of the Pacific station and was ordered to proceed thither by way of Quallah Battoo, Sumatra, and to obtain satisfaction from the piratical Malays at that place for the outrage they had recently committed on the American vessel *Friendship.* Downes reached Quallah Battoo in February 1832. Landing his sailors and marines, he stormed the town and destroyed the greater part of it. This battle, the first American action in the Orient, lasted two hours and a half and resulted in a loss to the Americans of two killed and eleven wounded, and to the Malays of 150 killed. At home the commodore was criticized by some of the newspapers for his severity, but not by President Jackson, who approved of the chastisement.

The cruise of the *Potomac,* which came to an end in 1834, was Downes's last sea service. The rest of his life he spent in shore duty, with several long intermissions when he was on waiting orders. From 1835 to 1842 and again from 1849

to 1852 he served as commandant of the Boston navy-yard. In 1843–45 he was port captain at Boston and in 1852–53 he was a lighthouse inspector. He died at Charlestown, Mass. On Oct. 30, 1821, he was married to Maria Gertrude Hoffman at Upper Red Hook, N. Y. Their son, John Downes, was an officer in the navy, rising to the rank of commander.

[Record of Officers, 1802–55, Bureau of Navigation; Navy Registers, 1814–54; D. T. V. Huntoon, *Hist. of the Town of Canton, Norfolk County, Mass.* (1893), pp. 450–57; G. W. Allen, *Our Navy and the Barbary Corsairs* (1905); David Porter, *Jour. of a Cruise Made to the Pacific . . . in the U. S. Frigate Essex* (2nd ed., 2 vols., 1822); C. J. Deblois, "Private Jour. kept on board the U. S. Frigate *Macedonian,* 1818–19," in Navy Dept. Lib.; *U. S. Naval Inst. Proc.,* XXXVI (1910), 481–500, 707–716.]   C. O. P.

DOWNEY, JOHN (*c.* 1765–July 21, 1826), educator and essayist, was one of five children of Capt. John and Sarah Downey of Germantown, Pa. In this vicinity he spent his early life. His father, who was head of the English School of the Germantown Academy, 1769–74 (Manuscript Minutes, Germantown Union School, Mar. 7, 1774), was killed in 1778 in an engagement near Crooked Billet (*Pennsylvania Packet,* May 4, 1778); but through his mother's efforts the son received a classical education at the celebrated Germantown Academy, where he distinguished himself. About 1795 he removed to Harrisburg, where he opened a school in 1796. There he resided till his death. On June 5, 1798, he married Alice Ann Beatty, daughter of James Beatty, an early settler of Harrisburg. He continued to teach school; served the city in the capacity of justice of the peace, 1807–26; was town clerk for many years; and a member of the legislature, 1817–18. While living at Harrisburg he served about a year as first cashier of the Harrisburg Bank; was active in the incorporation of the Harrisburg & Middletown Turnpike Company; and served as treasurer of the board of directors of the stock company authorized by the legislature in 1812 to build the Harrisburg bridge over the Susquehanna River.

As an educator, Downey is best known for his plan of an educational system, proposed in a letter to Gov. Thomas Mifflin, Feb. 24, 1797 (*Notes and Queries,* II, 223–26). He recommended a state system, comprising: first, two or more elementary schools in each township, supported by a tax on property; second, one school in each township, supported in the same way, in which more advanced studies should be taught; third, one academy in each county, supported by a "very moderate assessment," devoted to "more liberal science." He recommended furthermore that attendance in these schools "for a sufficient time should be strictly enjoined under an adequate penalty," and added the suggestion that it might "not be unworthy the attention of the legislature to raise agriculture from its present servilely imitative practice by encouraging scientific pursuits." That he was not visionary, however, is indicated in the shrewd observation that "perhaps the public mind is not ripe for the reception" of such a plan. Though Downey failed to gain the realization of his project, the system he proposed was later commended by Henry Barnard [q.v.] as having unusual merit. Besides this educational scheme, Downey is to be credited with the authorship of numerous humorous sketches, chiefly political, contributed by "Simon the Wagoner," "Simon Slim," and "Simon Easy" to the public press, and a compilation called the *Justice's Assistant*. His skill as a Latinist may be judged from his Latin poem on "A Republican Caucus or Democratic Assembly" (*Notes and Queries,* I, 219 ff.).

[Everett H. Brown and others, *A Hist. of the Germantown Academy* (1910); G. H. Morgan, *Annals of Harrisburg* (1858); Jas. P. Wickersham, *A Hist. of Education in Pa.* (1886); the *Commemorative Biog. Encyc. of Dauphin County, Pa.* (1896); W. H. Egle, *Hist. of the Counties of Dauphin and Lebanon* (1883); *Notes and Queries Hist. and Geneal. Chiefly Relating to Interior Pa.* (ed. by W. H. Egle), I, 218, 518; II, 221–27; and III, 200; and the Minutes of the Union School of Germantown (MS.), 1759–77. *The Oracle of Dauphin,* July 22, 1826, contains a notice of Downey's death.]　　　　　　　　　　　　T. W.

DOWNING, ANDREW JACKSON (Oct. 30, 1815–July 28, 1852), landscape gardener, architect, horticulturist, was born at Newburgh, N. Y. His father, Samuel Downing, originally a wheelwright, moved from Lexington, Mass., to New York shortly after 1800, and finally settled at Newburgh on the Hudson in 1801. Here he established a nursery, which he continued until his death twenty-one years later. Andrew, born late in the lives of his parents, was delicate in health and led a lonely life as a child, finding solitary enjoyment in the natural beauties that surrounded the Newburgh cottage. As he grew older he attended an academy at Montgomery, where he was later remembered as a quiet reserved boy, but proud in spirit. He completed his formal schooling at the age of sixteen, and refusing to be influenced by his mother, who sought to apprentice him as a dry-goods clerk, indicated his taste by joining his elder brother, Charles [q.v.], in operating the nursery. He began to make short excursions to the fine estates on the banks of the Hudson for purposes of observation and to better train himself in landscape design. With the Austrian Baron de Liderer, who had a summer home at Newburgh, he explored the hills and dales of the neighborhood, studying and discussing their mineralogical and botanical aspects. In the home of the Baron and that of his wealthy neighbor, Edward Armstrong, he first came in contact with a refined and polished society, and learned much of value for his self-development. Among the guests who came and went, he was most influenced by Raphael Hoyle, the young English landscape painter and Charles Augustus Murray, the English travel writer. Downing now began to write. His first essay was a description of the Danskamer or Devil's Landing Place, near Newburgh, published in the *New York Mirror.* It was followed by an account of Beacon Hill. He then wrote a discussion of novel-reading and several botanical papers which appeared in a Boston journal. Apparently dissatisfied with these efforts, however, he resolved not to publish again until he could write with authority, in the meantime devoting himself to hard work in the nursery, studying landscape gardening, and reading classical literature.

In his twenty-third year (June 7, 1838) he married Caroline Elizabeth DeWint, a young woman of congenial spirit, refinement, and intelligence, the daughter of John P. DeWint of Fishkill Landing on the Hudson. About this time he bought his brother's interest in the nursery and assumed control himself. Immediately following his marriage, he built a house of his own design upon a six-acre tract at Newburgh, molding into it the thoughts which he had evolved through the preceding years. Elizabethan in style, simple yet distinguished in character, with a landscape in harmony and the garden one of its most attractive features, the place was intended to show the possibilities of adapting European ideas to the needs of the New World. Here for years he played the part of gracious and hospitable host. According to George William Curtis, who met him for the first time in 1846, Downing was a tall, slight, Spanish-looking gentleman with a certain aristocratic hauteur and a constant sense of personal dignity, which comported well with his smile of quiet welcome.

Simultaneously with the establishment of his home, he plunged into the preparation of a work on landscape gardening. Completed and published in 1841 under the title, *A Treatise on the Theory and Practice of Landscape Gardening, Adapted to North America,* the book won immediate popularity, passed rapidly through numerous editions the latest being 1921 and was quickly ranked as a classic. Filled with the sense of beauty which is a notable characteristic of

Downing's writings, interesting in content and genial in style, it made a deep impression upon his contemporaries. Loudon, Lindley, and other foreign writers joined in its praise, and from the date of its publication until his death Downing was recognized as the chief American authority on "rural art." In 1841 also, in conjunction with Asa Gray, he brought out the first American edition of Lindley's *Theory of Horticulture*. In 1842 he published *Cottage Residences,* in which the principles of *Landscape Gardening* were applied to the needs of more humble folk. Following the publication of these works, he was elected an honorary member of most of the horticultural societies in America and a corresponding member of numerous foreign societies, and began an extensive correspondence with Loudon and other foreign notables who eagerly sought his opinions. In 1845, Wiley & Putnam published in New York and London, *The Fruits and Fruit Trees of America,* in the preparation of which Downing had been assisted by his brother Charles. This book, the most complete treatise of its kind up to that time, at once established his reputation as a pomologist, and like his other works, was widely read. Although criticized in some quarters because of minor errors in the first edition, due to the vastness of the subject, it nevertheless went through thirteen printings during the author's lifetime. The same year he also edited the first American publication of Mrs. Loudon's *Gardening for Ladies.* In 1846, at the request of Luther Tucker, Downing accepted the editorship of the *Horticulturist,* a new periodical. He continued in this position until his death, his influence upon his contemporaries becoming even more noticeable. His editorials attracted such attention that an extensive correspondence sprang up between him and his readers, and he was thus enabled to establish a personal relation with hundreds who never saw him. Many of these editorials were republished in a posthumous volume, *Rural Essays* (1853).

Downing's increased interest in architecture is shown in his writings and other activities after 1846. In 1849, he published *Additional Notes and Hints to Persons about Building in this Country,* in connection with a work by George Wightwick. This was followed the next year by Downing's *Architecture of Country Houses, Including Designs for Cottages, Farm Houses and Villas.* In 1850 he took a trip to England and France, a visit to which he had long looked forward, for he was a great admirer of the English rural scene. Here he met the notables of the day and was lionized on all sides, but did not neglect to obtain more information to add to his already large store. While abroad, he made an arrangement with Calvert Vaux, a young English architect, which led to a partnership for the purpose of building homes and preparing landscape gardens in America. The combination proved a happy one, and upon his return, with Vaux he designed and constructed the houses and grounds of a number of estates on Long Island, along the Hudson, and elsewhere. In 1851 he was engaged to lay out the grounds for the Capitol, the White House, and the Smithsonian Institution in Washington. His ideas and plans were carried into effect by his successors, but Downing did not live to complete the work. On July 28, 1852, he embarked from Newburgh for New York on the steamer *Henry Clay,* with members of his family and friends. Opposite Yonkers, the captain engaged in a race with another boat. The *Henry Clay* caught fire, and many of the passengers were burned or drowned. Downing, cool in the face of disaster, gave minute instructions to the frightened people about, calmly gathered chairs and threw them overboard to assist those already struggling in the water, and, himself an excellent swimmer, was attempting to save his friends who could not swim when he was last seen alive. His body was not recovered until the next day.

As the first great American landscape gardener, Downing created a national interest in the improvement of country homes and estates, which, as some one has said, made over the face of rural America in his own day. Although a representative of the English, or natural school, he adapted ideas to the requirements of his own land and succeeded in producing a distinctly American art. His influence upon his pupils and successors was marked. Frederick Law Olmstead, Calvert Vaux, and others, were much indebted to him for their inspiration. Downing's book on landscape gardening has probably been more influential in this country than any other work upon the subject. He is also considered by many the greatest single figure in American horticulture.

[Obituaries and other special notices of Downing, in periodicals and transactions of horticultural societies in 1852, especially the article by Mrs. Monell in the *Knickerbocker Mag.,* Oct. 1852; comments in the *Cultivator,* Sept. 1852, and the *Horticulturist,* Sept., Oct., Nov. 1852; sketch by Marshall P. Wilder in *Proc. Am. Pomological Cong.,* 1852; *N. Y. Times,* July 28, 1852; memorial by Geo. W. Curtis and letter of Frederika Bremer in the posthumous *Rural Essays,* mentioned above. For genus of plants named after him see Downingia.]

H. A. K.

DOWNING, CHARLES (July 9, 1802–Jan. 18, 1885), pomologist, horticulturist, and author, although not as well known to the public as his brother Andrew Jackson Downing [q.v.], won a sound reputation for his creative work in pomology. Born in Newburgh, N. Y., his taste for horticultural pursuits was early stimulated by close contact with a nursery owned by his father, Samuel Downing. Even while attending an academy in the neighborhood he worked a portion of the time in this nursery and upon the death of his father in 1822, he succeeded to the entire charge of the establishment. His younger brother, Andrew [q.v.], was admitted to a partnership in 1834, an arrangement which lasted until 1839, when Charles sold his interest and embarked in the same business elsewhere. About 1850 he discontinued his commercial nursery and henceforward until the end of his career devoted himself to extensive experiments with varieties of fruits. His research activities had much to do with placing nursery gardening on a scientific basis. The test orchard which he developed contained trees and grafts of 1,800 varieties of apples, 1,000 of pears, and other fruits in like measure. He had assisted his brother in the preparation of *The Fruits and Fruit Trees of America* (1845) and following the death of the latter reissued it in edition after edition, adding new material provided by himself, until the volume was twice as large in content as when it first appeared. Andrew had made the book the best publication of the kind in America; Charles by his additions and revisions made it well known abroad. He also wrote many articles upon horticultural subjects under the initials "C. D." His work throughout was conscientious and accurate, and he was internationally recognized as an authority upon pomology, horticulture, and tree growths. Quiet, modest, and retiring, although an active member of horticultural societies, he would never make a public speech. While in New York City in 1883, he was knocked down and run over by a horse-car and never completely recovered from the injuries which he received at that time. His death two years later, after a lingering illness, was a distinct loss in the horticultural world. His wife was Mary Wait, daughter of Samuel Wait of Montgomery, N. Y.

[For articles and notices of Downing see the *Am. Agriculturist, Cultivator, Country Gentleman, Prairie Farmer, Horticulturist, Am. Gardening,* and other agricultural and horticultural periodicals in his period, also L. H. Bailey, *Cyc. of Am. Horticulture* (1906), II, 1,573; *N. Y. Herald, N. Y. Times, N. Y. Tribune,* Jan. 20, 1885.]   H.A.K.

DOWNING, GEORGE (August 1623–July 1684), baronet, ambassador to the Netherlands from Cromwell and Charles II, member of Parliament, was the second graduate of the first class (1642) at Harvard College. He was born in Dublin, the son of Emmanuel Downing of the Inner Temple and his second wife, Lucy Winthrop, sister of John Winthrop [q.v.]. The family emigrated to New England in 1638 and settled at Salem, where young Downing came under the influence of the Rev. Hugh Peters [q.v.], from whom it is quite probable that he "sucked in [those] principles that, since, his reason had made him see were erroneous" (Beresford, p. 119). Soon he began to disquiet his mother by his desire to rove and his fondness for field sports. After his graduation from Harvard, on Dec. 27, 1643, he was appointed tutor on a yearly salary of four pounds. Restless and ambitious, he was soon scheming to return to England. In the summer of 1645, apparently as chaplain of a ship, he escaped to the West Indies and thence made his way to London. The rest of his career belongs to English history. Downing Street in London is named for him, and Downing College, Cambridge, owes its foundation to a bequest of his grandson.

[J. L. Sibley, *Biog. Sketches Grads. Harvard Univ.,* I (1873), 28–51, 583; C. H. Firth, article on Downing in the *Dict. of Nat. Biog.,* vol. XV (1888); John Beresford, *The Godfather of Downing Street* (1925).]

G.H.G.

DOWSE, THOMAS (Dec. 28, 1772–Nov. 4, 1856), bibliophile, was born in Charlestown, Mass., the seventh of the eight children of Eleazer and Mehitable (Brentnall) Dowse. His father was a leather-dresser. The family fled from Charlestown on June 17, 1775, when that village, including their house, was burned by the British during the battle of Bunker Hill. Soon afterward they settled in Sherborn, Mass. Thomas was a born reader, and it is said that before he was eighteen years of age he had read all the books he could procure in Sherborn. Doubtless this trait was intensified by his lameness, the result of a fall from an apple tree when he was a young child. Trained in his father's trade, he worked for ten years for a wool-puller and leather-dresser in Roxbury, and then set up for himself in that business in Cambridgeport. He was successful, became prosperous, and remained in business until about seventy-four years of age. His leisure hours, early morning and evening, were devoted to reading and to his garden. By buying good books he gradually acquired a remarkable library that was valued at $40,000. He had a special admiration for Sir Walter Scott, and he used to remark, "Lameness drove us both to books,—him to making them, and me to reading them." The only bust that adorned his library was one of Scott. About 1821, as a result of a lottery, he became the owner of a collection of foreign water-colors and engravings that were much admired in Boston.

In the summer of 1856, a few months before his death, he decided to donate his library to the Massachusetts Historical Society, though he was not a member of that organization. The only condition attached to the gift was that the books should be "preserved forever in a room by themselves, to be used only in said room" (*Proceedings Massachusetts Historical Society,* I ser. III, 100–09). The gift was accepted and the Dowse library was incorporated in the building of the Massachusetts Historical Society. Of the great figures in American history, Benjamin Franklin was one of Dowse's favorites. In commemoration of him Dowse erected a monument in Mount Auburn Cemetery, and built a tomb for his own remains on an adjacent piece of ground. Among the beneficiaries of his estate were the Massachusetts General Hospital, the city of Cambridge, and the town of Sherborn. His collection of water-colors was given to the Boston Athenæum. A series of lectures is given annually in Cambridge from a foundation known as the Dowse Institute. Socially Thomas Dowse was a recluse. "He kept no company, he joined no clubs, belonged to no mutual-admiration societies, talked little, wrote less, published nothing." He was unmarried. A portrait of him by M. Wight which hangs in the library of the Massachusetts Historical Society suggests that his countenance was serene, intelligent, and kindly. In stature he was tall—six feet or more—and well proportioned.

[The most detailed account of Dowse's life is Edward Everett's "Eulogy" in *Proc. Mass. Hist. Soc.,* I ser. III, 361–98; but see also: Wm. B. H. Dowse, *Lawrence Dowse of Legbourne, England, his Ancestors, Descendants and Connections* (1926); *Catalogue of the Private Library of Thos. Dowse Presented to the Mass. Hist. Soc., 1856* (1870).]   L. S. M.

DOYLE, ALEXANDER (Jan. 28, 1857–Dec. 21, 1922), sculptor, son of George and Alice (Butler) Doyle, was born in Steubenville, Ohio, and from earliest childhood was familiar with the practical aspects of monument-making, his father being engaged in an important quarrying business. His great-grandfather, Basil Doyle, was a civil engineer who in Revolutionary days removed from Maryland to Ohio, and became one of the first settlers of Steubenville. In 1869, the boy Alexander was taken by his parents to live in Italy, where he studied music, painting, and sculpture. Returning to the United States after about three years, he graduated from the Louisville High School, and in 1874 went back to Italy. He sometimes acted as organist in Italian churches. His studies in sculpture were pursued in the National Academies at Carrara, Rome, and Florence. His masters were Nicoli, Dupré, Pellicia. Whatever artistic training he received abroad was reinforced by his knowledge of the business side of a sculptor's work, especially as regards marble, granite, and limestone. Settling in New York City in 1878, and taking as partner a talented English sculptor named Moffitt, Doyle soon became widely known as a maker of monuments. His agreeable personality, his father's business connections, and the fact that his partner was a Roman Catholic were helpful in securing commissions. Though an honorary member of the Royal Raphael Academy at Urbino, Italy, he joined no American art societies and sent nothing to American art exhibitions. His works, however, are numerous, and are found in widely separated sections of the country—East, South, and Middle West—state committees rightly having confidence in his ability to complete his contracts. The assertion that "at thirty-three he had done more public monuments than any other sculptor, and was producer of more than a fifth of those standing in the country" (*Muncie Star,* Dec. 22, 1922) would seem to stress quantity rather than quality. In 1880, at Hallowell, Me., he married Fannie, daughter of Mark and Sarah Johnson.

Among his prominent works are the heroic seated bronze statue of Horace Greeley, given to the city of New York in 1890, the Soldiers' Monument in New Haven, Conn., a bronze equestrian statue of Gen. Albert Sidney Johnston, a bronze statue of Gen. Robert E. Lee, and a marble statue of Margaret Haughery [*q.v.*], "The Bread Giver," the last three being in New Orleans, La.; the National Revolutionary Monument at Yorktown, Va.; eight colossal marble figures in the State Capitol, Indianapolis; a bronze statue of Gen. Steedman in Toledo, Ohio, and a marble statue of Gen. Garfield in Cleveland. For Atlanta, Ga., he made the marble statue of Senator Benjamin H. Hill, and the bronze statue and monument to Henry W. Grady. In Statuary Hall of the National Capitol he is represented by statues of Thomas H. Benton and Francis P. Blair, given by Missouri, and by the statue of John E. Kenna of West Virginia. His marble portrait with pedestal at the grave of John Howard Payne and his marble portrait statue of the Rt. Rev. William Pinckney are in Washington, D. C.; his Francis Scott Key monument is in Frederick, Md. On the death of his father, Doyle devoted himself to the management of the Bedford (Ind.) limestone quarries which he had inherited. In 1906, when it was decided to erect in Steubenville a statue of Edwin M. Stanton, secretary of war under Lincoln, he undertook the work gratuitously, Steubenville being Stanton's native town as well as his own. He was engaged on this until his retirement in 1911. From that time until his death, eleven years later, he lived in Dedham, Mass., not wholly unoccupied, as he there completed a heroic statue of Lincoln, "to be erected somewhere in Europe after the close of the World War" (*Boston Transcript*, Feb. 6, 1918). He died in Boston, leaving a wife and a daughter.

[Obituaries were printed in the *Boston Transcript*, N. Y. *World, Muncie* (Ind.) *Star*, Dec. 22, 1922, and in other dailies. Chas. E. Fairman, *Art and Artists of the Capitol* (1927) gives a brief list of works and one illustration. The Art Library of the Metropolitan Museum, N. Y., has a more nearly complete list published in a folder issued by Doyle himself. See also Jos. B. Doyle, *20th Century Hist. of Steubenville and Jefferson County, Ohio* (1910); Thieme-Becker, *Allgemeines Lexikon der Bildenden Künstler*, IX, 531; *Am. Art Annual*, 1923.]
                                                A. A.

DOYLE, ALEXANDER PATRICK (Feb. 28, 1857–Aug. 9, 1912), Catholic missionary and editor, was one of a family of six children—two of whom became nuns—born to Richard and Matilda (Shea) Doyle of San Francisco. Educated at first in the public schools and later under the auspices of the Jesuits and Christian Brothers, Alexander was graduated from St. Mary's College, San Francisco, in 1875, and received his master's degree a year later. Aroused by a Paulist mission, he entered the Congregation of St. Paul in 1875 and on completion of his theological studies was ordained, May 22, 1880—the first native Californian raised to the priesthood. For twelve years he served on the mission band, giving lectures on Catholic dogma and practises to non-Catholics and retreats for preachers throughout the United States and even in Canada and Mexico. Although without special natural endowment for public speaking, he developed into a winning preacher and a popular confessor. As editor of *Temperance Truth* (1892–1903), founder and a director of the Temperance Publication Bureau, which distributed over a million tracts, and general secretary of the Catholic Total Abstinence Union of America (1894–1904), he contributed largely to the total abstinence movement. He was manager of the Paulist Press, and editor of the *Catholic World* (1893–1904), the leading Catholic magazine, for which he wrote reviews, editorials, and an occasional article; and he founded the Catholic Book Exchange for the dissemination of tractarian literature. As founder (1896) and secretary-treasurer of the Catholic Missionary Union, he collected money for the training of priests for domestic missions. With Father Walter Elliott [*q.v.*] he established in 1902 the Apostolic Mission House as an allied school of the Catholic University (Washington, D. C.) for the normal training of missionaries. As rector of this institution he taught homiletics and pastoral theology, and for the last fifteen years of his life (from 1896) he edited *The Missionary* which he himself had founded. He was superior of Catholic chaplains in the army and navy, and President Taft found him "most careful, conscientious, and candid in his recommendations." Chaplains learned that they could rely on his pastoral counsel.

Always active, seeking no rest save in rotation of labors, he finally suffered a breakdown in health, and he died in his native San Francisco. A devout priest, a liberal man, a friend of civic reform, and an ardent Republican, Father Doyle was widely acquainted among churchmen and political leaders. Archbishop Ireland saw him as a true disciple of Father Hecker's, a patriot and an apostle who was "priestly in every stepping." On his death Theodore Roosevelt who had known him for years wrote (*Catholic World*, September 1912): "It was with Father Doyle that I first discussed the question of my taking some public stand on the matter of race suicide, it having been developed in one of our talks that we felt equally strong on the matter. I have never known any man work more unweariedly for the social betterment of the man, woman, or child whose chance of happiness is least in our modern life. . . . Again and again in speeches which I made I drew largely on the great fund of his accumulated experience."

[*Who's Who in America*, 1912–13; *The Am. Cath. Who's Who*, 1911; *Outlook*, Aug. 31, 1912; *Cath. World*, Sept. 1912, Sept. 1913; *The Missionary*, Sept. 1912, Aug. 1913; *San Francisco Chronicle*, Aug. 10, 1912.]
                                                R. J. P.

DOYLE, JOHN THOMAS (Nov. 26, 1819–Dec. 23, 1906), lawyer, was of Irish descent. His family having been actively implicated in the Irish Rebellion of '98, John Doyle came to the United States in 1815, married Frances Glinden, and settled in New York City, where their son, John Thomas Doyle, was born. He obtained his early education at Columbia College Grammar School, proceeding thence to Georgetown College, D. C., where he graduated in 1838. He then studied law in New York City, and after his call to the bar in May 1842, practised his profession there for nine years. In 1851, when on a vacation in Central America, he met Commodore Vanderbilt and at the latter's instigation, abandoned practise and became general agent of the American Atlantic & Pacific Canal Company in Nicaragua. The company was engaged on Vanderbilt's project of constructing an interoceanic canal across Nicaragua, and Doyle remained there two years, assisting in the building of the transit road to the Pacific. During this period he commenced an investigation of Spanish colonial policy, particularly in its relations with the Catholic Church, in the course of which he unearthed much valuable information on the subject of the religious endowments under royal rule. In 1853 it became evident that the canal project would not be brought to a successful issue, and he resigned his position, proceeded to California, and opened a law office in San Francisco. At this time there were many important questions arising out of the former Spanish occupancy remaining to be settled, particularly relative to the property of the Catholic missions and the rights of the Church after the cession. He was retained by Archbishop Alemany [q.v.] of San Francisco in this connection, and succeeded in obtaining from the government a ratification of the original title of the Church and the Missions to much of the land which they had enjoyed under Spanish rule. His previous excursions into Spanish colonial history had apprised him of the existence of "The Pious Fund of the Californias," and under instruction from Archbishop Alemany, he made exhaustive researches which disclosed the origin and history of the Fund. In 1697 individual members of the Jesuit order had received royal authorization to undertake the conversion of California, and a fund contributed by private donors was established, the income from which formed a permanent endowment of the missionary church. This fund attained great magnitude and was administered by the Jesuits. In 1772 the missions of Upper California were confided to the Franciscans, and the income of half the fund was appropriated to them. The fund itself had been taken out of the control of the Jesuits and held by the Spanish Crown as a trust estate. On the declaration of Mexican independence, Mexico succeeded the Crown as trustee, and in 1842 by a decree of Santa Anna the trust properties were sold and the proceeds paid into the public treasury, the Mexican government recognizing an obligation to pay six per cent interest annually to the ecclesiastical authorities in order to implement the trust. Since that time nothing had been done and no payments whatever had been made. In 1857, on these facts, Doyle was retained by Archbishop Alemany and Bishop Thadeus Amat of Monterey to act on behalf of the Church. Ultimately he presented the claim before the mixed American and Mexican Commission at

Washington in 1870. The commission's jurisdiction was limited by the Treaty of Guadalupe Hidalgo to matters since Feb. 2, 1848. So conclusive was Doyle's presentation that the umpire awarded the Church of Upper California twenty-one years' income from that date, i.e., $904,700.79, calculated at half the total interest on the sum received by Santa Anna's government, which Mexico paid (*Thadeus Amat et al.* vs. *Mexico,* No. 493 Am. Docket, *United States and Mexican Claims Commission, 1869–1876*). In further proceedings before the Permanent Court of Arbitration at The Hague in October 1902, the Church was awarded $1,426,000 for subsequent interest and it was decreed that Mexico should thereafter pay on this account $43,050 per annum.

Doyle had no taste for public life, and consistently declined to be a candidate for office, but, being keenly interested in transportation problems, accepted a position on the State Board of Commissioners on Transportation in 1878, serving one term. He was opposed to arbitrary regulation of freights by the state, and held that railways are public highways and should be open to all upon equal terms. He led the opposition to the refunding of the debt of the Central Pacific Railway Company, publishing open letters on the subject, which attracted wide attention. In 1888 he retired from general practise, residing much of his time at Menlo Park, San Mateo, Cal., where he died. He was married in 1863 to Antonia Pons of Lyons, France. As a lawyer his chief claim to recognition rests on his remarkable work in connection with the "Pious Fund." He was a great student and reader, a good classical scholar, and had an intimate acquaintance with the Spanish and French languages. Devoting much of his time to a study of Shakespeare, he wrote an article on the trial scene in the *Merchant of Venice* which Furness designated as extremely valuable and the substance of which he included in his Variorum edition of Shakespeare. Doyle also wrote a history of the "Pious Fund" of California (printed in *Papers of the California Historical Society,* vol. I, 1887), and contributed articles on various subjects to local periodicals.

[See *Hist. of the Bench and Bar of Cal.* (1901), ed. by O. T. Shuck, p. 518. This work contains, p. 81, an article, "Recovery of the Pious Fund," written by Doyle. The litigation with Mexico over the Catholic Church claims is exhaustively dealt with in John Bassett Moore, *Hist. and Digest of the International Arbitrations to which the U. S. has been a Party* (1898), II, 1348–52; and *Papers Relating to the Foreign Relations of the U. S.,* 1902, pp. 738–86 and Appendix II thereto. An obituary appeared in the *San Francisco Chronicle,* Dec. 24, 1906.]   H.W.H.K.

DOYLE, SARAH ELIZABETH (Mar. 23, 1830–Dec. 21, 1922), teacher of girls and a leader in behalf of higher education for women, was one of the seven children of Thomas and Martha Dorrance (Jones) Doyle. She was born and spent the whole of her long life in Providence, R. I., of which city a brother, Thomas Arthur, was for sixteen years the mayor. After graduating from the high school she taught in a private school for girls. In 1856 she was appointed teacher in the girls' department of the high school, and in 1878, became its principal. With forty-six years' service as a teacher to her credit, she retired in 1892, and in 1894 Brown University conferred upon her the honorary degree of Master of Arts.

She was not only a gifted teacher, she was also fitted physically and mentally for leadership. Her keen eye betokened an alert brain, and her vigorous frame, unbounded energy. She was a woman of liberal and progressive views, a Unitarian theologically, and was accustomed to express her convictions frankly and firmly. People stood a little in awe of her, but recognized back of her strength and aggressiveness a generous and kindly personality. She was the first woman to preside over a session of the National Education Association, an event which occurred at the meeting in Madison, Wis., in 1884. In 1898 she was named by Mayor Baker of Providence one of a committee of five to investigate the management of the public schools, and served as its secretary. While her major concern was that of furthering the interests of women, she was active in promoting education in general. She was among those who took the lead in establishing the Rhode Island School of Design, which has become one of the principal educational institutions of the state; was a charter member of the corporation; and from 1877 to 1899 its secretary. In 1876 with three or four other women she called a meeting which resulted in the formation of the Rhode Island Woman's Club, and was its first president, continuing in office until 1884. She also took part in the founding of the Rhode Island State Federation of Women's Clubs in 1895. A delegate to the meeting held in New York Mar. 20, 1889, she was appointed on the committee to draft a constitution for the General Federation of Women's Clubs. She was a pioneer worker in behalf of woman's suffrage, believing that the suffrage would react beneficially upon women themselves; and a reason why she was so ardent an advocate of higher education for girls was her conviction that it would make them more eager to grasp civic responsibility. One of her most notable services was in connection with the establishment of a college for women in Rhode Island. Their admission to Brown University had been agitated for some years, but there was strong opposition to coeducation. In 1892, however, women were allowed to become candidates for degrees, and were permitted to take the examinations required of men, though, except as graduate students, they were not admitted to the classrooms. Encouraged by President E. Benjamin Andrews [*q.v.*], in 1895 Miss Doyle headed a committee to secure money to erect a college building for women. The following year this committee was incorporated as the Rhode Island Society for the Collegiate Education of Women, with Miss Doyle as president. Funds for the building were secured and the corporation of Brown then voted to establish a department to be known as the Women's College in Brown University. At her death, which occurred in her ninety-third year, she was honored as one of the leading citizens of the state.

[*Providence Jour.*, Dec. 22, 1922; *Who's Who in America*, 1922–23; Jane C. Croly, *The Hist. of the Woman's Club Movement in America* (1898); Mary I. Wood, *The Hist. of the Gen. Fed. of Women's Clubs* (1912); Walter C. Bronson, *The Hist. of Brown Univ.* (1914); Thos. Woody, *A Hist. of Women's Education in the U. S.* (1929).]   H.E.S.

DRAKE, ALEXANDER WILSON (1843–Feb. 4, 1916), art director of the *Century Magazine*, "was the foremost figure in the development of American illustrative art, and was so regarded by his contemporaries" (Johnson, *Remembered Yesterdays*, p. 99). The son of Isaac and Charlotte (Osborn) Drake, he was born in Westfield, N. J., and as a youth took up the study of wood-engraving. Being a good draftsman, he subsequently drew upon the wood blocks for engravers, and studied painting in oils and in water-colors. In 1865 he established himself as a wood-engraver in New York City. Five years later he joined, as head of the art department, the organization which was about to issue *Scribner's Monthly Magazine*. When the ownership and name of the publication were changed, in 1881, Drake's title became that of art director of the *Century Magazine* and of *St. Nicholas*. With the support of the publishers, Charles Scribner and Roswell Smith [*qq.v.*], and the collaboration of the managing editor, Richard Watson Gilder [*q.v.*], through the pages of the *Century* Drake led American illustration into a new era. Himself an artist with a thirsty love of beauty in any form, he had also the technical training of a wood-engraver and the discernment, optimism, and friendly sympathy of a born teacher. These qualities fitted him to recognize ability and, by unsparing criticism, to develop it in a great number of young artists. Under his guidance a new school of wood-engraving grew up, the aim of which was "the truer and more exact reproduction of the work of the artist" rather than its "translation" into other terms (Drake, "A Great Artist in Wood," in *American Magazine,* August 1915). Owing to his initiative, in 1881 and 1882 the *Century* held competitions for wood-engravers which were active in stimulating interest in magazine art. As photographic reproduction was introduced he was quick to study and make use of the new methods. In all of his striving for improvement he was aided by the understanding and hearty cooperation of Theodore L. De Vinne [*q.v.*], the printer, whose mastery of his craft made possible the realization of Drake's ideals. The opportunities afforded illustrators by the type of work which the *Century* demanded were in no small measure responsible for the number of Americans who attained eminence in the field of illustration in the last quarter of the nineteenth century.

Drake was well-known as a collector in several fields. "All beauty was his heritage," said one of his colleagues, "and to him collecting was not, as to many, a fad: it was a quiet, perpetual, glorified enthusiasm that enriched immeasurably his own life and thousands of other lives" (Clarke, *post,* p. 106). His collections included not only bottles and brasses, but ship-models—now in India House, New York—old fashioned bandboxes, chosen for the beauty of the paper with which they were covered, and bird-cages. This last collection is now in the Cooper Institute, where Drake studied drawing and later for a time was a teacher. During the early nineties he yielded to a literary inclination and wrote three short stories which were published in the *Century.* After his death these were gathered into a little volume, *Three Midnight Stories* (1916), containing also tributes from some of his associates. Those who knew him seemed to be unanimous in their affectionate recollection of his "genius for friendship," his "quiet effectiveness," his kindly, lovable spirit. He was married three times: to Hilah Lloyd; after her death, to her cousin, Anne Lloyd; and in 1901, to Edith True. He retired from active work in 1913, and died, three years later, in New York City.

[In addition to references above, see: *Who's Who in America,* 1914–15; articles by C. C. Buel and W. F. Clarke in the *Century Mag.,* May 1916, reprinted, with "A Memory," by A. B. Paine and "A Word of Tribute," by R. U. Johnson, in *Three Midnight Stories; R. U. Johnson, Remembered Yesterdays* (1923) and letter in *N. Y. Herald,* Feb. 5, 1916; H. F. Leighton, "The Home of a Veteran Collector," *Am. Homes and Gardens,* Feb. 1913; *Outlook,* Feb. 16, 1916; *N. Y. Times,* Feb. 5, 1916. Joseph Pennell, who felt that American illustration owed much to Drake, commented on him in

many places, notably *Modern Illustration* (1895); *Pen Drawing and Pen Draughtsmen* (1920); *The Graphic Arts* (1921); and *Adventures of an Illustrator* (1925).]

J.J.

DRAKE, BENJAMIN (1795–Apr. 1, 1841), lawyer, editor, and biographer, was a younger brother of Daniel Drake [*q.v.*]. He was born in Mays Lick, Ky., his father being Isaac Drake and his mother Elizabeth Shotwell, both of whom had migrated to Kentucky from near Plainfield, N. J., in 1788. Although Benjamin had only rudimentary schooling, yet by hard work and by virtue of the natural strength and honesty of his mind he acquired a style of writing remarkable for its grace, clarity, and accuracy. While still a youth he went to Cincinnati from his father's farm to be clerk in the drug store of his brother Daniel and later a partner in the general merchandise store financed by Daniel Drake and conducted as Isaac Drake & Company. After the failure of this enterprise Benjamin studied law, 1825–26, and practised this profession with great success until compelled to retire by ill health. He contributed special articles, editorials, and stories to the newspapers,—in 1825 to the *Literary Gazette,* published by John P. Foote and after the suspension of this journal to various others. He established with others the *Cincinnati Chronicle* of which he was editor from 1826 to 1834, being succeeded by E. D. Mansfield. In 1827, in conjunction with Mansfield, he published a statistical account of Cincinnati under the name *Cincinnati in 1826.* This was republished in London and Germany for the information of intending immigrants and probably played a considerable part in determining the immigration from those places toward the rapidly developing city and the valley of the Ohio. This book contained an account not only of Cincinnati but also of the agriculture and commerce of the valley at that time. It is a valuable source of historical information. Drake contributed articles also to the *Western Monthly Magazine* and the *Southern Literary Messenger.* His fictitious stories of life in Cincinnati were collected and published under the name of *Tales and Sketches from the Queen City* (1838). His most serious literary works are: *The Life and Adventures of Black Hawk, with Sketches of Keokuk, the Sac and Fox Indians, and the Late Black Hawk War* (1838), *Sketches of the Civil and Military Services of William Henry Harrison* (1840), with C. S. Todd; and *Life of Tecumseh and his Brother, the Prophet, with an Historical Sketch of the Shawanoe Indians* (1841). These are written clearly, plainly, and concisely. The facts he collected with great care as to their accuracy, and these lives remain important sources of historical information of this most interesting and rapidly changing period of our history. *The Life of Tecumseh* was passing through the press at the time of the author's death, in April 1841. According to contemporaries Drake was a man of strict integrity and unusually sound mind, seeking always accuracy of statement. He had polished and courteous manners, was kindly, fond of society, and well liked.

[See E. D. Mansfield, *Memoirs of the Life and Services of Daniel Drake* (1855); obituary by Mansfield in *Cincinnati Chronicle*, Apr. 2, 1841; article by Jas. Hall in the same journal, Apr. 7, 1841; *Cincinnati Gazette*, Apr. 2, 1841; L. A. Leonard, *Greater Cincinnati and Its People, A History* (1927), vol. II. The date given above for Drake's birth follows Mansfield. It is sometimes given as Nov. 28, 1794.]   A.P.M.

DRAKE, CHARLES DANIEL (Apr. 11, 1811–Apr. 1, 1892), lawyer, jurist, United States senator, was the son of Dr. Daniel Drake [*q.v.*] and Harriet Sisson. The boy received cultural and literary training in his home, supplemented by academic instruction in Kentucky and Cincinnati schools. In 1827 he entered the naval academy at Annapolis where he remained for three years, resigning because of his sudden decision to study law. Arriving at St. Louis in 1834, he entered the practise of law, but was not a recognized leader of the local bar. Following a brief residence in Cincinnati, he returned in 1850 to St. Louis and shortly became active in politics. In the confused and chaotic political situation of the fifties he appeared, successively, as a Whig, a Know-Nothing, and a Democrat. He was elected as a Democrat to fill a vacancy in the legislature in 1859 and served out the term. In the critical campaign of 1860, Drake supported Douglas for president and the pro-slavery candidate, C. F. Jackson, for governor. He opposed secession but was not active in the spectacular events of the spring and summer of 1861 which culminated in the military defeat and political elimination of the disloyalists and assured the ultimate success of the Unionist cause. Early in the war, however, he became a leader in the attack on slavery as a legalized institution, an issue which to most Missouri leaders had been distinctly secondary to the preservation of the Union. Drake energetically led the radical or "charcoal" wing of the Unionist party, but from 1861 to 1863 was unsuccessful in his demand for immediate and uncompensated emancipation; the conservatives, led by Gov. Gamble and supported by Lincoln, maintaining control of the situation. By 1863 the radical faction had become a distinct group, well organized under Drake and with a definite program, including immediate emancipation, a new constitution, and a system of drastic disfranchisement (*Proceedings of the Missouri State Convention Held in Jefferson City, June, 1863*). The Radicals increased in strength and were successful in securing the authorization of a constitutional convention. In this body Drake, the vice-president, was easily the most active and conspicuous member. He was the directing force in the formation of the new constitution and the author of the sections dealing with the elective franchise (*Journal of the Missouri State Convention, Held at the City of St. Louis, Jan. 6–Apr. 10, 1865*). He was peculiarly adapted to this position, for, as Carl Schurz wrote, "in politics he was inexorable . . . most of the members of his party, especially in the country districts, stood much in awe of him" (*Reminiscences,* vol. III, 1908, p. 294). So pervasive and masterful was his influence that the adopted constitution became known as the "Drake constitution." The Radicals maintained absolute control of the state from 1865 to 1871, with Drake as their leader.

Never personally popular, he was elected to the United States Senate in 1867 as a recognition and reward for his services to his party. He took his stand with Morton, Wilson, and other extreme Radicals, in enthusiastic support of the Reconstruction measures, which permitted him to give full play to his dogmatism and intolerance. He regarded the wide-spread political and social disorder in the South as a sinister expression of the rebellious spirit in the whites and of a fixed purpose to prevent by violence the operation of the Republican party in the reconstructed states. He acted in accordance with the view that he was "a representative of radical radicalism"; and supported with obvious enthusiasm the Reconstruction legislation of 1867–70 (*Congressional Globe,* 40 Cong., 1 Sess., pp. 41, 99, 109, 356). He regarded the Civil War as a social conflict, the South as a conquered province, and introduced proposals so radical that even his Republican colleagues refused to support them (*Ibid.,* pp. 2,600, 3,920). In the trial of Johnson and in the consideration of the Fifteenth Amendment, Drake took an active part. In the meantime, his dictatorship of the Radical party in Missouri had been questioned, then successfully challenged, by the election of Carl Schurz [*q.v.*] to the Senate in 1869, despite Drake's bitter opposition. The factional division thus created between radicals and liberals came to a decisive test in the state campaign of 1870, where a combination of bolting liberals and Democrats triumphantly carried the state, and so amended the constitution as to end the various discriminations. With the passing of his leadership and almost of his party, Drake's position became precarious. He was unwilling and unable to adjust himself to the changed conditions, and realized that the Democrats would shortly regain control of Missouri. He accepted, therefore, from Grant in December 1870 the appointment as chief justice of the United States Court of Claims, and announced his definite withdrawal from politics. He served with distinction until his retirement in 1885. During his latter years Drake abandoned many of his former extreme views.

[Drake's Autobiography, MS., is useful for his early life, but disappointing for his political career. His views on the issues of the Civil War are in *Union and Anti-Slavery Speeches* (1864). His rise as a leader of the Missouri radicals is traced in the *Missouri Democrat*, 1863–71. A comprehensive account of that period is T. S. Barclay, *Liberal Republican Movement in Mo., 1865–1871* (1926).]   T.S.B.

DRAKE, DANIEL (Oct. 20, 1785–Nov. 6, 1852), scientist and physician, was born on the farm of his grandfather, Nathaniel Drake, near Plainfield, N. J., the oldest child of Isaac Drake and Elizabeth Shotwell. His mother was a member of the Society of Friends. His parents were poor, and in April 1788 they migrated with some relatives and friends to Kentucky, landing at Limestone, now called Maysville, on the Ohio River, on June 10. The party bought a piece of forest at Mays Lick, a few miles from Maysville, and here Daniel's boyhood was spent in the hardships of the frontier, helping his father clear the land and farm and his mother with the spinning and dyeing of their clothing. His character of industry, honesty, temperance, accurate observation, and ambition, combined with a deeply poetical love of the beauties of nature, was formed under these influences. His parents early decided to make him a physician, and he was given all the schooling the wilderness afforded. At the age of fifteen, in 1800, he was sent to Cincinnati, or Fort Washington as it was then called, to enter the office of Dr. William Goforth, a leading physician of that small village, where he remained four years studying medicine and Latin. He then became a partner of Dr. Goforth. Feeling the need of more instruction, he went in 1805 for a term to the Medical College of the University of Pennsylvania where he heard Dr. Rush and others. He returned to practise medicine at first in Mays Lick, but in 1807 went back to Cincinnati and became again the partner of Dr. Goforth. In that year he married Harriet Sisson. The greater part of his life was spent at Cincinnati in the practise of medicine, with interludes of a few years during which he lived in Lexington, Ky., and Louisville. He was, by general consent, the leading practitioner in Cincinnati during his residence there.

In 1810, he published a small book entitled *Notices Concerning Cincinnati, its Topography, Climate and Diseases,* which was the germ of his great work on the diseases of the "Interior Valley of North America," published much later, and of the widely known account published in 1815 and called *Natural and Statistical View, or Picture of Cincinnati and the Miami Country, Illustrated by Maps, with an Appendix Containing Observations on the late Earth Quakes, the Aurora Borealis and Southwest Winds.* This small book of two hundred and fifty pages, more commonly known by its abbreviated title, *Picture of Cincinnati in 1815,* contains a careful account of the prehistoric mounds formerly existing on the present site of the city and is their principal record. It contains a great variety of other observations of all kinds, including those on medicinal plants, characteristics of the forest, meteorological data, and so on, and a brief historical account of the settlement of the city. It was widely circulated, and was translated abroad. About this time Drake entered commercial life, first as a proprietor of a drug store and later of a general store which was conducted by his father and brother Benjamin, under the title of Isaac Drake & Company. These ventures were not successful financially.

It was Daniel Drake's great ambition to be a teacher of medicine, and in order to equip himself he returned with Mrs. Drake in 1815 to Philadelphia and took a second course of lectures at the Medical School of the University of Pennsylvania, receiving the degree of M.D. from that institution. He resumed his practise in 1816, and from 1817 to 1818 taught materia medica in the medical department of Transylvania University, Lexington, Ky. His ideals of medical education, which were far ahead of his time, were published in a series of essays in the *Western Medical and Physical Journal* of which he was founder and editor, and were later gathered into a small volume under the title of *Practical Essays on Medical Education and the Medical Profession in the United States* (1832). In the hope of making Cincinnati a great medical center, in 1819 Drake obtained a charter and founded the Ohio Medical College (now the Medical College of the University of Cincinnati), in which he was president and professor of medicine. His efforts, however, were frustrated by the jealousy of some of his colleagues. He was expelled from the presidency by the faculty, on Mar. 6, 1822, was reinstated a week later upon the insistence of the people of Cincinnati, but promptly resigned and left the college. He returned to Transylvania University in 1823, after the failure of his plans in Cincinnati, and was dean of the school from 1825 to 1827 and professor for four years. During this period his wife died. After a brief period in Cincinnati, in 1828 he became a member of the faculty of Jefferson Medical College in Philadelphia, returning the following year to Cincinnati and taking with him various colleagues to found a new medical school, to be a department of Miami University. This school, however, existed for but a year, when Drake again became connected with the Ohio Medical College for one year. Once more bickerings led to his withdrawal. He afterward established the medical department of Cincinnati College, which collapsed in 1839. From 1840 to 1849 he resided in Louisville and was a professor at the Louisville Medical Institute, during which period he prepared his great work on the diseases of the Interior Valley. In 1849, the Ohio Medical College being in a critical state, he returned to take charge of it for one year but resigned again, disgusted with the wrangling, and returned to Louisville. In 1852 he returned for the last time to Cincinnati and took charge of the Ohio College, but he died shortly after its opening.

The work upon which Drake's reputation chiefly depends is, *A Systematic Treatise, Historical, Etiological and Practical, on the Principal Diseases of the Interior Valley of North America, as they Appear in the Caucasian, African, Indian and Eskimoux Varieties of its Population.* The first volume, about 900 pages in length, was published in 1850, and the second, of approximately the same length, in 1854, two years after the author's death. It is a mine of information on the topography, meteorology, character of population, customs and diseases, of the interior of North America. It is characterized by the most painstaking accuracy of statement, a graceful and clear style, a most unprejudiced and scientific weighing of evidence, and great caution in inferences. In the spring before he died, he delivered two addresses before the Cincinnati Medical Library Association, "Medical Journals and Libraries" and "Early Medical Times in Cincinnati," which are an accurate picture of early medical history in the United States. He was an honorary member of the Philadelphia Academy of Natural Sciences, the American Philosophical Society, the Wernerian Academy of Natural Sciences of Edinburgh, Scotland, and of the Medical Societies of Massachusetts and Rhode Island. In addition to his activities as a physician and a teacher, he was actively engaged in all public-spirited enterprises of Cincinnati, originating and having a share in the establish-

ment of the Commercial Hospital and Lunatic Asylum, the eye infirmary, the circulating library, the Teacher's College, as well as planning the scheme of canals of Ohio and promoting railway connection with the South, which afterward resulted in that most successful municipal enterprise, the Cincinnati Southern Railway. He was an active advocate of temperance and his private character was above reproach.

[Autobiographical material appears in Daniel Drake, *Pioneer Life in Ky.; A Series of Reminiscential Letters,* etc. (1870), ed. by his son, Chas. D. Drake. The principal biographies are: E. D. Mansfield, *Memoirs of the Life and Services of Daniel Drake* (1855), and O. Juettner, *Daniel Drake and his Followers* (1909). Contemporary accounts include: S. D. Gross, *A Discourse on the Life, Character, and Services of Daniel Drake* (1853), and a sketch in *Trans. Coll. of Phys. of Phila.,* n.s., vol. II (1853), by a personal friend, C. D. Meigs.]
A.P.M.

DRAKE, EDWIN LAURENTINE (Mar. 29, 1819–Nov. 8, 1880), railroad conductor, pioneer petroleum industrialist, was born on his father's farm at Greenville, Greene County, N. Y. He lived there for about eight years, and then his parents moved to Vermont, near Castleton. Here Drake obtained a common-school education and helped on the farm until he was nineteen, when he left home to go to an uncle in Michigan. He was seven months on the way, most of the time working as night clerk on a steamboat plying between Buffalo and Detroit. Always an exceedingly sociable fellow, after a lonely year on his uncle's farm, he sought work in town and became a hotel clerk in Tecumseh, Mich. After two years in this position he went East for a visit to his home and shortly thereafter became a clerk in a dry-goods store in which occupation he continued for four years, first in New Haven, Conn., and later in New York City. About 1845 he moved to Springfield, Mass., where for five years he acted as express agent for the Boston & Albany Railroad, resigning to take a conductor's position on the newly opened New York & New Haven Railroad and moving to New Haven. He continued in this capacity for almost eight years, when ill health required his resignation.

Several years before, he had bought a little stock in the Pennsylvania Rock Oil Company and about the time he gave up his railroad position the oil company engaged him to visit its property on Oil Creek, near Titusville, Pa., and to obtain some corrections in legal papers. His letter of introduction from the company referred to him as "Colonel," simply for the sake of the impression such a title might make. The trip was made by Drake in December 1857, and on the way he studied salt-well drilling operations near Syracuse and Pittsburgh as the original promoter of the oil company, George H. Bissell, had suggested that oil might best be secured by such method. On his return to New Haven within a few weeks Drake's enthusiasm to engage immediately in drilling for oil resulted in the Pennsylvania Rock Oil Company's executing a lease of their lands for this purpose to Drake and another stockholder, the terms of which were a royalty of twelve cents on each gallon of oil produced. Drake, as president of the new company (the Seneca Oil Company), although only a minor stockholder, was immediately employed to proceed with drilling operations, and after many difficulties had been overcome during the succeeding nineteen months he finally struck oil at a depth of sixty-nine feet on Aug. 27, 1859. This was the first time that petroleum was tapped at its source and the first proof of the occurrence of oil reservoirs within the earth's surface. Besides his faith and persistence in the undertaking Drake's foremost contribution was the use of pipe driven to bed-rock to prevent the overburden of clay and quicksand from filling in the drill hole. He failed, however, to patent the idea. Disregarding, too, the advice of friends, he was content for the succeeding four years to be an oil commission merchant and justice of the peace in Titusville. He saved about $16,000 and with it went to New York in 1863, lost almost every penny in oil speculations, broke down again physically, and retired to Vermont. His life from this time on was a search for relief from pain and a losing effort to keep his family from starving. The terrible conditions under which they were living in Long Branch, N. J., was discovered about 1870 and some measure of relief was afforded them through contributions of Titusville citizens. Three years later this help was augmented by a grant of $1,500 annually, made by the Pennsylvania legislature. In 1870 Drake and his family moved to Bethlehem, Pa., where a decade later Drake died and was buried.

Subsequently his remains were removed to Titusville, where a monument was erected to Drake and his wife by that city. He was married first about 1845 to a young woman of Springfield, Mass., who died in 1854. In 1857 he married Laura Dow of New Haven who, with four children, survived him.

[C. A. Babcock, *Venango County, Pa., her Pioneers and People,* vol. II (1919); J. H. Newton, *Hist. of Venango County, Pa.* (1879); Ida M. Tarbell, *Hist. of the Standard Oil Co.,* vol. I (1904); J. McLaurin, *Sketches in Crude Oil* (1896); obituary in *N. Y. Tribune,* Nov. 10, 1880; U. S. Nat. Museum correspondence.]

C. W. M.

DRAKE, FRANCES ANN DENNY (Nov. 6, 1797–Sept. 1, 1875), actress, although a native of New York State, having been born in Schenectady and brought up in Albany, was always regarded as a Western product, and was in fact sometimes called the "Star of the West." Of her family little is known except that the name was Denny and that it appears to have been in comfortable circumstances. She was educated in the Albany schools, but adopted the stage as a profession at the early age of seventeen when she joined the little band of actors, principally members of his own family, shepherded by Samuel Drake through the wilds to entertain the legislators of Kentucky. According to Noah M. Ludlow, at that time likewise a novice but later one of the theatre magnates of the West, she made her début as Julia in *The Midnight Hour,* in the small town of Cherry Valley, N. Y., one of the first halting-places of the troupe. It was not long before the young girl was demonstrating that she was endowed with far greater histrionic gifts than any of her associates, talented as several of them were, and, after two or three years in Kentucky and neighboring states, she returned to the East, going first to Canada and reaching New York in 1820. There she appeared on Apr. 17 at the Park Theatre, playing Helen Worret in *Man and Wife.* After a year or more in the East, she rejoined her former company, and in 1822 or 1823, according to Ludlow, was married to Alexander Drake, the second son of "Old Sam" and a comedian of unusual talent. Her reputation now grew rapidly, and in 1824 she returned to New York as a star. Although she continued to appear in comedy rôles, it was as a tragic actress that her fame was made, and for several years prior to the rise of Charlotte Cushman she was, despite the doubtless greater gifts of Mrs. Duff, generally regarded as the "tragedy queen" of the American stage. For a short time, she and her husband managed a theatre in Cincinnati, but this project was ended by his death in 1830, and she devoted the remainder of her professional life to starring. Although by 1836 her powers had begun to fail, she remained on the stage for a number of years. She was married a second time, to G. W. Cutter, but they were not happy together and separated shortly, the actress resuming the name of Drake. For a time, she lived at Covington, Ky., but died, at an advanced age, on the family farm near Louisville. She left three children, Col. A. E. Drake, U. S. A., Samuel Drake, and Mrs. Harry Chapman; a third son, Richard, was killed in the Mexican War. Mrs. Drake was undoubtedly an actress of great power and one who worked zealously to make the most of her gifts. Her figure and bearing were impressive and she acquired a very grand manner which proved exceedingly effective in the popular tragedies and melodramas. Yet she had her lighter side, and has been described as a "most joyous, affable creature, full of conundrums and good nature."

[Reliable first-hand information concerning Mrs. Drake is difficult to discover. Probably the best biographical sketch available is to be found in N. M. Ludlow's *Dramatic Life as I Found It* (1880). There is also material in: J. N. Ireland, *Records of the N. Y. Stage* (1866); Geo. C. D. Odell, *Annals of the N. Y. Stage* (1927–28); *The Autobiog. of Jos. Jefferson* (1889); Joe Cowell, *Thirty Years Passed among the Players in England and America* (1844); Mrs. Frances Trollope, *Domestic Manners of the Americans* (1832), and other works dealing with the early history of the American stage. An obituary published in the *Louisville Courier-Jour.* of Sept. 4, 1875, contains a number of serious errors.]
                      W. G. B. C.

DRAKE, FRANCIS MARION (Dec. 30, 1830–Nov. 20, 1903), railroad builder, philanthropist, governor of Iowa, the son of Judge John Adams and Harriet Jane (O'Neal) Drake, was born in Rushville, Schuyler County, Ill. His parents were North Carolinians and claimed descent from a brother of Sir Francis Drake. In 1837 the family moved to Fort Madison, Iowa, where Francis received a common-school education. From 1846 to 1852 he lived in Drakeville, Davis County, where he worked as a clerk in his father's store. The excitement following the gold discoveries in California induced him to organize two overland expeditions to Sacramento which he personally conducted with notable success in 1852 and 1854. On his return to Iowa he became a partner in his father's business and continued therein until the Civil War. He was married on Dec. 24, 1855, to Mary Jane Lord. In June 1861 he enlisted and became a captain in the "Appanoose Guards," later included in the Southern Iowa Brigade, with which he saw service in the region of St. Joseph, Mo. In 1862 he enlisted in the 36th Iowa Volunteer Infantry, being commissioned major, and saw service immediately in Kentucky and Tennessee. In January of the following year, his regiment went into winter quarters at Helena, Ark. He was advanced to the rank of lieutenant-colonel, took part in the Yazoo Pass expeditions, and on Apr. 4, 1863, commanded one wing in the battle of Shell Mound. He was absent for some weeks on sick leave but returned to take part in the battles about Little Rock in September. On Mar. 23, 1864, he left on the Camden expedition, a flanking movement to aid the Banks Red River expedition. He participated in the battles of Elkins's Ford, Prairie D'Ane, Camden, Marks's Mills, and Jenkins's Ferry. Of his work at Elkins's Ford on Apr. 4, his commanding officer reported: "Too much praise cannot be awarded

to Lt.-Col. Drake for his distinguished gallantry and determined courage." On the 25th, at Marks's Mills, his troop was overwhelmed; he was shot; and the regiment captured. Gen. Sterling Price deemed Drake mortally wounded and authorized his return North. After months in the hospital, however, he recovered and returned to his command. For his notable services he was given, on Feb. 22, 1865, the brevet rank of brigadier-general.

As soon as he was mustered out he returned to Iowa and entered upon the study of law, being admitted to practise in 1866. He had been attracted, by public interest, to the building of railroads, and almost immediately took an active part in their promotion, construction, and operation. In the year of his admission to the bar he became president of the Iowa Southern Railway, running from Alexandria, Mo., to Bloomfield, Iowa. That road, in 1870, was taken over by the Missouri, Iowa & Nebraska Railway, Drake continuing as president, and the line extending west to Van Wert. In 1880 he constructed the Centralia, Moravia & Albia road, which also was absorbed by the Missouri, Iowa & Nebraska. These roads in 1886 became known as the Keokuk & Western Railroad. Drake had all of the dramatic and strenuous experiences of a pioneer railroad builder in the West. His constant and energetic rival was the Chicago, Burlington & Quincy Railroad, and the clashes and competition were often intense. In 1882 he sold his railroad holdings in Iowa and from that year to 1898 was president of the Indiana, Illinois & Iowa Railroad (now a part of the Chicago & Alton), which he began constructing in 1881. His son-in-law, Theodore P. Shonts [*q.v.*], who later achieved distinction in railroad circles, was closely associated with him.

In 1881, the faculty and trustees of Oskaloosa College, of which Drake's brother-in-law, George T. Carpenter, was president, decided to move to Iowa's capital, Des Moines. Local opposition and court proceedings prevented the conversion and removal of capital funds. Carpenter appealed to Drake for aid, and the latter telegraphed a subscription of $20,000. As a result, Drake University was incorporated in May 1881 and opened its doors to students in September following. The institution slowly but steadily grew in stature and strength. Drake served until his death as president of the board of trustees. While not a lavish giver, he was generous of his time, energies, and funds; his gifts of money, all told, amounted to $225,000. In his attitude toward academic programs and instruction he was liberal, tolerant, and sympathetic.

About 1890 he sought the political arena, Congress being his objective, but conditions did not favor him. In 1893 his name was mentioned for the Republican nomination for governor of Iowa. Again others had the inside track. Undiscouraged, however, he began an energetic and systematic canvass for the nomination in 1895 and in what the *Des Moines Leader* characterized as "the most adroitly managed campaign" the state ever had, he entered the state convention at Des Moines, July 10, 1895, as the leading candidate. He was nominated on the sixth ballot, over six ardent and ambitious competitors, and was elected by a substantial plurality. In his inaugural address, Jan. 16, 1896, he pronounced himself in favor of the policy of "local option" which the General Assembly had recently adopted in opposition to the radical advocates of Prohibition, his stand in this matter alienating many of his supporters among churchmen. His administration was signalized chiefly, however, by his call of an extra session of the General Assembly for the revision of the Code of Iowa, in 1897. The legislature heeded his caution not to include educational institutions in the proposed drastic reforms to centralize the control of charitable and penal institutions. A serious illness that aggravated his old army wounds caused him to decline to run for another term, in the forepart of 1897, and on Jan. 11, 1898, he retired to private life. He died at Centerville, Appanoose County, in his seventy-third year.

[Memoranda supplied by Drake's daughter, Mrs. E. D. Goss of Pasadena, Cal., and by J. C. Barrows, Esq., for thirty-five years editor of *The Iowegian* of Centerville; A. A. Stuart, *Iowa Colonels and Regiments* (1865); Reports of the Adjutant-General of Iowa for 1864 and 1865; *Official Records* (*Army*), 1 ser. vol. XXXIV; *Roster and Record of Iowa Soldiers in the War of the Rebellion,* vol. V (1911); *The 19th Ann. Report of the Board of R. R. Commissioners for 1896 . . . State of Iowa* (1897); W. W. Baldwin, *Corporate Hist. of the Chicago, Burlington & Quincy R. R. Co.* (1921); *Annals of Iowa,* 3 ser.; B. F. Gue, *Hist. of Iowa,* vol. IV (1903); *Who's Who in America,* 1901–02; *Biog. Dir. Am. Cong.* (1928); *Register and Leader* (Des Moines), Nov. 21, 1903; and the writer's personal recollections.]   F. I. H.

DRAKE, FRANCIS SAMUEL (Feb. 22, 1828–Feb. 22, 1885), historian, son of Samuel Gardner [*q.v.*] and Louisa (Elmes) Drake, was born in Northwood, N. H., and died in Washington, D. C. In his earliest memory his family were already living in Boston. His father was the proprietor of the first antiquarian bookstore in Boston, and the prolific editor and author of many works of American history. By 1848, Francis was a lieutenant in the Boston Light Guards, and in that capacity he went to Washington for the ceremonies held in connection with the laying of the corner-stone of the Wash-

ington Monument. By 1856, he was married to E. M. Valentine. In 1862 he removed to Kansas. During the Civil War, he served in the army for a brief period in the capacity of adjutant. He was back in Boston by 1871. The next year he published in one bulky volume a *Dictionary of American Biography Containing Nearly Ten Thousand Notices* (1872). In the preface he complains of the difficulty of attaining correct proportions in such a work—there was so much available material about New England and New York, and about politicians, authors, and clergymen, that an editor of his kind was in danger of emphasizing those regions and callings at the expense of others. He had tried, he said, to avoid that error. This book went through subsequent editions in 1874 and 1879. In 1872 he published a *List of Members of the Massachusetts Society of the Cincinnati,* and in 1873, *Memorials of the Society of the Cincinnati of Massachusetts,* and *The Life and Correspondence of Henry Knox,* both objective, dependable, and dry. He was not a member of the Society of the Cincinnati, but was probably "employed" to arrange the *Memorials* in accord with the resolution of the Society (Drake, *Memorials,* iii). His history, *The Town of Roxbury,* was published in 1878. Two years later he contributed to Justin Winsor's *Memorial History of Boston* a series of three articles each on Roxbury and Brighton. He edited Schoolcraft's *Indian Tribes of the United States* in 1884, and in 1885 he published *Indian History for Young Folks,* a book which has since been three times copyrighted—1912, 1919, and 1927. *Tea Leaves, Being a Collection of Letters and Documents Relating to the Shipment of Tea to the American Colonies* appeared in 1884, the editor's introduction comprising half of the entire volume. During the last years of his life he was consistently referred to by the Boston Directories as a "stationer," and one of the newspaper obituaries concerning him said that he was the "proprietor of a large circulating library and periodical store in Boston." At the time of his quite unexpected death, he was in Washington as a representative of the Boston Light Guards at the dedication of the Washington Monument.

[S. G. Drake, *Geneal. and Biog. Account of the Family of Drake* (1845), *Drake of Hampton, N. H.* (1867); *Washington Post,* Feb. 23, 1885.]   J. D. W.

DRAKE, JOHN BURROUGHS (Jan. 17, 1826–Nov. 12, 1895), hotel man, was born in Lebanon, Ohio, the son of John Burroughs Drake, a harness-maker from Trenton, N. J., and of Nancy (Hurry) Drake, a Pennsylvanian. He was one of six children. When he was eleven his father died, and the mother's problem of meeting the needs of the family was not easy. John augmented their budget by working in a store, although he somehow obtained what was called a "common school" education. When sixteen he became boy-of-all-work at the Williamson House, the tavern in Lebanon. From this humble beginning in the hotel business he was destined to rise till he became one of the country's foremost landlords. He seems, moreover, to have chosen the vocation deliberately. In 1845 he went to seek his fortune in Cincinnati, seventy-five cents in one pocket and a letter of introduction from Tom Corwin, his fellow townsman, in another. For ten years he was a hotel-clerk, first at the Pearl Street House, then at the Burnett House. He managed to accumulate the capital necessary for his next venture. In 1855 he purchased a quarter interest in the leading hotel in Chicago, the Tremont House. His affairs prospered; in fifteen years he was the sole owner of the hotel. Then came the fire of 1871. The Tremont House was burned, but Drake was still a landlord. While the fire was at its height he made a payment on the Michigan Avenue Hotel at the corner of Michigan Ave. and Congress St. He gambled that it would not burn, although the fire was across the street. It was the only hotel on the South Side to escape the flames. In 1873 he took charge of the Grand Pacific Hotel and here he rose to nation-wide fame as a landlord. He was an ardent Republican and his hotel was the recognized headquarters of that party in the West, but it attracted epicures as well as politicians. As Drake's capital increased he diversified his financial interests. He was one of the organizers of the Union Stock Yards, a director of the Chicago & Alton Railroad, and vice-president of the Illinois Trust & Savings Bank. His foresight is shown in his heavy investments in the Chicago Telephone and the Chicago Edison Electric companies. Altogether, he was one of the aggressive citizens whose energy helped to make Chicago a great city. He was married on Feb. 24, 1863, to Josephine C. Corey, daughter of Francis Edward Corey, a prominent citizen of Chicago. They had five children, three sons and two daughters. The Drake and Blackstone hotels are controlled by their heirs.

[*Encyc. of Biog. of Ill.* (1894), II, 95 ff.; obituary in the *Chicago Daily Tribune*, Nov. 13, 1895.]

W. T. U—r.

DRAKE, JOSEPH RODMAN (Aug. 7, 1795– Sept. 21, 1820), poet, was the son of Jonathan Drake of Pelham Manor, N. Y., seventh in descent from John Drake, who came to Boston and settled in Windsor, Conn., in 1630. This original immigrant was the son of John Drake of Plymouth, England, who, in 1606, was appointed by James I member of a company to attend to the settling of New England. Jonathan Drake married Hannah Lawrence, daughter of Effingham Lawrence of Flushing, L. I. Their son, Joseph, was born in New York City. His early years were saddened by the death of his father and the removal of his three sisters and his mother, after her remarriage, to New Orleans. It was then to near relatives, the Hunts at Hunts Point on East River, and the Rodmans of Rodman's Neck, that he turned for companionship. These associations furnished the background and the immediate inspiration of many of his best poems. In 1813, while he was a student of medicine in a school on Barclay St., New York, through his friend James E. De Kay [*q.v.*], also a medical student, he met Fitz-Greene Halleck [*q.v.*] with whom he was associated in the closest of friendships for the rest of his brief life. In 1816 he received his medical degree—at the head of his class (data from Charles De Kay)—and in October of the same year married Sarah Eckford, daughter of the ship-builder, Henry Eckford [*q.v.*]. Shortly afterward, with her, he visited Europe, travelling in Great Britain and Ireland, France, and Holland. A miniature of Drake, painted by Metcalf about this time, shows golden hair, large, dark-blue eyes, a slender but well-knit figure, and suggests the powers of attraction that charmed his friends. Early in 1819, in partnership with William Langstaff, he opened a drug store. His health began to fail, however, owing, it is said, to overwork in his profession, and in the autumn of the same year he journeyed by coach to New Orleans to visit his mother. When he returned, in the spring of 1820, he was far advanced in consumption, and on Sept. 21, in his twenty-sixth year, he died. He was buried in the private burying ground of the Hunt family at Hunts Point. The spot has been set apart and protected by the City of New York.

The only work of Drake's to be published during his life was the "Croaker Papers," satirical and humorous poems, rich in local allusion, which with Halleck he contributed to the New York *Evening Post,* between Mar. 10 and July 24, 1819. On his death-bed he instructed his wife to destroy his unpublished verse as of no consequence; but his papers were preserved, and much later his daughter, Janet Halleck, who had become the wife of Commodore George Colman De Kay [*q.v.*], published a selection of nineteen poems as *The Culprit Fay and Other Poems* (1835). Of these, "The American Flag" and

"The Culprit Fay" are still well known, at least by name; although "Bronx" and "Niagara" deserve attention as nature pieces and the lines "To a Friend" are an interesting statement of his strong preference for indigenous themes in poetry. For several generations American pulses have been quickened by the magniloquent lines of "The American Flag," of which the last quatrain in the published version is by Halleck; and "The Culprit Fay" was long regarded as one of the best American poems. It was written during three days, in August 1816, and was prompted by the challenging remark that American rivers are too poorly furnished with mythological and legendary lore to be subjects for poetry. Its 640 lines display spontaneity and facility rather than mastery or deep originality. Its imperfections are chargeable to the modesty of the author, who thought too highly of poetry to think of himself as a poet and never subjected his powers to the discipline that they merited.

[Information from Drake's grandson, Charles De Kay; J. G. Wilson, *Life and Letters of Fitz-Greene Halleck* (1869), *Bryant and His Friends* (1886), and articles in *Harper's Mag.*, June 1874, and the *Century Mag.*, July 1910; M. A. De Wolfe Howe, *Am. Bookmen* (1898); fresh biographical and critical data, together with an indispensable bibliography by Victor H. Paltsits, in *Trans. Bronx Soc. of Arts and Sci.*, vol. I, pt. IV (1919); obituary in *National Advocate*, Sept. 22, 1820; *The Cambridge Hist. of Am. Lit.* (1917), I, 262, 280–81, 521–22; contemporary appreciation in *Am. Monthly Rev.*, Sept. 1835; comment by N. P. Willis in *Athenæum* (London), Jan. and Feb. 1835; review by E. A. Poe in *Southern Lit. Messenger*, Apr. 1836; other criticism in Burton's *Gentlemen's Mag.*, Jan. 1840, and *Graham's Mag.*, Feb. 1842. Certain fugitive poems not published elsewhere were included in E. A. Duyckinck, *Cyc. of Am. Lit.* (1856).]
A. L. B.

DRAKE, SAMUEL (Nov. 15, 1768–Oct. 16, 1854), pioneer actor-manager of the West, was a native of England, where, says Noah M. Ludlow in his *Dramatic Life as I Found It*, he was an actor and theatre manager in the provinces. His name was really Samuel Drake Bryant (statement of his daughter Martha, in 1819, at the time of her second marriage), but he dropped his surname when he went on the stage. In 1810 he came to the United States, bringing with him a large and talented family, composed of his wife (formerly a Miss Fisher), three sons, and two daughters. They landed at Boston, where the parents were during the season of 1810–11 members of the Boston Theatre Company. With it they apparently remained until 1813, when they moved to Albany to join the company of John Bernard, Drake himself becoming stage manager and playing such rôles as Cæsar in *Julius Cæsar*. The next year Mrs. Drake died. About this time, there appeared in Albany a young man named Noble Luke Usher

who was endeavoring to collect a band of actors to go to Kentucky, where he had theatres in Louisville, Lexington, and Frankfort. He succeeded in interesting the Drakes, and the following spring (1815) they set out for what was then the Far West. They were joined by two ambitious novices, Ludlow and Frances Ann Denny, a girl of seventeen who later married the manager's second son, Alexander [v. Frances Ann Denny Drake], and was for some years the great American "tragedy queen." The journey to Kentucky was a most difficult and dangerous one, as much of the country through which the travelers had to pass was but sparsely inhabited and really wild. The hegira was probably the most heroic in the annals of the American stage. In November, according to Ludlow, the company reached Pittsburgh, where they halted long enough to give a brief season, and then pushed on to their destination. Meeting with success there and completely dispossessing his predecessor, one William Turner, Drake sought to set up his hegemony in neighboring centers, St. Louis, Vincennes, and Cincinnati. In these towns, however, he was not so successful, and during the remainder of his professional career centered his attentions on Kentucky, which state he dominated theatrically for years. After his retirement, he settled on a farm in Oldham County, where he eventually died. While it cannot be said that Drake was the first man to carry the drama into the West, it was unquestionably he who brought the first company of really talented players beyond Pittsburgh and who set the drama on a firm basis in Louisville, Lexington, and Frankfort. Of his five children, all but the youngest son were for a time at least on the stage. Two, Alexander (1798–1830), who was a clever comedian, and Julia (1800–1832), achieved great popularity in the West, and the latter left behind her a daughter who, as Julia Dean [q.v.], was a generation later one of the greatest favorites on the American stage.

[N. M. Ludlow, *Dramatic Life as I Found It* (1880), which is the authority (p. 363), for the dates of birth and death; Sol Smith, *Theatrical Management in the West and South for Thirty Years* (1868); W. W. Clapp, Jr., *A Record of the Boston Stage* (1853); "Colley Cibber," *Dramatic Authors of America* (1845); H. P. Phelps, *Players of a Century, a Record of the Albany Stage* (1880); J. S. Johnston, *Memorial Hist. of Louisville* (preface, 1896); W. G. B. Carson, "The Beginnings of the Theatre in St. Louis," *Mo. Hist. Soc. Colls.*, Feb. 1928; C. R. Staples, "The Amusements and Diversions of Early Lexington" (unpublished MS. in the possession of Mr. C. R. Staples, Lexington, Ky.); private information.]
W. G. B. C.

DRAKE, SAMUEL ADAMS (Dec. 19, 1833–Dec. 4, 1905), historian, son of Samuel Gardner and Louisa (Elmes) Drake, was born in

Boston, and died in Kennebunkport, Me. He was educated in the public schools of Boston. On Sept. 14, 1858, he was married in Louisville, Ky., to Isabella G. Mayhew, and at about the same time he went to live in Kansas. There he worked with a newspaper and was correspondent for papers in the East. He was a soldier through most of the Civil War, attaining the rank of brigadier-general in the Kansas militia, and colonel in the Kansas volunteers. His wife died in Cincinnati in 1863, and in 1866 he returned to New England. Soon after returning he married, on Oct. 4, 1866, Olive N. Grant of Kennebunkport, Me. His father and his brother, Francis Samuel Drake [*q.v.*], were both historians, and if his own interests were not already similar to those of his family he was not long in making them so. One of his books, in fact, *The Border Wars of New England* (1897), is the completion of work originally undertaken by his father. Beginning in the early seventies he published books at the rate of about one a year for twenty-five years. Two of these, *Nooks and Corners of the New England Coast* (1875), dedicated to Longfellow, and *The Heart of the White Mountains* (1882), dedicated to Whittier, were little more than sumptuous guide-books. He wrote also a series of semi-popular but dependable histories, dangerously like text-books: *The Making of New England* (1886), *The Making of the Great West* (1887); *The Making of Virginia and the Middle Colonies* (1893); and *The Making of the Ohio Valley States* (1894). But apart from these, the region round Boston was dominant in nearly everything that he wrote, from the *Old Landmarks and Historic Personages of Boston* (1873), *Historic Fields and Mansions of Middlesex* (1874), *Our Colonial Homes* (1894), to his one novel, a boy's book, *The Young Vigilantes, a Story of California Life in the Fifties* (1904). He once referred to a book of his as an "historic-colloquial ramble" (*Old Landmarks of Middlesex,* V), and that characterization—if not too informal for so much imperturbability and so much scrupulous indexing—is fairly apt for most of his work. He was a born antiquarian, and in spite of his occasional respectful comments about the Future, it was the Past only which really interested him. "I think myself," he once wrote, with manifest restraint, "that the New Englander has some good qualities, one among others being his veneration for the things that have a history or embody a sentiment" (*Colonial Homes,* preface).

[S. G. Drake, *Geneal. and Biog. Account of the Family of Drake* (1845), *Drake of Hampton, N. H.* (1867); *Who's Who in America,* 1903–05; *N. Y. Times,* Dec. 5, 1905.]   J. D. W.

DRAKE, SAMUEL GARDNER (Oct. 11, 1798–June 14, 1875), antiquarian, historian, was the son of Simeon and Love Muchmore (Tucke) Drake of Pittsfield, N. H., in which place he was born. He was descended from a line of English ancestors, the first of whom settled in New Hampshire near Exeter about 1640. Samuel submitted to a few years of schooling in New Hampshire villages and at seventeen went to work for an uncle in Boston who removed to Baltimore soon after, taking Samuel and his older brother with him. The anticipated business success was not achieved and after six months Samuel went back to his father and studied for a short time under John Kelly, a lawyer. In 1818 he took charge of the school at Loudon, N. H., at eight dollars a month, and continued to teach, at various places for some years. In 1819–20 he was at Columbia, near Morristown, N. J. Ill health compelled his return home and in 1820–21 he studied medicine under Dr. Thomas Shannon of Pittsfield. He then went back to teaching until 1824, when he decided to become a bookseller. The next year he issued a reprint of Church's *History of King Philip's War* which proved profitable. From 1828 to 1830 he was a book-auctioneer and in 1830 opened a shop in Cornhill, Boston. Two years later he published his *Indian Biography* (1832), which went through several editions under varying titles, being enlarged into the much more important *Book of the Indians,* first published under that title in 1841. In 1836 he published his *Old Indian Chronicle,* and in 1839, *Indian Captivities.* Union College gave him an honorary A.M., in 1843, and soon after he was one of the five founders of the New-England Historic Genealogical Society, serving as its corresponding secretary for twelve years and as president in 1858. He also edited its publication, *The New-England Historical and Genealogical Register,* from its beginning, 1847, until the close of the fifteenth volume. He had long had in mind a history of New England, and, although he never wrote it, he spent the years 1858–60 in Europe, and in England, searching for material. He continued his bookselling business on his return and accumulated a fairly important private library of nearly 12,000 volumes and 50,000 pamphlets, mainly relating to Indians and early colonial history. In addition to many articles and the works already named, he wrote or edited, among others: *Genealogical and Biographical Account of the Family of Drake in America* (privately printed, 1845); *The History and Antiquities of Boston* (1856); Mather's *Indian War of 1675–6* (1862); Mather's *Early History of New England* (1864);

Hubbard's *History of the Indian Wars in New England* (1865); *The Witchcraft Delusion in New England* (3 vols., 1866); *Annals of Witchcraft in New England, and Elsewhere in the United States* (1869); *A Particular History of the Five Years French and Indian War in New England and Parts Adjacent* (1870). He first married on Apr. 12, 1825, Louisa Elmes of Middleborough, Mass., by whom he had five children, among them being Francis Samuel and Samuel Adams Drake [*qq.v.*]. After Mrs. Drake's death, when he was past middle life, he was married again, to a relative, Sarah Jane Drake.

[Rather oddly, the New-Eng. Hist. Geneal. Soc. published no memoir after his death, though they did issue one twelve years before that event (*New-Eng. Hist. and Geneal. Reg.*, vol. XVII, 1863, pp. 197–211), which is naturally incomplete. There is an account by Wm. B. Trask in *Potter's Am. Monthly*, Oct. 1875. See also Drake's own *Genealogical . . . Account*.]   J. T. A.

DRAPER, ANDREW SLOAN (June 21, 1848–Apr. 27, 1913), politician, educator, was born at Westford, N. Y., the son of Sylvester Bigelow and Jane (Sloan) Draper. His father was descended from James Draper, a Puritan who settled at Roxbury, Mass., about 1649, and his mother from a Scotch-Irish family which came to the United States from the north of Ireland in 1812. Andrew was educated in the Albany public schools, was graduated from the Albany Academy in 1866, and from the Albany Law School in 1871. From 1866 to 1870, while he was reading and studying law, he taught at the Albany Academy and at a private school at Westford, and was the principal of a grade school at East Worcester. In 1871 he was admitted to the bar, and in the following year married Abbie Louise Lyon of New Britain, Conn. Until 1887 he practised law in Albany in the firm of Draper & Chester. He was a member of the board of education of Albany from 1879 to 1881; in the latter year he became a member of the state legislature, and from then on he was active in New York Republican circles. In 1884 President Arthur appointed him a member of the court of commissioners on the *Alabama* claims.

From 1882 to 1886 he had been a member of the board of the New York State Normal School. In the latter year he was elected state superintendent of public instruction, in spite of opposition by the educational leaders of the state. The latter felt, and had no hesitation in declaring, that he was primarily a politician and only secondarily an educator. His new office was one given by a partisan legislature to one of its partisans, and in 1892 when the legislature became Democratic he lost it. In those six years, how-

ever, the educator in him conquered the politician. His skill as the latter enabling him to get bills through the legislature, he obtained for education increased appropriations, more equitable distribution of the school taxes, a first progressive step for more security and regularity for teachers in their contracts and salaries, licenses for teachers issued by the state on the basis of uniform examinations, and the removal—to a considerable extent—of the appointments of teachers from politics.

His former opponents supported him for re-election as superintendent in 1892, but to no avail. He announced the resumption of his law practise, but so well known had he become as a school administrator that he was called to Cleveland, Ohio, as superintendent of schools. For two years he remained there and put new life into the school system of that city. In 1894 he accepted the presidency of the University of Illinois. The skill which he had acquired in Albany in handling legislators came to his assistance so that appropriations scarcely to be hoped for were forthcoming for buildings and educational improvements. In 1904 the double-headed system of education in New York State was so consolidated as to put the whole educational system of the state under the Board of Regents. To the new office of commissioner of education the legislature elected him, and after six years—in 1910 —the Regents continued him in office during good behavior. Upon bases which he laid, the present organization of the New York State Department of Education is largely founded.

He was given the silver medal of the Paris Exposition in 1900 for his monograph, *Educational Organization and Administration in the United States* (1900), and received several medals and awards at the St. Louis International Exposition in 1904 for his writings and conspicuous services in the field of education. President Roosevelt appointed him a member of the United States Board of Indian Commissioners in 1902, and he later became its chairman. His educational writings are mainly in the form of magazine articles and addresses. These were collected in five volumes, published between 1904 and 1912. He published a book on the Spanish-American War entitled *The Rescue of Cuba* (1899), and another entitled *American Education* (1909), comprising his more notable addresses. He was editor of the department of education in the *Encyclopedia Americana,* of the volume, *Selections from Lincoln* (1911), in the Gateway Series; and editor-in-chief of a ten-volume work entitled *Self Culture for Young People* (1906–07). In manner, Draper was inclined to be somewhat brusque and severe. In his public addresses he gradually became a very forceful speaker. He was deliberate in arriving at his conclusions, but when he had reached them he seldom surrendered to opposition.

[The best estimates of Draper and his work are an article by C. W. Bardeen in *The School Bulletin*, XXXIX, 197 ff.; a memorial address by his former law partner, Judge Alden C. Chester, in *Proc. Fifty-Third Convocation Univ. of the State of N. Y.* (1917); Thos. E. Finegan, *Life and Public Services of Andrew S. Draper* (1914); and a memorial brochure *Andrew Sloan Draper, Commissioner of Education* (1913), issued by the Board of Regents, containing selections from its minutes. See also *Who's Who in America,* 1912–13; *N. Y. Times, N. Y. Tribune,* Apr. 28, 1913; and Allan Nevins, *Illinois* (1917).]   **J. S—n.**

DRAPER, EBEN SUMNER (June 17, 1858– Apr. 9, 1914), manufacturer and politician, was born in that part of Milford, Mass., which is now Hopedale, the youngest son of George and Hannah (Thwing) Draper. His father, and his uncle, Ebenezer D. Draper, had been among the leading members of the famous Hopedale Community and their withdrawal in 1856, while it brought an end to that experiment, opened the way for the rapid expansion in the manufacturing enterprises of Milford and a rapid rise in the fortunes of the Drapers. The chief concern of that region became the factories for the manufacture of cotton machinery operating under the name of E. D. & G. Draper, which in 1868 was changed to George Draper & Son upon the retirement of Ebenezer and the addition of William Franklin Draper [*q.v.*], and again in 1877 to George Draper & Sons upon the admission of George A., George Draper's second son. Into this concern Eben was admitted as a junior partner after study at the Massachusetts Institute of Technology and a short period of training in the machine-shops of Hopedale and the cotton-mills at Lowell and other textile centers. As this concern prospered under the able management of the Drapers, the business interests of the partners widened. Eben became a director in many companies manufacturing cotton machinery and cotton goods and in Milford and Boston banks. In 1907, upon the retirement of his brother, William Franklin, as senior partner, he assumed the management of the Draper mills.

For some twenty years Eben S. Draper divided his time between his business interests and a political career. He became in 1892 a member of the Republican state committee and soon after, its chairman; and as chairman of the Massachusetts delegation to the Republican convention at St. Louis in 1896 he wielded his influence in favor of the gold plank. A presidential elector in 1900, he was elected lieutenant-governor for the three terms 1906–08, and governor for two

terms, 1909 and 1910, but was defeated at the hands of Eugene M. Foss in the latter year in the nation-wide reaction against the conservative Taft administration. As governor, Draper gave the state an efficient and businesslike administration which included work for forest conservation and harbor improvement. His economic views were conservative; he twice vetoed a bill providing for stricter enforcement of an eight-hour law for public employees, which action, combined with the fact that he employed only non-union labor on a ten-hour schedule in his own mills, won for him throughout his administration the active opposition of organized labor.

The town of Hopedale was separated from Milford largely through the efforts of the Drapers, and the family gave frequently to the community. Eben S. Draper and his brother built the Unitarian church, and he and his wife presented a hospital to the town. Draper was also responsible for a model-cottage colony for his workers. In spite of these benefits, the Draper mills were the scene, in April 1913, of an exceedingly bitter strike, in which the workmen, mostly immigrant, were led by I. W. W. leaders in demands for a fifty-hour week and higher pay. Draper claimed that conditions in his mills were as good as any in the state, was uncompromising in his refusal to deal with the strike leaders, and eventually broke the strike.

In addition to his local charities, Draper was favorably known throughout the state for his work as president of the Massachusetts Volunteer Aid Association, which raised $400,000 for soldiers' relief during the Spanish-American War, and as head of the Massachusetts committee which raised $1,000,000 for San Francisco fire relief. He was at one time vice-president of the American Unitarian Association and a member of the corporation of the Massachusetts Institute of Technology. He married, on Nov. 21, 1883, Nannie Bristow, a daughter of Gen. Benjamin H. Bristow [*q.v.*] of Kentucky, and by her had three children. Death came to him at Greenville, S. C., as the result of a paralytic stroke.

[See T. W. Draper, *The Drapers in America* (1892), p. 114; Adin Ballou, *Hist. of the Town of Milford* (1882); S. A. Eliot (ed.), *Biog. Hist. of Mass.* (1917), vol. VII. The Boston papers for April 1913 contain the story of the strike and those for Apr. 10, 1914, have long obituaries.]   **H. U. F.**

DRAPER, HENRY (Mar. 7, 1837–Nov. 20, 1882), astronomer, pioneer in astronomical photography, was reared in an atmosphere of culture and scientific thought. His father was John William Draper [*q.v.*], from 1838 to 1882 professor of chemistry in the University of the City of

New York, and an early investigator of photography; and his mother was Antonia Coetana de Paiva Pereira Gardner, daughter of the court physician of Emperor Dom Pedro I of Brazil. Born in Prince Edward County, Va., where his father was teaching natural philosophy in Hampden-Sidney College, he was taken as an infant to New York City, which was his home for the rest of his life. After transferring, during his sophomore year, from the classical course in the University of the City of New York, he went on to a degree in medicine, completing the course in 1857 but not receiving his diploma until 1858, when he had attained his majority. His thesis, "On the Changes of Blood Cells in the Spleen" (*New York Journal of Medicine,* 1858), was illustrated with photomicrographs. He had spent the year 1857–58 in Europe with an older brother. After receiving his degree of M.D. he served for eighteen months on the medical staff of Bellevue Hospital but in 1860 he left Bellevue to become professor of natural science at his alma mater.

His active interest in astronomy began, apparently, during his year abroad, when he visited Parsonstown to see the great telescope constructed by the Earl of Rosse. On his return from Europe he cast a 15½ inch speculum and constructed a grinding and polishing machine. This was the start of many years of painstaking and ingenious work on the making of reflecting telescopes. In 1860 he built an observatory on his father's estate at Hastings-on-Hudson, where his investigations during the summer months were henceforth carried on. The first instrument placed here was a 15½-inch silver-on-glass reflector, on an alt-azimuth mounting, ingeniously fitted for photography. The plate-holder was at first driven by a sand-clock—the weight of the clock resting on a column of sand which ran out through a hole of variable size. Later, a clepsydra was substituted. Large numbers of photographs of the sun and moon were taken. At the invitation of Joseph Henry, Draper wrote a paper, "On the Construction of a Silvered Glass Telescope 15½ inches in Aperture, and its Use in Celestial Photography," which was published in the *Smithsonian Contributions to Knowledge, No. 180,* July 1864. In 1867 he began work on a 28-inch mirror. This took much of his spare time to 1869 when the telescope was mounted in a new dome. The defining power not proving entirely satisfactory, the mirror was repolished, and it was not until 1872 that the driving clock and accessories were completed. Later he built six other driving clocks before he had one that functioned to suit him.

It was largely with this instrument that Draper did his great work in stellar spectroscopy. In May 1872 he secured his first spectrum of a star —that of Vega. This work involved the design and construction of many spectrographs and the careful investigation of the entire subject of securing stellar spectra. He also photographed the spectra of the moon, Jupiter, and Venus. In his laboratory over the stable behind his New York City house, he accomplished the photographic reproduction of the spectrum of the sun, undertaken for the purpose of securing standards from which the wave-lengths in the stellar spectra could be determined. Here also he made the investigations leading to his interesting conclusion that oxygen made known its presence in the sun by bright lines, and started an animated discussion as to whether the solar spectrum was made up of dark lines on a continuous background or of dark and bright lines. The investigation of the spectra of the elements led to many new difficulties to be overcome. In the use of a carbon disulphide prism he adopted Rutherfurd's suggestion of a stirrer to do away with striæ and constructed an even-temperature box which did away with the shifting of the spectrum lines.

In 1874 Draper was chosen, because of his experience, to organize the photographic work of the government expedition to observe the transit of Venus. He worked so devotedly for three months, devising methods, testing instruments and materials, and training observers, that Congress ordered a special gold medal struck in his honor. In 1878 he organized an expedition to observe the total solar eclipse in Wyoming.

Though Draper's most notable work was in astronomy, he was active in other fields. During the Civil War, in 1862, he served three months as surgeon of the 12th Regiment, New York State Militia. From 1866 to 1873 he was professor of physiology in the medical school, University of the City of New York; dean of the faculty, and from 1870 professor of analytical chemistry. He was a member of the National Academy of Sciences, and of the American Philosophical Society. In 1874, on the death of his father-in-law, Courtlandt Palmer of New York, whose daughter, Mary Anna, he had married in 1867, he was left managing trustee of Palmer's large estate, and proved equal to the task. He was an enthusiastic sportsman, and it was his yearly custom to join his friends Generals Marcy and Whipple for a few weeks' hunting in the Rocky Mountains.

In January 1882 his father died, and until the end of the academic year Draper succeeded him in the chair of chemistry, but he himself died less than eleven months later. His widow, interested in the successful attempts at the Harvard College Observatory to photograph the spectra of many stars simultaneously, placed Draper's eleven-inch telescope at the disposal of that institution, and provided them with generous funds to carry out a great program of securing, for purposes of classification, the spectra of all the brighter stars. Many volumes of "The Henry Draper Memorial" have appeared, containing the positions, magnitudes, and spectra of 225,300 stars, and the survey is now being pushed to still fainter limits.

[G. F. Barker, "Memoir of Henry Draper," in *Biog. Memoirs Nat. Acad. Sci.*, III (1895), 83; "Prof. Henry Draper," in *N. Y. Tribune*, reprinted in *The Sidereal Messenger*, Jan. 1883; W. H. M. C., "Prof. Henry Draper, M.D.," in *The Observatory*, Jan. 1883; Thos. Waln-Morgan Draper, *The Drapers in America* (1892).]

R. S. D.

DRAPER, IRA (Dec. 24, 1764–Jan. 22, 1848), textile-machinery inventor and manufacturer, was born at Dedham, Mass., the son of Abijah and Alice (Eaton) Draper. Abijah, descendant of James ("the Puritan") Draper, who settled at Roxbury, Mass., about 1649, was a farmer and a soldier. He had held every office in the militia up to that of major, in which capacity he commanded Minute Men under Washington at Roxbury. Abijah Draper was very well-to-do for the period, and afforded Ira a good education, though it was mostly in the nature of personal instruction from the family and employed tutors. Ira remained at Green Lodge, Dedham, the family home, helping his father in the management of the estate. In his twenty-second year, on May 31, 1786, he married Lydia Richards of Dedham, and at his father's death he inherited Green Lodge. He began to dabble with mechanical improvement along with his farming, and in this connection constructed a threshing machine and a road scraper. The threshing machine, though one of the first in the country and apparently practicable, did not contribute to later development of the machine. Finding invention more interesting than farming, Draper turned to textile-manufacturing machinery as a field affording considerable opportunity for improvement. He made several minor improvements on looms, among them a "fly shuttle" attachment and a jaw temple. He then conceived and constructed the first rotary temple, the invention which has made his name remembered. The loom temple is a device for keeping cloth spread to its proper width, with the warp threads taut and parallel, to minimize the chafing of the selvage. The old form was a telescoping stick with points at the ends to catch the selvage at either side. It had

to be adjusted in length for the width of cloth and the weaver had, from time to time, to move it forward as the cloth was woven. The rotary temple patented by Ira Draper in 1816 was the first practical self-acting temple. In this the cloth was held by a horizontal wheel having a row of teeth set obliquely to its axis. This had the effect of doubling the capacity of the operative by allowing one weaver to attend two looms. The device was improved by a spring mounting in 1829, and in 1840 George Draper, the son of Ira, added another row of teeth to prevent it from marking the cloth. The rotary temple was immediately and almost universally adopted and formed the basis of a profitable and lasting business. By continually improving their temple and purchasing the rights of other inventors the successive Draper descendants built up the Draper Company into the largest temple manufacturer of the world. In 1907 they supplied practically all of the loom temples used in the United States. Ira Draper continued his connection with the business until he was well along in years, when he turned it over to his sons. In 1811 his first wife died and on Mar. 9, 1812, he married her sister Abigail ("Nabby") Richards. He had, by both wives, sixteen children. He died at Saugus, Mass.

[E. H. Knight, *Knight's American Mechanical Dictionary*, 3 vols. (1874–76); T. W. Draper, *The Drapers in America* (1892); T. M. Young, *Am. Cotton Industry* (1903); Patent Office records.]

F. A. T.

DRAPER, JOHN (Oct. 29, 1702–Nov. 29, 1762), journalist, was the seventh child of Richard and Sarah (Kilby) Draper. The *Boston News-Letter* of Jan. 4, 1733, contained this notice: "Mr. Bartholomew Green . . . being dead, . . . it will be carried on . . . by John Draper, (Son-in-law to the said Mr. Green) who has been an Assistant with him in the said News-Letter, . . . And all the Rev. Ministers, or other Gentlemen, both of Town and Country, who may at any time receive any thing worthy of publishing, are desired to send it to the said Draper, . . . And it will yet be endeavoured to render This Weekly Paper as informing and entertaining as possibly can be, to the Satisfaction of all who do or may encourage it." In this fashion did Draper announce that he had become the third publisher of the oldest and one of the best of colonial newspapers. With it, and the attendant printing business, his whole public life was concerned. He held no offices and evidently took no part in town affairs beyond that of the ordinary good citizen. The facts of his domestic life are equally simple. His father was a shopkeeper, selectman, and deacon. John married Deborah (or Dorathy) Green on May 24, 1726, and their one child, Richard, was born on Feb. 24, 1727. The mother died on Dec. 9, 1736, aged thirty-nine years, and the widower took Elizabeth Avery of Truro, as his second wife in October 1737. She survived him many years.

Draper served his apprenticeship under Green, but seems to have done some independent work before his father-in-law's death, since he printed the first forty-seven numbers of Jeremiah Gridley's *Weekly Rehersal,* a political paper which appeared in September 1731. Draper succeeded Green as printer for the governor and Council and passed the position on to his son; for about thirty years his imprint appeared on law and other official publications, as well as upon numerous broadsides and some more permanent output, such as *Ames Almanac.* He subscribed for six copies of Prince's *Chronology.* Under his control the *News-Letter* kept step with colonial progress. Interest in colonial news as well as in European; the growth of information from other colonies; new features, such as "letters to the publisher," clippings, some verse; and a steady enlargement of the space devoted to advertisements: these, and an increase in size, are features of the development. Under him, as under Green, the paper had a distinctly religious tone. When he died his son said of him: "By his Industry, Fidelity, and Prudence in his Business he rendered himself very agreeable to the Public—His Charity and Benevolence; his pleasant and sociable Turn of Mind . . . has made his Death as sensibly felt by his Friends and Relations, as his Life is worthy Imitation" (*News-Letter,* Dec. 2, 1762). Richard Draper [*q.v.*] continued the paper, and on his death his wife, Margaret (Green) Draper [*q.v.*], took charge; but the outbreak of the Revolution was fatal to it.

[Aside from the local records for family facts, the only source on Draper is the newspaper itself, of which complete files are available in photostat. J. T. Buckingham, *Specimens of Newspaper Literature: with Personal Memoirs, Anecdotes, and Reminiscences* (1850), I, 27–29, contains some notes and extracts. See also Mary F. Ayer, "Checklist of Boston Newspapers, 1704–1780," *Colonial Soc. Mass. Pubs.,* vol. IX (1907); and C. S. Brigham, "Bibliography of Am. Newspapers," in *Proc. Am. Antiquarian Soc.,* vol. XXV (Apr. 1915).]

D. M. M.

DRAPER, JOHN WILLIAM (May 5, 1811–Jan. 4, 1882), chemist, historian, was born at St. Helen's near Liverpool, England, the son of the Rev. John Christopher Draper, superintendent of the Wesleyan Methodist Society of the Sheerness Circuit. The latter came of an influential Roman Catholic family, but, attending one of John Wesley's revival meetings, was so effective-

ly converted that he joined the Methodists, was disowned by his people, and spent the rest of his life as a Wesleyan minister. His real name remains unrecorded, that of John Christopher Draper being an assumed one. He was interested in scientific subjects, particularly in chemistry and astronomy, and owned a telescope with which he frequently made observations. He married Sarah Ripley, and John William was the third of their four children. At Woodhouse Grove, an institution supported by the Wesleyans, John William received sound training in mathematics and the classics. Next he went to London University in 1829, where he majored in chemistry under Prof. Edward Turner with whom he maintained a life-long friendship. He also continued his studies in the humanities at London University which was at that time the only institution of its kind in England open to non-conformists. While still a student he married Antonia Coetana de Paiva Pereira Gardner whose family had been attached to the court of Emperor Dom Pedro I of Brazil, her English father being court physician. She was descended from two of Vasco da Gama's captains, Paiva and Pereira, each of whom furnished a vessel of the fleet which first rounded the Cape of Good Hope. The death of John Christopher Draper induced the family, consisting of Mrs. Draper, her daughters, and her son and his wife, to emigrate to the United States where Ripley relatives had been established in Virginia since before the Revolution. They settled in Christiansville, Mecklenburg County. John William Draper had expected to secure a post as instructor in natural history at a local Methodist college, but arrived too late to obtain the appointment. Before leaving England he and an associate had published three papers on geological subjects, and shortly after his arrival in Christiansville he set up his own modest laboratory and proceeded independently with scientific work. His first record from this laboratory appeared in the *Journal of the Franklin Institute* for September 1834 under the title: "Some Experimental Researches to determine the Nature of Capillary Attraction." This was prophetic rather than conclusive, but it set forth the author's belief in the existence of theretofore unrecognized fields of force which have since been made the subject of illuminating study by physical chemists who succeeded him, and it was later to form the basis of his first important book, *A Treatise on the Forces which Produce the Organization of Plants* (1844). Other contributions followed, on such subjects as galvanic batteries, the alleged magnetic attraction of light, analyses of certain minerals.

From an early age Draper had resolved on a scientific career, and his sister Dorothy saw to it that nothing should stand in the way of his fulfilment of this ambition. She had talent as an artist, and by giving lessons in drawing and painting, she had laid aside by 1835 some $4,000, which she advanced to her brother to enable him to continue his studies at the University of Pennsylvania. Here he worked under Robert Hare in chemistry and physics, besides taking the course in medicine, in which he graduated in 1836. His thesis was entitled "Glandular Action." In the work leading to it he engaged in ingenious experimentation in the field of osmosis. He observed the passage of gases through soap bubbles, and applied the principles of osmosis in physiology. His purpose was to ascertain what goes on in the cells of the lungs, how oxygen is introduced into the blood stream, and in what way carbon dioxide escapes from it. These experiments are said to have disclosed "a cardinal fact in modern physiology." Nearly a century later they formed the basis for the study and exposition of the physiological phenomenon called "acapnia," which describes a condition of diminished carbon dioxide content of the blood.

In the fall of 1836 Draper accepted the chair of chemistry and natural philosophy at Hampden-Sidney College, Virginia, which enabled him to "convert experimental investigation, thus far only an amusement, into the appropriate occupation of his life" (Barker, *post,* p. 354). In 1838 he became professor of chemistry in the undergraduate department of the University of the City of New York, where his scholarship, his inquiring mind, and his administrative ability were immediately recognized. The following year he participated actively in the organization of the school of medicine of the university, taking over its chairs of chemistry and physiology. The chancellor, Theodore Frelinghuysen, was on terms of close friendship with this young professor who took an active part in planning and operating the medical courses. In 1839–40 the medical school had from forty to fifty students in attendance; by the following year the number had grown to 239. In 1850 Draper became president of the medical school, continuing to lecture both there and in the undergraduate department. He was unmindful of taking credit to himself, but was ambitious to bring the work of the medical school and of the city of New York as a medical center, to the attention of the public and of physicians. To this end he collaborated with his friend James Gordon Bennett the elder, whom he induced to devote whole pages of occasional numbers of the *New York Herald* to reports of medical lectures and clinics at the university, and to publish a journal, the *Lancet,* to keep physicians informed of the activities of the school and of the progress of research. In 1865 the building of the school of medicine on Fourteenth St. was destroyed by fire, in which Draper lost his library, materials, apparatus, and notes— a catastrophe which, however, did not cause him to omit a single lecture to his classes.

As a man of science Draper is best known by his work on radiant energy. In 1843 he presented a paper "On the Decomposition of Carbonic-Acid and the Alkaline Carbonates by the Light of the Sun," and in 1847 one on "The Production of Light by Heat" which indicated the essential principle of the modern incandescent lamp. Following these came noteworthy contributions on the production of light by chemical action. In 1857 he made the observation that "the occurrence of lines in the spectrum, whether light or dark, is connected with the nature of the substances producing the flame," and that "if we are ever able to acquire certain knowledge respecting the physical state of the sun and other stars, it will be by the examination of the light they emit." Here we find spectrum analysis clearly outlined, and indeed this leadership was acknowledged by Bunsen and Kirchoff, who figured in its later development. Draper was probably the first in America to use a diffraction grating, one being made for him in 1843 by Joseph Saxton of the United States Mint.

He was also a pioneer in photography. In 1839 Daguerre achieved the first practical photography, but the time of exposure required was so long that he and his associates despaired of ever making portraits. Even after the ordeal of posing, the sitter's eyes were never more than blurs in the picture. Samuel F. B. Morse [*q.v.*], a portrait painter, at that time was professor of fine arts at the university, and he went over to Paris to study the technique of making daguerreotypes. He imparted this information to his colleague, Draper, with whom he was on terms of close friendship, and the latter immediately set himself to work on its problems. He subjected the iodine-treated silver plates of Daguerre to the fumes of bromine, and found that this mixture of silver iodide and bromide was especially sensitive to blue light. This early use of silver bromide is especially noteworthy as cutting down the time of exposure. On the roof of his house on Fourth St., adjoining the university, Draper built a glass tank, filled it with a solution of ammonia and copper sulphate, and waited for a bright sunny day. Then, with sunlight projected through his blue tank, he photographed his sister Dorothy, making the first complete portrait of a person ever recorded by the sun. He clamped the sitter's head gently in a vise which later became the head-rest of the professional photographer. The portrait, including the eyes, was very good. After considerable experiment Draper discovered the uselessness of the filter tank, and made his portraits without it, in still shorter time. He sent his original first portrait to his friend Sir John Herschel, the astronomer, who was also an important contributor to the art of photography. It still remains in possession of the Herschel family, and it was lent for exhibition at the World's Fair in Chicago in 1893. Draper forthwith published his findings in the *Philosophical Magazine* of June and September 1840, and this was the beginning of photographic portraiture. In addition to this he instructed men and women in the art on one or two evenings a week for a considerable time, thus giving us the first photographers in America.

Another important contribution was in connection with the electric telegraph. Following the work of Joseph Henry in this country, and of Michael Faraday in London, Morse developed his alphabet, and was able to send messages over short distances. It was generally held, however, that long-distance telegraphy was an impossibility, on the ground that the current would dwindle to insignificance before it had traveled very far. Draper made exhaustive experiments along these lines, and soon was able to demonstrate, by stretching wires on the grounds of a rope-walk, that the resistance of the wires to currents became markedly less as a certain distance was reached; that the initial resistance of the wire was far greater than that of its longer extension. This proved that long-distance telegraphy was feasible, and a great advance in the art was initiated.

Notwithstanding these and other scientific achievements, Draper was more widely known as an author than as a man of research. In 1856 his book, *Human Physiology, Statical and Dynamical,* was published. It presented entirely new and illuminating views of the subject and was speedily translated into many languages. The author held fast to the attitude that we can advance in understanding only by the close study of life-processes in their mechanical and physicochemical reactions, and that, irrespective of prevailing opinions, we should not hesitate to seek the truth. This was the leading text-book on physiology of its period. It contained the first photomicrographs ever published, and it expounded his researches on the relation of car-

bon dioxide to the portal blood which he likened to the flow of sap in trees. In 1878 he brought out his *Scientific Memoirs,* a collection of papers on radiant energy. But his writings were not confined to scientific matters. In 1860 he delivered a lecture at the meeting of the British Association for the Advancement of Science at Oxford, in which he applied the principles enunciated in his *Human Physiology* to the development of society, and which gave opportunity to Huxley and the Bishop of Oxford for their famous tilt. So profound was the impression made by this address that he was encouraged to set it forth in book form. It resulted in the publication, delayed by the Civil War until 1863, of his *History of the Intellectual Development of Europe,* his *magnum opus.* It remains to-day, after sixty-seven years, a work of prime importance. Draper was an evolutionist according to the type of his fellow leaders in the thought of his day, following the Lamarckian theory of the inheritance of acquired characteristics as this idea prevailed before the advent of Weismann. In regard to the effects of climate he was singularly observant, and he blazed the trail for modern views in regard to its influence on social organization. In historical research he was indefatigable, both at home and abroad, yet he reached his conclusions independently. His ideas have provided the basis for many popular books which have appeared since his time. His style is at once engaging and scholarly. The work ran rapidly through many editions, and was translated into nearly every known langauge. A contemporary review said of this work, "What Comte showed might and ought to be done for the whole world of men, what Buckle commenced for England, Scotland, France, and Spain, Draper has effected for the whole of Europe." The work had a profound influence on nineteenth-century thought.

In 1865 Draper published *Thoughts on the Future Civil Policy of America,* which elaborated his very modern views on geography, his observations on the effects of climate on man, the effects of immigration, the political force of ideas, and the prospective course of national development as he saw it. In 1867–70 there followed his authoritative *History of the American Civil War* in three volumes, for which all documents available in Washington were placed at his disposal by Secretary Stanton. Gen. William T. Sherman personally edited much of the manuscript at Draper's home at Hastings. Draper's *History of the Conflict between Religion and Science* was published in 1874, ran through numerous editions, and was translated into French,

Dutch, German, Spanish, Portuguese, Russian, Polish, Serbian, and Japanese. It has been called a rationalistic classic, and, in common with the *Intellectual Development of Europe,* was placed on the Index Expurgatorius at Rome. Not recognizing the claims of revelation, inspiration, or ecclesiastical authority, Draper was wholly at variance with the upholders of these. He was, however, somewhat of an eighteenth-century deist who sensed divinity in the general order of the universe. He was on terms of amity with liberal clergymen of all denominations except the Roman Catholic, and one of his grandchildren who knew him in his later years declares that, without identifying himself with any sect or order or congregation, he was "a thorough-going Unitarian." Influenced profoundly by the writings of the medieval Arabs, Draper could also be called an Averroist. His family life was happy. The household consisted of three sons and two daughters besides his wife and his sister Dorothy. For several years the Fourth St. house near the university was their home, but in 1840 he bought an estate at Hastings-on-Hudson where he passed the rest of his life.

His wife was a woman of fine mind and an enduring piety. Brought up in the Roman Catholic faith, she became after marriage a liberal Anglican and was in hearty sympathy with her husband in his work. As her health was always frail, the professor's sister, Dorothy Catherine Draper, a beloved member of the household, aided in bringing up the children. Dr. Maximilian Toch, who was Draper's last student, writes of him, "He was a short man, not over five feet two, and in my time he wore a close-cropped beard which was quite white. He spoke with a distinct North of England accent, which at times had a faint burr of the Scotch. He was by no means talkative, but his interest in the intellectual development of Europe and in the conflict between religion and science was so great that even in his chemical lectures he would occasionally bring in expository references to these subjects. While never irreverent toward religion, now that I have a good perspective of him, I realize what a doughty fight he would have waged against the fundamentalists, were he living to-day! His son Henry was very like him, and it was characteristic of both father and son that their lectures were delivered entirely without notes." Of Draper's children, John Christopher taught chemistry and physiology; Henry [*q.v.*] was not only a noted astronomer, but, during the lifetime of his father, was professor of analytical chemistry at the University of the City of New York, and, later on, head of the de-

partment up to the time of his death. He married a daughter of Courtlandt Palmer, and their house on Madison Ave., and country home at Dobb's Ferry were distinguished for the important social and scientific meetings held there. The third son, Daniel, was for many years director of the Meteorological Observatory in Central Park, New York. Of the two daughters, Virginia became Mrs. Mytton Maury, and Antonia, Mrs. Edward H. Dixon. The American Scenic and Historic Society recently received from Mrs. Dixon as a gift nine acres of her father's estate at Hastings, together with the Draper Observatory, which is maintained by the Society as a memorial to him.

[Memorial address by Geo. F. Barker, followed by bibliography of Draper's writings, published in *Nat. Acad. Sci. Biog. Memoirs,* vol. II (1886); obituary in *Proc. Am. Phil. Soc.,* Jan.–June 1882; Thos. Waln-Morgan Draper, *The Drapers in America* (1892); personal information from Dr. Maximilian Toch, and from Draper's grandson, Dr. John W. Draper of New York.]

              E.H.

DRAPER, LYMAN COPELAND (Sept. 4, 1815–Aug. 26, 1891), historian, collector, librarian, was a native of New York State, and a son of Luke Draper, of colonial English stock, who fought in the War of 1812 as his sire fought in the Revolution. The home atmosphere was redolent of Revolutionary and frontier lore, including that of the Indian fighting of the period 1740–1815. In Lockport, N. Y., Lyman Draper attended the village school, worked in stores, and performed heavy manual labor. He spent a winter in Mobile, Ala., at the home of Peter A. Remsen, who had married his cousin, and then passed two years in college studies at Granville, Ohio. A short course at Hudson River Seminary completed his formal training. His private reading, mainly historical, included all the books he could find which bore on the history of the frontier. Noting the deficiencies both in the quality and quantity of this literature he resolved, at the age of twenty-three, to devote his life to the writing of biographies of Western heroes and to seek from their living contemporaries and descendants the data needed to make his narrative complete and accurate. "This," said Reuben Gold Thwaites (*post,* p. xii), "at once became his controlling thought, and he entered upon its execution with enthusiasm which never lagged through a half century spent in the assiduous collection of material for what he always deemed the mission of his life." With the sympathy and patronage of Remsen who gave him a home at several different periods, he journeyed over the Allegheny frontier area from western New York south to Alabama and Mississippi, seeking out the pioneer survivors, usually very aged men, and taking down from their own lips the stories of perilous adventure and daring they had to tell. For a few months he was joint owner and editor of an unsuccessful weekly in northern Mississippi; for a season he planted sweet potatoes—unsuccessfully, in the same region; for a year or two he held a clerkship under a relative who was superintendent of the Erie Canal at Buffalo. Always, however, his major interest was the collection of material for frontier history. His interviewing was a process of gentle but unrelenting cross-questioning which sifted truth from error as far as that is possible. The reminiscences of the pioneers, carefully recorded, together with supplementary and corrective material gathered from court records, from contemporaneous or later newspaper narratives, from account books, letters, diaries, title deeds, etc., came to fill a long series of volumes. In addition to these notes, Draper also received from many custodians of old papers, original manuscripts which were believed to have an important relation to his quest. In 1852, at the suggestion of his classmate, Charles H. Larrabee [*q.v.*], who had also been his partner in the potato-growing venture, he moved to Madison, Wis., where in 1854 he became secretary of the Wisconsin State Historical Society. In 1858 and 1859 he served as state superintendent of public instruction, and in this capacity obtained the passage by the legislature of a bill providing for township libraries—the funds for which were diverted to meet the exigencies of the Civil War—and attempted to lay the foundation for a library for the state university.

Draper supplied many short biographies to Appletons' *Cyclopædia,* and he published a monumental work on King's Mountain (*King's Mountain and its Heroes,* 1881), but the extended biographies he contemplated were never produced. " 'I have wasted my life in puttering,' he once lamented, 'but I see no help for it; I can write nothing so long as I fear there is a fact, no matter how small, as yet ungarnered' " (Thwaites, p. xvii). His greatest service to history was through his collections. He was a self-trained historian, but in his special field—the dramatic phases of Western history—his critical command of the facts and sources went unchallenged. His interests as a document collector and a writer were restricted to the dramatic; he had no *flair* for political, economic, or social history. As secretary of the Wisconsin State Historical Society, 1854–86, however, he included all aspects of history, and laid broadly the foundations of one of the great historical libraries. He built up a manuscript collection relating to the early fur-trading period in Wiscon-

sin and the Northwest; he took advantage of the opportunity to gather in files of early newspapers; and he began the publication of the *Wisconsin Historical Collections,* now (1930) numbering thirty volumes, of which he edited ten. His editorial notes are of permanent historical value. At his death he bequeathed to the Wisconsin State Historical Society his own invaluable collection, which contains many volumes of Kentucky Papers, Tennessee Papers, Preston and Virginia Papers, Daniel Boone Papers, George Rogers Clark Papers, King's Mountain Papers, Sumter Papers, etc., in addition to Draper's notes.

In person he was diminutive—less than five feet in height and slender, but sturdy and with a marvelous power of endurance. His countenance was benevolent and his general attitude retiring and scholarly, but he was cleverly persistent in any quest he happened to be pursuing. He combined restless activity with painstaking scholarship and a diplomatic tactfulness which rarely failed of its object. Hundreds of the Western pioneers became his devoted helpers in collecting. Draper was married in 1853 to his cousin, the widow of his patron Remsen. After years of invalidism, she died in May 1888, and in October 1889, at Cheyenne, Wyo., he married Mrs. Catherine T. Hoyt, who survived him.

[*Descriptive List of Manuscript Collections, Wis. Hist. Soc.* (1906); *Pubs. State Hist. Soc. of Wis., Calendar Ser.,* vols. I, II and III (1915, 1925, 1930); R. G. Thwaites, "Lyman Copeland Draper: A Memoir," in *Wis. Hist. Colls.,* vol. I (reprint, 1903); Louise Phelps Kellogg, "The Services and Collections of Lyman Copeland Draper," in *Wis. Mag. of Hist.,* Mar. 1922; Jos. Schafer, "The Draper Collection of MSS.," *Pubs. State Hist. Soc. of Wis., Proceedings,* 1922; *Madison Democrat,* Aug. 27, 1891.]
J. S—r.

DRAPER, MARGARET GREEN (fl. 1750–1807), was the wife of Richard Draper [*q.v.*], Boston publisher and printer, whom she married on May 30, 1750. The printers of Boston offer a curious example of a trade carried on by what may be considered as almost a trade-clan owing to constant inter-marriages for several generations. Margaret may have been Richard Draper's cousin and the grand-daughter of Bartholomew Green, another publisher. On the death of her husband, June 5, 1774, she continued to publish *The Massachusetts Gazette and Weekly News-Letter* with her late husband's partner, John Boyle, but they separated before the beginning of the Revolution. She was strongly Loyalist and continued her husband's journalistic policy. After managing the paper alone for several months she formed a partnership with John Howe, and together they published it until Boston was evacuated by the British when it was suspended (Feb. 22, 1776) after a life of seventy-two years, during which time it had often changed its name. All the other papers had had to be published elsewhere after the siege of Boston began, so that the *Gazette,* which had been the first paper to be started in Boston, was the last to be published there before the Declaration of Independence. Margaret Draper left with the British, going first to Halifax and thence to England, where she lived until her death in London, where her will was proved Feb. 12, 1807. Her property in Boston, including land and several buildings, was confiscated by the Americans and sold on Feb. 7, 1783 (*Proceedings of the Massachusetts Historical Society,* 2 ser., X, 107), but she received a pension from the British government.

[Isaiah Thomas, *The Hist. of Printing in America* (1810); J. H. Stark, *The Loyalists of Mass.* (1910); L. Sabine, *Biog. Sketches of Loyalists of the Am. Revolution* (2 vols., 1864); "Checklist of Boston Newspapers, 1704–1780," *Colonial Soc. Mass. Pubs.,* vol. IX (1907).]   J.T.A.

DRAPER, RICHARD (Feb. 24, 1726/7–June 5, 1774), Boston printer, was the grandson of Richard Draper who emigrated from England to Boston in 1680, and the son of John Draper [*q.v.*] who married Deborah, the daughter of Bartholomew Green, the publisher of the *Boston News-Letter.* John Draper continued the publication after the death of his father-in-law in 1732, taking into silent partnership his son Richard, who had been brought up to the printing trade. On the death of John in 1762, Richard in turn continued the paper, now called *The Boston Weekly News-Letter and New England Chronicle.* On April 7, 1763, the title was suddenly changed to *The Massachusetts Gazette and Boston News-Letter.* He took a kinsman, Samuel Draper, into partnership in the paper but not in the printing business, the connection lasting several years until the death of Samuel. A little more than a month before his own death, Richard took John Boyle as a partner. Draper's own firm did very little book printing but he was concerned with Edes & Gill, and the Fleets, and in that way was interested in book publishing. On Dec. 2, 1762, he was appointed printer to the Governor and Council in place of his late father. From 1763 to 1766, Richard and Samuel, and from 1767 to 1770, Richard, printed the theses for Harvard, calling himself "Academiæ Typographus." This last position, to his no small mortification, was taken from him and given to Isaiah Thomas in 1771. His main interest, however, appears to have been in journalism and he continued the publication of his paper until his death, changing the name several times (*Publi-*

cations Colonial Society of Massachusetts, IX, 431). In May 1768 he entered into a singular arrangement with Green and Russell who published the *Boston Post-Boy.* Each continued to publish his own paper, the *Post-Boy* appearing on Mondays and the *News-Letter* on Thursdays, but a combined paper, the *Massachusetts Gazette,* appeared in two instalments, one-half with each of the other two. This "Adam and Eve" journal ceased in September 1769 and Draper continued the *Massachusetts Gazette and Weekly News-Letter* by himself. Draper acquired a competency and built a substantial brick house on what is now Washington St., Boston. He suffered from constant ill health but was of cheerful disposition and is said to have been "remarkable for the amiable delicacy of his mind, and gentleness of his manners." He was strongly in favor of the British government whose cause was espoused in his paper. On May 30, 1750, he married Margaret Green [*v.* Margaret Green Draper], but they had no children.

[Isaiah Thomas, *The Hist. of Printing in America* (1810); T. W. Draper, *The Drapers in America* (1892); J. H. Stark, *The Loyalists of Massachusetts* (1910); "Checklist of Boston Newspapers, 1704–1780," *Colonial Soc. of Mass. Pubs.,* IX (1907), and "The Printer of the Harvard Theses of 1771," *Ibid.,* XXVI (1927), 1–15.]   J.T.A.

DRAPER, WILLIAM FRANKLIN (Apr. 9, 1842–Jan. 28, 1910), soldier, manufacturer, diplomat, was born in Lowell, Mass., a grandson of Ira Draper [*q.v.*] and the eldest son of George and Hannah (Thwing) Draper. His boyhood was spent at Woonsocket, R. I., Ware, Mass., and finally Milford, Mass., where the family moved in 1853 when his father joined the Hopedale Community. Here his father and his uncle Ebenezer started the manufacture of cotton machinery, an enterprise which expanded rapidly after the break-up of the Hopedale Community. At Hopedale, William attended the Community school until the age of sixteen, after which he worked for three years in various New England mills, thoroughly acquainting himself with the process and machinery of cotton manufacture. Enlisting in 1861 in a Milford company which later became Company B of the 25th Massachusetts Regiment, he was elected second lieutenant and began a war experience which extended over nearly four years of active campaigning. He was on Burnside's staff at Roanoke Island, New Bern, and Fort Macon; was commissioned (Aug. 12, 1862) captain in the 36th Massachusetts with which he went through the Antietam campaign and the battle of Fredericksburg; was sent west with the IX Corps in 1863, participating in the capture of Vicksburg and the fighting around Jackson. As a major, he spent the winter of 1863 with his corps in East Tennessee, where they engaged in the siege of Knoxville, and joined Grant in the Virginia campaign in 1864. Promoted to a lieutenant-colonelcy, Draper commanded a regiment in the Wilderness, where he was seriously wounded by a bullet in the shoulder. He recovered sufficiently, however, to join the army before Petersburg, and commanded a brigade at the Weldon Railroad engagement. Troubled by a second wound received at Pegram Farm, he left the service on Oct. 12, 1864, later receiving, before his twenty-third birthday, the brevet ranks of colonel and brigadier-general "for gallant and meritorious services in the field during the war."

Upon his return from active service he entered the employ of the firm of his father and father's brother, E. D. & G. Draper, into which he was taken as partner three years later when his uncle sold out his interest to the young man. William remained as junior partner in the new firm, now known as George Draper & Son, until the death of his father in 1887, when he assumed the leadership. His brothers, George A. and Eben Sumner [q.v.], and his two eldest sons in due time became partners, but William F. Draper dominated the business until his resignation as president in 1907. George Draper & Sons (so-called after the admission of George A. Draper in 1877) was in reality a firm which acted as selling agent for other concerns which it controled, and which manufactured cotton machinery. It prospered enormously in the seventies and thereafter by the production of the Sawyer and Rabbeth spindles and many other improvements in spinning and weaving machinery. William F. Draper was well fitted to head such an enterprise, for he inherited to a full degree the inventive and mechanical genius of his father and grandfather, who had both been inventors of textile machinery. He personally patented more than fifty inventions in textile machinery, and these with other improvements promoted and controled by him are believed to have doubled the speed of spinning yarn and to have cut the cost in half (*Representative Men*, pp. 22–26; *Boston Herald*, Jan. 29, 1910). During his later years he turned his attention to weaving in the hopes of achieving similar results. He was counted by many "the leading expert in spinning machinery in this country" (*The Drapers in America*, p. 113) and testified frequently in important patent suits relating to such machinery. In 1891 he made an important contribution to the technical history of cotton spinning in a paper, "The History of

Spindles," read before the New England Cotton Manufacturers' Association.

Until 1892 Draper never held any elective office except that of member of the town school committee, although he was a member of the convention which nominated Hayes and an elector-at-large for Harrison. He had been given a large vote in 1889 in the Republican state convention for governor but two years later when the nomination was assured him he declined to be a candidate. In 1892, however, being particularly interested in the tariff he was persuaded to run for Congress, and he served the 11th Massachusetts District in that body until his appointment as ambassador at Rome on Apr. 5, 1897. His attitude on public business was, in general, conservative. He opposed the Wilson tariff, the withdrawal of the Hawaiian annexation treaty, the intervention in Cuba, and was one of a half-dozen Republicans in the House to oppose the censure of Bayard. In spite of his stand on Hawaii he declared strongly some years later against the annexation of the Philippines.

He was ambassador to Italy (1897–1900) during the period of the Spanish-American War and filled the post with satisfaction to both governments. Pressure of private business, however, forced his resignation and brought an end to his public service. He was twice married: first, on Sept. 15, 1862, to Lydia Joy, adopted daughter of David Joy of Nantucket; second, on May 22, 1890, to Susan Preston, daughter of Gen. William Preston of Kentucky. There were five children by the first marriage, and one by the second. Draper's last years were spent in travel and recreation. In 1908 he published a volume of memoirs, *Recollections of a Varied Career*. He died in Washington, where it had been his habit to pass the winter. After his death his widow presented a memorial park to the town of Milford, and in 1912 an equestrian statue of him designed by Daniel Chester French.

[In addition to Draper's *Recollections*, see T. W. Draper, *The Drapers in America* (1892), pp. 112–13; Adin Ballou, *Hist. of Milford* (1882), pp. 719 ff.; *Representative Men of Mass. 1890–1900* (1898); obituaries in Boston papers, Jan. 29, 1910. "History of Spindles" was published in *Proc. Twenty-Sixth Annual Meeting New England Cotton Mfrs.' Asso.* (Apr. 29, 1891), pp. 13–47.]

H.U.F.

DRAYTON, JOHN (June 22, 1766–Nov. 27, 1822), governor of South Carolina, jurist, author, was born at "Drayton Hall," near Charleston, the eldest child of William Henry Drayton [q.v.] and Dorothy Golightly. Generally with his distinguished father until the last year of the latter's life, he was then placed in the Nassau Grammar School, Princeton, N. J., and in September 1779 entered the freshman class of the College of New Jersey. He did not graduate from the College, but was sent to England to complete his education, probably at the Inner Temple. Returning to South Carolina, he began the practise of law in Charleston and was married, Oct. 6, 1794, to Hester Rose, the daughter of Philip and Hester Rose Tidyman, who before her death in 1816 bore him six children.

In accordance with the family tradition, he entered public life at an early age, serving as a member of the state House of Representatives during most of the years from 1792 to 1798, when he was elected lieutenant-governor. Following the death of Gov. Edward Rutledge [q.v.] on Jan. 23, 1800, he was in charge of the executive department, though not officially recognized as governor until his election in his own right, Dec. 4, 1800, for a term of two years. He is said to have been the first governor to pass over the whole upper country and review the militia (O'Neall, post, I, 428). Both as lieutenant-governor and governor he urged the establishment of a central institution of higher learning in order to further the political unification of the state and promote public intelligence. Following his recommendation to the General Assembly, Nov. 23, 1801, an act providing for the establishment of the South Carolina College (now University of South Carolina) at Columbia was passed, and approved by him on Dec. 19. The first meetings of the trustees were held at his home in Charleston, and he himself served as president of the Board until December 1802 (Green, post, pp. 10–15; Schaper, post, pp. 403–06). The college, which was opened Jan. 10, 1805, proved to be a potent factor in drawing together the sections of the state. Very appropriately, it conferred on John Drayton the degree of LL.D., at its first Commencement exercises, Dec. 7, 1807. This same year, he was among the eminent counsel who appeared before the Supreme Court of the United States in the important case, Rose vs. Himely (4 Cranch, 241). He served in the state Senate from 1805 to 1808, when increased representation was given the up-country and he was again elected governor for two years. Appointed in 1812 judge of the United States court for the District of South Carolina, by President Madison, he held this post until his death in Charleston.

Early in his career Drayton published Letters written during a Tour through the Northern and Eastern States of America (1794), containing a contrast between the schools of Boston and those of South Carolina which was most unfavorable to his native state. During his first term as governor he published A View of South Carolina, as Respects her Natural and Civil Concerns (1802), a valuable descriptive work which was probably inspired by Jefferson's Notes on Virginia. Late in his life appeared his Memoirs of the American Revolution, from its Commencement to the Year 1776, Inclusive; as Relating to the State of South-Carolina and Occasionally Refering (sic) to the States of North-Carolina and Georgia (2 vols., 1821). This useful work was based on manuscripts left by his father, but was given its form by the pen of John Drayton, who, not without vanity, allowed only his own name to appear on the title-page.

[Emily H. Drayton Taylor, "The Draytons of S. C. and Philadelphia," Pubs. Geneal. Soc. Pa., VIII (1923), 21–22; Princeton Commencement Program, 1779, in Archives of the State of N. J., 2 ser., III (1906), 669–71; J. B. O'Neall, Biog. Sketches of the Bench and Bar of S. C., vol. I (1859); Wm. A. Schaper, "Sectionalism and Representation in S. C.," in Ann. Report Am. Hist. Asso., 1900, vol. I (1901); E. L. Green, A Hist. of the Univ. of S. C. (1916); Manuscript Jours. Senate and House of Representatives of S. C., Columbia; Charleston City Gazette and Commercial Daily Advertiser, Nov. 1822; Charleston Courier, Nov. 29, 1822.]

J. H. E—y.
D. M.

DRAYTON, PERCIVAL (Aug. 25, 1812– Aug. 4, 1865), naval officer, son of the younger William Drayton [q.v.] and his first wife, Ann Gadsden, was born in South Carolina of an aristocratic and distinguished family. Appointed midshipman on Dec. 1, 1827, he was initiated into the theory of his profession at the New York Naval School, and into its practise on the frigate Hudson of the Brazil Squadron. He was advanced to the rank of passed midshipman in 1833, and to that of lieutenant in 1838. While in the latter grade he served successively in the Brazil, Pacific, and Mediterranean squadrons, and at the New York navy-yard on ordnance duty. In 1855 he was made commander and three years later was appointed aide to Commodore Shubrick [q.v.] in command of the Brazil Squadron and the Paraguay expedition. The outbreak of the Civil War found Drayton on ordnance duty at the navy-yard in Philadelphia, a city which had been his home for upwards of thirty years. Sympathizing with the North in the approaching conflict, he requested on Feb. 25, 1861, that his name be entered in the naval register as a citizen of Philadelphia. In October of that year, he was appointed to the command of the Pocahontas and participated in Du Pont's expedition against Port Royal, S. C., fighting against his brother, Gen. Thomas F. Drayton [q.v.], and other relatives who had cast in their lot with the Confederacy. Ardent in his devotion to the Union, he wrote that rather than interfere with the success of the war he was ready to sacrifice every relative that he had, painful as it would be. The South Carolina legislature proscribed him and declared him infamous (*National Republican*, Aug. 5, 1865).

Drayton was of great service to Du Pont while that officer was in command of the South Atlantic blockading squadron. He made reconnoissances of St. Helena Sound and adjacent waters and was present at the capture of Fernandina and St. Mary's and at the occupation of Stono River. Made a captain, taking rank from July 16, 1862, he was placed in command of the monitor *Passaic,* the second ship of her class. In this ironclad he bombarded Fort McAllister and took part in Du Pont's attack on Fort Sumter. In letters to the secretary of the navy he was highly commended by his commodore. In December 1863, he was appointed fleet captain of the West Gulf blockading squadron, then commanded by Farragut. On board the *Hartford* he participated in the operations in Mobile Bay, where his services were exceedingly valuable. Farragut warmly expressed his appreciation of them in a letter to Secretary Welles. He was now regarded as one of the ablest officers in the navy and was especially expert as an organizer and administrator. In April 1865, these qualities were recognized by his appointment to the office of chief of the Bureau of Navigation, the leading naval bureau. While holding this position he died in Washington after a few days of illness. He was unmarried. Tall and commanding in appearance, Drayton was the "beau ideal" of a naval officer. Endowed with exceptional mental powers, he ranked high as a naval scholar, reading and speaking several foreign languages. He left to the Naval Academy his coins, shells, and foreign arms, and a letter of Admiral Nelson's. The torpedo boat *Drayton* was named for him.

[Record of Officers, Bureau of Navigation, 1827–65; Navy Registers, 1827–65; *Official Records (Navy)*, 1 ser., vols. XIII, XIV, XXI; *Army and Navy Jour.*, Aug. 12, Dec. 16, 1865; *Naval Letters from Capt. Percival Drayton, 1861–1865* (1906); Emily H. Drayton Taylor, "The Draytons of S. C. and Philadelphia," *Pubs. Geneal. Soc. Pa.*, VIII (1923), p. 21.] C. O. P.

DRAYTON, THOMAS FENWICK (Aug. 24, 1808–Feb. 18, 1891), planter, railroad president, Confederate soldier, son of the younger William Drayton [*q.v.*] and his first wife, Ann Gadsden, was born in South Carolina, most probably at Charleston. In 1828 he was graduated from the United States Military Academy and commissioned in the 6th Infantry. One of his classmates was Jefferson Davis, with whom he formed a lasting friendship and to whom he wrote in later life letters which now constitute the chief source of information about him. After serving

in garrisons at Jefferson Barracks, Mo., and Newport, Ky., he was assigned (1832) to topographical duty. He participated in the unsuccessful project to build a Charleston, Louisville & Cincinnati Railroad; first as assistant surveyor and subsequently, following his resignation from the army (Aug. 15, 1836), as resident engineer. In 1838 he acquired a plantation in St. Luke's Parish, S. C., which he cultivated until the beginning of the Civil War. Though planting was his chief interest in this period, he occupied from time to time positions of a public, or semi-public, character. From 1842 to 1847 he was captain of a company of South Carolina militia, and from 1851 to 1852 a member of the state board of ordnance. For the next three years (1853–56) he represented his parish in the upper house of the General Assembly. In 1853 he was elected president of the Charleston and Savannah Railroad, which was constructed (see *First Report of the President of the Charleston and Savannah Railroad,* 1855) and successfully operated under his direction until 1861. He regarded the railroad as the most effective means of unifying the South, and he labored with this end in view (letter to Davis, Apr. 9, 1858, Rowland, *post*, III, 216–17). At about the time of his retirement from the army he was married to Catherine Pope. She bore him eight children.

Drayton was commissioned brigadier-general in the Provisional Army of the Confederate States on Sept. 25, 1861. As commander of the military district about Port Royal, S. C., he directed its defense during the successful Federal assaults of Nov. 4–7, 1861 (*Official Records, Army,* 1 ser., VI, 6–14). On this occasion his brother, Capt. Percival Drayton [*q.v.*], led one of the attacking vessels. In July 1862 he was sent to Virginia in command of a brigade which, soon after its arrival, was attached to Longstreet's corps. He took part in the engagements at Thoroughfare Gap, Second Manassas, South Mountain, and Sharpsburg but did not acquit himself creditably. In fact as early as the battle of Port Royal there are to be found in the reports of his superiors (*e.g.,* Brig.-Gen. R. S. Ripley, *Official Records, Army,* 1 ser., VI, 13–14; and Maj.-Gen. J. C. Pemberton, *Ibid.,* p. 110) hints of Drayton's inefficiency as a commanding officer. Hints in South Carolina were followed by positive accusations in Virginia (*e.g.,* Maj.-Gen. D. R. Jones, *Ibid.,* 1 ser., XII, pt. 2, p. 579). "He is a gentleman and a soldier in his own person," Lee wrote Davis, "but seems to lack the capacity to command" (*Ibid.,* 1 ser., XXI, 1,030). In consequence his brigade was broken up, and Drayton himself was detailed as a member of a military court. In August 1863 he resumed field duty but not on the active front. For a time he commanded a brigade in the District of Arkansas and later was in charge of a sub-district in Texas. His last service in the Confederate army was as president of a court of inquiry which investigated Price's Missouri expedition.

His plantation having been damaged by Union soldiers and in part confiscated by the Federal government, Drayton removed at the close of the war to Dooly County, Ga., where he undertook to develop a farm. Though assisted in this enterprise by a bequest of $27,000 from his brother Percival, his efforts were unsuccessful; and in 1871 he accepted a position as agent of the Southern Life Insurance Company, going shortly afterward to Charlotte, N. C. In 1878 he was appointed president of the South Carolina Immigrant Society. His death occurred in 1891 at Florence, S. C.

[*Confed. Mil. Hist.*, V (1899), 387–89; Emily H. Drayton Taylor, "The Draytons of S. C. and Phila.," in *Pubs. Geneal. Soc. Pa.*, VIII (1923), 23; G. W. Cullum, *Biog. Reg.* (3rd ed., 1891); *Official Records (Army)*, 1 ser., esp. vol. VI; Dunbar Rowland, *Jefferson Davis, Constitutionalist, His Letters and Speeches* (1923), vols. III, VII, IX, and X, containing several illuminating letters from Drayton to Davis ranging over the period from 1858 to 1889.]   J. H. E—y.

DRAYTON, WILLIAM (Mar. 21, 1732–May 18, 1790), jurist, was the great-grandson of Thomas Drayton, who came to South Carolina from Barbados in 1679 and became the founder of a prominent family. William's father, Thomas, the third of the name in South Carolina, served on the Council, was a justice of the province, and a member of the Commons House of Assembly. He married, on Dec. 26, 1730, Elizabeth, daughter of William Bull [*q.v.*], lieutenant-governor of South Carolina, 1738–55. William, their second son and eldest surviving child, was born at "Magnolia," a plantation on the Ashley River which was acquired by his grandfather, added to by his father, at length (1774) sold by him to his uncle, John, and which, as "Magnolia Gardens," has long been noted for its gorgeous vegetation. On Oct. 6, 1750, he was admitted to the Middle Temple and on June 13, 1755, called to the English bar (Jones, *post*, p. 64). By 1756 he had returned home, begun the practise of law, and become a justice of the peace for Berkeley County. Removing to East Florida after 1763, he was appointed chief justice of the province (warrant dated Feb. 10, 1767) and became *ex officio* a member of the Council. Personal differences between him and John Moultrie, also a South Carolinian, who became lieutenant-governor in 1771, assumed a political character when he advocated the extension of local self-government. In this

he had the support of his friend, Dr. Andrew Turnbull, founder of a colony of Greeks, Italians, and Minorcans at New Smyrna (Doggett, *post*, pp. 87–90). In the course of the dispute, Drayton was suspended from the Council, though he was present at its first meeting after Gov. Patrick Tonyn arrived in March 1774 (Siebert, *post*, I, 4). On Feb. 13, 1776, Drayton was suspended from the office of chief justice, the charges against him being: association with the attempt of Jonathan Bryan to make a "fraudulent purchase" of Indian lands; disloyal correspondence with his cousin, William Henry Drayton [*q.v.*], a South Carolina Patriot; and a sympathetic attitude toward the grand jury when critical of the administration (*Ibid.*, p. 34). Meanwhile, Turnbull and Drayton, whom Gov. Tonyn termed "Patriots for the cause of America," went without leave of absence to England to plead their cause, bearing with them resolutions of loyalty signed by many citizens. As a result of their representations, the reinstatement of Drayton without loss of salary was ordered. On Sept. 4, 1776, the governor swallowed the bitter pill and restored the chief justice. He and Turnbull returned to the province the following year to find that the latter's colony was largely broken up, by Tonyn's recruiting activities, they claimed. The chief justice continued to speak freely against Tonyn's measures and "blunders," and advocated capitulation to an invading army of Patriots under Col. Samuel Elbert [*q.v.*] in order that the province might gain freedom from molestation, which he felt the governor's policy would never secure. Though he gave evidences of zeal, his suspension was again voted by the Council on Dec. 16, 1777 (*Ibid.*, p. 64). In the following March he sold his property in East Florida, and on Apr. 1 was suspended as "the head of a faction against administration," which he undoubtedly was. He went to England, where his wife died and he failed to gain reinstatement. He continued to assert his loyalty to the British Empire, but felt that the revolt of the colonies was in no small part due to the conduct of their governors.

Before May 13, 1780, when Turnbull joined him, Drayton was again in South Carolina. Charleston was not evacuated for more than two years, so he could have done little there for the Patriot cause. Thanks to family connections, however, he was soon in good standing in the state. He became judge of the admiralty court, associate justice of the supreme court, and in the autumn of 1789 was appointed first judge of the United States court for the District of South Carolina. He served as such until his death about six months later. His first wife, Mary, daughter of Jacob and Elizabeth (Martin) Motte, bore him nine children, one of whom, William [*q.v.*], attained distinction. His second wife, Mary Gates, to whom he was married about 1780, bore him one child.

[Wm. Drayton, "An Inquiry into the present State, and Administration of Affairs in the Province of E. Fla., with some Observations on the Case of the late Ch. Justice There" (1778), MS. in Lib. of Cong.; warrant in Pub. Record Office, C. O. class 324, 51, p. 307, Lib. of Cong. Transcripts; Carita Doggett, *Dr. Andrew Turnbull and the New Smyrna Colony of Fla.* (1919); W. H. Siebert, *Loyalists in E. Fla., 1774 to 1785* (2 vols. 1929); E. A. Jones, *Am. Members of the Inns of Court* (1924); Emily H. Drayton Taylor, "The Draytons of S. C. and Philadelphia," *Pubs. Geneal. Soc. Pa.*, vol. VIII (1923).]
J. H. E—y.
D. M.

DRAYTON, WILLIAM (Dec. 30, 1776–May 24, 1846), lawyer, soldier, congressman, was born at St. Augustine, East Florida, the youngest child of William Drayton [*q.v.*], chief justice of the province, and his first wife, Mary Motte. When, in the spring of 1778, his parents went to England, where his mother died, the infant was left in the care of Dr. Andrew Turnbull and his Greek wife. He was taken by them to Charleston when they joined his father there in May 1780. Sent to school in England, the boy was called home by the death of his father in 1790, at which date his formal education ended. He became assistant in the clerk's office of the court of general sessions under his brother Jacob, studied law, was admitted to the bar, and before 1812 had attained the first rank in his profession. Mild and courteous in manner, he was a persuasive speaker, renowned for choice diction and precision of language. His practise is said to have brought him an annual income of from $15,000 to $18,000 a year, which enabled him to invest extensively in commercial enterprises (O'Neall, *post*, I, 306–07). A Federalist in politics, he regarded the War of 1812 as unnecessary and deplorable, but offered his own services to the government. He had been associated earlier with the Ancient Battalion of Artillery as an officer, and became lieutenant-colonel of infantry, Mar. 12, 1812, and colonel on July 6 of that year. By this title he was commonly known in later life. On Aug. 1, 1814, he became inspector general (F. B. Heitman, *Historical Register and Dictionary of the United States Army*, 1903). His acquaintance with military affairs was sufficient to cause Andrew Jackson to recommend to Monroe in 1816 his appointment as secretary of war and himself to offer him the same post in 1829 (J. S. Bassett, *The Life of Andrew Jackson*, 1911, I, 339; II, 537).

In 1819 he became recorder and judge of the city court of Charleston, a position which he filled with distinction until 1823. Elected as a Union Democrat to fill the vacancy created by the resignation of Joel R. Poinsett from Congress, he served continuously in that body from Dec. 15, 1825, to Mar. 3, 1833. Both in Washington and South Carolina, he was a vigorous opponent of the tariff, though not averse to compromise, and a strict constructionist of the Constitution, though an implacable foe of nullification. Opposing among others his foster-brother, Robert J. Turnbull [*q.v.*], he was one of the chief organizers of the Anti-Convention or Union party in South Carolina. His oration delivered on July 4, 1831, in Charleston, which contained a severe attack upon the Exposition, was widely circulated, and served as the platform of the Union party (Boucher, *post*, pp. 139–43). After the triumph of the nullifiers in the state, Drayton, though not disposed to yield to their threat of force, tried in Congress to further a compromise on the tariff. His support of the Union gained him wide acclaim in the North and severe criticism at home, where, however, his personal qualities continued to be held in high esteem.

Leaving Charleston in the summer of 1833, he settled in Philadelphia, where until his death he was chiefly engaged in the duties of private life. Succeeding Thomas Dunlap as president of the Bank of the United States in 1841, he closed out the affairs of that institution (Philadelphia *North American*, Apr. 12, 1841; *United States Gazette*, Jan. 4, Feb. 22, 1842). He was twice married: first, to Ann, daughter of Thomas and Martha (Fenwick) Gadsden, who bore him four children, among them Thomas Fenwick and Percival Drayton [*qq.v.*]; second, to Maria Miles, daughter of William and Hannah (Shubrick) Heyward, who bore him five children, two of them attaining maturity. He was buried at Laurel Hill, Philadelphia.

[Wm. Drayton, *An Oration Delivered in the First Presbyt. Ch., Charleston, on Monday, July 4, 1831* (1831); *Address to the People of the Cong. Dist. of Charleston* (1832); J. B. O'Neall, *Biog. Sketches of the Bench and Bar of S. C.* (1859), I, 305–23; C. S. Boucher, *The Nullification Controversy in S. C.* (1916); Carita Doggett, *Dr. Andrew Turnbull and the New Smyrna Colony of Fla.* (1919); Emily H. D. Taylor, "The Draytons of S. C. and Philadelphia," *Pubs. Geneal. Soc. Pa.*, vol. VIII (1923); obituaries in *Pennsylvanian* (Phila.), May 26, 1846; and *Charleston Courier*, May 28, 1846.]
J. H. E—y.
D. M.

DRAYTON, WILLIAM HENRY (September 1742–Sept. 3, 1779), Revolutionary leader, the son of John and Charlotte (Bull) Drayton, was born near Charleston, S. C. He was a double first cousin of Chief Justice William Drayton [*q.v.*]. Having completed his education in England, at Westminster School and Oxford, he returned to South Carolina, where he married on Mar. 29, 1764, Dorothy Golightly, an heiress, and became a planter. The son of two prominent families, young Drayton naturally turned his attention to politics. Entering the Assembly in 1765, he found himself out of accord with the rising opposition to British administration. In 1769 he contributed a number of able articles to the press, denouncing the non-importation movement, and defending the right of the individual to ignore rules set up without legal authority. Unable to check the popular movement, and having become personally unpopular, Drayton then went to England, where he was received at Court as a promising champion of British rights.

Drayton returned to Carolina to sit with his father and his uncle Thomas on the Council of the province (1772–75), and to serve as assistant judge. Appointed to the latter office by his uncle, Lieutenant-Governor William Bull, the young Carolinian soon realized that, according to custom, he would be superseded by a stranger from abroad. He indignantly denounced this practise in a charge to the grand jury which Lord North brought to the attention of Parliament. He also published *A Letter from "Freeman" of South Carolina to the Deputies of North America* (1774), in which he denied the right of Parliament to legislate for America, and proposed the establishment of a federal system. He suggested that an assembly for North America be empowered to tax the colonies for the Crown and pass general legislation, each province being left to regulate its own internal affairs.

Suspended from the Council (Mar. 1, 1775), Drayton embraced the American cause with zeal. A member of all the important revolutionary bodies in the province, and chairman of several, he performed valuable service in the spring of 1775 in preparing for armed resistance. In the summer he made a tour of the back country, trying to win the inhabitants to the American cause. His mission, however, was largely a failure, as this section felt itself more oppressed by the low country than by England. On his return to Charleston, Drayton was elected president of the provincial Congress, Nov. 1, 1775. He assumed the leadership of the progressives, and with great boldness and energy proceeded to involve the province in war. In the revolutionary councils he always urged the most aggressive measures upon his more conservative associates.

Having been elected chief justice under the state constitution of March 1776, Drayton delivered a series of charges to the grand juries which set Carolinians to thinking of independence,

rather than of reconciliation with England. His zeal sometimes misled him, as when he attempted to persuade the Georgians to agree to a union with South Carolina. He desired a military commission, but conservative leaders preferred to make use of him as a commissioner to treat with neighboring states and the Indians, or to answer British offers of peace. Although a man of action rather than a deep political thinker, Drayton's speech in the Assembly on Jan. 20, 1778, shows that he foresaw the operation of sectional forces in the United States, and wished to safeguard the interests of the South. A radical in his opposition to Great Britain and the Loyalists, Drayton was not a social radical, although he promoted the adoption of the state constitution of 1778, which involved the disestablishment of the Church. Still chief justice of South Carolina, he represented the state in the Continental Congress from Mar. 30, 1778, until his death from typhus fever, in September 1779. With the exception of Gouverneur Morris, Drayton was a member of more committees during this period than any other man. His reply to the British peace commission of 1778 was widely read.

[*Memoirs of the Am. Revolution*, vol. I (1821), by Drayton's son, John Drayton [*q.v.*], contains a sketch with portrait. The narrative, based on materials collected by William Henry Drayton, goes down to June 1776. See also: *The Speech of the Hon. Wm. Henry Drayton . . . Delivered on the Twentieth Jan., 1778 . . . upon the Articles of the Confed. of the U. S. of America* (1778); reprints of speeches and articles in Peter Force, *Am. Archives*, 4 ser. vol. IV, V (1843–44), and Hezekiah Niles, *Principles and Acts of the Revolution in America* (1822); MSS. in possession of the Hist. Commission of S. C., *Jours. of the Continental Congress, 1774–89*, vols. X–XV (1908–09); Edw. McCrady, *The Hist. of S. C. in the Revolution 1775–80* (1901); *Pennsylvania Gazette and Weekly Advertiser*, Sept. 15, 1779.] M. D.

DRESEL, OTTO (*c.* 1826–July 26, 1890), concert-pianist and composer, was born in Geisenheim-on-the-Rhine, the son of Johann Dietrich Dresel and Luise Ephardt. He grew up in a progressive, intellectual home, his father being a sympathizer with the German liberal movement of 1848. After he had studied piano and composition with Hiller in Cologne and Mendelssohn in Leipzig, Dresel came to the United States in 1848. He settled in New York, as a concert-pianist and teacher in that middle period when "French, Italian, and English opera companies boarded the swifter and safer steamers for experiments in the American marketplace, and singers and instrumentalists from Germany in particular surged in to exploit the concert and teaching field" (Charles A. and Mary Beard, *The Rise of American Civilization*, I, 798). Dresel, when he returned to America in 1852 after a visit to Germany, made Boston his permanent home, perhaps because in New York, as in New Orleans, the opera with its social corollaries was more esteemed than concert music, and he felt his talent would more quickly win recognition in a more conservative city. Nor was he mistaken in his choice; his merit was soon recognized, and for more than fifteen years he held his place as Boston's foremost resident pianist, whose interpretation of the masterpieces of the classic piano repertoire gave evidence of his taste and technique. His influence was all the more valuable because, as a concert pianist, he avoided the facile brilliancies of such Europeans as Henri Herz, who had toured the United States and Mexico immediately before Dresel established himself in Boston; and Sigismund Thalberg, who played in Boston during his tour of the country in 1856. These virtuosos, like their American contemporary, Louis Moreau Gottschalk, inculcated a worship of mere bravura which Dresel consistently opposed by a conscientious cult of what was qualitatively highest in the literature of his instrument. His exceptional culture, incidentally, prevented his confining his influence to the piano recital. He was instrumental in introducing to the American public the most classic German music. He had collaborated with Robert Franz in supplying accompaniments for the vocal scores of Bach and Handel, and he took special pains to make the Franz songs known. His original compositions include piano pieces, songs, chamber music, an "Army Hymn" for solo, chorus, and orchestra (Boston, Jan. 1, 1863), and a setting of Longfellow's "In Memoriam," soprano and orchestra, to commemorate the fiftieth birthday of Louis Agassiz.

[*Dwight's Jour. of Music* (esp. issues of June 4, 1859, Apr. 28, 1860, Dec. 22, 1861) affords a survey of Dresel's activities in his field. The *Folio*, Boston, Sept. 1890, contains an obituary; and Sebastian Schlesinger has contributed an appreciation of the artist in letter form to the *Am. Art Jour.*, Sept. 6, 1890. See also H. C. Lahee, *Famous Pianists of Today and Yesterday* (1900); obituaries in *Boston Advertiser*, July 29, 1890, and other Boston papers. Dresel's daughter supplied the names of her father's parents and information regarding his birthplace and early life.]   F. H. M.

DREW, DANIEL (July 29, 1797–Sept. 18, 1879), capitalist, speculator, son of Gilbert and Catherine (Muckelworth) Drew, was born at Carmel, N. Y., and spent his boyhood on his father's hundred-acre stock-farm with meager schooling. At fifteen he was left by his father's death to make his way, and, in order to earn the hundred dollars paid for substitutes, enlisted in the War of 1812, spending three months at Fort Gansevoort near Paulus Hook, N. J. After a brief service with the Nathaniel Howe menagerie, he found work suited to his temperament

as cattle drover and horse trader, collecting live stock in the Hudson and Mohawk valleys and driving it to New York City. His training made him sharp-witted, grasping, and unscrupulous, though his trickiness was combined with a sanctimonious devotion to Methodism. By shrewdness and enterprise he soon became preëminent as a cattle buyer, and with the help of capital supplied by Henry Astor he extended his operations westward, being the first to drive cattle from Ohio, Kentucky, and Illinois across the Alleghanies. In 1829 he took up a permanent residence in New York, making his Bull's Head Tavern at Third Ave. and Twenty-fourth St., with yards for 1,500 cattle, the principal headquarters and exchange for drovers. During 1834 he went into the steamboat business in competition with Cornelius Vanderbilt [*q.v.*], running "anti-monopoly" boats first to Peekskill and then between Albany and New York. Beginning with the steamboats *Westchester* and *Emerald,* he reduced the Albany fare from three dollars to one, added to his fleet a series of well-known vessels, the *Knickerbocker, Oregon, Isaac Newton* (the first 300-foot boat on the Hudson), and *New World,* carried passengers for as little as a shilling, and by adroit management overcame Vanderbilt's opposition. When the Hudson River Railroad opened in 1852 he held undaunted to his line; for twenty-two years he also controled the Stonington Line in Long Island Sound; and he established a profitable steamboat service on Lake Champlain. Having accumulated capital, he entered Wall St. in 1844, forming the house of Drew, Robinson & Company, which for ten years did a large stock-broking and banking business; and when the death of his partners dissolved the firm he became one of the boldest and craftiest of independent operators. "I had been wonderfully blessed in money-making," he said late in life. "I got to be a millionaire afore I know'd it, hardly" (*New York Tribune,* Sept. 19, 1879, p. 5). His connection with the Erie Railroad began in 1853, and in 1857, assisted by the panic, he forced his election as director. This fiduciary position enabled him to manipulate the Erie stock, and he did so shamelessly, becoming the first notorious type of speculative director. But in the famous Harlem Railroad corner which Cornelius Vanderbilt and John Tobin planned in 1864, he was outwitted, went short on large commitments as the stock rose in five months from 90 to 285, and lost a half million dollars, an episode which left him eager for revenge.

Drew's greatest business battle, affording numerous illustrations of the outrageous business practises permitted just after the Civil War, was the "Erie War" with Vanderbilt in 1866–68. As treasurer of the hard-pressed line, Drew, in the spring of 1866, advanced it $3,500,000, taking 28,000 shares of unissued stock and bonds for $3,000,000 convertible into stock. He simultaneously went short of Erie on a rising market, suddenly unloaded 58,000 shares on the bulls, and as the stock sank from 95 to 50 made enormous profits (C. F. and Henry Adams, *post*, pp. 6–7). Vanderbilt, determined to control the line, made an alliance with Boston speculators who held stock, threatened court proceedings, and frightened Drew and his allies, Jay Gould and James Fisk [*qq.v.*], into a treaty of peace—to which Drew shortly proved treacherous. The crisis came when, in 1868, Vanderbilt, with the aid of court injunctions to stop the Erie printing-presses, tried to corner Drew. But Drew, Gould, and Fisk succeeded, despite the courts, in dumping 50,000 shares of newly printed stock in the market, depressed the price from 83 to 71, and sheared Vanderbilt of millions. Judge Barnard ordered their arrest, and the trio retreated with $6,000,000 in greenbacks to Taylor's hotel in Jersey City, which they fortified. The combat was then transferred from the courts to the legislature at Albany. Gould bought the passage of a bill legalizing the stock issue, and Vanderbilt consented to a peace by which the plundered wreck of the Erie was handed over to Gould and Fisk. While the nation was still gasping at the depths of business dishonesty and political corruption revealed by the Erie War, Drew, Gould, and Fisk used their gains and the proceeds of fresh stock-water for an assault (October 1868) upon bank credit, stock prices, and foreign exchange which ruined thousands. Drew was at the height of his fortunes, but the press voiced general opinion in calling upon every one to treat him and his associates as infamous.

In 1870 Drew's luck failed him, and he was the victim of a combination managed by his former associates, Gould and Fisk, who sold enough Erie stock in England to produce an unexpected rise, cornered him, and were credited with mulcting him of a million and a half. His descent thereafter was rapid. Further stock losses were followed by ruin in the panic of 1873 and the resulting failure of Kenyon, Cox & Company, a firm in which he was largely interested. After many struggles, he filed a schedule in bankruptcy in March 1876, his liabilities exceeding one million and his assets being negligible. In his twenty-fifth year he had married Roxana Mead. Now a broken, illiterate, despised old man, he spent his last years dependent upon his son, William H. Drew, and

living at 3 East Forty-second St. In his days of wealth he had built Methodist churches at Carmel and Brewster, N. Y., and had spent roughly $250,000 on the Drew Theological Seminary at Madison, N. J., and a somewhat smaller sum for the Drew Seminary for Young Ladies at Carmel; but his pledges for an endowment for the Drew Theological Seminary and for Wesleyan University at Middletown, Conn., were involved in his bankruptcy. Throughout life he had the tastes and habits of a drover, and he was survived by many stories of his ignorance, naïveté, parsimony, and mixture of piety and rascality.

[Bouck White, *The Book of Daniel Drew* (1910), an incisive semi-fictional study; Robt. H. Fuller, *Jubilee Jim; The Life of Col. Jas. Fisk, Jr.* (1928); C. F. and Henry Adams, *Chapters of Erie* (1871); E. H. Mott, *Between the Ocean and the Lakes; The Story of Erie* (1899); E. P. Oberholtzer, *Hist. of the U. S. Since the Civil War*, II (1922), 560 ff.; Allan Nevins, *The Emergence of Modern America* (1927), 194 ff.; Gustavus Myers, *Hist. of the Great Am. Fortunes*, II (1910), 155 ff.; John Bigelow, ed., *Letters and Literary Memorials of Samuel J. Tilden*, I (1908), 299 ff.; and the press of the day.]   A. N.

DREW, GEORGIANA EMMA [See Barrymore, Georgiana Emma Drew, 1856–1893.]

DREW, JOHN (Sept. 3, 1827–May 21, 1862), actor, was born in Dublin, Ireland. His father, an artisan, emigrated to Buffalo, N. Y., and young Drew went to sea. He left his ship in Liverpool, however, and sought employment on the stage. His first American appearance seems to have been at the Richmond Hill Theatre, New York, in 1842. In 1845 he played O'Toole in *The Irish Tutor* at the Bowery Theatre, and there began his career as an actor of Irish rôles. The following year he went to the Chestnut Street Theatre, Philadelphia, and in 1853, with William Wheatley, he leased the Arch Street Theatre in that city. In the company with him here was his brother Frank, and they used to play the two Dromios, made up so exactly alike that the audience would frequently lay bets on which was which, and even the other actors could not tell them apart. Two years later he visited England, and on his return toured America with his wife, Mrs. John Drew [*v.* Louisa Lane Drew]. In 1859 he made a tour to Australia, returning through England, and going back to Philadelphia where his wife was wrestling with the financial problems of the Arch Street Theatre, of which she had assumed the sole management. His popularity as an actor was of much assistance, though for but a brief season. On May 9, 1862, he made his last appearance, in New York. He died in Philadelphia. He married Louisa Lane (Mrs. Mossop) in 1850, and they had three children, John, Georgiana [*qq.v.*], and Louisa (Mrs. Charles Mendum). John Drew was a man of short, rather slender figure, with a plain but jovial face, and he early in life became noted for his impersonations in the Irish plays which were extremely popular in America during the middle and latter half of the nineteenth century, as well as for comedy parts in such plays as *The Road to Ruin* and *London Assurance*. His plain-spoken wife, in her autobiography, says, "Had he lived to be forty-five, he would have been a great actor, but too early a success was his ruin.... Why should he study when he was assured on all sides (except my own) that he was as near perfection as was possible for man to be?" Opposed to this is the testimony of Joseph Jefferson (*Autobiography,* pp. 412–14) who found in his Irish Emigrant "a sincerity ... artistic treatment that wins for it a lasting remembrance in the minds of those who have witnessed it." Jefferson's description—and Jefferson had a keen and critical eye for acting—plainly indicates that Drew possessed no little power to suggest pathos, and that his art, even if natural and unstudied, was admired by other players. Perhaps his wife alone realized how much better it could have been with more work and study. Drew played Sir Lucius with Jefferson, and the latter watched him in other rôles, and says, "I think it has been generally conceded that since Tyrone Power there has been no Irish comedian equal to John Drew." He was, at any rate, the father of one of the most noted stage families of the United States, and as such, if for no other reason, is entitled to a niche in the American theatrical hall of fame.

[*Autobiog. Sketch of Mrs. John Drew* (1899); *Autobiography of Joseph Jefferson* (1890); John Drew, *My Years on the Stage* (1921); T. A. Brown, *Hist. of the Am. Stage* (1870); M. J. Moses, *Famous Actor-Families in America* (1906).]   W. P. E.

DREW, JOHN (Nov. 13, 1853–July 9, 1927), actor, was born in Philadelphia, Pa., the son of John Drew, Sr. [*q.v.*], at the time actor-manager of the Arch Street Theatre, and Louisa (Lane) Drew [*q.v.*], then and later a famous actress. His maternal grandparents had also been players. Young John was sent to boarding schools in or near Philadelphia, and was graduated from the old Episcopal Academy. Although his mother had been on the stage since childhood, and had been manager of the Arch Street Theatre since 1861, John did not show any juvenile interest in acting, and did not appear on the stage till his twentieth year. In 1873 he acted in a farce, *Cool as a Cucumber,* for the benefit of his sister, Georgie (later Mrs. Maurice Barrymore). He considered his début something of a joke, and wasn't even nervous, so that his mother, he says, "was greatly annoyed that I took the thing so lightly." She very soon showed him that acting is not as easy as all that, for he appeared in her company all the next season, acting with a young newcomer of sixteen, Miss Ada Rehan. In 1875, having proved his family aptitude for the stage, and disclosed something of the easy charm of manner, the man-of-the-world poise, which distinguished him in later life, he was offered a position in Augustin Daly's company in New York. His first New York appearance, at the Fifth Avenue Theatre, was as Bob Ruggles in *The Big Bonanza*. The *New York Times* commented on his "agreeable freedom from affectation," and his "frank and welcome heartiness of style." This "agreeable freedom from affectation," or naturalness of acting, characterized Drew's art consistently, and though it was a conscious process, deliberately followed, it caused many people to say that he "always played himself." Later the same year he was one of the company supporting Booth. He played Rosencrantz in *Hamlet,* and other minor rôles. He then supported Adelaide Neilson in *Twelfth Night* and *Cymbeline* (playing Cloten in the latter). The Daly venture having failed, he joined his mother's old friend, Joseph Jefferson, and doubled as the innkeeper and Henrick Vedder in *Rip Van Winkle*. An engagement as Charles Surface at his mother's theatre followed, and then he went on a barnstorming tour with his brother-in-law, the brilliant Maurice Barrymore [*q.v.*], Oxford graduate and noted wit, in a version of *Diplomacy*. There was more adventure than profit in the tour; Barrymore was wounded in a fight in Texas, and another member of the company was killed. In 1879 Daly began again, in the theatre which so long bore his name at Broadway and Twenty-ninth St., and John Drew once more joined his company. For the next fourteen years he acted only with this famous troupe, and soon became one of the "Big Four" of the company— the others being Ada Rehan, Mrs. Gilbert, and James Lewis—who shared in the profits at the end of each season. In spite of many tours through the country, and later, trips to England and even Germany and France, the Daly company was essentially a New York institution, and all its members were closely identified with the life of that city, and known to all the inhabitants. John Drew was both a popular actor in New York, and a figure in the social life. He was an adept in sports, a delightful companion, a sartorial model, and a punctilious gentleman. As an artist, he played in the entire round of

Daly dramas, which included numerous sentimental light comedies and farces adapted from the German, many of the standard old comedies in English, and several of Shakespeare's plays. In all these pieces, of course, he played opposite Miss Rehan, so that their styles became adapted one to the other like hand and glove, and their scenes together were often close to the perfection of comic art. Probably the most famous of their impersonations were those of Katherine and Petruchio. Daly produced *The Taming of the Shrew* in 1887, restoring the induction, and Miss Rehan's regal Kate, a superb creature, mettle for any man's taming, has never been forgotten by those who saw it. Drew's Petruchio was of less heroic proportions, but it was so full of crackling humor that the play became at once, and remained, the high point of the Daly productions. In 1888 Daly took his company to London, and this play was acted by them in the Memorial Theatre at Stratford. In 1888, also, Drew was one of the group of men, headed by Edwin Booth who founded the Players Club in New York.

On Oct. 3, 1892, Drew appeared for the first time as a star, under the management of Charles Frohman, at Palmer's Theatre (later Wallack's), on Broadway at Thirtieth St., New York. The play was *The Masked Ball,* adapted from the French by Clyde Fitch, and the leading woman was a slip of a girl named Maude Adams. In his autobiography (*My Years on the Stage*) Drew gives no reason for leaving Daly's company except the natural desire for a larger salary. The desire to be a star, of course, may naturally be inferred. But it is also true that theatrical styles and methods were changing. Daly's plays were becoming old fashioned and stock companies were giving way to touring companies, organized season by season. Frohman, Fitch, and Miss Adams were all young. They represented the new generation in the theatre, and Drew's own methods of acting and point of view were young, also. By leaving Daly's he aligned himself with the modern movement in the theatre, and for the next two decades his productions, under the Frohman management, always made at the Empire Theatre, New York, about Labor Day, marked, as it were, the official opening of the season, and usually disclosed the newest sample of contemporary polite comedy, staged and acted to the contemporary taste. Drew, during all this period, was the touchstone and standard of high comedy acting in America, and played an important part in the growth of our modern theatre.

After *The Masked Ball,* he produced *Butter-*

flies by Henry Guy Carleton, Henry Arthur Jones's *The Bauble Shop, Christopher Jr.,* by Madeline Ryley, another French adaptation, and then *Rosemary* by Louis N. Parker and Murray Carson (Sept. 14, 1896). This play was a huge success. Miss Adams was so popular in it that Mr. Frohman made her a star the following year. In it, too, Drew's niece, Miss Ethel Barrymore, appeared as a maid, for her New York début. Drew's next success, and a landmark of the new drama, was Henry Arthur Jones's comedy, *The Liars,* in 1898. He next produced C. Haddon Chambers's delightful comedy, *The Tyranny of Tears,* which he revived many years later, adding, at that time, Barrie's *The Will* as an afterpiece. An attempt to act a stage version of Richard Carvel was a failure; he was by now too closely identified with contemporary rôles. He had great success, however, with two plays by Captain Marshall, *The Second in Command,* and *The Duke of Killicrankie,* and also in *The Mummy and the Humming Bird,* when his nephew, Lionel Barrymore, supported him. He was also the producer of two plays by Somerset Maugham, *Smith* and *Jack Straw,* and of a translation, called *Inconstant George,* from the French play *L'Ane de Burridan.* His one attempt at Shakespeare after leaving Daly was *Much Ado,* in which Laura Hope Crews played Beatrice to his Benedict. It was not a succcess. "I had been away from this style of comedy too long," he says (*My Years on the Stage*), "more than twenty years." He also produced a serious Pinero drama, *His House in Order,* in which Margaret Illington made a name for herself.

Drew's relations with Charles Frohman were close. After the first year, there was only a verbal contract between them, and as Drew was his first star, the little manager had a sentimental interest in his success. Frohman went down on the *Lusitania,* leaving not only Drew but other of his actors at loose ends. Miss Maude Adams never acted again. Drew, now sixty-four years old, and beginning to suffer from failing eyesight, felt keenly the loss of his friend and manager. He attempted a dramatization of *Pendennis,* playing the Major, and revived *The Gay Lord Quex.* In 1921–23 he played the old man's part in Somerset Maugham's play *The Circle*—incidentally disclosing to a wider audience than saw him in *The Will* a capacity for character acting. He also appeared as Sir Peter in a Spring revival, made by the Players Club, of *The School for Scandal* (1923). In 1926 he joined an all star company in a revival of Pinero's *Trelawney of the Wells,* playing of course the part of Sir William. The company did an enormous business everywhere, and frequently three or four matinées had to be played a week. But John Drew made no complaints, and was the rock around which the company was built. Peggy Wood, in her little book, *A Splendid Gypsy,* describes the road tour of this company vividly, and gives a touching account of Drew's last days, when he struggled bravely to play, though suffering great pain. His last appearance was in Vancouver, in May 1927, when he got through on sheer grit, and was rushed to San Francisco for the extraction of teeth supposed to be poisoning him. He died in that city on July 9, 1927. How much the "all star" company had been John Drew was proved by the fact that it has to disband after his loss. It had been Drew the public really flocked to see.

John Drew was married in 1880 to Josephine Baker, daughter of Mrs. Alexina Baker, an actress and friend of his mother's. Mrs. Drew died in 1918. They had one child, a daughter, Louisa (Mrs. John Devereaux). Their home was at East Hampton, Long Island, and Drew's social position is further indicated by the fact that he was a member of the Brook and Racquet Clubs as well as being the third president of the Players, succeeding Edwin Booth and Joseph Jefferson. He was a man of medium height, athletic figure, and strong features—the most pronounced being his long nose, inherited from his mother. Early in life he lost the sight of one eye, which resulted in partial blindness during his last years, but his easy bearing, his skilled technique, his charm of character, overcame any handicaps. His artistic method was that of Charles Matthews, his predecessor in England; he sought for matter-of-fact naturalness in stage deportment, even a sort of casual nonchalance, but combined with it, cleverly disguised, the most careful enunciation and the most artful "pointing" of any speech or situation. Though in his younger days he acted many romantic and classic rôles, he is best remembered for his later work in polite contemporary comedy, where his acting method exactly fitted the material, and his ease, naturalness and polish could serve as a direct inspiration to the younger players of the modern stage. He may justly be said to have bridged the gap between the older acting and the new, carrying on the standards of technical proficiency and upholding the dignity of the actor's position, while at the same time adapting his technique to a more realistic theatre and creating, for the new generation, a more satisfactory illusion.

[John Drew, autobiography, *My Years on the Stage* (1923) ; Peggy Wood, *A Splendid Gypsy: John Drew* (1927) ; Walter Prichard Eaton, *At the New Theatre* (1912), pp. 103 ff.; Edward A. Ditmar, *John Drew* (1900) ; M. J. Moses, *Famous Actor-Families in America* (1906) ; *N. Y. Times,* July 10, 1927.]　W.P.E.

DREW, LOUISA LANE (Jan. 10, 1820–Aug. 31, 1897), actress, theatrical manager, was born in London. Her parents were actors, and she was carried on the stage at the age of twelve months. Her widowed mother (later Mrs. Kinloch) brought her to America in 1827, and she appeared at the Walnut Street Theatre, Philadelphia, as the Duke of York to the elder Booth's Richard III. She was a clever mimic and "quick study," and became famous as an "infant phenomenon" over the country, which she toured with her mother. She acted Little Pickle in *The Spoiled Child,* and a protean sketch in which she took five parts. In 1831 she and her mother were shipwrecked off Santo Domingo on the way to Jamaica. Returning to the United States, she joined the Ravel family for a tour. In 1836 she married Henry B. Hunt, an English tenor and actor, and soon after reached a greater maturity of parts, supporting Edwin Forrest and other leading players. When she and her mother had appeared in Boston, their joint salary was $16 a week, but in 1839–40 she alone received $20 ! For a time she was with Macready, and like most actresses of that period she played a great variety of parts. In 1847, at the Park Theatre, New York, she tore a leaf out of Charlotte Cushman's book, by acting Romeo, and then outdid her by acting Antony. In 1848, she was married a second time, to George Mossop, an Irish singing player. He lived but a year, and in 1850 she married, for a third husband, John Drew [*q.v.*], and bore him three children, John, Georgiana [*qq.v.*], and Louisa, all destined to carry on the stage tradition. After her marriage to Drew, she concentrated more on comedy rôles, for which she was best fitted, playing among many others Peg Woffington, Lydia Languish, Hypolita in *She Would and She Wouldn't,* Lady Teazle, and later her most famous part, Mrs. Malaprop. In 1853 Drew had become part proprietor of the Arch Street Theatre in Philadelphia where his wife had a glimpse of the trials of management, and was forced to take a hand in them. Later they toured together, and separately, and in 1861, while Drew was abroad, she alone assumed once more the management of the Arch Street house, attacking the job with the great resolution characteristic of her, and in the first season herself acting forty-two different rôles. A typical day in that busy theatre is described in their son John's memoirs (*My Years on the Stage*). Her husband died in 1862, and she continued for more than thirty-one years to conduct the Arch Street Theatre, making it one of the best-known stock houses in the country, and herself one of the best-known managers. She was not the first woman in America to manage a theatre and direct an acting company, but she was the first to do so on a considerable scale, and over a term of years. She had a working agreement with Lester Wallack in New York for the exchange of plays, and many visiting stars acted with her company. In this house her children made their débuts, and when she finally retired from the management, she had become the *grande dame* of the American theatre. Thereafter, in her last years, she most delighted to act Mrs. Malaprop, and it is said she would cheerfully journey a thousand miles for a chance to play it. In 1896, she acted in the famous all-star cast of *The Rivals* which Joseph Jefferson had assembled. Her last appearance was in *The Sporting Duchess*. Later she died, in Larchmont, N. Y., having already seen her son John take his place as star and her grand-daughter, Ethel Barrymore, make her début.

Mrs. Drew was not beautiful; quite the opposite. But her long life on the stage had given her a thorough command of her art, and she had a vivid sense of humor and a blunt, honest, energetic, and engaging personality. She was both loved and respected. William Winter called her Malaprop "incomparable." Henry Irving said to Ethel Barrymore, at the time of Mrs. Drew's death, "She was, in her line, the finest actress I have ever seen." Joseph Jefferson (*Autobiography*, p. 401) described how she invented the business of first handing Captain Absolute, by mistake, her own letter from Sir Lucius, and when the mistake was discovered simpered and blushed. "Her manner during this situation was the perfection of comedy," he adds. Her wit, her innate dignity, and her off-stage bluntness and simplicity of manner are described by Francis Wilson, in his *Life of Jefferson*. Perhaps the best testimony to her qualities, however, is found in her son's memoirs, for he tells how she deliberately deflated his pride at his first performance, to make him realize the need of humility and hard work, and how during all his years at Daly's Theatre he consulted with her about his rôles, in the older comedies especially, and how she knew all the traditional "business" of the parts and could tell him what was, and what was not, effective. She was a woman whose entire life and education had been the theatre; she understood it, respected it, gave it fresh dignity, and sent her children into it to carry on its best traditions. Her sharp-edged and racy gifts as a cosmic actress, combined with her keen mentality and her downright personality and worth

as a woman, made her for a generation "the grand old lady" of the American stage.

[*Autobiog. Sketch of Mrs. John Drew* (1899) ; John Drew, *My Years on the Stage* (1921) ; *The Autobiography of Joseph Jefferson* (1890) ; Francis Wilson, *The Life of Joseph Jefferson* (1906) ; Montrose J. Moses, *Famous Actor-Families in America* (1906) ; *N. Y. Times*, Sept. 1, 1897.]   W. P. E.

DREXEL, ANTHONY JOSEPH (Sept. 13, 1826–June 30, 1893), philanthropist, banker, the son of Francis Martin Drexel [*q.v.*] and Catherine (Hookey) Drexel, was born in Philadelphia. When he was thirteen years old, and his father's brokerage office had been in existence only two years, he was taken into the office, and his education was confined almost entirely to this office and his home. His cultural education as well as his business training was under the direct supervision of his father, and consisted largely of music and languages. His father was rigorous in his discipline and at the same time liberal in bestowing responsibility, as when he sent the boy by stage-coach to New Orleans for the transfer of a large deposit of gold. He made Anthony Joseph a member of the firm of Drexel & Company in 1847, when the house was ten years old and the new member twenty-one. The latter married Ellen Rozet, daughter of a Philadelphia merchant of French descent.

The death in 1863 of Francis Martin Drexel, founder of the firm, coincided roughly with the close of an era in the financial history alike of the country and of the house of Drexel. The organization of the national banking system, the increase of public debts, and the vast expansion of industrial securities following the war affected the operations of the Drexels both qualitatively and quantitatively. Connections were established with banking houses of San Francisco, New York, London, and Paris. The handling of the flood of investment securities connected with national and local public debts, the building of railways, the development of mining, the growth of the factory system, and the improvement of urban real estate led to the transformation of the firm into essentially a house of investment brokers. During this period of expansion of the firm when its distinctive characteristics and functions were being developed, Anthony J. Drexel was the directing genius. Having lived intimately in contact with the business from the age of thirteen, his native abilities found natural, spontaneous expression in a quick, decisive, and penetrating judgment concerning the feasibility of financing the most intricate of undertakings. His conservatism of judgment and desire to maintain financial stability as against speculative expansion found expression frequently, as in his opposition to the excessively rapid railway development following the Civil War. Although his influence had already been predominant, the death in 1885 of his older brother, Francis, left to him the entire direction of affairs. A magnificent new bank and office building was erected, in wholesome contrast with the prevailing tendency toward ugly and sprawling business architecture. The closing years of his life saw a new era of expansion corresponding to the internationalizing of American trade.

In addition to his banking interests, Drexel engaged in extensive real-estate operations in Philadelphia and its vicinity, adding vastly to his fortune and attempting with some success to improve housing conditions among the working classes. He was also connected with the publishing business, as part owner of the *Public Ledger* in association with his life-long friend, the noted journalist and publisher George W. Childs [*q.v.*]. As a philanthropist he was noted no less than as a banker. He made extensive donations of the conventional kinds, to hospitals, to charitable institutions, and to churches of various denominations. He was associated with Childs in the founding of the Childs-Drexel Home for Aged Printers at Colorado Springs, Colo. His particular interest, however, was in promoting industrial education. His various ideas and projects at length converged in the founding of Drexel Institute at Philadelphia, opened to students in February 1892. His gifts to the Institute totaled about $3,000,000. Distinctive features included an emphasis on technology, free scholarships, and low tuition, night classes, public lectures and concerts, and an unrestricted admissions policy in respect to religion, race, sex, and social class. Drexel was an influential member of the Union League, and of a small group of business men who exercised the controling influence in the régime of President Grant. Like most of the members of the group, he abstained from public office. He died while in quest of health at Carlsbad, Germany.

[*A New Home for an Old House* (Phila., 1927) contains an account of the company and its founders and some excellent illustrations. There are brief sketches in W. W. Spooner, *Historic Families of America* n.d.), and in E. P. Oberholtzer, *Philadelphia: A Hist. of the City and its People* (n.d.), vol. II. A laudatory article by Geo. W. Childs was published in *Harper's Weekly*, July 15, 1893, and reprinted in the *Public Ledger Almanac* for 1894. There is a brief biography in manuscript by J. P. Ryder in the library of Drexel Institute.]   W. B.

DREXEL, FRANCIS MARTIN (Apr. 7, 1792–June 5, 1863), banker, was born at Dornbirn in the Austrian Tyrol, near the Lake of Constance. His father, Franz Joseph Drexel, was a well-to-do merchant of Dornbirn, and his mother, Magdalen Willhelm Drexel, seems to have been a native of the same town. For the son of a merchant, Francis Martin was given somewhat unusual opportunities for study by being sent to Milan at the age of eleven. Here he studied Italian and other languages and began his career as an artist. This was the period of the Napoleonic Wars, and the boy's studies were interrupted by his father's financial difficulties and by efforts to avoid conscription in the armies raised to fight against Napoleon. For several years he continued his studies intermittently in different parts of Europe, painting portraits whenever opportunity afforded, and returning to Austria in 1815. Unsettled conditions in Austria, combined with his roving disposition, sent him once more to various countries of Europe, and in 1817 he set sail from Amsterdam for Philadelphia.

He remained in Philadelphia for nearly ten years, painting portraits, giving lessons in drawing, and establishing promising connections. In 1821 he married Catherine Hookey of Philadelphia. His progress as an artist was interrupted by a quarrel with his brother-in-law and by a return of his *wanderlust*, which took him in 1826 on the first of his South American adventures. Here he remained four years, traveling extensively, making numerous acquaintances among the notables of the Latin-American countries, painting portraits, collecting curios, and accumulating considerable wealth by trafficking in currency as well as by practising his profession. He later made another trip to South America and also visited Mexico. His travels in Europe and America during periods of political disturbance and violent fluctuations taught him the nature and importance of banking and exchange and enabled him to profit handsomely in the incidental buying and selling of notes and currency.

It was the influence of these experiences, combined, perhaps, with a realization that his artistic ability was not of the highest order, that led him to abandon the profession of art and to open a brokerage office, in Louisville, Ky., in 1837. In January of the next year, at 34 South Third St., Philadelphia, he established the brokerage office, for dealing particularly in "uncurrent money," which ultimately grew into the world-famous house of Drexel & Company. For the kind of business for which he was particularly equipped, conditions were propitious. The charter of the Bank of the United States expired in 1836, and securities, whether public or private, as well as ordinary currency, were in a chaotic condition. Drexel's experience and judgment enabled him to develop a prosperous business, and his wealth was further increased by a successful venture in far-western banking during the mid-century gold rush. In his seventy-second year he was struck by a railroad train and killed. The business which he founded was developed by his sons into a position of importance in the rapidly expanding economic life of the country.

[Drexel left a brief autobiography, "Life and Travels of Francis M. Drexel," written in later life for his children and as yet unpublished. Copies of this and of his "Journal of a Trip to South America" are in the archives of the company at Philadelphia. The best brief sketch is in *A New Home for an Old House* (Philadelphia, 1927), pp. 36–41. The frontispiece is an excellent portrait of the founder of the house. See also W. W. Spooner, *Historic Families of America* (n. d.), p. 190.]
W. B.

DREXEL, JOSEPH WILLIAM (Jan. 24, 1833–Mar. 25, 1888), banker, philanthropist, was born in Philadelphia, the third son of Francis Martin Drexel [*q.v.*] and Catherine (Hookey) Drexel. He attended high school in Philadelphia but was largely indebted to his father for his extensive knowledge of languages, art, and music, as well as for his training in banking. On Apr. 18, 1865, he married Lucy Wharton of Philadelphia. Before his business career began, he traveled in the Mediterranean countries, and soon after he became connected with his father's business he represented the firm in Germany. In 1861 he engaged in banking at Chicago, but two years later, upon the death of the elder Drexel, he returned to Philadelphia. As in the case of his father, his knowledge of foreign languages and countries proved to be an important factor in his success as a banker. In 1867 he became one of the partners of the firm of Drexel, Harjes & Company of Paris, and four years later he became associated with J. Pierpont Morgan in the firm of Drexel, Morgan & Company. Thereafter his principal activities were in New York. He was connected with a large number of other financial institutions, being director of eleven banks, including the Garfield National Bank of which he was one of the founders. As a business man his chief significance lay in his serving as a connecting link between the larger banking and brokerage institutions of Philadelphia and New York and between these and European investment bankers. He lived during a period of exceedingly rapid industrial expansion, and vastly increased his inherited fortune by the conservative promotion of the more stable industrial enterprises as well as by handling great quantities of securities issued by national and local governments.

In 1876 he withdrew from active direction of his business interests in order to devote his time to philanthropic, public, and artistic enterprises. He collected an extensive library of music, including noted manuscripts and autographs, and was also interested in etchings. Important collections were bequeathed to the Lenox Library and to the Metropolitan Museum. He was president of the Philharmonic Society of New York and director of the Metropolitan Museum. His interest in public health found expression in his study and promotion of sanitation and in his serving as treasurer of the New York Cancer Hospital. He was deeply interested in the condition of the poor, the unemployed, and the dependent classes. He investigated the conditions of the families of large numbers of prisoners, and spent considerable sums for their relief. In addition to conventional methods of relieving the poor, as by maintaining soup houses, he undertook remedial measures of a distinctive kind. Among his various projects was a "back to the land" movement. He proposed to purchase large tracts, divide them up into small farms, build five-room houses, and sell them at cost on easy terms to worthy but indigent people of the city. Naturally the results, except in cases of occasional individual relief, were insignificant, and there is little indication that Drexel gave serious thought to the underlying causes of the conditions he sought to relieve. He died at the relatively early age of fifty-five as a result of a complication of a disease of the heart and Bright's disease.

[For bibliographical data, see notes following the sketches of his father, Francis Martin Drexel, and his brother, Anthony Joseph Drexel. For his marriage, see A. W. Wharton, *Geneal. of the Wharton Family* (1880), p. 49. The principal obituaries were published in the *N. Y. Times* and the Philadelphia *Public Ledger* of March 26, 1888. Concerning his musical interests, see *Catalogue of Jos. W. Drexel's Musical Library* (1869).]
W. B.

DRINKER, CATHARINE ANN [See JANVIER, CATHARINE ANN, 1841–1922.]

DRINKWATER, JENNIE MARIA (Apr. 12, 1841–Apr. 28, 1900), writer of juvenile fiction and originator of the Shut-in-Society, was born in Yarmouth, Me., the daughter of Capt. Levi P. and Mary Jane (Angus) Drinkwater. She was educated in the public schools and at Greenleaf's Institute, Brooklyn, N. Y. On Mar. 17, 1880, she married Nathaniel Conklin, a Presbyterian minister of New Vernon, N. J., who died in 1892. Beginning to write for the religious press when she was young, she later became widely known through her novels for young people, especially for girls, published under her maiden name. Between 1880 and 1900 more than thirty of these came from her pen. They were written to further the moral and spiritual welfare of their readers, and were preeminently suitable for Sunday-school libraries. Young people of their day found them interesting, however, and some of them went through several editions of 30,000 each. Among them are: *Tessa Wadsworth's Discipline* (1879); *Electa* (1881); *Bek's First Corner* (1883); *The Fairfax Girls* (1886); *From Flax to Linen* (1888); *Marigold* (1889); *Second Best* (1891); *Looking Seaward* (1893); *Goldenrod Farm* (1897); *Shar Burbank* (1898). In 1874 she conceived the idea of sympathy, encouragement, and comfort for invalids through correspondence. This resulted in the Shut-in-Society, which grew rapidly and in 1885 was incorporated under the laws of the State of New York. Mrs. Conklin was its first president, and its honorary president at her death.

[Frederick Orr, "Jennie M. Drinkwater," *The Writer*, Aug. 1891; *The Open Window*, June and July 1900; *Who's Who in America*, 1899–1900; *N. Y. Times*, Apr. 30, 1900; and information furnished by Dr. E. D. G. Conkling of Newark, N. J.]   H. E. S.

DRIPPS, ISAAC L. (Apr. 14, 1810–Dec. 28, 1892), inventor, engineer, was born in Belfast, Ireland, of Scotch and Irish parents who emigrated to Philadelphia, Pa., with him when he was an infant. He attended the city public schools, completing the curriculum at the age of sixteen, and then was apprenticed to Thomas Holloway, at that time the largest builder of steamboat machinery in Philadelphia. Here he remained for a little over five years, rising rapidly until he was given full charge of fitting and erecting all machinery built by the company. The best customer that Holloway had was the Union Line operating steamboats on the Delaware River. In 1830 this company organized a subsidiary to operate a steam railroad between Camden and Amboy, N. J., and ordered an English locomotive. When the "John Bull," as it was named, arrived in Philadelphia in August 1831, Dripps, then a little over twenty-one, was induced to join the railroad company and was given the task of transporting the knocked-down locomotive from Philadelphia to Bordentown, N. J., and of erecting it there. He had never seen a locomotive before, but with the aid of meager drawings accomplished the job, constructing at the same time a tender and subsequently a cow-catcher for it, and finally served as engineer on its trial trip Nov. 12, 1831. For the succeeding twenty-two years he continued with the Camden & Amboy Railroad. At first he was in charge of locomo-

tive construction in the company's shops at Hoboken. He then was made superintendent of machinery with the additional duty of maintenance of all steamboats operated by the company, and toward the end of his service was superintendent of motive power and machinery. In 1853 he became a partner in the Trenton Locomotive & Machine Works at Trenton, N. J. Before the company dissolved five years later, on account of financial difficulties, he had designed and built a wide tread wheel locomotive for running on two different gaged tracks, and an iron freight-car truck, the first of the well-known diamond-framed pattern. In 1859 he accepted the position of superintendent of motive power and machinery of the Pittsburgh, Fort Wayne & Chicago Railroad and moved with his family to Fort Wayne, Ind. During the succeeding ten years he completely rebuilt the mechanical department. Not only the shops but also much of the machinery and tools were designed by him and, when completed, the establishment was looked upon as the model shop of the country, far superior to anything then extant in the United States. Because of the record he achieved at Fort Wayne, Dripps was made superintendent of motive power and machinery of the Pennsylvania Railroad on Apr. 1, 1870, with headquarters at Altoona, Pa. Here he undertook the construction of the most extensive railroad-shops in the country, when his health failed and he was compelled to resign on Mar. 31, 1872. He served in the company, however, for the succeeding six years as a special agent, devoting most of his time to experimental work, particularly on the determination of the frictional resistance of various classes of locomotives. His health failing to improve, he gave up his work entirely in 1878 and retired to his son's home in Philadelphia. In the course of his career he devised innumerable mechanisms, tools, and the like for use in the construction of locomotives, freight and passenger cars, and steamboat machinery, but never patented any of them. He designed for one of the early steamboats of the Union Line a unique type of screw propeller, and also for the first time on any vessel installed the rudder aft of the propeller. He was married shortly after 1830 at Bordentown, N. J., and was survived by his son William.

[Angus Sinclair, *Development of the Locomotive Engine* (1907); *Locomotive Engineering*, Jan. 1892; *Report of the Proc. . . . of the Am. Ry. Master Mechanics Asso.*, 1893; U. S. Museum records; U. S. Museum correspondence with Pennsylvania R. R. Date of birth from Wm. Dripps, Esq.]   C. W. M.

DRISLER, HENRY (Dec. 27, 1818–Nov. 30, 1897), educator, was born on Staten Island, N.

Y., and had his early schooling there. He entered Columbia College in 1835, and remained in close connection with that institution for the rest of a long life. Upon graduation in 1839, he became a classical master in the Columbia Grammar School, and four years later was made a tutor in Greek and Latin in the college; in 1845 he became adjunct-professor of Latin, and in 1857 he succeeded to the first professorship established at Columbia in Latin as a separate field. Ten years later he followed Charles Anthon [q.v.] as Jay Professor of Greek. At many times during his distinguished career as scholar and teacher he was called upon to serve the college in other capacities. Thus he was acting president during President Barnard's absence for the year 1878, and again in the interim, 1888–90, between the death of Barnard and the inauguration of Seth Low. At the latter date he became the first occupant of the newly created office of Dean of the College. In 1894, on his retirement as emeritus professor of the Greek language and literature after fifty years of service, he was the recipient of distinguished academic honors. A public reception was tendered by the Columbia alumni, a gold medal was struck in his honor, and a volume of essays on classical subjects was dedicated to him by his former students; the Henry Drisler Fellowship in Classical Philology was founded, and a sum of money was donated as the Henry Drisler Classical Fund for the purchase of books, casts, and other materials of classical study. His interest in the college remained warm and effective after his formal retirement and found expression particularly in generous gifts of valuable books to the library.

His varied activity was not confined to academic halls. As a young student he had felt the need of a public library in New York City, and his continuing interest in this project led to his selection as trustee of the Astor Library and of the New York Public Library. He was also a trustee of the American School of Classical Studies in Athens, and devoted considerable time to its concerns, especially during a year spent mainly in Greece in 1891. He was president of the association of Columbia alumni for eight years from 1872, and vice-president of the Archæological Institute of America for three years following 1886. Deeply religious in nature and always a strong churchman, he served also as trustee of the Trinity School, of the General Theological Seminary, and of the Leake and Watts Orphan Asylum; as a member of the standing committee for his diocese, and as vice-president of the Society for Promoting Religion and Learning. He was the founder of a Greek

Club which gathered about him fortnightly for forty years in tribute to the power of his personality and the ardor of his scholarship. Although he was given to certain crotchety conservatisms, as in his bitter enmity to walking-sticks and to tobacco, he brought to his varied activities a rugged strength of character and a broad humanity which made him greatly revered.

He was a profound and exact scholar. Rigorous instruction under Anthon trained his native genius for taking pains to an admirable fitness for linguistic work, especially in lexicography. At a time when a decline in classical scholarship in the United States had almost extinguished original production, he was one of the first Americans to recognize the achievement of the German school which was inaugurating a second renaissance in classical study; and the influence of the distinguished scholars whom he visited in Berlin at a period when Americans were rarely seen there combined effectively with the vital spirit of Anthon in all his maturer work. In collaboration with Anthon he published a number of text-books, and edited Riddle and Arnold's *Copious and Critical English-Latin Lexicon* (1849); and he assisted Anthon in the preparation of several editions of Smith's *Classical Dictionary*. In 1854 his name appeared as joint-editor of Liddell and Scott's recension of Franz Passow's *Greek-English Lexicon,* in acknowledgment of the copious aid unofficially given to the editors. He published a greatly enlarged edition of Charles D. Yonge's *English-Greek Lexicon* (1870), was associate editor of *Johnson's New Universal Cyclopædia* (1875–78), and in addition to many other labors, was general editor of Harper's series of classical texts.

[Articles on Drisler in *Harper's Weekly,* June 9, 1894, and Jan. 1898, both by Harry Thurston Peck; in *Harper's Weekly,* Dec. 11, 1897, by J. Howard Van Amringe; and in the *Columbia Spectator,* Nov. 30, 1897, by Edward Delavan Perry. Further material may be found in the archives of Columbia Univ.; in "Univ. of the State of N. Y. 112th Annual Report of the Regents," *Docs. of the Senate of the State of N. Y., 1899, No. 55;* and in the *Athenæum* (London), Dec. 18, 1897.]

E. H. W.

DROPSIE, MOSES AARON (Mar. 9, 1821–July 8, 1905), lawyer, was born in Philadelphia of parents who came from Amsterdam and settled in the United States in 1819. His father, Aaron Moses Dropsie, was a Jew and his mother a Christian, and there had been an agreement that the children were to be allowed to choose their own religion. Three of them chose the Jewish religion, Moses undertaking his obligations at the age of fourteen. He attended a private academy in Philadelphia in charge of Rev. William Mann and received his Jewish training from Isaac Leeser, minister of the Portuguese Congregation in Philadelphia, of whom he wrote a "Panegyric" after the latter's death in 1868. In 1837, he was apprenticed to a watchmaker, and after the expiration of the indenture, which was for a period of two years, he continued in the jewelry business until 1848. At the age of twenty-seven, he decided to study law and entered the office of Benjamin Harris Brewster [q.v.], later attorney-general of the United States. He was admitted to practise on Jan. 11, 1851, and rapidly secured an important place at the bar of Philadelphia. He had a commanding personality and a direct and convincing way of presenting an argument, which carried conviction to both judge and jury.

He collected an excellent law library and had a passion for original prints and editions, not for their sale value but because he thought first editions valuable as source books. He was not only a practitioner of the law, but interested in its history. He rendered into English and supplied with notes the *Hand Book of Roman Law* by Dr. Ferdinand Mackeldey, which was published in 1883, and passed through several editions. In 1892, he published a work entitled *The Roman Law of Testaments, Codicils and Gifts in the Event of Death* (*Mortis Causa Donationes*) based on the Corpus Juris Civilis, and he likewise published a pamphlet, *The Life of Jesus from and Including the Accusation until the Alleged Resurrection* (1890), in which he treated of the trial of Jesus from a lawyer's point of view.

He early evinced public spirit and an interest in the city of Philadelphia. He was one of the pioneers who aided in the establishment of street railways and was elected president of the Lombard and South Streets Railway in 1862, holding that office for twenty years. He was president of the commission in charge of the building of the bridge across the Schuylkill River at South St. (1870), and in 1888 became president of another railway, the Green and Coates Streets Passenger Railroad Company. He was an ardent Whig, a strong supporter of the anti-slavery movement, and in 1856 one of the organizers of the Republican party in the state of Pennsylvania. In 1852, two years prior to the consolidation of the City of Philadelphia under a single mayor, he was a candidate for mayor of the Northern Liberties, but failed of election.

He was an ardent adherent of the Synagogue and joined in much of its charitable work, but principally in work that had to do with religious education. He was secretary and president of the Hebrew Education Society of Philadelphia from 1848 to 1892. He aided the Russian Jews in their difficulties from 1881 on; was president of the board of trustees of the first Jewish College in America, the Maimonides College of Philadelphia, which, however, existed only seven years (1867–73). In 1893, he became president of the board of trustees of Gratz College which was the first Jewish teachers college in America, and he gave the final exhibition of his interest in Jewish learning in his will, by which he bequeathed his entire estate for the foundation of a college in the city of Philadelphia "for the promotion of and instruction in the Hebrew and Cognate languages, and their respective literatures and in the Rabbinical learning and literature," providing further that in the admission of students there should be no distinction on account of creed, color, or sex. Although his will contained no direction as to the name of the College, the Governors decided to call it the "Dropsie College for Hebrew and Cognate Learning." Dropsie was unmarried and during the last fifteen years of his life was blind. He had great vigor and independence of thought and character, and in the years of his blindness refused a companion, which his means would have allowed, going abroad by himself and continuing to take part in the work of the world about him.

[Henry S. Morais, *The Jews of Phila.* (1894); David Sulzberger, in *Pubs. Am. Jewish Hist. Soc. No. 16* (1907) and in *Jewish Encyc.*, vol. V; *Jewish Exponent* (Phila.), *Am. Hebrew* (N. Y.), and *Jewish Comment* (Baltimore), all for July 14 and 21, 1905; family papers and private information.]   C. A.

DROWN, THOMAS MESSINGER (Mar. 19, 1842–Nov. 16, 1904), chemist, educator, was the youngest of the three children of William Appleton and Mary (Peirce) Drown of Philadelphia. He attended the public schools of that city and was graduated from the Philadelphia High School in 1859. A keen interest in chemical science led him to establish in his home a laboratory which soon made the rest of the occupants of the house so uncomfortable that his understanding father caused the laboratory to be removed to a small out-building constructed for the purpose. Drown's pronounced liking for chemistry led directly to his study of medicine at the University of Pennsylvania, since at that time chemistry had scarcely begun to maintain an independent existence. He received the doctorate in medicine in 1862, his thesis, "An Essay on Urological Chemistry," being the subject of high commendation. He immediately obtained a coveted opportunity to serve as surgeon on a packet steamer plying between Philadelphia and an English port, but a single round-trip constituted his entire formal career as a medical practitioner, as he determined that happiness for him would be found in the fields of chemistry or metallurgy rather than medicine. He, therefore, devoted the next three years to study, first at the Sheffield Scientific School at Yale, where life-long friendships with Professors Brush and Johnson were begun, and later, at the Lawrence Scientific School, Harvard. His work there with Prof. Wolcott Gibbs had a profound influence upon his later career as a teacher. Gibbs referred to him as "a dexterous worker, attractive in personality, and a gentleman by nature."

Beginning in 1865, Drown spent three and a half years in Europe, studying first at the School of Mines, Freiberg, Saxony, in metallurgical chemistry, and later becoming a pupil of Bunsen at Heidelberg University, a teacher to whom he always paid a high tribute of gratitude for his influence. He married Helen Leighton, at her home in England, shortly before his return to America in 1868. At the age of twenty-seven he had acquired a "thorough theoretical and technical training in chemistry and metallurgy which was almost unique at that time and would be unusual now" (Raymond, *post*). After a brief instructorship at the Lawrence Scientific School, he opened, in 1870, a private analytical and consulting practise in Philadelphia. In 1874, however, he began his fruitful career as a teacher and administrator in the educational field, by accepting a professorship of chemistry at Lafayette College, Easton, Pa. Meanwhile, in 1871, the American Institute of Mining Engineers had been organized at Wilkes-Barre, Pa., and he was elected one of the managers at the first meeting. He resigned this managership in 1873 to accept the much more important secretaryship, with which were combined the duties of editor of the *Transactions,* an office which, while onerous, was congenial to him. He retained this position for ten years and during that time placed the secretarial office on a firm and lasting footing, and brought the *Transactions* to a degree of excellence which was widely acknowledged. Simultaneously with his work for the institute he was establishing a sound system of instruction in chemistry at Lafayette College, based upon a maximum of personal contact between student and teacher and the fundamental thesis that it is the student and not the subject which it is most essential to teach. At the same time he contributed much of value in the development of exact and yet rapid analyti-

cal processes for commercial use, which were much needed at that stage of metallurgical developments. A number of his papers were published in the *Transactions* of the institute.

In 1881 he was obliged to sacrifice temporarily his professional plans to meet complications in family affairs, consequent upon the death of his father. He resigned his professorship in 1881 and the secretaryship of the institute in 1883. Throwing himself completely into the new problem, sparing neither strength nor his own funds, and with mature judgment and a high integrity, he brought matters to such an issue that in 1885 he was able to accept a call to the Massachusetts Institute of Technology in Boston, at first as professor of analytical chemistry, and later (1888) as professor in charge of the chemistry department. Still later (1893) the department of chemical engineering was placed in his care. Here, as at Lafayette, he came into close and inspiring contact with his pupils and his previous years of critical survey of analytical work in metallurgical fields while editor served him in good stead. In 1887 he also assumed control of the analytical laboratories established by the Commonwealth of Massachusetts, as a part of a comprehensive plan to examine and protect the water supplies of the state, and also served in an advisory capacity with respect to the plan as a whole, a relationship which continued until his death. No such comprehensive undertaking had previously been attempted, and the pioneer work done in this field under Drown's direction has everywhere been recognized as classic, and has been the foundation for all later work of an allied nature. The results were nearly all published in the annual reports of the State Board of Health.

In 1895, yielding to the appeals of many of his friends and former associates, he accepted the presidency of Lehigh University. He entered upon the duties of the presidential office with exceptional qualifications, having already been successful in both teaching and administration, and possessing a gracious and sympathetic nature, a genial bearing, and a ripe culture. Notwithstanding that his sudden death, after nine years of service, occurred at a time when many of his plans for the university were just coming to fruition, he guided it through a difficult era and secured for it financial support which assured its continued success. His presidential reports, addresses, and other papers on educational topics were constructive and influential. In 1897 he was president of the American Institute of Mining Engineers.

[R. W. Raymond, in *Engineering and Mining Jour.,*

Nov 24, 1904, and in *Trans. Am. Inst. Mining Engineers*, vol. XXXVI (1906); H. P. Talbot, in *Technology Rev.*, Apr. 1905 and in *Proc. Am. Chemical Soc.*, 1905; Persifor Frazer, in *Jour. Franklin Inst.*, Dec. 1904; J. L. Stewart, in *Alumni Reg.* (Phila.), Jan. 1905; "Thirty-Sixth Ann. Report of the State Board of Health of Mass.," *Public Docs. of Mass. No. 34 (1904)*; *The Drown and White* (South Bethlehem, Pa.), special edition, Nov. 16, 1904; personal recollections of the writer, covering nineteen years of intimate acquaintance.]

H. P. T.

DRUILLETTES, GABRIEL (Sept. 29, 1610–Apr. 8, 1681), Jesuit missionary, envoy to New England, emigrated from France to Canada in 1643. During the ensuing eight years he endured the hardships of life among the wandering savages north of the St. Lawrence River. At one time he became totally blind because of smoke in the wigwam and sun on the snow. "Filth was my cook and constant companion," he complained. Nevertheless, he accomplished his duties, said mass each day, baptized many savages, and in 1648, was sent to establish a mission on the Kennebec River for the Abnakis. There he became a friend of the Plymouth agent, John Winslow. In 1648 he visited Boston, partly in answer to Winthrop's proposal of 1647 for intercolonial trade, chiefly to obtain help from New England to subdue the Iroquois Indians, whose hostilities were ruining the colony on the St. Lawrence. Received with cordiality by the Massachusetts and Plymouth authorities, he returned to Canada to obtain official authorization for his mission. In September 1651, with Sieur Jean Paul Godefroy, he journeyed to New Haven to appear at a meeting of the commissioners of the New England Confederation. There he plead his cause before the representatives of the four New England colonies. "M. Gabriel Drwellets," writes the chronicler, "Improved his abilities to the utmost to perswade the Commissioners that the English collonies might Joyne in the warr against the Mohauks," but after weighty consideration the Confederation denied his plea. This instance of intercolonial comity, however, throws a pleasing light on the character and manners of the French missionary.

After returning to Quebec in April 1652, he was on service in the neighboring missions until 1656 when he started for the West with the Ottawa Indians, but was driven back and his companion killed by Iroquois. In 1660 Father Dablon [*q.v.*] took Druillettes with him on an extended trip to the North by way of the Saguenay and Lake St. John. Ten years later Druillettes again essayed the voyage to the Northwest, this time successfully, and passed several years in charge of the mission at Sault Ste. Marie. There he was very popular with both white and red men, was present at the pageant of possession in 1671, and retired to Quebec (where he died) only when age rendered him unfit for life in the wilderness. He had a reputation for great sanctity, he was a remarkable linguist, and a man of deep charity and self-sacrifice. He was for a short time the teacher of Marquette [*q.v.*], and whether on the Kennebec, the Saguenay, or the St. Mary's, was beloved both by the Indians and by his fellow missionaries.

[An account by Druillettes of his first visit to New England is in R. G. Thwaites, *The Jesuit Relations* (1896–1903), XXXVI, 83–111. His visit to New Haven is described in *Records of the Colony of New Plymouth*, IX (1859), 199–203. The sketch in *Jesuit Relations*, XXIII, 327, is incomplete. T. J. Campbell, *Pioneer Priests of North America* (1911), III, 70–109, gives an excellent account of the events of his life.]

L. P. K.

DRUMGOOLE, JOHN CHRISTOPHER (Aug. 15, 1816–Mar. 28, 1888), Catholic priest, was born near Granard, County Longford, Ireland, and died in New York City. When he was eight years old, his widowed mother, who had preceded him to America, sent for him to join her in New York. There he took up the trade of a cobbler. Of a devout nature even in childhood, he attracted the notice of his priests and was after a while made teacher in a kind of mission Sunday-school. In 1844, on the invitation of one of his clerical friends, he became a sexton. For a short period around 1850, in addition to his work as sexton, he helped run a small bookstore near his church. This was the only break in the routine of his life till 1863 when he began a course of study preparatory to entering the ministry—first at St. Francis Xavier College in New York, next at St. John's College in Fordham, and finally, in 1865, at the Seminary of Our Lady of Angels, near Niagara Falls. He was ordained in May 1869 and sent as a priest to the church where he had formerly been sexton. His passion to be useful had long since put him in contact with the victims of squalor and wretchedness, and in the late sixties he considered devoting his life to mission work among the freedmen. In 1871, however, he found in New York a type of work for which he was superbly fitted. A lodging house for waifs and newsboys, inaugurated about a year before under Catholic auspices, was failing to accomplish what had been expected. The new priest volunteered to try his hand at making it justify itself. Before he assumed control in the fall of 1871 the number of lodgers had fallen to fifteen, but by the end of 1873 it was necessary to increase the original quarters three times. The value of his work was widely recognized, and in November 1875 his hold on the public confidence was attested by the fact that he raised nearly

$15,000. After this, money came so freely at his call that by the time of his death he had spent on his charitable enterprises about a million dollars, and was caring for from sixteen hundred to two thousand children. His most notable monument is the Mission of the Immaculate Virgin, built in 1881. It was his theory that no youngsters are incorrigible provided they have properly displayed before them as a model the life of one who is "poor, honest, industrious, hard-working and virtuous" (Dougherty, p. 327). "From my experience," he said, "I find that with proper care boys can all be reclaimed" (Dougherty, p. 327). His entire career derived its character and strength from his deep piety and expansive human sympathy.

[J. E. Dougherty, "John Christopher Drumgoole," in *The Charities Rev.*, Sept. 1898; *Cath. Encyc.* (1909); *N. Y. Herald*, Mar. 29, 1888.]   J. D. W.

DRURY, JOHN BENJAMIN (Aug. 15, 1838–Mar. 21, 1909), Reformed (Dutch) clergyman, editor, was born in Rhinebeck, N. Y., the son of Alfred and Maria Ann (Schultz) Drury. He graduated from Rutgers College in 1858 and from the New Brunswick Theological Seminary in 1861, was licensed to preach by the Classis of Poughkeepsie, and gained his first ministerial experience in home mission work in Davenport, Ia. In 1864 he returned to his native region as pastor of the First Reformed (Dutch) Church at Ghent, Columbia County, N. Y. On Sept. 2, 1869, he married Henrietta Wynkoop Keese, who outlived him. While attending year in and year out to the duties of a rural minister, he found time for study and reflection and grew steadily too in the esteem of his colleagues. In 1883 he was the Vedder lecturer at the College and Seminary in New Brunswick; in 1885 he taught in the summer school of the American Institute of Christian Philosophy; and in 1886 he was president of the General Synod of the Dutch Reformed Church. He had risen to a position of influence rather through his common sense and trustworthiness, his courtesy and friendly, helpful disposition, than through any showier gifts, for he was not a notably good speaker and had written but little. In 1884 he had published a small book on *Truths and Untruths of Evolution,* which was regarded as somewhat liberal in tendency, and which had shown many a Reformed clergyman that religion was not served by vilifying Charles Darwin and attempting to impugn solidly established facts. Two parish histories and a few articles had also come from his pen, but writing was for him arduous labor. To the end of his life he composed with difficulty, and his articles

were characterized more by an obvious effort to be clear and accurate than by any grace of style. His chief work, nevertheless, was to be in religious journalism. In 1887 he resigned his charge and, with the issue of Dec. 7, assumed the editorship of the *Christian Intelligencer.* The *Intelligencer* had recently passed through bankruptcy and, confronted by the growing competition of secular newspapers and magazines, faced a severe struggle for survival. Its continuance seemed essential to the welfare of the Reformed Church. Drury undertook to keep the paper alive. For a long time he had a deficit to deal with at the end of each year, but he persisted in spite of discouragements and ultimately made the paper self-supporting. On the literary side the *Intelligencer* maintained a high standard among religious journals. Drury was a delegate to the Council of Reformed Churches holding the Presbyterian System at London in 1888, at Toronto in 1892, at Washington in 1899, and at Liverpool in 1904. He died after a short illness at his home in New Brunswick, N. J.

[E. T. Corwin, *Manual of the Reformed Church in America* (4th ed., 1902); *Who's Who in America,* 1908–09; J. H. Raven, ed., *Biog. Record Theol. Sem. New Brunswick 1784–1911* (1912); *Cat. of the Officers and Alumni of Rutgers Coll. 1766–1909* (1909); *Christian Intelligencer,* Mar. 17, 24, 31, Apr. 7, 14, 21, 28, 1909.]
                                           G. H. G.

DRYDEN, JOHN FAIRFIELD (Aug. 7, 1839–Nov. 24, 1911), senator, pioneer of industrial insurance in America, was born on a farm, at Temple Mills, near Farmington, Me., the son of John and Elizabeth (Butterfield) Dryden. His paternal ancestors came to New England from Northamptonshire, England, in the seventeenth century. He entered Yale College in 1861, but his health broke down during the closing year of his course and he was compelled to abandon his studies. In recognition of his subsequent achievements the university conferred on him the degree of M.A. and entered his name as one of the graduates of the class of 1865. Possibly his ill health may have influenced the choice of his life-work, for soon after leaving Yale he became interested in life insurance in particular relation to the practical solution of the economic problems of the poor. He made a careful study of the methods of the Prudential Assurance Company of London, which had met with considerable success in writing industrial insurance. He himself defined industrial insurance as "life insurance for small amounts, chiefly on the lives of wage-earners and members of their immediate families, with premiums payable weekly and collected from the houses of the insured" (*Addresses and Papers,* p. 85). In 1873 he settled in

Newark, N. J., secured the cooperation of a small group of able men, including Leslie D. Ward, a young physician, and Noah F. Blanchard, a leading leather manufacturer, and wrote the first policy of the Prudential Friendly Society on Nov. 10, 1875. No time could have been less propitious for the launching of a new project, for it was the beginning of an era of depression in industry and commerce, and the discouragements that attended the opening years of this pioneer company would have been fatal to a man less sure of himself or less resolute of purpose than was Dryden. From an insignificant beginning in the basement of the State Bank Building on Broad St., Dryden lived to see The Prudential Insurance Company (so named in 1878) advance under his leadership to a foremost place among the life-insurance companies of the world. The secret of his success was his clear grasp of fundamental principles, combined with indefatigable industry and a remarkable capacity for details. He believed in the practical utility of his plans to provide for the American working people a better and more secure form of thrift than prevailed in 1875 and insurance history has proved the wisdom of his policy.

A Republican all his life, he took an active interest in public affairs. On Jan. 29, 1902, he was elected to the United States Senate, following the death of Senator Sewell. He was opposed by several of the strongest men of the Republican party in New Jersey and the contest resulting in his election was one of the most memorable in the political history of the state. He made a notable record in the Senate as a member of the Committee on the Isthmian Canal, and his speech of June 14, 1906, was a decisive factor in securing the adoption of the lock-canal plan. His expression in 1902 of his views on Chinese exclusion, and his bill providing for federal regulation of insurance were other outstanding evidences of his ability. In 1907, as a candidate for reëlection, he was the choice of the voters in the primary but his opponents were strong enough to produce a deadlock in the joint meeting of the legislature which continued for two weeks. Then, his health breaking down, Dryden yielded to the advice of his physicians and family and withdrew from the contest. In 1909 a collection of his writings was published, under the title, *Addresses and Papers on Life Insurance and Other Subjects.*

He was married on Apr. 7, 1864, to Cynthia Jennings Fairchild, and they were the parents of two children. In personal appearance he was tall, erect, and of distinguished bearing, with clear-cut, high-bred face, in his later years accentuated by silvery beard and moustache, and head crowned with snow-white hair.

[*Statement Addressed to the Republican Members of the Legislature of N. J.—Feb. 4, 1907* (Newark, 1907), by Senator J. F. Dryden; F. L. Hoffman, *Hist. of the Prudential Insurance Co. of America* (1900); W. S. Myers, *Fifty Years of the Prudential* (1927); *John Fairfield Dryden* (1912), pub. by The Prudential Co.; *Proc. N. J. Hist. Soc.,* 3 ser., IX (1914), 118–20; W. E. Sackett, *Modern Battles of Trenton* (1914), vol. II; *Obit. Record Grads. Yale Univ.* (1912); obituary notices in *N. Y. Herald, N. Y. Tribune,* and *N. Y. Times,* Nov. 25, 1911.]   C.R.E.,Jr.

DUANE, ALEXANDER (Sept. 1, 1858–June 10, 1926), ophthalmologist, was born in Malone, N. Y., the son of Gen. James Chatham Duane [*q.v.*], military engineer, by his wife Harriet, daughter of Gen. Henry Brewerton of West Point. Because of the uncertain life of an army officer, Alexander Duane was tutored at home, being guided in literature by his mother, a woman of taste and wide reading, and in mathematics by his father. He attended the high school at Portland, Me., while his father was stationed there, and later went to St. Mark's School from which, at the age of fifteen, he entered Union College. He was graduated in 1878 with highest honors, including election to the Phi Beta Kappa society. During his academic years he laid an excellent foundation in languages, especially in German and Latin, and to the end of his life he was able to read and write Latin with ease and pleasure. His son, while at college, often received from him letters in that tongue. He spent a year at the Albany Medical College but transferred to the College of Physicians and Surgeons of New York, where he received his medical degree in 1881. After a year as interne at the New York Hospital, during which he utilized his odd moments by writing medical terms for *Webster's Dictionary,* he began to practise in New York as assistant first to a Dr. Ranney and later to Dr. George Stevens. After a sojourn in Norfolk, Va., in 1888, he worked with Dr. Hermann Knapp [*q.v.*] of New York for two and a half years. Duane's thorough academic training in mathematics and the languages made it possible for him to render peculiar and valuable services to the science of ophthalmology. His mathematics fitted him for dealing with abstruse problems in physiological optics, refraction, and muscular weakness, and to all these subjects he made notable contributions (see especially: "Some New Tests for Insufficiencies of the Ocular Muscles," *New York Medical Journal,* August 1889; *A New Classification of Motor Anomalies of the Eye* (1897); "Paralysis of the Superior Rectus and its Bearing on the Theory of Muscular Insufficiency," *Ar-*

chives of Ophthalmology, 1884, XXIII, 61–84). He also contributed to G. E. de Schweinitz and B. A. Randall's *An American Text-Book of Diseases of the Eye, Ear, Nose and Throat* (1899) and to W. C. Posey and W. G. Spiller's *Eye and Nervous System* (1906), and to J. E. Weeks's *A Treatise on Diseases of the Eye* (1910). As a linguist his greatest service was the translation of the eight successive editions of Ernest Fuchs's *Textbook of Ophthalmology,* the first American edition appearing in 1892 and the eighth and last in 1924. He contributed medical terms to successive editions of *Webster's International Dictionary,* to Foster's *Encyclopedic Dictionary of Medicine,* and to Murray's *New English Dictionary* (Oxford). During the Spanish-American War he served in the navy as lieutenant (junior grade), and during the World War he was acting signal officer of the U. S. S. *Granite State.*

He was a quiet, retiring, and somewhat sensitive personality, much given to hard and persistent work but taking pleasure in the indulgence of his wide literary tastes and in his love of history, astronomy, botany, and music. His photographs show a clear-eyed, simple, kindly face. On July 14, 1891, Duane married Susan Williams Galt of Norfolk, Va., by whom he had three children. His oldest son was killed in action in the World War.

[Two excellent biographies of Duane appeared shortly after his death : J. W. White and others, *Arch. Ophthal.,* 1927, LVI, 66–73 ; C. Berens, *Am. Jour. Ophthal.,* 1926, 3 ser., IX, 917–22; see also *Who's Who in America,* 1924–25 ; *N. Y. Times, N. Y. Herald Tribune,* June 12, 1926.]

                   J.F.F.

DUANE, JAMES (Feb. 6, 1733–Feb. 1, 1797), jurist, was born in New York City, probably at the corner of the then King and Queen Sts. He was the son of Anthony Duane (1682–1747), a prosperous New York merchant of Irish birth who came to New York soon after 1700, and of Althea Kettletas, his second wife, daughter of Abraham Kettletas, of Dutch descent, also a well-to-do merchant. James Duane probably received his early education from the Rev. Richard Charlton, a classical tutor, catechist of Trinity Church and later rector of St. Andrews, Staten Island. Without college or university training, he studied law in the office of James Alexander [*q.v.*], presumably from 1747 till his admission to the bar, in August 1754. His private practise grew with astonishing rapidity and embraced a wide variety of cases in all the courts of the province. In the famous case of *Forsey* vs. *Cunningham* (1763), originally an assault and battery case with the enormous damages of £1,500, he successfully maintained that no appeal from the pro-

vincial supreme court, in civil cases, lay to the governor in council—long a moot question. This was a defeat for Lieut.-Gov. Colden, whom, however, Duane defended successfully some seven years later in an extraordinary case when the Crown, in the person of Lord Dunmore, sued Colden in chancery for half a year's fees while Colden had been acting in Lord Dunmore's stead. The latter, as chancellor, presided over the trial when he was himself the plaintiff. It was regarded as an extremely courageous act on Duane's part to undertake the defense, several other well-known lawyers having refused the case.

Prerevolutionary activities in New York found Duane definitely on the conservative side. He was one of the prominent citizens who went about among the people attempting to quell the Stamp Act mob in November 1765. In November 1766 he was "busily employed in a new remonstrance to the Parliament respecting our trade" (Duane to R. Livingston, Jr., Nov. 15, 1766, Redmond private collection of Livingston papers). In 1768 he successfully defended the Tory candidate for the Assembly, James Jauncey, from accusations of corruption brought by his radical rival, John Morin Scott. On May 16, 1774, he was appointed to the Committee of Correspondence (Committee of Fifty-one), which on July 4 nominated him one of five delegates to the forthcoming Continental Congress, to which he was subsequently elected after much radical opposition. At the Congress he was a member of the committee which drew the statement of the rights of the colonists, being largely responsible for the mildness of its tone, and on Sept. 28 he seconded Galloway's plan of union, defending his reactionary stand by stating his belief that the right of regulating trade lay with Parliament because of the "local circumstances of the colonies, and their disconnection with each other" (*The Works of John Adams,* 1850, II, 389). He did, however, sign the "Association" or non-importation agreement on Oct. 20, 1774, though he considered that it went too far. He sat in the New York Provincial Convention and was by it elected to the Second Continental Congress; was a member of the New York Committee of Sixty to carry out the "Association" and of the subsequent Committee of One Hundred. He sat in the Continental Congress almost continuously till 1783, serving on a large number and great variety of committees. His chief services were in connection with financial and Indian affairs and he assisted in making the final draft of the Articles of Confederation. During May and June 1781, violent attacks on his patriotism and accusations of loyalism appeared in the Philadelphia *Freeman's Journal,* but after statements were offered on his behalf by several of his colleagues, including John Jay, Alexander McDougall, William Floyd, and Philip Livingston, the New York Assembly (June 25) and Senate (June 27) passed votes of confidence in him. He entered New York City on its evacuation by the British, Nov. 25, 1783, with Washington and Gov. Clinton, as a member of the Council of the latter. On Feb. 4, 1784, he was appointed mayor of New York, serving till September 1789, during which time his chief duties, both as mayor and as *ex officio* presiding officer of the mayor's court, were in connection with the rehabilitation of the city after the ravages of the British. Washington appointed him the first federal judge of the district of New York in September 1789, which position he held till his permanent retirement from public life on account of ill health in March 1794. He served in the Poughkeepsie Convention of 1788, where he was an ardent advocate of ratification of the Constitution, and sat in the New York Senate almost continuously from 1782 till his resignation, Jan. 27, 1790, to become a federal judge. One of his most intensive interests throughout a long period was in connection with the Vermont-New Hampshire boundary difficulties, in the course of which he represented the "Yorkers" in many private suits, and was their constant advocate before Congress. At one time a reward of £15 was offered by the "Vermonters" for his capture (*Connecticut Courant,* Feb. 5, 1772).

Perhaps his greatest non-professional interest was in land development. Having inherited a large tract of land from his father in the present Schenectady County, he continued to purchase in that immediate neighborhood and elsewhere in the Mohawk Valley till late in life. He was also deeply interested in the Vermont lands and was a heavy loser in the final settlement of that controversy. He was unremitting and in the main successful in his efforts to colonize his Mohawk Valley lands, selling and renting farms on easy terms. He had already begun development before 1765 when he imported a group of Germans from Pennsylvania. The township of Duanesburg (created Mar. 13, 1765) was almost entirely owned by him (portions of it are still in possession of his descendants), but that town did not cover all his holdings.

During his entire life he was vitally interested in Trinity Church, New York, and in King's (later Columbia) College. His domestic life was peculiarly happy. He married, Oct. 21, 1759, Mary, daughter of Robert Livingston, Jr., "third lord" of Livingston manor, by whom he had ten children. Five of these grew to maturity and survived him. Retiring to Schenectady to live in 1795, Duane died there, very suddenly, on the morning of Feb. 1, 1797, and is buried beneath the church at Duanesburg.

[A memoir by Samuel W. Jones appeared in *Doc. Hist. of the State of N. Y., IV* (1851), 1,061. A few copies of this, privately printed (1852), are extant. Some Duane letters were published in *Southern Hist. Asso. Pubs.,* 1903–06, and some of his reports in regard to the boundary controversy in *N. Y. Hist. Soc. Colls.,* vols. II, III (1870–71). The mass of material concerning him is in manuscript form in the possession of the N. Y. Hist. Soc. Diaries, account books, ledgers, etc., privately owned by Mr. Wilmot Townsend Cox, Mr. Geo. Wm. Featherstonhaugh, and Mr. Wm. North Duane have also been consulted, and together with the MSS. in the N. Y. Hist. Soc., form the basis of this sketch.]   S.H.J.S.

DUANE, JAMES CHATHAM (June 30, 1824–Nov. 8, 1897), military and civil engineer, son of James and Harriet (Constable) Duane, was born at Schenectady, N. Y. His grandfather, James Duane [*q.v.*], was a member of the Continental Congress, first mayor of New York after the Revolution, member of the convention that adopted the Constitution, and judge of the United States district court at New York. James C. Duane graduated from Union College in 1844 and from the United States Military Academy in 1848. He served until the Civil War as a subaltern in the Corps of Engineers, United States Army, taking part in the famous Utah expedition under Gen. Albert Sidney Johnston in 1858. When McClellan was placed in command of the armies of the United States and began the organization of the Army of the Potomac, he assigned to Capt. Duane the organization of its engineer and bridge equipage. To this work Duane devoted himself in the winter of 1861–62 and designed the various types of ponton trains and the engineer equipment for the construction of fixed bridges, siege and field works which were so successfully operated during the war. He also organized the battalion of engineers authorized by Congress. With his battalion and equipment he took part in the Peninsular campaign and demonstrated its efficiency at the siege of Yorktown and in the subsequent operations.

When McClellan reorganized his army for the Antietam campaign, Duane was assigned as chief engineer of the army and remained with it until McClellan was relieved. In 1863 he was chief engineer of the Department of the South, until recalled in July again to become chief engineer of the Army of the Potomac, which position he held until the close of the war, taking part in all its operations from the Potomac to

Appomattox. He had never sought a commission in the volunteers and was therefore only a major in 1865, although he received the brevets of lieutenant-colonel, colonel, and brigadier-general in the regular army for distinguished professional services, especially in the siege of Petersburg.

After the war he was engaged in the construction of many of the more important works of the Corps of Engineers—fortifications, lighthouses, and river and harbor improvements, and was a member of the Board of Engineers for Fortifications and River and Harbor Improvements and of the Light House Board. In 1886 he was promoted to brigadier-general and chief of engineers, United States Army. After two years of service in this capacity he retired, June 30, 1888. Shortly thereafter he was appointed a member of the Croton Aqueduct Commission by the mayor of New York, and served as president of the commission until his death. In 1850 he married Harriet Whitehorn Brewerton, daughter of Gen. Henry Brewerton, then superintendent of the United States Military Academy. They had three sons. A distinguished fellow officer (Gen. Cyrus B. Comstock) who served with him during and after the war said: "General Duane possessed that sound good sense which can look at all sides of a question without prepossessions, and which can see the great features of it, without giving details too much importance, gifts that are rare. Of unchanging and inevitable modesty, he accepted the duty that was assigned to him and did it faithfully, instead of pushing his own merits on his superiors or on the public. One needed to know him well to know his full value, and then one classed him among the just, faithful, able men whom to know strengthens one's faith in mankind."

[Cyrus B. Comstock, in *Twenty-ninth Am. Reunion Asso. Grads. U. S. Mil. Acad.* (1898); G. W. Cullum, *Biog. Reg.* (3rd ed., 1891); *Official Records (Army)*.]
G. J. F.

DUANE, WILLIAM (May 17, 1760–Nov. 24, 1835), journalist and politician, was born near Lake Champlain, N. Y., of Irish parentage, his mother being a Sarsfield, descendant of the Irish patriot. On his father's death in 1765, he was taken by his mother to Ireland where, disinherited by her, a Catholic, because of his marriage to Catharine Corcoran, a Protestant, he learned the printer's trade. Going to India in 1787, he established the *Indian World* at Calcutta, which brought him both prestige and fortune. Because of his denunciations of the methods of the East India Company, and his espousal of grievances of army officers, he was ar-

rested without a charge, deported without trial, and his property was confiscated. Returning to London where he served as parliamentary reporter for the *General Advertiser,* later merged with the *Times,* he vainly sought the restitution of his property through Parliament and the courts. Finally despairing of justice, he left England in disgust, and took up his residence in Philadelphia, where he became associated with Benjamin Franklin Bache [*q.v.*] in editing the *Aurora.* In September 1798 Bache died; Duane succeeded him in the editorship and immediately made the *Aurora* the most powerful organ of the Jeffersonians. His genius in controversy and management, his courage and audacity, the sincerity and intensity of his convictions, and his virile style of writing, made him the most effective journalist of his time. Adams and Pickering, wincing under his lash, exchanged views on the possibility of his deportation under the Alien Law. In the spring of 1799 he was arrested on the charge of creating a seditious riot by offering for signatures, petitions for the repeal of the Alien Law, but he was promptly acquitted in the state courts. Because of his exposure of the brutality of the undisciplined and idle volunteer soldiery mobilized for the war with France, projected by the Hamiltonian wing of the Federalists, he was murderously assailed by armed men, and his property saved from destruction only by the timely arrival of a group of Democrats. In the fall of 1799 he was indicted under the Sedition Law, but the trial was postponed until the following June, and then again postponed, and the charge dismissed when Jefferson acceded to the presidency. All these desperate attempts at intimidation failed of their purpose, for he continued in his course with unabated energy. Perhaps his most important service to the nation was his exposure of the secret plan of the Federalists to prevent the election of Jefferson through the notorious Ross Election Bill. Copies of this measure, then pending in the Senate behind closed doors, were sent him under cover, and its publication with vigorous comments so aroused the public wrath that it was defeated. No single person did more to discredit the projected war with France over the X. Y. Z. incident, to make the Alien and Sedition Laws abhorrent, to arouse and munition the masses, and make the triumph of Jefferson in 1800 inevitable.

With Jefferson's election, the career of Duane moved toward an anti-climax. The removal of the capital to Washington deprived his paper of its advantage. The editor, encouraged by Jefferson and Gallatin, opened a store in Washington in expectation of the government contract for printing and stationery, but the plans miscarried, and Duane never forgave the slighting of his claims. He soon broke with Gallatin, and ultimately turned on Madison and Monroe. In local politics, where he remained a power, he led the radical or anti-judiciary faction against Gov. Thomas McKean [*q.v.*], whom he had earlier supported. To Jefferson, however, he remained a faithful follower and devoted friend. His idol sought in numerous ways to serve him, appointing him lieutenant-colonel of rifles in July 1808, and soliciting subscriptions to relieve him of financial embarrassment in 1811. Duane served as adjutant-general through the War of 1812, and continued in the editorship of the *Aurora* until 1822, when he retired to travel in South America. The result was a volume, *A Visit to Colombia in the Years 1822 & 1823* (1826). On his return, he was made prothonotary of the supreme court of Pennsylvania, for the eastern district, and he held this position until his death. In his last years he made an unsuccessful attempt to revive the *Aurora* to fight the National Bank. He wrote several books of indifferent merit on military science, including *Military Dictionary* (1810), *An Epitome of Arts and Science* (1811), *Handbook for Riflemen* (1813), *Handbook for Infantry* (1813). Jefferson, whose friendship he retained through the vagaries of his later years, described him with fidelity in a letter to William Wirt: "I believe Duane to be a very honest man, and sincerely republican; but his passions are stronger than his prudence, and his personal as well as general antipathies render him very intolerant" ("The Letters of William Duane," *post*, p. 259). His first wife died in 1798, a few months before the death of Bache, and in 1800 Duane married Margaret (Markoe) Bache, widow of his colleague and owner of the *Aurora*. By her he had five children.

[There are numerous references to Duane in Frederic Hudson, *Journalism in the U. S.* (1873); G. H. Payne, *Hist. of Journalism in the U. S.* (1920); *Writings of Thomas Jefferson* (1903), vols. XII and XIII; *Works of John Adams*, vols. IX and X (1856); C. G. Bowers, *Jefferson and Hamilton* (1925). Francis Wharton, *State Trials of the U. S.* (1849), pp. 345–91, gives an illuminating report on his trial for creating a riot. "The Letters of Wm. Duane," *Proc. Mass. Hist. Soc.*, 2 ser. XX, 257–394, and Allen C. Clark, "Wm. Duane" in *Records of the Columbia Hist. Soc.*, IX (1906), 14–62, throw an interesting light on his later career.]   C. G. B.

DUANE, WILLIAM JOHN (May 9, 1780– Sept. 26, 1865), lawyer, was born at Clonmel, County Tipperary, Ireland, the son of William Duane [*q.v.*] and his wife, Catharine Corcoran. His early youth was passed in London where his father was employed as a printer, but in 1787 the latter went out to Calcutta to engage in news-

paper work, and William John with his mother returned to Clonmel. There he attended a private school for fifteen months—the only schooling he ever received, his mother having been his first teacher. When his father returned from India to become a Parliamentary reporter in London, the family was reunited there, and the boy frequently visited the gallery of the House of Commons to listen to the debates. When in 1796 William Duane moved his family to Philadelphia and assumed editorial charge of the *True American,* William John entered its composing room. Two years later, when the elder Duane became editor of the *Aurora,* he joined the staff of that newspaper, and commenced actively to interest himself in public affairs. In 1806 he relinquished newspaper work, and became the partner of William Levis, a paper merchant. He soon came to the front in local politics and in 1809 was elected to the Pennsylvania House of Representatives on the Republican—later Democratic—ticket. In the same year he wrote, *The Law of Nations, Investigated in a Popular Manner: Addressed to the Farmers of the United States.* In the legislature he was a prominent figure, being chairman of the Committee on Roads and Inland Navigation, and the committee to consider the case of Gideon Olmstead, but on seeking reëlection in 1810 he was defeated owing to party dissensions. In the following year he published, *Letters, Addressed to the People of Pennsylvania Respecting the Internal Improvement of the Commonwealth by means of Roads and Canals,* which had appeared in the columns of the *Aurora.* In 1812 he retired from business to take up the study of law in Philadelphia, and was again elected to the legislature, where he resumed the chairmanship of the Committee on Roads and Canals. He was admitted to the bar June 13, 1815, and through his political associations and diverse public interests, soon acquired an extensive legal connection. He was a candidate for Congress in 1816 and for the state legislature in 1817, but the division in the Democratic party still continued and he was defeated on each occasion. In 1819, however, amity was again obtained and he was elected to the State House of Representatives where he became chairman of the Committee on Banks. He had in the previous year published, *Observations on the Importance of Improving the Navigation of the River Schuylkill for the Purpose of Connecting it with the Susquehanna,* and in the legislature he was indefatigable in promoting improvement of internal means of transportation and communication, becoming chairman of the select committee relating to domestic economy and general stagnation of business. In 1820 he was appointed prosecuting attorney for the mayor's court, a position which he retained for three years, his only fault, it was said, being his leniency to petty offenders. In 1824 he refused a nomination for Congress but later resumed his political activities, becoming a member of the Democratic Committee of Correspondence for Philadelphia in 1828. In 1829 he was chosen a member of the Select Council of Philadelphia. His standing in the party was now high, and in 1831 President Jackson nominated him one of the commissioners under the treaty with Denmark. In May 1833 he accepted the office of secretary of the treasury in Jackson's cabinet and entered upon his duties June 1. Some time previous the President had determined that the government deposits should be withdrawn from the United States Bank and placed with the state banks. This could only be effected by the secretary of the treasury for the time being; the previous incumbent, having declined to accede to Jackson's request, had been transferred to the State Department, and the vacant office conferred upon Duane in the hope that he would be more amenable. He refused, however, to make the transfer prior to the meeting of Congress, and was accordingly dismissed by the President, Sept. 23, having held office less than four months. Duane in 1834 vindicated his conduct in a pamphlet addressed to the people of the United States and subsequently published a well-documented statement of the history of his appointment, tenure of office, and the circumstances of his dismissal entitled, *Narrative and Correspondence Concerning the Removal of the Deposites [sic] and Occurrences Connected Therewith* (1838). He returned to Philadelphia and practically withdrew from public life but did not resume active practise, only occasionally accepting retainers in the orphan's court from old clients. He was an intimate friend of Stephen Girard [*q.v.*], acted as solicitor for him, drafted his will, in which he was nominated an executor, and after Girard's death in 1831 was actively engaged in the settlement of the estate. The last public office which he held was that of director of Girard College.

As a lawyer his skill in draftsmanship was demonstrated in the course of the contest anent Girard's will, and the trust he inspired was exemplified in the large testamentary and other administrations which he handled in his later days. He was resolutely opposed to litigation, invariably striving to compromise disputes, and only occasionally appeared in court. Despite his desultory education he possessed a broad,

though not profound, culture and a wide acquaintance with current thought. His wife was Deborah, daughter of Richard Bache [*q.v.*] of Philadelphia and grand-daughter of Franklin.

[*Biog. Memoir of Wm. J. Duane* (1868); *Biog. Encyc. of Pa. of the Nineteenth Century* (1874), p. 54; J. T. Scharf and T. Westcott, *Hist. of Phila.* (1884), II, 1,137; *Pa. Mag. of Hist. and Biog.*, Jan. 1930.]

H. W. H. K.

DUBBS, JOSEPH HENRY (Oct. 5, 1838–Apr. 1, 1910), clergyman of the Reformed Church (German), college professor, church historian, was a son of Rev. Joseph S. Dubbs and his second wife, Eleanor. His paternal grandfather and his great-grandfather were gunsmiths. The latter, of German stock, is said to have come to America from Switzerland in 1732, settling in Lower Milford Township, Lehigh County, Pa. Joseph Henry Dubbs was born in a rural parsonage, in North Whitehall Township, Lehigh County, about seven miles north of what is now the city of Allentown, his father being a minister of the Reformed Church of that place. Dubbs spoke both English and German from childhood. The reader of his autobiography receives the impression that his boyhood life was somewhat abnormal and lonely. At fifteen he was a sophomore in Franklin and Marshall College, Lancaster, Pa., where he graduated in 1856. In 1859 he graduated from the Theological Seminary of the Reformed Church, situated at that time in Mercersburg, Pa. When about twenty-one years of age he became assistant to his father in the pastorate and one year later the sole pastor of Zion's Reformed Church, Allentown. On Sept. 22, 1863, he married Mary Louisa Wilson of Allentown, daughter of Thomas and Elizabeth (Martin) Wilson. From 1863 to 1871 he was pastor of Trinity Reformed Church, Pottstown, Pa., and from 1871 to 1875, of Christ Reformed Church, Philadelphia. In the latter year he was elected to the professorship of history and archeology in Franklin and Marshall College, which position he held up to the time of his death. Here he was active for about thirty-five years as a teacher and research student, especially along the lines of denominational ecclesiastical history and of local history. His publications, both numerous and valuable, include: *Historic Manual of the Reformed Church in the United States* (1888); *Home Ballads and Metrical Versions* (1888); *Why Am I Reformed?* (1889); *History of the Reformed Church, German* (1895), in American Church History Series; *Leaders of the Reformation* (1898); *The Reformed Church in Pennsylvania* (1902); *History of Franklin and Marshall College* (1903); "Reformed Church in the United States," in

Hastings' Encyclopedia of Religion and Ethics, vol. X (1919), and fragments of autobiography, published in the *College Student* of Franklin and Marshall College (vol. XXVII, 1907, pp. 166–71; vol. XXVIII, 1908, pp. 149–62; vol. XXX, 1909, pp. 87–97). It was said of him at the time of his death that in his field of historical study he had few equals and no superiors, and it is to be added that he is still unexcelled.

Dubbs had a wide range of interests far beyond his specialty. His enthusiasm was unbounded and transmissive; his memory was remarkable for its retentiveness; and he worked with an industry that was sustained and unwearied almost to the close of his life. He had at ready command a rich and varied fund of witty and humorous stories which he could relate as few can. In his nature there was a marked poetic strain; his personality was attractive and winsome. His students admired him because of his enthusiasm and the wide range of his scholarship, and loved him because of his genial spirit and the personal interest he took in them, but they also at times took reprehensible advantage of his leniency.

[Obituary in the *Daily New Era* (Lancaster, Pa.), Apr. 1, 1910, containing the most complete list of his writings ever published; *Reformed Church Messenger,* Apr. 7, 1910; *Who's Who in America,* 1910–11; *Almanac for the Reformed Church in the United States,* 1911; "In Memoriam," by John S. Stahr, president of Franklin and Marshall College, in the *Reformed Church Rev.,* Oct. 1910; biographical sketch by G. T. Ettinger in the *Pennsylvania-German Soc. Proc. and Addresses,* XX (1911), 48–50.]   **I. H. DeL.**

DUBOIS, AUGUSTUS JAY (Apr. 25, 1849–Oct. 19, 1915), civil engineer, was born at Newton Falls, Ohio, the son of Henry Augustus and Catherine Helena (Jay) Dubois. Both his mother and father were of French Huguenot descent. His father was a physician, holding his degree in medicine from Columbia College, while his mother was the grand-daughter of Chief Justice John Jay. After attending the Hopkins Grammar School at New Haven, Conn., Augustus Dubois studied civil engineering in the Sheffield Scientific School at Yale, from which he was graduated in 1869. He continued his studies at Yale for four more years, securing his degree of C.E. in 1870 and that of Ph.D. in 1873. Eighteen months of advanced study at the Royal Mining Academy in Freiberg, Saxony, followed. From 1875 until his death in 1915 he was a teacher of engineering subjects. For two years he was professor of civil and mechanical engineering at Lehigh University. In 1877 he went to Sheffield Scientific School as a teacher of mechanical engineering but in 1884 he was appointed professor of civil engineering there, a position which he filled

until his death. He contributed to both the theory and literature of engineering. While doing graduate work at Yale, and later at Freiberg, he made a special study of graphical statics, a science which was new at that time. His *Elements of Graphical Statics and Their Application to Framed Structures* (2 vols., 1875) was the first comprehensive work on this subject to appear in the United States. It was followed by his translation of sections of Weisbach's famous *Mechanics of Engineering,* and of translations from both Weyrauch and Roentgen, in an effort to fill the gap in engineering literature which was being felt in American technical schools at that time. In 1883 his *Stresses in Framed Structures,* giving methods of computing stresses by analytic and graphic processes, was published. *Elementary Principles of Mechanics* (3 vols., 1894–95) followed. These both came into wide use as text-books in engineering schools, and many editions were published. He contributed papers on roof trusses, steam-engines, etc., to various technical publications.

The *Century Magazine* published, between 1889 and 1894, a series of six papers originally prepared as lectures, in which Dubois attempted to establish moral truths on the same fundamental principles which underlie mechanics. Shortly before his death he summarized the conclusions of these lectures in a paper which is to be found in the *Yale Review* for July 1913. The series shows his originality of thought, his conciseness of expression, and clear logic. As a man, he has been described by a colleague, Prof. John C. Tracy, who succeeded him at Sheffield, as having "a sympathetic interest, a ready wit," and added, "Breadth of culture and an unusual power of expression made him a brilliant and inspiring conversationalist. Underneath a quiet and undemonstrative exterior, there was a man chivalrous, sympathetic, always thoughtful of others, loyal and wholly lovable." On June 23, 1883, he was married to Adeline Blakesley, daughter of Arthur Blakesley of New Haven, Conn.

[Mansfield Merriam in *Trans. Am. Soc. Civil Engineers,* LXXXI (1917), 1,699–1,701; obituaries in *Trans. Am. Soc. Mechanical Engineers,* XXXVII (1915), 1,505–06; *Engineering News,* Oct. 28, 1915; *Obit. Record Grads. Yale Univ.,* 1915–16.] **K. W. C.**

DUBOIS, JOHN (Aug. 24, 1764–Dec. 20, 1842), Roman Catholic prelate, third bishop of New York, was born in Paris. His early education was received at home, whence he passed to the Collège Louis-le-Grand. On the completion of his secular studies he entered the Seminary of St. Magloire, conducted by the Fathers of the Oratory of St. Philip Neri, and was ordained priest on Sept. 22, 1787. He served on the staff of the Church of St. Sulpice in Paris and also acted as chaplain to a community of nuns; but these activities were cut short in less than four years by the French Revolution, and in the spring of 1791 he was obliged to make his escape from France. In August of that year he landed at Norfolk, Va., and through letters of introduction from Lafayette he soon became acquainted with some of the most prominent men in the United States, such as Patrick Henry and James Monroe. The former taught him English; the latter received him into his house in New York; while it was doubtless owing to the influence of Lafayette that Dubois was permitted to celebrate Mass in the State Capitol at Richmond, a courtesy the more remarkable because of the state of feeling toward Catholics in the Virginia of that day. At the earliest opportunity he became an American citizen.

For a while he supported himself by teaching French; then, as soon as he was fitted for active work in his adopted country, he was sent by Bishop Carroll to parochial work in Virginia, first at Norfolk and then at Richmond. In 1794 he was transferred to Frederick, Md., where he built the first Catholic church in western Maryland and ministered to the Catholics of that section and much of the region now comprising West Virginia. During most of this time he was the only priest between Baltimore and St. Louis, and his labors were such as would have broken a man not endowed with splendid health and vigor. In 1807 he withdrew to devote himself to a work that had always attracted him, the education of aspirants to the priesthood, and established a preparatory seminary at Emmitsburg, Md. The following year he joined the Society of St. Sulpice, a community of secular priests whose purpose was to conduct ecclesiastical seminaries, some members of which had left France during the Revolution and founded St. Mary's Seminary in Baltimore.

The curriculum at Emmitsburg was altered in a short time so as to include instruction for laymen as well as for clerics. By 1821, accommodations more substantial than the log structures which had housed the institution became necessary, and Dubois began the erection of a new stone building, but when on the point of completion it was destroyed by fire. Immediately he recommenced, and in a few years a better building rose on the ruins. His labors in this undertaking were prodigious; he was simultaneously president, treasurer and professor; and in addition to these cares he had to meet the opposition of some among Catholics who sought to have him discontinue the courses in theology and thus give up the training of priests. The result of this attempt was that he severed his connection with the Sulpicians (1826) and was busy with plans for the reorganization of Mount St. Mary's at Emmitsburg when he was appointed to the diocese of New York to succeed Bishop John Connolly [q.v.].

He was chosen by Propaganda on Apr. 24, 1826, and the choice was confirmed by Pope Leo XII the following Apr. 30; he was consecrated by Archbishop Maréchal in the Cathedral of Baltimore on Oct. 29, 1826, Charles Carroll of Carrollton presenting the ring and the pectoral cross. In his new post he was faced with trying difficulties. The diocese was much larger than it is now; the system of lay trustees, under which church finances were administered by laymen, had given rise to dissensions; and the spirit of nationalism threatened to disrupt the Catholic body. So antagonistic to the new bishop were some of the elements among the New York Catholics that one of his first acts on reaching his see was perforce the issuance of a pastoral letter refuting the charge that his appointment had been brought about by undue French influence.

To meet the urgent need for priests he went to Paris and Rome in 1829 and secured financial assistance from the Society for the Propagation of the Faith and the Congregation of Propaganda. On his return he took up the task of building another seminary, but in New York he had not the success that had been his in Maryland. He completed a seminary at Nyack, N. Y., that was burned down before it could be occupied; the project of one in Brooklyn was never realized; and the one he opened in La Fargeville, N. Y., had to be given up because of its remoteness. Then he had to encounter the problem of trusteeism. At one time the trustees of his own cathedral withheld his salary and appointed in charge of the school attached to the cathedral a priest whom he had suspended; and it was on this occasion that he uttered the words so often quoted: "I am an old man and do not need much. I can live in a basement or in a garret. But whether I come up from the basement or down from the garret, if I have to preach from the top of a barrel on the street corner, I am still your bishop." Amid this distressing situation he struggled bravely and successfully, but the labor wore him down and in 1837 he accepted as coadjutor John Hughes [q.v.], a former pupil under him at Mount St. Mary's and later fourth bishop and first archbishop of New York. Two years later he retired from active government, leaving the diocese in the hands of Bishop Hughes, and spent the remaining years of his life in private devotion. He died on Dec. 20, 1842, and was buried in the crypt of St. Patrick's Church (the "Old Cathedral"), New York, where his body now lies.

[F. X. Reuss, *Biog. Cyc. of the Cath. Hierarchy of the U. S.* (1898) ; John T. Smith, *The Cath. Church in N. Y., A Hist. of the N. Y. Diocese* (1905) ; M. M. Meline and E. F. X. McSweeny, *The Story of the Mountain* (Emmitsburg, Md., 1911), vol. I, *passim*; *Cath. World* (N. Y.), Jan. 1882 ; Célestin Moreau, *Les prêtres français émigrés aux États-Unis* (Paris, 1856) ; J. G. Shea, *A Hist. of the Cath. Church within . . . the U. S.* (1890), vol. III ; *N. Y. Daily Express*, Dec. 21, 1842.]

                                      E.R.

DU BOIS, WILLIAM EWING (Dec. 15, 1810–July 14, 1881), numismatist, fifth of the eight children of Uriah and Martha (Patterson) Du Bois, was born in Doylestown and died in Philadelphia, Pa. His father, a Presbyterian minister, was descended from the Huguenot Louis Du Bois, who settled on the Hudson River about 1660. His mother was the daughter of Robert Patterson, professor in the University of Pennsylvania and from 1805 to 1824 director of the United States Mint. William was a precocious child; at six he studied the classics, at sixteen he published essays in the weekly papers, and in his early twenties he became a lawyer. An affection of the voice made it impossible for him to talk a great deal, and even caused him to write instead of speak the answers to many of the questions addressed to him. In 1883 this disability made him give up law to become director's clerk in the mint. Two years later he went into the assay department under the direction of Jacob R. Eckfeldt. In 1841 he married Eckfeldt's sister, Susanna, and on Eckfeldt's death in 1872 he succeeded him as assayer. As long as both lived they were intimate friends and faithful collaborators. Eckfeldt, it is said, was mainly concerned with the scientific exactitude of their operations, but it was Du Bois who emphasized also the desirability of giving their findings a permanent record. In 1842 they published their *Manual of Gold and Silver Coins of All Nations,* and in 1850, *New Varieties of Gold and Silver Coins,* both intelligent, exhaustive works showing wide reading and original observations. In the years following, Du Bois published a number of other essays on coinage and related subjects— among them, *On the Natural Dissemination of Gold* (1861), and *Propositions for a Revised System of Weights* (1869). He published several volumes dealing with the genealogy of his own family—Pattersons on the one hand (1847), and Du Boises on the other (1860 and 1876). In this connection he was at pains to declare that an in-

terest in one's ancestors does not of necessity imply vanity. He was writing, he said, only for those directly concerned ; on the cover of the Du Bois record of 1860 one is requested, "Please not to leave this exposed to general perusal." In 1872 he published, *A Brief Sketch of Jacob R. Eckfeldt.* He was a member of various learned societies, and he corresponded with many celebrated people in Europe as well as in America. He was earnest and gentle, and among his intimate friends, humorous.

[P. Du Bois, *In Memoriam, Wm. E. Du Bois* (1881) ; Robt. Patterson in *Proc. Am. Phil. Soc.,* vol. XX (1882–83) ; *Press* (Phila.), July 16, 1881 ; *Phila. Record,* July 18, 1881.]

                                      J.D.W.

DuBOSE, WILLIAM PORCHER (Apr. 11, 1836–Aug. 18, 1918), theologian, was born near Winnsboro, S. C., at his father's plantation, the son of Theodore Marion and Jane (Porcher) DuBose, of Huguenot descent on both sides, his own being the sixth generation in this country. His grandfather was Samuel DuBose, adjutant on the staff of his uncle, Gen. Francis Marion, in the Revolutionary War. His education was begun at Mt. Sion Institute at Winnsboro, S. C. From there he was sent to the Military College of South Carolina, known as the "Citadel," graduating in 1855 with first honors. Here he received his grounding in mathematics which showed itself later in the accuracy of thought in his teaching and writings. From the "Citadel" he went to the University of Virginia where he received the degree of master of arts, after which he entered the theological seminary of the diocese of South Carolina at Camden, which he left in 1861 to enter the military service of the Confederacy. During the Civil War he served first as adjutant in the "Holcombe Legion" on the staff of his former commandant at the "Citadel" and later as chaplain after being exchanged as prisoner from Fort Delaware. He was wounded several times but never bore arms except on one occasion, a scouting party. After the war he was ordained priest in the Protestant Episcopal Church in 1865 by Bishop Davis of South Carolina and served in the parochial ministry of that diocese at his birthplace, Winnsboro, and then at Abbeville, S. C., until 1871, when he was elected chaplain and professor of ethics and Christian apologetics in the University of the South at Sewanee, Tenn., where he lived and taught until his death in 1918. He was elected dean in 1894 of the theological department of the University, which department he had founded and in which he held the chair of New Testament exegesis. He resigned active teaching and administration in 1908 and was made dean and professor emeritus. DuBose was small in stature, not over five feet eight inches in height, with massive forehead and deep-set gray eyes which betokened the thinker. He wore a full beard and was meticulously careful but simple in his dress, believing that clothes are an index to character. He was gentle, but had the strength of gentleness. His students felt that they were in the presence of a great and good man, but they could not stand in awe of him for he was as approachable as a friendly child and had a keen enjoyment of humor. His lectures were difficult for those who were not philosophically minded but even these never went empty away, for they were enriched by the man's spirit even though they did not grasp his subtleties of thought. His personality was impressive but never overpowering and he encouraged his students to think for themselves. He was affectionately known among them as "The Doctor." He lectured five times a week to the whole body of theological students and each lecture was prepared afresh. He had been teaching twenty years before his first book was published in 1892; as a result he never found it necessary to revise an edition, notwithstanding hostile reviews from the more conventionally minded critics. His positions had been taken after mature thought. In his own field, that of the philosophy of the Christian religion, he was the foremost thinker in the Episcopal Church in America, and, in the opinion of the late Prof. William Sanday of Oxford University, "the wisest Anglican writer . . . on both sides of the Atlantic" (*The Life of Christ in Recent Research,* 1907, chs. x and xi). He was twice married: first, in 1863, to Anne Barnwell Peronneau of South Carolina, who died in 1873, and after her death, to Louisa Yerger of Jackson and Washington County, Miss., in 1878.

Besides *Turning Points in My Life* (1912), a short autobiography consisting of addresses read at a reunion of his old students in his honor at Sewanee in 1911, and numerous essays in the *Constructive Quarterly,* he was the author of six works on philosophical theology. *The Soteriology of the New Testament* (1892) is an exegesis of the New Testament containing his philosophy of salvation; *The Ecumenical Councils* (1897) is a philosophical interpretation of Christian doctrine as set forth by the councils of the early church; *The Gospel in the Gospels* (1906) contains his theology in a systematic but original form. *The Gospel According to St. Paul* (1907) is a theological interpretation of the Pauline teaching, while *The Reason of Life* (1911) is his philosophy of Christianity based upon the Gospels and the Epistles of St. John. *High Priesthood and Sacrifice* (1908) is a philosophical appreciation of the Epistle to the Hebrews. With the exception of the Book of Revelation and one or two minor Epistles his writings cover the whole of the New Testament. He was asked on one occasion to explain the meaning of the Book of Revelation and he replied that he wished he knew. He was born a Platonist and spoke the language of Aristotle. His affiliations were with St. John, but St. Paul has had no more loyal interpreter and defender.

[DuBose's autobiography, *Turning Points in My Life*; family records furnished by his son and two daughters, including an account of his family; G. R. Fairbanks, *Hist. of the Univ. of the South* (1905); *Who's Who in America,* 1918–19; memoir by the Rt. Rev. Wm. A. Guerry, in the *Churchman* (N. Y.), Aug. 31, 1918; editorials, *Ibid.,* Sept. 7, 1918, and in the *Southern Churchman* (Richmond), Aug. 31, 1918; John O. F. Murray, "DuBose and the Problems of Today," in the *Constructive Quart.,* Dec. 1921, and *DuBose as a Prophet of Unity* (1924); personal acquaintance.]

G. B. M.

DU BOURG, LOUIS GUILLAUME VALENTIN (Feb. 13, 1766–Dec. 12, 1833), Roman Catholic prelate, was born at Cap Français, Santo Domingo, the son of Chevalier Pierre Du Bourg de la Loubère et St. Christaut, Sieur de Rochemont, and his wife, Marguerite Armand de Vogluzan. At the age of two he was placed in the care of his grandparents at Bordeaux, France. After completing his classical studies in the Collège de Guyenne, in 1784 he commenced to study theology at the "Petite Communauté des Robertins," an annex to the Seminary of St. Sulpice, Paris, whence, on Oct. 12, 1786, he entered the Seminary proper. He was ordained, probably about the end of 1788, and in the fall of that year he was sent to Issy, near Paris, as rector of a preparatory school. Forced by events of the French Revolution to send home his charges and seek refuge in Paris, in September 1792, he fled to Orense, in Spain, and later sailed for America. Landing at Baltimore on Dec. 14, 1794, he entered at once into relations with the Sulpicians of St. Mary's, petitioned admittance into their Society, and was received on Mar. 9, 1795. Records of the time relate that in Baltimore he gave Sunday religious instruction to the negroes of both sexes. On Sept. 20, 1796, Bishop John Carroll [*q.v.*] appointed him to the presidency of the newly founded Georgetown College, an office which he resigned at the end of 1798. On Jan. 24, 1799, he sailed for Cuba to assist in the direction of the Sulpician college lately founded there. When opposition brought about the closing of the institution, he returned to Baltimore, accompanied by a number of his pupils. An academy for West Indian boys, in charge of Du Bourg, was opened at St. Mary's with the sanction of Bishop Carroll; in 1803 this institution was succeeded by St. Mary's College for American boys, Du Bourg remaining its head until 1812. In 1806 he helped to raise funds with which to build the Baltimore cathedral and was instrumental in securing its location on its present commanding site. About this time he became acquainted in New York with Mrs. Elizabeth Ann Seton [q.v.], foundress of the Sisters of Charity, prevailed upon her to move to Baltimore, and fostered her incipient Community.

In 1812 he was nominated to the bishopric of New Orleans, but because of the captivity of Pius VII, the Pontifical Bulls were never issued. Accordingly, Archbishop Carroll appointed Du Bourg Administrator Apostolic of that diocese. The task confronting him was exceptionally difficult: for fifty thousand souls he had only fourteen priests, half a dozen of them crippled by old age, and others, led by the Capuchin friar, Anthony de Sedella [Père Antoine, q.v.], in open opposition to the new order of things created by the Louisiana Purchase. Later, these difficulties were increased when in January 1815 a British army stood at the gates of New Orleans. Du Bourg at once gauged the situation, and impressed upon all the patriotic duty of supporting the American general. He was tireless in his efforts to assist the people of the threatened city, animating them by his eloquence, giving them material aid, and making the Ursuline Convent a place of refuge. After the battle, in the public celebration of the victory, it is said that Du Bourg, assisted by a college of priests, received Gen. Jackson at the cathedral door and placed a crown of laurel on his head. By this time he had won the affection of many of the citizens but the local clergy continued to oppose him, and in the spring of 1815 he journeyed to Rome to plead for help for his distracted diocese. As a result, the Lazarists were prevailed upon to go to Louisiana; three priests and one lay brother were at once enlisted for the expedition; some secular priests and ecclesiastical students joined them, and other recruits were promised for future needs. On these assurances the Administrator consented to receive Episcopal consecration in the church of S. Luigi de' Francesi on Sept. 24, 1815. Early in 1816, he visited northern Italy, France, and Belgium, recruiting for his diocese five priests, twenty-six seminarians, nine Ursuline nuns, and a few religious of the Sacred Heart. In Lyons he interested charitable persons in his extensive mission (though he cannot be regarded as founder at Lyons of the Society for the Propagation of the Faith), and even enlisted the aid of the King, Louis XVIII, who gave orders for the transportation of his company on the flute *La*

Caravane of the French navy. Meanwhile, at home, Sedella, leader of the opposition, was denying the Bishop's vicar-general access to the cathedral. For the prelate to go to New Orleans in such circumstances was to invite riot; accordingly, after landing at Annapolis, Sept. 4, 1817, he settled, temporarily, at St. Louis. When he left for New Orleans, on Nov. 20, 1820, he had almost completed a large brick church and had founded an academy for boys; the religious of the Sacred Heart, under Mother Duchesne [q.v.], were carrying out at Florissant their work of female education; St. Mary's Seminary at "the Barrens" was providing for the training of the future clergy of the diocese; a number of parishes in Upper Louisiana had been supplied with pastors; and ways and means were being devised for sending missionaries to the Indians of Missouri. Du Bourg's arrival in New Orleans opened for a while an era of peace; Sedella himself paid him honor and swore allegiance. The Bishop's first foundations were a college for boys in New Orleans and an academy for girls under the sisters of the Sacred Heart at Grand Côteau (1821). In 1822 he went to Washington to obtain government support for an Indian mission. Again success rewarded his efforts: besides obtaining from Secretary Calhoun encouraging promises, by a remarkable coincidence he rescued from disbandment and transferred to Missouri for the work they had contemplated a colony of Jesuits, one of whom was Pierre-Jean De Smet [q.v.], the famous Indian missionary of later years.

For some time Du Bourg had petitioned for a coadjutor, and on July 14, 1823, Joseph Rosati [q.v.] was appointed to that office. Previously, however, Du Bourg had recommended the nomination of his whilom arch-opponent Anthony De Sedella; and at another time one Angelo Inglesi, whom through sheer infatuation he had rushed to the priesthood. Rumors of these requests caused disaffection among his clergy, and keenly sensitive of their loss of confidence in him, he tendered his resignation to Leo XII on Feb. 1, 1825. For a time he received no reply, but continued to insist upon his release. After Easter 1826 he returned to Europe, and shortly after landing at Havre (July 3), was advised that his resignation was accepted. A few weeks later he was appointed to the See of Montauban; after seven years he was transferred to the Archdiocese of Besançon; and there he died.

[R. H. Clarke, *Lives of the Deceased Bishops of the Catholic Church in the U. S.* (1872), vol. I; L Bertrand, *Bibliothèque Sulpicienne, ou Histoire Littéraire de la Compagnie de St. Sulpice* (1900), III, 206–14; C. G. Herbermann, *The Sulpicians in the U. S.* (1916), pp. 94–107 and 170–80; C. L. Souvay in *Cath. Hist. Rev.*, Apr.–July 1917, Apr. 1918, and *St. Louis Cath.*

Hist. Rev., Jan. 1920, Apr.–July 1923; F. G. Holweck in *Pastoral Blatt* (St. Louis), Feb. 1918, and *St. Louis Cath. Hist. Rev.*, Jan. 1923; G. J. Garraghan, *Cath. Hist. Rev.*, Jan. 1919; certain information as to family and early life from Trist Wood, Esq., of New Orleans.]
                                                    C.L.S.

DUBUQUE, JULIEN (Jan. 10, 1762–Mar. 24, 1810), first white settler of Iowa, was born of Norman parents, Noël Augustin Dubuque and his wife, Marie Mailhot, in the village of St. Pierre les Brecquets, county of Nicolet, in the province of Quebec. He received a good education in the parish schools of his native village and at Sorel, became polished in manner, and was able to express himself well both in speech and writing. Seeking fortune and adventure, he set out for the West, and as early as 1785 was located at Prairie du Chien, Wisconsin. Learning that a band of Fox Indians who had their village on Catfish Creek across the Mississippi in the Iowa country controlled the output of rich lodes of lead, he sought to win their favor. He made numerous presents to them, learned their language, flattered their vanity, and in due time secured permission to work the lead mines. He himself, it is said, drew up the document which Kettle Chief and his associates signed at Prairie du Chien on Sept. 22, 1788, giving "la petite nuit," as he was called, sole permission to work the mines on the Iowa side of the Mississippi (*57 U. S.*, 222–23). Thus secured in his occupancy, he opened new mines, built cabins for his French-Canadian helpers, erected a smelting furnace, and opened a store for trade with the Indians. He used his French-Canadian helpers as overseers, smelters, and rivermen. The actual labor of mining was performed by the squaws and old men of the tribe. Dubuque inaugurated the plan of smelting the lead into pigs for convenience in loading and carrying the metal to St. Louis. In the hope of making himself more secure in the possession of his property, he named his possessions "The Mines of Spain," and humbly petitioned Baron Carondelet, governor of Louisiana, for title to a tract of land seven leagues in length up and down the west bank of the Mississippi and extending three leagues into the interior. With the assent of Andrew Todd, to whom sole permission had been given by Spanish authorities to carry on trade with the Indians in what is now Iowa, the petition was granted (*Ibid.*, pp. 224–26).

Dubuque now redoubled his activities. Twice a year his boats, laden with furs and lead, made the trip to St. Louis where the cargo was exchanged for goods to be used in the Indian trade. His arrival at St. Louis was a welcome event for he was a favorite both with the merchants and the ladies. A man of a little below the usual stature, with black hair and eyes, wiry and well-built, he had all the politeness and grace of a cultured Frenchman.

Despite his monopoly of the trade in fur and lead of the eastern Iowa country, he was a poor manager and fell heavily in debt to Auguste Chouteau [*q.v.*], the merchant prince of St. Louis. In October 1804, Dubuque assigned to his creditor seven-sixteenths of his domain, and agreed that the remainder of his land at his death should go to Chouteau or his heirs. Out of this agreement grew a long controversy that was finally settled by the Supreme Court of the United States, which in 1853 held that Dubuque did not have actual title to the land, merely permission to work the mines (*Chouteau* vs. *Molony, 57 U. S.*, 226–42).

When Dubuque died, at the age of forty-eight, the Indians, whose confidence he retained to the last, buried him with all the honors due to a chief. In excavating for the monument to his memory in 1897, workmen discovered his bones and those of an Indian chief who was buried near-by. The bones of Dubuque were placed in a coffin of native walnut and sealed in a sarcophagus at the base of the tower.

[Moses M. Ham, "The First White Man in Iowa," was published in *Annals of Iowa*, 3 ser., II (1896), 329–44. In *57 U. S.*, 203–42, the decision of the Supreme Court of the United States in the case of *Chouteau* vs. *Molony* reviews the history of Dubuque's career in Iowa. See also Richard Herrmann, *Julien Dubuque, His Life and Adventures* (1922).]
                                                    B.E.M.

DU CHAILLU, PAUL BELLONI (July 31, 1835–Apr. 30, 1903), African explorer, is sometimes said to have been born in New Orleans, but his own statements indicate that the United States was his country only by adoption and that France was his native land. His father was the agent for Messrs. Oppenheim of Paris at the Gaboon on the west coast of Africa. There Paul spent his early years and received his education in a Jesuit Mission school. He showed a great fondness for natural history and early became acquainted with the native languages and customs. In 1852 he came to the United States and while here secured the support of the Philadelphia Academy of Natural Sciences for an exploring expedition into Central Africa. This trip which he undertook in 1856 lasted nearly four years, and in that time he traveled about 8,000 miles through tropical Africa. He collected many specimens of rare birds and animals and brought back to America the first gorillas ever seen here. He also determined that the Muni, Munda, and tributaries of the estuary of the Gaboon were mere coast rivers but that the St. Nazareth, Mexias, and Fernando Vaz were deltaic arms of the Ogowe, a vast river rising in the interior. Another important contribution was the discovery of the Fan tribe of cannibals. In 1861, two years after his return, he published an account of his journey under the title, *Explorations and Adventures in Equatorial Africa.* This was at first received with ridicule and distrust and led to many a bitter controversy among scientists. One by one, however, Du Chaillu's discoveries were confirmed by later travelers, and his reputation was established. But Du Chaillu was not satisfied with this vindication, and in 1863 he returned to Africa to prove some of his previous statements by scientific observations. His experiences of this two-year trip, including the story of his discovery of the pygmies of the Black Forest, are told in *A Journey to Ashango Land,* brought out in 1867. For the next few years he made his home in New York and devoted himself to lecturing and writing upon equatorial Africa. Chief among the books of this period are: *Stories of the Gorilla Country* (1868), *Wild Life Under the Equator* (1869), *Lost in the Jungle* (1869), *My Apingi Kingdom* (1870), and *The Country of the Dwarfs* (1871). All of these works are very readable and contain interesting, lively descriptions which indicate a keen sense of observation on the part of the author.

In 1871, he went to Sweden and Norway, where, after studying the people and their institutions for more than five years, he began writing *The Land of the Midnight Sun,* published in 1881. This was followed in 1889 by *The Viking Age,* his most ambitious work. His later years were spent quietly in writing and study; but in 1901 he again felt the wanderlust and journeyed to Russia to make a survey similar to the one that he had conducted in Scandinavia thirty years before. It was while on this trip that his death occurred at St. Petersburg.

[The chief sources of information concerning Du Chaillu are sketches of his life in the following magazines: *Bull. Am. Geog. Soc.,* vol. XXXV (1903), no. 2, p. 230; *Nat. Geog. Mag.,* July 1903; *Geog. Jour.,* June 1903; *Scientific American,* May 9, 1903; *Harper's Weekly,* May 16, 1903; and *Independent,* May 14, 1903. Obituaries appeared in the *Sun* (N. Y.), *N. Y. Times,* and *N. Y. Tribune* for May 1, 1903, and in *Novoe Vremya* (St. Petersburg, Russia), Apr. 18–May 1, 1903. See also Du Chaillu, "Last Letters from Russia," in *Lamp,* June 1903.]   G.H.B.

DUCHÉ, JACOB (Jan. 31, 1737/38–Jan. 3, 1798), Anglican clergyman, Loyalist, was the son of Col. Jacob Duché, a prosperous Philadelphian, at one time mayor of the city, and his wife Mary Spence. He was graduated with the first class of the College of Philadelphia, in 1757. After a year at Cambridge University, he returned to Philadelphia in 1759 with deacon's orders, and became teacher of oratory at the college and assistant rector of the united parishes of Christ Church and St. Peter's. On June 19, 1759, he was married to Elizabeth Hopkinson, the sister of his friend and classmate, Francis Hopkinson [*q.v.*]. In 1762 he went to England for ordination, and in 1775 he succeeded the Rev. Richard Peters as rector of the united churches. He soon became one of the most popular preachers in the city, but two of his early sermons, *The Life and Death of the Righteous,* and *Human Life, a Pilgrimage,* published in 1763 and 1771 respectively, suggest that his reputation owed more to fervor of delivery than to depth or originality of thought. He early displayed literary ambitions. As an undergraduate he wrote some verse, the most ambitious example of which is *Pennsylvania, a Poem,* published by Franklin Hall in 1756. In 1762 there was published *An Exercise* on the accession of George III, which he and Hopkinson had written for the college commencement of that year. Beginning in March 1772, he published in the *Pennsylvania Packet* a series of twenty letters over the signature "Tamoc Caspipina," a pseudonym derived from the initial letters of the words "the assistant minister of Christ Church and St. Peter's in Philadelphia in North America." Though trite and commonplace, these letters evidently found readers, for in 1774 he republished them in a volume entitled *Observations on a Variety of Subjects, Literary, Moral and Religious.* Later they were reprinted in Philadelphia, Bath, London, Dublin, and Leipzig, sometimes under the original title, sometimes as *Caspipina's Letters.* With some of the later editions was included another work, "The Life and Character of William Penn."

At the beginning of the Revolution, Duché showed such zeal for liberty that he was made chaplain of the Continental Congress. In 1775 he published two patriotic sermons, *The Duty of Standing Fast in Our Spiritual and Temporal Liberties,* and *The American Vine,* the former of which was dedicated to Washington. After the Declaration of Independence, however, he began to lose his enthusiasm, and when Howe took Philadelphia and put him in jail, he experienced a complete change of heart. On Oct. 8, 1777, he wrote Washington a letter in which he severely criticized the Americans and predicted their defeat. He advised the General to urge Congress to recall the Declaration of Independence, and if they should refuse, to negotiate for peace at the head of his army. Washington turned this letter over to Congress, and the members of that body soon disseminated the news of their chaplain's treachery throughout the thirteen colonies

(*Letters of John Adams to His Wife*, p. 320). Those whose hearts had thrilled to Duché's eloquence now cursed him as a traitor, and even Hopkinson wrote him a burning letter of protest. Finding life in Philadelphia unendurable, Duché sailed for England in December 1777. The following year the Pennsylvania Assembly proscribed him and confiscated his property, but allowed his family enough money to enable them to join him in England. There he was rewarded for his recantation by being made secretary and chaplain of an orphan asylum at St. George's Fields, Lambeth Parish, but he never ceased to pine for America. He wrote to Washington and to many prominent Philadelphians, begging for permission to return, but it was not until May 1792 that the exiles at last came home. Although Duché had suffered a stroke of paralysis before leaving England, he lived until Jan. 3, 1798. His wife died as the result of an accident, on May 22, 1797.

Duché's later publications were: *Discourses on Various Subjects* (2 vols., London, 1779); *Sermons Preached in America* (Philadelphia, 1788); and *A Sermon—for the Benefit of the Humane Society* (London, 1791). In his later days he became a convert to the teachings of Swedenborg. This second change of principles and certain eccentricities that he manifested as he grew older caused some of his acquaintances to question his sanity, and hence to judge him more leniently than they once had done. A portrait of Duché and his wife (now in the Hopkins Collection, Historical Society of Pennsylvania), painted by their son, Thomas Spence, gives one a very favorable impression of their appearance. Both had regular and handsome features, expressing kindliness and intelligence, and both had an unmistakable air of culture and refinement.

[See E. D. Neill, "Jacob Duché" in the *Pa. Mag. of Hist. and Biog.*, II (1878), 58–73; Geo. E. Hastings, *The Life and Works of Francis Hopkinson* (1926), esp. pp. 111–13 and 268–75; C. P. Keith, *The Provincial Councillors of Pa.* (1883); Lorenzo Sabine, *Biog. Sketches of Loyalists of the Am. Rev.* (1864); Benjamin Dorr, *A Hist. Account of Christ Church, Phila.* (1859); C. R. Hildeburn, *The Inscriptions in St. Peter's Church Yard* (1874); T. H. Montgomery, *A Hist. of the Univ. of Pa.* (1900); *The Washington-Duché Letters* (1890), ed. by Worthington C. Ford; M. C. Tyler, *The Lit. Hist. of the Am. Rev.* (1897); Francis Hopkinson, *Miscellaneous Essays* (1792), III, ii, 83–88. Tyler and Hastings both give bibliographies. The full titles of Duché's works published in America may be found in Chas. Evans, *Am. Bibliography*, vols. III–VII (1905–12). The most valuable collections of his letters are those of Edward Hopkinson, Esq., of Philadelphia, and Mrs. Francis Tazewell Redwood of Baltimore; others are owned by the Harvard Univ. Lib., the Hist. Soc. of Pa., the Am. Philosophical Soc., the Library Company, Phila., and the Lib. of Cong.]

                         G.E.H.

DUCHESNE, ROSE PHILIPPINE (Aug. 29, 1769–Nov. 18, 1852), religious, teacher, pioneer, was born in Grenoble, Dauphiné, France, the daughter of Pierre François Duchesne and Rose Euphrosyne Périer. From her earliest years she showed the characteristics that had won for her father's family prominence in commerce, law and politics, and that had made the Périers eminent in French finance. These characteristics: an indomitable will, a restless energy, and generous, ardent zeal, were her natural endowment for her work as a pioneer in the missions. Her education, begun at home, was continued in the Convent of the Visitation of St. Mary on the Alpine spur, Chalmont, overlooking Grenoble. On her return home she shared the studies of four of her boy cousins under a tutor, thus strengthening the sturdy qualities already remarkable in her character. Having become a novice in the Convent of St. Mary, Grenoble, she was there when the French Revolution began. The monastery was taken over by the government to be used as a prison for non-juring priests and for Royalists, and the religious whose home it had been were dispersed. During the Reign of Terror, Philippine Duchesne showed herself an angel of pity to its victims in Grenoble. At the close of the Revolution she hoped to rehabilitate the religious of the Visitation in the ruined old monastery, but this proving impossible, she offered herself and the house to the newly founded Society of the Sacred Heart. It was as a professed of that Order that she was sent to America in 1818 by the foundress, Mother Madeleine Sophie Barat.

Such a mission had been Philippine Duchesne's ambition since as a child she had heard a missionary speak of the New World and of the pagan Indians. The two months' voyage from Bordeaux to New Orleans was followed by another no less hazardous, that up the Mississippi to St. Louis, where the travelers were welcomed by Bishop DuBourg [*q.v.*]. In St. Charles, a village some seventeen miles from St. Louis, the religious of the Sacred Heart opened a boarding-school for the daughters of the pioneers of Missouri, and at the same time founded the first free school west of the Mississippi. Later on, at Florissant, Mo., they added to these two works the foundation of a school for Indian girls, the first of its kind to be established under Catholic auspices in the United States. The sisters suffered from hunger, illness, and cold, from opposition, misunderstanding, and failure; yet when her brother offered to send her passage back to France, Mother Duchesne replied: "Use that sum of money to pay the way of two more nuns coming from France to America."

In spite of privations, the pioneers and their wives were glad to confide their children to her and the school records bear well-known names, such as Chouteau, Mullanphy, Pratte.

In 1821 another convent was founded at Grand Côteau, La., and there, as at St. Michael's, La., founded four years later, the religious conducted a boarding-school for the daughters of the planters, a day school for the white children of the parish, and, in addition to these institutions, classes for the instruction of the negroes. Mother Duchesne when stationed in Missouri made two long voyages to Louisiana to visit these schools, and on one of the return journeys contracted yellow fever and was put ashore where she nearly died of exposure and neglect. In founding a convent in St. Louis, she fulfilled an ardent desire of the foundress of her Order, Mother Barat, and by opening a mission school among the Indians of Kansas she realized her own long-cherished hope. At that time she was over seventy and broken in health, but with spirit undaunted she had pleaded to be sent to the red men, and in 1841 she made the perilous voyage up the river to Westport, Kan. Her work among the Potawatomi at Sugar Creek was confined to example and prayer, so that the Indians picturesquely designated her as "the woman who always prays." She had hoped to be left at that post to the end of her life, but was recalled to St. Charles where she remained in humble hidden labor, in suffering and prayer, until her death in November 1852. The members of the Historical Society of Missouri, after discussing what their state owes to its pioneer women, in 1918 voted Mother Philippine Duchesne as the greatest benefactress. They put an account of her life and work into their archives and had her name inscribed on a bronze tablet, placed in the Jefferson Memorial Building, St. Louis.

[*Mother Philippine Duchesne* (1879), by Abbé Louis Baunard, translated from the French by Lady Georgiana Fullerton; M. T. Kelly, *A Life's Ambition* (1910); G. E. McGloin, *Venerable Philippine Duchesne* (1914); *A Grain of Wheat* (1918); Marjory Erskine, *Mother Philippine Duchesne* (1926); unpublished letters and journals.]   M.E.

DUDLEY, BENJAMIN WINSLOW (Apr. 12, 1785–Jan. 20, 1870), surgeon, one of the fourteen children of Ambrose Dudley, a captain in the Revolutionary army and later a well-known Baptist preacher, was born in Spotsylvania County, Va. When one year of age he was taken to Kentucky by his parents and grew up near Lexington. His somewhat meager early education was acquired at the Lexington schools and there he began the study of medicine under the direction of Dr. Frederick Ridgely, of whom he always spoke in terms of warmest praise. In 1804 he entered the University of Pennsylvania and there received the degree of M.D. (1806). He returned home and began practise, at the same time, in order to acquire funds for further study, engaging in trade. In 1810 he went to New Orleans on a flatboat and buying a shipload of flour sailed for Europe. In Gibraltar and Lisbon he sold his cargo and made his way through Spain to Paris. Here and in London he spent four years of study under such masters as Larrey, Cooper, and Abernethy. Returning, a member of the Royal College of Surgeons, to Lexington (1814) he began a long career of professional toil, taking no vacations and rarely leaving the city. At the founding of the medical department of Transylvania University (1817) he became professor of anatomy and surgery, his former fellow students, Daniel Drake [*q.v.*] and Richardson, also accepting chairs. Misunderstandings characterized the opening of the new school, followed by pamphleteering, and culminating in a duel in which Dudley wounded Richardson in the thigh and then saved his life by promptly (and with Richardson's permission) stopping the blood flow with his thumb. In 1836 he successfully removed a cataract and gave sight to a man who had been blind since birth, the first operation of its kind in what was then called the West. Lexington having proved too small to support a medical school, in 1837 an attempt was made to transfer the institution to Louisville, but Dudley declined to leave, and followed the waning fortunes of the school until it closed, his last lecture being delivered in 1850. He retired from practise in 1853 except for an occasional consultation. His last years were spent in comfort at "Fairlawn," his country place near Lexington, and there he died.

In many respects Dudley was in advance of his time. He condemned blood letting, saying that a man's life is shortened a year for each bleeding. He had great faith in the value of boiled water in surgery and used quantities of it at the time of his operations and in the after care of his cases. His technique was characterized by absolute cleanliness in every detail for, though bacteriology was an undreamed-of science, he realized that filth, dirt, and impure water in some way contain the seeds of disease. His fear of impure water was particularly valuable during the cholera epidemic in Lexington (1832) when those who followed his advice escaped. He was original in the use of the trephine in traumatic epilepsy and in the treatment (by gradual pressure) of fungus cerebri, and was particularly skilful in the use of the bandage in medical as well as surgical conditions. On the other hand his treatment of tuberculous diseases by wasting diet is hard to reconcile with his otherwise sound views. His chief claim to fame as a surgeon must rest on his operation for bladder stone, in which he was more successful than any surgeon up to that time. During his life he operated in 225 such cases with a loss of only three. His work was all done without anesthesia but the patients' suffering did not destroy his calm self-possession. His surgery was always conservative. He was a pioneer in the preparative treatment of patients requiring operation and not only attempted to return the body as nearly as possible to normal before operation, but also required of his assistants a minute examination of every organ—a forerunner of the medical surveys of the hospital of to-day. He had little taste for writing and had been a successful teacher for years before he published anything. Indeed it is not unlikely that the appearance of the *Transylvania University Journal of Medicine and the Associate Sciences* (1828), edited by his brother-in-law, Dr. Charles W. Short, which required something from his pen, was his only incentive, and apparently all his writings were published in this journal. In the first issue he described the technique of his trephining operation for traumatic epilepsy and in subsequent numbers his operations for fungus cerebri, hydrocele, fractures, calculus, ligation of the perineal artery, the use of the bandage, etc. Gross credits him with being the first in the West to ligate the subclavian artery (1825). He married, in 1821, Anna Maria, daughter of Maj. Peyton Short, who died in early life, leaving three children.

[L. P. Yandell, "A Memoir of the Life and Writings of Dr. Benj. W. Dudley," *Am. Practitioner,* Mar. 1870; Bedford Brown, "Personal Recollections of the late Dr. Benj. W. Dudley," *Trans. Southern Surgic. & Gynecol. Asso.,* 1892; Lewis and R. H. Collins, *Hist. of Ky.* (1874), I, 51, and II, 218; Robt. Peter, *The Hist. of the Medic. Dept. of Transylvania Univ.* (1905), being Filson Club Pubs. No. 20; Sketch by B. W. Dudley in H. A. Kelly and W. L. Burrage, *Am. Medic. Biogs.* (1920); Archibald H. Barkley, *Kentucky's Pioneer Lithotomists* (1913); obituary note in *N. Y. Tribune,* Jan. 25, 1870.]   E.E.H.

DUDLEY, CHARLES BENJAMIN (July 14, 1842–Dec. 21, 1909), railroad chemist, was born at Oxford, Chenango County, N. Y., the son of Daniel and Miranda (Bemis) Dudley. His youth was given over to rugged labor in field and shop with such educational opportunities as the country school and local academy afforded. On Aug. 6, 1862, he responded to Lincoln's call, enlisting in Company A, 114th Regiment, New York Volunteers and serving until he was severely wounded, Sept. 19, 1864, at the battle of Opequon Creek, near Winchester, Va., and invalided home. Longing for a college education, he carried text-books into camp and conned them as he could. He entered Yale College in 1867. Obliged to work his way through, he engaged largely in newspaper work, becoming managing editor of the *Yale Courant* and, later, night editor of the *New Haven Palladium,* but he maintained so high a standard of scholarship in college as to win an oration at Commencement and election to the Phi Beta Kappa. He achieved his Ph.D. at the Sheffield Scientific School in 1874, majoring in chemistry.

On Nov. 10, 1875, he was appointed chemist to the Pennsylvania Railroad Company, and he died in service. Although railroad officials had occasionally, and casually, had analyses, or tests, made by consulting chemists, Dudley was the first person appointed as chemist to a railroad corporation to give his full time to applying his knowledge to the solution of the problems of such an organization. His appointment to this position was made at a time when much skepticism prevailed as to the value of the services of a university-trained scientific man in the practical affairs of life. Dudley was burly in form, rugged of countenance, had a luxuriant growth of somewhat rebellious hair and beard, which early became grizzled. He chose durable garments of a grayish nature. Limping from the effects of his wound, which necessitated the constant use of a cane, he was a most wintrish looking man. But the crinkles about his eyes revealed his well developed sense of humor and his philanthropic disposition, which was confirmed by the kindliness and warmth of his greeting. Accustomed to mingling with all sorts and conditions of men and having diligently made himself master of his subject, he listened sympathetically to the points of view of those with whom he dealt and discussed the problem tactfully but with definiteness and determination. Entering on his duties at Altoona with enthusiasm, he soon disclosed a multitude of opportunities for the application of chemistry and physics in increasing the economy, efficiency and safety of railroad maintenance and operations. His first publication from this study, "The Chemical Composition and Physical Properties of Steel Rails" (*Transactions American Institute of Mining Engineers,* Vol. VII, 1878, pp. 172–201), created great excitement among steel manufacturers, who viewed with trepidation chemical and physical supervision of their products, and antagonized many metallurgists, but Dudley continued to publish comparisons of laboratory findings with results from practise and his fundamental ideas eventually prevailed.

A series of articles on "Chemistry Applied to Railroads," by Dudley, and his associate chemist, F. N. Pease (*American Engineering and Railroad Journal*, 1889–1902), made widely known the essential value of the chemist in this field. He early stressed purchase according to specifications and was the first to write into specifications descriptions of the tests to be applied. It was through his efforts that the Bureau for the Safe Transportation of Explosives and Other Dangerous Articles, of the American Railway Association, was created, and that Congress was led to enact legislation conferring regulatory powers on the Interstate Commerce Commission. He was twice president of the American Chemical Society; was president, 1902–09, of the American Society for Testing Materials; president of the International Association for Testing Materials; chairman of the National Advisory Board on Fuels and Structural Materials, and head of many other organizations. He was most active in the service of Altoona and the state of Pennsylvania. He married Mary Virginia Crawford, Apr. 17, 1906, but died without issue.

[*Memorial Volume Commemorative of the Life and Life-Work of Charles Benjamin Dudley* (n.d.), pub. by the Am. Soc. for Testing Materials; *Who's Who in America*, 1906–07; *Am. Men of Science* (1906); *Public Ledger* (Phila.), Dec. 22, 1909; personal knowledge.]

C.E.M.

DUDLEY, CHARLES EDWARD (May 23, 1780–Jan. 23, 1841), politician, was born in England during the American Revolution, the son of Loyalist parents. His father, Charles Dudley, an Englishman, was Collector of the King's Customs at Newport, R. I., where he married Catherine Cooke, of a Rhode Island colonial family. In November 1775, he abandoned his office at Newport and sought refuge on board a British ship of war. In the following year he took up his residence in England, where his wife joined him, and in 1780 at Johnson Hall, Stafford, their son, Charles Edward, was born. Ten years later the father died and in 1795 the mother returned to her native town, bringing with her the fifteen-year-old lad, whose schooling was obtained at Newport. Near the opening of the nineteenth century, young Dudley was making voyages from New York to the East Indies as supercargo. During the War of 1812, and probably several years earlier, he was living at Albany, N. Y., where he married Blandina Bleecker, a member of a substantial Albany family. He entered public life in his late thirties. Known as a successful and generous man of affairs and an affable gentleman, he was repeatedly chosen by the Common Council as mayor of Albany and sat in the state Senate from 1820 to 1825.

As a stepping-stone to a place of power in New York State politics, his membership in the "Albany Regency," headed by Martin Van Buren, was more important than any state or local office within his grasp. Like the other members of the Regency, he was a man of personal integrity and, unlike some of the most eminent among them, he had skill and address in dealing with individuals. The details of troublesome patronage problems might safely be left to him, while Van Buren, Marcy, Wright, and other leaders were busied with the big question of public policy. Accordingly, Dudley became and long remained a useful member of the conclave. While he had a seat in the state Senate the Regency had to face the most critical situation in its career—the fight with DeWitt Clinton [*q.v.*]. Dudley, and his fellow senator, Silas Wright, voted for the expulsion of Clinton from the Canal Board, and they also voted to postpone the provision for popular choice of presidential electors. Through their votes the Regency declared itself. Meanwhile, Dudley kept Van Buren, now a Senator at Washington, informed as to Albany developments.

When Van Buren resigned his United States senatorship to become governor of New York, Dudley, having been defeated for a seat in the House of Representatives, was sent to Washington in his place. He was an early example of the business man in the Senate, where he played an inconspicuous rôle, but loyally supported the Jackson administration by his votes. He retired at the end of his term and passed the rest of his life at Albany, retaining his interest in Democratic politics. He received no public recognition from Van Buren as President. In 1856, fifteen years after his death, his widow provided funds for an astronomical observatory at Albany which received her husband's name. She was actuated in this generous act partly by the interest in astronomy that Dudley had manifested during his lifetime.

[Dean Dudley, *Hist. of the Dudley Family* (1886–94), pp. 10 and 203–04 (data supplied by Dudley's widow); Lorenzo Sabine, *Biog. Sketches of Loyalists of the Am. Rev.* (1864), I, 394; Cuyler Reynolds, *Albany Chronicles* (1906); Joel Munsell, *Annals of Albany* (1850–59) and *Colls. on the Hist. of Albany*, vol. II (1867); eulogy by Gov. Washington Hunt, *Inauguration of the Dudley Observatory at Albany* (1856); *Biog. Dir. Am. Cong.* (1928); *Albany Argus*, Jan. 25, 1841.]

W.B.S.

DUDLEY, EDWARD BISHOP (Dec. 15, 1789–Oct. 30, 1855), congressman from North Carolina, governor, railroad president, was born in Onslow County, N. C., where his father, Christopher, was prominent in farming, business, and politics as other Dudleys had been for generations (*Onslow County Record*, Dec. 1, 1827, Jan. 5, 1828). Though his early education was defective, Onslow sent him to the House of Commons (1811, 1812), and the state Senate (1814) where he displayed interest in military affairs. During the War of 1812 he went to Wilmington second in command of the Onslow regiment, and there settled. Big and handsome, genial and generous, the young officer was soon in the House of Commons from Wilmington and manifesting intelligent interest in navigation companies and state banking enterprises. Soon he married Eliza Haywood, of the Raleigh banker-politician family, who eventually bore him five children. When the state board of internal improvements was reorganized in 1824, he became one of its three members. Five years later the death of his father put large financial resources under his control (letter of John Sprunt Hill). Early in 1824 he became the Jackson representative on the anti-Crawford electoral ticket which later cast the state's vote for Jackson; and in late 1829 he became a Jacksonian congressman. His independent spirit, however, soon made him violently anti-Jackson. He was now ready for his big rôle. Returning to the House of Commons from the Wilmington borough, he supported the West in its fight against the Democratic East for constitutional reform and, in turn, secured important legislation, notably for the building of the Wilmington & Raleigh Railroad with state aid. In 1836 he was nominated for governor on the Whig ticket by a series of county conventions, which emphasized national issues (as did his own brief letter of acceptance) but were obviously influenced also by considerations of business and personal liking (*Raleigh Register*, January-March 1836). The West elected him in August (though in November the state went for Van Buren), and two years later reëlected him by a large majority. The years of his governorship (1837-40) marked the beginning of "a new period of economic and social development" (Boyd, *post*, p. 229). To him as chairman of the Internal Improvement and Literary Fund Boards fell primarily the investing of large funds which distribution of the federal surplus brought so as to further banking, railroads and drainage and lay the fiscal foundation for public education; and, despite some complaint of preference to Whigs in the matter, the task was well performed. On the basis of an able report which he procured, he recommended a cautious beginning of state public schools. Keenly sensitive to the economic backwardness of North Carolina —"our Rip Van Winkle"—and captivated by

the possibilities in railroad development, he sought to commit the state to a vast scheme of internal improvements financed by a huge state bank (Message, 1838; letters to Swain, March, August 1839); but the legislature would not then follow him. His greatest achievement, however, was the Wilmington & Raleigh Railroad, later (1855) the Wilmington & Weldon, the longest in the world for several years. He secured its charter, led in subscribing its capital, served as its president (1836-37, 1841-47), saved it by his personal credit from bankruptcy, secured its first feeder (the Wilmington & Manchester), and mapped out extensions which, as the Atlantic Coast Line, it later followed "precisely" (Sprunt, *post*, p. 137). He held no public office after 1840. Wealthy and exceedingly hospitable—Webster found his Madeira excellent— he gave little attention to business after 1847. His health becoming poor, he turned toward religion and ultimately joined St. James's Church (letter of Manly to Swain, Nov. 5, 1855), from which he was buried with military honors. The state at large and Wilmington in particular pronounced him among the foremost of benefactors.

[J. H. Wheeler, *Reminiscences and Memoirs of N. C. and Eminent North Carolinians* (1884); J. G. deR. Hamilton, *Party Politics in N. C. 1835-60* (1916); and Jas. Sprunt, *Chronicles of the Cape Fear River* (1914), are most valuable for personal information. W. K. Boyd, *Hist. of N. C.* (1919), and S. A. Ashe, *Hist. of N. C.*, vol. II (1925), supply background and some detail. The *Wilmington Jour.*, Nov. 2, 5, 12, and the *Raleigh Reg.*, Nov. 5, 1855, contain complimentary obituaries. C. L. Coon, *The Beginnings of Public Educ. in N. C.* (1908), vol. II, contains many documents. Some personal letters are in the Swain Papers in possession of the N. C. Hist. Commission. See also Wm. H. Hoyt, *The Papers of Archibald D. Murphey* (1914), esp. I, 291; and, for his activities in the legislature, *Jours. of the Senate and House of . . . Commons of N. C.*, 1816, 1817, and 1834, esp. pp. 219-22.] **C.C.P.**

DUDLEY, JOSEPH (Sept. 23, 1647-Apr. 2, 1720), colonial governor, born at Roxbury, Mass., was the seventh child of a father already seventy years old, Thomas Dudley [*q.v.*], the second governor of the colony, and his second wife, Catherine (Dighton) Hackburn. The redoubtable Thomas died when Joseph was only five; and the child's mother marrying again, he was brought up by his step-father, the Rev. John Allin (or Allyn), minister of the chlrch at Dedham. Dudley graduated from Harvard in 1665 with the intention of becoming a clergyman but soon turned to politics. The marriages of his sisters, one of them to Simon Bradstreet [*q.v.*], the last governor under the charter, helped Dudley politically and he himself in 1668 married Rebecca (born July 13, 1651), daughter of Edward Tyng, who was an Assistant for thirteen years and afterward a member of the Council. By his wife, who died Sept. 21, 1722, Dudley had thirteen children. He became a freeman in 1672 and was a member of the General Court as representative from Roxbury, 1673–76. He took part in King Philip's War and was then elected to the upper house of the legislature every year, except 1684, until the revocation of the old charter. He frequently served on important committees and from 1677 to 1681 was one of the commissioners of the United Colonies. He also gained much skill and reputation as a negotiator with the Indians.

In 1682 he was chosen to go to England as one of two agents sent to avert the threatened *quo warranto* proceedings and the loss of the charter. The charter was practically lost, however, before he sailed from Boston on May 31. He himself, indeed, was not wholly opposed to an alteration in the form of the colonial government which would bring it more within the control of the imperial authorities. He had wider views than had most of "the faction" at home and, whether from ambition or a genuine belief that he could harmonize the relations between the mother country and the recalcitrant colony, he adopted a line that many of the "die-hard" party in the colony regarded as treasonable. On Oct. 23, 1684, the charter was declared vacated, and when a temporary government was erected Dudley was made president of the Council and governor of Massachusetts, New Hampshire, and the King's Province. The new government assumed office May 17, 1686, the members of the General Court protesting against its legality. It was avowedly of a temporary nature and after seven months gave way to the more comprehensive scheme of unification under Sir Edmund Andros [*q.v.*]. It was fortunate for Massachusetts that Dudley should have bridged over the transition from the old charter government rather than such a man as was first proposed by the English government, but radical Massachusetts felt that she had been betrayed by one of her own household.

His administration ended when Andros arrived at Boston, Dec. 19, 1686, but although superseded as governor he became the most prominent member of Andros's Council and held many offices. He was placed on important committees, made censor of the press, chief justice of the superior court, and had a hand in forcing obedience to the hated laws passed during the Andros régime. In consequence of the feeling against him, it was necessary for his own safety to place him in jail when the Andros government was overthrown in 1689, and he remained confined for ten months until the king ordered

him released and taken to England. There, 119 charges, mainly of illegal acts in the administration of justice, were preferred against him by a committee composed of seven of the leading colonists. Dudley made a dignified defense and in the end was properly acquitted of any wrongdoing. Although he apparently had acted in strict conformity with law in carrying out the new royal policy, he had nevertheless made himself the most hated man in New England, a title for which at that time, there was no slight competition.

Although exonerated, Dudley was in an unhappy position. He was distrusted in the land of his birth, which he loved, and the king whom he had served had been replaced by William III. He still had some friends in England, however, notably William Blathwayt, and through their influence was appointed chief of the Council of New York. He yet looked toward New England and an ultimate return there but did able and useful work in his new post. Always a strong "prerogative man," he became unpopular in his new province for much the same reasons that he had gained disfavor in his native one. He was chief justice during the Leisler troubles and took a leading part in Leisler's trial. Although his course was entirely legal it was vastly unpopular and still further damaged his American reputation. In 1692, he resigned office, returned to Massachusetts and settled once more at Roxbury. There he regained the trust of some of his former friends but by February 1693 he was again in England. In London he found old, and made some important new, acquaintances, notably Lord Cutts, who was soon appointed governor of the Isle of Wight and made Dudley his deputy. About this time the latter conformed to the Church of England. He had now become an English official in the homeland, had a recognized position in English society, corresponded with eminent men, among them Sir Richard Steele, and led a very different life from that of his compatriots in Massachusetts.

He still had his property in New England, his expenses were more than his income warranted, and he seemed always to retain a love for his native colony if not for all of its institutions. On Apr. 1, 1702, he received the long-coveted commission as governor of Massachusetts and sailed for Boston on the 13th. The day he landed he met the General Court and began the struggle which was to be continuous for the rest of his public life. With regard to his personal salary, always one of the bones of contention, Dudley compromised, but in all other matters during his administration he exhibited little of the compromising spirit and insisted on upholding the prerogative at the expense of personal popularity. He was more than once threatened with personal violence and on one occasion had to defend himself in England against accusations of serious wrong-doing. He came out of this successfully and, in reality, under the new conditions, had rendered considerable service to the colony. Perhaps his qualities appeared to the best advantage in the military expeditions against Canada. The colonial opposition, however, became too strong and in 1715 he was replaced by Gov. Shute. In the four years of private life still left to him he regained some of his early popularity.

Dudley was unmitigatedly damned by the earlier American historians. He thought in terms of empire rather than of his own province. By the standards of eighteenth-century political life he ranks high in personal integrity. In the broader views taken to-day of the colonial problems, his political ideals need not be harshly condemned. His character, however, remains an unsympathetic one. He was ambitious, self-seeking, cold, and ungrateful to his friends. He loved power for the influence which it gave, and was ambitious to be an English gentleman. The colony, whether from pride or relief, gave him one of the most ostentatious funerals of that funereal age.

[Although limiting itself closely to the aspect indicated in its title, *The Public Life of Joseph Dudley* (1911), by Everett Kimball, is a most excellent and scholarly biography. The bibliography at the end covers all the important source material relating to Dudley. For genealogy see also Geo. Adlard, *The Sutton-Dudleys of England and the Dudleys of Mass.* (1862) and Dean Dudley, *Hist. of the Dudley Family* (1886–94).]

J.T.A.

DUDLEY, PAUL (Sept. 3, 1675–Jan. 25, 1751), jurist, was born at Roxbury, Mass., with which place both his grandfather, Gov. Thomas Dudley, and his father, Gov. Joseph Dudley [*qq.v.*], were intimately associated. The latter married Rebecca, daughter of Judge Edward Tyng, and Paul was their fourth and eldest surviving son. He entered Harvard College in 1686 and graduated in 1690. After reading law for a short time in Boston, he went to England, became a student at the Middle Temple, Nov. 10, 1697, and was called to the bar Nov. 22, 1700. In 1702, having received a commission from Queen Anne as attorney-general of the province of Massachusetts Bay and advocate in the vice-admiralty court at Boston, he returned to America. On his arrival he was appointed attorney-general by the Governor and Council, it being considered expedient not to use the Royal commission in view of a sharp disagreement between

the Council and Assembly as to the right to appoint. For some years his position in Boston was difficult, partly because of his zeal in championing the claims of the Crown to interfere in the administration of provincial affairs, but chiefly by reason of the unpopularity of his father and the bitter animosity of the Mather faction. He fulfilled his duties, however, with much tact, and his absolute integrity and sincere patriotism became gradually recognized. One of his first official acts was to take proceedings against and arrest a body of pirates who were infesting the coasts, some of whom were subsequently executed in Boston (*Rex* vs. *Quelch et al., 5 American State Trials,* 330). He was later elected a member of the legislature and the Executive Council, and in that capacity introduced reforms which materially improved the machinery of justice. In 1718 he was appointed a judge of the superior court of judicature, and contemporaries without exception testify that on the bench he displayed great ability. A sound lawyer, energetic, industrious, and attentive to the dispatch of business, he acquired the confidence and respect of the public, and his appointment as chief justice of Massachusetts in 1745 met with unanimous approval. He retained this position till his death, which occurred at Roxbury, Jan. 25, 1751. In 1703 he had married Lucy, daughter of Col. John Wainwright of Ipswich.

He was an accomplished naturalist, deeply interested in the local antiquities, and wrote a number of pamphlets dealing chiefly with natural history, also contributing papers to the Royal Society, which were published in *Philosophical Transactions,* vols. XXXI, XXXII, XXXIII, XXXIV, and XXXIX. He was one of the few Americans to be elected members of that body. In his later years he became a pronounced Puritan in religious matters, and wrote *An Essay on the Merchandize of Slaves and Souls of Men* (1731) and a number of theological tracts. In his will he left a bequest to Harvard College for the purpose of providing an annual lecture or sermon dealing with one of four designated theological subjects. Generous, hospitable, and charitable, "he was apt to be a little antiquated and out of fashion in his dress. . . . When off the Bench he would often be seen conversing familiarly with the commonest people, having his hands upon their shoulders" (Dean Dudley, *post,* p. 526). He could, however, be imperious and even dictatorial, if he considered the occasion demanded it.

[A detailed account of Dudley's ancestry will be found in Dean Dudley, *Hist. of the Dudley Family* (1894), I, 16 ff., which also contains original material for his life and career. See also F. S. Drake, *The Town* of Roxbury (1878) ; Emory Washburn, *Sketches of the Judicial Hist. of Mass.* (1840) ; Edward Alfred Jones, *Am. Members of the Inns of Court* (1924), p. 65 ; *Calendar of State Papers, Colonial Ser. 1706–08* (1916).]

H. W. H. K.

DUDLEY, THOMAS (1576–July 31, 1653), governor of the colony of Massachusetts Bay, was the only son of a certain Captain Roger Dudley of whom we know nothing save that he was "slain in the wars," leaving Thomas and his sister orphans at a very early age. Thomas, who was born at Northampton, England, and is said to have inherited £500, was befriended by one "Mrs. Puefroy" during his earlier childhood and sent by her to a Latin school (Adlard, *post,* p. 24). He later became page in the household of the Earl of Northampton, where he was trained in the manners of a nobleman's family. When a young man he was taken as a clerk by a kinsman on his mother's side, Judge Nichols, and became acquainted with legal practise. A little later England went to the support of Henry IV of France, and many young men from Northampton went to the front, Dudley going with them as captain. Although he got as far as Amiens he saw no fighting, and after peace was declared returned to England and settled again in the neighborhood of Northampton. There he met and married, Apr. 25, 1603, Dorothy Yorke (*Colonial Society Massachusetts Publications,* vol. XXV, 1922, p. 18), a lady whom Mather described as "a gentlewoman both of good estate and good extraction" (Adlard, *post,* p. 26). By her he had five children.

About the time of his marriage he became more deeply religious and, probably under the influence of the Puritan clergy of his neighborhood, avowed himself what Mather calls a "judicious Dissenter." In some way he came under the observation of Lord Saye and Sele and certain other noblemen ; they recommended him as steward to the young Earl of Lincoln who had just inherited his title and property. The estate was in a very confused condition and encumbered with debts which proved to amount to almost £20,000. In the nine years during which he served the young earl, Dudley not only succeeded in paying off the debts, reducing the estate to order, and increasing the income, but also in arranging a marriage between him and the daughter of Lord Saye and Sele. Apparently Dudley himself, either through his marriage or his own savings, had become well-to-do; retiring from Lincoln's service, he moved to Boston in Lincolnshire where he took a house and became a member of the congregation of the Rev. John Cotton. However, he had proved so useful to the earl that he was requested to return to his service and did so, remaining until he emigrated to New England.

He had been interested in the formation of the Massachusetts Bay Company and had been in close touch with the leaders of that enterprise from at least 1629. In 1630 he sailed on the *Arbella* with Winthrop, Saltonstall, and others of the chief men. They arrived at Salem June 12 and at first settled at Newtown. Before leaving England, Winthrop had been elected governor and Dudley deputy-governor. A somewhat violent disagreement between the two men, the first of many owing to Dudley's touchy and over-bearing temper, occurred when Winthrop abandoned the chosen settlement and moved to Boston. Dudley subsequently moved to Ipswich but after a short time, in order to be nearer the seat of government, definitely settled at Roxbury. Although Dudley was fifty-four years of age when he landed in New England he had still a long public career ahead of him. Throughout the rest of his life he was almost constantly in public office. He was elected governor in 1634, 1640, 1645, and 1650. He was thirteen times made deputy-governor and when not occupying either of these offices was usually to be found in the House as an Assistant. When the Standing Council was inaugurated with the idea of forming a body of members for life, Dudley was one of the three first chosen. When the New England Confederation was formed in 1643 Dudley was one of the two commissioners chosen by Massachusetts to confer with those of the other colonies. He was one of the founders of the First Church at Charlestown, July 30, 1630. He was one of the committee appointed in 1637 to consider the establishment of a college at Cambridge; he was one of the first Overseers of Harvard, and in 1650, as governor, signed the charter for that institution. In fact, there is hardly an event in the life of the colony during his own in which he did not act a part. He was evidently as strong in body as he was unyielding in temper and unbreakable in will. His first wife died, aged sixty-one, at Roxbury on Dec. 27, 1643. On Apr. 14 of the following year he married Mrs. Catherine (Dighton) Hackburn, the widow of Samuel Hackburn of Roxbury. She survived him and took a third husband in the Rev. John Allin (or Allyn) of Dedham. By her, Dudley had three children, the most noted, Joseph [*q.v.*], being Dudley's seventh child, born when the old man was seventy years of age.

Dudley was an able man with marked executive and business ability. His integrity was unimpeachable. His eye, though somewhat religiously jaundiced, was single to the public interest as he saw it. He was something of a scholar and wrote poetry, read in his day though unreadable in ours. In him New England Puritanism took on some of its harshest and least pleasant aspects. He often won approval but never affection. He was positive, dogmatic, austere, prejudiced, unlovable. He dominated by sheer strength of will as a leader in his community. Like many of the others he was no friend to popular government and a strong believer in autocracy. Opposed to the clergy in one respect, he believed that the state should control even the church and enforce conformity as the superior, and not the handmaid, of the ecclesiastical organization. In a poem of his own, found in his pocket after his death, we have his last mesage. It was, "hate heresy" and

> "Let men of God in courts and churches watch
> O'er such as do a *toleration* hatch."

[There are several volumes on the genealogy of the Dudley family: Geo. Adlard, *The Sutton-Dudleys of England and the Dudleys of Mass.* (1862) ; Dean Dudley, *Hist. of the Dudley Family* (1886–94) ; and *The Dudley Genealogies and Family Records* (1848). Cotton Mather has a brief sketch in *Magnalia Christi Americana* (edition of 1853), I, 131–35. He also wrote a longer account which, long thought to be lost, was found and printed by Adlard.]   J.T.A.

DUDLEY, WILLIAM RUSSEL (Mar. 1, 1849–June 4, 1911), botanist, the son of Samuel William and Lucy (Chittenden) Dudley, was born at Guilford, Conn., where his ancestor, William Dudley, had settled about 1637. In early youth he became interested in the out-of-doors, especially in plants and birds, and when it came time to go to college he decided to be a botanist and chose Cornell, because at that time this newly founded university offered better facilities in science than did Yale. A letter of introduction brought him in contact with David Starr Jordan, who, although still an undergraduate, was instructor in botany in charge of the laboratory work. Dudley became the collector of plants for Jordan's class, and the two together, as Dr. Jordan says in his *Days of a Man* (I, 55), "roamed over all the hills and to all the waterfalls within thirty miles of Ithaca." On these tramps they began a catalogue of the Cayuga Lake region, which was later completed and published by Dudley. In his junior year he was given the instructorship in botany, which had been left vacant by the graduation of Jordan. In 1874 he was granted the degree of B.S. and two years later that of M.S. In the same year, 1876, he was promoted to assistant professor, a position he held until 1892 when he was called to Stanford University as professor of systematic botany. While at Cornell he was granted a year's leave of absence in 1880 to become acting professor of biology at the

University of Indiana, a chair held by Jordan, who was away on leave. Again in 1887 he was granted leave to study abroad at the universities of Berlin and Strassburg.

Stanford University was beginning its second year when Dudley became a member of the faculty, and he entered with enthusiasm into building up his department and especially the botanical collections in the new institution. As a student of trees he became interested in the conservation of the forests and was frequently called upon by the United States forester, Gifford Pinchot, for botanical information and advice in the early development of the national forests in California. He was an active and influential member of the Sempervirens Club, the pioneer organization interested in the preservation of the redwood (*Sequoia sempervirens*), and was instrumental in the establishment of the California Redwood Park, the first public preserve of the redwood. He was appointed on the park commission by the governor of California, and served as secretary of the commission for several years. He was a born teacher of rare quality; his quiet, dignified, courteous manner, his thoroughness and enthusiasm in his work, formed lasting impressions upon his students. Although Dudley was a diligent and thorough student, he wrote comparatively little. Of the approximately forty scientific papers which he published, the more important are : *The Cayuga Flora* (1886) ; *A Catalogue of the Flowering Plants and Vascular Cryptogams found in and near Lackawanna and Wyoming Valleys* (1892), with Clarence O. Thurston ; *The Genus Phyllospadix* (1893) ; and "The Vitality of Sequoia Gigantea" read in 1905 and published in the *Dudley Memorial Volume.*

Undoubtedly Dudley's most important contribution to science was the collection of the extensive herbarium to which he devoted so much time, labor, and money. All these collections were presented by him to Stanford and form the nucleus of the university's botanical collections, which have been named the Dudley Herbarium, a lasting and growing monument in his honor.

[*Who's Who in America,* 1910–11 ; *Dudley Memorial Volume* (Stanford Univ., 1911) ; D. S. Jordan, *Days of a Man* (2 vols., 1922) ; Dean Dudley, *Hist. of the Dudley Family,* nos. 1 and 4 (1886, 1890).]   L.R.A.

DUER, JOHN (Oct. 7, 1782–Aug. 8, 1858), jurist, the second son of William Duer [*q.v.*] and his wife, Catherine Alexander, was born at Albany, N. Y. His education was intermittent and scanty. His father's financial troubles undoubtedly reacted unfavorably on his prospects and in 1798 he enlisted in the United States army. Two years later he obtained his discharge and commenced the study of law in the office of Alexander Hamilton, who had been his father's friend, at the same time taking steps to remedy the deficiencies of his early education by self-instruction. He was admitted as an attorney in 1806, and started practise in Orange County, N. Y., where he soon acquired a good connection, becoming known as a careful adviser and successful advocate. In 1821 he was a delegate from Orange County to the state constitutional convention of that year, and took a distinguished part in its proceedings, being a member of the committee on the judiciary department and exhibiting a grasp of public law, fertility of resource, and capacity for argument which gave him a state-wide reputation. In 1825 he was appointed to fill the vacancy on the commission to revise the New York statutes, caused by the resignation of Chancellor Kent. His fellow commissioners were Benjamin F. Butler and later John C. Spencer, and by a "kind of inspiration . . . the idea came to them of replacing the mass of disconnected statutes by a new and complete system of original laws systematically and scientifically arranged" (Butler, *post*). A large and important section of this work was performed by Duer. (See *The Revised Statutes of the State of New York, 1827–28,* 3 vols., 1829, *1828–35,* 3 vols., *1835–36,* edited by J. Duer, B. F. Butler and J. C. Spencer.) He was actively engaged in the revision till 1827, when he withdrew on his appointment as United States district attorney for southern New York. This latter position he held till the change of administration in 1829, when he resumed practise in New York City. Devoting his attention particularly to commercial and insurance law, he was recognized as an expert in the latter subject. In 1844 he published, *A Lecture on the Law of Representations in Marine Insurance* which attracted wide attention. This was followed by *A Treatise on the Law and Practise of Marine Insurance* (vols. I and II, 1845, 1846), a monumental and exhaustive work, the plan of which contemplated a third volume, which, however, was never completed. He also published a *Discourse on the Life, Character and Public Services of James Kent* (1848). In 1849 he was elected a judge of the superior court of the City of New York, becoming chief justice, May 10, 1857. On the bench he was notable for his personal charm of manner and unvarying dignity, but his inclination occasionally prompted him to merge the judge in the advocate, and he was apt to be somewhat discursive (Butler, *post*). He was the author of six volumes of *Reports of Cases Argued and Determined in the Superior Court of the City of New York* (1–6

Duer, 1852–57). His standing as a lawyer was high; Judge Silliman spoke of him as "the very lofty, learned and accomplished John Duer," and Charles O'Conor regarded him as the ablest jurist of his time in America. His opinions carried great weight and were always expressed in a form and language which rendered them models of their kind. He died on Staten Island, in his seventy-sixth year. His wife was Anna Bedford Bunner, daughter of George Bunner.

[The best appreciation of Duer's life and character appeared in Wm. Allen Butler, *The Revision of the Statutes of the State of N. Y., and the Revisers* (1889); see also D. McAdam, *Hist. of the Bench and Bar of N. Y.* (1897), I, 314; "The Duers," N. Y. *Evening Post,* Apr. 27, 1901; *Green Bag,* Sept. 1892; "In Memoriam," 6 *Duer,* preface and p. vi.]   H. W. H. K.

DUER, WILLIAM (Mar. 18, 1747–May 7, 1799), merchant and financier, was born in Devonshire, England. His father, John Duer, who was wealthy, owning large plantations in Antigua and Dominica, married Frances Frye, and William was their third son. He was educated at Eton, obtained a commission as ensign in the British army, received an appointment as aide-de-camp to Lord Clive and accompanied the latter when he returned to India as Governor of Bengal in 1764. He was unable to withstand the climate, however, and returned to England. Shortly afterward, on his father's death, he inherited a share in the paternal plantations and went to the West Indies. In 1768, having obtained a contract to supply masts and spars for the British navy, he visited New York for the purpose of purchasing timber. There he met Philip Schuyler of Albany under whose advice he purchased an extensive tract of timber-land on the Hudson River above Saratoga, N. Y., and established large sawmills. He also made other investments. In 1773 he went to England, settled his affairs in that country, and on his return made the province of New York his permanent home. From his first arrival in New York he had associated with the leaders in its public life, and his liberal sentiments induced him to identify himself with the rapidly growing opposition to the home government. In 1775 he was a delegate to the Provincial Congress, being also appointed deputy adjutant-general of the New York troops, with the rank of colonel. In June 1776, he was a delegate to the New York constitutional convention and acted on the committee appointed to draft a constitution for the new state, his agile mind, fertility of expedients, and quick perception showing to advantage. In the same year he acted on the Committee of Public Safety, being designated at this period "as great a rebel as ever had an existence" (*post*). In March 1777, he was chosen as delegate from New York to the Continental Congress, where he was distinguished by his eloquence and extreme activity, serving on seven committees. He was on May 8 appointed first judge of common pleas of Charlotte (now Washington) County, N. Y., a position which he is credited with holding till 1786, *sed quaere*. In addition, he was a member of the Board of War, and a signer of the Articles of Confederation. His strong patriotism was signally displayed on the occasion of the Conway Cabal, when New York was temporarily deprived of its vote because of Duer's serious illness. This gave Washington's opponents in Congress a majority, and they planned to nominate a committee to remove the General from his command at Valley Forge. Word was sent to Duer, and despite his physician's warning that he could only be taken to Congress at the imminent risk of his life, he ordered his litter to be prepared and was about to make the journey, when the faction, hearing of his intent, abandoned the project (Dunlap, *post*, II, 133–34). He resigned from Congress in January 1779, in order to attend to his private affairs, but in July of the following year was appointed commissioner for conspiracies. He became immersed in many and varied commercial and financial projects, was engaged in furnishing supplies to the army, holding some of the largest contracts, and at the close of the war was in all probability a rich man. It was largely due to his efforts that in 1784 the Bank of New York was founded. In March 1786, he was appointed secretary to the Board of the Treasury, and established his residence permanently in New York City, becoming in the same year a member of the New York Assembly. In 1787 he was the prime mover in the Scioto speculation, he and his associates securing a right to purchase from the United States a huge tract of western lands, which they in turn designed to sell chiefly to capitalists abroad, particularly in France and Holland. He was also interested in an attempt to establish an international banking house which should supplant the great Dutch firms in the handling of loans and commercial business generally. In September 1789, the Treasury Department was organized, and Duer was appointed assistant secretary under his friend Alexander Hamilton, but resigned six months later, thus terminating his long connection with public life. Thenceforth he was continuously engaged in speculation on a large scale, involving purchases of lands in Massachusetts, Maine, and Vermont, contracts for army supplies during the Indian troubles of 1791, a project for a national manufacturing society in New Jersey, and large

dealings in stocks. He became seriously involved, and when suit was brought against him by the government, regarding two unbalanced charges when he was secretary of the Treasury Board, a catastrophe was precipitated. Hopelessly insolvent, he was arrested for debt on Mar. 23, 1792, and sent to prison. This circumstance caused the first financial panic in the history of New York. Despite strenuous efforts to extricate himself, except for a short period in 1797 when he was released at Alexander Hamilton's intercession, he remained in prison till his death on May 7, 1799.

In 1779 he married Catherine, commonly called "Lady Kitty," daughter of Maj.-Gen. William Alexander [*q.v.*], also known as Lord Stirling, Washington giving the bride away. Of their children, William Alexander Duer [*q.v.*] became chief justice of the superior court of the City of New York. Of tireless energy, persuasive eloquence, and far-sighted, he was a natural leader in his various spheres of activity. He possessed capacity for business, and his operations were always planned with skill and daring, but almost all his promotions failed. His powers of execution were not equal to his conceptions. He undertook too much to give efficient attention to details. The manner of his operations had been much criticized and questions raised as to how far, if at all, he used his official position to advance his private concerns. It is perhaps safe to state that, though many of his acts were ill-advised and lent themselves to misconstruction, there is no evidence to show that they transgressed the law or exceeded the limits set by the standard of the commercial morality of the times. His opinions and sympathies were democratic, and his devotion to the cause of the Revolution was sincere, but in his mode of living he was very much the aristocrat. A contemporary (Manasseh Cutler, *post*), describing a dinner at his house in his prosperous days, says: "Colonel Duer . . . lives in the style of a nobleman. I presume he had not less than fifteen different sorts of wine at dinner and after the cloth was removed."

[Two original authorities for the details of Duer's life are Thomas Jones, *Hist. of N. Y. During the Revolutionary War* (1879), ed. by E. F. De Lancey (1879), II, 587; and an anonymous article in *The Knickerbocker or New York Monthly Mag.*, Aug. 1852, said to be based on the Duer papers in the N. Y. Hist. Soc., but apparently untrustworthy in places. See also J. S. Davis, *Essays in the Earlier Hist. of Am. Corporations* (1917), containing copious references; Wm. Dunlap, *Hist. of the New Netherlands* (2 vols., 1839); *Minutes of the Commissioners for Detecting and Defeating Conspiracies in the State of N. Y. 1778–81* (1909); *Life, Jours. and Correspondence of Rev. Manasseh Cutler* (1888), I, 240–41; T. T. Belote, *The Scioto Speculation and the French Settlement at Gallipolis* (1907); and "The Duers," in N. Y. *Evening Post*, Apr. 27, 1901.]
                     H. W. H. K.

DUER, WILLIAM ALEXANDER (Sept. 8, 1780–May 30, 1858), jurist, educator, was born at Rhinebeck, N. Y., the son of William Duer [q.v.], a member of the Continental Congress, of the Revolutionary Committee of Safety, and of the committee that drafted the first constitution of the state of New York. His mother was Catherine Alexander, daughter of Gen. William Alexander [q.v.], claimant to the Scottish earldom of Stirling. As a very young child, Duer went with his parents to live in New York City, where they first rented the Philipse house at the corner of Pine and William Sts., and afterward settled permanently in a residence at "the upper extremity of Broadway," opposite St. Paul's Church. They were fain to content themselves "with this remote residence," Duer explained later, owing to the scarcity of houses. At the age of eleven he was sent to England to be educated, under the care of his maternal aunts, but in a few years he returned and enrolled at Erasmus Hall, in Flatbush, under Dr. Peter Wilson.

On leaving school he entered the law office of Pierre Étienne Du Ponceau [q.v.] of Philadelphia, and later that of Nathaniel Pendleton in New York. After interrupting his legal studies to enlist as midshipman against France, serving on the same ship with Decatur and in the same rank, he returned to the law and was admitted to the bar in 1802. He began practise in conjunction with Edward Livingston [q.v.], then United States district attorney and mayor of New York, but a little later he formed a partnership with his brother-in-law, Beverley Robinson. At this time he was a contributor to the *Corrector,* a newspaper edited by Dr. Peter Irving in support of Aaron Burr. His former partner Livingston having meanwhile opened a law office in New Orleans, Duer joined him there in a thriving practise in which he devoted himself to the study of Spanish civil law. But the climate disagreed with him and he returned to New York after his marriage, on Sept. 11, 1806, to Hannah Maria Denning, daughter of William Denning, a prominent New York Whig. His friend Irving was now editing the *Morning Chronicle,* and Duer contributed occasional literary articles to this newspaper.

After opening a law office at Rhinebeck, he was elected to the state Assembly in 1814 and served till 1820. As chairman of the Committee on Colleges and Academies he secured the passage of a bill which furnished the basis for ensuing laws on common-school income. He was also chairman of the committee that drafted the law investing Livingston and Fulton with navigation rights in the Hudson River, and in the controversy over this he published two pamphlets (1817, 1819) addressed to Fulton's biographer, Cadwallader D. Colden [q.v.]. He aided in legislation concerning the canal system and the abuses of the lottery system. In 1822 he was made a judge of the supreme court of the state, and remained on the bench until 1829, when he resigned to accept the presidency of Columbia College. He held this office until failing health forced him to retire in 1842. His attention was given particularly to certain curricular changes, notably the establishment of scientific courses in which Latin should not be required and the furthering of studies in the modern languages and in Hebrew. He secured the foundation of a number of scholarships and increased the enrollment of the college. Taking personal charge of the freshman course in composition, he also gave to the seniors a course of lectures on constitutional jurisprudence, later published as *A Course of Lectures on the Constitutional Jurisprudence of the United States* (1843). His wise and efficient administration won the admiring affection of his college associates and his eloquence in numerous addresses, largely of political concern, gave him a leading place in the community.

After retiring, Duer lived at Morristown, N. J., where he wrote a biography of his grandfather in *The Life of William Alexander, Earl of Stirling,* published in 1847 by the New Jersey Historical Society. He continued to make frequent public addresses, notably one on education delivered at Columbia College, and one on his early recollections of New York, with reminiscences of Washington's inauguration, before the St. Nicholas Society. These were published as: *The Duties and Responsibilities of the Rising Generation* (1848), and *New York as it Was, During the Latter Part of the Last Century* (1849). His *Reminiscences of an Old Yorker* (1867) was published posthumously.

[The best account of Duer is an article by Wm. A. Duer in the *Columbia Univ. Quart.,* Mar. 1902. See also D. McAdam and others, *Hist. of the Bench and Bar of N. Y.* (1897), vol. I; "The Duers," *Evening Post* (N. Y.), Apr. 27, 1901.]

E. H. W.

DUFF, MARY ANN DYKE (1794–Sept. 5, 1857), actress, was born in London, England, the daughter of an Englishman, about whom little is known, except that he died in the service of the East India Company and left his wife and three daughters with small means of support. The girls began their preparation for the stage under the tutelage of D'Egville, then ballet master in the King's Theatre in London. In 1809 they made their first public appearance as dancers in the Dublin Theatre, in Dublin. At a benefit performance at Kilkenny, during the same year, Mary Ann met Tom Moore, the Irish poet, and he fell deeply in love with her. She was said to have been the inspiration of many of his love poems, among which is "Mary, I believed thee true," but she did not return his affections and he married her sister, Elizabeth Dyke. Mary Ann married a young actor, John Duff, whom she had met during her engagement at Dublin Theatre, and with him sailed for America immediately after their marriage, in 1810. On Dec. 31 of that year she made her début in Boston at the Old Federal Street Theatre in the rôle of Shakespeare's Juliet. Her beauty attracted much attention. During the following eight years she studied her art diligently and in February 1818 she appeared again as Juliet and was then acclaimed a great tragic actress. On Dec. 4, 1827, she returned to London, where she played with some success at the Drury Lane Theatre. She remained in England only a short time, however, and on May 20, 1828, she was again back in America. On Apr. 28, 1831, John Duff died. The following year Mrs. Duff continued to play, but with little success. The death of her husband had left her in a state of melancholy and the weight of new responsibilities hindered her work on the stage. During this period she married a man by the name of Charles Young; the marriage, however, was never acknowledged by Mrs. Duff, and was legally dissolved soon after. Mrs. Duff continued to act in Philadelphia, Baltimore, and Washington, playing with her daughter, Mary Duff. She made her last appearance in New York, on Nov. 30, 1835, and shortly after returned to her home in Philadelphia. In this year she married a man by the name of Seaver, a young lawyer of Philadelphia. After a brief engagement in Washington, and her farewell benefit, she went with her husband to New Orleans where they lived for nearly twenty years, and where Seaver's law practise became very prosperous. Mrs. Seaver continued her work on the stage, appearing under her former name, Mrs. Duff, and playing throughout the South with great success. After her retirement from the stage, she was active in religious work. Although she had been brought up in the Catholic faith, she renounced Roman Catholicism for Methodism. After the death of her husband she went to live with her daughter in New York City. The rest of her life was spent in strict seclusion, and she was known only as a kind old lady devoted to her religion. At the age of sixty-three she died of cancer, at her daughter's home in New York. She was the mother of ten children; seven of these, four sons and three daughters, reached maturity. With this load of do-mestic responsibility she, nevertheless, was acclaimed one of the greatest tragic actresses of her time. Joseph Ireland said of her, "She was endowed by nature with every mental faculty and physical requisite for pure tragedy."

[Jos. N. Ireland's biography, *Mrs. Duff* (1882), written for the American Actor Series; W. W. Clapp, Jr., *A Record of the Boston Stage* (1853); W. D. Adams, *A Dictionary of the Drama,* I (1904), 433.]   M. S.

DUFFIELD, GEORGE (Oct. 7, 1732–Feb. 2, 1790), Presbyterian clergyman, prominent in Pennsylvania both in the affairs of his denomination and as an ardent supporter of the American Revolution, was of French Huguenot descent, the family name having been originally Du Fielde. He was the son of George and Margaret Duffield, who, migrating from the north of Ireland some time between 1725 and 1730, settled in Lancaster County, Pa. Here in the township of Pequea he was born. He prepared for college at the Academy of Newark, graduated from the College of New Jersey in 1752, and subsequently studied theology in Pequea under Rev. Robert Smith [*q.v.*]. From 1754 to 1756 he was tutor at the College of New Jersey, being licensed to preach in the latter year, Mar. 11, by the Presbytery of New Castle. Three days earlier he had married Elizabeth, daughter of Rev. Samuel Blair [*q.v.*], who died the following year, and on Mar. 5, 1759, he married Margaret Armstrong, a sister of Gen. John Armstrong [1717–1795, *q.v.*]. In 1757 he was called to the church of Big Spring in conjunction with a recently formed church at Carlisle. His connection with the latter continued until 1772, but his relationship with the former was dissolved in 1769 and he assumed charge of the congregation at Monaghan. He was a man of vigorous personality and aggressive courage. An ardent temperament and facility in extemporaneous speaking made him a popular preacher. His career fell in troublous times. Old Side and New Side Presbyterians were in acrimonious conflict. Duffield, sympathetic toward Whitefield's followers, was emphatically New Side, and his ordination and installation at Carlisle were delayed until September 1759, because of a long-drawn-out controversy with Rev. John Steel, who came to the Old Side church already existing there. The communities to which he ministered were at this period in constant danger of attacks by Indians, and both he and his rival, Steel, captained their parishioners in one or two expeditions against them. The turbulence preceding the Revolution was rising, and Duffield identified himself with the boldest advocates of independence. Having declined two calls to the Second Presbyterian Church, Philadelphia, because it was felt that he was more needed at Carlisle, in 1772 he accepted the pastorate of the newly formed Third, or Pine Street, Church, of that city.

His ministry here had a stormy opening. Both Old Side sentiment and Tory sentiment were against him. The First Church, which had had a hand in establishing the Third, opposed his settlement. The church edifice was once closed against him, and when it was opened by his supporters and he persisted in conducting service after the King's Magistrate had ordered the people to disperse and had been thrown out as a disturber of public worship, he was arrested for aiding and abetting a riot. He had many zealous adherents, however, and came to exert much influence in the city. During the sessions of the Continental Congress John Adams and other delegates sat regularly under his patriotic preaching. Referring to the pastor of the First Church, Mr. Adams wrote "Mr. Sproat is totally destitute of the genius and eloquence of Duffield." After the declaration of independence he was commissioned chaplain of the Pennsylvania militia, and rendered such service that the British offered fifty pounds for his capture. He also served with Rev. William White [q.v.] as chaplain to the Continental Congress. Subsequent to the War he served the Third Church as pastor until his death in his fifty-eighth year. He was trustee of the College of New Jersey from 1777 to 1790, active in the organization of the Presbyterian Church after the Revolution, and the first stated clerk of the General Assembly. An account of a two months' missionary tour to frontier inhabitants and the Indians which he made with Rev. Charles C. Beatty [q.v.] in 1766, was published by the latter in 1768. Duffield's thanksgiving discourse for the restoration of peace, *A Sermon Preached in the Third Presbyterian Church in the City of Philadelphia on Thursday, Dec. 11, 1783,* was published in 1784.

[*Gen. Cat. of Princeton Univ. 1746–1906* (1908); W. B. Sprague, *Annals Am. Pulpit,* vol. III (1858); Alfred Nevin, *Centennial Biog. Men of Mark of Cumberland Valley, Pa. 1776–1876* (1876); *The Centennial Memorial of the Presbytery of Carlisle* (1889); *Jour. Presbyt. Hist. Soc.,* June 1905; J. T. Headley, *The Chaplains and Clergy of the Revolution* (1864); Ashbel Green, *A Sermon Preached at the Funeral of Rev. George Duffield, D.D., of Philadelphia* (1790); Hughes O. Gibbons, *A Hist. of Old Pine Street Church* (1905).]
H. E. S.

DUFFIELD, GEORGE (July 4, 1794–June 26, 1868), Presbyterian clergyman, grandson of Rev. George Duffield [q.v.], and son of George and Faithful (Slaymaker) Duffield, was born in Strasburg, Lancaster County, Pa. His father was for many years comptroller of the state. In the

strict Presbyterian circle in which the younger George grew up he was considered "wayward" but outside that circle he probably would not have been regarded as displaying any particularly wicked tendencies. He was precocious enough to graduate from the University of Pennsylvania in his seventeenth year, and, having been converted from his waywardness, to be licensed to preach by the Presbytery of Philadelphia before he was twenty-one, Apr. 20, 1815, after four years' study of theology with Dr. John Mitchell Mason [q.v.]. Almost a year and a half later, Sept. 25, 1816, he was ordained and installed pastor of the Presbyterian church, Carlisle, Pa., in which town his grandfather had been a pioneer minister. Like the latter he was a man of strong convictions, outspoken and fearless, making stanch friends and some enemies. His piety and zeal in his calling were never questioned. A strict disciplinarian, he insisted on daily worship and religious instruction in the home, established a Sunday-school for those who did not receive such instruction there, and required all communicants to renounce attendance at dances and theatres, and to abjure worldly amusements in general. In 1832, as the conflict which in 1837–38 split the church was beginning, he became a theological storm center through the publication of *Spiritual Life: or, Regeneration,* in which, it was alleged, he departed from the doctrinal standards of the church. The language of the book is obscure and confusing. Dr. Alexander McClelland is reported to have said of Duffield that "he knew no man so effective and mighty in presenting the practical side of religion, but that when he turned, as he sometimes did, to metaphysics, he got so deep down in the mud that he did not know where he was, nor did anyone else." Charges were brought against him. The Presbytery of Carlisle condemned the book, but since he declared that it was misunderstood and that in reality he had not repudiated the established doctrines, the Presbytery did not discipline the author. The Synod of Philadelphia took exception to this action. Duffield appealed to the General Assembly, but the appeal was not prosecuted. *The Principles of Presbyterian Discipline, Unfolded and Illustrated in the Protests and Appeals of George Duffield, Entered during the Process of the Presbytery of Carlisle, against him April, 1833, in which his Strict Adherence to the Confession of Faith and the Standards of the Church is Shown,* was published in 1835.

The controversy had divided his church, however, and on Mar. 23, 1835, he was dismissed. After brief pastorates at the Fifth Presbyterian

Church, Philadelphia, and at Broadway Tabernacle, New York, on Oct. 1, 1838, he was installed pastor of the First Presbyterian, then known as the Protestant Church, Detroit. Here for thirty years he had a notable ministry; his interest in the cause of education, temperance, and good morals making him prominent in both city and state. He was active in the New School branch of the church, and at the request of its committee on publication prepared a statement of the New School theology. It was not acceptable to a majority of the committee, but was printed in the *Bibliotheca Sacra* in July 1863 under the title "Doctrines of the New School Presbyterian Church." He was also an early and consistent advocate of reunion. Among his numerous published sermons and books are: *The Immorality of the Traffic in Ardent Spirits* (1834); *Discourses on the Sabbath* (1836), in collaboration with Albert Barnes; *A Sermon on American Slavery: Its Nature and the Duties of Christians in Relation to it* (1840); *The Death of Gen. William Henry Harrison . . . or, The Divine Rebuke* (1841); *Dissertations on the Prophecies Relative to the Second Coming of Jesus Christ* (1842); *Millenarianism Defended: A Reply to Professor Stuart's "Strictures on the Rev. G. Duffield's Recent Book on the Second Coming of Christ"* (1843); *The Claims of "Episcopal Bishops," Examined in a Series of Letters Addressed to the Rev. S. A. McCoskry, D.D., Bishop of the Protestant Episcopal Church of Michigan* (1842); *The Bible Rule of Temperance: Total Abstinence from all Intoxicating Drink* (1868). A detailed account of a trip abroad made in 1852 appeared in a series of articles in the *Magazine of Travel*. This periodical, which ran for only a year, was published in book form under the title, *Travels in Two Hemispheres* (1858). While delivering an address before the International Convention of the Young Men's Christian Association at Detroit, June 24, 1868, he suddenly collapsed and died two days later. His wife was Isabella Graham Bethune, grand-daughter of Isabella Graham [q.v.], and sister of George Washington Bethune [q.v.].

[*The Centennial Memorial of the Presbytery of Carlisle* (1889); *Presbyt. Reunion: A Memorial Volume* (1870); Samuel J. Baird, *A Hist. of the New School and of the Questions Involved in the Disruption of the Presbyt. Ch. in 1838* (1868); *Detroit Free Press*, June 25, 27, 29, 1868.]   H.E.S.

DUFFIELD, SAMUEL AUGUSTUS WILLOUGHBY (Sept. 24, 1843–May 12, 1887), Presbyterian clergyman, hymnologist, was fourth in descent from Rev. George Duffield (1732–1790), grandson of Rev. George Duffield (1794–1868), and the son of Rev. George Duffield (1818–

1888) and Anna Augusta Willoughby. His father was a Presbyterian clergyman and writer of hymns, some of which are now widely used in public worship. Samuel was born in Brooklyn, N. Y., fitted for college with William FewSmith at Philadelphia, and graduated from Yale in the class of 1863. The following winter he was in charge of the Adrian, Mich., high school. He then studied theology under his father and grandfather, and was licensed to preach by the Knox Presbytery of Illinois in April 1866. After being in charge of the Mosely Mission, Chicago, for six months, and preaching and studying for a period in New York and Philadelphia, he was called to the latter city and ordained and installed pastor of the Kenderton Presbyterian Church on Nov. 12, 1867. The following year, Oct. 1, in Adrian, Mich., he was married to Hattie S., daughter of Isaac Haywood. He had a brief pastorate in Jersey City in 1870, and was subsequently pastor of the First Presbyterian Church, Ann Arbor, Mich. (1871–74), of the Eighth Presbyterian Church, Chicago (1874–76); acting pastor of the Central Presbyterian Church, Auburn, N. Y. (1876–78); pastor of the Second Presbyterian Church, Altoona, Pa. (1878–81); and thereafter pastor of the Westminster Presbyterian Church, Bloomfield, N. J., relinquishing active work in 1886 because of a heart affection from which he died less than two years later.

He was a man of literary tastes and poetic gifts. A volume of his poems, *Warp and Woof*, was issued in 1870. He had previously published, *The Heavenly Land* (1867), a translation in English verse of *De Contemptu Mundi* by Bernard of Cluny. Five of his hymns, four of them translations, appeared in Charles Seymour Robinson's *Laudes Domini* (1884). His greatest contribution to hymnology, however, is his elaborate work, *English Hymns: Their Authors and History* (1886). At the time of his death he was engaged on a similar work, *The Latin Hymn Writers and Their Hymns* (1889), which was completed and edited by Robert E. Thompson. In collaboration with his father he also prepared and published, *The Burial of the Dead* (1882).

[See *Triennial Meeting and Biog. Record of the Class of Sixty-Three, in Yale College* (1869); *Presbyterian*, May 21, 1887; *Obit. Record Grads. Yale Univ., 1880–90* (1890); John Julian, *A Dict. of Hymnology* (1915). Thompson's preface to Duffield's *The Latin Hymn Writers* contains biographical sketch.]   H.E.S.

DUFOUR, JOHN JAMES (c. 1763–Feb. 9, 1827), pioneer viticulturist and founder of the Swiss vineyards in America, eldest child of Jean Jacques Dufour, a Swiss vinedresser, was born in the commune of Chatelard, district of Vevay, Canton de Vaud, Switzerland. He came to America in 1796 with the definite purpose of founding a grape colony to cultivate the grape, for wine. After an extensive search for a suitable situation for the vineyard, he arrived at Lexington, Ky., on Aug. 28, 1798, where he organized a vineyard association. A tract of 630 acres, called the First Vineyard, was purchased on the Kentucky River about twenty-five miles from Lexington. After the vineyard was well started, Dufour sent for his brothers and sisters in Switzerland. They, with relatives and friends, a little band of seventeen, arrived at the First Vineyard in the summer of 1801. They were full of hope but their efforts were doomed to failure, as a fatal disease soon attacked the vines. Some members of the colony then started the Second Vineyard, down the Ohio River at a place now called Vevay, Ind. The subscribers to the Vineyard Association having become disheartened, the association was dissolved and the full burden of carrying on the vineyards rested on the Swiss colony. In 1806 Dufour was obliged to return to Europe. He left the vineyards in the hands of his younger brothers. The second war with England broke out in his absence and he was delayed in returning until 1816. In the meantime his brothers abandoned the First Vineyard and joined the other colonists at Vevay. Here Dufour joined them on his return to America and here he wrote his book, *The American Vine Dresser's Guide* (Cincinnati, S. J. Browne, 1826). He died at Vevay at the age of sixty-four, a few months after his book was published. He was a man of unusual intelligence, forethought, and perseverance. While his grape colony experiments ended in failure, he contributed an important chapter to the history of grape growing in America.

[L. H. Bailey, *Sketch of the Evolution of our Native Fruits* (1898), pp. 21–40; Perret Dufour, "The Swiss Settlement of Switzerland County, Ind.," *Ind. Hist. Colls.*, vol. XIII (1925); *Ind. Horticultural Soc. Ann. Report*, 1872, pp. 128–29.]   C.R.B.

DUGANNE, AUGUSTINE JOSEPH HICKEY (1823–Oct. 20, 1884), poet, miscellaneous writer, was born in Boston and first came to public notice through patriotic poems which he contributed to newspapers. After the appearance of *Massachusetts* (1843) and *Home Poems* (1844) he migrated to Philadelphia and set up as an author. His income, which in a few years was sufficient for him to marry and to live with apparent happiness in marriage, came chiefly, it is probable, from his stories of adventure, which he produced in quantity lots for several publishers, including Erastus Beadle. He also

compiled books on philosophy, economics, and government and ventured into tragedy with *The Lydian Queen,* which was produced at the Walnut Street Theatre in 1848. His address in 1849 (*McElroy's Philadelphia Directory*) was the southeast corner of Fourth and Walnut Sts. He moved to New York sometime around 1850. There he continued to concoct paper-backed novels; wrote book reviews that kindled the enthusiasm of Thomas Holley Chivers (information from Dr. Lewis Chase) for John Sartain's *Union Magazine* and other periodicals; lampooned his contemporaries in *Parnassus in Pillory* (1851); advanced the cause of Americanism in literature with *A Sound Literature the Safeguard of our National Institutions* (1853), and *Art's True Mission in America* (1853); won a hundred-dollar prize in 1854 with a turgid "Ode to Powers' Greek Slave"; agitated in prose and verse for free land in the West; declaimed, also in both prose and verse, before meetings of fraternal orders and workingmen's organizations; and between 1847 and 1854 brought out seven volumes of his poems. While he was seriously ill in 1855, a Philadelphia friend, James Lesley, Jr., edited a sumptuous volume of his *Poetical Works* (2nd ed., 1856; autograph ed., 1865), with a portrait engraved by Sartain. The head, with its broad, unfurrowed brow, full beard, and flowing hair, bears a simultaneous resemblance to Alfred Tennyson and E. Z. C. Judson. In the prefatory matter the poet alludes to recent bereavements. In the autumn of 1855 the success of the Know-Nothing party landed him in the Assembly as the member for the sixth district of New York, but his career as a statesman lasted for only one term. In the autumn of 1862 Duganne helped to raise the 176th New York Volunteers and was commissioned immediately as its lieutenant-colonel. The regiment was sent to Louisiana. Through no fault of his he and his command were compelled to surrender to a superior force at Brashear (now Morgan) City, La., June 23, 1863, and the rest of his military life was spent ingloriously in prison camps near Hempstead and Tyler, Tex. His *Camps and Prisons: Twenty Months in the Department of the Gulf* (1865), largely autobiographical, is honest, vivid, and packed with detail. Its account of life in Texas during the war is of historical value. Duganne was paroled July 24, 1864, and, having suffered much during his captivity, was mustered out for disability, Sept. 10. At the close of the war, Gov. R. E. Fenton appointed him chief of the bureau of military statistics, and thereafter he was connected with the *New York Tribune,* and the *Sunday Dispatch,* a Masonic sheet of sensational proclivities. *Utterances* (1865) and *Ballads of the War* (complete ed., 1865) contain his martial verse. *Fighting Quakers* (1866), *Governments of the World* (1882), and *Injuresoul* (1884), a dull satire addressed to both Ingersoll and Beecher, are among his last books. Duganne was affable, kindly, and of studious habits. During his last years he was afflicted with tuberculosis. He died at his home in New York of a complication of diseases and was buried in Cypress Hills Cemetery.

[*N. Y. Times* and *N. Y. Tribune*, Oct. 22, 1884; *N. Y. Dispatch*, Oct. 26, 1884; F. B. Hough, *N. Y. Civil List 1777–1863* (Albany, 1863); *Ann. Report Adj.-Gen. State of N. Y.*, 1905; private information.] G. H. G.

DUGDALE, RICHARD LOUIS (1841–July 23, 1883), social economist, was born in Paris of English parents, Richard John Dugdale and his wife, Anna, a descendant of Sir Thomas Cuddon of Shaddingfield Hall, Suffolk. When the boy was seven years old his father, who had been both a manufacturer and a journalist, suffered business reverses. The family returned to England, and Richard was sent for three years to the Somerset School. He came to New York City with his parents in 1851, and attended the public schools until, at the age of fourteen, showing ability in drawing, he was for a time employed by a sculptor. He already had symptoms of heart trouble, and at seventeen went to live with his parents on an Indiana farm. Being unequal to manual labor he learned shorthand, and when the family returned to New York in 1860 he was employed as a stenographer. He attended night classes at Cooper Union, being particularly active in the debating clubs. He had a consuming interest in sociological subjects and resolved to be a social investigator, but since it was before the day of research foundations and he lacked the formal equipment necessary for an academic position, he decided to enter business in order later to accumulate enough to indulge his curiosity. Dugdale lived successively in several houses in Greenwich Village, and in 1871 moved to No. 4 Morton St., which he made a rendezvous for many social reformers. In 1868 he became a member of the executive committee of the Prison Association of New York, to which he gave his hardest work. In 1874 he was appointed a committee of one to inspect thirteen county jails. Struck with the consanguinity of many of the criminals, he used private funds to make a detailed study of one large family connection and in 1875, in a report of the Prison Association, he published "The Jukes, a Study in Crime, Pauperism, Disease and Heredity." This, together with his *Further Studies of Criminals*, was re-

published in 1877. He found that of 709 persons —540 of "Juke" blood and 169 of other strains connected with the family by marriage or cohabitation—180 had been in the poorhouse or received outdoor relief for a total of 800 years, 140 had been convicted of criminal offenses, 60 were habitual thieves, 7 were murdered, 50 were common prostitutes, 40 women venereally diseased had infected at least 440 persons, and there had been 30 prosecutions in bastardy. These people had cost the State at least $1,308,000. Dugdale's findings created a sensation. He believed that inheritance was of more importance as a limiting factor in determining character than environment, but he tried to give full weight to the latter. In 1880 he became the first secretary of the Society for Political Education, which sought to inform the electorate on social questions. He was an active member of a large number of sociological and civic organizations, and wrote for the reviews and spoke before scientific bodies, particularly on criminology. He was a thin, fair-haired, diffident man, of almost no presence, but had a devoted circle of intimates. He died of his heart trouble, after a long illness. His work has been followed by other similar studies, particularly that of Arthur H. Estabrook, *The Jukes in 1915* (1916), made possible by the finding, in 1911, of Dugdale's manuscript.

[E. M. Shepard, *The Work of a Social Teacher* (1884), being No. VII of the Economic Tracts of the Soc. for Pol. Educ.; historical note in Estabrook, *op. cit.*; G. H. Putnam, *Memories of a Publisher, 1865–1915* (1915); *N. Y. Times*, July 24, 1883.] B. M—l.

DUGUÉ, CHARLES OSCAR (May 1, 1821– Aug. 29, 1872), Creole poet, was born in New Orleans of French ancestry, the son of François Dugué, a wealthy planter, and Jeanne Marie (Pligne). He was educated in France, principally at the Collège St. Louis in Paris, and perfected his English at Transylvania College in Kentucky. Attracted to the fields of journalism, literature, and law, he wrote for the New Orleans papers, *L'Abeille*, *La Lorgnette*, *Le Propagateur catholique*, became editor in chief of *L'Orléanais*, and served for some time as judge of the district court for the parishes of St. Bernard, Jefferson, and Plaquemines. During the years 1847–52, which marked the height of his literary powers, he published: *Philosophie morale* (1847), a volume of miscellany; *Essais poétiques* (1847), a collection of verse; *Mila ou là mort de La Salle* (1852), a romantic drama whose chief figure is La Salle; and *Le Cygne ou Mingo* (1852), a drama in which Tecumseh plays a part. Turning to teaching, he became an assistant superintendent of schools in New Orleans and later president of Jefferson College in St. James Parish. When the doors of the college were closed on account of the Civil War, Dugué was broken in health. He met disaster with fortitude, however; worked on a poem to be entitled *"Homo,"* which he believed was to be his masterpiece, and taught in the New Orleans Normal School. In quest of a publisher and in the vain hope of regaining his lost health he went to Paris, where he died, survived by his wife, Elodie Augustine de Livaudais. His body was brought to New Orleans to rest in the family tomb in St. Louis Cemetery No. 2. In the year of his death, 1872, his last work, *Homo,* was published in Paris by his brother. It is a didactic poem in the form of a dialogue wherein God and Man discourse on the fatality of destiny and the freedom of the will. The book presents philosophical ideas that seek to obtain harmony and conciliation by persuasion.

Dugué is chiefly interesting because of his poetry. He himself believed in the sacredness of his mission and his youthful efforts attracted the attention of Châteaubriand. In his verses written under the influence of both Musset and Vigny at times he reached lyrical heights, especially when melancholy turned his thoughts to his native land. His poetical powers were not sustained, however; he preached the utility of the poet as a benefactor of society, and in later years his poetry assumed a didactic tone which deprived it of spontaneity and lyrical qualities. As a dramatist he was a follower of the so-called *"École de bon sens"* whose chief exponent was Ponsard.

[Chas. Testut in *Portraits littéraires* (1850) penned an interesting study of Dugué. Adrien Rouquette wrote a preface to *Les Essais poétiques* which contains important data. E. Fortier gave a synopsis of *Mila* in *Mémoires du Premier Congrès de la langue français au Canada, Quebec 1915.* The play itself was reprinted by L'Athénée Louisianais in its *Comptes Rendus* (Oct. 1907, Jan. 1908). Dugué's daughter, Sophie Elisabeth (Mrs. John Bendernagel) has furnished some information. See also Grace King, *Creole Families of New Orleans* (1921); E. A. and G. L. Duyckinck, *Cyc. of Am. Lit.* (1856); J. W. Davidson, *Living Writers of the South* (1869); *Lib. of Southern Lit.,* XV (1909), 130; Ruby Caulfeild, *The French Lit. of Louisiana* (1929); brief obituary in *L'Abeille,* Sept. 19, 1872.] L. C. D.

DUHRING, LOUIS ADOLPHUS (Dec. 23, 1845–May 8, 1913), dermatologist, was the son of Henry Duhring of Mecklenburg, Germany, and Caroline (Oberteuffer) Duhring of St. Gall, Switzerland, who migrated to the United States in 1818. They were thrifty, and educated, and the father, who had been moderately successful at home, became a prominent merchant in Philadelphia and gained considerable wealth. The family was particularly interested in music and

devoted many of its evenings to concerts at home with friends. Louis was studious, quiet, and retiring in manner and had considerable taste and talent for music. A sister, Julia Duhring, to whom he was devoted, developed talent as a writer. The boy's early education was obtained in Philadelphia private schools; in 1861 he entered the freshman class of the college department of the University of Pennsylvania. At the end of his third year he enlisted, in July 1863, in the 32nd Regiment, Pennsylvania Volunteers; after serving for three months he was honorably discharged, and entered the medical department of the University of Pennsylvania, where he graduated after three years. He then became an interne in the Philadelphia Hospital (Blockley) where he remained fifteen months.

In the summer of 1868 he went for further instruction to Vienna, where he studied under the brilliant Ferdinand Hebra, who was developing dermatology as a special branch of medicine. There were no such specialists in Philadelphia at the time and indeed but few in the United States. After two years, Duhring returned to Philadelphia and began practise as a dermatologist. He immediately organized and opened the "Dispensary for Skin Diseases," with the eminent surgeon, Prof. Samuel D. Gross [*q.v.*], as president of the board of trustees. With this institution Duhring retained connection until 1890, being a consultant after 1880. In 1871 he was made lecturer on skin diseases in the University of Pennsylvania. At this time he was twenty-six years old. In 1876 he published the first part of his *Atlas of Skin Diseases,* a water-color portrayal of diseases with descriptive text. This was the first effort of the kind in the United States and gained for its author considerable distinction. Since the work was not of a remunerative character, Duhring was obliged to draw upon his own purse to finance the venture. In the same year he became visiting dermatologist to the newly opened department of skin diseases at the Philadelphia Hospital (Blockley), continuing in this capacity until 1887. In 1877, he published a *Practical Treatise on Diseases of the Skin.* This was the first American text-book on the subject and served to establish its writer as the leader of his specialty in America. The excellence of the work led to second and third editions within a few years, and the book was later translated into French, Italian, and Russian. After years of experience as a dermatologist he published *Cutaneous Medicine* (part I, 1895; part II, 1898). He was a frequent contributor to medical journals and his articles disclosed a keen insight into the subjects with which he dealt. His most important articles were on what he called "dermatitis herpetiformis," which was closely related to an extremely fatal dermatosis known as pemphigus. Although the great Viennese dermatologist Kaposi and others took opposite sides of the controversy, Duhring successfully maintained his position and trenchantly established dermatitis herpetiformis as a separate clinical entity. Throughout the world this is known to-day as Duhring's Disease, and sufferers from this disease have a far better chance of recovery than from the fatal pemphigus.

Throughout his student days Duhring was conspicuously well dressed and gentlemanly in bearing and exhibited a fondness for music, theatrical performances, public and private, and cotillion dances. About the time of his graduation, however, a shadow was cast upon his lighter nature by the death of a young lady who was looked upon as his fiancée. This caused him to withdraw from social contacts and become increasingly absorbed in his professional labors. The deaths of his two brothers and more particularly that of his beloved sister, in 1892, further saddened his life, and he became more and more an isolated recluse. He lived alone in his domicile and, although many could claim acquaintance with him, no one had the privilege of his intimacy or friendship. As a result, he developed certain eccentricities of manner. He was diffident, retiring, and secretive in conversation, very parsimonious, and expended little upon himself. As a result of judicious investments he acquired for his time considerable wealth. His estate which was largely bequeathed to the University of Pennsylvania and the College of Physicians of Philadelphia, amounted to more than a million and a quarter dollars.

[H. W. Stelwagon, "Memoir of Louis A. Duhring," in *Trans. Coll. Phys. of Phila.* (1914) ; J. L. Chamberlain, *Universities and Their Sons, Univ. of Pa., 1740–1900* (1901) ; *Public Ledger* (Phila.), May 9, 1913.]
J. F. S.

DUKE, BASIL WILSON (May 28, 1838–Sept. 16, 1916), Confederate soldier, was born in Scott County, Ky., the son of Nathaniel Wilson and Mary (Currie) Duke. Nathaniel Duke was a naval officer, descended from a Maryland family which established itself in Kentucky in the eighteenth century. His son was educated at Georgetown (Ky.), and Centre College, and at the law school of Transylvania University at Lexington. Admitted to the bar in 1858, he began the practise of law in St. Louis. An enthusiastic state-rights man, he took a very active part in the secessionist movement in Missouri,

and engaged in secret operations which exposed him to danger from friends as well as enemies. On one occasion he narrowly escaped summary execution at the hands of a secessionist vigilance committee, by whom he was "suspected of being a suspicious character." Later, his arrest within the Union lines was prevented only by the intervention of his old friend, John M. Harlan, then in the Union army and later a justice of the Supreme Court, who was convinced that Duke was not there in the capacity of a spy,—as, indeed, he was not on this particular occasion, for he was merely taking a short cut to Lexington to pay a visit to his wife. He had married, in June 1861, Henrietta Hunt Morgan, the sister of John Hunt Morgan [*q.v.*], who was soon to distinguish himself as a cavalry leader.

The secessionist movement in Missouri having been checked, Duke enlisted as a private in his brother-in-law's "Lexington Rifles," and was elected first lieutenant. When the Lexington Rifles became a part of the 2nd Kentucky Cavalry, Duke was appointed lieutenant-colonel of the regiment and later became its colonel. He took a conspicuous part in all the operations of Morgan's cavalry command, was wounded at Shiloh, was captured along with the rest of Morgan's men in his spectacular raid through Ohio in 1863, and for a year remained a prisoner of war. Exchanged and rejoining his regiment, Duke was appointed a brigadier-general in September 1864, and commanded a cavalry brigade in eastern Kentucky and western Virginia until Lee's surrender. The infantry in the little army was then disbanded, the guns were spiked, and the wagon train was abandoned; the cavalry, mostly mounted on the draft mules of the train, endeavored to join Johnston in North Carolina. Reaching Charlotte, it was assigned as escort to Jefferson Davis and the fugitive Confederate government. Its general officers, Duke among them, shared in Davis's last council of war, and unanimously declared that further resistance was hopeless. After the party broke up, Duke, with a small force, tried to lead the pursuit away from the direction in which Davis had fled, and then surrendered and was paroled. He eventually settled in Louisville, and resumed law practise. A member of the Kentucky House of Representatives in 1869, he served as commonwealth attorney of the fifth judicial district, 1875–80. For more than twenty years he was a member of the legal staff of the Louisville & Nashville Railroad. His interest in Civil War history was keen, and he wrote extensively on such parts of it as came within his own experiences. His *History of Morgan's Cavalry,* first published in 1867, was reprinted in 1906 with a briefer title. He was a frequent contributor to the *Southern Bivouac,* a magazine the editorship of which he shared for two years (1885–87). He later edited (1893–94) the *Mid-Continent Magazine* and the *Southern Magazine.* The *Reminiscences of General Basil W. Duke, C. S. A.,* appeared in book form in 1911, after having previously been published as separate magazine articles. He also wrote a *History of the Bank of Kentucky* (1895). From 1895 until his death he was a commissioner of Shiloh National Park.

Duke was small in stature and slight of frame. His face was distinguished by the mustache and goatee of the traditional Kentucky gentleman, and by a humorous eye. His cheerfulness was unquenchable. The *Reminiscences,* written in his old age, are full of boyish enthusiasm and enjoyment, as well as shrewd comemnt on political and military measures. He was boyish, too, in his frank hero-worship of Morgan. Strong in his conviction of the justice of the Confederate cause, he could yet clearly appreciate the point of view of his opponents; and four years of war roused in him feelings of warm friendship, rather than of hatred, toward those against whom he fought. Southerners would have described him as chivalrous, and in this instance that much-abused word is appropriate. As a soldier, he was not of the first rank, though an able cavalry commander; but his personality makes him one of the most attractive figures of his time.

[His books, mentioned above, and several papers published in *The Century* (1884–87) and reprinted in *Battles and Leaders of the Civil War* (1887–88) give the best account of his military career. There is a good brief sketch of his life in *Confed. Mil. Hist.* (1899), vol. IX, Ky., pp. 234–36. See also *Official Records (Army),* 1 ser., vols. XVI (pts. 1, 2), XX (pt. 1), XXIII (pt. 1), XXXIX (pts. 1, 3), XLV (pts. 1, 2), XLIX (pts. 1, 2) ; 2 ser., vol. VI ; H. Levin, ed., *Lawyers and Lawmakers of Ky.* (1897).]   T. M. S.

DUKE, BENJAMIN NEWTON (Apr. 27, 1855–Jan. 8, 1929), industrialist, philanthropist, was born on the farm of his father, Washington Duke, four miles north of Durham, N. C. Washington Duke, the son of Taylor and Dicie (Jones) Duke, was of English, Scotch-Irish, and Welsh descent. He married in 1852 his second wife, Artelia, daughter of John and Mary Roney of Alamance County. She died in 1858, when Benjamin, her elder son, was three years old. When they became rich, Benjamin and James B. Duke [*q.v.*] gave a science building to Elon College, N. C., in honor of their mother. The boys, with their sister, were cared for until 1863 by aunts who came into Washington Duke's home after his wife's death. In that year their father, though a Unionist, went into the Confederate army, and

the children went to live with their grandparents in Alamance. Ben went to neighborhood schools at Harden's and Pisgah Church, and was a playful, sturdy youngster, busy after school with chores about the farm. After the war, when not working at growing and manufacturing tobacco, he was a pupil in the academy of Dr. Morgan Closs in Durham, and later was sent to the Quakers' school at New Garden (now Guilford College).

The Dukes built a factory in Durham in 1874, and in 1878 formed the firm of W. Duke Sons & Company. The firm was one of the first to introduce cigarette machines; it boldly cut the price on their product and extended its market throughout the world. Branch factories having been established in New York in 1884, the Dukes entered the "cigarette war" which ended in a combination, the American Tobacco Company, formed in 1890. Benjamin N. Duke was one of the directors, while his brother James was president. Then followed a series of mergers which gave this corporation control of the industry in America, the Duke brothers being the dominant factors in the whole. On the dissolution of the combination by order of the Supreme Court in 1911, Benjamin Duke diverted his capital to a variety of other undertakings. Already in 1906 he had become president of the Citizens National Bank in Durham, and had reorganized a local railroad, the Cape Fear & Northern, extended its tracks to reach Durham, and changed its name to the Durham & Southern. He became heavily interested in hydro-electric power development in the South, in cotton manufacturing, and in real estate. He was a leader in the South's economic revival. His fortune at one time was estimated at $60,000,000. At the time of his death he had withdrawn from active management of most of these enterprises, his only business positions being those of director in the Southern Power Company, and director of the Durham Realty Corporation, the latter owning hotels and apartment houses in New York and New Jersey. Benjamin N. Duke was not so gifted as his brother James in business organization, but he earlier manifested an interest in educational and charitable work, and influenced members of his family in this direction. He relinquished his design of building an orphanage at Durham when it was suggested to him that Trinity College might be removed from the country to the location he had selected, and he forwarded plans which brought this about in 1892. Between 1898 and 1925 his gifts to the college grew progressively, totaling in excess of $2,000,000. It was undoubtedly Benjamin's example that induced James to make this school the chief object of his benefactions, which resulted in very large gifts by him in 1924 and 1925, and a change of name to Duke University. Benjamin gave to churches, to a negro hospital in Durham, and to many other institutions associated with his young manhood. He married in 1877 Sarah Pearson Angier of Durham, and had two sons and a daughter. He was modest, avoided publicity, and sought to keep his gifts secret. He died at his home in New York, after being confined to the house for months. His body lay in state at Duke University and was buried in Durham.

[See John W. Jenkins, *James B. Duke, Master Builder* (1927); Wm. K. Boyd, *The Story of Durham, City of the New South* (1925); *Who's Who in America,* 1928–29; *N. Y. Times,* and Raleigh (N. C.) *News and Observer,* Jan. 9, 1929.]   B. M—l.

DUKE, JAMES BUCHANAN (Dec. 23, 1856–Oct. 10, 1925), industrialist, was the youngest child of Washington Duke and Artelia (Roney) Duke, his mother dying when he was an infant. He and his brother Benjamin Newton [*q.v.*] were born on his father's small farm near Durham, N. C., and soon were plunged into the poverty brought by the Civil War. James attended school in a log house at Harden's and later at Pisgah Church. When the father returned on foot from the Confederate army with a single half-dollar and two blind mules, life was resumed on the home farm, which had been swept clean by the invading army. Luckily, however, a quantity of leaf tobacco had been overlooked, and this was seized upon as the one hope. James and Benjamin helped their father pound it out with hickory sticks in a small log barn on the place, and the tobacco was put in packages labeled "Pro Bono Publico." Hitching their blind mules and supplied with rations, they struck out with their product to the southern part of North Carolina where tobacco was scarce. Meeting with ready sales, they purchased more leaf tobacco, built a larger log house for the manufacture, and found themselves prospering in their venture. They sold 125,000 pounds in 1872, and were as substantial as any in the local industry. James for a time attended the academy in Durham taught by Dr. Morgan Closs, proving quick with figures; he was then sent to a boarding school in Guilford County, but longed for the activity of farm and factory, and went home before the first term was over. Later he completed the course at the Eastman Business College, Poughkeepsie, N. Y., in record time. He was manager of the colored boys in the tobacco factory at the age of fourteen, and at eighteen be-

came a member of the firm of W. Duke & Sons, and gained experience in all branches of the business.

In 1881 the Dukes began manufacturing cigarettes, for which the local "bright" tobacco was particularly adapted, and James soon displaced the hand workers by the new Bonsack machines, which with the aid of William T. O'Brien he perfected. When the law was passed reducing the government tax on cigarettes by two-thirds, Duke immediately reduced the price of his product from ten to five cents a package, two months in advance of the operation of the act. This bold stroke, coupled with world advertising, gave the Duke firm a lead. A new period in his career and in the American tobacco business began when he left Durham and set up a branch factory in New York City in 1884. His firm now invaded the Northern and Western markets, and largely through the pouring out of hundreds of thousands of dollars a year in advertising of every form, by 1889 came to furnish half the country's total production of cigarettes. Soon the five principal cigarette manufacturers were engaged in the celebrated "tobacco war," in which competitive advertising and price concessions ruined profits. The older companies finally offered to buy Duke out, but this was his signal to force the fighting, and in 1890 all were joined in the American Tobacco Company, with $25,000,000 capital and Duke as president. In 1895 the combination began aggressively to absorb companies making other tobacco products, such as all-tobacco cigarettes, chewing tobacco, and snuff. An attempt of capitalists to gain control of enough stock to oust Duke from the headship failed. In 1898 a combination of plug manufacturers was formed, the Continental Tobacco Company, with $75,000,000 capital issued, Duke being president. The two combinations were controlled by the same interests. Duke was voracious for further mergers. Having drawn about him a remarkable group of capitalists, manufacturers, and merchants, including Oliver H. Payne, P. A. B. Widener, Grant B. Schley, William C. Whitney, R. J. Reynolds, and Thomas F. Ryan, he was enabled to form the American Snuff Company in 1900, the American Cigar Company the next year, then the American Stogie Company, and entered the retail field with the United Cigar Stores Company. In 1901 the Consolidated Tobacco Company was formed as a holding company to concentrate control of the American & Continental. After the decision of the Supreme Court in the Northern Securities case, the holding company was discontinued and the three were merged under the original name of the American

Tobacco Company. Duke next began manufacture in England by acquiring Ogden's at Liverpool. Led by W. D. and H. O. Wills, British manufacturers formed the Imperial Tobacco Company to fight the invader. A new tobacco war ensued, marked by Duke's offer to distribute to dealers who bought his product in disregard of the attempted boycott, the entire profits of Ogden's and £200,000 a year for four years. The Imperial threatened to build a factory in America. The result was an agreement by which the Imperial restricted its sales to Great Britain, the Consolidated confined itself to America, and the trade of the rest of the world was the province of the British-American Company, the Duke interests owning two-thirds of its stock and the English one-third. Duke's combinations now controlled 150 factories with a capitalization of $502,000,000. In 1911, after almost five years of litigation, the Supreme Court ordered the American Tobacco Company dissolved as a combination in restraint of trade. Duke bore chief responsibility in the difficult task of setting up the constituent elements in the merger as competitors once more. In 1904 Duke began developing the water powers of the Southern Piedmont. The next year the Southern Power Company was formed, which in twenty years came to supply power to over 300 cotton-mills, to other factories, electric lines, and cities. Duke in 1924 created a trust fund, composed principally of his holdings in the Southern Power Company, which, it is estimated, will eventually amount to $100,000,000; the fund to be used principally in creating Duke University in North Carolina and for hospitalization in the two Carolinas, with as subordinate objects the relief of Methodist churches and ministers, and the care of orphans. Duke was forceful in appearance and manner, full of self-confidence. At the age of forty-eight he married Mrs. William D. McCready of New York. The next year he obtained a divorce, and in 1907 married Mrs. Nanaline Inman of Atlanta. They had one daughter.

[John W. Jenkins, *Jas. B. Duke, Master Builder* (1927); Meyer Jacobstein, *The Tobacco Industry in the U. S.* (1907); Wm. K. Boyd, *The Story of Durham, City of the New South* (1925); *N. Y. Times, N. Y. Herald Tribune*, Oct. 11, 1925.]   B. M—l.

DULANY, DANIEL (1685–Dec. 5, 1753), lawyer, descended from a medieval Irish family, the O'Dulaneys, was born in Queen's County, Ireland, in the year 1685. His father was Thomas Delaney. His mother, of whom not so much as her maiden name is known, died before his emigration with two brothers, William and Joseph, to Port Tobacco, Md., where he arrived, a well-

educated but penniless youth, about the year 1703. He received financial aid from George Plater, a former attorney-general of the province, studied law under his direction, and was admitted to the bar of Charles County in 1709. The following year he was admitted to plead before the provincial court, and in 1716 was enroled as a student of Gray's Inn, London. Prosperous in his profession, he acquired several thousand acres of wheat land in the valley of the Monocacy, and by encouraging German Palatines to settle there he promoted an industrial revolution in a province that had been producing little except tobacco.

In 1721 Dulany removed permanently to Annapolis and in the following year was chosen a representative of that city in the popular branch of the Maryland Legislative Assembly. He was at once appointed a member of the most important committee of that body, the Committee on Laws, and, holding also the office of attorney-general, he rapidly assumed the leadership of those in opposition to the measures of the proprietor, governor, and council. The chief controversy for ten years immediately following his entrance into the Assembly was regarding the extension of English statutes to Maryland. The proprietor, in 1722, vetoed a bill which he thought seemed by implication to introduce all the English statutes into the province, and he indicated his view that none should be introduced without his consent. Dulany contended that the people of Maryland could not without the English statutes enjoy the privileges which were guaranteed by the Maryland charter. In 1728 he published his arguments on this subject in a small pamphlet entitled, *The Rights of the Inhabitants of Maryland to the Benefit of the English Laws*. Four years later he offered a compromise which was accepted by the proprietor and regarded as favorable to the popular cause. With a view to winning Dulany from the leadership of the opposition, the proprietor, in 1733, appointed him his agent and receiver general, and the same year he and Benjamin Tasker were appointed jointly to the remunerative office of commissary general. In 1734 he was appointed judge of the admiralty, and, in 1736, he was made sole commissary general but was succeeded by Benjamin Tasker in the office of agent and receiver general. Having served for twenty years in the popular branch of the Legislative Assembly, he was sworn into the Governor's Council, Sept. 25, 1742, and was a member of that body until his death in Annapolis eleven years later. In 1743 he drafted an able address to the proprietor on the need of regulating the tobacco industry, and he successfully advocated the enactment of the inspection law of 1747 which improved the quality of Maryland tobacco and resulted in the floating of a stable paper currency. He was married three times: first, to Charity, daughter of Col. John Courts of Charles County; second, to Rebecca, daughter of Col. Walter Smith of Calvert County, and mother of his son, Daniel Dulany [*q.v.*]; and third, to Henrietta Maria, daughter of Philemon Lloyd of Talbot County, and widow of Samuel Chew.

[Nearly all that is known of Dulany is contained in the *Archives of Md.,* and the *Md. Hist. Mag., passim.* Consult also B. L. Dulaney, *Something about the Dulaney (Dulany) Family* (1921), and St. George L. Sioussat, "Economics and Politics in Maryland, 1720–1750, and the Public Services of Daniel Dulany, the Elder," in Vol. XXI of *Johns Hopkins Univ. Studies in Hist. and Pol. Sci.* (1903).]   N. D. M.

DULANY, DANIEL (June 28, 1722–Mar. 17, 1797), lawyer, was born in Annapolis, Md., the son of Daniel Dulany [*q.v.*], an able lawyer and political leader, and his wife Rebecca (1696–1737), a daughter of Walter Smith of Calvert County, Md. The younger Daniel was educated in England at Eton College and at Clare Hall, Cambridge University, studied law at the Middle Temple, and was admitted to the bar in Maryland in 1747. Two years later he married Rebecca Tasker, daughter of Benjamin Tasker, who was a member of the Governor's Council and the proprietor's agent and receiver general. In 1751 Frederick County elected Dulany one of its representatives in the popular branch of the Maryland Legislative Assembly. He served there for three years, defending the measures of the government and opposing the violence of the popular faction. In return for this service the governor urged his appointment to the Council. The proprietor preferred to have him continue in the House. He decided not to be a candidate for reelection in 1755, but was returned from Annapolis the following year. In 1757 he was appointed to the Council, where, continuing to serve until the overthrow of the proprietary government, he became, with the exception of the governor, the most influential of the proprietor's officers, several of whom were related to him by the ties of kinship. He was also commissary general from 1759 to 1761 and secretary of the province from 1761 to 1774.

When urging Dulany's appointment to the Council, the governor wrote that he was recognized as a gentleman of the best natural and acquired abilities of any in the province. A few years later Charles Carroll wrote his son that Dulany was a man of great parts and, though not overscrupulous, "indisputably the best lawyer on this continent." His opinions on points of law came to have much the same weight as court decisions. Though largely endowed, he suffered from ill health and haughtiness. His relations with the governor were not cordial.

Within eight months of the passage by the British Parliament of the famous act imposing a stamp tax on the colonies, Dulany produced a pamphlet entitled, *Considerations on the Propriety of Imposing Taxes in the British Colonies, for the Purpose of raising a Revenue, by Act of Parliament* (1765). In this essay he contended that the colonies were not represented in Parliament, could not be effectually represented in that body, and that taxation without representation was a violation of the common law of England. He maintained that the colonists by manufacturing for themselves would remove the danger of being oppressed and teach the mother country to regard her colonies as a part of herself and not merely as her possessions. His forceful arguments ranked foremost among the political writings of the period and were freely drawn upon by William Pitt when speaking for repeal. Another significant pamphlet from his pen, in the form of a letter dated Dec. 30, 1765, was published under the title: *The Right to the Tonnage, the Duty of Twelve Pence per Hogshead on all exported Tobacco, and the Fines and Forfeitures in the Province of Maryland* (1766). The popularity in Maryland which Dulany won by his *Considerations* was lost in 1773 in a controversy with Charles Carroll [*q.v.*] of Carrollton, conducted in the columns of the *Maryland Gazette,* Dulany, writing as "Antilon," defending a proclamation by the governor fixing the amounts of officers' fees, and Carroll, as "First Citizen," contending that as the fees were in effect the same as taxes their amounts should be fixed only by an act of the Legislative Assembly. Dulany was one of the protesters against a resolution passed at a meeting in Annapolis to the effect that Maryland lawyers should bring no suit for the recovery of any debt due from an inhabitant of Maryland to an inhabitant of Great Britain until the Boston Port Bill had been repealed. Having opposed radical factions from the beginning of his public career, he manifested no sympathy for the Revolution and at its outbreak retired to Hunting Ridge, near Baltimore. He resided there as a Loyalist, except during a brief visit to England, until 1781, when nearly all of his property was confiscated and he moved to Baltimore, where he died.

[The chief sources of information about Dulany are the *Md. Archives; Md. Hist. Mag.,* esp. vol. XIII (1918), p. 143; and the *Md. Gazette.* An obituary note appeared in the *Federal Gazette and Baltimore Daily*

Advertiser, Mar. 23, 1797. The Md. Hist. Soc. has a small collection of his private papers. Several of his opinions on points of law are published in Volume I of Thomas Harris's and John M'Henry's *Md. Reports* (1809). His controversy with Carroll, edited by Elihu S. Riley, was published as *Correspondence of "First Citizen" Charles Carroll of Carrollton, and "Antilon" Daniel Dulany, Jr.* (1902).]   N.D.M.

DULUTH, DANIEL GREYSOLON, Sieur

(1636–Feb. 25, 1710), French explorer, wrote his own name "Dulhut." He was born of noble parents at St. Germain-en-Laye near Paris, and because of his rank was early enroled in the company of the King's guard. He and his younger brother, Claude Greysolon, Sieur de la Tourette, were residents of Lyons, since they are called Lyonnais; they were also cousins of the Italian officer, Henry de Tonty [*q.v.*]. An uncle named Patron had gone to Canada and become prosperous, so the brothers Greysolon followed him to Montreal, and Daniel was probably there when Joliet [*q.v.*] in 1674 returned from his epoch-making voyage of the discovery of the Mississippi. The same year Duluth was summoned to France to resume military service, and in the battle of Seneffe was squire for the Marquis de Lassay who was thrice wounded. Duluth escaped unhurt and was soon in Montreal once more, where he bought a house in which he and his brother dwelt.

Duluth had long desired to explore the West and in 1678 set out, probably with secret instructions from the Count de Frontenac, governor of Canada, to explore Lake Superior and the routes from there westward. First it was necessary to make peace between two warring tribes of Indians, who had for several years closed Lake Superior to white men's enterprise. Having made friends with the more eastern tribe of the Chippewa, Duluth and his intrepid band of followers set out in the spring of 1679 on the hazardous mission to reconcile these tribesmen with their hereditary enemies, the Sioux. Nothing more dangerous could be conceived. Duluth, however, wrote to Frontenac that he "feared not death, only cowardice or dishonor." He was successful in his undertaking, meeting the Sioux chiefs somewhere near the site of the city that now bears his name, and forming a peace between them and the Chippewa. Then the Sioux bore him in triumph through the maze of portages and waterways that led to their great village on Lake Mille Lac in northern Minnesota. There Duluth made an alliance between the Siouan Confederacy and France and took possession of their territory for Louis XIV. In token of this ceremony he fastened the arms of France to a great oak tree (see picture of this tree on Hennepin's map of 1683). While among the Sioux, the explorer heard of salt water to the westward, probably an Indian account of Great Salt Lake; this he thought was the western ocean, and he planned to explore in that direction. First, however, he had to return to Lake Superior, where on its northwest shore he counseled with the Assiniboin, and where he passed the winter, probably building a fort in their territory.

Early in the spring of 1680 he advanced by the Brule-St. Croix route to the Mississippi, where he learned that the Sioux had broken the treaty he had made with them and were holding three Frenchmen prisoners. Hastening to his compatriots' aid, he rescued them from the Sioux, bitterly reproaching the latter for their faithlessness. One of the rescued captives proved to be Father Louis Hennepin [*q.v.*], also a veteran of the battle-field of Seneffe. Together the Frenchmen went eastward, Duluth abandoning his plans for further exploration. At Mackinac he learned that his enemies were charging him with illegal trading, a charge he indignantly repudiated. He was never a *coureur de bois*, or one who traded without a license, although he has been frequently accused of so being. Frontenac, however, defended Duluth and sent him to France where he obtained a royal commission.

The next decade Duluth spent in futile efforts to explore westward from Lake Superior, being called into service twice (1684 and 1687) to lead contingents in the armies that invaded the Iroquois territory. In 1686 he was in command of a fort on St. Clair River, and at one time brought to justice the Indian murderers of some Frenchmen in Lake Superior and made exploration safe for years thereafter (*Wisconsin Historical Collections*, XVI, 114–25). Wherever he went he was popular with his colleagues, and the loyalty of the Indians to his wishes was exceptional. He settled disputes in Wisconsin and in the Sioux country; no one did more to establish the empire of France in the Northwest.

In 1690 he was promoted to a captaincy and while in command at Fort Frontenac had the pleasure of receiving his brother La Tourette, laden with furs from a post on Lake Nipigon, where he had diverted trade from the English at Hudson Bay. About 1695 Duluth was forced to retire because of lameness brought on by exposure. His last years were spent quietly at Montreal, where (as his will shows) he lived the life of a gentleman of quality, with good books, fine clothing, faithful service, and, it may be believed, many friends. Among the great French explorers of the seventeenth century he deserves a high place. Since he was singularly modest and silent concerning his exploits, his fame has been somewhat obscured. His contemporaries considered him of great worth, reporting that he was a "highly honorable man, a brave and experienced officer, active in business matters, of high repute and devoted to the service." He gave his time for his king and country not from sordid motives of gain, but from a scientific desire to expand the boundaries of geographical knowledge, and from a patriotic hope to cross the continent for France.

[Because of his partiality for La Salle, Parkman belittled Duluth. Several of the latter's letters are extant, and are published in Pierre Margry, *Découvertes et Établissements des Français dans l'Amérique Septentrionale* (Paris, 1880–82), vol. VI; for a translation of one see L. P. Kellogg, *Early Narratives of the Northwest* (1917), pp. 325–34; see also by same author, *The French Régime in Wisconsin and the Northwest* (1925), *passim*. Two excellent articles are by Wm. McLean, "A Gentleman of the Royal Guard" in *Harper's Mag.*, Sept. 1893; "The Death of Dulhut" in *Proc. and Trans. Royal Soc. of Canada*, 2 ser., IX (1903), 39–47.   L.P.K.]

DUMMER, JEREMIAH (Sept. 14, 1645–May 25, 1718), silversmith, engraver, portrait-painter, magistrate, was born at Newbury, Mass., the son of Richard Dummer and his wife, Frances, widow of Rev. Jonathan Burr. Richard Dummer, said to have been a native of Bishopstoke, England, settled at Newbury and later at Boston, and in 1635–36 was one of the Governor's Assistants. He had dealings with John Hull, mint master (*Suffolk Deeds*, VI, 235), in whose shop he placed Jeremiah as apprentice. Hull wrote in his diary (Hull, *post*, p. 150), "1st of 5th [1659] I received into my house Jeremie Dummer and Samuel Paddy, to serve me as apprentices eight years. The Lord make me faithful in discharge of this new trust committed to me." Having learned his trade, Dummer set up his own shop and, tall, erect, thin-visaged, a typical Puritan of aristocratic bearing, he entered upon his career as a useful and high-minded citizen of Boston. He was married in 1672 to Anna, daughter of Joshua Atwater, merchant, later prominent at New Haven, Conn. He joined in 1671 the Artillery Company, in which he held offices, but in 1686 when the Massachusetts militia was reorganized he was one of four captains who were not reappointed. His civic services began when he was made constable in 1675. He was a member of the Council of Safety, 1689, and with others signed two petitions addressed to Gov. Andros (Massachusetts Archives, CXXVI, 63, 200). Dummer was a selectman of Boston, 1691–92; justice of the peace, 1693–1718; treasurer of Suffolk County, 1701; overseer of the poor, 1702. He was of the com-

mission appointed in 1700 by the Earl of Bellomont [*q.v.*] to visit Gardiner's Island in search of treasure supposed to have been hidden there by Capt. William Kidd.

Dummer saw his second son, Jeremiah, Jr. [*q.v.*], started in an honorable legal career in England, and he sat a proud man in his pew on Sept. 27, 1716 (as recorded by his first cousin Samuel Sewall) while Mr. Pemberton preached a sermon congratulating another son, William Dummer, upon becoming lieutenant-governor and acting governor of the province. In his social and business relationships he seems to have been fortunate. He died after a long illness. The *Boston News-Letter* of June 2, 1718, commended him as "having served his country faithfully in several public stations, and obtained of all that knew him the character of a just, virtuous, and pious man."

Appreciation of Dummer's exquisite workmanship in silver has been revived in this century by successive exhibitions of colonial silver at the Boston Museum of Fine Arts and the Metropolitan Museum, New York, in whose permanent collections he is well represented. His shop produced some of the finest ecclesiastical and convivial pieces of the period. He also engraved money for Connecticut. In 1921 Frank W. Bayley discovered inscriptions in Dummer's handwriting on portraits of himself and his wife, which suggest that he may have been the earliest native portrait-painter of the English colonies. These likenesses, owned during several generations by descendants of Samuel Dummer of Wilmington, Mass., Jeremiah's eldest son, had previously been attributed to Sir Godfrey Kneller. The backs of the canvases, however, bear these inscriptions in a hand tallying with many Jeremiah Dummer signatures preserved at the Massachusetts Historical Society:

> Jeremiah Dum̄er pinx
> Dei in Anno 1691
> Mei Effigies, Ætat 46
>
> and
>
> Effigies Anna Dum̄er Ætat 39
> Depicta a Jeremiah Dum̄er
> Anno Dom. 1691

Although no autobiographical or contemporary reference to Dummer's practise of the limner's profession has to date (1930) been found it is plausible and even probable that so clever a craftsman, perhaps having seen some itinerant painter at work, learned to do passable likenesses, such as these are. Likenesses of John Coney [*q.v.*], silversmith, and his wife, who was Mrs.

Dummer's sister, were discovered in 1929 to bear Dummer's signature, and several unsigned portraits in New England may well have come from his hand.

[F. H. Bigelow, *Historic Silver of the Colonies and its Makers* (1917); F. W. Bayley, "An Early New England Limner," in *Old-Time New England,* July 1922; E. E. Salisbury, *Family Memorials* (1885); O. A. Roberts, *Hist. of the . . . Ancient and Honorable Artillery Company of Boston,* vol. I (1895); "Diary of Samuel Sewall" and "Letter Book of Samuel Sewall," in *Mass. Hist. Soc. Colls.,* 5 ser., vols. V–VII (1878–82) and 6 ser., vols. I, II (1886–88), respectively; "The Diaries of John Hull," in *Trans. and Colls. Am. Antiq. Soc.,* III, 110–316 (1857); *New-England Hist. and Geneal. Reg.,* July, October 1881.]   F.W.C.

DUMMER, JEREMIAH (*c.* 1679–May 19, 1739), colonial agent, author, who also signed his name Jeremy, was born in Boston, the son of Jeremiah Dummer [*q.v.*], by his wife, Anna Atwater. Jeremiah second was the younger brother of William, lieutenant-governor of Massachusetts 1716–30, who married a daughter of Gov. Dudley. He attended Harvard, graduating in 1699, and then went to Utrecht where he received the degree of Doctor of Philosophy in 1703 (*Colonial Society of Massachusetts Publications,* vol. XVIII, 1917, p. 210). He returned to Massachusetts and took part in the Harvard Commencement of 1704 where he is said to have spoken fluently in Latin (*Ibid.,* p. 376n). After considering the ministry as a career, he decided to enter business, and finding no opening in Boston, went to England and never returned. In England, he made prominent friends and was employed by Lord Bolingbroke in secret negotiations. He received assurances of promotion to an office of honor and profit, but the death of Queen Anne in 1714 ruined that hope. Meanwhile, he had done well and had become a prominent lawyer and a man of fashion (*Ibid.,* vol. XII, 1911, p. 127). In 1710, Sir Henry Ashurst, the Massachusetts colonial agent, died, and his brother declined to accept the proffered post. He recommended that the General Court choose Dummer who, in spite of Gov. Dudley's opposition, received the appointment. Dummer was genuinely interested in New England and in 1711 wrote to the Rev. Mr. Pierpont of Connecticut that a Mr. Yale, formerly governor of Fort George in India, had returned with a prodigious estate and the idea of bestowing some of it on a college at Oxford, as he had no son. Dummer added that he was trying to get him to give some of it to a college in New England and that he would "take care to press it home." (F. B. Dexter, *Biographical Sketches of the Graduates of Yale College, With Annals of the College History,* I, 1885, p. 101.) He succeeded, and Yale's benefactions to the college now bearing his name

began. Dummer's interest continued and in 1714 he sent over some seven hundred or a thousand books he had collected for the new institution. Indeed, it was said that he tried, later, to divert some of Thomas Hollis's interest in Harvard College to its Connecticut rival. Meanwhile, in 1712, he had been appointed colonial agent for Connecticut. In that year, he published in London, *A Letter to a Noble Lord, concerning the Late Expedition to Canada,* in which he set forth the efforts made by Massachusetts in the unfortunate Canadian expedition, to counterbalance the charges made by its incompetent commander, Sir Hovenden Walker, who claimed that its failure was due to the lack of cooperation by the colonies. Dummer is said to have unsuccessfully solicited for himself the post of judge-advocate on the expedition (J. G. Palfrey, *A Compendious History of New England,* 1873, IV, 277n). Although he did not return to New England, he appears to have still had property there, as in 1713 he was one of the absentee proprietors of the town of Leicester, Mass. (Emory Wasburn, *Historical Sketches of the Town of Leicester,* 1860, p. 9).

In 1715, when an attack was being made in Parliament on the colonial charters, Dummer wrote his *Defence of the New England Charters* (printed in 1721; reprinted 1745 and 1765). He claimed that these charters had a higher validity than those of corporations in England, as they had been granted in consideration of services to be performed; and that the colonial governments had never forfeited them by any misdoing; also that if there were any ground for forfeiture it would not be to the interest of the crown to resume them; and any legal action should be taken by the lower courts and not by Parliament. Dummer was much opposed to the appointment of Elizeus Burges as governor of Massachusetts, and was mainly instrumental in having him replaced by Shute (*Colonial Society of Massachusetts, Publications,* vol. XIV, 1913, pp. 362 ff.). When Shute returned to England and presented his *Memorial* of grievances, the Massachusetts Assembly forced the appointment of Elisha Cooke as temporary agent to join Dummer in England in refuting the charges. Dummer felt that the Massachusetts government was going too far for its own good in the countercharges made against Shute and that, as a result, it would appear in England as though in reality Massachusetts wanted no English governor at all. He did not hesitate to tell the Assembly so and, as a consequence, in 1721 that body, against the protest of the Council, dismissed him from his agency. In 1730 he was similarly and very curtly dismissed by Connecticut. He died unmarried, at Plaistow, England, and was buried at West Ham, Essex. His services to New England were of high value, but the colonies were rarely grateful to their agents, and Dummer, in addition, seems never to have been wholly trusted. He is said to have had a "vollible tongue," was a skeptic in religion, and not always in sympathy with the extreme radicalism of the colonial Assemblies.

[The facts of Dummer's life must be found in scattered sources. Some of his manuscript letters are in the State Archives of Mass. and in the Mass. Hist. Soc. A few, not important, have been printed in *Mass. Hist. Soc. Colls.*, 1 ser., VI (1800), 78–79 and 3 ser., I (1825), 139–46. His will is printed in the article by J. L. Chester on "The Family of Dummer" in *New-Eng. Hist. and Geneal. Reg.*, XXXV (1881), 254–71 and 321–31, at p. 268.]   J. T. A.

DUN, ROBERT GRAHAM (Aug. 7, 1826–Nov. 10, 1900), head of a mercantile agency, was born in Chillicothe, Ohio. His parents were Robert Dun, the son of a clergyman of Glasgow, and Lucy Worthum Angus, whom he had married in Virginia. Robert Graham Dun received his schooling at the local academy at Chillicothe. He was early employed in a store, and shortly after reaching his majority became the proprietor of a small local business. In 1850, Benjamin Douglass, who had married Dun's sister Elizabeth, gave the young man an opportunity to join the organization of Tappan & Douglass, "The Mercantile Agency," in New York City. This business, the first of its kind, had been originated by Lewis Tappan [*q.v.*] after the panic of 1837. At first its service consisted in supplying facts relating to the credit standing of country storekeepers to a few wholesale firms in New York, which paid annual subscriptions to cover the cost of obtaining such information. Under the management of Douglass the scope of its service was being expanded. Dun's first marked success was achieved in dealing with the personnel of the central office. He quickly won the interest and loyalty of his colleagues, which in the later development of the business was an important factor. In 1854 the firm was reorganized as B. Douglass & Company, with Dun as a partner. On the withdrawal of Douglass in 1859, Dun succeeded to his interest, becoming the sole owner, although the profits were shared with various associates who were known to the public as partners in the enterprise; the New York office operated for a time as Dun, Boyd & Company and later as Dun, Barlow & Company. At the outbreak of the Civil War in 1861, R. G. Dun & Company had branches in the principal cities of the country, including several in the South. Like many other enterprises of national scope, "The Mercantile Agency" could do little more than mark time during the war, but the remaining years of the century were signalized by unexampled growth and adaptation to rapid changes in business methods. In that period of transformation, Dun's managerial abilities were severely tested. He had a special gift for associating with him in close sympathy and coöperation men of ability, and this group which shaped the company's policies quietly proceeded to fit them to the changing demands of the business world, taking advantage at the same time of every new device in the mechanism of trade that seemed to promise increased efficiency in the service that they were rendering to the business community. The problem of reaching distant states promptly and receiving needed information from them in time to be of service was vastly greater than in the early days. Speed was entering into every form of business activity. The new conditions called for new methods. The offices of R. G. Dun & Company were among the first to make large use of the typewriter for communications with subscribers. The publishing activities of the house were developed with the expansion of its interests. As early as 1859, the year of Dun's accession to ownership, the first of the series of reference books appeared. The printing required by the efforts to keep up with the clients' requests for information in time attained so great a volume that the company had to install its own plant, employing several hundred persons. On Aug. 5, 1893, *Dun's Review,* containing a weekly report of business conditions, was inaugurated. Dun's researches went everywhere, even beyond continental bounds. Offices were opened in Paris, in Germany—finally, in Australia and South Africa. Personally a retiring man, with domestic tastes, he avoided publicity. He was married twice: first, to Elizabeth Douglass, sister of Benjamin Douglass, and second, to Mary D. Bradford of Milwaukee.

[*Who's Who in America,* 1899–1900; *N. Y. Times, N. Y. Tribune,* Nov. 11, 1900; E. N. Vose, *Seventy-Five Years of the Mercantile Agency, R. G. Dun & Co., 1841–1916* (1916); oral statement by R. D. Douglass, of R. G. Dun & Co.]   W. B. S.

DUNBAR, CHARLES FRANKLIN (July 28, 1830–Jan. 29, 1900), editor, economist, was born in Abington, Mass., the youngest son of Asaph Dunbar (1779–1867) and Nancy Ford. The father made boots and shoes. Charles was educated at Phillips Exeter Academy and Harvard College, receiving the degree of A.B. in 1851. For a brief period he engaged in his father's and older brothers' business in New Orleans, New York, and Boston. Owing to ill health he bought a farm in Lexington where he remained for a short time, until fully recovered. In 1857 he entered the Harvard Law School and was admitted to the bar in the following year. During 1856, however, he had contributed articles to the *Boston Daily Advertiser,* and in 1859 an opportunity arose whereby he became part owner and associate editor of that journal. This relationship continued for ten years, during the latter half of which he was sole editor. His editorials were vigorous and commanded wide recognition. His support of President Lincoln's administration during the war was whole-hearted, but free from extravagant eulogy of his own party, or rancorous criticism of opponents. In 1869 owing to a return of poor health he sold his interest in the *Advertiser* and resigned his position as editor. Within a few months he was invited by President Eliot of Harvard University at the very beginning of his administration, to become the first professor of political economy at that institution. He hesitated, not only because of poor health, but also on the ground of inadequate preparation. Finally he accepted, after two years of travel in Europe. His scholarly instincts and thorough knowledge of current economic problems quickly proved the wisdom of the choice. For thirty years he was the head of the department; as such he gathered about him a staff of younger scholars which brought prestige to the university. He did much to awaken interest in economics as a science, and to develop sound reasoning. He was especially acquainted with economics of the seventeenth and eighteenth centuries and with Ricardo's school. Although his special interest was in practical problems of banking and finance, he avoided propaganda in the interest of any particular group. He took an active part in the general administration of the university, serving as dean of the college faculty, 1876–82; and upon a subsequent administrative reorganization, as the first dean of the faculty of arts and sciences, 1890–95. In 1886 he assumed the editorship of the *Quarterly Journal of Economics,* the first periodical exclusively devoted to economic science to be established in the United States. To this, until 1896, he gave much time. In addition to these responsibilities, he was a member of the Board of Trustees of Exeter Academy, 1885–98, and for the last five years, president of the board.

Owing to his numerous administrative duties, coupled with frail health, Dunbar did not leave a large legacy of written work. In 1891 he published a compilation, *Laws of the United States, relating to Currency, Finance and Banking from 1789 to 1891,* which served as a most useful compendium for students in banking and finance. In the same year he also published *Chapters on the Theory and History of Banking* (1891). Though a slender volume, this is generally recognized as a classic in economic literature, especially in the treatment of deposit currency and banking reserves. In 1904 appeared *Economic Essays,* edited by Prof. O. M. W. Sprague, which brought together twenty of Dunbar's articles, for the most part previously published in the *Quarterly Journal of Economics* and *North American Review,* together with five that the author left in manuscript form. Four of these essays dealt with the history and methods of economic science; two with taxation; eleven with monetary and banking history, and two with commercial crises. They reveal the careful and patient scholarship of the author; they are free from controversial dogma, and have a permanent place in the historical literature of finance and banking. Notable among them are "Economic Science in America, 1776–1876" (pp. 1–29); "Some Precedents followed by Alexander Hamilton" (pp. 71–93); and "The Bank of Venice" (pp. 143–67).

In appearance Dunbar was of sandy complexion and of good height; his constitution was frail and delicate. He was reserved in conversation and cautious in his judgments. His religious affiliation was with the Unitarian Church. Soon after graduation he married Julia Ruggles Copeland of Roxbury, Mass.; three sons and one daughter survived him. In 1893 he served as the second president of the American Economic Association. He was also a member of the Massachusetts Historical Society and a Fellow of the American Academy of Arts and Sciences.

[Brief memoirs of Dunbar may be found as follows: Remarks by S. A. Green and Chas. W. Eliot, *Proc. Mass. Hist. Soc.,* 2 ser., XIII (1900), 425–28; Memoir by E. H. Hall, *Ibid.,* XIV (1901), 218–28; F. W. Taussig, in *Proc. Am. Acad. Arts and Sci.,* vol. XXXVI (1900–01), and in Dunbar's *Economic Essays* (1904), introduction, pp. vii–xvii; the remarks by President Eliot are reprinted in the *Harvard Grads.' Mag.,* June 1900.]

D. R. D.

DUNBAR, MOSES (June 14, 1746–Mar. 19, 1777), the only person ever executed in Connecticut for treason, was born in Wallingford, Conn., the second of the family of sixteen children of John Dunbar and his wife, Temperance Hall. The father was a Congregationalist; and Moses wrote that "my joining myself to the church [of England] caused a sorrowful breach between my Father and myself." About 1760 the family removed to what was then a part of

Waterbury, Conn., now Plymouth. In 1764 Moses married Phebe Jerome (or Jearom) who lived in that part of Farmington, Conn., which is now within the city of Bristol; and they established there their marital home. In the same year, "upon what we thought sufficient and rational motives," he and his wife left the Congregational Church, in which both had been brought up, and declared themselves of the Church of England. In Connecticut at that time the little Episcopal churches, served by missionaries sent from England and feeling themselves oppressed by the dominant Congregational authorities of the state, were practically unanimous in opposing the movement for American independence, and in supporting the cause of the King. The record book of the early Episcopal Church, which is preserved in the Bristol Public Library, bears on its title-page the significant text: "Fear God; Honor the King." This church Moses and Phebe Dunbar attended, and in this book are recorded the baptisms of their children. On May 20, 1776, Phebe died, having borne seven children of whom four survived. Soon after, Moses married Esther Adams.

The Revolutionary War was now in full progress, and Dunbar was already an object of suspicion. "Having spoken somewhat freely on the subject," he says, "I was attacked by a mob of about forty men, very much abused, my life threatened and nearly taken away, by which mob I was obliged to sign a paper containing many falsehoods." Soon after he says that he was taken before a committee of the Sons of Liberty "and by them ordered to suffer imprisonment during their pleasure, not exceeding five months." When he was released he fled to Long Island where Lord Howe was in command of the royal army, enlisted in the King's service, and received a commission as captain. He was given the dangerous errand of persuading other young men to enlist for the King. He procured the enlistment of a youth bearing the patriotic name of John Adams, but was betrayed to the officers of the state of Connecticut, was committed to jail at Hartford, and was tried in January 1777, for treason. He was convicted and sentenced to be hanged, and the sentence was carried out, Mar. 19, 1777, on a hilltop near Hartford, where the buildings of Trinity College now stand.

After his death his wife with her step-children, and one child of her own, left Connecticut and went to Nova Scotia, as did many of the Loyalists of New England. More than a century after his death, an old house in Harwinton was pulled down, and in the débris of the garret were found two papers, copies of letters written by Dunbar in the Hartford jail on the night before his execution. One was a letter, of an intimate and tender character, to his children; the other was a longer document, and contained an account of his life and a defense of his religious and political faith. Both are heroic in temper and strongly charged with religious feeling.

[This article is condensed from an extended monograph by Epaphroditus Peck, published in the *Conn. Mag.*, VIII (1904), 129, 297. Jos. Anderson, *The Town and City of Waterbury, Conn.* (1896), I, 434–36, gives the full text of Dunbar's letters mentioned above.]

E. P—k.

DUNBAR, PAUL LAURENCE (June 27, 1872–Feb. 9, 1906), poet, was born in Dayton, Ohio. His father, Joshua Dunbar, was born a slave on a plantation in Kentucky, but before the Civil War escaped and made his way to Canada, where he learned to read. He returned to the United States to enroll in the 55th Massachusetts Infantry. After the war he worked in Dayton, Ohio, as a plasterer, and in 1871 married a young widow, Matilda Murphy, who also had been a slave in Kentucky. Of this union Paul Laurence was the only child. Joshua Dunbar died when his son was twelve years of age. Paul was educated in the public schools of Dayton. At the Steele High School he was the only negro student in his class. His gentle, modest demeanor as well as his talent made him popular with his associates; he served as president of the literary society and as editor of the monthly publication of the students; and he composed the song when his class was graduated in 1891. For a while he cherished the thought of being a lawyer; but the best immediate employment that he could find was that of running an elevator in Dayton at four dollars a week. Poems that he wrote appeared from time to time in newspapers issued in or near Dayton, and just before Christmas, 1893, a booklet, *Oak and Ivy,* was printed at the publishing house of the United Brethren at a cost of $125. It was some time before the small edition was exhausted, but at the close of two weeks, by the personal sale of copies on his elevator at a dollar each, Dunbar was able to pay the amount of his bill. In the following year he was employed by Frederick Douglass in the Haiti Building at the World's Columbian Exposition in Chicago. Returning after some months to Dayton, he faced one of the most discouraging periods of his life; but he was befriended and encouraged by Charles Thatcher, a lawyer of Toledo, and Dr. Henry A. Tobey, superintendent of the Ohio State Hospital at Toledo; and these two men assisted toward the printing of a second book of poems, *Majors and*

Minors. This appeared in 1895 and showed great progress, especially more originality in the handling of negro themes. Of the very popular piece, "When Malindy Sings," the poet's mother had been the inspiration. Dr. Tobey, who had bought and distributed a number of copies of *Oak and Ivy,* suggested that James A. Herne, who was appearing in the city in "Shore Acres," be given a copy of the new book. Herne passed this on to William Dean Howells, and the result was an enthusiastic full-page review in *Harper's Weekly* for June 27, 1896. Requests for copies of *Majors and Minors* now poured in; Howells brought Dunbar to the attention of Maj. J. B. Pond, the head of a lecture bureau; and in the same year (1896) Dodd, Mead & Company formally published *Lyrics of Lowly Life,* the author's best-known collection. It was in the introduction to this book that Howells spoke of Dunbar as the first man of African descent and American training who had felt the life of his people esthetically and expressed it lyrically. Within the next few years the poet's success was so great as to be a vogue; in rapid succession he brought out volumes of fiction as well as verse, and he was in great demand as a reader of his poems. His experience with the lecture bureau was not happy, but it took him to England for a memorable visit early in 1897. While there he wrote *The Uncalled* (1898), which reflects his thought of being a minister. On his return to the United States, through the assistance of Col. Robert G. Ingersoll, he was given a place as an assistant in the Library of Congress, where he served at an annual salary of $720 from Oct. 1, 1897, to Dec. 31, 1898. On Mar. 6, 1898, in New York, he married Alice Ruth Moore, a native of New Orleans, a teacher, and an author in her own right. Meanwhile the numerous public readings, the late hours of composition at fever heat, and the confining work at the library told on his strength; and he spent the winter of 1899–1900 in Colorado in a vain search for health. His last years were a record of intense application, of sincere friendships, and a losing fight against disease. He died in Dayton.

Dunbar was singularly beloved by his people; and the story of his life, with its yearning and striving, its love of song, and its irony, has never ceased to appeal to them. He wrote the school song for Tuskegee Institute. Numerous societies were named for him, and in Washington the Dunbar High School. In eminent degree he represented the lyric genius of his race; but, while his most distinctive work was that in dialect, he regretted that the public preferred "a jingle in a broken tongue." His work looked both backward and forward. On one hand it reflected the humor and the pathos of those who lived on old plantations in the South; on the other it struck the key-note of the restlessness of an age that was yet to be. In addition to his poems, collected in one volume, *Complete Poems* (1913), he wrote four novels, *The Uncalled* (1896), *The Love of Landry* (1900), *The Fanatics* (1901), *The Sport of the Gods* (1902), stories and sketches, and in 1900, *Uncle Eph's Christmas,* a one-act musical sketch.

[The *Cambridge Hist. of Am. Lit.,* II (1918), 614, contains a list of Dunbar's volumes, with the exception of *Oak and Ivy* and *Majors and Minors* which were privately printed. The most detailed biography is that by Lida Keck Wiggins in *The Life and Works of Paul Laurence Dunbar* (1907). See also the chapters in Benjamin Brawley, *The Negro in Literature and Art* (1918, 1921, 1929); J. W. Cromwell, *The Negro in Am. Hist.* (1914). Much of the most valuable information about Dunbar, however, was that appearing in newspapers and magazines about the time of his great success in 1896 and at his death in 1906. The writer of this article is indebted to a sketch written with painstaking effort by Prof. P. M. Pearson of Northwestern Univ., and appearing in the *Chicago Times-Herald* of Oct. 14, 1900.]   B. B.

DUNBAR, ROBERT (Dec. 13, 1812–Sept. 18, 1890), engineer, inventor, was born in Carnbee, a short distance inland from the coast of Fifeshire, Scotland. About the beginning of the nineteenth century his grandfather, also Robert Dunbar, emigrated from Scotland and settled in Pickering Township, about twenty miles east of Toronto, Canada, where he purchased a farm and built up around it a warehouse, tannery, wagon shop and blacksmith shop. Around this little group of industries there grew the village of Dunbarton. When young Dunbar was twelve years old his father, William, a mechanical engineer, left Scotland with his family to join his father in Dunbarton. Here Robert prepared for college and was educated as a mechanical engineer. He completed his course at the age of twenty and had the immediate opportunity of demonstrating his engineering skill in designing and building the mechanical equipment for a new shipyard dock at Niagara, Ont. Shortly after the successful completion of this task, he decided to branch out for himself and in 1834, when just twenty-two years old, he went to Buffalo, N. Y. His first jobs here were rebuilding old flour-mills, incorporating in them his ideas for improvements, especially in mechanical handling. From this he progressed until he effected a partnership with C. W. Evans to engage in the design and erection of grain elevators and warehouses. Little is known of the extent of the activities of this partnership during the approximate fifteen years of its existence. Upon its dissolution in 1853, however, Dunbar immediately, with a group of friends, organized the Eagle Iron Works Company in Buffalo to conduct a similar business. In the course of the succeeding fifteen years practically all of the grain elevators in the vicinity of Buffalo were either newly designed by Dunbar or improved by him in the name of the company. During the period of the financial panic of the early seventies the Eagle Iron Works was dissolved, but Dunbar and another partner bought out the establishment and carried on as Dunbar & Howell for a few years. With Howell's retirement the business was conducted as R. Dunbar & Son. During his sixty years' continuous connection with the grain-handling business, Dunbar built up a world-wide reputation as an expert in the design and construction of elevators. Through the almost exclusive employment of his services, Buffalo gained the position of one of the largest grain markets in the United States. Elevators of his design were also constructed by him in Liverpool and Hull, England, as well as in Odessa, Russia. He apparently did not attempt to patent any of his ideas until toward the close of his career, when in the early eighties four patents were granted him for both fixed and portable elevators and conveyors, as well as the operating machinery for them. Dunbar married Sarah M. Howell of Buffalo on Aug. 26, 1840; she with a son and daughter survived him at the time of his death in Buffalo.

[Henry Hall, *America's Successful Men of Affairs*, vol. II (1896); obituaries in *Buffalo Commercial*, Sept. 19, and *Buffalo Express*, Sept. 20, 1890; Patent Office Records; correspondence with N. Y. State Lib.]

C. W. M.

DUNBAR, WILLIAM (1749–October 1810), planter, scientist, the youngest son of Sir Archibald Dunbar, holder of an ancient Scottish earldom, was born in the manor house of Thunderton, near Elgin in Morayshire, Scotland. It is said that he finally inherited, but did not assume, his father's title and estate in Scotland. He is known, however, in the history of Mississippi, his adopted state, as Sir William Dunbar. He received the greater part of his education at Glasgow and then went to London for advanced study in mathematics and astronomy. Here his health failed, and he decided to seek health and fortune in the New World. In 1771 he arrived at Fort Pitt (Pittsburgh), with a supply of goods to the value of £1,000 which he had purchased in London for trade with the Indians. Two years later, he formed a partnership with John Ross, a prominent Scotch merchant of Philadelphia, and established a plantation in the British province of West Florida near Baton Rouge. In Jamaica he purchased a large number of African

slaves for use on his plantation. The unsettled condition of the times later resulted in a series of misfortunes which swept away his accumulations; in 1775 some of his most valuable slaves were lost to him through an insurrection; three years later his plantation was thoroughly plundered by Continental soldiers under Capt. Willing; and a short time afterward he was again raided by Spanish soldiers under Galvez. In 1792, with Ross, he opened another plantation called "The Forest," nine miles south of Natchez and four miles east of the Mississippi. Applying his knowledge of chemistry and mechanics to farming, he made his plows and harrows on scientific principles, improved the cotton-gin, first suggested the manufacture of cottonseed-oil, and improved the method of packing cotton by introducing the square bale, utilizing a screw press he invented for that purpose. A few years of prosperity enabled him to purchase his partner's interest in the plantation, and further success enabled him to devote much of his time to scientific investigation.

In 1798, he was appointed surveyor general of the District of Natchez, and served also as a representative of the Spanish government in defining the boundary between the United States and the Spanish possessions east of the Mississippi. Upon the completion of this survey he took the oath of allegiance to the United States and became a warm supporter of its government. During 1799, he made the first meteorological observations in the Mississippi Valley. His interest in science attracted the attention of Thomas Jefferson, to whom in 1799, Daniel Clarke wrote that "for Science, Probity, & general information [Dunbar] is the first Character in this part of the World." At Jefferson's solicitation they entered upon an active correspondence, and on Jefferson's recommendation Dunbar was elected to membership in the American Philosophical Society. In 1804, the President appointed Dunbar and George Hunter to explore the Ouachita River country, and as a result the former became the first man to give a scientific account of the Hot Springs and an analysis of their waters. His manuscript journal of the exploration came into the possession of the American Philosophical Society in 1817, and at the time of the centennial of the Louisiana Purchase was published in *Documents Relating to the Purchase and Exploration of Louisiana* (1904). In 1805 he was appointed to explore the region bordering on the Red River. Among his many contributions to the *Transactions of the American Philosophical Society* are reports on his explorations, on the delta of the Mississippi, and on the sign language by which distant tribes of Indians communicate with each other. He wrote about the animal and plant life that he saw, and he solved the problem of finding the longitude by a single observer without any knowledge of the precise time. He also wrote articles on the fossil bones of a mammoth that he found in Louisiana, and propounded the theory that a profound calm exists inside the vortex of a cyclone. From his own observatory, fitted with elaborate foreign instruments, he observed lunar rainbows and other astronomical phenomena. He was the first man to observe an elliptical rainbow and to make a suitable explanation thereof. His interest in science gained him a reputation as the foremost scientist of the Southwest. He corresponded with, and held as his close friends, Sir William Herschel, Bartram, Hunter, Rittenhouse, and Rush. Even though he was indifferent to politics he was at one time chief justice of the court of quarter sessions, and later a member of the territorial legislature of Mississippi. He died at his home, "The Forest," in October 1810, leaving a widow and several children, each of whom was rendered independent by his large estate. His widow continued on the plantation until her death in November 1821.

[See J. F. H. Claiborne, *Miss. as a Province, Territory, and State* (1880), I, 200–01; *Pubs. Miss. Hist. Soc.,* II, 85–111, 182–83, V, 222; Dunbar Rowland, *Mississippi* (1907), I, 663–65; *Biog. and Hist. Memoirs of Miss.* (1891), I, 1020–21; *Quart. of the Texas State Hist. Asso.,* Apr. 1904, p. 311. For Dunbar's Report to the Spanish Govt. on Boundary Survey, see *Pubs. Miss. Hist. Soc.,* III (1902), 185–205. Fifteen letters from Dunbar to Jefferson will be found in the Jefferson MSS., Lib. of Cong.]　　　　　　　　　　　F. L. R.

DUNCAN, ISADORA (May 27, 1878–Sept. 14, 1927), dancer, was the first in modern times to raise her profession to the level of a creative art, making it a medium of expression for such varied and profound experiences as had hitherto found utterance in music and literature. Her father, Joseph Charles Duncan, was something of a poet; her mother, Dora Gray, was a skilled musician; the three older children, Raymond, Augustine, and Elizabeth, were all creatively interested in the dance and drama. Shortly after Isadora's birth, in San Francisco, Mrs. Duncan divorced her husband, and the family fell into poverty, so that the child early became familiar with the ugliness of shabby lodgings, cheap meals, and the hard-faced creditor. Equally early she came to know what was always to be to her the more real world of ideal beauty, centered at first in her mother's music. At the age of six she danced and taught dancing, having a little school formed of the children of the neighborhood. In comparison, the drab courses of the public school were exceedingly distasteful to her, particularly

as she was much too original and sincere to be understood by the ordinary teacher. Thus, when ten, she decided that she could waste no more time in school but must be about her own work— dancing.

She and her sister, Elizabeth, now for some years taught what they called a "new system," based on improvised movements interpretive of poetry, music, and the rhythms of nature, which gradually brought them a considerable vogue in the drawing-rooms of San Francisco. Then, at the age of seventeen, Isadora decided to follow her star in the East. She and her mother journeyed, with the slenderest resources, first to Chicago, where Isadora, ever scornful of the accepted ballet, had scant success, and then on to New York City, where she obtained an engagement in Augustin Daly's company. Daly, then at the height of his ephemeral fame, had no comprehension of her genius, and after two years she resigned, permanently disillusioned with the popular stage. Joined by Elizabeth and Raymond, she and her mother then traveled on a cattle boat to London. There the whole family spent their days studying Greek art in the British Museum—a study which had an abiding influence on Isadora's dancing—until they were on the verge of starvation. From this they were saved by a chance acquaintance with Mrs. Patrick Campbell, who came upon them dancing in a public park, and who introduced Isadora to an intellectual circle capable of appreciating art inspired by Walt Whitman, Nietzsche, and the Greeks. Applauded private performances in London were succeeded by similar performances in Paris, and the young American, accepted by those who counted, became the artistic sensation of the season. Rejecting lucrative offers from music-halls, she joined the company of Loie Fuller [*q.v.*] for a trip through Germany and then went on alone to a triumphant progress through Budapest, Vienna, Munich, and Berlin, where she aroused the wildest enthusiasm, the students night after night drawing her carriage through the streets to her hotel. In recognition of the communal, almost religious, emotions expressed in her dancing, she was called in Germany, "die göttliche, heilige Isadora."

Suddenly, Isadora fled with her family to study for a year in Athens. There they bought the hill of Kopanos outside the city and attempted to build a temple of dancing on an elaborate scale. The scheme devoured all of Isadora's earnings, and the next year she returned to the stage. In 1904, with the assistance of Elizabeth, she opened a school of the dance for forty children at Grünewald in the outskirts of Berlin. But while she was the energizing spirit of the school, the routine of instruction always bored her and it was no part of her theory of education that the teacher should sink his own life in that of the pupils. In 1905 her daughter, Deirdre, was born, the child of Edward Gordon Craig, and grandchild of Ellen Terry. Essentially pagan, believing in free love and detesting marriage, Isadora disdained to accommodate her life to the demands of conventional morality. In 1906, after a successful American tournée, she met in Paris a generous and art-loving millionaire whom she called "Lohengrin," who was the father of her son, Patrick, born in 1908. Time and again in subsequent years "Lohengrin" came to her assistance in financial difficulties.

In 1913, at the summit of her career, her unusually beautiful and talented children, with their English nurse, were drowned in a closed automobile which rolled into the Seine. She tried to ease her sorrow, first by assisting Raymond in relief work in Albania, then by feverish journeyings in Italy until brought to Viareggio and nursed back to sanity by her friend Eleonora Duse, and, finally, by having another child, unfortunately still-born, whose father was an Italian sculptor. Resolved at last to forget herself in her work, she returned to her school, for which "Lohengrin" now bought the great hotel at Bellevue near Paris, but all her plans were interrupted by the outbreak of the World War. Henceforth, like a broken spar, she was to be tossed from shore to shore at the mercy of political tempests.

The children of the school were first sent to America where Isadora joined them in 1915, only to take them back to Europe almost immediately when she became disgusted with American indifference to the Allied cause. There followed unsuccessful tournées, in South America in 1916 and in the United States in 1917. Finally in 1920 she made another effort to establish her school permanently, this time in Athens at the invitation of Venizelos, but the overthrow of the latter led her to return to Paris where her far-wandering school at last broke up. But she was not yet through. In the summer of 1921 she received an invitation from the Soviet Government to open a school in Moscow, an invitation which she promptly accepted. After vexatious delays, she was given an empty palace in the heart of the city where she gathered about her fifty pupils. This, her last school, was destined to endure, though not under her own management. In May 1922 she was married—the Russian marriage laws being sufficiently liberal to meet her approval—to the half-mad "poet laureate of the revolution," Sergei Yessenin, seventeen years her junior. The education of this handsome peasant-genius now became more important to her than the fortunes of her school. She at once took her young husband to Germany anu Belgium and then, in an unlucky hour, decided to bring him to America. Arriving at the height of the panic over "Red" propaganda, they were everywhere suspected of being Bolshevist emissaries and subjected to petty persecution by officious officials. The trip was an utter failure. Isadora's last words to her fellow countrymen were: "You know nothing of Love, Food, or Art. . . . So goodbye America. I shall never see you again."

She and Yessenin returned penniless to Paris where they lived for a time by selling the furniture, article by article, in Isadora's house, after which they made their way with difficulty back to Russia. Meanwhile the unfortunate poet's attacks of madness had become more frequent and violent; soon after their arrival in Moscow he deserted Isadora, sank into the lowest debauchery, and finally took his own life in December 1925. The posthumous sale of his poems brought large royalties which Isadora declined to accept, returning the money to his family. She was beset by poverty, but she had not lost her pride. After her final departure from Russia in September 1924, in western Europe she met with unwonted coldness, owing partly to political prejudice and partly to a very real decline in her own powers. The once taut, exquisite dancer became indolent and flabby with only occasional returns of fiery energy. One more artistic creation remained for her, however: the writing in 1926–27 of her autobiography, *My Life*, in which she achieved a masterpiece of courage and sincerity. More clouded days in Paris and Nice followed and then, none too soon, the end, which came at Nice, in a fittingly individual fashion. Entering an automobile which she was planning to purchase, she cried to her friends, "Je vais à la gloire," and a minute later she was dead, her neck broken by her long scarf which caught in the first revolution of the wheels. Her body was taken to Paris and buried in Père la Chaise.

The special creations of Isadora Duncan's flaming personality such as her renditions of the "Marseillaise," Tschaikowsky's "Marche Slave," and Chopin's "Marche Funèbre" all perished with her, but none the less the influence of her teachings and example have permanently enriched the art of the dance, even the ballet, in every western land.

[Isadora Duncan, *My Life* (1927), and *The Art of the Dance* (1928), ed. with introduction by Sheldon Cheney; Irma Duncan and Allan Ross Macdougall, *Isadora Duncan's Russian Days and Her Last Years in France*

(1929); Mary Desti, *The Untold Story; The Life of Isadora Duncan 1921–1927* (1929); Constantin Stanislawsky, *My Life in Art* (1924), tr. from the Russian by J. J. Robbins; Walter A. Propert, *The Russian Ballet in Western Europe 1909–1920* (1921); Wm. Bolitho, *Twelve Against the Gods* (1929), pp. 305–27; *N. Y. Times*, Sept. 15, 1927.]

E. S. B—s.

DUNCAN, JAMES (May 5, 1857–Sept. 14, 1928), labor leader, played a prominent part in the American Federation of Labor during its formative period of uncertainty and its struggle toward a permanent place in the industrial world. He was born in Kincardine County, Scotland, the son of David and Mary (Forbes) Duncan. After serving an apprenticeship as a granite cutter, he came to the United States at the age of twenty-three years. Almost immediately he became interested in the labor movement. In July 1881 he joined the New York local of the Granite Cutters' National Union, now called the Granite Cutters' International Association. Later he moved to Baltimore and was elected secretary of the Baltimore local in 1885. The following year he attended the convention at Columbus, Ohio, at which the Federation of Organized Trades and Labor Unions in the United States and Canada (1881–86) was dissolved and the American Federation of Labor formed. For half a century he was a friend and associate of Samuel Gompers and of others who were active in building up the type of unionism which the American Federation of Labor represents. In 1894, he was elected second vice-president of the American Federation of Labor. Six years later, he became the first vice-president, which office he held until the time of his death. He attended every convention of the Federation from 1886 to 1927, in the latter year, being unable to attend the Annual Convention because of illness.

He also represented labor in several important private and official missions. He was a delegate to the British Trade Union Conference in 1898; in 1911 he represented the American Federation of Labor at the International Secretariat in Budapest; in 1913, he was a member of a United States Commission to study workman's compensation; in 1917, envoy extraordinary of the United States Government on the diplomatic mission to Russia, known as the Root Mission; and, in 1919, a member of the American Labor Mission to the Peace Conference in Paris.

Like many other labor leaders of his generation, Duncan seems to have received very little formal education; but he possessed the excellent qualities of courage, persistency, and love for fellow workers. President William Green, of the American Federation of Labor, said in his address delivered at the funeral service: "I know of no man who possessed a more indomitable will, a higher conception of truth, righteousness and justice, and it was because he possessed those qualities to such an unusual degree that he made such a great success in the organized labor movement." For more than a year preceding his death, he was ill and inactive, having failed to regain strength after a serious operation. In January 1887, he had married Lillian M. Holman of Baltimore. His home for many years had been in Quincy, Mass., where the Granite Cutters' Association has its executive office.

[Obituary statements may be found in the Boston papers, Sept. 15, 1928; *Granite Cutters' Jour.*, Oct. 1928, pp. 1, 3 ff.; *Am. Fed. of Labor Weekly News Service*, Sept. 22, 1928; *International Molders Jour.*, Oct. 1928, p. 597; and in other labor papers. The *Am. Federationist*, Nov. 1928, contains an editorial note. See also *Who's Who in America*, 1928–29.]

F. T. C.

DUNCAN, JOSEPH (Feb. 22, 1794–Jan. 15, 1844), frontier politician, governor of Illinois, was born at Paris, Ky. He was the son of Maj. Joseph Duncan, of the United States army, and Anna Maria (McLaughlin) Duncan, both of whom had removed to Kentucky from Virginia. He had little formal schooling and this lack may have been responsible for the keen interest he later displayed in the cause of popular education. Upon the outbreak of the War of 1812, he secured an ensign's commission and was assigned to the 17th United States Infantry. He saw service in the frontier campaigns of the war and participated in the defense of Fort Stephenson on Aug. 2, 1813. In 1818, he removed from Kentucky to Illinois. In the course of time he acquired tracts of land in various parts of the state. His main interest was agriculture before he entered politics, and he considered himself a farmer by occupation. As early as 1823, however, he was commissioned major-general of Illinois militia, and later, during the Black Hawk War, served for a time as brigadier-general of the state volunteer forces. In 1824 he was elected to the state Senate from Jackson County. His notable service in the Senate was his active support of a bill for the establishment of a free public-school system, which became a law in 1825. In state politics he was allied with the faction opposed to Ninian Edwards [*q.v.*]. In 1826, he was elected congressman from Illinois, and served from March 1827 until 1834. As a member of Congress he had the social and political outlook of the frontiersman. He was keenly interested in frontier defense; he advocated the immediate survey and sale of public lands in Illinois and the region to the northward, and favored the distribution among the states of the proceeds of public land sales, the money to be used for internal improvements and education. As time went on, he found himself in marked opposition to President Jackson on various issues, including the bank, internal improvements, and appointments to office. Lack of sympathy with the Jackson administration may have been in part responsible for his decision to return to the field of state politics. In his successful campaign for the governorship in 1834, he was supported by most of the Whigs, though party lines were not yet clearly drawn and his position was still a trifle ambiguous. He was governor of Illinois from 1834 to 1838, and strongly supported the construction of the Illinois and Michigan canal, though he ultimately assumed the position that, in general, internal improvements within the state should be left to private initiative. In 1842, four years after his retirement, he ran for governor a second time, being nominated by the Whigs, but was decisively defeated, and his public career was ended. On May 13, 1828, he had been married to Elizabeth Caldwell Smith of New York City. His residence after 1830 was at Jacksonville, Ill., where he died.

[Elizabeth Duncan Putnam, "The Life and Services of Jos. Duncan, Gov. of Ill., 1834–38," in *Trans. Ill. State Hist. Soc.*, 1919, pp. 107–87, in which a diary covering a part of Duncan's congressional career is printed as an appendix; *Biog. Sketch of Jos. Duncan* (1888), by his daughter, Julia Duncan Kirby, published as Fergus' Hist. Series No. 29 by the Fergus Printing Co., Chicago; E. W. Blatchford, *Biog. Sketch of Hon. Jos. Duncan* (n.d.), read in 1905 before the Chicago Hist. Soc.; obituary in the *Illinoisan* (Jacksonville), Jan. 19, 1844.]   W. E. S.

DUNCAN, ROBERT KENNEDY (Nov. 1, 1868–Feb. 18, 1914), chemist, was the son of Robert Augustus Kennedy Duncan, an Irishman who had settled at Brantford, Ontario, and of Susan Hawley, a Canadian. He became interested in science in his preparatory-school days, and later at the University of Toronto specialized in physics and chemistry. Following his graduation from Toronto, in 1892, with the degree of B.A., he secured a fellowship in Clark University, where he remained a year. He was then appointed instructor in physics and chemistry in the Academic High School at Auburn, N. Y. In 1895 he resigned to accept a better opportunity in Dr. Julius Sach's Collegiate Institute, New York City, where he took advantage of his location to pursue supplemental graduate work in chemistry at Columbia College in 1897–98. He was an instructor at the Hill School of Pottstown, Pa., in 1898; married Charlotte M. Foster of Brantford, Dec. 27, 1899; studied abroad in 1900–01; and was appointed professor of chemistry in Washington and Jefferson College, Washington, Pa., in 1901. He occupied this chair until 1906,

continuing his European studies at intervals during this period. His preparatory-school experience and his general educational observations had made clear to him that there existed a great need for writings on chemistry and other sciences that would acquaint the lay public with notable discoveries through plain, easily understood translations of technical papers. He gave special attention to this useful literary work and about 1900 became a contributor to several New York periodicals. In the summer of 1901, after his articles had commanded favor, he was sent abroad by *McClure's Magazine*, to study radioactivity, particularly in the laboratory of Pierre and Marie Curie, in Paris. Two years later A. S. Barnes & Co. assigned him to collect in Europe material that would be suitable for use in preparing the manuscript of a book on new scientific knowledge, and in 1905 and 1906 he made for *Harper's Magazine* a comprehensive study of the relations of modern chemistry to industry in various European countries. Through this literary work he became widely known to the public at large as an interpreter of science. His books, *The New Knowledge* (1905), *The Chemistry of Commerce* (1907), and *Some Chemical Problems of Today* (1911), were of the highest scientific accuracy, but were so composed as to hold the lay reader's attention. Through his studies abroad Duncan became aware of the relative inferiority of the American chemical industry in the utilization of scientific research, and in 1906 he decided to devote the rest of his life to the creation of a system of industrial fellowships. The first fellowship of the kind was established in January 1907 in the University of Kansas, where Duncan had become professor of industrial chemistry on his return from Europe in 1906. By 1910, his great work at Kansas created a demand for his services in Pittsburgh, which, as a large industrial center, offered him special opportunities. He therefore accepted an invitation from Dr. Samuel Black McCormick, then chancellor of the University of Pittsburgh, to inaugurate his system in this institution in a department of industrial research, and the operation of the fellowships was begun in a temporary building on Mar. 1, 1911. Duncan served the University of Pittsburgh as professor of industrial chemistry as well as director of industrial research from the fall of 1910 until his death. He was also director of industrial research at the University of Kansas, 1907–12, and visiting lecturer at Clark University, 1911–14. Andrew W. Mellon and Richard B. Mellon, citizens of Pittsburgh and sons of Judge Thomas Mellon of the class of 1837 at the University of Pittsburgh, noted the practical success of Duncan's educational experiment and saw in his system an apparently sound method of benefiting American industry by the study of manufacturing problems under suitable conditions and by training young men for technical service. In consequence of this interest, in March 1913, they founded Mellon Institute of Industrial Research at the University of Pittsburgh, and later placed the industrial fellowship system on a permanent basis, as a memorial to their father (1813–1908) and also to Duncan. The present home of the institute, which is adjacent to the central group of the University of Pittsburgh, was occupied in February 1915, a year after Duncan's death, by the twenty-three fellowships then in operation. The institute was incorporated in 1927, and its affairs are managed by its own board of trustees. At present (1930) the building is filled to approximate capacity with sixty fellowships. The industrial research is organized on a contract basis, the problem being set by a person, firm, or association interested in its solution, the scientific worker being found and engaged by the institute, and an industrial fellowship being assigned for a period of at least one year. Each holder (fellow) of an industrial fellowship is given for the time being the broadest facilities for accomplishing a defined piece of research, and all results obtained by him belong exclusively to the founder (donor) of the fellowship. Only one investigation is carried out on a particular subject at any one time, and hence there is no duplication of the research activities of the fellowships in operation. By the application of the industrial fellowship system, the institute has been successful in demonstrating to American manufacturers, irrespective of size, that industrial research, properly conducted, is profitable to them.

[Raymond G. Bacon, sketch in *Science,* Apr. 3, 1914; H. J. Haskell, sketch in *Am. Mag.,* Feb. 1911; *Harper's Weekly,* July 27, 1912; *Who's Who in America,* 1912–13; information in the archives of Mellon Institute; biographic notes made by Miss Lois Whittle, Duncan's secretary, 1910–14, who is now secretary to Dr. E. R. Weidlein, director of Mellon Institute since 1921.]

W. A. H.

DUNGLISON, ROBLEY (Jan. 4, 1798–Apr. 1, 1869), medical writer and teacher, was born at Keswick, Cumberland, England, the son of William and Elizabeth Dunglison. He received his early education at Brisco Hill in Cumberland and at Green Row Academy. He was apprenticed to an apothecary, but by the attendance on lectures in Edinburgh, Paris, and London he gained the doctor's degree in 1818 at the Royal College of Surgeons in the last-named city. He later received a diploma from the Society of Apothecaries and became a "surgeon-apothecary."

Later, he studied at Erlangen and in 1823 he obtained the M.D. degree from that university. On Oct. 5 of the following year, in London, he married Harriette Leadham. His earliest publication was an extensive compilation of existing views regarding children's diseases, entitled *Commentaries on the Diseases of the Stomach and Bowels of Children* (1824). This book attracted wide attention and resulted in the appointment of its author, on the invitation of Thomas Jefferson, as professor of medicine at the University of Virginia, a position which he held from 1825 to 1833. He was then called to the University of Maryland where for three years he lectured on a variety of medical subjects. It was with the Jefferson Medical College of Philadelphia, however, that he was mainly identified, serving there as professor of the institutes of medicine, 1836–68, and for some years as dean of the faculty. He was in many ways a remarkable man and he undoubtedly exercised a great influence on medical education in the United States. According to Gross (*Memoir,* p. 313), he was a pioneer in the systematic teaching of physiology. He was not, however, a profound thinker, and his knowledge of disease came mainly from reading the work of others rather than from personal observation or research. His wide acquaintance with books and his exceptional industry combined with a certain degree of practical sagacity and attractive methods of presentation gave him an outstanding position as a lecturer and writer. In his day, in America, creative scholarship or productive work based on research and critical observation was not common in medicine, and the ability to express forcefully and clearly the thoughts of others constituted the main ground upon which the reputation of a medical writer or teacher rested. From such a view-point, Dunglison was a great teacher. He was a voluminous writer on many subjects, not medicine alone, and he translated and edited many foreign works. He was looked upon as a close student of philology and general literature. His most noteworthy medical books were: *Human Physiology* (1832); *A New Dictionary of Medical Science and Literature* (1833); *Elements of Hygiene* (1835); *General Therapeutics, or Principles of Medical Practice; with Tables of the Chief Remedial Agents, etc.* (1836); *New Remedies; the Method of Preparing and Administering Them* (1839); *The Practise of Medicine* (1842). The *Dictionary* was extensively used for many years, and in 1874 was revised by his son, Richard J. Dunglison, M.D., and published under the title *Medical Lexicon: A Dictionary of Medical Science.* Most of his books passed through many editions and were widely used. He was active in promoting the printing of books with raised letters for the use of the blind and with William Chaplin prepared *A Dictionary of the English Language for the Use of the Blind* (1860). In many ways he exerted an influence helpful to the community in which he lived. He was a member of a number of medical and other societies, and vice-president for some years of the American Philosophical Society. In 1825 Yale College conferred on him the honorary degree of Doctor of Medicine.

[R. J. Dunglison, *Memoir of Dr. Robley Dunglison* (1870); S. D. Gross, "Memoir of Robley Dunglison," *Trans. Coll. of Physicians of Phila.*, vol. IV, No. 6 (1869), pp. 294–313; *Autobiog. of Samuel D. Gross ... With Sketches of his Contemporaries* (1887); Franklin Peale, *Memorial of the Late Robley Dunglison* (1869); S. H. Dickson, in *Am. Jour. Medic. Sci.*, July 1869; J. E. Mears, in the *Western Jour. of Medicine* (Indianapolis), Aug. 1869; F. P. Henry, *Hist. of the Medic. Profession in Phila.* (1897).] R. H. C.

DUNHAM, HENRY MORTON (July 27, 1853–May 4, 1929), composer, organist, educator, was the oldest of the three sons of Isaac A. and Augusta L. (Packard) Dunham of North Bridgewater (now Brockton), Mass., a younger brother, also a professional musician, being William H. Dunham, baritone, long of the faculty of the New England Conservatory of Music. Henry at an early age showed musical aptitude which was encouraged by his parents who sent him in 1872 to the New England Conservatory, then recently established in Boston by Dr. Eben Tourjée. Registered as an organ student of George E. Whiting, Dunham became one of a group of young men in the school who were known as "the Doctor's boys," special protégés of Dr. Tourjée, who exerted himself for their rapid advancement. Of these students, nearly all of whom became distinguished musicians, Dunham retained the closest connection with his Alma Mater, from which he was graduated in 1873 and of whose faculty he was a member continuously from 1875 to 1929. His musical education, nevertheless, was not confined to this school, for in 1876 he was graduated from the Boston University College of Music which at that time was closely affiliated with the New England Conservatory. While still an advanced student Dunham gave recitals on the great organ in the Music Hall, playing all the major works of Bach and Thiele. In 1875 he became organist at the Porter Congregational Church, Brockton. He later served at the Cathedral of the Holy Cross and the Church of the Immaculate Conception, Boston. In 1883 began his connection with the Ruggles Street Baptist Church whose musical programs he made famous. He

had been reared in the tradition of the English organ school, typified by the works of William T. Best, but during his many years of church playing he kept abreast of all developments in organ construction and composition. His programs in the eighties emphasized Rheinberger, Merkel, and other German composers; later, he became a skilled interpreter of the French masters such as César Franck, Guilmant and Widor. From Ruggles Street he went in 1896 to the Shawmut Congregational Church, Boston. Ten years afterward he became organist of the Harvard Congregational Church, Brookline, at which he served until waning strength compelled him to give up all but his teaching engagements. He had married, June 28, 1887, Helen Hammond of New London, Conn. Their home was at Brookline.

Dunham's sound attainments as organist made it natural that he should compose chiefly for the organ. His sonatas, based on profound contrapuntal knowledge, are known to all serious organists. His *Organ School*, a text-book, published by the New England Conservatory in 1893, has had wide distribution, as has his later *Manual and Pedal Technique* (1914). Becoming interested in his last years in the combination of organ and orchestra, in which some of the greatest composers have not achieved success, he composed several very effective pieces in this form. Notable among them was "Aurora," which depicts the gradual coming of dawn; it was first performed in Symphony Hall, Boston, thereafter at the Hollywood Bowl, and by several leading symphony orchestras. He was a friendly, lovable man, a patient teacher who endeared himself to his many pupils. He was long the oldest instructor, in years of service, at the New England Conservatory, but until his latest year he kept his youthful appearance and enthusiasm. At the Conservatory Commencement of 1925 the fiftieth anniversary of his teaching was celebrated by performance of several of his works, his former pupil Wallace Goodrich, dean of the faculty, conducting the orchestra.

[The *Am. Organist*, in Dec. 1929, commenced the publication of Dunham's memoirs, under the title, "The Life of a Musician." Supplementing a long obituary in *New England Conservatory of Music Bull.*, June 1929, Geo. W. Chadwick, director of the Conservatory, and life-long friend of Dunham's, contributed an appreciation to the *Bulletin*, July 1929. See also Arthur Foote in *Am. Organist*, Nov. 1929; brief sketches may be found in *A Hundred Years of Music in America* (1889), ed. by W. S. B. Matthews; and in Louis C. Elson, *The Hist. of Am. Music* (1904). The obituaries in Boston newspapers of May 5 and 6, 1929, contain inaccuracies.] F. W. C.

DUNIWAY, ABIGAIL JANE SCOTT (Oct. 22, 1834–Oct. 11, 1915), leader of the woman suffrage movement in the Pacific Northwest, was born on a farm near Groveland, Tazewell County, Ill. Her parents, born in Kentucky, were of mixed nationality; the father, John Tucker Scott, Scotch-Irish and English; the mother, Ann Roelofson, German, French, and English. In 1852 the Scott family, father, mother, and ten children, including Abigail and her fourteen-year-old brother, Harvey W. Scott [*q.v.*], set out in ox-team wagons for the Oregon country. The mother and a brother died on this long journey. The others arrived at Lafayette, Ore., in the fall, and Abigail taught a district school throughout the following winter. In the next August, with Benjamin Charles Duniway, she began married life on a "backwoods" farm. After nine years of farm life, an accident to her husband threw upon her the support of her family, increased by six children. After running a boarding-school at Lafayette for three years, she moved her family to Albany where she taught a private school for one year and then launched into trade with a millinery and notions store. Her experience as a business woman in an occupation that brought her into intimate contact with other women brought to her attention the legal inequalities imposed upon her sex and led her to devote her life to the cause of equal rights for women. In 1870 she helped to organize an "Equal Rights Society" at Albany and the next year, selling her store, she moved to Portland. There with the aid of her sons, ranging in years from ten to sixteen, she launched on May 5, 1871, a newspaper, *The New Northwest,* through the columns of which she unceasingly championed the equal rights of women. For sixteen years she continued this paper and at the same time was active in lecturing, and organizing societies throughout the Northwest. She endured many bitter personal attacks and even mob violence before securing a hearing for herself and her cause. Through her efforts, however, in 1873 the Oregon Woman Suffrage Association was organized, and county and local associations throughout the state were founded in the years that followed. During these years petitions were presented to each session of the state legislature. In 1882 that body for the second time enacted a resolution submitting to vote of the people a constitutional amendment which should give the vote to women. The amendment was defeated at the election of 1884 but the agitation continued. In 1883 the legislature of Washington Territory passed a measure, drafted by Mrs. Duniway, that gave the vote to women. From 1887 until 1895 she resided in Idaho, and she won another victory when woman suffrage was adopted there in 1896. She

returned to Oregon and revived the movement in that state, but success did not come until the election of 1912, when the suffrage amendment was carried by a vote of 61,265 to 57,104. Mrs. Duniway drew up with her own hand the proclamation signed by the governor of Oregon that announced the final triumph of her long years of devotion to a single cause. Two years later she published *Path Breaking: An Autobiographical History of the Equal Suffrage Movement in Pacific Coast States* (1914), somewhat inaccurate in details. She had previously published two novels: *Captain Gray's Company: or, Crossing the Plains and Living in Oregon* (1859), and, nearly half a century later, *From the West to the West* (1905). In 1876 she published *David and Anna Matson,* in verse.

[R. C. Clark, *Hist. of the Willamette Valley, Ore.* (1927), I, 702–24; Harvey W. Scott, *Hist. of the Oregon Country* (1924); John W. Leonard, ed., *Woman's Who's Who of America* (1914–15); *Morning Oregonian* (Portland), Oct. 12, 1915.]   R. C. C—k.

DUNLAP, JOHN (1747–Nov. 27, 1812), printer, was born in Strabane, County Tyrone, Ireland. At about ten years of age he was sent to Pennsylvania to be trained by his uncle, William Dunlap, a printer, who had just married a relation of Mrs. Benjamin Franklin and through this influence had been appointed postmaster of Philadelphia. William Dunlap, who had learned his trade as apprentice to William Bradford, had been engaged as printer in Lancaster, Pa., but in 1757 moved to Philadelphia, where he opened a shop as printer and bookseller. At this juncture it seems probable that he sent to Ireland for his young nephew, who was immediately apprenticed to him to learn the trade of typography. William Dunlap felt he had a call to the ministry, and accordingly, in the year 1766, sold his stock as bookseller, leaving the printing business in charge of John, whose apprenticeship was near its close, while he went to England to receive ordination. Two years later, in 1768, he was given a charge in the parish of Stratton, in King and Queen County, Va., and sold his shop and equipment to his nephew. At this time the business consisted mainly in the printing of books, but in November 1771 John Dunlap began the publication of a weekly newspaper, *The Pennsylvania Packet, or The General Advertiser.* From September 1777 to July 1778, during the British occupation of Philadelphia, he printed his paper in Lancaster, Pa. When he returned to Philadelphia, he changed the period of issue to three times a week, and on Sept. 21, 1784, he began its publication as a daily—the first daily newspaper in the United States. Through numerous changes of ownership and name its tradition has been continued, its present successor being the *Public Ledger* of Philadelphia, by which it was absorbed in 1924. The Declaration of Independence was printed in Dunlap's office from Jefferson's manuscript, and this broadside, signed by Hancock and the Secretary of Congress, was the form in which the Declaration was sent to the various colonial Assemblies and to Europe. From 1778 until the federal government was founded and the capital removed to New York, Dunlap was printer to Congress. Soon after he returned from Lancaster he took David C. Claypoole, who had been his apprentice, into partnership. The Constitution of the United States was printed in the office of Dunlap & Claypoole and was first published in their *Pennsylvania Packet and Daily Advertiser*. The senior partner retired from business in 1795. In the words of a fellow printer: "Dunlap executed his printing in a neat and correct manner. It is said that, whilst he conducted a newspaper, he never inserted a paragraph which would wound the feelings of an individual!" (Thomas, *post*, I, 259). "The amiableness of disposition which might be implied from that sentence was not, perhaps, his talent. However, *de mortuis nil* . . . Dunlap possessed till his death, a handsome fortune (McColloch, *post*, p. 197). In 1780, he was one of ninety-two subscribers to the National Bank for the United States, formed for the purpose of supplying provisions to the army. His subscription was for £4,000. He was also active in military affairs, was one of the original founders of the 1st Troop of Philadelphia City Cavalry, in 1774, and as cornet accompanied the command in the campaign of 1776–77, taking part in the actions at Princeton and Trenton. In 1781, he was elected first lieutenant, and in 1794, captain of this ancient military company. During the Whiskey Insurrection, in 1794, he served as major commanding all the cavalry during the campaign. From 1789 to 1792 he was a member of the Common Council of Philadelphia. He died of apoplexy on Nov. 27, 1812, and was buried with military honors in the burial ground of Christ Church, Philadelphia. He was married, Feb. 4, 1773, to Mrs. Elizabeth Ellison, *née* Hayes of Liverpool.

[Isaiah Thomas, *The Hist. of Printing in America*, repub. in *Trans. and Colls. Am. Antiquarian Soc.*, vols. V and VI (1874) ; and Wm. McColloch, "Additions to Thomas's Hist.," *Proc. Am. Antiquarian Soc.*, n.s., vol. XXXI, pt. I (1921) ; *Hist. of the First Troop Phila. City Cavalry* (1875) ; MS. Records of Christ Church, Phila.; J. H. Campbell, *Hist. of the Friendly Sons of St. Patrick* (1892), p. 109 ; Henry Simpson, *Lives of Eminent Philadelphians* (1859), p. 325 ; James Cheetham, *Life of Thomas Paine* (1809), pp. 72 ff.] J. J.

DUNLAP, ROBERT PINCKNEY (Aug. 17, 1794–Oct. 20, 1859), governor of Maine, was born at Brunswick, Me. His grandfather, Robert Dunlap, a native of Barilla, County Antrim, Ireland, was a Presbyterian minister and master of arts of the University of Edinburgh, who settled at Brunswick in 1747. Capt. John Dunlap, son of Rev. Robert, married as his second wife Mary Tappan of Newburyport, Mass., and by traffic in furs and pelts, by shipbuilding and overseas trading, became one of the richest men in the District of Maine. Robert, third son of John and Mary Dunlap, graduated from Bowdoin College in 1815, and was admitted to the bar in 1818. Wealthy, personable, well-liked, he forsook the law and Federalist tradition for a life-long political career as a Jacksonian Democrat. At twenty-six he was in the Maine legislature, serving as representative during the years 1821 and 1822, and as senator during 1824–28 and 1831–33. He presided over the Senate for four years with an unruffled fairness and tact that won commendation from all parties. He was for a time a member of the Executive Council. From 1834 to 1838 he was governor of Maine, having defeated his Federalist-Whig opponents on the Jacksonian platform of the Union with state's rights, opposition to the protective tariff and the banking interests, and persistent championship of the laboring and agricultural classes. He was instrumental in obtaining prison reforms, the first insane asylum in Maine, the first geological survey of the state, and—by the sale of state lands—Revolutionary pensions and a school fund. In June 1837, during Dunlap's term, a Maine census agent was arrested by the governor of New Brunswick in that northeastern territory which had been in dispute since the Treaty of Paris of 1783. Dunlap proclaimed the soil of Maine invaded, called out the militia, entered into correspondence with John Forsyth, secretary of state, and by his vigor and tact brought and kept the critical situation before the eyes of the national government, at the same time holding the long-standing boundary controversy in abeyance throughout his term. In August of the same year (1837) he also commanded national attention when, although a Democrat and sympathetic with the grievances of the South, he refused to extradite to Georgia the master and mate of a schooner on which a slave had stowed away. He served on the Board of Overseers of Bowdoin College, 1821–59, and was president of the Board from 1843 until his death. His advocacy of Freemasonry in the period of the powerful Anti-Masonic party and general disapprobation is significant of his character. In 1825 he married

Lydia Chapman of Beverly, Mass., who bore him three sons and one daughter. He served two terms in Congress, 1843–47; was collector of the port of Portland, 1848; and from 1853 to 1857 was postmaster at Brunswick. He was not prominent in national politics but his friendship and advice were esteemed by his colleagues. Throughout his public life he received an unusual share of respect and popularity. Tall, impressive, with a calm but commanding countenance, he united suavity of manners with an expert knowledge of parliamentary rules and dignified impartiality. He remained a loyal Democrat despite the disruptive slavery issue.

[J. S. C. Abbott, *The Hist. of Maine* (1875; rev. by E. H. Elwell, 1892), pp. 429–31; L. C. Hatch, ed., *Maine, a Hist.* (1919), I, 214 ff.; G. A. and H. W. Wheeler, *Hist. of Brunswick, Topsham, and Harpswell, Me.* (1878), pp. 209, 501, 730–33. Geo. E. Adams, in *Me. Hist. Soc. Colls.*, vol. VII (1876); *Me. Hist. Memoirs* (1922); E. Hamlin, *Life and Times of Hannibal Hamlin* (1899), pp. 61, 102, 110, 304. H. S. Burrage, *Maine in the Northeastern Boundary Controversy* (1919); *Eastern Argus* (Portland, Me.), Oct. 21, 1859; *Am. Freemason* (N. Y.), IV (1859), 478–81; *Freemasons' Monthly Mag.* (Boston), XIX (1859), 24.]

B. M—o.

DUNLAP, WILLIAM (Feb. 19, 1766–Sept. 28, 1839), playwright, theatrical manager, painter, historian, was the son of Samuel Dunlap, a young Irishman who was color-bearer in the regiment known as "Wolfe's Own" on the Plains of Abraham. At the close of the war the regiment was stationed at Perth Amboy, N. J., where Dunlap withdrew from the army, began keeping store, and married Margaret Sargeant. William, their only child, was born at Perth Amboy, where he was reared and educated during his first eleven years. In 1777 the father's Loyalist sympathies made it expedient for the family to take up residence in New York, the British headquarters. A year later, while playing war with other boys, William sustained an injury which completely destroyed the sight of his right eye. The accident brought his formal schooling to an end, but he now resolved to develop a talent for drawing that he had already shown. A local artist was engaged to give him a few lessons, and by the age of sixteen the boy had set up as a professional portraitist. Among his early sitters were George and Martha Washington, whose likenesses he made in pastel while he was visiting friends at Rocky Hill, N. J., near the General's headquarters. In May 1784, the elder Dunlap, now a prospering china importer, sent his son to London to study painting under Benjamin West. During a foreign residence of over three years William applied himself to almost everything except his studies. He took particular delight in the theatre and saw all the leading actors, including Mrs.

Siddons in her prime. Naturally he returned to New York scantily prepared to take up his profession. His success was commensurate with his preparation.

It was not long before the studio was deserted for a new interest—the stage. Fired by the recent success of Royall Tyler's *The Contrast,* the first American play to achieve anything like a run, Dunlap wrote a five-act comedy, which he submitted to the managers, but which perished in the greenroom. His second comedy, *The Father; or, American Shandyism,* brought out in 1789 and later reprinted as *The Father of an Only Child,* met with sufficient applause to focus his ambition upon the theatre, and new plays from his pen began to appear on the New York stage at the rate of about one a year. During this period he also ventured into the field of poetry by writing two narrative poems of some length, both of which were included in two contemporary collections of American verse. But such occupations were inadequate for the support of a family (Dunlap had married Elizabeth Woolsey, Feb. 10, 1789); consequently his father made him a partner in his business.

In the spring of 1796 Dunlap took the crucial step of his career when he purchased a one-quarter interest in the Old American Company, New York's sole theatrical concern. He thus entered into partnership with Lewis Hallam and John Hodgkinson, rival actors and sworn enemies of each other. Dunlap's duties as acting manager, treasurer, and bookkeeper of the company were rendered so distasteful by the hostility of his associates that he soon deeply regretted his venture. The second season brought a realignment of interests by Hallam's withdrawal from the firm. The improvement was imperceptible. A more exasperating business associate than the irresponsible Hodgkinson it would stretch the imagination to conceive. The business was being conducted at a steady loss, but when, in January 1798, the managers transferred their company from the old John Street house to the new Park Theatre, they hoped for a reversal of fortune. They hoped in vain. By spring Hodgkinson had decided that Boston offered a more lucrative field, and, disposing of his concerns to his partner, he left Dunlap sole director and manager of the New York theatre. Having discovered that his own plays were but a feeble stimulant to box-office receipts, Dunlap now began to translate French and German successes, particularly those of the then famous Kotzebue. This German dramatist so effectually caught the taste of the town that during the next few years no less than twenty of his pieces were produced, the majority of them translated or adapted by the manager. By the increased support thus gained he contrived to hold his excellent company together. But it was a losing struggle. Grasping associates, a fickle public, yellow fever, ill health, and his own lack of business foresight conspired against his prosperity. In February 1805, Dunlap declared himself a bankrupt and forfeited his entire property.

As a means of supporting his family he now turned to his long-neglected brushes. Miniature portraits being much in demand, he essayed this form of art, although knowing but little of its technique. The season of 1805–06 was spent as an itinerant miniaturist, and, if his returns were small, at least he picked up some knowledge of his craft. In the spring of 1806, T. A. Cooper, formerly a leading actor in Dunlap's company and now manager at the Park, offered his old employer a position as his general assistant at a fair salary. The arrangement continued for over five years. One consequence of this office was a close acquaintance with the distinguished English actor, George Frederick Cooke, whom Cooper brought to America late in 1810 for a tour of the principal cities. During a part of this tour the dissipated player was entrusted to the guardianship of the abstemious Dunlap, who, shortly after the death of the former, turned this contact to good account by writing the *Memoirs of George Fred. Cooke, Esq., Late of the Theatre Royal, Covent Garden* (1813). Upon quitting the theatre for the second time, about the end of 1811, Dunlap again turned to painting. When his custom was interrupted by the War of 1812, he undertook the founding of a magazine, but the *Monthly Recorder* (1813) died with the fifth issue, leaving its editor poorer than before. Fortunately he was appointed assistant paymaster-general to the state militia in 1814, and the problem of how to go on living was temporarily solved. While holding this appointment, he completed a *Life of Charles Brockden Brown* (1815). His governmental employment came to an end late in 1816, and for the last time Dunlap returned to portrait painting. New York was still his headquarters, but he was often forced to turn itinerant and to visit Norfolk, Montreal, Vermont, and various other places in his search for patrons. He now worked chiefly in oil with only an occasional miniature. In 1821 he began a series of large show pictures, a popular form of art of the time. His subjects were usually drawn from the Bible and were often deeply indebted to Benjamin West's canvases of a similar kind. By sending these paintings on tour, the artist somewhat increased his meager earnings and probably did something to educate artistic taste, especially in the rural districts, where they were frequently exhibited. When an insurrection broke out in New York against the reactionary American Academy of the Fine Arts, Dunlap, although a member of that organization, joined forces with the progressives and in 1826 helped to found the National Academy of Design. From its inception he was very active in the affairs of the new society; he was a regular contributor to its annual exhibitions, he held the professorship of historical painting for several years, and served as vice-president from 1831 to 1838.

His last years were marked by continued poverty and much illness. In this condition he was helped and heartened by two successful benefits, one theatrical and one artistic, held for him at New York in 1833 and 1838 respectively. He did comparatively little painting during this final period, but in spite of weakened vitality his pen was never more active. His *History of the American Theatre* was published in 1832, and his two-volume *History of the Rise and Progress of the Arts of Design in the United States* in 1834. Two years later a temperance novel, *Thirty Years Ago; or, the Memoirs of a Water Drinker*, was brought out. His last energy was given to research in the history of New York. A preliminary study, *A History of New York, for Schools*, appeared in 1837. The first volume of the completed *History of the New Netherlands, Province of New York, and State of New York, to the Adoption of the Federal Constitution*, was published in 1839, and the second volume, posthumously, in 1840. Dunlap died, after a stroke of paralysis, in New York and was buried in Perth Amboy. He was survived by his wife and his son John Alexander Dunlap. A daughter, Margaret Ann, had died in 1837.

Dunlap was a man of only moderate talent but of unusual versatility, and he touched the cultural life of his day at many points. As a playwright he was without original ideas, but his craftsmanship was competent, and by employing ideas current on the English stage he was able to manufacture plays that were theatrically interesting and that contributed toward fashioning the tastes of the public and the practise of other writers. For instance, he experimented with the comedy of manners of the sentimental type, then popular abroad, but before Dunlap, except for Tyler's *Contrast*, unattempted in America. In serious drama Dunlap made two important innovations: he was the first in this country to write Gothic or terroristic plays, a species well illustrated by his *Fontainville Abbey* (acted 1795) and *Ribbemont; or, the Feudal Baron* (acted 1796); and he broke away from the formal pseudo-classic manner of the typical eighteenth-century tragedy, to which his American predecessors had adhered. In the two plays just mentioned and also in *Leicester* (acted 1794) he created a definitely romantic atmosphere for tragedy and tragi-comedy. It is worthy of note that in these three particulars Dunlap's efforts were quickly followed by a succession of American plays of similar type. If he did not, in all such cases, provide the model for his fellow playwrights, at least he was in the forefront of those who took the unaccustomed path. As a translator he reworked numerous Continental successes both French and German, often with considerable skill. His knowledge of stage technique and his facile, colloquial style sometimes created an adaptation more effective than the original. By bringing these European plays, ephemeral though they were, before the audiences of provincial America, he helped in some measure to give the United States a more cosmopolitan view of contemporary culture. With occasional dramatic work as late as 1828, Dunlap wrote in all approximately thirty original plays and made about the same number of translations. In quality his achievement was far superior to the average of his time. *The Father of an Only Child, The Italian Father* (acted 1799), *Leicester,* and *André* (acted 1798), the last two written in smooth and forceful blank verse, are probably the four most actable American plays of the eighteenth century, and they are interesting reading even to-day. In quantity of output he immensely outranked all predecessors. He was the first man of his country to make a serious business of writing for the stage. Perhaps, then, the title of the father of American drama, which has been applied to him, is no misnomer.

In his office as theatrical manager Dunlap aspired to establish a truly moral and cultural theatre, but popular taste did not support his efforts and he was compelled to compromise. He at least succeeded in offering more encouragement to American playwrights than they had formerly received, and he gave Continental drama its first real hearing in the United States, as well as featuring most of the current British plays. As a painter he must be regarded as a minor figure in an age that produced several great artists. Both his miniatures and his oils commonly show some stiffness and flatness—perhaps because he saw with only one eye. At the same time his subjects look like actual men and women with definite personalities, and in an occasional portrait he displays a power that commands admiration. Of more lasting influence than his plays and paintings are, *A History of the American Theatre* and the *Arts of Design.* In spite of inaccuracies both are still regarded as indispensable authorities, for they contain a fund of first-hand information that could have been provided by no other writer, and in both, the personal side of the actors or artists is so stressed as to produce a readability seldom found in works of this nature.

Dunlap was a man who pursued many interests and championed many causes, and always with large energy and enthusiasm. In the midst of his busy managerial days he found time for effective work in behalf of the abolition of slavery, having already demonstrated the sincerity of his pretension by manumitting the family slaves. He was an ardent American and never lost a chance to defend republican institutions. One result of his numerous activities was that he enjoyed close association with some of the leading men of his day, among them Irving, Bryant, Cooper, Samuel F. B. Morse, Gilbert Stuart, James Kent, and in particular Charles Brockden Brown. He could be a good hater, but his generosity, his love of good-fellowship, and his varied intellectual interests gained him a multitude of friends. Despite many hardships he faced life with cheerful fortitude. Even the strain of his often acute poverty he bore philosophically, conscious that he had forsaken his father's profitable business for the harder service of arts that his age scantily rewarded, but that he honestly loved.

[Certain autobiographical writings of Dunlap's provide the chief source of information about his life. For many years he kept a diary, of which four volumes are extant in the N. Y. Hist. Soc. Lib., and six in the Yale lib.; they cover about ten years between 1786 and 1834. In addition autobiographical sketches are included in *A Hist. of the Am. Theatre* and the *Arts of Design.* A detailed treatment of Dunlap will be found in O. S. Coad, *Wm. Dunlap, a Study of his Life and Works and of his Place in Contemporary Culture* (1917). Special phases of his work are discussed by T. S. Woolsey in "Wm. Dunlap, Painter and Critic, or the Am. Vasari," *Yale Rev.,* July 1914; and by O. S. Coad, in "The Dunlap Diaries at Yale," *Studies in Philology,* July 1927. See also A. H. Quinn, *Hist. of the Am. Drama from the Beginning to the Civil War* (1923), ch. iv; M. J. Moses, *The Am. Dramatist* (1925), ch. iv; G. C. D. Odell, *Annals of the N. Y. Stage,* vols. I and II (1927); and Oscar Wegelin, *A Bibliographical Checklist of the Plays and Misc. Writings of Wm. Dunlap* (1916).]

O. S. C.

DUNLOP, JAMES (1795–Apr. 9, 1856), lawyer, author, was the great-grandson of William Dunlop of County Armagh, Ireland, who in 1738 acquired land grants at Shippensburg and Falling Springs, Pa., and whose descendants continued to be associated with that neighborhood. His father, Andrew Dunlop, a lawyer of Lancaster and Chambersburg, married Sarah Bella Chambers, grand-daughter of the founder of the latter town, on Nov. 13, 1790, and James was born at Chambersburg. The family was well-to-do, and he received a good private education after which he proceeded to Dickinson College, Carlisle, where he graduated in 1812. He then studied law with his father, and after his admission to the Franklin County bar in 1817, commenced practise in Chambersburg. His family connections and natural ability procured for him a flourishing practise, in addition to which he engaged in industrial business, becoming senior partner in the firm of Dunlop & Madeira, owners of the Lemnos Factory at Chambersburg, and manufacturers of edge tools and cutlery. He also took an active interest in local politics, identifying himself with the Jackson Democrats, and was elected to the state Senate for Franklin County in 1824, serving till December 1827. During this period he prepared, "A Memoir on the Controversy between William Penn and Lord Baltimore Respecting the Boundaries of Pennsylvania and Maryland," which was read before the Historical Society of Pennsylvania on Nov. 10, 1825, and published in its *Memoirs,* vol. I (1826). In 1831 he was elected to the state House of Representatives for Franklin County and served one term, but in 1833 the action of President Jackson in withdrawing the government deposits from the United States Bank caused him to dissociate himself from the Democratic party, and he thenceforth practically withdrew from political life. In 1837 he represented the District of Franklin, Cumberland, and Adams counties in the state convention which met at Harrisburg, taking a prominent part in the debates. Though he was a good lawyer and a successful advocate, his business interests had interfered seriously with his legal practise, and in 1838, when industrial conditions became stagnant, he removed to Pittsburgh and commenced practise anew in that city. In 1843 he published Part 1 of a *Treatise on the Duties of County and Township Officers of Pennsylvania,* which dealt with the county commissioners and the assessing and collecting of taxes; but the plan, which contemplated a subsequent volume, was never completed. He also prepared, *The General Laws of Pennsylvania, 1700–1846, Chronologically Arranged with Notes and References to all the Decisions of the Supreme Court of Pennsylvania, Giving Construction to Such Laws* (1847). This work met with immediate favor, and two subsequent editions were called for, the last of which, issued in 1858 after his death, included the state laws up to 1853. He built up a substantial practise in Pittsburgh but considerations of health induced him in 1855 to retire, and he then took up his residence in Philadelphia where he published his *Digest of the*

General Laws of the United States with References and Notes of Decisions (1856). A great student, he enjoyed a high reputation as an accomplished lawyer and advocate, though no details of his professional achievements have survived apart from his own legal writings. In person Dunlop was over medium height and somewhat spare in build. Gifted with a brilliant wit and caustic tongue, he was "red headed and humorous, and would rather have lost a fee than have missed a chance to relate an amusing anecdote" (Cooper, *post*). He died when on a visit to Baltimore, Md. His wife was Maria Madeira of Chambersburg.

[Particulars of Dunlop's ancestry will be found in W. M. Mervine, *Harris, Dunlop, Valentine and Allied Families* (1920), and the *Kittochtinny Mag.,* July, Oct. 1905, which latter also contains details of his life. See also John M. Cooper, *Recollections of Chambersburg, Pa.* (1900).]

H. W. H. K.

DUNMORE, JOHN MURRAY, Earl of (1732–Mar. 5, 1809), colonial governor, who held also the titles of Viscount Fincastle, Baron of Blair, of Moulin, and of Tillymont, was the eldest son of William Murray, third earl of Dunmore, and his wife Catherine Nairne, daughter of William, Lord Nairne. The Murrays were descended in the female line from the house of Stuart; and in 1745 the third earl took part in the uprising of the Young Pretender in Scotland. Later he was pardoned for his share in the rebellion, and at his death in 1756 his son John succeeded to the title and estate. Reared in the ancestral home in Scotland, the young earl was a sturdy youth, accustomed to life in the open, but not without knowledge of the amenities of good living, nor without a wide acquaintance with the men of his day. In 1759 he won the hand of Lady Charlotte Stewart, daughter of the Earl of Galloway; and in 1761 was elected one of the sixteen representative peers of Scotland to sit in the British Parliament. The next nine years were passed for the most part at London, in the society of statesmen and eminent men. In 1766, for instance, Dunmore dined with Earl Shelburne when David Hume and a noted poet were the other guests (Lord Edmond Fitzmaurice, *Life of William, Earl of Shelburne,* I, 1875, p. 270); such facts disprove the rumor that the earl was uncultivated and rude in manners and appearance. In 1768 he was again chosen a Scottish peer for Parliament and in 1770 he was appointed by the Earl of Hillsborough governor of the royal colony of New York, an appointment which promised to afford both honor and profit, since it was provided that the governor's salary should not be dependent upon the whims of the colonial legislature, but should be paid from the revenue arising from the duty on tea (*Documents Relative to the Colonial History of the State of New York,* VIII, 1857, p. 223). The earl and his family reached the port of New York on Oct. 19, 1770, and were quartered at the castle, part of the Battery fortifications. The new governor entertained lavishly and was popular with the élite of the city.

After about eleven months, promotion came to Dunmore in his appointment as governor of Virginia. At first he was very popular and the recipient of many courtesies there; his charming wife and children were much admired; a newborn daughter, named Virginia, was adopted by the colony; and the governor's name was given (February 1772) to the new counties of Dunmore and Fincastle. In the Governor's Palace at Williamsburg the colonial gentry dined, among them Washington and other leaders of the Patriot party. Dunmore's first clash with this party occurred in 1773 when he dissolved the House of Burgesses for proposing a committee of correspondence on colonial grievances; the next year he again dissolved the House when the burgesses appointed a day of fasting and mourning over the Boston Port Bill. In the midst of these disagreements the Governor issued a call for the colony's militia to put down hostile Indians upon the frontier. He was later accused of inciting this Indian war to divert the minds of the Virginians from their grievances; there is evidence, however, that the Governor was sincere in his desire to protect the outlying settlements from hostile raids. He had in 1773 visited the colony's northwestern frontier, had built Fort Dunmore at the forks of the Ohio, and was preparing to have surveys made and claims entered when the Shawnee Indians became hostile. Determining to subdue them, he summoned the militia of the southwestern counties to collect under Col. Andrew Lewis [*q.v.*] and advance down the Kanawha River while he in person led his contingent west from Fort Dunmore (or Pittsburgh). Lewis's division was surprised on Oct. 10, 1774, at Point Pleasant, and after hard fighting repulsed the Shawnee under their chief, Cornstalk. Thus Dunmore found them humbled and subdued, and on the plains of the Scioto made peace with them. In after years the American soldiers asserted that Dunmore had treacherously attempted to lead the militia into a trap; there is, however, no proof of such a purpose. At the close of the campaign the officers expressed their appreciation of Lord Dunmore's conduct, and the legislature offered him thanks for his defense of the frontier (P. Force, *American Archives,* 4 ser., I, 1837, pp. 962–63). Nevertheless most of

the Virginians in his troops were soon in the army of the American Revolution, and the battle of Point Pleasant has been called its first engagement. Meanwhile, as the revolutionary movement gathered force, Dunmore was soon opposed by almost the entire colony. He first removed colonial powder to a ship-of-war, then the Patriots gathered and compelled him to pay for it. Threats were openly made that the Governor should be hung, whereupon on June 1, 1775, he retired with his family to the warship *Fowey,* and continued to oppose the colonials. In November he declared martial law and incited the slaves to desert, actions which caused him to be execrated by the whole colony. The troops gathered for a pitched battle at Great Bridge, on Dec. 9, 1775, when the Governor's forces were defeated and he again fled to the ships. On Jan. 1, 1776, he bombarded and fired Norfolk. The last conflict in July was at Gwynne's Island, after which Dunmore finally left Virginia and returned to England, where once more he was one of the Scottish peers sent to Parliament. Several years later he was governor of the Bahamas (1787–96). His death occured at Ramsgate, England.

Dunmore was not fitted for times of revolution; a forthright man with a single-track mind, he had no vision of the colonists' cause, and met the emergency by force rather than by finesse. Had he lived in quiet times, he might have been one of Virginia's popular and successful governors. Personally brave, he showed weakness in the crises, and by rash measures brought about his own downfall.

[R. G. Thwaites and L. P. Kellogg, *Doc. Hist. of Dunmore's War* (1905) gives a sketch of Dunmore as well as of the operations on the frontier. H. J. Eckenrode, *The Revolution in Va.* (1916), is prejudiced and presents the Governor's activities as they appeared to his enemies. See also Jas. M. Rigg, in *Dict. Nat. Biog.,* XIII, 1,285, which gives month of death as May; and Jas. B. Paul, *The Scots Peerage,* vol. III (1906), which gives date of death as Feb. 25, 1809. The Draper MSS., Wis. Hist. Lib., contain some of Dunmore's letters, and correspondence of L. C. Draper with Dunmore's grandsons. One of the latter, Charles Augustus Murray, is authority for the statement that Dunmore died Mar. 5, 1809.]   L. P. K.

DUNN, CHARLES (Dec. 28, 1799–Apr. 7, 1872), lawyer and jurist, was the son of John and Amy (Burks) Dunn. His father was a native of Dublin, Ireland, and his mother was from Virginia. He was born at Bullitt's Old Lick, Bullitt County, Ky., where he spent his early life. He attended schools in Louisville for several years, and had business experience before studying law. He read law under the direction of two prominent lawyers of Louisville and Frankfort. Removing to Illinois in 1819, he completed his law studies and was admitted to the bar in 1820.

He then entered practise at Jonesboro, Ill., where in 1821 he was married to Mary E. Schrader, a daughter of Judge Otto Schrader. In 1829 Dunn was appointed acting commissioner of the Illinois and Michigan Canal, and with his associates surveyed and platted the first town of Chicago. During the Black Hawk War he served as captain of an Illinois company which he had raised. Resuming practise after the war at Golconda, Ill., he was elected in 1835 to the House of Representatives of the Illinois legislature.

In the spring of 1836, he was appointed by President Jackson chief justice of the newly created territory of Wisconsin. This position he held for twelve years, until Wisconsin became a state in 1848, when a state elective judiciary was organized. His office as territorial chief justice was no sinecure. Not only did he preside over the appellate court of three judges, but he served as well as *nisi prius* judge of one of the three districts into which the territory was divided. He was a member of the constitutional convention of 1847–48 which framed the constitution of Wisconsin, serving as chairman of the judiciary committee. The power reserved to the legislature to alter or repeal the charter of any corporation created by it was his work. After retiring from the bench, he served as a senator in the state legislatures of 1853–56. He was a Democratic candidate for Congress in 1858 and for justice of the supreme court in 1860, but as the candidate of the minority party without hope of election. On moving to Wisconsin, Dunn had made his home at Belmont, LaFayette County, for a short period the capital of the territory. In this hamlet in southwestern Wisconsin he lived the remainder of his life. After retiring from the bench he resumed the active practise of law. He died and was buried at Mineral Point, Wis.

In the opinion of his contemporaries, Dunn ranked high, both as a trial, and as an appellate, judge, and during his long practise of law after his retirement from the bench, he was regarded by all members of the Wisconsin bar who knew him as "a great man in a private station." His chief services were in giving to the highest court of a young midwestern state the high character which it has never lost.

[See J. R. Berryman, *Hist. of the Bench and Bar of Wis.* (1898), I, 68–77; *Green Bag*, Jan. 1897; H. A. Tenney and David Atwood, *Memorial Record of the Fathers of Wis.* (1880), pp. 203–11; J. B. Winslow, *The Story of a Great Court* (1912), pp. 33–36; *Report of the State Bar Asso. of Wis. for the Years 1878, 1881 and 1885* (1905), pp. 105–06; 30 *Wis.*, 21–40, and 35 *Wis.*, 21–26. Dunn's opinions as chief justice may be found in Vols. I and II of Pinney's *Wisconsin Reports* (1872–74).]
W. M. S.

DUNN, WILLIAM McKEE (Dec. 12, 1814–July 24, 1887), congressman, judge-advocate general of the United States army, was the son of Williamson Dunn [*q.v.*] and Miriam (Wilson) Dunn. His parents, both of whom were of Scotch-Irish descent, moved from Kentucky to Indiana Territory in 1809, settling on the site of the future town of Hanover, and there their fifth child, William, was born. When he was eleven years old, William rode on horseback behind his father to Bloomington and entered the State Seminary, later Indiana University. He graduated in 1832 and became principal of the preparatory department of the newly organized Hanover College. Elected professor two years later, he went to Yale in order better to fit himself for his new work. In 1837, after a year more of teaching, he resigned his professorship, studied law in the office of an attorney at Madison, and was admitted to the bar. He began practise in New Albany; but, having married Elizabeth Francis Lanier, eldest daughter of James F. D. Lanier [*q.v.*], a wealthy and influential citizen of Madison, he moved to that town, where he formed a partnership with Stephen C. Stevens, a former judge of the Indiana supreme court, and practised until the Civil War.

In 1848 he was elected to the lower house of the Indiana legislature and played an active part in the passage of an act levying a state tax for the support of public schools. His career in the legislature led, in 1849, to his nomination for Congress by the Whigs, but in the election he was beaten by his Democratic antagonist. He was, however, chosen a delegate to the convention that formulated the Indiana Constitution of 1851 and played an active part in the work of that body, especially in matters concerning education and banking. Though a resident of southern Indiana, where Southern influence was strong, he opposed the extension of slavery, and when the Kansas-Nebraska Act led to the formation of the Republican party, he joined it. In 1858 and again in 1860 he was elected by that party to Congress, where his course was marked by energy and decision. During 1861–63 he was a member of the important committee on military affairs of the House. Upon the slavery question and most other issues his opinions were in close harmony with those of President Lincoln. He enlisted in the Indiana Infantry in 1861, and from June to August of that year served as aide-de-camp to McClellan. Having been defeated for reëlection to Congress in 1862, he was after the expiration of his term, appointed judge-advocate for the Department of Missouri, and ultimately rose, in 1875, to be judge-advocate general of the army, retiring in 1881. He died at his summer home, "Maplewood," in Fairfax County, Va.

[W. W. Woollen, *William McKee Dunn: A Memoir* (n.d.), printed for private distribution soon after Dunn's death; *Ind. Univ. Bull. Reg. of Grads. 1830–1916* (1917); T. A. Wylie, *Ind. Univ., Its Hist. from 1820 when Founded to 1890* (1890); *Complete List of the Members of the Senate and House of Representatives of Ind., 1816–1903* (1903); F. B. Heitman, *Hist. Reg. and Dict. U. S. Army* (1903); *Biog. Dir. Am. Cong.* (1928); *Washington Post* and *Evening Star* (Washington), July 25, 1887.]   P. L. H.

DUNN, WILLIAMSON (Dec. 25, 1781–Nov. 11, 1854), Indiana pioneer, was born near Crow's Station, not far from Danville, Ky. His parents were Samuel Dunn, a soldier in Dunmore's War and in the Revolution, and Eleanor Brewster. In September 1806, Williamson Dunn married Miriam Wilson, and three years later the pair, with two young children, moved to southern Indiana and built the first house where the town of Hanover now stands. With him Dunn took three negro slaves whom he had inherited and whom he now freed. In 1811 he was made by Gov. Harrison justice of the peace and judge of the court of common pleas of Jefferson County. Soon after the outbreak of the War of 1812, President Madison commissioned him a captain of rangers, and the next year he participated in raids upon hostile Indian towns along the White and Wabash rivers. Later that year he took command of Fort Harrison near Terre Haute. Retiring from the army before the end of the war, he served for a time as associate judge of the circuit court of Jefferson County. Upon the admission of Indiana to statehood in 1816, he was elected a member of the state House of Representatives and was thrice returned to that body. In the third and fourth legislatures he was speaker of the House. In 1820 he was commissioned register of the land office for the Terre Haute district and three years later removed to Crawfordsville, which town he helped to lay out. He held the office until 1829, when he returned to Hanover. In 1837 he was chosen on the Whig ticket to fill a vacancy in the state Senate, and in 1846 was elected probate judge of Jefferson County and was subsequently reëlected.

Throughout his career he took a strong interest in the advancement of education. He donated fifty acres of land to help establish the academy which became Hanover College, and, later, he gave the ground at Crawfordsville on which Wabash College was erected. He was widely esteemed for his ability, probity, and public spirit. One of his sons, William McKee Dunn [*q.v.*], became judge-advocate general of the United States army. Of his family a writer on the early history of Indiana says that no other "equalled the Dunns in bravery and soldierly qualities." They were often called "the fighting Dunns," and were well worthy of the name. Williamson Dunn suffered a sunstroke in September 1854, and died from its effects some weeks later.

[T. M. Hopkins, *Reminiscences of Col. John Ketcham, of Monroe County, Ind.* (1866), pp. 18–22; Wm. W. Woollen, *Biog. and Hist. Sketches of Early Ind.* (1883); W. M. Dunn, *Early Hist. of Hanover Coll.* (1883); A. Y. Moore, *Hist. of Hanover Coll.* (1900); R. T. Burrell, *Complete List of the Members of the Senate and House of Representatives of Ind.* (1903); *Presbyterian Herald* (Louisville), Dec. 7, 1854; *Madison Daily Banner* (Madison, Ind.), Nov. 13, 1854.]   P. L. H.

DUNNING, ALBERT ELIJAH (Jan. 5, 1844–Nov. 14, 1923), clergyman, editor, was the only son of Elijah Starr Dunning, a farmer of Brookfield, Conn., and his wife, Abigail Emily Beach. When he was six years old, the family moved to the neighboring town of Bridgewater, where Albert's boyhood was spent in farm work and at the district school. He spent a year at the Institute at Fort Edward, N. Y., and graduated at Bryant & Stratton's Business College at Albany in 1862. He prepared himself for Yale and entered the class of 1867 in the spring of its freshman year. Graduating with high academic and social honors, he proceeded to Andover Seminary where he graduated in 1870. His only pastorate was that of the Highland Congregational Church in the Roxbury district of Boston, where he was ordained and installed Sept. 29, 1870. He was secretary of the Congregational Sunday School and Publishing Society from 1881 to 1889, and editor of *The Congregationalist* from 1889 to 1911. He received the degree of D.D. from Beloit College in 1889.

Dunning's remarkable aptitude as an interpreter of the Bible began to show itself during his pastorate, especially in connection with the Sunday-school, and his important work with men's Bible classes, begun then, continued in various connections throughout his life. As secretary of the Congregational Sunday School and Publishing Society he was active in Sunday-school promotion in various parts of the country, especially in frontier work in the West and in the Southern mountains. He was a member of the International Sunday School Committee from 1884 to 1891 and was for several years in charge of the Sunday-school normal work at Chautauqua. Through his varied activities in this department, his contribution toward bringing the instruction in the Sunday-schools of the country into line with modern biblical study was important.

The earlier years of Dunning's editorship of

The Congregationalist were a period of theological transition. The Congregational churches were passing from the older orthodoxy of the New England theology to a larger way of looking at the Bible and religious truth; and his true liberality, coupled with his rare tact and wisdom, did much toward bringing his denomination through this critical period without disruption. He was the author of the following books: *The Sunday School Library* (1883); *Bible Studies* (1886); *Congregationalists in America* (1894); and *The Making of the Bible* (1911). After the close of his editorship, he engaged in varied professional and literary labor till a few months before his death which occurred at his home in Brookline, Mass. During his latter years he served for several periods as acting pastor of the Congregational Church at Bowdon, Cheshire, England, performing an especially valuable wartime service there in 1916. He traveled extensively, making a trip around the world in 1911–12. He was endowed with the social graces, had a keen sense of humor, and his circle of friends was international. On Dec. 27, 1870, he married Harriet Westbrook of Kingston, N. Y., who survived him with their three sons and one daughter.

[In 1927, Mrs. Dunning issued *Albert Elijah Dunning: A Book of Remembrance*, containing biographical chapters by herself and contributions from many friends, as well as a number of portraits. There are also accounts of Dunning's life in the *Congreg. Year Book*, 1923, and in *Report of the Trigintennial Meeting . . . of the Class of 1867, Yale* (1897); *Supplementary Record of the Class of 1867 in Yale Coll.* (1914); *The Congregationalist* (Boston), June 17, 1911, Nov. 22, 29, Dec. 6, 1923; *Yale Univ. Obit. Record*, 1924.]

F. T. P.

DUNNING, WILLIAM ARCHIBALD (May 12, 1857–Aug. 25, 1922), historian, teacher, was born in Plainfield, N. J. His father, John H. Dunning, was a manufacturer, a man of wide and eager intellectual interests, a close student, and an artist of some talent. His mother was Catherine D. Trelease. Dunning entered Dartmouth in 1877, but remaining there only a year he went to Columbia, where he was graduated in 1881, receiving the degree of A.M. in 1884 and that of Ph.D. in 1885. He was also for a time a student at the University of Berlin. On Apr. 18, 1888, he married Charlotte E. Loomis of Brooklyn, N. Y., who died June 13, 1917. At Columbia he was in succession fellow, lecturer, instructor, adjunct professor, and professor. In 1904 he became the first Lieber Professor of History and Political Philosophy.

His reputation rests upon the twofold basis of his own work as an investigator and writer, and his genius as a teacher. Deeply interested in scholarship and in scholars, he was one of the founders of the American Historical Association, a regular attendant upon its meetings, long a member of its council, and its president in 1913. He was the president of the American Political Science Association at the time of his death. He was a member of the Massachusetts Historical Society and the New York Historical Society. The list of his writings is extensive. It includes: *Essays on the Civil War and Reconstruction* (1898); *Reconstruction, Political and Economic, 1865–1877* (1907); *A History of Political Theories: Ancient and Mediæval* (1902); *From Luther to Montesquieu* (1905); *From Rousseau to Spencer* (1920); with Frederick Bancroft, "A Sketch of Carl Schurz's Political Career" in *The Reminiscences of Carl Schurz*, vol. III (1908); *The British Empire and the United States* (1914); and many articles and reviews published chiefly in the *American Historical Review* and in the *Political Science Quarterly*, of which he was managing editor from 1894 to 1903. He was the first to make scientific and scholarly investigation of the period of Reconstruction, and no one did more than he to rewrite the history of the generation following the Civil War, his own writings being supplemented by the results of investigations in the same field made by his many students. His study of Anglo-American relations is a brilliant piece of writing and an admirable analysis of the subject. His *History of Political Theories* deals with the development of systematic political thought from the classical period to modern times. In it, excluding primitive political theory and limiting the scope of the work to the philosophy of the European Aryan peoples, "he indicated the relation of political philosophy to ethical and juristic concepts and also to the general history of ideas. Nor was he unmindful of the relation between political philosophy and the current institutional development" (Merriam, *post*).

Dunning wrote with great precision and restraint. Highly critical of his own work, he set a lofty standard with respect both to form and content. His ideal was "to remain detached in interest and objective in method. He seemed to fear nothing so much as to be considered prejudiced, unbalanced, immature in judgment, reckless in conclusion" (*Ibid.*). This restraint was, however, much more noticeable in his books than in his short articles and reviews where he allowed his sprightly wit and his human quality free rein. As a lecturer, both to graduate and undergraduate students, he was interesting and stimulating. He never nursed his students; his method was rather that of throwing them overboard to swim for themselves. When once they had shown ability and self-reliance, however, he was the most helpful of critical guides. With them, the "Old Chief," as they affectionately called him, established a relationship of personal friendship which became to many of them a decisive influence in their lives. In 1914, in honor of his presidency of the American Historical Association, sixteen former students published *Studies in Southern History and Politics,* and in 1924 another group celebrated his presidency of the American Political Science Association with *A History of Political Theories, Recent Times.* Dunning had a charming personality, full of enthusiasm and human sympathy, with "a unique quality of princely fellowship and Shakespearian wit." He was a notable figure in any group.

[Chas. E. Merriam, in H. W. Odum, ed., *Am. Masters of Social Science* (1927), also in *Social Forces,* Sept. 1926; *Who's Who in America,* 1922–23; *N. Y. Times,* Aug. 26, 1922; *Springfield Sunday Republican,* Aug. 27, 1922; *The Independent* (N. Y.), Sept. 30, 1922; *Am. Hist. Rev.,* Oct. 1922; personal association over many years.]   J.G.de R. H.

DUNSTER, HENRY (1609–Feb. 27, 1658/-59?), first president of Harvard College, was the son of Henry Dunster of the parish of Bury, Lancashire, England, where the younger Henry was baptized Nov. 26, 1609. The family were apparently yeomen or small copy-holders of Balehoult, in the parish of Bury, but the son received a university education at Magdalene College, Cambridge, where he was granted the degrees of B.A. (1630/31) and M.A. (1634). After graduation he taught school and became curate of Bury but, probably on account of non-conformity, emigrated to Massachusetts where he arrived in 1640. His reputation for learning, particularly in the Oriental languages, had preceded him and almost as soon as he arrived he was made president of Harvard, Aug. 27, 1640. The institution which had been but a struggling school soon became a college under his administration. Rules of admission and the principles according to which degrees should be granted were laid down, and scholastic forms established similar to those of the English universities. The establishing act of the General Court in 1642 was probably, and the charter of 1650 avowedly, obtained on Dunster's petition. He was indefatigable in his services, and, although a poor man, gave the college 100 acres of land at a crisis in its affairs. The first president's house and college hall practically owed their existence to him (*Publications of the Colonial Society of Massachusetts,* III, 420), and through the Commissioners of the United Colonies he tried to interest all of the colonies in support of the institution. It may be noted that he had to call the attention of the General Court to the need for influencing graduates to remain in America, as of the twenty who graduated prior to 1646 eleven emigrated to England and remained there permanently. The first printing-press within the present limits of the United States was established in 1639 and two years later transferred to Dunster's own house and placed under his direction. Although he had no means of his own, the colony made no provision for paying him a salary as president other than by the allotment to him of certain taxes, leaving him to do the work of collecting them, which not only threw a large burden upon him but caused him heavy loss. After his resignation there was about £40 still due him which the college asked the General Court to pay him in view of his invaluable services but the Court refused, although after his death it compromised by paying half the sum due to his widow. In 1653 Dunster adopted some of the principles of the Baptists and was forced to resign his presidency, Oct. 24, 1654. After petitioning twice he was allowed to remain in the house built largely by himself until March 1655. In April he was indicted by the grand jury for disturbing the ordinance of infant baptism, convicted, sentenced to public admonition, and put under bonds for good behavior. Either immediately or within a few months he moved to Scituate where he acted as minister for some years, dying there, probably, in 1658/59. He married first, June 22, 1641, Elizabeth (Harris) Glover who died Aug. 23, 1643; and second, in 1644, Elizabeth (Atkinson?) who died Sept. 12, 1690.

[Jeremiah Chaplin, *Life of Henry Dunster* (1872); Samuel Dunster, *Henry Dunster and his Descendants* (1876); Josiah Quincy, *Hist. of Harvard Univ.* (2 vols., 1840); *New Eng. Hist. and Geneal. Reg.,* Apr. 1907, p. 188, Jan. 1926, pp. 86–95; *Pubs. Col. Soc. Mass.,* vols. III (1900), XV (1925), *loc. cit.*]

J.T.A.

DUNWOODY, WILLIAM HOOD (Mar. 14, 1841–Feb. 8, 1914), merchant miller, financier, was born in Westtown, Chester County, Pa., of Scotch ancestry, the son of James and Hannah (Hood) Dunwoody. His father as well as three generations before him had been farmers in this county. William attended the country schools until he was fourteen, when he was sent to an academy in Philadelphia for four years. At the conclusion of his course there, he entered the office of his uncle, Ezekiel Dunwoody, who was in the grain and feed business in that city. This association continued for five years, when Dunwoody, at the age of twenty-three, set out for himself and became the senior member of the firm of Dunwoody & Robertson, flour merchants in Philadelphia. Aware of the growing flour industry of Minneapolis, Dunwoody went there in 1869 to purchase flour for eastern firms. Presumably he was very favorably impressed with Minneapolis, for two years later he moved there, making it his permanent home. It had always been his ambition to own and operate a flour-mill, and, immediately upon establishing his residence in Minneapolis, he became a partner in two milling firms in that city. In 1875 he helped to organize the Minneapolis Millers' Association for the purpose of buying wheat for local mills and acted as its general agent, but the association was rather shortlived, because of the ultimate establishment of elevators covering the wheat-growing territory. The experience derived from the association, however, suggested the application of a similar institution to the selling of flour to Europe. The plan was not favored by most of the association, so Cadwallader C. Washburn, the largest individual miller in Minneapolis and the governor of Wisconsin, decided to carry it out alone, and selected young Dunwoody as his foreign representative. Dunwoody spent the year of 1877 in England and Scotland and after many discouragements succeeded in founding a permanent trade between the Old and New Worlds on a very thorough basis. It is generally recognized that the vast volume of the flour business of today is the result of Dunwoody's efforts. Upon his return to Minneapolis in 1878, he devoted his attention to his own flour interests and in 1879 became a partner with Washburn, John Crosby, and Charles J. Martin in the firm of Washburn, Crosby & Company. From that time on he was continuously identified with the establishment. He had other large interests as well, chief of which were the director-presidency of the Northwestern National Bank of Minneapolis for thirty-eight years, followed by the chairmanship of the board from 1911 until his death. He was a director of the Great Northern Railway for twenty-five years, and until he retired from active business; president of the St. Anthony & Dakota Elevator Company and the Barnum Grain Company; and vice-president of the Minneapolis Trust Company. He was a member of the Committee of One Hundred to meet Prince Henry of Prussia in 1902, and of the Chamber of Commerce of Minneapolis and of New York. His philanthropies were many, the most important being the Dunwoody Industrial Institute at Minneapolis, with its endowment of $5,000,000; a million-dollar endowment to the Minneapolis Institute of Arts; and the gift, with an endowment of a million dollars, of his old home near Philadelphia as a home for convalescents. Dunwoody married Katie L. Patten of Philadelphia in 1864, who survived him.

[*Who's Who in America*, 1912–13; Wm. C. Edgar, *The Medal of Gold* (1925); C. B. Kuhlmann, *The Development of the Flour-Milling Industry in the U. S.* (1929); *Minn. Hist. Soc. Colls.*, XIV (1912), 192; obituary notice in *Minneapolis Tribune*, Feb. 9, 1914; U. S. Museum correspondence with the Washburn-Crosby Company.]   C. W. M.

DU PONCEAU, PIERRE ÉTIENNE (June 3, 1760–Apr. 1, 1844), lawyer and author, known in America as Peter Stephen Du Ponceau, was born at St.-Martin, Île de Ré, France. His father was of ancient lineage and held a command in the army at St.-Martin. His early education was obtained at the grammar school there, supplemented by private tuition, and he acquired a thorough knowledge of English and Italian from soldiers of those countries quartered in the town. It had been intended that he should undertake a military career but this had to be relinquished because of his weak eyesight, and in 1773 he entered a college of Benedictine monks at St. Jean Angely with a view to a classical education, but returned to the Île de Ré the next year on the death of his father. His family was Catholic and now desired him to become a priest. So he "took the tonsure" and became a regent in the Episcopal college at Bressuire in Poitou. At the end of 1775, however, he abandoned the idea of entering the Church. Going to Paris, he at first earned his living expenses by translating and teaching, and then became secretary to the philologist, Court de Gébelin. Shortly afterward he was introduced to Baron Steuben who needed a secretary familiar with the English language to accompany him on his approaching journey to America, and who, on learning of Du Ponceau's qualifications, at once engaged him. Embarking from Marseilles, they landed at Portsmouth, N. H., Dec. 1, 1777. Du Ponceau was appointed captain in the Continental Army Feb. 18, 1778, and on Baron Steuben's being appointed major-general and inspector general by Washington at Valley Forge a few days later, he became Steuben's aide-de-camp. Though ill qualified for military life through his nearsightedness, he remained in active service for two years, but in the fall of 1779 he was compelled by an affection of the lungs to retire to Philadelphia on sick leave. Later he recovered sufficiently to join General Greene, but had a relapse which necessitated his leaving the army.

He became a citizen of Pennsylvania, July 25, 1781. Recommended to Robert R. Livingston, secretary for foreign affairs, by Judge Peters, he became Livingston's under-secretary, Oct. 22, 1781, continuing as such till June 4, 1783, and fulfilling his duties with great ability. He had prior to the close of the war determined to enter the legal profession, and after two years of study was admitted an attorney of the court of common pleas at Philadelphia on June 24, 1785, becoming an attorney of the supreme court in the following year. He commenced practise in Philadelphia, the international situation at that period and his own unusual attainments combining to bring him to the front at the bar in a very short time. The United States was neutral in the European conflict, and complicated questions of the conflicting rights of neutrals and belligerents arose continually, which the local practitioners were generally incompetent to handle, whereas Du Ponceau's acquaintance with civil and foreign law and languages caused him to be frequently retained in matters involving international law and practise. He became recognized as a leading authority in this country on that subject and as such appeared constantly before the supreme courts of Pennsylvania and the United States. Much French and other foreign business came to him, and he had among his clients the diplomatic and consular agents of France in the United States. Later in life he was frequently consulted on questions of constitutional law. He never evinced any interest in politics, local or national, and passed a somewhat sequestered life, engrossed in his professional engagements and finding his only recreation in literature and linguistic studies, in which latter field he acquired wide fame. His publications on legal subjects included: a translation from the original Latin of Bynkershoek entitled, *A Treatise on the Law of War . . . Being the First Book of his Quaestiones Juris Publici* (1810) with notes; *A Dissertation on the Nature and Extent of the Jurisdiction of the Courts of the United States* (1824); and *A Brief View of the Constitution of the United States* (1834), the last-named being also translated into French. His contributions to historical and linguistic literature were numerous, particularly on philological subjects, his studies in the languages of the North American Indian being particularly original and suggestive. He was the author of: *English Phonology* (1817), and *A Discourse on the Early History of Pennsylvania* (1821); and also published, *Histoire, mœurs et coutumes des nations indiennes qui habitaient autrefois la Pensylvanie et les États Voisins* (Paris 1822), translated from the English of John Heckewelder; a "Notes and Observations on Eliot's Indian

Grammar" (in *Collections of the Massachusetts Historical Society*, 2 ser. IX, 1822); *A Short Description of the Province of New Sweden: Now Called, by the English, Pennsylvania, in America* (1834), translated from the Swedish of Thomas Campanius Holm; *Mémoire sur le système grammatical des langues de quelques nations indiennes de L'Amérique du Nord* (Paris 1838), which procured for him the award of the Volney prize of $2,000 from the French Institute; and *Dissertation on the Nature and Character of the Chinese System of Writing* (1838). His correspondence with John Heckewelder on the languages of the American Indian was published in the *American Philosophical Society, Transactions of the Historical and Literary Committee* (vol. I, 1819, pp. 351–448). His contributions to philology brought him international recognition. In addition, a number of his addresses to the Law Academy of Philadelphia, which he founded in 1821, and contributions to the *Proceedings* of the American Philosophical Society, of which latter body he was elected president in 1828, were republished in pamphlet form. In his later years he became almost blind, and an increasing deafness was an additional obstacle to the prosecution of his investigations. His mental faculties, however, remained unimpaired to the last, and he only relinquished study a few weeks prior to his death. On May 21, 1788, he was married to Anne Perry.

[Four of Du Ponceau's letters, published in the *Pa. Mag. of Hist. and Biog.*, Apr. 1916, give details of his experiences in the Revolutionary period. *A Public Discourse in Commemoration of Peter S. Du Ponceau*, by Robley Dunglison, delivered before the Am. Phil. Soc., Oct. 25, 1844, and republished in *Am. Law Mag.*, Apr. 1845, is comprehensive and eulogistic. An excellent review of his career appeared in 7 *Law Rep.*, 62. See also *Jour. Am. Oriental Soc.*, I (1849), 161; *Western Law Jour.*, May 1844; W. W. Story, *Life and Letters of Jos. Story* (1851); J. B. Linn, *Record of Pa. Marriages Prior to 1810* (1890), II, 584.]   H. W. H. K.

DU PONT, ELEUTHÈRE IRÉNÉE (June 24, 1771–Oct. 31, 1834), manufacturer, was born in Paris, the younger son of Pierre Samuel du Pont de Nemours, celebrated member of the physiocratic school of economists and active participant in French public affairs. Turgot was Irénée's godfather, and gave him his baptismal names. His mother was Nicole Charlotte Marie Louise Le Dée. The boy was brought up on his father's estate, "Bois des Fossés," adjacent to the village of Egreville, not far from Nemours. He was an indifferent student under private tutors, though his father's reproaches were probably due less to the boy's neglect than to the parent's solicitude. He early proved to be manly, fond of the out-of-doors, energetic, and capable of making up his own mind. Early in 1788

Lavoisier, his father's close friend, whom Turgot had appointed chief of the royal powder works, took Irénée into the laboratory at Essonne, promising that the boy should have his own post some day. In 1791, when earning only 1,260 francs, he wished to marry Sophie Madelaine Dalmas, daughter of a family beneath his own in station. His father violently opposed the match on every ground, but the young man was determined, fought two duels with another suitor, and was married (Nov. 26), he being twenty and the bride sixteen. About the same time Lavoisier lost his direction of the powder works because of the Revolution. His protégé left Essonne also, assuming active charge of his father's large printing-house in Paris, established earlier in the year to bolster the conservative cause. Father and son suffered several imprisonments, and were in especially grave danger on Aug. 10, 1792, when they went to the Tuileries to defend the king.

In 1797 the Jacobins suppressed the publishing business of the Du Ponts, and the father decided the fortunes of the family should be cast in America, where he had acquaintance with important statesmen, and whither his elder son Victor [q.v.] had gone a decade before. Du Pont de Nemours organized a company which was to exploit land in the valley of the James River in western Virginia, and with Irénée, his wife and three children, and other close relatives, took ship in the *American Eagle* in September 1799, arriving at Newport, R. I., the first day of the new year. They moved on to New York, where they received a letter from Thomas Jefferson advising that investment in land be delayed. A part of the company's capital was used to establish a commission business in New York, but this venture was never profitable. Irénée hit upon a project which offered much more. He chanced to go hunting with a Col. Toussard; shooting away all their powder, they bought more to finish out the day. Irénée was impressed with its bad quality and high price, and with Toussard's help made a study of the manufacture of powder in America. He concluded that an expertly conducted establishment, even though small (one stamping mill and one wheel mill) would give a profit of $10,000 a year. Irénée du Pont returned to France for three months at the beginning of 1801 to secure machinery and designs for the manufacture of powder, and received every assistance from the government works at Essonne. Two-thirds of the necessary capital was subscribed by his father's company. Jefferson had urged that the plant be placed near Washington, but Irénée after investigation decided "the country, the people, the location are all worthless." He tried without success to buy the powder works of William Lane at Frankford, near Philadelphia, and finally purchased the farm of Jacob Broom, on the Brandywine River four miles from Wilmington, Del., where there had formerly been a cotton-mill operated by the water power. Alexander Hamilton sought to be of assistance in the founding of the business by securing favor for it from the Delaware legislature.

Irénée du Pont and his family in July 1802 settled in a little log house on the property, and he pushed forward the construction of the mills in spite of many discouragements, particularly in the want of capital. In the spring of 1804 powder was ready for sale, and Jefferson, then president, promised orders from the government. Sales in this year amounted to $10,000, the next year to $33,000, and by 1807 were $43,000. For the first six years the profits, in spite of a bad explosion, averaged about $7,000 a year. In 1811 the profits were more than $40,000, and Irénée du Pont and Peter Bauduy, his active associate, invested in a woolen-mill near the powder works, to be conducted by Victor du Pont. The war between the United States and England put the powder business in an assured position. Du Pont became the principal manufacturer of powder for the government, and supplied large quantities to the American Fur Company and to South American countries. He was made a director of the Bank of the United States, to represent the government, and was widely consulted on problems of industry and agriculture. He continued in the New World his father's interest in farming, an avocation which his descendants have maintained. He was active in the American Colonization Society. He proved his loyalty to the government by refusing to sell 125,000 pounds of powder to the South Carolina Nullifiers in 1833 for $24,000 cash. He insisted, in opposition to Bauduy's wish, that the business should be known by his name, E. I. du Pont de Nemours & Company, which it has continued to this day. His establishment, like some others in America at the period, was semi-feudal in the relations between master and workmen, the latter being housed on the property and fed from the farm. Irénée du Pont, himself sensitive and taking responsibility seriously, was surrounded by persons nervous and high-strung; he lived, in France and America, under circumstances of care and stress; these things made him often abrupt or downcast, but his extraordinary affection for those near to him comes out in all his letters. He died in Philadelphia of cholera, after a brief illness.

[See Bessie G. du Pont, *Life of Eleuthère Irénée du Pont* (12 vols., 1923–26); this is mainly his correspondence, but there are illuminating introductory and connecting notes by the editor. The same author's *E. I. du Pont de Nemours and Co., a History, 1802–1902* (1920) gives more compactly the essential facts concerning the founder. See also Dumas Malone, ed., *The Correspondence between Thos. Jefferson and Pierre Samuel du Pont de Nemours, 1798–1817* (1930); *Del. State Jour. and Statesman* (Wilmington), Nov. 4, 1834; and *Del. Gazette and Am. Watchman* (Wilmington), Nov. 4, 1834.]   B. M—l.

DU PONT, HENRY (Aug. 8, 1812–Aug. 8, 1889), manufacturer, was born at Eleutherian Mills, Wilmington, Del., the second son of Eleuthère Irénée du Pont [*q.v.*] and Sophie Madelaine Dalmas. He was a student at Mount Airy Military School, Germantown, Pa., from 1823 to 1829, when he entered the United States Military Academy at West Point. He graduated in 1833, and was made second lieutenant in the 4th Artillery at Fort Monroe, Va. Shortly afterward he served in the Creek country of Alabama, but in June 1834 resigned his commission to join his father in the manufacture of gunpowder. He married Louisa Gerhard in 1837. He had served in the mills sixteen years when, in July 1850, he became head of the firm of E. I. du Pont de Nemours & Company, his partners being his brother Alexis and their nephew, Irénée du Pont. Profits flowing to the company as a result of the Crimean War in 1854 helped Henry du Pont in his policy of progressive management. His older brother Alfred, head of the firm before him, had maintained the tradition of the founder, but when Henry assumed charge a new economic era was dawning. The new farms, mining operations, and railroads needed power. In 1857 Lamont du Pont was granted a patent which enabled the firm to use nitrate of soda from Peru, and much cheaper than the Indian saltpetre, in the manufacture of blasting powder. In 1859 the company bought mills on Big Wapwallopen Creek, Luzerne County, Pa., near the anthracite coalfields, for the manufacture of this blasting powder, thus partially solving an old problem of transportation. This same year Henry du Pont had experiments conducted in the making of hexagonal cakes of powder of large grain for big guns, but this work was interrupted by the Civil War and was not resumed for fifteen years, when it was notably successful. The firm refused to furnish powder to Virginia while the state's loyalty to the Union was in doubt. In 1861 Du Pont was appointed major-general of the Delaware forces, and put down disaffection which, in a state containing the country's largest powder

mills, promised to be dangerous. The supply of saltpetre failing, the firm was made the agent of the government in purchasing enormous supplies in England, but the prospect of war demand for powder did not deceive Du Pont, who declared that "the extra demand for powder for war purposes will not equal the regular demand which would have existed had peace continued." The company lost its trade in the South, and, on account of possible capture of cargoes and use by the Confederacy, was prohibited from shipping powder from New York and Philadelphia, which meant that the West Indies, Mexico, and, for a time, California, went unsupplied. Independent mills were established in California in 1861 to meet the needs of the miners. Du Pont supplied army and navy with powder at low prices despite cash payments in the manufacture, high taxes, and very slow remittance on the part of the government.

The intense competition which led up to the panic of 1873 and the stagnation which followed the crisis brought on consolidation in the powder business. The Du Pont firm bought a controling interest in the Hazard Powder Company in 1876 and in the California Powder Works the same year. Du Pont as he grew older became more cautious. He discountenanced the experiments in "high explosives" which were increasingly successful after 1865, and not until 1876 did his firm begin the manufacture of Hercules powder. He gave his attention principally to the finances of the company, and conducted an enormous correspondence with 500 agents and a half-dozen associated companies, refusing to have a stenographer, and writing by hand 6,000 letters a year. At first a Whig, he became a Republican, and was prominent in Delaware politics. He was of autocratic manner with strangers, but his workmen were nevertheless on easy terms with him. He died following an illness of some months, after fifty-five years in the manufacture of explosives.

[G. W. Cullum, *Biog. Reg.* (3rd ed., 1891); B. G. du Pont, *E. I. du Pont de Nemours and Co., a History, 1802–1902* (1920), and *Life of Eleuthère Irénée du Pont*, vols. 9–11 (1925–26); *Every Evening and Wilmington Daily Commercial*, Aug. 8, 1889; *Wilmington Daily Republican*, Aug. 9, 1889.]   B. M—l.

DU PONT, HENRY ALGERNON (July 30, 1838–Dec. 31, 1926), soldier, industrialist, United States senator, was born near Wilmington, Del., the elder son of Henry du Pont [*q.v.*] and his wife Louisa Gerhard. After preparatory training at Dr. Lyons's school near Philadelphia, and one year at the University of Pennsylvania, he entered the United States Military Academy at West Point, graduating at the head of his class in

1861. In the several ranks up to that of major he was engaged in a large number of battles and skirmishes of the Civil War, usually in command of artillery, in northern Virginia and the Valley. The chief of these were the engagements at New Market, Halltown, Winchester, Fisher's Hill and Cedar Creek, all in 1864. He was under fire for the first time at the battle of New Market, when twenty-six years old. As captain of Battery B, 5th Artillery, he did spectacular work in covering the Union retreat. Du Pont retired by echelon of platoons, maintaining such a spirited fire that pursuing Confederates believed the enemy had rallied, and consequently, in drawing up to resist, permitted Gen. Sigel's men to make their escape. Du Pont accomplished this maneuver on his own initiative, other officers having left the field. He was brevetted major for gallant services at Opequon and Fisher's Hill, and received the rank of lieutenant-colonel (Oct. 19, 1864), and the Congressional Medal of Honor for distinguished services and extraordinary gallantry at Cedar Creek. After the war he commanded light artillery and was ranking officer in various army posts in Virginia, the District of Columbia, and Rhode Island. He was a member of the board of officers which assimilated the tactics for the three arms of the service.

His father, head of the firm of E. I. du Pont de Nemours & Company, had long urged him to resign his army commission and join other members of the family in management of the powder manufactory. He was reluctant to leave military life, but did so in 1875; in 1878, at the time of the readjustment following the death of the second E. I. du Pont, he became a member of the firm. His duties were in the office at first, assisting his father in the correspondence, but he was soon placed in charge of negotiations with the officials of other companies (this being the period in which the Du Pont firm was acquiring shares in other powder mills) and he made all arrangements touching the railway transportation of the products. Out of this last connection grew his election (May 1879) to the presidency of the Wilmington and Northern Railroad. After the death of his father in 1889, Du Pont had charge of the settlement of his estate, and this experience led him to urge that the partnership be changed to a corporation; after much discussion and the instituting of compromise to overcome opposition, a charter was taken out under the laws of Delaware in October 1899 and he became one of three vice-presidents. In 1902, following the death of Eugene du Pont, the president, he was asked to assume the presidency, but declined it and retired from the business because his personal affairs required all his time. He helped, nevertheless, to formulate the plan whereby the direction remained in the hands of the family, T. Coleman du Pont, Alfred I. du Pont, and Pierre S. du Pont purchasing the old company for $12,000,000.

His election by the Delaware legislature in 1895 to the United States Senate having been contested on a technical point, the Senate committee recommended that he be seated, but he lost in the general vote; he did not receive the unanimous support of his own party, it was believed, because of his espousal of the gold standard. He served in the Senate, however, from 1906 to 1917, and was chairman of the military affairs committee from 1911 to 1913. Du Pont was distinguished for gracious, courtly manners. In his last years he gave much attention to farming, a traditional interest in his family, and to literary work. Of chief importance among his books are, *The Early Generations of the Du Pont and Allied Families* (1923), *and Rear-Admiral Samuel Francis Du Pont, a Biography* (1926). He also wrote military reminiscences. He was married to Mary Foster.

[H. A. du Pont's *Campaign of 1864 in the Valley of Virginia* (1925) contains much autobiographical matter. See also *Official Records (Army)*, 1 ser., vols. XXXIII, XXXVII, XLIII, XLVI; B. G. du Pont, *E. I. du Pont de Nemours and Company, a History, 1802–1902* (1920); Wilmington *Evening Jour.*, Dec. 31, 1926; *Wilmington Morning News*, Jan. 1, 1927.]   B. M—l.

DU PONT, SAMUEL FRANCIS (Sept. 27, 1803–June 23, 1865), naval officer, was born at Bergen Point, N. J., the temporary home of his father, Victor Marie du Pont [*q.v.*], head of the importing house of V. du Pont de Nemours & Company of New York. His paternal grandfather was the distinguished French statesman and author, Du Pont de Nemours. His mother was Gabrielle Joséphine de la Fite de Pelleport, a French woman of unusual mental and literary ability, and the youngest daughter of the Marquis de Pelleport. On the failure of his father's firm in 1805, Samuel Francis was taken by his parents to Angelica, Genesee County, N. Y., where he remained until 1809 when he accompanied them to Delaware, of which state he was thereafter a citizen. From the age of nine to fourteen he attended a boarding school at Mount Airy, Pa., near Germantown.

In December 1815, Du Pont de Nemours, having emigrated to America on Napoleon's return from Elba, wrote to Thomas Jefferson requesting an appointment of midshipman for his grandson. Jefferson replied that he had written to Madison on the subject, and that he hoped that the grandson would in time become "one of our high admirals." On Dec. 19 Madison appointed young Du Pont a midshipman, on waiting orders, and accompanied the appointment with another to the Military Academy at West Point. The son was permitted by his parents to choose between the two services. Influenced, doubtless, by the popularity of the navy, following the War of 1812, the youth chose that service, notwithstanding the fact that his maternal ancestors had been soldiers for generations. Du Pont's first sea service was in 1817 on the *Franklin, 74,* Commodore Charles Stewart, under orders to proceed to the Mediterranean. As there was no naval academy at this time, young midshipmen were instructed in navigation and mathematics by naval schoolmasters on shipboard, and probably Du Pont was so instructed on his first cruise. A portrait of him painted at this time depicts him as a tall and strikingly handsome youth. At maturity his height was six feet, one inch. In 1820 he returned home on the *Erie.* In the following year he was again in the Mediterranean, this time on the *Constitution.* After serving in the West Indies and on the coast of Brazil, he was in 1824 for the third time sent to the Mediterranean where he served as sailing-master on the *North Carolina.* In 1826 at the age of twenty-two years and seven months he was promoted to a lieutenancy. From 1829 to 1832 he was employed on the *Ontario,* cruising in European waters. After his return home he was, on June 27, 1833, married to his first cousin, Sophie Madeleine du Pont, youngest daughter of Eleuthère Irénée du Pont de Nemours [*q.v.*], founder of the powder works. Of great strength of character and of deep sympathies, she was a worthy companion of her husband, whom she long survived, guarding to the end his professional reputation.

During the decade previous to the Mexican War, Du Pont was employed first in the Gulf of Mexico, part of the time in command, successively, of the *Grampus* and the *Warren,* and later in European waters on the *Ohio,* the flagship of Commodore Hull. Promoted commander on Jan. 10, 1843, taking rank from Oct. 28, 1842, he was assigned to the command of the brig *Perry,* which that year sailed for China. Stricken with illness, he was invalided home from Rio de Janeiro. After serving as a member of Secretary Bancroft's board on the organization of the naval school at Annapolis, he sailed from Norfolk in October 1845 as commander of the frigate *Congress,* flagship of Commodore Stockton, with the American commissioner and the consul-general to Hawaii on board. He arrived at San Francisco, by way of Honolulu, about July 1, 1846. The Mexican War was in progress, and

Stockton proceeded to Monterey where he took charge of the naval forces in the Pacific and placed Du Pont in command of the sloop-of-war *Cyane.* Taking on board John C. Frémont's battalion, Du Pont disembarked it three days later at San Diego. Proceeding thence down the coast, he reached San Blas, where a landing party spiked the guns of the Mexicans. Entering the Gulf of California, he seized La Paz and at Guaymas burned, or caused the Mexicans to burn, the small fleet there. Within a few months he cleared the Gulf of hostile ships, destroying or capturing thirty of them. On Nov. 11, 1847, he aided Commodore Shubrick, who had succeeded Stockton, in the occupation of Mazatlan. When later the enemy attempted to recover Lower California, Shubrick ordered Du Pont to proceed at once to the Gulf. At San Jose, on learning that a party of Americans were besieged in a mission house three miles inland, he organized a detachment of two provisional companies, led it against the besiegers, and rescued his fellow countrymen. Subsequently he organized several similar expeditions and succeeded in clearing the country of hostile troops. On his arrival at Norfolk in October 1848, the secretary of the navy congratulated him on his "safe return after a long cruise, in which the services of the officers and crew of the *Cyane* were so highly distinguished for gallantry, efficiency, and skill" (H. A. du Pont, *post,* p. 56).

Du Pont now began a tour of shore duty which lasted upward of ten years and which was concerned with some of the most important improvements in naval and marine affairs made in the two decades preceding the Civil War. In 1849 he served as a member of a board appointed by the secretary of the navy to consider a course of study appropriate to a naval academy and to prepare proper regulations for the government of the same. The report of this board, which went into effect on July 1, 1850, provided for a "Naval Academy" comparable to the Military Academy at West Point. Du Pont was appointed superintendent, but after a month the appointment was revoked. His lively interest in naval education led, however, to his frequent selection as a member of the examining board at Annapolis. In 1853 he was one of three naval officers chosen to represent the government at the World's Fair in New York.

In 1851 Du Pont made a valuable report to the secretary of war on the national defenses, in which he discussed the effect on them of the "new element," steam. This was highly commended by Sir Howard Douglas the British expert on naval gunnery. In the same year he was chosen by the secretary of the treasury as one of the members of a board provided for by Congress to inquire into the light-house establishment. The elaborate report of this board laid the basis of a new establishment, in which Du Pont played an important part during the years 1852–57 when he served as a member of the Light-House Board. At different periods he served on boards authorized to revise the rules and regulations of the navy, and he was frequently employed on courts martial and courts of enquiry. He was a member of the famous naval efficiency board of 1855, composed of fifteen naval officers and authorized to examine into the efficiency of all officers above the rank of midshipman. After deliberating for several weeks it reported that 201 officers were incompetent or incapacitated. Its report, which was approved by the secretary of the navy and the president, created a profound sensation. The cause of the affected officers was taken up by their friends both in and outside of Congress, by the public press, and by several state legislatures. The brunt of the criticism fell upon Du Pont. His zeal for naval reform, the excellence of his professional reputation, and his long and efficient service in the navy made him a shining mark for attack. Senator Houston of Texas championed the cause of the affected officers and assailed Du Pont in the Senate. The two Delaware senators, Clayton and Bayard, ably defended him. In the end the affected officers obtained a modification of the act creating the board and its objects were only partly attained.

On Sept. 14, 1855, Du Pont was promoted captain. In 1857 he was ordered to command the new frigate *Minnesota,* one of the largest vessels in the navy, and to proceed to China with William B. Reed, recently appointed American minister to that country. The *Minnesota* was at the mouth of the Peiho River when the combined English and French fleets attacked and captured the Chinese forts there, giving Du Pont an opportunity to acquire information that was to prove useful in similar undertakings of his own during the Civil War. After visiting China, Japan, India, and Arabia, he sailed homeward, reaching Boston in May 1859. In December 1860, he was made commandant of the Philadelphia navy-yard, a post that he held at the outbreak of the Civil War.

Du Pont's first service in the war was performed in Washington as the senior member of the Commission of Conference, appointed by the secretary of the navy to prepare plans for naval operations, to devise methods for rendering the blockade effective, and to collect useful informa-

tion. Meeting at various times during June–September 1861, it submitted several reports, then strictly confidential, embodying much information and many suggestions, and recommending the establishment of a large naval base on the Carolina or Florida coast, where naval supplies could be stored and warships could safely ride at anchor. Of the several locations that were suggested, Du Pont favored Port Royal, S. C. On Sept. 18 he was relieved from duty at the Philadelphia navy-yard and assigned to the command of the South Atlantic blockading squadron, at the time the most important post in the gift of the Navy Department. He was to have control of all naval operations on the Atlantic coast south of the boundary between the Carolinas. His official designation was "Flag Officer," and his courtesy title, "Commodore." The rendezvous of the squadron was Hampton Roads, where by the end of October a fleet of seventy-five vessels was assembled—the largest up to this time ever commanded by an officer of the navy. Du Pont's flagship was the steam frigate *Wabash,* Commander C. R. P. Rodgers [*q.v.*]; and his chief of staff Commander C. H. Davis [*q.v.*]. A combined naval and military movement against Port Royal was decided upon. The military force, consisting of 14,000 troops, was commanded by Brigadier-General Thomas W. Sherman [*q.v.*]. On Oct. 29 the expedition sailed from Hampton Roads, and, after suffering considerable loss from a gale off Hatteras, reached its destination. By Nov. 7 it was ready for battle. The defenses of the Confederates consisted of two forts, Walker and Beauregard, on opposite sides of the entrance to Port Royal, and of a small flotilla of schooners. Du Pont steamed up the channel in two columns. The main column, consisting of the ten larger vessels and led by the flagship, attacked the forts; the smaller one, consisting of five gunboats, engaged the flotilla. The battle lasted upward of five hours and ended with the abandonment of the forts by the Confederates and their occupation by the Federal troops. The loss of the Union forces was thirty-one; of the Confederates, sixty-three. Since forts have but seldom surrendered to ships, the capture of Port Royal is justly celebrated in the annals of naval warfare. It greatly encouraged the North, depressed by the misfortunes of the army. On Feb. 22, 1862, on the recommendation of President Lincoln, Congress passed a resolution thanking Du Pont for his victory, and on July 30 he was made a rear admiral, taking rank from July 16.

Following the success at Port Royal, Du Pont occupied Beaufort, S. C.; and later captured Tybee Island, thus giving the army a base, from which, with the aid of the navy, in April 1862, it reduced Fort Pulaski. In March of that year, Cumberland Island, Amelia Island, St. Marys, Ga., Fernandina, Fla., and Fort Clinch were captured, the last named being the first fort upon which the flag of the Union was restored. All the sounds of Georgia were occupied, and Jacksonville and St. Augustine were taken. On Feb. 28, 1863, one of the vessels of the squadron destroyed the privateer *Nashville,* a highly creditable performance. Du Pont, who was an excellent organizer, established fourteen blockading stations, on thirteen of which the blockade was effective. On the fourteenth, the Charleston station, however, the Confederates frequently at night eluded the Union vessels.

In the meantime an event had taken place which was destined to influence subsequent naval operations in the war, as well as to affect the rest of Du Pont's naval career. By the success of the *Monitor* over the *Merrimac* in Hampton Roads on Mar. 9, 1862, public attention was directed to the ironclad vessel, and many persons, including the secretary and the assistant secretary of the navy, were led to exaggerate its offensive powers. The capture of Charleston, strongly defended by Fort Sumter, now appeared feasible, and a fleet of monitors was assembled under Du Pont with a view to taking that city. With less faith than the Navy Department in the new vessels, Du Pont tested them in an engagement with Fort McAllister and reported that they were deficient in "aggression or destructiveness as against forts" and that in order to secure success in such operations troops were necessary. He and his officers, however, were of the opinion that Fort Sumter could be reduced (Du Pont, *post,* p. 223; Ammen, *post,* pp. 102–03). On Apr. 7, 1863, he attacked the defenses of Charleston. The battle fleet consisted of seven monitors, the ironclad *New Ironsides* (the flagship), and an armored gunboat. It advanced into action led by the *Weehawken,* Capt. John Rodgers [*q.v.*]. The battle began at 2:50 p. m. and ended at 4:30 p. m., when Du Pont signaled his ships to withdraw from action, intending to resume the attack the following morning. He had suffered a severe reverse, the worst naval defeat of the Civil War. The armored gunboat was so damaged that she sank the next day. Five of the monitors were temporarily put out of action. The fleet fired 139 projectiles and was hit 411 times, being struck almost three times for each round that it discharged (Wilson, *post,* I, 26). The loss of the fleet was about fifty; of the forts fourteen. When in the evening Du Pont learned from his captains the extent of the damage suf-

fered by their ships, he decided not to renew the attack, since it would be futile, a conclusion concurred in by all his leading officers.

The failure of Du Pont was a great disappointment to the North, which had entertained hopes of a brilliant success. On Apr. 13, and again on the following day, the President ordered him to hold his position off Charleston. Rendered unduly sensitive by his defeat and fancying that the President's order implied a censure, he wrote to the secretary of the navy requesting the department not to hesitate to relieve him by an officer who in its opinion was more able to execute the service in which he had failed, the capture of Charleston. While the department was choosing a relieving officer, Du Pont kept his station, and on June 17 two of his ships, the *Weehawken* and the *Nahant,* captured the ironclad *Atlanta,* one of the chief naval prizes of the war. On July 6, on the arrival of the new commander-in-chief, Rear Admiral John A. Dahlgren [*q.v.*], Du Pont hauled down his flag and with this act terminated not only his active service during the war but also the active part of his naval career. In taking official leave of him, Secretary Welles, after referring in complimentary terms to the capture of the *Atlanta,* added, "You may well regard this, and we may with pleasure look upon it, as a brilliant termination of a command gallantly commenced and conducted for two years with industry, energy, and ability" (Ammen, *post,* p. 121).

Meanwhile an acrimonious correspondence had been begun by Du Pont with the Secretary. He believed that Welles was trying to shift to the commander of the fleet the blame that should fall upon the Department. Later, Congress made an investigation. Neither the correspondence nor the investigation sheds much light. Naval officers hold, although not unanimously, that their colleague was badly treated. It would appear that the responsibility for the battle should be shared by Du Pont and the Navy Department, and that any other commander might have failed in the hazardous enterprise. The chances of success, however, would have been considerably increased with Farragut in command.

On leaving the squadron, Du Pont retired to his home at Louviers, on the Brandywine River, near Wilmington, Del. In March 1865, he was in Washington as a member of a naval board charged with recommending for advanced rank those officers who had distinguished themselves in the war. This was his last professional employment. His long service in the hot malarial climate off the Southern coast had impaired his health. His death occurred in Philadelphia, after a brief illness. Deeply religious, Du Pont was an active worker in the Protestant Episcopal Church. He was distinguished in appearance and polished in manners, a dignified gentleman and officer.

In 1882 Congress provided that the circle at the intersection of Massachusetts and Connecticut Avenues in Washington should be called Du Pont Circle and that a statue of the admiral should be erected thereon. Two years later a memorial statue, the work of Launt Thompson, was unveiled in the presence of the secretary of the navy, a committee of naval officers, and members of the Du Pont family. In 1921 this memorial was removed and an artistic fountain, executed by Daniel Chester French, was erected in its place.

[H. A. du Pont, *Rear-Admiral Samuel Francis du Pont* (1926); *Sketch of the Public Services of Rear Admiral S. F. du Pont* (1865); *Official Despatches and Letters of Rear Admiral du Pont* (1883); *Official Records (Navy)*, 1 ser., vols. XII–XIV; "Confidential Correspondence of Gustavus Vasa Fox," ed. by R. M. Thompson and R. Wainwright in *Pubs. Naval Hist. Soc.*, vol. IX (1918); Record of Officers, Bureau of Navigation, 1815–61; Navy Registers 1820–65; *Report of Secretary of the Navy*, 1861–63; Daniel Ammen, *The Atlantic Coast* (The Navy in the Civil War, vol. II, 1883); *U. S. Naval Inst. Proc.*, XXXIII (1907), 1468–73, XXXVIII (1912), 1323–24; G. E. Belknap, "Reminiscent of the Siege of Charleston," *Papers Mil. Hist. Soc. of Mass.*, XII (1902), 155–207; J. G. Nicolay and John Hay, *Abraham Lincoln*, VII (1890), 58–86; H. W. Wilson, *Battleships in Action*, I (1926), 23–27; *Diary of Gideon Welles* (1911), vols. I, II.]   C. O. P.

DU PONT, VICTOR MARIE (Oct. 1, 1767–Jan. 30, 1827), diplomat, manufacturer, was born in Paris, the elder son of Pierre Samuel du Pont de Nemours and Nicole Charlotte Marie Louise Le Dée. He was educated under private tutors at his father's country place, "Bois des Fossés," Chevannes, and at sixteen entered the bureau of commerce over which his father presided, his work of collecting trade statistics taking him over all parts of France. He was for a time attached to the bureau of agriculture, but abandoned the line of promotion at home in 1787 to become attaché to the first French legation in the United States. He returned to France two years later to become aide-de-camp to Lafayette when the general was commanding the national guard. In 1791 he was back in the United States as second secretary of legation, but the following year was ordered to France to obtain fuller instructions from the Committee of Public Safety. Genet had been dispatched to this country as minister by the time Du Pont arrived in France, and the latter was without an appointment. To escape being drafted for the army, which would have been distasteful to a conservative, he joined the constabulary as a gendarme, but pretended illness and was allowed to resign. He was married "before the municipality" to Gabrielle Joséphine de la Fite de Pelleport at Chevannes, Apr. 9, 1794. He was over six feet three inches, handsome, and of charming manners. In 1795 he came to America for the third time, now as first secretary of legation. In July 1796 he was stationed at Charleston as acting French consul for the Carolinas and Georgia, and in 1797 became consul. His work in this post received official commendation, so that his father was able, when the whole legation was recalled incident to the inauguration of the Directory (1798), to have Victor appointed consul-general in the United States. On reaching Philadelphia, however, Du Pont discovered that President Adams would not grant him an *exequatur* because of current controversy with France. Relinquishing his office, Du Pont, his wife, and two children hastily took ship for Bordeaux, where he found his father, his brother Irénée [*q.v.*], and others in the family connection planning to sail for America to make a new start after the disasters of the Revolution. Victor allowed himself to be persuaded to return to the United States with them, especially since his father had committed him to becoming a director in the land and trading company which was projected to rebuild the family fortunes in the new world.

After a delayed start, and a long and trying voyage, all the Du Ponts arrived at Newport, R. I., Jan. 1, 1800. While they were getting their bearings, they took up residence in a pleasant house at Bergen Point, N. J., opposite Staten Island. The firm of Du Pont de Nemours, Père et Fils et Cie remained without definite plans for almost a year, during which time the capital was being spent for maintenance of the family. Victor, in order to be naturalized and thus escape the higher import duties charged on goods consigned to aliens, bought a house and shop in Alexandria, Va. In 1801 he went to France and vainly tried to persuade the government to establish, with the Du Pont firm as agent, a packet line to the United States. Shortly after his return to America his father sailed for Europe, chiefly for business reasons. Victor formed a new firm, V. du Pont de Nemours & Company, of New York, nominally independent of the parent enterprise, which was to remain under the father with headquarters in Paris. Victor believed he might become financial agent of the French government in the United States if he could succeed with a commission business, and in the first year he did well despite inadequacy of capital. He sent cargoes to France and did a good business with the French West Indies, but in August

1805 he failed, largely because the French government refused to honor Santo Domingo drafts on the paymaster of the navy to the amount of 560,000 francs. In 1806 he joined Philip Church in a land development project at Angelica, Genesee County, N. Y., paying $3,000 from his wife's little fortune for 500 acres. This venture was not successful, and when Victor left Genesee three years later the land was assigned to his creditors. He joined his brother Irénée at the powder works of the latter on the Brandywine River near Wilmington, Del., where he became active manager of woolen-mills erected by his brother and Bauduy, the latter's partner. This undertaking was not more successful than others of Victor's; but, gentle and easily influenced, he enjoyed and needed association with his more vigorous brother. He received recognition as a director of the Bank of the United States and a member of the Delaware legislature. He died of heart failure in Philadelphia.

[See Gabrielle Joséphine du Pont de Nemours, *Souvenirs de Madame V. M. du Pont de Nemours* (1908); B. G. du Pont, *E. I. du Pont de Nemours & Co.* (1920), and *Life of Eleuthère Irénée du Pont* (12 vols., 1923–26); *Wilmingtonian and Del. Advertiser*, Feb. 1, 1827; *Am. Watchman and Del. Advertiser* (Wilmington), Feb. 2, 1827.]   B. M—l.

DUPRATZ, ANTOINE SIMON LE PAGE (fl. 1718–1758), pioneer, historian, is remembered for his account of Louisiana, which is almost the only source of information about him. The date of his birth is given variously by secondary authorities as 1689 or 1690; and the place, as Holland, the Low Countries, and Belgium. He is said to have seen military service in Germany (Eyries, *post*). His own narrative begins with 1718, in which year he obtained a concession and came to Louisiana to seek his fortune. He reached New Orleans when it had but one cabin. He settled first on Bayou St. John, but dampness and the likelihood of floods led him to take up his abode near Fort Rosalie among the Natchez. Later he was granted a duchy in the Arkansas region. He explored the interior of Louisiana, going as far as the "South Sea." In 1726 he became overseer of a plantation near New Orleans, belonging to the Company of the Indies. This tract, which soon passed into the king's hands, Dupratz managed to the best of his ability, but the venture proved too costly and the post was abolished. He refused Bienville's invitation to remain in Louisiana, and in 1734 returned to La Rochelle whence he had sailed sixteen years before. In 1758 he published in Paris a three-volume work: *Histoire de la Louisiane. Contenant la dècouverte de ce vaste pays, sa description géographique: un voyage dans les terres, l'Histoire naturelle, les mœurs, coutumes, et religion des Naturels avec leur origine; deux voyages dans le Nord du Nouveau Mexique dont un jusqu'a la Mer du Sud*, illustrated with two maps and forty copper-plate engravings. The author used the accounts of Louisiana by Carlevoix and Dumont to check his own. Certain aspects of the man himself appear in his writing. Devoted to his Church, he refused an opportunity to marry an Indian princess and urged the baptism of all slaves. He was apparently kind to his negroes and was highly esteemed by the Indians. He was ever loyal to his superiors, and had a genuine interest in Louisiana. He knew something of astronomy and engineering, and his account includes a consideration of the hydraulic problem at the mouth of the Mississippi.

As a historian, he told the story of the relations between French and Indians, depicted Bienville smoking the calumet with the Tchitimachas, described the massacre at Fort Rosalie, and recorded precious material on pioneer life. He had vision, and saw even at that early date the possibilities latent in the vast territory of Louisiana. As a geographer, he noted the prodigious fertility of the soil, the favorable climate, the abundant streams, the fur-bearing animals, the plant life, the salt mines. He studied the natives, their tribal organization, languages, religion, manners, customs, ceremonies, history. Although discursive in manner, the book is written in a pleasing style and abounds in personal anecdotes which hold the interest of the reader. Little is known of Dupratz after the publication of this volume. It is stated by Eyries (*post*) that his death occurred in 1775.

[The *Histoire de la Louisiane* was translated into English (London, 1763). The anonymous translator claimed to have improved the text, but in the main he followed Dupratz, except where British interests were concerned, especially the tobacco trade and boundaries. The *Gentleman's Magazine*, June 1763, contains a summary of this translation. Both the translator's preface and that of Dupratz repay reading. This work was used as a basis for a compilation entitled, *An Account of La., Exhibiting a Compendious Sketch of its Pol. and Natural Hist. and Topography* . . . (Newbern, 1804). There is a sketch of Dupratz by J. B. Eyries, the noted French geographer, in Michaud's *Biographie Universelle* (1842–65).]   L. C. D.

DUPUY, ELIZA ANN (1814–Jan. 15, 1881), novelist, was born in Petersburg, Va., the daughter of a merchant and ship-owner of that place and Norfolk. She was, on her father's side, of French ancestry, and was proud of being a descendant of the Colonel Dupuy who received a land grant on the James River from James II for the little band of Huguenot exiles whom Dupuy led to America. Her maternal grandfather was Capt. Joel Sturdevant, commander of a company in the American Revolution, but she was, as contemporary biographers are careful to state, only "distantly connected with that old pirate known as Commodore Sturdevant." Her early childhood was spent in Norfolk, but while still in her teens she removed with her father to Kentucky. Heavy financial losses at this time made it necessary for her to contribute to the family income, and for this reason she turned to writing. Her first novel, "Merton, a Tale of the Revolution," was at once accepted for publication. Her education had been extremely sketchy, and while in Kentucky she deliberately set about to educate herself in order to take up teaching. On the death of her father she accepted the post of governess with the family of Thomas G. Ellis in Natchez, Miss., and it was here that her first popular novel was written, "The Conspirator," based upon the character and career of Aaron Burr. This appeared in the *New World* when she was only twenty-two years old. Some ten years later Appletons published the novel in book form, when it sold to the extent of 24,000 copies. Her entire life was spent in the South, where she continued to teach and to write voluminously —novels and articles and short stories. Many of the latter were published in the *New York Ledger* under the pen name of Annie Young. Ardent, almost fiery in her Southern sympathies, she was yet able to place her writings in Northern journals even during the Civil War. All her novels are extremely melodramatic, the sensational promise of the titles being more than fulfilled both in plot and in style. She was a systematic worker, doing her writing in the morning and devoting the afternoon to revision. The critics of her own day varied widely in their estimate of her ability. At the one extreme her work was considered "full of scenes of most absorbing interest, while it exhibits the elegance of style and purity of diction which are among Miss Dupuy's characteristics" (Freeman, *post*, p. 377). At the other extreme she was dismissed as lurid and "Miss Braddonish." Her historical novels are the best: *The Conspirator* (1850), *The Huguenot Exiles* (1856), and *All for Love* (1873), although none of them escapes the blight of over-emotionalism. Some of her most popular novels were frankly thrillers: *The Cancelled Will* (1872); *The Clandestine Marriage* (1875); *The Discarded Wife* (1875). She died in New Orleans at the age of sixty-seven.

[J. W. Davidson, *The Living Writers of the South* (1869); *The South in the Building of the Nation* (Southern Hist. Pub. Soc., 1909), vol. XI; Ida Raymond (Mrs. Mary I. Tardy), *Southland Writers* (1870),

vol. I, and *The Living Female Writers of the South* (1872); Mary Forrest (Julia Deane Freeman), *Women of the South Distinguished in Literature* (1860); B. H. Dupuy, *The Huguenot Bartholomew Dupuy and his Descendants* (1908).]

G. G.

DURAND, ASHER BROWN (Aug. 21, 1796–Sept. 17, 1886), engraver and painter, was of French Huguenot ancestry. His great-grandfather, Jean Durand, fled from Toulouse to England in 1684, thence emigrated to America, and in 1705 was living at Derby, Conn. He had eight children; one of them, Samuel, moved from Connecticut to New Jersey, about 1740, and settled in Newark, where he married, and had six children. His second child, John, born in 1745, on reaching manhood, established himself at Jefferson Village, six miles from Newark; bought land, built a house, married Rachel (Meyer) Post, a young widow, and had eleven children. The eighth child was Asher Brown Durand. His father was a watchmaker, silversmith, farmer, and a "universal mechanic," so versatile that he could turn his hand to almost anything requiring mechanical skill. Asher was a delicate boy, but at the age of seven he was sent to the village school, where he was instructed in "reading, writing, and arithmetic, a little geography, and the whole of the Westminster Catechism (*Life and Times*, p. 20). At vacation time he busied himself with sundry operations in his father's work-shop, making metal trinkets and engraving designs on copper plates. Evidently he inherited some of his father's mechanical ingenuity, for he invented and made his own tools for these purposes. Sagaciously foreseeing the lad's manifest destiny, his father apprenticed him to Peter Maverick, a steel-engraver, in 1812. For five years he served diligently as apprentice in Maverick's shop, his principal employment being to make copies of the illustrations in English books for the use of American publishers. At this time he became acquainted with Samuel Waldo, the portrait painter, and, having received from him advice and instruction in regard to portrait work, he made his first crude essays in that line. When he became of age in 1817 his term of apprenticeship expired; thereupon he was taken into partnership by Maverick. One of the most important jobs given to the firm was the engraving of John Trumbull's historical painting, "The Signing of the Declaration of Independence," now in the rotunda of the Capitol at Washington—the picture alluded to as "the shin piece" by Randolph of Roanoke. Trumbull, judging that the erstwhile pupil now surpassed the master, insisted that this important commission should be executed by Durand, a stipulation which aroused the ire of

Maverick. This partiality brought about strained relations and eventually led to the dissolution of the partnership in 1820. Durand continued work on Trumbull's composition for about three years. When completed, 1823, it was received with general acclaim. It served to establish the reputation of the young engraver.

Encouraged by this success, Durand, never lacking self-confidence, produced an original drawing of a nude female figure in rustic surroundings, and proceeded to make an engraving of it, which he called "Musidora." The subject was suggested by lines from Thomson's *Seasons*. The print met with fair success, and does not appear to have caused any serious disturbance of the peace. A more successful effort in the same line, a reproduction of a nude piece by John Vanderlyn, "Ariadne," was engraved by Durand at a later period, and made a decided stir in artistic circles. It is still considered something of a landmark in the history of steel engraving in America. The plate is now preserved in the National Museum, Washington; the original painting by Vanderlyn, which was made in Paris, belongs to the permanent collection of the Pennsylvania Academy of the Fine Arts, Philadelphia; and Durand's reduced-size copy in oils hangs in the Metropolitan Museum of Art, New York, to which it was given by Samuel P. Avery.

Stimulated by the wide interest manifested in his plate after Trumbull's "Declaration of Independence," Durand now began the production of a long series of engraved portraits of eminent personages in the life of the time. The full list of these portraits, which in perfection of craftsmanship unquestionably excelled any previous work of the kind in America, includes thirty-two clergymen, twenty-three statesmen and publicists, ten popular actors, and seven noted physicians. Dunlap quotes from a letter written by Horatio Greenough, the sculptor, in respect to Durand's engraving after Chester Harding's portrait of Charles Carroll of Carrollton, which had been exhibited in Florence, that it "quite astonished the Italians; they would hardly believe that it was executed by an American." Not only were Durand's portrait plates excellent in point of workmanship, exactitude of likeness, and fidelity to the original paintings, they were and are rarely interesting by reason of the historical consequence of his subjects.

Incessantly active and resourceful, Durand, in the intervals of his more pressing labors, contributed generously to the Annuals, or gift-books, dear to the ladies of the time. In *The Token, The Gift, The Talisman, The Magnolia, The Atlantic Souvenir*, the outstanding features were the illustrations, reproductions of the genre pictures of Leslie, Ingham, Newton, Inman, Chapman, who were as romantic and sentimental as the authors of the tales illustrated. In *The Magnolia* for 1836, for example, two of the best pictures were engraved by Durand—"The Bride of Lammermoor" and "The White Plume." Commercial work of various kinds, especially banknote engraving, in which he engaged with his brother Cyrus [*q.v.*], also engrossed a share of his attention. To his burin are doubtless due many of those pretty vignettes of half-draped figures symbolizing liberty, justice, commerce, agriculture, art, and transportation, which then adorned and to some extent still adorn the paper currency of the nation. Much of the work done in the Bureau of Engraving and Printing since that time owes not a little of its character to the tradition established by Durand. The process does not lend itself to freedom or spontaneity; its limitations are recognized, but so far as its application to financial purposes is concerned, its stiffness, exactitude, and mechanical quality are more or less negligible, since its chief end and aim is to provide protection against the wiles of the counterfeiter. Samuel Isham has very justly pointed out that Durand was a thoroughly competent engraver; he had mastered a variety of technique from the cross-hatching of the school of Raphael Morghen to the stipple of Bartolozzi; his drawing was good, his line clear and strong, and he faithfully reproduced his models.

In 1830, he interested himself in an enterprise called *The American Landscape,* a serial publication of engravings after views of places by native painters, with descriptive text by William Cullen Bryant; but only one number was issued. It contained six plates, all by Durand. He was a member of a club called The Lunch, founded by James Fenimore Cooper and including Bryant, Hillhouse, Halleck, Sands, Vanderlyn, Morse, Jarvis, and Dunlap. He was also a member of a sketch club organized by the art students of New York. The evening meetings of this club were not wholly given over to serious sketching, evidently, for on one occasion we hear of Mr. Bryant frivolously maintaining that "the perfection of bathing is to jump headforemost into a snowbank," while at another conclave we find Mr. G. C. Verplanck throwing new light on the precise form and capacity of antediluvian butter-churns. The Century Club and the National Academy of Design both owed their establishment to the same men who formed the sketch club. Durand was a charter member of the Academy, which opened its first exhibition in 1826, and his first *envoi* was a picture of "Mary Magdalen at the Sepulchre." He continued to exhibit regularly for many years. In 1845 he was elected president of the Academy, and he served until 1861, during which period, a period of considerable difficulties and vicissitudes, he gave much of his time and energy to the duties of the office, and showed wisdom and shrewdness in his administration.

From 1836 he abandoned engraving for the painter's profession and devoted the rest of his long life to work in color. He soon became as successful and famous in this work as he had been in his former specialty. The earliest pictures were mainly portraits and figure pieces; of the latter class were illustrations of episodes in the Bible and several scenes from the pseudo-historical tales of Irving and Cooper, which were highly esteemed. These include "The Wrath of Peter Stuyvesant" (New York Historical Society), painted to order for Luman Reed, his first patron and firm friend; also, "Rip Van Winkle introduced to the Crew of Hendrik Hudson in the Catskill Mountains"; and an interesting incident in *The Spy* by Cooper, the "Last Interview between Harvey Birch and Washington." Of the Old Testament subjects, perhaps the most important was "God's Judgment upon Gog" (1852), now in the permanent collection of the Metropolitan Museum of Art, New York.

After this he did not attempt to paint any more *"machines,"* as the French artists call that kind of pictures, or, as Thackeray denominates them, "thundering big first raters"; he was content now to turn to nature. He traveled to the banks of the Hudson, the Catskills, Lake George, the Adirondacks, Vermont, the White Mountains, the Berkshires, and the valley of the Connecticut, and found ample scope for the exercise of his fine perceptive faculty and the expression of his love for the country. He was shortly entitled to share with Thomas Cole the renown of being the founder of the American school of landscape. The typical Durand landscape is a view of far-reaching fields, meadows, and valleys, with fine trees in the foreground drawn with conscientious care and fidelity in every detail; distant hills enveloped in a summer haze; and a sky which suggests real air and light. In spite of a certain conventionality in the design, the sentiment is genuine, and the work is not without a vein of lyricism. An example is "Summer Woods," engraved in steel by James Smillie and published in the excellent anthology edited by Charles A. Dana, the *Household Book of Poetry* (1875), evidently an illustration to a poem by Mary Howitt. Nothing could more exactly denote the taste of the period in landscape. It is

a panoramic view from a hillside overlooking a wide vale through which a stream meanders nearly to the horizon of gently undulating heights. The peaceful pastoral feeling of the scene is very nicely suggested; and not the least engaging part of it is the hint of sunlight on the gilded lower edges of the cirrus clouds floating lazily in the placid summer sky. No wonder that such canvases found favor with the collectors of the day. An idea of the importance attributed to his work by the critics of mid-nineteenth century is to be derived from the ten pages of almost rhapsodic eulogy in Henry T. Tuckerman's *Book of the Artists*. His landscapes are described as grand, true, tender, faultless, "the mirror of reality," and, in one instance, "perfectly Titian-like." Particular praise was due to his wood interiors, which are, indeed, among his most felicitous canvases, though to more modern eyes a thought too literal and niggling. Sound drawing is, however, never to be rated as less than a high merit. In a memorial address to the members of the National Academy, shortly after Durand's death, Daniel Huntington dwelt eloquently on his rendering of the "subtle and infinitely varying effects of atmosphere, of fleeting clouds, mist, sunshine, twilight obscurity, and the thousand wondrous phenomena which form the peculiar glory of landscape."

An interlude in Durand's busy life was his tour of Europe in 1840–41 in company with his friends Casilear and Rossiter. In London he met Wilkie and Leslie, saw Turner and his pictures, visited the current exhibitions, and incidentally attended a masquerade ball, which in his diary he calls a "licensed scene of folly and depravity." After seven weeks in England, he spent a fortnight in Paris, and a shorter time in Antwerp, where he witnessed the inauguration of the statue of Rubens in the Place Verte. Thence he proceeded to Italy and passed the winter in Rome, returning home in June 1841. On Apr. 2, 1821, he was married to Lucy, daughter of Isaac Baldwin of Bloomfield, N. J. She died in 1830, and in 1834 he married Mary Frank of New York, a daughter of Jacob Frank.

Living in New York for a period of fifty-four years, where he was closely identified with every organized movement to foster the arts, greatly loved and admired by a host of friends and colleagues, the intellectual and artistic élite of the city, at a peculiarly interesting stage of the development of native art, officially active for a long term of years as the president of the National Academy, and thriving steadily as one of the most popular landscape painters of his generation, his life was full of the wholesome satisfactions of creative work and friendly associations, and he played an important and honorable part in the arena of American art. His last years were spent in retirement, though they were not by any means inactive. He moved from New York in 1869 to a quiet country home in his birthplace, Jefferson Village, N. J., where he died in 1886, and was buried in Greenwood Cemetery, Brooklyn.

[The standard work on Durand is his own son's biography, *The Life and Times of Asher Brown Durand* (1894), by John Durand, a thorough and readable record, with fifteen illustrations. Other sources include Daniel Huntington, *Asher B. Durand* (1887); Wm. Dunlap, *Hist. of the Rise and Progress of the Arts of Design in the U. S.* (ed. by F. W. Bayley and C. E. Goodspeed, 3 vols., 1918); H. T. Tuckerman, *Book of the Artists* (1867); G. W. Sheldon, *Am. Painters* (1879); J. J. Jarves, *The Art Idea* (1864); Samuel Isham, *Hist. of Am. Painting* (1905); *Biog. and Geneal. Hist. of the City of Newark and Essex County, N. J.* (1898). The Grolier Club of New York has published a check-list of Durand's engraved work.]   W. H. D.

DURAND, CYRUS (Feb. 27, 1787–Sept. 18, 1868), engraver, inventor, was born at Jefferson Village, near Newark, N. J., the second child of John and Rachel (Meyer) Post Durand. His father was a watchmaker and silversmith possessing mechanical talent of great versatility, and was engaged in the manufacture of various metal and other trinkets, such as sleeve buttons, arrowheads, powder horns, and engraved copper plates. It was in this environment that Cyrus grew to manhood, his whole education being obtained in the village public school. As a young man he was accustomed to help in his father's shop, one of his particular duties being the engraving of monograms or other devices on the various articles manufactured. Some of his time, too, was occupied in the design and construction of unusual machinery. At the age of thirty-one he secured a patent for what he called a "grammatical mirror." This machine rendered the abstract rules of grammar and the definitions of the parts of speech intelligible by objective means through a combination of mirrors, slides, wheels, and other mechanical equipment. Four years before this, following the accidental death of his father, Durand had established himself as a silversmith in Newark and had served for a few months in the army during the War of 1812–14. In 1815 he was employed for about a year in Rahway, N. J., to construct machines for carding and weaving hair to be used in the manufacture of carpets. Following this period he continued in his own establishment in Newark, and on Sept. 22, 1818, obtained another patent for a machine to ornament columns. He continued in Newark for about six years after this, when at the suggestion of Peter Maverick, tutor of

his younger brother Asher [*q.v.*] in engraving, the brothers established the A. B. & C. Durand Company in New York City, to engage in banknote engraving. Asher made the designs and Cyrus executed them with machines of his own invention, which included one for ruling straight and wave lines, another for drawing water lines, and a third for making plain ovals. These machines are regarded as the beginning of geometrical lathes by which machine work on banknotes is universally executed. The company continued as a partnership until 1832, when Asher retired to devote his life to art. Cyrus continued alone, constantly devising new appliances, not only for bank-note engraving but also for engine turning and transfer printing-press work. While it is not definitely known just when, Durand gave up his engraving business in New York and went to Washington, D. C., as an engraver in the Treasury Department. It is presumed that he continued to serve in this capacity after the establishment of the Bureau of Engraving and Printing in 1862 but no record is to be found in that department except a notice of his death in Irvington, N. J. Durand married Mrs. Phœbe Woodruff of Newark.

[John Durand, *The Life and Times of Asher Brown Durand* (1894); *Twentieth Century Biog. Dict. of Notable Americans* (1904), vol. III; records of U. S. Patent Office and Treasury Dept.; *N. Y. Times*, Sept. 21, 1868.]   C. W. M.

DURAND, ÉLIE MAGLOIRE (Jan. 25, 1794–Aug. 14, 1873), pharmacist, botanist, usually known in America as Elias Durand, was born at Mayenne, France, the youngest of the fourteen children of André Durand, the local recorder of deeds. At school he developed an aptitude for chemistry; and in October 1808 he was apprenticed to a M. Chevallier, a distinguished chemist and pharmacist of the city, who won his pupil's enduring gratitude by giving him thorough, systematic instruction in laboratory technique and in the elements of the physical and biological sciences. Twenty years later Durand repaid his master in the only way possible, by giving the same excellent instruction to his own apprentices in Philadelphia. After completing his scientific training by a year's study in Paris, he was commissioned as pharmacist in the French army, Feb. 2, 1813, and was assigned to the 3rd Division of the V Corps. He was present at the battles of Möckern, Lützen, Bautzen, Hanau, the Katzbach and Leipzig. He was captured at Hanau but was released almost immediately by a Prussian officer aghast at the losses sustained by his enemy. Durand resigned his commission on Apr. 3, 1814, and secured congenial employment at Nantes, returned to the army for the "Hundred Days," and went back to Nantes after Waterloo. Because of his Napoleonic sympathies, however, he was kept under surveillance and required to report himself every morning to the police. Unable to brook such restraint any longer, he determined to emigrate. He sailed from Nantes on Apr. 16, 1816, in the brig *La Nymphe* and landed at New York the first of July.

For the next few years his life was somewhat nomadic. In Boston he was kindly received by his distant relative, Bishop John Lefebre de Cheverus [*q.v.*], was introduced to various men of science, and was employed by a druggist named Perkins to manufacture Rochelle salt, tartar emetic, ether, and other drugs according to French methods. In Philadelphia he worked for a German, Wesener, who was making chromates and mercurial salts, but the salts affected his health, and he was compelled to quit. During a three months' stay at Bel Air, Md., he studied English assiduously. For one winter he lived with Gerard Troost [*q.v.*] at Cape Sable, Md. Troost, all alone except for his negro laborers, was engaged in manufacturing copperas and was starved for civilized company. Although he had no employment to offer him, he insisted vehemently that Durand stay with him anyway. Finally, in Baltimore in 1817, Durand entered into partnership with his compatriot and fellow pharmacist, Edme Ducatel. In Baltimore, during these years, he began his study of American flora.

Withdrawing from the partnership in 1824, he went to France to purchase apparatus and supplies and in 1825 opened a drug store at the corner of Sixth and Chestnut Sts., in Philadelphia. Resplendent with huge French bottles and other heavy glassware, porcelain jars, mahogany drawers, and marble counters, the shop instantly became fashionable. There was more to it, however, than glitter. Its proprietor, possessing skill and knowledge of a high order, regarded pharmacy as no mere trade but as a learned profession and a public trust. He collected a valuable professional library and took in a number of foreign scientific journals. He introduced to the medical men of the city a long list of foreign medicines, previously unused in the United States, and originated a number of others. Some of these medicines were suggested first by Dr. Samuel Jackson [*q.v.*]. By putting up some of the prescriptions as proprietary remedies with Jackson's name on the labels Durand unintentionally involved his friend in a question of professional ethics. He was also the first to bottle

mineral water in this country and invented a machine for bottling it under pressure. Attracted by his social qualities, the physicians of Philadelphia used Durand's Drug Store as an informal club-house. Ultimately Durand's example affected the drug business of the entire country.

Botanists as well as physicians were attracted to his store. He advanced money to many a botanical traveler and often accepted their collections in payment. It was in this way that he acquired Thomas Nuttall's herbarium. Constantine Samuel Rafinesque's he discovered, somewhat the worse for rats, in an old loft and bought it for a small sum. He himself explored the Dismal Swamp of Virginia in 1837 and the mountains of Pennsylvania in 1862 and made numerous shorter excursions with Joseph Bonaparte, then living at Bordentown, N. J., and with other scientific friends. He was elected to the Philadelphia Academy of Natural Sciences (1825), the College of Pharmacy (1825, vice-president 1844), and the American Philosophical Society (1854).

On Nov. 20, 1820, he married Polymnia Rose Ducatel, the daughter of his Baltimore friend. She died Feb. 18, 1822. On Oct. 25, 1825, about the time when he established himself in Philadelphia, he married Marie Antoinette Berauld, whose father, a merchant of Norfolk, Va., was one of the French refugees from the Santo Domingo Insurrection. Her death in 1851 led Durand, in the following year, to make his business over to his son and to give the rest of his life to botanical studies. He was a good Latin scholar. His English was always French in accent and occasionally in idiom, but he wrote the language fluently and well. He was noted for his charities and for his helpful kindness to younger scientists. In 1860 he went to France for a second time and also visited England. In 1868 he took to Paris his own herbarium, containing over 10,000 species and over 100,000 specimens, and presented it to the museum of the Jardin des Plantes, where it was housed in a special gallery as the Herbier Durand. During his retirement he also rearranged and from his own collections supplemented the herbarium of the Philadelphia Academy of Natural Sciences. He gave his botanical library to the Academy and his chemical and pharmaceutical works, together with a herbarium of medical plants, to the Philadelphia College of Pharmacy. He had previously given the College a general herbarium of 12,000 specimens. He died, loved and venerated, in his eightieth year.

His first publication, in collaboration with Joseph Togno, M.D., was a translation with additions of H. M. Edwards and P. Vavasseur's *Manual of Materia Medica and Pharmacy* (1829). His articles on chemical and botanical subjects are listed in the *Catalogue of Scientific Papers Compiled by the Royal Society of London,* vols. II (1868), VII (1877), and IX (1891). He also wrote memoirs of François André Michaux [*q.v.*] and Thomas Nuttall [*q.v.*].

[W. Procter, Jr., memoir in *Am. Jour. of Pharmacy,* XLV (1873), 508–17 ; T. Meehan, "Obituary Notice of Elias Durand," in *Proc. Acad. Nat. Sci. of Phila.,* 1873, pp. 355–59 ; C. Des Moulins, *Notice Nécrologique sur M. Élie Durand (Extrait des Actes de la Société Linnéenne de Bordeaux,* t. XXIX, 2e liv., 1873) ; J. W. England, ed., *The First Century of the Phila. Coll. of Pharmacy 1821–1921* (1922) ; portrait in J. W. Harshberger, *The Botanists of Phila.* (privately printed, 1899), op. p. 176.]   G.H.G.

DURANT, CHARLES FERSON (Sept. 19, 1805–Mar. 2, 1873), aeronaut, scientist, was born in New York City, son of William and Elizabeth (Woodruff) Durant. When he was eighteen, he went to Paris with Eugene Robertson, a French aeronaut, who on July 9, 1825, made an ascension at Castle Garden in honor of the Marquis de Lafayette. With Robertson, Durant made two ascensions in Paris in the summer of 1829, then returned to America and tried to arouse interest in ballooning as a means of transportation. He can be regarded as the first citizen of the United States to make a profession of aeronautics. He was the first native-born American to make a balloon flight in this country. As early as Jan. 9, 1793, Blanchard (a Frenchman) had ascended in a balloon at Philadelphia before President Washington and a large crowd of people, but Durant's flight which took place at Castle Garden, Sept. 9, 1830, was the first in which homemade materials were used and which was performed without assistance from foreign aeronauts. This first balloon was made at the Durant home in Jersey City. Other ascensions at Castle Garden occurred on Sept. 22, 1830; Aug. 24, Sept. 7, 1831; May 29 and June 14, 1833. Durant later made ascensions at Albany, Baltimore, and Boston, all carefully planned and successfully carried out. In Chesapeake Bay he landed on the deck of the steamship *Independence.* He made one ascent in Albany and three from Boston Common. On the last of these (Sept. 13, 1834) he went out beyond the harbor in one air current and returned in another, and after passing the city continued to the west-northwest, landing at Lincoln. He had been in the air about two hours and had reached a height of 8,000 feet. This ascension gave the first direct evidence of the shallow character of the sea-breeze.

In all, Durant made thirteen ascensions but seems to have made none after his marriage to

Elizabeth Hamilton Freeland, Nov. 14, 1837. He was engaged for many years in the business of printing and lithographing and took an active interest in political matters, especially in Jersey City. He spent much time collecting and classifying sea-weed, doubtless because of a business connection with the fish and oyster trade of New York City. He prepared a book on "Algae and Corallines of the Bay and Harbor of New York," and made about thirty copies, each illustrated with actual specimens of sea-weed and other marine flora. One copy was put up for sale at the New York Sanitary Fair and was sold for $150. A copy is in existence in the Jersey City Public Library, and another in the Cryptogamic Herbarium of Harvard University. The American Institute gave him six or more gold medals, one in 1836 for the first silk known to be made in the United States, others for the best specimens of cocoons, raw and sewing silk, and for the successful propagation of silk worms and the utilization of their products. He imported the worms from China. Durant also devised a portable barometer.

He published in 1837 a book entitled *Exposition, or a New Theory of Animal Magnetism, with a Key to the Mysteries,* which attempted to expose the methods employed by the Fox sisters [*q.v.*], then attracting much attention by their so-called spiritualistic exhibitions. He also published a "physical astronomy" but for some reason bought up the entire edition and destroyed all but one copy. His balloon flights were described in the newspapers of New York, Boston, Philadelphia, and also in London and Paris papers.

[A scrap-book of clippings concerning Durant in the New York Public Library ; E. A. Dime, "America's First Aeronaut," *Air Travel,* Jan. 1918; Jersey City *Journal,* June 21, 1927 ; and personal memoranda from Miss Emma Durant.]   A.M.

DURANT, HENRY (June 18, 1802–Jan. 22, 1875), Congregational clergyman, first president of the University of California, was born at Acton, Mass., the son of Henry and Lucy (Hunt) Durant. He prepared for college at Phillips Academy, Andover, Mass., and graduated from Yale in 1827, in a class numbering among its members Horace Bushnell and Nathaniel Parker Willis. Following graduation, Durant took charge of the Garrison Forest Academy, Baltimore County, Md. He gave up this position at the end of two years in order to accept a Yale tutorship which he held for four years (1829–33), meanwhile completing the course in the Yale Theological Seminary. On Dec. 10, 1833, he was married to Mary E. Buffett, daughter of the Rev. Platt Buffett of Stanwich, Conn. Later in the same month he was ordained pastor of the Congregational church in Byfield, Mass., and continued in this work until 1849, when he became head of the Dummer Academy in Byfield. This was at the time of the California gold rush. Among the many who were drawn to the West were a few earnest men who went in the interest of the welfare of their fellows. Henry Durant was one of this number. Awake to the possibilities of aiding in the educational development of the new state, he left his position in the East, and arrived in California on May 1, 1853.

At a joint meeting of the Presbytery of San Francisco and the Congregational Association of California held in Nevada City, Cal., on May 10, a plan was formulated to establish an Academy in Oakland (then known as Contra Costa) under the direction of Durant. A month later the Contra Costa Academy opened, with three pupils, in a former fandango house rented by Durant for $150 per month, payable in gold coin in advance. Durant, however, had come to California with "college on the brain," and never for a moment forgot his supreme aim and desire. Consequently it was upon the petition of the Board of Directors of his Academy that the State Board of Education granted a charter to the College of California, Apr. 13, 1855. By the year 1860 an entering class had been prepared, and the College of California began its first session in July with a freshman class of nine and a faculty of two: Henry Durant and Martin Kellogg [q.v.]. In 1868 the legislature of California provided for the establishment and support of the state University of California, and in the next year all assets of the College of California were turned over to the University. On Aug. 16, 1870, Henry Durant, now sixty-eight years old, was elected the first president, but he was forced to resign at the end of two years, owing to ill health. Following his recovery, he was twice elected mayor of Oakland and was occupying this office at the time of his death.

Durant was essentially a teacher and an organizer. He left practically nothing in the way of writings. He made no original contribution to literature, to science, or to any other branch of human knowledge. His great contribution to the culture of the West was the part he played in the founding, first, of the College of California, and then later, of the University of California.

[John B. Felton, "A Memorial Address," *Bull. of the Univ. of Cal.*, no. 10, Mar. 1875; W. W. Ferrier, *Coll. and Univ.: The Story of the Coll. of Cal. and its Relation to the Univ. of Cal.* (1921); W. C. Jones, *Illustrated Hist. of the Univ. of Cal.* (1901); *Overland Monthly*, Mar. 1875; S. H. Willey, *Hist. of the Coll. of Cal.* (1887); *Obit. Record of Grads. of Yale Coll.* (1875).]   F.H.S.

DURANT, HENRY FOWLE (Feb. 20, 1822–Oct. 3, 1881), lawyer, evangelist, philanthropist, was descended from Edward Durant, an early settler of Newton, Mass. He was born in Hanover, N. H., to William and Harriet (Fowle) Smith, who christened him Henry Welles, but in 1851, owing to the fact that eleven Boston lawyers bore the name Smith, he adopted that of Durant. In his childhood the family moved to Lowell, where the father practised law for many years. Henry was sent to the Rev. and Mrs. Samuel Ripley of Waltham to be prepared for Harvard, which he entered in 1837. The learning, versatility, and character of Mrs. Ripley seem to have made upon him a more lasting impression than any of the influences of an undistinguished college career. Upon receiving his degree in 1842, he began the study of law with his father, and at the age of twenty-one, was admitted to the bar. After five years' practise in Lowell, he moved to Boston, and here for seventeen years, with a success that was the wonder and the envy of his fellow lawyers, he pleaded cases at the Suffolk Bar. His rapid rise is attributed not only to his merciless cross-examination, his dramatic ability and skill in presentation, but also to his unsparing attention to detail. His defense in the "Eliot School Case," which concerned the reading of the Bible in the public school, is one of his best-known arguments.

On May 23, 1854, he married his cousin, Pauline Adeline Fowle, and to them were born Henry Fowle, Jr., and Pauline Cazenove. The daughter lived but two months, the son to the age of eight. The loss of this child in 1863 brought about a great change in Mr. Durant's activities and purposes. Abruptly abandoning the law, he turned to the service of Christianity, and for some years conducted revival meetings in churches of eastern Massachusetts. Meanwhile, he and his wife had become interested in Mount Holyoke, of which he became a trustee in 1867. After much consideration they determined to devote their country home in Wellesley and the considerable fortune accumulated from his profession and from successful business ventures, to the education of young women. From the time of obtaining the charter of Wellesley (1870) until his death, Mr. Durant's history is identified with that of the college. In name, he was the treasurer; in fact, the physical plant, the faculty, the curriculum, and the health and conduct of the students, were the intimate concern of the founder, who brought to the college the same zest and emotional intensity which he had given to the law. To him higher education and the forming of Christian character were synonymous, but this did not lessen his appreciation of the necessity for laboratories and first-hand materials for scholarly work.

Durant's appearance was striking. His features were clear-cut, his eyes dark and brilliant, and his hair, black in his youth, was always worn longer than the mode. In character he was a perplexing combination of dreamer and master of of practical detail, of fanatic and man of affairs. His wit was keen, his courage undaunted, his love of beauty unfailing.

[Florence Morse Kingsley, *The Life of Henry Fowle Durant* (1924), written in a tone of extreme adulation; Charlotte Conant, *Address Delivered in Memory of Henry Fowle Durant in Wellesley Chapel, Feb. 18, 1906* (1906); Florence Converse, *The Story of Wellesley* (1915); Wm. T. Davis, *Bench and Bar of the Commonwealth of Mass.* (1895), I, 498–99; the *Congregationalist*, Oct. 12, 1881; G. W. Smalley's "Anglo-American Memories," *N. Y. Tribune*, Mar. 28, 1909.] E.D.

DURANT, THOMAS CLARK (Feb. 6, 1820–Oct. 5, 1885), builder of the Union Pacific Railroad, son of Thomas and Sybil (Wright) Durant, was born at Lee, Mass., of colonial and Revolutionary ancestry. He graduated from the Albany Medical College in 1840, but soon joined his uncle in the firm of Durant, Lathrop & Company, exporters of flour and grain. Given charge of the New York office, he expanded the business and also became known as a daring and successful speculator in stocks. Becoming interested in the West, Durant in 1851 joined Henry Farnam [q.v.] in constructing the Michigan Southern Railroad; they later contracted to build the Chicago & Rock Island, and then the Mississippi & Missouri. The question of a railroad to the Pacific was in the air, and Farnam and Durant sent Peter A. Dey and Grenville M. Dodge to make surveys. In 1863, Durant alone sent out three parties, including a geologist to report on coal and iron, and claimed to have influenced President Lincoln to choose Omaha as the beginning point of the road. The Pacific Railway Act of 1862 fixed the capital of the Union Pacific at one hundred millions, but permitted organization when two millions had been subscribed and ten per cent of this amount paid. Capital was timid, and only $2,180,000 had been subscribed on Oct. 30, 1863, when Gen. John A. Dix was elected president and Durant vice-president of the company. Durant declared afterward that he had provided or guaranteed the instalments on three-fourths of the subscription (*House Report No. 78*, 42 Cong., 3 Sess., p. 515).

From this time until the completion of the road Durant was the chief figure in the management of the Union Pacific. He was influential in securing the amended act of 1864, which doubled the land grant and permitted the company to issue bonds equal in amount to the United States bonds lent and to make them a prior lien on the road. In securing these and other favorable amendments much money was used, but no actual proof of bribery or of misappropriation was ever adduced. These expenditures were long carried in the famous "suspense account," which was the occasion of much controversy, but Durant's accounts were approved by Presidents Dix and Oliver Ames, and by Treasurer Cisco. During 1863–64, Durant built a few miles of road with the cash in hand and made advances from his personal funds. When H. M. Hoxie, who had contracted to build 100 miles, later extended to 247 miles, was unable to continue, Durant and several associates took over his contract and subscribed $1,600,000, one-fourth in cash, as a building fund. The associates became frightened and refused to pay further instalments. Evidently New York capitalists would not build the road, the failure of which was generally regarded as certain. Meanwhile Durant had secured the charter of the Crédit Mobilier of which he became the largest stockholder and the president. This corporation took over the Hoxie contract, agreeing to take the securities of the road as issued in payment. The Ames brothers, Oakes and Oliver [qq.v.], and other New England capitalists came into Crédit Mobilier, thereby becoming stockholders in the road, and secured representation in its directorate in 1866. For the next three years the Durant and Ames factions, or the "New York crowd" and the "Boston crowd," contended for control of the Union Pacific. Durant refused to give the Crédit Mobilier a second contract, and a period of wrangling between the factions ensued. He was ousted from the directorate of the Crédit Mobilier in May 1867, but the effort to drop him from the direction of the road in October failed. Meanwhile (Aug. 16, 1867), Oakes Ames had offered to build 667 miles, and Durant agreed, provided the consent of every stockholder of the road be secured. Later he became one of the seven trustees under the tripartite agreement which assigned the profits of the contract to the Crédit Mobilier. With large funds at his disposal and fortified by a resolution of the executive committee of the Union Pacific (July 3, 1868) which made him practically dictator, Durant drove the work furiously under this contract, and the later Davis contract, regardless of difficulties or cost. Speed had become an obsession. He spent most of his time on the line and said that sometimes he did not remove his clothes for a week. This haste probably doubled the cost of construction. Durant knew that the "Boston crowd" would finally accomplish his downfall, and wished to complete the road first. He joined with President Leland Stanford of the Central Pacific in driving the "last spike," May 10, 1869, but on May 25 was dropped from the directorate.

Broken in health, Durant spent most of his later years in the Adirondacks, where he owned much land. Though crippled financially by the panic of 1873, he promoted a grandiose scheme to develop the iron and timber resources of the Adirondacks, including a railroad from Saratoga across the St. Lawrence into Canada. He had married in 1847 an Englishwoman, Héloise Hannah Timbrel, who with a daughter and a son survived him. He died at North Creek, Warren County, N. Y. Durant was an unusual combination of dreamer and forceful executive. Reticent and quiet in manner, he was able to excite his subordinates to extraordinary exertion. In his associates he aroused deep antagonism or warm admiration.

[An appreciative sketch is in the *N. Y. Tribune,* May 29, 1869, and one, evidently from material furnished by himself, is in *Representative Men of New York* (1872). A sketch by L. O. Leonard, inaccurate in some particulars, is in the *Rock Island Magazine,* Oct. 1926. Information has also been furnished by his daughter and son, who have permitted limited access to his papers. See also *N. Y. Tribune,* Oct. 6, 1885, and references in sketch of Oakes Ames.]   H.T.

DURANT, THOMAS JEFFERSON (Aug. 8, 1817–Feb. 3, 1882), lawyer, politician, the son of John Waldo and Sarah (Heyliger) Durant, was born in Philadelphia, where he obtained his early education in the common schools. In 1830 he entered the University of Pennsylvania, but before completing his course, removed in 1834 to New Orleans, where for a short time he held a position in the post-office. He then studied law, was admitted to the Louisiana bar, and opened an office in New Orleans. He rapidly achieved distinction and acquired a lucrative practise, at the same time identifying himself with the Democratic party and becoming active in state politics. He was not a rabid partisan and opposed the annexation of Texas on constitutional grounds, but this did not prevent him from becoming an influential member of the state committee which in 1844 managed the Louisiana campaign of Polk for the presidency. Elected as a Democrat, he served in the state Senate in 1846. Later, President Polk appointed him United States district attorney. He was now recognized as an outstanding figure in local legal and political circles. His practise had brought him wealth, he was a slave-owner, and his reputation for integrity had gained for him the respect of the community, but the outbreak of the Civil War found him aligned against the preponderant sentiment of his fellow citizens. A conscientious and consistent Unionist, he supported Lincoln in the campaign of 1860. He fought strenuously against secession, and when that became a reality he remained in New Orleans, but during the Confederate régime abstained from all political activities. When the Federal forces under Butler occupied the city in 1862 he headed the movement to organize Louisiana as a free state and was offered the position of governor, which he declined. In 1863, however, after Banks had superseded Butler as commander of the Department of the Gulf, Durant became president of the Free State General Committee which was formed to procure the election of a convention to frame a new constitution, and the military governor, G. F. Shepley, appointed him attorney-general and commissioner for the purpose of carrying out the registration of loyal citizens entitled to vote. The constitutional convention of 1864 revised and amended the state constitution of 1852 and abolished slavery, and its work was approved by the president and ratified by the people. Durant, however, held the view that secession had abrogated the constitution of 1852 and that the work of the convention, most of which was not in harmony with his views, was invalid, and from thenceforth he was involved in a bitter controversy with Banks and a powerful section of the Northern sympathizers led by A. P. Dostie. The merits of the dispute, if any, are obscured by the intemperate pamphlet warfare which broke out. Durant evidenced his bitter disapproval of the course of events by removing to Washington, D. C., where he henceforth devoted himself to his profession. The resumption, after 1865, of litigation, suspended throughout the South during the war, had its effect upon the Supreme Court docket, and an abnormal number of appeals from Louisiana came before that Court, a majority involving novel points of constitutional law and military authority. Durant was retained in practically all of these and soon established himself as one of the leading members of the Washington bar. To a thorough theoretical and practical knowledge of the civil law he added a persuasive logic, a facility of language, and a dignity of manner which always assured him an attentive hearing, and he enjoyed a larger practise before the Supreme Court and the Court of Claims than any contemporary, appearing as counsel in no less than 154 reported cases. His sphere of action was narrow, confined almost entirely to civil and constitutional law, bankruptcy, and admiralty, but within these limits he had in his time no superior. His most conspicuous success was obtained in the Slaughterhouse Cases

(16 *Wallace,* 36), where his elaborate argument as leading counsel for the defendants in error was upheld by the Supreme Court. Among his other outstanding cases were: *Coppell* vs. *Hall* (7 *Wallace,* 173), holding that a contract of the British consul at New Orleans to protect cotton of the insurgents was void; *Handlin* vs. *Wickliffe* (12 *Wallace,* 173), deciding that the authority of a judge appointed by a military governor ceases of necessity after the civil constitution of a state functions independent of military control; *Holdane* vs. *Sumner* (15 *Wallace,* 600), where it was held that all statutes of prescription and limitation were suspended in the federal courts during the period of the Civil War; and the Confiscation Cases (7 *Wallace,* 454). In 1881 he was retained as counsel for the United States before the Spanish and American Claims Commission. He died in Washington in the following year. His wife was Mary Elizabeth Harper, a daughter of Robert Withers Harper of Marlboro, Md.

Durant was recognized as a man of great innate ability and the highest character and culture. In 1869, when the number of the Supreme Court judges was increased, and again in 1872, when a vacancy in the Court occurred through the resignation of Judge Nelson, the claims of "the sad-faced and thin featured New Orleans Unionist" (*Boston Daily Advertiser,* Apr. 27, 1867) were urged in many quarters, on the ground that a Southerner was greatly needed to strengthen the Supreme Bench.

[See *Am. Ann. Cyc. and Reg.,* 1863, 1864; John Rose Ficklen, *Hist. of Reconstruction in La.* (1910), *passim*; Charles Warren, *The Supreme Court in U. S. Hist.* (1922); *Letter of Thos. J. Durant to the Hon. Henry Winter Davis, 27 Oct. 1864* (New Orleans, 1864); *Evening Star* (Washington, D. C.), Feb. 4, 1882. For an unfavorable view of Durant's reconstruction activities see A. P. Dostie, *The Political Position of Thos. J. Durant* (New Orleans, 1865), being a reprint of a letter to the chairman of the Committee on Elections, House of Representatives, Dec. 29, 1864. Emily Hagen Reed, *Life of A. P. Dostie* (1868), also gives a bitter partisan picture of Durant.]   H. W. H. K.

DURBIN, JOHN PRICE (Oct. 10, 1800–Oct. 19, 1876), Methodist Episcopal clergyman, began his public career at the age of eighteen with no more preparation than a bit of frontier schooling and acquiring the trade of cabinetmaker could give. He was a Kentuckian, born in Bourbon County near Paris, the son of Hozier and Elizabeth (Nunn) Durbin, both children of some of the first settlers in that region. Left in his thirteenth year by his father's death to the care of his mother and the clemency of the world, the eldest of five sons, he was shortly apprenticed; but an urge to the ministry and a display of native talent led to his being licensed as a preacher,

Nov. 19, 1818. He began his itinerary on the Limestone Circuit of the Kentucky Conference, and during the next seven years held various charges in Indiana and Ohio, being ordained deacon in 1822, and elder in 1824. Conscious of his deficiencies he spent every minute available in the study of English, oratory, theology and the classics, managing, without interrupting his duties, to do work at Miami University, and at Cincinnati College, which in 1825 granted him a degree. Immediately he was appointed professor of languages at Augusta College, Ky., one of the earliest Methodist experiments in education. On Sept. 6, 1827, he married Frances B. Cook, the daughter of Alexander Cook of Philadelphia, her younger sister subsequently becoming his second wife. Excursions in behalf of the college brought him to notice in the East, and, having now taken up the study of the natural sciences, in 1831 he was appointed professor of these at Wesleyan University, Conn., an office he did not fill because of his election to the chaplaincy of the United States Senate. This same year he edited Thomas Wood's *Mosaic History of the Creation of the World.* He was now launched on a career of national prominence which included the editorship of the *Christian Advocate and Journal* (1832–34); the successful steering of Dickinson College through the opening years of its Methodist history (1834–45); pastorates and presiding eldership in Philadelphia (1845–50); and finally his most distinguished service to American Methodism, secretaryship of the Missionary Society (1850–72). A trip abroad in 1842 resulted in *Observations in Europe* (1844) and *Observations in the East* (1845), well-written books that went through numerous editions.

It was said of him that he lived two lives each so eminent that his fame in the one dimmed that of the other. In spite of physical limitations, for he was small of stature, unprepossessing in appearance, with a voice inclined to be thin and high-pitched, he early came to be regarded as one of the greatest preachers of his day. At his death, however, he was remembered chiefly for his wisdom and generalship in the councils of the church, and for his administrative genius. He was a member of seven General Conferences, covering twenty-eight years. At the first of these, 1844, in the case of Bishop Andrew [*q.v.*], which led to the disruption of the church, he made a long-remembered stand against the Southern delegation, supporting the resolution advising the Bishop to desist from the exercise of his office while connected with slaveholding; yet he was not a radical abolitionist, for he opposed the expulsion of slaveholders from the church (see his article in *Christian Advocate,* New York, July 26, 1855) and indorsed the Colonization Society (see *Addresses Delivered in the Hall of the House of Representatives, Harrisburg, Pa.,* 1852). He was also an early advocate of theological schools and lay representation. His administration of the Missionary Society was one of the great epochs in its expansion. His death from cerebral hemorrhage occurred in New York, and he is buried in Laurel Hill Cemetery, Philadelphia.

[John A. Roche, article in *Meth. Review,* May 1887, and *Life of John Price Durbin* (1889); Abel Stevens, editorial in *Nat. Mag.,* Feb. 1855, and *Hist. of M. E. Church,* vol. IV (1867); *Minutes of Phila. Conference* (1877); *Christian Advocate* (N. Y.), Oct. 26, 1876; *Harper's Weekly,* Nov. 11, 1876; *N. Y. Times* and *N. Y. Tribune,* Oct. 20, 1876, are authority for date of death given above.]   H.E.S.

DURELL, EDWARD HENRY (July 14, 1810–Mar. 29, 1887), jurist, traced his descent from Norman Huguenot ancestors whose domicile was in the Channel Islands. His father, Daniel Meserve Durell, a prominent New Hampshire lawyer and chief justice of the court of common pleas, married on June 1, 1800, Elizabeth Wentworth, a descendant of Elder William Wentworth, and Edward Durell was their third son. Born in the "Governor Wentworth house" at Portsmouth, N. H., he attended Phillips Exeter Academy and proceeded in 1827 to Harvard College. Graduating in 1831, he read law in his father's office at Dover, N. H., and was admitted to the bar in 1834. For a short time thereafter he practised law at Pittsburg (Grenada), Miss., but finally settled at New Orleans, Mar. 27, 1837. Combining a sound knowledge of law and a rare gift of incisive speech, he quickly acquired a prominent position at the local bar and influenced the adoption of much-needed reforms in domestic legislation. His outstanding achievement in this line was the statute whereby the Louisiana law that on the death of a father, mother, husband, or wife, the children immediately obtained possession of one-half of the acquits and gains of the matrimonial partnership, was changed so as to give the surviving parent, etc., the usufruct of such half. Elected a member of the New Orleans common council in 1854, he drafted the city charter which became law in 1856. He was a pronounced Unionist, strenuously opposed the ordinance of secession, and on its adoption in 1860 retired for a time from public life. However, when the Federal troops took possession of New Orleans in 1862, at the request of the military governor he drafted the bureau system of municipal government which was then inaugurated, and he was appointed presi-

dent of the bureau of finance. In 1863 he became mayor of the city by military appointment and the same year was appointed by President Lincoln United States judge of the eastern district of Louisiana, his jurisdiction being extended in 1866 to cover the entire state. He was president of the State Constitutional Convention of 1864, being in that year also a delegate to the Republican National Convention at Baltimore. In 1867 he was instrumental in procuring the abandonment of the confiscation policy as far as it applied to Louisiana. While at Washington on this mission he was offered by Seward and declined the post of minister to Austria as he had two years previously similarly declined an appointment to the Supreme Court of the United States tendered to him by Lincoln. He contemplated retiring from the bench in 1871, but a "respectful remonstrance" of the Louisiana bar, wherein he was referred to as "a tried, faithful, able, learned and incorruptible judge," induced him to reconsider his decision. He had, throughout the embittered reconstruction conflict, avoided open participation or partisanship up to 1872, but the incidents of the state election of that year procured for him an unenviable notoriety. Following the voting a serious situation had arisen owing to the fact that three distinct election boards claimed the right to canvass the returns. Since it appeared that the Governor's board, which in a sense represented the Democratic interests, had completed its canvass and would function prior to its opponents, Durell, out of court at his house on Dec. 5, at nine o'clock at night, issued an unsealed order to the United States marshal to take possession of the statehouse and to give entrance only to certain authorized persons. This "midnight order" was, with the aid of Federal troops, immediately carried into effect. On the following day in court Durell declared the Democratic board illegal and ordered the returns delivered to the "legal" board, thus enabling the Republicans to obtain control of the legislature and state government. To what extent, if any, he acted with the connivance or tacit approval of the Federal administration is not known, but the matter was taken up in Congress, and the proceedings were investigated by the Senate Committee on Privileges and Elections, whose reports condemned his action unreservedly, characterizing the interference of a Federal judge in a state election as "without parallel in judicial proceedings" (see *House Executive Document No. 91,* 42 Cong., 3 Sess.; *Senate Report No. 457,* 42 Cong., 3 Sess.). A move to institute impeachment proceedings against him was terminated by his resignation in 1874 (*Congressional Record,* 43 Cong., 2 Sess., 319–24). Taking up his residence at Newburgh, N. Y., he married, June 8, 1875, Mary Seitz Gebhart of Schoharie, N. Y., to which latter place he subsequently removed and lived until his death. His later years were passed in literary pursuits, including the preparation of a "History of Seventeen Years; from 1860 to the Retiring of the Federal Army from Louisiana and South Carolina," which he did not complete.

[An extended review of his career appeared in the *Granite Monthly,* April 1888. See also J. R. Ficklen, *Hist. of Reconstruction in La.* (1910) ; E. Lonn, *Reconstruction in La. after 1868* (1918) ; *Am. Annual Cyc. and Register,* 1872 and 1873, and obituary notice in *Albany Evening Jour.,* Mar. 30, 1887.]   H.W.H.K.

DURFEE, JOB (Sept. 20, 1790–July 26, 1847), jurist, author, descended from Thomas Durfee who came to New England in 1660 and settled at Portsmouth, R. I., was born in Tiverton in that state. His parents were Thomas Durfee of Tiverton, at one time chief justice of the court of common pleas of Newport County, and his wife Mary, daughter of Richard Lowden of Newport. His primary education was received at home and in the public schools at Tiverton and Bristol. Entering Brown University in 1809, he graduated with high honors in 1813. He then commenced the study of law with his father, at the same time becoming actively interested in state politics. As a Republican (Jeffersonian), he was elected to represent Tiverton in the General Assembly in the spring of 1816, while yet a law student, and retained the seat for four years, being called to the bar at Newport on Mar. 4, 1817. In 1820 he was elected a member of the federal House of Representatives and remained in Congress till 1825. In 1826 he was again returned to the state legislature, and the following year was speaker of the House, which position he retained till 1829. In 1832 he published *Whatcheer: or Roger Williams in Banishment,* a long poem, which, though favorably noticed in England, did not attract any considerable attention at home. In 1833 he was elected an associate justice of the supreme court of Rhode Island, and two years later, became chief justice, holding the office till his death in 1847. As chief justice he was distinguished for his dignity and courtesy of manner, and though not a great lawyer, his strong common sense, industry, and absolute impartiality commanded the confidence of the bar and the public. His firm stand during the stormy period of the Dorr Rebellion, his early declaration that the movement was illegal, without law and against law, and his subsequent charge to the grand jury on the subject of treason, had great influence in crystalliz-

ing public opinion. When open insurrection broke out, he offered his services with the military forces of the state. He was a delegate to the convention called by the legislature to frame a new constitution, and a powerful factor in the solution of its problems. He presided at the trial of Dorr. Inclined to corpulence, he was "physically indolent almost to a proverb" (Thomas Durfee, *post*). Simple and unpretending in manners and conduct, he was taciturn in social circles, for which he had no taste and in which he did not shine. His wife was Judith, daughter of Simeon Borden.

He was the author of *The Panidèa, or An Omnipresent Reason Considered as the Creative and Sustaining Logos by Theoptes* (1846), a somewhat pretentious philosophical work which nobody read. In addition he contributed addresses to various societies on: *Aboriginal History* (1838), *The Idea of the Supernatural among the Indians* (1839), *The Influence of Scientific Discovery and Invention on Social and Political Progress* (1843), *The Progress of Ideas* (1843), and *The Rhode Island Idea of Government* (1846). After his death, *The Complete Works of the Hon. Job Durfee, LL.D., Late Chief Justice of Rhode Island* (1849), edited by his son Thomas [*q.v.*], was published under the auspices of the Rhode Island Historical Society.

[Details of Durfee's ancestry are contained in W. F. Reed, *The Descendants of Thos. Durfee of Portsmouth, R. I.* (2 vols., 1902–05). The chief authority for his life and career is the Memoir by Thos. Durfee, prefixed to the complete edition of his works. See also R. G. Hazard, *A Discourse . . . on the Character and Writings of C. J. Durfee* (1848) ; Conrad Reno, *Memoirs of the Judiciary and Bar of New England for the 19th Century,* vol. II (1901), pt. 2, p. 2, and *Memorial Biogs. of the New-England Historic Geneal. Soc.,* vol. I (1880), p. 37.]
H.W.H.K.

DURFEE, THOMAS (Feb. 6, 1826–June 6, 1901), jurist, was the elder son of Chief Justice Job Durfee [*q.v.*] and Judith (Borden) Durfee. He was born at Tiverton, R. I., and obtained his early education at home. In 1842, having previously received two years' private tuition at East Greenwich, R. I., he entered Brown University, where he graduated in 1846. He then studied law at Tiverton and later at Providence where he was admitted to the Rhode Island bar in 1848. Commencing practise at Providence, he was in 1849 appointed reporter to the supreme court and in that capacity compiled and published *Reports of Cases Argued and Determined in the Supreme Court of Rhode Island,* vol. II (1854). He resigned in 1854 when he was elected by the General Assembly a member of the court of magistrates for the City of Providence. This position he retained by successive reëlections for six years, being presiding magistrate during his last five terms. In 1857 he completed and published *A Treatise on the Law of Highways,* which had been partially written by J. K. Angell [*q.v.*] prior to his death. For many years this remained the standard work on the subject. He retired from the magistracy in 1860 in order to devote himself to private practise, and on the outbreak of the Civil War came to the fore as a strong supporter of the war measures of the administration. In 1863 he was induced to return to public life, entering the General Assembly as representative for Providence. Although he had had no legislative experience he was elected speaker, continuing to act as such till the expiration of his term. In 1864 he headed the Rhode Island delegation to the Republican National Convention at Cincinnati, when Lincoln was nominated for a second term. In 1865 he was elected to the state Senate, but in June of the same year was chosen an associate justice of the supreme court of Rhode Island. He became chief justice on Jan. 28, 1875, and continued to occupy that position till his retirement, Mar. 4, 1891, having completed over twenty-five years of judicial service. An accomplished lawyer, he was, as a judge, inclined to be conservative, and his opinions, never brilliant but eminently sane, commanded respect in professional circles beyond the confines of his state.

Though in 1897 he acted as chairman of the commission to revise the state constitution, he passed the remainder of his life in comparative retirement, dying at Providence in his seventy-sixth year. His wife, whom he married on Oct. 29, 1857, was Sarah, daughter of John Slater.

Durfee's active interests were not confined to the law. He was throughout his life a devoted supporter of Brown University, and rendered notable service to that institution, of which he was successively trustee, chancellor, and fellow. In his leisure he was constantly drawn to literary work of a varied nature, in all of which he displayed fine qualities of scholarship. At the request of the Rhode Island Historical Society he edited, *The Complete Works of the Hon. Job Durfee, LL.D., Late Chief Justice of Rhode Island* (1849), prefixing a memoir of the latter's life. He was the author of *The Village Picnic and Other Poems* (1872), *Gleanings from the Judicial History of Rhode Island* (1883), and a number of occasional addresses on historical subjects which were published in pamphlet form.

[W. F. Reed, *The Descendants of Thos. Durfee of Portsmouth, R. I.,* II (1905), 282; Conrad Reno, *Memoirs of the Judiciary and the Bar of New England,* vol. II (1901); *Representative Men and Old Families of*

Rhode Island (1908), p. 1289; *Hist. Cat. Brown Univ., 1764–1914* (1915).]   H.W.H.K.

DURFEE, WILLIAM FRANKLIN (Nov. 15, 1833–Nov. 14, 1899), engineer and inventor, was born in New Bedford, Mass., the son of William and Alice Sherman (Talbot) Durfee. His father, a carpenter by trade, acquired a wide reputation for his ability in erecting buildings of large dimensions. A steel furnace, erected for Anderson & Woods in Pittsburgh, in 1868, was one of his achievements. The son, William, received a practical mechanical training under the tutelage of his father and then took a course of special study in the Lawrence Scientific School at Harvard. At the age of twenty he established himself as an engineer and architect in New Bedford, and soon received an appointment as city surveyor. In 1861 he served in the state legislature. As secretary of the military committee, he was active in forwarding legislation for the equipment of troops at the beginning of the Civil War. While holding this office he introduced a resolution requesting Congress to repeal "all laws which deprive any class of loyal subjects of the Government from bearing arms for the common defense" (Reed, *post,* pp. 206 f.). This is said to have been the first definite proposal for the arming of colored troops. In 1862, at the invitation of his cousin, Z. S. Durfee [*q.v.*] and the latter's partner, Capt. E. B. Ward, he went to the Lake Superior district to undertake to test the suitability of certain ores of that district for the manufacture of steel by the process invented by William Kelly [*q.v.*], and almost identical with the Bessemer process. He designed the machinery and apparatus necessary to test the merits of the Kelly process on a large scale, and superintended the construction of a plant at Wyandotte, Mich., ten miles from Detroit, which was opened in the fall of 1864. Here, in September of that year, he supervised the making of the first Bessemer steel produced in America. From this steel, on May 25, 1865, the first American steel rails were rolled. Durfee also established in connection with the plant at Wyandotte a steelworks analytical laboratory, the first ever built in the United States. This achievement alone would have made him a memorable figure in American industrial progress.

Upon leaving the Wyandotte works, he built the Bayview Merchant Mill at Milwaukee. Later he became connected with the Wheeler & Wilson Company at Bridgeport, building for them at Ansonia, Conn., the first furnace for refining copper by the use of gaseous fuel ever constructed in the United States. While he was at Bridgeport he became general manager of a company that controlled patents for the production of castings in wrought iron, and he helped to develop a machine for the production of horseshoe nails. He had a gift for machinery design which he could readily turn to practical advantage, and he found a place for it continually in the various later connections of his life, such as the Pennsylvania Drill Company at Birdsboro, Pa., and the C. W. Hunt Company on Staten Island for which he acted as shop superintendent.

Although an intensely practical man in the industrial world, Durfee was of a studious, scholarly disposition. He had an almost encyclopedic knowledge of the history and past achievements of engineering and combined a talent for research work with his more practical ability. This rare combination of talents made him valuable, in later life, as an expert witness at court in patent cases. Technical papers which he found time to write were published in the proceedings and publications of the societies to which he belonged, such as the Iron & Steel Institute, the Franklin Institute of Philadelphia, and the American Society of Mechanical Engineers. To this latter organization he bequeathed his extensive library, rich in mechanical antiquities collected throughout a lifetime, and it may now be found as a part of the Engineering Societies Library in New York City. He was married in 1880 to Annie Swift of Boston.

[*Jour. Iron and Steel Inst.*, vol. LVI (1899), pt. 2, p. 292; *Trans. Am. Inst. Mining Engineers*, vol. XXX (1901); *Trans. Am. Soc. Mech. Engineers*, XXI (1900), 1161; *Railroad Gazette*, XXXI, 799, 818; and W. F. Reed, *Descendants of Thomas Durfee* (2 vols., 1902–05), I, 528, II, 206.]

E. Y.

DURFEE, ZOHETH SHERMAN (Apr. 22, 1831–June 8, 1880), inventor and manufacturer, was born at New Bedford, Mass. His parents, Thomas and Delight (Sherman) Durfee, were members of the Free Will Baptist Church and had resided in Fall River, Mass., before moving to New Bedford in the early part of 1831. He was educated at Friends' Academy, New Bedford. In early youth he learned the blacksmith's trade and later was associated with his father and uncle in that business. Becoming interested in the process of manufacturing steel directly from pig iron, the invention of Joseph Dixon [*q.v.*], Durfee, sponsored by New Bedford capitalists, undertook investigations of the various processes for the manufacturing of iron and steel which led him to believe that William Kelly [*q.v.*] of Eddyville, Ky., was the real inventor of the "Bessemer process" instead of Henry Bessemer of England who had claimed the invention. On the basis of this belief, Durfee, in partnership with Capt. E. B. Ward of Detroit, Mich.,

obtained control of Kelly's patents in 1861. The same year he went to Europe to study the Bessemer process and to purchase, if possible, Bessemer's rights in the United States. He failed to accomplish the latter object, and on his return home organized a company to protect the use of the Kelly patents. Ward and Durfee, in 1862, invited William F. Durfee [*q.v.*], a cousin of Z. S. Durfee, to assist in erecting an experimental plant at Wyandotte, Wayne County, Mich., for the manufacturing of pneumatic steel; and in May 1863 they and their partners organized the Kelly Pneumatic Process Company, Kelly retaining an interest in any profits the company might make.

During his first visit to England (1861), Durfee had become familiar with the invention of Robert Mushet for using spiegeleisen as a recarburizing agent (patent granted in England, 1856; United States, 1857) and was convinced that it was essential to the "successful conduct of the Kelly and Bessemer processes." In 1863 he was sent to England to secure control of Mushet's patent in the United States, and procured an assignment on Oct. 24, 1864. While Durfee was in England, the experimental works at Wyandotte made its first blow, in September 1864, under the supervision of William F. Durfee—the first Bessemer steel made in the United States. In 1865 a plant at Troy, N. Y., built by Alexander L. Holley [*q.v.*], began to manufacture steel under Bessemer's patents, and the following year the two interests were combined in the Pneumatic Steel Association, a joint stock company organized under the laws of the State of New York, in which was vested the ownership of the patents of both Kelly and Bessemer. Of this company Durfee was made secretary and treasurer, and he held the office until his death in 1880. He is said to have been, also, for a time "previous to 1868, superintendent of the steel works of Winslow & Griswold" located at Troy, N. Y. Throughout his life he was interested in the manufacture of steel. He originated the idea of using the cupola instead of a reverberatory furnace for melting the pig iron for the converter charge, a practise which has become universal. He guarded Kelly's business interests and did more, perhaps, than any other person to get the rights of Kelly recognized in the United States. He was always held in the highest esteem by Kelly. He obtained numerous patents for steel manufacture and iron and steel products, sixteen of which are recorded in *The Official Gazette of the United States Patent Office* between 1862 and 1876. His work was prematurely ended in his fiftieth year, when he died of paralysis at the Butler Hospital, Providence, R. I.

[*Report of the Commissioner of Patents,* 1871 ; *Official Gazette of the U. S. Patent Office,* vols. I, II (1872), V, VI (1874), VII, VIII (1875), IX, X (1876) ; J. M. Swank, *Hist. of the Manufacture of Iron in all Ages* (2nd ed., 1892) ; J. N. Boucher, *Wm. Kelly: A True Hist. of the Bessemer Process* (1924) ; W. F. Reed, *The Descendants of Thos. Durfee of Portsmouth, R. I.,* vol. I (1902), which is the authority for date of Durfee's birth ; Records of Deaths in the City of Providence, R. I., Book 15, p. 30, which gives his age at death as 48 years, 1 mo., and 16 days ; information from J. G. Kelly of Braddock, Pa., a son of Wm. Kelly.]

C. M. J.

DURHAM, CALEB WHEELER (Feb. 6, 1848–Mar. 28, 1910), engineer, inventor, was born at Tunkhannock, Pa., the son of Alpha Durham and his third wife, Elizabeth B. Riggs. His father was a Presbyterian minister who, two years after Caleb's birth, went alone to California to seek his fortune in the gold rush, was unsuccessful, and returned in 1852. He contracted fever at Panama on the way and died shortly thereafter in New York City. Subsequently Mrs. Durham moved with her children to Reading, Pa., where Caleb received his early education. The Civil War interrupted his high-school work and he enlisted as a private, first, in Company C, 42nd Pennsylvania Militia, serving in the reserves at Gettysburg, and, second, in Company B, 195th Pennsylvania Volunteers, seeing active service in Maryland and Virginia. Discharged at the expiration of his two years' enlistment in 1864, he went home and entered the employ of the Philadelphia & Reading Railroad Company. In 1866, with the intention of preparing for college, he attended Williston Academy, Easthampton, Mass., and in 1867 entered the University of Michigan at Ann Arbor, to study civil engineering. Two years later he became engaged to marry, gave up his college work, and entered the engineering department of the New York Central Railroad. From 1869 to 1873 he continued in railroad work for several companies in the Middle West and Southwest, but after his marriage, on May 28, 1873, to Clarissa Safford Welles of Ann Arbor, he established himself in Chicago as a civil engineer specializing in sanitation. About 1875 he devised an improved hot-air heater and undertook its manufacture and sale. It proved too costly, however, for general use, and the business was abandoned. Durham meanwhile had turned his attention to house drainage and after much experimentation invented in 1880 what is still known as the Durham System. This consists in the use of a wrought-iron or steel screw-jointed pipe, the specially threaded fittings being designed in such a way as to provide the inclina-

tions necessary in house drainage as well as tight joints and a smooth inner channel. The whole installation, too, is sufficiently rigid to be self-supporting. After obtaining patents, Durham organized the Durham House Drainage Company and carried on business in Chicago for several years. One of his largest contracts at this time was the entire house drainage system for the new city of Pullman, Ill. In 1883 he moved with his family to New York, reorganized his company, and carried on the business there for the remainder of his life. Among the most important installations of his system were those in Carnegie Hall and the Hotel Majestic in New York and the National Capitol at Washington. The last fifteen years of his life were fraught with difficulties induced both by the panic of 1893 and by the failure of the courts to sustain his original patent against various infringers. He was a member of the Civil Engineers' Club of the Northwest, Chicago, and the Engineers' Club, New York. He died at his home in Peekskill, N. Y., survived by four sons.

[*Engineering News,* Apr. 7, 1910; *Univ. of Mich. Cat. of Grads.,* etc. (1923) ; Alumni records, Univ. of Mich.; Patent Office records ; family records and correspondence.]

C. W. M.

DURIVAGE, FRANCIS ALEXANDER (1814–Feb. 1, 1881), author, journalist, and playwright, was through a long period of years a voluminous contributor of poems, humorous articles, short stories, sketches, and miscellaneous material to many newspapers and magazines. The son of Francis and Lucy (Everett) Durivage and a nephew of Edward Everett [*q.v.*], he was born in Boston, but passed a considerable portion of his life in New York and Paris, in which latter city he served as a foreign correspondent of American newspapers. While there he became interested in the Delsarte system of stage procedure and calisthenics, and meeting Steele MacKaye [*q.v.*], who was then conducting a class at Delsarte's house, joined forces with him in disseminating Delsarte's doctrines. When Durivage returned to America he became an active member of a little group of Delsartean enthusiasts who helped to spread the gospel of their master. He signed an article on Delsarte in the *Atlantic Monthly* for May 1871 which he wrote in collaboration with MacKaye. Durivage was the author of several plays, none of which was successful, not even *Monaldi,* another of his collaborations with MacKaye. It was produced at the St. James Theatre in New York on Jan. 8, 1872, with MacKaye himself acting the principal character, its chief object being to exemplify the practical stage theories of the Delsarte system. His literary work was varied and versatile, but without any enduring quality. At one time he was a co-editor of *Ballou's Pictorial*. Among his books were a translation of *Lamartine's History of the Revolution of 1848* (1849), and in collaboration with George P. Burnham, *Stray Subjects Arrested and Bound Over, being the Fugitive Offspring of the Old Un and the Young Un that have been Lying Around Loose, and are now tied up for Fast Keeping* (1848). He also compiled a *Popular Cyclopedia of History* (1845) and *Life Scenes from the World Around Us* (1853). He is referred to by William Winter as one of those of his "early friends in the literary vocation among whom the custom of perfectly candid criticism prevailed." He was a man of many friendships and activities, but the memorials of his personality and the records of his work are widely scattered through many obscure and well-nigh forgotten sources. Durivage was married to Almira Alderworth. His death was due to paralysis.

[Percy MacKaye, *Epoch, the Life of Steele MacKaye* (1927); Wm. Winter, *Old Friends* (1909); O. F. Adams, *Dict. of Am. Authors* (1901); W. R. Alger, *Life of Edwin Forrest* (1877); T. A. Brown, *Hist. of the N. Y. Stage*, vol. III (1903); *New-Eng. Hist. and Geneal. Reg.*, July 1860, p. 219; *N. Y. Herald*, Feb. 3, 4, 1881.]
                                        E. F. E.

DURKEE, JOHN (Dec. 11, 1728–May 29, 1782), Revolutionary soldier, colonizer, was born at Windham, Conn., the son of William Durkee and Susannah Sabin. Not long after attaining his majority, he removed to Norwich, making his home on Bean Hill. At various times he was an innkeeper, a justice of the peace, and a member of the General Assembly. On Jan. 3, 1753, he married Martha Wood of Norwich. He served during the French and Indian War, rising from the rank of second lieutenant to that of major of militia. At the time of the Stamp Act he became an ardent Son of Liberty. Heading a body of several hundred armed men, he dramatically forced the Connecticut stamp agent, Jared Ingersoll, to resign at Wethersfield, Sept. 19, 1765; and at a meeting of the Sons of Liberty at Hartford, Mar. 25, 1766, was appointed, together with Israel Putnam, member of a committee to arrange a system of correspondence between the Connecticut Sons of Liberty and those of other colonies. At a town meeting in Norwich in December 1767, he was chosen member of a committee which recommended that in conformity with the example of Boston the inhabitants refrain from the importation of certain articles of British manufacture.

In the spring of 1769, under the auspices of the Susquehanna Company, in which he had ac-

quired an interest, he conducted from Norwich a band of over one hundred emigrants to Wyoming Valley and laid out a settlement surrounded by a stockade which was called Fort Durkee. Later he named the settlement Wilkes-Barré in honor of John Wilkes and Col. Isaac Barré, steadfast champions of colonial rights. He was for a time president of the governing committee. In 1769 and again in 1770 he was captured and taken prisoner to Philadelphia by agents of the proprietary government of Pennsylvania, which claimed the Wyoming Valley as against Connecticut. In 1772 he returned to Norwich but was back again in Wyoming for certain periods in 1773 and 1774, at which date his connection with the settlement ceased.

Word having reached Norwich that the British forces had attacked the people of Boston, he set out on Sept. 4, 1774, with four hundred and sixty-four men, armed and mounted, but returned on learning that the rumor was false. In May 1775, he helped to raise in Norwich a company of one hundred men, including his two sons, which was mustered into the 3rd Connecticut Regiment commanded by Israel Putnam. Despite a frail constitution, he saw extensive service during the war, being present at the battle of Bunker Hill, and in the campaigns conducted by Washington in the middle colonies. His right hand was rendered useless by a wound received at the battle of Monmouth. He served successively as major and lieutenant-colonel of the 3rd Connecticut Regiment; as lieutenant-colonel and colonel of the 20th Regiment, Continental Foot; as colonel of the 4th and 1st Connecticut Line. He died at Norwich "from exhaustion induced by the service" (H. P. Johnston, *Record of Service of Connecticut Men during the Revolution*, p. 315). Fearlessness and decision were his salient characteristics as attested by his popular designation as the "bold man of Bean Hill."

[Besides the work noted above, the chief sources are: F. M. Gaulkins, *Hist. of Norwich* (1866); E. D. Larned, *Hist. of Windham County, Conn.* (2 vols., 1874–80); O. J. Harvey, *Hist. of Wilkes-Barre* (2 vols., 1909); A. A. Browning, "A Forgotten Son of Liberty," in *New London County Hist. Soc. Recs.*, vol. III, pt. II (1912).]
                                        E. E. C.

DURRETT, REUBEN THOMAS (Jan. 22, 1824–Sept. 16, 1913), lawyer, historian, was descended from the French family, Duret, which was induced by the excesses of St. Bartholomew's to transfer its domicile to England and there altered the spelling and modified the pronunciation of the name (*Library of Southern Literature*, IV, 1457). From England a branch of the family migrated to Spottsylvania County, Va., and thence their descendants went to Henry County, Ky. Reuben Thomas, son of William and Elizabeth (Rawlings) Durrett, grew up on his father's farm, spent two years, 1844–46, at Georgetown College, Ky., and in 1849 acquired the degree of A.B. from Brown University. The following year, spent in the law school of the University of Louisville, brought him a degree and a sufficient knowledge of law to serve as the basis of a successful, though not uninterrupted, practise for thirty years. In 1852 he was married to Elizabeth H. Bates of Cincinnati; the following year he served as a member of the city council of Louisville; from 1857 to 1859 he was editor and half-owner of the Louisville *Courier,* exchanging expletives and pistol-shots with the redoubtable George D. Prentice, editor of the rival *Journal;* and in 1861 he spent a few weeks in military prison because of his outspoken approval of secession. In these formative years he found time to acquire a reputation as a writer of blank verse and a wider reputation as an orator.

Many of these things, however, appear in perspective as merely the excesses of youth. Durrett's greatest usefulness came after he gave up his practise in 1880. An extensive law business combined with fortunate investments in natural gas had by this time brought him a large fortune, so that thereafter he was able to give liberal indulgence to his tastes. Always a book lover, he now turned his energies to building up his library with the ambition of securing a copy of every book written by a Kentuckian or about Kentucky. His ambition gradually widened to include the entire Ohio Valley with the result that by the time of his death he had acquired what was probably the most valuable private library in the West. Counting some fifty thousand volumes, chiefly on western history, with unique collections of manuscripts and files of old newspapers, the Durrett library became a Mecca for workers in the field of western history. Durrett's reputation was chiefly made by his library but did not altogether depend on it. Utilizing the material he had himself collected, he began to write history, his first work appearing in the *Southern Bivouac* and his later works as publications of the Filson Club which he founded in 1884 and of which he was president until his death. His best-known books are, *John Filson, the First Historian of Kentucky* (1884) and *Traditions of the Earliest Visits of Foreigners to North America* (1908). He was painstaking in his writing and based his historical work on careful research. But his importance lay less in his own writings than in the encouragement he gave to others. For thirty years he was a Mæcenas to all history workers in the West. His

library was always open to the student, and his influence on historical work in Kentucky can hardly be overestimated. His interest in books was evidenced not only by his own collection but also by the fact that he established the Louisville Public Library and for many years directed its growth.

In July 1912 Durrett suffered a stroke of paralysis from which he never recovered. He lived for a year unable to talk and with the right side of his face paralyzed. Upon his death in 1913, his library, which he had offered to give to the city of Louisville provided it would build a fireproof building for the storing of it, was sold to the University of Chicago and was removed thither.

[Sketches more or less extensive are in the *Lib. of South. Literature,* vol. IV (1907); *Louisville Evening Post,* Sept. 16, 1913; Louisville *Courier-Journal,* Sept. 17, 1913; *Who's Who in America,* 1912–13; and in M. Joblin & Co., *Louisville, Past and Present* (1875), pp. 254–68. The last named is very full in regard to Durrett's legal qualifications and also gives specimens of his poetry and oratory. The best account of his library is E. A. Henry, "The Durrett Collection, now in the Lib. of the Univ. of Chicago," in *Bibliographical Soc. of America Papers,* VIII (1914), 57.]   R. S. C.

DURRIE, DANIEL STEELE (Jan. 2, 1819– Aug. 31, 1892), librarian, was born at Albany, N. Y., the son of Horace and Johannah (Steele) Durrie. He was a descendant of John Steele, first secretary of Connecticut Colony, and William Bradford, first governor of Plymouth Colony. His father died when Durrie was a boy of seven. His formal education was received in a select school at South Hadley, Mass., and at the Albany Academy. As a young man he entered the store of a maternal uncle at Albany and learned the bookselling trade, succeeding to the business in 1844. At Albany, on Oct. 15 of that year, he was married to Ann Holt; to them were born six children. Durrie's business and all his other property were swept away in the great Albany fire of 1848. Unable to resume business, he removed in 1850 to Madison, Wis., in which place he resided thenceforward. At Madison, then a small western town with a population of about 2,000, he resumed for a few years the occupation of a bookseller.

Durrie early made the acquaintance of Lyman C. Draper [*q.v.*], the virtual founder and for over thirty years, from 1854 to 1886, the secretary of the State Historical Society of Wisconsin. Draper interested Durrie in this pioneer work and, in 1856, the latter was elected librarian, a position which he held until his death. With small resources and against great obstacles, these two men devoted the remainder of their lives to the upbuilding of an organization which, finally adopted by the state, became ultimately one of Wisconsin's most highly valued institutions. While primarily occupied with the development and active management of its library, Durrie was interested as well in the other activities of the State Historical Society. He found time to prepare many papers dealing with Wisconsin and Midwestern history. His largest work was *A History of Madison, the Capital of Wisconsin, Including the Four Lake Country,* published in 1874. In the field of genealogy, his most important work was his very useful *Bibliographia Genealogica Americana; an Alphabetical Index to American Genealogies and Pedigrees, Contained in State, County, and Town Histories, Printed Genealogies, and Kindred Works,* the long title suggesting its exhaustiveness. This pioneer bibliographical tool in its field, first published in 1868, passed through several revised and enlarged editions. He also published a genealogy of his mother's family under the title, *Steele Family: A Genealogical History of John and George Steele and Their Descendants* (1857). In manner Durrie was somewhat reserved and retiring, yet he was interested in public matters and always anxious to be of service. In 1858 and 1859, while Draper was superintendent of public instruction of Wisconsin, Durrie was his assistant. Throughout his life he was a devoted and active member of the Presbyterian church. His greatest service was, in collaboration with Draper, the building up, in the pioneer period of a Midwestern state, of a great collection of its fundamental historical material, and in developing in a new commonwealth a vital consciousness of its history.

[J. D. Butler, "Daniel Steele Durrie," in *Proc. State Hist. Soc. of Wis.,* *1892* (1893), pp. 73–81; obituary notices in *Madison Democrat, Madison Times,* and *Wisconsin State Journal,* Sept. 1, 1892.]   W. M. S.

DURYEA, HERMANES BARKULO (Dec. 13, 1863–Jan. 25, 1916), sportsman, was born in Brooklyn, N. Y., the son of Hermanes Barkulo and Mary (Peters) Duryea. He was a descendant in the sixth generation of Joost Durie, who emigrated with his wife from Mannheim, in the Rhine Palatinate, about 1675 and settled first at New Utrecht and later at Bushwick, Long Island, N. Y. His father was a lawyer, corporation counsel of Brooklyn, member of the Board of Education, Republican assemblyman from Kings County, and major-general in the New York National Guard. The younger Duryea was married in April 1895, in St. George's Chapel, London, to Ellen Winchester, widow of William Weld of Boston, who survived him. He never engaged in business but, enjoying an ample for-

tune, gave his whole life to sport. As a young man he was interested chiefly in yachting; in later years he devoted almost his entire time to the breeding and management of race horses. In both fields he achieved genuine distinction due not merely to his money but to his personal qualities.

In his youth, during summers spent on the family estate near Red Bank, N. J., he acquired the rudiments of his yachtsmanship in races on the Shrewsbury River. With W. Butler Duncan he originated one-design boat races in the United States, using twenty-one footers built by the Herreshoffs. He also raced several forty-foot yachts. In 1891 he was elected to the New York Yacht Club. For two seasons (1895–96) he sailed a "two and a half rater" at Cowes in some fifty races each season and made the best record for those seasons in his class. For a number of seasons he also had the best record at Newport, R. I. He and Harry Payne Whitney built the seventy-foot sloop *Yankee,* which won many races with Duryea as her pilot. In 1895 the Earl of Dunraven selected Duryea to represent him in the *America's* Cup races of that year. As an amateur pilot he was highly esteemed. During these years he usually passed the winters in shooting on his estate at Hickory Valley, Tenn. He was a president of the United States Field Trial Club and for several years was the leading winner in field trials. Much of his work with horses was done in partnership with Harry Payne Whitney, who for some time after the death of his father, William C. Whitney, ran his horses under the Duryea colors. Duryea and Harry Payne Whitney owned Irish Lad, who won the Brooklyn Handicap in 1903 and the Metropolitan Handicap a year later. When Gov. Charles Evans Hughes of New York secured the enactment of his anti-betting measures, Duryea, seeing no future for racing in the United States, in 1910 took his horses to France. He maintained a breeding farm in Normandy and a racing stable at Chantilly. He won a number of important English and French races, notably the 10,000 Guinea Race in England with Sweeper II in 1912 and in 1914 the Derby, the Biennial of 25,000 francs, and the Prix Noarelles of 30,000 francs—all with his most famous horse, Durbar II. During the racing season it was Duryea's habit to be with his horses every morning soon after daylight and personally direct their training and care. A week before the 1914 Derby, Durbar II was sent by special train to Calais and was met at Dover by another special that made the run to Epsom in record time. All the water and forage for the stay in England were taken along. Duryea went over the Epsom course with his jockey, McGee, giving him detailed instructions for the race. In all he won about $250,000 on this race, which was his last. Early in the autumn, in London, he suffered a severe attack of the grippe; in November he returned to his Tennessee estate, where he grew steadily worse. He died at Saranac Lake, N. Y., and was buried in the family mausoleum at Santa Barbara, Cal.

[Letter to author from Benjamin R. Kittredge, Esq., of Carmel, N. Y., and Strawberry, S. C., Sept. 8, 1928; obituaries in the *N. Y. Times*, *N. Y. Herald*, and *N. Y. Tribune*, Jan. 26, 1916; T. G. Bergen, "Contribs. to the Hist. of the Early Settlers of Kings County, N. Y.," in *N. Y. Geneal. and Biog. Record*, XI (1880), 62–70; editorial in *N. Y. Herald-Tribune*, July 12, 1926.] G.H.G.

DURYÉE, ABRAM (Apr. 29, 1815–Sept. 27, 1890), merchant, soldier, was of warlike Huguenot ancestry, his grandfather, Abraham Durea, having fought in the Revolution, his father and two uncles in the War of 1812. Born in New York City, the son of Jacob and Eliza Duryée, he was educated at the Crosby Street school and the grammar school of Columbia College. Choosing a mercantile career, he made a fortune in mahogany. At the age of eighteen he enlisted in the 142nd Regiment of militia; the next year he was appointed sergeant, and two years thereafter, sergeant-major. In 1838 he married Caroline E. Allen who bore him a son and three daughters. That same year he enlisted in the 27th—later the 7th—Regiment. Soon promoted sergeant, his rise was rapid: captain in 1843, major in September 1845, lieutenant-colonel in November, colonel in 1849. After ten years' devoted service he resigned in 1859 and resisted all efforts to make him reconsider. He was twice wounded while in command of his regiment during the Astor Place riots of 1849, and helped suppress other insurrections. In April 1861 he raised a regiment of volunteers which became the 5th New York, or Duryée's Zouaves. This regiment saw service at Big Bethel, June 10. Shortly afterward Col. Duryée became acting brigadier-general in place of Gen. E. M. Pierce. His command was ordered back to the vicinity of Washington. In command of his old regiment, he fortified Federal Hill, at Baltimore. The President appointed him a brigadier-general in August and he was given charge of the instruction of fifteen regiments. In response to his plea for active service he was transferred to Alexandria in March 1862, and in August commanded a brigade in Ricketts's division in the Valley of Virginia. Duryée's brigade gave good account of itself at Cedar Mountain, Rappahannock Station, Thoroughfare Gap, Groveton, Second Bull Run—where Duryée was twice wounded—Chantilly, and South Mountain. During the Antietam campaign he received three wounds while in command of Ricketts's division. After a furlough of thirty days, he found (November 1862) that a junior officer had been promoted over his head. Unable to secure redress, he resigned in January 1863. After the war he was made brevet major-general of volunteers. Generals Ricketts, MacDowell, Pope, and Meade all commended him in their official reports. Mayor Havemeyer appointed Duryée police commissioner of New York, in 1873, a position which he filled with ability and fidelity. He became dockmaster in 1884 and rendered able service here also. He died of cerebral hemorrhage in his seventy-sixth year, survived by his three daughters.

[For Duryée's career consult F. B. Hough, *Hist. of Duryée's Brigade* (1864); *Official Records* (Army); Frederick Phisterer, *N. Y. in the War of the Rebellion* (3rd ed., 1912), vols. I, II; Emmons Clark, *Hist. of the Seventh Regt. of N. Y. 1806–89* (1890); Wm. Swinton, *Hist. of the Seventh Regt., Nat. Guard, State of N. Y.* (1870); W. L. Stone, *Hist. of N. Y. City* (1872); Appletons' *Ann. Cyc.*, 1888; C. E. Fitch, *Encyc. of Biog. of N. Y.* (1916); F. B. Heitman, *Hist. Reg. and Dict. U. S. Army* (1903); *N. Y. Tribune*, Sept. 28, 1890.] M.L.B.,Jr.

DU SIMITIÈRE, PIERRE EUGÈNE (c. 1736–October 1784), artist, antiquary, naturalist, was, according to his own statement, a native of Geneva, Switzerland (*Pennsylvania Archives*, 2 ser., III, 121). Of his life before he came to America in 1765, little is known excepting that he spent about ten years traveling and collecting natural history specimens in the West Indies, subsisting by painting portraits and cutting silhouettes. He landed in New York but soon made his way to Burlington, N. J., where he remained for a short time, and then, in 1766, went to Philadelphia. His first stay in that city seems to have been comparatively short, for he was in Boston in 1767–68 and on May 20, 1769, was back in New York, where he became a naturalized citizen (*Journals of the Legislative Council of New York*, 1861, p. 1708). Some years later, however, in 1777, when he was drafted into the Pennsylvania militia, he presented a petition to the Supreme Council claiming immunity because he was a foreigner, in the course of which memorial he said of himself: "Your memorialist is in no public way of business whatever, nor settled in any part of the Continent. . . . That he has resided for some time past in this city (Philadelphia) it has been entirely owing to the critical situation of public affairs. . . . That his long continuance here has also been extremely detrimental to his general pursuit of natural knowledge, the only object of his travel" (*Pennsylvania Archives*, 2 ser., III, 121). The greater part of his life in America was spent in Philadelphia. He was elected a member of the American Philosophical Society, and for about five years, 1776–81, was one of its curators. He designed the vignette for the title-page of the *Pennsylvania Magazine,* published in 1775–76 by Robert Aitken [*q.v.*], and the frontispiece for the *United States Magazine,* 1779. He submitted to the Continental Congress, at its request, designs for a medal to commemorate the Declaration of Independence and for a Great Seal for the United States, but neither of his designs was adopted. Du Simitière was one of the first good portrait-painters to come to America. He drew a portrait of Washington from a sitting in the year 1779, which was used in the design of the so-called Washington Cent of 1791. He drew a series of thirteen portraits of men prominent in the American Revolution, which were engraved and published in London in 1783. Among them were Washington, Steuben, Deane, Laurens, and Benedict Arnold. John Adams, writing to his wife in 1776, said of Du Simitière: "This M. Du Simitière is a very curious man. He has begun a collection of materials for a history of this revolution. He begins with the first advices of the tea ships. He cuts out of the newspapers every scrap of intelligence, and every piece of speculation, and pastes it upon clean paper, arranging them under the head of that State to which they belong, and intends to bind them in volumes" (*Letters of John Adams,* vol. I, 1841, p. 151). This collection was purchased by the Library Company of Philadelphia after Du Simitière's death. It includes an "almost unique collection of newspapers and rare pamphlets" (Potts, *post,* p. 351). A desire to form a museum appears to have been the chief aim in the artist's life, and in 1782 he advertised his collections of curiosities, under the title of "American Museum," as on view at his residence in Philadelphia. He may thus be considered the founder of the first museum in the United States, probably antedating Peale's Museum by two or three years. He was among the first to realize the importance of gathering collections illustrative of the life and customs of the American Indian, whom he regarded as doomed to extinction by the inroads of Europeans. Whether as antiquary, artist, or naturalist, he was thorough, energetic, intelligent, and talented. The exact date of his death is unknown, but he was buried on Oct. 22, 1784, in St. Peter's burial ground, Philadelphia. His grave is unmarked.

[The main source is a fairly exhaustive sketch of Du Simitière by W. J. Potts, in the *Pa. Mag. of Hist. and Biog.,* Oct. 1889. The date of burial is given from the manuscript Records of Christ Church, Phila., in the Hist. Soc. of Pa. See also Wm. Dunlap, *A Hist. of the Rise and Progress of the Arts of Design in the U. S.* (rev. ed., 1918), III, 297; *Early Proc. Am. Phil. Soc., 1744–1838* (1884).]

J.J.

DUSTIN, HANNAH (b. Dec. 23, 1657), pioneer, is said to have been the daughter of Michael and Hannah (Webster) Emerson of Haverhill, Mass. On Dec. 3, 1677, she was married to Thomas Dustin of that place, whose name was variously spelled as Duston and Durston. She bore him thirteen children before 1699, eight of whom were living at the time of the Indian raid on Mar. 15, 1697. Although the date of her death is unknown, she is supposed to have survived her husband, who was still living in 1729. The details of her noted exploit vary much in the forms in which it has been handed down but the main story is clear enough. Apparently Hannah was lying in the house with her week-old baby and the nurse, Mary Neff, while her husband and the other seven children were working and playing at some distance outside when the Indians swept down on the village. They entered the house and captured the three occupants in view of the husband. He rescued the seven children outside, carrying them off to safety but had to abandon his baby and wife, some accounts relating that he did so at her earnest entreaty to save the others. The next day, after killing or capturing forty of the inhabitants of the town, the Indians started their march northward carrying their captives with them. Hannah saw her house in flames as she left and one of the Indians took her infant and brained it by knocking it against a tree. After tramping for some days through the snow and without shoes, the party reached a small settlement of Indians living on an island (now called "Dustin's") at the confluence of the Contoocook and Merrimac rivers a few miles above Concord. There captors and captives halted for a few days before proceeding to the home of the chief, a long distance northward, where the victims were told they would be stripped and forced to run the gauntlet.

On the island was a young English boy who had been captured a year before and with him and Mary Neff, Hannah planned an escape. While the Indians were asleep Hannah and the lad killed ten of them, only a squaw and a small Indian boy escaping. Hannah, the English boy (Samuel Lennardson), and the nurse then started for the settlements but to have proof of the exploit Hannah returned and herself scalped the ten savages, of whom she had killed nine and the boy one. They finally made their way back to Haverhill to find the rest of the Dustin family safe. Hannah and her husband then went to

Boston, where they arrived on Apr. 21, and presented a petition to the General Court explaining the loss of all their property and Hannah's exploit. The Court awarded Hannah £25, and half of that sum each to Mary Neff and Samuel Lennardson. The family has many descendants.

[The best account is by G. W. Chase, *The Hist. of Haverhill* (1861), who reprints the account given by C. Mather, *Magnalia Christi Americana* (1702), who had the story from Hannah herself. R. B. Caverly, *Heroism of Hannah Duston* (1874), is a romantic account. The name Samuel Lennardson is so given on the tablet in Haverhill; in Caverly it appears as Leonardson.]

J. T. A.

DUTTON, CLARENCE EDWARD (May 15, 1841–Jan. 4, 1912), soldier, geologist, son of Samuel and Emily (Curtis) Dutton, was born at Wallingford, Conn. He received his elementary education at Ellington, Conn., entered Yale College in June 1856, and graduated with the degree of A.B. in 1860, at the age of nineteen. In September 1862 he was appointed adjutant of the 21st Connecticut Volunteers. On Mar. 1 of the following year he was promoted to a captaincy and in 1864 transferred to the Ordnance Corps of the regular army, in which he served through the remainder of the war. He was assigned in 1865 for duty at the Watervliet Arsenal, five years later was transferred to the Frankford Arsenal at Philadelphia, and later yet, to Washington, D. C. Here he became associated with Joseph Henry, S. F. Baird, J. W. Powell, and other scientific men of the period through whose influence he was induced to consent to a detail with the United States Geological and Geographical Survey. In this service he made his reputation as a geologist. In 1890 he returned to military duty but resigned his commission in February 1901 to reside for the remainder of his life at Englewood, N. J.

Beginning his geological career with service under Powell in 1875, he devoted the next ten years to a study of the plateau region of the western United States in Utah and Arizona. The results of this work are given in his *Report on the Geology of the High Plateau of Utah* (1879–80), a volume of 307 pages with atlas; his *Tertiary History of the Grand Canyon District* (1882); a quarto volume of 264 pages with a magnificent atlas of 23 plates from drawings by W. H. Holmes; and one on *Mount Taylor and the Zuñi Plateau* (1886), together with several important papers in the annual reports of the survey. In all these he dwelt with particular emphasis upon the physical problems of which the area afforded unusual examples, and became a leading advocate of the then little understood doctrine of isostasy. In the subjects of vulcanism and earthquakes Dutton had been interested from a very early pe-

riod, and in 1882 he paid a visit to the Hawaiian Islands to study the first-named phenomenon close at hand. Ever receptive of new ideas, he soon became an advocate of the possibilities of radioactivity in promoting vulcanism. His earthquake studies were given fresh impulse by the earthquake of Charleston, S. C., in 1886, of which he made an exhaustive study, subsequently setting forth his views on the general subject in an octavo volume of 314 pages entitled *Earthquakes in the Light of the New Seismology* (1904).

As a geologist he may be said to have inclined to speculation and philosophy. As a scientific writer he was one of the clearest, most impressive and entertaining America has produced. Of military bearing, he was companionable, a good speaker and raconteur and fond of alliterative expressions, as when in one of his public lectures on his return from his Hawaiian trip, he spoke of the native female portion of the population as comparing more than favorably with her "pale pious and pulmonary sisters of the effete east." It is stated that in writing his reports he made little use of notes, holding his subject wholly in mind until his problems were solved and his results fully attained. "When ready, he penned all his own manuscripts rapidly under stimulus of an enthusiasm begotten by a consciousness of his comprehensive and complete knowledge of the subject" (Diller, *post*). He was a member of the Philosophical Society of Washington, the American Academy of Political and Social Science, the Geological and Seismological Societies of America, and the National Academy of Sciences. He was married on Apr. 18, 1864, to Emeline C. Babcock of New Haven. He died of arteriosclerosis at the home of his son in Englewood, N. J.

[Memoir by Jos. S. Diller, with a bibliography of Dutton's most important geological publications, in *Bull. Geol. Soc. of America*, Mar. 1913; *Yale Coll. . . . Biog. Record Class of Sixty, 1860–1906* (1906); *Obit. Record Grads. Yale Univ.*, 1912; personal recollections.]

G. P. M.

DUTTON, HENRY (Feb. 12, 1796–Apr. 12, 1869), jurist, was born in Watertown, Litchfield County, Conn., the son of Thomas and Tenty (Punderson) Dutton. His father, a farmer in a small way, moved when Henry was a child to Northfield, where the boy attended the district school but more often assisted in the farm work. In 1812 he engaged in teaching, at the same time continuing his studies in order to enter Yale College, which he accomplished in 1816, graduating with honors in 1818. He was in debt when he left college, but proceeding to Fairfield, he became principal of the academy there and in two years had paid off all his liabilities. Concurrently with his scholastic work he read law. In 1821 he became a tutor at Yale, continuing his legal studies in his spare time, and was admitted to the Connecticut bar in 1823. In the same year he was married to Elizabeth Elliott Joy. He opened his law office at Newtown, Fairfield County, also undertaking private tuition of Yale students. He represented his district in the General Assembly for two terms, but in 1837 removed to Bridgeport. Here he quickly came to the fore, became state's attorney for Fairfield County, and represented Bridgeport in the legislature during two terms. In 1847 he was appointed Kent Professor of Law at Yale, and removed accordingly to New Haven, where he continued also to practise. In the same year he was appointed one of the commissioners to revise the state statutes, an undertaking which entailed great care and application since there had been no revision for twenty-five years. The task, however, was completed within a year. In 1849 he was elected to the state Senate, serving one term, at the conclusion of which he was elected representative for New Haven in the lower house. In 1852 he became judge of the New Haven County court, remaining such for one year. In 1854 the legislature appointed him governor of the state, the electorate having failed to make a choice at the preceding election, and he held the position for a full term. He had no interests other than the law and its amendment and thus by severe concentration was able to perform competently an enormous amount of work. In 1861 he was chosen judge of the supreme court of errors and of the superior court of Connecticut, to fill a vacancy, and continued to occupy a seat on the bench until Feb. 12, 1866, when, having reached the statutory age of seventy years, he retired. During his tenure of judicial office he had maintained his association with the Yale Law School and on his retirement from the bench devoted his energies chiefly to its affairs. He died at New Haven.

Dutton was not a learned lawyer but possessed an extensive and accurate knowledge of "case law," which he applied with remarkable facility. He was quick to grasp a point, fertile of resource, and at the bar, on the bench, and in the lecture room was adequate for any emergency. As an advocate his strength lay in his ability to present facts forcibly and lucidly to a jury from the practical commonplace standpoint, and as a judge he was expeditious, courteous, and eminently receptive. Somewhat advanced in his ideas on law reform, while he was a member of the legislature he procured the passage of a statute permitting in civil cases parties in interest to testify. He

was also sponsor of a bill giving the superior court sole jurisdiction in divorce. He was author of *The Connecticut Digest* (1833), and *A Revision of Swift's Digest of the Laws of Connecticut* (2 vols., 1848–53), in which he was assisted by N. A. Cowdrey.

[Louis H. Bristol, in 37 *Conn. Reports*, 620; John Livingston, *Portraits of Eminent Americans Now Living*, vol. II (1853); *Obit. Record Grads. Yale Coll.*, 1869; Gilbert Cope, *Geneal. of the Dutton Family of Pa. . . . With . . . a Short Accou::t of the Duttons of Conn.* (1871).]   H.W.H.K.

DUTTON, SAMUEL TRAIN (Oct. 16, 1849– Mar. 28, 1919), educator and peace advocate, was the eldest child of Jeremiah Dutton, farmer in the town of Hillsboro, N. H., and his wife Rebecca Hammond Train, daughter of a farmer in the same town. On both sides were ancestors in early colonial Massachusetts. Jeremiah Dutton was a stony, strictly orthodox, severely moral, unsocial, intolerant Puritan, respected and shunned by his neighbors. His wife was equally religious, but in her the hardness of Puritanism was absent. She had physical beauty and social charm. She freely gave and freely received sympathy, kindliness, and forbearance, and she had visions that transcended the Dutton farm. Samuel was like his mother, and it was with her encouragement that after completing the studies of the district school he went for a winter to the Francestown Academy and in the fall of 1867 entered the Literary and Scientific Institute at New London to prepare for Dartmouth. Two years later, in the midst of plans for going to Dartmouth, it occurred to him that a country boy ought to attend college in a city. He therefore chose Yale, and graduated in 1873. He expected eventually to enter the Christian ministry, but his funds were low. A part of the cost of his education had been met with borrowed money. The rest had been earned. In need of income he assumed charge of the schools in South Norwalk, Conn., in the fall of 1873. A year later he married Cornelia C. North of New Haven. Some wavering in the choice of a profession followed; for a time he turned to the study of law. The schools under his direction improved so rapidly, however, that he could not escape the consequences, and in 1877 he was elected principal of the Eaton Grammar School in New Haven. From 1882 to 1890 he was superintendent of the New Haven schools, and at the end of this period a national figure in education. Ten fruitful years as superintendent of schools at Brookline, Mass., followed, with numerous outside calls upon his services. He was lecturer on pedagogy at Harvard, 1895–97, at the University of Chicago, 1897–98, and at Boston

University, 1898. In 1900 he became superintendent of the Horace Mann Schools and professor of school administration in Teachers College, Columbia University. Here an interest in the peace movement began and grew to be his ruling passion. He was secretary of the New York Peace Society, chairman of the executive committee of the National Arbitration and Peace Congress, general secretary of the World's Court League, trustee of the World Peace Foundation, and member of the international commission on the Balkan War. He was also a trustee of the College for Women in Constantinople and of the Christian College in Canton, China. He retired from Teachers College in 1915 with the rank of professor emeritus, not to rest, but to work more effectively in the various organizations with which he was still connected.

Dutton was a pioneer in socializing the schools. Wherever he went he sought, and in a unique degree secured, cooperation between parents and teachers, not only for the training of children but for the improvement of the community, including parents. He had a profound interest in his fellow mortals and a genius for approaching all kinds of people and enlisting their support in any cause near his heart. He was also a pioneer in professionalizing the office of superintendent of schools. His views on public education are set forth in his annual reports as superintendent at New Haven and Brookline, and in various educational journals. His views on peace found frequent expression in periodicals, chiefly in *Christian Work,* the *Peace Forum* (later the *World Court*) and the *League of Nations Magazine.* He edited several school text-books and was author of, *Social Phases of Education in the School and Home* (1899) ; *School Management* (1903) ; and, in collaboration with David Snedden, *Administration of Public Education in the United States* (1908).

[C. H. Levermore, *Samuel Train Dutton, A Biography* (1922), contains numerous extracts from Dutton's correspondence and other writings, and a bibliography. See also *Obit. Record Yale Graduates,* 1918–19 ; *N. Y. Times,* Mar. 29, 1919.]

H.J.

DUVAL, WILLIAM POPE (1784–Mar. 19, 1854), lawyer, congressman, governor of Florida, was born near Richmond, Va., the son of William and Ann (Pope) Duval. His father was well-to-do and attempted to give his children a good education. William, however, did not complete his schooling, as he left his home at the age of fifteen or sixteen, and went to Kentucky alone. He spent the next two or three years on the frontier. When eighteen, he went to Bardstown to begin the study of law. In 1804 he married Nancy, a daughter of William Hynes, and began practising his profession. Later he served as a Republican in the Thirteenth Congress (1813–15).

A new period in his life began in 1821 when he was appointed by President Monroe as the first judge of the superior court of East Florida. Early in the following year he was made the first civil governor of the territory. His early life among frontiersmen, his legal studies and his experience as a lawmaker were valuable assets in the new position, and his temperament made him a fit leader in a pioneer community. He was courageous and determined, but also democratic and full of humor. Although only five feet seven inches in height, his cheerful and energetic personality nevertheless dominated in the presence of others. Duval took the lead in grappling with the numerous problems that faced the new government. In 1823 he appointed two commissioners to select a site for the future capital, which was finally located at Tallahassee. Duval then began the work which is probably his outstanding achievement, the peaceable removal of the Seminole Indians to South Florida. He was admirably successful, so that there was no serious outbreak by the natives while he was in office. While engaged in his pacification of the Indians, he visited almost every part of northern Florida, and in February 1826 made a long trip overland to Tampa Bay. He often urged the necessity of establishing schools, although the results were disappointingly meager. The chief enactment was the creation in 1831 of the first board of education for Florida. Due to his insistence, the territorial laws were compiled in 1828; and not satisfied with this, he urged in 1833 and 1834 another compilation which was eventually published in 1839. His interest in the conduct of elections was particularly keen so that many of the basic features of Florida's present electoral machinery were adopted during his administrations.

At first Duval was popular, but after some years the increasing electorate began to regard him as the irresponsible representative of the Federal Government. This feeling of discontent was augmented by his strong insistence on his executive prerogatives and his lukewarmness toward the chartering of state banks. Prior to 1833, he vetoed all bills incorporating banks, although many were passed over his veto. The disagreement of the executive and the legislature apparently reached its height in 1833 when he vetoed about one-fifth of the bills passed. Under such conditions it is not surprising that Jackson replaced him in 1834 by John Eaton. Continuing to reside in Florida, he was elected one of Calhoun County's representatives to the Constitutional Convention that assembled in St. Joseph in December 1838. He was defeated for the presidency of the body by one vote, but was chosen chairman of the committee on the executive department. When the legislature of Florida was made bicameral in 1839, he was elected a senator from the Middle District, a position which he held until 1842. He was president of the upper house in 1840. His last public office was that of commissioner in 1845 to settle the disputed northern boundary of the state. He was the unsuccessful Democratic nominee for Congress in 1848.

Duval's wife died of yellow fever on July 14, 1841, at St. Joseph. In May 1843 he took up his residence in St. Augustine, and in 1849 he followed his children to Texas, of which state he was a citizen at the time of his death. He died in Washington, D. C.

[Information about Duval's life before 1804 is derived chiefly from Washington Irving, *The Early Experiences of Ralph Ringwood in Wolfert's Roost* (1865). For his activities in Florida, see chiefly *Am. State Papers, Indian Affairs*, II (1834); *Acts of the Legislative Council of Territory of Fla.* (1831); *Jour. of the Proceedings of a Convention of Delegates to form a Constitution for the People of Fla.* (1838); *Jour. of the Proceedings of the Senate of the Territory of Fla.* (1840–42); John T. Sprague, *The Origin, Progress, and Conclusion of the Fla. War* (1847); and general histories of Florida. Some of his messages before 1832 may be found in the newspapers and, in part, in *Niles' Reg.* For a good description see *The Fla. Jour.* (Apalachicola), Mar. 17, 1841; for obituaries, *Nat. Intelligencer*, Mar. 25, 1854; *Tallahassee Floridian and Jour.*, Mar. 25, Apr. 1, 1854.]   J.O.K.

DUVENECK, FRANK (Oct. 9, 1848–Jan. 3, 1919), painter, etcher, sculptor, teacher, was an outstanding figure in the art of his time, and a leader of remarkable influence, numbering many gifted painters among his disciples. His parents were Germans. His father was Bernard Decker; and his mother's maiden name was Katherine Seimers. They came to America from a small town not far from Vechta, in Oldenburg, and settled in Covington, Ky., where, in 1849, Decker died while his son Frank was an infant in arms. The widow subsequently married Squire Duveneck, and her son took the name of his stepfather, being known as Frank Duveneck. In Covington, his birthplace, he left school at an early age to begin work on the interior decorations of Catholic churches; he was employed in the modeling, carving, painting, and gilding of altarpieces and the like, and the unusual merit of his work soon led to his regular employment by a successful ecclesiastical decorator in Cincinnati. As a method of training in craftsmanship this kind of practical experience had undeniable advantages, not

the least of which was the remarkable facility that it developed. It goes far to explain much of the character of Duveneck's later accomplishments, more especially the skill and freedom of his manipulation of various mediums. He continued this apprenticeship for several years, constantly gaining in technical knowledge and power.

At the age of twenty-two, when he went to Munich and became a student of the Royal Academy, he was already so well equipped as a painter that, after three months of study in the antique class, he was promoted to Wilhelm Dietz's painting class, where he distinguished himself by taking several prizes. In 1872 he won the composition prize, entitling him to the use of a studio of his own. To this period belongs one of his best-known canvases, the "Whistling Boy," also several other notable pieces of precocious brilliancy and breadth. "It was with the naturalists that he instantly aligned himself," writes his biographer, Norbert Heerman; "theirs was the spirit in which Duveneck approached his work." He approached it with superb confidence and ardor. Nothing is more apparent in his paintings than the hearty gusto with which they were made.

Returning to America in 1873, Duveneck busied himself at once with a church decoration in Chicago and some portrait commissions in Cincinnati, where he held a modest exhibition of a few portraits painted in Munich. The "Young Man with Ruff" was painted at that time; the portrait of Mr. William Adams followed in 1874. The year 1875 was signalized by a Duveneck exhibition in Boston, which proved to be a triumph for the young artist, owing to the vitality and spontaneity of his style. The five canvases shown at the Boston Art Club created a sensation; they were all sold; and the painter was urged to leave Cincinnati and come to Boston, where a dozen commissions for portraits were promised him. Much of this success was to be attributed to the influence of William Morris Hunt. Duveneck, however, was not yet inclined to forsake the training and surroundings of Europe; he went back to Munich, where he worked for two years, until 1877. Then he went to Venice, and a year later we find him again in Munich. The principal pictures of this time were the "Woman with Forget-me-nots," distinctly reminiscent of Rubens and not without a distant echo of Rembrandt; the "Red-haired Man with Ruff," the "Man in Spanish Coat," "Beeches of Polling," and the monochrome self-portrait of 1877.

His "Turkish Page" (1876), first shown at the National Academy, New York, 1877, and now belonging to the Pennsylvania Academy of the Fine Arts, Philadelphia, may be considered one of his most important early compositions. It is rich in color and textures, and the still life is rendered with marked ability. So striking, indeed, was the virtuosity of this and the succeeding works, that Duveneck ran some danger of establishing a reputation for science and manual skill, connoting superficiality and a lack of emotion, but if this be in a measure true of certain *tours de force* of the early days, it is far from being so in the typical examples of the maturer period, which owe much of their enduring worth and charm to their genuine human feeling and sympathetic quality.

To such personal characteristics as these, quite as much as to his knowledge and talent, Duveneck owed his notable success as an inspiring and beloved teacher. His own school of painting, which was started at Munich in 1878, became famous at once; some sixty students, of different nationalities, the majority of them Americans, were enrolled, and the enthusiasm, devotion, industry, and ambition which he knew how to evoke from these young followers proved that he had not mistaken his vocation. The names of a few of his pupils—John W. Alexander, William M. Chase, Frederick P. Vinton, Joseph R. De Camp, John Twachtman, Julius Rolshoven, Oliver D. Grover, Otto Bacher, Robert Blum, Theodore Wendel—are sufficient to show that he was fortunate in his pupils, and that, by the surprising diversity of their styles as well as by the general excellence of their achievements, they bore witness to the breadth and wholesomeness of his personal influence rather than the soundness of his methods of painting. All that he cared about, as Mr. Cortissoz has pointed out, was to see that they got hold of the root of the matter, to foster in them a love of the art of painting for its own sake. He instilled in his boys "a sense of the thrilling excitement, the joy and the dignity, to be got out of the reverent exercise of a painter's instruments." Almost all of them, however, wisely turned away from the fascinating but treacherous bitumen of the Munich school, and several, notably Twachtman, became brilliant exponents of high-keyed luminous impressionism in landscape art.

When Duveneck moved from Munich to Florence, toward the end of 1879, about half of his pupils accompanied him. They remained in Italy about two years, passing the winters in Florence and the summers in Venice, working and enjoying life as only care-free art students may. An interesting glimpse of their boyish ways is given in William D. Howells's *Indian Summer* (1886), wherein the badinage, mockery, and jollity of the

Bohemian party as seen in a trattoria are picturesquely described. What they thought about Botticelli and Michelangelo; of old Piloty's things at Munich; of the dishes they had served to them; of the quality of the Chianti; of the respective merits of German and Italian tobacco; of the "over-rated coloring of some of those Venetian fellows"; of the delicacy of Mino da Fiesole; and of many other matters—such were some of the themes of discussion overheard by the hero of the story. In his reminiscences of those student days in Italy, Oliver Dennett Grover has added his testimony to that of others of the group respecting the obligations they were under to the "Old Man." Those days were all too short, he says, but while they lasted they were more significant than a similar period in the lives of most students, because more intensified, more concentrated. It is necessary thus to emphasize Duveneck's influence as a teacher if we would rightly understand the important part he played in the development of art in America. Admirable as are his works in painting, etching, and sculpture, it may well be that in the final appraisal of his achievements his most valuable contribution to the cause of art will be found in his personal influence as a leader of his "boys." Their doings have become a legend and a tradition, not to be omitted in any history of American art.

It was in 1879 that Duveneck painted the portrait of John W. Alexander, the "Woman in Black Scarf," and "The Blacksmith"; but during the two ensuing years he was too much occupied with his school work to find much time for painting. He began to etch in 1880, at Venice, experimenting at first with some very small plates. Most of the dated prints, almost all of Venetian motives, were made in 1883, 1884, and 1885. Characteristic examples, of the highest order of excellence, are the two versions of the "Riva degli Schiavoni," the "Grand Canal," the "Palazzo Ca d'Oro," and "The Rialto." The first-named plates were shown at the first exhibition of the New Society of Painter-Etchers, in London, in the spring of 1881. Apparently, certain members of this society, including Seymour Haden and Alphonse Legros, suspected for a moment that these etchings were the work of Whistler, and that Whistler was trying to play a practical joke on the society. The particulars of this esthetic tempest in a teapot may be found in Whistler's *Gentle Art of Making Enemies* (1890) and in the biography of Whistler by E. R. and J. Pennell. As a matter of fact, Duveneck's etchings of the Riva degli Schiavoni were finished before Whistler made his plates of the same subject. Never did Duveneck succeed in bettering these beautiful plates, which remain his most artistic etchings. The later Venetian compositions, though interesting as fine drawings of architecture, are somewhat too much elaborated as to detail, and lack the stenographic suggestiveness that is proper to the process.

In 1886 Duveneck was married in Paris. His wife, Elizabeth Boott, had been a pupil of Thomas Couture and of William Morris Hunt and was a painter of distinct merit. She was a daughter of Francis Boott, of Boston and Cambridge; her mother was a Miss Lyman, of one of the old families of Massachusetts. Elizabeth Boott had lived and studied in Paris, Florence, and Boston. In 1879 she became a pupil of Duveneck in Munich. Their engagement followed, but the marriage did not take place until nearly seven years later. Two years after that time Mrs. Duveneck died. She was buried in the Allori Cemetery in Florence, where the noble memorial figure in bronze created by her husband marks her grave. This is a recumbent effigy in the mode of the Italian Renaissance, modernized, intimate, and imbued with the deepest personal sentiment. The original model belongs to the Cincinnati Museum. A marble version is in the Museum of Fine Arts, Boston. In the museums of Philadelphia, Chicago, and San Francisco are copies of the Boston marble. Copies from the original model are in the Metropolitan Museum of Art, New York, and in the John Herron Art Institute, Indianapolis. The only other sculptures of consequence made by Duveneck are the seated portrait statue of Ralph Waldo Emerson, now in Emerson Hall, Harvard University—a work in which Clement J. Barnhorn collaborated—and the bust portrait of Charles William Eliot. The superior quality of these few works, more particularly his *magnum opus,* the monument to his wife, gives rise to regret that Duveneck should not have elected to specialize in sculpture.

After his wife's death in 1888, he returned to his old home, Cincinnati, where he remained for the rest of his life. There his time and energy were mainly devoted to teaching, though he did some painting, and acted as adviser in artistic matters in connection with the Cincinnati Museum. He was never without a devoted following, and his influence as instructor during his last years did but continue and extend the extraordinary personal leadership that had been so conspicuous in Munich and Florence and Venice. Thus his last twenty-five years, spent in the Cincinnati Museum and the Cincinnati Art Academy, of which he was the dean of the faculty, were fruitful and busy years. It was his loyalty to the Museum and his many pupils that

led him to make the very unusual disposition of his work. He made over to the Museum by gift the great collection of paintings, etchings, sketches, etc., which he considered fit material for continuing to students such help as his own life-work had afforded. The value of such a gift, after a lifetime of useful personal achievement, may be realized only by a pilgrimage to Cincinnati.

The most complete exhibition of Duveneck's works ever made outside of Cincinnati was that at the Panama-Pacific exposition, San Francisco, in 1915. This collection contained thirty oil paintings, thirteen etchings, and a replica of the monument to his wife. A special gallery was set aside for the Duveneck exhibit. Prominent examples among the paintings were the "Whistling Boy," the "Woman with Forget-me-nots," the "Turkish Page," the portraits of William Adams, J. Frank Currier, Professor Loeffts, John W. Alexander, and Mrs. Francis Hinkle. The exhibit as a whole was so impressive that the occasion constituted a veritable apotheosis for the artist. In the words of Christian Brinton, it "served to rehabilitate his name and insure for him that position in the development of American painting which he so rightfully merits" (*Impressions of the Art at the Panama-Pacific Exposition,* 1916, p. 96). The foreign members of the international jury of awards unanimously recommended that in recognition of his distinguished contribution to American art a special medal of honor should be struck and awarded to him. This handsome proposal was promptly indorsed by the entire jury. The significance of the rare honor thus conferred on Duveneck only four years before his death lies not only in the fact that it gave expression to the deliberate opinion of experts, but also that it originated with foreign experts, who presumably could have no personal bias in the matter and were therefore able to take a purely detached view-point.

Duveneck died in the Good Samaritan Hospital, Cincinnati, on Jan. 3, 1919. In the tribute of the Cincinnati Art Club we find these words: "A father to all interested in art . . . He knew hard work in his early days, and it did not narrow him; he knew sorrow, but it did not embitter him. . . . His judgment was always of the best; he was gifted with wonderful vision. He had marvelous power." Temperament counts for so much more than schooling in Duveneck's paintings that it is safe to say he would have gone as far, done as well, and developed as richly, had he obtained his training elsewhere than in Munich. In other words, the Munich methods and the Munich palette formed no essential part of his artistic assets. He outgrew them, and eventually they were abandoned in favor of better methods. His debt was great to Rembrandt, Hals, and Rubens; and he learned more precious things in the Old Pinakothek than in Prof. Dietz's classroom. Naturally a rapid and skilful executant, with a hearty relish for the most rebellious of all mediums, oil paints, it would be little less than astounding that he did not fall a victim to his own wonderful facility, degenerating into a mere star performer of technical prodigies, were it not for the repeated proofs in his pictures of his fine moral qualities—his quick sympathy and the breadth and depth of his interest in human nature. He joined craftsmanship with a kindly disposition; virtuosity with magnanimity; knowledge with modesty. When John S. Sargent said of him that he was the greatest talent of the brush in this generation, he spoke truth, but "talent of the brush" tells only half the story. What makes Duveneck the honored figure that he is in American art is the richness and warmth of his temperament, the generosity of his nature; without these qualities, easily to be discerned in his best works, he would have made no original contribution of enduring value to the sum total of modern art.

[The chief source is Norbert Heermann's *Frank Duveneck* (1918), an excellent biography, containing twenty-two illustrations. The frontispiece is a print after Jos. R. De Camp's portrait of the artist in the Cincinnati Museum. A small anonymous book entitled *Frank Duveneck, 1848–1919,* was issued by the Cincinnati Museum Association at the time of the artist's death. Other references include "Frank Duveneck and His Munich Tradition," by Royal Cortissoz, in *Scribner's Mag.,* Feb. 1927; "Frank Duveneck: Artist and Teacher," by Anna Seaton-Schmidt, in *Art and Progress,* Sept. 1915; "Frank Duveneck," by D. Croal Thomson, in *Connoisseur,* Sept. 1921; "Blakelock and Duveneck," by E. V. Lucas, in *Ladies' Home Jour.,* Feb. 1927; *What Pictures to See in America,* by Lorinda M. Bryant (1915); *Biog. Sketches of Am. Artists* (Lansing, 1924); Samuel Isham, *Hist. of Am. Painting* (1905); *Am. Art Rev.,* Nov. 1880; *Arts and Decoration,* July 1911; *Scribner's Mag.,* Nov. 1915.]

W. H. D.

DUYCKINCK, EVERT AUGUSTUS (Nov. 23, 1816–Aug. 13, 1878), editor, biographer, descended in the seventh generation from Evert Duycking (*sic*) who came to New Amsterdam in 1638, was a son of Evert and Harriet June Duyckinck and a brother of George L. Duyckinck [*q.v.*]. His father was for about forty years a respected publisher of standard literature in New York. In this environment Evert Augustus naturally imbibed a love for good books. He graduated from Columbia College in 1835, where his studious habits, classical attainments, and taste for elegant literature were distinguished (*New York Tribune,* Aug. 15, 1878). He then studied law with John Anthon and was

admitted to the bar (1837), but did not practise. For a year (1838–39) he traveled in Europe. Returning home, he took up literature as a definite profession, toward which he had already contributed articles in the *New York Review* on George Crabbe, George Herbert, and Oliver Goldsmith. In April 1840 he married Margaret Wolfe Panton. They soon took up their life-long residence at 20 Clinton Place, which became the resort of the most eminent literary men of the country. Three sons were born, but all died young and without issue. In December 1840, Duyckinck began in company with Cornelius Mathews the editorship of *Arcturus, a Journal of Books and Opinion,* a monthly discontinued after May 1842. Five years later he edited for Osgood & Company, publishers of New York, their new periodical, the *Literary World, a Journal of American and Foreign Literature, Science, and Art.* He edited twelve numbers (Feb. 6–Apr. 24, 1847), then retired. No. 13 was issued by the publishers and Nos. 14–87 (May 8, 1847–Sept. 30, 1848) were edited by Charles Fenno Hoffman [*q.v.*]. The Duyckinck brothers, Evert and George, then bought the periodical, and edited it jointly from No. 88 (Oct. 7, 1848) to No. 361 (Dec. 31, 1853), completing the thirteenth volume. It was the best American literary weekly of its time, but financially unremunerative. The brothers then turned their attention to research and the editing of a *Cyclopædia of American Literature* (2 vols., 1855), which Evert, after George's death, revised and enlarged (2 vols. and supplement, 1866), and which was brought out in a final edition, edited by M. L. Simons, in fifty-two parts (1873–74). It was during this period that Evert Duyckinck edited for Wiley & Putnam a Library of Choice Reading. He also edited the first edition in book form of Thackeray's *Confessions of Fitz-Boodle* (1852), the first American edition of Thackeray's *Yellowplush Papers* (1852), Sydney Smith's *Wit and Wisdom* (1856), and an edition of Willmott's *Poets of the Nineteenth Century* (1857). In 1859 he compiled *Irvingiana,* anecdotes and traits of Washington Irving. Later he edited the *Salmagundi Papers* (1860); Philip Freneau's *Poems Relating to the American Revolution* (1865); Alexander Anderson's *Illustrations to Mother Goose* (1873), and a collection of Anderson's engravings (1873). He wrote the text for the following subscription works, which had a large sale: *National Portrait Gallery of Eminent Americans* (2 vols., 1861–62); *National History of the War for the Union* (3 vols., 1861–65); *Lives and Portraits of the Presidents of the United States* (1865); *History of the World*

(1869–71), largely compiled by his son **George** (1846–1873), and *Portrait Gallery of Eminent Men and Women of Europe and America* (2 vols., copyright 1873). He wrote memorials of John Allan (1864), Francis L. Hawks (1871), Henry T. Tuckerman (1872), and Fitz-Greene Halleck (1877). At the time of his death he was associated with William Cullen Bryant in editing Shakespeare (3 vols., 1886–88). He was domestic corresponding secretary of the New York Historical Society, and a trustee of Columbia College and the New York Society Library. Lowell (*Fable for Critics,* 1848) referred to him as a ripe scholar and a neat critic, with the soul of a gentleman. Those who knew him best declared with unanimity that he was "singularly free from blemish or blame, and equally exempt from enmity or detraction" (Butler, *post*). In disposition he was retiring, gentle, meditative, hesitant in debate but genial and interesting as a companion. His library of American and English literature and works on art, about 17,000 titles, exclusive of manuscripts, was given to the Lenox Library in two consignments, in 1878 and after his wife's death.

[The N. Y. Public Lib. has a copy of W. C. and C. J. Duyckinck, *The Duyckinck and Allied Families* (1908), with manuscript additions. Also in the N. Y. Pub. Lib. are the extensive Duyckinck Papers which include the correspondence of the brothers, their writings, notebooks, legal papers, and accounts. Diaries of Evert Duyckinck cover 1836–39, 1842–61. The literary letters are from most of the men and women writers of the United States from about 1840 to the close of the Civil War. See also Wm. Allen Butler, *Memorial Sketch* (read before the N. Y. Hist. Soc., Jan. 7, 1879, and reprinted); Samuel Osgood, memoir in *New Eng. Hist. and Geneal. Reg.,* April 1879 (also reprinted); *N. Y. Times, N. Y. Tribune,* and *World,* all for Aug. 15, 1878.]   V.H.P.

DUYCKINCK, GEORGE LONG (Oct. 17, 1823–Mar. 30, 1863), editor, biographer, younger brother of Evert Augustus Duyckinck [*q.v.*], attended Geneva (now Hobart College), and then the University of the City of New York, graduating in 1843. He studied law and was admitted to the bar, but never practised. "His organization, both bodily and mental, was of that delicate and sensitive order which finds nothing congenial in the conflicts and sharp issues of the busy world" (Morgan, *post*). He traveled in Europe in 1847–48 and 1857. His life was devoted to religion, literature, and art. He was associated with his brother Evert in editing the *Literary World, a Journal of American and Foreign Literature, Science, and Art* (Oct. 7, 1848–Dec. 31, 1853) and the *Cyclopædia of American Literature* (2 vols., 1855). In 1855 he was elected to the executive committee of the General Protestant Episcopal Sunday School

Union and Church Book Society, and in 1857 became its treasurer, devoting himself to wholesome literature for the children of his denomination. For this society he wrote biographies of George Herbert (1858), Thomas Ken (1859), Jeremy Taylor (1860), and Hugh Latimer (1861). He edited an American edition of Shakespeare, based upon J. Payne Collier's, with variorum notes (8 vols., 1853).

[Wm. F. Morgan, *Obituary Notice of the Late Geo. L. Duyckinck* (1863); *N. Y. Times,* Mar. 31, 1863; *N. Y. Tribune,* Apr. 1, 1863; references in bibliography of sketch of Evert Duyckinck.]   V.H.P.

DWENGER, JOSEPH (Sept. 7, 1837–Jan. 22, 1893), Roman Catholic prelate, was born in or near Stallotown (now Minster), Ohio, the son of Gerhard Henry Dwenger and Maria Catherina Wirdt. On his father's death in 1840, his mother moved to Cincinnati, where Joseph had his early schooling. Through the death of his mother he became an orphan at the age of twelve. Father Kunkler, a priest of the Community of the Most Precious Blood, who waited on Mrs. Dwenger in her last illness, took Joseph in charge, acted as a sort of guardian to him, and assisted him to pursue his studies for the priesthood. After some time as a student at Mount St. Mary's of the West, Cincinnati, Dwenger was ordained a priest by Archbishop Purcell on Sept. 4, 1859, as a member of the Congregation of the Precious Blood, of whose seminary at Carthagena, Ohio, he was later the founder and first president, and in which he taught as professor. In 1867 he became secretary of the religious congregation to which he belonged, and from that time until 1872 he also filled the rôle of missionary. His services were engaged by many priests, because he was a powerful and very effective pulpit orator. In the year 1872 Pius IX appointed him bishop of Fort Wayne to succeed Bishop John Henry Luers, the first incumbent of this See. Having experienced what it means to be deprived of both father and mother in early childhood, Bishop Dwenger soon became known as the "Orphans' Friend." He built an Orphan Asylum for boys at Lafayette, Ind. (1875), and another for girls at Fort Wayne (1886), both of which are still in use, accommodating some three hundred children. During his administration the diocese of Fort Wayne became renowned throughout the United States for its excellent and well-regulated parochial school system. Every parish of fifty families and upwards had its own school, examined twice a year by one of ten members of a school board, who exercised a very wholesome influence over the schools, contributing much toward their efficiency and progress.

Bishop Dwenger was director of the first official American pilgrimage to Lourdes and Rome, in 1874, leaving at the Shrine a bright American flag, which still ornaments a wall of the basilica. Following the Council of Baltimore, held in 1884, he was one of the three prelates designated to carry the report to Rome and to speak for the Church's approbation of the various decrees which this Council enacted. He died in his fifty-sixth year, and was buried in a crypt or mausoleum under the sanctuary of the Cathedral. Archbishop Elder of Cincinnati officiated at the obsequies. The funeral sermon was preached by Bishop Rademacher of Nashville, who became his successor in the See of Fort Wayne in the following year.

[Baptismal Record of St. Augustine's Parish, Minster (then Stallotown), Ohio; H. J. Alerding, *Hist. of the Diocese of Fort Wayne* (1907); *Cath. Hist. Rev.*, Oct. 1916; John H. Lamott, *Hist. of the Archdiocese of Cincinnati* (1921); *The Cath. Church in the U. S. A.* (1912), vol. I; Chas. Blanchard, *Hist. of the Cath. Church in Ind.* (1898), vol. I; *Sadlier's Cath. Directory*, 1893; *Cath. Encyc.*, VI, 150, and VII, 741; *Indianapolis Jour.*, Jan. 23, 1893.]   J.F.N.

DWIGHT, BENJAMIN WOODBRIDGE (Apr. 5, 1816–Sept. 18, 1889), educator, author, clergyman, the eldest son of Benjamin Woolsey Dwight and Sophia Woodbridge (Strong) and a brother of Theodore William Dwight [*q.v.*], was born in New Haven, Conn. A year later the family moved to Catskill, N. Y., where his father conducted a hardware business until 1831, when he moved to Clinton, N. Y., and set up as a gentleman farmer. He was elected treasurer of Hamilton College, from which Benjamin was graduated in 1835. After completing his course at the Yale Divinity School in 1838, he taught at Hamilton College for three years; in 1844 founded the First Congregational (now the Central Presbyterian) Church of Joliet, Ill., where he was ordained by the Presbytery of Chicago in 1845; and in 1846 established a commercial and classical school for boys, Dwight's High School, in Brooklyn, N. Y. He continued this school with success until 1858, when he founded a boarding-school in Clinton, maintained until 1863. In his own writings he hinted somewhat mysteriously that external forces caused him to close this institution. For the four years following he conducted a like school in New York City. He inherited the Dwight teaching ability, so prominent in his grandfather, President Timothy Dwight [*q.v.*] of Yale, and made innovations in the curriculum of his schools. He believed his school the first in the country to include German (1846); and he developed a method of encouraging and promoting the brighter pupils without

discouraging the duller. In the Clinton School, he included girls among the day students. He educated in all some 2,000 students. In 1854 he founded The Rural Art Association in Clinton, which did much to stimulate intellectual life and to beautify the town. In 1867 he gave up his New York school, retired from teaching, returned to Clinton, and for the rest of his life followed literary pursuits and supplied various pulpits. For a short time he was editor and owner of *The Interior,* a Presbyterian religious weekly in Chicago, Ill. His literary endeavors were in several fields. He published: *Higher Christian Education* (1859); *Modern Philology, First and Second Series* (1864); *History of the Descendants of Elder John Strong of Northampton, Mass.* (2 vols., 1871); *The History of the Descendants of John Dwight of Dedham, Mass.* (2 vols., 1874), a mine of information; *Higher Culture of Woman* (1887); *True Doctrine of Divine Providence* (1887).

Dwight was twice married: first, in 1846, to Wealthy Jane Dewey, daughter of Harvey and Betsey Maria (Harrison) Dewey, by whom he had three daughters and one son; and after her death in 1864, to Charlotte Sophia Parish, by whom he had one daughter. He was of smaller stature than many of the Dwights, but his engraved portrait shows that he had the comeliness characteristic of the family.

[Autobiographical sketches in Dwight's own genealogies of the Dwight and Strong families; W. W. Spooner, *Historic Families of America* (n.d.); *Eighth Gen. Cat. of the Yale Divinity School* (1922); *N. Y. Tribune,* June 13, 1846.]   E.W.F.

DWIGHT, EDMUND (Nov. 28, 1780–Apr. 1, 1849), merchant, manufacturer, philanthropist, descended from John Dwight who settled at Dedham, Mass., in 1635, was the seventh of eight children born to Jonathan and Margaret (Ashley) Dwight of Springfield, Mass. His father had been sent without patrimony at the age of ten to Springfield where he had become a leading citizen and merchant in that rising frontier community. Although the family was prosperous, Edmund was brought up to work on the farm and in the store. After a thorough preparation he entered Yale College, from which he graduated in 1799. He read law for some time in the office of Fisher Ames at Dedham, but upon the completion of his studies, decided on a more active career in business. His association with Ames, however, introduced him to the best society of Boston and brought him into contact with many of the keenest minds of eastern Massachusetts, an experience valuable in his education and helpful later in his business. Anxious to travel in Europe before settling down, he proposed to his father that his share of the inheritance be given to him at once. His father's willingness enabled the young man to spend the years 1802–04 abroad.

Returning to America, he associated himself with his father and his brothers, whose business interests now included banking enterprises and branch stores in several towns. In spite of the expanding activities of the Dwight family, Edmund Dwight found time to represent the town of Springfield in the General Court, 1810–13, and 1815, and his interest in politics continued throughout his life. His business during these Springfield years took him frequently to Boston and there he married, Apr. 19, 1809, Mary Harrison Eliot (May 15, 1788–Oct. 12, 1846), daughter of Samuel Eliot, a prominent merchant of that city. This marriage gave Dwight further contacts with the most distinguished merchant families of the seacoast, and in 1816 he removed to Boston.

Establishing a partnership with James K. Mills, he was soon placed by his energy and foresight among the foremost of the entrepreneurs who laid the foundations for New England manufacturing. His was the directing hand in the establishment of three manufacturing centers, Chicopee Falls, Chicopee, and Holyoke, all situated in the Connecticut Valley where he had lived for many years. In 1822 he and his brother Jonathan purchased most of the land later occupied by the village of Chicopee Falls, built a dam to harness the power, and by 1831 had erected four cotton-mills operating first under the name of the Boston & Springfield Manufacturing Company and then of the Chicopee Manufacturing Company. The first-named company in 1825 bought the water rights and land later covered by the city of Chicopee. These water rights were distributed by the Springfield Canal Company, organized in 1831, and along the canal operated by this corporation Dwight built huge mills himself and induced other manufacturers to establish themselves. It was also the Dwight concern which eventually, through the Hadley Falls Company, secured the water rights and built the dam and canals upon which the manufacturing of Holyoke is based. By 1841 his company had the principal direction of cotton-mills, machine-shops, and calico printing works, employing about 3,000 persons. Outside of manufacturing, Dwight's chief business interest was in the promotion of the Western Railroad from Worcester to Albany. He was a member of the first board of directors (1836–39), was elected by the legislature a director on the part of the state in 1842,

and until his death continued on the board as a representative either of the state or of the stockholders. He was president of the road in 1843 and during his entire service used his influence for the most durable and scientific construction.

Less spectacular than his business ventures was his notable contribution to the development of public education. Becoming keenly interested in that subject after reading a translation of Cousin's *Report of the State of Public Instruction in Prussia*, he was the center of a group who devised the School Law of 1837 passed under the governorship of Edward Everett [*q.v.*], and became a member of the board of education established by it. This law gave the board large powers to collect information and distribute school funds. To make the board an effective instrument it was necessary to have a secretary of the highest talent, and Dwight made this possible by paying for sixteen years part of the salary of Horace Mann [*q.v.*]. When the board decided that a system of normal schools should be established, he contributed $10,000 on condition that the state appropriate a similar amount, and later offered to raise $5,000 if the state would duplicate it. His generosity also allowed Horace Mann to make his first experiments with teachers' institutes. After Dwight's death, the *Thirteenth Annual Report of the Board of Education* in 1849 asserted that "it was through his exertions, perhaps, more than any other individual, that this Board was established, and through his liberality, more than that of all others, that it was enabled to prosecute the system of measures which has resulted in whatever of success it has achieved."

[B. W. Dwight, *The Hist. of the Descendants of John Dwight of Dedham, Mass.* (1874), II, 894–98; Francis Bowen, "Memoir of Edmund Dwight," in *Barnard's Am. Jour. of Educ.*, Sept. 1857; L. H. Everts, *Hist. of the Conn. Valley* (1879), II, 917, 971–73; L. L. Johnson, *Chicopee Illustrated* (1896); F. B. Dexter, *Biog. Sketches Grads. Yale Coll.*, vol. V (1911); *Boston Atlas*, Apr. 2, 1849.]
H.U.F.

DWIGHT, FRANCIS (Mar. 14, 1808–Dec. 15, 1845), lawyer, educator, was born in Springfield, Mass., the sixth in descent from John Dwight, who settled at Dedham, Mass., in 1635, and the eighth of the twelve children of James Scutt and Mary (Sanford) Dwight. His father, a wealthy, enterprising, benevolently inclined merchant, owned a large wholesale and retail emporium in Springfield and six branch stores in as many near-by villages. He imported his wares direct from Europe, his own sloops and schooners conveying them from New York to Hartford, where river boats, also of his ownership, carried them on to Springfield. Francis entered Phillips Exeter Academy in 1822 and Harvard College in 1824, graduated in 1827, and studied law for two years in the school at Northampton. When his brilliant young teacher, John Hooker Ashmun, was appointed to a professorship in the newly organized Harvard Law School, Dwight followed him to Cambridge for his final year (September 1829–July 1830) of study. Subsequently he spent a year or more in travel in England, France, and Germany, partly for the sake of his health, which had been weakened by too close application to his books. In 1834 he was admitted to the Massachusetts bar. On July 4 of that year he married Catharine Van Rensselaer Schermerhorn of Geneva, N. Y. She died on Aug. 20, 1840, and on Apr. 20, 1843, he married Catharine Waters Yates of Albany, N. Y., who outlived him. Although definite information is lacking, Dwight does not appear to have succeeded well with the law, in spite of the good opinion that Justice Joseph Story had formed of him at Cambridge, and probably lost interest in his profession. After a year's practise in Massachusetts he moved out to Michigan Territory, but in 1838 he returned East and settled at Geneva, N. Y., the home of his father-in-law. Meanwhile he had been interesting himself in the Lyceum movement and in popular education. With the encouragement of John Canfield Spencer, then secretary of state of New York and superintendent of common schools, he published in March 1840 the first number of the *District School Journal of the State of New York*, and soon after changed his headquarters to Albany. The paper gained official support and became the organ of the state common-school system. Dwight, by his enthusiasm and wide knowledge, was able to keep his little monthly on a high plane and so to make it of real service to the state. Not long after he was appointed superintendent of the schools of the city and county of Albany, was made a member of the board of directors of the Albany Normal School, and was looked upon as a leader in education. He was but entering on what should have been his real career when "inflammation of the bowels"—not then recognized as appendicitis—cut him short. He had already won the esteem, however, of educators throughout the eastern United States and had done notable work for the public schools of New York.

[B. W. Dwight, *The Hist. of the Descendants of John Dwight* (1874) ; article in *Barnard's Am. Jour. of Ed.*, Dec. 1858; *Quinquennial Cat., Harvard Univ., 1636–1915* (1915); *Dist. School Jour. of the State of N. Y.*, Jan. 1846.]   G.H.G.

DWIGHT, HARRISON GRAY OTIS (Nov. 22, 1803–Jan. 25, 1862), missionary, the son of Seth and Hannah (Strong) Dwight, and a descendant of John Dwight who settled at Dedham, Mass., in 1635, was born at Conway, Mass. Soon after his birth the family moved to Utica, N. Y., in the schools of which town he secured his early education. In his fifteenth year, he was "hopefully converted" in a religious revival at Utica, and became a member of the local Presbyterian church. He attended the academies in Fairfield and Utica in preparation for college, and in 1821 entered Hamilton College, graduating in the spring of 1825. In the fall of the same year he entered Andover Theological Seminary, Mass., where he took the full three years' course in preparation for foreign missionary service. Graduating in 1828, he secured appointment under the American Board of Commissioners for Foreign Missions and spent the ensuing fifteen months as agent of the Board traveling among the churches. On July 15, 1829, at Great Barrington, Mass., he was ordained to the ministry. On Jan. 4 following, he was married to Elizabeth, daughter of Joshua and Ruth Barker of North Andover, Mass., and on Jan. 21, with her, set sail from Boston on their journey eastward to Turkey. They arrived at Malta on Feb. 27, and leaving his wife there for a time, on Mar. 17 Dwight took ship for Smyrna in company with Dr. Eli Smith, an American Board missionary, to gather information about the Armenians in the interior of Asia Minor with a view to the opening of mission stations. Traveling on horseback, in Turkish costumes, they made a memorable journey of 2,400 miles, going as far as the Caucasus and northwestern Persia. They returned by way of Constantinople, arriving at Malta on July 2, 1831. The results of this important venture in missionary exploration were published by the two authors in 1833 in two volumes entitled *Researches of Rev. Eli Smith and Rev. H. G. O. Dwight in Armenia.*

In May of the following year (1834), Dwight with his wife and an infant son left Malta to take up permanent residence in Constantinople, at first in a suburb and then in Stamboul, the Turkish city proper. For nearly thirty years his special office was that of "missionary to the Armenians," of whom there were about a hundred thousand in Constantinople. He did much literary work, being one of the first American students of the Armenian language. He wrote a geography with special reference to Turkey, several tracts, and many articles in the *Avedaper* (Messenger), which he edited after 1854; and worked on various translations. In English, in addition to his share in the *Researches,* he wrote *Memoir of Elizabeth R. Dwight* (1840), *Christianity Revived in the East* (1850, reissued in

London in 1854 under the title *Christianity in Turkey*), and prepared a catalogue of Armenian literature for the *Journal of the American Oriental Society* (vol. III, 1853).

He sought and held interviews with inquirers, gave lectures on theology, preached frequently, helped in the organization of schools and churches, and was the chief founder of the Armenian Evangelical Church in Turkey. He made several tours of preliminary investigation for his mission, and many tours of inspection. In the summer of 1833 he sailed around the Sea of Marmora, and in the summer of 1834 journeyed into European Turkey. He visited Nicomedia often and aided in the work there. In 1837 Mrs. Dwight and John, one of their four sons, succumbed to plague. Dwight returned the following year to America. During his stay in Washington, D. C., he met Mary Lane of Sturbridge, Mass., who became his bride on Apr. 16, 1839, and who returned with him to Constantinople in the autumn of the same year. Five children, one of whom was Henry Otis Dwight [*q.v.*], were born of this union; four of them survived the death of their mother on Nov. 16, 1860. During the first nine months of 1861 Dwight made a tour of all the stations which had been established by the Board in Turkish and Persian areas, and then returned to America, where he journeyed among the churches on behalf of the Turkish Mission. His death occurred in a railroad accident near Bennington, Vt., and he was buried at Utica, N. Y.

[Many of Dwight's letters recounting his experiences were published in the *Missionary Herald* between 1830 and 1862. See also *Memoirs of Am. Missionaries* (1833); H. C. Haydn, *Am. Heroes on Mission Fields* (Am. Tract Soc., 1890); B. W. Dwight, *The Hist. of the Descendants of John Dwight* (1874); Julius Richter, *Hist. of Protestant Missions in the Near East* (1910); E. M. Bliss, *The Encyc. of Missions* (1891), I, 345; W. E. Strong, *The Story of the Am. Board* (1910); *Gen. Cat. Theol. Sem., Andover, Mass. 1808-1908*; *Essex Register* (Salem, Mass.), Jan. 4, 1830; obituary notice in the *Missionary Herald,* Mar. 1862; information from H. G. Dwight, Esq., and from Miss Cornelia P. Dwight.]   **J.C.A.**

DWIGHT, HENRY OTIS (June 3, 1843–June 20, 1917), missionary, editor, the son of Harrison G. Otis Dwight [*q.v.*] and Mary Lane, his second wife, was born in Constantinople. His entire early education, including the equivalent of high school training, was obtained in Constantinople, for the most part in his own home. When he was ready for college, he came to America and entered Ohio Wesleyan University. He was there only a year, for in September 1861 he enlisted as a private in the 20th Ohio Infantry. He was promoted successively sergeant, second lieutenant, first lieutenant, and brevetted captain.

At the close of the war he declined an appointment in the regular army. He served as *aide* on the staff of Maj.-Gen. M. F. Force of the 1st Division, XVII Army Corps, Army of the Tennessee, and was mustered out in July 1865. During 1866–67 he was treasurer of the Northampton, Mass., Street Railway Company. He had "dabbled in engineering" while in the army, and assisted in laying out the city's railway system.

In March 1867 he was married to Mary Bliss, daughter of the Rev. Elisha E. Bliss [*q.v.*], of the Western Turkey Mission, with whom he sailed on Nov. 23, 1867, for Constantinople, to serve under the American Board of Commissioners for Foreign Missions in connection with the mission's business department. He was "Secular Agent" until 1874, and from 1875 to 1899 was general editor of the Turkish publications of the mission. In the latter capacity he performed the great scholarly work of his life, the editing of the *Turkish and English Lexicon* (1890) of Sir James Redhouse.

From 1875 to 1892 he acted as special correspondent of the *New York Tribune,* supplying his paper with valuable news of events from the outset of the reign of Abdul Hamid II. Some of his letters to the *Tribune* formed the basis of a volume, *Turkish Life in War Time,* published in 1881. He also contributed articles on Turkey to magazines in the United States, often writing under an assumed name in order to avoid difficulties with the Turkish censorship. Throughout this period, his intimate understanding of affairs in Turkey made his letters to the United States minister on behalf of the mission useful to the State Department in shaping its policy in the Near East. In 1893 he published *Treaty Rights of American Missionaries in Turkey.* At one time he was mentioned for the post of United States minister at Constantinople, but he felt that he could be of greater use in a humbler but more permanent position. In 1899 he gave up his editorial connection with the mission and returned to America.

He was editor, in 1900, of the *Report* of the Ecumenical Missionary Conference held that year in New York City. In 1901 he resigned from the mission altogether, continuing the general editorial work upon which he had been engaged and devoting his time more fully to authorship. He published *Constantinople and its Problems* (1901); was editor in chief of the *Encyclopædia of Missions* in 1904; was the author of the *Blue Book of Missions,* issued in 1905 and 1907, and of *A Muslim Sir Galahad* (1913). From March 1904 he acted as secretary of the Bureau of Missions, in New York City, and from

Jan. 1, 1907, as recording secretary of the American Bible Society. As historian of this Society he published in 1916 their *Centennial History*.

Although he never held a pastorate, while in America on a furlough in 1880 he was ordained to the ministry by the Council of the Lamoille County (Vt.) Congregational Association. He was married four times. His first wife, Mary Bliss, died at Constantinople on Nov. 15, 1872, at the age of twenty-eight. On Apr. 18, 1874, he married Ardelle Maria Griswold, of the Turkey Mission, who had gone out to Cæsarea in 1869. She died at Constantinople on Dec. 28, 1884, in her thirty-seventh year. In 1887 he married Belle S. Bliss, who died in 1894, in her thirty-sixth year. On Dec. 26, 1900, he married Mrs. Frances Warner Mulford of Roselle, N. J. He died at Roselle shortly after his seventy-fourth birthday.

[*Who's Who in America*, 1916–17; B. W. Dwight, *The Hist. of the Descendants of John Dwight of Dedham, Mass.* (1874), vol. II; *Congreg. Year Book*, 1917; *Missionary Review of the World*, July 1917; *Missionary Herald*, Aug. 1917, and frequent mention, 1867–1901; *N. Y. Tribune*, June 20, 1917; *N. Y. Times*, June 21, 1917; *Foreign Relations of the U. S.*, esp. 1890–1900; information from a son, H. G. Dwight, Esq.] J.C.A.

DWIGHT, JOHN SULLIVAN (May 13, 1813–Sept. 5, 1893), music critic, editor, was born at Boston, Mass., eldest of the four children of Dr. John and Mary (Corey) Dwight. His father, who had studied for the ministry and then become a physician, was a radical freethinker. The boy, a sensitive, affectionate, gentle lad, early gave evidence of literary ability, and before he was sixteen, of an absorbing love of music. Prepared at the Boston Latin School, he entered Harvard College in 1829, maintained a "respectable standing" in his class, and was happily associated with the musical club, the Pierian Sodality. After graduation in 1832, when he delivered the class poem, he became a student in the Harvard Divinity School, where he formed lasting friendships with Theodore Parker and Christopher Pearse Cranch [*qq.v.*]. He completed his course in August 1836, giving a dissertation upon "The Proper Character of Poetry and Music for Public Worship" (*Christian Examiner*, November 1836), and entered upon a period of supplying various pulpits, writing literary reviews for periodicals, and studying and translating German poetry. In 1837 he was one of the leaders in the formation of the General Association of the Members of the Pierian Sodality, later the Harvard Musical Association. He was responsible for most of the translation and all of the notes in *Select Minor Poems translated from the German of Goethe and Schiller* (1839).

In 1840 he was called to the pastorate of the Unitarian church at Northampton. On May 20 he was ordained and installed, George Ripley [*q.v.*] preaching the sermon and William Ellery Channing delivering the charge. During the year that followed, two of his sermons, "The Religion of Beauty" and "Ideals of Every Day Life," were published in the first volume of the *Dial*. Although esteemed by his parishioners for his amiability and purity of soul, he did not have the power of disciplined thought which the Northampton congregation required of its preacher. Accordingly, after about a year he resigned, and before long "quietly dropped out of a profession which he felt was no longer congenial."

He had been a member of the Transcendental Club from its beginning and in November 1841 joined Ripley at Brook Farm, where he became one of the leaders. Here he was teacher of music and Latin, and in the former field he found his calling. Instilling in the children and awakening in the adults an appreciation of music and a conception of its power in the enlargement of the spiritual life, he organized Mass Clubs both at West Roxbury and in Boston to sing the great compositions of Mozart, Bach, and Beethoven, and made the *Harbinger*, the organ of Brook Farm and later of the American Union of Associationists, "one of the best musical journals the country has ever possessed" (Cooke, *Dwight*, p. 108). He was a constant contributor to the *Harbinger*, of articles on "Association," literary reviews, and poems, as well as musical criticism; for a while, with Ripley, he edited it, and after its removal to New York upon the break-up of the Brook Farm community in October 1847 he was one of its editorial contributors. During the next four years, residing in Boston, he directed the choir of W. H. Channing's Religious Union of Associationists; lectured on musical subjects; wrote reviews and musical criticisms for Boston and New York journals; contributed a series of monthly articles to *Sartain's Magazine* (1851–52); for a few months conducted in the Boston *Daily Chronotype* a department devoted to Association; and for the first six months of 1851 was musical editor of the *Boston Commonwealth*. On Feb. 12, 1851, he was married to Mary Bullard, a member of his choir.

In the next year, aided by the Harvard Musical Association, he issued the first number of *Dwight's Journal of Music: A Paper of Literature and Art*, of which he was publisher as well as editor and chief contributor until Oliver Ditson & Company took over the publishing in 1858. In the columns of his *Journal* he "translated music into literary form, showed the public what to find in it and how to discover its profound spiritual charm and power" (*Ibid.*, p. 236), and for nearly thirty years exerted an unparalleled influence on the formation of musical taste in America. At the end of that time its purpose had been to some extent accomplished; new schools of music, with whom the editor could not wholly sympathize, were coming into prominence; and the issue of Sept. 3, 1881, was the last.

Although the *Journal* absorbed most of his energy, Dwight found time to translate a number of lyrics and several works on music from the German, to lecture frequently, and to contribute to other periodicals. The *Atlantic Monthly* for September and November 1870 contained two parts of a notable lecture delivered earlier in that year: "Music a Means of Culture" and "The Intellectual Influence of Music." He wrote the chapter on music for Justin Winsor's *Memorial History of Boston* (1881); completed Vol. I (1883) of *The History of the Händel and Haydn Society of Boston, Mass.*, begun by Charles C. Perkins; from 1885 to 1890 assisted in the revision of musical definitions for *Webster's International Dictionary*; and in 1890, for six months, substituted for W. F. Apthorp as musical editor of the *Boston Transcript*. An essay, "Common Sense," in which he discussed philosophy, religion, and politics, written in 1885, appeared in the *Unitarian Review,* May 1890.

Dwight was for eighteen years a trustee of the Perkins Institution for the Blind, and gave to it enthusiastic service. He was one of the earliest members of the Saturday Club, and from 1877 had a large share in the handling of the Club's affairs. He was vice-president of the Harvard Musical Association from 1855 to 1873 and president and librarian from 1873 until his death. In 1865 he was instrumental in the formation among its members of the Philharmonic Society; in 1876 with the establishment of a professorship of music at Harvard he saw the accomplishment of the Association's stated object. After the death of his wife, in 1860, while he was in Europe on his only trip abroad, he made his home for a time with his mother and sister, then in an apartment near the *Journal* office, and after 1873, in the rooms of the Harvard Musical Association. Here he died, in his eighty-first year. Unpractical, gentle, visionary, Dwight "lived sunnily in life-long poverty, loved his friends, loved flowers and music," and by "his rare gift of appreciation and enthusiasm diffused a sense of beauty throughout a whole community" (Perry, *post*).

[Geo. Willis Cooke, *John Sullivan Dwight, Brook-Farmer, Editor, and Critic of Music* (1898) and *Early*

Letters of Geo. Wm. Curtis to John S. Dwight (1898); W. S. B. Mathews, in *Music* (Chicago), Sept. 1893; Wm. F. Apthorp, *Ibid.*, Oct. 1893, reprinted from the *Boston Transcript,* Sept. 5, 1893; Bliss Perry, in E. W. Emerson, *The Early Years of the Saturday Club, 1855–1870* (1918); B. W. Dwight, *Hist. of the Descendants of John Dwight, of Dedham, Mass.* (1874); *Boston Evening Jour.* and *Boston Advertiser,* Sept. 6, 1893.]

E. R. D.

DWIGHT, NATHANIEL (Jan. 31, 1770–June 11, 1831), physician, educator, tenth of the thirteen children of Maj. Timothy and Mary (Edwards) Dwight and seventh of their nine sons, was born in Northampton, Mass. His early education was probably in charge of his mother, the gifted daughter of Jonathan Edwards, who conducted a regular school for her children, and whose rare teaching ability was inherited by many of her descendants. He may also have attended the school at Greenfield Hill kept by his brother Timothy [*q.v.*], later president of Yale. Apparently he did not go to college, but he later said himself (Preface to *Geography*) that he was employed "several years in school-keeping." He studied medicine under an eminent Hartford physician, Dr. Mason F. Cogswell; practised in Hartford, and served for a time as assistant surgeon in the army at Governors Island. Resigning from the army, he practised in Westfield, Mass., and New London and Wethersfield, Conn. In 1812 he entered the ministry and settled in Westchester, Conn., returning, however, to medical practise in 1820, in Providence, R. I., and Norwich, Conn. Apparently not financially successful, Dwight was nevertheless accounted a good medical practitioner, "kind and generous to a fault," and a faithful and earnest preacher. Like his brothers, he was tall and well built, though not as fine-looking as most of them. He was married on June 24, 1798, to Rebecca Robbins of Wethersfield, Conn., the daughter of Appleton Robbins and Mary Stillman. Four of their eight children died in infancy.

In 1795 he published *A Short but Comprehensive System of the Geography of the World: by Way of Question and Answer,* which went through numerous editions over a period of years. This effort was enthusiastically received as "better calculated to impress the facts which it contains on the minds of children than any heretofore published," but it was not, as has often been stated, the first school geography issued in the United States, *The American Geography* (1789), by Jedidiah Morse having preceded it. Dwight wrote another schoolbook, *Sketches of the Lives of the Signers of the Declaration of Independence,* first published in 1830, which continued to appear with slightly varying title in subsequent editions up to 1895. His chief additional contribution seems to have been a constructive suggestion for improving the condition of the insane. "As early as 1812, Dr. Nathaniel Dwight of Colchester sent to the convention of the [Connecticut Medical] Society a communication upon the subject of a hospital for lunatics in this State, and a committee was appointed to collect proper information and report" (Speech by Dr. Gurdon W. Russell, Jan. 7, 1873, at the semi-centennial celebration of the Hartford Asylum, *Hartford Daily Courant,* Jan. 8, 1873). He died at Oswego, N. Y., while on a visit.

[B. W. Dwight, *The Hist. of the Descendants of John Dwight of Dedham, Mass.* (2 vols., 1874) ; Preface to Dwight's *Geography.*]   E.W.F.

DWIGHT, SERENO EDWARDS (May 18, 1786–Nov. 30, 1850), educator, clergyman, fifth of the eight sons of the elder Timothy Dwight [*q.v.*] and his wife, Mary Woolsey, was born at Greenfield Hill in Fairfield, Conn. His early education was conducted at home and in his father's school. From 1796 to 1799 he attended the Hopkins Grammar School in New Haven; in 1803, at the age of seventeen, he graduated from Yale, of which his father was then president, and began his teaching career at Litchfield, Conn. The following year he returned to New Haven as his father's amanuensis, acting at the same time as assistant to Benjamin Silliman [*q.v.*], professor of chemistry. After another year, spent in general study, he was a tutor at Yale, 1806–10, in sole charge of half a class in mathematics, rhetoric, and the classics, and simultaneously studied law, which he practised in New Haven from 1810 to 1816. He was over six feet tall, erect and dignified in his carriage, meticulous in details of dress, handsome and intellectual in countenance and altogether of commanding and striking presence. On Aug. 28, 1811, he was married to Susan Edwards Daggett, daughter of David Daggett [*q.v.*] and Wealthy Ann Munson. In 1812 he fell victim to a severe lung fever, the mercury treatment for which produced a painful eruption which was to torture him for the rest of his days. Though successful in his law practise, in 1815 he decided to enter the ministry and on Oct. 8, 1816, was licensed to preach by the West Association of Ministers of New Haven County. Shortly afterward he was appointed chaplain of the United States Senate, in which his father-in-law was representing Connecticut, and served during the session 1816–17. The following summer he accepted a call to the famous Park Street Church in Boston, being ordained and installed on Sept. 3, 1817. He remained there until 1826, except for the year 1824–25, which he spent in European travel and a vain search for medical help.

Forced by vocal trouble and ill health to resign his pastorate, he returned to New Haven, and in 1828, in partnership with his youngest brother, Henry, opened a boarding-school for boys, the New Haven Gymnasium, modeled on the German plan. This project was highly successful, but neither brother had sufficient strength to keep it up, and in 1831 it was discontinued. In 1833 he was called to the presidency of Hamilton College, of which his brother Benjamin Woolsey Dwight was then treasurer. As president of Hamilton he raised a $50,000 fund, and also taught metaphysics, moral philosophy, and natural theology. He resigned on Sept. 2, 1835, because of disagreement with the trustees (see *Documentary History of Hamilton College,* 1922), and he never accepted another office, except that of agent for the Pennsylvania Colonization Society which he held from 1835 to 1838. His wife died in 1839; deprived of her mental and spiritual companionship, he survived her in loneliness and suffering for eleven years, living chiefly in New York and engaged largely in reading. In 1850 he went to Philadelphia, hoping to benefit from hydropathic treatments; but he died there in November of that year. He was buried in New Haven.

Soon after his marriage, Dwight wrote his first book, *The Hebrew Wife,* published in New York many years later (1836), and republished in Glasgow (1837). In 1818 he prefaced a five-volume edition of Timothy Dwight's *Theology, Explained and Defended* (1818–19) with a memoir of his father. Assisted by his wife, he worked for many years editing the complete writings of his great-grandfather, Jonathan Edwards; Edwards's *Memoirs of the Rev. David Brainerd* was published in 1822, and ten subsequent volumes, one a memoir of the great divine, were published in 1830 as *The Works of President Edwards: with a Memoir of his Life.* Various sermons and addresses of his own were published, mostly in pamphlet form, during his lifetime, and after his death appeared a volume, *Select Discourses of S. E. Dwight, D.D.* (1851), with a memoir by his younger brother, Rev. William T. Dwight.

[B. W. Dwight, *Hist. of the Descendants of John Dwight of Dedham, Mass.* (2 vols., 1874) ; memoir by W. T. Dwight, in *Select Discourses,* mentioned above; *Park Street Church Centennial* (1909), ed. by A. Z. Conrad; Wm. B. Sprague, *Annals Am. Pulpit,* vol. II (1857) ; F. B. Dexter, *Biog. Sketches Grads. Yale Coll.,* vol. V (1911).]   E.W.F.

DWIGHT, THEODORE (Dec. 15, 1764– June 12, 1846), lawyer, author, editor, was born in Northampton, Mass., seventh of the thirteen children of Maj. Timothy and Mary (Edwards) Dwight, whose first-born was Timothy Dwight [*q.v.*]. His father was a well-to-do merchant, landowner, and local office-holder; his mother, a daughter of Jonathan Edwards [*q.v.*], was a woman of remarkable strength of character. Maj. Timothy Dwight died when Theodore was in his thirteenth year, and the boy was brought up by his mother on the farm in Northampton. When he was about twenty, an injury obliged him to give up farming. He studied law with his uncle, Pierpont Edwards [*q.v.*], of New Haven, was admitted to the bar in 1787, and began practise at Haddam, Conn. In 1791 he moved to Hartford and practised there until 1815. He is reported to have been at one time in the early period of his practise on the point of forming a partnership with his cousin, Aaron Burr, the agreement falling through because of a political dispute. He was married on Sept. 9, 1792, to Abigail, daughter of Richard and Mary (Wright) Alsop of Middletown, Conn., and sister of Richard Alsop [*q.v.*], the poet. Dwight soon acquired a reputation as a competent lawyer, an able writer, and an eloquent speaker. A number of his speeches on various occasions during his years at Hartford have survived. One of the most interesting was delivered May 8, 1794, before the Connecticut Society for the Promotion of Freedom, and is noteworthy as an early arraignment of slavery; it contains passages which resemble utterances of Garrison and Phillips. His political addresses show that he shared with most of his contemporaries the enthusiasm for the French Revolution which later turned to fear and aversion. It was during this same period that he became identified with the group of writers known as the "Connecticut Wits." He was himself the author of much verse, but his poetical effusions are of antiquarian rather than literary interest (Parrington, *post*). Some of the New Year addresses, however, contributed to the *Connecticut Courant* and *Connecticut Mirror* are clever imitations of Hudibras and have been frequently quoted by historians.

He was ultra-Federalist in politics, and his views of the opposing party and its doctrines are to be found in his published addresses and in frequent editorial contributions, essays, and verses in the *Connecticut Courant* and *Connecticut Mirror*. His journalistic writings are characterized by the scurrility and personal abuse which were so common in American newspapers of the period. In 1806–07 he served for a single session in Congress, in place of John Cotton

Smith, resigned; and from 1809 to 1815 was a member of the Council. He was less prominent as an office-holder, however, than as a party worker, pamphleteer, and editor. He was well known throughout New England, his writings were widely quoted, and he corresponded with leading Federalists in other states. In Connecticut he fought all the reforms proposed by the Republicans prior to the War of 1812, and was earnestly opposed to the latter contest. At the same time he had numerous business interests, maintained a law practise, and was active in various local societies. In 1814 he acted as secretary of the Hartford Convention and in 1833 published the journal of that ill-starred gathering together with a review of the steps leading up to the War of 1812. It is an able defense of the Federalist party, although somewhat too polemical for good historical writing, as is also *The Character of Thomas Jefferson as Exhibited in his own Writings* (1839). In 1815 he moved to Albany, N. Y., where he founded the *Daily Advertiser*; but he remained there less than two years. In 1817 he founded the *New York Daily Advertiser,* and continued in New York City in active management of the paper until 1836, when he returned to Hartford to spend his declining years. His death took place in New York, however, as had that of his wife less than three months earlier.

[W. W. Spooner, *Historic Families of America* (n.d.), p. 110; Dwight Loomis and J. G. Calhoun, *Judicial and Civil Hist. of Conn.* (1895), p. 236; B. W. Dwight, *Hist. of the Descendants of John Dwight* (1874), I, 227–31; V. L. Parrington, in *The Conn. Wits* (1926), pp. xxxiii–xxxv, giving a list of Dwight's principal writings; S. G. Goodrich, *Recollections of a Lifetime* (1856), II, 123; R. J. Purcell, *Conn. in Transition, 1775–1818* (1918), giving an excellent historical setting for Dwight's earlier career; obituary in *N. Y. Tribune,* June 13, 1846.]   W. A. R.

DWIGHT, THEODORE (Mar. 3, 1796–Oct. 16, 1866), author, educator, was born in Hartford, Conn., the son of Theodore [*q.v.*] and Abigail (Alsop) Dwight. His father was the secretary of the Hartford Convention; his mother was a sister of Richard Alsop [*q.v.*]. With such parents it was natural that Theodore should be fed from early childhood on unadulterated Federalism and Calvinism and that the diet should be topped off with a four-year course at Yale, where he graduated in 1814, under his uncle Timothy [*q.v.*], whose memory he revered and whose classroom utterances, taken down in shorthand, he published as *President Dwight's Decisions of Questions Discussed by the Senior Class in Yale College in 1813 and 1814* (1833). He had intended to study theology under his uncle, but an attack of scarlet fever followed by a hemorrhage of the lungs made him relinquish his plans and turn to less strenuous employment. He traveled abroad for his health in 1818–19 and in October 1820 went again to England and France for a longer stay. In Paris he engaged with the Rev. Francis Leo in distributing free copies of De Sacy's French New Testament and was arrested for collecting an unlawful number of persons on the streets. He spoke French, Spanish, and Italian well and had a fair command of German, Portuguese, and modern Greek. At home in New York and in Brooklyn, where he lived from 1833 till his death, he taught school, worked on his father's paper, the *New York Daily Advertiser,* busied himself as author, editor, and translator of English books into Spanish, and engaged in various philanthropic, religious, and educational enterprises. At one time or another he worked for the *Protestant Vindicator,* the *Family Visitor,* the *Christian Alliance and Family Visitor,* the *New York Presbyterian,* and the *Youth's Penny Paper.* A venture of his own was *Dwight's American Magazine and Family Newspaper,* 1845–52. On Apr. 24, 1827, he married Eleanor Boyd of New York. He has the distinction of having introduced vocal music into the New York public schools. From 1854 to 1858 he worked with George Walter to send Free-Soil settlers to Kansas; together they persuaded about 3,000 persons to emigrate to the new territory. His knowledge of the Romance languages, his republicanism, and his desire to protestantize Catholic countries led him to entertain many political exiles from the Latin countries of Europe and the Americas. Of these guests the most famous was Garibaldi, who intrusted to him his autobiography for publication in the United States. Dwight's more important books are: *A Journal of a Tour in Italy in the Year 1821* (1824); *The Northern Traveller, containing the Routes to Niagara, Quebec, and the Springs* (1825; 6th ed., 1841); *Sketches of Scenery and Manners in the United States* (1829); *A New Gazetteer of the United States of America* (1833, with William Darby [q.v.], Dwight being responsible for New York, New Jersey, and New England); *Lessons in Greek* (1833, an interesting attempt at a rational method of instruction); *The Father's Book, or Suggestions for the Government and Instruction of Young Children on Principles Appropriate to a Christian Country* (1834, also published in London), of considerable interest; *The School-Master's Friend, with the Committee-Man's Guide: Containing Suggestions on Education, Modes of Teaching and Governing, . . . Plans of School-Houses, Furniture, Apparatus, Practical Hints,*

and Anecdotes on Different Systems (1835); *Open Covenants, or Nunneries and Popish Seminaries Dangerous to the Morals and Degrading to the Character of a Republican Community* (1836); *Dictionary of Roots and Derivations* (1837); *The History of Connecticut* (1840); *Summer Tours, or Notes of a Traveler through some of the Middle and Northern States* (1847, originally published in 1834 as *Things as They Are;* republished in Glasgow in 1848 as *Travels in America*); *The Roman Republic of 1849* (1851); an edition with much new material of Maria Monk's *Awful Disclosures* (1855); *Life of General Garibaldi, Translated from his Private Papers with the History of his Splendid Exploits in Rome, Lombardy, Sicily, and Naples to the Present Time* (1861). Dwight's admiration for Garibaldi, it may be added, was unbounded. During his last years he worked in the New York Customs House. He died from shock and injuries received in jumping from a moving train in Jersey City.

[B. W. Dwight, *The Hist. of the Descendants of John Dwight of Dedham, Mass.* (1874); F. B. Dexter, *Biog. Sketches Grads. Yale Coll.,* vol. VI (1912).]

G.H.G.

DWIGHT, THEODORE WILLIAM (July 18, 1822–June 29, 1892), lawyer, educator, grandson of Timothy Dwight [q.v.], was born at Catskill, N. Y., the second son of Dr. Benjamin Woolsey Dwight and his wife, Sophia Woodbridge Strong, sister of Theodore Strong, the eminent mathematician. Benjamin Woodbridge Dwight [q.v.] was his elder brother. The family moved to Clinton, N. Y., in 1831. As a boy Theodore William was an omnivorous reader and possessed an exceptionally retentive memory. In 1837 he entered Hamilton College, graduating with honors in 1840. He then studied physics in New York City for a short time, later becoming instructor in classics at Utica Academy. He had discovered, however, that "as all roads lead to Rome, so all intellectual aspiration may lead to law," and in 1841 he entered the Yale Law School. He did not complete his course, being in 1842 appointed tutor in Hamilton College, a position which he held for four years, at the same time initiating and conducting an informal class for instruction in law. In 1845 he was admitted to the New York bar. In 1846 he was appointed to the Maynard Professorship of Law, History, Civil Polity, and Political Economy at Hamilton, and during his twelve years' tenure of this chair, laid the foundations for the work with which his name will always be associated. The instruction in law at Hamilton had been perfunctory and did not contemplate any graduate study, but he systematized and extended the course, obtained recognition of a regular department of law in 1853, and laid down the principles upon which it was to be conducted: "The great object aimed at is to store the mind of the student with the fundamental principles of law." His method involved an extensive use of authoritative text-books from which the student obtained a grasp of the principles, and then was taught how to apply them. Cases were only used as illustrations of the propositions formulated in the books. In 1855 the Hamilton Law School was incorporated and he became its head, continuing to hold the Maynard Professorship. Up to this time there had been no law school in New York City, and, in order to supply the want, the trustees of Columbia College in 1858 established the Columbia Law School, offering Dwight the professorship of municipal law in connection therewith. He accepted and in November of that year commenced his initial course of lectures, which were an immediate success, and students enrolled in large numbers. For fourteen years he continued unassisted to lecture on all the topics embraced in private law, justifying the comment that "he was himself the Columbia Law School," and though there was no progress during the Civil War, on its termination the classes became crowded. In addition to his heavy duties at Columbia, he lectured on constitutional law at Cornell, 1869–71, and at Amherst College, 1870–72. In 1873 he was assisted by George Chase [q.v.], who was that year appointed instructor, becoming assistant professor of municipal law in 1875. The reputation of the school had now spread far and wide, and the increase of students was such that five professorships were created in 1878, Dwight continuing as warden to direct the policy and superintend the teaching, in addition to lecturing. His method was always the same, and it was, to use his own term, "Socratic, illustrative and expository" (Strong, p. 259). He remained head of the school till June 1891. In that year the trustees of Columbia University determined upon a revolutionary change of policy, involving the adoption of the system, then in vogue at Harvard Law School, of studying law by considering principles as evolved from decided cases, i. e., the "case system." This was the antipodes of the method which he had successfully pursued for thirty-three years, and he accordingly resigned, being, however, appointed professor emeritus. The tradition of his teaching was perpetuated in the establishment of the New York Law School under the auspices of former pupils, with his colleague, George Chase, as dean.

His interests had not been confined to the Co-

lumbia Law School, and for years he was an active figure in state matters. In 1866 he and E. C. Wines were appointed a committee to examine the prison systems of the state of New York and the following year they published a *Report on the Prisons and Reformatories of the United States and Canada,* which was replete with valuable suggestions. In 1867 he was a delegate to the state constitutional convention and served upon its judiciary committee. He took a prominent part in the municipal reform movement in New York City consequent upon the operations of the Tweed Ring, and in 1873 was chairman of the legislative committee of the Committee of Seventy. In the same year he was appointed by Gov. Dix a member of the commission of appeals, which assisted the New York court of appeals in disposing of its badly congested cause list, and in this capacity his all-round legal learning showed to great advantage. Maintaining his interest in prison reform and social well-being, he became vice-president of the state board of public charities and president of the state Prison Association, and in 1878 was state commissioner to the International Prison Congress at Stockholm. In his early days at Columbia he had been associated as referee or counsel with important testamentary litigation, particularly the Rose and Hoyt Will Cases. In 1886 he was retained as counsel for five professors at Andover Theological Seminary against whom complaints of heterodoxy had been made, and the display of learning, historical and legal, in his argument on their behalf was impressive. His appearances as counsel were rare, however, and only in exceptional cases. There was a theoretical cast to his mind and an absence of the practical which would have been a serious obstacle to successful practise (Strong, *post*). In addition to a number of academic addresses which were later issued in pamphlet form, he published: *Cases Extracted from the Reports of the Commissioners of Charities, in England, and from the Calendars in Chancery* (1863); *James Harrington and his Influence upon American Political Institutions and Political Thought* (1887); and an Introduction to Maine's *Ancient Law,* prefixed to the first American edition of that work (1864). For a number of years he was associate editor of the *American Law Register,* and he was legal editor of *Johnson's Cyclopædia of Literature and Science,* contributing many articles thereto.

Of large build, five feet ten inches in height, with broad shoulders and florid complexion, he was dignified but not distant in manner. Sympathetic, courteous, and always accessible, he possessed a singularly attractive personality, and his influence over his pupils, during their academic careers and in after life, was extraordinary. He was married, on Aug. 24, 1847, to Mary Bond, daughter of Asa Olmstead of Clinton, N. Y. His death occurred in Clinton.

[N. Y. Geneal. and Biog. Record, Jan. 1886; W. W. Spooner, Historic Families of America (n.d.); B. W. Dwight, The Hist. of the Descendants of John Dwight of Dedham, Mass. (1874), I, 189; Theron G. Strong, Landmarks of a Lawyer's Lifetime (1914), p. 259; In Memoriam Theodore William Dwight (n.d.); Case and Comment, Apr. 1900; N. Y. Times, N. Y. Tribune, June 30, 1892.] H. W. H. K.

DWIGHT, THOMAS (Oct. 13, 1843–Sept. 9, 1911), anatomist of Boston, son of Thomas Dwight by his wife, Mary Collins Warren, daughter of —— John Collins Warren, *primus* [*q.v.*], was born in Boston. As a child he was taken abroad and attended school in Paris until about the age of twelve when he returned to complete his education in Boston. He entered Harvard College with the class of 1866, but after two years transferred to the Harvard Medical School where he obtained his degree of M.D. in 1867; he did not take his A.B. degree until 1872 when it was received as of the class of 1866. After completing his work at the medical school he again spent some time abroad, studying natural history and anatomy, and while in the laboratory of Rüdinger of Munich he learned the technique of examining frozen microscopical sections, which he introduced into the United States on his return. Between 1872 and 1877 he held instructorships in comparative anatomy and in histology at the Harvard Medical School, and a professorship of anatomy at Bowdoin from 1873 to 1876; he also served during the years 1873–78 as editor of the *Boston Medical and Surgical Journal*. In 1880 he again accepted an anatomical instructorship at Harvard, and three years later succeeded to the Parkman Professorship of Anatomy in the place of Oliver Wendell Holmes [*q.v.*], retaining this position until his death in 1911. He was president of the Association of American Anatomists in 1894, and was a member of the editorial board of the *American Journal of Anatomy* from its founding. For a number of years he practised surgery in Boston, being surgeon to out-patients at the Boston City Hospital (1877–80), visiting surgeon of the Carney Hospital (1876–83) and president of the staff of the Carney Hospital (1883–98). In 1900 he retired from active surgical work in order to devote his entire time to anatomical research and teaching.

Dwight was deeply interested in the minutiæ of human anatomy, and his chief contributions related to his meticulous studies of the anatomical variations of the skeleton and joints. He collected a notable series of specimens showing the chief variations of certain of the bones of the feet and hands (carpus, tarsus, and cuboid) and described a new element in the foot, the intercuneiform bone. Through his activity many additions were made to the Warren Pathological Museum of the Harvard Medical School. As a teacher he was forceful and eventually popular, though at first the task of filling the chair vacated by Holmes proved difficult. Throughout his life Dwight was an ardent follower of the Roman Catholic faith and supported actively such societies as the St. Thomas Aquinas Academy of Philosophy and Medicine of Rome and the Society of St. Vincent de Paul, of which he was vice-president in 1884 and president in 1887. His study of the variations of the human skeleton had led him to consider the problem of heredity, and he attempted, just before his death, to harmonize the theories of evolution and heredity with the teachings of the Church of Rome. His book, *Thoughts of a Catholic Anatomist*, the proof-sheets of which he corrected during his last illness, was published in 1911, just before his death. His devotion and loyalty to his creed were outstanding in his life and influenced his point of view and his scientific opinions. A list of his numerous anatomical papers is to be found in the *Index Catalogue* of the Surgeon General's Library. His most important contributions were: his Boylston Prize Essay, *The Intracranial Circulation* (1867); *The Structure and Action of Striated Muscle Fibers* (1873); *The Anatomy of the Head, with . . . Plates Representing Frozen Sections* (1876); *Frozen Sections of a Child* (1881); *Description of the Human Spine Showing Numerical Variations* (1901); *Notes on the Dissection and Brain of the Chimpanzee "Gumbo"* (1895); and his chapters in G. A. Piersol's *Anatomy* (1911) on bones and joints, and on the gastro-pulmonary system and accessory organs of nutrition.

[Articles by John Warren in Anatomical Record, Nov. 1911, and Boston Medic. and Surgic. Jour., Aug. 14, 1919, the first including a bibliography of Dwight's publications, the second reprinted in H. A. Kelly and W. L. Burrage, Am. Medic. Biogs. (1920); Boston Medic. and Surgic. Jour., Sept. 21, 1911; Jour. Am. Medic. Asso., Sept. 23, 1911; T. F. Harrington, The Harvard Medic. School (1905), III, 1415.] J.F.F.

DWIGHT, TIMOTHY (May 14, 1752–Jan. 11, 1817), Congregational divine, author, president of Yale College from 1795 to 1817, and throughout these years the dominant figure in the established order of Connecticut, was born in Northampton, Mass., a descendant of John Dwight who came from Dedham, England, in

1635 and settled in Dedham, Mass. His father, Major Timothy, was a successful merchant and the proprietor of a considerable estate. Some light is thrown on his character by the fact that although a graduate of Yale and destined for the law, he "had such extreme sensibility to the beauty and sweetness of always doing right, . . . and regarded the legal profession as so full of temptations to doing wrong, in great degrees or small," that he preferred not to be a lawyer (Benjamin W. Dwight, *History of the Descendants of John Dwight of Dedham, Mass.*, 1874, I, 130). His conscientiousness was indirectly the cause of his death. As judge of probate he had sworn fealty to the Crown, and therefore felt himself debarred from taking any part in the Revolution. To escape the situation to which his scruples gave rise, he bought part of a Crown grant to his deceased brother-in-law, Phineas Lyman, in West Florida, and, with the latter's widow and children and two of his own sons, in 1776 he went to take possession of it. In this unhealthful region he died June 10, 1777, although news of the fact did not reach his family in Northampton until a year later. Six feet and four inches tall and well proportioned, he was by actual test as strong as an ox. In contrast, his wife, Mary, daughter of Jonathan Edwards, was so petite that, according to tradition, he could hold her at arm's length on the palm of his hand. She bore him thirteen children, of whom Timothy was the first-born.

Mary Edwards Dwight was a woman of remarkable character and mental ability. At her death Timothy said that he owed all that he was to her, although in this statement he was not quite fair to his father to whom some of his spiritual traits, as well as his physical stature, may certainly be attributed. She was but seventeen years old at his birth, but almost from the cradle she proceeded to educate him according to ideas of her own. He early displayed a tenacious memory, acquisitiveness, and determination. He learned the alphabet in one lesson, and by the time he was four he was reading the Bible with ease and correctness. When he was six years old he was sent to grammar school, where, contrary to the wishes of his father, who thought him too young, and without the knowledge of his master, he acquired familiarity with Latin by studying the books of the other boys while they were at play. Had the school not been discontinued, he would have been ready for college at the age of eight. His mother continued his instruction, which was supplemented by a short period of schooling under Rev. Enoch Huntington of Middletown, Conn., and at thirteen he entered Yale,

having already done much of the work of the first two college years. He graduated in 1769, sharing highest honors with Nathan Strong, and at once became principal of the Hopkins Grammar School, New Haven, returning to Yale in 1771 to remain six years as tutor.

During the first half of his college course he seems to have been guilty of some of the ordinary frailties of humanity, card playing especially, but having reached the mature age of fifteen, he was converted to a more serious view of life, and his native ambition to make a conquest of all knowledge took full possession of him. A resolve to devote fourteen hours a day to study was rigorously kept, and although the college schedule began at 5:30 winters, and at 4:30 summers, he was up an hour earlier reading by candle light. He thus laid the foundation for an affection of the eyes, which subjected him to suffering and limitation for the remainder of his life. While a tutor, in order not to have to take time for exercise, he reduced his eating until his dinners consisted of twelve mouthfuls, asceticism which resulted in a physical breakdown. He recuperated by walking upward of 2,000 miles and riding on horseback 3,000 more, thus beginning the peregrinations and observations, the fruits of which appeared later in records of much value. In 1774 he united with the college church, and soon gave up his original intention to become a lawyer, and turned to theology. The conventional subjects of the day were not his only interest, however. He made a study of sacred music and wrote several anthems. With his fellow tutors, Joseph Howe and John Trumbull, he developed an interest in literature, composition, and oratory at Yale, and sought to broaden its curriculum. Upon receiving his master's degree in 1772 he delivered *A Dissertation on the History, Eloquence, and Poetry of the Bible* which was published that same year. To this literary interest at Yale may be traced the origin of the school known as the "Connecticut" or "Hartford Wits," of which Dwight was one of the most prolific members—a school devoted to the cultivation of belles-lettres, and ambitious to give to America a worthy body of poetry. As a tutor he was noted for his skill as an administrator and was extraordinarily popular. When in 1777 Naphtali Daggett resigned as president *pro tem.*, the students wanted Dwight appointed president. That others also had him in mind is revealed by the appointee, Dr. Stiles, who records: "I have heard of but one Gentleman that disapproves the Choice . . . and he is Hon. Col. Davenport of Stanford a Gent. of Learning & great Merit. He says the Corpora have done wrong in electing me; they should have chosen Mr. Tutor Dwight" (F. B. Dexter, *The Literary Diary of Ezra Stiles,* 1901, II, 231). Before leaving Yale Dwight broke an old tradition by marrying while a tutor, taking for his wife, Mar. 3, 1777, Mary, daughter of Benjamin Woolsey.

His resignation, September 1777, was due to the war. The preceding June he had been licensed to preach by a committee of the Northern Association of Massachusetts, and on Oct. 6, Congress appointed him chaplain of Gen. S. H. Parson's Connecticut Continental Brigade, and he soon joined the army at West Point. He threw himself into the work of instructing and inspiring the soldiery with his characteristic vigor, and according to tradition with notable practical results. He also wrote patriotic songs which became popular in the army, among them "Columbia, Columbia, to glory arise."

The death of his father and the necessity of taking charge of the family affairs in Northampton, compelled him to resign, Jan. 28, 1779 (F. B. Heitman, *Historical Register of Officers of the Continental Army,* 1914). The next five years spent in this Massachusetts town were full of strenuous and varied labors. He ran two large farms, constantly supplied churches, and established a school for both sexes which attracted so many students that he had to employ two assistants. He also became prominent in political affairs, representing his town in county conventions and in 1781 and 1782 in the state legislature, where his activities won him such favor that his friends wished to nominate him for the Continental Congress. Had he been willing to abandon the ministry for public life, he would undoubtedly have risen high. Calls came to him to settle over churches in the vicinity of Boston, which he declined. Connecticut attracted him more, and on July 20, 1783, he accepted an invitation to the pastorate of the Congregational church at Greenfield Hill, where on Nov. 5, he was ordained.

During his twelve years here his fame as an educator, preacher, author, and man of affairs spread. Again he established a school for both sexes to which, in addition to many other enterprises, he gave six hours a day. It became widely and justly celebrated, drawing its students from the Middle and Southern states as well as from New England. Approximately a thousand pupils were educated by him, many of them in all the studies of the college curriculum. Among the clergy his learning and force of character speedily gave him leadership. In 1785 *The Conquest of Canaan,* written several years before, was published, the first epic poem, according to the au-

thor, to appear in America. It consists of eleven books in rhymed pentameters, and was an audacious attempt to give the New World an epic such as the *Iliad* was to Greece, and the *Æneid,* to Rome. The Bible story is told with such changes as suited the writer's purpose, and interjected are allusions to contemporary characters and events. It is unbearably tedious to the modern reader, but increased Dwight's prestige, was republished in England in 1788, and was charitably reviewed by Cowper in the *Analytical Review* (III, 1789, 531). A second ambitious work, *Greenfield Hill,* appeared in 1794. In form imitative of eighteenth-century English poets, it describes the scenery, history, and social conditions of the country, and has the patriotic purpose of contributing to the moral improvement of the author's countrymen and of demonstrating to Europeans that America offers the makings for a native poetry of interest and excellence. A rigid Calvinist and a stanch Federalist, Dwight exerted all his personal influence, intellectual equipment, and literary ability against the rising tide of democracy and infidelity, the two being in his mind synonymous; a warfare which he was to continue with a stubborn closed-mindedness for the remainder of his life. He took up the weapon of satire and published, *The Triumph of Infidelity, a Poem* (1788), dedicated to "Mons. de Voltaire," in which he uncorks vials of abuse. Satire was not one of Dwight's gifts. "Probably there can now be left for us on this planet few spectacles more provocative of the melancholy and pallid form of mirth, than that presented by those laborious efforts of the Reverend Timothy Dwight to be facetious at the expense of David Hume, or to slay the dreadful Monsieur de Voltaire in a duel of irony" (Moses Coit Tyler, *Three Men of Letters,* 1895, p. 92). His own religious, social, and political views are set forth in sermons and addresses, among which are: *A Discourse on the Genuineness, and Authenticity of the New Testament* (1794); *The True Means of Establishing Public Happiness* (n.d.), delivered July 7, 1795; *The Nature, and Danger, of Infidel Philosophy* (1798); *The Duty of Americans, at the Present Crisis* (1798), and in Fast Day discourses delivered in 1812. At the request of the citizens of New Haven, on Feb. 22, 1800, he gave an address on Washington, with whom he had personal acquaintance, which was published that same year under the title: *Discourse . . . on the Character of George Washington, Esq.* After the duel between his cousin, Aaron Burr, and Hamilton he preached a sermon on the *Folly, Guilt, and Mischiefs of Duelling* (1805).

The height of his ambition was perhaps achieved when on June 25, 1795, a few weeks after the sudden death of Ezra Stiles, Dwight, having just declined a call to the presidency of Union College, was elected president of Yale. That he was ambitious for position and power he himself confessed shortly before his death. "Particularly," he says, "I have coveted reputation, and influence, to a degree which I am unable to justify." (Sereno E. Dwight's Memoir prefixed to T. Dwight's *Theology*, p. xliii). President Stiles, who had an extreme dislike for Dwight, accusing him of decoying students from Yale for his schools, and suspecting him of trying to undermine him in his own position, also states: "He meditates great Things & nothing but great things will serve him—& every Thing that comes in the Way of his preferment must fall before him. Aut Cæsar, aut nullus" (Dexter, *ante*, II, 531). For more than twenty-one years he administered the college with great ability, exerted an influence over the students such as few presidents achieve, instructed the senior class in rhetoric, logic, metaphysics, and ethics, acted as professor of theology, supplied the college pulpit, gave counsel of weight in the affairs of state, and was altogether the most conspicuous figure in New England. The unregenerate dubbed him "Pope Dwight," while the children of the elect were taught to regard him as second only to St. Paul.

His real greatness has been questioned. Even some of his contemporaries had difficulty in accounting for the exalted place he held in public regard. An admirer, S. G. Goodrich, admits that his greatness was not that of genius and that he was only a man of large common sense and a large heart, inspired by high moral principles, a "Yankee, Christian gentleman—nothing more—nothing less" (*Recollections of a Lifetime*, 1856, I, 355). Unquestionably he had serious limitations. His outlook was narrow; his views of life, his political and social doctrines, all his judgments and all that he wrote, were determined or colored by his theological system. He had a little of the bigotry and uncharitableness of Puritanism at its worst. His literary work was without originality, and of all his poetry, so laboriously constructed, the only bit now generally known is the hymn, "I love thy Kingdom, Lord." Theologically he belonged to the school of his grandfather, Jonathan Edwards, but here he displayed some independence. His views are set forth in a series of sermons, repeated every four years at Yale, that all the students might hear them, and published after his death, *Theology, Explained and Defended* (5 vols., 1818–19), pop-

ular in America and abroad. (For analysis of his system, see Williston Walker, *A History of the Congregational Churches in the United States*, 1894, pp. 301–03). His one work which is likely to survive is *Travels in New England and New York* (1821–22), in four sizable volumes, written to record how "New England appeared, or to my own eye would have appeared, eighty or a hundred years before," and to refute foreign misrepresentations of America. It is an astonishingly varied collection of descriptions of natural scenery, agricultural, political, religious, and social conditions, including historical, biographical, and statistical information, and is interlarded with shrewd practical comments.

"On account of his noble person," Goodrich was persuaded, "the perfection of the visible man —he exercised a power in his day and generation somewhat beyond the natural scope of his mental endowments" (*ante*, I, 353). In appearance "he was about six feet in height, and of a full, round, manly form. His head was modeled rather for beauty than craniological display. . . . Dr. Dwight had, in fact, no bumps : I have never seen a smoother, rounder pate than his, which being slightly bald and close shorn, was easily examined. He had, however, a noble aspect—a full forehead and piercing black eyes though partly covered up with large spectacles in a tortoise-shell frame. . . . His voice was one of the finest I have ever heard from the pulpit—clear, hearty, sympathetic—and entering into the soul like the middle notes of an organ" (*Ibid.*, I, 348–49). Dwight's reputation and influence, however, were not due to his looks and manner alone. They are to be attributed in part to his mental equipment. He had a tenacious memory, a wide range of interests, and capacity for keen and minute observation. His mind was stored with a wealth of information on the most diverse subjects. He could talk intelligently with men in almost every walk of life, and frequently demonstrated that he knew how to do a job better than those whose business it was. Forced, because of the condition of his eyes, to depend upon amanuenses, such was his power of concentration that he could dictate to several at one time, turning from one to the other and unaided beginning where he had stopped. With all else he also had sound judgment and common sense. In certain aspects of character, moreover, he was great. However open to criticism his social and political views, he displayed a noble devotion to his country's interests, and no one ever doubted his religious integrity. He had disciplined himself to inflexible conformity to duty, and his industry, perseverance, and self-command came well up to the height of human possibilities. Any one who could accomplish what he did, so handicapped as to be unable to use his eyes for close work for but a short time each day, forced often to get up in the night and walk miles to gain relief from intense pain, compelled to compose both prose and poetry through dictation, and finally keep on his way with fortitude through slow death from cancer, had in him the stuff that compels admiration. By all, too, he was conceded to have been a great teacher. He probably came nearer to exemplifying what the name Mark Hopkins symbolizes than did Hopkins himself. He not only inspired the interest of his students in the studies he taught, but he made his class-work a means of enriching them out of his own great stock of general knowledge, so that to be under him alone was a liberal education. As a college president he had qualities which would have given him high rank in any generation, and from his administration Yale dates her modern era. He made the faculty in cooperation with the president a part of the college government; abolished obsolete customs and methods of discipline; gathered about him able instructors; encouraged the teaching of science; established a medical department, and contemplated the establishment of theological and law departments. His interest in the extension of education and religion led him to give much thought and labor to the founding of institutions which have had permanence and wide influence. He was one of the projectors of Andover Theological Seminary; of the Misssionary Society of Connecticut; and of the American Board of Commissioners for Foreign Missions. His whole life in fact was devoted to great interests, and if he was the personification of the "venerable *status quo*," an exemplifier of Connecticut Puritanism, he was also the personification of all that was finest in it.

[F. B. Dexter, *Biog. Sketches Grads. Yale Coll.*, vol. III (1903) gives list of publications and a copious bibliography. See also Dexter, *Sketch of the Hist. of Yale Univ.* (1887), and "Student Life at Yale under the first President Dwight" in *Proc. Am. Antiquarian Soc.*, Oct. 1917; W. B. Sprague, "Life of Timothy Dwight" in Jared Sparks, *The Lib. of Am. Biog.*, 2 ser., IV (1845), 225–364; Henry A. Beers, *The Conn. Wits and Other Essays* (1920); Vernon L. Parrington, *The Conn. Wits* (1926), and *Main Currents in Am. Thought: The Colonial Mind* (1927); *Cambridge Hist. of Am. Lit.*, vols. I and II (1917–18); M. A. DeWolfe Howe, *Classic Shades* (1928); R. J. Purcell, *Conn. in Transition* (1918); Frank H. Foster, *A Genetic Hist. of the New Eng. Theology* (1907); A. P. Stokes, *Memorials of Eminent Yale Men* (1914), esp. vol. I; J. B. Reynolds, S. H. Fisher, H. B. Wright, *Two Centuries of Christian Activity at Yale* (1901).]　　　　　H.E.S.

DWIGHT, TIMOTHY (Nov. 16, 1828–May 26, 1916), Congregational clergyman, educator, president of Yale University, was born in Norwich, Conn., of a family noted for its achievements in literary and academic fields. His grandfather, Timothy [*q.v.*], one of the "Hartford Wits," and himself president of Yale for twenty-two years, was a grandson of Jonathan Edwards. The younger Timothy's father, James Dwight, although a successful business man, had the family taste for study. To his mother, however, Susan Breed, a woman of unusual intellectual power, Timothy felt himself above all indebted. "I owed more to her," he says, "in the matter of the awakening of my mental enthusiasm than to any or all the teachers of my childhood and youth" ("How I was Educated," *Forum*, November 1886, p. 251). She was a descendant of Allen Breed, who came to this country and settled at Lynn, Mass., about 1630, and the daughter of John McLaren and Rebecca (Walker) Breed, the former a lawyer, mayor of Norwich, and noted for enterprise, benevolence, and public spirit. Because his mother believed in home education, Timothy did not attend school until he was eleven years old, when he entered the academy in Norwich conducted by Calvin Tracy. He finished his preparation for college at the Hopkins Grammar School, New Haven, where his mother had gone that she might be with her sons during their period of study; entered Yale at the age of seventeen, although he was sufficiently prepared a year earlier; and graduated in 1849.

From boyhood he had looked forward to the life of a Congregational minister, and he was licensed to preach, May 22, 1855, and ordained, Sept. 15, 1861. It was to be his fortune, however, to spend his days in academic surroundings. His sermons were chiefly occasional. A volume of these, most of them preached to Yale students, was published in 1899, under the title, *Thoughts of and for the Inner Life*. From 1849 to 1851, having won the Clark Scholarship for the student who passed the best examination on the studies of the college course, he did graduate work at Yale. He then filled the office of tutor for four years, his fair-mindedness, tact, and humor making him extraordinarily popular. For the first two years of this period he was also enrolled in the Divinity School, where, after study at Bonn and Berlin (1856–58), he was appointed assistant professor of sacred literature, becoming full professor in 1861. On Dec. 31, 1866, he married Jane Wakeman Skinner of New Haven. He was an excellent New Testament scholar according to the standards of the time, and his accuracy and good sense were of much service to the American committee on the revision of the Bible, of which he was a member from 1873 to 1885. He also edited (1884–87) several volumes of the English translation of H. A. W. Meyer's commentaries on the books of the New Testament, and published in 1886 a translation with additional notes of Godet's *Commentary on the Gospel of John.* During his professorship the Divinity School was practically refounded. It was a task requiring great faith, wisdom, courage, and hard work. To all these Dwight contributed more perhaps than any one else.

In 1886 he succeeded Noah Porter as president of the college. From 1866 he had been one of the editors of the *New Englander,* and in 1870–71 had published in it a series of five articles on "Yale College—Some Thoughts Respecting its Future." The recommendations he had there made, he now proceeded to put into execution. An act was secured from the legislature authorizing the title "University"; the various schools were reconstructed and coördinated; and the college became a university in fact. The institution needed more money and buildings. The president did not personally solicit funds, but made clear the opportunity that was offered. He himself turned back his salary into the treasury, and from his inherited fortune contributed more, until the total amounted to over $100,000. He also undertook the duties of treasurer for a period, and supplied the college pulpit. The needed funds came, and the University had great expansion. At the age of seventy he resigned with the remark that he "proposed to do so while he still knew enough to know that he ought to." He was a genial, lovable, modest man, thoroughly human, capable of delightful flashes of humor, intensely practical, and displaying throughout his career indomitable faith and devotion to duty. Besides a number of addresses he published *Memories of Yale Life and Men, 1845–1899* (1903), which contains much autobiographical material.

[Autobiographical articles may be found in the *Forum*, Nov. 1886 and Jan. 1891. See also B. W. Dwight, *The Hist. of the Descendants of John Dwight of Dedham, Mass.* (1874), vol. I; *Timothy Dwight, President of Yale Univ. 1886–99, Memorial Addresses* (1917); *Who's Who in America*, 1916–17; *Record of the Graduated Members of the Class of 1849 of Yale Coll., Prepared for the Quarter Century Meeting* . . . 1874 (1875); *Obit. Record, Grads. Yale Univ.*, 1916; *Congregational Year-Book* (1916); *Outlook*, June 7, 1916.]

H.E.S.

DWIGHT, WILLIAM (July 14, 1831–Apr. 21, 1888), manufacturer, soldier, a descendant of John Dwight who helped to settle Dedham, Mass., in 1635, was born at Springfield, Mass., the son of William Dwight and Elizabeth Amelia, daughter of Daniel Appleton White. Three of his brothers became soldiers and two, railroad executives. He went from a private military school to West Point in 1849, but resigned in

1853 before graduation. He engaged in manufacturing, probably of cotton, first at Boston, then at Philadelphia. On Jan. 1, 1856, he married Anna Robeson. Upon the outbreak of the Civil War he entered the military service and was commissioned captain in the 13th United States Infantry in May 1861. The next month he was appointed lieutenant-colonel of the 70th New York Volunteers, of which D. E. Sickles was colonel. Upon the promotion of Sickles, Dwight became colonel in July 1861. At the battle of Williamsburg, May 5, 1862, he was wounded three times and left for dead upon the field. After a short sojourn in a Confederate prison hospital he was exchanged and commissioned brigadier-general, for gallantry at Williamsburg. Dwight's brigade was the first of Grover's division of Banks's army. He led it creditably in the campaigns about Baton Rouge, Bayou Têche, and Irish Bend in the spring of 1863, and through the siege of Port Hudson. It participated in the first assault upon the Confederate works, May 24, and led the attack upon one wing in the final attempt, June 14, to carry Port Hudson by storm. Dwight was a member of the commission which arranged for the surrender of Port Hudson, July 8. After the Texas expedition in the autumn of 1863, he was appointed chief of staff to Banks for the Red River expedition of the following year. In July 1864 he was transferred to the command of the 1st Division of the XIX Corps of Sheridan's army in Virginia. This division was described as "capable and well-disciplined." Winchester, Fisher's Hill, and Cedar Mountain were the chief engagements in which it participated. Dwight remained in the army until January 1866, when he removed to Cincinnati and associated himself with his brothers Daniel and Charles in the management of the White Water Valley Railroad. His death occurred in Boston.

[B. W. Dwight, *The Hist. of the Descendants of John Dwight of Dedham, Mass.* (1874); *Appletons' Ann. Cyc.*, 1888; *Official Records (Army)*, ser. 1 and 2; F. Phisterer, *N. Y. in the War of the Rebellion* (3rd ed., 1912); Edward Bacon, *Among the Cotton Thieves* (1867); M. L. Bonham, Jr., "Man & Nature at Port Hudson, 1863, 1917" in *Military Historian and Economist*, Oct. 1917, Jan. 1918.]

M.L.B.,Jr.

DYAR, HARRISON GRAY (Feb. 14, 1866–Jan. 21, 1929), entomologist, was born in New York City, the son of Harrison Gray Dyar and Eleonora Rosella Hannum. Both parents were of colonial descent, the American advent of the families dating from 1632 on the father's side and from 1677 on the mother's. He attended the Roxbury Latin School, and in 1889 took his bachelor's degree at the Massachusetts Institute of

Technology. He had been interested in general biology and especially in the study of insects from the age of nineteen; in 1892 he returned to Boston and took the last year of the biology course of the Massachusetts Institute under William T. Sedgwick and spent the summer at the Woods Hole Laboratory of Marine Biology. He then went to Columbia University, where he received his master's degree in 1894. His thesis, published in the *Annals of the New York Academy of Sciences* of May 1894, was an important paper on the classification of Lepidopterous larvæ which, from its originality and scope, established his reputation as an entomologist. His doctoral thesis, published in the same *Annals* for November 1895, was based upon bacteriological work and was entitled "On Certain Bacteria from the Air of New York City." This work was largely done under Dr. T. Mitchell Prudden, whom he assisted in the bacteriological laboratory of the College of Physicians and Surgeons. His main interest, however, continued to be in entomology, and in 1897 he was invited to Washington to fill an honorary position in the United States National Museum. This invitation he accepted, and became custodian of the Lepidoptera, a position he held until his death. After the death of William H. Ashmead [*q.v.*] in 1908, Dyar was placed in charge of the whole of the insect collections of the Museum, but held this position for a comparatively short period. He presented his very large private collection to the Museum, and continued his interest in the Lepidoptera for the rest of his life.

His main work, and the one in which he built up a lasting reputation, was with the mosquitoes. In 1901 he became interested in mosquito larvæ and later was associated with the late Frederick Knab and L. O. Howard in the preparation of a four-volume monograph, *The Mosquitoes of North and Central America and the West Indies.* The work on this monograph was supported by the Carnegie Institution of Washington for the years 1903 to 1906, and after that time the authors relied on help from various other sources. Dyar himself was financially independent and was able to make at his own expense many expeditions into out-of-the-way regions. The monograph was finally completed, the first volume being published in 1912 and the last in 1917, and for many years it has been constantly consulted by the entomologists and medical men of many nations. It was published by the Carnegie Institution of Washington. In 1927, the same institution having approved a plan for the preparation and publication of a single additional volume of taxonomic range only, Dyar with tireless energy prepared a monograph, *The Mosquitoes of the Americas,* including the South-American fauna. This volume was published in 1928, shortly before his death.

Dyar was an indefatigable worker, and published during the last thirty years of his life a constant stream of shorter papers, largely of a taxonomic character. In 1913 he started at his own expense a monthly journal which he called *Insecutor Inscitiae Menstruus,* of which fourteen volumes were issued, which was devoted largely to shorter entomological papers, for the most part taxonomic. He was editor of the *Journal of the New York Entomological Society* from 1904 to 1907 and of the *Proceedings of the Entomological Society of Washington* from 1909 to 1912. In 1924 he was commissioned captain in the Sanitary Department of the Officers' Reserve Corps of the army. He was twice married: on Oct. 14, 1889, to Zella Peabody, and on Apr. 26, 1921, to Wellesca Pollock Allen. He died in Washington, D. C.

[Biog. sketch by L. O. Howard, in *Science,* Feb. 8, 1929, repr. in *Technology Rev.,* July 1929; J. M. Cattell, *Am. Men of Science* (4th ed., 1927); *Who's Who in America,* 1928–29.]   L.O.H.

DYE, WILLIAM McENTYRE (February 1831–Nov. 13, 1899), soldier, staff officer of the Egyptian army, military adviser to Korea, was born in Pennsylvania. On July 1, 1853, he was graduated from the United States Military Academy as brevet lieutenant with a standing above the middle of his class. He had been appointed to West Point from Mansfield, Ohio, where his guardian was a John McCullough. Before the Civil War he served both on garrison duty and on the frontier, with regular promotions. In August 1862 he went to the front as colonel of the 20th Iowa Volunteers, and in the campaigns of the next year served in Missouri and Arkansas. For bravery at Vicksburg he was made brevet major in the regular army, and for gallantry and skill in handling a brigade in the Red River campaign of 1864 he was brevetted lieutenant-colonel. In September 1864 he commanded a brigade during the campaign against Mobile, and later served as assistant provost-marshal-general of Kansas, Nebraska, Colorado, and Dakota. On Mar. 13, 1865, he received the brevets of colonel in the regular army and brigadier-general in the volunteer army for gallant and meritorious service throughout the war. On July 8, 1865, he was mustered out of the volunteers, and on Jan. 14, 1866, was promoted to major and assigned to the 4th Infantry. The quiet life of an officer in time of peace was not to his taste, however, and he was honorably discharged from the army at his own request, Sept. 30, 1870.

On Feb. 18, 1864, he had married Ellen A. Rucker, the daughter of a Chicago judge, and after his resignation from the army he took his family to Marion, Ia., where he engaged in farming. He had one son and two daughters. Though he had a great fondness for agriculture as a hobby, it did not possess the romance of adventure, and when the opportunity came, in 1873, he went to Egypt with other American officers to join the staff of the Egyptian army. Later in 1875 he became assistant to the chief of staff, Gen. C. P. Stone, in the army of Khedive Ismail Pasha in the campaign against Abyssinia, where he was wounded. He returned to New York in June 1878. Two years later he published an account of his adventures under the title of *Moslem Egypt and Christian Abyssinia, or Military Service Under the Khedive* (1880).

After his return to the United States, he served for several years as chief of police of Washington, D. C.; but in 1888 adventure called again and he made haste to answer. Korea had been open to Americans since 1883, and the king of that country had urged the American government to send military advisers to organize his army on modern lines. Since Congress failed to pass legislation for the appointment of officers from the regular army, on the recommendation of Gen. Sheridan, Dye went to Korea in 1888 to become chief military adviser to the Korean government. His duties consisted chiefly in conducting a military academy for the training of Korean officers. He made a careful study of military systems, evolved a series of maneuvers best suited to Korean conditions and to command in a foreign tongue, and later published in the Korean language a small treatise on military tactics. His troops were so well trained as to arouse the commendation of visiting American naval officers, but he was immeasurably handicapped by the failure of Korean officials to cooperate with him and by the impossibility of holding Korean noblemen to strict military discipline. His influence extended only to a small portion of the army, while the rest of it was subject to numerous conflicting influences, both native and foreign. After the beginning of the Sino-Japanese war his men and their arms were tampered with, and when certain Japanese and Koreans murdered the Queen of Korea on Oct. 8, 1895, very few of Dye's men stayed to give their lives for their queen. Until the coming of Russian influence in the spring of 1896, the Korean king retained Dye as a sort of personal body guard. After the Russians came into power they took charge of the

army and the general was appointed by His Majesty to supervise the government experiment farm, where he had an opportunity to put his hobby into practical effect. From 1895 to 1898 he wrote a series of six articles on agricultural subjects for the *Korean Repository*. His last relations with the Korean government were marred by controversies over salary. On May 5, 1899, he left Seoul for Muskegon, Mich., where he was confined to his bed until his death in November. He had suffered severely with dysentery for many years.

[Documents concerning Dye's life in Korea may be found in the archives of the Dept. of State and in the archives of the former American legation in Seoul, Korea. There is a biographical sketch in *Thirty-first Ann. Reunion, Asso. Grads. U. S. Mil. Acad.* (1900). See also G. W. Cullum, *Biog. Reg.* (3rd ed., 1891); F. B. Heitman, *Hist. Reg. and Dict. U. S. Army* (1903); Edythe J. R. Whitley, *Hist. of the Rucker Family and Their Descendants* (1927); *Evening Star* (Washington), Nov. 14, 1899.]   H.J.N.

DYER, ALEXANDER BRYDIE (Jan. 10, 1815–May 20, 1874), soldier, was born in Richmond, Va., the son of William Hay and Margaret (Brydie) Dyer. Graduated from the United States Military Academy at West Point, July 1, 1837, and promoted to second lieutenant, 3rd Artillery, he was assigned to duty at Fort Monroe, Va., and served in the Florida War of 1837–38. Upon the enlargement of the Ordnance Corps he was transferred to that body in 1838, and served in various ordnance establishments until the outbreak of the Mexican War, when he was assigned to duty as chief of ordnance of the army invading New Mexico. In this campaign he was brevetted a captain "for gallant and meritorious conduct." He was engaged in the actions of Canada, Pueblo de Taos, and Santa Cruz de Rosales, and was wounded on Feb. 4, 1847. He was promoted captain in the Ordnance Corps, Mar. 3, 1853, after fourteen years' continuous service. At the outbreak of the Civil War, though he was a native Virginian, he remained loyal to the Union. On Aug. 21, 1861, he was assigned to the command of the National Armory, at Springfield, Mass., not without opposition, however, as some entertained misgivings of his loyalty. Later when Congress met, the question was raised of the advisability of permitting a Southerner to hold a position of such responsibility, involving, perhaps, the fate of the nation. All suspicions were soon dispelled, however, by the evidence of his tireless industry, and the efficiency with which he administered his new command. He entered at once upon his difficult task with systematic energy and excellent judgment. Workshops were reorganized, grounds enlarged, and buildings erected, thousands of mechanics were employed, and the production of the National Armory was increased to 1,000 rifles a day.

On Mar. 3, 1863, Dyer was promoted major, Ordnance Corps, and the following year, Sept. 12, 1864, was appointed chief of ordnance, United States army, with the rank of brigadier-general. Before he left Springfield to assume his duties at Washington, 3,000 employees of the armory presented him with an address offering him their congratulations for "the well deserved mark of public confidence" just bestowed upon him by his promotion to the head of his department, and assuring him that the termination of his late command was "a source of deep personal grief, and the end of official relations characterized by uninterrupted harmony and kindly feelings." The tremendous task, which the necessities of the nation imposed upon him as chief of ordnance, that of providing the Union armies with munitions of war, required his most watchful care and greatest efforts. His administration of the Ordnance Department won for him the admiration and respect of his fellow officers. He had, however, difficulties with inventors and dishonest contractors, who, failing to gain their ends, were embittered against him and his department, and finally carried their grievances to Congress. He asked for a court martial, which was refused, and then asked for a court of inquiry, which was granted. The inquiry, which was long and thorough, not only exonerated him but held him up as an example worthy of the imitation of all army officers. He was brevetted major-general, United States army, Mar. 13, 1865, for "faithful, meritorious, and distinguished services in the Ordnance Department during the Rebellion." Dyer invented a projectile for cannon which he offered to and which was accepted by the government. He was offered a large royalty on this projectile but refused it, preferring to give his invention to the country. He was married to Elizabeth Allen, on Feb. 6, 1840, and had six children. He was a man of generous and genial temper, of unaffected simplicity, candor, and dignity, and above all of uncompromising integrity. He retained the office of chief of ordnance until his death.

[G. W. Cullum, *Biog. Reg.* (3rd ed., 1891); *Jour. of the Mil. Service Institution,* Sept. 1894; T. H. Price, *The Dyer Family* (1906); *Evening Star* (Washington), May 22, 1874; records in the Adjutant-General's Office, Washington, D. C.]   C.F.C—y.

DYER, ELIPHALET (Sept. 14, 1721–May 13, 1807), jurist, was descended from Thomas Dyer, a cloth manufacturer of Shepton Mallet, Somersetshire, England, who in 1632 arrived in Boston and settled in Weymouth, Mass., where he was prominent in public life. His grandson, Col. Thomas Dyer of Windham, Conn., married Lydia, daughter of John Backus, and their son, Eliphalet, was born at Windham. He graduated at Yale College in 1740, then studied law, and having been admitted to practise before the Connecticut courts in 1746, opened an office in Windham, which remained his home during the whole of his life. Taking a lively interest in public affairs, he was in 1747 elected to represent his district in the General Assembly of which he remained a member by repeated reëlections for fifteen years. Becoming known as a capable and industrious lawyer he soon acquired a good practise, though he devoted much of his time to other interests. In 1753 he was prominent in the organization of the Susquehannah Company, the object of which was to found a Connecticut settlement in the Wyoming Valley, west of the province of New York; and he was a member of the committee which purchased the necessary lands from the Six Nations in 1754. Further progress was blocked by the outbreak of war between England and France and in August 1755 he was appointed lieutenant-colonel of a Connecticut regiment, taking part in the Crown Point operations. In 1758 he commanded a regiment in the expedition which was directed against Canada in that year. In 1762 he was elected a member of the governor's council, a position which he retained for twenty-two years. In 1763 the Wyoming land scheme again came to the front, settlers having commenced to take possession and the proprietaries of Pennsylvania having put forward an adverse claim under a previous Crown grant to William Penn of the area involved. In consequence of this Dyer was sent to England as agent of the Susquehannah Company to procure a confirmation of the title acquired from the Indians, but he was unsuccessful. After his return, he took a prominent part in the rising opposition to the colonial policy of the British government and was a Connecticut delegate to the Stamp Act Congress of 1765. In 1766 he was elected an associate judge of the superior court of Connecticut, continuing, after his elevation to the bench, in close association with the leaders of the colonial cause. In the meantime, efforts were made to settle the Wyoming controversy, and he visited Philadelphia twice with this object in view, going in June 1769 as agent of the Susquehannah Company and in October 1773 as one of three commissioners appointed in that behalf by the Connecticut legislature, but nothing was effected. In 1774 he was appointed delegate from Connecticut to the First Continental

Congress, and in 1775 was a member of the first Connecticut Committee of Safety. Throughout the Revolutionary period he rendered valuable services, acting as a member of Congress and attending the Hartford Convention in 1780 as one of the Connecticut commissioners. He had in 1776 declined an appointment as brigadier-general in the Continental Army, considering that he could serve the cause more effectually in Congress than in the field. In 1781 the dispute as to the Wyoming land title finally came before Congress, and a board of commissioners was appointed to settle the question of jurisdiction as between Pennsylvania and Connecticut. At its session, which was held at Trenton, N. J., Nov. 12, 1782, Dyer appeared as counsel for Connecticut, and after a hearing extending to forty-one judicial days, a unanimous decision was rendered to Connecticut. In 1789 he became chief justice of Connecticut and held that office till 1793. On leaving the bench he retired into private life, residing at Windham till his death. He married Huldah, daughter of Col. Jabez Bowen of Providence, R. I.

John Adams said of him: "Dyer is long winded and roundabout, obscure and cloudy, very talkative and very tedious, yet an honest worthy man, means and judges well." Another side of his character is exhibited in the record of expenses incurred by him as congressman in 1777 as rendered to and paid by Connecticut (*The Connecticut Magazine,* Jan.–Mar. 1906), which shows that he did not despise the good things of life.

[W. L. Weaver, *Hist. of Ancient Windham* (1864), p. 61 ; Cornelia C. Joy-Dyer, *Some Records of the Dyer Family* (1884) ; G. H. Hollister, *Hist. of Conn.* (1857), esp. p. 632 ; J. W. Barker, *Conn. Hist. Colls.* (1856), p. 447 ; F. B. Dexter, *Biog. Sketches Grads. Yale Coll.,* vol. I (1885).]   H. W. H. K.

DYER, ISADORE (Nov. 2, 1865–Oct. 12, 1920), physician, was born in Galveston, Tex., the son of Isadore Dyer, a native of Dessau, Germany, and his wife, Amelia Ann Lewis. After graduation at the Sheffield Scientific School of Yale (Ph.B., 1887), he began the study of medicine at the University of Virginia, but after a year there matriculated at Tulane University where he received his M.D. in 1889. His interneship was at the New York Skin and Cancer Hospital (1890–92) and in 1891 he was, in addition, lecturer at the Post Graduate Medical School. A part of 1892 was spent in graduate study in Paris and London. He became associate professor of dermatology at the Tulane University of Louisiana in 1905, was promoted to professor in 1908, and in that year was made dean: positions which he occupied until his death. From 1892

until its absorption by Tulane, he was also professor of diseases of the skin at the New Orleans Polyclinic. At the outset of his practise in New Orleans he began his life-long interest in leprosy, and not only accomplished much in the treatment of the disease, but also in the proper protection and care of its victims. In 1894 he founded and became president of the first board of control of the Louisiana Leper Home, later to become the National Leprosarium. In 1905 he married Mercedes Louise Percival of Havana, Cuba. His interest in the military service began in 1908 when he was commissioned first lieutenant in the newly organized Medical Reserve Corps of the army. He served on various examining boards from time to time and three days after the entrance of the United States into the World War was made a major. For a time he was inspector and later on duty in the Surgeon-General's Office, War Department. In 1919 he was commissioned colonel in the Reserve. He was a successful dermatologist and one of the foremost leprologists of his time, his contributions to the literature on this malady being very extensive. He was the author of more than a hundred papers on diseases of the skin, medical biography, and essays, some of which were collected in *The Art of Medicine and Other Addresses, Papers, etc.* (1913). He was editor of the *New Orleans Medical and Surgical Journal* from 1896 until his death and co-editor of the *American Journal of Tropical Diseases and Preventive Medicine* (1914–16). He was a man of great native ability and of diversified talents and culture, being internationally recognized not only as a specialist in his chosen field but also as an educator, an executive, and a philanthropist. He was a leader of medical thought and successful as an organizer of scientific and civic bodies. He was a charter member of the National Board of Medical Examiners, a body in which he took great interest as a pioneer in the standardization of medical education. He was a delegate to the International Leprosy Conference in Berlin (1897) and the Brussels Conference on Prophylaxis of Venereal Diseases (1899).

[*Southern Medic. Jour.,* XVIII (1925), 15 ; *Who's Who in America,* 1920–21 ; *Medic. Record,* XCVIII (1920), 740 ; *New Orleans Medic. and Surgic. Jour.,* LXXIII (1920–21), 157–59 ; *Am. Jour. Trop. Med.,* II (1922), 173 ; *Yale Univ. Obit. Record,* 1921 ; *New Orleans Times-Picayune,* Oct. 13, 1920 ; Records of the Dean's Office, Tulane Univ.]   E. E. H.

DYER, LOUIS (Sept. 30, 1851–July 20, 1908), classical scholar, writer, and lecturer, was born in Chicago, Ill., the son of Charles Volney Dyer, M.D., and Louisa Maria (Gifford) Dyer. His father was descended from William and Mary

Dyer [*q.v.*], who came from Somersetshire to Boston in 1635, became adherents of Mrs. Hutchinson, and were driven from Massachusetts Bay to Rhode Island, where they joined the Society of Friends. Charles Dyer practised medicine in Newark, N. J., in New York, and in Chicago, and was prominent in the anti-slavery movement and active in the work of the "Underground Railroad." In 1862 President Lincoln appointed him judge for the United States in the Anglo-American Mixed Court at Sierra Leone. Louis Dyer's independent habit of thinking, his quiet and efficient friendliness, and his interest in social problems, undoubtedly derived from these antecedents. Educated by private tutors in Geneva and near Lyons, he entered first the University of Chicago (1867), then the University of Munich, and finally the sophomore class at Harvard (September 1871). Older than most undergraduates, and matured by extensive travel, he was none the less liked by his classmates, and interested himself in many college activities. At graduation (June 1874) he obtained highest honors in classics. Entering Balliol College, Oxford, in the autumn of 1874, he won the Taylorian Scholarship for proficiency in Italian, and studied there until February 1877, when the illness of his father required his return to Chicago. He became tutor in Greek at Harvard, and in 1881 assistant professor of Greek, a post which he held until June 1887. During this period he published: *A Consideration of the Use of Form in Teaching* (1881); *The Greek Question and Answer* (1884); and an excellent edition of Plato's *Apology and Crito* (1886). After 1887 his life was spent mostly in Oxford, where he had been given the B.A. degree in 1878. In December 1889, he returned to Boston to deliver eight lectures in the Lowell Institute course, later published under the title *Studies of the Gods in Greece at Certain Sanctuaries Recently Excavated* (1891).

In 1893 he was made master of arts at Oxford, and appointed lecturer in German and French at Balliol; he was examiner of schools for the Oxford and Cambridge Schools Examination Committee. In 1893 he published *An Introduction to the Study of Political Economy,* translated from the Italian of Luigi Cossa. During the year 1895–96 he was acting professor of Greek at Cornell University, and in 1899 he delivered three lectures on Machiavelli before the Royal Institution of Great Britain, later published as *Machiavelli and the Modern State* (1904). In 1899 also he contributed to *Notes and Queries for Somerset and Dorset* a series of notes on the career of his ancestor, under the title, "William

Dyer, a Somerset Royalist in New England." Returning to the United States, he delivered in 1900 the Hearst Lectures on Greek art in the University of California, visiting, in the next year, many of the American universities, where he lectured on Mycenæ and Cnossus. *Oxford as it is,* published in 1902, was a small but useful volume for the guidance of Rhodes scholars. In 1904 he became a member of a committee of the Oxford Congregation interested in the maintenance of Greek as a compulsory requirement in the university. At the same time he engaged in the work of promoting the Egypt Exploration Fund, which was to yield papyri of inestimable worth, and he was also a prominent member of the council of the Hellenic Society. In all these enterprises his activities were untiring and fruitful. He married, in London (Nov. 23, 1889), Margaret Anne Macmillan, daughter of the publisher, Alexander Macmillan. In June 1890, he purchased Sunbury Lodge, which thereafter became known in Oxford as a center from which radiated kindness, hospitality, and helpfulness, "one of the first places to which cultivated American visitors in England turned, and where they met sympathetic Oxford colleagues." There he was the recognized intermediary between the university and the young American students who began to flock to Oxford under the Rhodes Foundation.

As a classical scholar, Dyer had read widely and with fine appreciation the literatures of Greece and Rome, and his exposition of them was enriched by illustrations from many modern writers of different tongues. His work as a teacher was sound and enduring. He contributed many reviews, letters, and articles to the *Nation* (N. Y.), *Athenæum, Classical Review, Journal of Hellenic Studies,* and *Harvard Studies in Classical Philology*; he preferred, however, to sacrifice further achievement as a scholar to the making of human contacts at Oxford, and his diversity of interests, the warmth of his enthusiasm for the young student's development, his devotion to social work connected with his church or with the succor of neglected children, drew friends to him wherever he went. Domestic affliction, which would have distracted lesser men, never closed his door to the service of others. Gifted with a wide knowledge of men and things, with a joyous wit and humor, and sweetness of disposition, he possessed a charm that few or none could resist.

[*Ninth Report of the Class Secretary of the Class of 1874,* Harvard Univ. (1909), pp. 34–37; *Harvard Coll. Class of 1874, Fiftieth Anniversary, Eleventh Report* (1924), pp. 91–95; *Educational Rev.,* Sept. 1908; *Na-*

tion (N. Y.), July 23, Oct. 15, 1908; London *Times*, July 21, 1908.]   C. B. G.

DYER, MARY (d. June 1, 1660), Quaker martyr, was the wife of William Dyer of Somersetshire, England, with whom she came to Massachusetts probably in 1635. According to Gov. Winthrop, Mrs. Dyer was "a very proper and fair woman" (*post*, I, 266), and both she and her husband were well educated and apparently of good family. On Dec. 13, 1635, they became members of Mr. Wilson's church in Boston. During the Antinomian controversy their open sympathy with Mrs. Anne Hutchinson and the Rev. John Wheelwright [*qq.v.*] alienated them from their orthodox neighbors. In November 1637 Dyer was disenfranchised and subsequently disarmed because of his support of Wheelwright, and later, when Mrs. Hutchinson was expelled from the church, Mary Dyer accompanied her as she withdrew from the assemblage. Rumors set afloat following this act, to the effect that Mary's still-born child of which she had been delivered the previous October was "a monster," subjected her to painful notoriety as an object of divine displeasure. From the hostile atmosphere of Boston the Dyers moved to Rhode Island, where in March 1638 William Dyer was among the founders of Portsmouth and where he became a man of consequence. Mary Dyer went to England in 1650 and was joined there the following year by her husband, sent on Colony business. He returned to Newport leaving her in England where she remained until 1657, meantime becoming a Quaker. Passing through Boston on her return to Rhode Island, she was arrested and imprisoned but released upon her husband's entreaty. In 1658 she was expelled from New Haven for preaching Quakerism. The next year, when certain Quakers were imprisoned in Boston, she went to visit them and to "bear witness to her faith," and was again imprisoned. Banished on Sept. 12, 1659, she returned to Rhode Island, but in the next month went back to visit other imprisoned Quakers at Boston, was seized by the authorities, and on Oct. 27 was condemned to be hanged. At the last moment, on petition of her son William, captain of a coasting vessel, she was reprieved and sent back to Rhode Island (Louis Dyer in *Notes and Queries*, December 1899). She again returned to Boston on the 21st of the following May, was again imprisoned and condemned to death, and finally, in spite of the supplications of her husband, she was hanged on the first day of June. When offered her life if she would leave Massachusetts and return no more she said: "Nay, I cannot; for in obedience to the will of the Lord God I came, and in His will I abide faithful to the death." A number of distinguished American families trace their descent to her through one or another of her seven children.

[Horatio Rogers, *Mary Dyer . . . the Quaker Martyr* (1896); C. C. Joy-Dyer, *Some Records of the Dyer Family* (1884); R. M. Jones, *The Quakers in the Am. Colonies* (1911); Geo. Bishop, *New England Judged not by Man's, but by the Spirit of the Lord* (1661, 1667); John Whiting, *A Call from Death to Life* (1660) and *Truth and Innocency Defended* (1702); Jos. Besse, *A Collection of the Sufferings of the People called Quakers* (2 vols., 1753); *Winthrop's Jour.* (2 vols., 1908), ed. by J. K. Hosmer; *Records of the Governor and Company of the Mass. Bay in New England* (1853–54), vol. IV, pt. 1; Louis Dyer, "Wm. Dyer, A Somerset Royalist in New England," in *Notes and Queries for Somerset and Dorset*, June, Sept., Dec. 1899.]   J. T. A.

DYER, NEHEMIAH MAYO (Feb. 19, 1839–Jan. 27, 1910), naval officer, was born at Provincetown, Mass., to Henry and Sally (Mayo) Dyer. He was educated in the local public schools, but being a true product of a seafaring town, soon turned to a nautical life. At the age of fifteen he entered the merchant marine. In 1861 he enlisted in the 13th Massachusetts Volunteers but on Apr. 4, 1862, he transferred to the volunteer navy as acting master's mate. About a year later (May 18, 1863) he was made an acting ensign and appointed to command the *Eugénie,* used for blockade work off Mobile. On Jan. 12, 1864, he was promoted to acting master and later this same year was assigned to the *Metacomet,* in which he participated in the battle of Mobile Bay, receiving in person the surrender of the Confederate ship *Selma.* After serving on the *Hartford,* Farragut's flagship, he was ordered North to command the *Rodolph.* After the close of the Civil War, he was one of the few volunteer officers to be retained. He was commissioned lieutenant on Mar. 12, 1868, and ordered to the *Dacotah* of the South Pacific Squadron. On Dec. 18, 1868, he was advanced to the grade of lieutenant-commander and ordered to command the *Cyane,* which was due to proceed to Alaska. In 1870, while on the *Ossippee,* he saved a sailor from drowning and for this act was given a medal and publicly thanked by his commanding officer. For several years thereafter, he performed the various duties to which a line officer is subject, including work at the Torpedo School at Newport in 1873 and lighthouse inspection in 1883. Dyer was advanced to the full grade of commander on Apr. 23, 1883, and after being lighthouse inspector for four years, he was ordered to command the *Marion* at an Asiatic station until 1890. He took the course at the Naval War College in 1894. On July 13, 1897, he was given his captaincy, and in October of the same year was placed in command of the *Baltimore*. After the outbreak of the Spanish-American War, he and his ship were in Dewey's squadron in the Philippines and participated in the battle of Manila Bay, May 1, 1898. For his conduct in this battle, he was advanced seven numbers in rank. His official report to Admiral Dewey shows some of the difficulties under which he worked (*House Document No. 3, 55* Cong., 3 Sess., pp. 78–79). The citizens of Baltimore presented him with a magnificent gold sword as a token of their esteem. He served throughout the war, and in 1900 was ordered to the Navy Yard at Boston. On Feb. 19, 1901, he was retired with the rank of rear-admiral. His services were duly recognized by the United States nearly twenty years later when on Apr. 13, 1918, the torpedo-boat destroyer *Dyer* was launched. After his retirement he took up his residence at Melrose, Mass. He kept up his interest in naval matters in his connection with the Massachusetts Nautical Training School, and in 1903 and 1904, he was chairman of the board of commissioners of this famous school. Perhaps he took this opportunity of passing on to posterity the love of the sea that he had developed, for he never married and had no sons to follow in their father's footsteps.

[*Who's Who in America*, 1908–09; Navy Register, 1863–97; L. R. Hamersly, *The Records of Living Officers of the U. S. Navy and Marine Corps* (7th ed., 1902); *U. S. Army and Navy Jour.*, Feb. 5, 1910; *Official Records (Navy)*, 1 ser., vols. XVII, XX, XXI, XXII; R. W. Neeser, *Ship Names of the U. S. Navy* (1921), p. 71; *Boston Post* and *Boston Jour.*, Jan. 28, 1910.]
        A. R. B.

DYLANDER, JOHN (*c.* 1709–Nov. 2, 1741), Lutheran clergyman, was assistant pastor at Börstil, Sweden, in 1737 when he was appointed by Archbishop Steuchius and the Consistory of Upsala to succeed Gabriel Falck as pastor of the Swedish Lutheran congregation at Wicacoa, Pa. (now Southwark, Philadelphia). Accompanied by William Malander of Rosland, a student of theology, he sailed from Stockholm on July 13 and landed at Philadelphia on Nov. 2. Four days later he was installed by his compatriot, the Rev. Peter Tranberg, as pastor of Gloria Dei Church. His ministry, though of only four years' duration, left a deep impression not only on his own people but on his English and German neighbors. Whereas most of the Swedish pastors regarded themselves as merely sojourning in America, Dylander identified himself with the country by marrying a daughter of the merchant, Peter Koch (Kock, Cook). He restored the discipline and finances of his congregation, catalogued the church library, which consisted

of thirteen folio and thirty-three quarto volumes of substantial Lutheran theology and church history, and established a fund for the relief of the poor. Holding that his duty extended to all whom he had strength to serve, he ministered in their own language to the Germans at Philadelphia, Germantown, and Lancaster, and with astonishing rapidity learned to preach acceptably in English. He often delivered as many as sixteen sermons a week. In his own church, for more than a year, it was his practise to have a service at 8 a. m. in German, the main service in Swedish, and vespers in English. It was the fashion for couples to come to Gloria Dei Church to be married by him; one English clergyman, alarmed by the inroads thus made in his perquisites, complained vainly to the governor to have the practise stopped. Peter Kalm, the famous Swedish naturalist, records that he found Dylander everywhere beloved. In 1741 Benjamin Franklin published a tract for him entitled *Free Grace in Truth: The XXIVth Meditation of Dr. John Gerhard Translated from Latin into English, with Notes for the Better Understanding of the Author's Meaning*. On the authorization of the Upsala Consistory he and Tranberg arranged to ordain Malander on Nov. 2, 1741, but on that very day Dylander died. He was buried under the chancel of his church.

[Pehr Kalm, *En Resa til Norra America* (Stockholm, 1756), translated by J. R. Forster as *Travels into North America* (2nd ed., London, 1772); Israel Acrelius, *Beskrifning om de Swenska Församlingars* (Stockholm, 1759), translated by W. M. Reynolds as *Hist. of New Sweden* (Phila., 1874); C. R. Hildeburn, *A Century of Printing: Issues of the Press in Pa. 1685–1784* (1885), Item 700; A. L. Gräbner, *Geschichte der Lutherischen Kirche in America* (St. Louis, 1892).]
        G. H. G.

DYMOND, JOHN (May 3, 1836–Mar. 5, 1922), Louisiana sugar-planter, inventor, editor, was born in Canada, a son of Richard and Anne (Hawkens) Dymond, Cornish emigrants. Richard Dymond was for a time a Methodist preacher and later a merchant. In John's childhood the family moved to Zanesville, Ohio. He was educated in the public schools, Zanesville Academy, and Bartlett's College, Cincinnati, worked for a time in his father's store, dabbled in cotton manufacturing, and in the spring of 1860 went to New York, where he at once secured a position as a traveling salesman. In 1862 he was married to Nancy Elizabeth Cassidy of Zanesville. In 1863 he became a broker in New York, in the firm of Dymond & Lally, which three years later opened a branch house in New Orleans and did a tremendous business in Louisiana sugar and molasses as well as in imported sugar and coffee. In the autumn of 1868 the firm purchased the "Belair" and "Fairview" sugar plantations on the Mississippi River, thirty miles below New Orleans, and Dymond began his career as a planter, gradually withdrawing from his city business. In the autumn of 1877 he led the movement resulting in the creation of the Louisiana Sugar Planter's Association, and from 1887 to 1897 was its president. He was one of the leaders in urging the expediency of research work in the culture and manufacture of sugar. This agitation culminated in the organization of the Louisiana Scientific Agricultural Association, of which he was president until his death, and in the establishment of the Audubon Sugar Experiment Station. When in 1888 the sugar-planters of New Orleans, in an endeavor to save the sugar industry from many preventable losses, formed a corporation to publish *The Louisiana Planter and Sugar Manufacturer,* Dymond was chosen as managing editor as well as general manager and president, and served for thirty-four years. He was quick to grasp new ideas in labor-saving devices and in processes, and to aid in their development. The only time in his life that he visited a moving-picture show was when he went to see the interesting picture of a new machine for harvesting sugar-cane. Conspicuous among the devices he helped introduce were the Mallon stubble digger and the McDonald hydraulics; and among the processes, double and triple milling in grinding the cane, the redivivus or multiple effect evaporation, and the so-called dry-vacuum in vacuum boiling. He installed the first nine-roller mill ever erected in Louisiana; patented a sulphur machine, the shelf or cascade machine, which is now in use everywhere; was the first man in the sugar world to weigh sugar-cane received at the mill as the basis for a comprehensive system of cost determination; and was also the first to purchase cane at the mill by weight. With the Hon. Henry McCall he was placed in charge of the experiments in diffusion conducted in the later eighties at Gov. Warmoth's Magnolia Plantation by Norman J. Colman [*q.v.*], then United States commissioner of agriculture. Inventors of new appliances of every sort for use in the sugar factory or in the field always received from him cordial interest and an opportunity to make at "Belair" such trials and experiments as they might wish to conduct. Louisiana then led the sugar world in industrial progress, and many distinguished men from distant lands came there to investigate and study. No visitor to the state ever went away without seeing Dymond at "Belair."

In 1888 he was a delegate to the National Democratic Convention and a member of the platform committee, where he energetically op-

posed extreme free-trade ideas. When, in September 1894, at a meeting of sugar-planters in New Orleans, the Lily White movement was inaugurated in protest against the Wilson-Gorman tariff act and the planters voted to go into a White Republican party, Dymond, as a protectionist and old-fashioned Democrat, cast the only dissenting vote. He was also involved in local politics, serving as president to the police jury of Plaquemines Parish and as chief executive on Levee Boards. In 1890 he became seriously interested in the anti-lottery movement and was the business manager of the party organ, the *New Delta.* He carried his parish against the lottery, and as president of its police jury declined the proffered gift of $3,000 of lottery money for the maintenance of the public levees during the high-water season of 1891. He was active in the campaign that led to the election of the anti-lottery candidates, Edward D. White and Murphy J. Foster, as United States senator and governor of Louisiana, respectively. In 1892 he sat in the legislature as representative from his parish, which had been under negro control since the Civil War. In 1896 the parish still had a negro sheriff and a negro clerk of the court, but under Dymond's lead white men were elected to all the parish offices, and he himself was reëlected to the legislature. He represented his parish in the state constitutional convention of 1898 and in the state Democratic convention of 1899, and was four times elected state senator, declining reëlection in 1920 on account of failing health.

After the burning of his "Belair" sugar house in 1907 and the sale of two of his large plantations, he gradually turned his attention to other industries. In New Orleans, where he resided most of the time, he edited the *Southern Farmer* and the *Trade Index of New Orleans,* and published *The Louisiana Planter and Sugar Manufacturer, El Mundo Azucarero,* and the *Lower Coast Gazette.* He was a member of the Unitarian church from boyhood, and was honorary president of the First Unitarian Church of New Orleans at the time of his death. He was buried in New Orleans.

[A brief biography, presumably contributed by Dymond, in Alceé Fortier, *Louisiana* (1914), III, 139-43; files of the *Proc. La. Sugar Planter's Asso.,* and the annual *La. Sugar Report,* both ed. by A. Bouchereau; files of *La. Planter and Sugar Manufacturer* and obituary in the issue of Mar. 11, 1922; annual *Reports* of the U. S. Commissioner of Agriculture, especially those for the years 1885-89; obituary and editorial estimate in the New Orleans *Times-Picayune,* Mar. 6 and 7, 1922.]

W. P.

DYOTT, THOMAS W. (1771–Jan. 17, 1861), patent medicine king, glass manufacturer, welfare worker, temperance advocate, came to Philadelphia from England in the nineties with a few shillings in his pocket. He was of Scotch-English parentage, and had been a druggist's apprentice and clerk in London. Renting a small room and basement in Philadelphia, he commenced polishing boots in the day time, and making liquid shoe-blacking at night and was soon selling all of the blacking that he could produce. Saving his earnings, he opened a drug-store and prospered. He soon became the largest maker and dealer in patent medicines in the country, advertising these nostrums and establishing agencies for the wares in remote frontier settlements. He used quantities of glass containers of various sizes and shapes for his drugs and medicines and eventually became an agent for several Pennsylvania and New Jersey glass houses making bottles, window-glass, chemical and "philosophical" apparatus, which he retailed at his drug-store. In 1833 Dyott purchased the Kensington Glass Works, established in 1771 by Robert Towars and James Leacock, buying it from the sons of James Rowland, and also took over an adjacent plant near Gunner's Run, the two properties covering between 300 and 400 acres along the Delaware River. He expanded the factories and was soon making five grades of glass in five separate furnaces. Nearly 450 hands, including 100 apprentices, were employed at the glass works. There were fifty different factory buildings on the premises, besides wharves, docks and farm buildings. Dyott improved the grade of bottle-glass, undersold importations, employed expert mold designers and chippers, and impressed more of his containers with his name, or that of the factory, than any other American glass manufacturer. Many sizes and shapes of bottles were manufactured, the fame of the Kensington output resting, from the glass collector's standpoint, on the fanciful and historical flasks decorated with ships, locomotives, trees, flags, various agricultural and symbolical devices, or with the likenesses of celebrities, including Dyott himself.

At this period of his life, success went to the head of "Dr." Dyott (he had appropriated the title "M.D." as was a custom of patent-medicine men of that era). He adopted an extravagant manner of living and a fantastic form of dress, and considered himself quite a personage. A unique community life was established at the glass works, which was called "Dyottville" and "Temperanceville," and no liquor was allowed upon the premises, although his patent nostrums contained a large percentage of alcohol. The man aimed at combining "mental and moral with manual labor." A twelve-month operating schedule

was inaugurated for the first time in the United States, and Dyottville became largely self-supporting, with artisans and farmers, a medical department containing a sick-room, a library, a singing-school, concerts, games, and recreational sports. Life was regulated with precision—a rising bell at daylight, stated hours for baths, crackers and biscuits served during working intermission, supper followed by an hour of leisure, night-school, and prayers. The younger folk were in bed by 8:30 p. m., and at 9:30 p. m. the gates of Dyottville were shut. Discipline, although strict, was nevertheless kindly, and the moral tone of the community high.

The versatile Dyott published *The Democratic Herald* for a time and issued a monthly advertising sheet. He was the author of a treatise called *An Exposition of the System of Moral and Mental Labor Established at the Glass Factory of Dyottville* (1833), and he opened "The Manual Labor Bank," an unchartered institution, maintained entirely upon his personal credit. His philanthropic ideas, however, were his undoing. In 1836 the Schuylkill Bank became financially involved and closed its doors; Dyott could then obtain no specie with which to pay his notes, and after his personal resources became completely exhausted, he failed, and the works were closed. He was indicted for fraudulent insolvency, found guilty, and sentenced to the Eastern State Penitentiary in 1837, but was pardoned before the expiration of his term. After release from prison, he went back to his drug-store, and again acquired considerable wealth. His death occurred in his ninetieth year.

[Jos. D. Weeks, "Reports on the Manufacture of Glass" (1874), in *House Misc. Doc. No. 42, pt. 2, 47 Cong., 2 Sess.*; Carmita de Solms Jones, in *Bull. Pa. Museum*, vol. XXII (1926); Charles Messer Stow, "Dr. Thos. W. Dyott—Welfare Worker in the Glass Industry," in *Boston Transcript*, July 23, 1927; Rhea Mansfield Knittle, *Early Am. Glass* (1927), ch. xviii; *Press* (Phila.), Jan. 19, 1861.]   R. M. K.

EADS, JAMES BUCHANAN (May 23, 1820– Mar. 8, 1887), engineer, inventor, was born in Lawrenceburg, Ind., the son of Thomas C. and Ann (Buchanan) Eads. His forebears were English and Irish gentlefolk, the Eads having settled first in Maryland, while his mother's people hailed from Ireland. Thomas Eads was a merchant but never a very prosperous one, and in the hope of bettering his condition periodically moved from one town to another. When James was three years old the family moved to Cincinnati; when he was nine, to Louisville; and when he was thirteen, finally settled in St. Louis, Mo. His schooling ceased here because of the immediate necessity of helping to support the family. He first peddled apples on the street, but in a short time entered the dry-goods store of Williams & Durings as clerk, and through the kindness of Mr. Williams spent most of his spare time in the latter's library. Five years later, in 1838, he became a purser on a Mississippi River steamboat. In this work he had the opportunity to satisfy somewhat his boyish interest in machinery and also to recognize the economic importance of reducing the heavy losses in boats and cargoes. For three years, therefore, while steaming up and down between St. Louis and New Orleans, he concentrated his attention on the invention of a diving bell. He patented it, and in 1842 gave up his purser's job and formed a partnership to engage in steamboat salvaging. The business was successful from the start. Eads personally supervised every job and was as often on the river bottom within his diving bell as on the bell tender. He continued in this work for three years and then sold his interest, married, and organized a glass manufactory in St. Louis, the first west of the Ohio River. This venture proved to be a failure, and Eads found himself in 1848 in debt to the amount of $25,000. With $1,500 advanced by his creditors, he then returned to the wrecking business and by 1857 had not only paid off his indebtedness but also had amassed a fortune which enabled him to give up an occupation requiring almost continual absence from home. During his twelve years on the river he had become more and more interested in the study of the laws which governed its flow and determined its deposits, and had become thoroughly satisfied in his own mind as to the proper manner of combating the destructive action not only of the Mississippi but of all rivers. As early as 1856 he proposed to Congress to remove all snags and wrecks from the Mississippi, Missouri, Arkansas, and Ohio rivers and to keep their channels open for a term of years, but the bill authorizing such action died in the Senate.

From 1857 to 1861 Eads lived in semi-retirement in the happy environment of his family, even indulging in a trip to Europe. In the latter year, however, he was summoned to Washington by President Lincoln to advise with him upon the best methods of utilizing the western rivers for attack and defense. He proposed a fleet of armor-plated, steam-propelled gunboats, of special construction to ward off shell fire, and when the government advertised for bids he submitted one in which he contracted to construct seven of these vessels of 600 tons each, ready for armament in sixty-five days. It was the contract of a bold and self-reliant man and seemingly impossible of execution in view of the existing chaotic industrial conditions; but within two weeks, over four thousand men, scattered all over the country, were engaged in various details of construction, and in forty-five days the first of the seven gunboats, the *St. Louis,* with her boilers and engines aboard, was launched. The other six followed in quick succession, while an eighth—one of Ead's wrecking boats—was rebuilt to incorporate his steam-operated gun mounting. In the course of the war he constructed fourteen armored gunboats, incorporating several new ordnance inventions which he patented; converted seven transports into what were called "tin-clads"; and built four heavy mortar boats, all of which were in active service. His was a most heroic undertaking, and before it was completed his health became seriously impaired, but his indomitable spirit pulled him through, and by 1865 he was again physically fit.

In that year a bill was introduced into Congress authorizing the construction of a bridge across the Mississippi at St. Louis. When the bill was passed it was amended so as to call for a 500-foot centre span and fifty feet of clearance. The project was thought to be impracticable and was so pronounced by a group of twenty-seven of the leading civil engineers in the country. Eads, however, who had been selected by one of the construction companies as its engineer, thought otherwise; and when his plan was finally approved in 1867 he proceeded with the construction of the bridge and successfully completed it in 1874. It is of steel and masonry construction and its center span is 520 feet long. The base of one pier is 136 feet below high water and was sunk through ninety feet of sand and gravel to bedrock. The conditions encountered during the construction were so extraordinary in many respects that only an inventive genius such as Eads possessed could provide the many appliances needed for the subaqueous work and for the superstructure. Known to-day as "Eads Bridge," it is still greatly admired.

Hardly had this work been completed when, in February 1874, Eads made a formal proposition to Congress to open one of the mouths of the Mississippi River into the Gulf and maintain the channel, agreeing to do it at the sole risk of himself and his associates. The proposition was attacked chiefly by army engineers, but after a considerable fight the proposal was accepted, Eads's work to be confined, however, to the small South Pass. Here he had his most desired opportunity to apply his knowledge of the river's currents, and by a system of jetties so arranged that the river deposited its sediments where he wanted them, he successfully accomplished the task four years later, in 1879. This achievement placed him in the foremost rank of hydraulic engineers as his great bridge had placed him in the first rank of bridge engineers. His papers, addresses, and communications to Congress and to the technical magazines, newspapers, and societies during his work at the South Pass are probably unsurpassed in value as engineering expositions on controlling the flow of water, the movements and dispositions of sediment, and the correct methods of river improvement.

The year this work was finished the first meeting of the Panama Canal Congress was held. Eads was opposed to a canal and conceived the idea of a ship railway. He selected the shortest possible route between the two oceans, by way of the Tehuantepec Isthmus, two thousand miles shorter than the Panama route, and from 1880 until his death he worked energetically for such a project. He appeared in Congress and replied to Count De Lesseps who advocated the canal. He obtained a valuable concession from the Mexican government for building the railway and proposed to Congress to build it at his own expense, provided the government would guarantee a dividend of six per cent for fifteen years when it had been proven practical. A bill embodying his suggestion passed the House but failed in the Senate. In 1885 he introduced a new bill in Congress, modified as a result of additional concessions granted by Mexico, and he spent considerable time in Washington for the next two years doing what he could to bring about passage of the bill. His health was far from good, however, and on the advice of physicians, in January 1887 he went to Nassau, Bahama Islands, where he died three months later.

Eads was an engineer of international reputation; his advice was sought not only by many municipalities in the United States but by foreign governments as well. He made plans for the improvement of the harbor of Toronto; advised on improvements for the harbors of Vera Cruz and Tampico; served in an advisory capacity to the Mersey Docks and Harbor Board of Liverpool, and many others. In 1877 the University of Missouri conferred upon him the honorary degree of LL.D., and in 1884 the British Society for the Encouragement of Art, Manufacture, and Commerce awarded him the Albert Medal "as a token of their appreciation of the services you have rendered to the science of engineering." He was the only American up to that time who had received this award. He was a member of the American Society of Civil Engineers, and vice-president in 1882; a fellow of the American Association for the Advancement of Science; a member of the British Institution of Civil En-

gineers, and of the British Association. Some of his writings, edited by Estill McHenry, were published in 1884 under the title, *Addresses and Papers of James B. Eads*. He was twice married, first to Martha Dillon of St. Louis, who died in 1855 leaving him with two daughters, and two years after her death, to Eunice Eads, the widow of his cousin Elijah, who had three daughters.

[Wm. Sellers, in *Nat. Acad. Sci. Biog. Memoirs,* vol. III (1895); Louis How, *Jas. B. Eads* (1900); sketch by Estill McHenry in *Addresses and Papers,* mentioned above; *Scientific American,* Apr. 23, 1887; *Washington Post, Evening Star* (Washington, D. C.), Mar. 11, 1887; Patent Office records; correspondence with Eads's descendants.]   C. W. M.

EAGELS, JEANNE (June 26, 1894–Oct. 3, 1929), actress, daughter of Edward Eagels, a carpenter, and Julia (Sullivan) Eagels, is said to have been born in Boston and to have moved at the age of two to Kansas City, Mo., but according to her own account (*Who's Who in America,* 1928–29) she was born in Kansas City. Her birth-date has also been given as 1890 (Edward Doherty). At an early age she commenced a stage career, appearing with O. D. Woodward's stock company as Puck in *A Midsummer Night's Dream.* The next eight years she spent touring through small towns of Kansas, Nebraska, and Oklahoma, principally with the Michelson and Levinsky tent company, and playing a wide variety of rôles in such plays as, *For Home and Honor, The Octoroon, Uncle Tom's Cabin,* and *Little Lord Fauntleroy.* Mrs. Eagels, a former school-teacher, accompanied and tutored her daughter, whose public school education had ended abruptly after her first stage appearance. Jeanne's experiences were colorful and exciting during this apprenticeship of barnstorming in cabooses.

Her facility at impersonating famous actresses of the day, a talent she always feared, brought her to the attention of Anna Held, who was greatly impressed by the slight, gawky girl, with her long yellow hair and gray eyes. In 1911 she came to New York and in a few weeks was engaged for a small part in *Jumping Jupiter,* a musical show. Her second part was Olga Cook in The *"Mind-the-Paint"* Girl, at the Lyceum in 1912. Her beauty caused Florenz Ziegfeld to offer her a place in the chorus of the *Follies* at $150 a week, but although she was receiving only $35 she declined, saying, "I am a dramatic actress." John Emerson, then in the Frohman offices, gave her the assignment in her second Broadway play, impressed by what she herself termed her "tremendous nerve." The first important part she played was in the Elsie Ferguson rôle of *The Outcast,* when that play went on tour in the season of

1915–16. After this she appeared as George Arliss's leading lady in three plays, and in David Belasco's success, *Daddies*. In 1922 began her four years' engagement, under the management of Sam H. Harris, as Sadie Thompson in *Rain,* one of the outstanding characterizations of the decade. She played her last legitimate stage rôle for Gilbert Miller in *Her Cardboard Lover,* the engagement ending in her suspension for eighteen months by the Actor's Equity Association, in April 1928, because of her failure to appear in the play in Milwaukee and St. Louis. When her tour thus came to a sudden close, she turned over her home at Ossining to her supporting English cast.

She was married to Edward Harris Coy, a former captain of the Yale football team, in August 1925 at the home of Fay Bainter in Stamford, Conn. Their marriage proved happy for a time, but in June 1928 she instituted divorce proceedings in Chicago, charging cruelty. The charges not being contested, she was granted a divorce on July 14. Her frail physique and an extremely nervous condition, which caused her to be treated by a nerve specialist for nine years before her death, were probably responsible for many of the scenes she created. In the summer of 1924, she had hysterics at Southampton when English customs inspectors questioned her. She twice interrupted performances in *Her Cardboard Lover*, once to have a stage door closed, the second time to have a drink of water. Her suspension by Equity and fine of two weeks' salary ($3,600), caused her to enter vaudeville for a time, and then motion pictures. She was the star of *Man, Woman and Sin,* directed by Monta Bell for Metro-Goldwyn Mayer, and of *The Letter* and *Jealousy* for Paramount. She was under contract to the latter company for another dialogue picture when she died at the Park Avenue Hospital, New York City. Her death was ascribed by her personal physician to "a nervous toxic disorder."

George Arliss said of her acting, "She has the vital sense of time." Ambitious and industrious, she told friends when she was being featured by Belasco, "I'm just beginning and this is not enough." During the sensational run of *Rain* for nearly 1,500 performances, she missed but eighteen. It has been said that off the stage she was, "if possible, more consummately the actress than on it" (Brock, *post*). She had a host of friends in the theatrical profession who mourned her death at the height of her career.

[J. B. Kennedy, "Jeanne Eagels," *Collier's Weekly*, Oct. 1, 1927; H. I. Brock, "Her Road from Yesterday," *Personality Mag.*, Mar. 1928; press books of George C. Tyler, David Belasco, Sam H. Harris, and Paramount; Jeanne Eagels, "The Actor is More Important Than the Play," *Theater Mag.*, Jan. 1928; obituaries in *N. Y.*

Times and *Chicago Tribune*, Oct. 4, 1929, and in *N. Y. Herald-Tribune*, Oct. 4, 5, 1929; information secured through the courtesy of Edward Doherty, who at the time this biography was written was preparing a series of articles for publication.]   H. B.

EAKINS, THOMAS (July 25, 1844–June 25, 1916), painter, sculptor, teacher, was born in Philadelphia, where his entire professional life was passed. His paternal grandfather was from the North of Ireland. His father, Benjamin Eakins, was a writing-master, a methodical and deliberate man, whose work as an expert engrosser of manuscripts was in constant demand. A portrait of him by his son, called "The Writing Master," shows him engaged in this kind of work, and is noteworthy for the admirable drawing of the hands, the form and action of which serve to reveal his character. Eakins's mother was Caroline Cowperthwait Eakins. On this side of the family the descent was from English and Dutch stock. As a lad in the Philadelphia high school, Eakins had the reputation of being independent but unobtrusive. An early likeness shows him to have been of a vigorous, determined character, and a portrait taken in middle life further emphasizes these personal traits. On graduation from the high school, he enrolled himself as a student in the Pennsylvania Academy of the Fine Arts, where he obtained a good groundwork for his training as a painter. Then, in 1866, at the age of twenty-two, he sought more advanced instruction in Paris. In the École des Beaux-Arts he came under three instructors, J. L. Gérôme, Léon Bonnat, and the sculptor A. A. Dumont. Spending three years there in arduous study, he became a favorite pupil of that efficient master Gérôme, for whom he had the greatest respect. It was characteristic of him that he should take his work in the school seriously; in fact, so severely did he apply himself that, late in 1869, his health was menaced, and he betook himself to Spain for a rest.

During the seven months that he remained in Spain he painted only two or three pictures and made a few studies. But the most important result of his sojourn was the impression made upon his mind by the great Spanish realists whose works he saw in Madrid, notably Velasquez, Ribera, Goya, and Herrera. There can be no doubt as to the confirmation given by these uncompromising masters to a latent tendency present in the temperament of the young man. He returned to his home in Philadelphia in 1870, the year of the outbreak of the Franco-Prussian War, and there he lived for the rest of his life, busily teaching, lecturing, painting, and making a few pieces of sculpture. Immediately upon his return he began the study of anatomy at the

Jefferson Medical College. This specialty always interested him, and he mastered it with the thoroughness that marked everything to which he directed his attention. It was his knowledge of anatomy that brought him his opportunity to teach in the schools of the Pennsylvania Academy of the Fine Arts in 1873. He became the dean of the faculty of that famous institution, the oldest art school in America, and for many years he was the principal instructor there. When a group of students founded the Art Students' League, they gladly accepted his offer to furnish instruction there also. He was as strong in drawing and perspective as in construction, and he had the happy faculty of making these difficult subjects vitally interesting to his pupils. He worked unsparingly, and in addition to his classes in anatomy, he lectured, painted many portraits, and presently busied himself with certain more elaborate compositions, including two unusually large pictures of surgical clinics,—the "Clinic of Dr. Gross" and the "Clinic of Dr. Agnew."

The first-named work, measuring 96x78 inches, was completed in 1875, and now belongs to the Jefferson Medical College. It was exhibited in Chicago, St. Louis, and Buffalo, and is generally regarded as his masterpiece. Both choice of subject and manner of treatment are indicative of the essentially scientific bent of Eakins's mind. The structure of the body was his lifelong hobby; the strength and the weakness of his art alike arise from this preoccupation. Nothing interested him more than a surgical operation or an autopsy, unless it were a boat-race or a boxing-match. He looked upon the clinic of Dr. Gross with precisely the same professional calm as that of the surgeon, the assistants, and the medical students in the background. The absence of all tension and all dramatic feeling is an unqualified merit, because it is true to the atmosphere of the occasion, and because it corresponds to Eakins's own mental habit. He was always deeply serious, but it would not have been possible for him to be sensational. To his interest in physiology is mainly due his masterly drawing of the human figure in repose or in action, and this is his chief title to distinction.

In the work in question the expression of character is typical of his best efforts. Dr. Gross, occupying the center of the composition, is explaining to the class each successive step in the operation, which is being performed by his colleague, Dr. White. The surgeon, the anesthetician, the nurses, and the students are intent, absorbed, business-like. The light is concentrated on the operating table, the white cloths, the flesh, the instruments, the wound and blood. One feels the momentous nature of the event—what issues of life and death are involved; yet one feels also the impressive atmosphere of expert knowledge, experience, and skill, pervading the scene. Two centuries and a half had passed since Rembrandt, then a young man, painted his "Anatomy Lesson," with much of the same detachment. His work was not more serious than that of Eakins; and it is probably true, as Charles H. Caffin has pointed out, that there is no other painter in America, and few elsewhere, who could have treated the "Clinic of Dr. Gross" at once so realistically and so pictorially. Yet the work was not received with approval; there was no order for it; and it is said that it brought Eakins only $300.

Among the many other pictures by Eakins, which sufficiently illustrate his choice of motives, may be mentioned the huge "Clinic of Dr. Agnew," belonging to the University of Pennsylvania; "Between Rounds" and "Salutat," scenes from the world of Fistiana; the "Pair-Oared Shell" and the "Biglen Brothers Turning the Stakeboat," depicting professional oarsmen in action on the Schuylkill River; and a long series of fishing subjects. In addition to painting, he made a certain number of pieces of sculpture. Two of the reliefs on the battle monument in Trenton, N. J., are from his hand. He modeled the horses ridden by Lincoln and Grant which form a part of the soldiers and sailors monument in Brooklyn, N. Y. He also collaborated with his pupil Samuel Murray in the making of the colossal figures of the prophets which adorn the Witherspoon Building in Philadelphia.

He was a slow, methodical workman, but he was indefatigable. Notwithstanding his intense devotion to work, he maintained his health by systematic outdoor exercise, hunting, fishing, boating, and riding, for he was an ardent sportsman. "He enjoyed the wild rush of his bronco across country, near his haunts in the Welsh Mountains of Pennsylvania," says Harrison S. Morris, "and I recollect one such episode when I found myself astride of a pony which in spite of me followed at a gallop the mad pace which Eakins set on his western nag." And Alan Burroughs recalls that in 1887, when Eakins took a few months' trip in the West, he engaged in a strenuous outdoor existence with ease, and rode horseback all the first day without showing a sign that he had not ridden for years.

To the Centennial Exposition of 1876 Eakins sent the "Chess Players," "Whistling for Plover," several portraits, and a water-color entitled "Baseball." The "Chess Players," which was subsequently acquired by the Metropolitan Museum of Art, New York, exemplifies his power of expression, and might be called a tangible embodiment of cogitation. His portraits are somewhat unprepossessing, certainly not flattering to the sitters, but they have the virtue of honesty, and some of them are memorable American types. Such beauty as they have is that of candid veracity. Some of his own remarks are illuminating: "That's the way it looked to me." "You can copy a thing to a certain limit, then you must use intellect." "Respectability in art is appalling."

In 1881 Eakins was married to Susan H. Macdowell, who had been an art student at the Academy. They had no children. They lived in a modest by-street, Mount Vernon St., and the studio was a plain and dusty third-floor back room, overflowing with pictures and studies. Eakins had another studio, in Chestnut St., below Broad St., at the top of an office building. In his dining-room he had installed a blackboard, so that he might elucidate his ideas at any time by a diagram or an outline. Modest, reticent, though not without consciousness of his own power, his manner of speech was slow and blunt. He was a man of unusual education, and could speak four or five languages. His "quiet but earnest spirit looked out at you from a face that was almost heavy with thought and invention." Toward the end of his life he lost his good health, took on weight, and appeared lethargic in contrast to the energy of his earlier years. He did scarcely any work in his studio during the last six years. His death occurred in 1916, when he was seventy-two. A few medals and a "small flurry of appreciation" were all the symbols of fame that had come to him.

The virility of his nature is evident from his selection of subjects; and his strength of characterization is proved by the truth of expression which makes of each portrait not only an individual personality but a racial type. An outstanding example of this is "The Thinker," a full-length standing figure painted in 1900, which is the most penetrating study of a native type produced by the painter. It is a type as purely American as Abraham Lincoln. Underneath the reserve and sobriety of the style are understanding and feeling. The dry manner of statement is in itself excellent, for it fits the man. It is unique in its plainness. This stark sort of realism, which preserves for us a certain something in America not recorded by any other painter, constitutes Eakins's authentic contribution to American art. It strikes a new note, not melodious, but memorable. It is the work of an unbiased historian who takes things as he finds

them and refrains from comment, letting facts speak for themselves, with a Spartan objectivity that in the last analysis becomes not only significant but in some way noble and universal. If the artist had no imagination, he knew how to stir the imagination of his audience. His negative merits are scorn for all that is adventitious, trivial, sensuously charming: the rejection of conventional beauty. In his work there are analogies to that of Walt Whitman and Winslow Homer, possibly to Emerson, too, in his homely moods. The underlying dignity and worth of common things and people are suggested, but without *parti pris*. The clear, cool light in which Eakins envisages the American scene is fatal to all glamour, almost cruel in its crudity, but his work is unique for its fidelity, and has a distinct historical value. In 1930 a collection of thirty-six of his paintings was given to the Pennsylvania Museum, in Philadelphia, by Mrs. Eakins and Miss Mary A. Williams.

[J. McLure Hamilton and H. S. Morris, "Thomas Eakins: Two Appreciations," in the *Bull.* of the Metropolitan Museum of Art, N. Y., Nov. 1917; Alan Burroughs, "Thomas Eakins, the Man," in *The Arts,* Dec. 1923; Alan Burroughs, "Catalogue of Work by Thomas Eakins, 1869–1916," in *The Arts,* June 1924; G. S. Parker, Introduction to the catalogue of the memorial exhibition at the Pa. Acad. of the Fine Arts, Phila., 1917; Henry McBride, "Modern Art," in the *Dial,* Jan. 1926; Louis Kalonyme, "New York Exhibitions from a Personal Angle," in *Arts and Decoration,* Jan. 1926; C. H. Caffin, "Some Am. Portrait Painters," in the *Critic,* Jan. 1904; Royal Cortissoz, "Thomas Eakins," in *Am. Artists* (1923), pp. 77–82; G. W. Eggers, *Bull.* of the Worcester Art Museum, Jan. 1930; F. J. Mather, *International Studio,* Jan. 1930; Bryson Burroughs, Introduction to the catalogue of the loan exhibition of works by Eakins at the Metropolitan Museum of Art, N. Y., 1917; Samuel Isham, *Hist. of Am. Painting* (1905), p. 525; articles by Bryson Burroughs, Robert Henri, and Joseph Brummer, in the catalogue of an exhibition held at Brummer's Galleries, N. Y., 1923; *Public Ledger* (Phila.), June 26, 1916.   W. H. D.

EAMES, CHARLES (Mar. 20, 1812–Mar. 16, 1867), lawyer, diplomat, was born at New Braintree, Worcester County, Mass. His mother was a descendant of Ebenezer Tidd, who emigrated from Lexington to New Braintree in 1768. After preparation at Leicester Academy, he entered Harvard from which he was graduated in 1831, the first in a class which included Wendell Phillips and Motley the historian, with both of whom he maintained a friendship until his death. Eames spent one year in the Harvard Law School and then studied law with John Duer in New York City, but whether or not he was admitted to the bar, he abandoned the profession in 1845 to accept a prominent position in the Navy Department at Washington under Secretary George Bancroft. A few months later he engaged in newspaper work and as associate editor of the Washington *Union* acquired a high reputation for his political writings. On Jan. 12, 1849, he was appointed by President Polk as commissioner to Hawaii, succeeding Anthony Ten Eyck. A letter from Secretary of State Buchanan, Feb. 16, 1849, authorized him "to conclude a Treaty with the Hawaiian Government similar in all respects to their Treaties with Great Britain and France" (*Works of James Buchanan,* VIII, 333). Accordingly, he met the Hawaiian plenipotentiary, Gerrit Parmele Judd [*q.v.*], in San Francisco, and there concluded a treaty with him—an accomplishment which had baffled his two predecessors. His work completed, he resigned on Oct. 22, 1849, and returned to newspaper work, first as editor of the *Nashville Union* for six months and then as editor of the Washington *Union* until sent by President Pierce in 1854 as minister resident to Venezuela to succeed Isaac Nevett Steele. A change in administration brought about his resignation and his return to Washington, where he devoted himself to the practise of international law. During the Civil War, Eames was counsel for the Navy Department and the captors in all the prize cases and for the Treasury Department in all the cotton cases. While arguing before the United States Supreme Court the great prize case of the *Sir William Peel,* in which William M. Evarts was the opposing counsel, he was stricken down with the disease that terminated fatally two months later. He rallied sufficiently in a month to appear again in the prize case of the *Grey Jacket,* involving a million dollars, which he won for the government. This was his last professional appearance before his death. During the last five years of his life "his management of prize cases showed him to be one of the best admiralty lawyers of this country, while his great knowledge of international law, supported by a remarkable memory and most acute and indefatigable intellect, won for him at the same time well-deserved distinction and respect" (*National Intelligencer,* Mar. 19, 1867). A fine linguist and a brilliant conversationalist, he made his home a great center for the celebrities of his day in politics, jurisprudence, letters, art, and society. Gov. Andrew, in a glowing obituary notice in a Boston newspaper (Hurd, p. 685), mentioned the home of Mr. and Mrs. Eames as the "most hospitable, agreeable and attractive house in Washington."

[D. Hamilton Hurd, *Hist. of Worcester County, Mass.* (1899), vol. I; Wm. T. Davis, *Bench and Bar of the Commonwealth of Mass.,* II (1895), 397; *Nat. Intelligencer* (Washington), Mar. 19, 1867; *Boston Advertiser,* Mar. 18, 1867.]   H. F. W.

EARLE, ALICE MORSE (Apr. 27, 1853–Feb. 16, 1911), author and antiquarian, was born in Worcester, Mass., the daughter of Edwin and Abigail (Clary) Morse, and the granddaughter of Benjamin and Elizabeth (Hoar) Morse. She was very proud of her ancestry, which later gave her membership in the Colonial Dames of America. She was educated at the Worcester High School and at Dr. Gannett's boarding-school in Boston. In 1874 she married Henry Earle, of Brooklyn, N. Y., and the remainder of her life was spent largely in that city and, during the summer, at her father's home in Worcester. After her husband's death, she traveled extensively in Europe with her sister, and was a passenger on the *Republic* when it was rammed in 1908 by the *Florida,* on which occasion she fell into the water accidentally from the life-boat and narrowly escaped drowning. She had four children, three of whom survived her. She died at Hempstead, L. I., N. Y., at the age of fifty-eight, and was buried at her early home in Worcester.

The author's life is mainly the story of the preparation and publication of book after book dealing with the colonial history of America, a subject of which she was an indefatigable student. Her first published writing was an article for the *Youth's Companion* upon some old Sabbath customs which had been related to her by her grandfather. The article in an enlarged form was accepted by the *Atlantic Monthly,* and, in the following year (1891) her book, *The Sabbath in Puritan New England,* was published by Scribners. This was the beginning of a long series of similar treatises: *China Collecting in America* (1892), *Customs and Fashions in Old New England* (1893), *The Diary of a Boston School Girl* (1894), *The Costume of Colonial Times* (1894), *The Life of Margaret Winthrop* (1895), *Colonial Dames and Goodwives* (1895), *In Old Narragansett* (1896), *Colonial Days in Old New York* (1896), *Curious Punishments of Bygone Days* (1896), *Home Life in Colonial Days* (1898), *Child Life in Colonial Days* (1899), *Stage-Coach and Tavern Days* (1900), *Old-Time Gardens* (1901), *Sun Dials and Roses of Yesterday* (1902), and *Two Centuries of Costume* (1903), a work in two volumes which she considered to be her most significant and valuable production. In addition, she assisted in the compilation of *Early Prose and Verse* (1893), and was a contributor to *Historic New York* (1897), and *Chap-Book Essays* (1897). Her articles frequently appeared in magazines, and she also lectured on her favorite topics.

Mrs. Earle owes her place in literature to the fact that she devoted herself to one phase of American history until she had mastered all the available material. Her books fostered the renewed interest in our colonial past which developed toward the close of the nineteenth century, and because she wrote in entertaining fashion, without pedantry or too obtrusive scholarship, her volumes had a considerable sale. It cannot be said that she added much new information to our knowledge of colonial times.

[*Who's Who in America*, 1910–11; the *Writer*, Apr. 1911, p. 48; *N. Y. Times, N. Y. Tribune*, Feb. 18, 1911; certain information supplied by members of the family.]
C. M. F.

EARLE, JAMES (May 1, 1761–Aug. 18, 1796), painter, son of Ralph and Phebe (Whittemore) Earle, was born in that part of Leicester now known as Paxton, Mass. He went to England as a young man, probably with his brother Ralph [*q.v.*], and after a period of study attained distinction as a portrait-painter. About 1789 he married, in London, Caroline Georgiana Pilkington Smyth, widow of Joseph Brewer Palmer Smyth of New Jersey, a Loyalist who returned to England during the Revolution. Earle's professional life was spent in London, England, and Charleston, S. C. In London he exhibited sixteen portraits at the Royal Academy of Art, during a period of nine years. In Charleston he painted many portraits, including those of General Charles Cotesworth Pinckney, Edward Rutledge, Mrs. Nellie Custis (Mrs. Lawrence Lewis), Lawrence Lewis, and the Right Reverend Robert Smith. Seven years after his marriage, he returned to America for a visit and concluded to make it his permanent home. He took passage to England to bring his family back, but the vessel first stopped at Charleston, S. C., and there he succumbed to an attack of yellow fever and died. It is unfortunate that Earle's death, in the prime of his life, prevented a wider knowledge of his work in his own country. His brush stroke conveyed a happy combination of grace and distinction of line. A contemporary appreciation ranked him with Copley, Savage, Trumbull, and West, and referred to his unusual ability in giving life to the eye and characteristic expression to every feature.

[W. Dunlap, *Hist. of the Rise and Progress of the Arts of Design in the U. S.* (new ed. 1918), II, 115; Pliny Earle, *The Earle Family* (1888), pp. 90–91; U. Thieme and F. Becker, *Allgemeines Lexikon der Bildenden Künstler*, X (1914), 281; Frick Art Reference Library portrait file; *S. C. State-Gazette and Timothy and Mason's Daily Advertiser*, Aug. 20, 1796.] J. M. H.

EARLE, MORTIMER LAMSON (Oct. 14, 1864–Sept. 26, 1905), educator, was born in New York City, the son of Mortimer Lent and Josephine (Allen) Earle. He was educated at the Ashland Public School in East Orange, N. J., and at Columbia College, where he graduated with high honors in 1886. From the beginning of his college studies he showed a marked proficiency in languages and literature, and a scholarly precision that distinguished all his later work. His principal devotion was to the Greek and Latin tongues, though he gave considerable attention also to French, German, Italian, and Sanskrit. At graduation he was awarded a fellowship in letters for three years. The first and third of these were employed in teaching and research at Columbia; the intervening year, 1887–88, was spent at the American School in Athens. While in Greece, he took part in excavations near Marathon and directed those at Sicyon, on the Gulf of Corinth, where he discovered an interesting theatre containing a statue of Dionysus which now belongs to the Museum at Athens. At the same time his incidental interests led him to an unusual proficiency in several dialects of modern Greek.

Proceeding to the doctorate at Columbia in 1889, Earle was given charge of the instruction in Greek in Barnard College, founded in that year. His sound scholarship at once placed the classical curriculum of the new college on a firm basis. With the exception of three years as associate professor at Bryn Mawr, from 1895 to 1898, he remained at Barnard continuously; and when the latter institution was united with Columbia in 1899 he succeeded to a professorship of classical philology, dividing his time between undergraduate teaching in Barnard and the direction of graduate students in the university. In both schools he showed distinguished gifts for teaching and administration as well as for scholarly production. He was rapidly coming to occupy an almost unique position among American classicists, with discoveries of importance already to his credit, with a paleographical and bibliographical knowledge hardly rivaled in the country, and with an unusual faculty for the interpretation of Roman and Hellenic life and art, when he met an untimely death from a virulent typhoid contracted during a scholarly expedition in Italy. He was survived by his wife, Ethel D. Woodward, whom he had married on June 4, 1892.

In addition to numerous important contributions to classical journals in America and Europe, he published an edition of the *Alcestis* of Euripides (1894), one of the *Œdipus Tyrannus* of Sophocles (1901), and one of the *Medea* of Euripides (1904). At the time of his death he was engaged upon a study of Thucydides, which appeared in the *American Journal of Philology* (October–December, 1905). A posthumous volume of studies was published in 1912 as *The Classical Papers of Mortimer Lamson Earle,* with a memoir by Sidney G. Ashmore.

[Ashmore's memoir; E. D. Perry, "Mortimer Lamson Earle," in the *Columbia Univ. Quart.,* Dec. 1905; *N. Y. Times,* Sept. 27, 1905; archives of Columbia Univ.]   E. H. W.

EARLE, PLINY (Dec. 17, 1762–Nov. 29, 1832), inventor, cotton-machinery manufacturer, the son of Robert and Sarah (Hunt) Earle, was born in Leicester, Worcester County, Mass. He traced his descent from Ralph Earle, a resident of Newport, R. I., who was one of the original twenty-nine who there organized themselves "into a civil body politicke" in April 1639. Brought up on his father's farm, he assisted in the farm work as well as the supplemental work which his father had undertaken, that of currying and washing leather. About 1785 Edmund Snow began the manufacture of cotton and wool hand cards in Leicester, and the following year young Earle, then twenty-four years old, started a similar manufactory in the same town. His inherent mechanical ingenuity presumably stood him in good stead for he successfully competed from the beginning with other manufacturers. In 1789 Almy & Brown, machinists of Providence, R. I., engaged him to cover a carding machine for them. This was opportune, for in a few months Samuel Slater became associated with that firm in the manufacture of cotton-spinning machinery, and Earle made for them the cards by which the first cotton was wrought which was spun by machinery in America. In 1791 Earle formed a partnership with two of his brothers to engage in manufacture of machine card clothing. The business became one of the most extensive of its kind in the United States and continued to be for more than twenty-five years. Earle's difficulties in furnishing cards for Slater's machinery directed his attention to the invention of a machine with which to prick the leather for cards, which theretofore had been done by hand. The device was in use in the late nineties, although the patent was not issued until Dec. 6, 1803. This formed the basis of all machines for pricking twilled cards until it was supplemented by the machine which not only pricked the leather but cut and set the teeth in one process. By 1802 the Pliny Earle & Brothers Company was considerably enlarged to include the building of machines for both wool and cotton cards, and by 1804 it had placed wool-carding machines for the accommodation of local farmers upon some stream in each of the several towns of Worcester County and one in Rhode Island. The business flourished during the War of 1812 despite the extremely high prices which had to be paid for

raw materials. The sudden termination of the war, however, found the company with a very large stock of expensive raw materials on hand but with no orders for cards. This embarrassed the organization financially to such an extent that it was dissolved. Earle retained what was left of the business and continued it until his death. In addition to his other activities, he was quite an agriculturist. As early as 1820 he engaged in sheep raising and in the cultivation of mulberry trees for the production of silk. He soon found, however, that the cost of culture was too great for the prices which could be secured on manufactured silk. On June 6, 1793, Earle married Patience, daughter of William and Lydia (Arnold) Buffum, in Smithfield, R. I., and was survived by five sons and four daughters.

[Pliny Earle, *The Earle Family* (1888); J. D. Van Slyke, *Representatives of New England Manufacturers* (1879); J. N. Arnold, *Vital Record of R. I.,* vol. VII (1895); Emory Washburn, *Hist. Sketches of the Town of Leicester, Mass.* (1860); *The Mass. Spy* (Worcester), Dec. 5, 1832.]   C. W. M.

EARLE, PLINY (Dec. 31, 1809–May 17, 1892), physician and psychiatrist, was born at Leicester, Mass., the brother of Thomas Earle [*q.v.*], and the son of Pliny Earle [*q.v.*] and Patience (Buffum) Earle. He studied at the Leicester Academy and later at the Friends' School, Providence, R. I., from which he graduated in 1828. He taught in this institution until 1835 when he was made principal, but in the meantime began the study of medicine under Dr. Usher Parsons and took his medical degree at the University of Pennsylvania in 1837. He then devoted a year to walking the general hospitals of Paris and a second year to a tour of inspection of European insane asylums from England to Turkey. Returning to the United States, he was made superintendent of the Friends' Hospital for the Insane at Frankford, Pa., in 1840. In 1841 he published a series of articles in the *American Journal of the Medical Sciences* which was reprinted with the title *A Visit to Thirteen Asylums for the Insane in Europe,* and in the same year also published a volume, *Marathon and Other Poems,* contributed originally to various newspapers. Three years later he left Frankford to become superintendent of the Bloomingdale Asylum, New York City, and in 1848 published his *History, Description and Statistics of the Bloomingdale Asylum for the Insane.* He resigned his position in 1845 to make a second tour of Europe and in 1853 there appeared his *Institutions for the Insane in Prussia, Austria and Germany.* On his return he settled in New York as a psychiatrist, was appointed visiting physician to the New York City Insane Asylum,

Blackwell's Island, and lectured on mental diseases at the College of Physicians and Surgeons. Owing to a breakdown in health, however, he retired from active practise in 1855 and for some years lived quietly at Leicester. After the outbreak of the Civil War he gave his services (1862–64) to the Government Hospital for the Insane at Washington, where insane soldiers were interned, and during 1863 also taught materia medica and therapeutics at the Berkshire Medical Institution. In 1864 he was made superintendent of the State Lunatic Hospital, Northampton, Mass., where he remained until his death, although he resigned from active service in 1885. After this period he made, despite his age, a third journey to Europe in the interest of psychiatry. In addition to writings already enumerated he published the following small volumes: *An Examination of the Practice of Bloodletting in Mental Disorders* (1854); *The Curability of Insanity* (1877); and *Popular Fallacies Concerning the Insane* (1890), as well as numerous minor contributions to periodical medical literature. His lifelong hobby was genealogy, and in 1888 he published *The Earle Family: Ralph Earle and His Descendants,* representing fifty years of research. He was a co-founder of the American Medical Association and the American Medico-Psychological Association, of which he was president in 1884. He was also the first president of the New York Psychological Association. A man of much originality and initiative, he led all his colleagues in familiarity with psychiatric institutions, and in the treatment of the insane he was ahead of his age. Incidentally, he delivered lecture courses on various subjects to his interned patients. Among the legal cases in which he was called upon for professional testimony was the trial of Guiteau for the assassination of President Garfield.

[F. B. Sanborn, *Memoirs of Pliny Earle with Extracts from His Diary and Letters, 1830–1892* (1898); *Medic. Record,* July–Dec. 1892; *Medico-Legal Jour.,* 1886, vol. IV, p. 189; H. A. Kelly and W. L. Burrage, *Am. Medic. Biogs.* (1920).]   E. P—e.

EARLE, RALPH (May 11, 1751–Aug. 16, 1801), painter, was the son of Ralph and Phebe (Whittemore) Earle, the brother of James Earle [*q.v.*], and the fifth in descent from Ralph Earle, the emigrant ancestor of the family who settled in Newport, R. I. He was born in Shrewsbury, Mass., and probably spent his boyhood in that vicinity. By 1774 he was in New Haven, painting portraits. In the autumn of that year he was again in Massachusetts, where he married his cousin, Sarah Gates, in Leicester. He then returned, unaccompanied, to the itinerancy for which his nature seems to have destined him. In

1775 he is reported to have visited Lexington and Concord, and to have made four paintings of the battles and scenery there. These were engraved by his companion and friend, Amos Doolittle [*q.v.*], who later advertised them for sale in New Haven. As works of art they deserve faint praise, but they have been celebrated as among the first historical paintings to be produced in this country.

From November 1776 until May of the following year, when their second child was born, Ralph and Sarah Earle kept house together in New Haven. Whether his roving nature led him to desert his wife, or whether, as has been written, "he was a Tory, and skedaddled, leaving her behind" (Gates, *post*), he was, at all events, painting portraits in England as early as 1779. There he became an artist of recognized standing. He studied under West, was made a member of the Royal Academy, painted the king and other personages, and, incidentally, married again. His second wife was Anne Whitesides (or Wheelock) by whom he had two more children. He seems to have deserted her on his return to America in the late eighties. Here, again, he busied himself painting portraits in New York, Connecticut, and Massachusetts, though his habits of intemperance and procrastination kept him from realizing his potentialities. Once, when he was imprisoned for debt in New York, Alexander Hamilton induced his wife and other women to sit to him in his cell in order that he might secure his release.

Earle was the best portrait-painter in Connecticut, and most of his subjects were well-known contemporaries. Although his work is uneven, varying both in style and technical perfection, it is almost invariably interesting. Some of his portraits are wooden; others, notably that of Mrs. Charles Jeffery Smith, show considerable vitality and a capacity for acute character portrayal. In his decorative use of flat surfaces, as in the canvases of William and Mary Carpenter (Worcester Art Museum), he suggests the schools of simplification of the early twentieth century. More often, however, he places his subjects in the conventional eighteenth-century setting, making use of draperies and minute cluttered landscapes as background.

Earle died, in 1801, a victim of his own indulgences. His son by his second marriage, Ralph E. W. Earle, was also an artist. After marrying a niece of Mrs. Andrew Jackson, he became, on her death, a protégé of her husband, and in the capacity of friend and portraitist, lived in the White House during the whole of Jackson's administration.

[Much confusion and error exist regarding the life of Ralph Earle, partly because the Earle brothers studied contemporaneously in England, married and had children there, were the fathers of artist sons (James was the father of Augustus Earle), and both died in the United States. The most reliable account of the subject of this sketch is to be found in the *Bull. of the Worcester Art Museum* for July 1916. See also *Ibid.*, Jan. 1917; Wm. Dunlap, *Hist. of the Rise and Progress of the Arts of Design in the U. S.* (1918); H. T. Tuckerman, *Book of the Artists* (1867), p. 54; Samuel Isham and Royal Cortissoz, *Hist. of Am. Painting* (1927), p. 76; Michael Bryan, *Dict. of Painters and Engravers,* I (1886), 451; Pliny Earle, *The Earle Family* (1888), pp. 87–88; C. O. Gates, *Stephen Gates . . . and his Descendants* (1898), p. 44; J. W. Barber, *Hist. and Antiquities of New Haven, Conn.* (1856), p. 157; Emory Washburn, *Hist. Sketches of the Town of Leicester, Mass.* (1860), pp. 207–09. There is a pen-sketch of Earle in Dunlap, I, 260.]   M.B.P.

EARLE, THOMAS (Apr. 21, 1796–July 14, 1849), lawyer, was the son of Pliny Earle [*q.v.*], a manufacturer of wool-carding machinery, and Patience (Buffum) Earle, who resided at Leicester, Mass. After attending the common schools and Leicester Academy, he passed several years in his father's employ, but as business was not prosperous he went to Worcester, Mass., in 1816, where he became a clerk in a store. In 1817 he removed to Philadelphia, and engaged in the commission business there for six years. He had no liking or capacity for a mercantile career, however, and in 1824 commenced the study of law. Meantime, in July 1820, he had married Mary Hussey of Nantucket, Mass. On his being admitted as an attorney, Apr. 2, 1825, he opened a law office in Philadelphia, at the same time engaging in literary and political work. His journalistic abilities were quickly recognized and he became editor successively of the *Columbian Observer* and *The Standard*. In the course of his legal studies he discovered that the Constitution of Pennsylvania was extremely defective and needed amendment. This he urged in the local newspapers, but it was not until he had acquired a proprietary interest in *The Mechanics' Free Press and Reform Advocate* and devoted its columns to the subject, that the public became aroused. His continued agitation at length procured the calling of the constitutional convention of 1837, to which he was a delegate. He took a leading part in its deliberations and many of the amendments which he advocated were accepted and embodied in the new constitution. Two reforms, however, which he ardently advocated, the democratization of the judiciary, and the extension of the suffrage to colored people, were rejected after long and acrimonious debate. His views on the franchise procured for him the lasting displeasure of a large section of the Democratic party, thereby destroying all chances of future political preferment. In 1840 at a conven-

tion of "Friends of Immediate Emancipation" held at Albany, N. Y., he was selected as candidate of the Liberty party for vice-president of the United States with James G. Birney [*q.v.*] for president, but he was repudiated by the abolitionists in whose name the Liberty party had made the nomination, and his name did not appear upon the ticket. He had been all his life an avowed opponent of slavery, and for a time was editor of *The Pennsylvanian,* the anti-slavery newspaper in the state. Henceforth, he took no active part in public affairs, but devoted himself to literary pursuits. He had in his earlier days published an *Essay on Penal Law in Pennsylvania* (1827) and a pamphlet, *The Right of States to Alter or Annul Charters* (1823). These were followed by his *Treatise on Railroads and Internal Communications* (1830), the first book written in the United States on this subject. His last completed work was *The Life, Travels and Opinions of Benjamin Lundy* (1847). He was an excellent linguist, well acquainted with French, German, Italian, and Spanish, and during his later years was engaged on the compilation of a "Grammatical Dictionary of the French and the English Languages" and a translation of Sismondi's *Italian Republics,* both of which were unfinished at his death.

[Pliny Earle, *The Earle Family* (1888); J. T. Scharf and T. Westcott, *Hist. of Phila. 1609–1884* (1884); *North Am. and U. S. Gazette* (Phila.), July 16, 1849; *Am. Courier* (Phila.), July 21, 1849.]   H.W.H.K.

EARLY, JOHN (Jan. 1, 1786–Nov. 5, 1873), Methodist bishop, was born in Bedford County, Va., the thirteenth child of Joshua and Mary (Leftwich) Early. The ancestors of both his father and mother came to Virginia from England about the middle of the seventeenth century. He had little formal education. His parents were Baptists, but in 1804 he joined the Methodist Church. After two or three years he was licensed to preach; in 1813 he became a presiding elder; and in 1832—but for his owning slaves—he would most likely have been made a bishop. The welfare of negroes was one of his chief interests throughout his life. His first work as a minister was among the slaves of Thomas Jefferson, and in 1825 he became president of the Colonization Society which existed in his home, Lynchburg, for the purpose of transporting negroes back to Africa. He was a pioneer advocate of free public education and of railways. He was repeatedly nominated for Congress, was offered the governorship of the territories of Illinois and of Arkansas, and was invited by John Tyler to be his comptroller of the treasury. But he kept himself to his ministry. At one camp-meeting which he conducted a thousand people were converted within a week, and it was "generally conceded that he traveled more, had more souls converted under his ministry, and received more persons into the church than any of his contemporaries" (Flood-Hamilton, p. 553). His primacy in these matters was not based on laxness of method. He refused even to pray for a penitent who would not first go down into the dust, literally, to show his anxiety for salvation (Flood-Hamilton, p. 550). It is probable that he more than any one else should be considered the founder of the Methodist Randolph-Macon College. He was a member of its first board of trustees (1830), and afterward president of the board for about forty years. In 1844 he took an active part in the General Conference of the Methodist Church which resulted in the formation of the Methodist Episcopal Church, South. He was for a while president of the first conference of this new organization, and became one of its first book agents. In 1854 he was made a bishop, but was superannuated in 1866, having suffered a railway accident which permanently injured his health. He died in Lynchburg after a long illness. Early was married twice: first, to Anne Jones, and again in 1822 to Elizabeth Browne Rives, daughter of Anthony Rives.

[A. Stevens, *Compendious Hist. of Am. Methodism* (1868) ; A. H. Redford, *Hist. of the Organization of the M. E. Ch., South* (1871) ; T. L. Flood and J. W. Hamilton, *Lives of Meth. Bishops* (1882) ; R. Irby, *Hist. Randolph-Macon Coll.* (1898) ; R. H. Early, *Family of Early* (1920) ; *Richmond Enquirer*, Nov. 6, 1873.]
J. D. W.

EARLY, JUBAL ANDERSON (Nov. 3, 1816–Mar. 2, 1894), Confederate soldier, was born in Franklin County, Va., the son of Joab and Ruth (Hairston) Early. He graduated at West Point in 1837, was commissioned in the 3rd Artillery, and served in Florida against the Seminoles. He was promoted to first lieutenant, July 7, 1838, but resigned, July 31, 1838, studied law, and was admitted to the bar in 1840. With occasional interruptions he practised at Rocky Mount, Va., until the Civil War. He was elected to the legislature as a Whig and served 1841–42, being the youngest member of the house. Volunteering in the Mexican War, he was appointed major of the 1st Virginia Regiment, Jan. 7, 1847, and went with it to northern Mexico. Taylor's campaign being already ended, the regiment saw no fighting but remained in garrison at Monterey. Early returned home on sick leave at one time, escaped uninjured when the steamboat on which he was traveling blew up, and returned to duty in Mexico. Mustered out of the army in April 1848, he resumed his law practise. He

was an unsuccessful candidate for election to the state constitutional convention in 1850, and to the legislature in 1853. He opposed secession in 1861, and as a delegate to the state convention voted against it, but immediately entered the Confederate army and fought at Bull Run as colonel of the 24th Virginia Infantry. He was then appointed brigadier-general, and for the next three years served constantly with the Army of Northern Virginia, advancing to the command of a division in 1862 and of a corps in 1864. He was appointed major-general in January 1863 and lieutenant-general in May 1864.

In June 1864 his corps was ordered into the Shenandoah Valley, and for the remainder of the war he was in independent command. In detaching so large a portion of his army Lee hoped that its operations would cause the withdrawal of a still larger force from the Army of the Potomac, now pressing him hard before Richmond. After driving the Union troops, greatly outnumbered, westward into the mountains, Early came down the Shenandoah, crossed the Potomac, levying heavy contributions in supplies and money, and marched on Washington. Though well fortified, the city was garrisoned by a force too small to man the works and consisting largely of recruits and convalescents. On the Monocacy River, Early encountered Lew Wallace, who brought up a small field force to certain defeat, but saved Washington by delaying the Confederate march several hours. As Early's advance came in sight of the fortifications, two army corps, which Grant had sent to the rescue, were landing at the city wharves. After some sharp skirmishing (July 11, 12), Early, recognizing that an assault was now hopeless, withdrew during the second night. Remaining in the lower Shenandoah Valley, he raided far and wide, obstructed communication between Washington and the West, and threatened Maryland and Pennsylvania. The burning of Chambersburg by his orders was an act which contrasts unpleasantly with Lee's conduct when operating over the same ground the year before. To dispose of Early and clear the valley, an army of over forty thousand men was assembled under Sheridan. Early was defeated at Winchester, and Fisher's Hill, but nevertheless assumed the offensive, attacking the Union army at Cedar Creek on Oct. 19, in Sheridan's absence, and for a time driving all before him. But Sheridan arrived on the field after his famous ride "from Winchester, twenty miles away," and the day ended with a Confederate defeat. Early retired up the valley and remained unmolested until March 1865, when his force was almost completely destroyed at Waynesboro. Feeling in the

South was bitter toward him. His disasters were contrasted with Jackson's earlier brilliant successes in the valley, without consideration of the fact that Early was fighting against greatly superior forces commanded by one of the most enterprising of the Union generals. Though Lee's belief in Early's ability was unshaken, he relieved him from duty, realizing that Early could no longer inspire confidence in his own troops. Undismayed by Lee's surrender a few days later, Early started west in disguise, meaning to join Kirby Smith beyond the Mississippi and keep up the struggle. But Smith had also surrendered, and Early continued on into Mexico and thence took ship for Canada, intending to quit the United States permanently. He abandoned a project to lead a Confederate exodus to New Zealand, for none would follow him, and eventually returned home, resuming law practise at Lynchburg in 1869. Later, he was employed by the Louisiana lottery at a large salary, but in the latter part of his life again resided at Lynchburg.

While in Canada, he published *A Memoir of the Last Year of the War for Independence in the Confederate States of America* (1866), useful as the narrative of a leading actor, but marred by the violence of its tone and its tendency to minimize the numbers under his command. Later in life he may have reconsidered his predictions that the negro race would meet a deplorable fate when deprived of the blessings of slavery, but his bitterness against the Federal government did not abate. Events of the war with Spain caused one Confederate veteran to remark that what he anticipated with greatest interest in the next world, was hearing "what Jubal Early would say when he met Fitz Lee wearing a Yankee uniform" (*The Reminiscences of General Basil W. Duke, C. S. A.,* 1911, p. 477). He remained "unreconstructed." Partly, no doubt, for that reason, partly because of his deep interest in the history of the Confederate States, manifested in his presidency of the Southern Historical Society, the disfavor with which he was regarded at the end of the war gave place to admiration, and even adulation, in the South. Personally, however, he was never popular. He consoled himself by the reflection that those who knew him best, liked him best (*Autobiographical Sketch,* p. xxv). A patriarchal beard gave distinction to his appearance, in spite of a stoop due to rheumatism acquired in the Mexican War. Though cold and unprepossessing in manner, he was highly charitable, in the financial sense, and gave liberally to the poor.

[*Lieut.-Gen. Jubal Anderson Early, C. S. A., Autobiographical Sketch and Narrative of the War between the States* (1912); "Gen. Jubal A. Early. Memorial Address by Hon. John W. Daniel," in *Southern Hist. Soc. Papers,* vol. XXII (1894) ; C. A. Evans, ed., *Confed. Mil. Hist.,* I (1899), 686–88 ; *Personal Memoirs of P. H. Sheridan* (2 vols., 1888) ; *Battles and Leaders of the Civil War* (1887), vol. IV ; *Official Records* (*Army*), 1 ser., vols. XXXVII, XLIII ; J. G. Barnard, *A Report of the Defenses of Washington* (1871), being no. 20 of the Professional Papers of the Corps of Engineers U. S. Army ; *Norfolk* (Va.) *Landmark,* Mar. 3, 1894.]

T. M. S.

EARLY, PETER (June 20, 1773–Aug. 15, 1817), politician, judge, belonged to that generation of Virginians who migrated to the frontier state of Georgia late in the eighteenth and early in the nineteenth century and left a deep impress on the young commonwealth. He was born in Madison County, Va., was graduated from Princeton in 1792, studied law in Philadelphia, and went with his father, Joel Early, to Greene County, Georgia, in 1795. As a young lawyer at a bar noted for its ability, he soon made a reputation by virtue of his native talent and unusual preparation. He entered politics in 1802, upon his election to Congress, and was a member of the House Committee appointed to conduct proceedings against Samuel Chase, the Federalist Supreme Court judge, whose impeachment he ardently favored. The only other matter of importance with which his name was associated seems to have been the bill to outlaw the African slave-trade, a measure which he supported. He was reëlected to the Eighth and Ninth Congresses and served until 1807. On the expiration of his third term he did not seek reelection, but returned to Greensboro where he was appointed first judge of the Ocmulgee Circuit, just then created. This position he held from 1807 to 1813. He was a model judge, unbending, inflexible, upright, always turning a deaf ear to demagogic appeals.

Elected governor in 1813 for a two-year term, Early was confronted with the problem of seeing that Georgia did her part in the war with Great Britain. He cordially supported the American cause and took great interest in various campaigns against the Indians on the frontier, who, under British instigation, harried the settlements. His administration was signalized by his courageous act in vetoing a stay-law for the relief of debtors. This law had already been in force six years and when the legislature sought to renew it, Early greeted the bill with a stinging veto. He opposed it not only as an unwise and inexpedient measure, but as an unconstitutional impairment of the validity of contracts. He called attention to the fact that the war demand had enabled the people to dispose of their products at good prices and that all who were so minded had been able to pay their debts; dishonest people were taking advantage of the law to defraud their creditors. The law "accustoms men to consider their contracts as imposing no moral obligations, and, by making fraud familiar, destroys the pride of honesty."

In 1815 Early was elected to the state Senate, serving until his death which occurred in Greensboro. In 1793 he had married Anne Adams Smith, daughter of Francis Smith, and sister of Gen. Thomas A. Smith. Two contemporaries, both of whom were friends of the governor, wrote in the same strain about him. He was described as devoid of wit, humor, and "what is called address." One of his friends said, "I never saw him smile . . . his lips were forever compressed and firm . . . his mind was in perfect correspondence with his body; and it never hesitated or faltered."

[The most comprehensive and apparently reliable account of Early's career is that by Joel Crawford in S. F. Miller's *Bench and Bar of Ga.* (1858), I, 345, although there is an error of five years in the date of his death. Later accounts, also erroneous in some respects, are found in W. J. Northen, *Men of Mark in Ga.* (1910), II, 358, and L. L. Knight, *Standard Hist. of Ga. and Georgians* (1917), I, 466, 471, IV, 2166. See also *Biog. Dir. Am. Cong.* (1928), and *Gen. Cat. Princeton Univ., 1746–1906.*]   R. P. B.

EASTMAN, ARTHUR MacARTHUR (June 8, 1810–Sept. 3, 1877), firearms manufacturer, promoter of a direct Atlantic cable, was born at Gilmanton, N. H., the son of Ebenezer and Deborah (Greeley) Eastman. His ancestry was distinguished: his grandfather, Ebenezer, served conspicuously as a lieutenant in Stark's brigade at the battle of Bunker Hill; his grandmother, Mary Butler Eastman, was the heroine of B. F. Taylor's poem, "Mary Butler's Ride," which describes one of the romantic episodes of the Revolution; his father was a major of militia. Educated at Gilmanton Academy, he began his business career as a clerk in the country store of Stephen L. Greeley and later opened a store on his own account at Gilmanton. In 1837 or shortly thereafter he moved to Boston, where he engaged with but indifferent success in the wholesale iron trade, and later in company with his brother did a large wholesale grocery business. In 1844 he commenced the manufacture of woolen underwear at Roxbury, Mass., and while engaged in this business acquired interest in a patent spinning-jenny which he took to England in 1849 and disposed of for a handsome sum to English manufacturers. With the outbreak of the Crimean War, Eastman turned his attention to the manufacture of munitions. Securing the patent for an improved breech-loading cannon, he sold it at a large profit to the British government. Fore-

seeing that the American Civil War would be a long one and learning that the country was especially deficient in cavalry equipment, Eastman bought up large quantities of old arms and made them over into carbines, which, with the expansion of the cavalry force, found a ready market at remunerative prices. In addition to the carbines he furnished other arms to the Federal government, and at the conclusion of the conflict continued to manufacture largely for foreign nations, contracting, in particular, with the French government for carbines.

About 1869 Eastman planned the enterprise which was to be the great work of his life, the laying of a direct ocean cable between Europe and the United States. The difficulties in his way were great. Not only was it necessary to raise $6,500,000 in gold, but also to overcome at every step the powerful opposition of the Anglo-American, the Western Union and the French companies. Securing a charter from New Hampshire and permission from the federal government, Eastman went to Europe, where he was well and favorably known, and there, after five years of tireless effort, he obtained the necessary funds. The American end of the new cable was laid at Rye Beach, N. H., in July 1874 with elaborate ceremonies, and it was in full working order in the next year. It provided the first competition from this country with the Anglo-American Telegraph Company (Bright, *post*, pp. 213–14). Overwork in connection with the cable project undoubtedly hastened Eastman's death, which followed a three weeks' illness. He has been described as a man of great judgment and tact "whose appearance at once arrested attention" (Manchester *Daily Mirror and American*, Sept. 3, 1877). Late in life he became interested in politics, serving as colonel on the staff of Gov. Weston in 1872 and as a member of the New Hampshire constitutional convention of 1876. In the late fifties he laid out a beautiful estate known as "Riverside" on the Merrimac River near Manchester. He married in 1836 Elizabeth H. Moulton of Gilmanton, who with two daughters survived him.

[G. S. Rix, *Hist. and Geneal. of the Eastman Family* (1901), pp. 106, 212; Chas. Bright, *The Story of the Atlantic Cable* (1903), pp. 213–14; *Appletons' Ann. Cyc. 1877* (1878), p. 579; Manchester *Daily Union*, Sept. 3, 1877.]   H. U. F.

EASTMAN, CHARLES GAMAGE (June 1, 1816–Sept. 16, 1860), journalist, politician, poet, was born in Fryeburg, Me., the son of Benjamin Clement and Mary Rebecca (Gamage) Eastman, and as a child was taken by his parents to Barnard, Vt. His father was a watchmaker who through accident or temperament never settled in a town large enough to give him steady work. Finally he heard a clear call to preach the gospel. His eleven year old son, deeming even watch-making more comfortable for the family than the Methodist itinerancy, undertook to expostulate with him and was righteously thrashed for his presumption. Charles then left home and there-after, as he phrased it, "cut his own fodder." He got a little schooling at Windsor, Vt., when he was thirteen, taught school himself for a while, attended the academy at Meriden, N. H., and then went to the diminutive University of Ver-mont, where he founded the Lambda Iota literary society. To support himself he wrote for the *Burlington Sentinel;* soon journalism engrossed his entire time, and his formal education broke off. His first independent venture, the *Lamoille River Express* (1838), at Johnson in Lamoille County, brought him commendation but no money, and did not last long. At Woodstock in 1840 he started the *Spirit of the Age* as an organ of Jacksonian Democracy. Its editor was young, handsome, and likable, and his terse, racy edi-torials got themselves read. In 1845 he sold out at an advantage and on Jan. 1, 1846, became editor and part-proprietor of the Montpelier *Vermont Patriot,* a four-page weekly that under his man-agement became the leading Democratic paper in the state. In that same year he married Mrs. Susan S. Havens, a widow, daughter of Dr. John D. Powers of Woodstock. In 1851 he became sole owner of the *Patriot,* which he continued to edit until his death. In 1848 he published a volume of *Poems,* of which 2,000 copies were sold or at any rate distributed, and which brought him many favorable notices and a local reputa-tion as a bard. A volume of selected *Poems* was published, long after his death, in 1880. His verse exhibits respectable metrical skill and at times a pleasing, songlike quality. Generous praise may be given quite honestly to the tense, restrained lines of the "Dirge" and to several others. He was also successful with humorous verses. Eastman was elected a state senator from Washington County in 1852 and again in 1853, was several times an unsuccessful candidate for Congress, and, on President Pierce's appoint-ment, was for six years postmaster at Montpelier. He attended the national Democratic conventions regularly from 1844 on, and was in his later years a member of the Democratic National Commit-tee. Stricken by a fatal disease in the spring of 1860, he nevertheless journeyed to the Democrat-ic conventions at Charleston and Baltimore, took his part in the work, and, in line with his Jack-sonian principles, supported Stephen A. Douglas,

himself a native Vermonter, against Abolition-ists on the one side and Secessionists on the other. He died peacefully at home in the midst of the campaign.

[*Vt. Patriot,* Sept. 22 (by F. A. Eastman), Sept. 29 (collection of obituaries), Oct. 13, Dec. 22, 1860; A. M. Hemenway, ed., *Vt. Hist. Gazetteer,* vol. IV (1882); G. S. Rix, *Hist. and Geneal. of the Eastman Family* (1901); *Gen. Cat. Univ. Vt. 1791–1900* (1901).]

G. H. G.

EASTMAN, ENOCH WORTHEN (Apr. 15, 1810–Jan. 9, 1885), lieutenant-governor of Iowa, state senator, was born at Deerfield, Rockingham County, N. H., the third of the seven children of John and Mary (James) Eastman. His grand-father, Ephraim Eastman, fought at Bunker Hill, and his father was a lieutenant in the War of 1812. As a boy, Enoch worked on his father's farm, was employed in a sawmill, and attended district school. Earning his own way by teach-ing, he later attended Pembrook and Pittsfield academies. In 1835 he began the study of law in the office of Moses Norris at Pittsfield, and in 1840 was admitted to the bar at Concord. Rec-ognizing the opportunities to be found in the Middle West, Eastman moved to Burlington, Ia., in 1844, and started to practise his profes-sion. Within a few months he was attracting attention throughout the territory by his speeches opposing the boundaries for Iowa as proposed by Congress. The constitutional convention of 1844 had selected the Missouri River as the western border for the new state, but when the constitu-tion came before Congress for approval, the boundary was changed to a line which cut off about one-third of the present state. Together with Fred D. Mills, Theodore S. Parvin, and others, Eastman stumped the territory making vigorous speeches. Largely through their efforts the constitution was rejected, and in no small measure was the acceptance of the Missouri River as the western boundary of Iowa due to Eastman's labors.

On Jan. 8, 1845, he married Sarah C. Green-ough of Canterbury, N. H. They lived succes-sively at Burlington, Oskaloosa, and Eldora, Ia. Four years after the death, in 1861, of his first wife, he married Amanda Hall. At Eldora East-man became a prominent attorney. He was coun-sel for the city in a successful county-seat contest with Point Pleasant, and participated in many important cases. He was a strong supporter of the Democratic party until the election of Presi-dent Buchanan, with whose doctrines he did not agree. Thereafter he affiliated with the Republi-can party, and in 1863 was nominated for the office of lieutenant-governor of Iowa. He was elected, with the largest majority which up to that time had been given to a candidate for this office in the state. His loyalty to his state and to the principles of his party found expression in the motto which he wrote for the Iowa stone in the Washington Monument: "Iowa, Her affections, like the rivers of her borders, flow to an inseparable Union." In 1883 he was elected to the Senate from Hardin County and served one term. This was his last political office.

[*"Enoch Worthen Eastman,"* by his friend, T. S. Parvin, was published in the *Iowa Hist. Record,* I, 49–57. Another biographical sketch, by a fellow townsman, W. J. Moir, appeared in the *Annals of Iowa,* 3 ser. VI, 416–24. A discussion of the origin of the inscription on the Washington Monument is found in the *Annals of Iowa,* 3 ser. I, 661–63.]   B. E. M.

EASTMAN, HARVEY GRIDLEY (Oct. 16, 1832–July 13, 1878), business man, politician, educator, was born near Waterville, Oneida County, N. Y., the son of Horace and Mary (Gridley) Eastman. His father was a farmer. Eastman began his career by teaching in a business college conducted at Rochester by his uncle, George Washington Eastman. He started a similar school of his own in Oswego in December 1855, married Minerva Clark of Canastota in 1857, and in the spring of 1858 moved his business college to St. Louis. There a bid for publicity turned swiftly into a boomerang. Uninformed of local sentiment, he guilelessly imported some noted Eastern abolitionists—Joshua Giddings, Gerrit Smith, Elihu Burritt, Charles Sumner—to lecture to his young Missourians. Amid the ensuing uproar he decided to try his luck elsewhere and conferred himself, apparently at random, on Poughkeepsie, N. Y., preceding his arrival with a generous quantity of advertising. On Nov. 3, 1859, in a room rented for seventy-five cents a week, with no equipment worth mentioning, he opened Eastman's National Business College to three enrolled students. As more pupils trickled in, their fees were invested in publicity. Eastman gave Horace Greeley $1,500 per insertion for a full page of the *Weekly Tribune,* and Greeley obligingly came up to Poughkeepsie to address the students on the subject of "The Self-Made Man." In one year Eastman spent $60,000 for advertising in five New York newspapers; he shipped catalogues, circulars, and prospectuses by the ton to all parts of the country and even abroad. At home he organized his students into a monster brass band, and celebrated —at suspiciously frequent intervals—the "anniversary" of the college with a huge banquet, music, and speeches. And it paid to advertise. He had 500 students in 1861, 1,200 in 1863, 1,700 in 1864–65. The town swarmed with young men seeking a commercial education and also board,

lodging, and sundries. Poughkeepsie prospered; Eastman grew rich. His college, known from the Atlantic seaboard to the Rockies, did its work well, for Eastman taught banking and commercial practise by a laboratory method as effective as it was then novel. Genial, dependable, sanguine, possessed of a magnetic personality and a torrential energy, he became the great man of the town. His castellated residence stood in a park of twenty-seven acres, which was generously thrown open to the public. He had his thumb in every local pie: the Poughkeepsie Ice Club, the First National Bank, a horse-racing association, the Poughkeepsie & Eastern R. R., and in several of them he lost a great deal of money. He built a row of pretentious houses on Eastman Terrace and finally disposed of them at a loss of $60,000. As mayor of the city 1871–74 and from 1877 till his death, he spent the taxpayers' money lavishly for improvements, was sharply criticized, but defended himself successfully. In 1872 and again in 1874 he sat as a Republican in the state Assembly, being sent there by his constituents in order to secure enabling legislation for a projected cantilever bridge across the Hudson. The bridge, it was believed, would put Poughkeepsie on a trunkline railway between Pennsylvania and New England and would make the city rich. Eastman was vice-president of the company that proposed to build it. He won the needed legislation, but engineering difficulties, lack of money, and the opposition of railway and steamboat companies delayed the completion of the bridge until ten years after his death, which took place in Denver, Colo., where he had gone for his health. A lone, broken bridge pier in the Hudson was known locally for years as "Eastman's monument."

[E. Platt, *The Eagle's Hist. of Poughkeepsie* (1905); *Commemorative Biog. Record of Dutchess County, N. Y.* (1897); J. H. Smith, *Hist. of Dutchess County, N. Y.* (1882); G. S. Rix, *Hist. & Geneal. of the Eastman Family* (1901), II, 802; obituary in *N. Y. Tribune,* July 15, 1878.]   G. H. G.

EASTMAN, JOHN ROBIE (July 29, 1836– Sept. 26, 1913), astronomer, was born in Andover, N. H. He was the son of Royal F. Eastman and Sophronia Mayo, descendants of Roger Eastman, who came to Salem in 1638, and of John Mayo, the first pastor of North Church in Boston. Soon after his graduation from Dartmouth, with the M.S. degree, in 1862, he obtained a position as assistant astronomer at the Naval Observatory. Three years later he was promoted to the rank of professor of mathematics. He remained there until his retirement in 1898. Some years later he was given the rank of rear admiral. He was one of that distinguished group of astronomers which included Newcomb and Hall and which gave substantial reputation to the Naval Observatory. From 1872 to 1882 Eastman edited the publications of the Observatory, but the greater part of his life-work in astronomy is represented by a single volume, called the *Second Washington Catalogue of Stars,* published in 1898. It is a peculiarity of this type of research that observations with a meridian circle, continued for many years, furnish material for very laborious and time-consuming computation but for only a thin volume of results. The few figures printed in each line of the catalogue represent many hours of work the value of which to astronomers and laymen is permanent and cumulative.

In 1869 Eastman went to Iowa to observe a total eclipse of the sun. A year later he went on a similar expedition to Sicily, and again, in 1878, to Colorado. The observations were made visually, and each observer recorded or sketched his impressions as best he could. In 1882 the government sent out eight expeditions to different parts of the world to observe the transit of Venus, an event which gave promise of yielding an accurate value for the distance of the sun. Eastman, in charge of one of the parties, was sent to Florida. He also took part in the determination of the longitudes of certain places in the United States. At various times Eastman was president of the Philosophical Society of Washington, president of the Washington Academy of Sciences, general secretary and vice-president of the American Association for the Advancement of Science. In addition to his scientific studies he published a *History of the Town of Andover, N. H., 1851–1906* (1910), containing genealogical as well as historical data. He was married, on Dec. 25, 1866, to Mary J. Ambrose, of Boscawen, N. H.

[R. H. Tucker, "John Robie Eastman," in the *Pubs. of the Astronomical Soc. of the Pacific*, Feb. 1914, pp. 41–42; an obituary in the *Jour. of the British Astronomical Asso.*, Nov. 1913; *Who's Who in America*, 1912–13; Eastman's history of Andover.] R. S. D.

EASTMAN, TIMOTHY CORSER (May 30, 1821–Oct. 11, 1893), cattle merchant, meat packer, was born in Croydon, N. H., the son of Joseph Eastman, a carpenter, and his wife Lucy Powers. He had to begin work at an early age and therefore had little formal instruction. His mother, however, taught a family fireside school in the long winter evenings so that he received an average elementary school education. His father taught him the carpenter's trade at which he worked until he had enough money to carry him through the high school at Meriden, N. H. He then taught school for a time and at the age

of twenty-one was able to buy a farm. Imbued with the western fever, he went to Wisconsin for a time, but returned, and in 1849 moved to Ohio. He settled near Cleveland, where he began operating a dairy farm. He was very successful, and in buying and selling cattle for his milk business he laid the foundation for the work which occupied the last forty years of his life. He developed a marvelous gift for judging cattle, and it was not long until he began bringing live stock from Ohio and Kentucky to the East, making his headquarters at Albany, N. Y. In 1859 his business had grown to such proportions that it was necessary to move to New York City. It was at this time that he made the acquaintance of Commodore Vanderbilt and was put in charge of all the cattle business handled by the New York Central Railroad. Soon after settling in New York he began shipping cattle and other live stock out of the country and revolutionized the methods of supplying England and Scotland, in particular, with American beef. He not only shipped thousands of live cattle but was the pioneer in the shipping of dressed meat in quantity as a commercial article in the refrigeration chambers of steamships. His first shipment of this nature was made on Oct. 1, 1875. Some of that beef was sent to Queen Victoria at Windsor Castle for which transaction Eastman's Ltd., his English agency, received the Royal Seal. For some time he was the only one shipping dressed meat in this manner, his weekly exports in 1877 averaging four thousand quarters of beef in addition to one thousand live cattle. In 1889 he promoted retail meat stores in all parts of the United Kingdom and in the same year incorporated The Eastman's Company to carry on his business in the United States and abroad. He served as the president of this concern until his death. He was also a director in the West Side Bank of New York and a member of the New York Produce Exchange. He married Lucy Putnam in 1845 by whom he had one son and one daughter. He died in Tarrytown, N. Y., after a brief illness.

Eastman was a man who started with nothing but who, through native ability in the judging and handling of live stock and through the possession of courage to undertake new things, rose to the leadership of the business in which he was engaged. When he died he was reputed to be one of the wealthiest men in New Hampshire.

[G. S. Rix, *Hist. and Geneal. of the Eastman Family* (1901), pp. 461–62; Edmund Wheeler, *Croydon, N. H., 1866* (1867), p. 99; R. A. Clemen, *Am. Livestock and Meat Industry* (1923), pp. 272, 276–79, 325–26; J. T. Critchell and Joseph Raymond, *Hist. of the Frozen Meat Trade* (1912), p. 190. Obituaries appeared in the

N. Y. Times, Oct. 13, 1893, and the *Independent States-man* (Concord, N. H.), Nov. 2, 1893.]   J. H. F.

EASTMAN, WILLIAM REED (Oct. 19, 1835–Mar. 25, 1925), engineer, clergyman, librarian, was born in New York City, the son of the Rev. Ornan Eastman and Mary Reed. He was graduated from Yale (A.B.) in 1854 with high honors, the youngest member of his class, and at his death was its sole surviving graduate member. He received the degree of A.M. from Yale in 1857. From 1854 to 1859 he was a civil engineer, working on the enlargement of the Erie Canal, the construction of the Michigan Southern and Northern Indiana Railroad, and on the survey of the first railroad from Vera Cruz to Mexico City. In 1859 he entered Union Theological Seminary and at graduation in 1862 was ordained a Presbyterian minister. From July 1862 to July 1864 he was in turn first sergeant of Company H, 22nd Regiment New York State Militia, chaplain of the 165th New York Volunteers, and from Jan. 1, 1863, chaplain of the 72nd New York Volunteers. From 1864 to 1888 he served continuously as pastor of Congregational churches in Grantsville, Mass., Plantsville and Suffield, Conn., and South Framingham, Mass. He was financial secretary for Howard University, 1888–90, living at Wellesley, Mass. In 1890 he executed a complete and rather surprising right-about face. Caught in the rapidly rising tide of the modern library movement and genuinely attracted by its opportunities, he embarked at the age of fifty-five upon a career in a new profession with all the enthusiasm and devotion of youth. More remarkable still, he won a national reputation in the field. He would accept nothing less than the best preparation, and so with the zest of a schoolboy he entered in 1890 the New York State Library School at Albany, completing the course in 1892 with the degree of B.L.S. Immediately appointed to the work of library inspection, supervision, and extension in New York State, for twenty years, in various capacities, as a veritable "library bishop" he shepherded the public libraries of his "diocese" with rare energy and judgment. His genial presence, his tolerance, quick sympathy, and ripe experience with men and affairs, contributed greatly to his success. After his retirement in 1913 he lived in New Haven, and continued to lecture on library subjects, especially to library schools. In 1907 he received the degree of M.L.S. from the New York State Library School.

Eastman came to be perhaps the first authority in his profession on library buildings and equipment. His principal publications (aside from numerous reports, journal articles, and addresses) are in this special field. His lectures in the various library schools, on the economic and efficient construction of library buildings and furniture, were widely influential. He was secretary of the New York Library Association, 1893–99, and its president, 1904–05. He married on Nov. 20, 1867, Laura Elizabeth Barnes, who survived him.

[A sketch in the *Lib. Jour.*, Jan. 1913, is reprinted in *N. Y. Libraries*, Feb. 1913. See also *Yale Univ. Obit. Record* (1925), and *Yale Alumni Weekly*, Apr. 17, 1925.]   J. I. W.

EASTON, JOHN (*c.* 1625–Dec. 12, 1705), governor of Rhode Island, was the son of Nicholas Easton [*q.v.*] and as a boy emigrated with him from Wales to Massachusetts. In 1680 he described himself as "aged fifty-five or thereabouts" (*Early Records*, VI, 10). Both father and son were Quakers. They were among the first settlers of Newport and became prominent in the colony of Rhode Island. John Easton frequently represented Newport in meetings of the General Assembly of the colony. In 1653 he was elected attorney-general and was repeatedly re-elected to that office. He served as Assistant under the charter of 1663 and in 1674 was elected deputy-governor, his brother Peter being elected to the combined offices of attorney-general and treasurer. John served as deputy-governor from May 1674 until April 1676, and as governor from 1690 to 1695. In 1694 he refused as governor to issue commissions to privateersmen, who, in many cases, were mere pirates, but the deputy-governor did so and involved the colony in difficulty with the home government by his action.

Easton wrote a *Narrative of the Causes which led to Philip's Indian War,* beginning with the death of Sassamon, which was not published until 1858, when F. B. Hough edited and printed it. Although Increase Mather expressed a contemptuous opinion of it (probably because it emanated from Rhode Island), it is now considered valuable evidence, and was again printed in 1913 (*Narratives of the Indian Wars,* C. H. Lincoln, ed.). Easton became an extensive landowner in the colony. He married Mehitable Gant on Jan. 4, 1660, who was the mother of five children. She died Nov. 11, 1673, and he married Alice ——, who died March 24, 1689 (*Vital Record of Rhode Island,* VII, 15, 99). Easton died Dec. 12, 1705, and was buried in the Coddington burial-place, Newport.

[*Early Records of the Town of Providence* (21 vols., 1892–1915); *Records of the Colony of R. I. and Providence Plantations, 1636–1706* (1856–58); *R. I. Court Records* (2 vols., 1920–22); *New-England Hist. and Geneal. Reg.*, XV (1861), 151 n.; S. G. Arnold, *Hist. of the State of R. I.*, vol. I (1859).]   J. T. A.

EASTON, NICHOLAS (1593–Aug. 15, 1675), governor of Rhode Island, was a tanner by trade who emigrated from Wales to Massachusetts in 1634, bringing his two sons with him on the *Mary and John.* He first settled at Ipswich, being admitted a freeman Sept. 3. The following year (1635) he was elected representative to the General Court but was dismissed as unduly chosen. In the same year he removed to Newbury. He was an adherent of Wheelright in the Antinomian controversy and was among those disarmed by order of the Court in 1637. With a few others he began a settlement at what is now Hampton, N. H., but was warned off and in 1638 settled at Pocasset (Portsmouth) in Rhode Island. He was almost at once elected one of the "Elders" who were to assist the "Judge" in governing the community, but, disputes having arisen, he joined the Coddington group in secession, and moved to what is now Newport. He built the first house there in April 1639, which two years later was burned by the Indians, probably by accident. He was always prominent in the life of the colony. In 1639 he was one of the two men instructed by the Coddington group to petition Henry Vane to use his influence in procuring for them a patent for the island. He was chosen an Assistant in 1640, was several times reëlected to that office, and served frequently as moderator at meetings of the General Assembly. He was one of the three men chosen in 1653 to see that the "State's [England's] part of all prizes be secured and accompt given." This gave him some trouble five years later in making a proper accounting. Under the first patent, the administrative head of the Colony was designated "president," and Easton held that office from May 1650 to August 1651 and again from May 1654 to Sept. 12, 1654. The charter of 1663 provided for a governor and deputy-governor. Easton held the latter office from 1666 to 1669, again from 1670 to 1671, and was governor from May 1672 to May 1674.

Apparently his first wife (unknown) had died before he left Wales. In 1638 he married Christian, widow of Thomas Beecher, who was probably the mother of seven of his nine children. She lived until Feb. 20, 1665. On Mar. 2, 1671, he was married to Ann Clayton, who survived him. Easton died Aug. 15, 1675, and was buried in the Coddington graveyard, Newport. In his will he named his son John residuary legatee.

[Jas. Savage, *Geneal. Dict. of the First Settlers of New England*, vol. II (1860) ; H. M. Chapin, *Documentary Hist. of R. I.* (2 vols., 1916–19) ; *Records of the Colony of R. I. and Providence Plantations, 1636–1677* (1856–57) ; S. G. Arnold, *Hist. of the State of R. I.* (2 vols., 1859–60) ; J. Callender, *Hist. Discourse* (1838) ; *R. I. Court Records* (2 vols., 1920–22.]   J.T.A.

EATON, AMOS (May 17, 1776–May 10, 1842), scientist and educator, son of Capt. Abel and Azuba (Hurd) Eaton, was born in Chatham, Columbia County, N. Y. His father was a farmer and descendant of John Eaton who came from Dover, England, about 1635 and settled in Dedham, Mass. Amos was graduated from Williams College in 1799 and fitted himself for the legal profession, but through association in New York with Dr. Samuel L. Mitchill and Dr. David Hosack [*qq.v.*] he became interested in the natural sciences, particularly in botany. After his admission to the bar in 1802 he settled in Catskill as a lawyer and land agent, though continuing his studies of the sciences. As early as 1810 he began a course of popular lectures in botany and published a small text-book on the subject. This was followed in 1817 by *A Manual of Botany for the Northern States,* which met with great popular favor and passed with much revision and many changes of title through eight editions, the last appearing in 1840. He abandoned his law practise altogether about 1815, "owing to a concurrence of circumstances, which our limits will not allow us to explain" (Durfee, *post*, p. 363), and placed himself under the tutelage of Professors Ives and Silliman of Yale College, where he is reported to have been a diligent student.

Having, as he felt, become sufficiently grounded in botany and geology, he moved to Williamstown, Mass., in 1817 where he began giving public lectures which aroused much popular interest and led to similar lectures in Amherst, Northampton, Middlebury, and other towns in New England and along the Hudson. In 1818 he was asked by Gov. Clinton to deliver a course of lectures before the members of the New York legislature. This was undoubtedly the beginning of the work which resulted in 1836 in the establishment of a State Geological Survey. In 1820 Eaton was appointed professor of natural history in the Medical School at Castleton, Vt., and in 1820 and 1821, under the patronage of Stephen Van Rensselaer, he made a geological and agricultural survey of Albany and Rensselaer counties, following it up in 1824, also at Van Rensselaer's instance, with a survey of the district along the Erie Canal. In the same year he was designated senior professor in the Rensselaer School (now Rensselaer Polytechnic Institute) at Troy, N. Y., a position which he retained until his death.

Eaton was a man of indefatigable industry and had to a remarkable degree the gift of arousing interest and enthusiasm in others. He was a vigorous thinker, writer, and compiler, issuing five works on botany, two on chemistry, six on geology, exclusive of a score or more brief notes, and others on educational subjects. Owing to the condition of science at the time much of his work was necessarily faulty in many respects. He failed often to realize possibilities beyond his own immediate observation and deductive reasoning. His successive geological writings became filled with bombastic repetitions of unfounded and erroneous statements, defects that sadly diminished his usefulness in later years. Nevertheless, through his enthusiasm he did more perhaps than any one man of his time in arousing a popular interest in science. He is described as a man of striking personality, of a large frame, portly, and dignified. His face was highly intellectual. "He had an easy flow of language, a popular address and a generous enthusiasm in matters of science which easily communicated itself to his pupils" (Ballard). He was four times married: first, on Oct. 16, 1799, to Polly Thomas, by whom he had one son; second, on Sept. 16, 1803, to Sally Cady, by whom he had five sons; third, on Oct. 20, 1816, to Anne Bradley, by whom he had three children; and fourth, on Aug. 5, 1827, to Alice Johnson, by whom he had one child, a son.

[See H. H. Ballard, "Amos Eaton," in *Colls. Berkshire Hist. and Sci. Soc.* (1897); Calvin Durfee, *Hist. of Williams Coll.* (1860); P. C. Ricketts, *Hist. of the Rensselaer Polytechnic Inst.* (1895); W. J. Youmans, *Pioneers of Science in America* (1896), pp. 112–13. A bibliography of Eaton's geological writings is given by John M. Nickles, *Geol. Lit. on North America, 1785–1918* (1923), in Bull. 746, U. S. Geol. Survey.]

G.P.M.

EATON, BENJAMIN HARRISON (Dec. 15, 1833–Oct. 29, 1904), agriculturist and pioneer in irrigation, was born on a farm near Zanesville, Ohio, where his parents, Levi and Hannah (Smith) Eaton, led uneventful lives. After receiving an elementary education he alternately taught school and farmed in Ohio and Iowa, until the even current of his life was disturbed by the news of the gold discoveries at Pike's Peak. Eaton joined the crowd of adventurers who flocked to the Rockies in 1859, but was, like most of them, unsuccessful as a miner. Leaving Colorado, he went to New Mexico, started farming on the Maxwell Land Grant, and there built his first irrigation ditch. He returned to Colorado in 1864, purchased a farm near the present town of Windsor, and remained in that vicinity for the rest of his life. Northern Colorado was in 1864 an unpromising region for agriculture. Here and there along the river bottoms were small farms; beyond these there stretched the prairie with its cactus and prairie-dog towns. But the young farmer saw promise in the land. Building an irrigation ditch, the first of its kind in the district, he brought water to his land and began to cultivate it. Thereafter his life was spent in acquiring more land and in developing it. He was always land-poor, but continued buying. At his death he held about fourteen thousand five hundred acres of cultivated land, and nearly seven thousand acres not under the plow. After some years of farming, he leased the greater part of his estate and lived in Greeley, the home of the Union Colony. As his holdings increased he constructed more reservoirs and ditches. Six reservoirs held water for his land; one of these, the Windsor Reservoir, was the largest at that time in the state. He built ditches everywhere. As contractor he built the Larimer and Weld Canal which was over sixty miles in length, Canal No. 2 of the Union Colony, the important High Line Ditch near Denver, and others. It was said of him in 1884 that he had "had more to do with the construction of irrigating canals in Colorado than perhaps any other five men in the State" (*Denver Tribune-Republican*, Sept. 15, 1884).

Though Eaton built the town of Eaton which was incorporated in 1888, owned a mill and a business house there, and raised some cattle, he was essentially a leader in agricultural development. Politics formed only an interlude in a busy life. A stanch Republican, he served in the territorial house in 1872, in the council in 1876, and as governor of the state in 1885–86. As legislator and governor he showed a great interest in agricultural matters. He was twice married. His first wife, Delilah Wolf, whom he married in Ohio on May 1, 1856, died in 1857. In 1864 he married Rebecca J. Hill, daughter of Abraham Hill, in Louisa County, Iowa.

[There is no extensive biography of Eaton. Brief accounts are to be found in W. F. Stone, *Hist. of Colo.*, III (1918), 22–25; *Portrait and Biog. Record of the State of Colo.* (1899), pp. 417–18; *Denver Times*, Oct. 31, 1904; *Denver Tribune-Republican*, Oct. 30, 1904. An article in the same paper for Sept. 15, 1884 (erroneously dated Sept. 14 on the first page), is a reprint from the *North British Agriculturalist* for Aug. 27, 1884.]

J.F.W.

EATON, DANIEL CADY (Sept. 12, 1834–June 29, 1895), botanist, was born at Fort Gratiot, Mich., the son of Gen. Amos B. Eaton and Elizabeth Selden. His grandfather, Amos Eaton [*q.v.*], author of botanical text-books, had been an inspiring and influential teacher of botany in America during the first half of the century; his father, though lacking a special scientific education, was keenly interested in natural history. Thus, during his undergraduate years at Yale, Eaton's ambition centered in fitting himself for a professorship of botany in that institution, in which his grandfather had studied. He corresponded freely with such authorities as Torrey, Gray, and Sullivant, and laid the foundation of the large and important herbarium which to-day bears his name. Cryptogamous plants claimed his special attention, and even in his junior year at college he described several new ferns from California in classical Latin form. Following his graduation from Yale in 1857, Eaton spent three successive years at Harvard College, carrying on his botanical studies under Asa Gray, especially in the ferns. During this time he contributed the fern text to Chapman's historic *Flora of the Southern United States* (1860), and published several papers dealing with fern collections from Cuba, Venezuela, Japan, and the Mexican boundary region. Then, with the outbreak of the Civil War, he served with the army commissary department in New York City. In 1864 he was elected to the newly founded professorship of botany in Yale College, and to the end of his active life continued his botanical studies and instruction there. He married, on Feb. 13, 1866, Caroline Ketcham of New York City.

Eaton is best known as a discriminating student of ferns. He not only contributed the fern text to several voluminous botanical reports of the transcontinental railroad survey expeditions, but also published numerous short papers. His most important publication, *The Ferns of North America* (1877–80), is a beautifully illustrated work in two volumes describing in detail the ferns then known from the area north of Mexico. In later years his attention was given mainly to mosses and hepatics. Other activities included the preparation of botanical definitions for *Webster's International Dictionary,* numerous reviews of botanical works for both technical and general periodicals, and genealogical studies for publication. Naturally conservative, his efforts were invariably characterized by precision, thoroughness, and keen insight. Above all, he was no "closet naturalist," but an excellent field student, a lover of outdoor sports, and a devotee of fishing and hunting. A man of simple tastes, his high ideals, culture, and wide technical knowledge combined to make him an inspiring instructor and helpful friend.

[*Bull. of the Torrey Botanical Club,* Aug. 31, 1895; *Botanical Gazette,* Aug. 1895; *Fern Bull.,* July 1890; *Science,* July 19, 1895; *Obit. Record of Grads. of Yale Univ., 1890–1900* (1900); *New Haven Evening Reg.,* June 29, 1895.]   W.R.M.

EATON, DORMAN BRIDGMAN (June 27, 1823–Dec. 23, 1899), lawyer, civil-service reformer, was born at Hardwick, Vt., the son of the Hon. Nathaniel and Ruth (Bridgman) Eaton, and educated at the University of Vermont, from which he was graduated in 1848.

Thereafter he entered the Harvard Law School, receiving the degree of LL.B. in 1850. A prize essay which Eaton wrote at the time of his graduation from the law school attracted the attention of Judge William Kent who was engaged in preparing a new edition of his famous father's *Commentaries.* Judge Kent invited the young lawyer to become his assistant in the work of editing and several years were devoted to this task, the assistant editor displaying such painstaking care and good legal judgment that Judge Kent took him into partnership. Meanwhile, in 1856 he had married Annie S. Foster of New York City and had been admitted to the New York bar. In active practise Eaton made rapid progress by reason of his ability, courage, and perseverance. He was appointed counsel for the Erie Railroad and became engaged in important legal controversies which grew so bitter that on one occasion he was set upon and severely injured by persons whose identity was never discovered. These injuries kept him from work for a time; but on recovery he plunged once more into active practise and became deeply interested in the movement for civil-service reform, of which he was one of the earliest American advocates. Indeed, he is entitled to share with George W. Curtis and Carl Schurz [*qq.v.*] the honor of having gained for the merit system its first real recognition in the national administration.

From 1870, when he gave up his law practise, to the end of his life in 1899, Eaton was a courageous and persistent fighter in two causes which he had much at heart, the abolition of the spoils system and the reform of city government. In 1873 President Grant appointed him chairman of the national Civil Service Commission, succeeding George W. Curtis, who had resigned; but in 1875 Congress cut off the appropriations for the Commission and caused its work to be suspended. President Hayes, in his inaugural (1877), urged Congress to renew the appropriation and meanwhile invited Eaton to make a study of the civil-service system in Great Britain. This necessitated an extended visit to Europe and resulted in the publication of his well-known volume, *The Civil Service in Great Britain: A History of Abuses and Reforms and their Bearing Upon American Politics,* which appeared in 1880. This book interested a wide circle of readers and proved to be of great value to the movement for civil-service reform in America. It enhanced the author's reputation so notably that he was called upon to draft the bill which became the Pendleton Act of 1883. This statute remains the basis of the federal civil-service system at the present day. Immediately after its enactment President Arthur placed Eaton once more at the head of the national Civil Service Commission, and President Cleveland reappointed him in 1885. On his return to New York City after the conclusion of his service on the Commission, Eaton threw his energies into successive campaigns for the reform of municipal government in the metropolis. He was particularly interested in the reform of the police judiciary and the improvement of public-health administration. He also made a study of city administration in general and finally embodied his program of civic improvement in a volume on *The Government of Municipalities* (1899), which appeared from the press a few months before his death. In its day this book was a notable contribution to the then scanty literature of municipal reform.

Throughout his public career, Eaton was a crusader by instinct, fearless and relentless in the battle for civic righteousness, a citizen with the spirit of a Roman consul. As an educator of public opinion he was determined that his work should not come to an end with his death, and in his will he provided for the establishment of professorships in two American universities, the Eaton Professorship of the Science of Government at Harvard, and the Eaton Professorship of Municipal Science at Columbia, both of which chairs have had distinguished occupants.

[A small memorial volume, *Dorman B. Eaton, 1823–1899*, containing a brief sketch of his life, with eulogies by Carl Schurz and others, was published in 1900. In addition to the books mentioned above, he was the author of various articles in magazines. Incidental data relating to his activities may be found in the various works relating to civil-service reform and to the municipal government of New York City during the last three decades of the nineteenth century. See also N. Z. R. Molyneux, *Hist. Geneal. and Biog. of the Eaton Families* (1911).]   W.B.M.

EATON, HOMER (Nov. 16, 1834–Feb. 9, 1913), clergyman of the Methodist Episcopal Church, for twenty-four years agent of its Book Concern, and long prominent among the leaders of his denomination, was born in Enosburg, Vt. His father, Rev. Bennett Eaton, a Methodist preacher, was a descendant of Francis Eaton, who came to America in the *Mayflower*; and his mother, Betsey Maria, daughter of Joel and Hannah (Billings) Webster, was a descendant of John Webster, one of the original proprietors of Hartford, Conn., and a colonial governor. He was educated at Bakersfield Academy, Vermont, and at the Methodist General Biblical Institute, Concord, N. H. In 1857 he joined the Troy Conference, of which he remained a member until his death, and the following year, Apr. 28, he

married Hannah, daughter of Jacob and Rowena Saxe of Sheldon, Vt. From 1857 to 1889 he was pastor of eleven churches, and served as presiding elder. In 1889 he was made an agent of the Methodist Book Concern in New York, and in 1912, when a new constitution for the Concern was adopted, he was elected general agent, with duties covering the entire field in this country.

Eaton was a rugged Vermonter of massive frame, with a noble head and clean-cut profile, always dignified in his bearing, and possessing a powerful voice. He had a statesmanlike mind, a large fund of native humor, and though not accustomed to indulge in prolonged debate, he had great capacity for bringing men into line with his purposes. He managed the enormous business of the Book Concern with notable sagacity. The extent to which his abilities were valued by his denomination is shown by the fact that he was a member of ten General Conferences, being first elected in 1872, and then continuously from 1880 to 1912. In 1881 and in 1901 he was delegate to the Ecumenical Methodist Conference in London, and in 1874, fraternal delegate to the General Conference of the Methodist Church in Canada. In addition to his other duties he was for seventeen years (1896–1913) treasurer of the Board of Foreign Missions. He was also a trustee of Syracuse University and of Drew Theological Seminary. His death occurred at his home in Madison, N. J., while his wife was reading to him from one of the denominational papers, and he was buried in the Albany (N. Y.) Rural Cemetery.

[*Christian Advocate* (N. Y.), Feb. 13 and 20, 1913; *Minutes of the Troy Annual Conference of the M. E. Ch.* (1913); Henry C. Jennings, *The Meth. Book Concern* (1924); *Who's Who in America*, 1912–13.]   H.E.S.

EATON, JOHN (Dec. 5, 1829–Feb. 9, 1906), educator, was born at Sutton, N. H., the son of John and Janet (Andrew) Eaton. He was reared on his father's farm, supplemented his scanty schooling by home reading, and taught school until he was sent to the Thetford Academy in Vermont. He then worked his way through Dartmouth, graduating in 1854, and went to Cleveland, Ohio, as principal of the Ward School. In 1856 he became superintendent of schools at Toledo, where he had opportunities to develop his marked administrative ability, and took a special interest in the compilation of educational statistics. He continued his earlier purpose of entering the ministry, however, and in 1859 resigned to attend Andover Theological Seminary. Ordained in 1861, he entered the army as chaplain of the 27th Ohio Volunteers, which served first in Missouri and then in Tennessee. In November 1862 Grant selected the young chaplain for the difficult task of caring for the negroes who flocked into the army camps. Under Grant's orders Eaton organized the freedmen into camps where provision was made for their physical needs and their education, and they were set to work picking cotton on abandoned plantations and cutting wood for the river steamboats. Eaton's jurisdiction as superintendent of freedmen was extended over the whole department of the Tennessee, including Arkansas. He was given suitable military rank as colonel of a negro regiment in October 1863, and in March 1865 he was brevetted brigadier-general. When the Freedmen's Bureau, for which Eaton's successful organization was an important precedent, was organized in the same month, he was appointed an assistant commissioner in charge of the District of Columbia, Maryland, and parts of Virginia. He resigned in December and was mustered out. On Sept. 29, 1864, he had married Alice Eugenia Shirley, the daughter of a Vicksburg Unionist.

Aside from his personal interest in the South, Eaton felt the need for a Unionist newspaper at Memphis, his old headquarters, and in 1866–67 he edited the *Memphis Post,* which supported Grant for the presidency and showed its editor's interest in education by advocating a system of free public schools. Under the school law of 1867 he was elected state superintendent for two years. "Eaton's system," however, was opposed by many who objected to spending money for this purpose, and it fell to the ground. Meanwhile he had been active in politics as an editor and as a member of the Republican state committee. Grant accordingly appointed him in 1869 to the board of visitors at West Point, and in 1870 made him Commissioner of Education.

The Bureau of Education, then three years old, was in danger of extinction from congressional neglect. It was Eaton's task to build up the organization and to demonstrate its usefulness. Fortunately, in addition to administrative talent, he had tact and a *flair* for the kind of publicity needed to convince the public and Congress that his bureau was worth while. Moreover, he had the president's cordial support. Eaton thought it the main duty of the bureau to collect educational information and to disseminate it as widely as possible. He stood for no particular educational dogma, but tried to familiarize educators with the best practises here and abroad. Believing in federal appropriations to aid the states in developing school systems, he supported Senator Blair's bill for federal aid. In 1886

he resigned because of his health. Almost immediately he began another phase of his career, as a college president, at Marietta College (1886–91), and then at Sheldon Jackson College at Salt Lake City (1895–99). In 1899 he was asked to organize a public-school system in Porto Rico during the military occupation, and served until May 1, 1900, when he resigned because of serious ill health. He was prominent in various learned societies and other organizations in which he was interested.

[John Eaton, in collaboration with Ethel Osgood Mason, *Grant, Lincoln, and the Freedmen* (1907), gives an autobiographical account of his Civil War experiences, and a biographical sketch by Miss Mason which is the best available. See also Paul S. Peirce, *The Freedmen's Bureau* (1904); the U. S. Bureau of Education *Circulars of Information* and the *Report of the Commissioner of Education, 1870–86; Report of the Commissioner of Education* for 1899–1900, I, 221–73, II, 1650; *Who's Who in America,* 1906–07.]

D. L. M.

EATON, JOHN HENRY (June 18, 1790– Nov. 17, 1856), lawyer, politician, was the son of John and Elizabeth Eaton. His father, a maker of chaises who resided at Halifax, N. C., during the Revolutionary period, was coroner of his county and a representative in the Assembly (*State Records of North Carolina,* XI, 1895, p. 712; XVII, 1899, pp. 407, 878; XX, 1902, p. 100). In 1796, as executor for Maj. Pinketham Eaton of the Continental Line, who had been killed in action, he acquired an estate of 4,800 acres of land in what came to be Williamson County, Tenn. (Tennessee Land Office Records, North Carolina Military Warrants, Book D, No. 4, p. 22). At the age of sixteen John Henry attended the University of North Carolina for a time. He afterward studied law and in 1808 or 1809 migrated to Tennessee, taking up his residence in Franklin, the seat of justice for Williamson County. During the War of 1812 he served a brief tour of duty as a private soldier (War Department Records). Just before this, his father died (Records of Halifax County, N. C., Wills, vol. III, p. 526), and his mother removed to Tennessee. Eaton purchased for her a home in Franklin which she occupied until her death in 1843. The family owned slaves and appear to have lived in comfort.

Young Eaton married Myra, daughter of one William Terrell Lewis, who had possessed much land. Another daughter of his married Maj. William B. Lewis. The two Lewises were not related, but both young women were wards of Gen. Andrew Jackson (Parton, *post,* II, 652–53; W. W. Clayton, *History of Davidson County, Tenn.,* 1880, pp. 72–73), a fact of far-reaching significance in the career of Eaton, for in making this marriage he also made his fortune. In 1816 a Nashville newspaper announced that the biography of Andrew Jackson which had been begun by John Reid would be completed by J. H. Eaton. Since the young author was not well known to the people of the community, the editor took occasion to call him to their favorable attention (*Nashville Whig,* June 4, 1816). Published in 1817, *The Life of Andrew Jackson, Major General in the Service of the United States* proved to be a dull, uncritical attempt to lionize the Hero of New Orleans, though it went through at least three English and two German editions. In 1817 Eaton became a speculator in Pensacola lands as a result, it appears, of a tip from Jackson (Parton, II, 407), and in 1818 he was appointed to the United States Senate to complete an unexpired term. In 1819 he became the defender of Jackson on the committee which was appointed to investigate the Seminole affair. The legislature presently elected him to fill the seat which he had originally acquired by appointment, and he held the office until his resignation in 1829.

When Jackson became a candidate for the presidency, Eaton and William B. Lewis were two of the principal members of a little group which formed in Nashville to promote his interests. As a senator in Washington, Eaton was the most influential of this clique and he served as its diplomatic representative to stir up favorable sentiment in various parts of the country. When Jackson's election had been accomplished, it was determined that the secretaryship of war should go to a Tennessean, either to Eaton or Hugh Lawson White. Eaton wrote to White explaining that they were being considered, that Jackson had discussed the matter with him, and that he would withdraw if White wished the place. White made no claim, and Eaton received the appointment. The dissolution of the cabinet, which was brought about partly through the refusal of Washington society to accept Eaton's second wife, Peggy O'Neill (see O'Neill, Margaret L.), served to draw Jackson and Eaton closer together. When Eaton helped to pave the way for the reorganization of the cabinet by resigning his office in 1831, it was Jackson's intention to give the secretaryship of war to H. L. White, and to secure the election of Eaton to the place which would thus be vacated by White in the Senate. But White, having been passed over once, was not now amenable and the plans for Eaton went awry. In 1833 a senatorial vacancy occurred and the president used his influence with the Tennessee legislature to have Eaton elected. But, ironically enough, it was

his chief's championship which caused Eaton's defeat (T. P. Abernethy, "The Origin of the Whig Party in Tennessee," in *Mississippi Valley Historical Review,* March 1926, pp. 507–08). Thwarted in this plan for his favorite, Jackson in 1834 made him governor of Florida. In 1836 he was appointed minister to Spain, where he remained for four years. At the time of his return to the United States, Martin Van Buren had just been elected president. Eaton, who had been ready to oppose Van Buren's pretensions to the vice-presidency in 1832 (Parton, III, 421), maintained the antagonism in 1840, thereby causing a break with Jackson and terminating his own political career. He continued to live in Washington until his death in 1856.

[The best of the fragmentary notices of John H. Eaton are to be found in John H. Wheeler, *Reminiscences and Memoirs of N. C.* (1884); James Parton, *Life of Andrew Jackson* (1887); and J. W. Caldwell, *Sketches of the Bench and Bar of Tenn.* (1898). See also Wm. Terrell Lewis, *Geneal. of the Lewis Family* (1893); *Biog. Dir. Am. Cong.* (1928). The date of Eaton's birth is taken from the inscription on his tombstone in Oak Hill Cemetery, Washington, D. C.]

T. P. A.

EATON, JOSEPH ORIEL (Feb. 8, 1829–Feb. 7, 1875), painter, was born at Newark, Licking County, Ohio, the son of William and Margaret (Adams) Eaton. Following his early years in the West, he went to New York City to secure his art education and in time attained distinction. He was a genre and portrait-painter in oil and water-colors and was particularly successful in his portraits of children. He had a fine and sensitive appreciation of nature and quick comprehension of personal characteristics shown in facial expression. It was doubtless this faculty that made him a master in portraying the elusive charms of childhood. The titles of his paintings suggest his versatility and range of interests. However, portraits remained the most important part of his work. His best paintings include: "Landscape,—View on the Hudson" (1868), "Moral Instruction" (1869), "Dawning Maternity" (1871), "Greek Water Carrier" (1872), "Lady Godiva" (1874), and portraits of R. S. Gifford (1869), E. J. Kuntze, and Rev. George H. Hepworth (1870). His own portrait (belonging to the National Academy of Design), and "Looking Through the Kaleidoscope" were exhibited after his death. He was elected an Associate National Academician and became a member of various other organizations.

In 1855 Eaton married Emma Jane Goodman of Cincinnati. He died at his home in Yonkers, N. Y., at the age of forty-six.

[N. Z. R. Molyneux, *Hist. Geneal. and Biog. of the Eaton Families* (1911), p. 759; F. A. Virkus, *Abridged Compendium of Am. Genealogy,* I (1925), 73; C. E.

Clement and L. Hutton, *Artists of the Nineteenth Century*, I (1879), 233; *N. Y. Times*, N. Y. *Evening Post*, Feb. 8, 1875; J. D. Champlin, Jr., *Cyc. of Painters and Painting*, II (1886), 2.]   J.M.H.

EATON, MARGARET L. O'NEILL [See O'NEILL, MARGARET L., 1796–1879.]

EATON, NATHANIEL (*c.* 1609–1674), first head of Harvard College, was a disreputable member of a reputable family. He was a son of the Rev. Richard Eaton, a clergyman of Coventry, England, who had a large family of children including Samuel and Theophilus [*qq.v.*], who were prominent in the settling of New Haven. Nathaniel matriculated at Trinity College, Cambridge, in 1629, but did not take a degree. Three years later he received a license to go to Leyden, and in the following year was studying under Dr. William Ames at Franeker. He emigrated to Massachusetts with his two brothers in 1637. Although they soon went to New Haven, Nathaniel remained in Boston. He was welcomed for his learning and was made head of the infant Harvard College, though he did not have the title of president. On June 6, 1639, the General Court granted him 500 acres of land on condition that he would continue there and teach during the remainder of his life. He was soon in trouble, however, and charged with avarice in withholding food he was supposed to provide for the students. He was also haled into court for having beaten his usher with a heavy club while two servants held the unfortunate man by the arms and legs. Eaton was removed from office, forbidden to teach in Massachusetts again, fined 100 marks and ordered to pay the usher £30, both fine and payment being lowered later to £20 each. Soon after he was tried by the church and excommunicated. Instead of making the payments ordered by the court, he fled to Piscataqua, where he was followed and captured. After giving his word that he would go back peaceably to Boston, he made an escape by force onto a vessel bound for Virginia, leaving his wife and children and £1,000 of debts in Boston. He had gained credit ɒy fraudulently drawing drafts on his brother Theophilus. In Virginia he secured a position as assistant rector in an Anglican church on the Eastern Shore and became a drunkard. He sent for his wife and children to follow him. Against the advice of her friends she did so, taking all but one of the children with her. They were lost at sea on the voyage. Eaton then married again, his second wife being the only surviving child of Thomas Graves of Virginia, formerly of Dorchester, Mass. He is supposed to have deserted her and returned to England. In 1647 he received the degrees of Ph.D.

and M.D. from the University of Padua (Venn, *post*). After the Restoration he conformed, was vicar of Bishop's Castle, Shropshire, in 1661, and in 1668, despite his continued bad habits, was made rector of Bideford, Devonshire. He died, a prisoner for debt, in King's Bench prison, Southwark, in 1674.

[D. C. Eaton, "The Family of Nathaniel Eaton," in *Papers of the New Haven Colony Hist. Soc.*, IV (1888), 185–92; John Winthrop, *Journal*, I (1908), 310–15; Thos. Hutchinson, *Hist. of the Colony of Mass. Bay*, I (1764), 90–91; *New-Eng. Hist. and Geneal. Reg.*, XL (1886), 295; J. and J. A. Venn, *Alumni Cantabrigiensis*, II (1922), 83. Eaton is mentioned in the histories of Harvard, and an account, with additional references, is in the *Dict. Nat. Biog.*]   J.T.A.

EATON, SAMUEL (1596?–Jan. 9, 1665), clergyman, was the third son of the Rev. Richard Eaton, vicar of Great Budworth, Cheshire. He was born in the hamlet of Crowley in that parish. The father became minister of the church at Coventry and it was there that Samuel's eldest brother, Theophilus [*q.v.*], later governor of New Haven, became acquainted with John Davenport. It is not known where Samuel went to school but he attended Magdalene College, Cambridge, where he received the degree of B.A. in 1624–25 and M.A. in 1628. He entered the church and took orders, but found himself unable to conform under Archbishop Laud, and in 1637 emigrated with his brother to New Haven, where he became the colleague of John Davenport. He seems to have been more liberal-minded than either Davenport or his brother, the chief leaders of the colony, for at a meeting held in June 1639 he objected to the article in the New Haven laws which prohibited all except church members from either voting or holding offices. The other two refused to consider any change, so he withdrew his objections. In 1640 he received from the colony a grant of the territory known as Totoket, now Branford, where he proposed to establish a new settlement under the jurisdiction of New Haven. He determined to go back to England to raise a new company of settlers of his own. On the way he stopped for some time in Boston where he declined an offer to remain permanently. When he reached England he found conditions improved and decided to give up all idea of returning to America. His subsequent life belongs to English biography. He continued as a clergyman and wrote a half-dozen small books on religious topics. During his brief sojourn in America he left no permanent mark, save, perhaps, his protest against the strictness of the theocratic government, and his work in establishing the church with Davenport. He died Jan. 9, 1664/5 without issue.

[There is an account in the *Dict. Nat. Biog.* which contains a bibliography of Eaton's writings. Further references are found in the general works dealing with the early ecclesiastical and political history of New Haven.]   J. T. A.

EATON, THEOPHILUS (1590–Jan. 7, 1658), merchant, colonizer, was born at Stony Stratford, England, and was one of the nine children of the Rev. Richard Eaton, later rector of a church at Coventry. There the young Theophilus went to school as a classmate of John Davenport, who was to be his life-long friend. His father wished him to be a clergyman, but since his own taste was for trade he went to London where he was apprenticed to a merchant. He finished his term and became a freeman of the city and a merchant on his own account, trading largely with the Baltic countries. So conspicuously successful did he become that he was elected deputy-governor of the great East-Land Company, visited the northern countries in order to enlarge its business, and according to Mather (*Magnalia*, I, 151) was also appointed agent of Charles I at the Court of Denmark. He resided for a time at Copenhagen and then returned to London. There he married his first wife, to whom he had been engaged for three years but whose name is unknown. After her death a few years later he was married to Ann, the daughter of George Lloyd, bishop of Chester, and widow of Thomas Yale.

Eaton took great interest in the plans for colonizing New England. He had become a strong Puritan and it may be that his interest in the new company was partly commercial and partly religious. In any event, he was one of the original patentees of the Massachusetts Company, and when it was determined to place the management of the company in the hands of ten men, five in New and five in Old England, he was chosen as one of the English five. Within a few years the colony became firmly established. It is not known what finally determined Eaton, then a rich and prosperous merchant in London, to transfer himself and his fortune to America, but he with some others, including John Davenport, emigrated in a body in 1637, forming the wealthiest and, commercially, the ablest group which had yet gone to the New World. They landed at Boston in June. Great efforts were made to keep so valuable an addition within the limits of Massachusetts, and they were offered various sites both there and in Plymouth, but they preferred to establish their own independent colony. Eaton, having heard of the special advantages of the territory about Quinnipiack, explored the country in the autumn, and there the company decided to settle. Accordingly, late in March 1638, they sailed from Boston and arrived, some two weeks later, at what is now New Haven. Thereafter, Eaton's life was bound up with that of the New Haven colony, he and his boyhood friend, John Davenport, being "the Moses and Aaron" of the community (Mather, *Magnalia*, I, 152). At a town meeting held June 4, 1639, the fundamental laws for the new colony were agreed upon, limiting the franchise and office holding to church members. The only dissenting voice was that of Eaton's brother Samuel, who was promptly overridden. From that time on there was no opposition in New Haven to the rule of Theophilus and John. On August 22 those two with five others were chosen to constitute "the church" and they proceeded to admit other members according to their own judgment. Eaton was elected civil governor of the colony and continued to be reëlected annually until his death. In 1643 he was one of the first body of commissioners of the United Colonies of New England. Two years later occurred the celebrated trial of his wife for lying as a result of which she was condemned by the church and excommunicated. His relations with her had not been happy before that time and were less so afterward. In 1655, the colony, having discovered the inadequacy of the laws of Moses, by which they had hitherto governed themselves, appointed Eaton to draw up a new code. This he did with Davenport's help. It was accepted and sent to London where it was printed in 1656.

Eaton had evidently expected to establish himself as a merchant and had entered upon various trading schemes. One of these, an attempt which he and his associates made to establish a fur trading post on the Delaware, brought on long and complicated troubles with the Dutch. As a result, the New Haven men finally had to abandon the enterprise, with the loss of £1,000. Constant diplomatic conflicts with New Amsterdam marked the whole of Eaton's service as governor. In 1646 another effort was made to establish the colony on a mercantile basis. A 150-ton ship was built, freighted, and dispatched to Europe, but was lost and never heard from. Some of the leading men then deserted the colony and returned to England, but Eaton remained, devoting himself thereafter to agriculture. He died suddenly in 1658, having governed the colony for nineteen years in a course marked by wisdom, justice, firmness, and prudence.

[Mather has an account of Eaton in his *Magnalia Christi Americana*, I (1853), 149–55. The Memoir by J. B. Moore in the *Colls. of the N. Y. Hist. Soc.*, 2 ser., vol. II (1849), 467–93, is excellent except for certain genealogical errors. Mrs. Eaton's trial is recorded in the article by Newman Smyth in the *Papers of the New Haven Colony Hist. Soc.*, V (1894), 133–48; her genealogy is given correctly in the *Col. Soc. Mass. Pubs.*, XXV (1924), 417–19. See also Leonard Bacon, *Thirteen Hist. Discourses* (1839); S. E. Morison, "New England and the Western Fur Trade, 1629–1675," in *Col. Soc. Mass. Pubs.*, XVIII (1917), 160–92.]

J.T.A.

EATON, WILLIAM (Feb. 23, 1764–June 1, 1811), army officer, diplomat, was born at Woodstock, Conn., the son of Nathan and Sarah (Johnson) Eaton. After a runaway enlistment in the army at sixteen, he underwent a series of hardships. He managed, however, to prepare himself for Dartmouth, and by alternately teaching and studying, succeeded in graduating in 1790. He then went to teach in Windsor, Vt., and, while holding this position, secured, through the influence of Senator Bradley from that state, the appointment of captain in the United States army. This was in March 1792. On Aug. 22, 1792, he married Eliza Sykes, the widow of Gen. Timothy Danielson, and in the fall of the same year was ordered to the Army of the West, on the Ohio. He was sent to Georgia in 1795, and while there made an enemy of his commandant and was court-martialed. The young officer plead his own cause to the secretary of state, Timothy Pickering, to such effect that he was ordered to Philadelphia without loss of rank. In July 1797, having been charged with a secret mission relating to the William Blount conspiracy, he returned in two days with prisoner and papers. By this time he had progressed so far in the esteem of the secretary of state that he was appointed consul to Tunis, and left for his post in December 1798, accompanied by the special diplomatic agent, James L. Cathcart [*q.v.*]. The government had made, through a French agent, Joseph E. Famin, a treaty with the piratical Bey of that North African country, which was unsatisfactory to the Senate. Eaton and Cathcart succeeded in rearranging this agreement and Cathcart proceeded to Tripoli, which country, in 1801, declared war on the United States. The situation there was unique; the reigning Pasha had usurped his brother's throne. Cathcart had formerly suggested that an attempt be made to effect a peace with the country by reinstating the exiled Hamet Karamanli. The proposition was placed before Congress by Eaton himself in the early part of 1804, some favorable attention was given to his scheme, and in September of the same year, with the title of "Navy Agent to the Barbary States," he returned to the Mediterranean to pursue his venture. On his arrival, he discovered that the exiled Pasha had fled to Upper Egypt. Undaunted, he sought out his charge and brought him to Alexandria. From there began a spectacular march through the Libyan Desert with a motley army of Greeks, Italians, and Arabs, collected along the way. After many seemingly unsurmountable difficulties this strange army arrived at Derne, a Tripolitan seaport. Eaton, with the aid of American gunboats, occupied the town. Victory seemed sure. Suddenly he was ordered to leave Tripoli and instructed that a treaty was being negotiated which would secure the illegal ruler on the Tripolitan throne and provide for the payment of ransom for imprisoned American officers.

Eaton was incensed and humiliated. He returned immediately to America, where his brilliant services had given him great prestige, but the warmth with which he defended himself after the government had supported the treaty-makers made him many political enemies. His feat was mentioned by the president in his annual message, but Eaton's complaints kept him from receiving a medal from the House of Representatives. The remainder of his life was none too happy. In 1807 he was summoned to witness in the Aaron Burr trial; he had been closely associated with Burr, but was able to clear himself before the court. In December of that year he took a seat in the Massachusetts legislature, but because of his too ready utterance of his opinions he was not reëlected. He retired to Brimfield, Mass., where he spent his last years. The fatigues of his active life, the disappointments in his cherished schemes, and his excesses had undermined his health, and he died at forty-seven years of age.

[Charles Prentiss, *Life of the Late Gen. William Eaton* (1813); C. C. Felton, *Life of William Eaton* (1838) in Sparks's Lib. of Am. Biog.; *Hist. Celebration of the Town of Brimfield ... 1876* (1879); Gardner W. Allen, *Our Navy and the Barbary Corsairs* (1905); *Am. State Papers, Foreign Relations*, II (1832), 281, 702–25; Preble Papers, Lib. of Cong.; C. W. Goldsborough, *The U. S. Naval Chronicle* (1824), pp. 254–56, 272–78; Commanders' Letters, Nos. 1 to 26, and Miscellaneous Letters, III, Nos. 36, 38, 48 (Navy Dept.); *Nat. Intelligencer*, Nov. 20, 1805. There is a popularly written sketch of Eaton in Meade Minnigerode's *Lives and Times* (1925).]

R.B.B.

EATON, WYATT (May 6, 1849–June 7, 1896), painter, was born at Philipsburg, province of Quebec, Canada. He was the son of Jonathan Wyatt and Mary (Smith) Eaton, the former a lumber and shipping merchant and native of New Hampshire. When about eighteen years old, he became a student at the National Academy of Design under Samuel Colman, Daniel Huntington, Leutze, and others, and painted in the studio of Joseph Oriel Eaton [*q.v.*], who became both instructor and friend. In 1872 he took a European trip which widened his horizon considerably. In London he became acquainted with Whistler, then, journeying to the continent, he sought the studio of Gérôme at the École des Beaux-Arts in Paris. Here valuable contacts with Munkácsy, Bastien-Lepage, Dagnan-Bouveret, and others stimulated him in his work in Paris and at Barbizon in the Forest of Fontainebleau, but of all his friendships, that with Millet was of most vital and lasting worth to him. The older artist cast a noticeable influence on the younger, and in his family, Eaton was treated as a son. In addition to required academic work, Eaton painted portraits, figures, and landscapes. At the Salon of 1874 his "Reverie" was exhibited and in 1876 his "Harvesters at Rest." Both were shown at the Universal Exposition of 1878. Later he exhibited a portrait of Mrs. Hawkins, said to be one of the finest canvases in the Salon that year. After returning to America in 1877, Eaton, with Augustus Saint-Gaudens, Walter Shirlaw, and others, founded the Society of American Artists, was its first secretary, and later its president. He was then a teacher at Cooper Institute, New York.

His portraits of the poets Emerson, Whittier, Longfellow, Bryant, Holmes, and Dr. Holland, engraved by T. Cole for the *Century Magazine*, were considered an innovation in magazine work. In 1884 and 1885, while in Europe, he painted a few peasant subjects but eventually became absorbed in portraiture. Notable examples of Eaton's work are his portraits of Bishop Horatio Potter, Roswell Smith, President Garfield (after his death), for the Union League Club of New York, John Burroughs, Senator Franklin Murphy of Newark, and Mrs. R. W. Gilder. The last has won a place among the best pictures produced in this country. During a trip to Canada, in 1892–93, Eaton painted some of the benefactors of McGill University, as well as Sir William Dawson of Montreal and other prominent people. His work there was so successful that other important commissions followed and he spent the remainder of his life chiefly in Canada. Among the best-known of his Canadian portraits are those of Sir William and Lady Van Horne, Sir Donald and Lady Smith, Mr. Angus, and Lady Marjorie and the Hon. Archie Gordon. Eaton's deft use of the brush gave his paintings an unusual delicacy and grace, while his portraiture reveals a rare skill in transcending the limitations of photographic likeness.

Being unequal to an anticipated summer trip abroad in 1896, Eaton went to Newport, R. I., instead, where he died of consumption. His first wife, whom he married on Sept. 24, 1874, was Laura Constance Papelard, born in Château-

Thierry, France. After her death, on Feb. 7, 1886, he married, July 23, 1887, Charlotte Amelia Collins.

[N. Z. R. Molyneux, *Hist. Geneal. and Biog. of the Eaton Families* (1911), p. 760; F. F. Sherman, *Am. Painters of Yesterday and Today* (1919), pp. 39–44; G. W. Sheldon, *Am. Painters* (enlarged ed., 1881), pp. 169–74; *Century Mag.*, Oct. 1902; certain information from the New England Hist. Geneal. Soc.] J.M.H.

EBERLE, EDWARD WALTER (Aug. 17, 1864–July 6, 1929), naval officer, was born at Denton, Texas, the son of Joseph Eberle, who came as a youth from Switzerland and was a major in the Confederate army, and Mary Stemler of Georgia. He later settled at Fort Smith, Ark., whither his parents had moved in 1865. In his eighteenth year he entered the United States Naval Academy, graduating about the middle of his class in 1885. Of his sea duty in the decade following, the most profitable, as a rigorous training in old-style seafaring, was three years of charting and survey work in the Fish Commission steamer *Albatross,* off Cape Horn, Alaska, and the west coast of the United States. After duty at the Naval Academy and promotion in 1896 to lieutenant (junior grade), he served three years in the *Oregon,* making the famous cruise around the Horn in the Spanish-American War and commanding her forward turret at Santiago (see Eberle, "The *Oregon* at Santiago," *Century Magazine,* May 1899). Later, at Manila, when Capt. Barker of the *Oregon* succeeded Dewey in command of the Asiatic Squadron during the Philippine Insurrection, he made Eberle his flag lieutenant and acting chief of staff (see Eberle, "The Navy's Cooperation in the Zapote River Campaign," *Proceedings of the United States Naval Institute,* March 1900). A specialist in ordnance, Eberle, then aide to the superintendent at the Naval Academy, wrote the first modern manual of *Gun and Torpedo Drills for the United States Navy,* and in 1901–02 was gunnery officer of the *Indiana.* Again flag lieutenant for Admiral Barker, in the Atlantic Fleet (1903–05), he drew up the first instructions and code for wireless on naval vessels. After study at the War College in 1905, and two years' service as recorder of the Board of Inspection and Survey, he accompanied the world cruise of 1907–08 as executive of the *Louisiana* as far as San Francisco, where he became commandant of the Training Station, 1908–10. During the next two years he commanded the *Wheeling* on a voyage around the world via Alaska, Japan, and the Mediterranean. Captain's rank came to him in 1912 while he was commanding the Atlantic Torpedo Fleet, in which he developed the use of smoke screens and the employment of aircraft against submarines. In the summer of 1914 he was senior officer at Santo Domingo during revolutionary disturbances, in which the navy was engaged in protecting property and arranging a settlement.

As superintendent he administered the Naval Academy, September 1915–January 1919, with marked success through the period of wartime expansion, when classes were tremendously increased, courses compressed, and many reserve officers were in training. At the close of the war he was awarded the Distinguished Service Medal, in February 1918 was made temporary rear-admiral, and on July 1, 1919, was given the permanent rank. In 1919–21 he commanded divisions of the Atlantic Fleet, and from June 1921 to June 1923, the Pacific Fleet, known after reorganization in December 1922, as the Battle Fleet. After this second highest sea command, his general popularity and a belief in his sound judgment and tact in dealing with political leaders prompted his promotion to the highest shore office, that of chief of naval operations, which he held from July 1923 to November 1927, a period when special problems were raised by the expeditionary forces in China and Nicaragua. Following a year on the Navy General Board he retired, Aug. 17, 1928. His death, at the Naval Hospital, Washington, came from an infection above the ear, the result of an injury years before. He was survived by his wife, Tazie, daughter of Randolph Harrison of Virginia, whom he married in San Francisco on Oct. 24, 1889, and by a son, Edward Randolph. Not a bookish man or a great reader, Eberle was successful chiefly because of his remarkable grasp of his profession in its every detail, combined with ability to win the trust and devotion of his subordinates. His whole life was in his work, and to his high rank he brought a frank manliness and a poise of manner which made him esteemed both within and without the service.

[*Everyday Life in the Navy: Autobiography of Rear Admiral Albert S. Barker* (1928); obituaries in the *N. Y. Times,* July 7, 1929; *Army and Navy Jour.,* July 13, 1929; *U. S. Bureau of Navigation* (*Navy Dept.*) *Bull. 108,* July 13, 1929.]   A.W.

EBERLE, JOHN (Dec. 10, 1787–Feb. 2, 1838), physician, was born probably at Hagerstown, Md., and taken by his parents at an early age to Lancaster, Pa., though it has been stated that he was born at the latter place. His father, a blacksmith, and his mother were both simple farmer folk of German birth or descent. John was twelve years of age before he could speak English. He had no early educational advantages, but, being a constant reader, he acquired suffi-

cient knowledge to enable him to begin the study of medicine with Abraham Carpenter of Lancaster, and enter the University of Pennsylvania in 1806, where three years later he graduated, his thesis being on *Animal Life.* He returned to his home and began to practise medicine. During this period he was drawn into political writing and became the editor of a newspaper. Toward the end of the War of 1812 he was appointed surgeon of the Lancaster militia and served at the battle of Baltimore (1814). Removing to Philadelphia, he helped to found, and for some two years devoted practically his whole time to editing, the *American Medical Recorder,* a quarterly journal first issued in 1818. The *Recorder* was well received in America and Europe and its editor received considerable recognition, for example, election to the German Academy of the Natural Sciences. In 1818 also, he published *Botanical Terminology,* a pocket "companion" for students of botany. His success as a writer encouraged him to publish his *Treatise of the Materia Medica and Therapeutics* (1823) which became a standard text-book and went through five editions. Through the meetings of the Philadelphia Medical Society he was brought in contact with an enthusiastic group of students and teachers, and together with Dr. George M'Clellan gave regular lectures at the Appollodorian Gallery. In 1824, with Dr. Joseph Klapp and Dr. Jacob Green, he proposed to the trustees of Jefferson College at Canonsburg, Pa., to establish a medical department of that college in Philadelphia. This proposal was accepted, and the Jefferson Medical College opened (1825) with Eberle as professor of materia medica, and afterward of the theory and practise of medicine (1825–31). He soon issued a small volume called "Eberle's Notes," a kind of *vade mecum* for the student. The work was sufficiently popular to justify a second edition (1832) and from this grew his *Notes of Lectures on the Theory and Practice of Medicine* (2nd ed., 1834, with four subsequent editions), a text characterized by original thought and not, as were many of that day, a mere compilation of foreign opinions. From 1824 to 1826 he was editor of the *American Medical Review.* Within a few years much litigation and controversy arose at the Jefferson Medical College, and, finances running low, Eberle became discouraged and in 1830 accepted the offer of Daniel Drake [*q.v.*] to organize the faculty for the medical department of Miami University, designed as a competitor of the Medical College of Ohio. Eberle arrived in Cincinnati in 1831 and learned that the old school and its would-be rival had consolidated so that he and his colleagues found themselves members of the conjoint faculty. In 1832 they founded the *Western Medical Gazette*. Shortly thereafter Eberle published his *Treatise on the Diseases and Physical Education of Children* (1833). On the outbreak of cholera in Cincinnati, Eberle and T. D. Mitchell were appointed special health officers. Their report was published in the *Cincinnati Daily Gazette,* June 26, 1832. In 1837 Eberle accepted the chair of the theory and practise of medicine at the reorganized medical department of Transylvania University in Lexington, Ky., where he became one of the editors of the *Transylvania Journal of Medicine*. His health was now beginning to decline so that he was able to do but little teaching. He resigned before completing a full school term, and died in Lexington after less than a year's residence.

He was a brilliant teacher and writer and successful in the debates with other medical men so characteristic of the period. He was a champion of the theory of physiological drug action as opposed to "solidism" as taught by Harrison and others. At the three medical schools at which he was professor he was always popular with the students, who liked his simplicity of manner while admiring his learning. He was an idealist and inclined to be a dreamer, but an incessant worker. Besides the works above mentioned, he was the author of numerous short articles. His *Treatise on the Practice of Medicine,* in two volumes, first appearing in 1830, was published with subsequent revisions, the last being in 1849 with additions by George M'Clellan. His *Treatise on the Diseases . . . of Children* was revised and republished in 1850 by his former colleague, Thomas D. Mitchell. These republications of his works long after his death are sufficient proofs of their popularity.

[Sketch from memory, by T. D. Mitchell, in *Lives of Eminent Am. Physicians* (1861), ed. by S. D. Gross; Robt. Peter, The *Hist. of the Medic. Dept. of Transylvania Univ.* (1905), being Filson Club Pub. No. 20; Otto Juettner, *Daniel Drake and his Followers* (1909); *Autobiog. of Samuel D. Gross* (2 vols., 1887); E. G. Eberle, "John Eberle, 1787–1838" (1924), MS. in Army Medical Lib.; Alexander Harris, *Harris' Biog. Hist. of Lancaster, Pa.* (1872); *Kentucky Gazette* (Lexington), Feb. 8, 1838.]   E. E. H.